P9-BIF-761

FROMMER'S
JAPAN &
HONG KONG

BETH REIBER

3RD EDITION

PRENTICE HALL

New York ☐ London ☐ Toronto ☐ Sydney ☐ Tokyo ☐ Singapore

Copyright © 1986, 1988, 1990
by Simon & Schuster Inc.

All rights reserved
including the right of reproduction
in whole or in part in any form

Published by Prentice Hall Trade Division
A Division of Simon & Schuster Inc.
15 Columbus Circle
New York, NY 10023

ISBN 0-13-332834-1
ISSN 1045-6899

Manufactured in the United States of America

CONTENTS

PART ONE

JAPAN

PART TWO

HONG KONG

MAPS

To Joan and Fritz, my parents in Kansas,
who always encouraged me
to look farther than my own backyard

ACKNOWLEDGMENTS

I would like to thank a number of fine and very special people who graciously offered their help in preparation of this book: Toshinobu Ikubo, Grace Herget, and Seiko Taniguchi of the Japan National Tourist Organization; Morris Simoncelli of Japan Airlines; Satoshi Misonoo of ANA enterprises; Jun Oda of Miyako Hotels; Karisa Yuen-Ha Lui, Stephen Wong, and Mary Testa Bakht of the Hong Kong Tourist Association; Debbie Howard and Evelyn Lenzen for their moral support and editorial advice; and Paul Pasmantier, Marilyn Wood, and all the other people at Frommer Books who helped make this book a reality.

INFLATION ALERT AND EXCHANGE RATE

We don't have to tell you that inflation and the fluctuation of the U.S. dollar on the international market has affected travelers' buying power abroad. While the exchange rate between the U.S. dollar and the Hong Kong dollar has been fairly stable, the rate between the U.S. dollar and the Japanese yen has been volatile. In researching this book, we have made every effort to obtain up-to-the-minute prices, but even the most conscientious researcher cannot keep up with the current pace of inflation. As we go to press, we believe we have obtained the most reliable data possible. Nonetheless, in the lifetime of this edition, the wise traveler will add 15% to 20% to the prices quoted throughout these pages and will check the exchange rates when planning a trip and again before departure.

A DISCLAIMER

Readers are advised that prices fluctuate in the course of time and travel information changes under the impact of the varied and volatile factors that affect the travel industry. The author and publisher cannot be held responsible for the experiences of the reader while traveling. Readers are invited to write the publisher with ideas, comments and suggestions for future editions.

Readers should also note that the establishments described under Reader's Selections or Suggestions have not in all cases been inspected by the authors and that opinions expressed there are those of the individual reader(s) only and do not in any way represent the opinions of the publisher or author of this guide.

A NOTE ON JAPANESE SYMBOLS

Many hotels, restaurants, and other establishments in Japan do not have signs showing their names in English letters. Appendix II lists the Japanese symbols for all such places appearing in this guide. Each establishment name in Japanese symbols is numbered, and the same number appears in an oval in the text following the bold-faced establishment name. For example, in the text Osaka's **Hotel Hokke Club** (164) is number 164 in the Japanese symbol list in Appendix II.

FROMMER'S JAPAN AND HONG KONG

Hardly a day goes by that you don't hear something about Japan, whether it's about trade or business, cars or computers. And yet despite the fact that Japan has become one of the most advanced industrialized nations in the world, it still remains something of an enigma to people in the Western world. What is Japan? Is it computers and robots, cars and cameras? Or is it still the land of the *geisha* and the *bonsai*, the tea ceremony and flower arranging? Has Japan become more Westernized than Japanese?

The fact is that Japan is a blend of both East and West, and it is not an easy nation for Westerners to comprehend. Discovering Japan is much like peeling an onion—you uncover one layer only to find many more. Thus no matter how long you stay in Japan you never stop learning, and to me that's one of the most fascinating aspects of being in Japan. One American journalist who has lived in Japan more than 20 years and is the author of several books on Japan told me that she still doesn't understand all the nuances of Japanese culture and customs, and that she is amazed to find new aspects of the country almost daily.

This book is designed as an aid to your own discoveries of this truly wonderful and interesting country. According to the Japan National Tourist Organization, the average length of stay for tourists visiting Japan is 10½ days. To see all the places I've listed in this book you would need approximately three months. It's obvious, therefore, that you must be selective in planning your itinerary. Decide beforehand what your priorities are, whether they're temples, hot-spring spas, landscape gardens, or mountain scenery. Although the Japanese archipelago consists of more than 3,000 islands, I've limited the scope of this book to Japan's four main islands, where you'll find all of Japan's major cities and historical sights.

One aspect of this guidebook that sets it apart from most others is that in Appendix II it lists the written Japanese equivalent for restaurants and hotels that do not have signs in English. After all, nothing is more frustrating than walking down a street where everything is written only in Japanese and not being able to distinguish one locale from the other. Most Japanese consists of pictographs called *kanji*, and with a little practice you can probably match up identical kanji. Appendix I, on Japanese vocabulary, should further help you in your travels through Japan.

But don't worry—even if you don't know the language, you'll find Japan navigable. Japan rates as one of the safest countries in the world, much safer than the United States or even European countries. You don't have to worry about muggers, pickpockets, or crooks. The Japanese are honest and extremely helpful toward foreign visitors. Indeed, it's the people themselves who make traveling in Japan such a delight.

Readers of this book will also find a chapter devoted to the British colony of Hong Kong, known throughout the world as a mecca for shopping bargains. Many airlines that fly to Hong Kong (such as Japan Airlines) allow stopovers in Japan, making it easy to combine a trip to both destinations. Seeing Japan and Hong Kong will give you the opportunity to observe both Japanese and Chinese culture, providing you with a well-rounded view of the Orient.

A WORD ABOUT COSTS

No doubt you've heard horror stories about how expensive Japan can be. The truth is, hardly anyone comes to Japan without suffering an initial shock at how expensive everything is—simply because almost everything *is* shockingly expensive. With the dramatic fall of the dollar against the yen in the last few years, Tokyo has emerged as one of the most expensive—if not *the* most expensive—cities in the world. Food and lodging, for example, are much costlier in Tokyo than they are in New York, and if you insist on living and eating exactly as you do back home, the costs will be astronomical.

The secret is to live and eat much as the Japanese do. This book will help you do exactly that, with descriptions of out-of-the-way eateries and Japanese-style inns that cater to the Japanese. By following the advice in this book and exercising a little caution on your own, you should be able to cut down on needless expenses and learn even more about Japan in the process. While you may never find Japan cheap, you will find it richly rewarding for all those other reasons that brought you here in the first place.

And how much should you expect to spend every day for food and accommodations? If you want to travel rock-bottom and are willing to stay in youth hostels and eat inexpensive Japanese food, you can travel in Japan on ¥5,500 ($44) a day, excluding transportation costs. It's best, however, to allow yourself at least ¥10,000 ($80) to ¥14,000 ($112) a day, plus extra for occasional splurges, shopping, and emergencies. That's the budget I follow when I travel in Japan, and by sticking to the recommendations in this book you should be able to do it too.

However, in this book I haven't neglected the finest and most expensive places—after all, even though you may flinch at spending $200 on a meal, many such restaurants do exist and you may be interested simply in reading about them. Recommendations in this book are generally listed in a descending order from the most expensive down to the cheapest—skip to the end of the list, therefore, for a rundown of budget recommendations.

Keep in mind, however, that although every effort was made to be as accurate as possible, prices do change—which means that they go up. Always inquire about prices before checking into a hotel to avoid embarrassment when it comes time to pay the bill. Furthermore, keep in mind that places do close and change ownership or management.

AN INVITATION TO READERS

In researching this book I have come across many wonderful establishments, the best of which I've included here. However, I being only one person and you readers being many, I'm sure that you'll run across other great hotels, inns, restaurants, shops, and attractions during your own travels in Japan and Hong Kong. Please don't keep them to yourself. Share them so that others might benefit from your experiences. You might also wish to comment on places I *have* covered in this book—especially if the place has changed for the worse. You can write to me, Beth Reiber, c/o Frommer Books, 15 Columbus Circle, New York, NY 10023. Thanks for your help!

Frommer's Dollarwise® Travel Club—How To Save Money On All Your Travels

---

In this book we'll be looking at how to get you your money's worth in Japan and Hong Kong, but there is a "device" for saving money and determining value on *all* your trips. It's the popular international Frommer's Dollarwise Travel Club, now in its 30th successful year of operation. The club was formed at the urging of numerous readers of the $-A-Day and Frommer Guides, who felt that such an organization could provide continuing travel information and a sense of community to value-minded travelers in all parts of the world. And so it does!

In keeping with the budget concept, the annual membership fee is low and is immediately exceeded by the value of your benefits. Upon receipt of $18 (U.S. residents), or $20 U.S. by check drawn on a U.S. bank or via international postal money order in U.S. funds (Canadian, Mexican, and other foreign residents) to cover one year's membership, we will send all new members the following items.

(1) Any *two* of the following books

Please designate in your letter which two you wish to receive:

Frommer $-A-Day Guides

Europe on $40 a Day
Australia on $30 a Day
Eastern Europe on $25 a Day
England on $50 a Day
Greece on $30 a Day
Hawaii on $60 a Day
India on $25 a Day
Ireland on $35 a Day
Israel on $40 a Day
Mexico (plus Belize and Guatemala) on $35 a Day
New York on $60 a Day
New Zealand on $45 a Day
Scandinavia on $60 a Day
Scotland and Wales on $40 a Day
South America on $35 a Day
Spain and Morocco (plus the Canary Is.) on $40 a Day
Turkey on $30 a Day
Washington, D.C., and Historic Virginia on $40 a Day

($-A-Day Guides document hundreds of budget accommodations and facilities, helping you get the most for your travel dollars.)

Frommer Guides

Alaska
Australia
Austria and Hungary
Belgium, Holland, and Luxembourg
Bermuda and The Bahamas
Brazil
California and Las Vegas
Canada
Caribbean
Egypt
England and Scotland
Florida
France
Germany
Italy
Japan and Hong Kong
Mid-Atlantic States
New England
New York State
Northwest

Portugal, Madeira, and the Azores
Skiing USA—East
Skiing USA—West
South Pacific
Southeast Asia
Southern Atlantic States
Southwest
Switzerland and Liechtenstein
Texas
USA

(Frommer Guides discuss accommodations and facilities in all price ranges, with emphasis on the medium-priced.)

Frommer Touring Guides

Australia
Brazil
Egypt
Florence
London
Paris
Scotland
Thailand
Venice

(These new, color-illustrated guides include walking tours, cultural and historic sites, and other vital travel information.)

Gault Millau

Chicago
France
Hong Kong
Italy
London
Los Angeles
New England
New York
San Francisco
Washington, D.C.

(Irreverent, savvy, and comprehensive, each of these renowned guides candidly reviews over 1,000 restaurants, hotels, shops, nightspots, museums, and sights.)

Serious Shopper's Guides

Italy
London
Los Angeles
Paris

(Practical and comprehensive, each of these handsomely illustrated guides lists hundreds of stores, selling everything from antiques to wine, conveniently organized alphabetically by category.)

A Shopper's Guide to the Caribbean

(Two experienced Caribbean hands guide you through this shopper's paradise, offering witty insights and helpful tips on the wares and emporia of more than 25 islands.)

Beat the High Cost of Travel

(This practical guide details how to save money on absolutely all travel items—

accommodations, transportation, dining, sightseeing, shopping, taxes, and more. Includes special budget information for seniors, students, singles, and families.)

Bed & Breakfast—North America
(This guide contains a directory of over 150 organizations that offer bed & breakfast referrals and reservations throughout North America. The scenic attractions, as well as major schools and universities near the homes of each, are also listed.)

California with Kids
(A must for parents traveling in California, providing key information on selecting the best accommodations, restaurants, and sightseeing attractions for the particular needs of the family, whether the kids are toddlers, school-agers, preteens, or teens.)

Caribbean Hideaways
(Well-known travel author Ian Keown describes the most romantic, alluring places to stay in the Caribbean, rating each establishment on romantic ambience, food, sports opportunities, and price.)

Frommer's Belgium
(Arthur Frommer unlocks the treasures of a country overlooked by most travelers to Europe. Discover the medieval charm, modern sophistication, and natural beauty of this quintessentially European country.)

Frommer's Cruises
(This complete guide covers all the basics of cruising—ports of call, costs, fly-cruise package bargains, cabin-selection booking, embarkation and debarkation—and describes in detail over 60 or so ships cruising the waters of Alaska, the Caribbean, Mexico, Hawaii, Panama, Canada, and the United States.)

Frommer's Skiing Europe
(Describes top ski resorts in Austria, France, Italy, and Switzerland. Illustrated with maps of each resort area. Includes supplement on Argentinian resorts.)

Frommer's Honeymoon Destinations
(A special guide for that most romantic trip of your life, with full details on planning and choosing the destination that will be just right in the U.S. [California, New England, Hawaii, Florida, New York, Pennsylvania, etc.], Mexico, and the Caribbean.)

Marilyn Wood's Wonderful Weekends
(This very selective guide covers the best minivacation destinations within a 200-mile radius of New York City. It describes special country inns and other accommodations, restaurants, picnic spots, sights, and activities—all the information needed for a two- or three-day stay.)

Manhattan's Outdoor Sculpture
(A total guide, fully illustrated with black-and-white photos, to more than 300 sculptures and monuments that grace Manhattan's plazas, parks, and other public spaces.)

Motorist's Phrase Book
(A practical phrase book in French, German, and Spanish designed specifically for the English-speaking motorist touring abroad.)

Paris Rendez-Vous
(An amusing and *au courant* guide to the best meeting places in Paris, organized for

hour-to-hour use: from power breakfasts and fun brunches, through tea at four or cocktails at five, to romantic dinners and dancing 'til dawn.)

Swap and Go—Home Exchanging Made Easy
(Two veteran home exchangers explain in detail all the money-saving benefits of a home exchange, and then describe precisely how to do it. Also includes information on home rentals and many tips on low-cost travel.)

The Candy Apple: New York with Kids
(A spirited guide to the wonders of the Big Apple by a savvy New York grandmother with a kid's-eye view to fun. Indispensable for visitors and residents alike.)

The New World of Travel
(From America's No. 1 travel expert, Arthur Frommer, an annual sourcebook with the hottest news and latest trends that's guaranteed to change the way you travel—and save you hundreds of dollars. Jam-packed with alternative new modes of travel that will lead you to vacations that cater to the mind, the spirit, and a sense of thrift.)

Travel Diary and Record Book
(A 96-page diary for personal travel notes plus a section for such vital data as passport and traveler's check numbers, itinerary, postcard list, special people and places to visit; a reference section with temperature and conversion charts; and world maps with distance zones.)

Where to Stay USA
(By the Council on International Educational Exchange, this extraordinary guide is the first to list accommodations in all 50 states that cost anywhere from $3 to $30 per night.)

(2) Any *one* of the Frommer City Guides
Amsterdam and Holland
Athens
Atlantic City and Cape May
Boston
Cancún, Cozumel, and the Yucatán
Chicago
Dublin and Ireland
Hawaii
Las Vegas
Lisbon, Madrid, and Costa del Sol
London
Los Angeles
Mexico City and Acapulco
Minneapolis and St. Paul
Montréal and Québec City
New Orleans
New York
Orlando, Disney World, and EPCOT
Paris
Philadelphia
Rio
Rome
San Francisco
Santa Fe, Taos, and Albuquerque
Sydney
Washington, D.C.

(Pocket-size guides to hotels, restaurants, nightspots, and sightseeing attractions covering all price ranges.)

(3) A one-year subscription to *The Dollarwise Traveler*

This quarterly eight-page tabloid newspaper keeps you up to date on fastbreaking developments in low-cost travel in all parts of the world, bringing you the latest money-saving information—the kind of information you'd have to pay $35 a year to obtain elsewhere. This consumer-conscious publication also features columns of special interest to readers: **Hospitality Exchange** (members all over the world who are willing to provide hospitality to other members as they pass through their home cities); **Share-a-Trip** (offers and requests from members for travel companions who can share costs and help avoid the burdensome single supplement); and **Readers Ask . . . Readers Reply** (travel questions from members to which other members reply with authentic firsthand information).

(4) Your personal membership card

Membership entitles you to purchase through the club all Frommer publications for a third to a half off their regular retail prices during the term of your membership.

So why not join this hardy band of international budgeteers and participate in its exchange of travel information and hospitality? Simply send your name and address, together with your annual membership fee of $18 (U.S. residents) or $20 U.S. (Canadian, Mexican, and other foreign residents), by check drawn on a U.S. bank or via international postal money order in U.S. funds, to: Frommer's Dollarwise Travel Club, Inc., 15 Columbus Circle, New York, NY 10023. And please remember to specify which *two* of the books in section (1) and which *one* in section (2) you wish to receive in your initial package of members' benefits. Or, if you prefer, use the order form at the end of the book and enclose $18 or $20 in U.S. currency.

Once you are a member, there is no obligation to buy additional books. No books will be mailed to you without your specific order.

PART ONE

JAPAN

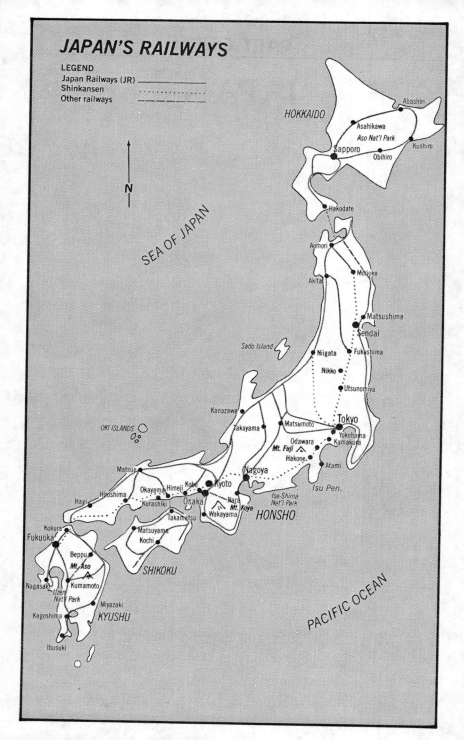

JAPAN'S RAILWAYS

LEGEND
Japan Railways (JR) _____
Shinkansen ··················
Other railways _____

N

HOKKAIDO

Abashiri
Asahikawa
Aso Nat'l Park
Sapporo
Kushiro
Obihiro

Hakodate

SEA OF JAPAN

Aomori
Morioka
Akita

Matsushima
Sendai
Sado Island
Niigata
Fukushima
Nikko
Utsunomiya
Kanazawa
Takayama
Matsumoto
Tokyo
OKI ISLANDS
Yokohama
Kamakura
Odawara
Mt. Fuji
Hakone
Atami
Matsue
Nagoya
Izu Pen.
Hiroshima
Okayama Himeji Kobe
Hagi
Kyoto
Kurashiki
Osaka
Nara
Ise-Shima
Mt. Koya
Nat'l Park
Takamatsu
Wakayama
HONSHO
Matsuyama
Kochi
Kokura
SHIKOKU
Fukuoka
Beppu
Mt. Aso
Nagasaki
Kumamoto
Uzen
Nat'l Park
Miyazaki
Kagoshima
KYUSHU
Ibusuki

PACIFIC OCEAN

GETTING TO AND AROUND JAPAN

1. GETTING THERE
2. TRAVELING WITHIN JAPAN
3. TIPS FOR THE TRAVELER
4. THE ABCs OF JAPAN

A holiday in Japan, for most readers of this book, must begin with a transpacific trip to Japan. That necessitates a brief examination of the available transportation.

1. Getting There

Although there is infrequent ferry service connecting ports in Japan with Shanghai, Nakhodka in the U.S.S.R., Taiwan, and South Korea, the overwhelming majority of visitors to Japan arrive by air. There are a number of carriers that fly from the U.S. to Japan. They include *All Nippon Airways* (tel. 800/235-9262), *American Airlines* (tel. 800/433-7300), *China Airlines* (tel. 800/227-5118), *Continental Airlines* (tel. 800/231-0856), *Japan Airlines* (tel. 800/525-3663), *Delta Air Lines* (tel. 800/241-4141), *Korean Air* (tel. 800/223-1155), *Northwest Airlines,* (tel. 800/225-2525), *Philippine Airlines* (tel. 800/435-9725), *Singapore Airlines* (tel. 800/742-3333), *Thai Airways International* (tel. 800/426-5204), and *United Airlines* (tel. 800/241-6522). Contact your travel agent or specific carriers for current information.

But to get a head start on your travel adventure it seems only appropriate to fly Japan's own *Japan Airlines,* known as JAL. An introduction to Japanese culture begins as soon as you enter the plane and are greeted with a bow and a smile by the flight crew. After your craft leaves the ground you are given a hot, steaming towel called an *oshibori* with which to refresh yourself, and, in first and business class, your meal will include both Japanese and Western cuisine selections. (Economy class is served only Western meals.)

JAL's gateways in the United States include New York, Chicago, Los Angeles, San Francisco, Seattle, Atlanta, Anchorage, and Honolulu. Almost all JAL international flights from North America arrive at the New Tokyo International Airport in Narita, about 40 miles from Tokyo's center. Another international gateway is Osaka, which is the most convenient gateway if you plan to go straight to either Osaka or Kyoto.

The flying time to Tokyo is about 14 hours from New York, 12 hours and 45 minutes from Chicago, 10 hours from Seattle, almost 11 hours from San Francisco, and about 11 hours 20 minutes from Los Angeles.

PLANE FARES

No matter which airline you fly, there are certain things you should know about airfare structures. While first, business and basic economy fares (those with no restrictions) are the same all year to Japan, most airlines charge different APEX (Advance Purchase Excursion) fares according to seasons. Peak season, usually during the summer months, is the most expensive; basic season, during the winter, offers the least expensive fares; and shoulder seasons are in between both price- and time-wise. Whatever the season, APEX fares are a little more expensive on weekends.

Listed below are some of the options in fares to Japan from New York, Chicago, and the West Coast as of Fall 1989. Be sure to contact the airlines or your travel agent for an up-date on prices once you've decided on your exact travel plans. If you plan to include Hong Kong on your trip to the Orient—and I strongly urge that you do—you should purchase a ticket that will allow you a stopover in Japan on your way to Hong Kong. Consult the Hong Kong "Getting There" section for fares to Hong Kong from North America.

First Class

All airlines provide some luxuries to their first-class passengers. JAL's royal treatment is typically Japanese and begins at their special first-class check-in counter, where your baggage will be loaded into a special container so it will be taken off first on arrival in Japan. You will also be invited to use the Sakura Lounge (at major gateways), a special waiting area with free alcoholic drinks, coffee and soda. On board the plane you'll have a comfortable, electronically operated seat that will incline to a 60° angle, and you'll be offered a Japanese *happi* coat and slippers for inflight wear. In addition to complimentary champagne and other alcoholic beverages, travel kits and the use of headphones, you will be offered a choice of five entrées of Western or Japanese cuisine. JAL's first-class, round-trip fares to Tokyo are $4,912 from New York, $4,792 from Chicago, and $3,984 from Seattle, San Francisco, or Los Angeles.

Business Class

While most carriers have business class, JAL's Executive Class also has its own check-in counter at the airport, a separate cabin with seats that recline 40°, complimentary champagne, cocktails and wine, free use of headphones, and a complimentary travel kit. Meals feature Western and Japanese cuisine, including *jubako* meals, which are typical Japanese home-cooked food, served in traditional lacquer containers. For health conscious passengers, there's a special low-calorie menu. JAL's business class round-trip fares to Tokyo are $2,744 from New York, $2,624 from Chicago, and $2,114 from Seattle, Los Angeles, or San Francisco.

Economy Class

As an example of economy-class round-trip fares to Tokyo, JAL's are $2,344 from New York, $2,224 from Chicago, and $1,714 from Seattle, Los Angeles, or San Francisco.

APEX (Advance Purchase Excursion) Fares

One way to cut the cost of your flight to Japan is to purchase your ticket in advance and comply with certain restrictions. Reservations, ticketing, and payment for the APEX fare usually must be completed no later than 21 days prior to departure, but rules vary depending on the airline. There's a minimum time you can stay in Japan, usually one or two weeks; the maximum stay may be up to six months. Rates vary according to the season, with peak-season rates applied June through August. APEX fares can run as high as $1,504 for flying on a weekend in summer from New York to as low as $850 during the week in winter from the West Coast.

The best strategy for securing the lowest airfare is to shop around. On a few airlines you can occasionally purchase a ticket at the very last minute that is lower in price (that is an APEX fare with all the restrictions except the advance purchase time limit), because if the flight is not fully booked, an airline will discount tickets to try to achieve full passenger capacity.

Discount Travel

There are also companies that provide deeply discounted tickets (some more than 50% less on economy fares and around 30% less on APEX) with no restrictions depending on availability. You can buy your ticket through them well in advance as well as at the last moment, if you're lucky. Among the firms that deal with travel to Japan are **Nippon Travel** (202/362-0039), **Japan Associates Travel** (202/939-8853), and **Japan Express Travel** (202/347-7730). Consolidators like **C. L. Thomson Express International** in San Francisco and **CNH International** and **Star Tours, Inc.,** in Los Angeles also sell discounted tickets, but only through travel agents.

Many airlines and tour operators also offer occasional promotional fares with tight restrictions as well as package tours, which might be the cheapest way to go because packages include hotels, transfers, some meals, and more.

A warning: Remember all fares, rules and regulations are subject to change. Be sure to contact your travel agent or the airlines for current information.

NARITA AIRPORT

Most likely you'll arrive at the New Tokyo International Airport in Narita. Once you've gone through Customs you'll exit through automatic doors into the arrival waiting lobby. The arrival lobby is divided into a south and a north wing, both of which have counters for hotel reservations, limousine bus service into Tokyo, and the Keisei Skyliner train to Ueno Station. If you've purchased a Japan Rail Pass, you can turn in your voucher at the arrival lobby at the JR Information and Ticket Office, which is open daily from 7 a.m. to 11 p.m.

The **Tourist Information Office** is located in the south wing and is open from 9 a.m. to 8 p.m. (closed on Sunday, holidays, and Saturday afternoon). You can pick up a map here and ask for directions to your hotel or inn.

If you need to change money, there is a **bureau de change** located just after you clear Customs and *before* you enter the arrival lobby. If you forget to change money here, there are also counters in the arrival lobby and a bank in the departure lobby up on the fourth floor.

Other facilities include a post office in the basement (open Monday through Friday from 9 a.m. to 5 p.m., on Saturday to 12:30 p.m., a post office on the fourth floor (departure floor) of the north wing (open daily from 9 a.m. to 8:30 p.m.), and a KDD (Kokusai Denshin Denwa) office on the fourth floor, where you can make an international call or send a telegram from 9 a.m. to 9 p.m.

Getting from Narita to Tokyo

Everyone grumbles about the Narita airport because it's so far away from Tokyo when compared to the airports of other capital cities. Obviously, jumping into a **taxi** and driving straight to your hotel is the easiest way to get to Tokyo, but it's also the most expensive—and may not even be the quickest if it's during rush hour. Expect to spend ¥22,000 ($176) or more for a taxi from the Narita airport for a ride that will take from one to two hours.

The most popular way to get from Narita to Tokyo is via the **Airport Limousine Bus.** Buses operate most frequently to the Tokyo City Air Terminal, and the trip takes about 70 minutes. Buses also go to Tokyo and Shinjuku stations and more than a dozen of Tokyo's major hotels, but service is less frequent. Check with the staff at the Airport Limousine Bus counter in the arrival lobby to inquire as to which bus is most convenient to your hotel. If you take a bus to the Tokyo City Air Terminal, there are plenty of taxis available that can deliver you to your final destination. Fares for the Limousine Bus range from ¥2,700 ($21.16) to ¥3,000 ($24), according to the distance.

There's another company that operates buses to more than 20 hotels in Tokyo, called **Airport Shuttle.** Fares for this service begin at ¥2,800 ($22.40), and the counter is in the arrival lobby.

Another way to reach Tokyo is the privately owned **Keisei Skyliner** train. It's the way I always get to and from the Narita airport, but keep in mind that you have to make several transfers—which may not be practical if you have lots of baggage. There are porters available, however, who charge ¥200 ($1.60) per bag. At any rate, there's a Keisei Skyliner counter in the north and south wings of the arrival lobby. The fare from the Narita airport to Ueno Station in Tokyo is ¥1,900 ($15.20) and includes the cost of the shuttle bus that takes you from the airport to Narita Airport Station. The bus stop is located just outside the arrival doors. The bus ride takes only five minutes and the ride on the Skyliner train to Ueno Station takes one hour. Trains depart approximately every 30 or 40 minutes between 7:52 a.m. and 10 p.m. At Ueno Station you can take either the subway or JR Yamanote Line to other parts of Tokyo (refer to "Orientation and Getting Around" in Chapter III). There are also plenty of taxis available.

If you've bought a voucher for a Japan Rail Pass (described more fully in the "Traveling Within Japan" section that follows), you can exchange it for the **train** pass right in the arrival lobby at the JR Information and Ticket Office, which is open from 7 a.m. to 11 p.m. Then you can use your pass to get to Tokyo via a shuttle bus from outside the arrival lobby to Narita Station (it takes 25 minutes) and from there by train to Tokyo Station. You can also go by shuttle bus to Narita Airport Station and from there take a train to Ueno Station. The route you choose should depend on which hotel you're staying in. Keep in mind, however, that these routes are not as convenient or fast as the modes of transportation listed above, and should be used only if you want to economize.

If you don't have a rail pass, the fare is ¥920 ($7.36) from Narita Airport Station to Ueno Station. The trip takes 75 minutes on the limited express and 90 minutes on the express. From Narita Station (in the city of Narita) to Tokyo Station the limited express costs ¥2,300 ($18.40) and takes 63 minutes; the rapid train costs ¥1,200 ($9.60) and takes approximately 75 minutes.

HANEDA AIRPORT

If you're connecting to a domestic flight, more than likely you'll need to transfer to Haneda Airport. The Airport Limousine Bus makes runs between Narita and Haneda airports. The fare is ¥2,900 ($23.20), and the trip takes an hour or more depending on the traffic. If perchance you're arriving at Haneda Airport, you can also take the Airport Limousine Bus to Shinjuku and Akasaka. The locals, however, are more likely to take the monorail from Haneda Airport to Hamamatsucho Station on the Yamanote Line, for which the fare is ¥300 ($2.40). The trip takes only 15 minutes, and if you have a validated rail pass you can use it here.

OSAKA AIRPORT

Osaka Airport is convenient to Osaka and Kyoto. Taxis to hotels in Osaka average about ¥4,500 ($36) and are the most convenient way to get into the city. There's also frequent bus service from the airport to Osaka Station and to Shin-Osaka, which is the terminus for the Shinkansen bullet train (more about that later).

The trip to Osaka Station takes about 30 minutes and costs ¥390 ($3.12), while the journey to Shin-Osaka takes 25 minutes and costs ¥300 ($2.40).

If you're going to Kyoto, there is frequent bus service from Osaka Airport directly to Kyoto Station and to major hotels. The trip takes from 60 to 90 minutes, depending on traffic and your destination, and fares average about ¥860 ($6.88).

---

2. Traveling Within Japan

BY TRAIN

The most convenient way to travel around Japan is by train. Whether you're being whisked through the countryside aboard the famous Shinkansen bullet train or are winding your way up a wooded mountainside in a two-car electric tram, trains in Japan are punctual, comfortable, dependable, and clean. And because train stations are usually located in the heart of the city next to the city bus terminal, arriving in a city by train is usually the most convenient way to begin your stay there. What's more, most train stations in Japan's major cities and resort areas have tourist offices that can help with directions to your hotel. The staff may not speak English, but they often have maps or brochures in English. Train stations also often have a counter where hotel reservations can be made free of charge. Most of Japan's trains are run by **Japan Railways (JR)**, which operates as many as 28,000 trains daily, including more than 500 Shinkansen bullet trains.

The **Shinkansen** is probably Japan's best-known train. With a front car that resembles a space rocket, the Shinkansen hurtles 140 miles per hour through the countryside on its own special tracks (new trains are being built now that will increase speeds up to 190 miles per hour).

There are three Shinkansen lines operating in Japan. The most widely used line for tourists is the **Tokaido-Sanyo Shinkansen,** which runs from Tokyo Station west to such cities as Nagoya, Kyoto, Osaka, Kobe, Himeji, Okayama, and Hiroshima before reaching its final destination of Hakata/Fukuoka, on the island of Kyushu. The **Tohoku Shinkansen** line runs from Ueno Station to Morioka in northern Japan, while the **Joetsu Shinkansen** connects Ueno with Niigata on the Japan Sea coast. There are two types of Shinkansen running along these tracks, one that stops only at the major cities and one that makes more stops and is therefore slightly slower. If your destination is a smaller city on the Shinkansen line, make sure the train you plan to take stops there. As a plus, telephone calls can be made to and from the bullet trains. To reach someone on a bullet train, you can call 107 from anywhere in Japan, provided you know the exact train; however, announcements are made only in Japanese.

In addition to the Shinkansen, there are also two long-distance trains that operate on regular tracks. The **limited express trains (Tokkyu)** are the fastest after the Shinkansen, while the **express trains (Kyuko)** are slightly slower and make more stops. To serve the everyday needs of Japan's commuting population, **local trains (Futsu)** stop at all stations and are the trains most widely used for side trips outside the major cities.

There are also some privately owned lines that operate from major cities to tourist destinations. No matter which train you ride, be sure to hang on to your ticket—you'll be required to give it up at the end of your trip as you exit through the gate.

As for finding out the various **train schedules,** the Tourist Information Center in Tokyo has a *Condensed Railway Timetable* giving details in English for the Shinkansen and some other major lines. If you plan to do a lot of traveling by train, however, I recommend that you purchase *JTB's Mini-Timetable* (*Speedo Jikokuhyo*) for ¥310 ($2.48); it is published monthly and available at bookstores or Japan Travel Bureau offices in big cities. It covers the schedules in both English and Japanese for all JR long-distance trains, including the Shinkansen, and for private trains, planes, ferries, and even express buses. It also has maps of Japan with various destinations served by trains written in both Japanese and English. I find this handy little guide invaluable during my trips through Japan.

Train Traveling Times and Distances

Distances in Japan can be deceiving, because the country is much longer than most people imagine. Its four main islands, measured from the north to the south, are roughly the same distance as the U.S. East Coast from Maine to northern Florida. Thank goodness for the Shinkansen bullet train.

The chart measures the distance and traveling time from Tokyo to principal Japanese cities. Since Tokyo is located approximately in the middle of Japan, you'll most likely change trains there when traveling from north to south and vice versa. Traveling times *do not* include the time needed for transferring and are calculated for the fastest trains available.

TRAIN RESERVATIONS

You can reserve a seat in advance for the Shinkansen, limited express, and express trains at any major JR station for a small fee. The larger stations have special reservation counters or offices that are easily recognizable by their green signs with "Reservation Tickets" written on them. They're open daily from 10 a.m. to 6 p.m. If you are at a JR station with no special reservation office, you can reserve your seat at one of the regular ticket windows. I recommend that you reserve your seats for your entire trip through Japan as soon as you know your itinerary, especially if you'll be traveling during peak times. However, all trains also have nonreserved cars that work on a first-come, first-served basis.

Japan Rail Pass

The Japan Rail Pass is without a doubt the most convenient and most economical way to travel throughout Japan by train. With the rail pass you don't have to hassle with buying individual tickets, and you can reserve all your seats on all JR trains for free. The rail pass entitles you to unlimited travel on all JR train lines, including the Shinkansen, and on JR buses and ferries.

The Japan Rail Pass is available only to foreigners visiting Japan as tourists and can be purchased only outside Japan. *You cannot buy a rail pass once you're in Japan.* You can purchase the pass from an authorized travel agent or from Japan Airlines. You'll be issued a voucher that you then exchange for the pass itself after you've arrived in Japan. This can be done at the JR Information and Ticket Office at the Narita airport or at any of the 12 JR Travel Service Centers in Japan, including Tokyo Station and JR stations in Osaka, Kyoto, Hiroshima, and Sapporo.

There are two types of Japan Rail Passes available—for ordinary coach class or for the first-class Green Car—and you can purchase passes good for one, two, or three weeks. Rates for the ordinary pass as of August 1989 are ¥27,800 ($222) for 7 days, ¥44,200 ($353) for 14 days, and ¥56,600 ($453) for 21 days. Rates for the Green Car are ¥37,000 ($296) for 7 days, ¥60,000 ($480) for 14 days, and ¥78,000 ($624) for 21 days. And how much can you save by purchasing a rail pass? Quite a bit if you plan to do even just a little traveling. If you were to buy a round-trip ticket on the Shinkansen from Tokyo to Kyoto, for example, it would cost you ¥25,940 ($207.52) which is almost as much as a week's ordinary rail pass. If you plan to see more than just Tokyo and Kyoto, it pays to use a rail pass.

JAL Room & Rail

If the idea of a rail pass appeals to you and you'd like to make life even simpler by paying for your hotels in advance, **Japan Airlines' Room & Rail package** may be the thing for you. Offered only to passengers of Japan Airlines, this do-it-yourself

FROM TOKYO TO PRINCIPAL CITIES

City	Distance in Miles	Traveling Time
Aomori*	458	4 hrs 43 min
Atami	65	52 min
Beppu*	762	7 hrs
Hakata	730	6 hrs
Hakodate	557	6 hrs 51 min
Hiroshima	554	4 hrs 37 min
Kamakura	32	56 min
Kanazawa*	386	4 hrs 20 min
Kumamoto*	803	7 hrs 15 min
Kyoto	318	2 hrs 39 min
Matsue*	571	6 hrs 25 min
Matsumoto	146	2 hrs 48 min
Matsuyama*	587	6 hrs 47 min
Miyazaki*	897	10 hrs 25 min
Nagasaki*	825	8 hrs 3 min
Nagoya	227	1 hr 49 min
Narita	42	1 hr 13 min
Niigata	207	1 hr 39 min
Nikko	93	1 hr 29 min
Okayama	454	3 hrs 51 min
Sapporo*	731	10 hrs 17 min
Shimoda	75	2 hrs 40 min
Shin-Kobe	366	3 hrs 12 min
Shin-Osaka	343	2 hrs 56 min
Takamatsu*	499	5 hrs
Takayama*	330	4 hrs 52 min
Toba*	289	3 hrs 59 min
Yokohama	18	27 min

* Destinations requiring a change of trains

package combines the Japan Rail Pass described above with hotel coupons good for more than 80 hotels in more than 50 cities in Japan. These hotel coupons are valid for one or two weeks. The coupons for seven nights cost approximately ¥46,000 ($368) per person for a twin room and ¥56,500 ($452) for a single. The 14-night coupons cost ¥92,000 ($736) per person for a twin room and ¥113,000 ($904) for a single.

You can combine the rail pass and hotel coupons in any combination you wish. For example, if you want to spend your time leisurely, you might want to purchase a one-week rail pass and combine it with two weeks of hotel coupons.

Hotel coupons can be purchased only in conjunction with the rail pass, and *the whole package must be purchased outside Japan* at least one week prior to your first night's stay in Japan. Contact your travel agent or JAL for more details.

BY AIR

Because it takes the better part of a day and night to get from Tokyo down to southern Kyushu or up to northern Hokkaido by train, you may find it more convenient to fly at least one stretch of your journey in Japan. You may, for example, take a leisurely two weeks to travel by train from Tokyo through Honshu and Kyushu, and then fly back to Tokyo from Kagoshima. I don't advise flying for shorter distances— say, from Tokyo to Osaka—because of the time spent getting to and from airports. By the way, departures on domestic flights from Tokyo leave from the much more conveniently located Haneda Airport, reached by monorail from Hamamatsucho Station on the Yamanote Line.

Two major domestic airlines are **Japan Airlines** and **All Nippon Airways (ANA),** with networks that stretch all the way from Okinawa to northern Hokkaido. ANA carries more than half of all domestic passengers in Japan and flies to 30 cities throughout the country, including Tokyo, Sapporo, Fukuoka, Hakodate, Takamatsu, Nagasaki, Kagoshima, and Osaka.

Although it's subject to change, the cost of flying from Tokyo to Sapporo in Hokkaido runs about ¥26,000 ($208) one way, while the flight from Tokyo to Kagoshima is about ¥32,000 ($256). It's cheaper, however, if you plan ahead and purchase your domestic flight in conjunction with your international flight to Japan. Contact your travel agent.

BY BUS

Buses often run where trains don't—and may be the only way to get to the more remote areas of Japan. Buses are used extensively, for example, in Hokkaido, and the only way to get to Shirakawa-go in the Japan Alps is by bus. Although the procedure may vary, there's generally a ticket machine by the entry door of the bus. Take a ticket, which is number-coded with a board displayed at the front of the bus. The board shows the various fares, which increase with the distance traveled. You pay your fare upon departure.

In addition to serving the remote areas of the country, buses also operate between major cities in Japan. There is, for example, a special bus that leaves Tokyo Station every night for Nagoya (¥6,200, or $49.60), Kyoto (¥8,030, or $64.24), and Osaka (¥8,450, or $67.60), arriving the next morning. Similarly, there's also a night bus from Osaka, Kyoto, and Nagoya to Tokyo. If you're on a budget, this is certainly the cheapest way to travel between Tokyo and Kyoto.

BY BOAT

Because Japan is an island nation, it has an extensive ferry network linking the string of islands. Although it takes longer to travel by ferry, it's also cheaper. You can, for example, take the ferry from Tokyo all the way to Hokkaido for ¥12,800 ($102.40). There are also many ferries plying the waters of the Seto Inland Sea. From Osaka you can take a ferry in late evening and arrive in Beppu on Kyushu the next morning for ¥6,200 ($49.60). Contact the Tourist Information Office for more details concerning ferries, prices, and schedules.

BY CAR
With the exception of perhaps the Izu Peninsula and Hokkaido, driving is not recommended as a means for touring Japan. For one thing, cars are driven British style, on the left side of the road; and for another, signs are often in Japanese only. (The government is slowly replacing Japanese signs with bilingual Japanese/ English ones on major highways, with expected completion sometime in 1990.) In cities, streets are often hardly wide enough for a rickshaw, let alone a car. Many roads do not have sidewalks, so you have to dodge people, streetlamps, and telephone poles. But that's not all—it's not even economical to drive in Japan. Not only does gas cost $3.50 a gallon, but all of Japan's expressways charge high tolls. The one-way toll from Tokyo to Kyoto, for example, is almost the same as the price of a ticket to Kyoto on the Shinkansen. But whereas the Shinkansen takes only three hours to get to Kyoto, driving takes about eight. So unless there are four of you to split the costs and you are not limited by time, it doesn't make sense to drive.

Car-rental rates vary, but the average cost for 24 hours with unlimited mileage (but not including gasoline) ranges from ¥8,000 ($64) for a subcompact to ¥17,000 ($136) for a standard-size car. Both **Hertz** and **Avis** can accept reservations for their affiliated car-rental companies in Japan.

Note: If you intend to drive in Japan, you'll need either an international or a Japanese driving license.

---

3. Tips for the Traveler

PLANNING YOUR ITINERARY
If you want to see everything Honshu, Hokkaido, Kyushu, and Shikoku have to offer, plan on spending at least a year traveling about. Barring that, it's obvious you'll have to be selective in planning your itinerary. Decide beforehand what your priorities are.

If you're interested in feudal castles, you'll find them in Osaka, Nagoya, Matsue, Matsumoto, Himeji, Kumamoto, Okayama, Hiroshima, and Matsuyama. Japan's most famous gardens are Kenrokuen Garden in Kanazawa, Korakuen Garden in Okayama, and Kairakuen in Mito. Other beautiful gardens are Ritsurin in Takamatsu on the island of Shikoku, and Suizenji in Kumamoto and Iso Garden in Kagoshima, both on the island of Kyushu. Japan's most famous rock garden is probably the one at Ryoanji Temple in Kyoto.

If you're a camera buff, my own personal list of picturesque towns and villages in Japan includes Kyoto, Kamakura, Takayama, Shirakawa-go, Tsumago, Kurashiki, Mount Koya, and the tiny village of Chiran, south of Kagoshima. As for towns with historical significance, nothing can beat Kyoto, Nara, or Kamakura, three ancient capitals of Japan. These three towns are also where you'll find a majority of the country's temples and shrines. Other important Shinto shrines in Japan include the Meiji Shrine in Tokyo, Ise Jingu Shrines located in Ise-Shima National Park, and Itsukushima Shrine on Miyajima Island. Mount Koya is the place to head if you're interested in spending the night in a genuine Buddhist temple.

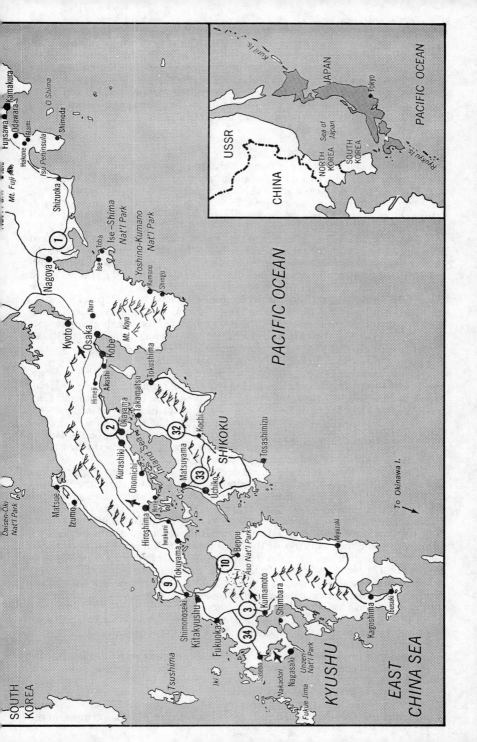

And last but not least, Japan is blessed with a number of hot-spring spas, from its southern to northern tips. In fact, tourism in Japan began when bathing enthusiasts started traveling to hot springs simply for the joys of the bath. There are open-air spas in forests, sand baths, gigantic public baths, mud baths, sulfur baths, and just plain hot tubs. The closest hot springs to Tokyo are in Hakone and Izu Peninsula. Other famous hot springs include Matsuyama's Dogo Spa on Shikoku island; Beppu, Ibusuki, and Unzen on Kyushu; and Noboribetsu, Toyako Spa, Sounkyo, and Akanko Onsen in Hokkaido.

One- and Two-Week Itineraries

If you have only one week in Japan—what can I say, I feel sorry for you. I suppose if I were faced with such a limited amount of time, I would spend it this way:

Day 1: Most likely you'll arrive at Narita airport, from which it's about a two-hour trip to your hotel in Tokyo. Spend the first day recuperating from your flight, settling in, and getting a feel for the city. Top off the day with a meal in a traditional restaurant.

Day 2: Because of the difference in time zones, most visitors from the Western Hemisphere find themselves wide awake in the wee hours of the morning. That's the perfect time to get up and head for Tsukiji Fish Market, the largest wholesale fish market in Japan. After a breakfast of fresh sushi at the market, take the Hibiya Line to Ueno, where you'll find the Tokyo National Museum. From Ueno, hop on the Ginza Line for Asakusa and its famous Nakamise Dori lane, with shops selling traditional products and the popular Sensoji Temple (also known as the Asakusa Kannon Temple). If you have time, take a stroll down Ginza's fashionable shopping district or head for Harajuku for its inexpensive clothing boutiques and Oriental Bazaar, one of the best places to shop for Japanese souvenirs. Spend the evening in Shinjuku, Roppongi, or another one of Tokyo's famous nightlife areas.

Day 3: Take the three-hour Shinkansen bullet train to Kyoto early in the morning. Spend the afternoon on a self-guided walk from Kiyomizu Temple to Heian Shrine and the Silver Pavilion, followed by shopping at the Kyoto Handicraft Center. Spend the night in one of Kyoto's many traditional Japanese-style inns.

Day 4: Take in Nijo Castle, Ryoanji Temple, the Golden Pavilion, and a few other sights of your choosing. If you want to see more temples in one of Japan's ancient capitals, head for Nara, where you'll want to spend at least two to three hours to see the Great Buddha, Nara Park, and Kasuga Shrine.

Day 5: From Kyoto there are several destinations good for a one-night trip, but you should leave Kyoto very early in the morning. If you want to spend the night in a Buddhist temple atop Japan's most sacred mountain, take the Kintetsu Railways private line (there are only a couple of departures daily, so plan ahead) to Kintetsu Namba Station, in Osaka, transferring there to the Nankai Koya Line for the two-hour trip to Mount Koya. If you'd rather spend the night in a quaint, picturesque town with some museums, board the Shinkansen for Kurashiki—less than two hours away, although along the way it's worth your while to make a two-hour stop-over in Himeji, where you'll find Himeji Castle, considered by many to be the most beautiful feudal castle in Japan. And finally, if all you want to do is relax at a hot-spring resort, take the Shinkansen back toward Tokyo to Odawara, where you should transfer to a local train bound for Hakone.

Day 6: Spend the day sightseeing, departing by late afternoon for Tokyo. If your plane leaves early the next morning, you may wish to spend the night at Narita.

Day 7: Departure.

If you have two weeks, I would expand the above schedule as follows:

Day 1: Arrival at Narita airport, settling into your hotel and becoming acclimated to Tokyo.

Day 2: Same as in the one-week itinerary.

Day 3: If you'd like to spend another day in Tokyo, refer to the Tokyo chapter. If you'd rather make an excursion to one of the sites outside Tokyo, foremost on the list are day trips to either Kamakura, with its many temples, or Nikko, which is famous for the colorful mausoleum of Shogun Ieyasu Tokugawa.

Day 4: Tokyo to Takayama. Early in the morning, take the Shinkansen to Nagoya (about two hours), from which it's a three-hour train ride to Takayama, in the Japan Alps. Take time to explore the picturesque, narrow streets of this old castle town.

Day 5: Takayama to Shirakawa-go. Before departing Takayama, be sure to visit the morning market by the river. Take the 2½-hour bus ride along a winding mountain road to Shirakawa-go, a tiny village of rice paddies and thatched farmhouses. Spend the night in one of these farmhouses.

Day 6: Shirakawa-go to Kyoto. Since Shirakawa-go is rather remote, it takes the better part of a day to reach Kyoto. Luckily, the scenery is magnificent. From Shirakawa-go you can take a bus either back to Takayama or to Nagoya. In any case, you must afterward transfer to a train for the rest of the journey to Kyoto.

Days 7 and 8: Same as those spent in Kyoto in the one-week itinerary above.

Day 9: Kyoto to Mount Koya. Early in the morning, set out for Nara, visiting the Great Buddha, Nara Park, and Kasuga Shrine. From Nara you can take the Kintetsu Railways private line (departing from Nara Kintetsu Station) to Kintetsu Namba Station in Osaka, transferring there to the Nankai Koya Line bound for Mount Koya. If you have a rail pass, you can take JR trains to Hashimoto, there transferring to the private Nankai Koya Line. Spend the night on Mount Koya, one of Japan's most sacred Buddhist retreats, in a Buddhist temple.

Day 10: Mount Koya to Kurashiki. After paying your respects at Okunoin, the burial grounds of Kobo Daishi, return to Osaka and transfer to the Shinkansen bullet train at Shin-Osaka Station or a JR train at Osaka Station bound for Kurashiki. It's worth your while to make a two-hour stopover in Himeji along the way to see the beautiful Himeji Castle. Spend the night in one of Kurashiki's varied accommodations and take an evening stroll along the canal.

Day 11: Take in Kurashiki's sights, including its many museums. Leave for Hiroshima late in the day (about an hour away by Shinkansen).

Day 12: Hiroshima to Beppu. Spend the morning at Peace Memorial Park, with its museum and statues erected in memory of those who lost their lives when an atomic bomb was dropped over Hiroshima on August 6, 1945. In the afternoon, take an excursion to the tiny island of Miyajima, with its famous Itsukushima Shrine. Take the overnight ferry from Hiroshima to Beppu.

Day 13: Spend a relaxing day in the hot-spring resort of Beppu, where you can visit the huge baths of Suginoi Palace or take a sand bath at Takegawara Bathhouse. Visit the Hells, boiling ponds created by volcanic activity.

Day 14: Beppu to Tokyo. Take an early-morning flight from nearby Oita (¥27,000, or $216) airport to Haneda Airport in Tokyo, transferring to Narita Airport for the flight home.

Needless to say, this is something of a whirlwind trip, but it allows you to take in some of the best that Honshu island has to offer. If you want to get off the beaten track or have more time, refer to the chapters on Shikoku, Kyushu, and northern Japan for more ideas in planning your itinerary.

THE LANGUAGE BARRIER

Without a doubt the hardest part of traveling in Japan is the language barrier. Suddenly you find yourself transported to a crowded land of 120 million people where you can neither speak nor read the language. To make matters worse, few Japanese speak English, and outside the major cities the signs are usually only in Japanese. Menus, signs at train stations, and shop names are often only in Japanese.

However, millions of foreign visitors before you who didn't speak a word of Japanese have traveled throughout Japan on their own with great success. In fact, I've talked to foreign tourists who told me they thought it was actually quite easy getting around in Japan. Much of the anxiety travelers have in other countries is eliminated in Japan because the country is so safe and the people are so kind and helpful to foreigners. In addition, the Japan National Tourist Organization (JNTO) does a super job of publishing brochures, leaflets, and maps on various aspects of Japan.

A Note on Japanese Characters

Many hotels, restaurants, and other establishments in Japan do not have signs showing their names in English letters. Appendix II lists the Japanese symbols for all such places appearing in this guide. Each establishment name in Japanese symbols is numbered, and the same number appears in ovals in the text following the boldfaced establishment name. For example, in the text Osaka's **Hotel Hokke Club** ⑯⑭ is number 164 in the Japanese symbol list in Appendix II.

If you need to ask directions of a stranger in Japan, your best bet is to ask younger people. They have all studied English in school and are most likely to be able to help you. Japanese businessmen also often know some English. And as strange as it sounds, if you're having problems communicating with someone, write it down so that he or she can read it. The emphasis in schools tends to be written rather than oral, with the result that Japanese who can't understand a word you say may know all the subtleties of syntax and English grammar. If you still have problems communicating, you can always call the Travel-Phone, a toll-free nationwide helpline set up by JNTO to help foreigners in distress or in need of information. (Information on the Travel-Phone is given in the following section, "The ABCs of Japan.")

If you're heading out for a particular restaurant, shop, or sight, it helps to have your destination written out in Japanese. Have someone at your hotel do that for you. If you get lost along the way, look for a police box. Called *koban*, these are spread throughout neighborhoods virtually everywhere in Japan. They have maps of the district and can pinpoint exactly where you want to go if you have the address with you. Remember, too, that train stations in major cities and tourist resort areas have tourist information offices (*kanko annaijo*), which can help you with everything from directions to hotel reservations. The staff may not speak any English, but I don't think you'll have trouble communicating your needs.

For specific words and phrases in Japanese, refer to Appendix I at the back of this book. In addition, *The Tourist's Handbook,* distributed free by JNTO, lists phrases in both English and Japanese for situations that may arise, from eating at a restaurant to staying in a Japanese inn.

WHAT TO BRING

A friend and I once spent the better part of an hour trying to list items travelers may need that they wouldn't be able to find in Japan. We finally gave up. With the exception of perhaps some medicines, we decided that virtually everything is available in Japan—the problem lies in choosing the brand. Even bleach to make your hair blond is available in this nation of black-haired people. It doesn't make sense, therefore, to pack king-size supplies of toothpaste, shampoo, and other daily necessities. If you run out of something, you'll have no problem finding it in Japan.

One item you should absolutely bring with you is a pair of good walking shoes. Shoe sizes in Japan are much smaller than in the West and chances are you won't be able to find Japanese shoes that fit. Keep in mind, too, that because you have to remove your shoes to enter Japanese homes, inns, shrines, and temples, you should bring a pair that's easy to slip on and off. And since you may be walking around in stockinged feet, save yourself embarrassment by packing socks and hose without holes.

As for traveling around Japan, you'll want to have a folding umbrella. It's also good to carry a supply of pocket tissues, since most public rest rooms don't have toilet paper. You can pick up pocket tissues at newspaper stands near and in train stations. In the summer when the weather is hot and extremely humid, you'll see women walking around with wet cotton handkerchiefs that they use to wipe their faces. Try it; it helps keep you cooler.

Although most hotels and Japanese-style inns provide guests with towels, soap, washcloths, toothbrushes and toothpaste, and a cotton kimono called a *yukata,* some of the budget-priced inns do not. If you're traveling on a budget, therefore, carry these items with you. Many hotels and inns also provide a thermos of hot water or a water heater as well as some tea bags. If you're a coffee addict, you can save money by buying instant coffee and drinking your morning cup in your hotel room.

And at the risk of sounding perverse, I also recommend traveling with your own portable cassette player and headphones. Buy them once you get to Japan— they're inexpensive, and they may help preserve your sanity. Many of the buses traveling scenic routes (and tourist boats as well) run continuous commentaries in Japanese at a pitch so high it drives me crazy. I'd much rather look at the scenery to the accompaniment of my own choice of noise. And if you're staying in budget accommodations, chances are there won't be a radio, but only a TV with programs in Japanese. You can buy all kinds of attachments for portable cassette players, including tiny speakers and even a cord with outlets for two headphones so that both you and your companion can listen to the music.

Although it might seem superfluous to say this, pack lightly. Struggling through crowded train stations with big bags is no fun, and stations often consist of multitudes of stairways and overhead and underground passageways. In addition, trains in Japan do not have large overhead racks.

While traveling, you'll probably pick up souvenirs, gifts, and other items. I deal with this problem of accumulation by mailing boxes home to myself every two weeks or so while I'm on the road. All international post offices in Japan sell three sizes of cardboard boxes that come with everything you need for mailing packages abroad, which makes sending packages a snap. I simply show up with my bag, empty it of all unneeded items, buy a box, and leave the post office feeling pounds lighter. And, believe me, traveling with a lighter bag is almost like getting a new lease on life.

BAGGAGE TRANSFER SERVICES

If you find yourself encumbered with luggage too heavy to handle, or you simply prefer to travel without bothering with bags, consider sending your luggage on ahead to your next destination through the services of a baggage transfer company. For assistance and information, ask your hotel porter or stop by one of numerous outlets throughout major cities. Among the companies providing this service are the **Kuroneko** company and the **Perikan-bin** company. The cost of transferring a bag from Tokyo to Kyoto is ¥1,240 ($9.92) for luggage weighing 5 to 10 kilos (11 to 22 pounds) and ¥1,450 ($11.60) for bags weighing 10 to 20 kilos (22 to 44 pounds).

POSTCARDS

Unless you have a photographic memory and can remember places, names, and how to spell them, chances are all those snapshots of temples, shrines, and gardens will look distressingly alike once you get your film developed. My mother's solution: buy postcards of every place you visit. That way you can match snapshots with postcards, many of which may have such useful information as name, location, and correct spelling of the object in question. And if your pictures don't turn out, well, you always have those postcards.

DATES TO AVOID

The Japanese have a passion for travel, and generally they all travel at the same time. Trains and hotels are jam-packed at these times. Refer to the section in Chapter II on festivals and annual events for dates you should avoid. The worst times of year are the New Year's period, from December 28 to January 4; the so-called Golden Week, from April 29 to May 5; and the Obon Festival time, in mid-August—avoid traveling at all costs on these dates.

CUTTING EXPENSES

During your first few days in Japan—particularly if you're in Tokyo—money will seem to flow out of your pockets like water. In fact, money has a tendency to disappear so quickly that many people become convinced they must have *lost* some of it somehow. At this point almost everyone panics (I've seen it happen again and again), but then slowly comes the realization that values are different here and that all it takes is a bit of readjustment in thinking and habits. Coffee, for example, is something of a luxury, and some Japanese are astonished at the thought of drinking four or five cups a day. By following the advice here, you'll be able to cut down on needless expenses, saving your money for those splurges that are really worth it.

If you're on a budget, avoid eating breakfast at your hotel. Coffeeshops offer what is called "morning service" until about 10 a.m., which generally consists of a cup of coffee, a small salad, a boiled egg, and toast for about ¥400 ($3.20). That's a real bargain when you consider the fact that just one cup of coffee usually costs ¥300 ($2.40) to ¥500 ($4). If you're addicted to coffee in the morning, you can save money by purchasing instant coffee and drinking it in your hotel room. Many hotels and inns in Japan provide a thermos of hot water or a water heater. Since jars of instant coffee tend to be heavy and bulky, you might want to buy individual packets of coffee, which come complete with powdered cream and sugar and are available at all large Japanese grocery stores. Called "coffee sticks," popular brands are Astoria and UCC.

Eat your biggest meal at lunch. Many restaurants offer a daily set lunch, called a *teishoku*, at a fraction of what their set dinners might be. Usually ranging in price from ¥700 ($5.60) to ¥1,500 ($12), they're generally available from 11 or 11:30 a.m. to 2 p.m. A Japanese teishoku will often include the main course (such as tempura, grilled fish, or the specialty of the house), soup, pickled vegetables, rice, and tea, while the set menu in a Western-style restaurant usually consists of an entrée, salad, bread, and coffee. Places to look for inexpensive restaurants include department stores (often one whole floor will be devoted to various kinds of restaurants), underground shopping arcades, around train and subway stations, and in nightlife districts. Some of the cheapest establishments for a night out on the town are the countless *yakitori-ya* across the nation, which are drinking establishments that also sell skewered meats and vegetables.

And if you really want to save money, you can avoid restaurants altogether. Japan is one of the most accomplished countries in the world when it comes to the preparation, packaging, and selling of pre-prepared foods. The *obento*, or box lunch, is a complete meal usually costing between ¥600 ($4.80) and ¥1,000 ($8) and commonly sold on express trains, at train stations, and in tiny neighborhood shops throughout Japan. In the basements of department stores you'll find counter after counter of pre-prepared foods, including grilled meats, salads, sushi, and desserts. More information on inexpensive meals is given in the food section in Chapter II.

Another way to cut costs is to cut short your time spent in Tokyo. Accommodations in Kyushu, for example, are much more reasonably priced than they are in the capital. Your best bet is to stay in a *minshuku,* a private home that offers rooms— usually Japanese style—to tourists. These average ¥5,000 ($40) to ¥6,000 ($48) per person and include both breakfast and dinner. And as for your travels in Japan, avoid taxis when possible and purchase a Japan Rail Pass if you plan on covering long distances.

ORGANIZED CITY TOURS

With the exception of Tokyo and Kyoto, few city tours are conducted in English. This book is designed for the individual traveler who prefers sightseeing on his or her own, but if you're pressed for time or don't want to deal with public transportation to sights that may be spread throughout a city, consider joining a Japanese tour. It's certainly the easiest way to get to the various attractions, and perhaps there will even be a Japanese along who won't mind providing some translations.

TOURIST BROCHURES

The Tourist Information Centers in Tokyo and Kyoto have a number of leaflets available on destinations throughout Japan, along with information on train, bus, and ferry schedules. Unfortunately, such leaflets are almost never available at the destination itself, so you must pick them up at the T.I.C. *before* leaving Tokyo or Kyoto. Below is a partial list of leaflets available:

Sapporo and Vicinity
Southern Hokkaido
Morioka and Rikuchu Kaigan
(Coast) National Park
Sendai and Matsushima
Nikko
Narita
Hakone and Kamakura
Mt. Fuji and Fuji Lakes
Izu Peninsula
Matsumoto and Kamikochi
Kanazawa and the Noto
Peninsula
Takayama and Vicinity
The Inland Sea and Shikoku

Nagoya and Vicinity
Ise-Shima
Tokyo, Walking Tour Courses
Kyoto, Walking Tour Courses
Nara, Walking Tour Courses
Okayama and Kurashiki
Matsue and Izumo-Taisha
Hiroshima and Miyajima
Fukuoka
Beppu and Vicinity
Nagasaki and Unzen
Kumamoto and Mt. Aso
Miyazaki and Vicinity
Kobe, Himeji, and
Takarazuka

4. The ABCs of Japan

Arriving in Japan for the first time can be rather overwhelming, primarily because of the language barrier. Just for starters: assuming that you don't know any Japanese, you won't be able to read any of the signs, which means that in the beginning you won't be able to tell the difference between even a post office and a bank, much less read the hours and days of the week they're open. In addition, few Japanese speak fluent English; therefore, if you make what's intended to be a quick and casual telephone inquiry, it's likely to turn into moments of pure frustration. In other words, finding information in Japan is sometimes a true test of ingenuity. To make your stay in Japan as problem-free as possible, this section is designed to answer some questions you might have before and during your trip with regard to such items as visa requirements, whether you should tip, business hours, and electric voltage of the country. For information pertaining to a particular city, be sure to check under the individual chapter headings. "The ABCs of Tokyo," for example, tells you where the main post office is, the address of the American Express office, and where in Tokyo you can buy books in English.

Remember also that much information can be gleaned from the staff of your hotel. Many of the larger first-class hotels even have guest relations officers who are there to answer any questions tourists may have. Finally, if you don't know where else to turn, the **Japan National Tourist Organization** has set up a tourist telephone helpline with English-speaking staff members who can help you with everyday problems you may encounter. I've used this telephone service for such diverse problems as how to find the Tokyo office of the Hong Kong Tourist Association, where to go for a visa extension, and the date and the time of the next sumo match. You can call them if you're bewilderingly lost, are having communication problems with a store clerk or hotelier, or simply want information about sightseeing. Look under the heading "Travel-Phone" (below).

Currency Note
The prices quoted in this book were figured at ¥125 = US$1. However, due to fluctuations in the exchange rate of the yen (it was ¥146 to the dollar at press time), the U.S. dollar equivalents given might vary during the lifetime of this edition. Be sure to check current exchange rates when planning your trip.

BANKS AND EXCHANGES: Banks are open Monday through Friday from 9 a.m. to 3 p.m.. They're closed on Saturday and Sunday. If you need to exchange money outside these hours, inquire at one of the larger first-class hotels—some of them will cash traveler's checks or exchange money even if you're not their guest. If you're arriving at the Narita airport outside Tokyo, you can exchange money there from 9 a.m. until the arrival of the last flight.

BUSINESS HOURS: Government offices and private companies are generally open Monday through Friday from about 9 a.m. to 5 p.m. In reality, however, Japanese businessmen in the private sector tend to work long hours and it's not unusual to find someone in the office as late as 7, 8, or even 10 p.m. To be on the safe side, however, it's best to conduct business before 5 p.m.

CALENDAR YEARS: The Japanese have their own system for counting years based on an emperor's reign. The Meiji period, for example, ran from 1868–1912, which translates in the Japanese calendar to Meiji 1–44. Thus Meiji 10 refers to the tenth year of Emperor Meiji's reign, or 1878. Subsequent periods are Taisaho (1912–26), Showa (1926–89) and Heisei, which began in January 1989, at the beginning of Emperor Akihito's reign.

CIGARETTES: A wide variety of both domestic and imported brands are readily available throughout Japan. There are even outdoor vending machines on what seems to be every major city street in Japan. The cost for Japanese brands, of which Mild Seven is among the most popular, is about ¥220 ($1.76) per pack, while imported brands, such as Marlboro, cost about ¥240 ($1.92).

Unfortunately for nonsmokers, Japan has never had much of an antismoking campaign. Few restaurants, therefore, have nonsmoking sections and only a few enlightened hotels have designated nonsmoking floors. If you want to sit in the nonsmoking car of the Shinkansen bullet train, ask for the *kinensha*.

CLIMATE: Most of Japan's islands lie in a temperate seasonal wind zone similar to the East Coast of the United States, which means that there are four distinct seasons. **Summer,** which begins in June, is heralded by the rainy season, which lasts from about mid-June to mid-July. Although it doesn't rain every day, it does rain a lot and umbrellas are imperative. As you walk through all those puddles, remember that this is when Japan's farmers are out planting their rice seedlings. After the rains stop it turns very hot (in the 80s) and uncomfortably humid throughout the country, with the exception of the northern island of Hokkaido, such mountaintop resorts as Hakone, and the Japan Alps.

The end of August and September is typhoon season, though most storms stay out at sea and generally vent their fury on land only in thunderstorms. **Autumn,** which lasts until about November, is one of the best times to travel in Japan. The days are pleasant and slightly cool, with the changing reds and scarlets of leaves giving brilliant contrast to deep-blue skies. A photographer I know says that autumn is the best season for landscape photography in Japan.

Lasting from December to March, **winter** is marked by snow in much of Japan, especially in the mountain ranges, where the skiing is superb. The climate then is generally dry, and on the Pacific coast the skies are often blue. Tokyo, where the mean temperature is about 40°F, doesn't get much snow.

Spring is brought in with a magnificent fanfare of plum and cherry blossoms in March and April, an exquisite time when all Japan is set ablaze in whites and pinks. The cherry blossom season starts in southern Kyushu toward the end of March and travels slowly northward until it reaches northern Japan in about mid-April. The blossoms themselves last only a few days, symbolizing to the Japanese the fragile nature of beauty and life itself.

Remember that because Japan's four main islands stretch from north to south at about the same latitudes as Boston and Atlanta, you can travel in Japan virtually any time of the year. Winters in southern Kyushu are mild and pleasant, while summers in Hokkaido in the north are cool. In addition, there is no rainy season in Hokkaido.

CLOTHING SIZES: Talking in stereotypes, the Japanese are generally of slighter build than most Westerners, with sizes to match. If you're a basketball player, of large build, or simply have big feet, you're going to be tormented by all the wonderful, well-made, and often bargain-priced merchandise you can't fit into. Be sure to pack accordingly.

CREDIT CARDS AND CHECKS: Major hotels, tourist shops, and well-known restaurants generally accept such credit cards as American Express, MasterCard, or VISA. The majority of Japan's smaller shops, however, do not. Traveler's checks can be exchanged for yen at banks and generally fetch a better exchange rate than cash. Personal checks, however, are virtually useless in Japan. Even if you have an account at a Japanese bank, it costs about $20 and takes a couple of weeks to process a personal check. Most Japanese pay with cash—and because the country has such a low crime rate, you can feel safe walking around with lots of money. When I worked as editor of a travel magazine in Tokyo, I was paid in cash; I often left the office for a night on the town with a whole month's salary in my purse and never once was I afraid I would be mugged, and I certainly wasn't the only one. Because the Japanese feel so safe in their own society and carry lots of cash with them, sadly enough they're often easy targets when they travel abroad. The only time you should be alert to possible pickpockets is when you're riding a crowded subway during rush hour.

CURRENCY: The currency in Japan is called the **yen,** symbolized by ¥. Coins come in ¥1, ¥5, ¥10, ¥50, ¥100, and ¥500. Bills come in ¥1,000, ¥5,000, and ¥10,000 denominations. Although the conversion rate varies daily, the prices in this book are based on ¥125 to $1. In your own rough calculations, therefore, you can generally approximate what things cost by figuring roughly $8 to every ¥1,000. If something costs ¥5,000, for example, you know it's around $40.

CUSTOMS: You can bring duty-free into Japan up to 400 non-Japanese cigarettes or 500 grams of tobacco or 100 cigars; three bottles (760 cc each) of alcoholic beverages; and two ounces of perfume. In addition to the items above, you can also bring in gifts and souvenirs whose total market value is less than ¥200,000 ($1,600).

A word of caution: Make sure you do not take any pornographic material with you; American magazines such as *Playboy, Penthouse,* and others are not allowed into Japan because it's prohibited to show pubic hair. The Japanese equivalents of these magazines are either much more modest or have the offensive parts blacked out. As for drugs, don't even think about it. A number of musicians, including Paul McCartney, have been busted at the Narita airport and are prohibited from returning to Japan. Penalties for offenders are severe and strict.

Upon returning to the United States, you're allowed to bring back free of duty $400 worth of goods purchased abroad. Beyond that, the next $1,000 worth of goods is assessed at 10% duty. If you're shipping purchases home by mail, you're allowed to send up to $50 per package duty-free.

READER'S CUSTOMS SUGGESTION: "I would highly recommend that fellow tourists keep a traveler's diary, especially regarding their purchases. When handed the customs slip en route to Honolulu, it was hard to remember all the things I bought and the dollar value of each. Travelers should keep all their papers—passport, customs slip, and receipts together, and if possible, all the purchases in one bag. It would help for a smoother exit from customs" (Sharon Nakata, Los Angeles, Calif.).

DOCUMENTS FOR ENTRY: Americans traveling to Japan as tourists need only valid passports to gain entry to the country and are allowed to stay up to three months. Although Americans once had to obtain visas for entry to Japan, visa requirements for American tourists have been waived in an experimental trial period that extends to the end of 1991. Whether visa requirements will then be abolished altogether or reinstated had not been announced at press time, so be sure to contact the Japanese embassy or tourist office if you plan on being in Japan beyond 1991.

Note that only American *tourists* do not need visas. No extensions of stays longer than three months are granted. Note also that American tourists cannot work in Japan. If you are coming to Japan to work or study, and plan on being in Japan longer than three months, you will need a visa; contact the Japanese embassy or consulate nearest you.

Australians must possess a passport and a three-month visa for entry to Japan and can apply for extensions for longer stays. Canadians do not need visas for stays up to 90 days, while citizens of the United Kingdom can stay up to 180 days without a visa.

If you qualify for an extension of stay in Japan (for example, you're on a working visa or are a Canadian on a tourist visa), you can apply for extensions at the nearest immigration bureau in Japan. In Tokyo the place to go is the **Tokyo Regional Immigration Bureau,** 1-3-1 Otemachi, Chiyoda-ku (tel. 03/213-8111), near the Otemachi subway station. Hours are 9 a.m. to 5 p.m. (closed from noon to 1 p.m.

for lunch) on weekdays and 9 a.m. to noon on Saturday. After you've extended your visa you must also apply for an alien registration card, which all foreigners must carry if they stay in Japan longer than three months. Apply at the ward office closest to your hotel. The registration card is free but you'll need two passport-size photos.

If you intend to drive in Japan, you'll need either an international or, if you stay longer than one year, a Japanese driver's license.

DRINKING WATER: The water is safe to drink anywhere in Japan, though some people claim it's too highly chlorinated. Bottled water is also readily available.

ELECTRICAL APPLIANCES: The electrical current throughout Japan is 100 volts A.C., but there are two different cycles in use. In Tokyo and to the northeast it's 50 cycles, while in Nagoya, Kyoto, Osaka, and all points to the southwest it's 60. Leading hotels in Tokyo often have two outlets, for 110 and 220 volts; many of them also have hairdryers that you can use for free. Actually, you can use many American appliances such as radios or hairdryers in Japan because the American current of 110 volts and 60 cycles is close enough that the only difference is that they'll run a little slower than back in the States. For sensitive equipment, either have it adjusted or see if it can run on batteries. The plugs are the same as in the U.S.

EMBASSIES: Embassies for most countries are located in Tokyo, and are generally open Monday through Friday from 8:30 or 9 a.m. to about 5 or 5:30 p.m. Most of them close for an hour or so for lunch, and the visa or passport sections are open only at certain times during the day. It's best to call in advance. The **American Embassy and Consulate** is located at 1-10-5 Akasaka, Minato-ku (tel. 03/224-5000), close to Toranomon subway station. The **Canadian Embassy** is at 7-3-38 Akasaka, Minato-ku (tel. 03/408-2101), near Aoyama-Itchome subway station. The **British Embassy and Consulate,** 1 Ichibancho, Chiyoda-ku (tel. 03/265-5511), is close to Ichigaya, Kojimachi, and Hanzomon stations. The **Australian Embassy,** at 2-1-14 Mita, Minato-ku (tel. 03/435-0971), has been undergoing renovation and is scheduled to reopen in June 1990. The telephone number above is the temporary number, but you can find out the new number by dialing the old and listening to the message.

EMERGENCIES: The national emergency numbers are 110 for **police** and 119 for both **ambulances** and **fire** reports. Be sure to speak slowly and precisely.

FILM AND CAMERAS: Probably no one is surprised to hear that Japan is one of the best countries to be in if you're nuts about photographic equipment, though prices are not cheap. Check the Tokyo shopping section in Chapter IV to find out where to shop. As for film, you won't have trouble finding Kodak or the Japanese brand Fuji in major cities for most types of film. Outside the big cities, however, and especially around tourist attractions, it's sometimes difficult to find anything other than Fuji film for color prints. If you prefer taking slides, be sure to stock up before setting out for more remote areas. You'll probably want to wait until you return to Tokyo or home to process Kodak film. Shops outside Tokyo often send Kodak film to the capital city for developing, which can take as long as a week.

GAS: Gas stations are found readily along Japan's major highways. As of this writing, the average cost for regular gasoline is about $3.50 per gallon.

HIKING: Day hiking and backpacking are popular summer recreation sports in Japan, particularly in the Japan Alps and in Hokkaido, where there are cabins in which hikers can stay overnight. Another popular trek is up to the summit of Mount Fuji, covered later in this book. Check with the Tourist Information Center about details for different parts of the country.

HITCHHIKING: Hitchhiking is not common in Japan; in fact, foreigners who have hitchhiked in Japan tell me that some drivers stop simply because they're curious as to what the foreigners could possibly want. But even though hitchhiking is uncommon, Japan is probably one of the safest and easiest countries in the world for hitchhiking. Stories abound of how drivers have gone hours out of their way to deposit passengers at their destination.

HOLIDAYS: National holidays are January 1 (New Year's Day); January 15 (Adults' Day); February 11 (National Foundation Day); March 20 or 21 (Vernal Equinox Day); April 29 (Greenery Day); May 3 (Constitution Memorial Day); May 5 (Children's Day); September 15 (Respect-for-the-Aged Day); September 23 or 24 (Autumn Equinox Day); October 10 (Health and Sports Day); November 3 (Culture Day); November 23 (Labor Thanksgiving Day); December 23 (Emperor's Birthday). When a national holiday falls on a Sunday, the following Monday becomes a holiday.

Although government offices and some businesses will be closed on public holidays, restaurants and most stores remain open. The exception is during the New Year's celebration from January 1 to 3, when almost all restaurants, public and private offices, and stores close up shop; during that time you'll have to dine in hotels. Keep in mind that the New Year's season is peak travel time for the Japanese, who all seem to make a mass exodus for their respective hometowns. Another peak travel time is so-called Golden Week, at the end of April and beginning of May, when there are three public holidays in a row. And finally, from about August 10 to 18 is Obon, a time when many Japanese will return to their hometowns to pay respects to their ancestors. Trains, ferries, and hotels are often fully booked during these three peak times, so be sure to plan far in advance.

As for regional peak travel times, be sure to check the section on festivals and annual events in the next chapter for dates when particular cities might be crowded due to festivals. Some festivals are so popular that you must book a hotel room at least six months in advance.

HONG KONG TOURIST ASSOCIATION: If you plan to go to Hong Kong from Japan, you might want to stop off at the Hong Kong Tourist Association, on the fourth floor of the Toho Twin Tower Building, 1-5-2 Yurakucho (tel. 03/503-0731), close to Hibiya subway station in Tokyo. Although its main function is to provide the Japanese with information on Hong Kong, it does have some publications in English and can answer questions you might have.

LAUNDRY: All the upper-bracket hotels and even some of the hotels for business travelers have laundry service. Since this tends to be expensive, you may want to wash your clothes yourself. Not everyone has a washing machine in Japan, so self-service laundries are abundant. The cost is about ¥150 ($1.20) to ¥300 ($2.40) per load for the washer; dryers are about ¥100 (80¢) for 10 minutes.

Some of the inexpensive Japanese inns described in this book that cater largely to young travelers also have coin laundry machines on their premises.

MAIL DELIVERY: Citizens of Canada, the United Kingdom, and Australia can have their mail forwarded to them at their respective embassies in Japan. The American Embassy, however, told me that they stopped such a policy in the 1970s and will no longer hold mail. If you don't know where you'll be staying, you can always have your mail sent to the central post office of the major cities you'll be visiting. In Tokyo, have your mail sent c/o *Poste Restante,* Central Post Office, Tokyo, Japan, which is located just southwest of Tokyo Station.

METRIC MEASURES: Japan uses the metric system.

Weights

U.S.		Japan
1 ounce	=	28.3 grams
1 pound	=	454 grams
2.2 pounds	=	1 kilo (1,000 grams)
1 pint	=	0.47 liter
1 quart	=	0.94 liter
1 gallon	=	3.78 liters

Measures

U.S.		Japan
1 inch	=	2.54 centimeters
1 foot	=	0.3 meters
1 yard	=	0.91 meters
1.09 yards	=	1 meter
1 mile	=	1.61 kilometers
0.62 mile	=	1 kilometer
1 acre	=	0.40 hectare
2.47 acres	=	1 hectare

Before the metric system came into use in Japan, the country had its own standards for measuring length and weight. There's no reason for you to learn these nowadays, but you will hear one way of measuring that is still common—rooms in Japan are still measured by the number of *tatami* straw mats that will fit in them. A six-tatami room, for example, is the size of six tatami mats. A tatami is roughly three feet wide and six feet long.

NEWSPAPERS AND PERIODICALS: Five English-language newspapers are published daily in Japan. They're the *Japan Times,* the *Mainichi Daily News,* the *Daily Yomiuri,* the *Asahi Evening News,* and the *International Herald Tribune.* Hotels and major bookstores also carry the international edition of such news magazines as *Time* and *Newsweek.* For regional publications detailing what's going on in a city, check with the local tourist information office listed in the individual city chapters.

PASSPORTS: Foreigners are required to carry with them *at all times* either their passports or their alien registration cards. The police generally do not stop foreigners, but if you're caught without the proper identification, you'll be taken to the local police headquarters. It happened to me once and, believe me, I can think of better ways to spend an hour and a half. I had to explain in detail who I was, what I was doing in Japan, where I lived, and what I planned on doing the rest of my life. I then had to write a statement explaining how it was that I rushed out that day without my passport, apologizing and promising never to do such a thoughtless thing again. The policemen at the station were very nice and polite—they were simply doing their duty.

POLITICS: Japan has both an emperor, who acts as head of state, and a prime minister, who is head of the government. The constitution, which was adopted in 1947, stipulates that the supreme power of the country resides with the people, who vote for members of the National Diet, the legislative body in Japan. The constitution also renounces war, which is at least one reason why the Japanese have been reluctant to build up their own military since World War II.

POSTAL SERVICE: Although all post offices are open from 9 a.m. to 5 p.m. Monday through Friday, international post offices are open much later, often until 7 or 8 p.m. It's only at larger post offices that you can mail packages abroad, and these are often found close to the city's main train station. Keep in mind also that these branches sell cardboard boxes in three sizes that come with the necessary tape and string, which is certainly much easier than going out and buying all that stuff. Packages mailed abroad cannot weigh more than 20 kilograms.

If you're mailing a letter, your hotel may be able to do it for you or direct you to the nearest post office. Airmail letters up to 10 grams cost ¥100 (80¢) to North America and ¥120 (96¢) to Europe. Postcards are ¥70 (56¢) to both. Domestic letters up to 25 grams are ¥62 (50¢); postcards are ¥41 (33¢).

Post offices are easily recognizable by the red symbol of a capital "T" with a horizontal line above it.

RADIO AND TELEVISION: For English-language radio programs, the Far East Network (FEN, 810 kHz) is the U.S. military station, with broadcasts of music, talk shows, sports broadcasts from the U.S., and Tokyo sumo matches. Upper-bracket hotels in Tokyo also have KTYO, a cable radio station broadcasting music, news, and sports around the clock.

If you enjoy watching television, you've come to the wrong country. Almost nothing is broadcast in English—even foreign films are dubbed in Japanese and the only way to hear them in English is if you have what's called a bilingual television. A few of the best hotels in Tokyo and other major cities do have bilingual televisions, and there are generally one to three English movies on television each week. Major hotels in Tokyo, Osaka, and Kyoto also have cable TV with English-language programs, including CNN broadcasts from America. But even if you don't understand the language, I suggest that you watch television in Japan at least once. Maybe you'll catch a samurai series, which is very popular. Commercials are also worth watching —often they're what I call "mood" advertising in which the scenery simply sets a mood that has very little to do with the actual product.

By the way, during your travels you may come across rooms in both Western- and Japanese-style establishments that offer video programs with their televisions. These programs are either coin-operated or are charged automatically to your bill. Since the explanations for these programs are usually in Japanese only, I will clear up the mystery—they're generally "adult entertainment" programs. Now you know.

REST ROOMS: If you're in need of a rest room, your best bet is at train and subway stations, big hotels, and department stores. Many toilets in Japan, especially those at train stations, are Japanese style. They're holes in the ground over which you squat facing the end that has a raised hood. Men stand and aim for the hole. Although Japanese lavatories may seem uncomfortable at first, they're actually much more sanitary because no part of your body touches anything. Who knows, you may even come to prefer them over Western-style toilets. To find out if a stall is empty, knock on the door. If it's occupied someone will knock back. Similarly, if you're inside a stall and someone knocks, answer with a knock back or else they'll just keep on knocking persistently and try to get in.

Don't be surprised if you go into some rest rooms and find men's urinals and individual private stalls in the same room. Women are supposed to simply walk right past the urinals without noticing them.

SAFETY: Japan is one of the safest countries in the world. Although crime is slowly on the increase, it's still negligible compared with that in the United States. Although it doesn't hurt to exercise caution, you'll notice shortly after arrival that the country is safe and the people are honest. Those are two of Japan's best attributes. However, whenever you're traveling in an unfamiliar city or country, stay alert. Be aware of your immediate surroundings. Wear a moneybelt and don't sling your camera or purse over your shoulder; wear the strap diagonally across your body. Men should carry their billfolds in an inner pocket. This will minimize the possibility of your becoming a victim of crime. Every society has its criminals: It's your responsibility to be aware and alert in even the most heavily touristed areas.

SHOP HOURS: Most stores in Japan don't open until 10 a.m. and they close about 8 p.m. Often they're closed one day a week, and it's not unusual for almost all the shops in a particular neighborhood to be closed on the same day. Some shops, especially those around major train stations and entertainment areas, stay open until 10 p.m. Some convenience stores are open 24 hours.

Department stores are open from 10 a.m. to 6 or 7 p.m. They close one day a week, but it's different for each store so you can always find one that's open, even on Sunday.

SHOPPING: It probably won't take you long to figure out that the number one hobby in Japan is shopping. Stores both mammoth and miniature are everywhere, offering everything you can and can't imagine. Traditional Japanese crafts and souvenirs that make good buys include woodblock prints (*ukiyoe*), toys and kites, bamboo window blinds, Japanese dolls, carp banners, swords, lacquerware, ceramics, fans, masks, knives and scissors, sake, and silk and cotton kimonos. Also popular are products made of Japanese paper (*washi*), such as umbrellas, lanterns, boxes, wallets and stationery. Japan is also famous for its workmanship in electronic products, including cameras, stereo and video equipment, computers and typewriters. However, because of the present exchange rate, you can probably find these products just as cheaply, or even more cheaply, in the United States. If you think you want to shop for electronic products, therefore, it pays to do some comparison shopping before you leave home so that you know what the prices are.

SKIING: With about 75% of Japan's land space consisting of mountains, you can bet that skiing is the country's most popular winter sport. The skiing is so good here that Hokkaido, Japan's big northern island, was selected as the site of the 1972 Winter Olympics. With the ski season generally lasting from about mid-December to early April, keep in mind that the slopes can be very crowded during weekends and holidays, especially those close to a large city. Also, although shops where you can rent skis, boots, and poles for about ¥4,000 ($32) to ¥5,500 ($44) a day are plentiful, most shops don't have shoes larger than about men's size 9. Day passes for ski lifts generally run between ¥3,200 ($25.60) and ¥3,500 ($28). For more information, the Tourist Information Centers in both Tokyo and Kyoto have a pamphlet called *Skiing in Japan,* which gives information about ski resorts in northern and central Japan. There are also a number of skiing areas within easy access to Tokyo and Sapporo. A great plus of many of Japan's ski resorts is that they're situated around hot springs—what could be better than soaking in a hot tub after a day out on the slopes?

TAXES AND SERVICE CHARGE: In 1989 the Japanese government introduced a 3% consumption tax on goods and services, including hotel rates and restaurant meals. If you stay overnight in accommodations that cost ¥10,000 ($80) or less per person, a 3% government consumption tax will be added to your bill; if your accommodations cost more than ¥10,000 per person, both a 3% consumption tax and a 3% local tax will be added to your bill. Some hotels, particularly business hotels, include the tax in their tariff, while others do not. Be sure to ask, therefore, whether rates include tax. In restaurants, a 3% consumption tax is levied on meals costing ¥5,000 ($40) or less per person, while meals costing more than ¥5,000 are subject to a 6% tax (which includes both consumption and local taxes).

In addition to these taxes, a 10% to 15% service charge will be added to your bill in lieu of tipping at most of the fancier restaurants and at many hotels. Thus the 16% to 21% in tax and service charge that will be added to your bill in the more expensive locales can really add up. Most *ryokan,* or Japanese-style inns, include service charge but not tax in their rates. If you're not sure, ask.

As for shopping, a 3% consumption tax is also levied on most goods (some of the smaller vendors are not required to levy tax). Travelers from abroad, however, are eligible for an exemption on goods taken out of the country, though only the larger department stores and specialty shops seem equipped to deal with the procedures. In any case, most department stores grant a refund on the consumption tax only when the total amount of purchases exceeds ¥10,000 ($80). You can obtain a refund immediately by having sales clerks fill out a list of your purchases and then presenting the list to the tax exemption counter of the department store. You will need to show your passport. Note that no refunds for consumption tax are given for food, drinks, tobacco, cosmetics, film, and batteries.

If you depart Japan from the Narita airport outside Tokyo, you will be charged a ¥2,000 ($16) service facility fee (there is no departure tax at any of the other international airports in Japan).

TELEGRAMS: Your hotel may be able to handle telegrams. If not, you can send a telegram from a **KDD (Kokusai Denshin Denwa)** office. Ask the hotel clerk where the office nearest your hotel is. If you need to send a telegram on a holiday or late at night, the Tokyo KDD office at 1-8-1 Otemachi (tel. 03/212-6430) is open Monday through Friday from 9 a.m. to 10 p.m. and on weekends and holidays from 9 a.m. to 5 p.m. In Osaka, a KDD office open the same hours is at 1-25 Bingo-machi, Higashi-ku (tel. 06/228-2151). Both offices can handle facsimiles and phototelegrams, and have booths for ISD calls and Telex. The cost of sending a telegram to the United States is ¥118 (94¢) per word.

TELEPHONES: If you're staying in a medium- or upper-range hotel, most likely you can make an **international call** from your room. The alternative is to go to a KDD office or purchase a disposable telephone credit card and use it in one of the international green telephones (described below). If you want to make a collect call or call through an operator, dial 0051. An operator-assisted, station-to-station call to the United States costs ¥1,890 ($15.12) for the first three minutes.

Cheaper are calls made without the assistance of an operator, either through an international public telephone or telephones that offer direct-dial service (most first-class and some medium-priced hotels now offer direct dialing). The direct-dial number for calls to the United States is 001 + 1 + area code + telephone number. These cost ¥450 ($3.60) for the first minute in a call to the United States and ¥220 ($1.76) for each minute after that. Between 11 p.m. and 5 a.m. Japan time, international direct calls are only ¥270 ($2.16) for the first minute to the United States. Rates are also cheaper on Sunday.

As for **local and domestic phone calls,** there are a number of different telephones, all color-coded. You can find these telephones virtually everywhere—on stands in front of little shops, on train station platforms, in restaurants and coffeeshops. There are even telephones in Japan's bullet trains. The red, pink, and blue phones take only ¥10 coins, while the yellow and green ones take both ¥10 and ¥100 coins. A local call costs ¥10 (8¢) for three minutes, and after that a warning chime will tell you to insert more coins or else you'll be disconnected. I usually insert two or three coins when I make a phone call so that I don't have to worry about being disconnected—coins that aren't used are always returned at the end of the call. If you don't want to deal with coins, you can purchase a disposable telephone credit card that can be inserted into a slot on most of the newer green telephones. These can be bought at vending machines, telephone offices, and at some station kiosks for values of ¥500 ($4) to ¥5,000 ($40). If the green telephone is equipped to handle international calls, there will be a sign that reads "International & Domestic Card/Coin Telephone." Note that not all green telephones that accept credit cards are capable of international calls.

Area codes for all of Japan's cities begin with a zero. Tokyo's area code, for example, is 03, while Osaka's is 06. For other area codes, check the "Orientation" section in each city. Use the area code only when dialing from outside the area.

TIME: Japan is 9 hours ahead of Greenwich Mean Time, 14 hours ahead of New York, 15 hours ahead of Chicago, and 17 hours ahead of Los Angeles. Since Japan does not go on Daylight Saving Time, subtract one hour from the above times if you're calling the United States in the summer. Because Japan is on the other side of the International Dateline, you lose one day when traveling from the United States to Asia. Returning to North America, however, you gain a day, which means that you arrive on the same day you left. In fact, it often happens that you arrive in the States at an earlier hour than you departed Japan.

TIPPING: One of the delights of being in Japan is that there is *no* tipping, not even to waitresses, taxi drivers, or bellboys. If you try to tip them, they'll probably be confused or embarrassed. Instead of individual tipping, a 10% to 15% service charge will be added to your bill at the higher-priced hotels and restaurants.

TOURIST INFORMATION: Nearly all of Japan's cities and towns have tourist offices, most of them located at or near the main train station. Although the staff does not always speak English and they may not have maps in English, they can point you in the right direction to your hotel, and in many cases even make bookings for you. Your best bet for information is at the **Tourist Information Centers (T.I.C.)** in Tokyo, Kyoto, and the Narita airport. Run by the Japan National Tourist Organization, they have literature and information not only on their own cities but on the rest of Japan as well. Before setting out on your travels, be sure to pick up any pamphlets or maps they may have on the areas you want to visit; in most cases these pamphlets are not available outside Tokyo or Kyoto. For more information on tourist information centers, see the individual listings for each city.

Overseas, you'll find the **Japan National Tourist Organization** offices at 630 Fifth Ave., New York, NY 10111 (tel. 212/757-5640); at 401 N. Michigan Ave.,

Suite 770, Chicago, IL 60611 (tel. 312/222-0874); at 1519 Main St., Suite 200, Dallas, TX 75201 (tel. 214/754-1820); at 2121 San Jacinto St., Suite 980, San Francisco, CA 94108 (tel. 415/989-7140); and at 624 S. Grand Ave., Los Angeles, CA 90017 (tel. 213/623-1952). Other offices are at 165 University Ave., Toronto, ON M5H 3B8, Canada (tel. 416/366-7140); 167 Regent St., London, W.1, England (tel. 01/734-9638); and 115 Pitt St., Sydney, N.S.W. 2000, Australia (tel. 02/232-4522).

TRAVEL-PHONE: If you're having problems communicating with someone in Japan, are lost, or need information, the Japan National Tourist Organization operates a nationwide system called "Travel-Phone" that provides service every day throughout the year from 9 a.m. to 5 p.m. If you're outside Tokyo or Kyoto, all you have to do is insert a ¥10 coin into a yellow, blue, or green phone (the coin will be returned to you at the end of the call) and dial one of the following two numbers: if you want to know something about eastern Japan (Tokyo, Yokohama, Matsumoto, Hokkaido, etc.), dial 0120-222800; if you have any questions that pertain to western Japan (Nagoya, Kanazawa, Kyoto, western Honshu, Shikoku, and Kyushu), dial 0120-444800. Toll-free calls can be made only if you're outside Tokyo or Kyoto. If you're in Tokyo, the number to dial is 502-1461; in Kyoto it's 371-5649. In these two cities you have to pay for the call, which is ¥10 (8¢) per three minutes.

VACCINATIONS: You don't need any inoculations for entry into Japan.

YOUTH HOSTEL CARDS: If you forgot to get your youth hostel card at home or have decided that you'll need one here, you can get a membership card for ¥2,200 ($17.60) from the Japan Youth Hostel Association in the Hoken Kaikan Honkan Building, 1-2 Sadohara-cho, Ichigaya, Shinjuku-ku, Tokyo 162 (tel. 03/269-5831). You can also buy one at YH information counters on the fourth floor of Keio Department Store in Shinjuku, the second basement of Sogo Department Store in front of Yurakucho Station, and on the seventh floor of Seibu Department Store in Ikebukuro. The Tourist Information Centers in Tokyo and Kyoto have a pamphlet called *Youth Hostel Map of Japan*. For more information about Japanese youth hostels, see Chapter II, Section 8, further on.

AN INTRODUCTION TO JAPAN

Being informed about Japan, its history, people, and culture, will greatly enhance your trip. This chapter should serve only as an introduction to the wealth of information available. At the end of the chapter is a recommended reading list for books on Japan.

1. Geography

Separated from mainland China and Korea by the Sea of Japan, the nation of Japan stretches in a sliver of an arc about 1,860 miles long from northeast to southwest. Only 250 miles wide at its widest point, Japan consists primarily of four main islands—Honshu, Hokkaido, Kyushu, and Shikoku—which account for 97% of its 145,000 square miles. Surrounding these four islands are more than 3,000 islands and islets, most of them tiny and uninhabited, as well as a group of islands much farther to the south known collectively as the Okinawan islands, perhaps best known because of the fierce fighting that took place there during World War II. If you were to superimpose Japan's four main islands onto a map of the United States, they would stretch all the way from Maine down to northern Florida, which should give you at least some idea of the diversity of Japan's climate, flora, and scenery.

Of the four main islands, **Honshu** is the largest, has always been the most important both historically and culturally, and is where most visitors to Japan spend the bulk of their time. Honshu is the home of the ancient capitals of Nara, Kyoto, and Kamakura, as well as such bustling metropolises as Osaka, Nagoya, Hiroshima, and the modern capital of Japan, Tokyo. **Hokkaido,** the next largest island, lies to the north of Honshu and is regarded as Japan's last frontier, with its wide-open pastures, wildlife, and national parks of mountains, woods, and lakes. The southernmost of the four main islands is **Kyushu,** with a mild subtropical climate, active volcanoes, and hot-spring spas. Because it's the closest to Korea and China, Kyushu served as a gateway to the continental mainland throughout much of Japan's history, later becoming the springboard for both traders and Christian missionaries from the West. **Shikoku,** the smallest of the four islands, remains fairly undeveloped and is famous for its 88 Buddhist temples founded by one of Japan's most interesting historical figures, the Buddhist priest Kukai, known posthumously as Kobo Daishi.

As much as 75% of Japan consists of mountains, most of them volcanic in origin. Altogether there are some 265 volcanoes in Japan, more than 30 of them still considered active. **Mount Fuji,** now dormant, is Japan's most famous volcano, while **Mount Aso** on the island of Kyushu is the largest volcano in the world. Because of its volcanic origins, Japan throughout the centuries has been plagued by earthquakes (the last huge earthquake struck in 1923). Today Japan's buildings are constructed to withstand the shakes, quakes, and tremors that used to leave towns and villages in ruins.

At any rate, even though Japan is only slightly smaller in size than California, it has more than half the population of the United States. And because three-fourths of the nation is mountainous and therefore uninhabitable, Japan's people are concentrated primarily in what amounts to only 10% of the country's land mass, with the rest of the land devoted to agriculture. Thus, in an island nation physically isolated from the rest of the world, struck repeatedly through the centuries by earthquakes, fires, and typhoons, and with only limited space for harmonious living, Japan's geography and topography have played major roles in the country's development and in shaping its culture, customs, and arts.

2. History

ANCIENT HISTORY (ca. 30,000 B.C. to A.D. 710)

According to Japanese mythology, the history of Japan began when the sun goddess, Amaterasu, sent one of her descendants down to the island of Kyushu to unify Japan. This unification was realized a few generations later when Jimmu, an offspring of this descendant, succeeded in bringing all of Japan under his rule. It's at this point that legend fuses with fact, for in the 4th century A.D. there was a family known as Yamato who did indeed succeed in expanding its kingdom and unifying Japan. At the core of this unification was the Japanese belief in Shintoism, a religion indigenous to Japan which worships nature and ancestors, and which believed in the divinity of the emperor. At any rate, considered to be descended from the gods, Jimmu became Japan's first emperor and his descendants have continued to occupy the throne ever since. Japan's imperial family is the longest-running imperial family in the world.

Of course, the real history of Japan begins before the emperor came to the throne. Although the exact origin of the Japanese people is unknown, we know that Japan was once connected to the Asian mainland by a land bridge and that the territory was occupied as early as 30,000 B.C. From about 10,000 to 300 B.C., hunters and gatherers called the Jomon people were thriving in small communities primarily in central Honshu. They are best known for their hand-formed pottery decorated with cord patterns. The Jomon Period was followed by the Yayoi Period, marked by metalworking, the pottery wheel, and the mastering of irrigated rice cultivation, a period that lasted until about A.D. 300. It was after this that the Yamato family succeeded in unifying the state for the first time. Yamato became the ancient name of Japan, which began turning its cultural feelers toward its great neighbor to the west, China.

In the 6th century, Buddhism, which originated in India, was brought to Japan via China and Korea. This was the beginning of many cultural and scholarly ideas imported from China, including Chinese characters for writing, art, and architecture. Although the Japanese subsequently adapted the Chinese form of art and architecture, and even Buddhism, into its own cultural mold, the influence that China had on early Japan cannot be overstated. In A.D. 604 the Prince Regent Shotoku, greatly influenced by the teachings of Buddhism and Confucianism, drafted a document calling for political reforms and a constitutional government. By A.D. 607 he was sending multitudes of Japanese scholars to China to study Buddhism. Under Shotoku's guidance a number of Buddhist temples were built, the most famous of which was Horyuji Temple near Nara, said today to be the oldest existing wooden structure in the world.

THE NARA PERIOD (A.D. 710–794)

Before the 700s, the site of Japan's capital changed every time a new emperor came to the throne. In 710, however, a permanent capital was established in Nara. Although it remained the capital for only 74 years, seven successive emperors ruled from Nara and the period was graced with the expansion of Buddhism and a flourishing of temple construction throughout the country. Buddhism also inspired the arts, including sculpture, metalcasting, painting, and lacquerware. It was during this time that the huge bronze statue of Buddha was cast and erected in Nara. Known as the Daibutsu, this huge statue remains Nara's biggest attraction.

THE HEIAN PERIOD (A.D. 794–1192)

In 784 the capital was moved from Nara to Nagaoka. Ten years later it was moved once again to Heiankyo (present-day Kyoto), where it remained until Tokyo was made the new capital in 1868. Following the example of cities in China, Kyoto was laid out in a grid pattern with broad roads and canals.

The Heian Period, which lasted from 794 until 1192, was a peaceful time in Japanese history, and in fact "Heiankyo" means "capital of peace and tranquillity." It was a glorious time, a time of luxury and prosperity, during which court life reached new heights in artistic pursuits. The Chinese alphabet was blended with a new Japanese writing system, allowing for the first time the flowering of Japanese literature and poems. The life of the times was captured in the works of two women: Sei-Shonagon, who wrote a collection of essays known as the *Pillow Book,* and Murasaki-Shikibu, who wrote the world's first novel, *The Tale of Genji.*

Because the nobles were completely engrossed in their own luxurious lifestyles, however, they failed to notice the growth of military clans in the provinces. The two most powerful warrior clans were the Taira and the Minamoto, who fought fierce civil wars that tore the nation apart until finally a young warrior named Yoritomo Minamoto triumphed and established supremacy.

THE KAMAKURA PERIOD (A.D. 1192–1333)

Wishing to set up rule far away from Kyoto, Yoritomo Minamoto established his capital in a remote and easily defendable fishing village called Kamakura, not far from today's Tokyo. He created a military government, ushering in a new era in Japan's history in which the power of the country passed from the aristocratic court into the hands of the warrior class. In becoming the nation's first *shogun,* or military dictator, Yoritomo laid the groundwork for military governments in Japan, which lasted for some 700 years, until the imperial court was restored in 1868.

The Kamakura Period is perhaps best known for the unrivaled ascendancy of the warrior caste, known as the *samurai*. Ruled by a rigid code of honor, the samurai were bound in loyalty to their feudal lord, and as the centuries wore on they became the only caste allowed to carry weapons. They were supposed to give up their lives for their lord without hesitation, and if they failed in their duty they could gain back their honor by committing ritualistic suicide, known as *seppuku*. Spurning the soft life led by the noble court in Kyoto, the samurai embraced a harsher and simpler set of ideals marked by a Spartan lifestyle. When Zen Buddhism with its tenets of mental and physical discipline was introduced to Japan from China in the 1190s, it appealed greatly to the samurai class.

In 1274 Mongolian forces under Kublai Khan attempted to invade Japan. They failed but returned in 1281 with an even larger fleet. Luck was on Japan's side, however, when a typhoon blew in and destroyed the whole fleet. Regarding it as a gift from the gods, the Japanese called it *kamikaze,* meaning "divine wind," a term that took on a different significance at the end of World War II when Japanese pilots flew suicide missions in an attempt to turn the tide of war. More important, however, is the fact that until American occupation forces entered Japan at the end of World War II, Japan was never once invaded or occupied by a foreign nation.

THE MUROMACHI AND AZUCHI-MOMOYAMA PERIODS (A.D. 1336–1603)

After the fall of the Kamakura shogunate, a new feudal government was set up at Muromachi in Kyoto. The next 200 years, however, were marred by bloody civil wars and confusion as *daimyo* (feudal lords) staked out their fiefdoms throughout the land. Similar to the barons of Europe, the daimyo owned tracts of land with complete rule over the people who lived on them. To help serve him each lord had his retainers, the samurai, who helped in waging war against his enemies.

But even though these centuries were characterized by strife, they also saw a blossoming of art and culture. Kyoto witnessed the construction of the extravagant Golden and Silver Pavilions as well as the artistic arrangements of the famous rock garden at Ryoanji Temple. *Noh* drama, the tea ceremony, flower arranging, and landscape gardening became the passions of the upper class. The end of the 16th century also saw a flurry of castles built across the land, both as a show of a daimyo's strength and might as well as a defense against the firearms that had been introduced in Japan around 1543.

In the second half of the 16th century, a brilliant military strategist by the name of Nobunaga Oda almost succeeded in ending the civil wars by unifying Japan. But in 1582, before he could succeed, he was assassinated by one of his own retainers. His campaign was taken up by one of his best generals, Hideyoshi Toyotomi, who had been born a peasant instead of a samurai but who had risen up in the ranks of Nobunaga's army. Hideyoshi built a magnificent castle in Osaka, crushed all rebellion, and was finally able to unify Japan before he died in 1598.

THE EDO PERIOD (A.D. 1603–1867)

Upon Hideyoshi's death, power was seized by Ieyasu Tokugawa, a statesman so shrewd and skillful in eliminating enemies that his Tokugawa heirs would continue to rule Japan for the next 250 years. In 1603 Ieyasu set up his shogunate government in Edo (present-day Tokyo), leaving the emperor intact but virtually powerless in Kyoto.

Meanwhile, Western influence in Japan was spreading. Japan had already had its first contact with the Western world back in 1543 with the arrival of the Portuguese, who were followed by Christian missionaries. In 1549 Saint Francis Xavier arrived in Kyushu, where he remained for two years, converting thousands of Japanese into

Christians. By 1580 there were perhaps as many as 150,000 Christians in Japan. Although the rulers of Japan at first welcomed the foreigners and trade, they gradually became alarmed at the influence of the Christian missionaries. Hearing about the power of the Catholic Church in Rome and fearing the expansionist policies of the European nations, the shogunate banned Christianity at the end of the 1500s. In 1597 some 26 Japanese and European Christians were crucified in Nagasaki.

The Tokugawa shogunate intensified the campaign against the Christians and carried it a step further when in 1633 it closed all its ports to foreign trade. Adopting a policy of total isolation, the Tokugawas subsequently forbade foreigners to land in Japan and forbade the Japanese to leave. Even those Japanese who had been living abroad in overseas trading posts were not allowed to return to their native homes and were therefore forced to live the rest of their days in exile. Those who defied the strict decrees paid for it with their lives. The only exception to this policy of isolation was in Nagasaki, where there was a colony of tightly controlled Chinese merchants and a handful of Dutch who were confined to a small trading post on a tiny island.

Thus began an amazing time in Japanese history, during which its doors were virtually closed to the rest of the world for more than 200 years. It was a time of political stability but also a time when personal freedom was strictly controlled by the Tokugawa government. Japanese society was divided into four distinct classes: the court nobles, the samurai, the farmers, and the merchants. Although the nobles occupied the most exalted social position, the real power lay with the samurai, and it was probably during the Tokugawa Period that the samurai class reached the zenith of its glory. At the bottom of the social ladder were the merchants, but as peace reigned on and they began accumulating wealth, new forms of entertainment arose to occupy their time. *Kabuki* drama and woodblock prints became the new rage, while stoneware and porcelain, silk brocade for elaborate and gorgeous kimonos, and lacquerware improved in quality.

To ensure that no daimyo in the distant provinces might grow powerful enough to usurp the shogun's power, the Tokugawa government ordered that each daimyo leave his family in Edo to serve as a kind of hostage. Furthermore, each daimyo was required to spend every other year in Edo. In exerting so much time and money traveling back and forth and maintaining residences both in the provinces and in Edo, the daimyo was left with nothing extra with which to wage a rebellion. To serve these elaborate processions as the daimyo traveled with his retainers back and forth between Edo and the provinces, inns and townships sprang up along Japan's major highways. What a sight these constant processions must have been with their palanquins, samurai, and footmen as they made their way through the rough terrain of Japan's mountains.

But even though the Tokugawa government took measures to ensure its supremacy, by the mid-19th century it was clear that the feudal system was outdated. With the economic power in the hands of the merchants, money rather than rice became the primary means of exchange. Many samurai families found themselves on the brink of poverty, and discontent with the shogunate grew widespread.

In 1853 Commodore Matthew C. Perry of the U.S. Navy sailed to Japan to force the nation to grant America trading rights. Returning a year later, he finally succeeded in forcing the shogun to sign an agreement despite the disapproval of the emperor, thus ending Japan's two centuries of isolation. In 1867 some powerful families succeeded in toppling the Tokugawa regime and restoring the emperor as ruler. The feudal era drew to an end.

MODERN JAPAN (A.D. 1868–PRESENT)

In 1868 Emperor Meiji moved his imperial government to Edo, renamed it Tokyo (which means "Eastern Capital"), and made it the official capital of the nation. The ensuing years, known as the Meiji Restoration, were nothing short of amazing as Japan rapidly progressed from a feudal agricultural society of samurai and peasants to an industrial nation in only a few decades. The samurai were stripped of their power and no longer allowed to carry swords, a prime minister and cabinet were appointed, a constitution was drafted, and a parliament, called the Diet, was elected. With the enthusiastic support of Emperor Meiji for the modernization and Westernization of Japan, all the latest in technology and know-how was imported to Japan, including the railway and postal systems, and even specialists and advisers. Between 1881 and 1898 as many as 6,177 British, 2,764 Americans, 913 Germans, and 619 French were retained by the Japanese government to help in the transformation of Japan into a modern society.

Meanwhile, Japan was testing its new wings with forays into neighboring lands. In 1894 Japan fought China and won, and in 1905 Japan attacked and defeated Russia. In 1910 Japan annexed Korea. After militarists gained control of the government in the 1930s, these expansionist policies continued when Japan went to war with China in 1937. On December 7, 1941, Japan attacked Pearl Harbor, entering World War II against the United States. Although victories continued as Japan conquered Hong Kong, Singapore, Burma, Malaysia, the Philippines, the Dutch East Indies, and Guam, the tide eventually turned. American bombers reduced to rubble every major city in Japan with the exception of Kyoto. On August 6, 1945, the United States dropped over Hiroshima the world's first atomic bomb, followed on August 9 by a second atomic bomb over Nagasaki. Japan submitted to unconditional surrender on August 14 and soon thereafter American occupational forces arrived in Japan, where they remained until 1952. For the first time in Japan's history it had suffered defeat and occupation by a foreign power.

Adopting a new constitution that renounced war and set up a democratic government, Japan quickly began rebuilding its cities and economy. By the time the Olympic Games were held in Tokyo in 1964, Japan had become an economic phenomenon. Considering the fact that today Japan is one of the most industrialized nations in the world, its progress in the past century is indeed nothing short of remarkable. What's more, Japan is ready, eager, and able to lead the rest of the world into the 21st century.

---

3. The People

As an island nation with few natural resources, Japan has as its greatest asset its 120 million people. Hard-working, honest, and proud about performing a task well no matter how insignificant it might seem, the Japanese are well known for their politeness and helpfulness to strangers. Hardly anyone returns from a trip to Japan without stories of the extraordinary goodness and kindness extended to them by the Japanese.

With approximately 99% of the population consisting of Japanese, Japan is one of the most homogeneous nations in the world. Originally of Mongoloid stock with strains of a few other Asian peoples thrown in, the Japanese have had remarkably little influx of other gene pools into the country since the 8th century. That, coupled with Japan's actual physical isolation as an island nation, has more than anything else led to a feeling among the Japanese that they belong to one huge tribe different from any other people on earth. You'll often hear a Japanese preface a statement or opinion with the words "We Japanese," the implications of which are that all Japanese think alike and that all people can basically be divided into two worlds, Japanese and non-Japanese.

One characteristic of the Japanese that has received much publicity in recent years, and that is regarded as at least one reason why their nation has become so powerful economically, is their group mentality. In Japan, consideration of the group—whether it be family, friends, co-workers, or Japanese society as a whole—always wins out over the desire of the individual. In fact, I have had Japanese tell me that they consider individuality to be synonymous with selfishness and a complete disregard for the feelings and consideration of others.

Whereas in the West the attainment of "happiness" seems to be the elusive goal for a full and rewarding life, in Japan it's the satisfactory performance of duty and obligation. From the time they are born the Japanese are instilled with a sense of duty that extends toward their parents, their husbands or wives, their children, their bosses and co-workers, their neighbors, and the rest of Japanese society as a whole.

In a nation as crowded as Japan, such consideration of others is essential. The average Japanese family lives in what Westerners would regard as intolerably tiny living quarters, especially in the larger cities like Tokyo or Osaka, where space is at a premium. And in most cases it's still customary for retired parents to live with their eldest son.

The son, however, has very little time to spend at home. If he lives in Tokyo he probably spends two to three hours a day commuting on the city's trains and subways to and from work. Commonly called a "salary man," he works long hours, sometimes until 7 or 8 p.m., often followed by an evening out with his fellow workers, which he considers necessary for promoting understanding, closeness, and a more harmonious working condition. Most likely he'll work for the same company his entire life, taking only national holidays and one week's vacation a year. In return he is assured of lifetime employment (unless his company goes bankrupt, which is not too terribly uncommon), a pay raise according to his age, and promotion according to the number of years he has worked for the company. Although he may secretly complain of the long hours he has to work, he basically accepts it because everyone else is doing the same thing.

Being a housewife and full-time mother is considered the most honored position a woman can have. Although more and more women are working outside the home than ever before, they are generally confined to low-paying menial and part-time jobs. Take a look at the employment opportunities in the classified section of the *Japan Times*. There you'll see that employers can discriminate on the basis of sex, age, and race. Jobs for women are typically as secretaries, waitresses, and teachers, with few jobs open to those over 30. It's still pretty much a man's society when it comes to business in Japan, and a woman's primary obligation and function are in the home. With few exciting career opportunities easily open to them, it's perhaps understandable why the main goal of most Japanese women is to get married and have children. Those who fail to find a mate during college or the early working years can always find one through an arranged marriage. Such marriages still make up about 30% of the matches in Japan. The Japanese go all out when it comes to marriage ceremonies—believe it or not, the cost of an average wedding in Japan, including the honeymoon, is a whopping $30,000.

Of course, the situation is changing in Japan, as elsewhere, and it's no longer safe to talk in stereotypes. In 1986 a new law, the Equal Employment Opportunity Act, went into effect, thereby overturning an earlier law that had limited the number of hours women could work overtime—and if you don't work overtime in Japan, there's hardly any chance for promotion. Day-care centers for children are on the increase, young people are moving away and living far from their hometowns, and some young couples are determined to lead different, and separate, lives from their parents. Although rare, you can now find female politicians, doctors, and lawyers who juggle both family and career.

But change evolves slowly in Japan. Those who advocate change are in danger of ridicule or, even worse, rejection from the group. It's especially difficult for Japanese who have lived abroad and then return home—unless they slip back quietly into their old mold they are regarded with suspicion and resentment, as though they have somehow become tainted and are no longer quite Japanese.

As for foreigners, even though treated with extreme kindness during a visit, they soon realize that they will never be totally accepted in Japanese society: they will always be considered outsiders, even if they speak fluent Japanese. In fact, Japanese-speaking foreigners will tell you that they are sometimes met with suspicion and coldness simply because, to the Japanese mind, foreigners aren't supposed to be able to speak their language. Among the groups most discriminated against are probably the Koreans, many of them second and third generation and the descendants of Koreans who were brought to Japan in forced labor before World War II.

On the positive side, the Japanese on a personal level are among the most likeable people in the world. They are kind, thoughtful, and adept in perceiving another's needs. The fact that the country is so safe from violent crime speaks highly of the people. And as for aestheticism, the Japanese have an unerring eye for pure beauty, whether it be in food, architecture, or landscaped gardens. I don't think it would be possible to visit Japan and not have some of the Japanese appreciation of beauty rub off. Having produced both the bonsai and the Toyota, as well as the robot, the sumo wrestler, and the geisha, the Japanese are such a fascinating people that it's impossible not to get hooked. Quite a few foreigners living in Japan originally come to the country with the intention of staying only a short while—and they end up living here for years. I was one of them.

In short, Japan, like every nation in the world, has both its good and bad sides, and the informed visitor should be aware of both. On the whole, however, the visitor will be overwhelmed by the wonderful aspects of the country and the kindness of the people, which makes traveling in Japan such a delight. By the time you go home, no doubt you'll have your own extraordinary stories to tell.

4. The Language

No one knows the exact origins of the Japanese language, but we do know that it existed only in spoken form until the 6th century. It was then that the Japanese borrowed the Chinese characters, called *kanji*, and used them to develop their own form of written language. Later, two additional character systems, *hiragana* and *katakana*, were added to kanji to form the existing Japanese writing system. Thus both Chinese and Japanese use some of the same pictographs, but otherwise there is no similarity between the two languages. While they may be able to recognize some of each other's written language, the Chinese and Japanese cannot communicate verbally.

A Note On Japanese Symbols

Many hotels, restaurants, and other establishments in Japan do not have signs showing their names in English letters. Appendix II lists the Japanese symbols for all such places appearing in this guide. Each establishment name in Japanese symbols is numbered, and the same number appears in an oval in the text following the boldfaced establishment name. For example, in the text **Osaka's Hotel Hokke Club** ⑯ is number 164 in the Japanese symbol list in Appendix II.

There are at least two ways of pronouncing most kanji in Japanese—one is a Chinese pronunciation from the 6th century and the other is a Japanese pronunciation. This leads to the problem that one often can't tell by looking at the characters which pronunciation is the proper one except by context. Similarly, if you don't know the characters of, say, a restaurant, it may be impossible to find out the telephone number.

There are about 10,000 Japanese characters, but the average adult knows only

2,500 or so, which is enough to read newspapers, most books and novels, etc. Hiragana and katakana, phonetic alphabets consisting of 46 symbols each, came into use because kanji was considered inadequate to express everything in Japanese thought. Hiragana is used for writing words not expressed in kanji and for verb endings. Katakana is the alphabet used for all foreign words and for telegrams. As a foreigner, for example, if you have visiting cards made up in Japanese, your name will be written in the katakana syllabary.

The Japanese written language—a combination of kanji, hiragana, and katakana—is probably one of the most difficult systems of written communication in the modern world. And as for the spoken language, there are all kinds of levels of speech and forms of expression that relate to your own social status and whether you're male or female. It's little wonder that Saint Francis Xavier, a Jesuit missionary who came to Japan in the 16th century, wrote that Japanese was an invention of the devil designed to thwart the spread of Christianity. And yet the most astounding thing is that literacy in Japan is estimated at around 99%.

But despite the fact that Japanese are able to learn their own complicated language, they have much difficulty when it comes to English. Although most students are required to take English for six years in school, these studies lean primarily toward entrance exams at universities, which require extensive reading comprehension of the language and grammar but almost no practical application. Thus while many Japanese can read English, few are able to understand spoken English. As I've mentioned elsewhere, if you're having problems communicating with a Japanese, it sometimes helps to write everything down.

Realizing the difficulties foreigners have with the language barrier in Japan, the Japan National Tourist Organization has put out a nifty booklet called *The Tourist's Handbook* with sentences written in English and Japanese equivalents for everything from asking directions to shopping to ordering in a restaurant and staying in a Japanese inn. Foreigners traveling around Japan on their own should pick up a copy of this valuable booklet at the Tourist Information Center in either Tokyo or Kyoto. Appendix I in the back of this guide also lists some common phrases and words in Japanese to help you get around on your own.

Finally, if you are having difficulty communicating with a Japanese, it may help to pronounce an English word in a Japanese way. Foreign words, especially English, have penetrated the Japanese language to such an extent that they are now estimated to make up 20% of the words used by the Japanese. The problem is that these words change in Japanese pronunciation because words always end in either a vowel or "n," and because two consonants in one syllable are usually separated by a vowel. Would you recognize *terebi* as "television," *koohi* as "coffee," or *rajio* as "radio"?

I'd like to mention here that English words are quite fashionable in Japanese advertising, with the result that you'll often see English on shop signs, posters, shopping bags, and T-shirts. However, words are often wonderfully misspelled or used in such unusual contexts that you can only guess at the original intent. I don't know how many times my day has been brightened with the discovery of some zany or unfathomable English. What, for example, could possibly be the meaning behind "Today birds, tomorrow men," which appeared under a picture of birds on a shopping bag? In Matsue there's a "Beauty Saloon," which conjures up all kinds of images of beauties getting their hair cut while chugging down mugs of beer, and in Gifu one can only guess at the pleasures to be had at the Hotel Joybox. In Okayama I saw a shop whose name was a stern admonition to its customers to "Grow Up," while in Kyoto there's the "Selfish" coffeeshop and the "Pitiful Pub." How about a "sandwitch" or "Creap" coffee creamer? Popular advertising slogans such as "I feel Coke" and "Speak Lark" have puzzled many a resident foreigner.

Certainly the best sign I've seen was at the Narita airport. At all the check-in counters was a sign telling passengers that they would be required to pay a service facility charge at "the time of check-in for your fright." Unable to control my giggles, I explained the reason for my breakdown to the perplexed man behind the counter. Two weeks later when I came back through the airport, all the signs had been corrected. That's Japanese efficiency.

5. Meeting the Japanese

If you've been invited to Japan by some organization or business, you will receive the royal treatment, most likely being wined and dined so wonderfully and thoroughly that you'll never want to return home. If you've come to Japan on your own as an ordinary tourist, however, chances are your experiences will be much different. Except for those who have lived or traveled a lot abroad, few Japanese have had much contact with foreigners. In fact, even in Tokyo there are Japanese who have never spoken to a foreigner and would be quite embarrassed and uncomfortable if suddenly confronted with the possibility. And even though most of them have studied English, few of them have had the opportunity to use it and most feel totally unable to communicate in it. That's one reason why the empty seat beside you in the subway is the last one to be occupied—most Japanese are deathly afraid you'll ask them a question they won't be able to understand.

In many respects, therefore, it's much harder to meet the inhabitants here than in many other countries where the people tend to be more gregarious, openly curious, and forward. The Japanese are simply much more shy. Although they will sometimes approach you to ask whether they might practice some English with you, for the most part you are left pretty much on your own unless you make the first move. And for the most part your experiences in Japan will depend on you and your own initiative.

Recognizing the difficulty foreigners may face in meeting the Japanese, the Japan National Tourist Organization has launched a super program called the **Home Visit System,** which offers overseas visitors the chance to visit an English-speaking Japanese family in their home. It doesn't cost anything and the visit usually takes place for a few hours in the evening (dinner is *not* served). It's a good idea to bring a small gift, such as flowers, fruit, or something from your hometown. The system is operating in the following 15 cities, for which I've provided the contact telephone numbers: Tokyo (tel. 03/502-1461); Sapporo (tel. 011/211-3341); Narita (tel. 0476/32-8711 or 24-3198); Yokohama (tel. 045/641-5824); Nagoya (tel. 052/581-5678); Otsu (tel. 0775/23-1234); Kyoto (tel. 075/752-0215); Osaka (tel. 06/345-2189); Kobe (tel. 078/303-1010); Okayama (tel. 0862/32-2255); Kurashiki (tel. 0864/22-5141); Hiroshima (tel. 082/247-6738); Fukuoka (tel. 092/291-0777); Nagasaki (tel. 0958/24-1111); and Kagoshima (tel. 0992/24-1111 or 53-2500). To apply, call the appropriate city at least one day in advance of the intended visit. If you have any other questions, the Tourist Information Center in Tokyo (tel. 03/502-1461) can answer them.

Another good way to meet the Japanese is to stay in a minshuku, inexpensive lodging in a Japanese home. Usually small with only a handful of rooms, minshuku often afford the opportunity to meet both the family running the place as well as the other guests, since meals are usually served in a communal dining room. More information is given about minshuku in the section on accommodations later in this chapter.

I've found that one of the best ways to meet Japanese is to visit a so-called **English conversation lounge.** These are informal affairs, often attached to English schools for the Japanese to give them the opportunity for unstructured conversations in English with anyone who is there. Most are open in the evenings and offer the chance to play games or read magazines and have drinks of coffee or beer. Usually foreigners are admitted free of charge; at some lounges you must pay an entrance fee of ¥500 ($4) or so, but it's always less than what the Japanese pay. At any rate, the Japanese who come to these lounges often speak excellent English and will be delighted to talk to you. When I first came to Japan I visited one of these lounges about five times, learning much about Japanese society as we talked about everything from the role of women in Japan to homosexuality to opinions about interracial marriages. I was told that the Japanese feel much more comfortable talking about such subjects in English and would be unable to express themselves as openly in Japanese. Regardless, it's an excellent way to meet Japanese and learn about the country. The *Tokyo Journal*, published monthly to describe what's going on in the capital city, lists conversation lounges in its classified section.

And finally, another way to meet Japanese is to go where they play, namely the country's countless bars and eateries. There you'll often encounter Japanese who will want to speak to you if they understand English, and even some slightly inebriated Japanese who will speak to you if they don't. If you're open to it, such chance encounters may prove to be the highlight of your trip, or at the very least an evening of just plain fun.

---

6. Japanese Etiquette and Manners

Much of Japan's system of etiquette and manners stems from its feudal days, when the social hierarchy dictated how a person spoke, sat, bowed, ate, walked, and lived. Failure to comply with the rules could bring severe punishment, sometimes even death.

Of course, nowadays it's quite different, though the Japanese still attach much importance to proper behavior. As a foreigner, however, you can get away with a lot. After all, you're just a "barbarian" and as such can be forgiven for not knowing the rules. There are **two cardinal sins,** however, that you should never commit. One is that you should never wear your shoes inside a Japanese home, traditional inn, or temple, and the other is that you should never, ever wash with soap inside a Japanese bathtub. Except for committing either of these two horrors, you will probably be forgiven for any other social blunder.

As a sensitive traveler, however, you should try to familiarize yourself with the social etiquette for Japan, the basics of which are given below. The Japanese are very appreciative of foreigners who take the time to learn about their country and are quite patient in helping you learn. And, remember, if you do commit a faux pas, apologize profusely and smile. They don't chop off heads anymore.

BOWING

The main form of greeting in Japan is the bow rather than the handshake. Although at first glance it might seem simple enough, the bow and its implications are actually quite complicated, with the depth of the bow, the number of seconds, and the total number of bows dependent on who you are and whom you're bowing to. In addition to bowing in greeting, the Japanese also bow upon departing and to express deep gratitude. The proper form for a bow is to bend from the waist with a straight back and to keep your arms at your sides, but as a foreigner a simple nod of the head is enough. Knowing that foreigners shake hands, a Japanese may extend his hand, though he probably won't be able to stop himself from giving a little bow as well. In my travels in Japan I've even seen Japanese businessmen shake hands among themselves, although it is still quite rare.

VISITING CARDS

You're a nonentity in Japan if you don't have a visiting card, called a *meishi* in Japanese. Everyone from housewives to plumbers to secretaries to bank presidents carries meishi with them to give out during introductions. If you're trying to conduct business in Japan, you'll be regarded suspiciously—even as a phony—if you don't have business cards. As a tourist you don't have to have business cards, but it certainly doesn't hurt and the Japanese will be greatly impressed by your preparedness. The card should have your address and occupation on it. You might even consider having your meishi made in Japan with the Japanese syllabic script (katakana) written on the reverse side.

DINING

One of the great customs in Japan is that as soon as you're seated in a Japanese restaurant you'll be given a wet towel, which will be steaming hot in winter or pleasantly cool in summer. Called an oshibori, it's for wiping your hands. In all but the fancy restaurants men can get away with wiping their faces as well, but women are not supposed to (I ignore this one if I'm hot and sweaty). The oshibori is one custom you'll wish would be adopted back home.

The next thing you'll probably be confronted with are chopsticks. The proper way to use them is to place the first chopstick between the base of the thumb and the top of the ring finger (this chopstick remains stationary) and the second one between the top of the thumb and the middle and index fingers. This second chopstick is what you move to pick up food. The best way to learn is to have a Japanese show you how. It's not difficult to learn, but if you find it impossible, some restaurants might have a fork as well. How proficiently foreigners handle chopsticks is a matter of great curiosity for the Japanese and they're surprised if you know how to use them; even if you were to live in Japan 20 years, you would never stop receiving compliments on how talented you are with chopsticks.

As for etiquette involving chopsticks, if you're taking something from a communal bowl or tray you're supposed to turn your chopsticks upside down and use the part that hasn't been in your mouth. After transferring the food to your plate, you turn the chopsticks back to their proper position. Never stick your chopsticks down vertically into your bowl of rice and leave them there—that is done only when a person has died. Similarly, you're not supposed to pass anything between chopsticks, since that's how cremated bones are passed in a Buddhist funeral.

If you're eating soup you won't use a spoon but, rather, will pick up the bowl and drink from it. It's considered in good taste to slurp with gusto, especially if you're eating noodles. Noodle shops in Japan are always well orchestrated with slurps and smacks. And, by the way, it's considered bad manners to walk down the street in Japan eating or drinking. You'll notice that if a Japanese buys a drink from a vending machine, he'll stand there, gulp it down, and throw away the container before going on.

If you're drinking in Japan, the main thing to remember is that you never pour your own glass. Bottles of beer in Japan are so large that people often share one. The rule is that, in turn, one person pours for everyone else in the group, so be sure to hold up your glass when someone is pouring for you. Only as the night progresses do the Japanese get sloppy about this rule. It took me a while to figure this one out, but if no one notices that your glass is empty, the best thing to do is to pour everyone else a drink so that someone will pour yours. If someone wants to pour you a drink and your glass is full, the proper thing to do is to take a few gulps so that he or she can fill your glass. Because each person is continually filling everyone else's glass, you never know exactly how much you've had to drink, which (depending on how you look at it) is very good or very bad.

SHOES

Nothing is so distasteful to the Japanese as the bottoms of shoes, and as such they are taken off before entering a home, a Japanese-style inn, a temple, and even some museums and restaurants. Usually there will be some plastic slippers at the entranceway for you to slip on, but whenever you encounter tatami you should take off even these slippers—only bare feet or socks are allowed to tread upon tatami.

Rest rooms present a whole other set of slippers. If you're in a home or Japanese inn, you'll notice another pair of slippers—again plastic or rubber—sitting right inside the rest room at the door. Step out of the hallway plastic shoes and into the bathroom slippers, and wear these the whole time you're in the rest room. When you're finished, change back into the hallway slippers. If you forget this last change-over, you'll regret it—nothing is as embarrassing as walking down the hall in the bathroom slippers and not realizing what you've done until you see the mixed looks of horror and mirth on the faces of the Japanese. Although it might seem like a lot of bother to go through all this ritual with the shoes, it actually does make sense once you get used to it.

THE JAPANESE BATH

On my very first trip to Japan I was certain that I would never get into a Japanese bath. I was under the misconception that men and women bathed together and I couldn't imagine getting into a tub with a group of smiling and bowing Japanese men. I needn't have worried. The good news (or, I suppose, bad news for some of you) is that in almost all circumstances bathing is segregated for men and women in Japan. There are some exceptions, primarily outdoor hot-spring spas in the country-side, but the women who go to these are usually grandmothers who couldn't care less. Young Japanese women wouldn't dream of jumping into a tub with a group of male strangers. And, by the way, whoever said that the Japanese are very good at averting their eyes and don't stare must have been blind. I once went to an outdoor sulfurous hot-spring spa with a group of friends where there were little pools spread throughout the hillside. We finally found a deserted pool and bathed, but as we were getting dressed we discovered a group of hikers in the distance observing us with binoculars. Honestly!

Anyway, Japanese baths are delightful—and I, for one, am addicted to them. You find them at Japanese-style inns, hot-spring spas, and at neighborhood baths (not everyone has his or her own bath in Japan). Sometimes they're elaborate affairs with many tubs, plants, and statues, and sometimes they're nothing more than a tiny tub. The procedure at all of them is the same. After completely disrobing in the changing room and putting your clothes in either a locker or basket, hold your wash cloth in front of you so that it covers the vital parts and walk into the bath area. There you'll find a plastic basin (they used to be wood), a plastic stool, and faucets along the wall. Sit on the stool in front of the faucet and repeatedly fill your basin with water, splashing it all over you. If there's no hot water from the faucet, it's acceptable to dip your plastic basin into the hot bath. Soap yourself down and completely— and I mean *completely*—rinse away all traces of soap. After you're squeaky clean you're ready to get into the bath. After your bath, do not pull the plug.

Your first attempt at a Japanese bath may be painful—simply too scalding for comfort. It helps if you ease in gently and then sit perfectly still. You'll notice all tension and stiffness ebbing away, a decidedly relaxing way to end the day. The Japanese are so fond of baths that many take them every night, especially in the winter, when a hot bath keeps one toasty warm for hours afterward. Who knows, with time you'll probably become addicted too.

TIPS ON BEHAVIOR

Most forms of behavior and etiquette in Japan developed to allow relationships to be as frictionless as possible, a pretty good idea in crowded Japan. The Japanese don't like confrontations, and although I'm told they occur, I've never seen a fight in Japan.

The Japanese are an emotional people but they're very good at covering almost all unpleasantness with a smile. Foreigners find the smile hard to read, but a smiling Japanese face can mean happiness, sadness, embarrassment, even anger. My first lesson in this happened on a subway in Tokyo where I saw a middle-aged Japanese woman who was about to board the subway brutally knocked out of the way by a Japanese man rushing off the train. She almost lost her balance but she gave a little laugh, smiled, and got on the train. A few minutes later as the train was speeding through the tunnel, I stole a look at her and was able to read her true feelings on her face. Lost in her own thoughts, she knitted her brow in consternation and looked most upset and unhappy. The smile had been a put-on.

Another aspect of Japanese behavior that sometimes causes difficulty for foreigners is that the Japanese find it very difficult to say no. They're much more apt to say that your request is very difficult to fulfill or they'll simply beat around the bush without giving a definite answer. At this point you're expected to let the subject drop. Showing impatience, anger, or aggressiveness rarely gets you anywhere in Japan. Apologizing sometimes does. And if someone does give in to your request, you can't say thank you enough.

MISCELLANEOUS ETIQUETTE

If you are invited to a Japanese home, you should know that it is a rarity and an honor. Most Japanese consider their homes too small and humble for entertaining guests, which is why there are so many restaurants, coffeeshops, and bars. If you are invited to a home, don't show up empty-handed. Bring a small gift such as candy, fruit, or flowers. Alcohol is also appreciated. You don't have to fly to Japan more than once to realize that—it seems as if every Japanese on board is laden down with his or her three-bottle quota of alcohol. Take your cue from them and stock up on a few bottles on the flight over if you know you'll be visiting someone. Whisky and brandy seem to be the favorites.

When the Japanese give back change, they hand it back to you in a lump sum rather than counting it out. Trust them. It's considered insulting for you to sit there and count it in front of them because it insinuates that you think they might be trying to cheat you. The Japanese are honest. It's one of the great pleasures of being in their country.

Don't blow your nose in public if you can help it and never at the dinner table. It's considered most disgusting. On the other hand, even though the Japanese are very hygienic they are not at all averse to spitting on the sidewalk. And, even more peculiar, the men urinate when and where they want, usually against a tree or a wall and most often after a night of carousing in the bars.

This being a man's society, men will walk in and out of doors and elevators before women, and in subways will often sit down while their wives stand. Some Japanese men who have had contact with the Western world and who know that in the West it's women before men will make a gallant show of allowing a Western woman to step out of the elevator, etc., first. For the sake of Western women living in Japan, such men should be warmly thanked and their behavior greatly encouraged.

---

7. A Word About Japanese Inns

Even though it can be very expensive, it's worth it to splurge at least once during your trip to Japan to spend the night in an old Japanese-style inn. Nothing conveys the mood, simplistic beauty, and atmosphere of old Japan better than these small enclaves of gleaming polished wood, tatami floors, rice-paper sliding doors, meticulously pruned Japanese gardens, and kimono-clad hostesses. Personalized service and exquisitely prepared meals are the trademarks of a Japanese inn, called ryokan in Japanese, and staying in one of these is like taking a trip back in time.

Ideally made of wood with tile roofs, most ryokan are small, only one or two stories high with about 10 to 30 rooms. The entrance is often through a gate and small garden, whereupon you are met by a bowing woman in a kimono. Take off your shoes, slide on the plastic slippers, and follow your hostess down long wooden corridors until you reach the sliding door of your room. After taking off your slippers, step into your tatami room, which is almost void of furniture—a low table in the middle of the room, floor cushions, an antique scroll hanging in an alcove, a simple flower arrangement, and best of all, a view past rice-paper sliding screens of a Japanese landscaped garden with bonsai, stone lanterns, and a meandering pond filled with carp. You notice that there's no bed in the room.

Almost immediately your hostess brings you a welcoming hot tea and a sweet, served at your low table so that you might sit there for a while and appreciate the view, the peace, and the solitude. Next comes your hot bath, either in your own room (if you have one) or in the communal bath. (Be sure to follow the procedure outlined in the previous section on Japanese etiquette, soaping and rinsing yourself *before* getting into the tub.) After bathing and soaking away all tension, aches, and pains, change into your yukata, a cotton kimono provided by the ryokan.

When you return to your room, you'll find the maid ready to serve your dinner, which consists of locally grown vegetables, fish, and various regional specialties all spread out on many tiny plates. There is no menu in a ryokan but, rather, one or more set courses determined by the chef. Admire how each dish is in itself a delicate piece of artwork, adorned with slices of ginger, a maple leaf, or a flower. It all looks too wonderful to eat, but finally hunger takes over. If you want, you can order sake or beer to accompany your meal.

After you've finished eating, your maid will return to clear away the dishes and to lay out your bed. Called a *futon*, it's a kind of mattress with quilts and is laid out on the tatami floor. The next morning the maid will wake you up, put away the futon, and serve a breakfast of fish, pickled vegetables, soup, dried seaweed, rice, and a raw egg to be mixed with the rice. Feeling rested, well fed, and pampered, you are then ready to pack your bags and pay your bill. Your hostess sees you off at the front gate, smiling and bowing as you set off for the rest of your travels.

Such is life at a good ryokan. Sadly enough, however, the number of upper-class ryokan diminishes each year. Unable to compete with the more profitable high-rise hotels, many ryokan in Japan's large cities have had to close down, with the result that there are very few left in such cities as Tokyo or Osaka. If you want to stay in a Japanese inn, it's best to do so at a resort or hot-spring spa. Altogether there are approximately 90,000 ryokan still operating in Japan in a variety of different price ranges. Although ideally a ryokan is an old wooden structure at least 100 years old and perhaps once the home of a samurai or a wealthy merchant, many—especially those in hot-spring resort areas—are modern concrete affairs with as many as 100 or more rooms. What they lack in intimacy, however, is made up for in modern bathrooms and the added attractions of perhaps a bar and outdoor recreational facilities. Most guest rooms are fitted with color television, phone, and a safe for locking up valuables.

Unlike Western-style hotels, rates in a ryokan are based on a per-person charge rather than a straight room charge, and they include breakfast, dinner, and service charge. Tax is usually extra. Although rates can vary from ¥8,000 ($64) to ¥60,000 ($480) per person, the average cost is generally ¥10,000 ($80) to ¥20,000 ($160). Even within a single ryokan the rates can vary greatly, depending on the room you choose, the dinner courses you select, and the number of people in your room. If you're paying the highest rate, you can be certain you are getting the best view of the garden, or perhaps even your own private garden, as well as a better meal than the lower-paying guests. All the rates for ryokan in this book are based on double occupancy; if there are more than two of you in one room, you can generally count on a slightly cheaper per-person rate.

Although I have heartily recommended that you try spending at least one night in a ryokan, there are a number of disadvantages to this style of accommodation. In my estimation, however, the experience itself far outweights the disadvantages. The most obvious problem may be that you will find it uncomfortable sitting on the floor. And because the futon is put away during the day, there's no place except the hard tatami-covered floor on which to lie down for an afternoon nap or rest. In addition, some of the older ryokan, though quaint, are bitterly cold in the winter and may have only Japanese-style toilets. As for breakfast, some foreigners might find it difficult to swallow raw egg, rice, and seaweed in the morning. Sometimes you can get a Western-style breakfast if you order it the night before, but more often than not the fried or scrambled eggs will arrive cold, leading you to suspect that they were cooked right after you ordered them.

A ryokan is also quite rigid in its schedule. You're expected to arrive sometime after 4 p.m., take your bath, and then eat at around 6 or 7 p.m. Breakfast is served early, usually by 8 a.m., and check-out is by 10 a.m. That means you can't sleep in late, and because the maid is continually coming in and out, you have a lot less privacy than you would in a hotel.

The main drawback of the ryokan, however, is that the majority of them will not take you. They simply do not want to deal with the problems inherent in accepting a foreign guest, including the language barrier and differing customs. I saw a number of beautiful old ryokan that I would have liked to include in this book, but I was turned away at the door. The ryokan in this guide, therefore, are ones willing to take in foreigners, but because management and policies can change, it's best to call beforehand. In fact, you should always make a reservation if you want to stay in a first-class ryokan, and even in most medium-priced ones, because the chef has to shop for and prepare your meals. They do not look kindly upon unannounced strangers turning up on their doorstep.

You can book a reservation for a ryokan through any travel agency in Japan, such as the Japan Travel Bureau (JTB), or by calling a ryokan directly, though it's best if the call is conducted in Japanese, and you may be required to pay a deposit.

8. Other Types of Accommodations

Besides ryokan there are a number of other kinds of accommodations available in Japan, ranging from inexpensive Japanese-style to large Western-style hotels. Although theoretically you can travel throughout Japan without making reservations beforehand, it's essential to do so if you're traveling during peak travel seasons, and recommended at other times. These peak times are the end of April through the first week of May (called Golden Week), New Year's holiday from about December 27 to January 4, and mid-July through August, particularly around mid-August.

If you find all my recommendations for a certain city fully booked, there are several ways to find alternative accommodations. Easiest is to book through a travel agency, such as the Japan Travel Bureau. If you arrive at your destination and need help obtaining accommodations, most major train stations in Japan have a hotel and ryokan reservation office that will find you a place to stay. Although policies may differ from office to office, you generally don't have to pay a fee for their services, though you usually do have to pay a percentage of your overnight charge as a deposit. The disadvantage is that you don't see the locale beforehand, and if there's space left here even in peak tourist season, you can guess that there's probably a pretty good reason for it. The two worst places I've stayed in in Japan were booked through one of these reservation offices at a train station (don't worry, I don't recommend them in this book). Although these offices can be a real lifesaver in a pinch and in most cases may be able to recommend quite reasonable and pleasant places in which to stay, it certainly pays to plan in advance.

JAPANESE-STYLE ACCOMMODATIONS

If you want to experience a Japanese-style inn but can't afford the prices of a ryokan, there are a number of other types of accommodations available. Though they don't offer the personalized service and beautiful setting of a ryokan, they do offer the chance to stay in a simple tatami room, sleep on a futon, and in some cases eat Japanese food. As at a ryokan, prices are per person and include service charge and often two meals as well. English is rarely spoken.

Japanese Inn Group

The Japanese Inn Group is a special group of more than 60 Japanese-style inns throughout Japan that offer inexpensive lodging and cater largely to foreigners. Although at first thought you may balk at the idea of staying at a place filled mainly with foreigners, you must remember that most of the cheap Japanese-style inns in Japan are not accustomed to guests from abroad and may be quite reluctant to take you in. I have covered many of these Japanese Inn Group members in this guidebook and have found the owners for the most part to be an exceptional group of friendly people eager to offer foreigners the chance to experience life on tatami and futon. In many cases these are good places in which to exchange information with other world travelers, and they are popular with both young people and families.

A Note On Japanese Symbols

Many hotels, restaurants, and other establishments in Japan do not have signs showing their names in English letters. Appendix II lists the Japanese symbols for all such places appearing in this guide. Each establishment name in Japanese symbols is numbered, and the same number appears in an oval in the text following the boldfaced establishment name. For example, in the text Osaka's **Hotel Hokke Club** ⑯ is number 164 in the Japanese symbol list in Appendix II.

Although they call themselves ryokan, they are not ryokan in the true sense of the word because they do not offer personalized service and many of them do not serve food. However, they do offer simple tatami rooms that generally come with a coin-operated TV and sometimes with a coin-operated air conditioner as well. Some of them have towels and the cotton yukata kimono for your use. Facilities generally include a coin-operated washer and dryer and a public bath, and the average cost of a one-night stay is about ¥4,000 ($32) per person, without meals.

Upon your arrival in Japan, you can pick up a pamphlet at the Tourist Information Center in Tokyo called *Japanese Inn Group*, which lists the members of this organization. You should make reservations directly with the ryokan in which you wish to stay. In some cases you will be asked to pay a deposit (equal to one night's stay), which you can do with a personal check, traveler's check, money order, or bank check, but the easiest way is with American Express. If you want more information, the Inn Group's office headquarters is at 314, Hayao-cho, Kaminoguchi-agaru, Ninomiyacho-dori, Shimogyo-ku, Kyoto 600 (tel. 075/351-6748). If you're in Tokyo, there's a liaison office at 03/822-2251, but the T.I.C. may be able to answer your questions.

Minshuku

Technically, a *minshuku* is an inexpensive lodging in a private home. The average per-person cost for one night is about ¥5,000 ($40) to ¥6,000 ($48), including two meals. Because minshuku are family-run affairs, you are expected to lay out your own futon at night, supply your own towel and nightgown, and tidy up your room in the morning. Rooms do not have their own private bathroom, but there is a public bath. Meals are served in a communal dining room. Minshuku can range from thatched farmhouses to old rickety wooden buildings to modern concrete structures. Although, officially, the difference between a ryokan and a minshuku is that the ryokan is supposedly more expensive and provides more services, the difference is sometimes very slight. I've stayed in cheap ryokan that provided almost no service at all and in minshuku too large and modern to be considered private homes.

Since minshuku cater primarily to Japanese travelers, they're often excellent places in which to meet the locals, and I've included in this guide a number of minshuku willing to take in foreigners. For more information, contact the **Japan Minshuku Center,** Kotsu Kaikan Building, Basement 1, 2-10-1 Yurakucho, Chiyoda-ku, Tokyo (tel. 03/216-6556). It's open from 10 a.m. to 6:30 p.m. (to 5 p.m. on Saturday) every day except Sunday and holidays, and you can make reservations here for member minshuku across the country.

Kokumin Shukusha

A *kokumin shukusha* is public lodging found primarily in resort and vacation areas. Established by the government, there are more than 300 of these facilities throughout Japan. Catering largely to Japanese school groups and families, they offer basic, Japanese-style rooms at an average daily rate of about ¥6,000 ($48) per person, including two meals. Although you don't have to have a reservation to stay in these places, they are usually quite full during the summer and peak seasons. Reservations can be made through a travel agency. The drawback to many of these lodges is that because they are often located in national parks and in scenic spots, the best way to reach them is by car.

Kokumin Kyuka Mura

Similar to kokumin shukusha, the *kokumin kyuka mura* is a "vacation village" that is government-run and located in a national park, but the difference is that it is more expensive, generally around ¥8,500 ($68) per person with two meals, and offers more recreational facilities. Apply through a travel agency.

Shukubo

These are lodgings in a Buddhist temple. Japanese-style rooms, they are similar to inexpensive ryokan except that they're attached to temples and serve vegetarian food. There is usually an early-morning service at 6 a.m. in which you are welcome to join. Probably the best place to experience life in a temple is at Mount Koya (described in Chapter VIII). Prices at a *shukubo* range from about ¥5,000 ($40) to ¥11,000 ($88) per person, including two meals.

WESTERN-STYLE ACCOMMODATIONS

Lodging in this category ranges from large first-class hotels to inexpensive ones catering primarily to Japanese businessmen. Remember in figuring out your bill that accommodations costing more than ¥10,000 ($80) per person per night will add a 6% local/consumption tax, while accommodations costing less than ¥10,000 will add a 3% consumption tax. There will also be a 10% to 15% service charge added to your bill. Although ryokan and some of the less expensive types of lodging include service and sometimes tax in their price, most hotels do not. Unless otherwise stated, therefore, you can assume that 16% to 21% will be added to the prices quoted in this book for hotels costing more than ¥10,000 ($80) per person per night. Incidentally, a twin room refers to a room with twin beds and a double room refers to one with a double bed.

Hotels

Both first-class and medium-priced hotels in Japan are known for their excellent service and cleanliness. The first-class hotels in the larger cities can compete with the best hotels in the world, and offer a wide range of services, which may include a health club and massage services (for which there's an extra charge), an executive business center with secretarial services, a guest relations officer to help with any problems you may have, a travel agency, a shopping arcade, cocktail lounges with live music, and fine Japanese- and Western-style restaurants. Rooms have their own private bathroom and color television, and usually a radio, a hot-water thermos with tea bags, and a minibar. Because they're accustomed to foreigners, most hotels in this category employ an English-speaking staff. The most expensive hotels in Japan are in Tokyo, where you will pay at least ¥18,000 ($144) for a single room in a first-class hotel. Outside Tokyo, single rooms in this category generally range from about ¥10,000 ($80) to ¥14,000 ($112), while in medium-priced hotels rooms are usually about ¥2,000 ($16) less.

Business Hotels

Catering primarily to traveling Japanese businessmen, a "business hotel" is a no-frills establishment with tiny, sparsely furnished rooms, most of them singles, but usually with some twin or double rooms also available. Primarily just a place to crash for the night, these rooms usually have everything you need but in miniature form—minuscule bathrooms, tiny bathtubs, small beds, and barely enough space to unpack your bags. After a while these business hotels all start to look alike. If you're a large person you may have trouble sleeping in a place like this. There are no bellboys, no room service, and sometimes not even a lobby or coffeeshop, although usually there are vending machines that dispense beer and soda. The advantages to staying in business hotels is that they're inexpensive—often starting at ¥5,000 ($40) for a single—and are often conveniently located next to train and subway stations. Although check-in is usually not until 3 or 4 p.m. and check-out is usually at 10 a.m., you can leave your bags at the front desk. The most sophisticated business hotels can be found in Tokyo, where because of high prices they make up the bulk of medium-priced accommodations.

Pensions

If you see an accommodation listed as a pension, you know that it is the Western equivalent of a minshuku. Usually containing no more than ten rooms, these Western-style lodges come with beds and, on the average, charge ¥6,000 ($48) to ¥8,000 ($64) per person, including two meals. Many seem geared to young Japanese girls and are thus done up in rather feminine-looking decor with lots of pinks and flower prints. They're most often located in ski resorts and in the countryside, sometimes making access a problem.

Youth Hostels

There are more than 450 youth hostels in Japan, most of them privately run and operating in locations ranging from temples to concrete blocks. There is no age limit, and although most of them require a youth hostel membership card from the Japan Youth Hostel Association, they often let foreigners stay without one for about ¥500 ($4) extra per night. Although there are usually such restrictions as a 9 or 10 p.m. curfew, meals at fixed times, and rooms with many bunk beds or futons, youth hostels are quite cheap, costing about ¥3,000 ($24) per day, including two meals. They're certainly the cheapest places to stay in Japan, though one Norwegian I met compared life in a youth hostel to that in the military. They're not quite that regimented, but you get the picture.

I've included youth hostels throughout my guide just in case you want to try some of them to keep down costs. If you plan on staying exclusively in youth hostels, however, you should pick up a pamphlet available at the Tourist Information Centers in Tokyo or Kyoto called *Youth Hostel Map of Japan.* You should also get a youth hostel membership card. If you fail to get one in your own country, you can get one in Japan for ¥2,200 ($17.60). The **Japan Youth Hostel Association** is located in the Hoken Kaikan Honkan Building, 1-2 Sadohara-cho, Ichigaya, Shinjuku-ku, Tokyo 162 (tel. 03/269-5831). Other places in Tokyo where you can buy a youth hostel card are at YH information counters on the fourth floor of Keio Department Store in Shinjuku, the second basement of Sogo Department Store in front of Yurakucho Station, and on the seventh floor of Seibu Department Store in Ikebukuro.

9. Food and Drink

Whenever I leave Japan it's the food I miss the most. Sure, there are *sushi* bars and other Japanese specialty restaurants spread throughout the United States, but they don't offer nearly the variety you can get in Japan. For just as America has more to offer than hamburgers and steaks, Japan has more than just sushi and *tempura*. For both the gourmet and the uninitiated, Japan is a treasure trove of culinary surprises.

Altogether there are more than a dozen different and distinct types of Japanese cuisine, as well as countless regional specialties. A good deal of what you eat may be completely new to you as well as completely unidentifiable. No need to worry. I've found that sometimes the Japanese don't even know what they're eating, so varied and so wide is the range of Japanese edibles. The rule is simply to enjoy, and the joy of Japanese food begins even before it enters your mouth. To the Japanese, presentation of food is as important as the food itself, and dishes are designed to appeal to the eye as well as to the palate. In contrast to the American way of piling as much food as possible onto a single plate, the Japanese use lots of small plates, each arranged artfully with bite-size morsels of food. After you've seen what can be done with maple leaves, flowers, bits of bamboo, and even pebbles to enhance the appearance of food, your relationship with what you eat may be changed forever.

The biggest problem facing the hungry foreigner in Japan is ordering, because few restaurants have English menus. This book alleviates that problem to a large extent by giving some sample dishes and prices for specific restaurants throughout Japan. Another custom in Japan that simplifies ordering is the use of plastic food models in glass display cases either outside or just inside the front door. Sushi, tempura, daily specials, spaghetti—they're all there in mouthwatering plastic replicas, along with the corresponding prices. The use of such food models began after Japan opened its doors a century ago and was inundated by all kinds of strange, foreign things. Food was one of them, and the models eased the problems of ordering. Today those plastic dishes work in reverse by saving the hungry lives of visiting foreigners. Simply decide what you want and point it out to your waitress.

Unfortunately, not all restaurants in Japan have plastic display cases. When that's the situation, the best thing to do is to look at what people around you are eating and order what looks best. An alternative is to simply order the teishoku, or the daily special. These are set courses and often include an entire meal with soup, rice, appetizer, and main dish. Although some restaurants have special set courses for dinner as well, lunch is the usual time for the teishoku, and you can help keep your costs down by eating your big meal in the middle of the day. Even a restaurant that may be prohibitive to your budget at dinnertime may be perfect for a lunchtime splurge, when specials may cost as little as a fourth of what a dinner would be. The usual time for the teishoku is from about 11 or 11:30 a.m. to 2 p.m.

Keep in mind that restaurants will add a 3% tax to your bill. First-class restaurants will also add a 10% to 15% service charge.

For those of you who may not want to eat Japanese food every day, I've included suggestions throughout this book for non-Japanese restaurants as well. The most popular Western-style restaurants in Japan are Italian and French, although more often than not they cook for the Japanese rather than the Western palate. French nouvelle cuisine matches well the Japanese style of cooking, since both stress presentation, textures, and flavor, and the most expensive foreign restaurants in Japan are nearly all French. Other popular restaurants in Japan include Indian and Chinese, as well as numerous steakhouses.

Below are explanations of some of Japan's most common types of cuisine and foods. Generally speaking, only one type of cuisine is served in a given restaurant—that is, only raw seafood is served in a sushi bar. There are some exceptions to this, especially in those restaurants where raw fish may be served as an appetizer. In addition, some of Japan's drinking establishments offer a wide range of foods, from soups to salads to sushi to skewered pieces of chicken.

RICE
There are no problems here—everyone is familiar with rice. The difference, however, is that in Japan it is quite sticky, making it easier to pick up with chopsticks. It's also just plain white rice (called *gohan*)—no salt, no butter, no soy sauce. Like other Asians, the Japanese have used rice as a staple in their diet for about 2,000 years, though not everyone in the old days could afford the expensive white kind. The peasants had to be satisfied with a mixture of white and brown rice, millet, and greens. Today some Japanese still eat rice three times a day, though the younger ones are now just as apt to have bread and coffee for breakfast.

KAISEKI CUISINE
Kaiseki is the king of Japanese cuisine, the epitome of delicately and exquisitely arranged food, the ultimate in Japanese aesthetic appeal. It's also among the most expensive and can cost ¥20,000 ($160) or more per person. Some restaurants, however, do offer mini-kaiseki courses that are much more affordable. The reason kaiseki is expensive is that much time and skill are involved in preparing each of the many dishes, with the ingredients cooked so as to preserve their natural flavor. Even the plates are chosen with great care, meant to enhance the color, texture, and shape of each piece of food.

Kaiseki cuisine is based on the four seasons, with the selection of food and its presentation dependent on the time of the year. In fact, so strongly does a kaiseki preparation convey the mood of a particular season that the kaiseki gourmet can tell what season it is just by looking at his meal. The roots of kaiseki go back to the development of the tea ceremony, when monks ate small morsels of food to protect the stomach against the effects of strong tea.

A kaiseki meal is usually a lengthy affair, with various dishes appearing in set order. First comes the appetizer, clear broth, and one uncooked dish. These are followed by a boiled, broiled, fried, steamed, heated, and vinegared dishes, and finally by another soup, rice, pickled vegetables, and fruit. Since kaiseki is always a set course, there's no problem in ordering. Let your budget be your guide.

SUSHI AND SASHIMI
It is estimated that the average Japanese eats 70 pounds of seafood a year, six times the amount Americans do. Although this seafood may be served in any number of ways, from grilled to boiled, a great deal of it is eaten raw. Granted, the idea of eating raw fish might seem a little strange at first, but if you'll just try it you'll probably like it.

Sashimi is simply raw seafood. A good choice to start out with if you've never eaten it is *maguro,* or lean tuna. Contrary to what you might think, it doesn't taste fishy at all and is so delicate in texture that it almost melts in your mouth. The way to eat sashimi is first to mix *wasabi* (pungent green horseradish) into a small dish of soy sauce and then dip the raw fish into the sauce.

Sushi, also called *nigiri-zushi,* is raw fish, seafood, or vegetables placed on top of vinegared rice with just a touch of wasabi. It's also dipped into soy sauce. Use chopsticks or your fingers to eat sushi; remember that you're supposed to eat each piece in one bite—quite a mouthful but about the only way to keep it from falling apart. Another trick is to turn it upside down when you dip it into the sauce so that only the fish and not the rice touches the sauce.

Typical sushi includes flounder (*hirame*), sea bream (*tai*), squid (*ika*), octopus (*tako*), shrimp (*ebi*), and omelet (*tamago*). Ordering is easy because you usually sit at the sushi bar, where you can see all the food in a refrigerated glass case in front of you. You also get to see all the action of the sushi chefs at work. The typical meal begins with sashimi and is followed by sushi, but if you don't want to order separately, there are always various set courses.

TEMPURA

Today a well-known Japanese food, tempura was actually introduced by the Portuguese, who came to Japan in the 16th century. *Tempura* is deep-fried food that has been coated in a batter of egg, water, and wheat flour and is served piping hot. To eat it, dip it into a soy sauce that has been mixed with a fish stock base and flavored with radish (*daikon*) and grated ginger. Various tempura specialties may include eggplant, mushroom, sweet potato, green pepper, slices of lotus root, shrimp, squid, and many kinds of fish. Again, the easiest thing to do is to order the set course, the teishoku. If you're still hungry you can always order something extra à la carte.

SUKIYAKI

Until about a hundred years ago the Japanese could think of nothing so disgusting as eating the flesh of animals (fish was okay). Considered unclean by the Buddhists, meat consumption was banned by the emperor way back in the 7th century. Imagine the horror of the Japanese to discover that Western "barbarians" ate bloody meat! It wasn't until Emperor Meiji himself made a public announcement a century ago that he was going to eat meat that the Japanese accepted the idea. Today the Japanese have become skilled in preparing a number of beef dishes. And according to a survey conducted a couple of years back by the Japan Fisheries Association, grilled meat, curried rice, and hamburger were the three favorite dishes among senior high school boys living in Tokyo. The girls, by the way, still preferred sushi.

Sukiyaki is one of Japan's best-known beef dishes and is one many Westerners seem to prefer. Actually its origins are more Western than Japanese (it was introduced in the last century as a new Western cuisine). To the Western palate, however, it seems distinctly Japanese and today enjoys immense popularity in Japan. Whenever I'm invited to a Japanese home, this is the meal most often served. Like fondue, it's cooked at the table, which makes for an intimate and cozy setting.

Sukiyaki is thinly sliced beef cooked in a broth of soy sauce, stock, and sake, along with scallions, spinach, mushrooms, tofu, bamboo shoots, and other vegetables. All diners serve themselves by taking what they want out of the simmering pot and then dipping it into their own bowl of raw egg. You can skip the raw egg if you want, but it adds to the taste and also cools the food down enough so it doesn't burn your tongue.

SHABU-SHABU

Similar to sukiyaki, *shabu-shabu* is also prepared at your table and consists of thinly sliced beef cooked in a broth with vegetables. The main difference between the two is the broth. Whereas in sukiyaki it consists of stock flavored with soy sauce and sake and is slightly sweet, the broth of shabu-shabu is relatively clear and has little taste of its own. The pots used are also different.

Named for the swishing sound the beef supposedly makes when it's cooking, shabu-shabu is a meal in which you hold your own piece of meat in the watery broth with your chopsticks until it cooks, usually only a few seconds. Vegetables are left in longer to swim around until you fish them out. Sauces are either sesame with diced green onions or a more bitter sauce made from fish stock. Restaurants serving sukiyaki usually serve shabu-shabu as well.

TEPPANYAKI

A *teppanyaki* restaurant is a Japanese steakhouse. As in the famous Benihana restaurants in many cities in the United States, the chef slices, dices, and cooks your meal of tenderloin or sirloin steak and vegetables on a smooth hot grill right in front of you. Because beef is relatively new in Japanese cooking, some people categorize teppanyaki restaurants as "Western" cuisine. However, I consider its style of cooking and presentation unique enough that throughout this book I generally refer to such restaurants as Japanese.

ROBATAYAKI

Robatayaki refers to restaurants in which seafood and vegetables are cooked over a *robata* grill. In the olden days an open fireplace (robata) in the middle of an old Japanese house was the center of activity for cooking, eating, socializing, and simply keeping warm. So today's robatayaki restaurants are like nostalgia trips back into Japan's past. They are often decorated in rustic farmhouse style with the staff dressed in traditional clothing. Many robatayaki restaurants are open only in the evenings and are popular among office workers for both eating and drinking.

There's no special menu in a robatayaki restaurant—rather, it includes just about everything eaten in Japan. The difference is that most of the foods will be grilled. Favorites of mine include gingko nuts, asparagus, green peppers, mushrooms, potatoes, and just about any kind of fish. You can also usually get skewers of beef or chicken as well as a stew of meat and potatoes (*nikujaga*), delicious in cold winter months. Since ordering is à la carte, you'll just have to look and point.

YAKITORI

Yakitori is chunks of chicken or chicken parts basted in a sweet soy sauce and grilled over a charcoal fire on thin skewers. A place that serves yakitori (sometimes called a *yakitori-ya* and often identifiable by a red paper lantern outside its front door) is technically not a restaurant but, rather, a drinking establishment. It usually doesn't open until 5 p.m., and most are extremely popular with the working crowd as inexpensive places to drink, eat, and be merry.

Although you can order a set dish of various yakitori, I usually refrain because this will often include various parts of the chicken like the skin, heart, and liver. You may like such exotica but they're definitely not for me. If you're ordering by the stick, you might want to try chicken meatballs (*tsukune*), green peppers (*piman*), chicken and leeks (*negima*), mushrooms (*shitake*), gingko nuts (*ginnan*), or chicken breast (*sasami*).

KUSHIAGE

Kushiage foods (also called *kushikatsu* or *kushiyaki*) are deep-fried on skewers and include chicken, beef, seafood, and lots of seasonal vegetables (snowpeas, gingko nuts, lotus root, and the like). The result is delicious and I highly recommend trying it. I don't understand why this style of cooking isn't better known— maybe someday it will be. Ordering the set menu is easiest, and what you get is often determined by both the chef and the season.

TONKATSU

Tonkatsu is the Japanese word for "pork cutlet" and it's made by dredging pork in wheat flour, moistening it with egg and water, dipping it in bread crumbs, and deep-frying it in vegetable oil. Restaurants serving tonkatsu are generally inexpensive and therefore popular with office workers and families. The easiest order is the teishoku, and the most common is with either the pork filet (*hirekatsu*) or the pork loin (*rosukatsu*). In any case, your tonkatsu is served on a bed of lettuce or shredded cabbage, and two different sauces will be at your table.

FUGU

Known as the blowfish, pufferfish, or globefish in English, *fugu* is perhaps one of the most exotic and adventurous foods in Japan, primarily because if it's not prepared properly it means almost certain death for the consumer. In the past decade or so as many as 200 people in Japan have died from fugu poisoning, usually because they tried preparing it at home. The ovaries and intestines of the fugu are deadly and must be entirely removed, without puncturing them. So why eat fugu if it can kill you? Well, for one thing it's delicious, and for another, fugu chefs are strictly licensed by the government and greatly skilled in preparing fugu dishes. You can eat fugu raw (*sashimi*) or in a stew (*fugu-chiri*) cooked with vegetables at your table. The season for fresh fugu is from October or November through March, but some restaurants serve it throughout the year.

UNAGI

I'll bet that if you ate *unagi* without knowing what it was, you'd find it very tasty. In fact, you'd probably be very surprised to find out that you had just eaten eel. Popular as a health food because of its high vitamin A content, eel is supposed to help fight fatigue during the hot summer months but is eaten year-round. Broiled eel (*kabayaki*) is prepared by grilling filet strips over a charcoal fire; the eel is repeatedly dipped in a sweetened barbecue soy sauce while cooking. A favorite way to eat broiled eel is on top of rice, in which case it's called *unaju*. Do yourself a favor and try it.

NOODLES

The Japanese love eating noodles but I suspect that at least part of the fascination stems from the *way* they eat them—they slurp and suck them in with a speed that defies gravity. If you ask me, Gone in 60 Seconds could describe the way a businessman attacks his lunchtime bowl of noodles. At any rate, you're *supposed* to slurp noodles: it's considered proper etiquette. Fearing that it would stick with me forever, however, slurping is a technique I never quite mastered.

There are many different kinds of noodles—some are eaten plain, some in combination with other foods; some hot and some cold. *Soba,* made from buckwheat flour, is eaten hot or cold. *Udon* is a thick, white noodle originally from Osaka and is usually served hot. *Somen* is a fine, white noodle that is eaten cold in the summer and dunked in a cold sauce.

Noodle shops are generally inexpensive, ranging from stand-up stalls seen around train stations to more traditional restaurants, where guests sit at low tables on tatami.

OKONOMIYAKI

Meaning literally "as you like it," *okonomiyaki* originated in Osaka and is sort of like a Japanese pizza. Basically it's a kind of pancake to which meat or fish, shredded cabbage, and vegetables are added. Since it's a popular fare of street vendors, restaurants specializing in this type of cuisine are very reasonably priced. At some locales the cook makes it for you, but in others it's do-it-yourself, which can be quite fun if you're with a group.

OTHER TYPES OF CUISINE

During your travels you might also run into other types of Japanese cuisine. *Kamameshi* is a rice casserole with different kinds of toppings that might include seafood, meat, or vegetables. *Nabe* cuisine is a stew cooked in an earthenware pot at your table with ingredients that might consist of chicken, sliced beef, pork, or seafood, and vegetables. *Oden* is fish cakes, *tofu,* and vegetables steeped in broth, served with hot mustard.

Although technically Chinese fast-food restaurants, *ramen* shops are so much a part of dining in Japan that I feel compelled to include them here. Serving what I consider to be generic Chinese noodles, soups, and other dishes, ramen shops can be found everywhere in Japan, easily recognizable by their red signs, flashing lights, and quite often pictures of various dishes displayed right by the front door. In addition to ramen (noodle and vegetable soup) you can also get such things as *yakisoba* (fried noodles) or—my favorite—*gyoza,* which are fried pork dumplings. What these places lack in atmosphere is made up for in price: most dishes average about ¥500 ($4).

BUDGET CHOICES

Although some of the above types of restaurants (such as noodle and ramen shops) are already rock-bottom choices, you can save even more money by avoiding restaurants altogether. There are all kinds of pre-prepared foods you can buy, and some of them are complete meals in themselves, perfect for picnics in the park or right in your hotel room.

Perhaps the best-known is the obento, or box lunch, commonly sold on express trains, on train station platforms, and at counter windows of tiny shops throughout Japan. Costing usually between ¥600 ($4.80) and ¥1,000 ($8), the basic obento contains a piece of meat (generally fish or chicken), rice, and pickled vegetables. Sushi boxed lunches are also available.

Department stores usually sell pre-prepared foods in their basements in their food and produce sections, including such items as tempura, yakitori, sushi, salads, and desserts. These places are very popular with housewives. By the way, most department stores also have inexpensive restaurants, usually on one of the top floors. Since they almost always have plastic food displays, ordering is easy.

Street vendors are also good sources for inexpensive meals. They sell a variety of foods, including oden, okonomiyaki, and fried noodles (yakisoba). And finally, if you find yourself in real financial woes, you can always subsist on "cup noodle," which you can buy in any food store. Eaten by poor students and workingmen who don't have the time to sit down to a real meal, it's a dried soup that springs to life (well, sort of) when you add hot water—usually readily available if you're staying in a ryokan. It comes in a variety of choices, such as curry or chili tomato, and usually costs less than ¥250 ($2). Eat too much of it, though, and you'll probably disintegrate.

In case you're interested, Japan also has American fast-food chains such as McDonald's (where Big Macs cost about ¥400 ($3.20), Wendy's, and Kentucky Fried Chicken, as well as Japanese chains—Morninaga, Lotteria, and First Kitchen among them—which also sell hamburgers and french fries.

DRINKS

All Japanese restaurants serve complimentary Japanese green tea with meals. If that's a little too weak, Japanese *sake* made from rice is an alcoholic beverage, served either hot or cold, that goes well with most forms of Japanese cuisine. Japanese beer is also very popular. The biggest sellers are Suntory, Kirin, and Sapporo, but ironically enough Budweiser is a big hit among young Japanese. Japanese businessmen are fond of whisky, which they usually drink with ice and water. Although cocktails are available in discos, hotel lounges, and fancier bars, most Japanese stick with beer, sake, or whisky. Popular in recent years is *shochu*, an alcoholic beverage usually made from rice but sometimes from wheat or sweet potatoes. It used to be considered a drink of the lower classes, but its sales have increased so much that it's threatening the sake and whisky business. A clear liquid, it's often combined with soda water in a drink called *chu-hi*, but watch out—the stuff can be deadly.

---

10. Religion, Shrines, and Temples

The main religions in Japan are Shintoism and Buddhism, and many Japanese consider themselves believers in both. Whereas a Westerner might find it difficult to belong to two completely different religious organizations, the Japanese find nothing unusual about it and incorporate both into their lifestyles. Most Japanese, for example, are married in a Shinto ceremony, but when they die, they'll probably have a Buddhist funeral.

Unlike Westerners, whose churches have religious services weekly, the Japanese generally visit a temple or shrine only for a specific purpose. On New Year's, for example, many Japanese throng to shrines to pray for good fortune in the coming year, while in mid-July or mid-August they go to pay respect to their ancestors. As such, neither religion has a great influence in the everyday life of the Japanese. Rather, religion is more a way of thinking, a way of relating to one's world, environment, and family. The Japanese appreciation of natural beauty and strong sense of duty and obligation, for example, have religious roots.

SHINTOISM

A native religion of Japan, Shintoism is the worship of ancestors and national heroes, as well as all natural things, both animate and inanimate. These natural things are thought to embody gods, called *kami,* and can be anyone or anything: mountains, trees, the moon, stars, rivers, seas, fires, animals, a rock, even vegetables. In this respect it resembles beliefs of some American Indian tribes. Shintoism also embraces much of Confucianism, which entered Japan in the 5th century and stressed the importance of family and loyalty. There are no scriptures in Shintoism, no set of morals or ethics.

The most important goddess in Shintoism is Amaterasu, the sun goddess, who is considered the progenitor of the Japanese imperial family. Central to the principles of Shintoism through the centuries, therefore, was the belief that the emperor was a living god. The emperor held this revered position for more than 1,500 years, until the end of World War II. It was then that the emperor was forced to renounce his claim to divinity and admit that he was a regular human being just like everyone else. At this time Shintoism also lost its official status as the national religion, a position it had held since the Meiji Restoration (1868). However, Shintoism has not lost its popularity and claims more than 80 million followers in Japan. As for the imperial family, they still occupy a special place in the hearts of the Japanese.

The place of worship in Shintoism is called a shrine, *jinja* in Japanese. Every city, town, village, and hamlet has at least one shrine, and to most inhabitants they embody the soul of their district. The most famous shrines are Meiji Shrine in Tokyo, the Ise Shrines in the Ise-Shima National Park (dedicated to the sun goddess), and Itsukushima Shrine on Miyajima Island.

The most obvious telltale sign of a shrine is its *torii,* an entrance usually of wood that consists of two tall poles topped with either one or two crossbeams. Sometimes there will be several of these torii spread out over the pathway leading to the shrine, reminding visitors that they are approaching a shrine and giving them time to achieve the proper frame of mind. Before reaching the shrine itself you'll pass a water trough with communal cups where the Japanese will rinse out their mouths and wash their hands. Purification and cleanliness are important in Shintoism because they show respect to the gods, aspects that have carried over even today in the Japanese custom of bathing and removing shoes indoors.

At the shrine itself the worshipper will throw a few coins into a money box, clap his hands three times to get the attention of the gods, and then bow his head and pray. Sometimes there will be a rope attached to a gong that's even louder in calling the gods. And what do worshippers pray for? Good health, protection, safe delivery of a child, that sons get into good universities and that daughters get good husbands. Some shrines are considered lucky for love while others are good against certain ailments. You can ask any favor of the gods. Shrines are also the sites of many festivals and are visited on important occasions throughout one's life, including marriage and on certain birthdays.

BUDDHISM

Whereas they're called shrines in Shintoism, in Buddhism they're called temples (*otera* in Japanese). Instead of torii, temples will often have an entrance gate with a raised doorsill and heavy doors. Temples may also have a cemetery on their grounds, which Shinto shrines never have, and a pagoda.

Founded in India in the 5th century, Buddhism came to Japan in the 6th century via China and Korea, introducing to Japan the concept of eternal life. By the end of the 6th century Buddhism had gained such popularity that Prince Shotoku, one of Japan's most remarkable historical figures, declared Buddhism the state religion and based many of his governmental policies on its tenets. Another important Buddhist leader to emerge was a priest called Kukai, known posthumously as Kobo Daishi. After studying Buddhism in China in the early 800s, he returned to Japan, where he founded the Shingon sect of Buddhism and established his mission atop Mount Koya. The temples he built throughout Japan, including the famous 88 temples on Shikoku Island and those on Mount Koya, continue to attract millions of pilgrims even today.

Probably the Buddhist sect best known to the West, however, is Zen Buddhism. Considered the most Japanese form of Buddhism, Zen is the practice of meditation and a strictly disciplined lifestyle in the belief that it helps rid oneself of desire so that one can achieve enlightenment. There are no rites in Zen Buddhism, no dogmas nor a theological conception of divinity. You do not analyze rationally but, rather, are supposed to know things intuitively. The strict and simple lifestyle of Zen appealed greatly to Japan's samurai warrior class, and many of Japan's arts, including the tea ceremony, arose from the practice of Zen.

Visitors to Japan who are interested in Buddhism and temples should try to spend at least one night in a temple. The best place for this is Mount Koya, known as Koyasan to the Japanese, where approximately 50 temples have opened their doors to overnight guests, offering them simple tatami rooms, vegetarian meals, and the opportunity to join in the 6 a.m. service. (For more information, see Chapter VIII, Section 6.)

11. Festivals and Annual Events

With both Shintoism and Buddhism as the major religions in Japan, it seems as though there's a festival going on somewhere in the country almost every day. Every major shrine and temple in the land has at least one annual festival, with events that might include traditional dances, archery, or colorful processions in which portable shrines are carried through the streets by groups of chanting Japanese dressed in traditional costumes.

There are also a number of national holidays observed throughout the country, as well as such annual events as cormorant fishing and cherry-blossom viewing. During the summer, festivals are held seemingly everywhere, and you may stumble onto a neighborhood festival just by accident.

As for the larger, better-known festivals, they may be exciting for the visitor but do take some planning, since hotel rooms may be booked six months in advance. If you haven't made prior arrangements, you may want to let the following schedule be your guide in avoiding certain cities on certain days. You won't find a hotel room anywhere near Takayama, for example, on the days of its two big festivals. If you plan your trip around a certain festival, be sure to double-check the exact dates with the Japan Tourist Office, since these dates can change. And remember, if a national holiday falls on a Sunday, the following Monday becomes a holiday.

January
1—New Year's Day. This is the most important national holiday in Japan. Like Christmas in the West, it's a time of family reunions, and it's a time when friends get together to drink sake and eat special New Year's dishes. Streets and homes are decorated with straw ropes and pine or plum branches. Because this is a time that Japanese spend together with their families, and because almost all businesses, restaurants, and shops close down, it's not a particularly rewarding time of the year for foreigners.

3—Tamaseseri (Ball-Catching Festival), held at Hakozakigu Shrine in Fukuoka on Kyushu. The main attraction here is a struggle between two groups of youths who try to capture a sacred wooden ball. The team that wins is supposed to have good luck the whole year.

6—Dezome-shiki (New Year's Parade of Firemen), held in Harumi Chuo Dori in Tokyo. Agile firemen dressed in traditional costumes prove their worth with acrobatic stunts atop tall bamboo ladders—you'd certainly feel safe being rescued by one of them.

7—Usokae (Bullfinch Exchange Festival), at Dazaifu Temmangu Shrine outside Fukuoka City. The trick here is to get hold of the bullfinches made of gilt wood that are given away by priests—they're supposed to bring good luck.

9 to 11—Toka Ebisu Festival, held at Imamiya Ebisu Shrine in Osaka. Ebisu is considered the patron saint of business and good fortune, so this is the time when businesspeople pray for a successful year. The highlight of the festival is a parade of women dressed in colorful kimonos and carried through the streets in palanquins.

15—Adults' Day. A national holiday in Japan, this day honors young people who have reached the age of 20, when they can vote and assume other responsibilities.

15—Grass Fire Ceremony, on Wakakusayama Hill in Nara. As evening approaches Wakakusayama Hill is set ablaze and fireworks are displayed. The celebration marks a time more than a thousand years ago when a dispute over the boundary of two major temples in Nara was settled peacefully.

15—Toshi-ya, a traditional Japanese archery contest held at Sanjusangendo Hall in Kyoto.

February

Wednesday to Saturday of the first week—Snow Festival, in Sapporo. This famous festival features huge, elaborate statues and figurines carved of snow and ice.

First Sunday—Oyster Festival, held in Matsushima at the seaside park along the bay. Matsushima is famous for its oysters, and this is the time they're considered at their best. Booths are set up and oysters are given out free.

3 or 4—Setsubun (Bean-Throwing Festival), held at leading temples throughout Japan. According to the lunar calendar this is the last day of winter, and people throng to temples to participate in the traditional ceremony of throwing beans to drive away imaginary devils.

3 or 4—Lantern Festival, at Kasuga Shrine in Nara. This is a beautiful sight in which more than 3,000 stone and bronze lanterns are lit.

11—National Foundation Day (*Kigensetsu*), a national holiday.

March

1 to 14—Omizutori (Water-Drawing Festival), at Todaiji Temple in Nara. This festival includes a solemn rite performed in the evenings in which young ascetics brandish large burning torches and draw circles of fire. The biggest ceremony takes place on March 12th, and on the 13th the ceremony of drawing water is held to the accompaniment of ancient Japanese music.

3—Hinamatsuri (Doll Festival). Observed throughout Japan, it's held in honor of young girls to wish them a future of happiness. In homes where there are girls, dolls dressed in ancient costumes representing the emperor, empress, and dignitaries are set up on a tier of shelves along with miniature household articles.

13—Kasuga Matsuri, at Kasuga Shrine in Nara. This festival has a history stretching back 1,100 years and features traditional costumes and classical dances.

20 or 21—Vernal Equinox Day, a national holiday. Throughout the week Buddhist temples hold ceremonies to pray for the souls of the departed.

Late March to May—The cherry-blossom season begins in late March on the southern islands of Kyushu and Shikoku, travels up Honshu through April, and reaches Hokkaido by the beginning of May. Early to mid-April is when the blossoms burst forth in Tokyo and Kyoto. Popular cherry-viewing spots in Kyoto include Maruyama Park, the garden of Heian Shrine, the Imperial Palace, Nijo Castle, Kiyomizu Temple, and Arashiyama, while in Tokyo people throng to Ueno Park, Yasukuni Shrine, and the moat encircling the Imperial Palace.

April
8—Buddha's Birthday. Ceremonies are held at all Buddhist temples.
Second to third Sunday—Kamakura Matsuri, at Tsurugaoka Hachimangu Shrine in Kamakura. This festival honors heroes from the past, including Yoritomo Minamoto, who made Kamakura his shogunate capital back in 1192. Highlights are horseback archery (truly spectacular to watch), a parade of portable shrines, and sacred dances.
13 to 17—Yayoi Matsuri, at Futarasan Shrine in Nikko. This festival features a parade of decorated floats.
14 and 15—Takayama Festival, at Hie Shrine in Takayama. This festival supposedly dates back to the 15th century and features a procession of huge, gorgeous floats.
Mid-April—Gumonji-do (Firewalking Ceremonies). These rites and ancient shrine dances called *bugaku* are held atop Mount Misen on Miyajima. Walking on fire is meant to show devotion and is also for purification.
29—Greenery Day, a national holiday.
April 29 to May 5—Golden Week. Many Japanese offices and businesses close down and families go on vacation. It's a crowded time to travel, making reservations a must.

May
3—Constitution Memorial Day, a national holiday.
3 and 4—Hakata Dontaku, in Fukuoka. Citizens dressed as deities ride through the streets on horseback to the accompaniment of flutes, drums, and traditional instruments.
5—Children's Day, a national holiday. This festival honors young boys, and the most common sight are colorful streamers of carp flying from poles throughout Japan. These fish symbolize attributes desirable for young boys—perseverance and strength.
11 and 12—Takigi Noh performances, at Kofukuji Temple in Nara. Noh plays are presented onstage after dark under the blaze of torches.
11 to October 15—Cormorant fishing, on the Nagara River near Gifu. Visitors board small wooden boats at night to watch cormorants dive into the water to catch *ayu*, a kind of trout. Cormorant fishing is also held on the Katsura (also called Oi) River outside Kyoto.
15—Aoi Matsuri (Hollyhock Festival), of Shimogamo and Kamigamo shrines in Kyoto. This is one of Kyoto's biggest festivals, a colorful pageant commemorating the days when the imperial procession visited the city's shrines. It supposedly dates from the 7th century, when a ceremony was held to appease the gods following severe storms.
Saturday and Sunday closest to the 15th—Kanda Festival, held at Kanda Myojin Shrine in Tokyo every other year. Portable shrines are carried through the district.
Mid-May—Kobe Matsuri, in Kobe. This relatively new festival celebrates Kobe's international past with fireworks at Kobe Port, street markets, and a parade on Flower Road, with participants wearing native costumes.
17 and 18—Grand Festival of Toshogu Shrine, in Nikko. This festival commemorates the day in 1617 when Ieyasu Tokugawa's remains were brought to his mausoleum in Nikko, accompanied by 1,000 people. This festival re-creates the dra-

ma with more than 1,000 armor-clad people escorting three palanquins through the streets.

Third Saturday and Sunday—Sanja Matsuri, at Asakusa Shrine in Tokyo. About 100 portable shrines are carried through the district on the shoulders of men and women in traditional garb.

Third Sunday—Mifune Matsuri, held on the Oi River outside Kyoto in Arashiyama. In a reproduction of an ancient boat festival, the days of the Heian Period are reenacted, when the imperial family used to take pleasure rides on the river.

June

1 and 2—Takigi Noh performances, at Heian Shrine in Kyoto. Evening performances of Noh are presented on an open-air stage in the shrine's compound.

10 to 16—Sanno Festival, at Hie Shrine in Tokyo. This festival, which first began in the Edo Period (1603–1867), features the usual portable shrines transported through the busy streets of the Akasaka district.

14—Rice-planting Festival, at Sumiyoshi Shrine in Osaka. In hopes of a successful harvest, young girls in traditional farmers' costumes transplant rice seedlings in the shrine's rice paddy to the sound of music and traditional songs.

Mid-June—Hyakuman-goku Festival, in Kanazawa. Held only since 1952, the Hyakuman-goku Festival commemorates the arrival of Maeda, a feudal lord who laid the foundations of the Kaga clan, in this castle town. The highlight of the festival is a procession, and in the evening paper lanterns float down the Asano River.

July

1 to 15—Hakata Yamagasa, at Fukuoka. The main event takes place on the 15th, when a giant fleet of floats topped with elaborate decorations is paraded through the streets.

7—Tanabata (Star Festival), celebrated throughout Japan. According to myth, the two stars Vega and Altair, representing a weaver and a shepherd, are allowed to meet once a year on this day. If the skies are cloudy, however, the celestial pair cannot meet and must wait another year.

13 to 15—Obon Festival. This festival takes place in either mid-July or mid-August, depending on the area in Japan, and is held in memory of the dead, who, according to Buddhist belief, revisit the world during this period. Many Japanese return to their hometowns for the event, especially if a member of the family has died recently. As one Japanese, who grandmother had died a few months before, told me, "I have to go back to my hometown—it's my grandmother's first Obon."

17—Gion Matsuri, at Yasaka Shrine in Kyoto. This festival is one of the most famous festivals in Japan. It dates back to the 9th century, when the head priest at Yasaka Shrine organized a procession in an attempt to ask the gods' assistance against a plague that was raging in the city. Although the festival is actually celebrated the whole month of July, the highlight is on the 17th, when spectacular floats wind their way through the city streets. Many foreigners plan their trip to Japan around this event.

25—Tenjin Matsuri, at Temmangu Shrine in Osaka. This is one of Osaka's biggest festivals. It dates back to the 10th century, when the people of Osaka visited Temmangu Shrine to pray for protection against the diseases prevalent during the long, hot summer. They would take pieces of paper cut in the form of human beings and, while the Shinto priest said prayers, would rub the paper over themselves in ritual cleansing. Afterward the pieces of paper were taken by boat to the mouth of the river and disposed of. Today the festival reenacts the boat procession with a fleet of more than 100 sacred boats making its way down the river, followed by a fireworks display.

Late July or early August—Kangensai Music Festival, at Itsukushima Shrine in Miyajima. There's classical court music and bugaku dancing and three barges carrying portable shrines, priests, and musicians across the bay, along with a flotilla of other boats. Because this festival takes place according to the lunar calendar, the actual date changes each year.

Late July or early August—Fireworks display over the Sumida River in Asakusa, Tokyo. This is Tokyo's largest, and everyone sits on blankets along the banks of the river. Great fun!

August

First Saturday and Sunday—Oshiro Matsuri, in Himeji. This festival is famous for its Noh dramas performed on a special stage constructed on the Himeji Castle grounds. On Sunday there's a procession from the castle to the city center, with participants dressed in traditional costumes.

6—Peace Ceremony, in Hiroshima. Held at Peace Memorial Park, this annual ceremony is in memory of the victims who died from the atomic bomb dropped over Hiroshima on August 6, 1945. A similar ceremony is held on August 9 in Nagasaki.

5 and 6—Waraku Odori, in Nikko. This is a good opportunity to see some of Japan's folk dances.

6 to 8—Tanabata Festival, at Sendai. Sendai holds its Star Festival one month later than the rest of Japan. It's the country's largest, and the whole town is decorated with colored paper streamers.

11 to 13—Matsuyama Festival, in Matsuyama on Shikoku. Festivities include dances, fireworks, and a night fair.

12 to 14—Takamatsu Festival, in Takamatsu on Shikoku. About 6,000 people participate in a dance procession which threads its way along Chuo-dori Street. Anyone can join in.

15—Toronagashi and Fireworks Display in Matsushima. Held in the evening, first there's a fireworks display, followed by the setting adrift of about 5,000 small boats with lanterns on the bay. Another 3,000 lanterns are lit on islets in the bay, which illuminate the water. The lanterns are to console the souls of the dead.

16—Daimonji Bonfire, on Mount Nyoigadake in Kyoto. A huge bonfire in the shape of the Chinese character *dai*, which means "large," is lit near the peak as part of the Obon festival.

September

15—Respect-for-the-Aged Day, a national holiday.

16—Yabusame, at Tsurugaoka Hachimangu Shrine in Kamakura. Archery performed on horseback recalls the days of the samurai.

23 or 24—Autumnal Equinox Day, a national holiday.

October

7 to 9—Okunchi Festival, at Suwa Shrine in Nagasaki. This festival illustrates the influence Nagasaki's Chinese population has had on the city through the centuries. A parade of floats and dragon dances are highlights.

8 to 10—Marimo Matsuri, on Lake Akan, Hokkaido. *Marimo* is a spherical green weed that grows in Lake Akan. This festival is put on by the native Ainu population.

9 and 10—Takayama Matsuri, of Hachiman Shrine in Takayama. Similar to the festival held here in April, huge floats are paraded through the streets.

10—Health-Sports Day, a national holiday.

9 to 11—Great Festival of Kotohiragu Shrine, near Takamatsu on Shikoku. The climax of this festival is a parade of *mikoshi* (portable shrines).

14 and 15—Mega Kenka Matsuri (Roughhouse Festival), at Matsubara Shrine in Himeji. Portable shrines shouldered by youths jostle each other as the youths attempt to show their skill in balancing the heavy shrines.

17—Autumn Festival, at Toshogu Shrine in Nikko. Armor-clad parishioners escort a sacred portable shrine.

22—Jidai Matsuri (Festival of the Ages), at Heian Shrine in Kyoto. Another of Kyoto's grand festivals, this is one of the most interesting because it features a procession of more than 2,000 people dressed in ancient costumes representing different epochs of Kyoto's 1,200-year history. The festival is held in commemoration of the founding of Kyoto in 794.

22—Fire Festival, at Yuki Shrine, Kyoto. Long rows of torches are embedded along the approach to the shrine to illuminate a procession of children.

November

2 and 3—Ohara Matsuri, in Kagoshima. About 15,000 people parade through the town in cotton yukata, dancing to the tune of popular Kagoshima folk songs. A sort of Japanese Mardi Gras, this event attracts several hundred thousand spectators a year.

3—Culture Day, a national holiday.

3—Daimyo Gyoretsu, in Hakone. The old Tokaido Highway that used to link Kyoto and Tokyo comes alive again with a long parade that is a faithful reproduction of a feudal lord's procession in the olden days.

15—Shichi-go-san (Children's Shrine-Visiting Day), held throughout Japan. *Shichi-go-san* literally means "seven-five-three," and refers to children of these ages who are taken to shrines by their elders to express thanks and pray for their future.

23—Labor Thanksgiving Day, a national holiday.

December

17—On-Matsuri, at Kasuga Shrine in Nara. This festival features a parade of people dressed as courtiers, retainers, and wrestlers of long ago.

23—Emperor's Birthday, a national holiday.

31—New Year's Eve. At midnight many temples ring huge bells 108 times to signal the end of the old year and the beginning of the new. Many families visit temples and shrines on New Year's Eve to pray for the coming year.

---

12. Cultural Activities

Japan is known around the world for its aestheticism, apparent in everything from its food to its gardens to its art. Rich in its cultural history, the nation has produced widely divergent forms of expression—the tea ceremony, *sumo, Kabuki,* and flower arranging, to name a few—all of which command a large audience even today. In fact, the Japanese think so highly of their artists and performers that masters in many fields have been designated National Living Treasures.

Although it's possible to see the performing arts as well as sumo and the tea ceremony in other parts of Japan, Tokyo is your best bet for offering the most at any one time. Several of the larger first-class hotels in Tokyo, for example, offer a few hours' instruction in English in the tea ceremony, and sumo matches and Kabuki performances are held several times during the year. For specific information on cultural entertainment in the capital city, refer to Chapter IV, Section 8.

KABUKI

Probably Japan's best-known traditional stage art, *Kabuki* theater is also one of the country's most popular forms of entertainment. Visit a performance and it's easy to see why. In a word, Kabuki is *fun!* The plays are dramatic, the costumes are gorgeous, the stage settings are often fantastic, and the themes are about things everyone can identify with—love, revenge, and conflicts between duty and personal feelings. Probably one of the reasons Kabuki is so popular even today is that it developed centuries ago as a form of entertainment for the common people in feudal Japan, particularly the merchants. And one of the interesting aspects of Kabuki is that all roles—even those of women—are portrayed only by men.

It didn't start out that way. Kabuki was actually originated by a group of women in Kyoto in the early 1600s who began by giving performances of erotic dances. Needless to say, the dances were enthusiastically received by the audience and it wasn't long before there were troupes of women of rather questionable repute giving all kinds of lewd performances. Finally, the shogun decided that the dances were too vulgar and he banned all women from performing. Kabuki was then taken over by all-male companies, who transformed it into the drama it is today.

Kabuki has changed little in the past century. Altogether there are more than 300 Kabuki plays, all written before this century. One of the most interesting things about going to a Kabuki play lies in watching the audience. Because this has always been entertainment for the masses, the audience can get quite lively, with yells from spectators, guffaws, and laughter. In fact, old woodcuts showing cross-eyed men apparently stem from Kabuki—actors would stomp their feet and strike a cross-eyed pose in an attempt to get the audience's attention when things got a little too rowdy.

Of course, you won't be able to understand what's being said, but it doesn't matter. Because much of Kabuki drama dates from the 18th century, even the Japanese have a hard time understanding the language. This has led to a good system of programs and/or earphones that describe the plots in minute detail, often available in English as well. Thus you can follow the story and enjoy Kabuki just as much as everyone around you.

NOH

Whereas Kabuki developed as a form of entertainment for the masses, *Noh* was a much more traditional and aristocratic form of theater. In contrast to Kabuki's extroverted liveliness, Noh is very calculated, slow, and restrained. Noh is the oldest form of theater in Japan and there has been very little change in Noh presentations in the past 600 years. In fact, the language is so archaic that Japanese cannot understand it at all today, which explains in part why Noh does not have the following that Kabuki does. Don't expect programs in English.

As in Kabuki, all the performers in Noh are men. The subject matter of Noh's some 240 surviving plays is usually about supernatural beings, beautiful women, mentally confused people, or tragic-heroic epics. Performers usually wear masks.

Because the action in Noh is so slow, watching an entire evening can be quite tedious unless you are particularly interested in Noh dance and music. You may just want to drop in for a short while. In between Noh plays are short comic reliefs called *kyogen,* which usually make fun of life in the 1600s.

BUNRAKU

Bunraku is traditional Japanese puppet theater. But contrary to what you might expect, Bunraku is for adults rather than children, with themes centering on love and revenge, sacrifice and suicide. Many dramas now used in Kabuki were first written for the Bunraku stage.

Popular in Japan since the 17th century and at times even more popular than Kabuki, Bunraku is fascinating to watch because the puppeteers are right onstage with their puppets, dressed in black and wonderfully skilled in making the puppets seem like living beings. Usually there are three puppeteers for each puppet, which is about three-fourths the size of a human being. One is responsible for the head, the expression on the puppet's face, and the right arm and hand. The second operates the puppet's left arm and hand, while the third one moves the legs. Although at first the puppeteers are somewhat distracting, after a while you forget they're even there as the puppets assume personalities of their own. All the talking of Bunraku is provided by a narrator, who tells the story and speaks all the various parts as well.

The narrator is accompanied by the *shamisen,* a three-stringed traditional Japanese instrument. By all means try to see Bunraku if possible. The most famous Bunraku presentations are at the Osaka Bunraku Theater, but there are performances in Tokyo and other major cities as well.

TEA CEREMONY

Brought to Japan from China more than 1,000 years ago, tea first became popular among Japanese Buddhist priests as a means to stay awake during long hours of meditation. Gradually its use filtered down among the upper classes, and in the 16th century the tea ceremony was perfected by a merchant by the name of Sen-no-Rikyu. Using the principles of Zen and the spiritual discipline of the samurai, the tea ceremony became a highly stylized ritual with exact detail given on how tea was prepared, served, and drunk. The simplicity of movement and tranquillity of setting were meant to free the mind from everyday life and allow the spirit to enjoy peace.

The tea ceremony, *cha-no-yu,* is still practiced in Japan today and is regarded as a form of disciplinary training for mental composure as well as a good way to learn etiquette and manners. There are many schools with different methods for performing the tea ceremony throughout the country (see Chapter IV, Section 9). Several of Japan's more famous landscape gardens have tea houses on their grounds where you can sit on tatami, drink the frothy green tea and eat some sweets (meant to counteract the bitter taste of the tea), and contemplate the view.

IKEBANA

Whereas a Westerner is likely to put a bunch of flowers into a vase and be done with it, the Japanese consider the arrangement of flowers tantamount to an art. Most young girls have at least some training in flower arranging, known as *ikebana* in Japanese, and there are various schools and differing methods on the subject (see Chapter IV, Section 9, for a list of schools). First becoming popular among the aristocrats during the Heian Period (8th to 12th centuries) and spreading to the common people in the 14th to 16th centuries, traditional ikebana in its simplest form is supposed to represent heaven, man, and earth. Department store galleries sometimes have ikebana exhibitions; otherwise, check with the local tourist office.

GARDENS

Nothing is left to chance in a Japanese landscape garden. The shape of hills and of trees, the placement of rocks and waterfalls—everything is skillfully arranged by the gardener in a faithful reproduction of nature. To the Westerner, perhaps, it may seem a bit strange to arrange nature to look like nature. But to the Japanese even nature can be improved upon to make it more beautiful and more pleasing, with the best possible use of limited space. The Japanese are masters at this, as a visit to any of their famous gardens will testify.

The Japanese have been sculpting gardens for more than 1,000 years. At first the gardens were designed as pleasure gardens for walking and boating, with ponds, man-made islands, and pavilions. As with almost everything else in Japanese life, however, Zen Buddhism exerted an influence on the style of Japanese gardens, making them simpler and attempting to create the illusion of boundless space within a small area. To the Buddhist a garden was not for merriment but rather for contemplation, an uncluttered and simple landscape on which to rest the eyes.

Basically there are three styles of Japanese gardens. One style uses ponds, hills, and streams to depict nature in miniature. Another uses stones and raked sand in the place of water and is often seen at Zen Buddhist temples. The third style emerged with the tea ceremony and is built around a tea house with an eye toward simplicity and tranquillity. Japanese gardens often use the principle of "borrowed landscape," that is, using the surrounding mountains and landscape by incorporating them into the overall design and impact of the garden.

Famous gardens in Japan include Kenrokuen and Suizenji parks in Kanazawa,

Korakuen Park in Okayama, and Ritsurin Park in Takamatsu. Kyoto alone has about 50 gardens, including the famous Zen rock gardens at Daitokuji and Ryoanji temples, the gardens at both the Golden and Silver Pavilions, and those at Heian Shrine, Nijo Castle, and the Katsura Imperial Villa.

ZAZEN

Zazen, or meditation, is practiced by Zen Buddhists as a form of mental or spiritual training. Laymen meditate to relieve stress and clear the mind.

Zazen is accomplished sitting down in a cross-legged lotus position, with the neck and back straight and the eyes slightly open. Usually done by a group in a semidark room with cushions facing the wall, meditation is helped along by a monk who stalks noiselessly behind the meditators—if someone squirms or moves, that person is whacked on the shoulders with a stick, which is supposed to help him get back to meditating.

There are several Zen temples at which foreigners can join in zazen (see Chapter IV, Section 9). Through a notice in the *Japan Times,* I spent a weekend at a Zen temple outside Tokyo and tried zazen, ate vegetarian meals, and helped in household chores. If you'd like to try zazen yourself, contact the Tourist Information Center in either Tokyo or Kyoto. Check the *Japan Times* also to see whether a session of zazen is being organized with instruction in English for foreigners.

SUMO

The Japanese form of wrestling known as *sumo* began perhaps as long as 2,000 years ago, becoming immensely popular by the 6th century. Today it's still popular, and the best wrestlers are revered as national heroes in Japan, much as baseball players are in the United States. Often taller than six feet and weighing well over 200 pounds, sumo wrestlers follow a vigorous training period that usually begins in their teens. Unmarried wrestlers even live together at their training schools, called sumo stables.

A sumo match takes place on a sandy-floored ring less than 15 feet in diameter. The object of sumo is for a wrestler either to eject his opponent from the ring or cause him to touch the ground with any part of his body other than his feet. This is accomplished by shoving, slapping, tripping, throwing, and even carrying the opponent. Altogether there are 48 holds and throws, and sumo fans know all of them.

There are six 15-day sumo tournaments in Japan every year. Three are held in Tokyo (in January, May, and September), and the others are held in Osaka (March), Nagoya (July), and Fukuoka (November). Matches are widely covered on television as well as on the American armed forces FEN radio station. If there's no match being held during your stay, you may want to drop in on a sumo stable to watch the training. See Chapter IV, Section 9, for more details.

---

13. Recommended Reading

Japanese history, culture, life, society, and the arts are so rich and extensive that I have been able to give only a short overview in this book. Fortunately, there are vast numbers of books in English covering every aspect of Japan, so you shouldn't have any problem reading up on subjects in more detail. In particular, Kodansha International, a Japanese publishing company, has probably published more books on Japan in English than any other company. Available at major bookstores in Japan, its books are distributed in the United States through Harper & Row, 10 E. 53rd St., New York, NY 10022.

For an introduction to Japan's history, a standard work is George B. Sansom's *Japan: A Short Cultural History* (Prentice-Hall, 1962), which covers the country's history from antiquity to modern times. A former United States ambassador to Japan, Edwin O. Reischauer gives a detailed look at Japan's history in *Japan: The Story of a Nation* (Knopf, 1974). If you're interested in Japan since World War II, *A History of Postwar Japan* (Kodansha, 1982), by Masataka Kosaka takes in the enormous changes that have occurred in the country in the past few decades.

A general overview of Japanese history, politics, and society is provided in Edwin O. Reischauer's *The Japanese* (Harvard University Press, 1977). Delving deeper into Japanese society and psychology are Kurt Singer's *Mirror, Sword and Jewel: The Geometry of Japanese Life* (Kodansha, 1981) and Chie Nakane's *Japanese Society* (University of California Press, 1970).

A classic in describing the Japanese and their culture is the brilliantly written book by Ruth Benedict called *The Chrysanthemum and the Sword: Patterns of Japanese Culture* (New American Library, 1967), first written in the 1940s but reprinted many times. A more contemporary book on the Japanese is *The Japanese Mind: The Goliath Explained* (Linden Press/Simon & Schuster, 1983), by Robert C. Christopher. I consider this book compulsory reading for anyone traveling to Japan because it describes so accurately the Japanese, the role history has played in developing the Japanese psyche, and problems facing the nation today.

In a more lighthearted vein, a delightful account of the Japanese and their customs is given by the irrepressible George Mikes in *The Land of the Rising Yen*. Because it was published in the early 1970s and is now out of print, I doubt you'll be able to find a copy in the United States; it's in major bookstores in Japan, however, and would make light and enjoyable reading during your trip.

Likewise, the Japan Travel Bureau puts out some nifty pocket-size booklets on things Japanese, including *Eating in Japan* and *Festivals of Japan*. My favorite, however, is *Salaryman in Japan* (JTB, 1986), which describes the private and working lives of those guys in the look-alike business suits, Japan's army of white-collar workers who receive set salaries. The book is illustrated throughout and includes a picture of the typical salaryman, from his metal-framed square-rimmed glasses down to his dark-red necktie with diagonal stripes and black leather shoes. The endearing thing about this book is that it was written in complete seriousness, with chapters devoted to life in the salaryman's company, the etiquette of business cards, company trips, the wife of a salaryman, and even the "salaryman blues." Easy to read, this book is both entertaining and enlightening.

If you're interested in women's issues in Japan, read Alice Cook's and Hiroko Hayashi's *Working Women in Japan: Discrimination, Resistance and Reform* (ILR Press, 1980). A book seemingly from another era is *Geisha* (Kodansha, 1983), written by Liza C. Dalby and describing her year living as a geisha in Kyoto as part of a research project.

For information on Japanese religions, two beautifully illustrated books are *Shinto: Japan's Spiritual Roots* (Kodansha, 1980) and *Buddhism: Japan's Cultural Identity* (Kodansha, 1982), both by Stuart D. B. Picken with introductions by Edwin O. Reischauer.

If you find yourself becoming addicted to Japanese food, you might want to invest in a copy of *Japanese Cooking: A Simple Art* (Kodansha, 1980), by Shizuo Tsuji. Written by the proprietor of one of the largest cooking schools in Japan, this book contains more than 220 recipes as well as information on food history and table etiquette. The history and philosophy of the tea ceremony, beginning with its origins in the 12th century, are given in *The Tea Ceremony,* by Sen'o Tanaka (Kodansha, 1983).

An introduction to Japanese art is provided in Langdon Warner's *Enduring Art of Japan* (Grove Press, 1958). *Japan, A History of Art* (Doubleday, 1971) by Bradley Smith offers a beautifully illustrated overview and makes an elegant coffee table book as well. *A Net of Fireflies: Japanese Haiku and Haiku Paintings* (Charles E. Tuttle, 1960) is a charming collection of these typical Japanese art forms. Kabuki and other stage arts are covered in Faubion Bowers's *Japanese Theater* (Greenwood Press, 1976).

Two other informative charmers are *The World of the Shining Prince: Court Life in Ancient Japan* (Knopf, 1964), by Ivan Morris, and, if you are planning to stay at a ryokan, in *The Japanese Inn: A Reconstruction of the Past* (UH Press, 1982), Oliver Statler will take you through 400 years of Japanese social history with the family that owned one.

Reading fiction is certainly one of the most relaxing and fun ways to learn about a country. Whenever I travel in Japan I especially enjoy reading fictional accounts of the country because it puts me more in tune with my surroundings and increases my awareness and perception. The world's first novel was written by a Japanese woman, Murasaki-Shikibu, whose classic *The Tale of Genji* (Knopf, 1978) was written in the 11th century and describes the aristocratic life of Prince Genji. Lafcadio Hearn, a prolific writer of things Japanese in the late 1800s, describes life in Japan around the turn of the century in *Writings from Japan* (Penguin, 1985), while Isabella Bird, an Englishwoman who traveled alone to Hokkaido in the 1870s, writes a vivid account of what life was like for rural Japanese in *Unbeaten Tracks in Japan* (Virago Press Limited, 1984). An overview of Japanese classical literature is provided in *Anthology of Japanese Literature* (Grove Press, 1955), edited by Donald Keene. In Tokyo book-stores, you'll find whole sections dedicated to English translations of Japan's best-known authors, including Yukio Mishima, Soseki Natsume, Kobo Abe, Junichiro Tanizaki, and Nobel Prize-winner Yasunari Kawabata.

And finally, because it was also made into a television miniseries, most Western-ers are familiar with James Clavell's *Shogun* (Dell, 1975), a fictional account based on the lives of Englishman William Adams and military leader Ieyasu Tokugawa around 1600. In addition, a vivid history of Japanese woodblock prints from the 17th to 19th centuries comes alive in a first-person account written by James Miche-ner in *The Floating World* (University of Hawaii Press, 1983).

For more recent, personal accounts of what it's like for Westerners living in Ja-pan, two entertaining novels are *Ransom* (Vintage, 1985), by Jay McInerney, and *Pictures from the Water Trade* (Harper & Row, 1986), by John D. Morley.

GETTING SETTLED IN TOKYO

To the uninitiated, Tokyo may seem like a whirlwind of traffic and people, so confusing that visitors might swear they had somehow landed on another planet. This chapter should make getting settled in Tokyo not only less confusing but more enjoyable as well.

1. Introducing Tokyo

First-time visitors to Tokyo are almost invariably disappointed. They come expecting an exotic and Oriental city, but instead they find a city that has been Westernized and modernized to the point of ugliness, much of it a drab concrete jungle of unimaginative buildings clustered so close together there's hardly room to breathe.

Simply stated, Tokyo is a crush of humanity. Its subways are often packed, its sidewalks are crowded, its streets are congested, and its air is filled with an irritating amount of noise, pollution, and what can only be called "mystery smells." Almost 12 million people live in Tokyo's 770 square miles, many of them in so-called bedroom towns where they have to commute to work an average of two to three hours every day. No matter where you go in Tokyo, you are never alone. After you've been here for a while, Paris, London, and even New York will seem like deserted cities.

Tokyo's crowdedness and ugliness, however, are what you'll see only if you don't bother to scratch beneath its surface. Beautiful in its own way, Tokyo is most definitely a state of mind, and if you open yourself to it you'll find a city humming with energy and vitality, a city unlike any other in the world. People rush around here with such purpose, with such determination, it's hard not to feel that you're in the midst of something important, that you're witnessing history in the making.

But before I begin discussing Tokyo's merits, it might help to put the city into historical perspective.

Although today the nation's capital, Tokyo is a relative newcomer to the pages of Japanese history. For centuries it was nothing more than a rather unimportant village called Edo, which means simply "mouth of the estuary." Then, in 1603, Edo was catapulted into the limelight when the new shogun, Ieyasu Tokugawa, made the sleepy village the seat of his shogunate government. From then on the town grew quickly, and by 1787 the population had grown to 1.3 million, making Edo even then one of the largest cities in the world.

The Tokugawas ruled Japan for about 250 years, following a policy of isolation from the rest of the world. When the Tokugawas were overthrown in 1868, the Japanese emperor was restored to power. Although the imperial family had been living in Kyoto all these years, they decided to move their capital to Edo, which they renamed Tokyo, "Eastern Capital." Thus Japan's feudal era came to an end. Its policy of isolation from the rest of the world ground to an abrupt halt and its doors were flung open to the West in a scramble to modernize itself.

As the nation's capital, Tokyo was the hardest hit in this new era of modernization as fashions, architecture, food, department stores, and even people were imported from the West. West was best, and things Japanese were forgotten or ignored. It didn't help that Tokyo was almost totally destroyed twice in the first half of this century. In 1923 a huge earthquake struck the city, followed by tidal waves. Almost 150,000 people died and half of Tokyo was in ruins. Disaster struck again during World War II in 1945, when incendiary bombs destroyed most of the city.

I guess that's why most visitors are disappointed with Tokyo—there's almost nothing of historical importance to match Kyoto or Kamakura. So put your notions of "quaint Japan" out of your mind and plunge headfirst into the 21st century. Because that's what Tokyo is all about. The city is so wired and electric you can feel it in the air.

As the financial nerve center of Japan, Tokyo is where it's happening in Asia. In a nation of overachievers, Tokyo has more than its fair share of intelligentsia, academics, politicians, and artists, and it's the country's showcase for technology, fashion, art, music, and advertising.

But even though Tokyo has a fast-paced, somewhat zany, and sometimes crazy side to it, it also has a quieter and often overlooked side that makes the city both loveable and liveable. Although formidable at first glance, Tokyo is nothing more than a series of small towns and neighborhoods clustered together, each with its own narrow, winding streets, ma-and-pa shops, fruit stands, and stores. Look for the small things and you'll notice the carefully pruned bonsai sitting on the sidewalks, women in kimonos bowing and shuffling down the streets, old wooden houses, neatness and order.

Tokyo is both new and old, both Western and Japanese—but it's definitely more Japanese than Western. I myself love Tokyo. Despite the fact that it's over-crowded and that it's sometimes frustrating being a foreigner here, I find Tokyo exhilarating, often exciting, and always interesting. And perhaps best of all, Tokyo is one of the safest cities in the world. In a city of almost 12 million, it's remarkable indeed that you can walk safely anywhere, anytime, night or day. The only thing you usually have to watch out for are those Japanese businessmen who have had too much to drink—reserve thrown off, they may want to practice their English on you.

2. Orientation and Getting Around

Your most frustrating moments in Tokyo will probably occur when you find that you are totally lost. Maybe it will be in a subway or train station when all you see are signs in Japanese. Or perhaps it will be on a street somewhere as you search for a

museum, restaurant, or bar. At any rate, accept here and now that you *will* get lost if you are at all adventurous and strike out on your own. It's inevitable. But take comfort in the fact that Japanese get lost too. Even taxi drivers get lost and bewildered in Tokyo.

TOKYO NEIGHBORHOODS

Taken as a whole, Tokyo seems formidable and unconquerable. It's best, therefore, to think of it as nothing more than a variety of neighborhoods scrunched together, much like the pieces of a jigsaw puzzle.

The financial heart of the city is **Hibiya,** where you'll also find the Imperial Palace and—important for tourists—the Tourist Information Center. Within walking distance of Hibiya is the **Ginza,** the swankiest and more expensive shopping area of all of Japan. Ginza is where you'll find a multitude of department stores, boutiques, exclusive restaurants, hostess clubs, and drinking establishments. On the edge of Ginza is **Kabukiza,** venue for Kabuki productions. And only two subway stops from Ginza is **Tsukiji,** Japan's largest wholesale fish market.

If you're interested in seeing something of old Tokyo, you'll want to include **Asakusa** on your itinerary, located in the northeastern part of central Tokyo. Here you'll find the famous Sensoji Temple, as well as a wealth of tiny shops selling traditional Japanese crafts. Not far from Asakusa is **Ueno,** also considered part of the old downtown section of Tokyo. Considered the playground of Tokyo families, Ueno boasts Uneo Park, a huge green space which also contains a zoo, a concert hall and several acclaimed museums. Among them is the Tokyo National Museum, considered to have the largest collection of Japanese art in the world. North of Ueno is **Nippori,** a residential area of old traditional homes and temples.

Harajuku is the mecca of Tokyo's younger generation, and swarms throughout the week with teenagers in search of fashion and fun. Other important shopping areas are **Ikebukuro, Shinjuku, Shibuya** and of course, Ginza, all of which have scores of department stores and boutiques. If you're interested in electronics, you'll no doubt want to go to **Akihabara,** Tokyo's center for electronic and electrical appliances.

And for evening, the most important nightlife areas are Shinjuku, Akasaka, Shibuya, Ginza and **Roppongi,** all of which offer countless opportunities for eating, drinking and dancing.

For more information on Tokyo's various neighborhoods, refer to Chapter IV, "What to Do in Tokyo."

TOKYO ADDRESSES

One factor that makes finding your way around difficult is that hardly any streets are named. Think about what that means in Tokyo—12 million people living in a huge metropolis of nameless streets. Oh, major thoroughfares and some well-known streets in areas like Ginza or Shinjuku might have names that they received after World War II on the insistence of American occupation forces, but for the most part Tokyo's address system is based on a complicated number scheme that must make the postman's job here a nightmare. To make matters worse, most streets in Tokyo aren't straight but rather zigzag around—an arrangement apparently left over from olden days to confuse any enemies that might attack. Today streets in Tokyo confuse not only foreign tourists but even the Tokyo residents themselves.

A typical Tokyo address might read 7-8-4 Roppongi, Minato-ku, which is the address of the Inakaya restaurant. Minato-ku is the name of the ward, which encompasses a large area (altogether there are 23 wards, known as *ku,* in Tokyo). Within that area is the district, in this case Roppongi. Roppongi is further broken down into *chome,* here 7-chome. Number 8 refers to a smaller area within the chome, and 4 is the actual building. Addresses are usually posted on buildings, beside doors, and on telephone poles.

As you walk around Tokyo, you will notice maps posted beside sidewalks giving a breakdown of the number system for the area. The first time I tried to use one I stopped first one Japanese, and then later another, and asked them to point out on the map where a particular address was. They both studied the map and pointed out the direction. Both turned out to be wrong. Not very encouraging, but if you learn how to read these maps, they're invaluable.

Another invaluable source of information are the numerous police boxes, called koban, spread throughout the city. The policemen have maps of their areas and are very helpful. You should also never hesitate to ask a Japanese the way, but be sure to ask more than one. You'll be amazed at the conflicting directions you'll receive. Apparently the Japanese would rather hazard a guess than impolitely shrug their shoulders and leave you standing there. The best thing to do is ask directions from several Japanese and then follow the majority opinion. You can also duck into a shop and ask someone where a nearby address is, although it's been my experience that employees may not even know the address of their own store.

GETTING AROUND

The first rule of getting around Tokyo is: It will always take longer than you think. Tokyo is huge and its attractions are far-flung. It takes a long time to gauge how much time is needed to get from point A to point B. In fact, Tokyo's old hands pride themselves in being able to calculate perfectly the amount of time necessary to reach any destination. Arriving late is an unpardonable sin in Tokyo.

For short-time visitors, calculating travel times in Tokyo is tricky business. Taking a taxi can be expensive and involves the probability of getting stuck interminably in traffic. Taking the subway is usually more efficient, even though it's more complicated and harder on your feet, because there are often various routes that can be taken, and transfers between lines are sometimes quite a hike in themselves. However, if I'm going from one end of Tokyo to the other by subway, I usually allow anywhere from 30 to 60 minutes, depending on the number of transfers and the amount of walking necessary once I get there. The journey from Roppongi or Shibuya to Ueno, for example, takes approximately a half hour because it's a straight shot on the subway. But the trip from Toranomon to Ueno can take an hour because it requires transfers.

Before setting out on your own, arm yourself with a few maps. Maps are so much a part of life in Tokyo that they're often included in a shop or restaurant advertisement, brochure, on a business card, and even in private party invitations. Even though I've spent several years in Tokyo, I rarely venture forth without a map. One I find particularly useful is issued free by the Tourist Information Center; it's called *Tourist Map of Tokyo* and includes smaller, detailed maps of several districts (such as Shinjuku) as well as subway and greater Tokyo train maps. With this map you should be able to locate at least the general vicinity of every place mentioned in the Tokyo chapters of this book.

At any rate, the best policy for getting around Tokyo is to take the subway to the station nearest your destination. From there you can either walk, asking directions along the way, or take a taxi.

By Subway

To get around Tokyo on your own it's imperative that you learn how to ride its subways. Fortunately, Tokyo's subway system is efficient, modern, clean, and easy to use, and all station names are written in English. Altogether there are ten subway lines crisscrossing underneath the city, and each line is color-coded. The Ginza Line, for example, is orange, which means that all its coaches are orange. If you're transfering to the Ginza Line from another line, just follow the orange signs and circles to the Ginza Line platform.

Vending machines at all subway stations sell tickets, which begin at ¥120

(96¢) for the shortest distance and increase according to how far you're traveling. Vending machines give change and some even accept ¥1,000 notes. A large subway map above the vending machines will tell you your fare, but it's in Japanese only. Major stations also post a smaller map listing fares in English, but you may have to search for it. An alternative is to look at your T.I.C. subway map—it lists stations in both Japanese and English. Once you know what the Japanese characters look like, you may be able to locate your station and the corresponding fare on the huge subway map above the vending machines.

If you still don't know the fare, just buy a basic fare ticket for ¥120 (96¢). When you exit at the other end, the ticket collector will tell you how much you owe. In any case, be sure to hang on to your ticket since you must give it up at the end of your journey. If you're confused about which exit to take from the station, ask the ticket collector. Taking the right exit can make a world of difference, especially in Shinjuku, where there are more than 60 exits from the station.

If you think you're going to be using the subways a lot, you can purchase a one-day ticket (¥620 or $4.96 for an adult; ¥310 or $2.48 for children), which allows unlimited travel on the Ginza, Marunouchi, Hibiya, Tozai, Chiyoda, Yurakucho, and Hanzomon subway lines. These lines pass through 137 stations in Tokyo, including Hibiya, Ginza, Shinjuku, Tsukiji, Ueno, and major sightseeing destinations. One-day tickets are valuable, however, only if you plan on using the subways for very long distances or more than five times in one day. If so, you can purchase this one-day ticket at more than two dozen subway stations, including Ginza, Shinjuku, Shibuya, and Akasaka-mitsuke. Contact the T.I.C. for more information.

Most subways run from about 5 a.m. to midnight, though the times of the first and last trains depend on the line, the station, and whether it's a weekday or weekend. There are schedules posted in the stations, and through most of the day trains run every three to five minutes. Avoid taking the subway during the morning rush hour, from 8 to 9 a.m. The stories you've heard about commuters packed into trains like sardines are all true. There are even "platform pushers," men who push people into compartments so that the doors can close. If you want to witness Tokyo at its craziest, go to Shinjuku station at 8:30 a.m.—but go by taxi unless you want to experience the crowding firsthand.

By Train

In addition to subway lines, there are also electric trains operated by Japan Railways that run above ground. These are also color-coded and fares also begin at ¥120 (96¢). Buy your ticket the same as you would for the subway. The Yamanote Line (green-colored coaches) is the best-known and most convenient JR line. It makes a loop around the city, stopping at 29 stations along the way. In fact, you may want to take the Yamanote Line and stay on it for a roundup view of Tokyo. The entire trip around the city takes about an hour, passing stations like Shinjuku, Tokyo, and Ueno on the way.

Another convenient JR line is the Chuo Line, whose coaches are orange-colored. It cuts across Tokyo between Shinjuku and Tokyo stations.

Transfers: You can transfer between subway lines without buying another ticket. Likewise, you can transfer between JR train lines on one ticket. However, your ticket does not allow a transfer between subway lines and JR train lines. You usually don't have to worry about this, though, because if you exit through a wicket and have to give up your ticket, you'll know you have to buy another one. There are instances, however, when you pass through a ticket wicket to transfer between subway lines (for example, when you transfer from the Yurakucho Line to the Hibiya Line at Hibiya Station). In this case, simply show your ticket when you pass through the wicket. The general rule is that if your final destination and fare are posted above the ticket vending machines, you can travel all the way to your destination with only one ticket. But don't worry about this too much—the ticket collector will set you straight if you've made a miscalculation.

By Bus

Buses are difficult to use in Tokyo because their destinations are written only in Japanese and most bus drivers do not speak English. If you're feeling adventurous, board the bus at the front and drop the exact fare into a box by the driver. If you don't have the exact fare (usually ¥160 or $1.28), another machine located next to the driver will accept coins only. Your change will come out below, minus the fare.

By Taxi

Taxis are fairly expensive in Tokyo, starting at ¥470 ($3.76) for the first 1¼ miles (2 kilometers) and increasing ¥80 (64¢) for each additional 1,221 feet (370 meters). You can hail a taxi from the street or go to a taxi stand. A red light will show above the dashboard if a taxi is free to pick up a passenger; a green light indicates the taxi is already occupied. Be sure to stand clear of the door—it will swing open automatically. Likewise, it will automatically shut once you're in.

Unless you're going to a well-known landmark or hotel, it's best to have your destination written out in Japanese, since most taxi drivers do not speak English. But not even that may help. Tokyo is so complicated that even taxi drivers are not familiar with much of it, although they do have detailed maps with them. If a driver doesn't understand where you're going, he may refuse to take you, however. Notice the taxi drivers' white gloves and the way the drivers are always writing things down on a roster—Japanese taxi drivers must write down more information than any other taxi drivers on earth.

There are so many taxis cruising Tokyo that one is always around and available —except when you need it most. That is, when it's raining and late at night on weekends after all subways and trains have stopped. Nightlife areas such as Shinjuku, Roppongi, Ginza, and Akasaka are especially bad, and I've waited as long as an hour in each of these places for a taxi after midnight. So if you're out past midnight on Friday or Saturday, you might as well stay out until about 2 or 3 a.m., when it's easier to get a taxi. And from 11 p.m. to 5 a.m., an extra 20% is added to your fare.

The telephone numbers of major taxi companies are 586-2151 for Nihon Kotsu; 491-6001 for Kokusai; 563-5151 for Daiwa; and 814-1111 for Hinomaru. Note, however, that only Japanese is spoken and that you will be required to pay extra (usually not more than ¥550, or $4.40, extra).

By Car

Driving a car in Tokyo can be a harrowing experience. For one thing the streets are crowded and unbelievably narrow, street signs are often only in Japanese, and driving is on the left side of the street. Parking spaces can be hard to find, and garages are expensive. However, if you're still not convinced, see "The ABCs of Tokyo" below for car-rental agencies.

---

3. The ABCs of Tokyo

As one of the most modern and efficient cities in the world, Tokyo has just about every facility and service you might need. Listed below are practical information and addresses for the capital city. If you can't find what you're looking for here, check "The ABCs of Japan" in Chapter I.

AMERICAN EXPRESS: The American Express office handling currency exchanges is located in the Mitsui Building at 3-8-1 Kasumigaseki, Chiyoda-ku (tel. 03/508-2400). Hours are 9 a.m. to 4:30 p.m. Monday through Friday, and 9 a.m.

TOKYO SUBWAYS

Line		Line	
▬▬▬	Toei Mita Line	▨▨▨	Ginza Line
⊪⊪⊪	Toei Asakusa Line	═══	Yurakucho Line
⊪⊪⊪	Tozai Line	∷∷∷	Toei Shinjuku Line
●●●●	Hibiya Line	▬ ▬ ▬	Hanzomon Line
◉◉◉◉	Chiyoda Line	┼┼┼┼	Private RR Line
▨▨▨	Marunouchi Line	●	Interchange Station
▬ ▬	JR Line		

to noon on Saturday; closed Sunday and public holidays. Closest subway station: Toranomon. An additional American Express office is located in the Four-Stars Building, 4-4-1 Ginza (tel. 564-4381). It's open Monday through Saturday from 10 a.m. to 5 p.m.

BANKS: Banking hours are 9 a.m. to 3 p.m. Monday through Friday. You can exchange money in major banks throughout Tokyo, often indicated by a sign in English near the front door. The **Bank of America** is located in the Arc Mori Building, 1-12-32 Akasaka, Minato-ku (tel. 587-3111), and the **Chase Manhattan Bank** is at 1-2-1 Marunouchi, Chiyoda-ku (tel. 287-4000). Generally speaking, banks give a better exchange rate on traveler's checks than they do on cash.

BOOKSTORES: There are several very good bookstores in Tokyo where there's a large selection of books written in English about Japan, as well as novels and reference materials. On Shinjuku Station's east side on Shinjuku Dori, there's the **Kinokuniya Bookstore,** 3-17-7 Shinjuku (tel. 354-0131). Books in English are located on the sixth floor, and this large store is open from 10 a.m. to 7 p.m. (closed the third Wednesday of the month). Another good bookstore is **Maruzen,** 2-3-10 Nihombashi, Chuo-ku (tel. 272-7211), with its foreign books located on the second floor. Hours are 10 a.m. to 6 p.m.; closed Sunday. The **Yaesu Book Center,** 2-5-1 Yaesu, Chuo-ku (tel. 281-1811), located close to Tokyo Station, is a five-story bookstore with about a million books, including books in English on the fourth floor. It's open Monday through Saturday from 10 a.m. to 7 p.m.; closed Sunday. **Jena,** 5-6-1 Ginza, Chuo-ku (tel. 571-2980), is conveniently located in the heart of Ginza on Harumi Dori Avenue. Open Monday through Saturday from 10:30 a.m. to 7:50 p.m. and on Sunday from 12:30 to 6:45 p.m., it has English paperbacks, magazines, special-interest books, maps, and travel guides. It's located between the Ginza and Hibiya subway stations. Another place to look for books in English is the area of **Jimbocho-Kanda,** with its many kinds of bookstores, described more fully in the Tokyo shopping section.

CAR RENTALS: As I've stressed before, driving a car in Tokyo can make a roller-coaster ride at the local amusement park seem like tame stuff. If you're still not convinced, there are approximately a dozen major car-rental companies in Tokyo with branch offices spread throughout the city and at Narita airport. The **Nissan Reservation Center** is in the Landick Iikura Building, 1-5-7 Azabudai, Minato-ku (tel. 03/587-4123); the **Nippon Rent-A-Car Service** is in the Nippon Rent-A-Car Building, 5-5 Kamiyacho, Shibuya-ku (tel. 03/468-7126); and **Toyota Rent-A-Lease** is at 1-1-8 Fujimi, Chiyoda-ku (tel. 03/264-2834). Prices start at around ¥8,000 ($64) for 24 hours. You'll need either an international or Japanese driver's license.

DOCTORS AND DENTISTS: Your embassy can refer you to English-speaking doctors, specialists, and dentists. Otherwise, there are a few clinics popular with foreigners living in Tokyo where some of the staff speak English. The **Tokyo Medical & Surgical Clinic,** close to Tokyo Tower in the 32 Mori Building, 3-4-30 Shiba-koen, Minato-ku (tel. 436-3028), is open on weekdays from 9 a.m. to 4:45 p.m. (closed 1 to 2 p.m. for lunch) and on Saturday from 9 a.m. to 12:45 p.m. Appointments are necessary. The **International Clinic** is within walking distance of Roppongi Station at 1-5-9 Azabudai, Minato-ku (tel. 582-2646), and is open Monday through Friday from 9 a.m. to noon and 2:30 to 5 p.m. and on Saturday from 10 a.m. to noon. Only walk-ins accepted here. You can also make appointments to visit doctors in the hospitals listed below under "Hospitals."

DRUGSTORES: There is no 24-hour drugstore in Tokyo, but there are convenience stores throughout the city that carry things like aspirin. (If it's an emergency, I suggest going to one of the hospitals listed below.) If you're looking for specific pharmaceuticals, a good bet is the **American Pharmacy,** in the Hibiya Park Building, 1-8-1 Yurakucho, Chiyoda-ku (tel. 271-4034). Open every day except Sunday from 9 a.m. to 7 p.m., it has most of the drugs you can find at home, many of them imported from the United States, and can fill American prescriptions. This handy drugstore is located just a minute's walk from the Tourist Information Center at Hibiya Station.

EMERGENCY: The same all over Japan, the national emergency numbers to call are 110 for police and 119 for an ambulance or to report a fire.

HELPLINE: At the end of your rope? Have some problems? The **Tokyo English Life Line** (tel. 03/264-4347) gives free confidential counseling over the telephone, will listen to your problems, and will let you blow off steam.

HOSPITALS: In addition to going to a hospital for an emergency, you can also make an appointment at a hospital's clinic to see a doctor. The **International Catholic Hospital (Seibo Byoin),** 2-5-1 Naka-Ochiai, Shinjuku (tel. 951-1111), has clinic hours from 8:30 to 11 a.m. Monday through Saturday. The cost for a first visit is about ¥4,400 ($35.20); special tests or treatments cost more. The closest subway station is Meijiro on the Yamanote Line.

Other hospitals include **St. Luke's International Hospital (Seiroka Byoin),** 1-10 Akashicho, Chuo-ku (tel. 541-5151), with clinic hours from 8:30 to 11 a.m. Monday through Saturday (closest subway: Tsukiji on the Hibiya Line); and the **Japan Red Cross Hospital** (Nisseki Iryo Center), 4-1-22 Hiroo, Shibuya-ku (tel. 400-1311), with hours from 8:30 to 11 a.m. on weekdays and from 8:30 to 10:30 a.m. on Saturday (closest subway stations are Roppongi, Hiroo, and Shibuya, from which you should take a taxi). No appointments taken here.

LOST PROPERTY: If you've forgotten something on a subway, in a taxi, or on a park bench, you don't have to assume it's gone forever. In fact, if you're willing to trace it down, you'll probably get it back. If you've lost something along a street or outside, go to the nearest police box, called a koban. Items found in the neighborhood will stay there for about three days. After that you should contact the Central Lost and Found Office of the **Metropolitan Police Board,** 1-9-11 Koraku, Bunkyo-ku (tel. 581-4321, ext. 4542 or 4543).

If you've lost something in a taxi or subway, you need to contact the appropriate office: for taxis it's the **Taxi Kindaika Center** at 7-3-3 Minamisuma, Koto-ku (tel. 648-0300); for JR trains it's the **Lost and Found Section** at Tokyo JR Station (tel. 231-1880) or at Ueno Subway Station (tel. 841-8069); and for Tokyo Metropolitan buses, subways, and streetcars it's at 1-35-15 Hongo, Bunkyo-ku (tel. 818-5760). If you've lost something on one of the subways belonging to the Teito Rapid Transit Authority (for example, the Ginza, Marunouchi, Yurakucho, Tozai, or Hanzoman Line), call 834-5577. The Japanese are generally honest, so don't assume you will never see your lost belongings again.

POST OFFICE: If your hotel cannot mail letters for you, ask the concierge where the nearest post office is. The Central Post Office is located just southwest of Tokyo Station. If you need information on postage or mail, contact the Information Office of the **Tokyo International Post Office** at 2-3-3 Otemachi (tel. 241-4891), located north of Tokyo Station.

RAILWAY INFORMATION: You can obtain information and buy tickets for Japan Railways trains going throughout Japan at any JR station, including those along the Yamanote Line, which loops around Tokyo. For specific train times, call the Tourist Information Center at 502-1461 or call JR directly (best if you have a Japanese speaker with you) at 212-7051.

TELEGRAMS AND TELEPHONES: You can make long-distance calls from your room in most tourist hotels in Tokyo. Otherwise, there are telephone and telegraph offices throughout the city. The **Tokyo Telegraph & Telephone (KDD) office** at 1-8-1 Otemachi (tel. 211-5588), close to Tokyo Station, is open Monday through Friday from 9 a.m. to 10 p.m.; on Saturday, Sunday, and holidays from 9 a.m. to 5 p.m. and can handle facsimiles, phototelegrams, ISD calls, and Telex in addition to telegrams and telephone calls. In Shinjuku there's a telephone and telegraph office at 2-3-2 Nishi Shinjuku (tel. 347-5000).

There are several English telephone directories available that provide addresses and telephone numbers for many businesses, companies, shops, and restaurants in Tokyo. They're *City Source,* the *English Telephone Directory,* the *Japan Times Directory,* and the *Japan Telephone Book Yellow Pages.* If your hotel does not have one of these and you're interested in buying one, they're available at the bookstores listed above. For assistance on directory telephone listings in Tokyo, English-speaking operators can help you if you call 201-1010.

If you're calling a number in Tokyo from outside the city, the **area code for Tokyo** is 03.

TOURIST INFORMATION: The **Tourist Information Center (T.I.C.),** 1-6-6 Yurakucho, Chiyoda-ku (tel. 502-1461), can answer all your questions regarding Tokyo and can give you a map of the city as well as various sightseeing materials. It also has more information than any place else on the rest of Japan, including pamphlets and brochures on major cities and attractions across the nation. Be sure to stop off here if you plan to travel to other destinations, since in many cases information in English is not available at the destination itself. Check the travel tips section in Chapter I for various pamphlets available on Japan.

The tourist office is open weekdays from 9 a.m. to 5 p.m. and on Saturday from 9 a.m. to noon. Although it doesn't make sense in a city as large as Tokyo, it is closed on Sunday and national holidays. The office is located close to both Hibiya and Yurakucho subway stations (if you're arriving at Hibiya Station, take the A4 or A5 exit). There's also a tourist office at the Narita airport where you can pick up a map and ask how to get to your hotel.

In addition, the Tokyo Metropolitan Government maintains the **Information Bureau of Tokyo,** located at JR Tokyo Station in a corner of the Travel Plaza at the Yaesu Entrance (tel. 211-7391). It provides all kinds of information on Tokyo, including transportation, shopping, accommodations, and sightseeing. It's open Monday through Saturday from 9 a.m. to 6 p.m.; closed Sunday and holidays.

If you want to have a quick rundown of what's happening in Tokyo, you can call 503-2911 for a taped recording in English of what's going on in the city and the vicinity in the way of special exhibitions, performances, festivals, and events.

And finally, the Nippon Telegraph Corp. (NTT) and Kokusai Denshin Denwa Co. (KDD) sponsor a telephone service that answers questions relating to Japan. Called the **Japan Hotline** (tel. 586-0110) it advises callers on Japanese customs and etiquette, gives tips on such aspects of Japanese daily life as education and health services, and can answer questions ranging from the availability of instruction on flower arranging to obtaining tickets for Kabuki. Advisers are on duty Monday through Friday, except holidays, from 10 a.m. to 4 p.m.

TOURIST PUBLICATIONS: The best publication for finding out what's going on in Tokyo in terms of contemporary and traditional music and theater, exhibitions in museums and galleries, films, and special events is the *Tokyo Journal*. Published monthly and available for ¥500 ($4) at foreign-language bookstores, restaurants, and bars, it also has articles of interest to foreigners in Japan. It even lists department store sales, photography exhibitions, apartments for rent, schools for learning Japanese, and many other services. I don't know how foreigners survived in Tokyo before this publication made its debut in the early 1980s.

Another English publication of interest to tourists is the *Tour Companion's Tokyo City Guide,* a weekly distributed free to hotels, travel agencies, and the T.I.C. It tells of upcoming events and festivals, as well as other information useful to the traveler. *Weekender* is also a free weekly and is found in supermarkets, hotels, and other places where foreigners hang out. It's best known for its classified ad section, but has articles and features as well. English-language newspapers such as the *Japan Times* also carry information on the theater, films, and special events.

4. Accommodations

Tokyo has no old, grand hotels. In fact, it doesn't have many old hotels, period. But what Tokyo's hotels may lack in quaintness or old grandeur is more than made up for in the excellent service for which the Japanese are legendary, and in cleanliness and efficiency. Be prepared, however, for small rooms. Space is at a premium in Tokyo, so with the exception of some of the upper-range hotels, rooms seem to come in only three sizes: minuscule, small, and adequate.

Unfortunately, Tokyo does not have many ryokan, or Japanese-style inns. So I suggest that you wait for your travels around Japan to have your ryokan experience. However, realizing that not all visitors have the opportunity to travel outside Tokyo, I've listed medium- and budget-range ryokan that are enthusiastic and willing to take in foreigners. In fact, if you're traveling on a budget, a ryokan is often the cheapest way to go. As for upper-range ryokan in Tokyo, none of them accept foreigners. They prefer that guests be introduced through someone they know and simply do not want to deal with the inconveniences and difficulties caused by cultural and language barriers.

Most of the upper-bracket hotels offer at least a few Japanese-style rooms, with tatami mats, Japanese bathtubs (which are deeper and narrower than Western ones), and futons. Although these rooms tend to be expensive, they are usually large enough for four people.

For each hotel or ryokan listed I've given the nearest subway station and the walking time required. Remember that in addition to the prices quoted below, upper-class hotels and most medium-range hotels will add a 10% to 15% service charge. Further, rates of more than ¥10,000 ($80) per person per night will require an additional 6% tax; rates of less than ¥10,000 per person will require an additional 3% tax.

A word about costs: Because of the unfavorable dollar/yen exchange rate, the price of a hotel room in Tokyo is truly astronomical. Recognizing the difficulty foreigners have making ends meet, some hotels that cater largely to Americans have kept their tariffs at the same level for the past two years. Some hotels have even lowered their rates. Hopefully, the yen amount given here is the most you'll have to pay.

Currency Note

The prices quoted in this book were figured at ¥125 = US$1. However, due to fluctuations in the exchange rate of the yen (it was ¥146 to the dollar at press time), the U.S. dollar equivalents given might vary during the lifetime of this edition. Be sure to check current exchange rates when planning your trip.

THE UPPER BRACKET

The hotels in this category can rival upper-range hotels anywhere in the world. Although many of Tokyo's best hotels may not show much character from the outside, inside they are oases of subdued simplicity where service and hospitality reign supreme. Rooms in this category are adequate in size, some of them even large by Tokyo's standards, and they all come with such amenities as minibar, bilingual television with English-language cable and CNN broadcasts from the States, clock, radio, cotton kimono, hot water for tea, and countless other personal touches that make staying in Japan a pleasure. Note, however, that even though many hotels in this bracket have health clubs and swimming pools, an extra fee is charged for their use.

The **Imperial Hotel,** 1-1-1 Uchisaiwaicho, Chiyoda-ku (tel. 03/504-1111), is one of Tokyo's best-known hotels. About 50% of its guests are foreigners, mostly business executives. Located across from Hibiya Park within walking distance of Ginza, the Imperial's trademark is excellent and impeccable service: Guests are treated like royalty and the atmosphere throughout is subdued and dignified. Although the present hotel dates from 1970, with a 31-story tower added in 1983, the Imperial's history goes back to 1922, when it opened as a small hotel made of brick and stone with intricate designs carved into its facade—all designed by Frank Lloyd Wright. The Imperial won lasting fame when it survived almost intact the 1923 earthquake that destroyed much of the rest of the city. Although the old structure was torn down in 1968 to make way for a larger building, part of it was moved to Meiji-Mura, a museum village outside Nagoya.

The Imperial's 1,143 rooms are located in both the main building and the tower. Rooms in the main building are quite large for Tokyo, running from ¥24,750 ($198) to ¥46,000 ($368) for one person and ¥29,000 ($232) to ¥50,000 ($400) for two. They are currently being renovated, a process that will be completed by 1990. Tower rooms, while slightly smaller, are higher up, bright and cheerful, and from their floor-to-ceiling bay windows offer fantastic views of either the Imperial Palace or Ginza and the harbor. Prices here run ¥26,500 ($212) to ¥46,000 ($368) for one person and ¥30,800 ($246) to ¥50,000 ($400) for two. Facilities at the hotel include 13 restaurants and four bars, an impressive shopping arcade, and Tokyo's most dramatic swimming pool, located on the 20th floor with a breathtaking view of Tokyo Bay (fee: ¥1,000 or $8). The closest subway station is Hibiya Station, about a minute's walk away.

Another venerable hotel in Tokyo is the **Hotel Okura,** 2-10-4 Toranomon, Minato-ku (tel. 03/582-0111), built just before the 1964 Olympic Summer Games were held in Tokyo. Located across the street from the American Embassy, it's the favorite hotel of visiting U.S. dignitaries as well as such celebrities as rock star David Bowie and pianist Vladimir Horowitz. Conservative and traditional in decor, the

Okura combines Western comfort with Japanese design in the use of *shoji* screens, flower displays, and a beautifully sculptured garden. The hotel has both indoor and outdoor swimming pools (¥1,200 or $9.60 for both), eight restaurants and four bars, and a shopping arcade of exclusive boutiques from Hanae Mori to Mikimoto pearls.

Rooms here are ¥26,500 ($212) to ¥38,000 ($304) for one person and ¥35,000 ($280) to ¥43,500 ($348) for two. The more expensive rooms are on the fifth floor just off the lobby. Conveniently located, they have good-size balconies overlooking the Japanese garden. The Okura also has 11 Japanese-style rooms with tatami floors, shoji screens, and Japanese tubs, costing ¥37,000 ($296) to ¥73,000 ($584). Nearest subway stations: Toranomon and Kamiyacho, each about ten minutes away.

Since its grand opening in 1986, the **ANA Hotel Tokyo,** 1-12-33 Akasaka, Minato-ku (tel. 03/505-1111), has given the Hotel Okura stiff competition. A gleaming white building rising 37 stories high above the crossroads of Akasaka, Roppongi, Toranomon, and Kasumigaseki, the ANA Hotel is Tokyo's newest luxury hotel. Its lobby, located on the second floor and of cool, cream-colored marble with a water fountain serving as a focal point, is both impressive and spacious, and the lobby lounge is a favorite among Tokyoites for people-watching. Restaurants, rooms, and even corridors are superbly decorated with artwork and vases. Facilities at the hotel include a business center with secretarial services, a travel desk, shopping arcade, barbershop and beauty salon, sauna (for men only), an outdoor swimming pool (fee: ¥1,500 or $12), and a babysitter's room. Restaurants serve Japanese, Chinese, and Western cuisine; the Astral bar on the 37th floor provides fantastic views of the city.

Rooms are large, with views of Tokyo Bay, Mount Fuji, or the Imperial Palace and come with TV, pay video, minibar, English-language newspapers delivered twice a day, and other thoughtful amenities. Various types of rooms and suites are available, with prices starting at ¥22,000 ($176) for single occupancy and ¥29,000 ($232) for double occupancy. For ¥4,000 ($32) more, you can opt to stay on the executive floor, which offers the services of a concierge, free continental breakfast, and an evening cocktail hour. Nearest subway stations: Roppongi, Akasaka, Kamiyacho, Toranomon, and Kokkai Gijido-mae.

The **Capitol Tokyu,** 2-10-3 Nagata-cho, Chiyoda-ku (tel. 03/581-4511), is another one of Tokyo's hotels built just before the Olympics. It used to be the Tokyo Hilton, but in 1984 the current owner, the Tokyu hotel chain, took over the management. A cozy establishment, it has only 459 guest rooms—a small hotel by Tokyo's standards—and has the unique ability of making foreign guests feel as if they are in the Orient and at home all at the same time. With more than 892 full-time employees, service is at a premium. There are, for example, no cigarette machines in the hotel—instead, guests are requested to ask any hotel employee to fetch them a pack of cigarettes. The hotel boasts a meticulously pruned Japanese garden complete with a pond and golden carp, an outdoor swimming pool, a small shopping arcade, and Japanese, Chinese, and Western restaurants. The hotel is located in the Akasaka district within walking distance of the moat-encircled Imperial Palace. If you stay here, be sure to check out Hie Shrine, next door.

Double and twin rooms, which are comfortably large, start at ¥29,000 ($232) for single occupancy and ¥33,000 ($264) for double. There are also 50 single rooms available for ¥25,000 ($200) to ¥25,000 ($179), but they're smaller and it may be worth springing for the additional couple of thousand yen for a double room. Nearest subway station: Kokkai Gijido-mae, one minute away.

The **Miyako Hotel Tokyo,** 1-1-50 Shiroganedai, Minato-ku (tel. 03/447-3111), is an affiliate of the famous Miyako Hotel in Kyoto and was designed by Minoru Yamasaki, the architect of the World Trade Center in New York and the Century Plaza in Los Angeles. The Japanese themselves account for 70% of its guests, and although it's a bit inconveniently located, it offers a free bus shuttle to and from Meguro Station and to Ginza. The lobby overlooks 5½ acres of lush gardens that once belonged to the father of a foreign prime minister. The hotel's rooms are large, with huge floor-to-ceiling windows that have views of either the hotel's own garden, a garden next door, or Tokyo Tower. All rooms were recently recarpeted, and all single beds are semidouble in size. There are nine restaurants and bars, a huge indoor pool that is great for swimming laps, and even a chapel. Double rooms start at ¥21,000 ($168) for single occupancy and ¥24,000 ($192) for double, while twin rooms start at ¥20,000 ($160) and ¥23,000 ($184) respectively. Although there are nine single rooms, each for ¥18,500 ($148), these are usually booked. Five Japanese-style rooms are available for ¥23,000 ($184) for one person and ¥26,000 ($208) for two. Closest subway station: Takanawadai, about an eight-minute walk.

Hotel Seiyo Ginza, 1-11-2 Ginza, Chuo-ku (tel. 03/535-1111), opened in 1987 as Ginza's newest luxury hotel. Its room rates, which begin at ¥42,000 ($336) for a single or double and go all the way up to ¥275,000 ($2,200) for its premier suite, are the most expensive in Tokyo, if not in all of Japan. Its market is targeted at foreign executives, and with only 80 guest rooms, service is at a premium. The hotel is not open to the public—that is, you must either be a hotel guest or have a reservation at one of its exclusive restaurants to enter the main entrance. A hush prevails throughout the hotel, and instead of a front desk there is a comfortable reception room that resembles a living room. As one hotel employee explained, "The hardware is a Western-style hotel, but the software is traditional Japanese service."

Rooms are large for Japan and come with safes, humidity-control dials, and videocassette players. With the busy executive in mind, telephones have two lines and there are computerized "Do Not Disturb" and "Maid Service" buttons linked to hotel personnel so that they can respond immediately to the desires of their guests. Bathrooms are huge, with separate shower and tub units and even mini-TVs. The hotel is located about a five-minute walk from the Ginza 4-chome Crossing and two minutes from the Ginza-Itchome subway station.

Also new in Ginza but much more reasonably priced is the **Ginza Tobu Hotel,** 6-14-10 Ginza, Chuo-ku (tel. 03/546-0111). Small and personable, it employs a full-time staff of 250 to service guests in its 206 rooms. About 40% of its guests are foreigners, half of which are Americans (no group tours are accepted). In addition to the usual minibar, laundry rope in the bathroom, massage shower head, and free *Japan Times* delivered in the morning, each room comes equipped with bilingual TV with CNN and a radio/music system with—get this—440 different music channels. There are also hookups for facsimile machines, which you can use free of charge. Facilities include an upscale French restaurant, a Japanese restaurant, and a coffeeshop open 24 hours a day. Singles range from ¥14,000 ($112) to ¥20,000 ($160), doubles are ¥27,000 ($216), and twins start at ¥26,000 ($208). Located behind the Ginza Matsuzakaya department store, the hotel is a four-minute walk from Ginza Station or one minute from Higashi Ginza Station.

Japan's largest hotel is the **Hotel New Otani,** 4-1 Kioi-cho, Chiyoda-ku (tel. 03/265-1111), with more than 2,000 rooms. Its facilities are incredible: more than 35 restaurants and bars, 120 stores, medical offices, a post office, health club, tea ceremony room, outdoor swimming pool (fee: ¥1,200 or $9.60) and tennis courts, and a babysitting room. Most splendid of all, however, is its 400-year-old Japanese garden that sprawls over ten acres of ponds, waterfalls, bridges, bamboo groves, and manicured bushes. Standard single rooms, which are extremely small, begin at ¥22,000 ($176), while double and twin rooms go for ¥28,000 ($224) to ¥32,000 ($256). If you're booking a standard double or twin room, request that it be in the 40-story tower (it was built in 1974 and has slightly larger rooms). Japanese suites start at ¥49,000 ($392). Nearest subway stations: Akasaka-mitsuke, about three minutes away, and Yotsuya, about five.

Across the street from the New Otani is the **Akasaka Prince Hotel,** 1-2 Kioi-cho, Chiyoda-ku (tel. 03/234-1111), a 40-story, gleaming white skyscraper of remarkable modern design. Its lobby is intentionally spacious and empty, lined with almost 12,000 slabs of white marble. When the hotel opened in 1983, it caused quite a stir: some Tokyoites complained that it was too cold and sterile. In my opinion, however, the Akasaka Prince is just ahead of its time. Japanese style, after all, has always called for simplicity—and this hotel's design is a projection of that Japanese simplicity into the world of the 21st century.

Designed by Kenzo Tange, the hotel's 761 rooms are set on a 45° angle from the center axis of the core of the building, giving each room a corner view with expansive windows overlooking the city. Room color schemes are a soothing powder-blue and white, bright with a lot of sunshine. The single rooms, which start at ¥22,000 ($176), are among the nicest in Tokyo, with three windows forming a pleasant alcove around a sofa. Sinks and vanity desks are located away from the toilet and bath area. Twin rooms start at ¥32,000 ($256) and doubles at ¥35,000 ($280). Request a room overlooking the Akasaka side and you'll have a view of neon lights down below and Tokyo Tower off in the distance. Facilities include 12 international restaurants and bars. Nearest subway station: Akasaka-mitsuke, a three-minute walk.

Also located in Akasaka, but with slightly lower prices, is the **Akasaka Tokyu Hotel,** 2-14-3 Nagata-cho, Chiyoda-ku (tel. 03/580-2311). Built in 1969 and easily recognizable from the outside by its candy striped exterior, this 566-room hotel boasts an 89% average occupancy, attributed in part to its ideal location. Its 200 single rooms go for ¥18,000 ($144) to ¥22,000 ($176), but the lower-priced ones are pretty small. Double rooms are ¥28,000 ($224), while twins start at ¥27,000 ($216) and go to ¥39,000 ($312). Try to get a twin or double room facing Akasaka —the windows can open, a rarity in Tokyo. There are more than 14 restaurants in the building, and the first and second floors are devoted to shops and boutiques. The lobby is on the third floor—and be prepared for the huge poster of a seminude woman in the lobby lounge. Nearest subway station: Akasaka-mitsuke, one minute away.

Because of its proximity to Tokyo's business district, the **Palace Hotel,** 1-1-1 Marunouchi, Chiyoda-ku (tel. 03/211-5211), is a favorite among foreign businessmen, and foreigners account for 65% of its hotel guests. Located across the street from the Imperial Palace and gardens, the hotel's deluxe twin rooms—which are large, face the gardens, and have balconies—are highly recommended. They go for ¥46,500 ($372). Otherwise, the standard single rooms, which are adequate in size, start at a low of ¥18,500 ($148) and double rooms start at ¥29,000 ($232). Built in 1961, the hotel is small, with only 404 rooms, and repeat guests are rewarded with monogram slippers. Of its seven restaurants, the French Crown Restaurant on the tenth floor is the best, offering superb views of the Imperial Palace. Nearest subway station: Otemachi Station, three minutes away.

Shinjuku's newest deluxe hotel is the **Tokyo Hilton International,** 6-6-2 Nishi-Shinjuku, Shinjuku-ku (tel. 03/344-5111), which opened in 1984. As with all Hiltons, its room decor reflects traditional native style: shoji screens instead of curtains and simple yet elegant furniture. The largest Hilton in the Asia/Pacific area, the S-shaped, 38-story structure houses 808 rooms, which offer views of either Shinjuku's skyscrapers (a pretty sight at night) or (on clear days) Mount Fuji. Room rates are based on both size and location, with the more expensive rooms higher up. Single occupancy runs ¥24,000 ($192) to ¥32,000 ($256), while double occupancy costs ¥27,500 ($220) to ¥36,000 ($288). Japanese-style rooms range from ¥49,000 ($392) to ¥60,000 ($480). The hotel boasts an excellent fitness center, tennis courts, indoor pool (fee: ¥1,000 or $8), and seven restaurants and bars. Nearest subway station: Shinjuku, a ten-minute walk.

Across the street from the Hilton is the **Century Hyatt Tokyo,** 2-7-2 Nishi-Shinjuku, Shinjuku-ku (tel. 03/349-0111). Its lobby is an impressive seven-story atrium with three massive chandeliers and an inlaid marble floor. Its adequately sized rooms are attractively appointed in soft pastels, and the bathrooms feature bright lights that are great for applying makeup. There are single rooms available for ¥18,500 ($148), but the windows are at such an angle in the corner of the rooms that you can hardly see out of them. The twin rooms are better, with big windows that let in a lot of sunshine. These range from ¥25,000 ($200) to ¥30,000 ($240). Diversions here include a swimming pool on the 28th floor, a disco, and 12 restaurants and bars. Closest subway station: Shinjuku, a ten-minute walk.

The **Keio Plaza Inter-Continental Hotel**, 2-2-1 Nishi-Shinjuku, Shinjuku-ku (tel. 03/344-0111), has the distinction of being the first skyscraper built in Japan, and at 47 stories it's still Tokyo's tallest hotel. Built in 1971, its brilliant white exterior is composed of precast concrete panels, the first application of this technique in Japan. With almost 1,500 rooms and 20 restaurants and bars, it's one of Tokyo's largest hotels. The room rates are based on size rather than location, so ask for a room higher up where the view is better. Singles range from ¥23,000 ($184) to ¥33,000 ($264), and doubles cost ¥25,000 ($200) to ¥36,000 ($288). The hotel is just a few minutes' walk from Shinjuku Station.

A subsidiary of Air France, the **Hotel Pacific Meridien**, 3-13-3 Takanawa, Minato-ku (tel. 03/445-6711), is built on grounds that once belonged to Japan's imperial family and has a coffee lounge that looks out onto a peaceful and tranquil garden. Its Blue Pacific lounge on the 30th floor has dynamite views of Tokyo Bay. Restaurants include those serving Japanese, Chinese, and excellent French cuisine, and there's an outdoor pool (free for hotel guests). The hotel's 954 rooms are of adequate size and begin at ¥20,000 ($160) for singles and ¥23,000 ($184) for doubles and twins. Nearest subway station: Shinagawa, only two minutes away.

The **Takanawa Prince Hotel**, 3-13-1 Takanawa, Minato-ku (tel. 03/447-1111), has a subdued, comfortable lobby with dark colors and low ceilings. Known for its beautiful ten-acre traditional Japanese garden, this hotel caters largely to Japanese, both businessmen and tourists. Single rooms begin at ¥20,000 ($160), doubles and twins at ¥24,000 ($192). The guest rooms are slightly small but are quiet and comfortable and were renovated in 1986. Eighteen Japanese tatami rooms and suites are also available for ¥44,000 ($352) to ¥70,000 ($560). There are two outdoor swimming pools and French, Chinese, and Japanese restaurants. Nearest subway station: Shinagawa, a five-minute walk.

The **Roppongi Prince Hotel**, 3-1-7 Roppongi, Minato-ku (tel. 03/587-1111), opened in 1984—a welcome event in Roppongi, which still woefully lacks in hotels. The Roppongi Prince attracts young Japanese vacationers aged 20 to 25 and caters to them throughout with a young and cheerful staff, modern designs, and bold colors. The hotel is built around an inner courtyard, which features an outdoor swimming pool with a heated deck; a solar mirror on the hotel's roof directs the sun's rays down on sunbathers below. The pool is open year-round and charges ¥2,000 ($16). Rooms are small, but are bright and colorful and come with the usual minibar, desk, color TV, clock, and radio. Singles here are ¥20,000 ($160); twins, ¥22,000 ($176) to ¥26,000 ($208); and doubles, ¥24,000 ($192) to ¥26,000 ($208). A good place to be if you want to be close to the action in Roppongi. Roppongi Station is a 15-minute walk away.

Another relatively new hotel on the Tokyo scene is the **Asakusa View Hotel**, 3-17-1 Nishi-Asakusa, Taito-ku (tel. 03/847-1111), which opened in the fall of 1985. It's the only upper-bracket and modern hotel in the Asakusa area and looks almost out of place rising among this famous district's older buildings. This is a good place to stay if you want to be in Tokyo's old downtown rather than in the spanking newness of its business districts. The lobby exudes cool elegance, with a marble floor, atrium, and hanging chandeliers. Its 350 guest rooms are very pleasant, with contemporary Japanese furnishings of sleek lines and wallpaper with a fan motif. Bay windows give rooms plenty of sunshine, and rooms that face the front have views of the famous Asakusa Kannon Temple. Facilities include an indoor swimming pool (fee: ¥3,000 or $24) and French, Chinese, Italian, and Japanese restaurants. Singles are ¥15,500 ($124), doubles start at ¥23,000 ($184), and twins start at ¥26,000 ($208). If you want to stay in a Japanese-style room, eight are available; they start at ¥33,000 ($264) and sleep up to five persons. Nearest subway station: Tawaramachi Station on the Ginza Line, an eight-minute walk away.

THE MEDIUM BRACKET

Accommodations in this price range vary from Western-style hotels to business hotels to ryokan, with business hotels making up the majority in this category. Popular with Japanese businessmen, business hotels are generally quite small and offer just the basics but are usually situated in a convenient location. There's very little to differentiate one business hotel from another—they all look pretty much the same. If you're more interested in a clean and functional place to sleep rather than in roomy comfort, a business hotel may be the way to go, although the distinction between a hotel and a business hotel is sometimes a fine one. Unless otherwise stated, all rooms in this category come with private bath and toilet and air conditioning. Remember, too, that unless otherwise stated, a tax and service charge will be added to the quoted room rate.

Hotels

The 212-room **President Hotel,** 2-2-3 Minami Aoyama, Minato-ku (tel. 03/497-0111), is one of the best deals in town. Although a small hotel, it offers some of the same conveniences as the larger and more expensive hotels (like Telex and room service) and has a great location between Akasaka, Shinjuku, and Roppongi. Its rooms are small but clean, comfortable, and pleasant. They come with minibar, hot water for tea, hairdryer, TV with English cable, radio, and cotton kimono. The lobby is pleasingly elegant but unpretentious and has a somewhat European atmosphere. The President has two very good restaurants, one Japanese and one French. Foreigners constitute 50% of the hotel's clientele. Room rates begin at ¥10,500 ($84) for a single, ¥14,000 ($112) for a twin, and ¥15,500 ($124) for a double. Nearest subway station: Aoyama-Itchome, one minute away.

The **Fairmont Hotel,** 2-1-17 Kudan Minami, Chiyoda-ku (tel. 03/262-1151), is another good choice in this category. It's beautifully located on a quiet street opposite the Imperial Palace moat, which is lined with cherry trees—a real treat when the blossoms burst forth in spring. Guests like the Fairmont because it's an older hotel (built in 1952) with only 211 rooms and because it's conveniently located, yet away from the hustle and bustle of downtown Tokyo. Both of the hotel's restaurants look out onto a pleasant small garden with a waterfall. Singles here range from ¥10,600 ($85) to ¥12,200 ($98), twins run ¥14,000 ($112) to ¥23,000 ($184), and doubles cost ¥14,000 ($112) to ¥20,000 ($160). Prices include tax and service. The more expensive rooms are larger and face the palace moat—definitely worth it during cherry-blossom season. Nearest subway station: Kudanshita, a ten-minute walk.

The **Hilltop Hotel,** 1-1 Surugadai, Kanda, Chiyoda-ku (tel. 03/293-2311), is located, as the name implies, on a hill. It's an old-fashioned, unpretentious hotel with character. Its main building dates back to 1937 and, together with its annex, contains a total of only 75 rooms. The hotel's brochure maintains that "oxygen and negative ions are circulated into the rooms and its refreshing atmosphere is accepted by many, including prominent individuals, as most adequate for work and rest." I'm not sure exactly what that means but it probably doesn't do any harm. Its double rooms are fairly small, and although nothing fancy, they're pleasant and come with cherry-wood furniture, color TV, radio and clock, desk, table and chairs, and old-fashioned heaters with intricate grillwork. Prices are ¥21,000 ($168) to ¥22,000 ($176) for a double and ¥20,000 ($160) to ¥26,000 ($208) for a twin. There are also small singles starting at ¥12,000 ($96). The hotel's seven restaurants are all tastefully decorated and offer steaks as well as Italian, Chinese, and Japanese cuisine.

Closest subway stations: Ochanomizu and Shin-Ochanomizu, each eight minutes away; Jimbocho, five minutes.

The **Tokyo Holiday Inn**, 1-13-7 Hatchobori, Chuo-ku (tel. 03/553-6161), is similar to Holiday Inns back home. As many as 30% of its guests are Americans, mainly individual travelers. A red-brick building with the familiar Holiday Inn sign, it's located on Shin Ohashi-dori Avenue. The rooms are what you'd expect and come with the usual minibar, desk, clock, radio, and TV with CNN. They're priced at ¥15,500 ($124) for one and ¥22,500 ($180) for two persons. The hotel is small, with only 120 rooms, and has an outdoor swimming pool free for hotel guests. It's about a 20-minute walk to Ginza. Nearest subway station: Hatchobori, a three-minute walk.

The 800-room **Ginza Dai-ichi Hotel**, 8-13-1 Ginza, Chuo-ku (tel. 03/542-5311), is located on the southern edge of Ginza and offers such facilities as a sauna, beauty salon, barbershop, shopping arcade, travel agency, bar, coffeeshop, and sushi bar. French and Japanese restaurants are located on the 15th floor, with good views of Tokyo Bay by day and the lights of Ginza by night. The lobby is on the second floor. The guest rooms are unexciting but comfortable enough, and the bathrooms are tiny, one-piece plastic units. Those with the best views face Tokyo Bay. The price for one person is ¥15,000 ($120), twins start at ¥18,500 ($148), and triples start at ¥25,000 ($200). Nearest subway station: Shimbashi, five minutes away.

Located right next to Tokyo Station near its Yaesu North Exit, the **Hotel Kokusai Kanko**, 1-8-3 Marunouchi, Chiyoda-ku (tel. 03/215-3281), is convenient for visitors who are staying in Tokyo only one or two nights before departing for southern Japan on the Shinkansen from Tokyo Station. With a total of 94 rooms, it's a combination business and tourist hotel and caters primarily to the Japanese. Rooms are fairly quiet despite its noisy location, though higher-priced rooms are more shielded from traffic noise. Room rates start at ¥12,500 ($100) for a single, ¥21,500 ($172) for a double, and ¥22,000 ($176) for a twin. Restaurants serve both Western and Japanese food. Nearest station: Tokyo Station, one minute away.

An older, rather eccentric-looking hotel, the **Gajoen Kanko Hotel**, 1-8-1 Shimo-Meguro, Meguro-ku (tel. 03/491-0111), was built in the early 1930s. It has a decidedly Oriental atmosphere, with wood paneling and Japanese prints on its lobby ceiling and intricately inlaid shell and mother-of-pearl designs in its two old elevators. In its early years it was a hospital; after World War II American army personnel were stationed here for ten years. Now the hotel caters to a large Chinese clientele. In any case, for several years the hotel was becoming more and more rundown, but in 1986 extensive renovations cleaned up the lobby and guest rooms and added a new wing, bringing the total number of rooms to 104. Singles start at ¥10,000 ($80) and twins begin at ¥15,500 ($124). The best rooms are those on a corner or those facing the backyard, where there are trees. Nearest station: Meguro, an eight-minute walk.

Business Hotels

An attractive hotel, the **Mitsui Urban Hotel Ginza**, 8-6-15 Ginza, Chuo-ku (tel. 03/572-4131), is a cross between a business hotel and a regular hotel. Because of its location, convenient to Ginza and to the Kasumigaseki and Marunouchi business centers, it caters to both businessmen and tourists. The lobby is on the second floor and is manned by a friendly staff. The guest rooms are small and come with hot water for tea, alarm clock, radio, cotton kimono, and color TV offering English programs and adult entertainment for an extra ¥1,000 ($8) a day. The bathrooms are larger than in other business hotels. Rooms vary in size, beginning at ¥12,500 ($100) for a single and ¥18,300 ($146) for a twin or double. I suggest asking for a room away from the highway overpass beside the hotel. Nearest subway station: Shimbashi, only one minute on foot.

The **Ginza Capital Hotel**, 3-1-5 Tsukiji, Chuo-ku (tel. 03/543-8211), and its newer annex, called the New Ginza Capital Hotel, offer a total of 528 rooms within a ten-minute walk of Ginza. A modern and efficient establishment with a friendly staff, it has rooms that are clean and bright even though they are minuscule in size. If being able to look out a window is a big deal to you, stay away from the annex rooms that face north—they have a glazed covering about a foot out from the building so you can't see anything (heaven knows why). Rooms come with the usual hot water for tea, cotton kimono, and TV with adult movies, but a plus here is the full-length mirrors. The annex has both a Western and a Japanese restaurant and the main building a Western one. Rates in the main building start at ¥8,200 ($66) for a single and ¥13,700 ($110) for a twin; in the annex it's ¥8,400 ($67) for a single, ¥14,400 ($115) for a double, and ¥14,600 ($117) for a twin. Prices include service charge and tax. Nearest subway station: Shintomicho, two minutes away.

A red-brick building, the **Hotel Ginza Dai-ei,** 3-12-2 Ginza, Chuo-ku (tel. 03/541-0111), is a typical business hotel with minuscule rooms and the usual TV, hot-water heater, cotton kimono, and desk. A plus, however, is that its windows open. It also has Japanese-style rooms available at ¥16,500 ($132) for one person, ¥19,000 ($152) for two, and ¥21,500 ($172) for three. Otherwise, rooms start at ¥9,600 ($77) for one and ¥14,300 ($114) for two. Prices include tax and service. One restaurant serves Chinese food. The hotel is just a few minutes' walk from Higashi-Ginza Station.

There's nothing fancy or out of the ordinary about the **Ginza Nikko Hotel,** 8-4-21 Ginza, Chuo-ku (tel. 03/571-4911), but it's clean and conveniently located in southern Ginza. A small and personable business hotel with only 112 rooms, it's more than a quarter of a century old, making it one of the oldest hotels in the area. Facilities include a coffeeshop, one restaurant, and a bar. Singles start at ¥13,800 ($110), doubles at ¥20,000 ($160), twins at ¥24,000 ($192), and triples at ¥29,700 ($238). It's a four-minute walk to Shimbashi Station.

Miyako Inn Tokyo, 3-7-8 Mita, Minato-ku (tel. 03/454-3111), is a combination business and city hotel rising 14 stories high in southern Tokyo. Rooms on the top floor have the best views and face either Tokyo Bay or Tokyo Tower in the distance. All rooms come with the usual refrigerator, TV with extra charges for movies, cotton kimono, alarm clock, and hot-water thermos and tea. Facilities include Japanese, Chinese, and Western restaurants. Prices, including tax and service, range from ¥10,300 ($82) to ¥10,900 ($87) for a single and ¥16,200 ($130) to ¥22,300 ($178) for a twin. Differences in room rates are reflected in the size of the room and the bed. Double rooms are ¥16,200 ($130). Nearest stations: Tamachi, Mita, and Sengakuji, all within a six-minute walk.

The bottom ten floors of the **Shinjuku Prince Hotel,** 1-30-1 Kabuki-cho, Shinjuku-ku (tel. 03/205-1111), include shopping arcades and restaurants, while the 10th through 24th floors hold the hotel's 571 rooms. A smart-looking, streamlined brick building in the heart of Shinjuku, this business hotel has ten restaurants and bars and 24-hour room service. The standard rooms go for ¥13,200 ($106) for a single and ¥15,900 ($127) for a double or a twin. Deluxe rooms are twice as large as the standards and start at ¥22,000 ($176) for a twin and ¥24,000 ($192) for a double. This hotel has a great location, just a five-minute walk north of Shinjuku Station. The Seibu Shinjuku Line begins in the hotel itself.

The **Hotel Sunroute Tokyo,** 2-3-1 Yoyogi, Shibuya-ku (tel. 03/375-3211), attracts a 40% foreign clientele and calls itself a "city hotel," but its rooms resemble business-hotel rather than tourist accommodations. A 15-story white building, it has four restaurants serving Italian, Chinese, and Japanese cuisine. The guest rooms are small but clean, cozy and attractive and start at ¥10,300 ($82) for a single, ¥15,400 ($123) for a double, and ¥14,500 ($116) for a twin. Nearest train station: it's a two-minute walk south of Shinjuku Station.

In 1985 the **Hotel Sunlite,** 5-15-8 Shinjuku, Shinjuku-ku (tel. 03/356-0391), moved across the street from its old location into a spanking new building. As for the older building, it was turned into the Hotel Sunlite Annex and offers much lower rates than the newer location does. At any rate, all 192 rooms are cheerful and clean, though those in the Annex are small and its singles are minuscule. Feelings of claustrophobia are somewhat mitigated, however, by the fact that all windows can be opened. The best rooms are the new building's twin rooms that are situated on the corners, which have windows on two sides. Rates in the Annex start at ¥7,000 ($56) for a single and ¥10,500 ($84) for a twin. Charges in the new building start at ¥8,000 ($64) for a single, ¥14,000 ($112) for a twin, and ¥13,000 ($104) for a double. All rates include tax and service charge. Incidentally, if you like to stay out late, beware. Doors here close at 2 a.m. and don't reopen until 5:30 a.m. It's about a 15-minute walk to Shinjuku Station.

If you like electronic gadgetry and the benefits of the Space Age, you might like staying at the **Shinjuku Washington Hotel**, 3-2-9 Nishi-Shinjuku, Shinjuku-ku (tel. 03/343-3111). Opened in West Shinjuku in 1984, with an annex added in 1987, this huge white building reminds me of an ocean liner—even the hotel's tiny windows look like a ship's portholes. It has an interesting interior design with a lot of open spaces, and everything is bright and white. Make your way up to the third floor to the lobby—a row of machines provides for automated check-in and check-out. There are a few humans there, however, to help you with the process. You'll receive a "card key" resembling a credit card, which also activates the bedside controls for such things as the TV, radio, and room lights. There are no bellboys here, no room service. The guest rooms remind me of cabins in a ship and are small, but everything you need is there—fridge, TV with video programs, and radio. It's rather comical to see older women shuffling down the corridor of this thoroughly modern and automated hotel, but the place seems to attract all kinds. It also has a reputation for serving as a "love hotel" for young couples—an interesting place. Prices include tax and service. Singles start at ¥9,400 ($75), doubles at ¥16,400 ($131), twins at ¥15,800 ($126), and triples at ¥27,000 ($216). Prices in the annex are slightly different, starting at ¥10,000 ($80) for a single, ¥15,800 ($126) for a double, and ¥18,600 ($149) for a twin. The annex has its own check-in desk, and be sure to check out the annex toilets. Instructions are in Japanese only, but with the right push of a switch a spray of water is sent shooting into the air. A Japanese version of the French bidet. Nearest subway station: Shinjuku, about ten minutes away.

A pleasant, small business hotel, the **Hotel Yoko Akasaka**, 6-14-12 Akasaka, Minato-ku (tel. 03/586-4050), caters primarily to Japanese. In a handy location close to the nightlife in both Roppongi and Akasaka, its singles start at ¥8,200 ($66) and twins begin at ¥15,000 ($120). Prices include tax and service charge. For a couple of dollars more in each category you can get a slightly larger room, which may be worth it if you're claustrophobic. In any case, the bathrooms are barely large enough for even one person. Nearest subway station: Akasaka Station, five minutes away, on Akasaka Dori Street.

Not far from the Hotel Yoko Akasaka is **Shanpia**, 7-6-13 Akasaka, Minato-ku (tel. 03/586-0811). The special feature of this hotel is that 228 of its 250 rooms are singles. The other 22 rooms are twins only—no double beds. Singles go for ¥8,200 ($66) and twins run ¥14,800 ($118), including tax and service charge. Closest subway station: Akasaka is about a five-minute walk.

The **Hotel Tokyukanko**, 2-21-6 Akasaka, Minato-ku (tel. 03/583-4741), is located close to the ANA Hotel, about a ten-minute walk from either the Roppongi or Akasaka subway station. An older, 48-room hotel built at the time of the Olympics, in 1964, it's a bit worn in places and shows its age but is still popular because of its location. Single rooms with showers are ¥7,000 ($52), but these face an inner courtyard and have glazed windows. If you like the light of day, spring for a single with bath for ¥9,000 ($72). Twins start at ¥13,700 ($110), while doubles are ¥14,000 ($112). Rooms are larger than in some other business hotels, and bathrooms are tiled instead of being the usual plastic units.

If you want to stay closer to the night action of Roppongi, the **Hotel Ibis**, 7-4-14 Roppongi, Minato-ku (tel. 03/403-4411), is about as close as you can get, and you can't beat it for its location. It caters to both businessmen and to couples who come to Roppongi's discos and don't make (or want to make) the last subway home. Prices, which include tax and service, start at ¥13,000 ($104) for a single room, ¥17,000 ($136) for a double, and ¥21,500 ($172) for a twin. The lobby is on the fifth floor. On the 13th floor is the Sky Restaurant, an inexpensive French restaurant offering a good view of the surrounding area. Closest subway station: Roppongi, one minute away.

All 1,016 rooms in the main building of the **Shinagawa Prince Hotel**, 4-10-30 Takanawa, Minato-ku (tel. 03/440-1111), are singles. In 1986 an annex of 257 twin and double rooms was added. The best feature of this huge hotel complex is its adjoining sports complex, where you can use tennis courts, an ice-skating rink, bowling lanes, and an outdoor pool for an extra charge. The hotel has 13 restaurants and bars, and in the summer it has an outdoor beer garden. Catering to Japanese businessmen on weekdays and students on weekends and holidays, the Shinagawa Prince charges ¥8,400 ($67) for singles. If there are two of you but you still want to stay in the hotel's main building, an extra bed can be added for a total of ¥10,600 ($85). That gives you hardly room to walk, but the price is certainly reasonable. Ask for a room above the tenth floor, where you have a view of either mountains on the west side or the sea on the east. As for rooms in the annex, twins go for ¥13,700 ($110) and doubles for ¥14,300 ($114); all of these have the extra benefit of a refrigerator. The views, however, are unexciting. Nearest subway station: Shinagawa, a one-minute walk.

A Note On Japanese Symbols

Many hotels, restaurants, and other establishments in Japan do not have signs showing their names in English letters. Appendix II lists the Japanese symbols for all such places appearing in this guide. Each establishment name is numbered, and the same number appears in an oval in the text following the boldfaced establishment name. For example, in the text Osaka's **Hotel Hokke Club** (164) is number 164 in the Japanese symbol list in Appendix II.

Ryokan

Seifuso ①, 1-12-15 Fujimi, Chiyoda-ku (tel. 03/263-0681), is an excellent choice for travelers wishing to experience a ryokan for the first time. It's run by Setsuko Fukushima, a friendly woman who doesn't speak a lot of English but who compensates for it with warmth and with a sheet of instructions written in English about such things as etiquette of the Japanese bath and where and when to wear slippers. More than 30 years old, Seifuso has a total of 17 rooms, most of which have their own small alcove with chairs overlooking a small Japanese garden. If you'd like to have the experience of staying in a ryokan but don't relish the idea of sleeping on the floor, there's one Western-style room with a double bed available. There are also public baths that are separated for men and women.

Rooms without bath begin at ¥6,600 ($53) for one, ¥11,000 ($88) for two, and ¥16,500 ($132) for three. If you want a room with private bath, it's ¥12,000 ($96) for one, ¥22,000 ($176) for two, and ¥26,000 ($208) for three. These prices include service charge, but no meals or tax. Meals range from ¥1,320 ($10.56) for tempura to ¥10,000 ($80) for a Japanese-style dinner, and are served in a dining area that looks out onto the garden. Nearest subway station: Iidabashi, about a seven-minute walk. However, because Seifuso is a bit hard to find and has a sign only in Japanese, I suggest taking a taxi from Iidabashi.

Shimizu Bekkan ②, 1-30-29 Hongo, Bunkyo-ku (tel. 03/812-6285), is another ryokan that accepts foreigners and has had American guests. It has a variety of rooms available, and its prices, which include service charge only, are on a per-person rather than per-room basis. A variety of meal options are offered. Rooms without bath and toilet are ¥6,600 ($53) with no meals, ¥7,700 ($62) with breakfast only, ¥10,000 ($80) with dinner only, and ¥11,000 ($88) with dinner and breakfast. For rooms with private bath and toilet, add ¥1,000 ($8) to the charges above. Meals are served in your room, and there are separate public baths for men and women. Nearest subway station: Hongo Sanchome is about eight minutes away; it's best to take a taxi.

A bit far from the station, but a good medium-price ryokan as far as Tokyo goes, is **Tokiwa,** 7-27-9 Shinjuku, Shinjuku-ku (tel. 03/202-4321). An older building surrounded by a white wall and gate on Meiji Dori Street, this place is divided into two parts, a hotel and a ryokan, but all its 50 rooms are Japanese style. I suggest staying in the ryokan part—it's more than 40 years old and has a lot more character, with wooden beams, the earthy smell of tatami, and an old rock-enclosed and quaint public bath. Like most older Japanese buildings, it's cold and drafty in winter, but rooms have a *kotatsu*—a low table with a heating element underneath and a blanket spread all around it. By sitting at the table with your legs stuck under the quilt, you can stay pretty toasty. Rates are per person and include tax and service charge. The charge is ¥6,200 ($50) for a room without bath or meals, ¥7,500 ($60) for a room without meals but with its own bathroom. Rooms with their own private bath and meals are ¥13,200 ($106). Nearest subway station: Shin-Okubo, a ten-minute walk.

THE BUDGET CATEGORY

It's difficult to find inexpensive lodging in Tokyo the way you can in other big cities in Asia. The price of land is simply too prohibitive. You can, however, find rooms—tiny though they might be—for less than $35 a night, which is pretty good considering that you're in one of the most expensive cities in the world. Accommodations in this category are basic: a bed and usually a phone, television, heating, and air conditioning. Facilities are generally spotless, and prices often include tax and service charge. Inexpensive Japanese-style rooms make up the majority of this category.

Western Style

Asia Center of Japan, 8-10-32 Akasaka, Minato-ku (tel. 03/402-6111), is top choice in this category if you're looking for Western-style accommodations in the center of town. The only problem is that it's so popular it's often fully booked. Everyone from businessmen to students to travelers to foreigners teaching English stay here. (I know one teacher who has lived here for years.) Resembling a college dormitory, it has 172 rooms with and without private bath; a cafeteria and a lobby are located on the second floor. Rooms are basic, no frills, and in the singles you can almost reach out and touch all four walls. They come with bed, desk, telephone, air conditioner, heater, and pay TV. Rooms without bath are ¥5,000 ($40) for a single, ¥5,900 ($47) for a twin, and ¥10,000 ($80) for a triple. If you want your own bath, it's ¥5,000 ($45) for a single, ¥9,400 ($75) for a twin, and ¥12,300 ($98) for a triple. Prices include tax and service. The average price of meals served in the cafeteria is ¥600 ($4.80) for breakfast, ¥700 ($5.60) for lunch, and ¥1,400 ($11.20) for dinner. Nearest station: Aoyama-Itchome, about three minutes away. It's about a 15-minute walk to Roppongi, where all the night action is.

The **Tokyo City Hotel,** 1-9 Nihombashi Honcho, Chuo-ku (tel. 03/270-7671), is a fine, no-nonsense business hotel with all the usuals. Its one restaurant serves Western food. Although the single rooms are quite small, the twin rooms are adequate. Prices include tax and service. Singles start at ¥7,500 ($60), doubles at ¥11,300 ($90), and twins at ¥12,400 ($99). Each room has a private bathroom. Nearest subway station: Mitsukoshi-mae, two minutes away.

If you prefer to stay in the old downtown district of Asakusa, the **Asakusa Pla-**

za Hotel, 1-2-1 Asakusa, Taito-ku (tel. 03/845-2621), is located just a few minutes' walk from the famous Asakusa Kannon Temple. Its 90 rooms, 40 of which are singles, are simple but adequate and come with private bathroom, TV, hot-water pot and tea, and cotton kimono. The front desk is up on the second floor. Singles range from ¥5,500 ($44) to ¥7,000 ($56), but keep in mind that the cheapest singles don't have windows. Rooms with slightly smaller than double-size beds begin at ¥8,200 ($66) for double occupancy, doubles begin at ¥10,000 ($80), and twins begin at ¥10,500 ($84). Closest subway station: Asakusa, about a minute away.

Also located in northern Tokyo—but this time near Ueno and its attractions— is the **Hotel Ohgaiso**, 3-3-21 Ikenohata, Taito-ku (tel. 03/822-4611). Although rather unimaginative, it's inexpensive and clean. Its 85 rooms, all with private bath and toilet, come with desk, coin-operated TV, refrigerator, radio, and clock. There's no closet but there's a bar for hanging up clothes. Front doors close at 2 a.m. Rates are ¥6,000 ($48) for a single and ¥10,700 ($86) for a twin, including tax and service. The hotel is located close to Ueno Park and has bicycles for rent. Its one restaurant serves both Japanese- and Western-style breakfasts, as well as tempura, sashimi, and sukiyaki. Closest subway stations: the Ohgaiso is a three-minute walk from Nezu and a five-minute walk from the Ikenohata Exit of the Keisei (Skyliner) Ueno Station.

The Ys

The **YMCA Asia Youth Center**, 2-5-5 Sarugaku-cho, Chiyoda-ku (tel. 03/ 233-0611), is a relatively new and modern-looking facility, which opened in 1980. Its concrete structure houses a total of 55 rooms, each with its own private bathroom. Both men and women of any age are accepted, and about 30% of its guests are Korean. Rooms are very simple and go for ¥6,700 ($54) for a single, ¥11,300 ($90) for a twin, and ¥14,800 ($118) for a triple, tax extra. YMCA members receive a discount of ¥500 ($4) on the above rates. Western- or Japanese-style breakfasts are available for ¥800 ($6.40), lunches start at ¥1,000 ($8), and dinners start at ¥1,500 ($12). Facilities include an indoor swimming pool (fee: ¥700 or $5.60). Closest subway stations: Suidobashi and Jimbocho, each about a five-minute walk away.

Close to Ichigaya Station are two YWCAs. If you've already made reservations, make sure you're headed for the right one. The **National YWCA of Japan** ③, 4-8-8 Kudan-Minami, Chiyoda-ku (tel. 03/264-0661), is located about two minutes by foot from the Kudan exit of the station. It accepts women only. An exceptionally clean, cheerful, and rather modern establishment, it has nine Western-style rooms (eight singles and one twin) and two Japanese-style rooms, all without private bath. The charge is ¥5,000 ($40) for one person staying in a room, and ¥10,000 ($80) for the twin room, including tax. There's a small living room with a kitchenette for personal use and a TV. There's no cafeteria, and front doors close at 11 p.m.

At the opposite end of Ichigaya Station, close to the Ichigaya exit, is the **Tokyo YWCA Sadowara Hostel** ④, 3-1-1 Ichigaya Sadowara-cho, Shinjuku-ku (tel. 03/ 268-7313). It accepts married couples as well as single women. The rates, excluding tax, here are ¥5,200 ($42) for one person and ¥10,500 ($84) to ¥11,500 ($92) for two.

Ryokan

Ryokan Mikawaya Bekkan, 1-31-11 Asakusa, Taito-ku (tel. 03/843-2345), is located just off Nakamise Dori, a colorful, shop-lined pedestrian street leading to the famous Asakusa Kannon Temple. This is a pleasant area in which to stay because it gives you more of a feel for older Japan. Owned by Katsuo Tobita, who speaks good English, Mikawaya Bekkan has been a ryokan for more than half a century. Its 12 tatami rooms are all different and come with pay TV, floor cushions with backrests, and Japanese-style vanity mirrors. The ryokan is built around a small inner courtyard with a goldfish pond, where you can sit outside in warm weather. Room rates are ¥5,000 ($40) for one person and ¥9,500 ($76) for two. A Japanese breakfast is available for ¥700 ($5.60), but if you're tired of fish, rice, and vegetables in the morning, a Western-style breakfast of eggs, toast, salad, fruit, and coffee can be arranged for the same price. Doors close at 11:30 p.m., and guests are requested to leave their rooms from 10 a.m. to noon daily for cleaning. Nearest subway station: the ryokan is just a few minutes from Asakusa.

If the above ryokan is full, another place to stay in Asakusa is **Kikuya Ryokan,** 2-18-9 Nishi Asakusa, Taito-ku (tel. 03/841-6404). A modern red-brick building with ten Japanese-style rooms, it's located just off Kappabashi Dori Avenue, lined with shops selling those plastic-food displays you see in restaurants throughout Japan. Sensoji Temple is about a ten-minute walk away. Rates for rooms without private bathroom are ¥4,000 ($32) for one person, ¥7,000 ($56) for two, and ¥9,500 ($76) for three. Rooms with private bathroom range from ¥4,900 ($39) to ¥5,300 ($42) for one person, ¥7,700 ($62) to ¥8,800 ($70) for two persons, and are ¥11,000 ($88) for three persons. The front doors close at midnight, and the closest station is Tawaramachi, about an eight-minute walk away.

Another great place to stay if you want to get away from the glitter and neon of Tokyo is the area around Ueno Park. **Ryokan Sawanoya,** 2-3-11 Yanaka, Taito-ku (tel. 03/822-2251), is located northwest of Ueno Park. Although the ryokan itself is relatively modern-looking and unexciting, it's surrounded by a delightful part of old Tokyo—narrow streets lined with potted plants and bonsai, temples and old wooden houses tucked behind walls with wood gates, ma-and-pa shops selling everything from Japanese paper to rice crackers. To help in your exploration of the area, the ryokan will give you a map outlining places of interest.

As for the ryokan itself, it has a nice feeling to it. It has pamphlets and lots of information on other inexpensive ryokan and accommodations throughout Japan, and if you pay for the call, the owner here will even make your next reservation for you. It's a good place to meet other travelers and exchange information. There are instant coffee and tea available free in the lobby/dining area throughout the day. The place is different from most ryokan in that you wear your shoes inside, taking them off only before entering your tatami room. All 12 rooms are Japanese style, but only two come with private bath. Along with the usual pay TV, phone, heater, and air conditioner, each room has its own sink. The best rooms, in my opinion, are those on the third floor because they have their own small balcony. A breakfast of toast and fried eggs is available for ¥300 ($2.40), and if you order it the day before, you can have a Japanese-style breakfast for ¥800 ($6.40). Facilities include a vending machine dispensing beer and soda, a coin-operated washing machine and dryer (with free laundry detergent), a refrigerator, and a public bath. Room rates begin at ¥4,000 ($32) for one person, ¥7,500 ($60) for two, and ¥10,200 ($82) for three. Nearest subway station: the Yanaka exit of Nezu Station is about a seven-minute walk.

In the same neighborhood but located a few minutes farther south is **Katsutaro,** 4-16-8 Ikenohata, Taito-ku (tel. 03/821-9808). All of its seven rooms are Japanese style, and four of these have their own private bathroom. Rooms are quite large and have coin-operated TV, but try to avoid rooms that face the main street, as these can be quite noisy. The building itself is about 35 years old, and at least half the guests staying here are Japanese. A continental breakfast costs ¥400 ($3.20). Rooms without bath are ¥4,200 ($34) for one person, ¥7,700 ($62) for two, and ¥10,500 ($84) for three. Rooms with bath are ¥4,800 ($38), ¥8,800 ($70), and ¥12,000 ($96), respectively.

A third ryokan close to Ueno Park is **Suigetsu,** 3-3-21 Ikenohata, Taito-ku (tel. 03/822-4611). It's located next to the Hotel Ohgaiso, a Western-style hotel described above. The two places are under the same management but have their own front desks. Suigetsu has 66 Japanese-style rooms (some with balconies) in a hotel-like setting, and caters mainly to Japanese families and tour groups. The rooms come with coin-operated TV with adult video, refrigerator, safe, mirror, and table. There are three public baths: one for women, one for men, and one for families. You can rent bicycles here. A restaurant serves Japanese food and Japanese- and Western-style breakfasts. Most rooms are without bath and start at ¥5,500 ($44) for a single, ¥8,800 ($70) for a twin, and ¥11,800 ($94) for a triple. Rooms with private bath are for four or five people only and cost ¥9,500 ($76) per person. Nearest subway stations: the Ikenohata exit of Keisei (Skyliner) Ueno Station (a ten-minute walk) and Nezu Station (a five-minute walk).

The small (only nine rooms) **Sansuiso** is at 2-9-5 Higashi Gotanda, Shinagawa-ku (tel. 03/441-7475). The friendly and accommodating couple who run this place don't speak any English but they have a poster answering all pertinent questions, such as how many nights will you be staying, etc. The ryokan is very clean and rooms come with the usual hot water and tea bags, cotton kimono and towel, mirror, heater and air conditioner, and pay TV. Some rooms have Japanese toilet and bath. Rooms start at ¥4,400 ($35) for one, ¥7,700 ($62) for two, and ¥10,700 ($86) for three. Nearest subway station: Sansuiso is a five-minute walk east of Gotanda Station.

Inabaso Ryokan, 5-6-13 Shinjuku, Shinjuku-ku (tel. 03/341-9581), first began receiving foreign guests during the 1964 Olympics and since then has had many travelers from North America, Australia, and Europe. All 13 rooms (2 of them Western style) have their own private bath and Western-style toilet, TV, and refrigerator. A Japanese breakfast of rice, bean-paste soup, fish, and ham and eggs is available for ¥650 ($5.20); coffee, toast, and eggs cost ¥300 ($2.40); and a Japanese dinner runs ¥1,650 ($13.20). Room rates here begin at ¥4,400 ($35.20) for one person, ¥8,000 ($64) for two, and ¥9,900 ($79) for three. Nearest subway stations: it's ten minutes from Shinjuku, three minutes from either Shinjuku Sanchome or Shinjuku Gyoen-mae.

Kimi Ryokan, 2-1034 Ikebukuro, Toshima-ku (tel. 03/971-3766), underwent extensive remodeling in 1986 and reopened as a completely new structure. In place of the old, rambling building that used to stand here is a five-story cement building with whitewashed walls, wooden corridors, and tatami-style guest rooms. The place is spotlessly clean, and although it's modern in every sense of the word, care has been given to add such Japanese touches as sliding screens and traditional Japanese music playing softly in the hallways. Owned by three brothers who speak excellent English, Kimi began attracting overseas visitors in the late 1970s and now caters exclusively to foreigners, many of whom are working in Tokyo as English teachers or in other professions and some of whom are living here while searching for more permanent places to stay. There's a bulletin board with various jobs available (mainly as English teachers). This place is so popular, in fact, that there's sometimes a waiting list to get in. All rooms are without private bath but are cheerful and clean and come with telephone and coin-operated heater and air conditioner. Prices start at ¥2,800 ($22) for a dormitory bed, ¥3,800 ($30) for a single, ¥5,500 ($44) for a double, and ¥6,000 ($48) for a twin. Facilities include a lounge with TV, a vending machine for drinks, and a pay telephone from which you can make international calls. Free tea is available throughout the day. Nearest station: about a five-minute walk from the west exit of Ikebukuro Station. The tiny police station located to your right as you exit the station has maps available that will guide you to Kimi.

One of the least expensive places to stay in Shinjuku is **Keiunso Ryokan** Ⓢ, 2-4-2 Yoyogi, Shibuya-ku (tel. 03/370-0333 or 370-0650). However, the English-speaking woman who runs this place expressed some reluctance about taking in foreigners who had never stayed in a ryokan before. Another disadvantage to staying here is that guests are requested to leave during the day from 10 a.m. to 5 p.m. However, this place has such a good location that it's worth a try. There are a total of 25 rooms and all are Japanese style with just the basics of pay TV and phone. Most also have their own sink, but the bath is communal. The price per person is ¥6,000 ($48) if there's one of you and ¥5,000 ($40) if there are two. Nearest station: the south exit of Shinjuku Station is only three minutes away.

If the ryokan listed above are full, you might try **Okubo House,** 1-11-32 Hyakunincho, Shinjuku-ku (tel. 03/361-2348). You have to leave during the day from 9:30 a.m. to 5 p.m., the front doors are locked at 11 p.m., and the people who run this place are sometimes curt and gruff, but it's one of the cheapest places to stay in Tokyo. The rooms are the smallest I've seen—just two- or three-tatami-mat rooms—but at least they all have windows. Room prices are ¥3,000 ($24) for one person and ¥4,200 ($34) for two. There are also two dormitory-style rooms with bunk beds, for men only, for ¥1,700 ($14). Children are not accepted in this ryokan. Cotton kimonos and Japanese tea are provided, but there's no kitchen or meals. There are separate public baths for men and women. Nearest subway station: Shin-Okubo, about a two-minute walk. To get there, turn left out of the station's only exit, then turn left again on the first side street, which runs right past the station and parallels the train tracks. Okubo is on this street and is easy to identify, having a sign in English.

Youth Hostels

Opened in 1984, the **Tokyo International Youth Hostel,** 21-1 Kaguragashi, Shinjuku-ku (tel. 03/235-1107), is definitely the best place to stay in its price range. The lobby is on the 18th floor of the new Central Plaza Building. You just can't beat this place—it's new, spotlessly clean, modern, and offers a great view of Tokyo. And the best thing is that you don't even need a youth hostel card to stay here, and there is no age limit. All 138 beds are dormitory style, with two, four, or five bunk beds to a room. The rooms are very pleasant, with big windows and wooden and metal bunk beds of modern design. Each bed even has its own curtain you can draw around it for privacy. Lodging costs ¥2,800 ($22) without meals, ¥4,100 ($33) with two meals.

There are, however, some restrictions and rules. Officially you can stay here a maximum of only three days, although if there are vacancies you can stay longer. The place is so popular in summer that it's necessary to make reservations about three months in advance. At 10:30 p.m. the front door is locked and it's lights out. The hostel is closed during the day from 10 a.m. to 3 p.m. A plus, however, is that you have free use of a washer and dryer. Nearest subway station: Iidabashi is one minute away.

The **Tokyo Yoyogi Youth Hostel,** National Olympic Memorial Youth Center, 3-1 Yoyogi-Kamizono, Shibuya-ku (tel. 03/467-9163), is on the west side of Meiji Shrine Outer Garden. Located in an enclosed complex of buildings surrounded by a fence, the hostel is in Building 14. The whole compound used to house American occupation troops after World War II and was then used to accommodate athletes during the 1964 Olympics. It's now devoted to a number of youth activities. There are 150 beds here and the cost is ¥1,850 ($15) per night. Nonmembers pay ¥2,300 ($18). No meals are served but there are cooking facilities. There's a large Japanese-style bath in a neighboring building. The hostel is closed daily from 10 a.m. to 5 p.m., and the front gate closes at 10 p.m. Closest subway station: Sangubashi, about five minutes away.

Capsule Hotels

So-called capsule hotels became popular in the early 1980s and are used primarily by Japanese businessmen who have spent an evening out drinking with fellow workers and missed their last train home—a capsule hotel is cheaper than a taxi home. At any rate, accommodation in one of these establishments is a small unit no larger than a coffin consisting of a bed and private color TV, alarm clock, and radio. These units are usually stacked two deep in rows down a corridor, and the only thing separating you from your probably inebriated neighbor is a curtain. A cotton kimono and locker are provided, and bath and toilets are communal.

Most capsule hotels do not accept women; the two listed here are no exception. **Fontaine Akasaka,** 4-3-5 Akasaka, Minato-ku (tel. 03/583-6554), is located right in the heart of Akasaka's nightlife. It offers a total of 332 capsule beds, a sauna and public bath, and nonsmoking floors. Check-in is after 5 p.m., check-out is at 10 a.m., and the charge is ¥4,700 ($38) per person for a bed and sauna. Closest subway stations: a two-minute walk from Akasaka Station and a five-minute walk from Akasaka-mitsuke.

Capsule Inn Akasaka, 6-14-1 Akasaka, Minato-ku (tel. 03/588-1811), is located just off Akasaka Dori Street, about a five-minute walk from Akasaka subway station. It also offers a sauna and public bath and has the same check-in and checkout times as the capsule hotel listed above. The charge here is ¥3,800 ($30) per weeknight, ¥3,500 ($28) on weekends.

ACCOMMODATIONS AT NARITA

If you find yourself on a stopover at Narita International Airport for one or two nights, you may not want to take the one- to two-hour trip to a hotel in Tokyo. There are a number of Western-style hotels close by that operate free shuttle buses to and from the airport. Rooms are soundproofed and have the usual conveniences of private bath and toilet, TV, phone, and radio, but otherwise there's nothing that really distinguishes one hotel from the next. Reservations for these hotels can be made at the hotel counter located in the arrival wing of the airport. The telephone prefix for Narita is 0476, which you needn't dial if you're calling from the airport.

If you find yourself with some spare time, be sure to visit Shinshoji Temple, popularly known as Narita-san, which is located close to the train station in downtown Narita. It's a Buddhist temple dedicated to Fudo, god of fire, and is visited by more than seven million people each year—usually when they have a favor to ask, whether it be good health, a happy marriage, or success in passing a university entrance exam. Behind the temple is a 40-acre Japanese garden that has three ponds and many flowering trees and bushes, including wisteria, plum, and cherry.

Narita International Hotel, 650-35 Nanae, Tomisato-mura Inba-gun, Chiba (tel. 0476/93-1234)—an affiliate of Northwest Airlines—is located 15 minutes away from the airport via shuttle bus. Its 212 rooms are large for Japan, and the hotel is surrounded by greenery, woods, and fields. Facilities include an outdoor swimming pool, tennis courts, and Japanese and Western restaurants. There's free shuttle bus service daily to Narita-san temple. Room rates are ¥13,000 ($104) for a single, ¥18,000 ($144) for a double, and ¥21,000 ($168) for a twin.

Narita Airport Rest House (tel. 0476/32-1212) is a square white building located right beside the airport terminal. Its singles are ¥12,900 ($103), and twins and doubles start at ¥16,200 ($130), including tax and service. The 210 rooms are rather sterile but have everything you need. Four TV screens in the hotel give all the latest information on arrival and departure times for all airlines. There are a Japanese and a Western restaurant and a bar in the hotel.

Holiday Inn–Narita, 320-1 Tokko, Narita-shi, Chiba (tel. 0476/32-1234), is located just a mile away from the airport and is similar to Holiday Inns in the United States. Its rooms are pleasantly decorated in powder blue and white. Facilities include an outdoor swimming pool, a sauna, restaurants serving Japanese, Chinese, and Western cuisine, and a bar/restaurant on the ninth floor with views of the airport. Rates begin at ¥13,000 ($104) for one person and ¥16,500 ($132) for two.

Narita View Hotel, 700 Kosuge, Narita City (tel. 0476/32-1111), is located ten minutes away from both the airport and Narita train station. Facilities here include four restaurants and one bar, a sauna, tennis courts, indoor and outdoor pools, a garden, and a gym. Singles are ¥13,000 ($104), doubles run ¥15,500 ($124), and twins cost ¥19,800 ($158).

Hotel Nikko Narita, 500 Tokko, Narita (tel. 0476/32-0032), is located about five minutes from the airport by free shuttle bus. It offers an outdoor swimming pool, tennis courts, and two bars and four restaurants serving Japanese, French, Chinese, and Western cuisine. Its 525 rooms cost ¥14,800 ($118) for a single,

¥22,300 ($178) for a double, and ¥22,300 ($178) to ¥32,000 ($256) for a twin, including tax and service.

---

5. Where to Dine

From stand-up noodle shops at train stations to rustic farmhouses serving country cooking Japanese style, restaurants in Tokyo number at least 45,000, which gives you at least some idea of how fond the Japanese are of food and of eating out. In a city where apartments are so small and cramped that entertaining at home is almost unheard of, restaurants serve as places for socializing, meeting friends, and wooing business associates—as well as excuses for drinking a lot of beer, sake, and whisky. I know people in Tokyo who claim they haven't cooked in years—and that doesn't mean that they're millionaires (though it could mean that they're bad cooks). It just means that they take advantage of one of the best deals in Tokyo, the teishoku, or set lunch course. Even the most prohibitive restaurants in Tokyo often offer set lunch menus by which you can dine in style at very reasonable prices. To keep your costs down, as I have suggested, try eating your bigger meal at lunch.

Although Japanese food is varied, healthy, and delicious, even the most dedicated Japanophile starts craving Western food after a while. In fact, even the Japanese themselves crave Western food, as shown by the increase in Western restaurants in Tokyo in the past decade. So I have included a goodly number of restaurants serving food other than Japanese. The most popular Western restaurants are French and Italian, which can be quite expensive. Other international cuisines tend to be more reasonably priced, including Mexican, Chinese, Thai, Greek, and American. Ethnic restaurants have literally mushroomed in popularity in the past few years and have become somewhat of an epidemic. The result is that you can dine at French, Indian, and other international restaurants that rival ethnic restaurants anywhere else in the world.

In addition to the restaurants recommended in this section, there are a number of bars and nightspots listed in the Chapter IV "After Dark in Tokyo" section that serve food. And remember that a 3% consumption tax will be added to your bill. Many first-class restaurants also add a 10% to 15% service charge. Unless otherwise stated, the prices I've given do not include the extra tax and charges.

Street maps for the Ginza, Asakusa, Shinjuku, Akasaka, and Roppongi areas are also provided in Chapter IV. Use them to plan your restaurant journeys.

NOTE: See "A Note on Japanese Symbols" on page 99, which explains how to identify places whose signs have only Japanese symbols.

RESTAURANTS AT A GLANCE

Below is a partial list of restaurants covered in the Tokyo dining section, divided into various areas for easy reference. You may, for example, find yourself in Asakusa with an appetite for sukiyaki but not a desire to read through the entire restaurant section to find a sukiyaki restaurant in Asakusa. I've therefore selected eight of the most commonly visited areas in Tokyo and listed restaurants in those areas, along with each locale's price bracket (upper, medium, or budget) and the type of cuisine served. More information on these restaurants is given in the extensive dining section that follows, which also covers restaurants outside these eight areas. (See the "Food and Drink" section in Chapter II for explanations of the cuisine.)

Name of Restaurant	Price Bracket	Type of Cuisine
GINZA		
Japanese Food		
Kisso	Upper	Kaiseki
Kinsen	Upper	Kaiseki

Ten-ichi	Upper	Tempura
Sushiko	Upper	Sushi
Sushi Sei	Medium	Sushi
Ohmatsuya	Medium	Grilled foods
Suehiro	Medium	Steaks, sukiyaki
Benihana of New York	Medium	Teppanyaki
Kushi Colza	Medium	Yakitori, kushiyaki
Ginza Benkay	Medium	Teppanyaki, sushi, kaiseki
Ohmatsuya	Budget	Rice casseroles
Munakata	Budget	Mini-kaiseki
Torigin	Budget	Yakitori, rice casseroles
Atariya	Budget	Yakitori
Donto	Budget	Varied, including noodles, tempura, sashimi

Non-Japanese Food

Maxim's	Upper	French
Shakey's	Budget	Pizza

AKASAKA
Japanese Food

Hayashi	Upper	Grilled foods
Inakaya	Upper	Grilled foods
Sekishin-tei	Upper	Teppanyaki
Zakuro	Upper	Shabu-shabu, sukiyaki, teppanyaki
Suehiro	Medium	Steaks
Hayashi	Budget	Rice casseroles
Torijoh	Budget	Yakitori
Kushinobo	Budget	Kushikatsu

Non-Japanese Food

Tour D'Argent	Upper	French
Kana Uni	Upper	French
Trader Vic's	Upper	Seafood, steaks
Le Chalet	Medium	French
Victoria Station	Medium	Hamburgers, steaks
Tiger Seafood Restaurant	Medium	Seafood
Moti	Budget	Indian

ROPPONGI
Japanese Food

Takamura	Upper	Kaiseki
Kisso	Upper	Kaiseki
Inakaya	Upper	Grilled foods
Fukuzushi	Upper	Sushi
Seryna	Upper	Shabu-shabu, sukiyaki
Sushi Sei	Medium	Sushi
Momiji-ya	Medium	Seafood
Hassan	Medium	Shabu-shabu, sukiyaki
Shabu Zen	Medium	Shabu-shabu, sukiyaki
Gonin Byakusho	Medium	Varied, including grilled foods, obento
Chisen	Medium	Kushiage
Roppongi Colza	Medium	Teppanyaki, seafood

Ganchan	Medium	Yakitori
Bikkuri Sushi	Budget	Sushi
Torigin	Budget	Yakitori, rice casseroles
Kamakura	Budget	Yakitori
Tanuki	Budget	Noodles
Ichioku	Budget	Original creations

Non-Japanese Food

Chianti	Upper	Italian
Spago	Upper	Californian
Atantot	Medium	French
Zest	Medium	Mexican/American
Metropole	Medium	Chinese
Tong Fu	Medium	Chinese
Victoria Station	Medium	Hamburgers, steaks
Nicola	Budget	Italian
Moti	Budget	Indian
Samrat	Budget	Indian

SHINJUKU
Japanese Food

Kakiden	Upper	Kaiseki
Shirakawago	Upper	Regional specialties
Mon Cher Ton Ton	Upper	Shabu-shabu, teppanyaki
Hayashi	Medium	Grilled foods
Tsunahachi	Medium	Tempura
Suehiro	Medium	Steaks
Irohanihoheto	Budget	Yakitori

Non-Japanese Food

La Primavera	Medium	Italian
Shakey's	Budget	Pizza
Spaghetti Factory	Budget	Spaghetti
Ban-Thai	Budget	Thai
Healthmagic	Budget	Sandwiches, salads
Negishi	Budget	Ox-tail soup, boiled wheat with grated yam

HARAJUKU and AOYAMA
Japanese Food

Genrokusushi	Budget	Sushi

Non-Japanese Food

L'Orangerie de Paris	Upper	French, Sunday brunch
Sabatini	Upper	Italian
Mominoki House	Medium	Japanese/French
Selan	Medium	Japanese-style French
Zest	Medium	Mexican/American
Beer Market Doma	Budget	Pao foods, Asian casseroles and salads
Bamboo Sandwich House	Budget	Sandwiches
Sabatini Pizzeria Romana	Budget	Italian
Shakey's	Budget	Pizza

Central Park	Budget	Chinese
El Pollo Loco	Budget	Chicken
El Amigo	Budget	Mexican
Health Magic	Budget	Sandwiches, salads
Brasserie D	Budget	Sunday brunch
Spiral Cafe	Budget	Sunday brunch

TSUKIJI
Japanese Food

Tamura	Upper	Kaiseki
Edogin	Medium	Sushi
Tentake	Medium	Blowfish
Sushi Dai	Budget	Sushi

ASAKUSA
Japanese Food

Chinya	Medium	Shabu-shabu, sukiyaki
Komagata Dojo	Medium	Dojo (a sardine-like river fish)
Mugitoro	Medium	Yam
Tatsumiya	Budget	Varied, traditional dishes
Keyaki	Budget	Eel
Namiki	Budget	Noodles

Non-Japanese Food

| Kamiya Bar | Budget | Steaks, grilled food |

UENO
Japanese Food

| Izu'ei | Budget | Eel |

SHIBUYA
Japanese Food

Seiyo Hiroba	Medium	Mediterranean
Irohanihoheto	Budget	Yakitori
Tenmi	Budget	Macrobiotic vegetarian

Non-Japanese Food

| The Prime | Budget | Sandwiches, salads, curries, Chinese, sushi |

THE UPPER BRACKET

Japanese patrons in Tokyo's top restaurants almost never spend their own money. Most of them are on expense accounts, without which many of these establishments would dry up and die out tomorrow. If you're not on an expense account, however, don't despair. The restaurants I've listed in this category will allow you to splurge and experience some of Japan's most exquisite and finest cuisine without having to mortgage your house upon your return home. And don't forget about those set lunch courses—great bargains by any standards.

Japanese Food

Takamura ⑥, 3-4-27 Roppongi (tel. 585-6600), is a must for everyone who can afford it. Located on the edge of the hot spot that is Roppongi, this wonderful

42-year-old house is like a peaceful oasis that time forgot. Each of the eight rooms in this house is different, with windows looking out onto miniature gardens and bamboo, and with charcoal hearths built into the floor. Takamura has a very Japanese feel to it, a feeling that expands proportionately with the arrival of your meal—seasonal kaiseki food arranged so artfully that you almost hate to destroy it. Your pleasure increases, however, as you savor the various textures and flavors of the food. Specialties here may include quail, sparrow, or duck, grilled on the hearth in your own private tatami room. Seating, by the way, is on the floor, as it is in most traditional Japanese restaurants. Reservations are a must, and with dinners ranging from ¥16,500 ($132) to ¥22,000 ($176), the price of dinner here usually averages about ¥25,000 ($200) to ¥30,000 ($240) by the time you add drinks, tax, and service charge. If you are a party of four or more, you can also come here for lunch if you make reservations one day in advance. Special lunches cost ¥11,000 ($88) to ¥14,000 ($112). Hours here are noon to 3 p.m. and 5 to 10:30 p.m., with last orders taken at 8 p.m. It's closed Sunday. Nearest subway station: Roppongi is about five minutes away by foot. There are two entrances to Takamura, marked by wooden gates complete with little roofs. The sign on the restaurant is in Japanese only, but look for the credit card signs.

At the other extreme from Takamura is the thoroughly modern **Kisso** (tel. 582-4191), located in the basement of the Axis Building, at 5-17-1 Roppongi. A combination shop/restaurant, Kisso sells Japanese gourmet cookware, including expensive ceramics, utensils, and lacquerware of contemporary design. The dining area is simple but elegant, with sprigs of flowers, heavy tables, and soft lighting. The food is kaiseki and comes only in set courses, served (as you might guess) in beautifully lacquered bowls, trays, and ceramic plates. I love eating here because to me Kisso represents all the best that is modern Japan—understated elegance, a successful marriage between the contemporary and the traditional. There should be more places like this in Tokyo. Dinner courses range from ¥8,800 ($70.40) to ¥13,200 ($105.60), with a complete meal consisting of an appetizer, soup, sashimi, a seasonal dish, baked dish, boiled dish, tea, rice, and dessert. If you want to come here for lunch, it's very reasonable, with set courses ranging from ¥1,300 ($10.40) to ¥5,500 ($44). Lunch is served from 11:30 a.m. to 2 p.m. and dinner from 5:30 to 10 p.m.; closed Sunday. Closest subway station: Roppongi. From Roppongi Station, walk toward Tokyo Tower; after about four minutes the Axis Building will be on your right.

If you're in Ginza, there's a second branch of Kisso at 4-6-18 Ginza (tel. 535-5035), with courses similar to those described above. Complete set lunches here start at ¥1,000 ($8), while set dinners start at ¥6,500 ($52). Hours are 11:30 a.m. to 2 p.m. and 5 to 9 p.m. daily. Very modern in decor, it's located on Chuo Dori Avenue between Mitsukoshi and Matsuya department stores and is up on the fifth floor. Closest subway station: Ginza.

Another kaiseki restaurant is **Kakiden** ⑦, 3-37-11 Shinjuku (tel. 352-5121), on the eighth floor of Yasuyo Building on the east side of Shinjuku Station next to My City shopping complex. This is a sister restaurant to one in Kyoto that was founded more than 260 years ago as a catering service for the elite. Although located in a rather uninspiring building, Kakiden has a relaxing tea house atmosphere, with low chairs, shoji screens, bamboo trees, and soothing traditional Japanese music playing softly in the background. The menu is in Japanese only, but since meals are set courses, simply pick out to fit your budget. Dinners range from ¥6,600 ($52.80) to ¥16,500 ($132); as with all kaiseki, meals vary daily according to what's available and fresh. Some of the more common dishes here will include fish, vegetables, eggs, sashimi, shrimp, and mushrooms, but don't worry if you can't identify everything. I've found that even the Japanese don't always know what they're eating. Special lunches are available until 5 p.m. for ¥3,300 ($26.40) to ¥5,500 ($44). Kakiden is open daily beginning at 11 a.m.; the last order is at 9 p.m.

Tamura ⑧, 2-12-11 Tsukiji (tel. 541-2591), is a modern kaiseki restaurant with four floors of smiling and bowing kimono-clad waitresses and hostesses. The very friendly staff here make you feel as though they've been waiting all this time just for you. Although the menu is only in Japanese, they'll help you decide what to order, and you have your choice of either tatami or table-and-chairs dining. Dinner, served daily from 5:30 to 10 p.m. (last orders taken at 7:30 p.m.), starts at ¥33,000 ($264) and reservations are necessary.

If you want to come for lunch, however, reservations are not necessary. This place is popular with Japanese housewives, and there's even a tatami room for women only and a special menu for ladies only for ¥5,500 ($44), including tax. Men can order it too, but for some reason have to pay an additional 10%. Other courses are available for ¥7,700 ($61.60) and ¥11,000 ($88). Lunch is served daily from noon to 3 p.m. Closest subway station: Tsukiji, about a two-minute walk.

A conveniently located, modern kaiseki restaurant in the heart of Ginza is **Kinsen** ⑨, 4-4-10 Ginza (tel. 561-8708). It's located on Harumi Dori Avenue on the fifth floor of the Ginza Kintetsu Building, just across the street from Jena Bookstore. There's no English menu, but various courses are available so simply choose one to fit your budget. Lunch courses range from ¥2,600 ($20.80) to ¥5,200 ($41.60), while dinners cost from ¥10,000 ($80) to ¥13,000 ($104). Food is served artistically arranged in various bowls and boxes. Kinsen is open every day from 11:30 a.m. to 2 p.m. and from 5 to 8:30 p.m. Nearest subway: one minute from Ginza Station.

One of the most delightful old-time restaurants I've been to is **Hayashi** ⑩, on the fourth floor of the Sanno Kaikan Building, 2-14-1 Akasaka (tel. 582-4078). Serving home-style country cooking, this cozy, rustic-looking restaurant specializes in grilled food, which you do yourself over your own square hibachi. Altogether there are ten grills in this small place, some of them surrounded by tatami mats and some by wooden stools or chairs. As the evening wears on, the one-room main dining area can get quite smoky, but somehow that just adds to the atmosphere (sorry, couldn't resist saying that), and nice touches are the big gourds and memorabilia hanging around and the waiters in traditional baggy pants. The owner of Hayashi, which opened in 1965, is almost always present and told me that it was his philosophy that the fire in the grills brought people more in touch with their basic feelings. "All mankind loves fire," he said. "For many years man has had a close relationship with fire. It opens our hearts and makes us relax."

Open every day except Sunday from 5:30 to 11 p.m., Hayashi serves just three set menus, which change with the seasons. The ¥5,500 ($44) meal—which will cost about ¥8,800 ($70.40) by the time you add drinks, tax, and service charge—may include such items as sashimi and vegetables, chicken, scallops, and gingko nuts, which you grill yourself. The ¥7,700 ($61.60) and ¥10,000 ($80) meals have more items, and may include oysters, abalone, beef, or fresh fish. Since this place is small it's safest to make a reservation. You can also come here for lunch from 11:30 a.m. to 2 p.m. Monday through Friday, when only *oyakodomburi* is served. Literally "parent and child," it's a simple rice dish with egg and chicken on top costing only ¥850 ($6.80). Nearest subway: Akasaka Station, only one minute away, near the Akasaka Dori and Misuji Dori intersection.

Shirakawago ⑪, 2-29-10 Kabuki-cho, Shinjuku-ku (tel. 200-5255), is a 300-year-old farmhouse brought to Tokyo from the Shirakawa region in the Japan Alps (minus the thatched roof, which would probably be a major fire hazard in crowded Tokyo). A massive house with heavy wooden beams and tatami floors, this place serves food native to the Hida Shirakawa region, chiefly river fish, such as rainbow trout, from Nagara River, as well as wild fowl and game. Other items on the menu, which is written in English, include chicken teriyaki, a one-pot tofu dish, green-tea buckwheat noodles, sashimi, tempura, grilled smelt, and deep-fried whole river crab. It may be easier to order one of the set courses. These start at ¥4,400 ($35.20) for five dishes and go up to ¥6,500 ($52) for nine dishes. Expect to spend at least ¥7,000 ($56) per person once you add tax, service charge, and drinks, and don't neglect to visit the upstairs floor with its eclectic collection of kitsch and antiques, including farm implements, straw shoes, a bowling trophy, and even a statue of the Virgin Mary. Hours are 1 to 11 p.m. daily. Nearest subway station: it's about a 10- to 15-minute walk from Shinjuku Station on the northern edge of Kabuki-cho, but it may be best to go by taxi. There's no sign in English, but the farmhouse is easy to recognize and there are credit cards displayed outside.

Whenever I'm playing hostess to foreign visitors in Tokyo, I always take them to **Inakaya** ⑫, 7-8-4 Roppongi (tel. 405-9866), and they've never been disappointed. What I like about this place is the drama of it. You sit at a counter and in front of you are mountains of fresh vegetables, beef, and seafood. In the middle of all the food are two male cooks (cooks in Japan are almost always male), who can sit for inordinate amounts of time on pillows with their legs tucked neatly underneath them. They cook on a grill in front of them in a style called robatayaki. To order, simply point at what you want. Your waiter shouts it out and then all the other waiters repeat it in shouted unison, with the result that there is always this excited yelling going on. No way to order quietly here. Food offerings may include yellowtail, red snapper, sole, king crab legs, giant shrimp, steak, meatballs, gingko nuts, potatoes, eggplant, and asparagus, all piled high in wicker baskets. Sometimes there are tiny, crunchy crabs you pop whole in your mouth—they tickle all the way down. A meal here costs at least ¥12,000 ($96) per person and no reservations are accepted. Hours are 5 p.m. to 5 a.m. daily. Inakaya is about a five-minute walk from Roppongi Station toward Aoyama-Itchome on Gaien-Higashi Dori Avenue.

If you want to make reservations, you can do so at the two other Inakaya restaurants up to 7 p.m. (whenever a restaurant proves successful in Japan, branches open immediately). The **Roppongi East Branch**, 5-3-4 Roppongi (tel. 408-5040), is also open from 5 p.m. to 5 a.m. **Inakaya in Akasaka,** 3-12-7 Akasaka (tel. 586-3054), is open only until 11 p.m.

Ten-ichi, 6-6-5 Ginza, on Namiki Dori Street (tel. 571-1949), is the main shop of a restaurant chain that first began serving tempura in Tokyo more than 50 years ago and helped this style of cooking gain worldwide recognition by serving important foreign customers. Today there are more than ten Ten-ichi restaurants in Tokyo. Hours may vary, but generally run from 11:30 a.m. to 9:30 p.m.—it's best to call beforehand and make a reservation. Ten-ichi has one of the best reputations in town for serving the most delicately fried foods. Set menus start at ¥5,500 ($44) for lunch and ¥7,700 ($61.60) for dinner, and you can sit at a counter to watch the chef prepare your food. Closest subway station: Ginza is a few minutes away.

Other Ten-ichi restaurants can be found in the Ginza Sony Building (tel. 571-3837), the Imperial Hotel's Tower basement (tel. 503-1001), Akasaka 3-chome, Misujidori (tel. 583-0107), and both the Shibuya and Ikebukuro Seibu department stores.

Fukuzushi ⑬, 5-7-8 Roppongi (tel. 402-4116), is one of the classiest sushi bars in town. Tucked underneath Spago's restaurant behind the Roi Building in Roppongi, this sushi bar has an entrance through a small courtyard and an interior of red and black. Some people in town swear it has the best sushi in Tokyo, although with 7,000 sushi bars in the city I'd be hard-pressed to say which one is tops. Certainly you can't go wrong here. Open for dinner daily from 5:30 to 11 p.m., it has an English menu that opens up like a fan and offers a variety of choices of sashimi and nigiri-zushi. Dinner will cost anywhere from ¥8,800 ($70.40) to ¥11,000 ($88), although if you're careful about your drinks and the amount you order, you can do it for much less. Another alternative is the set lunch, served from 11:30 a.m. to 2 p.m. every day except Sunday and holidays in two courses costing ¥2,750 ($22). Nearest subway station: Roppongi.

If you're in pursuit of exclusive sushi shops in Tokyo, your search will eventually take you to **Sushiko** ⑭, 6-3-8 Ginza (tel. 571-1968). There's no menu and its counter seating is for 11 customers only, so reservations are imperative. Owned by a fourth-generation restaurateur, this establishment doesn't display its fish as in most sushi bars but rather keeps the fish freshly refrigerated until the moment it meets the swift blade of the expert chefs. A meal here averages about ¥15,000 ($120), and hours run from noon to 2 p.m. and from 5 to 9:30 p.m.; closed Sunday and public holidays. Nearest subway station: Ginza.

Seryna, 3-12-2 Roppongi (tel. 403-6211), is the name usually associated with this well-known large, modern establishment, but actually there are four restaurants here, all under the same ownership. Japanese often entertain foreign visitors here, and menus are in English. Seryna Honkan serves Kobe beef shabu-shabu and sukiyaki. Saraebo, on the third floor, specializes in *yaki-shabu* and Chinese cuisine. Mon Cher Ton Ton, in the basement, serves Kobe beef, shrimp, fish, shellfish, and vegetables grilled teppanyaki style right before your eyes. Kani Seryna offers crab and seafood dishes, including crab shabu-shabu, Maine lobster, and steamed fish. It also has the famous Kobe beefsteak that is cooked at your table on a heated stone. The average dinner at these places will range from ¥14,000 ($112) to ¥20,000 ($160). All restaurants are open from 5 to 11:30 p.m. (10:30 p.m. on Sunday and holidays) with the exception of Kani Seryna, which opens at noon (12:30 p.m. on Sunday and holidays). Nearest subway station: Roppongi is three minutes away.

If you're in Shinjuku, there's another branch of Seryna and Mon Cher Ton Ton on the 52nd floor of the Shinjuku Sumitomo Building, 2-6-1 Nishi-Shinjuku (tel. 344-6761). It serves Kobe sirloin steaks starting at ¥7,000 ($56) and shabu-shabu starting at ¥6,000 ($48), and there's an English menu. Set lunches begin at ¥2,000 ($16). Hours here are 11:30 a.m. to 10:30 p.m., and needless to say the view is great. It's a good place to stop off if you're exploring the west side of Shinjuku. Nearest station: Shinjuku is about a seven-minute walk.

Sekishin-tei, 4-1 Kioi-cho, Chiyoda-ku (tel. 265-1111), located in the New Otani Hotel's 400-year-old garden, is a glass-enclosed teppanyaki restaurant where Kobe beef, fish, lobster, and vegetables are cooked on a grill right in front of you. Meals begin at ¥4,000 ($32) for lunch and ¥8,200 ($65.60) for dinner, and if you order a salad, try the soy sauce dressing—it's delicious. This place, with peaceful views surrounding you, is open daily from noon to 2 p.m. and 6 to 9 p.m. Nearest subway stations: Yotsuya and Akasaka-mitsuke.

Serving shabu-shabu, sukiyaki, teppanyaki, and tempura, **Zakuro** ⑮ is conveniently located in the basement of the TBS Kaikan Building, 5-3-3 Akasaka (tel. 582-6841). Open every day from 11 a.m. to 11 p.m. (last order at 10 p.m.), it has an English menu which lists a special sukiyaki lunch for ¥1,800 ($14.40) and shabu-shabu, sukiyaki, and teppanyaki beginning at ¥7,400 ($59.20). Japanese-style set courses, which might include such items as sashimi, charcoal-broiled fish, soup, rice, and pickled vegetables, begin at ¥8,500 ($68). By the time you add tax, service charge, and drinks, most dinner checks average ¥10,000 ($80). Nearest subway station: Akasaka, a minute from the TBS exit.

Although Japanese restaurants usually specialize in only one type of cooking, **Yamatoya Sangen,** in the Miyako Hotel, 1-1-50 Shiroganedai (tel. 445-0058), serves a variety of foods, from shabu-shabu, tempura, kaiseki, and sushi to eel. This is a good place to come if there are several of you and you can't make up your mind what you want to eat. The restaurant overlooks the hotel's Japanese garden and is simply decorated with shoji screens and slats of wood. Set dinners range from ¥8,000 ($64) to ¥20,000 ($160), and are served daily from 5 to 10 p.m. There are also special lunch menus averaging ¥3,000 ($24) to ¥8,800 ($70.40), served from 11:30 a.m. to 2 p.m. If you've been intimidated by the thought of eating eel, this may be the best place to try it for the first time, although it's available only for lunch. Closest subway station: Takanawadai.

Another hotel restaurant with a good selection of Japanese food served in a charming setting is the **Unkai,** in the ANA Hotel Tokyo, 1-12-33 Akasaka (tel. 459-6921). With its stone pathway leading through the restaurant and a replica of a thatch-roofed house built as a façade into one of the walls, the atmosphere is one of a country village. The restaurant, open from 11:30 a.m. to 2:30 p.m. and from 5:30 to 10 p.m., overlooks a pond and a waterfall. There are various set courses available for lunch beginning at ¥3,800 ($30.40), as well as à la carte selections of tempura, sashimi, seasonal vegetables, and other dishes. Dinner will probably cost at least ¥7,500 ($60) per person. Nearest subway stations: Roppongi, Akasaka, Kamiyacho, Toranomon, and Kokkai Gijido-mae.

Western Food

When **Tour D'Argent**, 4-1 Kioi-cho, Chiyoda-ku (tel. 239-3111), opened in the New Otani Hotel in 1984, there were rumors flying around Tokyo that it was the most expensive restaurant in town. I doubt it, especially when I consider those exclusive and highly elusive Japanese restaurants with geisha entertainment patronized by Japan's top corporate management. Still, the cost of a meal here with wine ranges from ¥28,000 ($224) to ¥33,000 ($264) per person. Tour D'Argent is the sister restaurant to the one in Paris, which opened back in 1582 and was visited twice by Japan's former emperor, Hirohito.

Entrance to the Tour D'Argent in Tokyo is through an impressive hallway with a plush interior and displays of tableware that have been used in the Paris restaurant through the centuries. The dining hall looks like a Parisian drawing room, with an elegance a bit too overstated for my taste. The service, however, is superb and the food is excellent. The specialty here is duckling—it meets its untimely end at the age of three weeks and is flown to Japan from Brittany. Other dishes on the menu, which changes with the seasons, may include sea bass, médaillons of veal in light curry sauce, young pigeon, beef tenderloin, or fricassee of lobster and morels. For appetizers, I recommend either duck or goose foie gras. The restaurant opens at 5:30 p.m. daily, with the last order taken at 9:30 p.m. If you can afford to come here, you probably won't come by subway, but the nearest stations are Akasaka-mitsuke and Yotsuya.

It's hard to imagine a more romantic setting than the **Rose Room** in the ANA Hotel Tokyo, 1-12-33 Akasaka (tel. 459-6921). Small and intimate, with a huge vase of roses in the center of the dining room, this French restaurant is perfect for a tête-à-tête as classical music plays softly in the background. The menu changes twice a year but may include such selections as Beluga caviar, turtle soup lightly seasoned with curry, lobster, rack of lamb, chicken, and steak. Meals here cost upward of ¥4,500 ($36) for lunch and ¥15,000 ($120) for dinner, and are served daily from 11:30 a.m. to 2:30 p.m. and from 5:30 to 10 p.m. After dinner you may wish to retire to the Astral lounge up on the 37th floor, where you have a good view of the city. The lounge is open until 2 a.m. Nearest subway stations: Roppongi, Akasaka, Kamiyacho, and Kokkai Gijido-mae.

It may seem kind of strange to find a top-class restaurant in the third basement of the Sony Building, but then this is Japan. **Maxim's**, 5-3-1 Ginza (tel. 572-3621), opened in 1966 and is an exact copy of Paris's famous Maxim's, which opened its doors in 1893. Decorated in art nouveau style, the small dining room is one of the most romantic in town—very French, with gilded mirrors, cut-glass panels, mahogany paneling, and crimson cushions. Service is discreet and professional as waiters bring you such specialties as goose liver pâté, sole cooked in French vermouth, sautéed tenderloin with truffle sauce, roast duckling with peaches, or grilled prime rib of Kobe beef. If you order à la carte it will cost around ¥25,000 ($200). There is also a set dinner for ¥22,000 ($176) and a set lunch menu for ¥7,000 ($56), both of which change daily and include tax and service charge. Maxim's is open for lunch from 11:30 a.m. to 2:30 p.m. and for dinner from 5:30 to 11 p.m.; closed Sunday. Nearest subway station: Ginza is a minute away.

Another French restaurant with a sister in Paris is **L'Orangerie de Paris**, 3-6-1 Kita-Aoyama, Minato-ku (tel. 407-7461), located in the chic area of Omote Sando, on the fifth floor of the Hanae Mori Building, which houses fashion designer Hanae Mori's entire collection. The building was designed by Kenzo Tange, who also designed the controversial Akasaka Prince Hotel as well as a score of other buildings around town. Check out the front shop windows—they're always interesting.

There's a set dinner menu here for ¥8,800 ($70.40) and a set lunch menu for ¥4,400 ($35.20), which change every two weeks. Hours are 11:30 a.m. to 2:30 p.m. and 5:30 to 10 p.m. (last order: 9:30 p.m.) every day except Sunday. Very popular, Sunday brunch is held here from 11 a.m. to 2:30 p.m. It costs ¥3,700 ($29.60), including tax and service, and seems to attract half the foreign population in Tokyo. Nearest subway station: Omote Sando is one minute away.

One more French restaurant, this one not far from Akasaka's nightlife district, **Kana Uni,** 1-1-16 Moto-Akasaka (tel. 404-4776), is a cozy and intimate restaurant/bar. It's owned and managed by a brother and sister who speak excellent English and who love to have foreign guests. In fact, because the place is a little hard to find they'll even come and fetch you if you call from Akasaka-mitsuke Station. Open since 1966, it has an English menu, and entrées include sliced raw tenderloin, steaks, beef stew, grilled fish, sautéed scallops, and poached filet of sole with sea urchin sauce. Expect to spend about ¥8,000 ($64) for dinner. It's open only in the evening from 6 p.m. to 2:30 a.m.; closed Sunday and national holidays. It's one of the few restaurants in Akasaka still serving food after midnight, and there's even live jazz nightly from 7 p.m. to 2:30 a.m. After dinner, relax with cocktails and enjoy the ambience. Cocktails run from ¥1,000 ($8) to ¥1,400 ($11.20). Nearest subway station: Akasaka-mitsuke.

Sabatini, located in the basement of the Suncrest Building, 2-13-5 Kita-Aoyama, Minato-ku (tel. 402-3812), is owned by three Italian brothers who have had a restaurant in Rome for more than 30 years. They take turns overseeing the Tokyo store, so one of them is always here, serving food or helping out in the kitchen. This restaurant, with its Italian furniture and tableware and strolling musicians, seems like it was moved intact from the Old World. In fact, the only thing to remind you you're in Tokyo are the Japanese waiters. The menu includes soups, spaghetti, seafood, veal, steak, lamb, and a variety of vegetables. Dinner ranges from about ¥15,000 ($120) to ¥21,000 ($168), but you can do it cheaper at lunch with the ¥4,500 ($36) set menu, which gives you a choice of soup or pasta, fish or meat, and salad and coffee. Hours are 11:30 a.m. to 2:30 p.m. and 5:30 to 11 p.m. daily. Nearest subway station: Sabatini is two minutes from Gaienmae.

Established in 1960, **Chianti,** 3-1-7 Azabudai (tel. 583-7546), is one of the oldest Italian restaurants in Tokyo. Founded by two Japanese who had been living in Europe and who wanted to introduce Western food to the Japanese, it also became popular with Tokyo's foreign community through the years. Dining is in two separate areas, although the menu is the same. On the second floor it's the requisite red-and-white-checkered tablecloth—an informal atmosphere. In the basement it's more formal, more intimate, better for couples. The menu includes such entrées as grilled chicken in spicy tomato sauce, veal scallop sautéed with vegetables, Milanese veal cutlet, Hungarian beef stew, and braised veal shank in tomato sauce. The average price per dish runs between ¥3,500 ($28) and ¥4,400 ($35.20), though most people end up spending about ¥10,000 ($80) including wine and appetizers. On the ground floor there's a coffeeshop where you can have snacks, salads, and sandwiches. There's also an additional restaurant that opened a few years back called **Chianti Nishi-Azabu,** 3-17-26 Nishi-Azabu (tel. 404-6500), where the food is about 20% cheaper, with entrées under ¥3,000 ($24). It caters to a slightly younger crowd. Hours for both are noon to 1:45 a.m. daily (last order), and the nearest subway station is Roppongi.

Spago, 5-7-8 Roppongi (tel. 423-4025), serves California cuisine created by its owner, Wolfgang Puck, an Austrian-born chef who has a similar restaurant in Los Angeles. The atmosphere here is bright, airy, and cheerful, very Californian, with huge bouquets of flowers, potted palms, ferns, white walls, and a colorful mural. The menu changes every three months to reflect what's in season, but examples of what's been offered in the past include spicy fettuccine with grilled shrimp and fresh basil; sliced breast of duck with Japanese *oba* leaves and plum wine sauce; angel hair noodles with goat cheese, broccoli, and thyme; grilled spicy chicken with garlic and

Italian parsley; and roasted baby lamb with a cabernet, mustard, and rosemary sauce. If you order pizza, it will come not with tomato sauce but with olive oil, making it much lighter, so the emphasis is on the toppings. Needless to say, the entrées are always imaginative, and the service is great. Dining here is a pleasure, and as you might expect, Spago has the largest selection of California wines in town. For dessert try the restaurant's homemade ice cream. An average meal here, including wine, runs about ¥11,000 ($88), but there's also a set course offered Monday through Saturday for ¥8,800 ($70.40). Spago is open daily from 5:30 to 11 p.m., with last orders taken at 10:30 p.m. Nearest subway station: two minutes from Roppongi, located behind the Roi Building.

Trader Vic's, in the New Otani Hotel, 4-1 Kioi-cho, Chiyoda-ku (tel. 265-4708), is part of an American chain operating out of California. The decor, as always, is Polynesian, and there are views of the hotel's 400-year-old landscaped garden from a few of the tables. The extensive menu offers salads, seafood, Chinese dishes, curries, and steak, fish, and chicken dishes, with entrées running about ¥5,000 ($40) to ¥9,000 ($72). Hours are 11:30 a.m. to 2:30 p.m. and 5 to 10 p.m. Its bar is open throughout the day, from 11:30 a.m. to 2 a.m. Cocktails start at ¥1,500 ($12). Nearest subway station: Otemachi Station, three minutes away.

THE MEDIUM-PRICED RANGE

So many of Tokyo's good restaurants fall into this category that it's tempting simply to eat your way through the city—and the range of cuisine is so great that you could eat something different with each meal. Be sure to read the list of restaurants in the upper-bracket category—many have great set courses for lunch at very reasonable prices.

Japanese Food

Sushi Sei ⑯, 7-14-15 Roppongi (tel. 401-0578), is a typical medium-priced sushi bar serving tender cuts of raw fish, making it a good place to go for both novice and appreciative sushi fans. The decor is simple here—just a long counter with stools for about 25 people sitting elbow to elbow. Behind a glass case on the counter you can see what's fresh and available, and on the other side of that the sushi experts deftly slice fish and make sushi according to your instructions. Just point at what you want. Ordering à la carte is the fun way to do it, and an evening spent here drinking sake or beer won't cost more than ¥5,000 ($40). If that's too formidable, however, take the easy way out and order a *seto,* or set meal. This costs only ¥1,300 ($10.40), is available anytime night and day, and comes with six pieces of sushi with various selections of raw fish and six pieces of *makizushi* (raw fish, cucumber, and rice rolled inside a sheet of seaweed). The chef will prepare your food and place it on a raised platform on the counter in front of you. This is your plate, and it's proper etiquette to use your fingers. Hours are noon to 2 p.m. and 5 to 11 p.m.; closed Sunday and holidays. Nearest subway station: Sushi Sei is one minute from Roppongi. There are many branches of this restaurant throughout the city, and a couple more addresses are: Dainana Kanai Building, 8-2-13 Ginza (tel. 572-4770), and 3-11-14 Akasaka (tel. 586-6446).

Close to Tsukiji's famous fish market is **Edogin** ⑰, 4-5-1 Tsukiji (tel. 543-4401). Actually there are four Edogin sushi restaurants in Tsukiji, all located within walking distance of one another, and in any of them you can be assured that the fish is fresh, since it's close to the market. There's nothing aesthetic about Edogin—the lights are bright, it's packed with the locals, and it's noisy and busy, with waitresses constantly bustling around. Open every day except Sunday from 11 a.m. to 9:30 p.m., it's particularly packed during lunch- and dinnertime. All this points to one thing: the food is dependably good and plentiful. The menu is in Japanese only, but there's a glass case outside with some of the dishes displayed. As an alternative, look at what the people around you are eating. The lunch teishoku range from ¥1,000 ($8) to ¥3,000 ($24), and if you come here for dinner, you can eat a satisfying meal with beer or sake for less than ¥4,000 ($32). Nearest subway station: three minutes from Tsukiji Station. Anyone in the neighborhood will be able to point you in the right direction; look for the building with a string of Japanese lanterns adorning its facade.

People who really know their fugu, or blowfish, will tell you that the only time to eat it is from October through March, when it's fresh. You can eat fugu all year round, however, and a good place to try this Japanese delicacy is at **Tentake** ⑱, 6-16-6 Tsukiji (tel. 541-3881). This is also a popular place with the Tsukiji working crowd. The menu is in Japanese, so if you want suggestions, try the fugu sushi, which costs ¥2,800 ($22.40), or fugu-chiri for the same price. The latter is a do-it-yourself meal whereby you cook raw blowfish, cabbage, dandelion leaves, and tofu in a pot of boiling water in front of you. This is what I had and it was more than I could eat. There are also fugu dishes for ¥4,500 ($36) and ¥6,500 ($52) that come with a variety of other dishes as well. You can also order tempura, eel, and crab dishes here. The restaurant is open from noon to 10 p.m. (from April through September it's closed on Sunday, and from October through March it's closed the first and third Wednesdays of the month). Nearest subway station: Tsukiji is about a seven-minute walk.

Momiji-ya, Asano Building, 6-1-12 Roppongi (tel. 479-0400), is one of Roppongi's newest seafood restaurants. A gigantic round fish tank adorns the front façade, along with a list of the fresh catches of the day. Inside, the dominant feature is another fish tank in the middle of the dining room. Fish is scooped directly from this tank, so you know your meal is fresh. Other seafood selections available include cuttlefish, scallops, live lobster, and, of course, sashimi. Dinner courses start at ¥7,500 ($60), while a special lunch menu is only ¥1,100 ($8.80). It's open daily from 11:30 a.m. to 2 p.m. and from 5 to 11 p.m. Last order is at 10 p.m. Closest subway station: Roppongi Station, about two minutes away.

Hassan ⑲, in the basement of the Denki Building, 6-1-20 Roppongi (tel. 403-8333), serves shabu-shabu and sukiyaki. Seating is either in chairs or on tatami, waitresses wear kimonos, and *koto* (Japanese zither) music plays in the background. Open seven days a week from 11:30 a.m. to 2 p.m. and 4:30 to 11 p.m. (last order: 10 p.m.), Hassan has an all-you-can-eat beef shabu-shabu full-course meal for just ¥6,300 ($50.40) per person. Sukiyaki starts at ¥4,100 ($32.80). It also serves kaiseki menus for ¥7,500 ($60) to ¥11,000 ($88), but you need reservations for these. For lunch you can order the all-you-can-eat shabu-shabu menu for ¥4,000 ($32) per person. There's also a sukiyaki plate or a shabu-shabu selection for ¥2,200 ($17.60). Kaiseki lunches begin at ¥4,000 ($32), and lunch boxes are ¥2,200 ($17.60). The menu is in English, so it's easy to order here. Closest subway: one minute from Roppongi Station. If you take the road toward Shibuya, Hassan will be on your left.

Shabu Zen ⑳, 5-17-16 Roppongi (tel. 585-5388), has an English-speaking staff and a menu in English along with color illustrations. For ¥4,700 ($37.60) you can eat all the shabu-shabu or sukiyaki you want. Shabu Zen also has a seafood shabu-shabu for the same price. If you're hungry you might want to order the ¥7,000 ($56) shabu-shabu menu, which includes an unlimited amount of meat and vegetables, plus two appetizers, sashimi, egg custard, salad, and dessert. There are also kaiseki menus for ¥5,500 ($44), ¥8,800 ($70.40), and ¥11,000 ($88), but you must order these at least two days in advance. The restaurant is open daily from 5 p.m. to midnight. Closest subway station: a five-minute walk from Roppongi Station; it's located behind the Axis Building.

Established in 1880, **Chinya** ㉑, 1-3-4 Asakusa (tel. 841-0010), is an old sukiyaki restaurant with a new home in a seven-story building. It's located to the left of the Kaminarimon Gate if you stand facing the famous Asakusa Kannon Temple; look for the sukiyaki sign. The entrance to this place is open-fronted, where all you'll see is a man standing there, waiting. Take off your shoes and step up onto the tatami floor, and a kimono-clad waitress will take you upstairs to one of the restaurant's many rooms. The menu is in Japanese only, but there are pictures to choose from. Most courses are ¥5,800 ($46.40) and up, although there are sukiyaki and shabu-shabu dishes available for ¥2,900 ($23.20). The best time to come is for lunch, when you can order sukiyaki or shabu-shabu for just ¥2,400 ($19.20). If you want to eat even more cheaply, there's another dining area in the basement with slightly lower prices. Hours are 11:30 a.m. to 9:30 p.m.; closed Wednesday. Closest subway station: Asakusa, a couple of minutes away.

Also relatively close to the Kaminarimon Gate of Asakusa Kannon Temple is **Komagata Dojo** ㉒, 1-7-12 Komagata, Taito-ku (tel. 842-4001). Following a tradition that has spanned more than 185 years, this old-style dining hall specializes in *dojo,* a tiny sardine-like river fish. It's served in a variety of styles, from grilled to stewed. Teishoku, available throughout the day, range in price from ¥2,200 ($17.60) to ¥6,000 ($48). The dining area is simply one large room of tatami mats, with waitresses moving quietly about dressed in kimonos. Nearest subway station: about a five-minute walk from Asakusa Station. To reach the restaurant, walk south with your back towards Kaminarimon Gate. The restaurant, a large, old-fashioned house on a corner with blue curtains at its door, is located on the right side of the street past the Bank of Tokyo. Hours run from 11 a.m. to 9 p.m. daily.

In the same neighborhood as Komagata Dojo is **Mugitoro Shiori** ㉓, 2-2-4 Kaminarimon (tel. 842-1066). This restaurant, founded about 60 years ago but now housed in a new building, specializes in *tororo-imo,* which is yam. Popular as a health food, yam is featured in most all the dishes and the menu changes monthly. Most courses range from about ¥4,500 ($36) to ¥10,000 ($80), served daily from 11:30 a.m. to 9 p.m. Nearest subway station: Asakusa. If you're walking here from Asakusa Kannon Temple, walk south with your back to the temple until you reach the first big intersection. Komagatabashi Bridge will be to your left, and Mugitoro is located right beside the bridge. Look for the big white lanterns hanging outside.

In the midst of all the chic discos in the Roppongi Square Building is **Gonin Byakusho** ㉔, 3-10-3 Roppongi (tel. 470-1675), which is on the fourth floor. Its name means "five farmers," and the atmosphere here is of a farmhouse in the countryside with the usual heavy beams and thick wooden tables; there's a huge hearth and oven off to one side. You take off your shoes before entering this restaurant and place them in lockers. Most of the food here is charcoal-broiled, and dinner courses that may include grilled fish or shrimp, sashimi, and vegetables begin at ¥4,000 ($32). A la carte items such as yakitori, charcoal-broiled shrimp, assorted sashimi, *kamameshi* (rice casserole), or tempura begin at ¥700 ($5.60). Dinner à la carte will probably cost about ¥5,000 ($40) per person. At lunchtime there are special box lunches for ¥1,650 ($13.20) and ¥2,750 ($22), as well as tempura courses. This place is open from 11:30 a.m. to 2 p.m. and 5 to 10:30 p.m.; closed Sunday and holidays. Nearest subway station: three minutes from Roppongi Station.

With a rustic interior imported intact from the mountain region of Takayama, **Hayashi** ㉕, Hide Building, 2-22-5 Kabuki-cho (tel. 209-5672), specializes in Japanese set courses cooked over your own hibachi grill. A companion restaurant to the Hayashi restaurant described under the upper bracket and budget category sections but under a different ownership, it's a small, cozy place with only five hibachi grills. Women in kimonos oversee the cooking operations like mother hens, taking over the operation if customers seem the least bit hesitant. Four set courses are offered, ranging in price from ¥3,300 ($26.40) to ¥7,700 ($61.60). I chose the ¥4,400 ($35.20) course, which came with sashimi, yakitori, tofu steak, scallops cooked in their shell, shrimp, and vegetables, all grilled one after the other. Open from 5 to 11:30 p.m. every day except Sunday and public holidays, this restaurant is about a ten-minute walk from Shinjuku Station on the northern edge of Kabuki-cho.

Another country-style restaurant in the heart of Ginza is the delightful **Ohmatsuya** ㉖, 5-4-18 Ginza (tel. 571-7053). Located on Sony Street, the small side street behind the Sony Building that parallels Namiki Dori Street, it's up on the second floor of a very ordinary-looking building. Once inside the restaurant, however, you're greeted instantly by waitresses clad in countryside costumes and by an atmosphere that very much evokes the feeling of an old farmhouse. Little wonder: part of the decor was brought from a 17th-century samurai house in northern Japan. Even the style of cooking is traditional, as customers grill their own food over a hibachi and charcoal flame. Sake is served in a length of bamboo and is drunk from bamboo cups. Dinner courses, very reasonably priced from ¥4,000 ($32) to ¥7,000 ($56), include such delicacies as grilled fish, skewered pieces of meat, and vegetables. Lunches are even cheaper, with oyakodomburi (rice with morsels of chicken laid on top) costing just ¥850 ($6.80). The buckwheat noodles for ¥1,000 ($8) are a special treat—you're given a fresh chunk of wasabi that you grate yourself and add to the soy sauce. Ohmatsuya is open from 11:30 a.m. to 2 p.m. and from 5 to 10 p.m. every day except Sunday. Closest subway station: Ginza.

Kushiage, which literally means "skewered cutlets," is a little-known style of cooking whereby food is breaded, deep-fried, and served on skewers. An excellent restaurant serving this delicious food is **Chisen,** 4-12-5 Roppongi (tel. 403-7677), open daily from 5:30 to 11 p.m.—it has more than 25 different kinds of kushiage (also called kushikatsu). What's available will change according to the season, but common items include mushrooms, asparagus, shrimp, squid, oysters, and onions. The breading is very light and flaky. There's a menu in English with a few à la carte selections, but I'd advise you to select one of the set meals. The Chisen Set for ¥4,600 ($36.80) gives you 11 kushiage sticks, fresh vegetables, and rice or soba (noodles). If you choose the Zen menu, kushiage will be served to you one after the other until you say stop, and this option includes small seasonal dishes as well. The Zen menu is what I opted for, and I had three sticks of kushiage, two types of salad, and a bottle of beer for less than ¥3,000 ($24). If you're hungrier, of course, it will cost more. There's another Chisen shop not far away at 7-16-5 Roppongi (tel. 478-6241) in case the first one is full. Nearest subway station: just a few minutes from Roppongi Station.

A restaurant serving tempura, **Tsunahachi** ㉗, 3-31-8 Shinjuku (tel. 352-1012), first opened in 1923. There are now more than 40 branch restaurants in Japan, including three in Shinjuku Station alone, and others in Ginza and Akasaka. Hours may vary, but most shops are open daily from 11:30 a.m. to 10 p.m. Tempura à la carte ranges from about ¥350 ($2.80) to ¥1,000 ($8). The least expensive set meal begins at ¥1,150 ($9.20) and includes deep-fried shrimp, three kinds of fish, a vegetable, and a shrimp ball. Nearest subway station: this branch is about a five-minute walk east of Shinjuku Station.

Another successful chain restaurant, **Suehiro** ㉘, has 23 stores throughout Japan. A steak-and-sukiyaki chain, the main store is at 6-11-2 Ginza (tel. 571-9271) behind the Matsuzakaya department store. Established in 1933, it claims to be the first restaurant in Tokyo to serve sukiyaki and it has its own cattle ranches for its Matsuzaka beef. There are various courses, from sirloin steak for ¥2,700 ($21.60) to Matsuzaka beef sukiyaki for ¥4,500 ($36). Open from 11 a.m. to 10 p.m. daily, Suehiro is about a five-minute walk from Ginza Station. Other conveniently located Suehiro shops are located at 3-16-7 Akasaka (tel. 585-9855), in the heart of Akasaka on Hitosugi Dori Street, and on the 29th floor of the NS Building (tel. 343-3982), one of Shinjuku's skyscrapers on the west side of Shinjuku Station.

With about 50 Benihana restaurants in the United States, I'm not sure whether anyone is interested in seeking out the one in Tokyo—which, by the way, calls itself **Benihana of New York,** 6-3-7 Ginza (tel. 571-9060). Specializing in teppanyaki steak, this is the place where the cook prepares your meal in front of you with lots of theatrical bravado and karate-like knife chops. Dinner courses range from ¥3,800 ($30.40) for a combination plate of seafood and steak and side dishes to ¥22,000 ($176) for sirloin steak and the works, with most choices in the ¥7,000 ($56) range. A steak lunch costs ¥2,750 ($22). Benihana is open daily from 11 a.m. to 10 p.m., except on Sunday, when it closes at 8 p.m. Nearest subway stations: about a five-minute walk from Hibiya Station and a ten-minute walk from Ginza Station.

Kikkoman is a well-known brand of soy sauce in Japan, and the Kikkoman company maintains a few restaurants as well. **Kushi Colza** ㉙, 6-2-1 Ginza (tel. 571-8228), is one of these, and it serves yakitori and kushiyaki (also grilled meats and vegetables served on skewers) delicately seasoned with—what else, Kikkoman soy sauce. This place is modern and pleasant, and you can watch the chefs at work preparing your food. Open for dinner from 5 to 10 p.m. daily, it serves three dinner menus beginning at ¥3,300 ($26.40). If you come for lunch (between noon and 1:30 p.m.), you will have six courses to choose from, ranging in price from ¥850 ($6.80) to ¥2,700 ($21.60). These consist of various skewered filets of beef, fish, eel, or pork, and include salad, rice, and bean-paste soup. À la carte selections include skewered beef, pork, chicken, prawn, squid, and such vegetables as asparagus and bacon, gingko nuts, and mushrooms. Nearest subway stations: about five minutes from Hibiya and ten minutes from Ginza. It's located in the basement of the Riccar Building, across from the Gekkoso Museum. A sign above the door reads, "Kushi & Wine."

Another Kikkoman restaurant, this time in Roppongi, is **Roppongi Colza,** 7-15-10 Roppongi (tel. 405-5631). Located in the basement of the Clover Building, this locale specializes in teppanyaki steaks and seafood, flavored with Kikkoman condiments. Open daily from 11:30 a.m. to 2 p.m. and from 5 to 10 p.m. (noon to 9 p.m. on Sunday and holidays), it features courses ranging from ¥8,800 ($70.40) to ¥13,200 ($105.60) for various cuts of Matsuzaka beef and seafood, along with side dishes and dessert. Lunch set menus begin at ¥1,300 ($10.40). Roppongi Station is about a minute's walk away.

Ginza Benkay, 7-2-17 Ginza (tel. 573-7335), is a Japan Airlines affiliate and specializes in teppanyaki, sushi, and kaiseki, each served in its own special dining area. Coolly decorated with a stone-and-pebble floor, bamboo, wood, and shoji screens, it offers a variety of set courses in many price ranges. Lunch is the most economical time to come, when teppanyaki courses, an assorted plate of sushi, or a small kaiseki lunch box range from ¥1,300 ($10.40) to ¥3,800 ($30.40). Dinner courses of teppanyaki, sushi, or kaiseki begin at around ¥7,000 ($56), while a shabu-shabu course is ¥8,800 ($70.40). An especially good deal is the dinner "lunch box" for ¥3,800 ($30.40). Closest station: Yurakucho, near the International Arcade. Another Ginza Benkay is located in the basement of the President Hotel in Aoyama (tel. 402-0246).

Ganchan ㉚, 6-8-23 Roppongi (tel. 478-0092), is one of my favorite yakitori-ya. It's small, intimate, and is owned by a friendly and entertaining man who can't speak English worth a darn but keeps trying with the help of a worn-out Japanese-English dictionary he keeps behind the counter. He also keeps an eclectic cassette collection—I never know whether to expect Japanese pop tunes or mellower Simon and Garfunkel. Seating is just along one counter with room for only a dozen or so people. Though there's an English menu, it's easiest to order the *yakitori seto* for ¥2,500 ($20). It comes with salad and soup and eight skewers of such items as chicken, beef, meatballs, green peppers, and asparagus with bacon wrapped around it. When I've ordered à la carte, my meal has come to about ¥4,000 ($32), including beer. This place is open daily from 6 p.m. to 3 a.m., except on Sunday and holidays, when it closes at midnight. Nearest subway station: about four minutes from Roppongi. Take the small street going downhill on the left side of the Almond Coffee Shop; Ganchan is at the bottom of the hill on the right—look for the big white paper lantern.

Non-Japanese Food

I'm not sure how to categorize **Mominoki House,** 2-18-5 Jingumae (tel. 405-9144). Although the menu (written only in Japanese, up on a huge blackboard) is French, the dishes are the special creations of the chef, who uses lots of soy sauce, ginger, and Japanese vegetables. Suffice it to say that Mominoki House is in a category all by itself and is somewhat of a rarity in Tokyo. Serving macrobiotic foods, this alternative restaurant features hanging plants and split-level dining, allowing for more privacy than one would think possible in such a tiny place. Its recorded jazz collection is extensive, and on weekends there's live music. The menu changes according to what's fresh and what the chef himself feels like eating, but dishes may include tofu steak, duck, sole, escargots, eggplant gratin (baked in a delicious white sauce), salads, and homemade sorbet. At any rate, this place seems to always satisfy both vegetarians and meat eaters, and you'll probably spend about ¥4,000 ($32) for dinner. An especially good deal is the daily lunch special for ¥850 ($6.80), which gives you brown rice, miso soup, salad, fish or other entrée, and a glass of wine. It's open every day except Sunday and holidays from 11 a.m. to 11 p.m. (last order is at 10 p.m.). Closest stations: Harajuku and Meiji-Jingu-mae, from which you're best off taking a taxi.

Selan, 2-1-19 Kita Aoyama (tel. 478-2200), is another restaurant that's difficult to classify. An elegant place with outdoor seating overlooking a tree-lined street, it offers well-known Western fare such as steak, chicken, fish, lobster, and duck—all prepared with Japanese ingredients. Serving what may be described as nouvelle Japonesque cuisine, this innovative establishment may offer such unusual combinations as flounder stuffed with chopped shrimp and calamari and topped with sea urchin and vegetables, or seared bonito salad with soy sauce, garlic, and oil dressing. Set lunches start at a reasonable ¥1,700 ($13.60), while dinner entrées range from ¥2,700 ($21.60) to ¥3,300 ($26.40). Since Selan is fast becoming one of Tokyo's favorite mealtime retreats, be sure to make reservations for lunch or dinner. Hours here are 8 a.m. to 10 p.m., with breakfast served until 11:30 a.m., lunch served from 11:30 a.m. to 2:30 p.m., and dinner served from 6 p.m. Tea time is 4 to 6 p.m. Located just off Aoyama Dori, it is about a five-minute walk from either Gaienmae or Aoyama-Itchome subway station.

Chez Figaro, 4-4-1 Nishi Azabu (tel. 400-8718), has been serving traditional French cooking for more than 20 years. A small and cozy place popular with both foreigners and Japanese, its specialties include homemade pâté, escargots, fish soup, stuffed quail with grapes, steak, and braised sweetbreads with mushrooms. À la carte entrées range from about ¥3,300 ($26.40) to ¥4,900 ($39.20), and there are two dinner courses offered for ¥6,500 ($52) and ¥8,800 ($70.40). Lunch is reasonable, with three set menus beginning at ¥2,700 ($21.60), served from noon to 2 p.m. Dinner is from 6 to 9:30 p.m. (last order). The restaurant is closed on Sunday. Chez Figaro is about a 15-minute walk from Roppongi Station. From Roppongi Crossing, walk toward Shibuya until you come to the second major intersection, at the bottom of a hill. Turn left and after about four minutes you'll see Chez Figaro on your right. Hiro Station is seven minutes away.

Another French restaurant is the chic **Atantot,** 5-17-1 Roppongi (tel. 586-4431), located on the third floor of the Axis Building. Its interior is sparse, with black, brown, and white marble walls and floors and only eight tables. The center attraction is the open kitchen, where you can watch the chefs prepare your food. The menu changes weekly, and there's a set dinner menu for ¥4,600 ($36.80), served daily from 6 to 10 p.m. Personally, I prefer to come here for lunch when the weather is warm and I can sit outside on the terrace. The set lunch is ¥2,500 ($20) and is served from 11:30 a.m. to 3 p.m. Nearest subway station: Roppongi.

Le Chalet, in the basement of the Shimizu Building, 3-14-9 Akasaka (tel. 584-0080), is a pleasant and modestly priced French restaurant in the heart of Akasaka. With seating for only 30 persons and decorated in an opulent pink and red, Le Chalet serves set lunches starting at ¥1,600 ($12.80) and set dinners ranging from ¥4,900 ($39.20) to ¥7,000 ($56). The ¥4,900 course includes an hors d'oeuvre, soup, fish, a meat dish, dessert, and coffee. Hours here are 11:30 a.m. to 2 p.m. and 5 to 10 p.m. daily. Nearest subway station: a minute away from Akasaka Station.

La Patata, 2-9-11 Jingumae, Shibuya-ku (tel. 403-9664), is an Italian restaurant specializing in seafood. It's a cheerful place with lots of windows, plants, and warm, blond furniture, reminding me of health-food restaurants in the States.

Served from 6 to 10:30 p.m., the dinner menu includes a fish of the day, broiled shrimp, sole, lamb, sliced veal, and beef filet, with the average dinner costing about ¥8,000 ($64), including wine. Lunch specials are ¥1,700 ($13.60) and ¥2,700 ($21.60), available from noon to 2 p.m. Wednesday through Sunday. The restaurant is closed on Monday and reopens Tuesday at 6 p.m. Nearest subway station: about ten minutes from Gaienmae, La Patata is on a street with the intimidating name of Killer Dori Avenue.

The discovery of **La Primavera**, Sanko Building, 2-5-15 Shinjuku (tel. 354-7873), has been a cause for celebration for many an Italian-food lover in Tokyo. The food is great, the prices are reasonable, and the bread is among the best in town. Since it opened in 1985, its faithful clientele has been growing steadily. An intimate locale with only half a dozen tables, each with candles, and Botticelli reproductions on the wall, it serves pastas starting at ¥750 ($6), pizzas from ¥1,000 ($8), and main entrées of steak, scallops, or fish, most costing ¥2,200 ($17.60). Customers are requested to order more than one dish per person for dinner. Set lunch courses, which include steak, stew, homemade sausage, or pasta, range in price from ¥1,000 ($8) to ¥2,200 ($17.60). It's open from 11:30 a.m. to 3 p.m. and from 6 to 11 p.m.; closed every first and third Sunday. Nearest subway station: Shinjuku Gyoen-mae, about a four-minute walk away.

If you have a big appetite, you'll benefit from the all-you-can-eat buffet at **Seiyo Hiroba** ③, located on the fifth floor of the Prime Building, 2-29-5 Dogenzaka (tel. 770-1781), in Shibuya. Its lunch buffet, served daily from 11:30 a.m. to 2 p.m., costs ¥2,200 ($17.60), while the dinner buffet, available from 6:30 to 10:30 p.m., goes for ¥5,500 ($44). The cuisine is French and Spanish Mediterranean, with an emphasis on fish, salads, and vegetables. Even if you don't eat a lot, this is a great place to come just for the atmosphere. Billing itself as a "resort restaurant," it tries to make customers feel as though they've embarked on a minivacation, with turquoise lighting, potted palms, a spacious dining area, and candles on the table. This place manages to look romantic even in the middle of the day. What's more, every evening there's free entertainment, ranging from music to pantomime. There are also occasional top-quality jazz performances, in which case there's an extra entertainment charge. Nearest subway station: Shibuya, about two minutes away.

If you're hit with a craving for Mexican food, try **Mexico Lindo**, 2-20-7 Akasaka (tel. 583-2095). It has a one-room dining area with Mexican knickknacks, pleasant waitresses, and Mexican music. The dinner menu includes tacos, flautas, tostados, and enchiladas, soups, and nachos. Most dishes are about ¥1,700 ($13.60), and if you're really hungry you'll probably want to order two. A set lunch for two persons costs ¥2,200 ($17.60) per person. Tacos come in a soft tortilla with only the meat inside—there are then separate bowls of tomatoes, green peppers, onions, cottage cheese, lettuce, and sauce, which you put on the way you like it. Mexico Lindo is open every day but Monday for lunch from 11:30 a.m. to 3 p.m. (last order at 2 p.m.) and for dinner from 5:30 to 10 p.m. (last order); open Sunday from noon to 8 p.m. Nearest subway stations: Akasaka and Roppongi, both about ten minutes away (near the ANA Hotel).

Looking nothing like the usual Mexican restaurant is the group of breezy, trendy **Zest** restaurants, which specialize in Mexican and Southern Californian cuisine. Newest of these is the Zest at 2-13-15 Nishi Azabu (tel. 400-3985), located near the intersection of Roppongi Dori and Gaien Nishi Dori streets, about a ten-minute walk from Roppongi Station. Its menu lists burgers, salads, and Mexican dishes, with most priced around ¥1,000 ($8) to ¥2,000 ($16). Tacos are rather expensive: three shells and sauce are ¥500 ($4), with fillings costing ¥900 ($7.20) and up. This place makes California a bargain. But the food is good, the ambience is even better, and it's open daily from 11:30 a.m. to 5 a.m. (last order at 4:15 a.m.). There's a minimum charge of ¥800 ($6.40) after 6 p.m., but that's not difficult to meet considering the prices. Cocktails average ¥900 ($7.20). If you want to eat Mexican but don't want to spend a fortune, consider coming for lunch, when specials are offered for less than ¥800 ($6.40) until 2 p.m. every day except Sunday and holidays. Other Zest restaurants are at 4-11-13 Roppongi (tel. 478-0222), open from 5 p.m. to 5 a.m.; and at 6-7-18 Jingumae in Harajuku (tel. 409-6268), open from 11:30 a.m. to 5 a.m.

With its black marble walls and innocuous decor, there's little to tip you off that **Z Greek Tavern**, 6-9-11 Minami Aoyama (tel. 499-4958), is a Greek restaurant. No Greek music (at least not during my visit) and no obligatory pictures of the Acropolis. The main menu includes souvlaki, moussaka, roast lamb, and home-style chicken, with most entrées priced under ¥2,300 ($18.40). Dinner courses start at ¥3,800 ($30.40). The special lunch menu lists set meals starting at ¥1,000 ($8), which may include a choice of pork, fish, lamb, or vegetable entrée along with salad, soup, rice, and coffee or tea. It's closed on Sunday and holidays, but otherwise the hours here are noon to 2 p.m. and 6:30 to 11 p.m. Nearest subway station: Omote Sando. Z is located on Roppongi Dori Street, which runs between Roppongi and Shibuya, near the Fuji Film building.

Metropole, 6-4-5 Roppongi (tel. 405-4400), gets my vote as having the most interesting, eclectic decor in town. A hip Chinese restaurant, it has everything from an old-fashioned double-door entryway to Roman statues and a bar area that looks like an old-world library. Large mirrors on the walls allow you to watch the action even if your back is turned, and the waiters are correct and trendy. All in all, the whole scene looks like a set for a Fellini movie. Open daily from 11:30 a.m. to 3 p.m. and from 6 to 11:30 p.m., it has a menu with more than 80 offerings, including beef in a lettuce roll, jellyfish, shrimp in spicy chili sauce, braised shark's fin with crab meat, crispy duck, and shredded pork with bamboo shoot. A meal here averages ¥7,000 ($56) to ¥10,000 ($80), though set lunches start at ¥1,300 ($10.40). Nearest subway station: Roppongi, about a ten-minute walk away.

Tong Fu, 6-7-11 Roppongi (tel. 403-3527), is another trendy Chinese restaurant, this one with ceiling fans; tablecloths of lime green, orange, purple, or bright yellow, and a fantasy-provoking mural covering one whole wall. In the summertime, there are even a couple of tables outside in a small courtyard under a weeping willow (make a reservation if you want to sit here). Dishes from Shanghai include shark's fin soup, shrimp in chili sauce, Beijing duck, crabmeat omelet, simmered chili tofu and eggplant, and shredded pork. Dinner here averages about ¥10,000 ($80) per person excluding drinks, but lunch courses start at a low ¥2,000 ($16). Hours here are 11:30 a.m. to 2:30 p.m. (last order at 2 p.m.) and 5 to 10:30 p.m. (last order). Closed on Sunday, it is open on holidays from 11:30 a.m. straight through to 10:30 p.m. Nearest subway station: Roppongi, two minutes' walk away. From Roppongi Crossing, take the small diagonal street that leads downhill beside the Almond Coffee Shop; Tong Fu will be on the right side of the street.

If you're hungering for American steaks, salads, and soups, **Victoria Station**, 4-9-2 Roppongi (tel. 479-4601), may be the closest you can come. Similar to the approximately 100 Victoria Stations in the United States, it's decorated like a railroad station and has one of the best salad bars in town. The price for prime rib ranges from ¥3,800 ($30.40) to ¥6,800 ($54.40) and includes as many trips as you want to the salad bar. I prefer to come for lunch, at which time they also serve hamburgers. A hamburger plus a trip to the salad bar costs only ¥1,100 ($8.80). If you're interested mainly in beverages, there's a cocktail bar upstairs with drinks starting at ¥600 ($4.80). It has its own menu, with spaghetti, sandwiches, and snacks available throughout the day. For ¥960 ($7.68) you can go to the salad bar as many times as you wish. Victoria Station is open from 11 a.m. to midnight, except on Sunday and holidays, when it closes at 11 p.m. It's located close to Roppongi Crossing almost catercorner from the Almond Coffee Shop. Another Victoria Station is located in Akasaka at 3-15-13 Akasaka (tel. 586-0711), on a tiny side street off Hitosugi Dori (the small street in front of the Fontaine Akasaka Capsule Hotel). This branch is open daily from 11 a.m. to 11 p.m.

Tiger Seafood Restaurant, 3-11-3 Akasaka (tel. 582-0105), is an American

West Coast chain restaurant serving seafood the way you're used to it back home (that is, cooked instead of raw). Entrées start at ¥2,200 ($17.60), averaging ¥3,500 ($28) for most seafood dishes. Lobster halves cost ¥3,300 ($26.40), and there are also steaks at ¥3,800 ($30.40) and up. Hours are 11 a.m. to 2 p.m. and 5 to 10 p.m., and the nearest stations are Akasaka-mitsuke and Akasaka. There's another Tiger Seafood Restaurant at 3-5-12 Kita-Aoyama (tel. 478-1222) on Aoyama Dori Avenue between Omote Sando and Gaienmae subway stations.

The **Terrace Restaurant** is a pleasant café-style restaurant and coffeehouse in the venerable Okura Hotel, 2-10-4 Toranomon (tel. 582-0111). There are so few restaurants in Tokyo with good views that you might want to come here just to relax and unwind, looking out on a landscape garden with a waterfall and a little stream. The best time to come is at lunch, when there are set meals from ¥2,700 ($21.60). Otherwise, à la carte dishes generally cost about ¥1,500 ($12) to ¥2,500 ($20) and include such things as spaghetti, sandwiches, filet of sole, salmon steak, beef Stroganoff, and shrimp or chicken pilaf. For the weight-conscious there's also a diet menu with the calorie count and nutritional value listed beside each dish. It's open daily from 7:30 a.m. to 9 p.m.

THE BUDGET CATEGORY

Many of Tokyo's most colorful, noisy, and popular restaurants fall into this category, frequented by the city's huge working population as they catch a quick lunch or socialize with friends after hours. Be sure to read over the restaurants listed in the upper- and medium-range categories—most of them offer great lunches at reasonable prices, which means that you may be able to splurge in style. For the most part, however, keep in mind that you can generally eat more economically at Japanese restaurants than at Western establishments. Remember to check the nightlife section for more suggestions on inexpensive drinking places that serve food.

Japanese Food

Hayashi ⑩, on the fourth floor of the Sanno Kaikan Building, 2-14-1 Akasaka (tel. 582-4078), was described at length as an upper-bracket restaurant, but I mention it again here simply because I don't want those of you on a budget to miss it. This is one of the coziest and most delightful restaurants in town, and although dinner here can cost you ¥5,500 ($44) and up, you can go for lunch and enjoy the same atmosphere for only ¥850 ($6.80). There's only one dish served at lunch and it's called oyakodomburi (rice with chunks of chicken and omelet on top). Served with your meal are pickled vegetables, clear soup, and tea. Hours are 11:30 a.m. to 2 p.m. Monday through Friday only.

Similar to Hayashi in atmosphere and food is **Ohmatsuya** ㉖, 5-4-18 Ginza (tel. 571-7053), also described earlier in the medium-range category of restaurants. It too serves oyakodomburi for ¥850 ($6.80), as well as buckwheat noodles for ¥1,000 ($8), every day except Sunday from 11:30 a.m. to 2 p.m. Nearest subway station: Ginza.

Another wonderful restaurant, and a great place to stop off for lunch or dinner on your visit to Asakusa, is **Tatsumiya** ㉜, 1-33-5 Asakusa (tel. 842-7373). Serving home-style cooking, this old farmhouse is jam-packed with antiques—old chests, pots, bags, gourds, hibachis, clocks, cups, rice buckets, and more. You could spend an hour here just looking at everything. Seating is on the floor in a room elevated from the rest of the house and partitioned with sliding shoji screens and wooden-slatted doors. There are two dinner courses: ¥2,500 ($20) is for sashimi, boiled vegetables, and grilled fish; ¥4,200 ($33.60) gets you soup, sashimi, boiled vegetables, grilled fish, pickled food, and rice porridge. Lunch is much cheaper, with set meals ranging from ¥750 ($6) to ¥1,500 ($12) for fried chicken, rice porridge with either crab or chicken, a lunch box, and rice with either beef or chicken. Hours are noon to 2 p.m. and 5 to 10 p.m.; closed Monday. The closest subway station is Asakusa. Tatsumiya is located on a pedestrians-only street that parallels Nakamise

Dori Avenue to the east, just off the covered arcade. There's no English sign, but look for the shop windows packed with antiques and blue curtains hanging in front of the door.

Technically a drinking establishment and every bit as interesting as Tatsumiya but a lot more boisterous, **Irohanihoheto** ㉝, 1-19-3 Jinnan, Shibuya-ku (tel. 476-1682), is extremely popular with university students. It seats 400 people at tables, counters, and on tatami mats, and if you get here after 7 p.m. you may have to wait for a place to sit. The atmosphere is country—Japanese style—with dark-stained heavy wooden ceiling beams held together with big thick ropes (purely for show, since this establishment is located in the basement of a modern building). All in all, it's a fun place to go.

The extensive menu of both Japanese and Western food is in Japanese but has pictures, making it easy to order. Try nikujaga (potato and meat stew), fried tofu, or oden (a tofu, fishcake, and vegetable stew). You can also order yakitori, fried noodles, potato salad, sashimi, or grilled meatballs. The list is almost endless, and most items are only ¥350 ($2.80) to ¥450 ($3.60). You'll probably want to order several dishes per person. This place is open every day from 5 p.m. to 4 a.m. Less than ten minutes from the Shibuya subway station near the Parco I and II department stores, it's a little hard to find. Once you get to Parco you'll probably have to stop someone on the street and ask.

There's another Irohanihoheto more conveniently located in Shinjuku, at 3-15-15 Shinjuku (tel. 359-1682). On the sixth floor of a building next to Isetan Kaikan on Yasukuni Dori Avenue, it bills itself as an "Antique Pub," the meaning of which becomes even more evasive once you're inside. The main hall looks imitation barn to me, with rafters, hurricane lamps, and glass lanterns everywhere. A second room is more traditional Japanese, with tatami seating and folkcrafts hanging about. People don't come here for the decor, however, but because of the prices. Its menu is similar to the Irohanihoheto described above, with draft beer starting at ¥380 ($2.71), and hours are the same. Nearest subway stations: Shinjuku and Shinjuku-Sanchome.

Kaiseki cooking is one of the most expensive meals you can have in Japan, but there are some lunch specials that make it quite reasonable. **Munakata**, a Japanese restaurant in the basement of the Mitsui Urban Hotel in Ginza, 8-6-15 Ginza (tel. 574-9356), serves a small mini-kaiseki lunch for ¥2,750 ($22) from 11:30 a.m. to 4 p.m. In addition, both **Kisso** and **Kakiden** (described as upper-range restaurants) offer inexpensive kaiseki lunches. Nearest subway station: Shimbashi, only one minute on foot.

Uogashi ㉞, 2-2-3 Nihombashi (tel. 271-8833), is a sushi bar for the adventurous. It's difficult to find but the rewards are great—it's one of the cheapest and best sushi places in town. First, look for the restaurant with the number 2-3 on it. You'll see display cases with plastic food in front of it and short blue curtains hanging in front of the sliding door. This is the main restaurant, but not the one you want. The sushi bar is located at the end of a short alley on the right side of this main restaurant.

Uogashi is tiny, just two small counters, and since there are no stools you have to stand. The people around you will be serious sushi eaters. They put away their food with astonishing speed, usually out of consideration for the people who are waiting in line for their turn at the counter. There are no chopsticks, so you just eat with your fingers. Whatever you order will usually come in a set of four, costing a total of only ¥240 ($1.92). When it's time to pay, go to the small closet-like room beside the side door. The man there will give you your change from the shop's cash register, just an old wooden box. Closed on Sunday and holidays, Uogashi is open from 11:30 a.m. to 2 p.m. and again from 4 to 10 p.m. Nearest subway stations: three minutes from Nihombashi Station and five minutes from Tokyo Station, near Maruzen and Takashimaya.

Located right in the Tsukiji fish market, **Sushi Dai** ㉟, (tel. 542-1111) boasts some of the freshest fish in town. Nestled in a barrack-like building with other tiny shops and restaurants, Sushi Dai consists of just one counter, filled usually with people who work in the vicinity or at the market. This is one of the few places I've seen Japanese drink beer in the morning when they weren't on holiday. The easiest thing to order is one of the seto for ¥1,000 ($8) or ¥1,500 ($12), which usually comes with tuna, eel, shrimp, and other morsels of sushi, along with six rolls of tuna and rice in seaweed (*onigiri*). Sushi Dai is open every day except Sunday and holidays from 5 a.m. to 1:30 p.m. Closest subway station: Tsukiji Station. If you're walking from the station, take your first right once you've crossed the bridge leading onto the market grounds (don't enter into the market building itself). If you're uncertain, there's a little guard's box right after the bridge to the left where you can ask for directions. Otherwise, turn right as described above and then take your first left. To your right will be a row of several barrack-like buildings and tiny alleyways. Sushi Dai is located in Building 6 on the third alley and is the third shop on the right side. Look for the blue curtains hanging outside the door.

A sushi bar that's a bit easier to navigate is **Genrokusushi** ㊱, 5-8-5 Jingumae (tel. 498-3968). Located in Harajuku, this is actually just one of a chain of fast-food sushi bars. The gimmick here is plates of food conducted along the counter on a conveyor belt. Seated at the counter, you simply take the plate you want when it comes by, which makes dining a cinch because you don't have to know the names of anything. Each plate costs ¥120 (96¢) and when you go to pay, just tell the cashier how many plates you had. Hours are 11 a.m. to 9 p.m. daily. Nearest subway stations: one minute from Meiji-Jingumae and five minutes from Harajuku Station. Genrokusushi is on Omote-Sando Dori Avenue close to Oriental Bazaar.

Another conveyor-belt sushi establishment, but this time in Roppongi, is **Bikkuri Sushi,** 3-14-9 Roppongi (tel. 403-1489). One of the cheapest places to eat in this nightlife district, it offers plates of sushi starting at ¥120 (96¢). White plates are all priced at ¥120, while the colored dishes run ¥240 ($1.92) and ¥300 ($2.40). It's open from 11 a.m. to a late 5 a.m. Closest subway station: Roppongi. From Roppongi Crossing, walk toward Tokyo Tower; Bikkuri Sushi will be on your left, opposite the Roi Building on a corner.

Another chain restaurant, but this time a yakitori-ya, **Torigin** ㊲ has one of its shops located at 4-12-6 Roppongi (tel. 403-5829). The decor in this one is simple, typical of so many of the smaller Japanese restaurants, and the older men working behind the counter look like they've been here since the Edo Period. The *yakimono* ("grilled things") begin at ¥130 ($1.04) a stick, but after 9 p.m. prices rise about ¥10 (8¢) to ¥100 (80¢) per item. Yakimono listed in the English menu include gingko nuts, green pepper, quail eggs, and chicken. Not on the menu are some salads, as well as grilled bacon and asparagus (my favorite). Torigin also has kamameshi, a rice casserole cooked and served in its own little pot and topped with such things as chicken, bamboo shoots, mushroom, crab, salmon, or shrimp. Prices for these begin at ¥750 ($6). Open every day except Sunday from 11:30 a.m. to 2 p.m. and from 5 p.m. to 1 a.m. (last order at 12:30 a.m.), Torigin is about a two-minute walk from Roppongi Station.

Much more refined than most yakitori-ya is **Kamakura,** 4-10-11 Roppongi (tel. 405-4377). Open from 5 p.m. to midnight (to 1 a.m. on Friday and holidays) every day except the first and third Tuesdays of the month, it's decorated with paper lanterns and sprigs of fake but cheerful spring blossoms, with traditional koto music playing softly in the background. Its English menu lists yakitori courses starting at ¥2,200 ($17.60). Sticks à la carte include those with shrimp, meatballs, squid, eggplant, and mushrooms, most in the ¥150 ($1.20) to ¥300 ($2.40) range. Beer is ¥550 ($4.40). Closest subway station: Roppongi, about a minute away. Kamakura is located across from the Ibis hotel, on a side street.

Another yakitori-ya is **Atariya** ㊳, 3-5-17 Ginza (tel. 564-0045). You have your choice of table or counter seating on the first floor, while up on the second floor you take off your shoes and sit on split-reed mats. Wearing colorful twisted headbands, the employees here will bring either a yakitori course beginning at ¥1,500 ($12) or individual skewers starting at ¥150 ($1.20). Since courses will include most parts of the chicken including its liver, gizzard, and skin, you might wish to order à la carte for your favorites. The shop's name means to be right on target, to score a bull's eye, and according to its English pamphlet, eating here is certain to bring you good luck. "If you are a businessman, your business will prosper. If you are an artist, your art will become famous. If you are ball players, you will hit many home runs," the pamphlet promises. I'm still waiting. Closed on Sunday, it's open the rest of the week from 5 to 10:30 p.m. Closest subway station: Ginza.

Torijoh ㊴, 3-1-10 Akasaka (tel. 583-7600), is another yakitori-ya, this one in Akasaka. I stumbled on it once when I was wandering through the area looking for a cheap place to eat, and I was so overwhelmed by the enthusiastic and friendly reception given by the waiters that I've been back several times since. The only way to describe the atmosphere is primitive—the lights are too bright, the place looks like some greasy spoon back home, and there's absolutely nothing about it that's aesthetically appealing. But look around you. It's packed with Japanese businessmen in suits and ties stopping in for food, conversation, and a bottle of beer before battling it on the trains back to the suburbs. What's more, Torijoh has been serving yakitori from this spot for more than 100 years. Skewers begin at ¥130 ($1.04) and include the usual fare of chicken, gingko nuts, meatballs, or green peppers. If you want to try a variety of grilled items, ask for the ¥1,000 ($8) platter, which includes chicken, meatballs, and quail eggs. Closest subway station: Akasaka-mitsuke in the heart of Akasaka. It's open from 5 to 10:30 p.m. every day except Sunday.

Not far away, on the third floor of the Akasaka Plaza Building (connected to the Akasaka Tokyu Hotel on the same floor as the lobby), is a kushikatsu restaurant called **Kushinobo** ㊵, 2-14-3 Nagato-cho (tel. 581-5056). Serving skewers of shrimp, vegetables, and meats deep fried in oil, it's a tiny, popular place and customers will wait in line to eat here. I like ordering the *Omakase* course, or cook's choice, with the cook supplying skewer after skewer until you simply say stop. I've been able to eat mint leaf, beef, mushroom, fish, asparagus, chicken, crab, shrimp, green peppers, and pumpkin before crawling away from the table. You'll have various sauces in which to dip your skewered goodies, including soy sauce, mustard, and vinegar. Lunch courses begin at ¥1,300 ($10.40), while dinner courses start at ¥2,700 ($21.60). If you opt for the Omakase, your bill will probably be between ¥3,000 ($24) and ¥5,000 ($40), a splurge that's worth it. Nearest subway station: Akasaka-mitsuke, one minute away. Hours here are 11:30 a.m. to 10 p.m. daily.

Tonki ㊶, 1-1-2 Shimo Meguro, Meguro-ku (tel. 491-9928), is probably the best-known tonkatsu (pork cutlet) restaurant in town, and most likely you'll have to wait to get a seat at the long U-shaped counter. At any rate, as soon as you walk in the door a man will ask you which you want, the hirekatsu (a filet cut of lean pork) or rosukatsu (loin cut). If you're uncertain he'll hold up the two slabs of meat and you just point to one. No matter which slab you decide on, ask for the teishoku, the set meal, which costs ¥1,480 ($11.84) and includes soup, rice, cabbage, pickled vegetable, and tea. He'll scribble your order down on a piece of paper and put it with all the other scraps of paper, miraculously keeping track not only of which order belongs to whom but also which customers have been waiting for a seat the longest.

The open kitchen behind the counter takes up most of the space in the restaurant, and as you eat you can watch the dozen or so cooks scrambling around turning out orders. Never a dull moment. You can get free refills on tea and cabbage, and when you're ready to go, just pay at the counter where you're sitting. This place is closed Tuesday and open the rest of the week from 4 to 11 p.m. (last order at 10:30 p.m.). Nearest station: one minute from Meguro. Take the west exit from the station and then the first left after the Mitsui Bank building and just before McDonald's. Tonki has blue curtains hanging in front of its sliding glass doors.

Put aside all your prejudices about eels and head for **Izu'ei** ㊷, 2-12-22 Ueno (tel. 831-0954). A modern yet traditionally decorated restaurant with a 260-year history dating back to the Edo Period, it boasts its own charcoal furnace in the mountains of Wakayama Prefecture, which produces the best charcoal in Japan.

Since eels are grilled over charcoal, the Japanese place a lot of stock in the quality of the charcoal used. *Unagi donburi* (rice with strips of eel on top) is ¥2,200 ($17.60), and tempura and sushi are also available. Hours are 11 a.m. to 9:30 p.m. daily. Closest subway station: it's located across the street from Shinobazu Pond and the Shitamachi Museum, a three-minute walk from JR Ueno Station.

Another eel restaurant is **Keyaki** �43, 1-34-5 Asakusa (tel. 844-9012). It's located on the second street that parallels Nakamise Dori Avenue to the east—look for the brown flag with an eel on it and for the fish tank just inside the door. Small with just a counter, a couple of tables, and an adjoining tatami room, it offers a set eel course (*unagi seto*) for ¥2,000 ($16) as well as tempura or sashimi courses for ¥1,600 ($12.80). Try the house specialty, a sake called *ginjo-shu*. Hours here are 11:30 a.m. to 3 p.m. and 5 to 10 p.m., closed Monday. Nearest subway station: Asakusa.

If you're in the vicinity of the Tourist Information Center in Hibiya and are looking for an inexpensive place to have lunch, across the street from the T.I.C. is **Donto** ㊹, located in the basement of the Denki Building, 1-7-1 Yurakucho (tel. 201-3021). Popular with the local working crowd, it's pleasantly decorated with shoji screens, wooden floors, and an open kitchen. Choose what you want from the plastic display case, which shows various teishoku for ¥930 ($7.44). Everything from noodles, sashimi, and tempura to kaiseki is available. Closed on Sunday and holidays, it's open the rest of the week from 11 a.m. to 2:30 p.m. and from 5 to 11 p.m. Nearest subway station: Hibiya.

Soba (noodle) shops are among the least expensive restaurants in Japan, and one of Tokyo's most famous noodle places is **Yabu-Soba** ㊺, 2-10 Awajicho, Kanda (tel. 251-0287). Established in 1880, it's surrounded by a wooden gate and has a small bamboo and rock garden. The house is Japanese style, with shoji screens and a wooden ceiling, and although it looks old it dates only from the 1940s, the previous building having been flattened during World War II. You'll find the restaurant filled with middle-aged businessmen and housewives, and if you come during lunchtime you may have to wait for a seat. One big room, the dining area is divided into tatami mats and tables; and since there's a menu in English, ordering is easy. Listen to the woman sitting at a small counter by the kitchen—she sings out orders to the chef as well as hellos and good-byes to customers. Hot and cold noodles start at ¥600 ($4.80), and you can also get noodles with shredded yam, topped with crispy shrimp tempura, or served with grilled eel. Noodles and beer here will cost you less than ¥2,000 ($16). Hours are 10:30 a.m. to 7 p.m.; closed Monday. Nearest subway stations: about five minutes from Awajicho and ten minutes from Akihabara. Located between these two stations, it's on a side street east of Sotobori Dori Avenue. A good place to stop off for a meal or snack if you're in Akihabara looking at electronics.

Tanuki Soba ㊻, 3-5-6 Azabudai, Minato-ku (tel. 583-0545), is another soba restaurant, this time a wonderful respite from the concrete of Roppongi. Tanuki means "racoon" and there's a stuffed animal in the window vaguely resembling the real thing, but get past that and you'll find yourself in an old farmhouse that looks out onto a walled garden—you can even sit outside when it's warm. The friend who showed me this place said she was here once over New Year's and witnessed distinguished-looking businessmen coming in to bow deeply to the old woman in a kimono who runs this place, clearly a sign of deep respect and admiration. Prices start at ¥600 ($4.80) for buckwheat noodles, and the menu includes warm noodles (*kake soba*), cold noodles (*mori soba*), noodles with tempura (*tempura soba*), with sushi (*soba sushi*). This place is closed Sunday and holidays, but otherwise is open from 11:30 a.m. to 4 p.m. and 5 to 8 p.m. Nearest subway station: less than ten minutes from Roppongi Station, across the street from Azabu Post Office as you walk toward Tokyo Tower.

Asakusa's best-known noodle shop is **Namiki** ㊼, 2-11-9 Kaminarimon (tel. 841-1340). It's a one-room place with tatami and tables and an English menu. Noodles range in price from ¥500 ($4) for plain noodles in cold or hot stock to ¥1,400 ($11.20) for tempura and noodles. Hours are 11:30 a.m. to 7:30 p.m.; closed Thursday. Nearest subway station: about three minutes from Asakusa. To reach Namiki, take the road that leads south away from Asakusa Kannon Temple and Kaminarimon Gate. Namiki is a brown building on the right side of the street with some bamboo trees by the front door.

Also in Asakusa is **Kamiya Bar**, 1-1-1 Asakusa (tel. 841-5400). Established in 1880, this inexpensive eatery serves both Japanese and Western fare in its three floors of dining. It's open every day except Tuesday from 11:30 a.m. to 10 p.m., but the best time to come is for lunch, when the teishoku (which changes daily) is offered for ¥600 ($4.80) until 2 p.m. There's also a mixed grill for ¥2,200 ($17.60). A plain, brown-tiled building, Kamiya Bar is located almost on top of the Asakusa subway station, on Edo Dori Street.

Ichioku ④⑧, 4-4-5 Roppongi (tel. 405-9891), is one of my favorite restaurants in Tokyo for casual dining. Ichioku opened in the early 1970s and its name means "one-hundred million," supposedly the amount of money the owner hopes to earn eventually. Open from 6 to 11:30 p.m. every day, it's a tiny, cozy place with only eight tables, and you fill out your order yourself. The menu is in English, comes complete with pictures, and is glued onto your table underneath clear glass. The food is difficult to describe and categorize—maybe you could call it Japanese nouveau cooking. There's tuna and ginger sauté, mushroom sauté, shrimp spring rolls, and a dish of crumbled radish and tiny fish. I recommend the tofu steak (fried tofu with flakes of dried fish on it), as well as the cheese gyoza (a fried pork dumpling with cheese melted on it). The average meal here will cost ¥3,000 ($2.40) or less. The nearest station is Roppongi, about three minutes away.

If you're a vegetarian or looking for a Japanese health-food restaurant, **Tenmi** ④⑨, on the second floor of Daiichi Iwashita Building, 1-10-6 Jinnan, Shibuya-ku (tel. 496-9703), serves traditional Japanese macrobiotic vegetarian food from 11:30 a.m. to 2:30 p.m. and 5 to 8 p.m. except on Sunday and holidays, when it's open from 11:30 a.m. to 6 p.m. Tenmi is closed the third Wednesday of the month. Dishes and set menus range from ¥650 ($5.20) to ¥1,700 ($13.60) and include various vegetable, tofu, noodle, and rice combinations. I found the set menu for ¥1,000 ($8) that included brown rice, an assortment of boiled vegetables, seaweed, and miso soup very satisfying and delicious. There's a health-food shop on the ground floor. Nearest subway station: about five minutes from Shibuya.

Non-Japanese Food

If you find yourself in Shibuya, it's worth checking out **The Prime**, 2-29-5 Dogenzaka (tel. 770-0111). Opened a few years back by the Seibu conglomeration, The Prime is a great building filled with restaurants and amusements, including movie theaters, a dance and aerobics studio, and a concert and theater-ticket agency. The second floor is a large cafeteria, with various counters offering dishes from around the world. You can pick up everything from bagels and sandwiches to Indian curries, Chinese food, sushi, salads, and pastas. Most dishes are priced less than ¥1,000 ($8), and you pay the cashier at each counter. It's open daily from 10 a.m. to 10 p.m. In the basement are a number of noodle shops serving Chinese, Singaporean, Kyushu, and Hokkaido styles, with huge bowlfuls priced at ¥600 ($4.80) and up. The Prime is located about two minutes away from Shibuya Station, on Dogenzaka.

One of my favorite restaurants in Harajuku is **Beer Market Doma,** located in the basement of the Ga-Z Building at 6-5-3 Jingumae (tel. 498-7251). A true gem in terms of prices, quality, and atmosphere, it's decorated with an earthen floor (*doma*) and silk cloth draped from the ceiling, which looks like a tent—or harem—belonging to the nomads of mainland Asia. The food is a mixture of Chinese, Japanese, Thai, and other Asian cuisine, along with pao dishes. Pao foods, originally from the Middle East, feature such morsels as beef with *kimchi* (spicy Korean cabbage) or fish and curry wrapped in lettuce. Cheapest, however, are the cafeteria offerings, with a dozen or so dishes ranging from salads, soups, and main entrées to desserts, most in the ¥300 ($2.40) to ¥750 ($6) range. Simply get a wooden tray and go through the line. Hours are 11:30 a.m. to 2 p.m. and 5 to 11:30 p.m. daily, and cafeteria prices are even cheaper during lunch. Closest subway stations: Meiji-Jingumae and Harajuku. It's located on Meiji Dori in the direction of Shibuya, just off Omote Sando.

If you miss a decent sandwich, head for **Bamboo Sandwich House**, 5-8-8 Jingumae (tel. 406-1828), located off Omote Sando on a side street beside the Paul Stuart shop. It offers more than 20 sandwich fillings, most in the ¥450 ($3.60) to ¥750 ($6) range, and you have your choice of white or rye bread. What's more, it's probably the only place in town to offer a bottomless cup of coffee for a mere ¥200 ($1.60), a price that hasn't changed in a dozen years. A cheerful place that even boasts outdoor seating, it's open daily from 11 a.m. to 9 p.m. Closest subway stations: Omote Sando, Meiji-Jingumae, and Harajuku.

The 1984 opening of **Sabatini Pizzeria Romana**, located in the basement of the Suncrest Building, 2-13-5 Kita-Aoyama, Minato-ku (tel. 402-2027), was a cause for rejoicing among pizza-lovers in Tokyo. It's owned by three brothers from Rome who operate an expensive Italian restaurant (also located in the Suncrest Building) and offers the closest thing to real Italian pizza in town. Many ingredients are flown in from Italy, including olive oil, huge slabs of parmesan and other cheeses, as well as the restaurant's large wine selection; they even shipped in a pasta machine. Pizzas here start at ¥1,000 ($8), and there's also spaghetti, lasagne, and fettuccine. The ¥2,000 ($16) lunch special gives you a pizza, salad, coffee, and choice of beer or wine. À la carte meals should average about ¥2,500 ($20) to ¥3,000 ($24). Hours are 11:30 a.m. to 2:30 p.m. and 5:30 to 11 p.m. daily. The pizzeria is one minute from Gaienmae, at the intersection of Aoyama Dori and Killer Dori Avenues.

One of the oldest, if not *the* oldest, pizzerias in town is **Nicola**, 3-12-6 Roppongi (tel. 401-6936). It claims to have been the first to bring pizza to Japan, more than three decades ago. At any rate, it offers more than 50 different kinds of pizza, starting at ¥600 ($4.80) in 6-inch, 9-inch, or 12-inch pans, as well as spaghetti, beginning at ¥770 ($5.50). With its dimmed lighting and comfortable booths and chairs, it's a good place to relax—if you can just ignore the fake grapes hanging from the ceiling. Nicola is open every day of the week from 5 p.m. to midnight. Nearest subway station: Roppongi. From Roppongi Station, walk toward Tokyo Tower; Nicola is on the first alley to the left on the third floor of Roppongi Plaza Building. Look for Nicola's sign.

If you want to gorge yourself on pizza, the best deal in town is at one of the 20 or so **Shakey's** around town. They offer a great all-you-can-eat pizza lunch every day except Sunday and holidays from 11 a.m. to 2 p.m.—for just ¥600 ($4.80) per person. One German I know prides himself on being able to put away 27 pieces in one sitting, but you don't have to eat that much for it to be a bargain. In Shinjuku there's a Shakey's across the street from Isetan department store at 3-30-11 Shinjuku (tel. 341-0322). Others are in Harajuku at 6-1-10 Meiji-Jingumae (tel. 409-2405), on Omote Sando Dori Avenue close to the Oriental Bazaar, and in Ginza at 3-5-8 Ginza (tel. 563-2008), on Chuo-Dori Avenue across the street from Matsuya department store.

Spaghetti with a view is what you'll get at the **Spaghetti Factory,** located on the 29th floor of the N.S. Building in Shinjuku at 2-4-1 Nishi Shinjuku (tel. 348-1393). Open every day from 11 a.m. to 9 p.m. (last order), it offers spaghetti dishes starting at ¥1,000 ($8) with a wide variety of sauces and toppings. Nearest subway station: about an eight-minute walk west of Shinjuku Station.

A good place for hamburgers is **Ari's Lamp Light,** 7-8-1 Minami Aoyama (tel. 499-1573). Actually a piano bar where Ari himself plays easy-listening music every evening from 9:30 on, this place has hamburgers, sandwiches, and salads for about ¥1,000 ($8). There's also a large cocktail selection with drinks costing about ¥1,000 ($8). Hours are 5:30 p.m. to 2 a.m. daily, except Sunday. Nearest subway station: about a 15- to 20-minute hike from Roppongi. From Roppongi Crossing, walk toward Shibuya. After you pass the big Fuji Film building on your right, look for the "Lamp Light" sign on your left. It's in the basement of the Odakyu Building.

Central Park, 4-30-6 Jingumae (tel. 478-6200), is an interesting restaurant serving Cantonese Chinese dishes, sandwiches, and snacks, with most items costing less than ¥1,200 ($9.60). It has a good selection of juices and cocktails. The interesting thing about this place is that it's located in the middle courtyard of a tall office building, with palm trees and open sky above. In winter a plastic tarp covers the restaurant. Another noteworthy item is that an aerobics class adjoins the restaurant —which means that you can watch women working out as you eat. Hours here are 11:30 a.m. to 10 p.m. daily. Nearest subway station: one minute from Meiji-Jingumae in Harajuku. Central Park is located in Central Apartment Building on the corner of Omote Sando and Meiji Dori Avenues.

Not far from Central Park in Harajuku, **El Amigo,** 4-30-2 Jingumae (tel. 405-9996), is one of the cheapest Mexican restaurants in town. To cut corners they use cabbage instead of lettuce, but otherwise it's the usual tacos and enchiladas, margaritas and Mexican beer. Unless you become addicted to those margaritas (a lot of people come here just for those), your meal will probably cost less than ¥2,000 ($16). A plus here is that there's an outdoor patio of sorts, below street level and smothered in plants. The place is cheerful and often crowded. Hours are 5 p.m. to midnight daily. Nearest subway station: Meiji-Jingumae, one minute away off Omote Sando Dori Avenue on a side street beside Wendy's hamburger shop.

If you're crazy about charbroiled chicken at reasonable prices, head straight for **El Pollo Loco,** 1-13-12 Jingumae (tel. 408-4024). A fast-food chain imported from the shores of California, El Pollo Loco specializes in charbroiled chicken served with tortillas and mild salsa. A two-piece combo, which comes with two pieces of chicken, two tortillas, salsa, rice, and a small side dish, is ¥640 ($5.12). Hours are 10 a.m. to 10 p.m. daily, and it's located on Omote Sando Dori Street, near Harajuku and Meiji-Jingumae subway stations in Harajuku.

My favorite Indian restaurant in town is **Moti,** 6-2-35 Roppongi (tel. 479-1939), and judging by how crowded it sometimes gets, it must be a lot of other people's favorite as well. Vegetable curries begin at around ¥1,100 ($8.80), chicken and mutton curries at ¥1,300 ($10.40). I usually opt for the sag mutton (lamb with spinach). There are also tandoori chicken dishes beginning at ¥1,700 ($13.60). An especially good deal are the lunches, which are ¥990 ($7.92) and give you a choice of vegetable, chicken, or mutton curry, along with Indian bread (*nan*) and tea or coffee. Moti is open seven days a week from 11:30 a.m. to 10 p.m. (lunch is served until 2:30 p.m.). Moti is about three minutes from Roppongi Station, on the left side of the street as you walk from Roppongi Crossing toward Shibuya.

There are also two other Moti restaurants, both in Akasaka: on the second floor of the Akasaka Floral Plaza, 3-8-8 Akasaka (tel. 582-3620), and on the third floor of the Kinpa Building, 2-14-31 Akasaka (tel. 584-6640).

Samrat, Shojikiya Building on the third floor, 4-10-10 Roppongi (tel. 478-5877), is another Indian restaurant, this one located across from the Ibis hotel. Its curries average ¥1,400 ($11.20), while the tandoori mixed grill is ¥1,900 ($15.20). For ¥2,700 ($21.60) you can have either a vegetarian or meat set course, which gives you three dishes and nan. Open seven days a week from 11 a.m. to 5 a.m. Until 3 p.m. there's a special lunch set for ¥1,050 ($8.40), with a choice of curries and nan. Closest subway station: a minute away from Roppongi.

Thai food has surged in popularity in recent years, and riding the crest of the wave is **Ban-Thai,** 1-23-14 Kabuki-cho (tel. 207-0068). Its Thai staff prepares and serves excellent and authentic Thai dishes, with 40 mouthwatering items listed on the menu; for the timid, red dots signify the most fiery foods. My favorites are the cold and spicy meat salad, the chicken soup with coconut and lemon grass, and the *pat Thai* (Thai fried rice). There are also lots of pork, shrimp, chicken, and beef dishes from which to choose, with most items priced between ¥1,100 ($8.80) and

¥1,800 ($14.40). Monday through Friday, it's open for dinner only from 5 p.m. to midnight, while on weekends it's open throughout the day from 11 a.m. to midnight. Closest subway station: Shinjuku. Ban-Thai stands in the seediest part of Kabuki-cho, on a neon-lit pedestrian street that connects the Koma Building with Yasukuni Dori Street. Located on the third floor, it's a bit difficult to find, so look for the numbers of the address on the building.

Popular with the young Japanese crowd is **Healthmagic,** 3-16-4 Shinjuku (tel. 352-4062). Billing its food as "high-protein, high-mineral, high-vitamin, low-fat, and low-sugar," this restaurant serves salads, soups, pita-bread sandwiches, low-calorie desserts, and fruit and vegetable drinks, with most items ranging in price from ¥600 ($4.80) to ¥1,000 ($8). Some foods on the menu sound a bit interesting, such as seaweed salad, pita bread filled with peanut butter and banana, tofu au gratin, and the spinach cake. Open daily from 11 a.m. to 11 p.m. (to 10:30 p.m. on Sunday), this is a pleasant restaurant with potted palms and large windows. However, the music tends to be too loud, and for some reason everyone here seems to be a fiendish cigarette smoker. About five minutes from Shinjuku's east exit, Healthmagic is located on a back alley to the west and behind the Isetan department store. A second Healthmagic opened recently in Harajuku at 6-10-4 Jingumae (tel. 407-5710); open daily from 11:30 a.m. to 10 p.m. It's located in Meiji Dori, on the left side of the street if you're walking from Omoto Sando crossing toward Shibuya.

It would be easy to overlook **Negishi** ⑤⓪, 2-45-2 Kabuki-cho (tel. 232-8020), a tiny hole-in-the-wall with just a counter and a few tables. It would be a shame, however, to miss its healthful, low-calorie foods. It specializes in stews, ox-tail soup, and *mugi-toro* (boiled wheat with grated yam). You might also want to try grilled ox-tongue, which is low in calories and fat but rich in protein. The lunch special here is ¥1,200 ($9.60), while set dinners are ¥1,500 ($12). It's open daily from 11 a.m. to 10:30 p.m., except on Sundays and holidays, when it closes at 9:30 p.m. Closest subway station: either Shinjuku or Seibu Shinjuku. It's located near America Boulevard, on a tiny side street that runs beside Green Plaza.

Sunday brunches are finally catching on in Tokyo, and one restaurant that serves a very reasonable Sunday brunch is **Brasserie D,** Ecsaine Plaza Aoyama, 3-15-14 Kita Aoyama, Minato-ku (tel. 470-0203). Served on Sunday from 11:30 a.m. to 3 p.m., brunch here gives you a choice of either beer, wine, kir, or juice, and a choice of either omelet, croque, or eggs Benedict. On the buffet table are a variety of salads, side dishes, and desserts. The cost is ¥3,000 ($24) per person. The nearest subway station is Omote Sando, about two minutes away. It's located on the left side of Aoyama Dori Avenue as you walk from Omote Sando toward Gaienmae.

Also in Omote Sando but on the other side of Aoyama Dori Avenue is **Spiral Cafe,** located in the Spiral building, 5-6-23 Minami Aoyama (tel. 498-5791). A beautifully designed white building that opened in 1985, Spiral houses galleries, a concert hall and theater, a shop on the second floor that specializes in well-designed kitchenware and household gadgets, and several restaurants. On Sunday from 11 a.m. to 2 p.m., Spiral Cafe also offers a brunch for ¥2,700 ($21.60), which includes a choice of cocktails and one egg dish and a trip to the buffet. My one complaint is that the eggs almost always arrive cold, but a consolation is the live classical music that accompanies you as you eat. Nearest subway station: less than a minute from Omote Sando Station.

There are ramen (Chinese noodle) shops all over Tokyo, easily recognizable by their red signs, flashing lights, and pictures of various dishes displayed by the front door. In addition to ramen you can also order gyoza (fried dumplings), fried noodles, and other Chinese fast food. Since **ramen shops** are found on almost every corner in Tokyo, it seems pointless to single any out, but if you want specific addresses there is one in Roppongi that is easy to find. If you walk from Roppongi Crossing toward Tokyo Tower, within a minute there will be a ramen shop on your left at 3-14-10 Roppongi (tel. 408-9190). Look for the red signs and pictures (outside by the door) of the various dishes served.

WHAT TO DO IN TOKYO

Tokyo hasn't fared very well over the centuries. Fires and earthquakes have taken their toll, old buildings have been torn down in the zeal of modernization, and World War II left most of the city in ruins. The Tokyo of today has very little remaining of historical significance. Save your historical sightseeing for places like Kyoto, Nikko, and Kamakura, and consider Tokyo your introduction to Japan's economic miracle, the showcase of the nation's accomplishments in the arts, technology, fashion, and design. Go shopping, explore mammoth department stores, experiment with restaurants, visit museums, walk around the city's various neighborhoods, and take advantage of the city's glittering nightlife. There are plenty of things to do in Tokyo. I can't imagine being bored even for a minute.

If you're so unfortunate as to have only one day in Tokyo, I suggest you spend it going to Tsukiji Fish Market in the wee hours of the morning, followed by a trip to the Tokyo National Museum, the country's largest and most important museum. In the afternoon you could go to Ginza for some shopping and dinner, and then spend your evening in either Roppongi or Shinjuku. You might be exhausted by the end of the day but at least you'd have seen a few of the city's highlights and visited a few of its different areas.

Assuming that you have more than one day to spare, however, I am including in this chapter six districts in Tokyo that offer the most to tourists in terms of sightseeing and variety. This chapter also covers shopping, a few offbeat suggestions for sightseeing, Tokyo's nightlife, and cultural events such as sumo and Kabuki.

1. The Imperial Palace

The Imperial Palace can be considered the heart of Tokyo, where Japan's imperial family lives. Built on the very spot where Edo Castle used to stand during the days of the Tokugawa Shogunate, it became the imperial home at its completion in 1888. The present palace, however, isn't even the original—that was destroyed along with almost everything else during air raids in 1945. The palace was rebuilt in 1968, but you can't see much of it. Except on New Year's and on the emperor's birthday (December 23), when the grounds are open to the public, the palace remains off-limits to visitors. You'll have to console yourself with a camera shot of the palace taken from the southeast side of Nijubashi Bridge, with the moat and the palace turrets showing above the trees.

But despite the fact that you can't really see the palace, tourists still like to make a brief stop here. Surrounding the palace is a wide moat lined with cherry trees, beautiful in the spring and popular all year round with jogging enthusiasts. If you feel like taking a stroll at a more leisurely pace, you can walk the three miles around the palace and its moat in about an hour.

Probably the most worthwhile thing to do in the vicinity of the palace is to visit its **East Garden (Higashi Gyoen),** located just to the east of the palace grounds and open free to the public from 9 a.m. to 4 p.m. (you must enter by 3 p.m.); closed on Monday and Friday. It takes about an hour to wander through this pleasant green oasis in the middle of the city. Be sure to stop by the little pond with its wisteria, stepping stones, and croaking frogs.

In the garden is also what's left of the central keep of old **Edo Castle**—the stone foundation. Built in the first half of the 1600s, Edo Castle was once the largest castle in the world, with an outer perimeter stretching ten miles. The central keep towered 168 feet above its foundations, offering an expansive view of Edo. As you stand there on top of what's left of the keep's foundation, consider how different things used to look back then—a marsh surrounding the Sumida River, a fishing village where Hibiya now stands. You could see the shore of the bay; what's Ginza today used to be completely under water.

North of the Imperial Palace lies **Kitanomaru Koen Park,** formerly the private grounds of the imperial guard and today the home of several museums. The most important museum here is the **National Museum of Modern Art** (Tokyo Kokuritsu Kindai Bijutsukan; tel. 214-2561), with an excellent collection of modern Japanese art, dating from the Meiji Period. A few Western artists are also represented in the displays of paintings, sculptures, prints, watercolors, and drawings. Open from 10 a.m. to 5 p.m. (you must enter by 4:30 p.m.) every day except Monday and during exhibition changes, the museum charges a ¥360 ($2.88) admission fee.

Not far from the art museum is the **Crafts Gallery** (Bijutsukan Kogeikan; tel. 211-7781). Housed in a Gothic-style brick building constructed in 1910 as headquarters of the imperial guard, the gallery has in its custody contemporary crafts including lacquerware, ceramics, textiles, and dolls. Usually, however, the gallery is used for special exhibitions, and while the hours are the same as those of the modern art museum, the admission charge here is from ¥360 ($2.88) up, depending on the exhibit. The **Japan Science Museum** (tel. 212-8471) is also in Kitanomaru Koen Park, open daily from 9:30 a.m. to 4 p.m., with a ¥515 ($4.12) admission fee. However, because exhibits are mostly in Japanese only, the museum doesn't have much of interest to the foreigner.

If you have the time and inclination to cover more in this area, northwest of

Kitanomaru Koen Park is **Yasukuni Shrine,** built in 1869 and dedicated to the Japanese war dead. Famous for its cherry blossoms in the spring, the shrine is built in classic Shinto style and becomes a center of controversy every August, when World War II memorials are held here and the prime minister shows up. Some people think it improper that a prime minister should visit a shrine so closely tied to Japan's nationalistic and militaristic past.

2. Ginza

Ginza is without a doubt the most chic, most sophisticated, and swankiest area in all of Japan. Ginza is Tokyo's Fifth Avenue, its Champs-Élysées. But rather than just a street, Ginza is a whole area of expensive boutiques, the city's largest concentration of department stores and galleries, excellent restaurants, hostess bars, and coffeeshops. Elegant and glamorous, Ginza is worth a browse even if you can't afford to buy anything.

Ginza means "silver mint," a name that goes back to the days of Ieyasu Tokugawa, when the area was reclaimed from the sea and became the home of a silver mint in 1612. After Japan opened itself up to the rest of the world in 1868, Ginza was the first place to become modernized, with Western-style buildings, and to display goods from abroad. There were brick buildings, gas streetlamps, and planted trees, a popular place for the upwardly mobile to shop and be seen.

The buildings have changed since then, but Ginza remains the hub of Japan's affluence and the most expensive area in which to shop and entertain. There's no longer a silver mint here, but the coins keep rolling in.

For a tour through Ginza, I suggest that you begin not in Ginza itself but rather in neighboring **Hibiya** on the north side of the Imperial Hotel. If you've been touring the vicinity of Imperial Palace, walking to Hibiya and then on to Ginza can all be combined in an easy day's self-guided tour. By the way, the Tourist Information Center is also located in Hibiya, so you may want to stop by there first before beginning your tour of this area.

At any rate, the **Imperial Hotel,** located above Hibiya Station, is easy to find and is one of the city's landmarks. Today a modern first-class hotel, it used to be much smaller and was originally designed by Frank Lloyd Wright. Pressures of space, however, brought the grand old hotel's demise. The original façade is now in Meiji Mura, an architectural museum outside Nagoya. The present Imperial Hotel houses expensive boutiques, such as Gucci, Hanae Mori, Mikimoto, Chanel, Dunhill, and other imported brands, favorites of wealthy Japanese. This is a great place for window shopping.

Across the street on the north side of the Imperial Hotel are two small shops selling woodblock prints. The **Sakai Kokodo Gallery,** at 1-2-14 Yurakucho (tel. 591-4678), claims to be the oldest woodblock print shop in Japan. The first shop was opened back in 1870 in the Kanda area of Tokyo by the present owner's great-grandfather, and altogether four generations of the Sakai family have tended the store. This is a great place for original prints as well as for reproductions of such great masters as Hiroshige. (If you're really a woodblock print fan, you'll want to visit the Sakai family's excellent museum in the small town of Matsumoto in the Japan Alps.) As for this shop, it's open daily from 10 a.m. to 7 p.m. Almost next door is another shop selling woodblock prints called **Nakazawa,** 1-2-15 Yurakucho (tel. 591-1553). It also deals in old and new prints and is open from 10 a.m. to 6 p.m. every day except Sunday.

As you leave the print shop and head east toward Ginza, you'll see overhead the tracks of the Yamanote Line. Underneath these tracks is the **International Arcade,** a long arcade of shops where you can look for such tax-free items as watches, kimonos, Noritake china, woodblock prints, pearls, cameras, and other souvenirs, as well as

clothing, shoes, and accessories. Although you can find cheaper prices elsewhere, this may be a good place to wander through if you're in a rush and don't have time to hunt around. Who knows, you might find a bargain or two. Be sure to have your passport with you so you qualify for duty-free prices. Stores are open daily from 10 a.m. to 6 p.m.

Located next to the International Arcade and also under the tracks is the **Nishi Ginza Electric Center,** where you can shop for radios, cassette players, calculators, compact disk players, and televisions. It's closed on Sunday but open the rest of the week from 9:30 a.m. to 7 p.m.

Just on the other (east) side of the tracks is the **Riccar Art Museum,** 6-2-3 Ginza (tel. 571-3254), a delightful little museum devoted exclusively to ukiyoe, or woodblock prints, located on the seventh floor of the Riccar Building (note that the entrance to the museum is not through the main entrance of the Riccar Building but rather through a much smaller entrance on a side street called Miyuki Dori). It has approximately 6,000 prints in its collection, which it displays on a rotating basis. Open from 11 a.m. to 6 p.m. every day except Monday, it changes exhibits monthly. The place is so tiny it won't take you long to walk through, but it's certainly worth the ¥300 ($2.40) to ¥500 ($4) admission.

Ready for some more art? There are lots of galleries in the Ginza area, some of them dealing with old paintings or screens and some in modern art. Right next to the Riccar Art Museum on Miyuki Dori Street is the **Gallery Center Building,** 6-3-2 Ginza, with several art and antiques galleries. Gallery Hiragi, on the third floor, deals in old scrolls and paintings.

From Gallery Center Building, walk one more block east to a large street called Sotobori Dori Avenue, where you should take a right and walk a few blocks until you find the **Takumi Craft Shop** on your left (if you reach Ginza Nikko Hotel you've gone too far), located at 8-4-2 Ginza (tel. 571-2017). This crafts store stocks Japanese folk art including ceramics, some kites, umbrellas, lacquerware, textiles, and paper objects. Hours are 11 a.m. to 7 p.m. (to 5:30 p.m. on national holidays); closed Sunday. You'll pass many art galleries on this street.

Paralleling Sotobori Dori a couple blocks east is Namiki Dori Street. A narrow tree-lined lane, it alternates art galleries and exclusive boutiques with pubs and hostess bars, giving it a wholly different perspective if you were to return here at night. **Tokyo Gallery,** on the second floor of the Dai Go Shuwa Building, 8-6-18 Ginza (tel. 571-1808), is a one-room gallery that specializes in avant-garde art. Since the gallery is so small, it may be that only one artist's work is displayed. Hours are 10 a.m. to 7 p.m.; closed Sunday and holidays. Almost right next door to Tokyo Gallery is **S. Watanabe,** 8-6-19 Ginza (tel. 571-4684), an interesting small shop that deals mostly in modern and old woodcut prints. The staff is friendly and used to foreigners, and the hours here are 9:30 a.m. to 10 p.m. weekdays (to 5 p.m. on national holidays and to 8 p.m. on Saturday); closed Sunday. One more gallery you might want to drop in on is **Yoseido Gallery,** 5-5-15 Ginza (tel. 571-1312), also on Namiki Dori just off Harumi Dori Avenue. Open from 10 a.m. to 6:30 p.m. (closed Sunday and holidays), it specializes in modern Japanese woodblock prints, silkscreens, lithographs, copper plates, and etchings.

Next on the agenda is Harumi Dori Avenue, a busy street that runs from Hibiya through the heart of Ginza. As you come out on this busy avenue you might want to turn left and go two blocks, to the **Sony Building,** 5-3-1 Ginza (tel. 573-2371). This place is always crowded because it acts as a meeting place in Ginza, especially in early evening when couples or friends meet after work to go for a meal or drink. As you might expect, Sony displays its products in showrooms on the first, third, and fourth floors. Stop here to see all the latest in everything from the Walkman to computers to television. It's open daily from 11 a.m. to 8 p.m.

Catercorner from the Sony Building are two relatively new department stores in Ginza, **Hankyu** and **Seibu,** both of which opened in the mid-1980s with a lot of fanfare. Altogether there are eight large department stores in the Ginza area. They're closed one day a week, but it's staggered so you can always find department stores open.

To see more department stores, walk east on Harumi Dori Avenue until you come to Chuo Dori Avenue. This intersection, called the **Ginza 4-chome Crossing,** is the heart of Ginza, and the subway station here is serviced by three subway lines—the Hibiya, Ginza, and Marunouchi lines. The older building with the clock tower is **Wako** department store, famous for its innovative shop windows (and high prices). Across the street is **Mitsukoshi,** and other department stores in the area are **Matsuya, Matsuzaka,** and **Printemps.** (Check the Tokyo shopping section further on in this chapter for more information regarding department stores.) There are also many boutiques and shops along Chuo Dori Avenue, including **Mikimoto,** 4-5-5 Ginza (tel. 535-4611), Japan's most famous distributor of cultivated pearls.

Near Ginza Crossing is also the **Nihonshu Center,** 5-9-1 Ginza (tel. 575-0656), which sells something dear to my heart—the Japanese rice wine, sake. This is a good place to go to learn more about the brew, and you can sample five different kinds of sake for only ¥300 ($2.40)—and you get to keep the sake cup. A great deal. It's located on Harumi Dori in the direction of Higashi Ginza, on the right side of the street (look for a sign that says "Sakespo 101"). Closed on Thursday and holidays, it's open the rest of the week from 10:30 a.m. to 6:30 p.m.

Feel like a snack? **Le Carrefour,** on the second floor of Mitsukoshi department store, is a coffeeshop that dishes up bowls of ice cream, cakes, scones, and other desserts. Open daily from 8 a.m. to midnight, this place with large windows right above the busy intersection of Ginza 4-chome Crossing affords a vantage point from which to watch the bustling crowds, and if you're here at dusk you can witness Ginza explode into colors with the bright lights of neon and signs. It's one of my favorite places to end a successful shopping day in Ginza, though be warned that coffee here is ¥600 ($4.80) a cup.

---

3. Ueno

Ueno, on the northeast edge of the Yamanote Line, is one of the most popular places in Tokyo for Japanese families on a day's outing. In contrast to the chic sophistication of Ginza, Ueno has always been favored by the common people of Tokyo, workers, and immigrants from the north. The atmosphere is more down-to-earth, more casual. The main drawing card is Ueno Park, one of the largest parks in Tokyo and a cultural mecca with a number of museums, including the prestigious Tokyo National Museum, a zoo, and a pond with a bird sanctuary. And close to Ueno Station, the terminus for trains departing for northern Japan, is a large and lively produce and goods market popular with housewives of the area. Plan on spending at least half a day here to see all the sights, but if you're pressed for time, head straight for the Tokyo National Museum.

UENO PARK

Opened in 1873, Ueno Park was Tokyo's first public park and the first place in Japan to see the establishment of a museum and a zoo. It's not a very large park, especially compared to New York's Central Park, but families and school groups come here for a bit of culture, relaxation, and fun. By the way, along with Shinjuku, Ueno is also a favorite place for Tokyo's down-and-out population. (Yes, even Tokyo has its bums, mainly alcoholics who live tucked away in corners of parks or sleep at entrances to subway stations on sheets of cardboard. They stay politely out of people's way and are left pretty much on their own.)

A landmark in the park is a **statue of Takamori Saigo,** a samurai born in 1827 near Kagoshima on Kyushu island. After helping restore the emperor to power after the downfall of the Tokugawa Shogunate, Saigo subsequently became disenchanted with the Meiji regime when rights enjoyed by the military class were suddenly rescinded. He led a revolt that failed and ended up taking his own life in ritualistic suicide. The statue was erected in 1898 and became the center of controversy when Gen. Douglas MacArthur, leader of the occupation forces in Japan after World War II, demanded that the statue be removed because of its ties to nationalism. The Japanese people protested in a large public outcry and MacArthur finally relented. Today the statue is one of the best known in Tokyo.

The busiest time of the year at Ueno Park is in April, during the cherry blossom season. There's nothing like the bursting forth of cherry blossoms to make one feel that spring is finally here, and people come en masse to Ueno Park to celebrate the birth of the new season. It's not the spiritual communion with nature that you might think, however. In the daytime on a weekday Ueno Park may be peaceful and sane enough, but on the weekends and in the evenings during cherry blossom season, havoc prevails as officeworkers break out of their winter shells. Whole companies of workers converge on Ueno Park to sit under the cherry trees on plastic or cardboard. They drink sake and beer, and they get drunk and rowdy. The worst offenders are those who sing loudly into microphones accompanied by cassettes playing the appropriate instrumental music to each song; a popular entertainment called *karaoke,* also found in special clubs devoted to it. At any rate, visiting Ueno Park during cherry blossom season is an experience no one should miss. More than likely you'll be invited to join one of the large groups—by all means do. You'll all sit there drinking, being merry, and seemingly totally oblivious to the pink and fragile blossoms shimmering above.

TOKYO NATIONAL MUSEUM

In addition to being the largest museum in Japan, the Tokyo National Museum (Tokyo Kokuritsu Hakubutsukan; tel. 822-1111) has the largest collection of Japanese art in the world. This is where you go to see antiques of Japan's past—old kimonos, samurai armor, priceless swords, lacquerware, pottery, scrolls, screens, ukiyoe woodblock prints, and more. Altogether the museum has about 86,000 items in its collections, including more than 10,000 paintings, 1,000 sculptures, 15,500 metalworks, 3,000 swords, 3,700 pieces of lacquerware, 27,000 archeological finds, and 7,500 works of foreign Eastern art. Needless to say, it's all too much to be displayed at once, so only about 4,000 items are shown at any one time and are moved on a rotating basis. Thus no matter how many times you visit the museum you'll always see different things.

There are four main buildings with museum displays. The **Main Gallery (Honkan),** the building straight ahead as you enter the main gate, is the most important one. Just inside the building's entrance is a desk where you can buy the *Tokyo National Museum Handbook* if you want a room-by-room account with explanations of various periods in Japanese art history. You'll feast your eyes on Buddhist sculptures dating from about 538 to 1192; armor, helmets, and decorative sword mountings (armor worn by the nobility was *heavy*—imagine walking around, or worse yet, fighting, with all that stuff on); swords, which throughout Japanese history were considered to embody spirits all their own; textiles; ceramics from prehistoric times; and paintings, calligraphy, and scrolls.

The **Gallery of Eastern Antiquities (Toyokan)** houses art and archeological artifacts from everywhere in Asia outside Japan. There are Buddhas from Pakistan from the 2nd and 3rd centuries; Egyptian relics, including a mummy dating from around 751–656 B.C. and wooden objects from the 20th century B.C.; bronze weapons from Iran; stone reliefs from Cambodia; embroidered wall hangings and cloth from India; Korean bronze and celadon; and Thai and Vietnamese ceramics. The largest part of the collection consists of Chinese art, including jade, glass, stone reliefs, paintings and calligraphy, mirrors, lacquerware, ceramics, and bronzes. Throughout the centuries China played a tremendous role in the development of Japan's art, architecture, and religion.

The **Hyokeikan Gallery** is where you'll find archeological relics of Japan, including pottery and objects found around old burial mounds. One room is devoted to items used in daily life by the Ainu, an indigenous ethnic group now confined mainly to Hokkaido (refer to Chapter XI for more information regarding the Ainu). The fourth building is the **Gallery of Horyuji Treasures,** open only on Thursday if the weather permits. It houses treasures from the Horyuji Temple in Nara, including gilt bronze Buddhist statuettes, religious objects, and paintings.

The Tokyo National Museum is open from 9 a.m. to 4:30 p.m. (you must enter by 4 p.m.) every day except Monday and charges ¥360 ($2.88) admission. Sometimes it hosts special exhibitions as well, for which it charges a special admission.

THE OTHER MUSEUMS

Not far from the Tokyo National Museum, the **Tokyo Metropolitan Art Museum (Tokyo-to-Bijutsukan;** tel. 823-6921) displays modern Japanese works, usually with a number of temporary exhibitions. There are separate admission fees for each exhibit, so unless you're familiar with the particular artists it's just a hit-and-miss thing as far as choosing which exhibit to see. Hours here are 9 a.m. to 5 p.m.; closed Monday and during the changing of exhibits.

Nearby is the **National Museum of Western Art (Kokuritsu Seiyo Bijutsukan;** tel. 828-5131), the main building of which was designed by Le Corbusier. As the name implies, it features Western art, with a concentration on French impressionism. Artists include Renoir, Monet, Sisley, Manet, Delacroix, Cézanne, Degas, El Greco, and Goya. Open daily from 9:30 a.m. to 5 p.m. (except on Monday and during exhibition changes), the museum is famous for its 50 some sculptures by Rodin, the third-largest Rodin collection in the world.

Also in Ueno Park is the **National Science Museum (Kokuritsu Kagaku Hakubutsukan;** tel. 822-0111), open from 9 a.m. to 4:30 p.m. every day except Monday. This sprawling complex covers everything from the evolution of life to electronics in Japan to aircraft and automobiles. Unfortunately not all displays are explained in English but there's an English handbook available for ¥310 ($2.48). The museum is worth visiting because of its exhibits relating to Japan. For example, there are displays on the origin and development of the Japanese people, examples of architecture (no nails were used to join heavy wooden beams), the process of making Japanese lacquerware and paper, a "Zero" fighter plane built during World War II, and an excellent collection of antique Japanese clocks. It charges a ¥360 ($2.88) admission.

TOSHOGU SHRINE

Erected in 1651, Toshogu Shrine is dedicated to Ieyasu Tokugawa, founder of the Tokugawa Shogunate. Stop here to pay respects to the man who made Edo (present-day Tokyo) the seat of his government and thus elevated the small village to the most important city in the country. The pathway to the shrine is lined with massive stone lanterns that were donated by various feudal lords.

UENO ZOO

Opened back in 1882, Ueno Zoo (tel. 828-5171) is small but very popular with Japanese families. The main attractions are two giant pandas that were donated by the Chinese government. These two celebrities are so popular that there are always long lines to their cages on weekends, and there are all kinds of souvenirs you can buy with pandas on them. The zoo also has an aquarium and a large aviary filled with tropical plants that you can walk through, enabling you to observe birds in their natural surroundings. Open from 9:30 a.m. to 4:30 p.m. (enter by 4 p.m.) every day except Monday, the zoo charges ¥400 ($3.20) admission.

SHINOBAZU POND

This marshy pond was constructed in the 17th century so that visitors to the various shrines in the area had a nice view of water on which to rest their eyes; tea houses used to line the pond's banks. Now part of the pond has literally gone to the birds: it's a bird sanctuary. The pond is filled with lotus plants, there are small boats for rent in a corner, and there's also a small temple in the middle of the water attached to the bank with walkways.

SHITAMACHI MUSEUM

At the southeastern edge of Shinobazu Pond is the Shitamachi Museum (Shitamachi Fuzoku Shiryokan; tel. 823-7451). Shitamachi means "downtown" and refers to the area of Tokyo in which commoners used to live, mainly around Ueno and Asakusa. There's very little left of old downtown Tokyo, and with that in mind, this museum seeks to preserve for future generations a way of life that was virtually wiped out first by the great earthquake of 1923 and then by World War II.

On display is a Shitamachi tenement house that was common at the turn of the century, a long narrow building with one roof over a series of dwelling units. The only thing separating one family from another was a thin wooden wall. These were homes of the poorer people, confined to the narrow back alleys. Everyone knew everyone else's business—there were few secrets you could keep in such crowded conditions as these. The alleyways served as communal living rooms. Children played in them and families sat outside in them in the summertime to catch whatever breeze there might be. The museum also displays relics relating to the life of these commoners, including utensils, toys, costumes, and tools, most of which are not behind glass cases but are simply lying around so that you can pick them up and inspect them more closely. There are also shops set up as they might have looked back then, including a merchant's shop and a candy shop.

Admission is ¥200 ($1.60) and hours are 9:30 a.m. to 4:30 p.m. every day except Monday.

AMEYA YOKOCHO

On your way back to Ueno Station you may want to walk through Ameya Yokocho, a narrow shopping street along the west side of the elevated tracks of the Yamanote Line between Ueno and Okachimachi Stations. Originally a wholesale market for candy and snacks and later becoming a black market in U.S. Army goods after World War II, Ameya Yokocho today consists of approximately 400 shops selling discounted items of everything from fish to vegetables to handbags and clothes. Early evening is the most crowded time as workers rush through on their way home and hawkers shout out their wares. The scene retains something of the shitamachi spirit of old Tokyo.

4. Asakusa

East of Ueno is an area called Asakusa, the heart of old downtown Tokyo. It's where the merchants settled back when the Tokugawas made Edo the seat of their shogunate government. In those days merchants were considered quite low on the social ladder and were restricted as to where they could live and even what they could wear. Gradually, however, the merchants acquired wealth, and whole new forms of popular entertainment arose to occupy their time. Theaters for Kabuki and Bunraku were built and flourished in Asakusa. Ukiyoe (woodblock prints) became the latest artistic rage, with scenes depicting daily life in Edo, Kabuki stars, and beau-

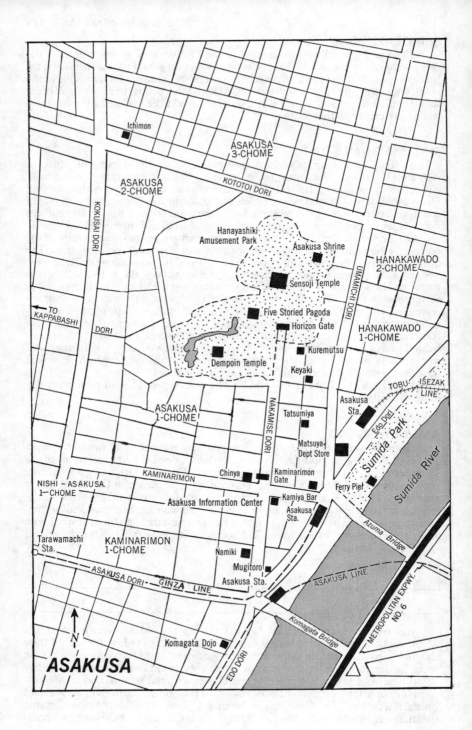

ASAKUSA

ties. To the north of Asakusa was Yoshiwara, the most famous geisha and pleasure district in the city. What a sight Asakusa must have been back then, with its carnival atmosphere of stalls, theaters, and amusements, its bustling crowdedness and liveliness.

Unfortunately, Asakusa has not escaped the modernization that swept through Japan over the past century, but more than anywhere else in Tokyo it still retains the charm of old downtown Edo. It still has a festive atmosphere, crowded with stalls and people. For Japanese, visiting Asakusa evokes feelings of nostalgia. For tourists, it provides a glimpse of the way things were.

HOW TO GET THERE

The most dramatic way to arrive in Asakusa is **by boat.** Departing from Hi no de Sanbashi Pier (closest subway station: Hamamatsucho), the small ferry makes its way along the Sumida River just as in past centuries boats carried wealthy townsmen to the pleasure district of Yoshiwara. Although much of what you see along the river today is only concrete embankments, I recommend the trip because it affords a different perspective of Tokyo—barges making their way down the river, high-rise apartment buildings with laundry fluttering from balconies, warehouses, and superhighways. The boat passes under approximately a dozen bridges during the 40-minute trip, each bridge completely different. Ferryboats ply the waters between Asakusa and Hamamatsucho about every hour, but because schedules change it's best to call ahead (tel. 841-9178 or 457-7830). Cost of the ferry one way is ¥560 ($4.48). The same ferry also makes a stop at Hama Rikyu Garden, described in the "Sightseeing Miscellany" section later in this chapter. Cost of the ferry one way from the garden is ¥520 ($4.16); entrance to the garden itself is another ¥200 ($1.60).

If you're combining both Ueno and Asakusa into a day's trip, transportation between the two districts is served by either the Ginza **subway** line or a special double-decker **bus.** If you arrive in Asakusa via Ueno, you might want to take the boat trip back home.

If you need information on Asakusa upon arrival, stop by the **Asakusa Information Center,** located catercorner from the Kaminarimon Gate. Open daily from 9:30 a.m. to 8 p.m., it's staffed by English-speaking volunteers until 5 p.m.

SENSOJI TEMPLE

The most famous attraction in Asakusa, Sensoji Temple is the oldest temple in Tokyo. You'll know you've reached the main entrance when you see a huge lantern hanging from the front gate, named the Kaminarimon Gate after the god of thunder. Once inside the gate, a pedestrian lane, called Nakamise Dori, leads straight to the temple. This lane is lined on both sides with stalls selling fabrics, shoes, toys, trinkets, bags, umbrellas, Japanese dolls, clothes, fans, masks, and traditional Japanese accessories. How about a brightly decorated straight hairpin? A black hairpiece? A wooden comb? Old Japanese women dressed in kimonos shuffle slowly down the lane, bent over their canes. Perhaps there's a Buddhist monk in gray robes and straw hat, begging and thereby learning humility. At the end of the lane is another gate, and then a square filled with pigeons, and then there's the temple itself.

Founded in the 7th century, Sensoji Temple is dedicated to Kannon, the Buddhist goddess of mercy, and is therefore popularly called the Asakusa Kannon Temple. According to legend, the temple was founded after two fishermen pulled up a golden statue of Kannon from the sea. The sacred statue is still housed in the temple, carefully preserved inside three boxes, and even though it's never on display and none of the public has ever seen it, people still flock to the temple to pay their respects. In front of the temple is a large incense pot where worshippers "wash" themselves to ward off or help against illness. If, for example, you have a sore throat, be sure to rub some of the smoke over your throat for good measure. On the right side of the temple is a shrine, the Asakusa Jinja Shrine.

VICINITY OF THE TEMPLE

West of Sensoji Temple (the area to the left if you stand facing the temple) is a small but interesting area of Asakusa popular among Tokyo's older working class. In addition to tiny shops and more stalls, the area also has pubs, a rather corny amusement park called **Hanayashiki** (open 10 a.m. to 6 p.m.; closed Friday) and inexpensive strip shows. One of the most famous strip shows is **France-za**, located on a small street that leads west from Sensoji Temple. With four shows daily, beginning at 11 a.m. and the last show at 7 p.m., it charges a ¥3,300 ($26.40) entrance fee—and leaves nothing to the imagination. At any rate, the area of Asakusa is fun just to wander through. If you keep walking west, within ten minutes you'll reach Kappabashi Dori Street, Tokyo's wholesale district for restaurant items. Yes, this is where you can buy models of all that plastic food you've been drooling over in restaurant displays. Mugs foaming with beer, ice cream, pizza, fish, sushi—it's all here, looking like the real thing. Surely you know someone back home who would get a kick out of receiving a gift of plastic food. My favorite is one of spaghetti with a fork hovering above it, supported by a few strands of noodles. In addition to plastic food there is also kitchenware, including frying pans, knives, lunch boxes, lacquerware, and ceramics. This is where restaurant owners come to purchase items wholesale, but retail sales are made to the public as well.

If you want to return to the center of Tokyo by subway, the nearest station to Kappabashi Dori is Tawaramachi, on the Ginza Line. However, if you have the energy, you should take advantage of the number of interesting traditional restaurants (check the restaurant section) and bars in Asakusa. **Kuremutsu** ⑤, 2-2-13 Asakusa (tel. 842-0906), is a unique watering hole located just southeast of Sensoji Temple. It's actually a tiny house, tucked behind an inviting courtyard with a willow tree, a millstone covered with moss, and an entrance invitingly lit with lanterns. Inside it's like a farmhouse in the countryside, filled with farm implements, old chests, masks, cast-iron tea kettles, hibachis, and other odds and ends. Traditionally dressed to match the mood, waitresses will bring you a dish of hors d'oeuvres (otsumami) whether you want it or not—perhaps some roasted soybeans or a small river fish. The food is expensive, so you're best off ordering noodles for ¥850 ($6.80) or a platter of assorted sashimi for ¥3,800 ($30.40). My one beer and the otsumami came to ¥1,600 ($12.80). Closed Thursday, it's open the rest of the week from 4 to 10 p.m.

Ichimon �52, 3-12-6 Asakusa (tel. 875-6800), takes its name from *mon*, which was the lowest piece of currency used by the common people during the Edo Period. Ichimon means "one mon." At any rate, this establishment has a unique system whereby each customer is required to purchase ¥5,000 ($40) worth of mon, issued here in wooden tokens, which are then used to pay for your sake and meal. It's usually enough to cover a couple of small flasks of sake, a tray of appetizers, and a dish or two that might include sashimi, steak, *nabe* (a one-pot stew of meat and vegetables), or chicken. Mon you don't use can be exchanged for the real thing when you leave. Open every day except Sunday from 5:30 to 10:30 p.m. (last order), this place is cozy and decorated like an old farmhouse, with wooden beams, shoji screens, and koto music playing in the background. The specialty of the house is its 45 different kinds of sake. When you order some, a basket filled with sake cups is brought to your table so you can select the one you want to drink from. Nearest subway station: about a 15-minute walk from Asakusa Station or 5 minutes from Tawaramachi.

---

5. Shinjuku

A few hundred years ago Shinjuku was nothing more than a fork in the road, a small community with lodgings, painted ladies of the night, and other amusements for passing travelers. Today Shinjuku is a burgeoning satellite center of skyscrapers, office buildings, shops, bars, and sex shows. Such deluxe hotels as the Keio Plaza, Century Hyatt, and Hilton International are found in Shinjuku, as well as the famous department stores **Isetan, Odakyu, Keio,** and **Mitsubishi.**

The nucleus of Shinjuku is **Shinjuku Station,** the largest station in Japan, handling a whopping two million passengers a day. No matter what time of the day or evening you pass through Shinjuku Station you'll find it unbelievably congested, as shoppers and commuters surge through it in rivers of humanity. In fact, it can probably be argued that you haven't seen Tokyo unless you've witnessed its trains and subways during rush hour, and Shinjuku Station is the best place to see it. The most crowded time is around 8:30 a.m., when workers are rushing to their jobs. If you go to the platform of the Yamanote Line, you'll see people packed into train compartments like sardines in a can, and just when you think a compartment is filled to capacity ten more people will push their way in. On the platform, uniformed men rush up and down pushing arms, legs, and umbrellas far enough in so that the doors can close. Imagine going through that every day. And yet it's not unusual for Tokyo's workers to commute two to three hours a day going to and from their jobs.

As for the station itself, I find myself lost here more than any other place in Tokyo. Nine train and subway lines pass through Shinjuku Station. There are more than 60 exits leading out of the station, made even more confusing by a maze of underground shopping arcades. Your best bet is to head toward either the east or west exit and then go above ground as soon as possible to get your bearings. On the west side of Shinjuku Station is a modern area of skyscrapers and deluxe hotels. The east side features shopping by day and a somewhat seamy but fascinating entertainment district by night.

THE WEST SIDE

In the early 1970s Shinjuku's first skyscraper appeared on the scene with the opening of the 47-story Keio Plaza Hotel. Now there are more than a dozen highrises tickling the clouds on Shinjuku Station's west side, including office buildings and a couple more hotels. On the top floors of several of the skyscrapers are restaurants providing panoramic views of the city, while in between the buildings are open-air plazas of brick and tile. Shinjuku is Tokyo's newest business hub, an upstart rival of Tokyo's older established business districts around Marunouchi and Akasaka.

This is the area to head to if you're interested in 20th-century architecture. My favorite building is the **Sumitomo Building,** a triangular building that's hollow on the inside. Stand in the middle of the ground-floor lobby and look up—you'll see past the glass roof and more than 50 stories to the sky above. On the ground floor is **Jewel Palace,** with individual boutiques selling everything from gold and diamonds to pearls and coral. On the 49th to 52nd floors are coffeeshops and restaurants, most of them open from 10 a.m. to 10 p.m., providing outstanding views of the huge metropolis and on clear days of Mount Fuji beyond.

Another interesting building in Shinjuku is the Nihon Seimei Building, popularly called the **N.S. Building.** It also has a hollow interior atrium extending all the way to the top floor. The large open lobby has a 24-foot-tall Seiko clock, and the top two floors sport a number of Japanese and Western restaurants. Computer buffs will enjoy the fifth floor, called the **O.A. Center,** where more than a dozen computer companies have showrooms displaying all the latest in computers, telephones, printers, copiers, and software. Exhibitors include NEC, Toshiba, Epson, Fujitsu, Hitachi, and Riso, and the hours are generally from about 9:30 or 10 a.m. to 5 or 6 p.m.; closed Saturday and Sunday.

Shinjuku is also the best place in Tokyo to shop for camera equipment, though because of the high yen cameras are no longer the bargain they once were. **Yodobashi,** on Shinjuku's west side, has probably the lowest prices around,

with about 30,000 items in stock including every imaginable kind of camera, calculator, watch, and more. Buy your film here. **Doi** and **Sakuraya** are other camera shops worth checking out. Refer to Section 10, "Shopping," in this chapter for more information.

THE EAST SIDE

With department stores and countless boutiques and shops, Shinjuku is a shopping mecca by day. Come night, however, the emphasis shifts to pleasures of a different kind. Located northeast of Shinjuku Station past Yasukuni Dori Avenue, the area of **Kabukicho** is one of the raunchiest, wildest, and most fascinating nightlife districts in all of Japan. There are pachinko pinball parlors, bars, discos, jazz clubs, pornographic shops, sex shows, and things going on you wouldn't believe. The best way to enjoy the atmosphere of this area is simply by walking around. (For specific dining and entertainment recommendations, refer to the dining section in Chapter III and the nightlife section in this chapter.)

In addition to shopping and entertainment, Shinjuku's east side is home also to **Shinjuku Gyoen,** a wonderful park that amazes me every time I go there. Its 144 acres provide changing vistas of Japanese classic gardens, as well as French- and English-style gardens. Each bend in the pathway brings a completely different garden—ponds and sculpted bushes give way to a promenade lined with sycamores which opens up into a rose garden. Cherry blossoms, azaleas, chrysanthemums, and other flowers provide splashes of color from spring through autumn, and also in the park is a greenhouse filled with tropical plants. Formerly the private estate of a feudal lord and then of the imperial family, the park is open every day except Monday from 9 a.m. to 4:30 p.m. (enter by 4 p.m) and charges admission of ¥150 ($1.20). Although you can walk to Shinjuku Gyoen from Shinjuku Station in about 15 minutes, if you're feeling tired you can also take the Marunouchi Line to Shinjuku Gyoenmae Station.

6. Harajuku

An area south of Shinjuku on the Yamanote Line, Harajuku is one of my favorite neighborhoods in Tokyo. Sure, I'm too old to really fit in. If you're over 25 you're apt to feel ancient here, since this is Tokyo's most popular and trendy place for Japanese high school and college students. But I like Harajuku for its vibrancy, its sidewalk cafés, its street hawkers and fashionable clothing boutiques. Harajuku is where the young come to see and be seen, and there are Japanese punks, girls dressed all in black, and young couples in their fashionable best. Harajuku is also the home of Tokyo's most important Shinto shrine, as well as a woodblock print museum, an excellent souvenir shop of traditional Japanese items, and a park with wide open spaces. Formerly the training grounds of the Japanese army and later the residential area of American families during the Occupation, Harajuku was also the site of the 1964 Olympic Village.

SUNDAY ATTRACTIONS

If at all possible, come to Harajuku on a Sunday. That's when the main thoroughfare, a tree-lined venue bisecting the heart of Harajuku called Omote Sando Dori, is closed to vehicular traffic and becomes a pedestrian promenade. Young Japanese dressed to kill walk up and down holding hands (a rather new phenomenon) and in the shadows of the Olympic stadiums is where the crowds are the thickest—for that's where Sunday's most unusual attraction takes place, an open stage for anyone who wants to perform.

Every Sunday from about noon to 5 p.m., everyone from rock 'n' rollers and breakdancers to roller skaters, rock bands, and pantomime artists converges on

Omote Sando Dori just south of Yoyogi Park to do their thing on the street. It all started in the 1970s when a group of kids got together and began dancing to music they brought with them on their portable cassette players. Gradually the number of young dancers grew, until by the mid-1980s there were as many as several hundred teenagers dancing in the street, dressed either in styles of the 1950s or in colorful circus-like clothing.

Although today the number of dancers has dwindled, a few diehards are still here. Contrary to what you might imagine, however, this isn't just wild and random dancing in the street. Similar to most undertakings in Japan, this is group participation. In other words, you have to belong to one of the dancing groups. Individual dancing is out, and if by chance you simply joined in, the other dancers would regard you with astonishment and consider you slightly weird. Each group has its own cassette player, own music, own leader, and own costumes. The fun consists in simply wandering about, observing group after group. In addition to dancers, you might also come across a roller skating club putting on stunts, young boys performing on trick bicycles, a pantomimist, and, in recent years, lots of rock bands. In this carnival-like atmosphere there are also stalls selling everything from fried noodles to roasted corn on the cob to a kind of Japanese omelet. In nearby Yoyogi Park, families spread their picnic lunches.

If it's the first or fourth Sunday of the month, you might also want to drop by Togo Shrine off Meiji Dori Avenue in the heart of Harajuku. A **flea market** is held here these two days of the month. Everything from old chests, dolls, and inkwells to kitchen utensils and kimonos are for sale, spread out on cloths on a sidewalk that meanders under trees to the shrine. Beginning early in the morning, it usually goes on until about 4 p.m.

Another flea market, held once a month on a Sunday but not a specific Sunday, takes place on a tree-lined pedestrian lane between the Olympic Stadiums and the NHK broadcasting building. It's mainly old clothes and second-hand kitsch. To find out when the next market is, call 226-6800.

Incidentally, you may want to begin your Sunday in Harajuku with brunch at L'Orangerie, Brasserie D, or Spiral Cafe, all described under the Tokyo restaurant section in Chapter III.

MEIJI JINGU SHRINE

The most venerable shrine in Tokyo, Meiji Jingu Shrine opened in 1920, dedicated to Emperor and Empress Meiji, who were instrumental in opening Japan to the outside world a hundred years ago. A fine example of dignified and refined Shinto architecture, this shrine is made of Japanese cypress topped with green copper roofs. Two large torii built of cypress wood more than 1,700 years old mark the entrance to the shrine on a shaded pathway lined with trees and dense woods. Almost all of the 100,000 shrubs and trees on the shrine grounds were donated by people from throughout Japan, which means that you can find flora from all over the country. Huge crows like to hang out around here, and on the way to the shrine you can stop off at the **Iris Garden,** spectacular for its irises in late June. A stream meanders through the garden, and if you follow it to its source, you'll find a spring where you can drink the cold water and refresh yourself. North of the shrine complex is the **Treasure Museum** with garments and personal effects of Emperor Meiji and the empress.

OTA MEMORIAL MUSEUM OF ART

This museum, at 1-10-10 Jingumae (tel. 403-0880), just off Omote Sando Dori not far from Harajuku Station, features the private ukiyoe (woodblock prints) collection of the late Ota Seizo. Exhibitions of the museum's 12,000 prints are changed monthly, and hours are 10:30 a.m. to 5:30 p.m. The museum is closed on Monday, New Year's, and from the 24th to the end of every month. Admission is ¥500 ($4).

JUST WALKING AROUND

Across the street from the south exit of Harajuku Station is a small area called **Green Hill Park,** where young vendors set up stalls of clothing and accessories. You can find bargains here, though some of the leather-studded items might be too bizarre for the folks back home.

From the north exit of Harajuku Station there's a narrow street extending east that bisects Meiji Dori Avenue. Called **Takeshita Dori Street,** it's always jam-packed with pedestrians—usually young Japanese girls—out hunting for bargains in the shops with doors flung open wide to the crowds. If you're looking for a refuge, a good place to stop for a break is a small café/flowershop located at the top of Takeshita Dori Street next to McDonald's. Called **Sterling Silver** (tel. 404-8787), this glass-enclosed café filled with plants and flowers is a pleasant place from which to contemplate the shoulder-to-shoulder stream of shoppers rushing by. Serving coffee, iced or hot chocolate, beer, and snacks, it's open from 11 a.m. to 11 p.m. (to 7 p.m. on Sunday and holidays).

Continuing on Takeshita Dori Street, you'll pass boutiques, record shops, shoe stores, and coffeeshops—it's all there if you can only find it through the crowds. At the end of Takeshita Dori is Meiji Dori Avenue, where you should turn right and walk until you come to the first major intersection. This crossroad of Meiji and Omote Sando Dori streets is the heart of Harajuku. On the corner is **La Foret,** a building filled with trendy shoe and clothing stores. If you cross Omote Sando Dori and turn right, you'll arrive almost immediately at a shop with the unlikely name of **Chicago,** which nonetheless stocks what looks like thousands of used and new kimonos and yukatas in a corner of its basement.

Take a left on Omote Sando Dori, and on your right you'll soon come to **Kiddy Land,** which sells gag gifts and a great deal more than just toys, and to **Oriental Bazaar,** 5-9-13 Jingumae (tel. 400-3933), one of Tokyo's best places to shop for Japanese souvenirs. Three floors offer antique chinaware, old kimonos, Japanese paper products, fans, jewelry, woodblock prints, screens, and more. Shopping hours are 9:30 a.m. to 6:30 p.m. every day except Thursday. Other interesting shops along Omote Sando Dori include **Vivre 21,** open daily from the 11 a.m. to 8 p.m. and boasting boutiques showcasing fashions of designers Kenzo, Takeo Kikuchi, and Kensho Abe, and the **Hanae Mori Building,** with a shop of fashions by this famous fashion designer. In the basement of the Hanae Mori Building is the **Antique Market,** with individual stallkeepers selling china, jewelry, clothing, watches, swords, and items from the 1930s. It's open daily from 11 a.m. to 8 p.m. Near the Hanae Mori Building is **Shu Uemura,** which features cosmetics, blush, and eyeshadow in incredible rainbow colors.

More fashionable—and expensive—stores can be found along nearby Aoyama Dori Avenue.

SIDEWALK CAFÉS

After you've seen the Sunday dancers of Harajuku, visited Meiji Jingu Shrine, and fought your way through the crowds, you're probably ready to imbibe a drink or two. Although Tokyo does not have many sidewalk cafés, Harajuku is blessed with several of them, all on Omote Sando Dori Avenue. Closest to the Meiji-Omote Sando Dori intersection is **Café de Rope,** 6-1-8 Jingumae (tel. 406-6845). The oldest outdoor café in Harajuku, this has long been a place popular with Tokyo's "beautiful people." In the wintertime a plastic tarp and heaters keep the place in operation. Beers start at ¥550 ($4.40), cocktails at ¥900 ($7.20), and coffee at ¥500 ($4). There are also cakes and sandwiches. This place is open every day from 11 a.m. to 11 p.m.

Farther east on Omote Sando Dori, right next to Shakey's pizza parlor, is **Café Haus Vie Ben** (called **Café B Haus**), 5-10-1 Jingumae (tel. 498-2655), a slick sidewalk café that opened in 1985. It features white-tiled floors and sleek black furniture. Hours are 9 a.m. to 11 p.m., and a coffee here is ¥450 ($3.60). The most economical place for a coffee, however, is farther up Omote Sando, where you should take a right at the Paul Stuart shop. There you'll find **Bamboo Sandwich House,** where a bottomless cup of coffee is a mere ¥200 ($1.60). If it's raining and you feel like splurging, walk in the opposite direction on Omote Sando in the direction of Harajuku Station, where you'll eventually come to a relatively new building called Quest. There you'll find the exclusive **Demel,** modeled after Vienna's famous coffeeshop, where a cup of the dark substance will set you back ¥1,000 ($8).

Although Harajuku is tremendously popular during the day, it's rather empty in the evenings, primarily due to zoning restrictions (if you look past the shops on Omote Sando Dori, you'll see that all of Harajuku is actually residential). There are, however, a few bars and restaurants in the area in case you feel like spending the evening in Harajuku. For more information, refer to the dining section in Chapter III and the nightlife section in this chapter.

---

7. Sightseeing Miscellany

In addition to the six districts described above, there are a number of other attractions, museums, and sights to lure you to other parts of Tokyo. In planning your itinerary, try to coordinate your sightseeing, shopping, and dining choices so that you cover Tokyo a section at a time. It takes more time than you think to crisscross the wide expanses of this metropolis.

ADDITIONAL MUSEUMS
In addition to the museums described previously in the sections on the Imperial Palace, Ginza, Ueno, and Harajuku, there are a number of other museums worth checking out if you have the time. Be sure to pick up a copy of the Japan National Tourist Organization's pamphlet *Museums and Art Galleries* for more information on museums in Tokyo and throughout Japan.

Note that most museums are closed on Monday and during New Year's celebrations. If Monday happens to be a national holiday, however, most museums will remain open but will close the next day—Tuesday—instead. Call beforehand to avoid disappointment.

Museums of the Arts
The **Gotoh Art Museum (Gotoh Bijutsukan),** 3-9-25 Kaminoge, Setagaya-ku (tel. 703-0661), houses fine arts and crafts of ancient Japan, China, and other Asian countries, including calligraphy, paintings, ceramics, and lacquerware. Surrounding the museum is a garden with a tea house. Hours are 9:30 a.m. to 4:30 p.m. (you must enter by 4 p.m.); closed Monday and during exhibit changes. Admission is ¥500 ($4). Nearest subway station: Kaminoge.

The **Hara Museum of Contemporary Art (Hara Bijutsukan),** 4-7-25 Kita-Shinagawa, Shinagawa-ku (tel. 445-0651), is open every day except Monday from 11 a.m. to 5 p.m. Featuring paintings and sculptures mainly from the 1950s and 1960s by Japanese and foreign artists, this is a pleasant museum housed in a building that used to be the Hara family home. The museum holds exhibitions regularly for rising young artists. Admission: ¥700 ($5.60). The nearest station is Shinagawa.

Hatakeyama Collection (Hatakeyama Kinenkan), 2-20-12 Shiroganedai, Minato-ku (tel. 447-5787), is behind the garden of the Hannya-en Restaurant, a six-minute walk from Takanawadai subway station. With an emphasis on tea-ceremony ceramics and objects, it also has some paintings and calligraphy, sculptures, and lacquerware from ancient Japan and China. Charging ¥500 ($4) admission, it's open from 10 a.m. to 5 p.m. (until 4:30 p.m. from October through March); closed Monday and the last two weeks in March, June, September, and December and the first week in January.

The **Nezu Art Museum (Nezu Bijutsukan),** 6-5-36 Minami Aoyama, Minato-ku (tel. 400-2536), has a fine collection of Oriental art, including Chinese bronzes, Japanese calligraphy, Korean ceramics, and other artwork. The museum is surrounded by a delightful small garden with several tea houses. Hours are 9:30 a.m. to 4:30 p.m.; closed Monday, the day after a national holiday, during exhibition changes, and the whole month of August. Admission is ¥500 ($4) and the closest station is Omote Sando Station, from which it's about a ten-minute walk.

The **Suntory Museum of Art (Suntory Bijutsukan)** is on the 11th floor of the Suntory Building, 1-2-3 Moto-Akasaka (tel. 470-1073), only a few minutes' walk from the Akasaka-mitsuke subway station. Exhibitions change regularly and feature ceramics, kimonos, screens, glass objects, lacquerware, paintings, and prints. Closed on Monday and during exhibition changes, it's open otherwise from 10 a.m. to 5 p.m. (until 7 p.m. on Friday). That means you could begin an evening in Akasaka with a visit to this museum. Admission is ¥500 ($4).

Specialized Museums

Opened in 1986, the **Fukagawa Edo Museum (Fukagawa Edo Shiryokan),** 1-3-28 Shirakawa, Koto-ku (tel. 630-8625), is a delightful museum which captures life in Tokyo during the Edo Period. This indoor museum contains an entire neighborhood—11 houses, shops, and buildings that were brought here from their original locations in Fukagawa and reconstructed. Among them are shops belonging to a vegetable dealer and a fishmonger, two inns, and tenement homes. This museum is open daily from 10 a.m. to 5 p.m., and admission is ¥300 ($2.40). Nearest station is Monzen-Nakacho or Morishita Station. From either station you can catch bus 33 going in the direction of Kiyosumi Garden; get off at Kiyosumi Teien-mae bus stop, from which it's a three-minute walk.

The **Japan Folk Crafts Museum (Nippon Mingeikan),** 4-3-33 Komaba (tel. 467-4527), has folk art from all over Japan and includes furniture, pottery, and textiles, many dating from the Edo and Meiji eras. Crafts from other Asian and European countries are also displayed. Admission is ¥700 ($5.60) and hours are 10 a.m. to 5 p.m.; closed Monday. The museum is about a five-minute walk from Komaba-Todaimae Station on the Keio-Inokashira Line.

The **Furniture Museum (Kagu no Hakubutsukan),** 3-10 Harumi, Chuo-ku (tel. 533-0098), features—as you might have guessed—old Japanese furniture. On the second floor of the JFC Building, it charges ¥200 ($1.60) and is open from 10 a.m. to 4:30 p.m.; closed Wednesday and national holidays. The closest station is Tsukiji, but from there you should take a taxi. There's also a bus from Ginza.

The **Kite Museum (Tako no Hakubutsukan),** on the fifth floor of the Taimeiken Building at 1-12-10 Nihombashi (tel. 271-2465), has kites from Japan and other countries. Hours here are 11 a.m. to 5 p.m. (closed Sunday and national holidays), and the entrance fee is ¥200 ($1.60). Closest station: Nihombashi.

If you're interested in Japanese paper, the **Paper Museum (Kami no Hakubutsukan),** 1-1-8 Horifune, Kita-ku (tel. 911-3545), displays products and utensils used in making Japanese paper by hand. Open from 9:30 a.m. to 4:30 p.m. (closed Monday and national holidays), it charges ¥200 ($1.60) admission and is located across from the south exit from Oji Station.

The **Sword Museum,** 4-25-10 Yoyogi, Shibuya-ku (tel. 379-1386), pays tribute to Japanese swords, long considered an art form in the highest degree. Sword makers were respected as masters in feudal Japan. Hours are 9 a.m. to 4 p.m.; closed Monday. Admission is ¥515 ($4.12). The nearest station is Sangubashi Station on the Odakyu Line.

The **Sumo Museum,** 1-3-28 Yokoami, Sumida-ku (tel. 622-0366), is located in the Kokugikan sumo stadium, about a minute's walk from Ryogoku Station. It shows the history of sumo since the 18th century, with portraits and mementos of past grand champions. It's open from 9:30 a.m. to 4:30 p.m.; closed Saturday, Sunday, and national holidays. Admission is free, but during tournaments you must have sumo tickets to enter the stadium.

Daimyo Clock Museum, 2-1-27 Yanaka, Taito-ku (tel. 821-6913), houses 260 clocks made during the Edo Period. Only about 50 can be shown at any one time, however, and exhibitions are changed annually. Closed on Monday and from July 1 to September 30 and December 25 to January 15, it's open the rest of the time from 10 a.m. to 4 p.m. Admission is ¥300 ($2.40). It's about a ten-minute walk from Nezu Station in an interesting neighborhood filled with temples and old homes.

The **Sugino Costume Museum,** 4-6-19 Osaki, Shinagawa-ku (tel. 491-8151), exhibits clothing of Western Europe from around the 18th century, as well as clothing worn in Japan and other Asian countries. Included are kimonos, samurai outfits, and costumes worn in Noh plays and kyogen comic skits. It's open from 10 a.m. to 4 p.m.; closed Sunday and national holidays. Admission is ¥200 ($1.60). It's about a seven-minute walk from Meguro Station.

TOKYO STOCK EXCHANGE

Established in 1878, the Tokyo Stock Exchange vies with that of New York as one of the busiest stock exchanges in the world. It's located in the Nihombashi/Kyobashi district, a commercial area even during the Edo Period and known today as the Wall Street of Japan. At any rate, with one of the shortest trading hours in the world, the Tokyo Stock Exchange is open free to the public from 9 to 11 a.m. and from 1 to 3 p.m. Monday through Friday except during national holidays. In addition to watching the frenetic trading floor from a glass-enclosed observation deck, visitors can also visit an excellent display called Exhibition Plaza. On the first floor is a historical hall that traces the history of the Japanese securities market, while the second floor contains an array of audio-visual displays to enhance the visitor's knowledge of securities and the stock market. What's more, the entire Plaza has explanations in English. A three-dimensional display explains the intricacies of what you see on the trading floor and how it all works, while a robot demonstrates the various hand signals used on the trading floor. Computors simulate the actual experience of investing in stock by asking questions and leading the viewer through various procedures. All in all, a visit to the Tokyo Stock Exchange is a fascinating experience, and if you want to learn more about the exchange, you will want to join one of the free English tours offered Monday through Friday at 9:30 a.m. and again at 1:30 p.m. The tour lasts approximately an hour. For more information, call the exchange at 666-0141. Closest stations: a five-minute walk from Kayabacho Station (take Exit 11) or a five-minute walk from Nihombashi Station (take Exit A2).

TSUKIJI FISH MARKET

This huge wholesale fish market—the largest in Japan—is a must for anyone who has never seen such markets in action, and the action here starts *early*. About 3 a.m. boats begin arriving from the seas around Japan, from Africa, and even from America with enough fish to satisfy the demands of a nation where seafood reigns supreme. The king is tuna, huge and frozen, unloaded from the docks, laid out on the ground, and numbered. Wholesalers then walk up and down the rows, jotting down the numbers of the best-looking tuna. By 6 a.m. auctions are well under way, but they're not open to the general public. The wholesalers then transfer the fish they've bought to their own stalls in the market, which they subsequently sell to their regular customers, usually retail stores and restaurants.

This wholesale market is held in a cavernous hangar-like covered building, which means that you can visit it even on a dismal rainy morning. Stall after stall stretches in front of you, selling everything from the sea that the Japanese eat—salmon, shrimp, mackerel, tuna, sardine, squid, octopus, and countless other varieties of fish. This market handles almost all the seafood consumed in Tokyo, which should give you at least some idea of its enormity. There's a lot going on—men in black rubber boots rushing wheelbarrows and carts through the aisles, hawkers shouting, knives chopping and slicing. This is a good place to bring your camera if you have a flash—the people working here burst with pride if you single them out for a photograph.

This is also a good place to come if you want sushi for breakfast. Beside the covered market are rows of barrack-like buildings divided into sushi restaurants and shops related to the fish trade. Sushi Dai, for example, described in the restaurant section in Chapter III, offers a seto for ¥1,000 ($8) and is open every day except Sunday and holidays from 5 a.m. to 1:30 p.m.

The Tsukiji Fish Market takes place every day except Sunday, holidays, New Year's, and August 15 and 16. You can find something going on anytime between 3 and 10 a.m., but the best hours are between 4 and 8 a.m. Because the floors are wet, leave your fancy shoes at the hotel. The nearest subway station is Tsukiji Station on the Hibiya Line; take the Honganji Temple exit.

As you walk the distance between the Tsukiji subway station and the fish market, you'll find yourself in a delightful district of tiny retail shops and stalls where you can buy the freshest seafood in town, plus dried fish and fish products, seaweed, vegetables, and cooking utensils. In this area and beside the wholesale market are stalls selling cheap sushi, noodles, and fish, catering mainly to buyers and sellers at the market who come for a quick breakfast. There are also a lot of pottery shops and stores that sell plastic and lacquered trays, bowls, and cups. Although they usually sell in great quantities to restaurant owners, shopkeepers will usually sell to the casual tourist as well.

HAMA RIKYU GARDEN

Not far from Tsukiji Fish Market is the Hama Rikyu Garden, making it a logical next stop on your day's itinerary. Open every day except Monday from 9 a.m. to 4:30 p.m., this garden is considered by many Tokyoites to be the best in the city. Once the site of a villa of former Tokugawa shoguns, the garden passed to the imperial family in 1871 and was opened to the public after World War II. Come here to see how the upper classes enjoyed themselves during the Edo Period. In the center of the garden is a tidal pond, spanned by three bridges draped in wisteria. There are also other ponds, a beach lined with pine trees, moon-viewing pavilions, and tea houses. Admission is ¥200 ($1.60). Note that once inside the garden, you can board a ferry that will continue up the Sumida River all the way to Asakusa, the fare for which is ¥520 ($4.16). Otherwise, the closest station to Hama Rikyu Garden is Shimbashi, about a ten-minute walk.

OBSERVATION PLATFORMS

If you like getting an overview of things, you might want to take a trip to one of the observation decks high above the city. Most famous is **Tokyo Tower,** built in 1958 and modeled after the Eiffel Tower in Paris. Lit up at night, this 1,089-foot tower is a familiar landmark in the city's landscape but has lost its popularity over the decades with the construction of Tokyo's skyscrapers. It's open from 9 a.m. to 8 p.m. (to 6 p.m. from November to March), and the best time of year to go up is supposedly during Golden Week at the beginning of May. With many Tokyoites gone from the city and most plants and businesses closed down, the air is thought to be the cleanest and clearest at this time, affording views of the far reaches of the city —and exactly how far this city stretches will amaze you. Admission to the main observatory (492 feet high) costs ¥720 ($5.76). If you want to go farther up—to the highest place in Tokyo—the special observatory (820 feet) costs ¥510 ($4.08) more. Nearest subway station: Onarimon or Kamiyacho.

If you don't want to dish out money for a view, the **Kasumigaseki Building** at 3-2-5 Kasumigaseki, Chiyoda-ku, has a free observatory on its top floor, the 36th floor. Back when this building was constructed in the 1960s, it was Japan's first skyscraper. From here you have a superb view of the Imperial Palace, the harbor, Ginza, and even Shinjuku off in the distance, and there are free binoculars you can use. On the 36th floor is also a restaurant serving such items as pizza, spaghetti, tempura, or desserts from 10:30 a.m. to 10 p.m. Nearest subway station: Toranomon. It's across from the American Express.

At the other end of Tokyo is the city's tallest building, the 60-story-high **Sunshine City Building,** near Ikebukuro Station at 3-1-1 Higanshi. On the top floor is an observatory, open from 10 a.m. to 7:30 p.m. at a charge of ¥650 ($5.20). Even better is Le Trianon Lounge on the 59th story of this building, where you can sit and relax over a cup of coffee or a cocktail while looking out over the city. Coffee, tea, and desserts are served from 10 a.m. to 5 p.m., while cocktails starting at ¥800 ($6.40) are served from 5 p.m. to 2 a.m. Coffee is ¥500 ($4).

TOKYO DISNEYLAND

I'm not sure why anyone coming to Japan from the United States would want to spend time visiting Tokyo Disneyland, but in case you do this one is virtually a carbon copy of the back-home versions. Here you can find the Jungle Cruise, Pirates of the Caribbean, Haunted Mansion, and Space Mountain (okay, I admit that I've been to Tokyo Disneyland three times). The hottest attractions are the park's newest: Big Thunder Mountain, a roller-coaster mining train that winds through a gorge; *Captain EO,* the 3-D space opera video starring Michael Jackson; and Star Tours, a joint venture between George Lucas Productions and Walt Disney Productions that takes visitors on a flight through the *Star Wars* universe.

Opened in April 1983, this Disneyland had already had more than 60 million visitors by the end of its sixth year.

Tickets for Tokyo Disneyland can be purchased in advance at Tokyo Station near the Yaesu-guchi exit and at travel agencies, such as JTB. The Disneyland Passport, which includes entrance and use of all attractions, is ¥4,600 ($36.80) for adults, ¥4,100 ($32.80) for junior high and high school students, and ¥3,100 ($24.80) for children. Disneyland is open daily from 8:30 or 9 a.m. to 9 or 10 p.m. in summer, with slightly shorter hours in winter.

The easiest way to reach Tokyo Disneyland is via the shuttle buses that run at 10-minute intervals from Tokyo Station directly to Disneyland's front gate in 35 minutes. The bus stop is behind the Tekko Building on the Yaesu-guchi side of Tokyo Station, and the one-way fare is ¥600 ($4.80) for adults and ¥300 ($2.40) for children. Another shuttle bus makes runs between Ueno Station's Iriya exit directly to Disneyland's front gate in 40 minutes; the fare is the same.

A less expensive way is to take the Yurakucho subway line to Shinkiba Station, where you transfer to the JR Keiyo Line for the six-minute ride to Maihama Station right in front of Disneyland's main gate.

Another way to go is to take the Tozai subway line from either Nihonbashi or Otemachi Station to Urayasu Station. From Urayasu you have to walk five minutes to the Disneyland bus terminal and catch a bus that costs ¥200 ($1.60) for adults and half that for children.

NATIONAL CHILDREN'S CASTLE

If you have children, you'll want to bring them to the National Children's Castle (Kodomo no Shiro), 5-53-1 Jingumae, Shibuya-ku (tel. 797-5666). Conceived by the Ministry of Health and Welfare to commemorate the International Year of the Child in 1979, the Children's Castle opened in 1985 with activity rooms designed to appeal to children of all ages. A video library offers videos on everything from fairy tales and Golden Book series to *Sesame Street* and even rock videos. There's an English list of videos from which to choose, and viewing is in your own private little cubicle. A Play Hall features building blocks, jungle gym, table tennis and football for older kids, a large doll house, and computer games. Children can make their own creations in a supervised art room, and on the roof there is a playground. Closed on Monday, the Children's Castle is open from 1 to 5:30 p.m. on weekdays and from 10 a.m. to 5:30 p.m. on Saturday, Sunday, and holidays. The entrance charge is ¥410 ($3.28) for those older than 18, ¥310 ($2.48) for children aged 6 to 18, and free for children under 6. Closest station: Omote Sando (take the B2 Exit), about a five-minute walk.

WORLD'S MAGAZINE GALLERY

If you're a voracious reader of magazines and miss your favorite publications, chances are you can find them at World's Magazine Gallery, located on the mezzanine floor of the Magazine House, 3-13-10 Ginza (tel. 545-7227). Magazine House is a flashy pink-and-gray-striped building located behind the Kabukiza theater (nearest subway station: Higashi-Ginza). You can't take the magazines out of the gallery, but there are tables and chairs there as well as an adjacent coffeeshop. Altogether there are approximately 1,300 current magazines from about 50 countries, including the United States, Germany, France, England, Italy, Spain, Korea, U.S.S.R., China, and countries in Africa and South America. Publications include *The New Yorker, Foreign Affairs, Advertising Age, Billboard, Chicago, Vogue, Bazaar, House and Garden, Ellery Queen's Mystery Magazine, Dog Fancy, Teen Machine, Fly Fishing* —and all kinds of publications you never knew existed. Use of the gallery is free. It's a good place to come if you want a few quiet hours spent catching up on what's going on in the rest of the world. It's open from 10 a.m. to 7 p.m.; closed on Sunday and holidays.

NATIONAL FILM CENTER

If you're a fan of Japanese movies, no doubt you'll be disappointed to discover that the big box office favorites are usually imported from Hollywood. If you're interested in seeing Japanese classics, your best bets are movies shown Saturday and Sunday at the **National Museum of Modern Art**, located in Kitanomaru Koen Park. Movies include both Japanese and foreign films (some with English subtitles), and programs change often; so the best thing to do is call the National Film Center (a branch of the museum) to see what's playing (tel. 561-0823) and to check the times. Admission to the movies is ¥360 ($2.88). Nearest subway station: Takebashi Station.

PACHINKO

No doubt you'll notice so-called pachinko parlors as you walk around Tokyo. Usually brightly lit and garish, they're packed with upright pinball-like machines, with row upon row of Japanese businessmen, housewives, and students sitting intently and quietly in front of their machines. Becoming popular after World War II, pachinko is a game in which ball bearings are flung into the machine, one after the other. Humans control the strength with which the ball is released, but otherwise there's very little to do. Points are amassed according to which holes the ball bearings fall into. Just ¥100 (80¢) gives you 20 ball bearings, which don't last for long. If you're good at it, you win ball bearings back, which you can subsequently trade in for food, cigarettes, watches, calculators, and the like. It's illegal to win money in

Japan, but outside many pachinko parlors along back alleyways are tiny windows where you can trade in the watches, calculators, etc., that you won for cash. Police just look the other way. At any rate, there are probably more pachinko parlors in Tokyo than there are streetlights, so you won't have any problems finding one.

SIGHTSEEING TOURS

Although this book is designed to make it possible for individual travelers to explore Japan on their own, your schedule might make it more advantageous to join a sightseeing tour group. Unsurprisingly, there are a number of tour operators offering group tours of Tokyo and its environs, including companies such as the **Japan Travel Bureau** (JTB, tel. 276-7777), **Japan Gray Line** (tel. 433-5745), and **Fujita Travel Service** (tel. 573-1417), with bookings easily made at most tourist hotels. Day tours may include such sights as Tokyo Tower, the Imperial Palace district, Asakusa Sensoji Temple, Meiji Shrine, and Ginza. Night tours may take in such things as a Japanese dinner, a visit to a Kabuki theater, and a trip to a geisha party— but keep in mind that it's very touristy. Prices for tours range from about ¥4,300 ($34.40) for a half-day tour to about ¥14,000 ($112) for a night tour with dinner.

One tour you might consider joining because you can't do it on your own is the "Industrial Tokyo" tour offered by JTB twice a week. Plants toured may include the Japan Airlines maintenance plant, Isuzu Motors factory, or the Tokyo Stock Exchange. The price of this tour is ¥10,900 ($87.20), including lunch.

---

8. Cultural Entertainments

While these entertainments—Kabuki, Noh, Bunraku, and Sumo—are described in Chapter II, Section 12, this section will tell you where to see them.

To find out about Kabuki and Noh performances, as well as other information relating to the performing arts, check either *Tour Companion's Tokyo City Guide* or the *Tokyo Journal,* or contact the Tourist Information Center.

KABUKI

Among the several theaters in Tokyo with regular showings of Kabuki, **Kabukiza,** at 4-12-15 Ginza (tel. 541-3131), is the most famous and best known. Located above the Higashi-Ginza subway station, this theater has about eight or nine Kabuki productions a year, each of which runs 25 days (there are no shows in August). Usually there are two different programs being shown; matinees run from about 11 or 11:30 a.m. to 4 p.m., and evening performances run from about 4:30 or 5 to about 9 p.m. It's considered perfectly okay to come for only part of a performance. In addition to English programs explaining the plot, which cost ¥800 ($6.40), there are also English earphones you can rent (¥650, or $5.20, plus a deposit) that provide a running commentary on the story, the music, actors, stage properties, and other aspects of Kabuki. I strongly suggest that you either buy a program or rent earphones; it will add to your enjoyment of the play immensely.

Tickets generally range from about ¥2,000 ($16) to ¥12,000 ($96), depending on the program and the seat location. Advance tickets can be purchased at the Advance Ticket Office, to the right side of the Kabukiza's main entrance, from 10 a.m. to 6 p.m. Otherwise, tickets for each day's performance are placed on sale one hour before the opening of each matinee and evening performance. For more information, call 541-3131.

If you want to come for only part of a performance (say, for an hour or so), you can do so for as little as ¥600 ($4.80) to ¥900 ($7.20) if you're willing to sit up on the fourth floor. No earphones are available, but you can still buy a program. These seats are on a first-come, first-served basis.

Kabuki performances are also held several times a year at the **National Theater**

of Japan (Kokuritsu Gekijo), 4-1 Hayabusacho, Chiyod
est stations are Hanzomon, Kojimachi, and Nagatacho.

NOH

Noh performances are given at a number of locations in To
generally ranging from ¥3,000 ($24) to ¥8,000 ($64). Following i
Noh theaters:

Ginza Nohgakudo, on the eighth floor of the Ginza Nohgakudo Bu
15 Ginza (tel. 571-0197). Nearest station is Ginza, and it's about 100 ya
Sukiyabashi intersection toward Shimbashi.

Hosho Nohgakudo, about a five-minute walk from Suidobashi Station at 1-
Hongo, Bunkyo-ku (tel. 811-4843).

Kanze Nohgakudo, 1-16-4 Shoto, Shibuya-ku (tel. 469-5241), a 15-minute
walk from Shibuya Station in the area behind the Tokyu Main Department Store.

Kita Nohgakudo, 4-6-9 Kami-Osaki, Shinagawa-ku (tel. 491-7773). This theater is a ten-minute walk from the JR Meguro station toward Gajoen.

National Noh Theater (Kokuritsu Nohgakudo), 4-18-1 Sendagaya, Shibuya-
ku (tel. 423-1331). Near Sendagaya Station.

Tessenkai Butai, 4-21-29 Minami Aoyama, Minato-ku (tel. 401-2285). About
a five-minute walk from Omote Sando Station (take the A4 exit from the station).

Umewaka Nohgakudo, 2-6-14 Higashi-Nakano, Nakano-ku (tel. 363-7748),
about a five-minute walk from Nakano Sakaue Station on the Marunouchi subway
line, or a seven-minute walk from Higashi-Nakano Station on the JR Sobu Line.

Yarai Nohgakudo, 60 Yaraicho, Shinjuku-ku (tel. 268-7311). This theater is
up the hill from the Yarai exit of Kagurazaka Station on the Tozai subway line.

BUNRAKU

The **National Theater of Japan (Kokuritsu Gekijo),** 4-1 Hayabusacho,
Chiyoda-ku (tel. 265-7411), stages about three Bunraku performances a year with
two to three plays daily. Nearest stations are Kojimachi, Nagatacho, and Hanzomon.

SUMO

A new sumo stadium was completed in 1985 at 1-3-28 Yokoami in Sumida-ku,
just north of Ryogoku Station. Matches are held in Tokyo in January, May, and September for 15 consecutive days, beginning at around 10 a.m. and lasting until 6
p.m. The top wrestlers compete after 4 p.m. The best seats are ringside box seats, but
they're bought out by companies and friends and families of sumo wrestlers. Balcony seats, which start at about ¥6,700 ($53.60), are usually available and so are bench
seats, way up in the back, for ¥1,200 ($9.60). Sumo matches are broadcast on Japa-
nese television as well as on the American military FEN radio station.

If no tournament is going on, you might want to visit a sumo stable to watch
the wrestlers train. There are more than 30 stables in Tokyo, many of which are located in Ryogoku close to the sumo stadium. Call first to make an appointment and
make sure the wrestlers are in town. Stables include **Dewanoumi Beya,** 2-3-15
Ryogoku, Sumida-ku (tel. 631-0090); **Izutsu Beya,** 2-2-7 Ryogoku, Sumida-ku (tel.
633-8920); **Kasugano Beya,** 1-7-11 Ryogoku, Sumida-ku (tel. 631-1871); and
Takasago Beya, 1-22-5 Yanagibashi, Taito-ku (tel. 861-3210). The Tourist Information Center has a list of other stables as well.

9. Cultural Experiences

Just walking down the street in Japan can be considered a "cultural experience." However, there are a number of places, aside from museums, where you can
get further exposure—as a participant—to this country's fascinating cultural life.

ribes what the tea ceremony, ikebana, and zazen
where you can experience these and other dis-

E MASSAGE

heard about acupuncture, they may not be fa-
e-point massage). Many first-class hotels in Ja-
s listed below.

erywhere in Tokyo, and the staff of your hotel
arest you. If you want a specific recommenda-
econd floor of the Kur House Building at 4-2-
-7561). Hours here are 9:30 a.m. to 9 p.m.;
time fee is ¥7,210 ($57.68) for acupuncture
assage.

Seibu Shinjuku Ekimae Clinic, located above
a pharmacy on the fourth floor of the Chiyoda Building, 2-45-6 Kabuki-cho (tel.
209-9217). It's located near Seibu Shinjuku Station, across the street from a group
of shops called American Blvd. Open weekdays from 10 a.m. to 7 p.m. and on Saturday from 9 a.m. to 2 p.m., it offers treatments in acupuncture, shiatsu and
moxibustion (small cones of wormwood, used on specific points for heat stimula-
tion). A doctor trained in Western medicine is also in residence. A treatment of both
acupuncture and shiatsu is ¥3,500 ($28).

VISITING A PUBLIC BATH

If you won't have any other opportunity to visit a communal bath in Japan, I
suggest you go at least once to a neighborhood *sento* (public bath). Altogether Tokyo
has an estimated 2,000 sento, which may sound like a lot but is nothing compared to
the 20,000 the city used to have. Easily recognizable by a tall chimney and shoe lockers just inside the door, a sento usually costs about ¥300 ($2.40) and is generally
open from about 4 to 11 p.m. You can buy almost everything you need at the
bathhouse—soap, shampoo, towels, and even underwear.

Since there are so many public baths spread throughout the city, it's best simply
to go to the one most convenient to you. If you prefer a suggestion, however, the
Azabu Juban Onsen, at 1-5 Azabu Juban in Minato-ku (tel. 404-2610), is the one I
used to go to when I lived for a while in an apartment without a tub or shower.
Closed on Tuesday but open the rest of the week from 3 to 11 p.m., it has brownish
water that actually comes from a hot spring. The nearest station is Roppongi, from
which it's about a ten-minute walk.

The **Asakusa Kannon Onsen,** 2-7-26 Asakusa in Taito-ku (tel. 844-4141), is
located just west of the Sensoji Temple described in the Asakusa section above. This
one also boasts water from a hot spring and has the atmosphere of a real neighborhood bath. Closed every first and third Thursday, it opens early at 6:30 a.m. and
closes at 6 p.m. The fee is also slightly higher, at ¥500 ($4).

IKEBANA

Instruction in ikebana—or flower arranging—is available at a number of
schools in Tokyo. Information can be obtained from **Ikebana International,** in the
Ochanomizu Square Building, 1-6 Surugadai, Kanda (tel. 293-8188). Otherwise,
one school particularly good for foreigners is the **Ichiyo School Nakano,** 4-17-5
Nakano (tel. 388-0141). It provides instruction in English at various sites around
Tokyo and will give certifications. Other well-known schools include the
Sogetsuryu Ikebana School, 7-2-21 Akasaka (tel. 408-1126), located close to the
Aoyama-Itchome Station, with instructions in English every Tuesday from 10 a.m.
to noon for ¥3,300 ($26.40); and the **Ohararyu Ikebana School,** 5-7-17 Minami
Aoyama (tel. 499-1200), close to Omote Sando Station, where you can join in les-
sons Monday through Friday from 10 a.m. to noon for ¥3,300 ($26.40) per lesson.

Appointments must be made in advance. Flower arranging is also taught for ¥1,650 ($13.20) per lesson at **Sakura Kai**, 3-2-25 Shimoochiai, Shinjuku-ku (tel. 951-9043), described above in the tea ceremony section.

TEA CEREMONY

Several first-class hotels in Tokyo hold tea ceremonies with instruction in English. Since they are often booked by groups, be sure to call in advance to see whether you can participate.

The **Seisei-an** is on the seventh floor of the Hotel New Otani, 4-1 Kioi-cho, Chiyoda-ku (tel. 265-1111, ext. 2567), where instruction is given on Thursday, Friday, and Saturday from 11 a.m. to noon and again from 1 to 4 p.m. Cost of the instruction is ¥1,000 ($8). Closest station: Yotsuya or Akasaka-mitsuke.

The **Chosho-an,** on the seventh floor of the Hotel Okura, 2-10-4 Toranomon, Minato-ku (tel. 582-0111), gives instruction anytime between 11 a.m. and noon or 1 and 5 p.m. The cost is also ¥1,000 ($8). Nearest subway station is Toranomon.

Toko-an is on the fourth floor of the Imperial Hotel, 1-1-1 Uchisaiwaicho, Chiyoda-ku (tel. 504-1111), close to Hibiya Station. Instruction here is from 10 a.m. to 4 p.m. daily except Sunday and holidays. The cost is ¥1,100 ($8.80).

Another place you can enjoy the tea ceremony is at **Sakura Kai**, the Tea Ceremony Service Center, 3-2-25 Shimoochiai, Shinjuku-ku (tel. 951-9043), a short walk from Mejiro Station on the Yamanote Line. Instruction is on Thursday and Friday from 11 a.m. to noon and 1 to 4 p.m. There are various fees, and you can even combine a tea ceremony with a lesson in ikebana (flower arranging) for ¥2,700 ($21.60).

ZAZEN

Sitting meditation is occasionally offered with instruction in English by a few temples in the Tokyo vicinity. **Eiheiji Temple,** 2-21-34 Nishi-Azabu Minato-ku (tel. 400-5232), holds a zazen every Monday from 7 to 9 p.m. and charges ¥100 (71¢). Instruction here, however, is only in Japanese. For more information, contact the Tourist Information Center. The *Japan Times* also carries announcements of zazen instruction.

---

10. Shopping

One of the delights of being in Japan is shopping, but it's not only the tourists who go crazy shopping in Japan. The Japanese themselves are avid shoppers, and it won't take you long to become as convinced as I am that shopping is the number one pastime in Tokyo. Women, men, couples, and even whole families go on shopping expeditions in their free time, making Sunday the most crowded shopping day of the week. With such a discriminating, knowledgeable, and enthusiastic domestic market, it's little wonder that Japanese products have earned respect in international markets around the world. Today the label "Made in Japan" is synonymous with quality, reliability, and superb craftsmanship. Japanese workers take great pride in the products they produce, whether toys, lacquerware, computers, or cars.

As for Tokyo, it's the country's showcase for everything from the latest in camera or stereo equipment to original woodblock prints. You don't have to spend a fortune shopping either. You can pick up Japanese handmade paper products or other souvenirs, for example, for a fraction of what they would cost in import shops in the United States. In Harajuku it's possible to buy a fully lined dress of the latest fashionable craze for $40, and I can't even count the number of pairs of shoes I've bought in Tokyo for a mere $16. Used cameras can be picked up for a song, reproductions of famous woodblock prints make great inexpensive gifts, and many items —from pearls to electronic video and audio equipment—can be bought tax free.

If you have only a few hours to spare for shopping in Tokyo—what can I say, I feel sorry for you!—head for either a department store or a shopping arcade. With a wide selection of goods under one roof, they're the most convenient places to shop if you can't afford to waste a single minute. If your time *is* limited, a good choice among these is the International Arcade near the Imperial Hotel, with its wide range of everything from cameras to kimonos to watches and chinaware, while the Oriental Bazaar in Harajuku is excellent for traditional Japanese items. Those of you with more time on your hands might want to explore districts in Tokyo that specialize in certain products—Akihabara, for example, for electronic equipment or Kanda for used books.

DEPARTMENT STORES

Japanese department stores are institutions in themselves. Usually enormous, well designed, and chock-full of merchandise, they have about everything you can imagine, including art galleries, pet stores, rooftop playgrounds or greenhouses, travel agencies, restaurants, grocery markets, and flower shops. You could easily spend a whole day in a department store, eating, attending cultural exhibitions, planning your next vacation, and exploring the various departments. Microcosms of Japanese society, these department stores reflect the affluence of modern Japan, offering everything from a wedding kimono to fashions by the world's top designers. And one of the most wonderful aspects of the Japanese department store is its courtesy and its service.

If you arrive at a store as its doors open at 10 a.m., you will witness a daily Japanese rite: Lined up at the entrance, the entire staff will bow in welcome. Some Japanese shoppers arrive just before opening time so as not to miss this favorite ritual. Sales clerks are everywhere ready to help you. In many cases you don't even have to go to the cash register once you've made your choice. Just hand over the product along with your money to the sales clerk, who will return with your change, your purchase neatly wrapped, and an *"arigatoo gozaimashita"* (thank you very much). A day spent in a Japanese department store could spoil you for the rest of your life.

Department stores are good and convenient places to shop for traditional Japanese items, including lacquerware, china and kitchenware, trays, gift items, toys, furniture, sporting goods, shoes, cosmetics, jewelry, clothing, sweets, lingerie, belts, hats, and household goods. The basement is usually devoted to foodstuffs: fresh fish, produce, and pre-prepared snacks and dinners. Many department stores include boutiques of such famous Japanese and international fashion designers as Issey Miyake, Rei Kawakubo (whose line is called "Comme des Garçons"), Hanae Mori, Christian Dior, Calvin Klein, and Brooks Brothers, as well as a department devoted to kimonos. To find out what's where, stop by the store's information counter close to the front entrance. Many in the Ginza and Shinjuku areas have floor-by-floor guides in English.

Hours are generally 10 a.m. to 6 or 7 p.m., and since department stores close on different days of the week, you can always find several that are open, even on Sunday and holidays.

The *Tokyo Journal,* the monthly guide to what's going on in Tokyo, lists department store sales where you can pick up great bargains in everything from men's suits and electric goods to second-hand cameras, golf clubs, and brand-name clothing. In fact, most of the people I know living in Tokyo buy Japanese designer clothing only during these sales at department stores (usually held in June and December). You can pick up fantastic clothing at cut-rate prices—but be prepared for the crowds. Items on sale are usually on one of the top floors, with sometimes an entire floor devoted to the sale. Whenever I go to a department store, I can't resist riding the escalators up and up until I finally reach the bargain floor. I've come upon sales I never knew existed and ended up buying things I never really needed—but what the heck, it's great fun anyway. The *Tokyo Journal* also lists the various exhibitions being held at department store art galleries.

Remember that a 3% consumption tax will be added on to the price marked, but all major department stores in Tokyo will refund the tax on purchases amounting to more than ¥10,000 ($80). Ask at the store's information counter (usually located near the main entrance) for the special form to be filled out by the sales clerks and for the location of the refund counter. Be sure to bring your passport.

In Ikebukuro

If you want to visit a department store simply for the cultural experience, you might be interested in knowing that Seibu in Ikebukuro claims to be the second-largest department store in the world (the largest is Sogo in Yokohama). Just imagine—there are 47 entrances to Seibu, 8,000 sales clerks, 63 restaurants, 12 floors, 31 elevators, and 8 escalators. On an average weekday 190,000 shoppers pass through the store, a number that swells to 300,000 on a Sunday.

Located practically on top of Ikebukuro Station, **Seibu**, at 1-28-1 Minami Ikebukuro (tel. 981-0111), devotes two basement floors to foodstuffs alone—you can buy everything from taco shells to octopus to seaweed. Dishes are set out so that you can nibble and sample the food as you move along, and hawkers yelling out their wares give the place a market-like atmosphere. Fast-food counters sell salads, grilled eel, chicken, sushi, and other dishes ready to eat. The rest of the floors are devoted to clothing, furniture, art galleries, kitchenware, and a thousand other things, and many of the best Japanese and Western designers have boutiques here. It's closed on Thursday.

Other department stores easily spotted from Ikebukuro Station include **Tobu** (tel. 981-2211), which is closed on Wednesday; **Mitsukoshi** (tel. 987-1111), closed on Monday; and **Parco** (tel. 981-2111), open every day.

In Ginza and Nihombashi

The fashionable district of Ginza, along with Nihombashi east of Tokyo Station, has the largest concentration of top-quality department stores in Tokyo. **Wako**, 4-5-11 Ginza (tel. 562-2111), on the corner of Ginza 4-chome Crossing, is one of the few buildings in the area to have survived World War II. Its distinctive clock tower and innovative window displays are Ginza landmarks. Closed on Sunday and holidays, it specializes in imported fashions, luxury items, and Seiko timepieces. Certainly one of the classiest stores around with prices to match.

Also located on Ginza 4-chrome Crossing, **Mitsukoshi**, 4-6-16 Ginza (tel. 562-1111), is a branch of the famous Mitsukoshi in Nihombashi. Popular with young shoppers, it's closed on Monday. **Matsuzakaya**, 6-10-1 Ginza (tel. 572-1111), is located one block from Ginza 4-chome Crossing on Chuo Dori Avenue in the direction of Shimbashi. An older, more established mart, it was the first department store in Japan that did not require customers to take off their shoes at the entrance. It's closed on Wednesday. In the opposite direction from Ginza 4-chome Crossing, on Chuo Dori Avenue, **Matsuya**, 3-6-1 Ginza (tel. 567-1211), is one of my favorite department stores in Tokyo. It has a good selection of Japanese folkcraft items, kitchenware, and beautifully designed contemporary household goods in addition to the usual clothes and accessories. It's closed on Tuesday.

Relative newcomers in the Ginza scene are **Printemps**, 3-2-1 Ginza (tel. 567-0077), closed on Wednesday and a branch of Paris's fashionable Au Printemps; and **Seibu** (tel. 286-0111) and **Hankyu** (tel. 575-2233), two department stores located side by side in Yurakucho between the Hibiya and Ginza subway stations, both closed on Thursday.

In Nihombashi, **Mitsukoshi**, 1-7-4 Nihombashi Muromachi (tel. 241-3311), is one of Japan's oldest department stores. First opened as a kimono shop back in the 1600s, today it has many name-brand boutiques, including Givenchy, Dunhill, Chanel, Hanae Mori, Oscar de la Renta, Christian Dior, and Tiffany. Its kimonos, by the way, are still hot items. The building itself is old, stately, and attractive, making shopping here a pleasure. It's closed on Monday. The nearest station is Mitsukoshimae, which means "In Front of Mitsukoshi."

Takashimaya, 2-4-1 Nihombashi (tel. 211-4111), provides stiff competition for Mitsukoshi, with a history just as long. Closed on Wednesday and located close to Nihombashi Station, it also has boutiques by such famous designers as Chanel, Laroche, Dunhill, Celine, Lanvin, Louis Vuitton, Gucci, Christian Dior, Issey Miyake, and Kenzo.

In Shinjuku

Isetan, 3-14-1 Shinjuku (tel. 352-1111), is a favorite among foreigners living in Tokyo. It has a good line of conservative clothing appropriate for working situations, as well as contemporary and fashionable styles. It's closed on Wednesday and is located about a five-minute walk west of Shinjuku Station on Shinjuku Dori Avenue.

Odakyu, 1-1-3 Nishi Shinjuku (tel. 342-1111), is hard to miss since it's located right above Shinjuku Station. It's closed on Thursday. Another department store right over the station is **Keio,** 1-1-4 Nishi Shinjuku (tel. 342-2111), which specializes in everyday products and is closed on Thursday.

In Shibuya

In recent years, Shibuya has emerged as a shopping mecca for the fashionable young, and so many stores have opened in the last few years that there is a bona fide store war going on. Tokyu and Seibu are the two big names, both of which keep opening more and more shops around Shibuya Station.

Tokyu, 2-24-1 Dogenzaka (tel. 477-3111), is a conservative, middle-of-the road department store appealing greatly to middle-aged well-to-do women. It's closed on Thursday. Other Tokyu-affiliated stores include a smaller shop right above Shibuya Station, **Tokyu Hands** (everything imaginable for the hobbyist and the home), and **109** and **109-2** (filled with clothing boutiques).

Seibu, 21-1 Udagawacho (tel. 462-0111), is closed on Wednesday. Similar to the main store in Ikebukuro, it carries everything from accessories and art to stationery and wine. Designer boutiques here include for Comme des Garçons, Giorgio Armani, Issey Miyake, Jun Ashida, Kenzo and Yohji Yamamoto. Other Seibu stores include **Loft** (with items for the home and hobbyist, a stiff competitor of Tokyu Hands), **Parco** and **Seed,** two fashion stores described below.

MORE JAPANESE FASHION

The department stores listed above are all good places for checking the latest in fashion from Japan. A couple more places worth looking into are Parco and Seed in Shibuya and La Foret and Vivre 21 in Harajuku. **Parco,** 15-1 Udagawacho Shibuya (tel. 464-5111), a division of Seibu, is divided into three buildings called Parco 1, 2, and 3. Parco 1 and 2 are filled with designer boutiques for men and women, including such avant-garde Japanese designers and designs as Kansai, Yohji Yamamoto, Nicole, Comme des Garçons, and Issey Miyake, while Parco 3 is devoted to household goods and interiors. Parco has two sales a year that you shouldn't miss if you're here—one in January and one in July. It's open daily from 10 a.m. to 8:30 p.m.

Seed, 21-1 Udagawacho (tel. 462-0111), is one of Seibu's newest ventures and consists of eight floors devoted to the newest of the new in design talent. There will be a lot of names you're probably not familiar with, along with such notables as Paul Smith, Missoni, Katharine Hamnett, Takeo Kikuchi, Jean Paul Gaultier, and Junko Shimada. Closed on Wednesday, it's open the rest of the week from 10 a.m. to 7 p.m.

Another good place to shop is **La Foret,** 1-11-6 Jingumae (tel. 475-0411), near Harajuku's main intersection of Omote Sando Dori and Meiji Dori avenues. It is the most fashionable clothing store in the area. Although some of the boutiques are expensive, there are some great deals to be found here, particularly in the shops in the basement. Shops are open every day from 11 a.m. to 8 p.m.

Not far from La Foret is **Vivre 21,** 5-10-1 Jingumae (tel. 498-2221), a sleek white building filled with fashionable boutiques selling designer clothing and jewelry. Nicole, Kenzo, Takeo Kikuchi, Jean Paul Gaultier, and Junko Shimada are just a few of the designers with concessions here, and in the basement is an interesting shop selling kitchenware and interior design products for the home and office. It's open every day from 11 a.m. to 8 p.m.

If you want to pick up some fashions that have the Japanese-designer look without the corresponding price tags, the whole area around Harajuku has hundreds of shops selling inexpensive clothing. Takeshita Dori, a street described in the sightseeing section on Harajuku, is lined with shops catering to young, fashion-conscious Japanese.

ARCADES AND TAX-FREE SHOPS

Shopping arcades are found in several of Tokyo's first-class hotels. While they don't offer the excitement and challenge of going out and rubbing elbows with the natives, they are convenient, sales clerks speak English, and you can be assured of top-quality merchandise. The **Imperial Hotel Arcade** is one of the best, with shops selling pearls, woodblock prints, toys, antiques, and expensive name-brand clothing like Hanae Mori. The Okura and New Otani hotels also have extensive shopping arcades.

Underground shopping arcades are found around several of Tokyo's train and subway stations, the biggest of which are Tokyo and Shinjuku stations. Serving commuters on their way home, they often have great sales and bargains on clothing, accessories, and electronics.

Another good place to shop if you're short of time are duty-free stores. To qualify, you must present your passport, whereupon you'll be issued a piece of paper which you surrender at the Customs desk when departing Japan (the Customs desk at the Narita airport is well marked, so you can't miss it). At that time you may also be requested to show the product to Customs officials.

The best-known tax-free arcade is the **International Arcade,** 1-7-23 Uchisaiwaicho, Chiyoda-ku (tel. 571-1528), located close to the Imperial Hotel in Hibiya under the train tracks. Stores here are open daily from 10 a.m. to 6:30 p.m. and include merchandise from pearls and cameras to kimonos, china, woodblock prints, and electronics.

ART GALLERYS AND ANTIQUES

Antiques and Curios

One place to go for one-stop antique shopping is **Tokyo Antique Hall,** called Komingu Kottokan in Japanese. Located on Meiji Dori Street at 3-9-5 Minami Ikebukuro, Toshima-ku (tel. 982-3433 or 980-8228), this building has more than 35 antiques dealers' stalls. Although most articles are marked, it's okay to try bargaining. You could spend hours here, looking over furniture, ceramics, woodblock prints, jewelry, lacquerware, swords, china, hair combs, Japanese army memorabilia, kimonos and fabrics, scrolls and screens, samurai gear, clocks, watches, dolls, and other items too numerous to list. Antiques are both Japanese and Western, and dealers here work the flea markets across the country. Hours are 10 a.m. to 7 p.m. every day except Thursday, but it's best to get here before 5 p.m. because some of the stalls close down early if business is slow. The nearest station is Ikebukuro, a seven-minute walk.

One of the best-known names in fine antiques, **Mayuyama,** 2-5-9 Kyobashi, Chuo-ku (tel. 561-5146), was first established in 1905 and is one of Tokyo's oldest antique shops. A distinguished-looking stone building between Kyobashi and

Takaracho, within walking distance of Tokyo Station, Mayuyama deals in ceramics and pottery, scrolls and screens from Japan, China, and Korea—at expectedly high prices. Hours are 9:30 a.m. to 6 p.m.; closed Sunday and national holidays.

Kurofune, 7-7-4 Roppongi (tel. 479-1552), is owned by an American who has made his home in Japan for more than 20 years. Located in a house about a five-minute walk from Roppongi Station, it specializes in Japanese antique furniture which has not been refinished but, rather, left in its original condition. The stock also includes fabrics, prints, maps, and folk art. It's open from 10 a.m. to 6 p.m.; closed Sunday and national holidays.

Other places to look for antiques include both the Oriental Bazaar, described below, and the **Antique Market** in the basement of the Hanae Mori Building, 3-6-1 Kita-Aoyama, Minato-ku, on Omote Sando Dori. Individual stall holders here sell china, jewelry, clothing, swords, watches, woodblock prints, and 1930s kitsch; open daily from 11 a.m. to 8 p.m. Prices here are high.

Art Galleries

Ginza has the highest concentration of art galleries in Tokyo, with shops dealing in everything from old woodblock prints to silk screens to contemporary paintings. Refer to the Ginza sightseeing section for more information regarding particular stores.

Woodblock Prints

Originals and reproductions of the famous ukiyoe woodblock-print masters are available at **Sakai Kokodo Gallery** and at **Nakazawa,** both located across from the Imperial Hotel and described along with other woodblock print shops in the Ginza sightseeing section. Another good place to look for prints is at the Oriental Bazaar, listed in the "Traditional Arts and Crafts" section below.

TRADITIONAL ARTS AND CRAFTS

If you want to shop for traditional Japanese folkcraft items, a number of stores in Tokyo offer such craftwork as fans, paper products, chinaware, lacquerware, kimonos, and bamboo products. In addition to the shops listed below, remember that department stores have crafts sections with wide selections of everything from kitchenware to lacquerware to kimonos. Also, Nakamise Dori Street (described in the section on Asakusa) is packed with stalls selling everything from wooden *geta* shoes to hairpins worn by geishas.

Even if you can't afford to buy anything, it's worth a trip to the **Japan Traditional Craft Center (Zenkoku Dentoteki Kogeihin Senta),** on the second floor of the Plaza 246 Building, 3-1-1 Minami Aoyama (tel. 403-2460). Just a three-minute walk from the Gaienmae subway station, it's located at the corner of Gaien-nishi Dori Avenue and Aoyama Dori Avenue above a Häagen-Dazs ice-cream parlor. This store is devoted to beauty in all forms of Japanese traditional crafts and is a good introduction to Japanese design. Established to publicize and distribute information on Japanese crafts, the Craft Center has permanent exhibitions as well as items for sale. There's lacquerware, ceramics, fabrics, paper products, bamboo items, dolls, writing brushes, metalwork, and more. Prices are high but rightfully so. In a corner of the shop is a video screen where you can watch the making of Japanese swords, lacquerware, woodblock prints, and other traditional crafts, and some of the displays carry explanations in English about the origin and production of the craftwork exhibited. Crafts include those of traditional design as well as those that are strikingly contemporary. Hours are 10 a.m. to 6 p.m.; closed Thursday.

About a 15-minute hike from the Craft Center is the **Oriental Bazaar,** 5-9-13

Jingumae (tel. 400-3933), located on Omote
Oriental-looking façade of orange and green, it
oriented, I've always been partial to this store a
used kimonos. With hours from 9:30 a.m. to
offers three floors of souvenir and gift items,
woodblock prints, paper products, fans, Japa
chinaware, sake sets, Japanese dolls, and pearls
buy for office co-workers, neighbors, or friend
wallets (good for checkbooks) in a corner of the
apiece and would easily cost $4 or $5 in the
include cardboard coasters with woodblock p
small prints, all of which are inexpensive and
guests to this shop and they always leave wit
store will also ship things home for you.

shop at this location since
and kokeshi, as well as
5:30 p.m.; closed Su
tion, one minute a

Japanese
Fol
Ishizu

In the Ginza area, **Takumi Craft Shop,** 8-4-2 Ginza (tel. 571-2017), is on Sotobori Dori Avenue, close to Hibiya and Ginza stations. Stocking a variety of Japanese folk art, including rustic ceramics, paper products, fabrics, furniture, and lacquerware, it's open from 11 a.m. to 7 p.m. every day except Sunday. On holidays it closes early at 5:30 p.m.

Also on Sotobori Dori Avenue, but this time almost in front of Tokyo Station, is **Ishizuka,** 1-5-20 Yaesu, Chuo-ku (tel. 275-2991). Open from 10 a.m. to 7:30 p.m. daily except Sunday and holidays, it has folkcrafts from various regions around Japan, including ceramics, a wonderful selection of toys, clay idols, paper products, Japanese workers' pants (called *mompe*), products made of cherry bark, wooden dolls, chopsticks, bamboo products, and glassware. You can even buy the tiny spoon-like sticks the Japanese tradtionally use for cleaning out their ears. An attractive tea room is on the second floor.

If you're in Shinjuku, head for **Bingoya,** 10-6 Wakamatsucho (tel. 202-8778), located about a 15-minute walk from Akebonobashi Station (it's probably easiest to go by taxi from either Shinjuku or Akebonobashi Station). Its five floors hold toys, baskets, rustic furniture, pottery, lacquerware, and fabrics from all over Japan. Hours are 10 a.m. to 7 p.m.; closed Monday.

Cloisonné

At 5-6-2 Ginza (tel. 572-2261), **Ando** has what is probably the largest selection of cloisonné in town. Opened in 1880, it's located on Harumi Dori Avenue not far from the Ginza subway station. Hours are 9 a.m. to 6 p.m. daily; closed Sunday and holidays.

Flower Arranging and Tea Ceremony Accessories

Tsutaya, 5-10-4 Minami Aoyama, Minato-ku (tel. 400-3815), has everything you might need for ikebana (flower arranging) or the Japanese tea ceremony, including vases of unusual shapes and sizes and tea whisks. Hours here are 9 a.m. to 6:30 p.m.; closed the first and fourth Sundays of the month. Nearest station: Omote Sando.

Japanese Dolls

Japanese dolls range from elegant creatures with delicately arranged coiffures and silk kimonos to wooden dolls called *kokeshi.* One of the biggest doll shops in Japan is **Kyugetsu,** 1-20-4 Yanagibashi, Taito-ku (tel. 861-5511). Open daily from 9 a.m. to 6 p.m., it's located in front of Asakusabashi Station.

Yoshitoku Dolls, 1-9-14 Asakusabashi, Taito-ku (tel. 863-4419), has had a

1711. It sells a variety of Japanese dolls, including Hakata
souvenirs and some antiques. It's open from 9:30 a.m. to
nday and national holidays. Nearest station: Asakusabashi Sta-
way.

Paper Products

craft shops such as Takumi in Ginza, the Oriental Bazaar in Harajuku, and
ka near Tokyo Station all have items made of Japanese paper.

For a store dealing almost exclusively in handmade Japanese paper and
andcrafts from various parts of Japan, visit **Washikobo**, 1-8-10 Nishi Azabu,
Minato-ku (tel. 405-1841). It's located about seven minutes on foot from Roppongi
Station on the right side of the street as you walk toward Shibuya. Open from 10
a.m. to 6 p.m. every day except Sunday and national holidays, it sells paper and cardboard boxes, paper wallets, notebooks, paper lamps, toys, and sheets of beautifully
crafted paper.

If you're visiting Asakusa, you might want to stop in at **Kurodaya**, 1-2-5
Asakusa (tel. 844-7511), located right beside Kaminarimon Gate just a few minutes'
walk from Asakusa Station. First opened back in 1856, it sells traditional Japanese
papers, kites, papier mâché masks, boxes, and other products made of paper. It's
open from 11 a.m. to 7 p.m. every day except Monday.

Kimonos

The Oriental Bazaar, described earlier, has a good selection of new and used
kimonos, including elaborate wedding kimonos. An even larger selection can be
found in nearby **Chicago**, 6-31-21 Jingumae (tel. 409-5017), located on Omote
Sando Dori in Harajuku. Open seven days a week from 10 a.m. to 10 p.m., it stocks
thousands of kimonos and cotton yukatas in the very back of the shop, past the
1950s clothing. There are many used kimonos in the ¥2,000 ($16) to ¥5,000
($40) price range.

Stone Lanterns

Some people are so enamored of the huge stone lanterns they see at shrines and
landscaped gardens that they want to take one home. If that's you, a good place to go
is **Ishikatsu**, 3-4-7 Minami Aoyama (tel. 401-1677). In operation since 1706, they
have a catalog of various stone lanterns to choose from and they'll ship one to you.
Hours are 9 a.m. to 5 p.m.; closed on Sunday and holidays. The nearest stations are
Roppongi and Omote Sando, from which you should take a taxi.

Swords

The best-known sword shop in Tokyo, **Japan Sword**, 3-8-1 Toranomon (tel.
434-4321), which also deals in sword accessories, sword guards, and kitchen cutlery, is open from 9:30 a.m. to 6 p.m.; closed Sunday and holidays. The closest stations are Toranomon and Kamiyacho.

Other places to look for swords include the Oriental Bazaar, the Tokyo Antique
Hall, and the Antique Market in the basement of the Hanae Mori Building in
Omote Sando.

BOOKS

In addition to the bookstores listed in the Tokyo "ABCs" section in Chapter
III, there's a whole slew of bookstores along Yasukuni Dori Avenue in Jimbocho-
Kanda that no bookworm should pass up. A mecca for both new and used books,

there are more than 50 bookstores here, several of which deal in books written in English. The closest station is Jimbocho.

Tuttle Book Shop, 1-3 Jimbocho, Kanda (tel. 291-7072), has a wide selection of books on Japan and the Far East written in English, as well as Japanese-language books. The Tokyo branch of a Vermont firm, it's open from 10:30 a.m. to 6:30 p.m. Monday through Friday and from 11 a.m. to 6 p.m. Saturday and national holidays. Closed on Sunday.

Kitazawa, 2-5 Jimbocho, Kanda (tel. 263-0011), has an overwhelming selection of books on Japan. This is a good place to come if you're looking for the latest books published about this country. It also has old and rare books. Hours here are 10 a.m. to 6 p.m.; closed Sunday.

Another shop in Kanda is **Ohya Shobo**, 1-1 Jimbocho, Kanda (tel. 291-0062), open from 10:30 a.m. to 6:30 p.m. every day except Sunday and holidays. It claims to have the largest stock of old Japanese illustrated books, woodblock prints, and maps in the world.

CAMERAS

You can purchase cameras at many duty-free shops, including those in Akihabara, but if you're really serious about photographic equipment, you should make a trip to a shop dealing specifically in cameras. Shinjuku is the photographic equipment center for Tokyo, and the biggest store there is **Yodobashi Camera**, 1-11-1 Nishi Shinjuku (tel. 346-1010). Just a block west of Shinjuku Station, it ranks as one of the largest discount camera shops in the world with around 30,000 items in stock and reputedly sells approximately 500 to 600 cameras daily. In addition to cameras it also has watches, calculators, typewriters, and cassette players. Its duty-free section is on the second floor, and even though prices are marked, you can bargain here. Come here to stock up on film. Hours are 9:30 a.m. to 8:30 p.m. daily.

Another camera shop nearby is **Doi Camera**, 1-15-4 Nishi Shinjuku (tel. 344-2310). On the east side of Shinjuku Station is another Doi Camera shop, as well as three **Sakuraya** camera shops.

If purchasing a new camera is too formidable an expense, you should consider buying a used camera. New models in just about everything come out so frequently in Japan that older models can be grabbed up for next to nothing. **Camera no Kimura**, 1-18-8 Nishi Ikebukuro (tel. 981-8437), is west of Ikebukuro Station and has a good selection of used cameras. It's open every day from 8 a.m. to 8 p.m. (10 a.m. to 7 p.m. on Sunday). Another shop that deals in used Japanese and foreign cameras is **Matsuzakya Camera**, 1-27-34 Takanawa, Minato-ku (tel. 443-1311), about a 20-minute walk from Shinagawa Station. Hours here are 10 a.m. to 7 p.m. (only until 5 p.m. on Sunday and holidays).

ELECTRONICS

The largest concentration of electronic and electrical shops in Japan is in an area of Tokyo called **Akihabara**. Although you can find good deals on video and audio equipment elsewhere, Akihabara is special simply for its sheer volume. With more than 600 stores, shops, and stalls, Akihabara accounts for one-tenth of the nation's electronic and electrical appliance sales. An estimated 50,000 shoppers come here on a weekday, 100,000 per day on a weekend. It may surprise you to learn that 80% of Japan's consumer electronics market is domestic.

Even if you don't buy anything, it's great fun walking around (and if you do intend to buy something, make sure you know what it would cost back home—with the present exchange rate there are few bargains in Japanese electronic products, but you may be able to pick up something unavailable back home). Most of the stores and stalls are open-fronted, many of them are painted neon green and pink, and inside, lights are flashing, fans are blowing, washing machines are shaking and shimmying, stereos are blasting music. Salesmen yell out their wares, trying to get customers to look at their rice cookers, computers, video equipment, cassette players, TVs, calculators, and watches. This is the best place to go to see the latest models of everything electronic, an educational experience in itself.

If you purchase anything, make sure it is made for export—that is, that there are instructions in English, there's an international warranty, and it has the correct electrical connectors. All the larger shops in Akihabara have duty-free floors where the products are designed for export. Some of these shops include **Yamagiwa,** 3-13-10 Soto-Kanda (tel. 253-2111); **LAOX,** 1-2-9 Soto-Kanda (tel. 253-7111); and **Hirose Musen,** 1-10-5 Soto Kanda (tel. 255-2211). Simply look for signs saying "duty free." Good buys in Akihabara include cassette players, stereo equipment and compact disk players, watches, calculators, video equipment, and portable electronic typewriters. Be sure to bargain, and don't buy at the first place you go to. One woman I know who was looking for a portable cassette player bought it at the third shop she went to for ¥4,000 ($32) less than what was quoted to her at the first shop.

The easiest way to get to Akihabara is via the Yamanote Line or Keihin Tohoku Line to the JR Akihabara Station. You can also take the Hibiya subway line to Akihabara Station, but it's farther to walk. Most shops are open daily from about 10 a.m. to 7 p.m.

If you don't have time to go to Akihabara, in Shinjuku there's a branch of **LAOX** at 3-15-16 Shinjuku (tel. 352-5611), close to the Isetan department store on Shinjuku Station's east side. It also has duty-free prices on video cameras, stereo components, compact disk players, and VCRs. In Ginza there's the **Nishi-Ginza Electric Center,** 2-1-1 Yurakucho (tel. 503-4481), located next to the International Arcade under the train tracks. Shops here sell radios, cassette players, calculators, compact disk players, and other electrical and electronic gadgets duty free. It's open every day except Sunday from 9:30 a.m. to 7 p.m.

FLEA MARKETS

Flea markets, of course, are also good opportunities to shop for antiques as well as for delightful junk. Don't expect to find any good buys in furniture, but you can pick up second-hand kimonos, kitchenware, small chests, dolls, household items, and odds and ends. The markets usually begin as early as 6 a.m. and last until 4 p.m. or so, but go early if you want to pick up bargains. Bargaining is expected.

Togo Shrine, described in the Harajuku section, has a flea market on the first and fourth Sundays of the month. Nearest stations are either Meiji-Jingumae or Harajuku. **Nogi Shrine,** located at Nogizaka Station, has a flea market the second Sunday of the month. In Roppongi, the steps of the **Roi Building** (closest station: Roppongi) become a market as dealers lay out their wares on the fourth Thursday and Friday of every month.

On the second and third Sundays of the month, **Hanazono Shrine,** behind the Isetan department store on Yasukuni Dori in Shinjuku, is the site of a flea market, as is the basement of the Sunshine City's **Alpha Shopping Arcade** in Ikebukuro, on the third Saturday and Sunday of every month.

INTERIOR DESIGN

The **department stores** listed above have furniture and interior design sections, of which Seibu in Ikebukuro has an especially popular and well-known example. My favorite is Ginza's Matsuya department store's Design Collection on the seventh floor, which displays items from around the world selected by the Japan Design Committee as examples of fine design. Included may be such goods as the Alessi teapot from Italy, Braun razors and clocks, and Porsche sunglasses.

A very good place for studying the latest in contemporary Japanese interior design is the **Axis Building,** 5-17-1 Roppongi. Altogether there are more than two dozen shops here, most devoted to high-tech interior design. The majority of the products are Japanese but there are also selected goods from the United States and Europe. Shops feature various aspects of contemporary design, from sleek and unusual lighting fixtures to textiles and linen, clocks, kitchenware, office accessories, and lacquered furniture. Most of the stores are closed on Monday, and don't forget to check out the shops in the basement. Nearest subway station is Roppongi, and the Axis Building is on your right as you walk toward Tokyo Tower.

KITCHENWARE AND TABLEWARE

In addition to the department stores listed above, there are two areas in Tokyo with a number of shops filled with items related to cooking and serving. In Tsukiji along the streets stretching between Tsukiji Station and the Tsukiji Fish Market are shops selling pottery, serving trays, bowls, dishes, and lunch boxes. On Kappabashi Street near Tawaramachi subway station are many stores selling cookware, including sukiyaki pots, woks, lunch boxes, pots and pans, and disposable wooden chopsticks. Although stores in Tsukiji and Kappabashi are wholesalers selling mainly to restaurants, you're welcome to browse and purchase as well.

PEARLS

The first really good cultured pearl was produced back in 1913 by a Japanese man named Koichi Mikimoto. Today Mikimoto is one of the most famous names in the world of cultured pearls. The main **Mikimoto** shop is located at 4-5-5 Ginza (tel. 535-4611), not far from Ginza 4-chome Crossing. Closed on Wednesday, it's open from 10:30 a.m. to 6 p.m.

Another good place to shop for pearls is in the **Imperial Hotel Arcade** at 1-1-1 Uchisaiwaicho. Mikimoto has a branch shop here (tel. 591-5001), and there's also the **K. Uyeda** pearl shop (tel. 503-2587). In business since 1884, this shop has a wide selection of pearls in many different price ranges. **Asahi Shoten** (tel. 503-2528) is another pearl shop in the Imperial Hotel Arcade with a good selection in the modest-to-moderate price range. There are also pearl shops in the Hotel Okura shopping arcade and the International Arcade.

PLASTIC FOOD

As described in the Asakusa sightseeing section, Kappabashi near Tawaramachi subway station is also the place to go if you want to buy the plastic food you see in restaurant displays. Simply wander up and down the street—there's no mistaking stores selling plastic sushi, spaghetti, beer, and more. Buy something here for the person who has everything.

RECORDS

Department stores sell records and cassettes, with the largest selection available at Seibu in Ikebukuro. The largest record shop in town, however, happens to be a branch of Seibu called **Wave**, 6-2-27 Roppongi (tel. 408-0111). This innovative store has a computerized record reference system and a comprehensive selection of records, cassettes, and videos. On the first floor are headphones where you can select from 200 of the top hits, which is one way to keep abreast of what's hot in the music industry. Come to Wave for jazz, German new wave, reggae, heavy metal, classical, vintage, or the latest in Japanese music. In the basement is Cine Vivant, a 194-seat minitheater that shows foreign films four or five times daily for ¥1,500 ($12). Wave is open every day except every first and third Wednesday from 11 a.m. to 10 p.m. (to 8 p.m. on Sunday). It's about three minutes from Roppongi Station, on the left side of the street as you walk in the direction of Shibuya. If you're in Ikebukuro, there's a second Wave located across from Seibu department store at 1-19-6 Minami-Ikebukuro (tel. 980-0111). Closed on Thursday, it's open the rest of the week from 10 a.m. to 7 p.m.

If for some reason you're desperate for the latest U.S. releases, **Tower Records,** on the second floor of the Village 80 Building, 39-2 Udagawacho (tel. 496-3661) in Shibuya, is usually among the first places in town to get them. It's about a ten-minute walk from Shibuya Station and is open from 10 a.m. to 10 p.m. daily.

SAKE

Don't forget the **Nihonshu Center,** 5-9-1 Ginza (tel. 575-0656), recommended in the Ginza sightseeing section.

---

11. After Dark in Tokyo

By day Tokyo is arguably one of the least attractive cities in the world. A congested mass of concrete, it has too many unimaginative buildings, too many cars and people, and not enough trees and greenery.

Come dusk, however, Tokyo comes into its own. The drabness fades and Tokyo blossoms into a profusion of giant neon lights, paper lanterns, and millions of overworked Japanese out to have a good time. If you ask me, Tokyo at night is unequivocally one of the craziest cities in the world. It's a city that never gives up and never seems to sleep. The entertainment district of Roppongi, for example, is as crowded at 3 a.m. as it is at 3 p.m. Many establishments stay open until the first subways start running after 5 a.m. Whether it's jazz, reggae, gay bars, sex shows, discos, mania, or madness that you're searching for, Tokyo has it all.

To understand Tokyo's nightlife, you first have to know that there is no one center of nighttime activity. Rather, there are many nightspots spread throughout the city, each with its own atmosphere, price range, and clientele. Most famous are probably the centers of Ginza, Akasaka, Roppongi, and Shinjuku. Before visiting any of the locales suggested in this guide, be sure to walk around and absorb the atmosphere. The streets will be crowded, the neon lights will be overwhelming, and you never know what you might discover on your own.

Although there are many bars, discos, and restaurants packed with young Japanese men and women, nightlife in Japan is still pretty much a man's domain, just as it has been for centuries. At the high end of this domain are geisha bars, where highly trained women entertain by playing traditional Japanese instruments, singing, and holding witty conversations—and nothing more risqué than that. Generally speaking, such places are outrageously expensive and closed to outsiders. As a foreigner you'll have little opportunity to visit such a place unless you're invited by a business associate, in which case you should consider yourself extremely fortunate.

A Note on Japanese Symbols

Many hotels, restaurants, and other establishments in Japan do not have signs showing their names in English letters. Appendix II lists the Japanese symbols for all such places appearing in this guide. Each establishment name in Japanese symbols is numbered, and the same number appears in an oval in the text following the boldfaced establishment name. For example, in the text Osaka's **Hotel Hokke Club** (164), is number 164 in the Japanese symbol list in Appendix II.

More common than geisha bars, and generally not quite as expensive, are the so-called hostess bars, many of which are located in Ginza and Akasaka. And what do you get at a hostess bar? A woman who will sit at your table, talk to you, pour your drinks, listen to your problems, and boost your ego. You buy her drinks as well, which is one reason the tab can be so high. Hostess bars in various forms have been a part of Japanese society for centuries. Most foreigners will probably find the cost of visiting a hostess bar not worth the price as the hostesses usually only speak Japanese, but such places provide Japanese males with sympathetic ears and the chance to escape the world of both work and family. Men usually have their favorite hostess bar, often a small place with just enough room for regular customers. In the more exclusive hostess bars, only those with an introduction are allowed entrance. And in almost all cases, Japanese companies are picking up the tab.

At the low end of the spectrum are Tokyo's topless bars, sex shows, massage parlors, and pornography shops, with the largest concentration of such places in Shinjuku.

Keep in mind that taxis—which are seemingly everywhere during the day—suddenly become very scarce after midnight, especially on weekends. In great demand after the subways stop running, they are often impossible to flag down in all entertainment districts of Tokyo, and I've had the unpleasant experience of having to wait two hours in the dead of winter before an empty taxi would finally stop to pick me up. If it's a weekend night, you should plan either to catch the last subway home or else resign yourself to staying out someplace until 2 or 3 a.m., when it becomes easier to catch a taxi. And, of course, you can also simply stay out all night until the first subways start running after 5 a.m. In the section that follows, I've listed a number of establishments that stay open until such an ungodly hour.

In addition to the establishments listed here, be sure to check the Tokyo dining section. If you're counting your yen, for example, the Japanese restaurants listed under the budget category in Chapter III are your best bet for a relatively inexpensive night out on the town. Many places serve as both eateries and watering holes, especially those that dish out skewers of yakitori.

And finally, one more thing you should be aware of is the "table charge" that many bars and cocktail lounges charge their customers. Included in the table charge is usually a small appetizer—maybe nuts, chips, or a vegetable. At any rate, the charge is usually between ¥300 ($2.40) and ¥500 ($4) per person. Some establishments levy a table charge only after a certain time in the evening; others may add it only if you don't order food from their menu. If you're not sure and it matters to you, be sure to ask. Some locales call it an *otsumami*, or snack charge. Remember, too, that a 3% consumption tax will be added to your bill.

GINZA

A chic and expensive shopping area by day, at night Ginza transforms itself into a dazzling entertainment district of restaurants, bars, and first-grade hostess bars. Ginza is the most sophisticated of Tokyo's nightlife districts and also one of the most expensive. So you have to exercise great caution in choosing a place in which to settle down for the evening—otherwise, you might be paying for the experience for a long time to come. Ginza clubs are notorious for being ridiculously expensive, supported solely by business executives out on expense accounts. Remember that—hardly any of the Japanese businessmen you see out carousing in Ginza's expensive hostess bars are paying for it out of their own pockets. The cost is simply too prohibitive, with bills running from $100 to $500 per person. Since I am not wealthy, I personally prefer Shinjuku and Roppongi to Ginza for nighttime entertainment. However, because Ginza does have some fabulous restaurants, I am including some suggestions of things to do in the Ginza area if you find yourself here after dinner. Remember, the cheapest way to absorb the atmosphere in Ginza is to simply wander about, particularly around Namiki Dori Street.

If you are interested in visiting a hostess bar, one in Ginza that is receptive to foreigners and not too prohibitively expensive is **Club Maiko** ⑤③, located in the heart of Ginza on the fourth floor of the Aster Plaza Building, 7-7-6 Ginza (tel. 574-7745), on Suzuran Dori Street. The hostesses here are geisha and *maiko*, who are young women still training to be geisha. This is a small bar, consisting of a few tables and a long counter. The women here put on dancing shows, talking and sitting with customers in between performances. With its traditional music and atmosphere, this may be the closest you'll get to Japan's geisha bars. Open every night except Sunday and holidays from 6 p.m. to midnight, performances are given by the geisha four times nightly. Foreigners are charged a special package deal of ¥8,800 ($70.40), which includes entrance and show charge, snacks, and three free drinks. Additional drinks are ¥1,000 ($8) each.

If you're looking for a quiet place for a drink, you can't find a more subdued place than **Lupin** ⑤, 5-5-11 Ginza (tel. 571-0750). Located in a tiny alley behind Ketel, a German restaurant, this tiny basement bar first opened back in 1928 and has changed little over the decades. Featuring a long wooden bar and wooden booths and cabinets, it's so quiet here you can hear yourself think. As though the world of jukeboxes and stereos has passed it by, no music is ever played here, making it a good place to come if you want to talk. Open every day except Sunday and holidays from 5 to 11 p.m., it charges from ¥1,000 ($8) to ¥1,650 ($13.20) for cocktails and ¥880 ($7.04) for a bottle of beer.

If you're looking for a more boisterous drinking atmosphere, I recommend **Yagura Chaya** ⑤, 7-2-22 Ginza (tel. 571-3494). This dining-drinking establishment is in the basement of the Riccar Building not far from the Imperial Hotel. Look for a traditional-looking restaurant with lockers just inside the door where you're supposed to deposit your shoes. Popular with businessmen, couples, and large groups, this place has a large menu that includes sashimi, yakitori, fish, oden, and pizza, so technically you could come here for both drinks and dinner. Prices are very reasonable; the average cost of most dishes is about ¥600 ($4.80), beer starts at ¥500 ($4), and sake starts at ¥580 ($4.64). Decorated with antiques and traditional craft objects, this pleasant spot is open from 5 p.m. to midnight.

Another lively watering hole is **Nanbantei**, 5-6-6 Ginza (tel. 571-5700), which is actually a chain of yakitori-ya. Open daily from 5 to 11:30 p.m., it combines the modern with the traditional in its decor. Its à la carte menu lists skewers of pork with asparagus, Japanese mushroom, large shrimp, quail eggs, gingko nuts, and chicken meatballs, among many other items, with pairs of skewers ranging from ¥500 ($4) to ¥1,000 ($8).

If you feel like dancing and twisting the night away to tunes of the '50s and '60s, head for the newly opened **Kento's,** located on the top floor of the Takiyamacho Building at 6-7-12 Ginza (tel. 572-9161). One of a chain of live-band entertainment houses that virtually created the current rage for oldies nostalgia, Kento's is open daily from 6 p.m. to 2:30 a.m. and charges a ¥1,400 ($11.20) cover. Beer starts at ¥550 ($4.40).

Sapporo beer is the lure of **Sapporo Lion**, 7-9-20 Ginza (tel. 571-2590). Located on Chuo Dori Avenue not far from Matsuzakaya department store, this beer hall with its mock Gothic ceiling is open daily from 11:30 a.m. to 11 p.m. Draft beer starts at ¥480 ($3.84), and the English-language menu lists snacks ranging from yakitori to salads, spaghetti, and shrimp with chili sauce.

Another beer hall, this one featuring Kirin beer, is **Kirin City,** 8-8-1 Ginza (tel. 571-9694). Open daily from 11 a.m. to 11 p.m., this relatively new and modern establishment offers beer starting at ¥425 ($3.40) and snacks that include assorted sausages, chili beans and crackers, and salads. There's also a daily lunch special available for ¥770 ($6.16).

Tokyo is filled with so-called cafébars, which are combination coffeeshops and bars popular with young Japanese women and couples. One such cafébar in Ginza is **Skyair Pronto,** 8-6-25 Ginza (tel. 571-7864), easy to find because it's on Namiki Dori Street. Open every day from 8 a.m. to 11 p.m. (to 9:30 p.m. on Saturday and Sunday), it serves as a neighborhood coffeehouse until 5 p.m., with a cup of coffee going for a mere ¥150 ($1.20) and cakes starting at ¥140 ($1.12). Starting at 5:30 p.m. it's bar time, with Suntory draft beer priced at ¥400 ($3.20).

Although the Takarazuka theater is actually in neighboring Yurakucho, taking in a show there could be part of an evening in Ginza, since it's not far away. **Takarazuka Kagekidan** is a world-famous all-female troupe that stages elaborate musical revues with dancing, singing, and gorgeous costumes. The first Takarazuka troupe formed back in 1912 in a resort near Osaka and gained instant notoriety because it was all women just as Kabuki is all men. When I went to see this troupe perform, I was surprised to see that the audience consisted almost exclusively of women.

Performances are held in Tokyo at the Tokyo Takarazuka Gekijo, 1-1-3 Yurakucho (tel. 591-8100), about six or seven months of the year, generally in March, April, July, August, November, and December and sometimes in June. Occasionally a performance is held in the Kabukiza theater in Higashi-Ginza. Inquire at the Tourist Information Center for more information. Tickets generally range from about ¥1,500 ($12) to ¥5,000 ($40).

And finally, if you're in Hibiya or Yurakucho, you might like to stop at the **Rainbow Lounge,** located on the 17th floor of the Imperial Hotel's main wing, 1-1-1 Uchisaiwaicho (tel. 504-1111), for a quiet drink and a view of the city lights. It's open from 11:30 a.m. to midnight and cocktails start at ¥1,200 ($9.60).

AKASAKA

Not quite as sophisticated as Ginza, Akasaka nonetheless has its share of exclusive geisha and hostess bars, hidden away behind forbidding walls and exquisite front courtyards. More accessible are the many drinking bars, cabarets, restaurants, and inexpensive holes-in-the-wall. Popular with both executive tycoons and ordinary office workers, as well as foreigners staying in one of Akasaka's many hotels, this district stretches from the Akasaka-mitsuke subway station along a couple of narrow streets to the Akasaka subway station and beyond.

Cocktail Lounges and a Beer Garden

Whenever I go to Akasaka, I like to start out the evening with a quiet drink at **Top of Akasaka,** on the 40th floor of the Akasaka Prince Hotel, 1-2 Kioi-cho (tel. 234-1111). From here I can watch the day fade into darkness as millions of lights and neon signs twinkle on in the distance. Fancy and romantic, this cocktail lounge with the city of Tokyo as a dramatic backdrop is open daily from 5 p.m. to 2 a.m., with most drinks averaging ¥1,300 ($10.04).

If you'd rather rest your eyes on a Japanese landscape garden than on neon lights, the **Garden Lounge,** across the street at the Hotel New Otani, 4-1 Kioi-cho (tel. 265-1111), looks out over a 400-year-old garden complete with waterfall, pond, bridges, and manicured bushes. Cocktails, which start at ¥1,400 ($11.20), are served every evening from 6 to 10 p.m. There's live-music entertainment every night except Sundays, for which there's a ¥300 ($2.40) cover charge Monday through Friday and a ¥600 ($4.80) charge on Saturday.

If the prices at these two places are a bit out of your range, you can still enjoy a view from the beer garden atop the **Suntory Building,** 1-2-3 Moto-Akasaka (tel. 470-1970), at Akasaka-mitsuke's main intersection above the subway station. Open during the summer months from 5 to 9:30 p.m., it has prices similar to those of most beer gardens, with various sizes of foaming mugs starting at ¥650 ($5.20). You can also come here for a meal or snack, with barbecued steak, which you cook at your own table, going for ¥2,400 ($19.20) per person. Classier than most rooftop beer gardens, this one is closed on Sunday and holidays.

The nearest subway station for all three of these establishments is Akasaka-mitsuke.

A Nightclub

A well-known nightclub in Akasaka is **Cordon Bleu,** 6-6-4 Akasaka (tel. 582-7800 in the evening and 448-0651 before 6 p.m.). Small and intimate, this 150-seat

AKASAKA

establishment is actually a dinner theater. Former guests have included boxer Muhammad Ali and the late John Lennon. It opens at 6 p.m. daily, and shows are performed two times a night, featuring topless Japanese and foreign dancers and singing. Full-course dinners, including free drinks, show, and service charges, run ¥19,800 ($158.40) per person. There's also an hors d'oeuvre course that includes snacks, drinks, and service charge for ¥15,800 ($126.40) per person. Closest subway station: Akasaka.

Bars

This **Henry Africa,** on the second floor of the Akasaka Ishida Building, 3-13-14 Akasaka (tel. 585-0149), is one of several Henry Africa pubs in Tokyo. Decorated in the theme of the African hunt, with elephant tusks, potted palms, and Tiffany-style lampshades, this place is very popular with young Japanese male and female office workers. Snacks, averaging ¥900 ($7.20) per dish, include sandwiches, tofu steak, and salads, and cocktails begin at ¥900 ($7.20). This place is open daily from 11:30 a.m. to 11:30 p.m., except on Saturday and Sunday, when it's open from 6 to 10:30 p.m.

Henry Africa is just a 30-second walk from the Akasaka subway station across from the TBS Kaikan television building on Hitotsugi Street.

Similar to Skyair Pronto in Ginza, this **Pronto,** 3-12-1 Akasaka (tel. 582-3717), serves as an inexpensive coffeehouse by day and a bar by night. Located on Tamachi Dori, it serves ¥150 ($1.20) cups of coffee from 8 a.m. to 5 p.m., thereafter serving alcohol until 11 p.m. Beer starts at ¥400 ($3.20), while cocktails begin at ¥470 ($3.76). It's closed Sunday and holidays.

ROPPONGI

Although perhaps not as well known to the outside world as Ginza and Shinjuku, Roppongi has emerged as the most fashionable and hip place to hang out for Tokyo's younger crowd. It's also a favorite with Tokyo's foreign community, including the many models in the city, businessmen, and English teachers. With more discos than any other place in town, Roppongi also has more than its fair share of jazz houses, restaurants, expatriate bars, and pubs. Some Tokyoites complain that Roppongi is too crowded, too trendy, and too commercialized, but for the casual visitor I think Roppongi offers an excellent opportunity to view what's new and hot in the capital city.

For orientation purposes, the center of Roppongi is Roppongi Crossing intersection, at the corner of which sits the garishly pink **Almond Coffee Shop.** The coffeeshop itself has mediocre coffee and desserts at terribly inflated prices, but the sidewalk in front of the store is the number one meeting spot in Roppongi. If you're going to meet a friend in Roppongi, this is probably where it will be.

If you need directions, there's a conveniently located koban (police box) cater-corner from the Almond Coffee Shop and next to the Mitsubishi Bank. They have a big map of the Roppongi area showing the address system, and someone is always there.

Live-Music Entertainment

Down-to-earth and featuring good jazz, **Birdland,** 3-10-3 Roppongi (tel. 478-3456), is a welcome refuge from Roppongi's madding crowd. It's located in the basement of the Square Building, well known for its eight discos on the upper floors. Small and cozy with candles and soft lighting, this jazz house features live music performed by Japanese musicians every day of the week. The doors open at 5:30 p.m., with live entertainment running from 7 p.m. to about 11:30 p.m. (from 8:30 p.m. to 1 a.m. on Saturday). Cover and music charges here total ¥2,700 ($21.60), and drinks start at ¥900 ($7.20).

Satin Doll, on the third floor of the Haiyuza Building, 4-9-2 Roppongi (tel. 401-3080), is a comfortable and established locale featuring Japanese jazz singers and musicians seven nights a week. It's open from 5:30 p.m. to midnight, and there are three or four sets each night. The table charge here ranges from ¥1,300 ($9.60) to ¥1,800 ($14.40) depending on who is appearing. Beer is ¥800 ($6.40), while cocktails begin at ¥770 ($6.16).

After Six, 3-13-8 Roppongi (tel. 405-7233), is different from the above jazz houses in that its musicians are imported from America. Opened more than 20 years ago, this tiny basement establishment offers live music every night except Sunday from 8 p.m. to 2 a.m. The cover charge here is ¥2,700 ($21.60), beer is ¥650 ($5.20), and cocktails start at ¥1,000 ($8).

Another well-known music house is **Pit Inn,** 3-17-7 Roppongi (tel. 585-1063). A no-frills basement establishment catering to a younger crowd, it boasts some of the finest in native and imported fusion and jazz rock. With doors opening every evening at 6:30 p.m., its first concert is at 7:30 p.m. and the second is at 10:30 p.m. Cover charge is ¥2,700 ($21.60) and up, depending on the band. Beer is ¥550 ($4.40).

Completely different from the establishments listed above, **Lollipop,** on the second floor of the Nittaku Building, 3-8-15 Roppongi (tel. 478-0028), features a house band that plays hits from the 1960s, Motown, and twist tunes. The dance floor is small and usually crowded, and there are even mirrored disco balls hanging from the ceiling. It's open from 6 p.m. to 3 a.m. every night except Sunday, when it closes earlier at midnight. There's a ¥2,000 ($16) cover charge, and you're required to order one food dish from the menu—mixed nuts are the cheapest at ¥660 ($5.28). Beer is ¥550 ($4.40), and the house wine is ¥650 ($5.20) a glass.

Similar to Lollipop but in business many more years, **Kento's,** in the basement of the Daini Building at 5-3-1 Roppongi (tel. 401-5755), is where enthusiasts of yesterday come to hear bands play music of the '50s and '60s. It's decorated with posters of such stars as Elvis and Connie Francis, has waiters with slicked-back hair, and even the microphones here are decades old. Although there's hardly room to dance, that doesn't stop the largely over-30 Japanese audience from doing a kind of rock 'n' roll twist in the aisles. Open daily from 6 p.m. to 2:30 a.m. (to midnight on Sunday), it charges ¥1,400 ($11.20) as a cover. Beer starts at ¥550 ($4.40), while drinks are around ¥700 ($5.60). If you get hungry you can order such snacks as chicken, pizza, spaghetti, sausage, salads, and a rather peculiar treat consisting of butter and raisins, all within the ¥600 ($4.80) to ¥1,000 ($8) price range.

Right next door and owned by the same company but with a slightly different twist, the **Cavern Club,** 5-3-2 Roppongi (tel. 405-5207), has bands performing exclusively Beatles music. Named after the famous Cavern Club in Liverpool where the Beatles got their start, the bar is an example of how good the Japanese are at imitation. Close your eyes and you might even be inclined to think you've been transported back in time to the real thing. Extremely popular with both Japanese and foreigners, it's packed on weekends—with long waiting lines—and unfortunately, reservations are not possible. Filled with photos and memorabilia of the famous foursome, the Cavern Club has a ¥1,400 ($11.20) music charge plus a 20% service charge. Beer starts at ¥550 ($4.40), cocktails are ¥770 ($6.16), and such snacks as mixed pizza, various salads, pasta, and rice dishes range from ¥770 ($6.16) to ¥1,100 ($8.80). Hours here are 6 p.m. to 2:30 a.m. daily (to midnight on Sunday and holidays).

If you like your music loud, you won't be disappointed at **Hot Co-Rocket,** 5-18-2 Roppongi (tel. 583-9409), located across from the Porsche dealership as you walk from Roppongi Crossing toward Tokyo Tower. Live reggae bands regale the crowds here, and there's a tiny dance floor. Cover charge, including two drinks, is ¥2,700 ($21.60). After that, all drinks start at ¥770 ($6.16). It's open from 7 p.m. to 3 a.m. every night except Sunday, when it's a disco only and closes earlier, at midnight.

One of my favorite places to watch live music and dance is at the **Malibu Club,** 3-3-29 Roppongi (tel. 588-8344). It has changed names and hands several times in

ROPPONGI

the few years of its existence, due partly to the wild crowd that tends to gather here (and thereafter create havoc in this otherwise rather quiet residential area—a sign outside Malibu's front door pleads with customers to refrain from urinating in the area, giving some indication of the kind of clientele that sometimes gathers here). Hours are 6 p.m. to midnight daily (the early closing hour is an offering of peace to the neighborhood), and there's a live *gaijin* (foreigner) band playing everything from rock 'n' roll to reggae nightly. The cover charge is ¥2,200 ($17.60) and cocktails are ¥850 ($6.80).

Discos

Roppongi is disco heaven, with approximately two dozen clustered in the vicinity. Since the set cover charge often includes drinks and food, they're usually the cheapest way to spend an evening.

The most famous disco building in Tokyo is the **Square Building,** at 3-10-3 Roppongi, with its eight discos on various floors. You can check them all out to see which one fits your tastes, but the current favorite seems to be the immensely popular (and very crowded) **Java Jive** in the basement (tel. 478-0088 or 478-0087). It's actually a two-level establishment, with loose-limbed Jamaican cutouts dancing in silhouettes along the wall (I think you'll have to see this for yourself to understand what I mean). Tropical palms and the flicker of electric candles add to the atmosphere—the dance floor even used to be sand, but it was covered over when it proved too difficult to writhe upon. At any rate, even though I list Java Jive here under the disco section, it actually features a live reggae and salsa band every night except disco night on Sunday (this place is so cavernous and crowded, however, that friends who have been here swear they never even realized there was a live band, though that was probably due to the condition they were in). Officially open every night from 6 p.m. to midnight and unofficially to 4 a.m., it charges men ¥4,000 ($32) and women ¥3,000 ($24), which includes ten tickets that can be used toward food or drinks. (Is the lesser charge for women a recognition of the fact that in Japan they earn less than men, or simply a way to lure women in?) A beer takes three tickets.

Also in the Square Building up on the fifth floor is **Buzz** (tel. 470-6391). Using the catchwords "Video & Dance," the gimmick here is the presence of screens that show rock videos, allowing you to dance while watching your favorite performer. For some reason, it's decorated "like a New York rooftop," whatever that is, complete with clouds painted on the walls and—get this—giant flies hanging from the ceiling! Open from 6 p.m. to 3 a.m. Sunday through Thursday and until 5 a.m. on Friday and Saturday, it charges ¥4,000 ($32) for men and ¥3,000 ($24) for women. Included in the admission are ten tickets; cocktails require four tickets.

Lexington Queen, located in the basement of the Daisan Goto Building at 3-13-14 Roppongi (tel. 401-1661), opened back in 1980 and has been swinging ever since. The list of its guests reads like a Who's Who of foreign movie and rock stars who have visited Tokyo—Stevie Wonder, Rod Stewart, Liza Minnelli, Sheena Easton, Joe Cocker, Dustin Hoffman, John Denver, Jacqueline Bisset, Spandau Ballet, Duran Duran, and Jennifer Beals, to name a few. One night when I was there the two lead musicians of Wham walked in. Another night it was Duran Duran. Popular with foreign models working in Tokyo, Lexington Queen is managed by Bill Hersey, who, appropriately enough, writes a gossip column for the *Weekender.* Evidently the best place to be on Halloween and New Year's if you can stand the crowds, this disco is officially open from 6 p.m. to midnight but usually doesn't shut down until 2 or 3 a.m. The cover charge of ¥4,000 ($32) for men and ¥3,000 ($24) for women includes free drinks and ¥1,000 ($8) worth of sushi.

Not far from Lexington Queen is a relatively new disco called **Area,** 3-8-15 Roppongi (tel. 479-3721), an appropriate name for a disco with the highest ceiling in town. Its spaciousness also belies the fact that it's actually in the basement of the Nittaku Building (the same building as Lollipop, described above). This is one of the best discos for dancing and observing—there are elevated blocks for the nerviest of dancers who like showing off what they can do. The lighting is good, curtains lower and rise on the dance floor, and the ceiling is mirrored. All in all, this place somehow seems a bit wilder than most, and it's popular mainly with young Japanese women. The charge here is ¥4,000 ($32) for females and ¥4,500 ($36) for males, which includes tickets for about six drinks. On Friday and Saturday and the eve before a national holiday, cover charges increase by ¥500 ($4). This place opens at 5 p.m. and closes at midnight.

I rather like the entrance to **Neo Japonesque**—through an inner courtyard past slinking black panthers with eyes glowing in the dark. The disco itself, however, located in the basement of the Roppongi Forum Building at 5-16-5 Roppongi (tel. 586-0050), is plainly decorated in black and white. The main attraction is laser beams, which are shot through the crowd and bounced off the walls to create a fantastic light show. Messages and designs of dots and lines are flashed against the wall. Catering to a slightly older disco crowd than the usual 20-year-olds, this place is also slightly more expensive, at ¥5,500 ($44) for men and ¥4,400 ($35.20) for women, which includes three free drinks. After that, drinks are ¥1,000 ($8) apiece. Hours are 7 p.m. to 3 a.m. daily. *Note:* The sign on the door says that no jeans are allowed and that men unaccompanied by women are not admitted.

Bars

Although popular nightspots in Tokyo seem to come and go with both the brilliance and durability of a shooting star, it's worth mentioning that the hottest place this moment seems to be **Déjàvu**, 3-15-24 Roppongi (tel. 403-8777). Some people find the chaotic and colorful walls gaudy, others find them interesting, but everyone seems to be trying to get into this small place—they'll even line up outside and wait. There's no cover charge, and most drinks are around ¥900 ($7.20). It's open daily from 8 p.m. to 4 a.m., and the clientele is mainly foreign.

Much larger is **Paradiso**, 3-13-12 Roppongi (tel. 478-4211), located in the basement of a building next to Lexington Queen disco. Popular, chic, and very avant garde, it goes on and on like some underground cavern. It closes early on Sunday at 11:30 p.m. but is open the rest of the week from 7 p.m. to 4 a.m. It has a ¥1,000 ($8) table charge, but for some reason it's more expensive if you want to sit at one of the counters: ¥2,200 ($17.60). Cocktails start at ¥1,300 ($10.40). Good for people-watching, but expensive.

Although it's a bit of a hike from Roppongi Crossing, **Bohemia**, 3-17-25 Nishi Azabu (tel. 401-8143), is worth the trek because of its music—jazz—and innovative interior. The brainchild of fashion designer Takeo Kikuchi and styled by British design revolutionary Nigel Coates, it's located in the basement of the Takeo Kikuchi Building, which made its debut back in 1986. High-tech and eccentric, Bohemia is decorated in what might be called "airplane," complete with old airplane seats on its lower level and metal parts of a plane built into a wall. The music selection is good, the atmosphere is relaxed and dignified, and on the last Saturday of each month there's even live jazz, for which there's a cover charge of ¥1,000 ($8). Otherwise, there's no entry fee and drinks start at ¥900 ($7.20). Hours here are 7 p.m. to 2 a.m.; closed Sunday. Bohemia is located in Nishi Azabu, about a ten-minute walk from Roppongi Crossing in the direction of Shibuya.

Similar to its counterpart in Akasaka, **Henry Africa**, at 3-15-23 Roppongi (tel. 405-9868), is devoted to the spirit of the hunt and even has a real rhinoceros head, purchased in Hong Kong. The first of the Henry Africa chain bars (there are now four), it's open from 6 p.m. until 2 a.m. Monday through Thursday, until 4 a.m. on Friday and Saturday, and until 11:30 p.m. on Sunday and holidays. Popcorn is served free, there's no table charge, and cocktails start at ¥850 ($6.80).

Charleston, 3-8-11 Roppongi (tel. 402-0372), has had its ups and downs in the years it's been open. Starting out as a hip place filled with foreign models, it now has a clientele and corresponding atmosphere that are different every time I've come here. Sometimes it's filled with U.S. military men on leave, sometimes with foreign businessmen dressed in suits, and sometimes with characters that must have dragged themselves up from the deep. At any rate, it's almost always filled with men, which may be just what you're looking for, but the recent opening of Déjàvu has given Charleston some pretty tough competition and has stolen away much of its clientele. Who knows, we may be witnessing the demise of one of Roppongi's oldest establishments. Hours are 6 p.m. to 6 a.m. daily. There's no cover charge, and cocktails start at ¥880 ($7.04).

Run by an Australian woman who knows almost all of her customers by name, **Maggie's Revenge,** at 3-8-12 Roppongi (tel. 479-1096), is another expatriate bar that is also popular with the Japanese. There's live music here every night, usually provided by a guitar or piano soloist. Sometimes the music's good, sometimes not —you take your chances, but since the music charge is only ¥660 ($5.28), what the heck. With hours from 6:30 p.m. to 3 a.m. every day except Sunday, Maggie's charges ¥660 ($5.28) for its smallest beer and ¥880 ($7.04) for most cocktails. It also has a good selection of liqueurs, brandies, and champagnes.

For a bit of old Germany right in the heart of Tokyo, pay a visit to **Ex,** 7-7-6 Roppongi (tel. 408-5487). Its name, appropriately enough, means "bottoms up," and although this is primarily a beer-drinking establishment, owner Horst serves hearty helpings of German food. There's no menu, so you just have to ask Horst what's cooking; but common dishes are schnitzel, various kinds of wurst, boiled ribs of pork, sauerkraut, and fried potatoes. Ex is a tiny place, just a half circle of a bar with enough seating for 15 people, but it's usually packed with German businessmen and expatriates who don't mind standing to drink their favorite brand of German beer. Eating is usually done good-naturedly in shifts. Hanging from the ceiling and on the walls are such German paraphernalia as beer mugs, soccer pennants, and photos of German celebrities who have visited Ex. A meal and beer here will cost an average of ¥3,000 ($24) to ¥4,000 ($32), and the hours are 5 p.m. to 2 a.m.; closed Sunday and holidays. The nearest subway station is Roppongi, from which it's about a five-minute walk.

If you like your music loud, the **Hard Rock Café,** at 5-4-20 Roppongi (tel. 408-7018), easily recognizable by King Kong scaling an outside wall, is the place for you. The inside looks like a modern Yuppie version of the local hamburger hangout joint. Cocktails start at ¥900 ($7.20), and the food includes barbecued chicken, burgers, and chili. Hours are 11:30 a.m. to 2 a.m. (11:30 p.m. on Sunday).

A very civilized yet casual meeting place is **Inter-National Station,** 6-1-5 Roppongi (tel. 423-4667), located on the diagonal street down from the Almond Coffee Shop on the right side (across from With disco). The owner, Hiro, speaks English and serves as the amiable bartender. There are little gadgets and toys to play with if you don't feel like talking, and the music is at a level that allows for conversation if you do. You can come here as a single female and not feel weird. Closed on Sunday, it's open from 7 p.m. to 5 a.m. every night except Friday and Saturday, when it remains open until 6 a.m. Beer starts at ¥700 ($5.60), and the extensive cocktail selections start at ¥900 ($7.20).

SHINJUKU

Northeast of Shinjuku is an area called Kabuki-cho, which undoubtedly has the craziest nightlife in all of Tokyo. A world of its own, it's sleazy, chaotic, crowded, vibrant, and safe—block after block of strip joints, massage parlors, pornography shops, peep shows, bars, restaurants, and lots of drunk Japanese men. I wouldn't be surprised to hear that (with the possible exception of Munich's Oktoberfest) there are more drunk people per square meter in Shinjuku than anywhere else in the world.

Shinjuku's primary night hot spot is called **Kabuki-cho** but it has nothing to do with Kabuki. Apparently at one time there was a plan to bring some culture to the area by introducing a Kabuki theater. The plan never materialized but the name stuck. To the east of Kabuki-cho is a smaller district called "Goruden Gai," which is pronounced "Golden Guy." It's a neighborhood of tiny alleyways leading past even tinier bars, each consisting of just a counter and a few chairs. Closed to outsiders, these bars cater to regular customers. On hot summer evenings the "mama-san" of these bars sit outside on stools and fan themselves, soft red lights melting out of the open doorways. Things aren't as they appear, however. These aren't brothels, they are simply bars, and the mama-san—well, more likely than not they're men instead of women.

Unfortunately, Goruden Gai sits on such expensive land that many of the bar owners are being forced to sell their shops. Some of them are already boarded up, awaiting land developers who are itching to build a high-rise. It's a shame, because this tiny neighborhood is one of the most fascinating in all of Tokyo. If you feel like a drink, the most accessible establishment in the area is **Bon's**, 1-1-10 Kabuki-cho (tel. 209-6334). It's located on the very eastern edge of Goruden Gai near Hanazono Shrine. Open from 6 p.m. to 5 a.m. every day except Sunday and holidays, when it closes at 3 a.m., it boasts a Mickey Mouse collection behind a glass case. Drinks are under ¥1,000 ($8), and the table charge is ¥600 ($4.80).

Even farther east is Shinjuku 2-chome, officially recognized as the gay bar district of Shinjuku. It's here that I was once taken to a host bar featuring young men in crotchless pants. Strangely enough, the clientele included both gay men and groups of young, giggling office girls. The place has since closed down, but Shinjuku is riddled with places bordering on the absurd.

The best thing to do in Shinjuku is simply walk around. In the glow of neon light, you'll pass everything from smoke-filled restaurants to hawkers trying to get you to step inside so they can part you from your money. If you're looking for strip joints, topless or bottomless coffeeshops, peep shows, or pornography shops, I leave you to your own devices, but you certainly won't have any problems finding them. In Kabuki-cho alone there are an estimated 200 sex businesses in operation, including so-called Turkish baths. A Turkish bath is a bathhouse where women are available for sex, usually at a cost of around ¥25,000 ($200) to ¥30,000 ($240). Although prostitution is illegal in Japan, everyone seems to ignore what goes on behind closed doors.

In 1985, however, a new law went into effect stipulating that sex-related businesses must close by midnight. Before then, Shinjuku's bright lights flamed until the crack of dawn and about 400,000 people visited Kabuki-cho nightly. Now things are closing up early and businesses are complaining about losing customers. Whether the law will continue to be enforced is anybody's guess.

A word for women traveling by themselves—forgo the experience of Shinjuku. Although you're relatively safe here with so many people milling about, you won't feel comfortable with so many inebriated fellows stumbling around. If there are two of you, however, you'll be okay. I took my mother to Kabuki-cho for a spin around the neon and we escaped relatively unscathed.

Besides walking around and dining in Shinjuku (check the Tokyo dining section in Chapter III), you can also hear music and visit inexpensive drinking establishments. **Shinjuku Pit Inn**, 3-16-4 Shinjuku (tel. 354-2024), is one of Tokyo's most famous jazz, fusion, and blues clubs, and features both Japanese and foreign musicians. An institution for more than 20 years, this basement locale with exposed pipes and bare concrete walls places more emphasis on good music than on atmosphere. There are three programs daily, at 11:30 a.m., 2:30 p.m., and 7:30 p.m., making it a great place to stop for a bit of music in the middle of the day. Prices range from ¥880 ($7.04) for the 11:30 a.m. show— ¥1,400 ($11.20) on weekends—to ¥2,700 ($21.60) and up for the evening show and include one drink. After that, all drinks cost ¥450 ($3.60). Since only a few snacks (like potato chips and sandwiches) are available, eat before you come.

If you're young and don't have much money, head for **Irohanihoheto**, 3-15-15 Shinjuku (tel. 359-1682), located on Yasukuni Dori Avenue next to Isetan Kaikan on the sixth floor. Described earlier in the budget category of restaurants in Chapter III, it has draft beer that starts at ¥380 ($3.04), and most food items are less than ¥450 ($3.60).

Although most of the night action in Shinjuku is east of the station, the west side also has an area of inexpensive restaurants and bars. Try **Volga** ⑤⑥, 1-4 Nishi Shinjuku (tel. 342-4996), an ivy-covered two-story brick building on the second alley behind the Odakyu-Halc department store. A yakitori-ya, it has an open grill facing the street. Open from 5 to 11 p.m. every night except Sunday and holidays, this smoky and packed drinking hall is typical of older establishments across the country. Rooms are tiny and simply decorated with wooden tables and benches, and the clientele is middle-aged. Very Japanese, it charges ¥650 ($5.20) for a beer.

Down the street from Volga is **Vagabond**, 1-4-20 Nishi Shinjuku (tel. 348-9109), owned by the effervescent Mr. Matsuoka, who can be found either here or over at Volga. Vagabond features a jazz pianist nightly beginning at 7:30 p.m.; astoundingly, there's no music charge, though there is a snack charge of ¥300 ($2.40) per person. Small and cozy, it's popular with foreigners who live close to Shinjuku Station and with Japanese who want to rub elbows with foreigners. The only drawback is its one bathroom, but as one customer pointed out, the queue is a good place to meet people. Beer starts at ¥550 ($4.40) and cocktails are ¥650 ($5.20). It's open every day from 5:30 to 11:30 p.m. except on Sunday, when it's open from 4:30 to 10:30 p.m.

If you feel like dancing, try **Java Bay**, 3-14-20 Shinjuku (tel. 225-5657), located on the fifth floor of the Theater Building on Yasukuni Dori east of Isetan department store. Brought to you by the same folks who operate the popular Java Jive in Roppongi, this disco also features black silhouettes, candles at the bar, tiny lights hanging from the ceiling as though they're stars, and water sprayed from the ceiling into a pond below. The music ranges from rap to reggae, and the crowd seems to be overwhelmingly female Japanese. The entry fee is ¥3,500 ($28) for guys and ¥2,500 ($20) for gals, which includes tickets for about two drinks.

After midnight foreigners in Shinjuku gravitate toward **69**, located in the basement of the Daini Seiko Building at 2-18-5 Shinjuku (tel. 341-6358). In the heart of the gay district, the clientele here is mostly heterosexual as far as I can tell. Playing primarily reggae music, this dive is tiny, and often so packed it reminds me of the Yamanote Line during rush hour. It usually has a healthy mix of both foreigners and Japanese, with an atmosphere unlike that of any other place in Tokyo. Hours are 8 p.m. until midnight.

After 69 closes, many who refuse to call it quits migrate around the corner to **New Sazae**, 2-18-5 Shinjuku (tel. 354-1745), located on the second floor of the Ishikawa Building. It's open from 10 p.m. to 6 a.m. Your first drink here will cost you ¥800 ($6.40), except on Saturday and the eve before a national holiday, when the first drink costs ¥1,000 ($8). Thereafter drinks cost ¥650 ($5.20). The crowd is a bit rowdy, but if you get this far you're probably where you belong.

Much more civilized is **Kinsmen,** located in the building next to 69 up on the second floor at 2-18-5 Shinjuku (tel. 354-4949). A gay bar, it welcomes customers of both persuasions and is a good place to come if you want to hear yourself talk. A beer here is ¥650 ($5.20) and hours are 9 p.m. to 5 a.m.; closed Tuesday.

Located right above Kinsmen is a tiny, one-room disco called **Boogie Boy** (tel. 354-3848), which, despite its name, seems to draw mainly a straight crowd. It opens every evening at 9 p.m. and closes at 5 a.m.; its ¥1,000 ($8) admission includes one drink.

HARAJUKU

One of the most popular districts among young Japanese by day, Harajuku doesn't have much of a nightlife district because of the city zoning laws. There are a few places scattered through the area, however, that are good alternatives if you don't like the crowds or the commercialism of Tokyo's nightlife districts.

One of the newest—and most expensive—nightclubs to open in Aoyama in recent years is **Blue Note,** 5-13-3 Minami Aoyama (tel. 407-5781). About a five-minute walk from Omote Sando Station on the street across from the Kinokuniya grocery store, it's cousin to the famous Blue Note in New York and manages to draw top-notch jazz musicians. Oscar Peterson, Sarah Vaughan, Tony Bennett, Betty Carter, Lou Rawls, Sergio Mendes, and the Milt Jackson Quartet have all performed here. The seating is for a mere 200 people, and everything is decorated in a blue haze in a near-exact replica of the New York original. Tickets generally range from about ¥7,000 ($56) to ¥13,000 ($104)—and they're still packing them in. If it's any consolation, you get one free drink. Blue Note is open every day except Sunday from 6 p.m. to 2 a.m., with two shows nightly at 7:30 and 10 p.m.

Oh God, 6-7-18 Jingumae (tel. 406-3206), is one of the best places to go if you find yourself in Harajuku after nightfall. Located at the end of an alley behind the Café de Rope, this mellow, dimly lit bar features a mural of a city at sunset. Open daily from 6 p.m. to 6 a.m., it shows free foreign films every night beginning at 6 p.m. (9 p.m. on weekdays). I've seen everything from James Bond to Fassbinder to grade B movies here. Drinks start at ¥700 ($5.60). A plus here is the two pool tables.

Upstairs on the second floor of the same building as Oh God is **Café la Bohème** (tel. 400-3406). As you'd expect, the atmosphere is rather Bohemian, with lots of plants, ceiling fans, antiques, and Tiffany-style lampshades. This bar-restaurant has a long cocktail list—most drinks cost around ¥900 ($7.20)—and serves inexpensive pizza, pastas, and salads. It's open seven days a week from 11:30 a.m. to 5 a.m.

In an attempt to lure adults back to teenybopper-overrun Harajuku, NTT created the Harajuku Quest building in 1988. In its basement is one of the slickest bars to hit the Harajuku scene, **Libre.** Decorated in extravagant marble, strange metal parts, and giant-size tables and benches hewn from Canadian walnut, this bar-restaurant is run by Asahi Beer and features a great lunch and dinner menu. Draft beer is ¥600 ($4.80), cocktails are ¥1,000 ($8). Located on Omote Sande Dori Avenue not far from Harajuku Station at 1-13-14 Jingumae (tel. 470-7870), it's open daily from 11:30 a.m. to 2 p.m. and 5 to 11 p.m.

Located on Meiji Dori Avenue in the direction of Shibuya, **Crocodile,** 6-18-8 Jingumae (tel. 499-5205), is popular with the young and describes itself as a casual rock 'n' roll club with live bands ranging from rock to blues to jazz-fusion, reggae, and experimental. With an interesting interior and a good atmosphere, it opens daily at 6 p.m.; live music is played from around 8:30 to 11 p.m. The cover charge usually ranges from about ¥1,500 ($12) to ¥2,500 ($20).

NIGHTLIFE MISCELLANY

There are a number of organized **evening tours** that take in such activities as Kabuki or a geisha party (see the description in the Tokyo sightseeing sections). If your time is limited you might be interested in such a tour, though be warned that they are very tourist-oriented. Prices range from about ¥6,500 ($52) to ¥14,000 ($112).

If you're here in the summer months, a lovely place to go for either a meal or drinks is the **Hanezawa Beer Garden,** 3-12-15 Hiro, Shibuya-ku (tel. 400-6500). An outdoor beer garden spread under paper lanterns and trees, this pleasantly traditional-looking place is open daily from 5 to 9:30 p.m., April through September. A mug of foaming beer starts at ¥600 ($4.80), and such meals as sukiyaki, shabu-shabu, and Mongolian barbecue can be cooked at your table for ¥2,700 ($21.60) to ¥4,400 ($35.20) per person. Note that if you want shabu-shabu or sukiyaki, however, you should notify the restaurant the day before. The nearest station is Ebisu, from which you should take a taxi.

Finally, word should be mentioned here about Tokyo's so-called **love hotels.** Usually found close to large entertainment districts and along major highways, such hotels do not provide sexual services themselves but, rather, offer rooms for rent by the hour to lovers. Altogether there are an estimated 35,000 such love hotels in Japan, usually gaudy structures shaped like ocean liners or castles and offering such extras as rotating beds or mirrored walls. The most famous love hotel in Tokyo is the Meguro Emperor, a white castle with turrets that resembles Cinderella's castle at Disneyland. Located beside a river not far from Meguro Station at 2-1 Shimo-Meguro (tel. 494-1211), it has been undergoing extensive renovation and is slated for reopening in the summer of 1990. Other love hotels can be found near the pleasure districts of Shibuya, Shinjuku, and Asakusa. You'll know you've wandered into a love-hotel district when you notice discreet entryways and—a dead giveaway—hourly rates posted near the front door.

EXPLORING THE ENVIRONS OF TOKYO

If your stay in Tokyo is long enough, you should consider taking excursions to some of the sights in the vicinity. Kamakura and Nikko, for example, rank as two of the most important historical sites in Japan, while the Fuji-Hakone-Izu National Park serves as a huge recreational playground for the residents of Tokyo. The Tourist Information Center has a color brochure called *Side Trips from Tokyo* with information on Kamakura, Nikko, Hakone, and the Mount Fuji area. The T.I.C. also has a map of Tokyo's vicinity.

1. Kamakura

If you take only one trip to the environs of Tokyo, it should be to Kamakura, especially if you're unable to include the ancient capitals of Kyoto and Nara in your travels. Located about an hour south of Tokyo by train, Kamakura is a delightful hamlet with no fewer than 65 Buddhist temples and 19 Shinto shrines spread throughout the village and in the surrounding wooded hills. Most of these were built centuries ago, when a warrior named Yoritomo Minamoto seized political power and established his shogunate government in Kamakura back in 1192. Wanting to set up his seat of government as far away as possible from what he considered to be the corrupt imperial court in Kyoto, Yoritomo selected Kamakura because it was easy to defend. The village is enclosed on three sides by wooded hills and on the fourth by the sea, a setting that lends dramatic background to the many temples and shrines.

Although Kamakura remained the military and political center of the nation for 1½ centuries, the Minamoto clan was in power for only a short time. After Yoritomo's death, both of his sons were assassinated, one after the other, after taking up military rule. Power then passed to the family of Yoritomo's widow, the Hojo family. They ruled until 1333, when the emperor in Kyoto dispatched troops to crush the shogunate government. Unable to halt the imperial troops, 800 soldiers retired to the Hojo family temple at Toshoji, where they all disemboweled themselves in ritualistic suicide known as seppuku.

Today a thriving seaside resort with a population of 175,000, Kamakura, with its old wooden homes, temples, shrines, and wooded hills, makes a pleasant one- or two-day excursion from Tokyo.

The beach of Kamakura, called Yuigahama Beach, is nothing special, however, consisting of muddy-looking sand often strewn with litter and unbelievably crowded in summer. (One friend of mine told me he came to Kamakura Beach on a hot weekend day and couldn't find enough space in which to spread his towel, the beach was so packed with bodies. Perhaps he was exaggerating but you get the general idea.) Most amusing are the surfers. The waves are usually nothing more than ripples but that doesn't stop the surfing fanatics, who promptly fall off if a big wave does roll along unexpectedly.

ORIENTATION

Before departing from Tokyo, be sure to pick up a pamphlet entitled *Hakone and Kamakura* from the Tourist Information Center. It has a map of Kamakura and tells how to get to some of the village's most important sights by bus. You can reach Kamakura by train on the Yokosuka Line, which departs about every 10 to 20 minutes from the Yokohama, Shinagawa, Shimbashi, and Tokyo JR stations. The trip from Tokyo Station takes one hour, while the trip from Shinagawa takes 49 minutes.

If you have a full day for sightseeing, I suggest getting off the train at Kita-Kamakura Station, which is just before Kamakura Station. If you have only a few hours, head straight for Kamakura Station and begin your sightseeing there. The tourist information window (tel. 22-3350) is located immediately to the right as you exit from Kamakura Station's east exit in the direction of Tsurugaoka Hachimangu Shrine. Open daily from 9 a.m. to 6 p.m., it has a map in both Japanese and English, and the staff can direct you to the sights you want to see. Transportation in Kamakura is by bus, as well as a wonderful two-car train that will take you to Hase Station where you can see the bronze statue of the Great Buddha.

The **telephone area code** for Kamakura is 0467.

THE SIGHTS

Because Kamakura has so many temples and shrines, it's obvious that visitors must limit their sightseeing to those that offer the most in terms of historical and architectural importance. The most worthwhile places of interest in Kamakura are generally considered to be Tsurugaoka Hachimangu Shrine, the Great Buddha, and Hase Temple, while visitors with more time on their hands should take in a few other temples as well. Keep in mind that most temples and shrines open about 8 a.m. and close around 5 p.m.

Around Kita-Kamakura Station

If you leave the train at Kita-Kamakura Station, within a minute's walk you can reach **Engakuji Temple.** Founded in 1282, this Zen temple was once one of the most important and imposing temples in Kamakura, and although it's been reduced in grandeur by fires and earthquakes through the centuries, it's still considered by many to be the best remaining example of architecture from the Kamakura period. A

sacred tooth of Buddha is enshrined in a wooden structure called *Shari-den* on the precinct grounds. This temple sponsors a five-day Zen training course at the end of July, as well as intensive zazen meditation courses several times a year.

A five-minute walk from Kita-Kamakura Station is **Tokeiji Temple,** a Zen temple founded in 1285. Visited now for its flower blossoms of plum (mid-February), magnolias and peach (late March/April), peonies (late April/May), and irises (May/June), visitors back in feudal times came to Tokeiji for quite another reason. Known as the Divorce Temple, it was a place of refuge for women fleeing from cruel husbands and disagreeable mothers-in-law. Back in those days only men could divorce their wives. Women had no legal recourse, but if they could make it to Tokeiji they were given protection from their husbands and allowed to live among the nuns.

If you feel like walking, you can go on to Tsurugaoka Hachimangu Shrine in about 30 minutes, stopping in at **Kenchoji Temple** on the way, which along with Engakuji is considered to be among the five best Zen temples in Kamakura. Note the magnificent cedars surrounding the temple, as well as the ceremonial gate held together with wooden wedges. If you don't feel like walking, return to Kita-Kamakura Station and go one more stop to Kamakura Station.

Around Kamakura Station

About a ten-minute walk from Kamakura Station, **Tsurugaoka Hachimangu Shrine** is the spiritual heart of Kamakura. It was built by Yoritomo and dedicated to Hachiman, the Shinto god of war who served as the clan deity of the Minamoto family. The pathway to the shrine is along Wakamiya Oji, a cherry tree-lined pedestrian lane that was also constructed by Yoritomo back in the 1180s so that his oldest son's first visit to the family shrine could be accomplished in style with an elaborate procession. Along the pathway are souvenir and antique shops selling lacquerware and folk art, and three massive torii gates set at intervals along the route to signal the approach to the shrine.

As you ascend the steps to the vermillion-painted Hachimangu Shrine, note the gingko tree to the left. This is supposedly the site where Yoritomo's second son was ambushed and murdered back in 1219. The gingko tree itself is thought to be about 1,000 years old.

On the shrine grounds are the **Kanagawa Prefectural Modern Art Museum,** which exhibits contemporary art from 10 a.m. to 5 p.m. every day except Monday, and the **Kamakura Municipal Museum,** which displays a collection of carvings, bronzes, swords, calligraphy, lacquerware, and other historical objects from neighboring shrines and temples. This museum is open from 9 a.m. to 4 p.m.; closed Monday.

Although it's a little bit far out of the way, it might pay to make a visit to **Zeniarai-Benten Shrine,** about a 20-minute walk west of Kamakura Station. This shrine is dedicated to the goddess of good fortune, and on Oriental zodiac days of the snake, worshippers believe that if you take your money and wash it in spring water in a small cave on the shrine grounds, your money will double or triple itself later on. Of course, this being modern Japan, don't be surprised if you see a bit of ingenuity. My Japanese landlady told me that when she visited the shrine she didn't have much cash on her, so she washed something she thought would be equally as good—her plastic credit card.

Around Hase Station

To get to the attractions around Hase Station, you can go by bus, which departs from in front of Kamakura Station, or you can go by the Enoden train line, a two-car train that putt-putts its way seemingly through backyards on its way from Kamakura Station to Hase and beyond to Enoshima and Fujisawa. Since there's only one track, trains have to take turns going in either direction. I would suggest taking the bus from Kamakura Station directly to the Great Buddha, walking to Hase Shrine, and then taking the Enoden train back to Kamakura Station.

Probably the most famous attraction in Kamakura is the **Great Buddha,** the Daibutsu, which at 37 feet and 93 tons is the second-largest bronze image in Japan. The largest Buddha is in Nara, but in my opinion the Kamakura Daibutsu is much more impressive. For one thing, whereas the Nara Buddha sits enclosed in a wooden structure that reduces the effectiveness of its size, the Kamakura Buddha sits outside in a dramatic backdrop of wooded hills. Cast in 1252, the Kamakura Buddha was once housed in a temple, but a huge tidal wave destroyed the wooden structure and the statue has sat under the sun, snow, and stars ever since. I also prefer the face of the Kamakura Buddha. I find it more inspiring and divine, as though with its half-closed eyes and calm, serene face it's somehow above the worries of the world—wars, natural disasters, calamities, and sorrow. It's as though it represents the plane above human suffering, the point at which birth and death, joy and sadness, merge and become one and the same. If you want, you can go inside the statue—it's hollow.

Nearby, **Hase Temple,** constructed on a hill with a sweeping view of the sea, is the home of an 11-headed gilt statue of Kannon, the goddess of mercy. At more than 30 feet it's the tallest wooden image in Japan and was made from a single piece of camphorwood back in the 8th century. The legend surrounding this Kannon is quite remarkable. Supposedly two wooden images were made from the wood of a huge camphor tree. One of the images was kept in Hase not far from Nara, while the second image, if you can imagine, was given a short ceremony and then duly tossed into the sea to find a home of its own. The image drifted 300 miles eastward and washed up on shore but was thrown back in again because all who touched it became ill or incurred bad luck. Finally, the image reached Kamakura, where it gave the people no trouble. This was interpreted as a sign that the image was content with its surroundings and Hase Temple was erected at its present site.

As you climb up the steps to Hase Temple and its Kannon, you'll encounter statues of a different sort. All around you will be statues of Jizo, the guardian deity of children. Although originally parents came to Hase Temple to set up statues to represent their children in hopes that the deity would protect and watch over them, through the years the purpose of the Jizo has changed. Now they represent miscarried, stillborn, or, most frequently, aborted children. Altogether there are more than 10,000 of these statues here, and some of them, which you can buy on the temple grounds for as much as $400, are fitted with hand-knitted caps and sweaters. The effect is quite chilling.

WHERE TO DINE

A lovely spot for taking lunch is at **Raitei** ⑤⑦, Takasago (tel. 32-5656), which you can reach by taking a bus departing from platform 3 in front of Kamakura Station (make sure the bus is going to the Takasago bus stop, since not all buses from this platform go there). The wonder of this restaurant is that you can have either an inexpensive meal of soba (Japanese noodles) or a princely feast of kaiseki. Situated on the edge of Kamakura in verdant countryside, Raitei commands a fine view of a garden, stone and wooden pagodas, and a wooded ridge in the distance. There's a path circling through the garden that will lead you past a house serving snacks (how about stopping off for a beer here after lunch? There are benches outside where you can enjoy the view), a bamboo grove, stone images, and a miniature shrine. The stroll along the pathway takes about 20 minutes.

But back to your meal. At the entrance gate to the restaurant you pay an entrance fee of ¥500 ($4), which counts toward the price of your meal at the restaurant. Noodles are served daily from 11 a.m. "until the sun goes down" (about 6:30 p.m. in summer) on the bottom floor of an old house—walk around to the back entrance. There's an English menu, and dishes available include plain soba for ¥650 ($5.20), soba with chicken for ¥1,200 ($9.60), tempura soba for ¥1,600 ($12.80), and a soba teishoku (set meal) for ¥2,400 ($19.20). Obento lunch boxes are available for ¥4,400 ($35.20).

If you feel like splurging you can also eat kaiseki cuisine here, but you must make a reservation beforehand. Kaiseki here costs ¥5,500 ($44), ¥7,700 ($61.60), and ¥11,000 ($88) for full meals. Kaiseki meals are served until 8 p.m.

A Note on Japanese Symbols

Many hotels, restaurants, and other establishments in Japan do not have signs showing their names in English letters. Appendix II lists the Japanese symbols for all such places appearing in this guide. Each establishment name in Japanese symbols is numbered, and the same number appears in an oval in the text following the boldfaced establishment name. For example, in the text Osaka's **Hotel Hokke Club** ⑯⑭ is number 164 in the Japanese symbol list in Appendix II.

Monzen ㊽, Yamanouchi 407 (tel. 25-1121), is a modern-looking kaiseki restaurant located just across the tracks from Engakuji Temple in Kita-Kamakura. Open daily from 11 a.m. to 7:30 p.m., the main dining hall is on the second floor and seating is on tatami mats at low tables. Although there's no English menu, there are pictures of various meals available, which start at ¥2,700 ($21.60) for the obento teishoku. Vegetarian *shojin-ryori* dishes can be ordered, and prices begin at ¥4,400 ($35.20).

Located close to Yuigahama Beach on the main road leading from the beach to Kamakura Station is **Miyokawa** ㊾, 2-22-5 Yuigahama (tel. 23-0911), a modern restaurant constructed to resemble a country farmhouse with heavy crossbeams and latticed windows. It specializes in shabu-shabu and steaks. The menu is in Japanese only, but there's a pamphlet with pictures of set meals. Shabu-shabu starts at ¥3,500 ($28), while a full-course shabu-shabu meal with sashimi appetizer and dessert costs ¥5,000 ($40). Steak courses are ¥3,600 ($28.80). There are also obento lunch boxes costing ¥2,200 ($17.60) and up, which include various items from sashimi to tempura. Hours are 11 a.m. to 10 p.m. daily.

There's a second Miyokawa located on the road between the Daibutsu and Hase Temple, about a four-minute walk from both, at 1-16-17 Hase (tel. 25-5556). Specializing in kaiseki, this modern restaurant offers an obento lunch box for ¥2,200 ($17.60), a Japanese steak for ¥3,300 ($26.40), and mini-kaiseki starting at ¥4,900 ($39.20). Hours are 11 a.m. to 10 p.m. daily.

Closer to Kamakura Station, **Kayagi-ya** ㉑, 2-11-16 Komachi (tel. 22-1460), is situated on Wakamiya Oji Street next to a lumberyard. This modest, older-looking restaurant serves seven different kinds of inexpensive eel dishes. My favorite is the *unagi donburi* (eel served on top of rice) for ¥1,300 ($10.40). Closed on Friday, it's open the rest of the week from noon to 6:30 p.m.

Nakamura-an ㉖, 1-7-6 Komachi (tel. 25-3500), is a noodle restaurant located on a side street off Wakamiya Oji Avenue between Kamakura Station and Hachimangu Shrine. Open from 11:30 a.m. to 6 p.m. daily except Thursday, it's easy to spot because of the front window where you can watch noodles being made. There's also a front window display of plastic food, so it's easy to make your selection. Noodles start at a low ¥600 ($4.80).

WHERE TO STAY

A cheerful, elegant, and cozy ryokan, **Kaihinso**, 4-8-14 Yuigahama (tel. 0467/22-0960), is in a quiet neighborhood not far from the beach. It was formerly the Western-style house of a baron; new additions have been grafted onto the old house in a very unobtrusive way and provide a total of 20 guest rooms. Most of the rooms are in Japanese style with tatami mats and deep Japanese bathtubs, but a few

Western-style rooms with beds are also available. The management here is very friendly and receptive to foreigners, a tremendous help if you need directions for your sightseeing tours. Rates average ¥16,000 ($128) to ¥18,000 ($144) per person but depend on the number of people per room and whether it's peak season in summer or on weekends. Prices include two meals and service, and Western breakfasts are available. You can also experience communal bathing in the ryokan's public baths, which are separated for men and women.

Kamakura Hotel ⑥, 2-22-29 Hase (tel. 0467/22-0029), is an older hotel built around 1920. Located between Hase Station and the sea, some of its rooms have balconies and the more expensive rooms have good views of the sea. Japanese-style rooms range from ¥14,000 ($112) to ¥22,000 ($176) per person, which always including two meals; the higher-priced rooms are very cheerful, with lots of windows and shoji screens. Western-style rooms with either twin or double beds are the same price. If you'd rather not take your meals at the hotel, Western-style rooms range from ¥7,500 ($60) to ¥12,000 ($96) per person.

---

2. Nikko

Since the publication of James Clavell's *Shogun,* many people have heard of Ieyasu Tokugawa, a real-life powerful shogun of the 1600s on which Clavell's fictional shogun was based. Quashing all rebellions and unifying Japan under his leadership, Tokugawa built such a military stronghold that his heirs continued to rule Japan for the next 250 years without serious challenge.

If you'd like to join the millions of Japanese who through the centuries have paid homage to this great man, travel 87 miles north of Tokyo to Nikko, where a mausoleum was constructed in his honor in the 17th century and where his remains were laid to rest. Nikko means "sunlight," an apt description of the way the sun's rays play upon this sumptuous mausoleum of wood and gold leaf. Surrounding the mausoleum are thousands of cedar trees in a 200,000-acre national park. A trip to Nikko can be combined with a visit to Lake Chuzenji, a jewel of a lake about an hour's bus ride from the mausoleum.

ORIENTATION
Before leaving Tokyo, pick up a leaflet called *Nikko* from the Tourist Information Center. It gives the train schedule for both the Tobu Line, which departs from Asakusa Station, and JR trains that depart from Ueno Station. The T.I.C. also has some color brochures with maps of the Nikko area. The easiest and fastest way to get to Nikko is on the Tobu Line's limited express, which costs ¥2,280 ($18.24) one way and takes almost two hours. If you have a rail pass you'll probably want to take one of the JR trains departing from Ueno, in which case you'll have to change trains in Utsunomiya.

At any rate, the Tobu and JR stations in Nikko are located almost side by side in the village's downtown area. Tokugawa's mausoleum is on the edge of town, which you can reach by foot in about a half hour or by bus from either the Tobu or JR station in about ten minutes. When I last checked, no one at the **Nikko Tobu Station tourist information counter** spoke English, but they do have an English map. An additional tourist office is located about halfway to Toshogu Shrine from the train stations on the main road leading through town (tel. 0288/54-2496). Closed on Wednesday, it's open the rest of the week from 9 a.m. to 5 p.m.

The **telephone area code** for Nikko is 0288.

THE SIGHTS
The first indication that you're nearing Tokugawa's mausoleum, which is called Toshogu Shrine, is a vermillion-painted bridge arching over the rushing Daiyagawa

River. It was built in 1636, and for more than three centuries only shoguns and their emissaries were allowed to cross it. Even today mortal souls like us are prevented from completely crossing it because of a barrier at one end.

As you climb the steps opposite the bridge and across the road which leads into a forest of cedar, the first major group of temple buildings you'll come across belong to **Rinnoji Temple,** whose Sanbutsudo Hall contains three images of Buddha. You can buy a combination ticket here for ¥580 ($4.64), which allows entry to Rinnoji, Toshogu Shrine, and neighboring Futarasan Shrine, and another Tokugawa mausoleum. The combination ticket is also sold at Toshogu Shrine. At Rinnoji Temple there's also a small garden and museum, which you can visit for an additional fee of ¥300 ($2.40).

The most important and famous structure in Nikko, of course, is **Toshogu Shrine,** which contains the tomb of Ieyasu Tokugawa. Although Ieyasu died in 1616, construction of the mausoleum did not begin until 1634, when his grandson, Iemitsu Tokugawa, undertook the project as an act of devotion. It seems that no expense was too great in creating the monument. Some 15,000 artists and craftsmen were brought to Nikko from all over Japan, and after two years' work they had succeeded in erecting a group of buildings more elaborate and gorgeous than any other Japanese temple or shrine. Rich in colors and carvings, Toshogu Shrine is bedecked with an incredible amount of gold leaf used in gilding. Altogether 2.4 million sheets of gold leaf (that would cover an area of almost six acres) were used. The mausoleum was completed in 1636, almost 20 years after Ieyasu's death.

Toshogu Shrine is set in a grove of magnificent ancient Japanese cedars planted by a feudal lord named Masatsuna Matsudaira. It took him 20 years to plant these cedars back in the 1600s, and 13,000 of the original trees are still standing. They add a sense of dignity to the mausoleum and the shrine, standing as silent sentinels over Ieyasu's tomb. They seem timeless, adding a continuity to the individual struggles of the men who have passed beneath them and to the faces that come and go.

You enter Toshogu Shrine via a flight of stairs that pass under a huge stone torii gateway, one of the largest in Japan. On your left is a five-story, 115-foot-high pagoda. Although normally pagodas are found only at temples, this pagoda is just one example of how both Buddhism and Shintoism are combined at Toshogu Shrine. After climbing a second flight of stairs, turn left, where you'll presently see the Sacred Stable, which houses a sacred white horse. Look for the three monkeys carved above the stable door fixed in the pose of "hear no evil, speak no evil, and see no evil."

At the next flight of stairs is **Yomeimon Gate,** considered to be the central showpiece of Nikko. It's popularly known as the Twilight Gate, implying that it could take you all day until twilight to see everything carved onto it. Painted in red, blue, and green, and decorated with gilding and lacquerwork, this gate has about 400 carvings of flowers, dragons, birds, and other animals. It's almost too much to take in at once.

To the left of the gate is the hall where the portable shrines are kept, as well as **Honchido Hall,** famous for its dragon painting on the ceiling. If you clap your hands under the painting, the echo supposedly resembles a dragon's roar. You can visit the shrine's main hall, where guides will explain its history and main features in Japanese. To the right of the main hall is a gate with a carving of a sleeping cat above it. Beyond that are 200 stone steps leading past cedars to Ieyasu's tomb, which costs an additional ¥330 ($2.60).

Directly to the west of Toshogu Shrine is **Futarasan Shrine,** the oldest building in the district (from 1617), which has a pleasant garden. On the shrine's grounds is the so-called ghost lantern, enclosed in a small wooden structure. According to legend it used to come alive at night and sweep around Nikko in the form of a ghost. It apparently scared one of the guards so much that he struck it with his sword, the marks of which are still visible on the lamp's rim.

Past Futarasan Shrine is the **second mausoleum,** that of Iemitsu, grandson of

Ieyasu and the third Tokugawa shogun. Completed in 1653, it's not nearly so ornate as the Toshogu Shrine. It's also not as crowded, making it a pleasant last stop on your tour of Nikko.

After touring Nikko's shrines, you can catch a bus not far from the vermillion-painted bridge for **Lake Chuzenji** (you can also board it in front of Tobu Station). The ride takes about 50 minutes, winding higher and higher along hairpin roads. The view is breathtaking—I've even seen bands of monkeys along the side of the road. On Lake Chuzenji are many ryokan, souvenir stores, and coffeeshops, making it a popular holiday resort. Things to do include visiting Chuzenji Temple beside the lake, going on an hour-long boat cruise, and visiting nearby Kegon Falls, a stunning 250-foot waterfall considered to be one of the most beautiful falls in Japan.

FOOD AND LODGING

The most famous hotel in Nikko is the **Nikko Kanaya Hotel,** 1300 Kami-Hatsuishi (tel. 0288/54-0001). First established back in 1873, it has played host to a number of VIPs—Charles Lindbergh, Indira Gandhi, Helen Keller, Eleanor Roosevelt, David Rockefeller, Shirley MacLaine, and Albert Einstein, to name a few. A distinguished-looking, old-fashioned hotel secluded on a hill above the red sacred bridge, it combines the rustic heartiness of a European country lodge with elements of old Japan.

All rooms are Western-style twins and doubles, the differences in their prices based on room size and view. Room rates range from ¥7,500 ($60) to ¥22,000 ($176) for single occupancy and ¥9,000 ($72) to ¥27,000 ($216) for double. During the peak seasons of New Year's, Golden Week in early May, summer vacation in July and August, and in October, rates rise an additional ¥5,000 ($40) to ¥8,000 ($64). Rooms are rather old-fashioned but cozy, giving you the feeling that things haven't changed all that much around here in the past 50 years. Facilities at this grand old hotel include a small outdoor swimming pool, an outdoor skating rink, and a Japanese garden.

Even if you don't spend the night here you might want to come for a meal in the hotel's quaint dining hall. Since it's only a ten-minute walk from Toshogu Shrine, you can easily combine it with your sightseeing tour of Nikko. Lunch is served from noon to 2 p.m. and dinner from 6 to 7:30 p.m. I suggest Nikko's specialty, locally caught rainbow trout, available for ¥3,000 ($24) in three different styles of cooking. I had mine cooked Kanaya style, covered with soy sauce, sugar, and sake, grilled and served whole. Other items on the menu include veal cutlet Cordon Bleu, lobster thermidor, king salmon steak, and tenderloin with goose liver and truffle, all in the ¥3,000 ($24) to ¥9,000 ($72) price range. There are also sandwiches, spaghetti, and pilaf, averaging ¥1,600 ($12.80) per item.

A member of the Japanese Inn Group, **St. Bois,** 1560 Tokorono (tel. 0288/53-3399), is a country-style lodge located atop a hill and nestled in among pine trees on the edge of Nikko. About a 15-minute walk north of Tobu Station and a 30-minute walk from Toshogu Shrine, it's very pleasant and peaceful here, making it an inexpensive getaway from Tokyo. Rooms without private bath are ¥4,400 ($35) for one person and ¥8,300 ($66) for two. Rooms with private bathroom go for ¥4,700 ($38) and ¥9,000 ($72) respectively. Of the 11 rooms here, 9 are Western style, with beds, and 2 are Japanese style. Five of the rooms that face the front have their own balconies. Breakfast is available for ¥500 ($4) if you let the manager know the night before, and dinner is also available for ¥2,000 ($16) if you order it by 3 p.m.

Pension Turtle, 2-16 Takumi-cho (tel. 0288/53-3168), is also a member of the Japanese Inn Group. Although it's not as picturesque as St. Bois, it's closer to Toshogu Shrine and is run by the very friendly Fukuda family. A new two-story house on a quiet side street beside the Daiyagawa River, this 11-room establishment charges ¥3,600 ($29) to ¥5,200 ($42) for a single and ¥7,200 ($58) to ¥9,400 ($75) for a double; the higher prices indicate rooms with a private bathroom. Rooms are bright and cheerful, in both Japanese and Western styles. Dinners for

¥1,200 ($9.60) to ¥2,000 ($16) and breakfasts for ¥500 ($4) to ¥800 ($6.40) are available if you order them in advance.

There are also a couple of youth hostels in Nikko, both about a 20-minute walk from the train station. **Nikko Youth Hostel,** 2854 Tokorono (tel. 0288/54-1013), charges ¥2,300 ($18.40) for both members and nonmembers. **Nikko Daiyagawa Youth Hostel,** 1075 Nakahatsuishi (tel. 0288/54-1974), accepts only card-carrying members, who pay ¥2,000 ($16) a night. Meals are extra.

Most ryokan are strung along the shores of Lake Chuzenji. Keep in mind, however, that the majority of them are closed during the winter months and are open only from about mid-April to mid-November. It's best to reserve a room in advance if you want to stay in one of these ryokan, which you can do at a travel agency. You can also make a reservation upon arrival at Nikko at the accommodation-reservation window inside Nikko Tobu Station; they'll charge a ¥200 ($1.60) to ¥500 ($4) fee but will take care of all arrangements for you. Ryokan owners in this area do not speak English and aren't likely to take you in if you simply show up at their door (I've done it this way but I had to try several places before I finally found a sympathetic manager). If it's peak season, you should definitely reserve a room before leaving Tokyo at a travel agency such as the Japan Travel Bureau. Most ryokan start at ¥10,000 ($80) per person and include two meals; rates rise to ¥15,000 ($120) on holidays. There's little difference in what they offer: basically a tatami room, coin-operated TV, hot tea, breakfast and dinner served in your room, and a cotton kimono. Be sure to specify if you want a lakeside view.

If you want to stay at Lake Chuzenji but prefer a Western-style hotel, the **Nikko Lakeside Hotel,** 2482 Chugushi (tel. 0288/55-0321), is a conveniently located, modern 100-room hotel on the rim of the lake not far from Kegon Falls. It's open throughout the year. Each room comes with a private bathroom and begins at ¥18,500 ($148) for a twin or double during the winter months, rising to ¥33,000 ($264) during peak seasons. Facilities include tennis courts and a pleasant restaurant with a view of the lake where you can enjoy a meal of lake trout for ¥2,500 ($20).

3. Mashiko

Mashiko is a small village known throughout Japan for its *Mashiko-yaki,* distinctive, heavy, country-style pottery. A visit to Mashiko is usually combined with a trip to Nikko, since both are located not far from the town of Utsunomiya, north of Tokyo. Getting to Mashiko involves taking the train from either Asakusa or Ueno to Utsunomiya, and from there transferring to a bus. You can also reach Mashiko by taking the Tohoku Line from Ueno as far as Oyama, changing there for a local train to Mashiko. In any case, the trip from Tokyo to Mashiko takes three hours or more. Since the major attraction in Mashiko is its pottery shops and kilns, and there's little in the way of restaurants and accommodations, I suggest coming here just for the day, returning to Tokyo or traveling on to Nikko before nightfall.

Mashiko gained fame back in 1930 when the late Shoji Hamada, designated a National Living Treasure, built a kiln in this tiny village and introduced Mashiko ware throughout Japan. Other potters have since taken up his technique, producing ceramics for everyday use, including plates, cups, vases, and tableware. Altogether there are about 50 pottery shops in Mashiko, along with a number of kilns, where you can simply wander in, watch the craftsmen at work, and even try your own hand at throwing or glazing a pot.

The whole process of making pottery, for example, can be seen at **Tsukamoto Pottery** (tel. 2-3223), and visitors can try their hand at kneading clay, turning the potter's wheel, or hand-molding a pot. At the **Mashiko Reference Collection Museum (Mashiko Sankokan)** (tel. 2-5300), open from 9:30 a.m. to 4:30 p.m. every day except Monday, New Year's, and the month of February, you can see works by Hamada as well as a collection of Eastern and Western glass, ceramics, fabrics, furniture, and paintings. Charging an admission of ¥500 ($4), the museum is housed in several thatch-roofed structures, which served as Hamada's workshop. His kilns are still there, built along a sloping hill and once heated with wood.

The **telephone area code** for Mashiko is 02857.

WHERE TO EAT

There are a number of inexpensive restaurants spread along Mashiko's main street, where the pottery shops are located. They all sell the same types of dishes, including tempura, curry rice, and noodles ranging from about ¥600 ($4.80) and up. The **Yamani Restaurant** (tel. 2-4783), for example, located next to the Mashiko Pottery Center, serves the usual tempura starting at ¥1,000 ($8), curry rice for ¥600 ($4.80), and noodles for ¥500 ($4). Since there's little difference between the restaurants, however, you may want to try the one closest at hand when hunger strikes.

---

4. Yokohama

There are few attractions in Yokohama to warrant a visit by the short-term traveler to Japan. However, if you find yourself in Tokyo for an extended period of time, Yokohama is a pleasant and easy destination for an afternoon or one-day excursion.

A rather new city in Japan's history books, Yokohama was nothing more than a tiny fishing village when Commodore Perry arrived in the mid-1800s and demanded that Japan open its doors to trade. Nevertheless, the village was selected by the shogun as one of several ports to be opened for international trade, and in 1859 the first foreign settlers arrived. To accommodate them, Yokohama was divided into two parts—Outside the Barrier (Kangai) and Inside the Barrier (Kannai). A canal was dug between the two and the foreigners were placed in Kannai, ostensibly to protect them from irate samurai who were disgruntled with these foreign intruders and might try to assassinate them. It's probably not too far-fetched to assume, however, that this separation between foreigner and Japanese was also meant to isolate the strangers. After all, following more than two centuries of isolation from the rest of the world, the Japanese were bound to be at least a little cautious of foreigners and their habits. But as Japan entered the Meiji Period in full swing, relations relaxed and the foreigners moved to a nearby hill known as The Bluff.

Even so, throughout the 19th century the foreigners in Yokohama continued to be a source of great curiosity for the Japanese, who came from as far away as Tokyo to look at them and to see the Western goods that were being imported and unloaded at Yokohama's port. Serving as the capital city's port, Yokohama grew by leaps and bounds, becoming so important that the first railroad in Japan linked Tokyo with Yokohama, reducing the ten-hour journey by foot to less than an hour.

Today Yokohama is still an important international port and still supports a large international community, with many foreigners continuing to reside on The Bluff. Yokohama also has a large Chinese population, descendants of immigrants who moved here shortly after Japan opened itself to trade. With a population of almost three million, Yokohama is Japan's second-largest city.

ORIENTATION

Yokohama is easily reached by train from Tokyo, Shimbashi, Shinagawa, Yurakucho, and Shibuya stations, and most trains take 30 minutes or less. The majority of attractions in Yokohama are centered in the old part of town around Kannai Station, which is connected to Yokohama Station by subway, train, bus and even boat. If you want to go directly to Kannai Station, the Keihin Tohoku Line from Tokyo Station, with stops in Yurakucho, Shimbashi and Shinagawa, reaches Kannai in about 45 minutes.

The **Yokohama Municipal Tourist Association** is located in the Silk Center, 1 Yamashita-cho, Naka-ku (tel. 045/641-5824), close to the harbor and an easy walk from Kannai Station. The Silk Center also contains the Silk Museum, an attraction you shouldn't miss. The Yokohama Tourist Association is one of the best and most efficient I've come across in Japan, and its English map is excellent. The staff speaks English and can give you all kinds of brochures on the city. Yokohama also has the Home-Visit System whereby you can visit with a Japanese family. Be sure to call the Yokohama Tourist Association to set up the appointment at least a day in advance of your intended visit. The tourist office is open Monday through Friday from 8:45 a.m. to 5 p.m. and on Saturday from 8:45 a.m. to 12:45 p.m. Next door to the city tourist office is the **Kanagawa Prefectural Tourist Office,** where you can also obtain information on Hakone and Kamakura.

The **telephone area code** for Yokohama is 045.

THE SIGHTS

Because Yokohama is a relatively new city by Japanese standards, it doesn't have ancient temples or shrines, a castle, or a centuries-old landscape garden. In fact, most Japanese come to Yokohama for the same reason they've always come here—to soak up the cosmopolitan atmosphere created by the city's foreign population. They visit The Bluff, the nearby Foreign Cemetery where many of Yokohama's first international residents are buried, Yokohama port, and Chinatown, where there are a number of fine Chinese restaurants. For the foreigner visiting Yokohama, I would say that Kannai with its Silk Museum, the historical museums, the port, and neighboring Chinatown hold the most attraction, along with a superb park on the outskirts of town.

Around Yokohama Station

Just across the street from Yokohama Station's east exit is **Sogo** (tel. 465-2111), Japan's largest department store (before this store opened a few years back, Tokyo's Seibu in Ikebukuro claimed first place). Its 92,665 square yards of retail space and restaurants could occupy your entire day. There are lots of restaurants up on the tenth floor that stay open until 10 p.m. Otherwise, hours for the store are 10 a.m. to 7 p.m.; closed on Tuesday.

Incidentally, right beside Sogo are **shuttle boats** called Sea Bass, which deposit passengers at Yamashita Park, described later in this chapter. Boats leave about three times an hour and afford a view of the city from the water. The fare is ¥450 ($3.60), considerably cheaper than the harbor cruises.

Around Kannai and Sakuragicho

Your first stop in Kannai should be the Silk Center, in which you'll find both the tourist office and the **Silk Museum,** 1 Yamashita-cho, Naka-ku (tel. 641-0841). For many years after Japan opened its doors, silk was its major export, and most of it was shipped to the rest of the world from Yokohama, the nation's largest raw silk market. In tribute to the role silk has played in Yokohama's history, this museum has displays showing the metamorphosis of the silkworm and how silk is obtained from cocoons and has exhibits of various kinds of silk fabrics as well as gorgeous kimonos. I was astonished to learn that as many as 10,000 cocoons are needed to make just one kimono. By the way, today Japan produces about 33% of the world's silk, but the

Japanese are such avid fans of the expensive fabric that they use 50% of the world's total, which means that they must import silk to satisfy the demand. The Silk Museum is open from 9 a.m. to 4:30 p.m. every day except Monday and admission is ¥300 ($2.40).

Just a minute's walk from the Silk Center is the **Yokohama Archives of History,** 3 Nippon O-dori (tel. 201-2100), with exhibits and pictures relating to the opening of Japan and the establishment of Yokohama as an international port. It's a very small museum and can be toured quickly just to get an idea of early Yokohama. Hours are 9:30 a.m. to 4:30 p.m.; closed Monday and days following public holidays. The entrance fee is ¥200 ($1.60).

If you're really a museum buff, you should wander over to the **Kanagawa Prefectural Museum (Kanagawa Kenritsu Hakubutsukan),** 5-chome Minaminaka-dori (tel. 201-0926). It's close to Sakuragicho Station, about a 20-minute walk from the Silk Center. In a Western-style building constructed in 1904 to house the nation's first modern foreign-exchange bank, it exhibits items related to natural science, archeology, history, and folklore in Kanagawa Prefecture. Yokohama, incidentally, is Kanagawa Prefecture's chief town. The museum is open from 9 a.m. to 4 p.m. (closed on Monday and the last Friday of the month), and the entrance fee is ¥200 ($1.60). Included in the collection are rooms of a traditional Japanese farmhouse, tools for farming and silk production, and models of both Perry's ships and of Japan's first train, which ran between Tokyo and Yokohama.

Also near Sakuragicho Station is the newly opened **Yokohama Museum of Art,** 1-4 Midoricho (tel. 221-0300). With an emphasis on works by Western and Japanese artists since the 1850s, the museum's ambitious goal is to collect and display art that reflects the mutual influence between the modern art of Europe and Japan since the opening of Yokohama's Port in 1859. Hours here are 9:30 a.m. to 5:30 p.m. daily; admission is ¥300 ($2.40) and up depending on the exhibit.

Not far from the Silk Center is **Yamashita Park,** laid out after the huge earthquake in 1923 that destroyed much of Tokyo and Yokohama. Japan's first seaside park, Yamashita Park is a pleasant place for a stroll along the waterfront, where you have a view of the city's mighty harbor. At one end of the park is the 348-foot-high Marine Tower, with an observation platform which provides an excellent view of the city, port, and sometimes even Mount Fuji. It's open from 10 a.m. to 9 p.m. (6 p.m. in winter) and charges ¥650 ($5.20). Moored at a pier off the park is the *Hikawa Maru,* an old transoceanic liner built in 1930. Its maiden voyage was to Seattle, after which it crossed the Pacific 238 times until it was retired in 1960. Today it houses a restaurant and beer garden.

From Yamashita Park you can also take a sightseeing **tour of Yokohama harbor** by boat that, according to the boat company's English brochure, "will fill up your complete satisfactions." Tours, conducted only in Japanese, are operated approximately every half hour or hour from 10:30 a.m. to 6:30 p.m. The 40-minute cruise costs ¥750 ($6), the 60-minute tour costs ¥1,200 ($9.60), and the 90-minute cruise costs ¥2,000 ($16).

If you're interested in visiting **The Bluff** and the **Foreign Cemetery,** they're located south of Yamashita Park across the Nakamura River. From The Bluff you have another view of the harbor from Harbor View Park. Also of interest is **Chinatown,** with about 100 Chinese restaurants and shops selling Chinese foodstuffs and souvenirs. Refer to the dining section below for information on Chinese restaurants.

Sankei-en Garden

In my opinion Sankei-en Garden is the best reason for visiting Yokohama. Although it's not old, it's a lovely park with a number of old historical buildings that were brought here from other parts of Japan, all situated around streams and ponds. It was laid out back in 1906 by Tomitaro Hara, a local millionaire who made his fortune exporting silk. As you wander along the gently winding pathways, you'll see a villa built in 1649 by the Tokugawa Shogunate clan, tea arbors, a 500-year-old pagoda, and a farmhouse built in 1650 without the use of nails. No matter what the season, the views here are beautiful.

The easiest way to reach Sankei-en Garden is by bus 8, which departs from Yokohama Station and winds its way through Kannai and past Chinatown before reaching the Sankei-en-mae bus stop. It's therefore easy to combine Sankei-en and Kannai in a day's sightseeing tour. In fact, you may want to come first to Sankei-en Garden and then take the bus back to Kannai, ending up in Chinatown for dinner. Sankei-en is open from 9 a.m. to 4:30 p.m. and admission is ¥400 ($3.20).

WHERE TO EAT

Chinatown consists of one main street and dozens of offshoots, with restaurant after restaurant serving Chinese food. Most of them have plastic food displays or pictures of their menu, so let your budget be your guide.

If you feel like splurging, **Kaseiro** ⓺, at 164 Yamashita-cho (tel. 661-0661), is much more elegant than most other Chinese restaurants, though it hasn't escaped the stereotypically ornate decor of reds and golds. It serves Pekinese food and you should expect to spend at least ¥4,000 ($32) and up per person. Hours are 11:30 a.m. to 8 p.m. daily.

One note I'd like to add is that unless you arrive by taxi it's a bit frustrating searching for a particular restaurant in Chinatown because there are so many of them. You may want simply to wander around and choose one that suits your fancy.

If you'd rather have Japanese food, head for **Janomeya** ⓺, 126 5-chome Isezaki-cho (tel. 251-0832). It's located toward the end of the Isezaki-cho pedestrian shopping street, which stretches south from Kannai Station. At night this area lights up as one of Yokohama's nightlife districts. The plastic food display in its front window shows various dishes available, which include sukiyaki, shabu-shabu, sashimi, and tempura. Since there's no English menu, you might want to make your choice before going inside. Open every day (except the second Wednesday of the month) from 11:30 a.m. to 9:30 p.m., it serves sukiyaki beginning at ¥2,400 ($19.20) and shabu-shabu at ¥3,600 ($28.80). Set meals range from ¥5,500 ($44) to ¥7,700 ($61.60).

5. Kawasaki

With a population of almost one million, Kawasaki has pretty much been swallowed up by the Tokyo-Yokohama metropolis, and as you travel by train it's virtually impossible to see where Tokyo ends and Kawasaki begins. A sprawling industrial complex with some of the largest Japanese manufacturing plants located here, Kawasaki is one of those cities better left unseen. However, tucked away in a corner of woods and hills is a delightful open-air museum called **Nihon Minka-en** (tel. 044/922-2181), where traditional thatched houses and other historical buildings have been preserved. If you don't have the chance to visit Takayama or Shirakawa in the Japan Alps or a similar museum in Takamatsu, on the island of Kyushu, this may be your only chance to examine closely the way rural Japanese lived in centuries past.

Altogether 22 structures have been brought here from other parts of Japan and have been artistically situated on various wooded hills. Most of them are heavy-beamed thatched houses, but there are also warehouses, a shrine, and a Kabuki stage from a small fishing village. All the buildings are open to the public so that you can wander in and inspect the various rooms. The oldest houses date from about 300 years ago and were usually homes for extended families. Imagine how it must have been to live back then, with the family gathered around the central hearth on cold winter nights. An English pamphlet tells about each of the buildings, and there are many explanations throughout in English.

The Nihon Minka-en is open every day except Monday from 9:30 a.m. to 4:30 p.m. and charges ¥300 ($2.40) admission. To reach the open-air museum, take the Odakyu Line from Shinjuku to the Mukogaoka-yuen Station, which is the 18th stop. Minka-en is about a 15-minute walk from the south exit of the station. Because there are no special restaurants in this area, I suggest you either bring a picnic lunch to eat at the open-air museum or return to Shinjuku to take advantage of the many wonderful restaurants there.

In addition to Nihon Minka-en, there's one other attraction in Kawasaki you might like to know about, though it takes place only once a year, in mid-April. That's when the **Jibeta Matsuri festival** takes place. This rather unusual festival extolls the joys of sex and points out perhaps better than anything else the differences in attitude that the Japanese and Westerners have had about sex throughout the centuries. Whereas in the West sexuality has a long history of repression expressed largely through religious beliefs, the Japanese have always taken a rather open and natural attitude toward sex without the burden of guilt and without treating it as a moral issue.

At any rate, this festival takes place at Kanayama Shrine, which has on display huge phalluses as well as various sexual objects, and the highlight of the festival is a parade in which various phallic objects are carried through the streets. As with many festivals in Japan, this one is tied to a legend. According to a well-known Japanese myth, a long time ago there was a beautiful maiden who was afflicted by a terrible demon. Twice she tried to marry, but on both wedding nights her grooms died while they tried to consummate the marriage—the demon had bitten off the symbol of their manhood. As you can imagine, the father of the poor girl was unsuccessful in securing her another husband. Finally, a blacksmith heard about her story and, taking pity, he resolved to help her and applied to the protective deities of metalsmiths at his local shrine for assistance. There he had a vision in which he was instructed to create a metal phallus and use that to deflower the girl. The plan worked, the demon broke its teeth on the metal phallus, and everyone lived happily ever after. In gratitude to the deities the smith presented the metal phallus to the shrine and from that time on the deities were known as the Deities of the Metal Phallus.

You can get some unusual photographs at this annual event. Inquire at the Tokyo Tourist Information Center for the exact date. To get to Kanayama Shrine, also known as the Shrine of Kanamara-sama, take the Keihin Kyuko Line from Shinagawa Station to Keihin Kawasaki Station, and transfer to the Kawasaki Daishi Line for the ten-minute trip to Kawasaki Daishi Station. From there it's only a few minutes' walk.

6. Mount Fuji

Mount Fuji, affectionately called "Fuji-san" by the Japanese, has been revered as sacred since ancient times. Throughout the centuries Japanese poets have written about it, painters have painted it, pilgrims have flocked to it, and more than a few people have died on it. Without a doubt Mount Fuji has been photographed more than anything else in Japan.

Visible on a clear day from as far as 100 miles away, Mount Fuji is stunningly impressive. At 12,388 feet it towers far above anything else around it, a symmetrical cone of almost perfect proportions. Mount Fuji is majestic, grand, and awe-inspiring. To the Japanese Mount Fuji symbolizes the very spirit of Japan. However, even though Mount Fuji is something every visitor to Japan should see, few ever do. Unfortunately, Fuji-san is almost always cloaked in clouds. If you catch a glimpse of this mighty mountain (which you can do from the bullet train between Tokyo and Nagoga), consider yourself extremely lucky.

The most popular thing to do regarding Mount Fuji is to climb it. Several well-

marked trails leading to the top are open throughout the year, but because of snow and inclement weather from fall through late spring, the "official" climbing season from July 1 to August 31 is considered the best time to make an ascent. It's also the most crowded time of the year. Ask any Japanese where he would go if he could travel to only one place in his lifetime, and most likely he will answer Mount Fuji. Consider the fact that there are approximately 120 million Japanese, most of whom wouldn't dream of climbing the mountain outside the "official" two months it's open, and you begin to get the picture. More specifically, about 400,000 people climb Fuji-san every year, mostly in July and August and mostly on weekends. In other words, if you plan on climbing Mount Fuji on a Saturday or Sunday in the summer, go to the end of the line, please. I've seen pictures of a trail leading up to Fuji's summit taken on a hot summer's day and it was a solid, unbroken line of hikers stretching all the way up the face of the mountain, one right behind the other. It was as though everyone were waiting in a queue to get into a movie being shown at the top, but I have no doubt in my mind that these Japanese hikers were enjoying themselves immensely, reveling in the togetherness, happy that they were all sharing in the spirit of the climb up old Fuji-san.

In other words, unless you climb Mount Fuji outside the summer months it will not be a solitary venture. Rather, the experience should be viewed as something you can do together with a determined group of Japanese who are following in their fathers' footsteps by making pilgrimages to the top (women, incidentally, weren't allowed to climb Mount Fuji until 1868). Climbing Mount Fuji is not difficult, but it *is* extremely strenuous. You'll be amazed by the number of children and old people doggedly making their way to the top of the highest mountain in Japan.

ORIENTATION

As part of a larger national park called Fuji-Hakone-Izu National Park, Mount Fuji is only 60 miles away from Tokyo. Of the handful of trails leading to the top, Kawaguchiko is the one most often used by Tokyoites. All trails are divided into ten different stages, and Kawaguchiko Fifth Stage is the starting point for most climbs to the top. It takes about five hours to reach the summit and three hours to descend back to the Fifth Stage.

The easiest way to reach Kawaguchiko Fifth Stage is by direct bus from Hamamatsucho or Shinjuku Bus Terminal, in operation several times daily from July 13 to August 31. The fare from Hamatsucho Bus Terminal is ¥2,500 ($20) one way, and from Shinjuku Bus Terminal it's ¥2,300 ($18.40). Reservations for the bus are required and can be made through a travel agency, such as the Japan Travel Bureau. You can also reach the Fifth Stage by taking the bus or train to Kawaguchiko Station and then transferring to a bus. Bus service to the Fifth Stage is suspended, however, from November to April, a time when Mount Fuji is blanketed in snow and should be considered too dangerous for the novice climber.

More information regarding train and bus schedules to Mount Fuji and its surrounding area can be obtained from the Tokyo Tourist Information Center in leaflets called *Mt. Fuji and Fuji Five Lakes* and *Climbing Mt. Fuji*.

CLIMBING MOUNT FUJI

Don't be disappointed when your bus deposits you at Kawaguchiko Fifth Stage, where you'll be bombarded with an overflow of souvenir shops, restaurants, and busloads of tourists. Most of these tourists aren't climbing to the top, and as soon as you get past them and the blaring loudspeakers, you'll find yourself on a steep rocky path surrounded only by scrub brush and hikers on the path below and above you. After a couple of hours you'll probably find yourself above the roily clouds, which stretch in all directions. It will be as if you're on an island, barren and rocky, in the middle of an ocean.

You needn't have had climbing experience to ascend Mount Fuji, but you do need stamina. It goes without saying that you also need good walking shoes. It's possible to do it in tennis shoes, but if rocks are wet they can get awfully slippery. You should also bring a light plastic raincoat (which you can buy at souvenir shops at the Fifth Stage), a sun hat, and a sweater for the evening. It gets very chilly on Mount Fuji at night.

As for sleeping, there are about 30 mountain huts along the Kawaguchiko Trail above the Fifth Stage, but they're very primitive, providing only a futon and toilet facilities. The cost without meals is ¥3,800 ($30.40) per person, and with meals it's ¥6,000 ($48). When I stayed in one of these huts, dinner consisted of dried fish, rice, bean-paste soup, and pickled vegetables; breakfast was exactly the same.

The usual procedure for climbing Mount Fuji is to start out in early afternoon, spend the night near the summit, get up early in the morning to watch the sun rise, climb the rest of the way to the top, and then make the descent. In recent years, however, a new trend has started in which climbers arrive at the Fifth Stage late in the evening and then climb through the night to the top with the aid of flashlights. After the sunrise they then make their descent. That way they don't have to spend the night in one of the huts.

Climbing Mount Fuji is definitely a unique experience, but there is a saying in Japan: "Everyone should climb Mount Fuji once; only a fool would climb it twice."

7. Hakone

As part of the Fuji-Hakone-Izu National Park, Hakone is one of the closest and most popular resorts for residents of Tokyo. Blessed with beautiful scenery, Hakone has about everything a vacationer could wish for—hot-spring resorts, mountains, lakes, breathtaking views of Mount Fuji, and diversions in the form of interesting historical sites. It's located about 50 miles southwest of Tokyo, and you can tour Hakone as a day trip. But adding an overnight stay near Lake Hakone, or in the mountains, where you can soak in the water of hot springs, is much more pleasant. If you plan to return to Tokyo, I suggest leaving your luggage in storage at your Tokyo hotel and traveling to Hakone with only an overnight bag.

ORIENTATION

Before leaving Tokyo, pick up the *Hakone and Kamakura* leaflet available from the Tourist Information Office. It lists the time schedules for the extensive network of trains, buses, cable cars, and pleasure boats throughout the Hakone area. In fact, it's Hakone's transportation system that makes a trip here so pleasurable. Starting out by train from Tokyo, you can then switch to a small two-car train that zigzags up the mountain, change to a cable car and then a smaller ropeway, and end your trip with a boat ride across Lake Hakone, stopping off to see major attractions along the way. From Lake Hakone (from either Togendai or Hakone-machi), you can then board a bus bound for Odawara Station (an hour's ride), where you can then take the train back to Tokyo. If you're spending the night in Hakone, you can take a bus from Hakone Lake to the accommodations described later in this section in Tonosawa, Miyanoshita, and Sengoku.

The most economical way to see Hakone is to purchase the Hakone Free Pass, which despite its name isn't free but does give you a round-trip ticket from Shinjuku Station to Odawara or Hakone Yumoto on the Odakyu Romance Car and includes almost all other modes of transportation in Hakone, including the two-car train, cable car and ropeway, boat ride and Hakone Tozan bus. Valid for four days, it costs ¥5,380 ($43.04) if you take the nonstop Romance Car and ¥4,760 ($38.08) if you take the slower, ordinary train. If you have a rail pass, you should take the Shinkansen bullet train from Tokyo Station to Odawara. From there, you can travel on the private railways, cable cars, buses, and boats for the ¥3,500 ($28) Hakone

Free Pass, also valid for four days. Both passes—which also provide discounts on several of Hakone's attractions, including a ¥100 (80¢) discount to the Hakone Open-Air Museum—can be purchased at any station of the Odakyu Railway, including Shinjuku Station.

The **telephone area code** for Hakone is 0460.

WHAT TO DO

If you plan on spending only one day in Hakone, you should leave Tokyo by 9 a.m. Otherwise, you can arrange your itinerary in a more leisurely fashion and devote more time to Hakone's attractions, reaching your hotel or ryokan by about 5 or 6 p.m.

The Train Trip

If you leave Tokyo via the Shinkansen, make sure your train stops in Odawara, the gateway to Hakone. In Odawara, transfer to the Hakone Tozan Railway, a small tram that winds its way through forests and over streams as it travels upward to Gora, making several switchbacks along the way. If you're on the Romance Car, you should switch to the Hakone Tozan Railway at Yumoto Station. At any rate, between Odawara and Gora the Tozan Railway makes about a dozen stops along the way, including Tonosawa and Miyanoshita, two hot-spring spa resorts with a number of old ryokan and hotels (refer to my food and lodging recommendations). Some of these ryokan date back several centuries, from the days when they were on the main thoroughfare to Tokyo, the old Tokaido Highway. If the train trip has worn you out, you can stop for some open-air bathing at the public baths behind Yumoto Station, called **Kappa Tengoku** ⑥⑤ (tel. 0460/5-6121). Probably the closest outdoor baths in the vicinity of Tokyo, they're open from 10 a.m. to 10 p.m. and charge a ¥500 ($4) admission.

The next-to-the-last stop on the Tozan Railway is Chokoku-no-mori, the first stop on our sightseeing itinerary. Here is where you'll find the **Hakone Open-Air Museum** (tel. 0460/2-1161), with more than 100 sculptures by artists from around the world, including Rodin, Henry Moore, Imoto Atusushi, and Yodoi Toshio. Using nature itself as a dramatic backdrop, this museum spreads through glens and gardens and over ponds. There's also an indoor exhibit of paintings and sculpture, including a museum of Picasso's works. Open from 9 a.m. to 5 p.m. (to 4 p.m. in winter), it charges ¥1,500 ($12) admission.

By Cable Car and Ropeway

From Gora you can travel by cable car, which leaves every 15 minutes and arrives 9 minutes later at the end station of Sounzan, making several stops along the way. One of the stops is Koen-Kami, which is only a minute away from the **Hakone Art Museum** (tel. 2-2623). Open from 9 a.m. to 4 p.m. every day except Thursday, it displays ancient Japanese pottery and ceramics, from the Jomon Period (around 4000 B.C.) to the Edo Period. Included are water jars, terra-cotta taken from burial grounds which date from before the 7th century, Bizen ware from Okayama, and Imari ware of the 17th century. A lovely Japanese landscape garden of moss and bamboo is on the museum grounds. Admission is ¥800 ($6.40).

From Sounzan you board a small ropeway for a long haul down the mountain to Togendai, which lies beside Lake Hakone, known as Lake Ashinoko in Japanese. Before reaching Togendai, however, get off at the first intermediary station, Owakudani, the ropeway's highest point. Here you can take a 30-minute hike along a nature path through Owakudani, which means "Great Boiling Valley." Sulfurous steam escapes from fissures in the rock, testimony to volcanic activity still present here. In Owakudani there's also the **Natural Science Museum** (tel. 0460/4-9149), with displays on the fauna, flora, geology, and volcanic origins of Hakone. It's open from 9 a.m. to 5 p.m. and charges an admission of ¥350 ($2.80). Before starting back down on the ropeway, stop off for a drink at the second floor of the ropeway station, where you have fantastic views of Hakone and of Mount Fuji if it's not being fickle about showing itself.

Lake Ashinoko (Lake Hakone)

From Togendai you can take a pleasure boat across Lake Ashinoko, referred to as "Lake Hakone" in English brochures. Believe it or not, one of the boats crossing the lake is a replica of a centuries-old man-of-war. The trip takes about half an hour to cross the lake to Hakone-machi and Moto Hakone, two resort towns right next to each other on the southern edge of the lake. This end of the lake affords the best view of Mount Fuji, a view often depicted in tourist publications.

In Hakone-machi you should visit the **Hakone Barrier Gate** (Hakone Sekisho), a reconstructed guardhouse. Originally built in 1618, it served as a checkpoint on the famous **Tokaido Highway,** which connected Edo (present Tokyo) with Kyoto. In feudal days, local lords, called daimyo, were required to spend alternate years in Edo, and their wives were kept in Edo as hostages so that the lords wouldn't plan rebellions while in their homelands. This was one of the points along the highway where travelers were checked. Although it was possible to sneak around it, violators who were caught were promptly executed. A nearby museum illustrates the history of the Tokaido Highway.

Between Hakone-machi and Moto-Hakone is part of the Tokaido Highway itself. Lined with ancient and mighty cedars, 1¼ miles of the old highway follows the curve of Lake Ashinoko and makes a pleasant stroll (unfortunately, a road of the 20th century has been built right beside it). In Moto-Hakone is **Hakone Shrine,** revered by samurai until the Meiji Restoration in 1868. Especially picturesque is its red torii gate standing in the water.

FOOD AND LODGING

Japan's ryokan sprang into existence to accommodate the stately processions of daimyo and shogun as they traversed the roads between Edo and the rest of Japan. Many of these ryokan were built along the Tokaido Highway, and some of the oldest are found in Hakone.

Ichinoyu ⑥⑥, 90 Tonosawa (tel. 0460/5-5331), first opened more than 350 years ago and is now in its 14th generation of owners. It claims to be the oldest ryokan in the area and was once honored by the visit of a shogun. Located about a five-minute walk from Tonosawa Station (on the Hakone Tozan Line), this delightful, rambling wooden ryokan is located on a tree-shaded winding road that follows on the track of the old Tokaido Highway. On the one side of the ryokan is a roaring river.

There are 22 rooms here, the oldest dating from the Meiji Period, more than 100 years ago. The two rooms I like the most are called Seseragi and Matsu (rooms are usually named in ryokan). Old-fashioned, they face the river and consist mainly of seasoned and weathered wood. Old artwork, wall hangings, and paintings decorate the ryokan, and some of the rooms have old wooden bathtubs. Both the communal tubs and the tubs in the rooms have hot water supplied from a natural spring. As with most ryokan, prices include two meals, tax, and service, and range from ¥17,000 ($136) to ¥20,000 ($160) per person for rooms with private bath and toilet. Rooms without private bathroom begin at ¥15,000 ($120) per person.

The **Fujiya Hotel,** 359 Miyanoshita (tel. 0460/2-2211), is one of Japan's oldest Western-style hotels and is located within a five-minute walk of Miyanoshita Station on the Hakone Tozan Line. Established in 1878, it's the grandest and most majestic old hotel in Hakone, a lovely establishment with a Japanese-style roof, lots of windows, and wooden corridors. It consists of five separate buildings, each different and added on at various times in its 112-year history. One is shaped like a pagoda, while another has turrets and a roof shaped like a Japanese temple. In the back of the hotel are a garden with a waterfall and a pond full of carp. There's an outdoor swimming pool as well as an indoor thermal pool fed by water from a hot spring.

The hotel even has its own greenhouse. As expected, rooms are old-fashioned with high ceilings and wooden furniture, and all 146 rooms come with a private bathroom. Accustomed to foreign guests, the front-desk personnel speak very good English. The room charge starts at ¥15,000 ($120) for weekdays, increasing to ¥22,000 ($176) on Saturday, the day before a national holiday, and during Golden Week, from April 28 to May 4. During New Year's and the July/August vacation periods, rooms cost ¥27,000 ($216).

The Fujiya Hotel is also a good place to come for a meal. Its main dining room, open from noon to 2 p.m. and 6 to 8:30 p.m., is very bright and cheerful, with a high ceiling, large windows with Japanese screens, and a wooden floor. The views are nice and the service is attentive. For lunch you can have such dishes as pilaf, spaghetti, sandwiches, chicken, rainbow trout, and hamburger steak, with most dishes averaging ¥2,000 ($16). The dinner menu is more expensive and includes steaks, fish, grilled chicken, and stews, most in the ¥2,500 ($20) to ¥10,000 ($80) price range.

Across the street from the Fujiya Hotel is the **Naraya,** 162 Miyanoshita (tel. 0460/2-2411), a traditional Japanese inn with tiled roof, wooden walls, shoji screens, and hot-spring baths. Although the inn's history stretches back several hundred years, the present building is about a century old. The tatami rooms here, all with bath and toilet, have inspiring views of a large landscape garden and mountains beyond. This is a great place to relax and revel in nature's beauty. Prices begin at ¥30,000 ($240) per person, including two meals and service charge.

Situated right on Lake Ashinoko on secluded property is the luxurious **Hakone Prince Hotel** ⑥⑦, 144 Motohakone, Hakone-machi (tel. 0460/3-7111). The various types of rooms available here are in several differently styled complexes that sprawl over the well-tended grounds, which include gardens, tennis courts, an outdoor pool, and an arboretum. The public baths overlook the lake. The **Ryuguden** complex ⑥⑧, with its Japanese-style tatami rooms, resembles an Oriental palace, a grand structure built in 1936 with iron lanterns hanging from its wooden upturned eaves and sculptured bushes gracing its manicured lawns. Rooms here begin at ¥28,000 ($224) per person, including two meals, tax, and service charge. During peak seasons (New Year's and summer vacation) the rates increase to ¥35,000 ($280).

Not far from the Ryuguden is the Prince's Western-style hotel complex, designed by Japanese architect Togo Murano in a circular shape so that each room has a different panoramic view, complete with balcony. Room rates here start at ¥32,000 ($256), rising to ¥49,000 ($392) during the summer season.

And finally, you can also stay in your own pine log cabin, the wood imported from Finland. Spread underneath the trees in a kind of village, the Western-style cabins range in price from ¥17,000 ($136) to ¥35,000 ($280). Summer rates are ¥27,000 ($216) to ¥35,000 ($280).

Located at the southern tip of Lake Hakone is **Sugiyoshi Ryokan** ⑥⑨, 56 Moto-Hakone, Hakone-machi (tel. 0460/3-6327). All 12 rooms are in Japanese style and come with the usual coin-operated TV and fridge, and some of them have lake views. The public baths here are natural hot springs. Rates per person, including two meals and service charge, are ¥10,000 ($80) for rooms without bath or toilet and ¥14,000 ($112) for rooms with a private bathroom. During peak season rates start at ¥20,000 ($160).

Although it's a bit isolated, **Fuji-Hakone Guest House,** 912 Sengoku (tel. 0460/4-6577), is a member of the Japanese Inn Group and offers inexpensive lodging in nine tatami rooms. Opened in 1984 and kept spotlessly clean, this modern house in tranquil surroundings set back from a tree-shaded road is run by a man who speaks very good English. Some of the rooms face the Hakone mountain range. Facilities include a public hot-spring bath, coin-operated laundry and dryer, a large lounge area, and a communal refrigerator. Rates range from ¥4,500 ($36) to ¥5,000 ($40) for one person, and ¥8,500 ($68) to ¥10,000 ($80) for two. Triples range from ¥12,000 ($96) to ¥14,000 ($112). To reach the guest house, take a Hakone Tozan bus from Odawara Station for 45 minutes to Sengoku, getting off at the Senkyoro-mae bus stop (the stop is announced in English). From there it's a one-minute walk. This bus is included in the Hakone Free Pass and continues on to Togenda (only a ten-minute ride), from which you can catch either the ropeway or the boat across Ashinoko (described above).

---

8. The Izu Peninsula

Whenever Tokyoites want to spend a few days at a hot-spring spa on the seashore, they head for the Izu Peninsula. Jutting out into the Pacific Ocean, Izu boasts some fine beaches, verdant and lush countryside, and a dramatic coastline marked in spots by high cliffs and tumbling surf. However, even though the scenery is at times breathtaking, there is little of historical interest to lure the short-term visitor to Japan; make sure you've seen both Kamakura and Nikko before considering coming here. Keep in mind also that Izu's resorts are terribly crowded during the summer vacation period from mid-July to the end of August.

ORIENTATION

The fastest way to reach Izu is by the Shinkansen bullet train from Tokyo Station, which whisks you in less than an hour to Atami, Izu's main gateway on the east side of the peninsula. From Atami you can travel farther south to Shimoda by limited express train.

The west side of the peninsula is much less developed and in my opinion offers the best scenery in Izu. Since there is no rail service here, transportation is either by bus or by boat. A good choice of a place to stay on the west side is Dogashima, a small fishing village with a good beach, clear waters, and interesting rock formations. A pleasant way to reach Dogashima is either by boat from Numazu or by bus along the coast from Shimoda.

But the best way to enjoy Izu is to drive, making this one of the few times when it may be worth it to rent your own car. There's a road that hugs the coast all the way around the peninsula which you can drive easily in a day. If you're traveling by public transportation, an interesting route is to take the Shinkansen to Atami, travel by limited express to Shimoda, take the bus from Shimoda to Dogashima, and from there take a boat to Numazu, where you can catch a train back to Tokyo. Before leaving Tokyo, be sure to pick up the leaflet *The Izu Peninsula* at the Tourist Information Center.

PLACES OF INTEREST IN IZU

If you're traveling during the peak summer season, you should make reservations at least several months in advance. Otherwise, there are hotel, ryokan, and minshuku reservation offices in all of Izu's resort towns which will arrange accommodations for you, but be aware that if a place has a room still open at the last minute in August, there's probably a reason for it—poor location, poor service, or unimaginative decor. I took my chances one August and arrived in Atami without prior arrangements. The "ryokan" arranged by the accommodations office at the Atami train station was the worst I've ever stayed in. It pays to plan ahead. Below are recommendations for accommodations in Atami, Shimoda, and Dogashima, three towns that provide a good overview of what the peninsula has to offer.

Atami

Atami means "hot sea." Legend has it that a long time ago there was a hot geyser spewing forth in the sea, killing a lot of fish and marine life. The concerned fishermen asked a Buddhist monk to intervene on their behalf and to pray for a solution to the problem. The prayers paid off when the geyser moved itself to the beach. Not only was the marine life spared, but Atami was blessed with hot-spring water the townspeople could henceforth bathe in.

Today Atami, with a population of more than 50,000, is a conglomeration of hotels, ryokan, restaurants, pachinko parlors, souvenir shops, and a sizable red-light district. The city itself is not very interesting, but it's the most easily accessible hot-spring resort from Tokyo. Be sure to see the **MOA Art Museum** (tel. 0557/84-2511), located on top of a hill a short bus ride away from Atami Station. Housed in a modern building at the headquarters of the Church of World Messianity, this museum includes ukiyoe woodblock prints, ceramics, lacquerware, and artwork from the collection of Mokichi Okada, leader of this relatively new religion in Japan. Closed on Thursday, it's open the rest of the week from 9:30 a.m. to 4 p.m., and admission is ¥1,500 ($12).

The **Atami Tourist Information Office** is located at the train station (tel. 0557/81-6002) and is open daily from 10 a.m. to 6 p.m.

The **telephone area code** for Atami is 0557.

Food and Lodging: One of Atami's oldest ryokan, **Kiunkaku** ⑦, 4-2 Showacho (tel. 0557/81-3623), has a beautiful garden with a meandering stream, manicured bushes, and stunted pine trees. Although rooms encircle the garden, they are artfully concealed from one another and give optimum privacy through the clever use of bushes and mounds. Facilities include hot-spring baths, one of the most pleasant coffeeshops I've seen in a ryokan, and an outdoor pool. There are various styles of rooms available, ranging in price from ¥29,000 ($232) to ¥50,000 ($400) per person, including two meals, and service charge. The most expensive rooms are those with the best view, the most space, and the best meals.

However, there are a few rooms in the lower price range that are comparative bargains. Tamahime, for example, is the name of one of the ryokan's two Western-style rooms and it's changed little over the decades. It sports stained-glass windows, a paneled ceiling, a fireplace (no longer used), a monstrous old dresser, and cozy furniture—plus a good view of the garden. The only reason it's available for ¥29,000 ($232) is that there is no private bathroom.

The **Hotel New Akao** ⑦, Atami-cho 1993-250 (tel. 0557/82-5151), is one of the most conspicuous resort hotels on the Izu Peninsula. A large pleasure hotel hemmed in on one side by cliffs and on the other by the blue sea, it has about everything most Japanese want in a vacation: a swimming pool, a fancy dining hall affording an unusual view of surf crashing into cliffs, two discos, a large hot-spring public bath, an outdoor garden complete with Corinthian pillars and arbors, and a small miniature golf area. It even has a roped-off area in the sea where you can swim. Rooms in both Japanese and Western style are available, simply but tastefully done, all with large windows facing the water and a private bath. Obviously, what you're paying for here is use of the facilities rather than luxurious rooms. Per-person rates are ¥23,000 ($184) on weekdays and ¥25,000 ($200) on weekends, including two meals, tax, and service charge. My only complaint about this hotel is that it's so popular and crowded during peak season that the front desk seems too busy to be very accommodating.

On a less grand scale but recently renovated, the **New Fujiya Hotel,** 1-16 Ginza-cho (tel. 0557/81-0111), was built just before the 1964 Olympics. The staff here is friendly and efficient and used to foreigners. Although the hotel is located a few blocks inland, its top-floor rooms have partial views of the water. The cheapest rooms are those that face an inside courtyard. Facilities include an indoor pool, a rooftop playground, a public bath and sauna, and even an outdoor hot-spring spa. In the evening there's a nightclub—usually with performances by women rather scantily clad. Both Japanese- and Western-style rooms are available, beginning at ¥23,000 ($184) per person, including two meals, tax, and service charge. If you want a room without meals, they begin at ¥11,000 ($88) for a single and ¥22,000 ($176) for a twin.

Shimoda

Located on the southeast end of the Izu Peninsula, Shimoda is famous as the site where Commodore Perry set anchor in 1854 on his trip to Japan to force the nation to open its doors to trade. Shimoda is also where the first American diplomatic representative, Townsend Harris, lived before setting up permanent residence in Yokohama.

Ryosenji Temple, located about a 15-minute walk from Shimoda Station, is where Perry and representatives of the Tokugawa shogunate government agreed upon and signed the treaty to open up Japan. Strangely enough, the temple also houses a small museum of erotica. **Hofukuji Temple,** about a five-minute walk from Shimoda Station, is dedicated to Tojin Okichi, the mistress of Townsend Harris while he lived in Shimoda. Although today no one is exactly certain how it came about that she was chosen, we do know that she ended her life by drowning herself after he left. This temple contains both her tomb and personal artifacts. About 20 minutes south of Shimoda by bus is **Yumigahama Beach,** considered by many to be the best public beach in Izu.

The **Shimoda Tourist Office** is located just outside the train station and is open daily from 9 a.m. to 5 p.m. (tel. 05582/2-1531). They have very good brochures and a map in English.

The **telephone area code** for Shimoda is 05582.

Food and Lodging: A large white hotel situated on top of a hill, the **Shimoda Tokyu Hotel,** 5-12-1 Shimoda-shi (tel. 05582/2-2411), is about a ten-minute taxi ride from Shimoda Station. In addition to a hot-spring spa, it also has an outdoor swimming pool and a bathing area in the sea. From mid-July through August there's outdoor barbecue. Western-style rooms range from ¥12,400 ($99) to ¥20,600 ($165) for a single, and from ¥19,200 ($154) to ¥38,200 ($306) for a twin or double. The higher prices indicate rates during peak season. Japanese-style rooms start at ¥24,700 ($198), rising to ¥46,000 ($368) during peak season.

Shimoda Onsen Hotel, 6-12 Takegahama (tel. 05582/2-3111), is a reasonably priced ryokan that opened in 1954 with 63 tatami rooms. Located an eight-minute walk from Shimoda Station, it has friendly front-desk personnel and features a small outdoor swimming pool and hot-spring baths. Rooms, all with private bathroom, begin at ¥20,000 ($160), rising to ¥27,000 ($216) in summer. Rates are per person and include two meals; tax, and service charge are extra. Western-style breakfasts are available if ordered the night before.

If you're on a budget, head for Sotoura, a small bay on the edge of Shimoda with about 60 minshuku and pensions. It has its own small beach and is popular with young people and families. **Haji** ⑦ (tel. 05582/2-2597) is a small, clean, and simple minshuku with seven rooms, four of which have their own toilet. The owner spent a year in England more than a decade ago but doesn't have much opportunity to practice his English, so he's happy to see foreign guests. Rates are ¥6,500 ($52) per person and include two meals.

If Haji is full, you might try the nearby **Shimoda Pension Ohban** (tel. 05582/2-2953), a new three-story building with "Shimoda Pension" written on the front. I find this place rather impersonal and its dorm-like rooms dull, but it's conveniently located. The charge here is ¥9,000 ($72) per person, including two meals, during summer season.

Dogashima

With its fishing boats, tiny lanes and back alleyways, sandy beach, clear water, and rock formations jutting out of the sea, Dogashima is one of my favorite villages on Izu's west side. There's not much to do here except relax, swim, and walk around —which may be exactly what you're looking for. The **tourist office** (tel. 0558/52-1268) is located across the street from the bus terminal in a tiny one-room building not far from the boat pier. It's open from 8:30 a.m. to 5 p.m. on weekdays, from

8:30 a.m. to noon on Saturday, and is closed on Sunday and national holidays. During the peak season of July and August, it remains open every day from 8:30 a.m. to 5 p.m.

The **telephone area code** for Dogashima is 0558.

Food and Lodging: Dogashima's most exclusive luxury resort ryokan is **Ginsuiso** ⑦, 2977-1 Nishina, Nishi-Izu-cho (tel. 0558/52-2211). Service here is excellent and begins as soon as you arrive, with staff personnel on hand at the door to greet you. This stunningly white hotel sprawls along a cliff over the sea and has its own private beach and outdoor swimming pool. All 90 rooms are tatami and come with a private bathroom and views of the sea. There's a cabaret show beginning nightly at 8 p.m. The off-season price is ¥22,000 ($176) per person including two meals (tax and service charge are extra), but because it's popular with large Japanese tour groups, you should book well in advance, particularly in summer, when rates go up to ¥33,000 ($264).

Kaikomaru ⑦, Nishi-Izu-cho, Sawada (tel. 0558/52-1054), is a tiny family-run minshuku on Dogashima's main road. There are only eight Japanese-style rooms here and they go for ¥6,500 ($52) per person, including two meals. Use of the hot-spring bath costs ¥200 ($1.60) extra. No one speaks English, but the family, which seems to include everyone from small children to grandparents, is friendly if a bit shy. If you're gregarious and outgoing, you'll like this place.

KYOTO

As your Shinkansen bullet train glides into Kyoto Station, your first reaction is likely to be one of great disappointment. There's Kyoto Tower looming in the foreground, looking like some misplaced spaceship. Modern buildings and hotels surround you on all sides, making Kyoto look like just any other Japanese town.

But nestled in between all those buildings are an incredible 1,700 Buddhist temples and 300 Shinto shrines, narrow alleyways and willow-lined canals, gardens of rock and moss, and enough history to fill the pages of 1,000 years. If you stay here long enough, you'll grow to understand why I consider Kyoto to be Japan's most romantic city.

In fact, if you go to only one place in all of Japan, Kyoto should be it. As the only major Japanese city spared bombing attacks during World War II, Kyoto is charming, captivating, and spellbinding. As you walk its narrow streets and along its tiny canals, you will be struck with images of yesterday. Old women in kimonos bend over their "garden," which may consist only of a couple of gnarled bonsai beside their front door. An open-fronted shop reveals a man making tatami mats, the musty smell of the rice mats reminiscent of earth itself. Perhaps you'll see a geisha shuffling to her evening appointment in Gion, a small enclave of solemn-brown wooden houses where the sounds of laughter and traditional Japanese music escape through shoji screens. Nijo Castle is still here, built by the Tokugawas and famous for its creaking floorboards designed to warn of enemy intruders. The famous Ryoanji rock garden is here, a Zen garden of pebbles and stones. A pleasant stroll is from Kiyomizu Temple to Heian Shrine, with tea gardens, pottery shops, and temples along the way. In the evening in the summertime, couples sit along the banks of the Kamo River, which cuts through the heart of the city.

But as I said before, Kyoto has not escaped the afflictions of the modern age. Kyoto, too, has its share of ugly concrete buildings, the flashing neon of pachinko parlors, telephone lines, and traffic. But, then, Kyoto has always led a rather fragile existence, as a look at any of its temples and shrines will tell you. Made of wood, they have been rebuilt countless times, destroyed through the years by man, fires, and earthquakes.

So perhaps that is the lesson of Kyoto. Life is fleeting, ever-changing, and nothing lasts forever. As a product of the past and the present, Kyoto is a synthesis of all that is Japan in the 20th century. No one who comes to this country should miss the wealth of experience this ancient capital has to offer.

A BRIEF HISTORY

Kyoto served as Japan's capital for more than 1,000 years, from 794 to the Meiji Restoration in 1868. It was laid out in a grid pattern borrowed from the Chinese, with streets running north and south and east and west. Its first few hundred years, from about 800 to the 12th century, were perhaps its grandest, a time when culture blossomed and the court nobility led luxurious and splendid lives. If you have any fantasies about old Japan, perhaps they fit into this time period, known as the Heian Period. There were poetry-composing parties and moon-gazing events. Buddhism flourished and temples were built. A number of learning institutions were set up for the sons and daughters of aristocratic families, and scholars were versed in both Japanese and Chinese.

Toward the end of the Heian Period, however, military clans began clashing for power, resulting in a series of civil wars that eventually pushed Japan into the feudal era of military government that lasted nearly 680 years—until 1868. The first shogun to rise to power was Yoritomo Minamoto, who set up his shogunate government in Kamakura. With the downfall of the Kamakura government in 1336, however, Kyoto once again became the seat of power for the country. The beginning of this era, known as the Muromachi and Azuchi-Momoyama Periods, was marked by extravagant prosperity and luxury, expressed in such splendid villas as Kyoto's Gold and Silver Pavilions. Lacquerware, landscape paintings, and the art of metal engraving came into their own. Zen Buddhism was the rage. And despite the civil wars that rocked the nation in the 15th and 16th centuries and destroyed much of Kyoto, culture flourished. It was during these turbulent times that Noh drama, the tea ceremony, flower arranging, and landscape gardening gradually took form.

Emerging as victor in the civil wars, Ieyasu Tokugawa established himself as shogun and set up his military rule in Edo (present Tokyo), far to the east of Kyoto. For the next 250 years Kyoto remained the capital in name only, and in 1868 (which marked the downfall of the Tokugawa shogunate and the restoration of the emperor to power), the capital was officially moved from Kyoto to Tokyo. Thus Tokyo mushroomed into the concrete megalopolis it is today. Kyoto, with a population of about 1½ million people, remains very much a city of the past.

ORIENTATION

One of the major stops on the Shinkansen bullet train, **Kyoto** is three hours away from Tokyo and only 20 minutes from Osaka. If you're arriving in Japan at Osaka International Airport, you can reach Kyoto in about an hour by a special airport bus, for which the fare is ¥860 ($6.88). Most of Kyoto's attractions and hotels lie to the north of Kyoto Station. The largest concentration of restaurants, shops, bars, and nightlife activity spreads in a radius from the Kawaramachi–Shijo Dori intersection and includes a narrow street called Pontocho and the geisha district of Gion. Temples are sprinkled throughout Kyoto. Be sure to stop off at the **Kyoto Tourist Information Center (T.I.C.)** (tel. 075/371-5649) upon arrival. Located across the street from Kyoto Station's north side (take the Karasuma Central Exit out of Kyoto Station), it has great maps of the city as well as information on sightseeing. Keep in mind, however, that it's closed on Sunday, Saturday afternoon, and weekdays after 5 p.m., so plan your arrival accordingly. Otherwise, there's the local **Kyoto City Information Office,** also located on the station's north side. No one here speaks English, but you can pick up a map and get directions to your hotel. It's

open every day from 8:30 a.m. to 5 p.m. You can also call the **Japan Travel-Phone** for any questions you might have regarding Kyoto and the surrounding area at 371-5649 between 9 a.m. and 5 p.m., seven days a week. More information regarding Kyoto is given in Section 1, "The ABCs of Kyoto."

Kyoto's address system is actually quite simple once you understand what the directions mean. Many of its streets are named. Those north of Kyoto Station that run east-west are numbered; for example, the *shi* of Shijo Dori Avenue means "four." *Agaru* means "to the north," *sagaru* means "to the south," *nishi-iru* means "to the west," and *higashi-iru* means "to the east." Thus an address that reads Shijo-agaru means "north of Shijo Dori (or Fourth) Avenue." In addition, many addresses indicate which cross streets a building is near. Therefore, the address for Hotel Gimmond, which is Takakura Oike Dori, means that the hotel is near the intersection of Takakura Dori and Oika Dori.

GETTING AROUND

The easiest way to get around Kyoto is by bus. The city map given out by the T.I.C. shows major bus routes too. Some of the buses travel in a loop around the city, while others go back and forth between two destinations. At any rate, get on at the back of the bus. If the bus travels a long distance, there will be a ticket machine right beside the back door—take the ticket and hold on to it. It has a number on it and will tell the bus driver when you got on and how much you owe. You can see for yourself how much you owe by looking for your number on a panel at the front of the bus. Unsurprisingly, your fare rises the longer you stay on the bus. If you're on a loop bus, the fare is the same no matter how long you stay on—¥170 ($1.36)—and you pay when you get off. There are no transfer tickets, so you have to pay separately for each ride.

In addition to buses there's also one subway line completed, which is useful only for going to the Imperial Palace. It runs from Kitaoji in the north through Kyoto Station to Takeda.

Taxis in Kyoto come in three different sizes with correspondingly different fares. Small ones are ¥460 ($3.68) for the first two kilometers (1¼ miles), medium-size ones are ¥470 ($3.76), and large ones are ¥490 ($3.92). You can also hire taxis by the half hour, which may not be a bad idea if there are several of you and you don't have much time. Small taxis are available for ¥1,400 ($11.20) per 30 minutes, medium-size ones are ¥1,750 ($14), and large ones are ¥2,000 ($16). Make sure your taxi driver understands how long you want him for, and make sure of the price. Note that fares may have changed by the time you arrive in Kyoto.

A popular way to get around Kyoto is by rental bike, made easy by the fact that there are few hills and that most streets are named. **Rental Pia Service,** located across the street from Kyoto Station's south exit next to the Nippon Rent-A-Car, rents bicycles for about ¥1,000 ($8) a day (tel. 672-0662). Another rental service is available from **Taki Renta Bike** (tel. 341-7586).

---

1. The ABCs of Kyoto

Below is some practical information on Kyoto that you may need to know during your stay. Remember too that the concierge of your hotel, as well as the Kyoto Tourist Information Center, can probably answer any other questions you may have regarding Kyoto.

BANKS AND MONEY EXCHANGE: Banks are open Monday through Friday from 9 a.m. to 3 p.m. An establishment with longer hours is the **High Touch Plaza** of the **Kyoto Shinyo Kinko Bank,** located on Shijo Dori Avenue, Yanagino-banba, Shimogyo-ku (tel. 211-2111). It's open every day except Wednesday from 10 a.m. to 6 p.m., including weekends and holidays. In addition, another place to exchange money is at the large department stores like Takashimaya, Daimaru, and Kintetsu. If you need to cash a traveler's check outside these hours and your hotel doesn't have the facilities to do so, both the Grand and New Miyako hotels will cash traveler's checks even if you are not a hotel guest.

BOOKSTORES: There are two conveniently located stores selling books in English. **Maruzen,** Kawaramachi Takoyakushi-agaru, Nakagyo-ku (tel. 241-2161), is part of a national bookstore chain and has novels as well as books on Japan. Located north of the Shijo–Kawaramachi intersection, it's open from 10 a.m. to 7 p.m. (until 6:30 p.m. on Sunday); closed Wednesday. **Izumiya Book Center** is in the Avanti department store just south of Kyoto Station (tel. 671-8998). It's open every day except Thursday from 10 a.m. to 8 p.m.

CAR RENTAL: There are many car-rental agencies in Kyoto. Among them are: **Mazda Rent-A-Car,** Kawaramachi-Nishi-Iru, Gojo-dori, Shimogyo-ku (tel. 361-0201); **Nippon Rent-A-Car,** Higashi-Kujo Muromachi (tel. 671-0919); **Nissan Rent-A-Car,** 26, Nishi-Kujo-Inmachi, Minami-ku (tel. 661-2161); and **Toyota Rent-A-Lease,** Sanjo-agaru, Karasuma Dori Avenue, Nakagyo-ku (tel. 241-0100).

CREDIT CARDS: Credit cards are accepted by major tourist shops, restaurants, and hotels. If you need to use your credit card to obtain cash, there are several banks that handle specific credit cards. **Sanwa Bank,** Karasuma Shijo, Shimogyo-ku (tel. 211-1111), has a card-cashing service for American Express; **Tokai Bank,** Shijo Karasuma-agaru, Nakagyo-ku (tel. 221-7061), handles MasterCard; and **Sumitomo Bank** has two locations for those who wish to use VISA—Karasuma Sanjo-agaru, Nakagyo-ku (tel. 221-2111), and Shijo Kawaramachi-nishi, Shimogyo-ku (tel. 223-2821).

DOCTORS AND DENTISTS: The **Kyoto T.I.C.** (tel. 371-5649) has a list of approximately a dozen doctors and half a dozen dentists who speak English. If the T.I.C. is closed or you'd rather talk to a doctor directly, **Dr. Sakabe,** Gokomachi, Nijo-sagaru, Nakagyo-ku (tel. 231-1624), is an internist who speaks excellent English, and he can refer you to other doctors as well.

ELECTRICAL CURRENT: In both Kyoto and Nara it's 100 volts, 60 cycles, almost the same as in the United States (110 volts and 60 cycles).

EMERGENCY: The same all over Japan, the national emergency telephone numbers are 110 for **police** and 119 for both calling an **ambulance** and reporting a **fire.**

HOSPITALS: Most hospitals are not equipped to handle emergencies 24 hours a day, but a system has been set up in which hospitals handle emergencies on a rotating basis. If you go by ambulance, it must take you to one of these. The **Kyoto Second Red Cross Hospital (Daini Sekijuji Byoin),** Marutamachi-sagaru, Kamanza Dori, Kamikyo-ku (tel. 231-5171), is staffed 24 hours a day, but referral by a doctor who knows your problem is expected. English is spoken at **Japan Baptist**

Hospital (Nihon Baputesuto Byoin), 47 Yamanomoto-cho, Kitashirakawa, Sakyo-ku (tel. 781-5191).

LOST PROPERTY: If you left something on the Shinkansen bullet train, the number to call to see whether it's been found is 691-1000. Items lost at Kyoto Station are turned in to the lost and found office (tel. 371-0134). If you lost something along a street or outside, contact the Shichijo Police Station (tel. 371-2111). Forgetting something in a taxi is a bit more complicated because there are several different taxi companies—which means you have to know which taxi company to call. The MK Taxi Company number is 721-4141; the privately owned green taxis all report to 314-4481 and 661-2244. Another number to call for items left in taxis is 691-6518. Because it's so difficult to track down items left in taxis, the T.I.C. suggests you visit their office if you have any problems.

POST OFFICE: The **Kyoto Central Post Office** is located just west of Kyoto Station at 843-12 Higashi-shiokoji-cho, Shimogyo-ku (tel. 365-2471). It's open from 9 a.m. to 7 p.m. Monday through Friday, to 5 p.m. on Saturday, and to noon on Sunday and holidays. You can mail packages bound for international destinations here. You can also have your own mail delivered *Post Restante* here, but you have to pick it up within one month if it's international mail and within ten days if it's domestic.

RAILWAY INFORMATION: For information on train schedules, call the Travel Service Center at Kyoto Station at 361-5786 from 10 a.m. to 6 p.m.

SHOP HOURS: Department stores in Kyoto stay open from 10 a.m. to 6 p.m., while smaller shops in the downtown area remain open from about 10 a.m. to 8 p.m.

STUDENT GUIDES: Students of Kyoto University, Doshisha University, and Kyoto Women's University are happy to act as voluntary guides to tourists in Kyoto (it gives them practice with their English). You must apply at the Tourist Information Center one or two days in advance, and you're expected to pay for the student's transportation, entrance fees to shrines and temples, and lunch.

TELEPHONE AREA CODE: If you're calling from outside Kyoto, the area code for Kyoto is 075.

TOURIST INFORMATION: The **Tourist Information Center (T.I.C.)** is about a minute's walk from Kyoto Station's north side in the Kyoto Tower Building, Higashi-Shiokojicho, Shimogyo-ku (tel. 075/371-5649). Open from 9 a.m. to 5 p.m. Monday through Friday, to noon on Saturday, it has a staff that speaks excellent English and can help you with all your questions regarding Kyoto. The T.I.C. distributes a great map in English of the city, and has brochures and leaflets not only on Kyoto but on other destinations in Japan as well. Be sure to pick up the leaflet *Walking Tour Courses in Kyoto.*

If the T.I.C. is closed, you can get a map at the **Kyoto City Information Office,** located between the taxi stand and the bus stands on Kyoto Station's north side. Open daily from 8:30 a.m. to 5 p.m., it doesn't have an English-speaking staff but it does have maps in English.

To find out what's going on in Kyoto in terms of festivals, special events, Kabuki or Noh performances, or exhibitions, call the **Teletourist Service** at 361-2911. This 24-hour service provides 90 seconds of recorded information in English on what's going on during the week.

TOURIST PUBLICATIONS: In addition to the brochures and leaflets distributed by the T.I.C., there are a couple of publications with information on Kyoto. *Discover Kinki,* a monthly distributed free to hotels, travel agencies, and the T.I.C., tells of upcoming events and festivals in Kyoto and the neighboring cities of Osaka, Kobe, and Nara. Another monthly tabloid distributed free at hotels and restaurants is *The Kyoto Visitor's Guide,* which contains maps, a calendar of events, and information on sightseeing and shopping. In addition, a monthly English magazine called *Kansai Time Out* carries information and articles on Kyoto, Kobe, Osaka, and Nara. It's available in Kyoto at both the Maruzen and Izumiya bookstores and at the Gimmond and Miyako hotels, and costs ¥300 ($2.40).

2. Accommodations

There are many types of accommodations available in Kyoto, ranging from exclusive Japanese inns to business hotels to rock-bottom dormitory-like lodgings. If you've never stayed in a ryokan, Kyoto is probably the best place to do so. With the possible exception of some hot-spring resorts, Kyoto has more choices of ryokan in all price categories than any other city in Japan. Small, usually made of wood, and often situated in delightfully quaint neighborhoods, these ryokan can enrich your stay in Kyoto by putting you in direct touch with the city's traditional past. Remember that in upper- and medium-price ryokan the room charge is per person and includes two meals and service. Ryokan listed in the budget category, on the other hand, usually do not serve meals unless stated otherwise.

But even if you decide to stay in a hotel, Kyoto has a number of excellent choices in all price ranges (many hotels also have Japanese-style rooms available). Whichever type of accommodations you select, make reservations in advance. Kyoto is a favorite holiday destination for the Japanese, receiving as many as ten million visitors each year. Keep in mind that whereas ryokan include service charges and sometimes tax in their prices, hotels in the upper and medium price ranges will add a 6% tax and a 10% service charge to your bill.

Because Kyoto is relatively small and is served by such a good bus system, no matter where you stay you won't be too far away from the heart of the city. Most hotels and ryokan, however, are concentrated either in the center section of Kyoto not far from the Kawaramachi–Shijo Dori intersection (called Nakagyo-ku), east of the Kamo River (called Higashiyama-ku), or around Kyoto Station (called Shimogyo-ku).

THE UPPER BRACKET

The service and hospitality at Kyoto's first-class hotels and ryokan are legendary. After all, Kyoto has had centuries of practice catering to members of the imperial court, feudal lords, shoguns, and their emissaries. Following in their footsteps, you too will be treated like royalty. Western-style hotels in this category have the extra benefit of English-language television broadcasts, with CNN newscasts from the United States and information on local sightseeing attractions.

Western Style

One of the newest hotels in Kyoto is the centrally located **ANA Hotel Kyoto,** Nijo-Castle-Mae, Horikawa-dori Avenue, Nakagyo-ku (tel. 075/231-1155). Located just across the street from Nijo Castle—some rooms possess views of the castle grounds—this 303-room property has one of the most stunning lobbies in town, complete with a glass wall overlooking an impressive waterfall and tiny landscape garden. There's a service desk to help you make travel plans for the city and beyond, and facilities include an indoor swimming pool and sauna (which you can use at an extra charge of ¥2,200 [$17.60]); a nursery room; a beauty salon; and first-rate restaurants serving Japanese, Chinese, and Western cuisine. Rooms are attractive and comfortable, with lots of space in the bathrooms for spreading out cosmetics and toiletries. Singles, none of which face the castle, range from ¥10,000 ($80) to ¥16,500 ($132). Twins start at ¥18,000 ($144), with those facing the castle starting at ¥24,000 ($192).

Another new hotel in Kyoto is the **Kyoto Takaragaike Prince Hotel,** Takaragaike, Sakyo-ku (tel. 075/712-1111). Although it's a bit inconveniently located on the northern fringes of the city, about a 30-minute taxi ride from Kyoto Station, it's useful for those attending conferences in the Kyoto International Conference Hall across the street. Another advantage to staying here is nearby Takaragaike Park, complete with jogging paths, pond, botanical garden, and wood-covered hills. If you want the benefits of being in the countryside but don't want to give up the comforts of a first-class hotel, this may be the place for you. In any case, there are free shuttle buses that depart for Kyoto Station about five times a day.

Designed by the famous architect Togo Murano, this imposing circular hotel has the unmistakable touches of a Prince Hotel, including its excellent service, cheerful staff, and its bright color schemes of white, pink, and purple. Restaurants serve French, Chinese, and Japanese cuisine; on the hotel grounds is a traditional tea house, where you can observe a tea-ceremony demonstration for free. For ¥800 ($6.40) you can even partake of the green frothy mixture, along with Japanese sweets. As for the rooms, they are positively spacious, with a sink and vanity area separated from the bathroom. Upon arrival at the hotel, you will be treated to a complimentary tea and sweet, brought to your room by a kimono-clad hostess. Should you have any questions regarding the hotel or Kyoto during your stay, there's a guest relations officer on duty to help. Rates here start at ¥33,000 ($264) for a double or twin.

And finally, the newest deluxe hotel to open in Kyoto is the **Kyoto Brighton Hotel,** Nakadachiuri, Shinmachi-dori, Kamigyo-ku (tel. 075/441-4411), located near the Imperial Palace. Named after England's seashore resort to evoke a sense of light, airy brightness, the Brighton Hotel flaunts space, with a huge, six-story atrium and glass-enclosed elevators. With space at a premium in Japan, the air in this atrium is very expensive! All 183 rooms face the walkways that ring the atrium, so even women traveling alone should feel very safe here. All rooms are large, with a separate couch and lounging area, and range from ¥20,000 ($160) to ¥28,000 ($224) for twins and ¥18,500 ($148) to ¥33,000 ($264) for doubles. There are no single rooms, but rates for one person occupying a double room begin at ¥16,500 ($132). Facilities include an outdoor swimming pool open only in July and August, and restaurants serving French, Japanese, and Cantonese food.

If you're looking for an older, more established hotel with a lot more history, one of the best-known hotels in all of Japan is the **Miyako Hotel,** Sanjo Keage, Higashiyama-ku (tel. 075/771-7111), which spreads like an eagle on top of a hill at the north-eastern end of the city, commanding a good view of the city. First opened back in 1890, it has boasted a guest list that reads like a Who's Who of visitors to Japan—Queen Elizabeth II, Prince Charles, Anwar El-Sadat, Edward Kennedy, Rosalynn and Amy Carter, Albert Einstein, Charles Lindbergh, Dwight D. Eisenhower, Robert Kennedy, the Dalai Lama of Tibet, Gerald Ford, and Ronald Reagan, to name just a few. In fact, the Miyako Hotel is so well known around the world that half of its guests are foreigners.

Located about a 20-minute taxi ride from Kyoto Station or just a minute's walk from Keage Station on the Keihen Electric Railway Keishin Line, the Miyako Hotel is spread over 16 acres, including landscaped gardens, a pool, and a sauna. Its Western-style rooms come in a variety of decors and price ranges, but all are cozy, comfortable, and large. English-language newspapers are delivered to your room both morning and evening. Twenty Japanese-style rooms are available in an annex (connected to the main hotel by a covered passageway) that manages to maintain the atmosphere of a traditional ryokan with views of a Japanese garden. Rooms in this Japanese annex range from ¥26,400 ($211) to ¥49,500 ($396), with most in the ¥28,500 ($228) range. Rates for Western-style rooms range from ¥8,200 ($66) to ¥15,400 ($123) for a single and ¥15,400 ($123) to ¥36,000 ($288) for most twins and doubles.

The **Kyoto Grand Hotel,** Shiokoji-Horikawa, Shimogyo-ku (tel. 075/341-2311), was built in 1969 just before Expo was held in Osaka and has been one of Kyoto's grand hotels ever since. I like the architecture of this building—with its flat roof and railed ledges it resembles traditional Japanese architecture. The inside is a successful blend of traditional and modern. The rooms, for example, have shoji screens and fresh-flower arrangements, yet come with remote-control bilingual TV with CNN, soundproof windows, clock, radio, and other modern conveniences. Rates range from ¥8,800 ($70) to ¥17,500 ($140) for a single, ¥15,400 ($123) to ¥26,000 ($208) for a twin, and ¥17,500 ($140) to ¥26,000 ($208) for a double. Japanese-style rooms are available for ¥30,000 ($240). Located about a ten-minute walk east of Kyoto Station, the hotel maintains a shuttle-bus service to the south side of Kyoto Station every 15 minutes from 8 a.m. to 9 p.m. Facilities include an indoor swimming pool and sauna, as well as nine superb restaurants popular with Kyoto's residents, including Kyoto's only revolving restaurant. There's an English-language guest relations coordinator ready to assist you, and the hotel also issues its own maps and sightseeing information on Kyoto in English.

Japanese Style

Hiiragiya Ryokan, on the corner of Fuyacho (also spelled Huyacho) and Oike Streets in the heart of old Kyoto, Nakagyo-ku (tel. 075/221-1136), is a fine example of an old Japanese inn. Opened more than 150 years ago as a seafood merchant's shop and becoming an inn in 1861 to cater to visiting merchants, this exquisite ryokan is an excellent choice for foreigners unfamiliar with Japan. The staff is very efficient and accommodating and quite helpful in initiating visitors to the joys of the traditional inn. Surrounded by walls of wood and earth-toned yellow topped by tile roofs, this ryokan makes artful use of wood, bamboo, screens, and stones in creating a haven of simple design. The best room in the house is number 30, with magnificent views of the garden. At ¥88,000 ($704) per person, however, this room is probably a bit out of range for most of us. The next most expensive room is the one I find the most beautiful, a corner room with antiques and plenty of sunshine. It goes for ¥65,000 ($520) per person. Other rooms, with bath and toilet, start at ¥28,000 ($224) per person. All prices include two meals, of course, and Western-style breakfasts are available upon request. The three public baths here, as well as the tubs in the guest rooms, are of Chinese pine, soft to the touch. Guests who have stayed here include princes of the Japanese royal family, former Prime Minister Tojo, Charlie Chaplin, and designer Pierre Cardin.

Across the street from the Hiiragiya is another distinguished and venerable old inn, the **Tawaraya,** Fuyacho, Oike-Sagaru, Nakagyo-ku (tel. 075/221-5566). Since it opened in the first decade of the 1700s, it has been owned and operated by the same family. The present owner is Mrs. Toshi Okazaki Sato, who represents the 11th generation of innkeepers. Unfortunately, fire consumed the original building, so the oldest part of the ryokan now dates back only 175 years. This inn also has an impressive list of former guests, including the king of Sweden, former prime minister of Canada Pierre Trudeau, Leonard Bernstein, Edward Albee, Marlon Brando, Jean-Paul Sartre, Simone de Beauvoir, Walter Cronkite, Alfred Hitchcock, Candice Bergen, and Barbra Streisand. With tranquillity and refined taste reigning supreme, the ryokan has 19 rooms, each one different and exquisitely appointed. Some rooms, for example, have glass sliding doors opening up to a mossy garden of bamboo, stone lanterns, and manicured bushes, with cushions on a wooden veranda from which you can soak in the peacefulness. Rates for a room only begin at ¥44,000 ($352) for single or double occupancy. Meals are extra, with dinner ranging from ¥20,000 ($160) to ¥30,000 ($240) and breakfast ranging from ¥2,000 ($16) to ¥2,700 ($21.60). Tax and service charge extra.

Sumiya, Fuyacho-dori, Sanjo-sagaru, Nakagyo-ku (tel. 075/221-2188), is another traditional Japanese inn located on Fuyacho-dori Street south of the two ryokan described above. Like other ryokan in this price range, it offers excellent service amid simple yet elegant surroundings. Some of its 25 rooms have wonderful views of tiny private gardens, with outdoor benches or platforms for sitting. Rates here range from ¥33,000 ($264) to ¥75,000 ($600) per person, including two meals but not tax or service; off-season rates are cheaper. Western breakfasts are available.

THE MEDIUM BRACKET

Accommodations in this category are numerous and offer excellent value for the money, with prices lower than in Tokyo. All the hotels listed below have private bathrooms connected to all their guest rooms. Some of the ryokan, on the other hand, do not, especially the older ones. However, all ryokan have communal baths and toilets.

Western Style

With the Miyako name behind it, the **New Miyako Hotel,** Hachijo-guchi, Kyoto Station (tel. 075/661-7111), is one of the most popular hotels in this category. Opened in 1975, it's a sister hotel to the older first-class Miyako Hotel and is conveniently located just across the street from Kyoto Station's south side. With lower prices than the first-class Miyako Hotel, a modern exterior, and simple decor, it appeals widely to younger Japanese, group tours, and individual tourists. A ten-story white building shaped like an H, it has 714 rooms and eight restaurants. A beer garden is open on the roof from April to September every evening from 5 to 9 p.m. Rooms are what you'd expect in this price range, coming with TV with CNN English-language broadcasts, radio, refrigerator, and hot-water pot for tea. Single rooms range from ¥6,600 ($53) to ¥10,000 ($80); twins, from ¥12,000 ($96) to ¥23,000 ($184); and doubles, from ¥15,400 ($123) to ¥23,000 ($184). Triples, if you need one, begin at ¥23,000 ($184).

Across the street from Kyoto Station's north side is the **Kyoto New Hankyu Hotel,** Shiokoji-dori, Shimogyo-ku (tel. 075/343-5300), built in 1981 and offering 320 rooms. About 20% of its guests are foreigners, and of particular help to visitors is its information desk in the lobby, where the English-speaking staff can answer any questions you might have regarding your stay in Kyoto. The front-desk staff is very efficient and polite. Restaurants include a steakhouse and a Chinese restaurant, as well as a branch of the famous Minokichi Restaurant. Rooms are pleasant, with a decor of subdued colors, and come equipped with the usual fridge, radio, alarm clock, and hot water for tea, as well as a TV with CNN and coin-operated video. Rates begin at ¥8,500 ($68) for singles, ¥15,400 ($123) for twins, ¥18,500 ($148) for doubles, and ¥33,000 ($264) for Japanese-style rooms.

Another centrally located hotel is the **Kyoto Century Hotel,** 680 Higashishiokoji-cho, Shiokoji-sagaru, Shimogyo-ku (tel. 075/351-0111). Just east of Kyoto Station, this 243-room brick hotel features a four-story atrium lobby, Western and Japanese restaurants, a shopping arcade, and an outside swimming pool, which charges ¥1,500 ($10.71). All rooms include TV with CNN broadcasts and fridge and start at ¥9,300 ($74) for a single; twins range from ¥16,500 ($132) to ¥22,000 ($176), and doubles, from ¥13,700 ($110) to ¥24,000 ($192). Spacious Japanese-style rooms are available, starting at ¥38,000 ($304) for a two-room suite with kitchenette. Ask for a room facing east towards Higashiyama-ku. Although the view is nothing special, it's a lot better than the view toward the west, which looks squarely at the rooms of a neighboring hotel.

Located across the street from the National Museum, the **Kyoto Park Hotel,** Sanjusangendo Side, Higashiyama-ku (tel. 075/525-3111), is a good starting point for strolls throughout the eastern part of Kyoto, including the pleasant walk from nearby Kiyomizu Temple to Heian Shrine. With its stained-glass windows, plants, and statues, it's reminiscent of a European hotel, and there are two gardens on the hotel grounds. One is a rock garden, while the other is a lovely garden with a waterfall, cliff, and pond. Flowered wallpaper brightens up the rooms, which come with TV, hot-water pot, fridge, and clock. Especially nice are the more expensive twin rooms on the fifth floor, which have balconies overlooking the garden. Singles in this hotel are ¥8,500 ($68) to ¥10,700 ($86), doubles are ¥19,200 ($154), and twins run ¥14,800 ($118) to ¥23,600 ($189). To reach the Kyoto Park Hotel, take bus 206 or 208 from Kyoto Station to the Sanjusangendo-mae bus stop.

In the heart of Kyoto on Kawaramachi Dori Avenue, the **Kyoto Royal Hotel,** Kawaramachi, Sanjo, Nakagyo-ku (tel. 075/223-1234), is a typical tourist hotel and is easily reached by taking one of several buses from Kyoto Station to the Kawaramachi-Sanjo bus stop. In addition to Japanese and Chinese restaurants, it also has a Western restaurant on the tenth floor with panoramic views of the city and surrounding hills. Rooms are simple but bright and pleasant and feature bedside panels for the TV, an alarm clock, hot-water pot, and fridge. Most single rooms and some doubles face an inner courtyard, which cuts down on noise but also on sunshine. Room rates are ¥8,800 ($70) to ¥12,000 ($96) for singles, ¥14,800 ($118) to ¥22,000 ($176) for doubles, ¥14,800 ($118) to ¥20,900 ($167) for twins, and ¥23,000 ($184) for a triple.

Right up the street from the Royal Hotel is the **Kyoto Hotel,** Kawaramachi-Oike, Nakagyo-ku (tel. 075/211-5111). First opened in 1888, the present hotel consists of three different parts, the oldest stemming from 1927 and the newest from 1970. Altogether there are more than 500 rooms and seven restaurants catering to tourists (25% of which are foreigners). On the roof is a beer garden, open from mid-May to the end of August. Rooms have bilingual TV, hot-water pot, and fridge, and half the rooms have balconies. The cheapest singles face an inner courtyard. The older rooms have huge bathrooms—almost larger than the rooms themselves. Singles range from ¥8,200 ($66) to ¥25,000 ($200), twins run ¥15,400 ($123) to ¥33,000 ($264), and doubles cost ¥20,300 ($162) to ¥27,000 ($216). Japanese tatami rooms are also ¥25,000 ($200).

Situated on Oike Dori Avenue, the **Hotel Gimmond,** Takakura Oike Dori, Nakagyo-ku (tel. 075/221-4111), is a smaller hotel, with 145 rooms. Although it calls itself a tourist hotel, its rooms are rather plain and bare, resembling those in business hotels. They come with fridge, alarm clock, and TV with pay video. All rooms are soundproof, but I still think those that face away from Oike Dori Avenue are quieter. Singles begin at ¥7,700 ($62), and doubles and twins at ¥13,200 ($106). The easiest way to reach the Hotel Gimmond from Kyoto Station is to take the subway to Oike Station; from there it's just a few minutes' walk.

Located near the new Museum of Kyoto is the equally new **Dai-ichi Hotel Kyoto,** Higashino-toin, Sanjo-sagaru, Nakagyo-ku (tel. 075/252-4411). Located in the heart of old Kyoto, this pleasant and modern hotel has a bright, marbled lobby that features a large ikebana flower arrangement as its focal point. Although it calls itself a tourist hotel, I consider it more a business hotel, since 96 of its 117 rooms are singles. Rooms are of adequate size and come with stocked fridge, hot-water pot and tea, TV, radio, alarm clock, hairdryer, phone, and cotton yukata. There are five restaurants and bars, unusual for a hotel of this size. Singles range from ¥7,500 ($60) to ¥9,300 ($74), twins from ¥17,500 ($140) to ¥24,000 ($192); doubles are ¥17,500 ($140).

First opening more than 30 years ago, the **International Hotel Kyoto** (called the Kyoto Kokusai Hotel in Japanese) is located on Horikawa-dori Avenue across from Nijo Castle, Nakagyo-ku (tel. 075/222-1111). Despite its name, approximately 90% of the hotel guests are Japanese, and the hotel has been somewhat overshadowed by more modern hotels that have opened in Kyoto in the last three decades. Its lobby overlooks a pleasant, lush garden, and rooms are decorated with traditional shoji screens. Singles, none of which face the castle, start at ¥8,500 ($68). You can have a double or twin facing the castle for ¥21,000 ($168). Otherwise, doubles begin at ¥13,000 ($104) and twins at ¥14,000 ($112). Facilities include five restaurants and bars, as well as a beer garden open in summer from 5 to 9 p.m.

Although it's rather inconveniently located in the northeast corner of Kyoto, far from most of the city's sights, the **Kyoto Holiday Inn,** 36 Nishihiraki-cho, Takano, Sakyo-ku (tel. 075/721-3131), makes up for it by providing facilities normally found only at resort hotels, including indoor and outdoor swimming pools, tennis courts, an indoor ice-skating rink, a sauna and solarium, a golf-driving range, and a 100-lane bowling alley. A restaurant mall features a dozen different restaurants ranging from McDonald's to Chinese to steak, and a rooftop beer garden (open from 5 to 9 p.m. in the summer) has barbecued dishes you can cook at your own table. As with all Holiday Inns, the beds are all doubles and children under 12 can stay with their parents free. A number of different kinds of rooms are available, beginning at ¥10,000 ($80) for one person and ¥17,500 ($140) for two. The hotel maintains a shuttle-bus service, with runs to Kyoto Station every hour between 8:40 a.m. and 8:40 p.m. You can also take public bus 206 from Kyoto Station to the Takano bus stop.

Japanese Style

First opened almost 200 years ago in the early 1800s, **Kinmata** ⑦, 407 Gokomachi, Shijo-agaru, Nakagyo-ku (tel. 075/221-1039), is a beautiful, traditional wooden inn in the heart of Kyoto. Its earliest customers were medicine peddlers, and in the hallway hangs an old sign announcing the house rules of past centuries— among them no gambling, no prostitution, no mah-jongg, and no noisy parties. The present owner represents the seventh generation of innkeepers here. With only seven rooms, Kinmata is exquisite inside and out, complete with an inner courtyard and peaceful garden. The public bath is of cypress. Rates per person start at ¥22,000 ($176), with two meals, tax extra. You can also stay here for ¥8,800 ($70) per person if you opt to take meals elsewhere—but you'll be missing great meals prepared by the owner himself.

Seikoro, Toiyamachi Gojo, Higashiyama-ku (tel. 075/561-0771), is less than a minute's walk from Gojo Station on the Keihan Electric Railway. Accustomed to foreigners, the manager here speaks good English. The ryokan itself is about 100 years old but its history stretches back 160 years. After passing through a front gate and small courtyard, you'll find yourself in a cozy parlor, which holds an eclectic mixture of both Japanese and Western antiques, including an old grandfather clock. The rooms, also decorated in antiques, are very homey and comfortable and come with a private bathroom. Some rooms overlook a garden. An annex built just before the 1964 Olympics has rooms that are high enough up that you can see over the surrounding rooftops. Per-person rates, including two meals, and service charge (tax extra), range from ¥22,000 ($176) to ¥50,000 ($400). The management doesn't mind, however, if you prefer to take your meals elsewhere, especially if you're going to be here for a while. The charge for two people without meals, tax, or service charge is ¥22,000 ($176) to ¥44,000 ($352).

Located on the approach to Nanzenji Temple, the **Yachiyo Inn,** Nanzenji, Sakyo-ku (tel. 075/771-4148), has a large foreign clientèle. Formerly a villa (it became a ryokan after World War II), the building is about 100 years old but has been remodeled so that it seems almost new. All the rooms on the ground floor open onto a small garden. Less expensive rooms are located on the second floor. There are wooden bathtubs in most rooms, along with showers and Western toilets. Rooms also boast transom carvings and ikebana flower arrangements. This ryokan, which you can reach by taking bus 5 from Kyoto Station, doesn't mind if you prefer to take your meals elsewhere. If you're staying in Kyoto for a few days, you might want to first take breakfast and dinner at the ryokan and then later start going out to Kyoto's many restaurants. Room rates, including service charge only, range from ¥14,300 ($114) to ¥23,000 ($184) for one person and ¥17,600 ($141) to ¥26,400 ($211) for two. Rates including two meals and service range from ¥20,000 ($160) to ¥34,000 ($272) for one person and ¥28,500 ($228) to ¥49,500 ($396) for two.

Located on Shinmonzen shopping street in a quaint neighborhood of small wooden homes and antique shops, **Yoshi-ima,** Shinmonzen Street, Gion (tel. 075/561-2620), is within easy walking distance of both Gion and the Kawaramachi district, with its many restaurants and bars. Much of the ryokan, however, is relatively new and modern, although there are a few older rooms available in a wooden building for the same price. Most of the guests here are booked through the Japan Travel Bureau, including foreigners. In fact, sometimes the whole ryokan is filled with only foreigners. Once a year, for example, a group of writers and artists come from the Soviet Union. There are a total of 20 rooms, all with private bathroom, which start at ¥16,500 ($132), including two meals and service charge.

A sister ryokan of the exclusive Hiiragiya Ryokan, the **Hiiragiya Bekkan,** on Gokomachi Dori Street, Nijosaguru, Nakagyo-ku (tel. 075/231-0151), is a very good choice among Kyoto's medium-priced Japanese inns. Run by a very friendly and accommodating staff, this small 14-room ryokan has a warm and home-like feel to it. Opened 25 years ago, it's relatively new by ryokan standards but manages to transmit a traditional atmosphere, as most of the rooms open onto a small garden. The management prefers that you take your meals here, and per-person rates, including breakfast and dinner, and service, run ¥11,000 ($88) to ¥22,000 ($176).

Ryokan Rikiya ⑯, Ryozen Kannon-mae, Higashiyama-ku (tel. 075/561-2814), is located in front of Ryozen Kannon between Kiyomizu Temple and Maruyama Park. To reach it, take bus 206 from Kyoto Station to the Yasui bus stop, from which it's a four-minute walk. With ten rooms located in a modern building, this is a quiet, family-run ryokan. The best room is named Daiyu, has its own bathroom, and faces toward the front courtyard. Charges per person with breakfast are ¥11,000 ($88) for rooms without bathroom and ¥13,000 ($104) for those with bathroom. Japanese dinners are ¥8,000 ($64).

THE BUDGET CATEGORY

Kyoto abounds in accommodations in this price range, due in part to the large percentage of students and young people who flock to this cultural mecca. The majority of establishments in this category are Japanese style, while the Western hotels are all business hotels. Unless otherwise stated, you can expect the business hotel rooms to have a private bath, but rooms in Japanese-style ryokan do not. Remember also that unless otherwise stated, a 3% tax and often a 10% service charge will be added to your bill in Western-style accommodations. Japanese-style ryokan, on the other hand, often include tax and service charges in their rates.

Western Style

Kyoto Central Inn, Shijo Kawaramachi, Nishi-iru, Shimogyo-ku (tel. 075/211-1666), as the name implies, is centrally located in the heart of the city near the intersection of Shijo and Kawaramachi Streets. Although it's a business hotel, because it occupies one of the best spots in town, about 50% of its guests are tourists. Rooms are small but adequate, and come with TV and radio. The hotel's restaurant and coffeeshop is open from 7 a.m. to 9:30 p.m. Singles are ¥6,000 ($48), twins and doubles start at ¥12,000 ($96). Triples begin at ¥15,700 ($126). Remember, tax and service are extra. You can reach the hotel on a number of bus lines from Kyoto Station, including buses 4, 5, 14, and 205.

Located on Kawaramachi Dori Avenue not far from where it meets Sanjo Dori Avenue, the **Hotel Alpha**, Kawaramachi, Sango-agaru (tel. 075/241-2000), is a pleasant business hotel that opened in 1982. To reach it from Kyoto Station, take bus 4, 5, 14, or 205 to the Kawaramachi-Sanjo bus stop. Entrance to the hotel is on a side street called Anekoji Dori. Semidouble-size beds are in almost all 120 rooms, which also have the usual TV with video, hot-water pot, and fridge. Hairdryers are available on request. Since the cheapest singles face an inner courtyard and are fairly dark, it may be worthwhile to dish out the extra yen for a brighter room. Singles range from ¥7,000 ($56) to ¥8,500 ($68); twins, from ¥12,000 ($96) to ¥15,900 ($127); and doubles are ¥13,200 ($106). A few Japanese-style rooms are available beginning at ¥24,000 ($192).

It's hard to miss the **Kyoto Tower Hotel**, located right across the street from Kyoto Station's north side at Karasuma Shichijo (tel. 075/361-3211). Topped by a tall tower with an observation platform, this hotel was built just before the 1964 Olympics and is now a kind of cross between a tourist hotel and business hotel. Because of the tower and connecting shops there's a lot of traffic through the hotel's ground floor, but the lobby and restaurant on the eighth floor are a bit more peaceful. Rooms are soundproof and feature shoji screens, refrigerator, hot-water pot, TV, and alarm clock. The bathrooms and tubs are tiny. Room rates are ¥6,500 ($52) to ¥8,500 ($68) for singles, ¥11,000 ($88) to ¥20,000 ($160) for twins, and ¥12,000 ($96) to ¥16,500 ($132) for doubles. Triples begin at ¥18,000 ($144) and Japanese-style tatami rooms are ¥22,000 ($176).

Also located across from Kyoto Station's north side is the **Hotel Hokke Club**, Higashi-Shiokojicho, Shimogyo-ku (tel. 075/361-1251). Part of a business-hotel chain, this one caters to tourists because of its favorable location. Take off your shoes before entering; the front desk is on the ground floor and the lobby is on the second floor. On the ground floor there is also a large tatami room used for Buddhist ceremonies twice a day for the hotel's employees, which you're welcome to observe. There are two public baths, large and bright with windows extending along the length of one wall. You're better off asking for a room on a higher floor. The cheapest Japanese-style tatami rooms without private bathroom go for ¥11,500 ($92) for two persons. Western-style singles without bath are ¥5,700 ($46). They tend to be rather small with tiny windows, but have TV with video, radio, cotton kimono, hot-water pot, and sink. Twins without bathroom are ¥10,000 ($80); with bathroom they're ¥12,700 ($102). Other rooms available include triples without bath beginning at ¥11,900 ($95) and Japanese-style rooms with bathroom at ¥13,300 ($106). All rooms are very simple, with only the basics.

Opened in 1985, **Pension Higashiyama**, Sanjo-sagaru, Shirakawa-suji (tel. 075/882-1181), is a clean and cheerful establishment on a small street banked by the Shirakawa River not far from the Miyako Hotel on Kyoto's east side. Its 14 rooms, some of which overlook the willow-lined stream, are mainly Western style with flowered wallpaper and quilts on the bed, but three Japanese-style tatami rooms are also available. A few rooms have their own private bathroom. Rooms come with coin-operated TV and there's a coin-operated laundry on the premises. Rates, including tax and service, are ¥3,900 ($31) for one person, ¥7,900 ($63) for two, and ¥11,000 ($88) for three. Twins or triples with private bathroom run about ¥1,500 ($12) more. If you want to use a cotton kimono here, you can rent one for ¥200 ($1.60). The front doors are locked at 11:30 p.m. To reach it, take bus 206 from Kyoto Station to the Chion-in-mae bus stop, from which it's a two-minute walk.

Under the same ownership as Pension Higashiyama and charging the exact same rates is **Pension Station Kyoto**, Hichijo-agaru, Shinmachi, Shimogyo-ku (tel. 075/882-6200). As its name implies, it's much closer to the train station, about a five-minute walk away just west of Higashi Honganji Temple. It offers both Japanese- and Western-style rooms, two of which have private bath. Although this place overdoes it on fake flowers, it is nevertheless cheerful and spotlessly clean. Rooms come with coin-operated TV, air conditioner, and heater, and there's a coin-operated laundry. Western breakfasts are available for ¥800 ($6.40), while Japanese dinners cost ¥1,800 ($14.40).

Kuwacho Ryokan, 231 Shichijo-agaru, Akezu-dori, Shimogyo-ku (tel. 075/371-3191), has both Western- and Japanese-style rooms despite its name. Very conveniently located just a five-minute walk north of Kyoto Station and east of Higashi Honganji Temple, this modern concrete building has 14 rooms, all with private bathroom, coin-operated TV, and cotton kimono. Rooms facing the front even have a small balcony. No meals are served, and rates start at ¥4,900 ($39) for single occupancy, ¥7,700 ($62) for double, and ¥11,500 ($92) for triple.

Japanese Style

There isn't much variation in rooms in this category. After all, a tatami room is a tatami room and at this price there usually isn't much else in them. Rooms are fairly bare, with perhaps only a low table, a TV, some cushions, and a futon in the closet that you lay out yourself before retiring. Imparting a feeling of traditional Japan, however, these accommodations are highly recommended and include tax and service.

Matsubaya Ryokan, Nishi-iru, Higashitouin, Kamijuzuyamachi Dori Avenue, Shimogyo-ku (tel. 075/351-3727), is conveniently located about a ten-minute walk north of Kyoto Station just east of Higashi Honganji Temple. A member of the Japanese Inn Group, this traditional, 180-year-old ryokan offers excellent value for the money, with singles going for ¥3,800 ($30) to ¥4,000 ($32) and twins for ¥7,500 ($60) to ¥8,000 ($64). There are 11 Japanese-style tatami rooms here, the best ones facing an inner courtyard. These rooms come complete with wooden balconies and a couple of chairs, great places to relax. Another good choice in rooms are those that face a tiny enclosed garden. If you wish to make a reservation here, you must pay a deposit equal to one night's lodging, payable in the form of a cashier's check, international money order, traveler's check, or American Express credit card. Towels and cotton kimonos are provided, and rooms have a coin-operated TV. Facilities include two public baths and a coin-operated laundry. If you want to try a Japanese-style breakfast, you can order one for ¥1,000 ($8). Ham and eggs are available for ¥300 ($2.40). A Japanese dinner costs ¥2,200 ($17.60) and up. Matsubaya Ryokan is owned and managed by the friendly and irrepressibly energetic Mrs. Hayashi, representing the fifth generation of innkeepers. She'll talk on and on to you in Japanese even if you don't understand, making you wish you did. Highly recommended.

Not far from Matsubaya is **Ryokan Murakamiya,** 270 Sasaya-cho, Shichijo-agaru, Higashinotouin-dori, Shimogyo-ku (tel. 075/371-1260). Small and clean, its seven rooms are nicely decorated, some with old-style ceilings and woodwork. The building itself is about 50 years old. Rates here are ¥3,900 ($31) for a single, ¥7,900 ($63) for a twin, and ¥9,900 ($79) for a triple. Japanese breakfasts are ¥1,000 ($8).

Another inexpensive ryokan in the same general vicinity is **Ryokan Kyoka,** Seisinji-cho, Kaminoguchi-agaru, Kiyamachi Dori (tel. 075/351-7920), about a seven-minute walk from Kyoto Station. Although it doesn't have quite the charm of the other two described above, it also has good prices at ¥3,800 ($30) for one person and ¥7,500 ($60) for two in Japanese-style rooms. Some of the rooms are in a nearby annex, where you have a view of the Takase Canal. Although the annex, called Riverside Takase, is farther from the station (about a 15-minute walk away), its location is actually much prettier than at the Kyoka. Japanese- or Western-style breakfasts are available for ¥1,000 ($8).

Finally, one more place to try in this same vicinity east of Higashi Honganji Temple is **Takigawa** ⑦, Rokujo-sagaru, Higashinotouin-dori, Shimogyo-ku (tel. 075/351-1782). A bit impersonal because of its size, it offers 25 Japanese-style rooms, all without bathroom. Rooms are simple but pleasant with all the basics of TV, telephone, air conditioner, and heater. Rates here are ¥4,400 ($35) for a single, ¥7,700 ($62) for a twin, and ¥11,500 ($92) for a triple. Japanese breakfasts start at ¥1,000 ($8), while Japanese dinners start at ¥2,500 ($20).

Hiraiwa Ryokan, 314 Hayao-cho, Kaminoguch-agaru, Ninomiyacho-dori, Shimogyo-ku (tel. 075/351-6748), is one of the best-known ryokan in the Japanese Inn Group. Several feature stories have been published about this inexpensive Japanese inn and the couple who run it. They speak almost no English and yet have been welcoming foreigners from all over the world for many years. Spread through the main building and a new annex, rooms are spotless and come with TV, towel, and cotton kimono. Facilities include coin-operated washer and dryer and even heated toilet seats! Breakfasts are communal affairs around the kitchen table, where toast and coffee are available for ¥250 ($2). There are a small public bath and showers, but better still is the neighborhood public bath just around the corner, which charges ¥250 ($2). Single rooms cost ¥3,800 ($30) and twins are ¥7,500 ($60). This ryokan is about a 15-minute walk from Kyoto Station, but you can also take bus 17 or 205 and get off at the third stop, Kawaramachi Shomen. From there it's a three-minute walk.

In the vicinity of Hiraiwa is another inexpensive Japanese-style accommodation. **Yuhara** ⑦⑧, Kiyamachi-dori, Shomen-agaru, Shimogyo-ku (tel. 075/371-9583), has been a ryokan for more than 30 years, welcoming guests from all over the world. Pleasantly located beside a tree-lined narrow canal, it's run by an enthusiastic woman who speaks English. Of its nine rooms, one is Western style and three have their own sinks. The rate here is ¥3,300 ($26) per person.

Nashinoki Inn, Agaru Imadegawa Nashinoki Street, Kamikyo-ku (tel. 075/241-1543), in a quiet, peaceful neighborhood north of the Kyoto Imperial Palace, is run by a warm and friendly older couple who speak some English and have had the ryokan for about 20 years. There are eight tatami rooms here, some of them quite large and adequate for families. The rate for one person is ¥4,800 ($38) and for two people it's ¥8,800 ($70). A Japanese or Western breakfast is served for ¥1,000 ($8), with Japanese dinners available for ¥3,800 ($30.40). To reach this inn, take the subway from Kyoto Station to Imadegawa Station. From there it's about a ten-minute walk.

Rokuharaya Inn ⑦⑨, 147 Takemuracho Rokuhara, Higashiyama-ku (tel. 075/531-2776), is a basic, inexpensive ryokan located on a small street typical of Kyoto. There are only seven rooms here, and in my opinion the best ones are on the second floor. More foreigners stay here than Japanese. Each room has a coin-operated TV but not much more—just your average Japanese tatami room. Per-person rates are ¥3,800 ($30) without meals, ¥4,900 ($39) with breakfast, and ¥6,500 ($52) with two meals. To reach it, take bus 206 from Kyoto Station to the Gojozaka bus stop, from which it's a three-minute walk.

Another inexpensive lodging is **Hinomoto,** 375 Kotake-cho, Matsubara-agaru, Kawaramachi Dori, Shimogyo-ku (tel. 075/351-4563). Not far from the Kawaramachi-Shijo intersection, its front façade is brick but the rest is wood. It's a three-minute walk from Kawaramachi Matsubara bus stop, which can be reached by taking bus 17 or 205 from Kyoto Station. Although the couple running this six-room ryokan does not speak much English, they welcome foreigners. Rooms are pleasant, the location is quiet and convenient, and the public bath is made of wood. Rates are ¥3,800 ($30) for one person, ¥7,500 ($60) for two, and ¥9,900 ($79) for three. Western breakfasts cost ¥450 ($3.60) and Japanese breakfasts are ¥1,000 ($8).

Teradaya Inn, Gojo-bashi Higashi, Higashiyama-ku (tel. 075/561-3821), is located near the sloping approach to Kiyomizu Temple in east Kyoto. A concrete building with only five rooms, it charges ¥3,800 ($30) per person for a room only, ¥4,500 ($36) with breakfast, and ¥6,000 ($48) if you take a room with two meals. Yukata are provided, and televisions and air conditioners are coin-operated. Rooms on the second floor are the brightest. Facilities include a public bath and coin-operated laundry. From Kyoto Station, take bus 206 to Gojozaka bus stop.

Although it's not as conveniently located as the ryokan listed above, **Rakucho,** Higashihangi-cho, Shimogamo, Sakyo-ku (tel. 075/721-2174), offers pleasant, clean rooms for ¥3,600 ($29) for single occupancy and ¥7,200 ($58) for a double. All rooms have heating and air conditioning and a view of a small, peaceful garden. Rakucho is a ten-minute walk from Kitaoji subway station. You can also reach it by taking bus 205 from Kyoto Station to Furitsu-Daigakumae bus stop, from which it's a one-minute walk away. Entrance to the ryokan is through a well-tended tiny courtyard filled with plants.

Ryokan Mishima Shrine, 539 Kamiuma-machi, Higashioji Higashi-iru, Shibutani-dori, Higashiyama-ku (tel. 075/551-0033), is located on the grounds of Mishima Shrine, a Shinto shrine visited by women who desire children and by women already pregnant who wish to ensure a safe delivery. You can have your picture taken in traditional shrine garb, free if you have your own camera and ¥240 ($1.92) if you have it taken with the shrine's Polaroid. Although the shrine was founded about 150 years ago, the nine Japanese-style rooms are located in a new building that opened in the mid-1980s. Spotless and simple, it caters largely to foreigners in the summer and to Japanese in the winter. Cotton kimonos and towels are provided, and rooms have a coin-operated TV as well as a private toilet. Facilities include four public baths and a coin-operated washing machine. The family running this place speaks some English. If you're alone you'll be charged ¥3,800 ($30), two people are charged ¥7,500 ($60), and three people are charged ¥10,000 ($80). To reach the shrine, take bus 206 from Kyoto Station and get off at the Higashiyama-Umamachi bus stop, from which it's a five-minute walk.

If you want to stay in a Buddhist temple, **Myorenji Temple** ⑧⓪, Teranouchi Horikawa, Kamigyo-ku (tel. 075/451-3527), was founded more than 650 years ago, though the present buildings stem from about two centuries ago. To reach it, take bus 9 from Kyoto Station and get off at the Teranouchi bus stop. From there it's a few minutes' walk. Once you enter the temple grounds, the building open to guests lies straight ahead. Very peaceful, it's run by a jolly woman named Chizuko-san who speaks a little English. She requests that you make reservations to stay here at least a week in advance, preferably a month before. Sleeping is on futons spread out in large rooms, and the charge of ¥3,300 ($26.40) includes breakfast, dinner, and a ticket to use the neighborhood public bath (there are no bathing facilities on the temple grounds). If you're interested in attending services, they're held every morning at 6:30 a.m. Be sure to check out the rock garden in back of the temple.

If you're looking for lodging at rock-bottom prices, the best place in town is **Tani House,** 8 Daitokujicho, Murasakino, Kita-ku (tel. 075/492-5489). Located close to Daitokuji Temple on the route of several buses from Kyoto Station, including bus 206 (get off at the Kenkunjinja bus stop), the entrance of this 50-year-old wooden house is smothered with bamboo. Mrs. Tani keeps this place tidy and clean, and sleeping is either in private rooms or in communal tatami sleeping rooms separate for men and women. This place has a reputation that extends far beyond Japan's borders. One European staying here told me he had heard about Tani House when he was traveling through Russia. Mrs. Tani speaks some English and somehow seems able to cope with the many foreigners who pass through her life daily. You're supposed to leave during the day from 11 a.m. to 3 p.m., but rules are otherwise fairly lenient. The rate is only ¥1,500 ($12) per person whether you sleep in the dorm or in a private room (if you're the only one in the private room, however, she'll charge you double, since they're meant for two people). Although Tani House is a bit far north, the price more than makes up for it.

If you want to stay closer to the action, Mrs. Tani also rents out two rooms in the center of town above a shop where her English-speaking daughter works. **Tani Annex** is located at Nishi-minami Kade Gokomachi, Nakagyo-ku (tel. 075/211-5637), just off the covered shopping arcade. Often rented out by the week or for longer periods of time, both rooms here come with bathroom and color TV, and there's also a coin-operated laundry. The rate is ¥5,500 ($44) for two people.

Of the several youth hostels in and around the Kyoto area, **Higashiyama Youth Hostel,** 112 Shirakawabashi-goken-cho, Sanjo-dori, Higashiyama-ku (tel. 075/761-8135), is the most convenient and the closest to Kyoto Station. A 20-minute bus ride from Kyoto Station on bus 5 to the Higashiyama-Sanjo bus stop, this youth hostel is a modern concrete building that sleeps 130 people in bunk beds. You have to take breakfast and dinner here, and the charge is ¥3,000 ($24) for youth hostel members and ¥3,200 ($25.60) for nonmembers. Be sure to call in advance because this place is sometimes booked full with school groups.

Also in Kyoto but a bit farther from the station is **Kyoto Utane Youth Hostel,** 29 Nakayama-cho, Uzumasa, Ukyo-ku (tel. 075/462-2288). It's located in the northwestern part of the city near Ryoanji Temple, which is famous for its Zen rock garden. To reach it, take bus 26 from Kyoto Station or bus 10 from Shijo-Kawaramachi and get off at Youth Hostel-mae bus stop, from which it's a one-minute walk. Both members and nonmembers are charged ¥2,300 ($18.40), breakfast is ¥400 ($3.20), and dinner is ¥600 ($4.80).

A Note on Japanese Symbols

Many hotels, restaurants, and other establishments in Japan do not have signs showing their names in English letters. Appendix II lists the Japanese symbols for all such places appearing in this guide. Each establishment name in Japanese symbols is numbered, and the same number appears in an oval in the text following the boldfaced establishment name. For example, in the text Osaka's **Hotel Hokke Club** ⑯₄ is number 164 in the Japanese symbol list in Appendix II.

---

3. Where to Dine

Most of Kyoto's traditional Japanese restaurants are located in the heart of the city in Nakagyo-ku, spreading to the east in areas called Higashiyama-ku and Sakyo-ku. I have therefore divided Kyoto's restaurants according to district, adding some Western-style restaurants as well. In addition to the restaurants listed here there are also some establishments described in the nightlife section that serve food.

EASTERN KYOTO

Many of the restaurants in this part of town sprang up in connection with the Buddhist temples in the area, serving either vegetarian fare to Buddhist monks and worshippers or traditional Japanese food to sightseers. Kaiseki cuisine and tofu dishes are offered by the majority of restaurants in this area.

Japanese Food

Formerly a villa, **Minoko** ㉛, 480 Kiyoi-cho, Shimogawara-dori, Gion, Higashiyama-ku (tel. 561-0328), is an enclave of traditional Japan. With its simple, austere exterior and an interior of winding wooden corridors, tatami rooms, and a garden, it's the kind of building that excites curiosity from anyone passing by, making them want to pause and explore further. Opened about 70 years ago by the present owner's father, Minoko does its best to retain the spirit of the tea ceremony. For lunch, for example, you can order an informal box lunch called *chabako-bento,* named after the lacquered box it's served in which is traditionally used to carry tea utensils to outdoor tea ceremonies. Served from 11:30 a.m. to 2:30 p.m., it costs ¥3,300 ($26.40). For lunch you can also order the *hiru-kaiseki,* a mini-kaiseki set, for ¥8,800 ($70.40). Lunch is served communally in a large tatami room with a view of a beautiful tea garden. If you come here for dinner, available by reservation only, you'll eat in your own private tatami room. Elaborate kaiseki dinners begin at ¥11,000 ($88), including a special kind of kaiseki, called *cha-kaiseki*, usually served at tea ceremony gatherings. Hours here are from 11:30 a.m. to 10 p.m., with the last order at 8 p.m. It's closed the second and fourth Wednesdays of every month. Minoko is located just a couple of minutes' walk south of Yasaka Shrine.

Located right next to the stone torii gate of Yasaka Shrine is **Nakamuraro** ⑧, Yasaka-jinja-uchi, Gion (tel. 561-0016). Opened 400 years ago to serve worshippers on their way to the shrine, the tiny one-room tea house is said to be the oldest restaurant in Japan. It specializes in *tofu dengaku*, skewers of tofu smothered in miso sauce, and is now in its 12th generation of restaurateurs. Best is the tofu dengaku obento for ¥3,000 ($24), served from 11:30 a.m. to 6 p.m. every day except the last Thursday of every month. If you feel like splurging, beside the tea house is a handsome wooden restaurant, added in the 19th century, where meals are served in lovely rooms overlooking a magnificent garden. It specializes in kaiseki and serves a mini-kaiseki lunch until 3 p.m. If you come here for dinner, served until 7 p.m., expect to spend at least ¥20,000 ($160) per person for a kaiseki feast.

If you're the least bit shy about going into a Japanese restaurant and ordering something without being able to read the menu, the easiest place to enjoy Japanese food is in the internationally known Miyako Hotel, Sanjo-Keage (tel. 771-7111). In its Japanese restaurant, **Hamasaku,** open from noon to 2 p.m. and from 5:30 to 10 p.m., you can have a variety of dishes ranging from tempura, sushi, and eel to kaiseki cuisine. For lunch, why not try a special box lunch of, say, combination sushi or eel and rice for ¥3,300 ($26.40)? Tempura meals range from ¥4,700 ($37.60) to ¥6,300 ($50.40), while kaiseki menus, which change with the seasons, range from ¥8,800 ($70.40) to ¥13,200 ($105.60).

If you want to come to the Miyako for dinner, another place you can try is **Hagoromo.** It's open nightly from 5:30 to 9 p.m., serving pork, beef, or chicken sukiyaki beginning at ¥7,000 ($56), or *tobanyaki* (beef, chicken, pork, shrimp, and seasonal vegetables grilled on a porcelain plate) for ¥7,000 ($56).

Minokichi of Kyoto, Sanjo-agaru, Dobutsuen-mae Street, Sakyo-ku (tel. 771-4185), is one of Kyoto's best-known restaurants. First established more than 260 years ago, Minokichi now has several branches in Japan, including a handful in Kyoto, Osaka, and Tokyo. This flagship restaurant consists of various rooms in several buildings, the most enjoyable of which is tatami seating in the oldest building with an open square hearth and views of a graceful bamboo garden. The specialty of the restaurant is Kyoto kaiseki, reflecting the gourmet dining style of the upper classes during the Heian Period more than 800 years ago. Emphasis is on the appearance of the food, with great care given to the selection and preparation of seasonal food from field, mountain, river, and ocean. Although the dishes themselves change, a kaiseki meal here always consists of eight dishes: an appetizer, raw fish, soup, food cooked in delicate broth, steamed food, broiled food, deep-fried food, and vinegared food. Kaiseki meals start at ¥9,900 ($79.20). Other dishes available include sukiyaki for ¥7,000 ($56) or shabu-shabu beginning at ¥4,900 ($39.20). Set meals of tempura or eel begin at ¥3,300 ($26.40). There are also special box lunches available with a variety of seasonal dishes, beginning at ¥2,700 ($21.60) for lunch and ¥3,800 ($30.40) for dinner. Since there's a menu in English, ordering is no problem. This restaurant is open daily from 11:30 a.m. to 8 p.m. (last order), and if you plan on coming for dinner or eating kaiseki, be sure to make a reservation. Minokichi is located just a few minutes' walk northwest of the Miyako Hotel.

Another restaurant serving Kyoto kaiseki cuisine is **Awata Sanso** ⑧, Awataguchi Sanjo Bocho 2-15, Higashiyama-ku (tel. 561-4908). An old Japanese villa, this elegant restaurant, whose private rooms overlook a beautiful garden with flowering bushes, rocks, moss, ferns, and streams, is tucked away on a back street south of Sanjo Dori Avenue not far from the Miyako Hotel. A restaurant since 1937, it has been owned by the Kyoto Hotel since 1950. Entrance to the restaurant sets the mood as you walk past a wooden gate, stone lanterns, and an old well and are ushered into your own private tatami room. If you come here for lunch (served daily from 11 a.m. to 2 p.m.), you can order a mini-kaiseki meal starting at ¥11,000 ($88) or an obento box lunch for ¥6,500 ($52), tax and service charge included. Dinners (served from 5 to 9 p.m.) are much more elaborate affairs and include various kaiseki meals ranging from ¥16,500 ($132) to ¥36,000 ($288). Although dishes change according to the season, a typical meal may consist of dried mullet roe and sea urchin, halibut, bean-paste soup with grilled rice cake, sea bream with spring vegetables, pork, tempura, cooked crab, turnip and quail egg, turtle soup, assorted Japanese pickles, and fruit. You can also order shabu-shabu for ¥9,300 ($74.40). Reservations are a must.

Hyotei ⑧④, Kusakawa-cho 30-5, Nanzenji (tel. 771-4116), is on the main road leading to Nanzenji Temple (look for a plain façade hidden behind a bamboo fence with a sign shaped like a gourd). This restaurant consists of two parts, one serving expensive kaiseki and the other serving seasonal obento box lunches. Kaiseki meals, which start at ¥16,500 ($132) for lunch and ¥22,000 ($176) for dinner, are served in separate, tiny houses situated around a beautiful garden with a pond, maple trees, and bushes. The oldest house, which resembles a small tea house, is 350 years old. Seating is on cushions on a tatami floor in your own private room, and your food is brought to you by women in kimonos. The other part of the restaurant serves obento lunch boxes starting at ¥4,400 ($35.20); the menu depends on the season, and seating is at tables and chairs. Obento is served from noon to 4 p.m. every day except Thursday, while kaiseki is served from 11 a.m. to 7:30 p.m. except every second and fourth Tuesdays of the month.

Also on the road leading to Nanzenji Temple is **Junsei,** 60 Kusakawa-cho, Nanzenji (tel. 761-2311). A restaurant specializing in tofu dishes opened here in 1961, but the grounds and garden were originally part of a private institution established during the shogun era in the 1830s. Although Junsei is popular with tour groups and is tourist-oriented, the food is good and an English menu makes ordering easy. There are several buildings spread throughout the grounds and what you eat determines where you go—as soon as you arrive you will be given a menu and asked what you want to eat. I chose the *yudofu* (tofu) set meal for ¥2,200 ($17.60) and was directed to an older building filled with antiques and tatami mats. My meal came with vegetable tempura and various tofu dishes, including fried tofu on a stick and tofu boiled in a pot at my table. Other dishes available include kaiseki, starting at ¥6,600 ($52.80); turtle dishes, starting at ¥11,000 ($88); beef shabu-shabu, beginning at ¥6,500 ($52); sukiyaki, from ¥5,500 ($44); and tempura for ¥4,400 ($35.20). There are also obento lunch boxes beginning at ¥2,700 ($21.60). Meals are served daily from 11 a.m. and the last orders are taken at 8 p.m. After your meal be sure to take a stroll through the garden.

Located just north of Nanzenji Temple's main gate (called the San Mon Gate), **Okutan** ⑧⑤, 86-30 Fukuchi-cho, Nanzenji, Sakyo-ku (tel. 771-8709), is one of the oldest, most authentic, and most delightful tofu restaurants in Kyoto. Founded about 350 years ago as a vegetarian restaurant serving Zen dishes to Buddhist monks, this wooden place with a thatched roof serves just one thing, a tofu meal, with the finishing touches provided by a pond, a garden, and peacefulness. Okutan is very simple and rustic, with seating either in tatami rooms or outdoors on platforms. Women dressed in traditional rural clothing bring your food. The tofu set meal for ¥3,300 ($26.40) includes boiled tofu, fried tofu, vegetable tempura, yam soup, and pickled vegetables. If you're still hungry you can order some of the above items à la carte. This restaurant is especially delightful in fine weather. It's open from 10:30 a.m. to 5:30 p.m.; closed Thursday.

On the same road as Okutan (just around the corner to the north) is another vegetarian restaurant, **Koan** ⑧⑥, this one located on the grounds of the Shotekiin Temple, Fukuchi-cho, Nanzenji (tel. 771-2781). Open from 11:30 a.m. to 4:30

p.m. every day except Wednesday, it offers vegetarian and tofu dishes characteristic of Zen temple meals usually served to monks. The English menu lists yudofu set meals for ¥2,200 ($17.60) and ¥2,700 ($21.60), as well as other vegetarian dishes beginning at ¥3,300 ($26.40).

Goemonjaya ⑧⑦, 67 Kukasawa-cho, Nanzenji, Sakyo-ku (tel. 751-9638), is an inexpensive restaurant serving tofu dishes, tempura, and noodles. Located across the street from Yachiyo Ryokan on the road leading to Nanzenji Temple, this informal place is easily recognizable by a red lantern beside the road and a display case of plastic food. The restaurant itself is back off the main road past a small garden and a waterfall. Noodles start at ¥500 ($4), and other dishes average around ¥2,000 ($16). Hours here are 10 a.m. to 8 p.m.; closed the first and third Tuesdays of each month.

Mikaku ⑧⑧, Kawabata Dori, Shijo-agaru, Gion, Higashiyama-ku (tel. 525-1129), is a Japanese steak restaurant in the heart of Gion. Established about 50 years ago by the present owner's grandfather, the restaurant is located in a 100-year-old building that was once a private house. The specialty of the house is its *aburayaki* meal, which consists of beef filet cooked with various vegetables and seasoned with soy sauce and wine. Sukiyaki, *mizudaki* (similar to shabu-shabu but stronger in taste), and teppanyaki are also served. Meals average ¥8,000 ($64). If you order teppanyaki, you'll sit at a counter where the chef will prepare your food in front of you on a hot griddle. Outside the window is a pleasant view of a canal. If you order sukiyaki or mizudaki, you'll sit in your own private tatami room on the second floor. This restaurant is open from noon to 10 p.m. (last order is at 9 p.m.) every day except the second and fourth Sundays of the month, and there's an English menu.

Not far from Mikaku and also in Gion is **Beniya** ⑧⑨, located on Nawate Street north of Shijo (tel. 541-2370). This small and informal restaurant up on the second floor specializes in Kyoto cuisine, focusing on fresh vegetables and fish. The menu changes with the season but may include such items as snapper sashimi, pumpkin with sour cream, or oden stew simmered with radishes and vegetables. Set courses, which are served on tableware created by local craftsmen, begin at ¥5,500 ($44). Closed on Sunday and holidays, it's open the rest of the week from 6 to 10 p.m.

Isobe ⑨⓪, located on the southeastern edge of Maruyama Park, Ikenohata, Higashiyama-ku (tel. 561-2216), is a convenient place to stop for lunch if you're walking from Kiyomizu Temple to Heian Shrine. Easily recognized by its outdoor red umbrella (the logo also used for its sign), it's open daily from 10 a.m. to 10 p.m. The same menu is available day and night and includes an obento for ¥2,700 ($21.60), shabu-shabu or sukiyaki for ¥5,000 ($40), a tempura set meal for ¥3,300 ($26.40), or kaiseki from ¥7,700 ($61.60). This modern, pleasant restaurant offers a nice view of the park from its dining room.

In addition to the restaurants above, there are a lot of informal and inexpensive locales in and near Kiyomizu Temple, so you shouldn't have any problems finding a place to eat. If the weather is fine, you might wish to stop for noodles and a beer on Kiyomizu Temple grounds, where you'll find several tatami-mat pavilions.

Western Food

There aren't many Western restaurants in eastern Kyoto from which to choose, but if you're walking from Kiyomizu Temple to Heian Shrine, there's an informal restaurant called **Chorakukan** ⑨① located near the south entrance of Maruyama Park (tel. 561-0001). Tucked away in a corner of a large stone and brick Western-style building with a huge stone lantern in its driveway, this restaurant is nothing fancy but is restful: classical music plays in the background and there is a view of some maple trees. The dishes, most in the ¥900 ($7.20) to ¥1,700 ($13.60) range, include fried or grilled shrimp, grilled chicken with bacon, spaghetti, beef or chicken curry, and sandwiches. There are also lunch specials starting at ¥1,400 ($11.20). Hours are 11 a.m. to 7:30 p.m. every day of the week.

If you desire more formal dining, try **Le Grand Rêve,** in the Kyoto Park Hotel,

Sanjusangendo, Higashiyama-ku (tel. 525-3111). There aren't many restaurants in this vicinity, and it's the best place to go for lunch or dinner if you're visiting Sanjusangendo Hall or the Kyoto National Museum. Small and intimate, the restaurant overlooks a beautiful garden with a waterfall and pond. It specializes in French kaiseki meals, which is French food prepared with the imagination of kaiseki and eaten with chopsticks. The menu changes with the seasons, with lunch courses starting at ¥2,700 ($21.60) and dinner courses at ¥6,500 ($52). Service is from 11 a.m. to 3 p.m. and 5 to 9 p.m. (last order) daily.

NAKAGYO-KU (CENTRAL KYOTO)

The central part of Kyoto west of the Kamo River and embracing the nightlife district around Kawaramachi-Shijo intersection is called Nakagyo-ku. This area of town has a wide selection of both Japanese and Western restaurants.

Japanese Food

Izumoya ⑨, Pontocho, Shijo-agaru (tel. 211-2501), is a large, many-storied restaurant on Shijo Dori Avenue right beside the bridge spanning the Kamo River. The backside of the restaurant faces the river, and in the summer months a wooden veranda built on stilts is constructed over the water. Popular with tourists and groups, it serves a wide variety of dishes on its various floors. On the third floor, shabu-shabu and sukiyaki beginning at ¥3,300 ($26.40) are available, while on the second and fourth floors you can dine on set meals of tempura, sashimi, or eel for ¥2,200 ($19.20) and up. Only kaiseki meals, ranging in price from ¥5,500 ($44) to ¥7,700 ($61.60), are served on the outdoor veranda, open from 5 to 9:30 p.m. The restaurant itself is open daily from noon to 9:30 p.m.; closed Thursday.

Kyoshiki, Fuyacho-Dori Street, Sanjo-agaru (tel. 221-4866), is a reasonably priced kaiseki restaurant located just north of Sanjo Dori Avenue on Fuyacho Dori Street. Formerly a private home, it was turned into a restaurant about 15 years ago by English-speaking Shoichi Hirayama, who makes it easy on foreign guests by presenting them with an English menu. Various meals are available, averaging about ¥2,700 ($21.60) for lunch and ¥3,800 ($30.40) to ¥6,500 ($52) for dinner. If you're coming for lunch I recommend the Hisago lunch, which is a variety of seasonal food served in individual dishes that stack neatly on top of one another to form a gourd. You take the bowls apart to eat. The atmosphere here is relaxed and comfortable, with regular customers stopping in for a chat with Mr. Hirayama. The restaurant opens at 11 a.m. and the last order is taken at 8:30 p.m. On Monday and Wednesday free tea and sweets are served with lunch.

If you're hungering for tempura, **Tempura Yoshikawa** is easy to find on Tominokoji Dori Street near Oike Avenue (tel. 221-5544)—its sign is in English. It's a tiny, intimate place with a traditional atmosphere, and the counter seats only 12 so you should make a reservation to eat here. Open every day except Sunday, it serves a tempura lunch for ¥2,200 ($17.60) from 11 a.m. to 2 p.m. and dinner for ¥6,500 ($52) from 5 to 9 p.m. You can order side dishes of sashimi to go with your meal.

Nestled in an inner courtyard off busy Shijo Dori Avenue, **Tagoto** ⑨, Shijo-Kawaramachi, Nishi-iru, Kitagawa (tel. 221-1811), has been serving a variety of Japanese food at moderate prices for about 100 years. Its entrance is near the Kyoto Central Inn (look for a tiny door with a white sign; step through it and follow the passageway to the back courtyard). It's open from 11 a.m. to 8:30 p.m. (closed the third Wednesday of every month) with set meals ranging from ¥2,500 ($20) to ¥8,800 ($70.40). The menu includes tempura, eel dishes, obento lunch boxes, seasonal kaiseki courses, and sashimi. You can also have noodles beginning at ¥550 ($4.40).

There's a branch of **Minokichi** in the basement under the Bank of Tokyo, Kyoto Fukutoku Building, Karasuma Shijo-agaru (tel. 255-0621). Open for more than a decade, it's the largest Minokichi branch and has prices slightly lower than those of the main restaurant. With low lighting and latticed wood separating the dining tables from one another, this pleasant restaurant is open daily from 11:30 a.m. to 9 p.m. (last order) and serves a variety of typical Japanese cuisine, including shabu-shabu, beginning at ¥4,900 ($39.20); tempura, from ¥2,700 ($21.60); and eel dishes, from ¥2,000 ($16). If you want steak, beef teriyaki costs ¥3,800 ($30.40). Kaiseki courses range from ¥5,500 ($44) for a mini-meal to ¥15,000 ($120). I selected the mini-kaiseki course. Although the kaiseki menu changes monthly, my meal was typical of the variety of dishes you get: appetizer vegetables and sashimi; Japanese potato filled with crabmeat; gelatin with chicken, salmon, and asparagus inside; pumpkin soup; buckwheat noodles with eel and mushroom; a small river fish; tempura; dessert; and Japanese frothy green tea.

Unkai, located on the ground floor of the ANA Hotel Kyoto, Nijo-Castle-Mae, Horikawa-dori Avenue (tel. 231-1155), has a convenient location across from the main entrance of Nijo Castle. With a modern and refined decor, ceiling-to-floor windows, and kimono-clad waitresses, it also has an English menu, making ordering an easy task. What's difficult is deciding what to eat. The varied menu includes a shabu-shabu meal for two persons for ¥7,700 ($61.60); kaiseki starting at ¥8,800 ($70.40), a vegetarian set meal for ¥4,400 ($35.20); tempura from ¥6,600 ($52.80); and sushi à la carte. Special set lunches start at ¥2,200 ($17.60). Hours here are from 11:30 a.m. to 2:30 p.m. and 5 to 10 p.m.

Ganko Sushi ⑨④, Sanjo-Kawaramachi, Higashi-iru (tel. 255-1128), is a popular, lively sushi restaurant located just to the west of the Kamo River on Sanjo Dori Avenue. The English menu makes ordering here a cinch, with sushi à la carte beginning at ¥330 ($2.64) for two pieces. Available are the usual tuna, eel, bonito, squid, and fish selections, as well as such items as grilled yakitori, grilled asparagus wrapped in bacon, shabu-shabu, tempura, and shrimp or crab dishes. Behind the sushi counter is a fish tank with some rather large specimens, swimming around happily until their number comes up. Hours here are from 11:30 a.m. to 10:30 p.m.; closed the first Monday and third Tuesday of every month. Meanwhile, up on the second floor and in the basement are two robatayaki restaurants, with an English menu listing various kinds of grilled vegetables and meats. Popular with office workers when work is over, they're open only in the evenings, from 4:30 to 10:30. At any rate, you can eat at either the sushi or the robatayaki parts of the restaurant for less than ¥3,000 ($24), and even cheaper than that if you lay off the beer.

If money is a great concern, however, an even cheaper place for a meal of raw fish can be found at **Musashi,** located on the northwest corner of the Kawaramachi/Sanjo intersection (tel. 222-0634). Open daily from 11 a.m. to 10 p.m., it offers morsels of sushi via a conveyor belt that moves along the counter. Simply reach out and take what you want. Plates with pieces of tuna, octopus, sweet shrimp, eel, or crab salad all cost ¥140 ($1.12).

Another inexpensive, conveyor-belt sushi establishment is **Kuru Kuru Zushi** ⑨⑤, located in the Teramachi covered shopping arcade not far from Shijo Dori (tel. 221-8429). Plates of sushi here are ¥120 (96¢), and you're charged according to the number of plates you take off the conveyor belt. Closed on Wednesday, it's open the rest of the week from 11:30 a.m. to 9 p.m.

Misoka-an Kawamichiya, Sanjo-agaru, Fuyacho-dori (tel. 221-2525), is a charming, delightful noodle shop with a history that stretches back about 300 years. A tiny affair with a central courtyard and cubbyhole rooms, it offers plain buckwheat noodles for ¥450 ($3.60), as well as noodles with such adornments as tempura or chicken and onions. Its specialty is a one-pot noodle dish called *Hokoro,* which includes such items as chicken, tofu, mushrooms, and vegetables and costs ¥3,300 ($26.40). Closed on Thursday, it's open the rest of the week from 11 a.m. to 8 p.m.

Down the street from Kawamichiya is another noodle shop, **Gontaro** ⑨⑥, (tel. 221-5810), an upstart that has been serving its own handmade noodles for a mere 70 years. It's located on Fuyacho Dori Street just north of Shijo Dori Avenue—look for a tiny recessed courtyard, white curtains, and a lone pine tree. A small place, with a modern yet traditional interior, it offers various noodle (soba) dishes beginning at ¥650 ($5.20). Items you might try include tempura soba, chicken soba, potato soba, and soba sushi. Hours here are 11:30 a.m. to 11 p.m.; closed Wednesday.

One more place you might want to check out for inexpensive Japanese restaurants is the seventh and eighth floors of the **Hankyu department store,** on the corner of Shijo and Kawaramachi. There are lots of restaurants on these two floors serving both Japanese and Western cuisine, and because they have plastic food displays outside their front doors, it's easy to choose both a restaurant and what you want to eat. Simply wander around and decide what looks best. These restaurants are open daily from 11 a.m. to 10 p.m.

Western and Foreign Food

Misogi-gawa ⑨, Sanjo-sagaru, Pontocho, Nakagyo-ku (tel. 221-2270), is a lovely French restaurant on a narrow street called Pontocho, which parallels the Kamo River and is one of Kyoto's most famous nightlife districts. Located in a century-old wooden building that used to belong to a geisha as her entertainment house but has since been renovated, this exclusive restaurant successfully blends both French and Japanese cuisine into dishes artfully prepared and served on Japanese tableware. In fact, part of the delight of eating here is in receiving the various courses, each one exquisitely arranged as though a work of art. Dining is either at a counter or in private tatami rooms, and you have a choice of eating with either chopsticks or knife and fork. The menu changes monthly and ranges from ¥6,500 ($52) to ¥22,000 ($176) for dinner, served daily from 4:30 to 9 p.m. There's also a lunch special for ¥7,700 ($61.60), which includes a glass of wine; it's served daily from 11:30 to 2 p.m. If you want to order à la carte, the menu (written in French) includes such selections as lobster, sole, scallops, and various beef dishes—expect to spend about ¥10,000 ($80) to ¥18,000 ($144) per person. Reservations are strongly recommended.

If you prefer French dining in a Western atmosphere, the **Manyoken,** Fuyacho Shijo, on Shijo Dori (tel. 221-1022), is one of Kyoto's best-known restaurants and has more than 70 years of experience serving French cuisine. With its chandeliers, fresh roses, white tablecloths, and drawing-room atmosphere, this elegant restaurant serves a set lunch for ¥7,700 ($61.60) and set dinners for ¥11,000 ($88) to ¥18,000 ($144), all of which change monthly. À la carte selections include such dishes as steak, lobster, fish, and chicken. Perhaps you want to start out with escargots in bourguignonne sauce, followed by onion soup, sirloin steak cooked with a special house sauce, and then baked Alaska or soufflé in Curaçao or chocolate. Expect to spend about ¥15,000 ($120) or more per person, excluding wine. Hours are 11:30 a.m. to 3 p.m. and 4:30 to 8:30 p.m. (last order) daily.

If you're looking for French food with a twist, visit **Nijo,** in the basement of the ANA Hotel, which is located across the street from Nijo Castle on Horikawa-dori Avenue (tel. 231-1155). In a successful marriage of French cuisine and kaiseki philosophy, it serves one dish after the other rather than all at once. Portions are small, and each dish is so elegantly and artistically arranged that soon you find yourself enjoying the presentation of the food as much as you enjoy eating it. Receiving each course is kind of like opening presents; dining becomes a slow and joyous affair. Ordering is easy because only three set courses, which change with the seasons, are available, beginning at ¥8,800 ($70.40) for dinner. Lunch courses are offered for ¥4,400 ($35.20) and ¥6,600 ($52.80). If you prefer steaks, there's a separate room with a teppanyaki counter, with a set-lunch course costing ¥4,400 ($35.20) and dinner courses beginning at ¥8,800 ($70.40). Hours at Nijo are from 11:30 a.m. to 2:30 p.m. and from 5 to 10 p.m.

Although it's obviously tourist-oriented, **Suehiro,** at the Shijo-Kawaramachi intersection (tel. 221-7188), is dependable for its charcoal-broiled Kobe beef steaks. It has an English menu that makes ordering a snap. You can start with appetizers that might include shrimp or crab cocktail, oysters, and beef sashimi, then move on to various steak dishes ranging from ¥5,000 ($40) for filet mignon to ¥7,700 ($61.60) for a 270-gram sirloin steak. Steak dinner courses start at ¥6,700 ($53.60). Lunch specials, starting at ¥2,500 ($20), are served until 5 p.m. Turning out steaks in Kyoto since 1939, this restaurant, which has several floors of dining space, is open daily from 11:30 a.m. to 9 p.m.

It's difficult to classify **Beer Market Ichiba Coji,** located in the basement of the Withyou Building in the Teramachi covered shopping arcade just north of Shijo Dori (tel. 252-2008). It calls itself a "Kyoto mini-brewery," and even though it does serve its own original beer and has more beer on tap than any other establishment in Kyoto, it is certainly much more than that. Visually it's the most interesting and exciting new-age restaurant I've seen in Kyoto and reminds me of high-tech establishments in Tokyo. In fact, it looks an awful lot like Doma in Harajuku, so I wasn't too surprised to learn that both were designed by the same architectural firm. Ichiba Coji features bare cement walls, white pebbles on the floor, black furniture, and an elevated dining platform practically on top of a running stream. The waitresses and cooks are all decked out in Asian baggy pants and box hats, looking as if they had just stepped out of the pages of a fashion magazine. And as for the food, it's eclectic as well, though I guess it's more Chinese than anything else; the menu includes spring rolls, fresh fish, sweet-and-sour pork, steamed chicken in peanut sauce, and a large variety of salads. The specialty of the house is pao food, morsels wrapped in lettuce leaves. For fillings you can choose such delicacies as eggplant and pork in miso, boiled duck, white fish in pungent sauce, shrimp in chili sauce, dry curry pilaf, and much more. All the food is seasonal and fresh. Most dishes cost less than ¥1,000 ($8). If you like the newest of the new, come here any day of the week between 11:30 a.m. and 10:15 p.m. (last order).

Tohkasaikan, Shijo Ohashi, Nishizume (tel. 221-1147), is a Peking-style Chinese restaurant on Shijo Dori Avenue just west of the bridge that spans the Kamo River. A large yellow stone building that dates back more than 60 years, it started out as a Western restaurant and features an ancient elevator, lots of wood paneling, high ceilings, and old-fashioned decor. You have several choices of where to dine. From June to mid-September you can sit outside on a wooden veranda supported by stilts that extends over the Kamo River. If it's winter or raining, consider sitting in the dining room on the fifth floor, which has nice views of the city. The best views, however, are from the rooftop garden, open during the summer months—draft beer here costs ¥500 ($4) for a medium and ¥800 ($6.40) for a large. As for food, the English menu lists such dishes as sweet-and-sour pork, cooked shrimp with arrowroot, fried pork meatballs, chicken and green pepper, and pork and vegetable rolled with egg. Most entrées range from ¥1,000 ($8) to ¥2,700 ($21.60). It's open daily from 11 a.m. to 9 p.m.

Even cheaper is **Dim Sum,** located on the north side of Shijo Dori Avenue just east of Karasuma (tel. 255-6775). It's up on the second floor. As its name implies, it serves dim sum, which is finely chopped meat and vegetables wrapped in dough and then steamed or fried. A bamboo basket of dim sum starts at ¥380 ($3.04). There are also set lunches starting at ¥800 ($6.40) and dinner courses beginning at ¥1,100 ($8.80). Hours here are 11:30 a.m. to 9 p.m. every day but Wednesday.

If you want spicier food, try **Ashoka,** located on the third floor of the Kikusui Building on Teramachi Dori Street just off Shijo Dori Avenue (tel. 241-1318). One of Kyoto's most popular Indian restaurants, Ashoka serves both vegetarian and meat curries including mutton, chicken, fish, vegetable, and shrimp selections. I started out my meal here with mulligatawny Madrasi, a South Indian soup, and followed it with Indian bread stuffed with minced meat along with mutton *sagwala* (mutton and spinach). A meal here averages about ¥2,500 ($20) or more. Set lunches start at ¥990 ($7.92), while dinners start at ¥2,500 ($20). Hours are 11:30 a.m. to 2:30 p.m. and 5 to 9 p.m. every day (on Sunday and holidays, from 11:30 a.m. to 3 p.m. and 5 to 8:30 p.m.).

Although it's a bit difficult to find, **Sancho** ⑱, Fuji Ginko Yoko-agaru (tel.

211-0459), is worth a visit for its hearty portions of inexpensive salads. A small establishment with only a long counter and six tables, it's located just north of Shijo Dori Avenue on the first side street that parallels Kawaramachi to the west, which is the same street that runs beside Fuji Bank. Look for the sign that says "Salada House," as well as the plastic display case of salads. Salads cost ¥550 ($4.40) to ¥930 ($7.44) and include such combinations as asparagus and crab salad, shrimp salad and chicken salad. The English menu also lists hamburgers, teriyaki steak, and chicken. Sancho is open from noon to 9 p.m. every day except Wednesday.

From Monday through Saturday from 11 a.m. to 3 p.m., **Shakey's,** Teramachi Higashi-iru, Ishibashi (tel. 255-1325), offers an all-you-can-eat pizza buffet for only ¥600 ($4.80). Shakey's is conveniently located in the covered shopping arcade running along Sanjo Dori Avenue, just west of Kawaramachi Dori Avenue.

SHIMOGYO-KU (AROUND KYOTO STATION)

Restaurants around Kyoto Station cater to tourists, commuters, and shoppers. Most of these establishments are in the area's many hotels.

Japanese Food

In the basement of the Kyoto Grand Hotel, Shiokoji Horikawa (tel. 341-2311), are six restaurants offering a variety of cuisines, all with English menus. Most interesting is **Gourmond Tachibana,** which serves Japanese-style French cuisine every evening from 5 to 9:30 p.m. It has three set menus for ¥8,000 ($64), ¥11,000 ($88), and ¥13,000 ($104), which change twice a month. Other restaurants, all open from 11:30 a.m. to 2:30 p.m. and 5 to 9:30 p.m., serve teppanyaki steaks, tempura, eel, sukiyaki, shabu-shabu, traditional Kyoto cuisine, and Chinese food. The average dinner in these restaurants costs about ¥5,000 ($40) and up.

In the New Hankyo Hotel, north of Kyoto Station (tel. 343-5300), is a branch of the famous **Minokichi** restaurant. Designed to resemble a lane in a typical traditional Japanese village, it features waitresses in kimonos and Japanese music playing in the background. The menu includes kaiseki cuisine from ¥8,800 ($70.40) and typical Kyoto dishes from ¥3,300 ($26.40), as well as such Japanese favorites as tempura, obento lunch boxes, eels, and shabu-shabu. A mini-kaiseki course is available for ¥6,500 ($52). Hours here are from 11:30 a.m. to 9 p.m. (last order).

Izusen ⑨⑨ is an inexpensive restaurant located on the second floor of the Surugaiya Building on Karasuma Dori Avenue just north of the Tourist Information Center (tel. 343-4211). Although the decor is simple, the food is great and beautifully presented and features local Kyoto and vegetarian dishes. There's an English menu, and seating is either at tables or on tatami mats. The best thing to order is one of the specials. A vegetarian meal for ¥1,600 ($12.80), for example, is a light meal usually served at a tea ceremony. I opted for the Matsu for ¥2,500 ($20), which features Kyoto cuisine and included tempura, sashimi, various vegetables, broiled fish, rice, and soup. Other vegetarian dishes and Kyoto specialties start at ¥2,000 ($16). Closed on Thursday, it's open the rest of the week from 11 a.m. to 8 p.m.

If you're waiting for a train or want something inexpensive and fast, head for **Kinmei Town,** located on the southern edge of Kyoto Station near the Kintetsu Line. There are about two dozen enterprises here, most with plastic display cases offering everything from tempura and sashimi to okonomiyaki, obento, noodles, spaghetti, and desserts. Most prices fall between ¥600 ($4.80) and ¥1,500 ($12), and restaurants are open daily from 7:30 a.m. to 10 p.m.

Western Food

On the 14th floor of the Kyoto Grand Hotel, Shiokoji Horikawa (tel. 341-2311), is **Top of Kyoto,** the city's only revolving restaurant. On clear days you have excellent views over the tops of Kyoto's temples to the mountains surrounding the city. Recently remodeled with marble and decor imported from Italy, this trendy restaurant offers a set lunch menu for ¥4,400 ($35.20) and set dinners beginning at

¥10,000 ($80). A la carte orders will average ¥15,000 ($120) for meals, which might include steak, duckling, rack of spring lamb, veal, sole, lobster, or scallops. Adjoining the restaurant is a comfortable cocktail lounge, where you can relax with a drink after dinner. Food is served daily from noon to 11:30 p.m. And if you like Sunday brunch, you'll want to come here on Sunday between 11 a.m. and 2:30 p.m., when a brunch buffet is offered for ¥3,300 ($26.40).

Next to Kyoto Station is a relatively new building called the Renaissance Building, which features several restaurants. On the second floor, for example, is **Gio Giono** (tel. 365-0200), an Italian restaurant. Open from 11:30 a.m. to 10 p.m. (last order is 9:30 p.m.), it serves pizza starting at ¥900 ($7.20), pasta at ¥900 ($7.20), and seafood. A special lunch menu, available until 2 p.m., gives you a choice of pizza or spaghetti, a salad, dessert, and coffee for ¥880 ($7.04). Other food outlets in the Renaissance Building include a Chinese restaurant, a beer hall with lunches starting at ¥800 ($6.40), and a coffeeshop where you can order the "morning service" for ¥550 ($4.40), which includes coffee, toast, egg, and salad.

---

4. The Sights

Because Kyoto has 1,700 Buddhist temples, 300 Shinto shrines, and numerous gardens, museums, and other worthwhile sights, it's obvious that you must tailor your itinerary to gain the most satisfaction and enjoyment from your stay. Even the most avid sightseer can become jaded after days of visiting yet another temple or shrine—and after a while how much can your memory retain? Be sure to temper your visits to cultural and historical sights with time spent simply walking around. Kyoto is a city best seen on your own two feet, exploring small alleyways and curio shops, pausing to soak in the beauty of its carefully landscaped gardens. If you spend your days in Kyoto racing around in a taxi or a bus from one temple to another, the essence of this ancient capital and its charm may literally pass you by.

Ideally, you should allow at least four days in Kyoto, allotting a fifth day for a side trip to the even more ancient capital of Nara. Depending on how much you want to cover, that would allow you to select from the list I've compiled below the sights most interesting to you, with time left over for your own explorations. If perchance you have only one day to spend in Kyoto, I recommend that you spend it in East Kyoto, including the stroll from Kiyomizu Temple to Heian Shrine, topping it off with a visit to the Silver Pavilion, and, if time permits, a short stop at the Kyoto Handicraft Center for some shopping—and then start planning for your next trip back to Kyoto. If you have a second day, add Nijo Castle, Ryoanji Temple with its famous rock garden, and the Golden Pavilion, all in western Kyoto, plus a few other sights of your choosing. Such a two-day tour would present you a well-rounded view of Kyoto by giving you the chance to see temples, a shrine, gardens, and a former shogun's palace.

Before setting out on your walking tours, be sure to stop by the Kyoto Tourist Information Center, located across from Kyoto Station in the Kyoto Tower Building, Higashi-Shiokojicho, Shimogyo-ku (tel. 075/371-5649), to pick up a leaflet called *Walking Tour Courses in Kyoto*. It has four detailed maps for strolling tours of Kyoto, including the walk from Kiyomizu Temple to Heian Shrine and on to the Silver Pavilion, which I've outlined below. The T.I.C. also has city maps and a colorful brochure listing Kyoto's most important sites.

EAST KYOTO

The eastern part of Kyoto, embracing the area of Higashiyama-ku and stretching up all the way to the Silver Pavilion (Ginkakuji Temple), is probably the richest in terms of culture and charm. Although the walking-tour leaflet distributed by the T.I.C. claims you can walk from Kiyomizu Temple to Heian Shrine in 50 minutes, I don't see how it would be possible unless you put on your jogging shoes and ran the whole way. I've walked this route four times and it's always taken me the better part of a day—perhaps I'm slow, but it's a pace I've found does justice to this wonderfu area of Kyoto.

The two strolls I've listed below, through Higashiyama-ku and the Philosophers' Stroll, are logical continuations of each other. If you don't finish Higashiyama-ku in one day, therefore, you could start where you left off on the following day and then continue on with the Philosophers' Stroll.

In any case, since East Kyoto has some of the city's most traditional and beautiful restaurants, be sure to read through the dining section on eastern Kyoto to decide beforehand where you might want to eat lunch or dinner. The majority of the traditional restaurants are in the vicinity of Nanzenji Temple.

A Stroll Through Higashiyama-ku

Sanjusangendo Hall is the name popularly given to Rengeoin Temple, which is just south of Shichijo Dori a block or so east of the river. It is a 20-minute walk east of or a short ride on bus 206 from Kyoto Station. The hall is only 50-some feet wide but it stretches almost 400 feet long—and it's filled with more than 1,000 images of the thousand-handed Kannon. There are row upon row of these gold figures glowing in the dark hall, and in the middle is a large seated figure of Kannon, flanked by her 28 disciples. The large Kannon was carved in 1254 by Tankei, a famous sculptor from the Kamakura Period, and the hall itself dates from 1266. At the back of the hall is a 130-yard-long archery range, where a competition is held every January 15. Sanjusangendo is open daily from 8 a.m. to 4:30 p.m. (3:30 p.m. in winter) and admission is ¥400 ($3.20).

Across the street and to the northeast of Sanjusangendo Hall is the **Kyoto National Museum** (open from 9 a.m. to 4 p.m.; closed Monday). Established in the latter half of the last century as a repository for art objects and treasures that belonged to both Kyoto's temples and individuals, it displays historical items, artwork, and handcrafts, including a great collection of ceramics, paintings and sculptures. Admission is ¥350 ($2.80).

From the National Museum, either hop back on bus 206 or walk for about 15 minutes north on Higashioji Dori Avenue to the Gojo-zaka bus stop, where you should take a right and begin climbing up the gradual slope to **Kiyomizu Temple.** You'll pass some pottery shops on your way, but don't go crazy shopping yet—there are many more shops to come. Kiyomizu Temple, first founded in 798 and rebuilt in 1633 by the third Tokugawa shogun, Iemitsu, occupies one of the most exalted spots in all of Kyoto, with a grand view of the city below. The main hall is built over a cliff and features a large wooden veranda supported by 139 pillars, each 49 feet high. The magnificence of the height and view is so well known to the Japanese that the idiom "jumping from the veranda of Kiyomizu Temple" means that they're about to undertake some particularly bold or daring adventure. To appreciate the grandeur of the main hall with its pillars and dark wood, walk the few minutes to the three-story pagoda, which affords the best view of the main hall, built without the use of a single nail. From the pagoda, descend the steps down to Otowa Fall, where you'll see Japanese lined up to drink from the refreshing spring water. Here you'll also find some small pavilions where you can stop for a bowl of noodles and a beer. By all means do (and now you know why this walk takes me all day). If you're lucky to be here in fall, the fiery reds of the maple trees will set the whole place on fire. Kiyomizu Temple is open from 8 a.m. to 6 p.m. Admission is ¥300 ($2.40).

Before departing Kiyomizu Temple, be sure to make a stop at **Jishu Shrine,** particularly if you're in need of finding a good mate or thankful that you've found one. This vermillion-colored Shinto shrine is easy to spot and is located just north of Kiyomizu's main temple building, to the left. It's regarded as a dwelling place of the deity in charge of love and a good match, a deity you certainly should not slight. There's an explanation of the shrine in English, and you can buy various good-luck

EASTERN KYOTO

charms for everything from a happy marriage to easy delivery of a child to success in passing an examination. On the shrine's grounds are two stones placed about 30 feet apart—if you're able to walk from one stone to the other with your eyes closed, you're supposedly guaranteed success in your love life. It sure doesn't hurt to try.

From Kiyomizu Temple, take the road leading downhill directly in front of the temple's main gate, where you'll find shop after shop selling sweets, pottery, and curios. It's okay to go crazy shopping here, but remember you're going to have to carry whatever you buy. After a few minutes take a right at some steps leading downhill. Called Sannenzaka Slope, it leads past lovely antique and curio shops and wooden buildings reminiscent of old Kyoto. After passing Ryozen Kannon Temple, with its huge white statue dedicated to Japan's unknown soldiers who died in World War II, look for a tea house on your right called **Kodaiji Rakusho Tea Room** ⑩ (tel. 561-6892) (if you get all the way to Maruyama Park or the pagoda with the crane on top, you've gone too far). This tea house, one of my favorites in Kyoto, has a 100-year-old garden, which you can glimpse through a gate from the street. There's a pond with some of the largest carp I've ever seen, some of which are 20 years old. Stop for some noodles, tea, or dessert, and refresh yourself with views of the small but beautiful garden. It's open from 9:30 a.m. to 6 p.m.

After you've taken your time strolling through **Maruyama Park** with its ponds, pigeons, gardens, and vendors, you'll come to **Chion-in Temple,** founded in 1234 as a center of the Jodo sect of Buddhism. Famous for its enormous gate rising almost 80 feet, the temple also has Japan's largest bell, weighing 74 tons. Entrance to the temple precincts is free; and the hours are 9 a.m. to 4 p.m. Just north of Chion-in is **Shoren-in Temple,** built as a villa for the abbots of a Buddhist sect. The present buildings date from 1895. The temple has a very impressive garden, constructed in the 15th century and considered to be one of the best in Kyoto. Open from 9 a.m. to 4:30 p.m., it charges an admission of ¥400 ($3.20).

After crossing Sanjo Dori, Niomon Dori, and Nijo Dori, you'll know you're getting close to Heian Shrine when you see the vermillion-colored torii gate straddling a street busy with traffic. Before continuing on to the shrine, however, there are a few museums you might want to stop in on—the **Kyoto Municipal Museum of Art**, the **National Museum of Modern Art**, and the **Kyoto Municipal Museum of Traditional Industry.** The Museum of Traditional Industry is my favorite. Not only is it free, but it sells many of the items displayed. Crafts range from pottery to lacquerware to textiles, bamboo products, damascene jewelry, knives, and dolls. Prices are high, but so is the quality of workmanship. There are also frequent demonstrations by local artists. It's open from 9 a.m. to 4:30 p.m.; closed on Monday.

Directly north of the museums is **Heian Shrine.** If orange and green are your favorite colors, you're going to love this shrine. Although it was built only in 1895 in commemoration of the 1,100th anniversary of the founding of Kyoto, Heian Shrine is a replica of the first imperial palace, built in Kyoto back in 794, giving you some idea of the architecture back then. The most important thing to see here, however, is the garden, the entrance to which is on your left as you face the main hall. Admission is ¥500 ($4) and hours are 8:30 a.m. to 4:30 p.m. (5:30 p.m. in summer). Typical of gardens constructed during the Meiji era, it's famous for its weeping cherry trees, which blossom in spring; its irises and water lilies in summer; and changing maple leaves in fall.

After visiting Heian Shrine you may want to stop off to do some shopping at the **Kyoto Handicraft Center,** located behind the shrine on its north side. It's open from 9:30 a.m. to 6 p.m. (until 5:30 p.m. December through February). More information is given in the "Shopping" section.

Philosophers' Stroll

North of Nanzenji and Eikando temples is a narrow canal that runs almost a mile to Ginkakuji Temple, the Silver Pavilion. Lined with cherry, willow, and maple trees, the canal and a small pathway flanking its side are known as "The Path of Philosophy," referring to the fact that throughout the ages philosophers and priests have strolled along the tranquil canal thinking deep thoughts. Allow about two hours to see the sights below and to think your own deep thoughts as you stroll the philosophers' pathway.

Nanzenji Temple, a 20-minute walk southeast of Heian Shrine, is a Rinzai Zen temple set amid a grove of spruce. One of Kyoto's most famous Zen temples, it was founded in 1293. Attached to the main hall is a Zen rock garden, sometimes called "Leaping Tiger Garden" because of the shape of one of the rocks (can you tell which one?). In the building behind the main hall is a famous sliding door with a painting by Kano Tanyu of a tiger drinking water in a bamboo grove. Spread throughout the temple precincts are a dozen other lesser temples and buildings that you can explore if you have the time, including Nanzen-in, which was built about the same time as Nanzenji Temple and served as the emperor's vacation house whenever he visited the temple grounds. As you wander around, here's food for thought: Nanzenji is where a famous outlaw named Goemon Ishikawa hid before being captured and boiled alive along with his son (they certainly didn't fool around back in those days). Admission to the temple grounds is free, but entrance to the main hall, with its Zen rock garden and famous sliding door of the tiger, costs ¥350 ($2.80). For ¥300 ($2.40) more you can have ceremonial green tea and a Japanese sweet served in a tatami room off the main hall with a peaceful view of a waterfall. Hours are 8:30 a.m. to 4:30 p.m.

Eikando Temple, also known as Zenrin-ji Temple, was founded in 856. Things to see here include a statue of a Buddha who is turned so that he looks backward instead of forward, a garden, and maple trees. Hours are 9 a.m. to 4 p.m., and entrance is ¥400 ($3.20).

Ginkakuji, the Silver Pavilion, is the crown jewel of this walk—but it isn't silver at all. It was built in 1482 as a retirement villa of Shogun Yoshimasa Ashikaga, who intended to coat the structure with silver in imitation of the Gold Pavilion built by his grandfather. He died before this could be accomplished, however, which is just as well because the wood of the Silver Pavilion is beautiful just as it is. The whole complex is designed for the enjoyment of the tea ceremony, moon viewing, and other aesthetic pursuits, with a beautiful garden of sand, rocks, and moss. One Kyoto resident told me that this was his favorite temple in the whole city (the residence became a temple after Ashikaga's death). At any rate, the splendor, formality, and grandeur of the life of Japan's upper class can easily be imagined as you wander the grounds. Admission is ¥400 ($3.20), and hours are 9 a.m. to 4:30 p.m.

NORTHWESTERN KYOTO

The inspiration for the Silver Pavilion described above was **Kinkakuji, the Gold Pavilion,** which you can reach by taking bus 205 from Kyoto Station (platform B3) to the Kinkakuji-michi bus stop. One of Kyoto's best-known attractions, it was constructed in the 1390s as a retirement villa for Shogun Yoshimitsu Ashikaga and features a three-story pavilion covered in gold leaf and topped with a bronze phoenix on its roof. If you come here on a clear day, the Gold Pavilion shimmers against a blue sky, its reflection captured in the waters of a calm pond. Apparently the retired shogun lived in shameless luxury while the rest of the nation suffered from famine, earthquakes, and plague. Even today Ashikaga is not kindly remembered, but his Gold Pavilion is now enjoyed by the masses of a now-prosperous nation. However, the Gold Pavilion is not the original. In 1950 a disturbed student monk burned the pavilion to the ground, a story told by author Yukio Mishima in his *The Temple of the Golden Pavilion*. The temple was rebuilt in 1955. Be sure to explore the surrounding park with its moss-covered grounds and tea houses. Hours are 9 a.m. to 5 p.m., and admission is ¥300 ($2.40).

About a half-hour walk southwest of the Gold Pavilion is **Ryoanji Temple,** with what is probably the most famous Zen rock garden in all of Japan. Fifteen rocks set in waves of raked, white pebbles are surrounded on three sides by a wall and on the fourth by a wooden veranda. Sit down here and contemplate what the artist was trying to communicate. The interpretation of what the rocks are supposed to represent is up to the individual (to my mind they look like mountains rising up from the sea). My only objection to this peaceful place is that unfortunately it's usually not peaceful—a loudspeaker extols the virtue of the garden, destroying any chance for peaceful meditation. If you get here early enough, you may be able to escape both the crowds and the noise. After visiting the rock garden, be sure to take a walk around the 1,000-year-old pond. At one corner is a beautiful little restaurant with tatami rooms and screens where you can eat yudofu (boiled tofu with vegetables) for ¥1,500 ($12) or drink a beer and enjoy the view. Note, however, that if you order only a beer, which costs ¥550 ($4.40), an extra ¥300 ($2.40) will be added to the bill. The view, however, is well worth it. Ryoanji is open 8 a.m. to 5 p.m. (4:30 p.m. in winter) and admission is ¥350 ($2.80).

Ready for some fun? How about going to the **Toei Uzumasa Eiga Mura (Uzamasa Movie Village),** where many of Japan's samurai flicks are made? Open from 9 a.m. to 5 p.m. (9:30 a.m. to 4 p.m. from November 16 to March 15) and closed December 21 to January 1, it charges ¥1,550 ($12.40) admission for adults and ¥650 ($5.20) for children. Popular with school groups and resembling an amusement park more than a movie studio, it does have both outdoor and indoor sets, and if you're lucky you'll see a movie in the making. Reconstructed houses re-create the mood, setting, and atmosphere of feudal Japan, while indoor museums show miniature castles, houses, and items from the history of Japanese film. Who knows, you may even see a famous star walking around dressed in samurai garb. You can also have a photo taken of yourself decked out in a kimono or samurai gear. Since the Movie Village is clearly a commercial venture, come here only if you have a lot of time or are sick of temples.

CENTRAL KYOTO

Much of central Kyoto has been taken over by the 20th century but there are a few interesting sites worth investigating. **Kyoto Imperial Palace,** near the Imadegawa subway station, was where the imperial family lived from 1331 until 1868, when they moved to Tokyo. The palace was destroyed several times by fire, and the present buildings date from 1855. You need special permission to see the palace grounds, but that can be obtained the day of your intended visit by dropping by the Imperial Household Agency on the palace grounds. A 30-minute tour is held every morning at 10 a.m.—except Sunday and the second and fourth Saturdays of every month—and you must apply to join this tour by 9:40 a.m. Be sure to bring your passport. Another tour in English is held Monday through Friday at 2 p.m., and for this one you must apply by 1:40 p.m. The tours are free.

Whereas the Imperial Palace was where the royal family resided, **Nijo Castle** (to the southwest on Horikawa Dori) is where the Tokugawa shogun stayed whenever he left Edo and came to Kyoto for a visit. It was built by the first Tokugawa shogun, Ieyasu, and is considered the quintessence of Momoyama architecture. With delicate transom wood carvings and paintings on sliding doors, the castle has an understated elegance, especially when compared to the castles Europe was building at the same time. The castle has 33 rooms and a total of about 800 tatami mats. All the sliding doors on the outside walls of the castle can be removed in summer, allowing cool breezes to sweep through the building. Winters, on the other hand, must have been dreadfully cold. There was no heating and light was provided only by candles. Typical for Japan at the time, rooms were unfurnished, the mattresses stored in closets.

To protect the shogun from real or imagined enemies, the castle was protected by a moat and stone walls. How deep the shogun's paranoia ran, however, is apparent by the installation of the so-called nightingale floor inside the castle itself. Corridors were fitted with floorboards that squeaked when trod upon to alert against infiltrating assassins, and there were hidden alcoves for bodyguards.

Outside the castle is a garden famous in its own right, designed by famous gardener Kobori Enshu. The original grounds of the castle, however, were without trees—supposedly because the falling of leaves in autumn reminded the shogun and his tough samurai of life's transitory nature, making them terribly sad.

Nijo Castle is open from 8:45 a.m. to 4 p.m.; the garden remains open until 5 p.m. The ¥450 ($3.60) admission covers both the castle and the garden.

Incidentally, I prefer Nijo Castle because you can explore its interior on your own. The tours of the Imperial Palace cover only the palace grounds, and there's not much time for dawdling.

The newest attraction in central Kyoto is the **Museum of Kyoto,** Sanjo-Takakura (tel. 222-0888), which opened in 1988. It's housed in two buildings—a modern, slick building with polished granite walls, and an imposing Meiji-era brick building that used to be a bank. Through the use of video displays, slides, and even holograms, the Museum of Kyoto attempts to present the 1,200 years of Kyoto's history. Included are displays of prehistoric relics, glassware, fans, crafts, and artwork. The third floor is an exhibition hall to display the works of contemporary artists and craftsmen. A special feature of the museum is its film library with hundreds of titles of Japanese classics (the Japanese movie industry was based in Kyoto for decades). Movies are shown twice daily (at last check at 2 and 6:15 p.m., but you'd be wise to confirm the time) and admission is included in the museum entry fee. The movies shown range from silent movies to those filmed up to 20 years ago.

All in all, the museum is a welcome addition to Kyoto's cultural scene, and considering the city's historical importance, it's amazing Kyoto has managed this long without it. My only complaint is that explanations are only in Japanese—if enough people complain, maybe this will be corrected. Be sure to check out the holographic display of workers constructing the vermillion-colored shrine.

About a mile north of Nijo Castle is the **Nishijin Textile Hall (Nishijin-Ori Kaikan)** (tel. 451-9231), dedicated to the centuries of weavers who produced elegant textiles for the imperial family and the nobility. The history of Nishijin textiles began with the history of Kyoto itself back in 794, and by the Edo Period there were an estimated 5,000 weaving factories producing the famous material. The museum has regularly held weaving demonstrations, historical displays, and kimono shows. Admission to the hall itself is free; the kimono show costs ¥210 ($1.68). Hours for the textile hall are 9 a.m. to 5 p.m. daily, and it's located on Horikawa-dori Avenue, Imadegawa-minami-iru, Kamigyo-ku.

If you're interested in learning more about the Kyo-Yuzen method for dyeing silk for kimonos, visit **Kodai Yuzen-en** (tel. 811-8101), located a couple of minutes' walk northwest of the Horikawa-dori and Gojo Street intersection. It has displays and demonstrations showing the 300-year history of Yuzen dyeing and a shop where Yuzen goods are sold. It's open daily from 9 a.m. to 5 p.m. and charges a ¥500 ($4) admission. Although it's not as conveniently located—about a five-minute walk from Nishikyogoku Station on the Hankyu electric railway line in the west part of Kyoto—the **Yuzen Cultural Hall (Yuzen Bunka Kaikan)** (tel. 311-0025) also demonstrates the method of Yuzen dyeing. It's open every day except Monday from 9 a.m. to 4 p.m., and admission is ¥310 ($2.48).

Just north of Kyoto Station are two massive temple compounds, **Nishi-Honganji and Higashi-Honganji temples.** They were once joined under one huge religious center called Honganji but split after a disagreement several centuries ago. Higashi-Honganji is Kyoto's largest wooden structure, while Nishi-Honganji is the older temple and represents an outstanding example of Buddhist architecture. Only parts of both temples are open to the public.

If you've never been to a market in Japan, you'll probably want to take a stroll down **Nishiki-Koji Dori,** a fish and produce market right in the heart of town. A covered pedestrian lane stretching west from Teramachi Dori (and just north of Shijo Dori), Nishiki-Koji has been Kyoto's principal food market for more than three centuries. This is where the city's finest restaurants and inns buy their food, and you'll find open-fronted shops and stalls selling seasonal vegetables, fish, beans, seaweed, pickled vegetables, seafood, and more. Shops are open from the early morning hours until about 7 or 8 p.m.; many close on either Wednesday or Sunday.

IN KYOTO'S ENVIRONS

If this is your first visit to Kyoto and you're here only a short while, your sightseeing priorities should lie in Kyoto itself, concentrating on the sites described above. If, however, this is your second trip to Kyoto or you're here for an extended period of time, there are a number of worthwhile attractions in the region surrounding Kyoto you should make an effort to see.

Note: Katsura Imperial Villa, Shugakuin Imperial Villa, and **Saihoji** (popularly called the Moss Temple) all require advance permission to visit. To see the imperial villas you can telephone the Imperial Household Agency (tel. 211-1211) at least one week to three months in advance to make an appointment to join a tour—but unfortunately no one at the office speaks English, so you'll have to find someone to make the call for you in Japanese. If applying by mail, do so one to three months in advance and include your name, age, sex, occupation, passport number, nationality, and home address. You must be more than 20 years old, and the maximum number of people allowed in your group is four. Tours—in Japanese only—are given at Katsura at 10 a.m. and 2 p.m. and at Shugakuin at 9, 10, and 11 a.m. and 1:30 and 3 p.m. Note that no tours are given on Sunday, national holidays, the second and fourth Saturdays of every month and Saturday afternoon. When specifying your desired date and time, be sure to include several choices. The address of the Imperial Household Agency is 3, Kyoto-Gyoen, Kamigyo-ku, Kyoto, and once you arrive in Kyoto you should drop by the agency (located at the Kyoto Imperial Palace) at least one day prior to the tour to fill out a formal application. Be sure to bring your passport. The tours of the villas are free. For information about applying for a tour of Saihoji, please see the description of the temple further on in this section.

Obviously, it's somewhat of a hassle to visit the imperial villas, and according to the Tourist Information Office, applications by mail are not always acknowledged or successful. Applying by phone is much easier if you can find someone to do so in Japanese. If you're going to be in Japan longer than a week before arriving in Kyoto, you might try calling the Imperial Household Agency as soon as you arrive in Japan. If perchance all time slots are already booked, don't be too disappointed—there are many other sites that are equally enjoyable to visit.

Katsura Imperial Villa

Located about a 15-minute walk from Katsura Station on the Hankyu railway line or a 30-minute bus ride from Kyoto Station (take bus 33 to Katsura Rikyu Mae bus stop), Katsura villa is considered the jewel of traditional Japanese architecture and landscape gardening. It was built between 1620 and 1624 by Prince Toshihito, brother of the emperor, with construction continued by Toshihito's son. The garden, markedly influenced by Kobori Enshu, Japan's most famous garden designer, is a "stroll garden" in which each turn of the path brings an entirely new view.

The first thing you notice upon entering Katsura is its simplicity—the buildings are all made of natural materials in which everything was taken into consideration, including the slopes of the roof, the type of various woods used, their grain, texture, and color. A pavilion for viewing the moon, a hall for imperial visits, a tea house, and other buildings are situated around a pond, and as you walk along the pathway you are treated to views that literally change with each step you take. Islets, stone lanterns, various scenes representing the seashore, mountains, and hamlets, manicured trees, and bridges of stone, earth, or wood that arch gracefully over the water—everything is perfectly balanced. No matter where you stand, the view is complete and in harmony. Every detail was carefully planned, down to the stones used in the pathways, the way the trees twist, and how scenes are reflected in the water. Little wonder that Katsura villa has influenced architecture not only in Japan but around the world.

Shugakuin Imperial Villa

Located about a 15-minute walk from the Shugakuin Rikyu Michi bus stop (take bus 5 from Kyoto Station), the Shugakuin Imperial Villa was built in the mid-1600s for Emperor Go-Mizunoo, who became a monk after his abdication. Its stroll garden is among Kyoto's largest and is divided into three levels. The upper garden with its lake, islands, and waterfalls is the largest of the three and uses the principle known as "borrowed landscape," in which the surrounding landscape is incorporated into the overall garden design. The gardens are more spacious than most Japanese-style gardens, and the view of the surrounding countryside is grand.

Saihoji, the Moss Temple

Popularly known as Kokedera, the Moss Temple, Saihoji is famous for its velvety-green moss garden spread underneath the trees. Altogether there are more than 40 different varieties of moss through the grounds, giving off an iridescent and mysterious glow that is at its best just after a rain. Because the monks are afraid that huge numbers of visitors would trample the moss to death, prior permission is needed to visit Saihoji, which you can obtain by writing the temple at least one month in advance. The address is Saiho-ji Temple, Matsuo Kamigaya-cho, Nishikyo-ku, Kyoto (tel. 075/391-3631), and you should give your name, address, nationality, age, sex, and when you'd like to visit. Include a self-addressed return envelop and International Reply Coupons for return postage for the reply. The cost of a visit to the temple, which includes Sutra writing demonstrations, is ¥3,000 ($24) and can be paid when you pick up your ticket.

Enryakuji Temple

Along with Mount Koya, south of Osaka, Enryakuji Temple is considered one of the most important centers of Buddhism in Japan. Located atop Mount Hiei, Enryakuji Temple was founded back in 788 at the order of Emperor Kammu to ward off evil spirits that might come from the northeast. At one time Enryakuji Temple consisted of as many as 3,000 buildings and maintained an army of warrior monks that made raids of rival temples. Because of the temple's political and military power, an army organized by Oda Nobunaga attacked Enryakuji and destroyed the temple in 1571. Although some of the temple was subsequently rebuilt, it never again reached its former powerful position. However, there are a number of fine buildings spread out under large cedar trees and a peaceful atmosphere reigns. Enryakuji Temple can be reached either by bus or rail from Kyoto; the trip takes approximately an hour.

Byodoin Temple

Located in the town of Uji about 11 miles southeast of Kyoto, Byodoin Temple is a good example of temple architecture of the Heian Period. Most famous is the main hall, known as Phoenix Hall, which was built in 1053. It has three wings, creating an image of the mythical bird of China, the phoenix, and on the gable ends are two bronze phoenixes. On the temple grounds are one of the most famous bells in Japan, as well as a monument to Yorimasa Minamoto, who took his own life here after being defeated by the rival Taira clan.

Fushimi-Inari Shrine

Just a minute's walk from the JR Inari Station, Fushimi-Inari Shrine has long been popular with merchants and tradesmen who come here to pray for success and prosperity. One of Japan's most celebrated Shinto shrines, it was founded back in 711 and is dedicated to the goddess of rice. The 2½-mile-long pathway behind the shrine is lined with more than 10,000 red torii gates, presented by worshippers throughout the ages, and there are also stone foxes that are considered messengers of the gods. It's a glorious walk, as you wind through the woods and then gradually climb a hill, from where you have a good view of Kyoto spreading out below. At several places along the path are small shops where you can sit down for a bowl of noodles or refreshment.

Note: Both Byodoin Temple and Fushimi-Inari Shrine are on the same JR line that continues to Nara. If you plan on spending the night in Nara, you could easily take in these two attractions on the way.

Cormorant Fishing in Arashiyama

If you're lucky enough to be in Kyoto during July and August, I highly recommend that you spend one evening drifting in a wooden boat on the Oi River and watching men fishing with trained cormorants (seabirds). Cormorant fishing is held in Arashiyama every evening (except when there's a full moon and during and after a heavy rain) from July 1 to August 31. You can reach Arashiyama by bus from Kyoto Station or electric tram from Shijo Omiya Station in central Kyoto. You should arrive in Arashiyama shortly before 7 p.m. For a fee of ¥1,300 ($10.40) you can board a narrow wooden boat gaily decorated with paper lanterns. Along with dozens of others, your boatman will pole you down the river so that you can see the fishing boats lit by blazing torches. The cormorants, with rings around their necks so that they don't swallow the fish they catch, dive under the water for ayu, a small river fish. Water taxis ply the river offering snacks and beer. I find the whole experience of watching the cormorants and being a part of the flotilla of wooden boats and paper lanterns terribly romantic. It's a lovely way to spend a warm summer's evening.

A Maze

Trying to find your way around Japan is so difficult that I can't imagine anyone seeking out added aggravation, but if you enjoy frustration at every turn, you might want to visit the **Kyoto Daigo Granmaze**, a specially constructed maze for humans. Opened in 1985, the Kyoto Granmaze was the start of the maze craze that has since spread to other parts of Japan. Covering an area about half the size of a football field, this maze features wooden walls about 6½ feet tall, with lookout towers posted every so often to let you survey your position. Although the record time for finding one's way out is eight minutes, it takes most humans about an hour to complete the maze. If you take longer, don't feel bad. The longest time to date belongs to some hapless soul who wandered around for four hours and 34 minutes before reaching the finish line. To get to the Granmaze, take the Keihan Uji Line to Rokujizo Station, from which it's about a seven-minute walk north of the station (make sure you have the right line—otherwise you might well end up in Osaka, with more frustration than you bargained for). The Granmaze opens daily at 9 a.m., and lost souls are flushed out at sunset. Cost of all this fun: ¥500 ($4).

ORGANIZED TOURS

Although I believe that being herded around Kyoto's temples in a large group can never compete with the experience of wandering around at leisure on your own, you may find yourself so short of time that you feel compelled to join an organized tour of Kyoto. Both morning and afternoon tours are offered by **Japan Travel Bureau** (tel. 341-1413), and **Kintetsu Gray Line** (tel. 691-0903). Sites visited may include the Imperial Palace, Nijo Castle, the Golden Pavilion, Heian Shrine, Sanjusangendo Hall, and Kiyomizu Temple.

For those who want a more personalized tour, student guides are available through the T.I.C. For more information, see "The ABCs of Kyoto" earlier in this chapter.

One tour that you may consider joining if you have some extra time and you're tired of temples (Kyoto does seem to have more than its fair share of temples) is the

Rapids Shooting Tour. Flat-bottomed wooden boats depart from Kameoka six times daily March through November, with fewer departures in heated boats during the winter months. The trip lasts about two hours and covers approximately ten miles of the Hozu River, ending in Arashiyama. The rapids are not dangerous (in fact, most of them are nothing more than small riffles), and the trip is a very pleasant and relaxing way to see something of the surrounding countryside with its changing vistas of wooded hills and winding gorge. Cost of the trip is ¥3,400 ($27.20). For more information on the tour or how to get to Kameoka, contact the T.I.C.

---

5. Notes on Shopping

As the nation's capital for more than 1,000 years, Kyoto became home to a number of crafts and exquisite art forms that evolved to cater to the elaborate tastes of the imperial court and upper classes. Today you can shop for everything from Noh masks to silk to cloisonné and lacquerware in Kyoto.

KYOTO HANDICRAFT CENTER

For one-stop shopping under one roof your best bet is the Kyoto Handicraft Center, Kumano Jinja Higashi, Sakyo-ku (tel. 761-5080), located just north of Heian Shrine on Marutamachi Dori Street. Seven floors of merchandise contain almost everything Japanese imaginable—pearls, lacquerware, dolls, kimonos, woodblock prints, pottery, cameras, cassette players, items made of Japanese paper, swords, lanterns, silk and textile goods, painted scrolls, and music boxes. And that's just for starters. You can even buy socks to be worn with *geta* wooden shoes and *obi* sashes worn with the kimono. You can easily spend an hour or two here wandering around, and there are also demonstrations set up showing artisans at work on various crafts including hand-weaving, woodblock printing, and the production of damascene. The center is open from 9:30 a.m. to 6 p.m. (until 5:30 p.m. December through February); closed December 31 through January 3.

KYOTO CRAFT CENTER

Whereas the Kyoto Handicraft Center described above is good for souvenirs and inexpensive gifts for the folks back home, the Kyoto Craft Center, 275 Gion, Kitagawa, Higashiyama-ku (tel. 561-9660), features beautifully designed and crafted items by local and famous artisans. Located on Shijo Dori Avenue east of the Kamo River in the heart of Gion, the Kyoto Craft Center has a wide range of products, including jewelry, scarves, pottery, glass, fans, damascene, baskets, and much more. This is the place to shop for wedding gifts or something very special for yourself. It's open from 10 a.m. to 6 p.m.; closed Wednesday.

KYOTO MUNICIPAL MUSEUM OF TRADITIONAL INDUSTRY

Described earlier under the walking tour of East Kyoto, the Kyoto Municipal Museum of Traditional Industry is a craft museum but also sells many of the items displayed. Lacquerware, textiles, bamboo products, cloisonné, damascene jewelry, knives, dolls, and more are for sale. Admission to the museum is free, and it's open every day except Monday from 9 a.m. to 4:30 p.m.

DEPARTMENT STORES

Other good places to shop for Japanese items and souvenirs, including pottery, lacquerware, and kimonos, are department stores. They're open from 10 a.m. to 6 p.m., closed one day of the week. **Takashimaya** (tel. 221-8811), closed on Wednesday, and **Hankyu** (tel. 223-2288), closed on Thursday, are both located at the intersection of Shijo and Kawaramachi in the heart of Kyoto; **Daimaru** (tel. 211-8111), closed on Wednesday, is located farther west on Shijo Dori Avenue; **Kintetsu** (tel. 361-1111), closed on Thursday, is located across the street from Kyoto Station's north exit.

SPECIALTY SHOPS

There are a number of tiny specialty shops in Kyoto, the majority situated in Gion, along **Shijo Dori Avenue** and in the area of Kawaramachi Dori Avenue. The square formed by **Kawaramachi Dori, Shijo Dori, Sanjo Dori,** and **Teramachi Dori,** for example, includes a covered shopping arcade and specialized shops selling lacquerware, combs and hairpins, knives and swords, tea and tea ceremony implements, and more. If you're looking for antiques, woodblock prints, and art galleries, head towards **Shinmonzen Street** in Gion, which parallels Shijo Dori to the north on the east side of the Kamo River. Pottery shops are found in abundance on the roads leading to Kiyomizu Temple in Higashiyama-ku.

If you're interested in Japanese dolls, a good place to go is **Tanakaya**⑩, Yanaginobanba-higashi, on Shijo Dori Avenue (tel. 221-1959), where the shopkeeper speaks English. You can browse for Kyoto-style dolls, Noh masks, and inexpensive miniature animals. It's open from 10 a.m. to 6:30 p.m.; closed Wednesday.

Miyawaki Baisen-an ⑩, Tominokoji-nishi, Rokkaku-dori (tel. 221-0181), has specialized in fans since 1823, especially fans characteristic of Kyoto. It's open daily from 9 a.m. to 5 p.m., and English is spoken.

Located on Kawaramachi Dori Avenue next to Maruzen Book Store, **Yamato Mingei-ten,** Takoyakushi-agaru, Nakagyo-ku (tel. 221-2641), has been selling folkcrafts and folk art from all over Japan for more than four decades. For sale are ceramics, glassware, lacquerware, textiles, paper products, baskets, and other handcrafted items. It's open every day except Friday from 10 a.m. to 8:30 p.m.

Handcrafted boxwood hair combs and ornamental hairpins are on display at **Jusan-ya,** Otabi-cho, Shijo Dori, Shinkyogoku Higashi-iru, Shimogyo-ku (tel. 221-2008), on Shijo Dori Avenue west of Kawaramachi Dori Avenue. Opened in 1930 by the fifth generation of comb makers, it's open daily from 10 a.m. to 9 p.m.

If you want to decorate your garden back home with a Japanese stone lantern, drop by the **Sawakichi Stone Store,** 551 Gojozaka, Higashiyama-ku (tel. 561-2802). Located on a large intersection just west of the approach leading to Kiyomizu Temple, it offers a variety of styles and sizes in stone lanterns and is open daily from 9 a.m. to 6 p.m.

Zohiko Lacquerware, located in Okazaki Park not far from Heian Shrine (tel. 761-0212), carries on the tradition of Kyoto lacquerware, which has been produced in the ancient capital for 1,000 years. The showroom, with various lacquer products for sale, is open from 9:30 a.m. to 5:30 p.m.; closed Sunday and national holidays.

Inaba Cloisonné, Sanjo Shirakawabashi (tel. 761-1161), is one of Japan's most famous shops and has been dealing in cloisonné and artistic enamelware for about a century. Its showroom displays jewelry, vases, trays, and other products. Hours are 9 a.m. to 5:30 p.m.; closed Sunday and holidays. There's a workshop here where you can watch women producing various cloisonné wares. The shop is located west of the Miyako Hotel on Sanjo Dori Avenue not far from the Shirakawa River.

TOJI TEMPLE FLEA MARKET

On the 21st of each month a flea market is held at Toji Temple, located about a 15-minute walk southwest of Kyoto Station. Japan's largest monthly market, it's also one of the oldest, with a history stretching back more than 700 years. The market began in the 1200s as pilgrims began flocking to Toji Temple to pay their respects to Kobo Daishi, who founded the Shingon sect of Buddhism. Today Toji Temple is

still a center for the Shingon sec
booths selling antiques, old kimo
before a statue of Kobo Daishi and
temple calligraphers. Even if you d
market and booths makes a trip her

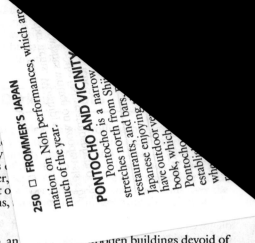

6. After

Nothing beats spending a fine su
From the geisha district of Gion to the
of Pontocho, Kyoto at night is a city
evening with a walk along the banks
young couples in love. In the summer,
and south of Shijo Dori Avenue erect o
water. Illuminated with paper lanterns,

mation on Noh performances, which are
much of the year.

PONTOCHO AND VICINITY
Pontocho is a narrow
stretches north from Shi
restaurants, and bars
Japanese enjoying
have outdoor ve
book, which
Pontocho
establi
wh

GION

Gion is a small district of Kyoto, an ....wooden buildings devoid of flashing neon signs. In fact, as the geisha entertainment district of the city, there's something almost austere and solemn about Gion, as though its raison d'être were infinitely more important and sacred than that of mere entertainment. Gion is a shrine to Kyoto's past, an era when geisha numbered thousands in the city. Now there are only a mere couple of hundred. After all, in today's world of technology, computers, and space travel, few women are willing to undergo the years of training to learn how to conduct the tea ceremony, to play the **samisen** (a 3-stringed musical instrument), or to perform ancient court dances. And contrary to popular Western misconceptions, geisha are not prostitutes. Rather, they are trained experts in conversation and coquettishness, and their primary role is to make men feel like kings while in the soothing enclave of the geisha house.

As you stroll the narrow streets of Gion, perhaps you will see a geisha or maiko (a young woman training to be a geisha) clattering in her wooden shoes on her way to her evening appointment. She will be dressed in a brilliant kimono, her face a chalky white and her hair adorned with hairpins and ornaments. From geisha houses music and laughter lilt out from behind paper screens, but you can only surmise the merry scene inside because you cannot enter without being invited. Not even the Japanese will venture inside without proper introductions. If it will satisfy your curiosity, however, I will tell you that on my fourth visit to Kyoto I was finally invited to one of Gion's geisha houses—and found it to be much like any other hostess bar in Japan. The women pour the drinks, the men drink, and everyone is lighthearted and happy.

After strolling around, the best thing to do in Gion is to visit **Gion Corner,** located on the first floor of Yasaka Hall, Hanamikoji Shijo-sagaru (tel. 561-1119), in the heart of Gion. This is where special variety programs are held every night from March 1 to November 29 with demonstrations of the tea ceremony, flower arrangement, *koto* (Japanese harp) music, *gagaku* (ancient court music and dance), *kyogen* (Noh comic play), *kyomai* (Kyoto-style dance) performed by maiko, and *Bunraku* (puppetry). This is an excellent way to see a variety of ancient Japanese entertainment in a short period of time. Admission is ¥2,100 ($16.80) and there are two shows nightly, at 7:40 and again at 8:40 p.m. Reservations are not necessary, but get there early since the 250 seats are on a first-come, first-served basis. Tickets are available at most hotels, travel agencies, and at Gion Corner itself.

The **Minamiza Theater,** on Shijo Dori Avenue just east of the Kamo River, stages Kabuki drama several times a year. Inquire at the Kyoto Tourist Information Center for information on performances, cost, and times. The T.I.C. also has infor-

street that parallels the Kamo River's west bank and
o Dori Avenue. Riddled with geisha houses, hostess bars,
ontocho is interesting to walk along and to watch groups of
themselves. Although many of these restaurants lining the river
randas in summer, I was able to include only a couple of them in this
you'll find listed in the restaurant section. Most of the restaurants in
are unfortunately unreceptive to foreigners, and I was turned away from
shment after establishment with the excuse that the place was full—even
n I could see that it was not. The Kyoto T.I.C. informed me that they do not
ecommend Pontocho to foreigners simply because of the cold reception. However,
I think it's worth walking through Pontocho because the area is so interesting and so
Japanese. Although most of the bars and clubs are virtually impossible to enter without an introduction, you might want to come here for a meal at one of the recommended restaurants in this book. And if you're feeling adventurous and are
determined to find seating under the paper lanterns on one of the open verandas,
maybe you'll be lucky. Once in a while, restaurants that do not want the publicity of
a guidebook will accept the occasional lone foreigner.

If you don't feel like eating but would still like to sit under the stars beside the
river, the best thing to do is to go to the north end of Pontocho where it joins Sanjo
Dori Avenue and drink a cup of coffee at **Karafuneya**, Pontocho, Sanjo-sagaru (tel.
255-1414). A coffeeshop with an outdoor veranda overlooking the river, it's open
24 hours a day every day, and offers various kinds of coffee, tea, sandwiches, ice
cream, sundaes, and desserts, with most items costing ¥600 ($4.80). No alcoholic
beverages are served, but it's a pleasant place to sit and watch couples strolling along
the riverbanks. Note that the veranda itself is open only during the summer in the
evenings, from 5 to 11 p.m.

Also on Pontocho, but facing away from the river, **Suishin Honten** ⑩③ (tel.
221-8596) is an inexpensive yakitori-ya very popular with young Japanese. Part of a
chain of Suishin yakitori restaurants, it has small mugs of beer that start at ¥400
($3.20). Three skewers of chicken yakitori or grilled fish (yakizakana) cost only
¥270 ($2.16), while a platter of assorted sashimi (called moriawase) costs ¥1,300
($10.40). Open every day from 4 to 11:30 p.m., it's located on the west side of
Pontocho just south of Sanjo Dori Avenue. Look for a big white sign, red curtains
hanging outside the front door, and a large display case. This is a good place to stop
off for a beer. Be sure to remove your shoes at the entryway and place them in one of
the lockers provided.

Finally, one more friendly place on Pontocho is **Zu Zu** ⑩④, Takoyakushi (tel.
231-0736), located just north of the playground that splits Pontocho in half and also
on the inland side of the street. Look for a white stucco façade and a sign that pro-
claims, "Welcome to the Oriental Restaurant." Closed on Thursday but open the
rest of the week from 6 p.m. to 2 a.m., this small, intimate place offers beer, wine,
cocktails, spirits, and Japanese, Chinese, and French dishes. A rack of roast spare rib
is ¥1,050 ($8.40), chicken steak is ¥630 ($5.04), and a draft beer is ¥450 ($3.60).

If you like your entertainment in one spot, head for the **Imagium** building,
located just north of Shijo and west of Kiyamachi in the nightlife district. It offers
eight floors of evening activity, from eating, drinking, and playing pool to dancing.
Most locales are open only in the evenings from about 6 p.m. Imagium is the
glitziest thing to hit Kyoto in a long time and looks like it was imported straight out
of Tokyo—and Kyoto purists grumble that Tokyo is exactly where it belongs.

Skewer of Nan-Zan, Kawaramachi-Sanjo, Futasugi-agaru (tel. 221-6930), is a
friendly yakitori-ya close to the Alpha and Kyoto Royal hotels and just a few steps

southeast of the Kawaramachi Catholic Church. It's located on Anekoji Dori Street in a basement and is open from 5 p.m. to 1 a.m.; closed the third Sunday of the month. The owner has studied English, is a big baseball fan, and is delighted to have foreign guests. The English menu lists various kinds of yakitori, including skewers of beef, chicken, squid, bell pepper, mushroom, and eggplant, with prices averaging ¥330 ($2.64) to ¥1,000 ($8) for three to five skewers. Also available is beef sushi, salads, soups, and beefsteak cooked Japanese style. I recommend trying grilled wrapped potato—mashed potato with egg, onions, and bacon in it. Beer starts at ¥500 ($4) and sake at ¥380 ($3.04).

A comfortable and pleasant bar that caters to a 20- to 30-year-old crowd, **Africa,** Shijo-Kawaramachi (tel. 255-4518), is located on a side street just east of Kawaramachi and north of Shijo avenues. Open daily from 6 p.m. to 2 a.m., it's filled with all kinds of knickknacks, stuffed animals, masks, junk, and stained-glass lamps. A video screen shows old and recent American movies, TV shows, and rock videos, and there are also a Foosball table and backgammon sets you can use. Beer and cocktails start at ¥550 ($4.40). Snacks include pizza, gratin, spaghetti, seafood, roast beef, fried chicken, and pilaf.

If you want to hear live music, head for **Taku Taku** ⑩⑤, Tominokoji-Bukkoji (tel. 351-1321). Featuring heavy metal, rock, soul, blues, reggae, jazz, and punk rock, this live-entertainment house is located in an old sake warehouse and its decor is rudimentary and plain. It caters mainly to Kyoto's college students and is open every evening from 6 to 11 p.m. Live music is usually from 7 to 9 p.m., and the cover charge averages ¥1,600 ($12.80) with one drink, rising to as much as ¥5,000 ($40) for bands from England or the U.S.A. Beer is ¥550 ($4.40), and sandwiches and various snacks are available. To find Taku Taku, walk south from Shijo Dori Avenue on Tominokoji Dori Street. It's just past the red-and-white spiral of a barbershop on the right-hand side of the street behind a small parking lot. Listen for the music.

Another popular place among Kyoto's college crowd is **Irohanihoheto** ⑩⑥, Shingoken-cho, Sanjo-kudaru, Yamato-dori, Higashiyama-ku (tel. 541-1683). It's located on Nawate Dori Street on the fifth floor of a white-tiled building just south of Sanjo-Keihan Station (look for a sign on the building's ground floor that says Colorado Coffee Shop). Open daily from 5:30 p.m. to 3:30 a.m. (to 5 a.m. on weekends), this is one of a chain of drinking establishments with headquarters in Hokkaido. Irohanihoheto is known for its rustic decor, which always includes heavy wooden beams held together with ropes to give it a country atmosphere, shoji screens, and crafts hanging down from the ceiling. It's also known for its low prices. Beer starts at ¥380 ($3.04), and the extensive Japanese menu with pictures includes yakitori, sashimi, salads, and vegetables. Most items cost less than ¥400 ($3.20).

Around the corner from Irohanihoheto and directly behind (south of) the Sanjo-Keihan Station is the **Jazz Club Sunnyside,** located on the fifth floor of the Kyoto Art Center Building, Furumonzen Dori Street, Yamato-oji, Higashiyama-ku (tel. 525-0910). Informal and cozy with room for only 15 or so people, it's owned by Fumhiro Watanabe, who also provides the entertainment by singing and playing the piano. His repertoire centers on American jazz and popular hits of the 1940s, and there's a tiny dance floor. Closed on Monday, it's open the rest of the week from 7 p.m. to 1 a.m. The ¥2,000 ($16) music charge includes one drink, snack, and tip. After that, beer costs ¥600 ($4.80). Note that Mr. Watanabe is hoping to move to a new location in the heart of Gion sometime during the life of this edition of this book, so it would be prudent to call first.

Catering to a much younger crowd is **China Express,** a disco located in the basement of the Sanjo Terrace Building, Sanjo Kiyamachi-sagaru (tel. 241-3870). It's on the first street south of and paralleling Sanjo Dori Avenue, between Kawaramachi and Kiyamachi streets. Open from 5:30 p.m. to midnight, it features a wooden dance floor, mirrors in which you can watch yourself dance, and an interesting Chinese-like decor. Admission is ¥3,800 ($30.40) for males and ¥3,300 ($26.40) for females, except on weekends and nights before a holiday, when prices go up ¥500 ($4). Included in the admission are 20 tickets you can exchange for drinks; beer costs six tickets, while cocktails are six or seven.

If you like to listen to reggae, one more place worth mentioning is **Rub a Dub,** Sanjo-sagaru, Kiyamachi (tel. 256-3122). It's located on the east side of Kiyamachi Street just a couple shops south of Sanjo Dori Avenue, below a drugstore. A tiny establishment open from 6 p.m. to 2 a.m. every day except Sunday, this bar is unpretentious and primitive. Beer and cocktails are all a low ¥550 ($4.40). The music isn't live, but prices are cheap.

If you're interested in a quiet place for a cup of coffee or a drink after dinner, the **François Salon de Thé** is on a small street running along the west side of the tiny canal about a minute's walk southwest of the Shijo Avenue Bridge, spanning the Kamo River (tel. 351-4042). More than 50 years old, the outside of the building resembles a miniature castle, while the inside has an atmosphere similar to that of an old Viennese coffeehouse. A domed ceiling, dark-wood paneling, stained-glass windows, heavy red-cushioned chairs, and classical music make drinking a cup of coffee here a pleasant and relaxing experience—a good place to escape the crowds. Tea and coffee start at ¥450 ($3.60), cakes start at ¥380 ($3.04), and beer is available for ¥550 ($4.40). It's open daily from 9:30 a.m. to 11 p.m. (to 11:30 p.m. on Saturday).

BEER GARDENS

A pleasant and inexpensive way to enjoy a warm summer's night is to spend it under the stars at a rooftop beer garden. On the roof of a restaurant called **Kikusui** ⑩, Shijo Ohashi (tel. 561-1001), is a beer garden open throughout the summer from 5 until 9 p.m. It's atop a five-story stone building right on Shijo Dori Avenue on the east side of the Kamo River and across the street from the Kabuki theater. It's easy to spot because the rooftop is lined with lanterns and has palm trees peeking over the ledge. Beer ranges from ¥450 ($3.60) to ¥800 ($6.40), and various snacks such as yakitori, pizza, and grilled squid are also available.

The **Kyoto Hotel** on Kawaramachi Dori Avenue also has a rooftop beer garden open mid-May to the end of August from 5 to 9 p.m. nightly. It offers a good view of the city, with a nightly buffet of all you can eat and drink for ¥2,900 ($23.20). Included items are yakitori, fried chicken, fried fish, fried noodles, smoked salmon, as well as such drinks as beer, whisky, and sake.

On top of the **ANA Hotel** is another beer garden, open from May to the end of August from 5:30 to 9 p.m. nightly. Beer here begins at ¥550 ($4.40) for a small. And finally, close to Kyoto Station is one more rooftop beer garden, this one atop the **New Miyako Hotel**. It's open throughout the summer months from 5 to 9 p.m.

7. A Side Trip to Nara

In the beginnings of Japanese history, the nation's capital was moved to a new site each time a new emperor came to the throne. In 710, however, the first permanent Japanese capital was set up in Nara. Not that it turned out to be so permanent —after only 74 years the capital was moved first to Nagaoka and shortly thereafter to Kyoto, where it remained for more than 1,000 years. What's important about those 74 years is that they witnessed the birth of Japan's arts, crafts, and literature. Turning to its more advanced neighbor to the west, Nara imported everything from religion to art to architecture from China. Even the city itself was modeled after Chinese concepts, laid out in a rectangular grid pattern. It was during the Nara period that Japan's first historical account, first mythological chronicle, and first poetry anthology (with 4,173 poems) were written. Buddhism flourished and Nara grew as the political and cultural center of the land.

Today Nara is celebrated as the cradle of Japanese culture. Japanese flock here because Nara gives them the feeling that they are communing with their ancestors. Foreigners come here because Nara gives them a glimpse of a Japan that was. For, remarkably enough, many of Nara's buildings and temples remain intact, and long ago someone had enough foresight to enclose many of its historical structures in the quiet and peaceful confines of a large and spacious park. Although most visitors come to Nara on only a day trip from Kyoto, there is more than enough here to occupy two full days. For that reason I've included some recommendations in accommodations. If you stay here overnight, be sure to take advantage of an evening or early-morning stroll through Nara Park.

ORIENTATION

You can pick up brochures and information on Nara before leaving Kyoto at the Kyoto T.I.C. The Kyoto map distributed there also has a map of Nara on the reverse side. Be sure also to pick up the leaflet *Walking Tour Courses in Nara*. In Nara itself there are **tourist information offices** at both the JR Nara Station (tel. 0742/22-9821), open daily from 8 a.m. to 6 p.m., and the Kintetsu Nara Station (tel. 0742/24-4858), open daily from 9 a.m. to 5 p.m. These offices have another good brochure and map of Nara issued by the Nara City Tourist Office, with useful information on how to get around Nara by bus. Incidentally, if you'd like to have your own personal guide to show you around, there are volunteer Goodwill Guides who will be glad to show you the sights in exchange for the practice it gives them with their English. One guide each is posted at both the JR and Kintetsu station tourist offices and is available to the first tourists who show up every day except Sunday. If you'd rather not take chances and would like to reserve a guide in advance, call the day before at 0742/44-2207 to arrange a time. The free guide service is available Monday through Saturday from 9:30 a.m. to 3 p.m.

There's a third tourist office located in the center of town about equidistant from both train stations. The **Nara City Tourist Center,** 23-4 Kamisanjo (tel. 0742/22-3900), is open daily from 9 a.m. to 9 p.m.

To find out what's going on in Nara by way of festivals and exhibitions, you can call 27-1313 for a two-minute taped recording in English. If you're calling outside Nara, the area code is 0742.

Only 26 miles south of Kyoto, Nara is easily reached in about 33 minutes from Kyoto Station on the Kintetsu Limited Express of Kinki Nippon Railways, which whisks you directly to Nara Kintetsu Station. If you have a rail pass you can take the slower JR train from Kyoto Station to the Nara JR Station in about an hour. You can also reach Nara from Osaka in about 30 to 50 minutes, depending on the train and the station from which you leave.

Nara's Kintetsu and JR stations are within a few minutes' walk of each other. Most of Nara's sites are located to the east of the two stations, within easy walking distance. To visit the areas of Horyuji and Nishinokyo, take bus 52 from either the JR or Kintetsu Station. It has announcements of its stops recorded in English. Other buses bound for the Horyuji and Nishinokyo temple areas are shown on the brochure of Nara available at the Nara tourist offices.

The **telephone area code** for Nara is 0742.

THE SIGHTS

The best way to enjoy Nara is to arrive early in the morning before the first tour buses start pulling in. If you don't have much time, the most important sites to see are Todaiji Temple, Kasuga Shrine, and Horyuji Temple.

Around Nara Park

With its ponds, grassy lawns, trees, and temples, Nara Park covers about 1,300 acres. It's home to more than 1,000 deer roaming freely through the park. As you walk east from either the JR or Kintetsu train station, the first temple you reach is **Kofukuji Temple,** founded in 710 as the family temple of the Fujiwaras, the second most powerful clan after the imperial family. At one time as many as 175 buildings were erected on the Kofukuji Temple grounds, but through centuries of civil wars and fires most of the structures were burned. Only a handful of buildings still remain, but even these were rebuilt after the 13th century. Its five-story pagoda, first erected in 730, was burned down five times. The present pagoda dates from 1426 and is an exact replica of its original form. At 164 feet tall, it's the second-tallest pagoda in Japan (the tallest is at Toji Temple in Kyoto). The temple's Treasure House, charging an admission of ¥400 ($3.20) and open from 9 a.m. to 5 p.m., displays many statues and works of art originally contained in the temple's buildings, the most famous of which is a statue of Ashura carved in the 8th century.

To the east of Kofukuji is the **Nara National Museum,** which houses invaluable Buddhist art and archeological relics. Many statues and other items originally contained in Nara's many temples are now housed here. Open every day except Monday from 9 a.m. to 4:30 p.m., it charges ¥360 ($2.88) admission.

Todaiji Temple, along with its **Daibutsu (Great Buddha),** is Nara's greatest attraction. When Emperor Shomu ordered construction of both the temple and the Daibutsu back in the mid-700s, it was his intention to make Todaiji the headquarters of all Buddhist temples in the land. In his plans to create a Buddhist utopia, he commissioned work on an overwhelmingly huge bronze statue of Buddha. It took eight castings to finally complete the Great Buddha, a remarkable work of art that remains the largest bronze statue of Buddha in Japan. At a height of more than 50 feet, the Daibutsu is made of 437 tons of bronze, 286 pounds of pure gold, 165 pounds of mercury, and 7 tons of vegetable wax. However, because of Japan's frequent natural calamities, the Buddha of today isn't quite what it used to be. In 855, in what must have been a whopper of an earthquake, the Buddha lost its head. It was repaired in 861, but, alas, the huge wooden building housing the Buddha was burned down twice during wars, melting the Buddha's head. The present head dates from 1692, but there's no telling how long he'll be able to hold on to it.

As for the wooden structure, called Daibutsuden, which housed the Great Buddha, it was destroyed several times through the centuries; the present structure dates from 1709. Measuring 161 feet tall, 187 feet long, and 164 feet wide, it's the largest wooden structure in the world. If you can imagine, however, the building is only two-thirds its original size. Be sure to walk in a circle around the Great Buddha to see it from all different angles. Behind the statue is a huge wooden column with a small hole in it near the ground. According to popular belief, if you can manage to crawl through this opening you will be sure to reach enlightenment. The Daibutsuden is open from 7:30 a.m. to 5:30 p.m. from April through September, from 8 a.m. to 4:30 p.m. in winter. Admission is ¥300 ($2.40).

A stroll through Nara Park will bring you to **Kasuga Shrine,** one of my favorite Shinto shrines in all of Japan. Originally the tutelary shrine of the Fujiwara family, it was founded in 768 and, according to Shinto concepts of purity, was torn down and rebuilt every 20 years in its original form until 1863. Nestled in the midst of verdant woods, it's a shrine of vermillion-colored pillars and an astounding 3,000 lanterns, some of them stone and others cast in bronze. The most spectacular time to visit the shrine is in mid-August or the beginning of February, when all 3,000 lanterns are lit. One of the fun things to do at Kasuga Shrine is to pay ¥100 (80¢) for a slip of paper in English with your fortune on it. If the fortune is unfavorable you can conveniently negate it by tying the piece of paper to the twig of a tree.

A ten-minute walk to the southwest of Kasuga Shrine brings you to **Shin-Yakushiji Temple,** built in the middle of the 8th century by the Empress Komyo to obtain the gods' help in the recovery of Emperor Shomu from an eye disease (Yakushi is the name given to the Healing Buddha). Only the main hall remains, the other buildings having been destroyed and rebuilt after the 13th century. The main hall contains a statue of Yakushi-nyorai surrounded by 12 pottery figures, 11 of which are originals and are considered national treasures. Admission is ¥400 ($3.20), and it's open from 8:30 a.m. to 6 p.m.

Horyuji Temple Area

Founded in 607 by Prince Shotoku as a center for Buddhism in Japan, Horyuji Temple is one of Japan's most significant gems in terms of both architecture and art. It was from here that Buddhism blossomed and spread throughout the land. Today about 45 buildings remain, some of them dating from the end of the 7th century and comprising what are probably the oldest wooden structures in the world. At the western end of the grounds is the Golden Hall (**Kondo**), a two-story structure 58 feet high which is considered the oldest building at Horyuji Temple. Next to the main hall is a five-story pagoda, which dates from the foundation of the temple. It contains four scenes from the life of Buddha, including Buddha's cremation and entry into Nirvana. The **Great Treasure House** (**Daihozoden**), a concrete building constructed in 1941, contains temple treasure, including statues and other works of art from the 7th and 8th centuries. On the eastern precincts of Horyuji Temple is an octagonal building built in 739 called **Yumedono Hall,** or Hall of Dreams. Supposedly Prince Shotoku used this building for quiet meditation.

Admission to Horyuji Temple, the Treasure House, and Hall of Dreams is ¥500 ($4). The grounds are open from 8 a.m. to 5 p.m. (until 4:30 p.m. in winter), but you must enter at least 30 minutes before closing time.

East of Yumedono is **Chuguji Temple,** a nunnery built for members of the imperial family. It contains two outstanding works of art. The wooden statue of Miroku-bosatsu dates from the 7th century and is noted for the serene and compassionate expression on its face. The Tenjukoku Mandala is the oldest piece of embroidery in Japan. It's a fragment of embroidery originally 16 feet long created by Shotoku's window and her female companions with scenes depicting life of the times. Only a replica of the fragile embroidery is now on display. Admission here is ¥300 ($2.40).

Nishinokyo Area

If you still have time to spend in Nara, it's worth making a trip to the vicinity of Nishinokyo Station to visit two more temples. **Toshodaiji Temple** was founded in 759 by Ganjin, a high priest from China who was invited to Japan by the emperor to help spread Buddhism. Ganjin's first attempts to reach Japan were thwarted by pirate attacks, storms, and five shipwrecks. During one of these voyages Ganjin lost his sight through disease. He finally reached Japan in 754 at the age of 66 and set to work constructing this magnificent temple. Its main hall and lecture hall still stand and are both national treasures. The main hall contains various statues and its front pillars are thought to resemble Greek architecture, the concept of which may have been brought to Japan via the Silk Road. Also on the temple's grounds is Ganjin's tomb.

About 800 yards south of Toshodaiji is **Yakushiji Temple,** which contains more Buddhist statues. Its three-story pagoda is believed to date from 698. It looks as if it has six stories because of the intermediate roofs.

FOOD AND ACCOMMODATIONS

With a population of more than 300,000, Nara has a number of fine hotels and ryokan in all price categories. One of the most famous is the **Nara Hotel,** Nara-Koen-nai (tel. 0742/26-3300), which was built in 1909 and sits like a palace on top of a hill above several ponds near Nara Park. You have your choice of staying in the old section of the hotel, with its high ceilings and comfortable old-fashioned decor, or in a new addition which opened in 1984, offering pleasant and modern rooms with verandas. Rates range from ¥9,000 ($72) to ¥10,500 ($84) for singles, ¥16,500 ($132) for doubles, and ¥16,500 ($132) to ¥30,000 ($240) for twins. The higher rates are for rooms in the new addition.

The dining room of the Nara Hotel is a good place to come for lunch or dinner. Decorated in old drawing-room fashion with heavy curtains, wood paneling, and a view of a peaceful pond, it has Western-style lunches starting at ¥3,800 ($30.40) from 11:30 a.m. to 2 p.m. and dinner beginning at ¥4,700 ($37.60) from 5:30 to 8 p.m.

If you can't afford to stay at the Nara Hotel, the prices of its **Nara Hotel Annex** (tel. 0742/26-3101) may be more within your budget. Its 34 rooms are located in a building directly above the Kintetsu Station on floors six and seven. Remodeled in 1985, the rooms are bright and cheerful and feature double-paned windows to shut out noise, a hot-water pot for tea, TV, clock, radio, and fridge. Singles cost ¥7,900 ($63) and twins are ¥15,000 ($120).

On the eighth floor of the Nara Hotel Annex is the hotel's restaurant, Sky Grill. If you can get a table at the north corner of the restaurant, you'll have a good view of Nara Park and the top of Todaiji Temple. Its changing set lunch menu starts at around ¥1,000 ($8), and dinners cost ¥2,700 ($21.60) to ¥11,000 ($88). À la carte items include sandwiches, spaghetti, lobster, sirloin steak, stewed beef, and pork cutlets. It's open from 11:30 a.m. to 9:30 p.m. During the summer months, from the end of May to the beginning of September, there's a rooftop beer garden open daily from 5 to 9 p.m.

If you want to stay in a Japanese-style ryokan, **Kikusuiro** ⑩, 1130 Takahata Bodaimachi (tel. 0742/23-2001), is a lovely 100-year-old inn. An imposing structure surrounded by a white wall not far from Nara Park, it makes good use of various woods to create pleasing forms of decoration in its tatami rooms. It also has a beautiful garden. There are 17 rooms here, 8 of which have private bath and toilet. Rates start at ¥33,000 ($264) per person, including two meals. Adjacent to the ryokan are both Western- and Japanese-style restaurants. The Japanese restaurant, open daily from 11 a.m. to 8:30 p.m., is new and decorated with bamboo and paper lanterns, and features sukiyaki or shabu-shabu starting at ¥6,500 ($52), obento lunch boxes starting at ¥4,400 ($35.20), and kaiseki from ¥16,500 ($132).

If you're looking for a business hotel, the **Hotel Sunroute Nara,** 1110 Takabatake-cho (tel. 0742/22-5151), is in a residential area south of Kofukuji Temple. With a cheerful lobby, the Sunroute offers a good-size single, including couch and chairs, for ¥7,000 ($56). Twins range from ¥13,200 ($106) to ¥15,000 ($120). Tax and service are extra. All rooms offer TV, refrigerator, a one-cup water heater with tea bags, private bath, and phone. This 95-room hotel features a pleasant restaurant serving Western breakfast, lunch, and dinner.

For budget travelers, **Furuichi** ⑩, 630 Higashitera Hayashimachi (tel. 0742/ 22-2440), offers 15 rooms, most of them Japanese style and some even with bathroom. There is a sink in all rooms, as well as TV, telephone, heater, air conditioner, and safe. Rooms are very pleasant, with traditional shoji screens and seating space beside the windows. The only drawback is that no one here speaks English. Rates per person are ¥3,800 ($30) for rooms without private bathroom and ¥4,500 ($36) for rooms with. It's located about a 10-minute walk from Kintetsu Station and a 15-minute walk from the JR Station, close to Sarusawano-ike Pond and the Hotel Sunroute.

A good place for lunch is **Harishin** ⑩, 15 Nakashinya-cho (tel. 22-2669). It's located near Gangoji Temple in a lovely part of old Nara, a part of town many tourists never see. The restaurant itself is a 200-year-old house of ochre-colored walls and a wood-slat façade, and dining is on tatami with a view of a garden. The specialty here is its Kamizumichi Obento, a one-pot dish for ¥2,700 ($21.60), and it's open only for lunch from 11:30 a.m. to 3:30 p.m. It's closed on Monday unless Monday happens to be a national holiday, in which case it remains open and closes on Tuesday instead. It's located about a 15-minute walk from Kintetsu Station—ask for directions at the tourist office.

THE JAPAN ALPS

Lying in the central part of Honshu, the Japan Alps consist of several volcanic mountain ranges. With the exception of Japan's tallest mountain, Mount Fuji, all of Japan's loftiest mountains are in these ranges, making the Japan Alps a popular destination for hikers and nature-lovers. Some of the villages nestled in the mountains remain relatively unchanged in architecture, giving visitors the unique opportunity to see how mountain people have lived through the centuries.

1. Takayama

Located in the Hida Mountains of the Japan Alps, Takayama is surrounded by 10,000-foot peaks, making the train ride here breathtaking no matter whether you approach it from the north or the south. The village, located on a wide plateau, was founded back in the 16th century by Lord Kanamori, who selected the site because of the impregnable position afforded by the surrounding Hida Mountains. For centuries Takayama was so remote and difficult to reach that travelers despaired of ever making it here alive.

Because of its isolation, Takayama developed its own architecture, food, and craftsmanship, much of it still preserved even today. The heart of Takayama is delightful, with homes of classical design typical of Hida in the 18th century. The streets of the old town are narrow and clean, flanked on both sides by tiny canals of running water. Rising up from the canals are one- and two-story homes and shops of gleaming dark wood with overhanging roofs. Latticed windows and slats of wood play games of light and shadow in the white of the sunshine. Strips of blue cloth flutter in the breeze of open shop doors. As you walk down the streets, you'll notice huge cedar balls hanging from the eaves in front of several shops, indicating a sake factory. Altogether there are eight sake factories in Takayama, most of them small affairs. Go inside, sample the sake, and watch men stirring rice in large vats. Takayama is a village that invites exploration.

ORIENTATION
You no longer have to despair of ever reaching Takayama alive. The easiest way to get here is by direct train from Nagoya, which takes about three hours. There are also a few direct trains from Osaka and Kyoto. Train schedules are listed in a leaflet, *Takayama and Vicinity,* distributed free by the Tourist Information Centers in Tokyo and Kyoto.

Upon arrival in Takayama, stop by the local **tourist office** (tel. 0577/32-5328), located in a wooden booth on the east side of Takayama Station. You can pick up an English brochure and a map of the village. It's open daily from 8:30 a.m. to 6:30 p.m. (until 5 p.m. in winter).

Most of Takayama's attractions lie to the east of the train station and are easily reached on foot. An alternative is to rent a **bicycle** from one of the many rental shops ringing the station, the cost of which averages ¥250 ($2) per hour or ¥1,300 ($10.40) for the whole day. To reach the Hida Minzoku Mura Folk Village, take bus 4 from Takayama Station.

The **telephone area code** for Takayama is 0577. It lies in Gifu Prefecture.

THE SIGHTS
Takayama's main attraction is its old merchant houses, which are found clustered around Sannomachi and Furuimachinami streets. Be sure to allow time just for wandering around. Shops in the area sell Takayama's specialties, including sake, yew woodcarvings, and a unique lacquerware called *shunkei-nuri*. Almost all the attractions listed below are closed during the New Year's holidays.

Hida Minzoku Mura Folk Village
Hida Minzoku Mura Folk Village (popularly called Hida no Sato) is an open-air museum where more than 30 old thatched farmhouses have been set up to show how farmers and craftsmen used to live in the Hida Mountain region. The whole village is very picturesque, with swans swimming in the central pond, green moss growing on the thatched roofs, and flowers blooming in season. Some of the houses have roofs in the *gassho-zukuri* style, built steeply to withstand the heavy snowfalls that often measure six feet deep. The tops of the roofs are said to resemble hands joined in prayer. There are shingle-roofed homes, houses with earthen floors, a woodcutter's hut, a grain storehouse, and a house where the second floor was used as a silkworm nursery. All the structures, which range in age from 100 to 500 years, are open to the public and are filled with utensils, tools, and furniture used in daily life. On display, for example, are old spindles and looms, utensils for cooking and dining, instruments used in the silk industry, farm tools, sleds, and straw boots and capes worn to fend off wet snow.

On one corner of the village grounds is a section devoted to folkcrafts and art where workshops have been set up to demonstrate such crafts as textile dyeing and weaving, lacquerwork, and wood sculpture. Within walking distance of the folk village is the **Hida Folklore Museum (Hida Minzoku-kan),** with more displays on life in the Hida region. Next to the folklore museum is the **Museum of Mountain Life,** with displays on the history of mountaineering in the Japan Alps and flora and fauna of the region.

Entrance to all the museums and the folk village is included in the one ticket price of ¥500 ($4). Hours are 8:30 a.m. to 5 p.m. daily.

Morning Markets
One of the things you should be sure to do in the morning is to head for the east bank of the Miyagawa River, where a colorful local market brings splashes of color as women sell flowers, vegetables, and local produce. Another market takes place every

morning also in front of Takayama Jinya. Both markets are held daily from 6 a.m. (7 a.m. in winter) to noon.

Merchants' Houses

In stark contrast to the thatched farmhouses in the Folk Village are two merchants' mansions, which show how the upper class lived. Located side by side on the north end of Ninomachi Street, the **Yoshijima House** and **Kusakabe Mingeikan** once belonged to two of the richest families in Takayama. Of the two, the Yoshijima House is my favorite. With its exposed attic, heavy cross-beams, sunken fireplace, and sliding doors, it's a masterpiece of geometric design. It was built in 1907 as both the home and factory of the Yoshijima family, well-to-do brewers of sake in Takayama. Notice how the beams and wood of the home gleam, attained through decades of polishing as each generation of women did her share in bringing the wood to a luster.

Not quite as rustic, the Kusakabe Mingeikan merchant house is more refined and imposing, built in 1879 for a merchant dealing in silk, lamp oil, and finance. Its architectural style is considered unique to Hida, and on display are items handed down through the generations.

Both merchant houses are open from 9 a.m. to 5 p.m. (to 4:30 p.m. December through February). From December through February, Yoshijima House, which charges ¥250 ($2), is closed on Tuesday while the Kusakabe mansion, which charges ¥300 ($2.40), is open daily.

More Museums

Not far from the merchants' houses is the **Takayama Yatai Kaikan,** an exhibition hall where you can see some of the elaborate floats used for Takayama's famous parades, held twice a year in April and October. These are huge floats, most of them from the 17th century and built by famous craftsmen of the village. The exhibition hall is open daily from 8:30 a.m. to 5 p.m. (9 a.m. to 4:30 p.m. December through February) and charges a ¥460 ($3.68) admission.

Other sites of interest in the vicinity of the exhibition hall are **Hachiman Shrine** and **Shishi Kaikan,** an exhibition hall with displays of lion masks used during festivals around Japan.

The **Hida Folk Archeological Museum (Hida Minzoku Kokokan),** in the heart of Takayama on Sannomachi Street, is an interesting old house that once belonged to a doctor and contains a number of trick devices, including secret passageways and a hanging ceiling. Imagine inviting an enemy to your home, offering him the best room in the house, and then secretly sneaking upstairs to chop the rope that has been holding up the suspended ceiling. The ceiling plunges down with a loud thud, neatly crushing your enemy to death. Rather dramatic, don't you think? And, of course, very effective. Back in the old days of Japan's constant civil wars, trickery was sometimes the only way to survive the constant power struggles. This museum, with its collection of earthenware and folk tools, is open daily from 7 a.m. to 7 p.m. (8 a.m. to 5 p.m. in winter). The entrance fee is ¥300 ($2.40).

Just down the street from the Folk Archeological Museum is the **Fujii Art Gallery (Fujii Bijutsu Mingei-kan),** which contains a good and varied collection of furniture, clothing, combs, dolls, pottery, and lacquerware, most dating from the Edo Period. Included are some beautiful *tansu* (chests), smoking utensils, belt pouches with *netsuke*, swords, paper-covered lamps, farming tools, and spinning wheels. Many items are identified in English. A very worthwhile museum, it's open daily from 9 a.m. to 5 p.m. (to 8 p.m. in summer) and charges ¥250 ($2) admission.

The **Takayama Museum of Local History (Takayama Kyodokan),** on Kami-Ichi-no-Machi Street, is another good museum, displaying antiques and folklore items handed down from generation to generation and work by Hida craftsmen. It charges a ¥200 ($1.60) admission and is open every day except Monday from 8:30 a.m. to 5 p.m. (to 4:30 p.m. December to March).

Across the street from the history museum is the **Toy Museum (Kyodo Gangu-kan),** with a collection of toys from around the country. From April through November the museum is open from 8:30 a.m. to 5 p.m., opening at 9 a.m. the rest of the year. Admission is ¥200 ($1.60).

Takayama Jinya, open from 8:45 a.m. to 5 p.m. (to 4:30 p.m. in winter), was once a manor house for administrators in Takayama. It contains a rice granary (rice was collected as a tax), chambers and courts, and historical records. Admission here is ¥300 ($2.40).

WHERE TO STAY

There are by far more minshuku and ryokan in Takayama than hotels, making Takayama the perfect place to stay in a traditional Japanese inn. In fact, staying in a tatami room and sleeping on a futon is the best way to immerse yourself in the life of this small community and partake of its lifestyle. And the best news is that there are places to fit all budgets. All rates below for ryokan and minshuku follow the Japanese system in that they are on a per-person basis and include breakfast, dinner, and service charges. Tax is extra. Although the rates given here represent the normal rates, you should be aware that in peak season (August and during festival times in April and October), prices will be higher, generally between 10% and 20% more.

A Note on Japanese Symbols

Many hotels, restaurants, and other establishments in Japan do not have signs showing their names in English letters. Appendix II lists the Japanese symbols for all such places appearing in this guide. Each establishment name in Japanese symbols is numbered, and the same number appears in an oval in the text following the boldfaced establishment name. For example, in the text Osako's **Hotel Hokke Club** ⑯ is number 164 in the Japanese symbols list in Appendix II.

Ryokan

Built a little more than a decade ago and possessing all the grace and charm you'd expect from a first-class ryokan, the **Ryokan Hishuya** ⑪ Kami-Okamoto-cho (tel. 0577/33-4001), is just a minute's walk from the Hida Minzoku Mura Folk Village on the quiet outskirts of town. Its rooms have views of either the garden surrounding the ryokan or the distant mountain peaks. Five of its 15 rooms here have wooden bathtubs and are more expensive, beginning at ¥18,500 ($148) per person. The other rooms all have the smaller unit bathrooms typically found in business hotels and begin at ¥13,200 ($106), costing about ¥1,000 ($8) more during peak season. Dinner is served individually in the guest rooms, while breakfast is served in a communal dining hall. If you request it in advance, you'll be greeted in the morning with a Western breakfast of scrambled eggs, toast, ham, coffee, and juice. Shabu-shabu is served to guests who stay a second night.

Another ryokan close to the Folk Village is **Hida Gasshoen** ⑫, 3-829 Nishinoishiki-cho (tel. 0577/33-4531). Secluded on a hillside, its approach has one of the most impressive stone walls I've ever seen—massive boulders, some of which measure ten feet high, all neatly piled on top of one another. The main building housing most of the guest rooms was built in 1980 and was designed to resemble an old gassho-zukuri farmhouse. Meals are served in a genuine 200-year-old thatched farmhouse. Per-person rates range from ¥7,000 ($56) for rooms without bathrooms to ¥13,200 ($106) for a room in a separate ancient house with its own private bath and toilet. Rates go up here only during festival times.

Kinkikan ⑬, 48 Asahimachi (tel. 0577/32-3131), is right in the center of old Takayama, set back from a small side street and surrounded by a wall. The entryway of this ryokan is 100 years old, with a small lobby full of furniture made of shunkei-nuri lacquerware crafted in Takayama. The lobby opens up over a running stream and a delightful century-old garden, just the kind of place that invites relaxation. Most of the 15 guest rooms were built about a decade ago, each one utilizing Japanese craftsmanship with its own distinctive interior design. One room, for example, has shoji screens and wall trimmings in shunkei-nuri lacquer, while another room is decorated with the wood of local trees. Three rooms on the ground floor have peaceful views of the garden. Rooms here start at ¥16,500 ($132), rising to ¥22,000 ($176) in August. All rooms have private toilet, and all but four have private bath as well. As with all ryokan, however, there's a public bath for communal bathing, this one brand new.

Down the street from Kinkikan in the center of Takayama is **Seiryu** ⑭, 6 Hanakawa-cho (tel. 0577/32-0448). A modern ryokan, it has 24 rooms, three of which are combination rooms with both beds and a separate tatami section. Although dinner is served in your own room, breakfast is served in a dining hall with each person receiving his own little tray. Western breakfasts are available on request. Rates here start at ¥8,800 ($70), rising to ¥15,000 ($120) in peak season.

Another modern ryokan is **Asunaro** ⑮, 2-96-2 Hatsuda-cho (tel. 0577/33-5551), located about a five-minute walk northeast of Takayama Station. Its 30 rooms are fairly standard; 11 of them come with their own bath and all have their own toilet. Rates for tatami rooms range from ¥6,500 ($52) to ¥16,500 ($132), and Western breakfasts are available. In August and during festivals, rates begin at ¥13,000 ($104), with the big increase due in part, the management says, to more elaborate meals.

Minshuku

Minshuku Sosuke, 1-64 Okamoto (tel. 0577/32-0818), is a delightful 13-room minshuku about an eight-minute walk southwest of Takayama Station across the street from the Green Hotel. Its entryway resembles those of farmhouses on display at the Folk Village, filled with country knickknacks and exuding a warm and friendly atmosphere. There's an old open-hearth fireplace, called an *irori,* in the communal room to the left as you enter—if it's chilly you'll be invited to sit down and warm yourself. The couple running this minshuku are outgoing and friendly. Mealtimes are especially fun. Everyone is seated around one long table where each person introduces himself. Since most of the guests are Japanese from other parts of the country, this is a good opportunity to learn about other places in Japan. Although the building housing the minshuku is 150 years old, the inside has been remodeled and all 13 rooms are spotlessly clean. The charge throughout the year is ¥6,000 ($48) to ¥8,000 ($64) per person and includes two meals.

Yamakyu, 58 Tenshoji (tel. 0577/32-3756), has a deserved reputation for serving the best meals in town in its price range. Although it's located a bit far from the station—about a 20-minute walk or a 5-minute taxi ride—it's only a 10-minute walk to the old part of town. As with most minshuku, all 28 Japanese-style rooms are without private bathroom, but the public baths are large and pleasant. Display cases line the corridors, showing off a collection of glass bowls, vases, clocks, and lamps. Per-person rates here with two meals are ¥5,800 ($46), with an additional ¥500 ($4) charged in peak season.

Another good minshuku is **Hachibei** ⑯, 2561 Kami-Okamoto-cho (tel. 0577/33-0573), a few minutes' walk from the Hida no Sato Folk Village. A big old house with a new addition and a rather nice and overgrown garden, it also has a pleasant open hearth where guests can sit and socialize in the evening. Most of the guests staying here are young Japanese. The public baths are large and are lined with rock walls. Rates here are ¥5,500 ($44).

Matsuyama, 5-11 Hanazato-cho (tel. 0577/32-1608), is conveniently located about a minute's walk from Takayama Station. Its 23 rooms are rather bare and plain, coming with just the basics of coin-operated TV, heater, and fan. Rates are ¥5,500 ($44) per person, rising ¥500 ($4) during peak season. If you decide to take your meals elsewhere, you can stay here for ¥3,500 ($28) per person.

Youth Hostel

The **Youth Hostel Tenshoji Temple,** 83 Tenshoji-machi (tel. 0577/32-6345), is located in a temple about 20 minutes east of the station by foot. Unfortunately, there is no bus to the hostel. Rooms here are tatami and rates are ¥2,900 ($23) for members and ¥3,500 ($28) for nonmembers, including two meals.

Hotels

The largest hotel in town is the **Takayama Green Hotel,** about an eight-minute walk from Takayama Station at 2-180 Nishinoishiki-cho (tel. 0577/33-5500). This is the place to stay if you like all the conveniences in one building—restaurants, bar, beer garden, shopping, beauty and barber salons, bike rentals, tennis courts, public bath, tea lounge, and sushi bar. All Western-style rooms here are twin-bedded rooms and start at ¥6,500 ($52) for the cheapest twin with toilet and sink only. Standard twins with private bathrooms start at ¥16,500 ($132). If you feel like splurging, Japanese-style tatami rooms here are available for ¥24,000 ($192). Keep in mind that none of the rates above include tax or service charge.

About four blocks northeast of Takayama Station is the **Hida Hotel Plaza,** Hanaoka-cho 2 (tel. 0577/33-4600). It consists of an older annex and a newer, contemporary high-tech addition—it's in the new wing where you'll find the front desk. All rooms come with TV, radio, refrigerator, hot-water pot and tea bags, and private bathroom. The newer addition has Western-style rooms, with singles going for ¥7,500 ($60), twins for ¥14,000 ($112), and doubles for ¥12,000 ($96). During peak season, rates are ¥8,500 ($68), ¥18,500 ($148), and ¥16,500 ($132), respectively. If you prefer to sleep on tatami and don't mind eating breakfast and dinner here, per-person rates with two meals are ¥14,000 ($112), rising to ¥20,000 ($160) during peak season. Tatami rooms are clean and simple, the way Japanese-style rooms should be; note, however, that meals are served in a communal dining hall.

Facilities at the Hida Hotel include an attractive wood-beamed shopping arcade, rental bicycles, a black marble and stainless-steel public bath, an indoor swimming pool, sauna and steambaths (extra fees charged), five restaurants, and a bar. During the summer months there's a rooftop beer garden open nightly from 5 to 9 p.m., which offers panoramic views of Takayama and surrounding hills.

WHERE TO DINE

For the big splurge, you should dine at **Kakusho** ⑰, 2-98 Babacho (tel. 32-0174), a restaurant serving local vegetarian fare called *shojin-ryōri*. Situated on the slope of a hill on the eastern part of town, this 250-year-old building with heavy wooden beams and ochre-colored walls is surrounded by a mossy garden and clay wall. Only lunch is served here, and hours are 11:30 a.m. to 1:30 p.m.; closed Thursday (sometimes Wednesday). You must make a reservation to dine here, and there's only one meal available, for ¥9,000 ($72), tax and service charge extra. Meals are served in private tiny tatami rooms in a separate old building in the back with its own view of the mossy garden. This place is worth every bite of the various mountain vegetables, mushrooms, nuts, and tofu you'll be served.

A popular restaurant in the center of Takayama is **Suzuya** ⑱, 24 Hanakawa-cho (tel. 32-2484). Closed on Tuesday but open the rest of the week from 11 a.m. to 8 p.m., it's easy to recognize by its curtains hanging above the front door and the cedar ball hanging from its eaves. Inside, it's darkly lit, with shoji screens covering the windows, wooden beams above, and traditional decor in keeping with the country atmosphere of Takayama. This place is so popular that if you come for lunch be tween noon and 1 p.m., you'll probably have to wait for a table. There's an English menu, with local specialties of mountain vegetables, fresh river fish, and noodles ranging from ¥660 ($5.28) to ¥2,700 ($21.60). One specialty of Takayama you should try is *hoba-miso*. Usually served for breakfast, it consists of soy-bean paste mixed with dried scallion, ginger, and mushrooms, and cooked on a dry magnolia leaf above a small clay burner. If you're staying at a ryokan or minshuku you'll proba bly get this for breakfast. Other dishes available include shabu-shabu and *tobanyaki*, a stew of leek, okra, mushrooms, and various chicken parts including liver, gizzard, skin, and meat. Mountain vegetable teishoku begin at ¥1,450 ($11.60).

If Suzuya is closed or crowded, a restaurant close by is **Bandai Kado Mise** ⑲, Hanakawa-cho (tel. 33-5166). Located across the street and a few shops down, it doesn't have an English menu so the easiest thing to do is to order one of the obento box meals beginning at ¥1,500 ($12) or the mountain vegetable teishoku for ¥2,200 ($17.60). Tempura or pork teishoku are also available. Bandai is open from 11:30 a.m. to 8 p.m.; closed on Wednesday.

If you're looking for an inexpensive meal, there's a homey, pleasant noodle shop just a few minutes' walk from the station called **Kofune** ⑫⓪, Hanasato-cho 6-6 (tel. 32-2106). To reach it, exit from the station and keep walking straight toward the river; the noodle shop will be on your left. It has an English menu, with prices ranging from about ¥550 ($4.40) to ¥1,200 ($9.60) for such dishes as noodles served plain or in combination with river fish, tempura, or mountain vegetables. It's open every day from 10:30 a.m. to 5 p.m.

If you're staying in a ryokan or minshuku and are hungering for something different from what you had for breakfast and dinner, maybe homemade pizza at **Ichoo,** Sowacho, (tel. 33-8913), will hit the spot. This small coffeeshop is located on Kokubunji Dori Street, about halfway between the station and the river. Pizzas are large, with a generous amount of cheese, and range from ¥700 ($5.60) to ¥900 ($7.20). Hours here are 8 a.m. to 10 p.m.; closed Monday.

Technically a drinking place because of the dozen different varieties of sake it sells, the **Jizake-ya** ⑫①, Suehiro Nibangai (tel. 34-5001), also serves a wide variety of Japanese food, including tofu steak, tempura, noodles, steamed dumplings, and river fish. Most items cost ¥600 ($4.80) to ¥1,400 ($11.20). A large room with tatami and low tables, this place has a convivial drinking-hall atmosphere. Hours are 5 p.m. to 2 a.m.; closed the third Sunday of the month.

---

2. Shirakawa-go

With its thatch-roofed farmhouses, rice paddies trimmed with flowerbeds, roaring river, and pine-covered mountains rising on all sides, Shirakawa-go is one of the most picturesque regions in Japan. Sure, it has its share of tour buses, especially in May, August, and October. However, because of its rather remote location and because it's accessible only by car or by bus, Shirakawa-go still remains off the beaten path for most tourists in Japan. A visit to this rural region could well be the highlight of your trip.

Stretching almost five miles long beside the Shokawa River and squeezed to a width of only 1.8 miles between towering mountains, Shirakawa-go is a tiny region with a population of 2,000 living in several small communities. The most important village for visitors is Ogimachi, with its 800 residents. It has minshuku, a couple of museums, and an open-air museum of old thatched farmhouses depicting how life used to be in the region before roads opened it up to the rest of the world.

Because Shirakawa-go is hemmed in by mountains, land for growing rice and other crops was always scarce and valuable. As a result, farmhouses were built large enough to hold extended families, sometimes with as many as several dozen family members living under one roof. Because there was not enough land available for young couples to marry and build houses of their own, only the oldest son was allowed to marry. The other children were required to spend their lives living with their parents and helping with the farming. The loss of even one family member meant hardship for the whole family. But even though younger children were not allowed to marry, a man was allowed to choose a young woman, visit her in her parents' home, and father her children. The children then remained with the mother's family, where they would become valuable members of the labor force.

Before the roads came to Shirakawa-go, winter always meant complete isolation as snow six feet deep blanketed the entire region. Open-hearth fireplaces (irori) were commonplace in the middle of the communal room. They were used both for cooking and for warmth, and because there were no chimneys, smoke simply rose into the levels above. So the family lived on the ground floor, with the upper floors used for silk cultivation and storage of utensils. Because of the heavy snowfall, roofs were constructed at steep angles, known as gassho-zukuri in reference to the fact that the tops of the roofs look like hands joined in prayer.

Today there are about 150 thatched farmhouses, barns, and sheds in Shirakawa-go, most of them built about 200 to 300 years ago. The thatched roofs are about two feet thick and last about 50 years. The old roofs are replaced in Shirakawa-go every April, when one to four roofs are replaced on successive weekends. The whole process involves about 200 people, who can replace one roof in a couple days.

ORIENTATION

The most common way of reaching Ogimachi is by bus from Takayama, with a change of buses in Makido. The entire trip takes about three hours along winding mountain roads and costs ¥2,900 ($23.20) one way. If you have a JR rail pass, however, you can use it between Makido and Ogimachi, in which case you'll need to buy a ticket only for the stretch between Takayama and Makido. Buses run throughout the year, with about three to five departures from Takayama daily, depending on the season. You can also reach Takayama by bus from Nagoya and Kanazawa during peak season.

As for getting around Ogimachi, your own two feet can do it best. You can walk from one end of the village to the other in about ten minutes. There's a **tourist office** (tel. 05769/6-1751) located in a small square in the center of the town. You can reserve a room in a minshuku here if you have not already done so, as well as pick up a pamphlet in English. If you want to make the tourist office your very first stop upon arrival in Shirakawa-go, get off at the bus stop called Gassho-Shuraku. The tourist office is about a minute's walk away and is open daily from 8:30 a.m. to 5 p.m.

The address for all establishments listed below is Shirakawa Mura, Ogimachi, Ono-gun, Gifu. The **telephone area code** is 05769.

THE SIGHTS

To see how rural people lived in past centuries in the Japan Alps, visit the **Shirakawa-go Gassho no Sato Village,** an open-air museum with 25 gassho-zukuri houses and sheds filled with implements and tools. Many of the old houses were moved to their present site some 20 years ago when construction of a dam threatened to destroy them. In some of the buildings are demonstrations and displays of local crafts, with artisans engaged in woodworking, pottery, basket-weaving, and toy-making. The village is located about a five-minute walk from Ogimachi along a footpath which takes you over a suspension bridge and through a narrow tunnel. Hours are 8:30 a.m. to 5 p.m. most of the year; in the winter from December through March the opening hours are from 9 a.m. to 4 p.m., while in August they're from 8 a.m. to 6 p.m. The entrance fee is ¥500 ($4).

In addition to the open-air museum, there are several other old farmhouses in Ogimachi open to the public. The **Seikatsu Shiryokan** ⑫, open daily from 8 a.m. to 5 p.m. March through November, displays farm implements and folkcrafts, including cooking utensils, lacquerware, household items, and clothing. The upstairs is crammed with all kinds of farming tools and items used in everyday life, including mountain backpacks, hatchets, handmade skis, saddles, and implements for silk cultivation. Charging an admission of ¥200 ($1.60), Seikatsu Shiryokan is located on the southern edge of town, past the Juemon minshuku (described under "Food and Lodging" further on).

Myozenji �123, is a 170-year-old house with farm equipment, straw raincoats, palanquins, and other relics on display. You can walk around upstairs and inspect how the roof looks from the inside. If a fire is burning in the downstairs irori, you can also see how smoky the upstairs can get. Attached to the house is the main hall of Myozenji Temple, which is more than two centuries old. Hours here are generally 7 a.m. to 5 p.m., with shorter hours in winter, and admission is ¥200 ($1.60). Myozenji is located in the heart of Ogimachi.

Not far from Myozenji is a relatively new museum, **Doburoku Matsuri no Yakata** �124, erected in honor of the **Doburoku Matsuri Festival** held in Shirakawa-go every year from October 14 to 19. Centering on a locally produced potent sake made from rice, the festival is held just outside the museum's grounds at Hachimanjinja Shrine. The ¥310 ($2.48) entrance fee allows you to see some of the costumes worn during the festival and to try some of the festive sake. The highlight of the museum, however, is the hour-long video that shows the festival activities, including dances, parades, and plenty of drinking. Although the video is kind of corny in parts, it's probably the next best thing to being at the festival itself. The museum is open daily from 8:30 a.m. to 4:30 p.m. (from 9 a.m. to 4 p.m. in winter).

And finally, for an overview of the entire village, walk along the gently sloping road that leads from the north of Ogimachi to the **Ogimachi Viewing Point.** There's a restaurant up here, but in my opinion the best thing to do is bring your own snack and walk to the hill's westernmost point (that is, toward the river, where there are some secluded benches). From here you have a marvelous view of the whole valley.

FOOD AND LODGING

Because huge extended families living under one roof are a thing of the past, many residents of Ogimachi have turned their gassho-zukuri homes into minshuku. There are more than two dozen minshuku in Ogimachi, giving visitors the unique chance to stay in a thatched farmhouse with a family that might consist of grandparents, parents, and children. English is limited to the basics of "bath," "breakfast," and "dinner," but smiles go a long way. Most likely the family will drag out their family album with pictures of winter snowfall and the momentous occasion when their thatched roof was repaired. All minshuku charge approximately ¥5,500 ($44) per person, including two meals. Tax is extra. Most of them are fairly small affairs, with about five to nine rooms open to guests. Rooms are basic, without bath or toilet, and you're expected to roll out your own futon. Although there's little difference between the minshuku, some of them do not have thatched roofs. Below is a list of those that do.

Magoemon �125 (tel. 05769/6-1167) is located by the suspension bridge on the way to the open-air museum. One of its six rooms overlooks the Shokawa River. About 300 years old, it features a cozy living room with open-hearth irori, wooden communal bathtub, and Western-style flush toilets.

Kandaya �126 (tel. 05769/6-1072) is a 200-year-old house with an irori. The largest minshuku in Ogimachi, it has nine rooms, some of which are in a separate building. It's located in the middle of the village and has a nicely remodeled bathroom and toilet area with wooden floors and walls.

Close by is **Yosobe** �127 (tel. 05769/6-1172), small, with only five guest rooms. The communal dining area is also small and friendly, with an irori in the middle of the room. The rooms facing the front of the house open onto wooden verandas, polished smooth by years of wear. In case it matters, the toilets here are nonflush in the Japanese style.

Otaya �128 (tel. 05769/6-1172) is located on the northern edge of the village, giving it a little more privacy. A couple of the rooms face a small river that cuts deep into a ravine. A pond outside the front door contains the fish you'll have for dinner.

Juemon ⑫⑨ (tel. 05769/6-1053), located on the other end of the community on the south edge of Ogimachi, features an irori in the dining room and recently remodeled bathroom facilities. This minshuku is a favorite place for young foreigners traveling in Japan, and the outgoing woman who runs this place is quite a character.

Since all minshuku and ryokan serve breakfast and dinner, the only meal you have to worry about is lunch. **Irori** ⑬⓪ (tel. 6-1737) is on Ogimachi's main street and is easy to spot because of a huge block of gnarled wood beside its front door. The inside of this gassho-zukuri house is appropriately rustic and even has an irori where you can fry your own fish on a skewer. The menu, in Japanese only, includes fresh river fish, wild mountain vegetables called *sansai,* hoba miso (soybean paste cooked on a magnolia leaf over a small clay pot), unagi donburi (eel on rice), yakisoba (fried noodles), and *sansai-soba* (mountain vegetables and noodles). I opted for the tofu teishoku set meal, which consists of fried tofu covered with fish flakes, vegetables, rice, and soup. All items on the menu range from ¥450 ($3.60) to ¥1,600 ($12.80). Because this place is open daily from 10 a.m. to 11 p.m., you might also want to come here for a nightcap. Beer starts at ¥550 ($4.40) and sake at ¥440 ($3.52).

Another large thatched farmhouse that has been turned into a restaurant is **Kitanosho** ⑬① (tel. 6-1506). It also has an irori, this one in the middle of a large tatami room. From the dining hall you can look out over the Shokawa River. When you finish your meal, climb the steep stairs to have a look at the second floor, where the heavy wooden beams are held together only with rope. Open only from April through November from 10 a.m. to 5 p.m., it offers river fish, bear stew (called *kumanabe teishoku* and available only in spring and autumn), *sansai udon* (noodles and mountain vegetables), curry rice, hoba miso, and *oyakodon* (chicken and egg on rice). The menu is only in Japanese, so look around at what others are eating. Prices range from about ¥600 ($4.80) for noodles to ¥1,700 ($13.60) for teishoku. Kitanosho is located on the southern edge of town, across the street from Juemon minshuku.

Finally, if you're visiting the open-air museum and want a quick lunch or snack, there are a couple of thatch-roofed combination modern restaurant/souvenir shops next to the museum's entrance. With hours similar to those of the museum, they offer noodles, obento box lunches, and sansai or hoba miso teishoku, most in the ¥600 ($4.80) to ¥1,300 ($10.40) price range.

---

3. Matsumoto

Located in the middle of a wide basin about 660 feet above sea level and surrounded on all sides by mountain ranges, Matsumoto boasts a fine feudal castle with the oldest existing *donjon* (keep) in Japan, as well as an outstanding ukiyoe woodblock print museum. Although the city itself, with a population of 200,000, is modern with little remaining from its castle days, I find the town pleasant, the air fresh, and its people among the nicest I've encountered in Japan. Most travelers pass through Matsumoto on their way to more remote regions of the Japan Alps. Encircled with towering peaks, sparkling mountain lakes, and colorful wild flowers, Matsumoto serves as the gateway to hiking trails in the Japan Alps and in nearby Chubu Sangoku National Park.

ORIENTATION

There's a direct JR line to Matsumoto from Tokyo's Shinjuku Station. The Limited Express Azusa reaches Matsumoto in about three hours, while the Express

Alps takes a bit longer at about five hours. There's also a direct train from Nagoya, which takes about two hours and 15 minutes.

Before departing Tokyo, be sure to pick up a sheet at the Tourist Information Center called *Matsumoto and Kamikochi*. It gives the latest train schedules as well as information on sights in and around Matsumoto. It also gives recommended hiking trips lasting two to four hours from Kamikochi, a small village which you can reach in a little over two hours via train and bus from Matsumoto.

Once in Matsumoto, stop by the **tourist information window** on the east side of Matsumoto Station (tel. 0263/32-2814). Open daily from 9:30 a.m. to 6 p.m. (9 a.m. to 5:30 p.m. in winter), it has a good pamphlet with a map of the city with destinations written in English, and its English-speaking staff will also help with accommodations. As for getting around Matsumoto itself, you can walk to Matsumoto Castle, just a mile northeast of the station, but you'll have to go by bus or taxi to the other sights.

The **telephone area code** for Matsumoto, located in Nagano Prefecture, is 0263.

THE SIGHTS

Originally built in 1504, when Japan was in the throes of bloody civil wars, **Matsumoto Castle** is a fine specimen of a feudal castle with the oldest existing donjon in the country. Surrounded by a willow-lined moat with ducks and white swans, the outside walls of the donjon are black, earning it the nickname of Karasu-jo, or Crow Castle. It's a rather small castle, dark and empty inside. Take your shoes off at the entrance and walk in stocking feet over worn wooden floors and up steep and narrow steps until you finally reach the sixth floor, from which you have a nice view of the city. The castle grounds are open from 8:30 a.m. to 4:30 p.m. Its entrance fee of ¥500 ($4) includes admission to the **Japan Folklore Museum**, located next to the castle. A rather eclectic museum, it has displays relating to archeology, history, and the surrounding region, including armor, an ornate palanquin, clothing, farming equipment, butterflies from around the world, insects, animals of the Japan Alps, and a wonderful collection of old clocks from Japan and other nations.

The **Japan Ukiyoe Museum**, 2206-1 Koshiba, Shimadachi (tel. 47-4440), is one of the best museums of woodblock prints in Japan. Privately owned, the museum is in a futuristic and airy building of glass and cement, built in 1982. Inside is the ukiyoe collection of Tokichi Sakai, a collection that dates back five generations to his great-great-grandfather, who was a friend and patron of Hokusai and Hiroshige, two of Japan's greatest woodblock-print artists. The collection contains more than 100,000 prints, including representative masterpieces of all known ukiyoe artists, and is believed to be the largest of its kind in the world. The exhibition changes every two months, so there's always something new to see. On one of my visits, for example, the masterpieces of Hokusai were being shown, including his series on famous Japanese bridges and waterfalls. A ten-minute slide show with explanations in English introduces the current exhibition, and a pamphlet in English describes the history of the collection and how woodblock prints are made. Closed on Monday, the museum is open from 10 a.m. to 5 p.m. and charges ¥600 ($4.80) admission. Unfortunately, there's no convenient way to get to the museum by public transportation, but the ¥1,000 ($8) taxi ride is worth it.

One more museum worth visiting if you have time is the **Matsumoto Folkcraft Museum**, (Mingei-kan) ⑬, located about 15 minutes by bus or taxi from Matsumoto Station (if going by bus, get out at the Shimoganai Mingeikan Guchi bus stop). Open every day except Monday from 9 a.m. to 5 p.m., it contains products of wood, glass, bamboo, and porcelain from Japan and foreign countries. Particularly beautiful are its wooden chests, and part of the collection is housed in a 100-year-old storehouse. Admission is ¥200 ($1.60).

If perchance you studied violin when you were young, maybe you were one of the countless children around the world who learned by the well-known Suzuki

Method. In Matsumoto is the famous **Suzuki Shin-ichi Talent Education Institute,** where young and old alike from around the world come to learn violin, piano, cello, and flute. Dr. Suzuki, founder of the method, is now in his 90s but is still actively involved in the daily lessons of his pupils. Group and private lessons for both pupils and teachers of the Suzuki Method are held throughout the week, and guests are welcome to watch. There are also periodic concerts given by graduating musicians of the institute. For more information, call the institute any time between 9 a.m. and 5 p.m. Monday through Saturday at 32-7171. Dr. Suzuki's group lesson is generally held from 9 to 10:30 a.m., but it would be wise to check the time beforehand.

If you find yourself with extra time on your hands, you might want to take a trip to **Alps Park,** located on one of Matsumoto's surrounding wooded hills, where you'll find the Alps Dream Coaster. I don't know who thinks up these names, but this one is a toboggan run and doesn't allow much time for dreaming. The race down the hill and around curves takes only a few minutes, during which time you swear you're going to fly off course. Being the conscientious researcher that I am, I raced down without applying the brakes to check its safety for you—it was terrifying and fun! Closed in the winter, it's open the rest of the year from 9 a.m. to 5 p.m., and one trip down costs ¥300 ($2.40). To reach Alps Park, take the bus from Matsumoto Station bound for Alps Koen; the trip takes about 25 minutes. Since there are only five buses daily, ask for the timetable at the tourist office. A restaurant and hiking trails are located in the park.

WHERE TO STAY

Because Matsumoto is popular primarily with hikers who are used to roughing it along nature trails, there are no luxury hotels in the city. Rather, facilities are geared mainly toward convenience.

The Medium-Priced Range

Matsumoto Tokyu Inn, 1-3-21 Fukashi (tel. 0263/36-0109), is a practical, clean, and pleasant business hotel conveniently located close to Matsumoto Station. The front desk is on the second floor. Four kinds of rooms are offered: a nicely decorated single with semidouble-size bed for ¥8,000 ($64); a double-bedded room for ¥13,800 ($110); a twin for ¥13,800 ($110); and a deluxe twin with sofa and chairs and a separate vanity area with its own sink for ¥25,000 ($200). Prices include service; tax is extra. Similar to other business hotels in the nationwide Tokyu Inn chain, it has 158 rooms that are decorated in beige and brown and come with desk or table, clock, fridge, tea server, and TV with pay video, including movies from the United States. Facilities include the Shangri-La restaurant, serving Western and Japanese meals, a bar/lounge, and vending machines on the fifth and eighth floors. As a service to the forgetful, rugs in the elevator tell what day of the week it is and are changed daily.

Hotel New Station, 1-1-11 Chuo (tel. 0263/35-3850), is about a two-minute walk from Matsumoto Station. Opened in mid-1985, this 103-room hotel offers a very pleasant and good-size single for ¥6,500 ($52), with print comforter, large desk, and hot-water heater for tea. Twins and doubles start at ¥10,000 ($80). A Japanese-style room with a six-tatami sleeping area is available for two or three persons for ¥13,200 ($106). Prices include tax and service. All rooms have coin-operated TV. The front-desk personnel are very helpful and accommodating, but not much English is spoken here.

The Budget Range

Matsumoto Tourist Hotel, 2-4-24 Fukashi (tel. 0263/33-9000), is a business hotel about a six-minute walk from the station. Its facilities include a restaurant serving both Western and Japanese food, a public bath, and a vending area. Its staff are very friendly, but again no one speaks much English. All rooms are simple but tastefully decorated, and include TV and hot-water heater for tea. Singles without a bathroom are ¥4,800 ($38), ¥5,800 ($46) with bath. Twins, all with private bathroom, start at ¥10,500 ($84). Also available are Japanese-style tatami rooms, all without private bath but with sink, which go for ¥5,000 ($40) for one person, ¥8,800 ($70) for two, and ¥11,500 ($92) for three. As with most budget accommodations, prices include service but not tax.

A bit on the old side, but very reasonably priced and run by friendly people, **Hotel Ikyu** ⑬, 1-11-13 Honjo (tel. 0263/35-8528), is a concrete building about a ten-minute walk from the train station and is popular with young Japanese. Rates per person are ¥4,000 ($32) without meals and ¥6,000 ($48) including breakfast and dinner. Some of the rooms have a private toilet. Both Japanese-style tatami rooms and Western-style rooms are available, and all rooms come with coin-operated TV, air conditioner and heater, fridge, and hot-water pot for tea. There are lots of windows in this place and added touches like plants in the stairwell. Meals are served in a small dining hall adjoining the hotel. Tax is extra.

Nishiya Ryokan ⑭, 2-4-12 Ote (tel. 0263/33-4332), is about a six-minute walk from Matsumoto Station in the direction of Matsumoto Castle. No meals are served here and rooms are just basic tatami without private bathrooms. At only ¥3,300 ($26.40) per person a night, no one is complaining.

The closest youth hostel is the **Asama Onsen Youth Hostel,** 302-1 Asama-Onsen (tel. 0263/46-1335), roughly 20 minutes from Matsumoto Station by bus. There's room for about 150 people here, and the cost of an overnight stay is ¥2,200 ($17.60) for members and ¥2,700 ($21.60) for nonmembers. No dinner is served, but Japanese breakfasts are available for ¥450 ($3.60).

WHERE TO DINE

If you feel like treating yourself to a wonderful French meal in rustic yet elegant surroundings, **Taiman,** 4-2-4 Ote (tel. 32-0882), is an excellent choice. Located not far from Matsumoto Castle, it looks as though it were once the hunting château of some European lord but somehow ended up in the Japan Alps. The inside of this ivy-covered building has heavy wooden beams, high ceilings, fresh flowers on the tables, and elaborate cutlery. Full dinners with changing menus are available for ¥10,000 ($80) to ¥16,500 ($132). There are also less expensive meals of either sole or stewed beef for ¥5,000 ($40). If you want to go à la carte for such dishes as roast lamb, steak, chicken, or sole, expect to spend at least ¥8,500 ($68).

One way to eat inexpensively is to come for the special lunch for ¥5,000 ($40). As an example, my luncheon included bread or rice, and started with an hors d'oeuvre plate of marinated squid, lox, cream cheese, capers, and grated onion. The next course was crab gratin, cooked in a cheese and tomato base, resembling lasagne. The main dish was sautéed pork wrapped in bacon and topped with cheese. Also included in the price were salad, dessert, and coffee. The restaurant is open from 11 a.m. to 9 p.m.; closed the first and third Wednesdays of the month.

If you'd rather have Japanese fare, **Kajika** ⑮, 1-2-21 Fukashi (tel. 35-7632), is on the fourth floor of the Cosmo Building behind the bus terminal, about a three-minute walk from Matsumoto Station. Open every day except Sunday from 11:30 a.m. to 2 p.m. and 4:30 to 10 p.m. (last order is 9 p.m.), it's a modern restaurant decorated in stained dark wood and cool white walls. The lunch menu is quite reasonable, with various kinds of teishoku available, ranging from ¥1,600 ($12.80) for an obento lunch box to ¥1,000 ($8) and ¥1,600 ($12.80) for steaks. Other teishoku offer sashimi, tempura, or soba. At dinnertime kaiseki meals are served, costing from ¥5,500 ($44) to ¥11,000 ($88). Reservations are required for dinner.

For inexpensive Japanese fare close to Matsumoto Station, try **Shikimi** ⑯, 1-5-5 Chuo (tel. 35-3279), just a three-minute walk away. Although relatively new, it manages to evoke an atmosphere of old Japan with its traditional tiled roof and cast-iron lanterns hanging from its outside eaves. The inside is a successful blend of the old and new, tastefully decorated with wooden sliding doors, small tatami rooms, a wooden counter, and paper lanterns. Open every day except Thursday from noon to 10 p.m., it specializes in eel and sushi. Its unagi donburi (eel on rice) costs ¥1,500 ($12) and comes with soup and pickled vegetables, while a platter of assorted sushi, called moriawase, is available for ¥2,000 ($16).

If you're a vegetarian or fan of natural foods, head for **Naja,** 4-3-20 Ote (tel. 36-9096). A tiny place with only three tables, it looks and sounds as if it had been transported from a commune in the woods of California—dried flowers hanging from the walls, music of the '60s. Its English menu lists a daily brown-rice set meal for ¥600 ($4.80), as well as such offerings as soy-bean curry with yogurt, noodles, tofu dishes, and brown-rice porridge. Prices range from about ¥400 ($3.20) to ¥800 ($6.40). Closed on Sunday, it's open the rest of the week from noon to 3 p.m. and from 5 to 9 p.m. It's located about a ten-minute walk from Matsumoto Station, in the direction of the castle. Since it's on a tiny alley, ask the tourist office to pinpoint its exact location on your map.

4. Magome and Tsumago

If you're traveling between Nagoya and Matsumoto, you'll most likely pass through the Kiso Valley in Nagano Prefecture, the most mountainous prefecture in central Japan. Surrounded by the towering peaks of the Japan Alps, the deep valley formed by the Kiso River has always served as a natural passageway through the hills. In fact, it was one of the two official roads that linked Kyoto with Edo, present-day Tokyo, back in the days of the Tokugawa shogunate (the other route was the Tokaido). Known as the Nakasendo Highway, it was the route of traveling daimyo (feudal lords) and their entourages of samurai retainers as they journeyed between Japan's two most important towns. To serve their needs, 11 post towns sprang up along the Nakasendo Highway. Back then, it took three days to travel through the valley.

Of the old post towns, Magome and Tsumago are two that still survive, with many of the old buildings left intact. What's more, there's a five-mile pathway skirting the Kiso River that links the two villages, providing hikers with the experience of what it must have been like to travel the Nakasendo Highway back in the Edo Period. Visits to the villages and the hike can easily be accomplished in a one-day excursion from Nagoya or Matsumoto.

ORIENTATION

Since neither Magome nor Tsumago is directly on a train line, you'll have to make the final journey by bus. To reach Magome, take the Chuo Honsen Line (which connects Nagoya and Matsumoto) to Nakatsugawa Station, from which it's a 35-minute bus ride to Magome. Nakatsugawa Station is one hour from Nagoya and about an hour and 15 minutes from Matsumoto.

Tsumago is only a seven-minute bus ride from Nagiso Station, which is also on the Chuo Honsen Line. Note, however, that not all trains stop in Nagiso or Nakatsugawa. Make certain, therefore, that your train stops where you want to go. Note also that buses are not very frequent, so you might want to inquire about bus schedules beforehand (because it's in the same prefecture, the Matsumoto Station tourist office has information on bus schedules). If you don't feel like walking the distance between Magome and Tsumago, there's also a bus that travels between the two villages.

If you have luggage, you might be interested in knowing that a luggage-transfer service between Magome and Tsumago is available daily from July 20 through August and on Saturday, Sunday, and national holidays from March 19 to July 19 and September through November. Luggage is accepted at either town's tourist office no later than 9 a.m. for morning delivery and no later than 1 p.m. for afternoon delivery. It would be prudent, however, to verify this beforehand. Call the **Magome tourist office** at 0264/59-2336 or the **Tsumago tourist office** at 0264/57-3123, but note that only Japanese is spoken on the telephone.

For more information on Magome and Tsumago, drop by the Tourist Information Center in Tokyo or Kyoto for a pamphlet called *Kiso Valley*. It provides a rough sketch of the five-mile hiking path between the two villages.

THE SIGHTS

Magome, the southernmost post town, has old inns and souvenir shops that line both sides of a gently sloping road. It takes about 20 minutes to stroll through the town. Halfway up the slope you'll see a museum dedicated to Shimazaki Toson (1872–1943), a noted novelist and poet born in Magome.

Tsumago, the second post town from the south, is in my opinion the more beautiful and authentic. Threatened with gradual decline and desertion after the Chuo Line was constructed in 1911, thus bypassing Tsumago, the town's decades of neglect are probably what ultimately saved it. Having suffered almost no modernization in the zeal of the 20th century, Tsumago was a perfect target for renovation and restoration in the early 1970s. In a rare show of insight (I say rare because this has hardly ever happened in Japan), electrical wires, TV antennae, and telephone poles were hidden from sight along the main road. Tsumago looks much as it did back in the days of Edo.

On the main street of Tsumago, be sure to stop off at the **Waki-honjin Okuya,** an officially appointed inn, once serving as an inn for daimyo and court nobles. It was also home of a sake brewery. The present house dates from 1877, rebuilt with *hinoki* cypress trees—for centuries all the way through the Edo Period (1603–1867), the people of the Kiso Valley were prohibited from cutting down trees, even if they were on private property. This house was rebuilt, therefore, during the Meiji Period in the style of a grand old castle. The Emperor Meiji himself stopped at the house in 1880. The house serves as a local museum, with displays of rice bowls, hair combs, books with ukiyoe prints, and other items relating to the Edo era. Be sure to check out the daimyo's bathtub and toilet.

The Hike

Allow about three hours for the hike between Magome and Tsumago, though you can probably do it in two. It's a beautiful walk, tracing the contours of the Kiso Valley and crisscrossing the stream with a series of bridges. The trail is mainly a footpath, though at times it follows a paved road. In any case, the signs are in Japanese, so familiarize yourself with the kanji for Tsumago ⑬⑦ and Magome ⑬⑧. As the trail does go up some steep inclines, be sure to wear your walking shoes. And have fun—this is a great walk.

THE REST OF HONSHU

In addition to Tokyo, Kyoto, and the Japan Alps, Honshu has numerous other towns and attractions well worth a visit. From the bustling modern cities of Osaka and Nagoya to the sacred shrines of Ise-Shima National Park and Miyajima, Honshu has more than enough to satisfy the whims of every traveler.

1. Nagoya

As Japan's fourth-largest city, Nagoya is a place most foreigners never stop to see. True, it doesn't have the attractions of many of the nation's cities, but it does have a castle originally built by the first Tokugawa shogun, as well as one of Japan's most important Shinto shrines. You can visit the world-famous Noritake chinaware factory, and in the area surrounding Nagoya you can observe cormorant fishing during the summer months and visit an open-air architectural museum with structures dating from the Meiji era. Nagoya also serves as the gateway to Toba and Ise-Shima National Park. Incidentally, Nagoya is the birthplace of pachinko, the upright Japanese pinball machine now found in the farthest corners of the islands.

ORIENTATION

Located two hours west of Tokyo by Shinkansen bullet train, Nagoya has a population of 2.1 million people and supports a wide range of industries, including automobile manufacture, chinaware, shipbuilding, and aircraft construction. Almost completely destroyed during World War II, it was rebuilt with wide and straight streets, many of which actually have names. The city's downtown area is called Sakae and has many shops, restaurants, and department stores.

The area around Nagoya Station is an important center because of its bus terminals, many hotels, and its huge underground shopping arcade. Clustered around the JR Nagoya Station are the Shinkansen station, the Meitetsu Bus Terminal, the Meitetsu Shin-Nagoya Station, the city bus terminal, and Kintetsu Station.

The easiest way to get around is via the city's subway system, which is simple to use because stations have names written in both English and Japanese. Probably the most important line for tourists is the Meijo Line, which runs through Sakae. It takes you to both Atsuta Jingu Shrine (subway stop: Jingu-Nishi) and to Nagoya Castle (subway stop: Shiyakusho); and if you take this line all the way to the end you'll end up in Ozone—no kidding!

Nagoya has one of the best facilities for foreign tourists of any city I've seen in Japan. Called the **Nagoya International Center,** it's on the third floor of the Nagoya International Center Building, 1-47-1 Nagono (tel. 052/581-5678), about a ten-minute walk from the train station. Open daily from 9 a.m. to 8:30 p.m., this modern and up-to-date facility features an English-speaking staff, cable TV newscasts from the States (a great way to catch up on the news from back home), and a free publication called *Nagoya Calendar,* published monthly with information on what's going on in Nagoya in the way of music, cinema, the stage, sports, art, and more. The center can also tell you anything you need to know regarding sightseeing, shopping, and accommodations. In addition to helping visitors, the center also helps foreign residents by advising them on how to get a visa, where to find an apartment, and which doctors speak English. In short, this facility really makes foreigners feel welcome in Nagoya. Be sure to pick up a map of the city, as well as a map of the underground shopping arcade radiating out from Nagoya Station.

There's also a **tourist information office** at the east exit of Nagoya Station (tel. 541-4301), open from 9 a.m. to 5 p.m. Although it doesn't have as many pamphlets as the center does, its staff speaks English and distributes maps and information about Nagoya.

The Tourist Information Center in Tokyo or Kyoto distributes a leaflet called *Nagoya and Vicinity,* which has a map of the city and a list of attractions in Nagoya and the surrounding area.

The **telephone area code** for Nagoya, capital of Aichi Prefecture, is 052.

THE SIGHTS

Built for his ninth son by Ieyasu Tokugawa, the first Tokugawa shogun of Japan, **Nagoya Castle** was completed in 1612 and served as both a stronghold and a residence for members of the Tokugawa family for almost 250 years, until the Meiji Restoration ended Tokugawa rule in 1868. As proof of Ieyasu's shrewd wisdom, he forced feudal lords around Japan to contribute to the castle's construction, thereby depleting their resources and making it harder for them to stage rebellions.

Although Nagoya Castle was destroyed in World War II, it was rebuilt in 1959 and is almost a carbon copy of the original. On top of the donjon roof are two golden dolphins, thought to protect the castle from dreaded fires. The dolphins each weigh about 2,650 pounds and are made of cast bronze covered with 18-karat gold scales. The castle is open daily from 9:30 a.m. to 4:30 p.m. and entrance is ¥400 ($3.20).

The 154-foot donjon houses treasures that escaped the bombing during World War II, including beautiful paintings on sliding doors and screens. Like most reconstructed castles in Japan, this one is made of ferroconcrete, and even has an elevator which will zip you up to the fifth floor, from which you have fine views of Nagoya and beyond.

East of the castle is **Ninomaru Garden,** noted as one of the few remaining castle gardens in Japan. Besides providing a beautiful setting, it served as an emergency shelter for the lord in case of enemy attack. Be sure to stop by the Ninomaru Tea House—it's said that if you drink tea here, five years will be added to your life.

If you're interested in seeing personal items that once belonged to the Tokugawa family, the **Tokugawa Art Museum,** 1017 Tokugawa-cho, Higashi-ku (tel. 935-6262), houses thousands of documents, armor, swords, helmets, pottery, lacquerware, and paintings of the shogun and his family. The museum's most famous exhibits are picture scrolls of *The Tale of Genji* (*Genji Emaki*)—but they're displayed only one week a year in November (the next showing will be November 17–25, 1990). However, there are plenty of other treasures to warrant a visit. Closed on Monday and during exhibition changes, the museum is open from 10 a.m. to 5 p.m.; entrance is ¥1,000 ($8).

Because it contains one of the Three Sacred Treasures belonging to the emperor, **Atsuta Jingu Shrine** is revered as one of the three most important shrines in Japan. It enshrines the Kusanagi-no-Tsurugi (Grass-Mowing Sword), and even though the sword isn't on public display, Japanese make pilgrimages here to pay their respects. (By the way, the other two sacred treasures are the Sacred Mirror, which is in the Ise Jingu Shrines, and the Jewels, which are kept in the Imperial Palace in Tokyo.)

Atsuta Shrine was founded in the 3rd century and was rebuilt in 1935. According to legend, the Grass-Mowing Sword was presented to an ancient prince by the name of Yamato-Takeru who used it during a campaign against rebels in eastern Japan. The rebels set a field of grass on fire and the prince used the sword to mow down the grass, thereby quelling the fire. *Atsuta* means "hot field" in Japanese.

If you like high places, you may be interested in knowing that the **Nagoya TV Tower** was the first such tower in Japan. Since its opening in 1954, more than 25 million visitors have ridden its glass-enclosed elevators to its observation platform, approximately 300 feet above the ground, for a bird's-eye view of the sprawling city. Used jointly by Nagoya's five television stations, the tower is located about a two-minute walk from Sakae subway station in the heart of Nagoya. Open daily from 10 a.m. to 5:50 p.m. (to 7 p.m. on Sunday and holidays), it charges ¥600 ($4.80) for a visit to the observation platform.

Factory Visits

For centuries Nagoya has been a pottery and porcelain production center, and today the city and its vicinity manufacture 50% of Japan's total export chinaware. The largest chinaware company in Japan is Noritake, known the world over for its fine tableware. Founded in 1904, Noritake now exports to 110 nations around the world. The **Nagoya Noritake Factory,** located about a ten-minute walk north of Nagoya Station, offers two free tours daily Monday through Friday. Conducted in English, the tours are at 10 a.m. and 1 p.m. and last about one hour, but you must make reservations by calling beforehand (tel. 562-5072). The tour begins with an excellent film that depicts the history of Noritake and describes the manufacturing and decorating process of porcelain. After the film ends, you're led on a trip through the various production stages of the Diamond Collection, Noritake's best porcelain line. Unlike most modern-day factories where work is largely automated, almost all the work here is still done by hand. You'll be amazed to see how much attention is given to each piece as it moves through the production process. If you're interested in buying some porcelain, there are two shops located next to the plant that sell Noritake ware at reduced prices. Ask your guide to point you in the right direction. Otherwise, if you're a real Noritake fan you might want to make a trip to the company's largest store in Japan, located at 2-1 Shinsakae-Machi, Naka-ku (tel. 951-

0561). The closest subway station is Sakae and the store is open 10 a.m. to 5:30 p.m.; closed on national holidays only.

In addition to its chinaware, Nagoya and its vicinity also rank first in the nation in the production of cloisonné. If you're interested in seeing demonstrations of how cloisonné is made, the Nagoya International Center has a 14-minute videotape showing its production. You can also visit the **Shippo-Cho Industrial Hall** (Shippo Sangyou Kaikan), Tojima Shippo-cho (tel. 441-3411). Open every day (except Tuesday and national holidays) from 9 a.m. to 5 p.m., it's free of charge to the public and contains exhibits of cloisonné ware. If you want to see demonstrations of how cloisonné is made, the Industrial Hall can arrange an appointment with one of the area's many cloisonné factories. To reach the Industrial Hall, take the Meitetsu bus from the Meitetsu terminal next to Nagoya Station to the Yasumatsu bus stop. From there it's a 15-minute walk.

Sights in the Vicinity

Meiji Mura: If architecture's your bag, you'll find a lot to delight in at the open-air museum called Meiji Mura. It features more than 50 buildings and structures from around Japan that were constructed during the Meiji Period (1868–1912). Before Japan opened its doors in the mid-1800s, unpainted wooden structures dominated Japanese architecture. After Western influences began infiltrating Japan, however, the nation witnessed a surge in new architectural techniques and materials. Stones, brick, painted wood, towers, turrets, and Victorian features came into play. Contained on the grounds of this 250-acre museum are Western homes that once belonged to foreigners living in Nagasaki and Kobe; official government buildings and schools; two Christian churches; a post office; a Kabuki theater; a brewery; even a prison. One of the most outstanding structures on display is the front façade and lobby of the original Imperial Hotel in Tokyo, designed by American architect Frank Lloyd Wright.

To get to Meiji Mura, you can take a direct bus from the Meitetsu Bus Station's third floor in the Melsa Building. Buses leave every 30 minutes (even more frequently on weekends) and the trip to Meiji Mura takes just over one hour. The ¥3,000 ($24) fee includes a round-trip bus ticket and entrance to Meija Mura. Meiji Mura is open from 10 a.m. to 5 p.m., closing one hour earlier from November through February.

Cormorant Fishing: There are two places in the vicinity of Nagoya where you can watch cormorant fishing every night (except during a full moon) throughout the summer months. Cormorant fishing is an ancient fishing method in Japan in which trained cormorants (seabirds) dive into the water in search of ayu, a small Japanese trout. To ensure that the cormorants don't swallow the fish, the birds are fitted with rings around their necks.

The city of **Gifu** features cormorant fishing on the Nagaragawa River from May 11 to October 15, and you can view the whole spectacle aboard a small wooden boat. To reach Gifu, take the Meitetsu Main Line train from Meitetsu Shin-Nagoya Station to Shin-Gifu Station. From there, switch to a local train or bus heading for Nagara Kitamachi and get off at Nagarabashi Station. You'll be able to see the ticket office (call Nagarabashi Kanransen Jimusyo) after exiting the station. Ticket sales begin at 6 p.m., but you can call in advance to reserve your ticket (tel. 0582/62-0104). The price of a ticket is ¥2,600 ($20.80) during May, September, and October, and ¥2,800 ($22.40) in June, July, and August.

The other site for cormorant fishing is in the town of **Inuyama,** where the event takes place from June 1 to September 30. To reach Inuyama, take the Inuyama Line of the Meitetsu railways from Meitetsu Shin-Nagoya Station to Inuyama Yuen Station. From there it's a five-minute walk. Tickets are sold throughout the day beginning at 9 a.m. and the action starts after 5:30 p.m. Call ahead to make reservations at 0568/61-0057. Tickets here cost ¥2,400 ($19.20) during June and September, and ¥2,600 ($20.80) in July and August.

Inuyama City: There are several attractions in Inuyama that might interest you —which means you could come here for the day and top it off with the cormorant fishing described above. Just a ten-minute walk from Inuyama Yuen Station, for example, is **Inuyama Castle,** which was constructed in 1537 and remains Japan's oldest castle. Admission is ¥300 ($2.40) and it's open every day from 9 a.m. to 5 p.m. Another popular activity is to **shoot the rapids** of the Kiso River. Boats depart approximately every 30 or 60 minutes for the one-hour trip, priced at ¥2,900 ($23.20). For more information, call the Nihon-Rhine Kanko Company at 0574/26-2231).

WHERE TO STAY

The greatest concentration of hotels is found close to Nagoya Station, with the rest of them spread east of the station close to Sakae and Nagoya Castle. In case you'd rather stay in a ryokan, I've listed a couple of inexpensive Japanese inns. As with most cities in Japan, Nagoya does not have many ryokan—the cost of personal service and the price of land are simply too prohibitive.

The Upper Bracket

One of Nagoya's newest hotels, the **Nagoya Hilton International,** 1-3-3 Sakae (tel. 052-212-1111), is a gleaming, white-tiled building that soars above the heart of the city. Twenty-eight stories high, it's Nagoya's tallest building with more than 400 rooms, seven restaurants and bars, and an indoor swimming pool and health club (extra fees charged for the pool and gym). Not surprisingly, room rates are based on height. The cheapest twins and doubles, for example (there are no singles), start at ¥14,300 ($114) for one person and ¥20,000 ($160) for two—which are rooms up to the 16th floor. If you want a view, therefore, ask for the highest floor available in this price category, preferably the 15th or 16th floor. All rooms are luxuriously appointed, with traditional shoji screens, bilingual TV with CNN broadcasts from the United States, minibar, hairdryer, and a phone in the bathroom.

Located between Nagoya Station and Sakae, the **Nagoya Kanko Hotel,** 1-19-30 Nishiki, Naka-ku (tel. 052/231-7711), is a first-class hotel offering many conveniences in one place. Facilities include a shopping arcade, five restaurants serving French, Japanese, and Chinese cuisine, and two lounges. The Aurora restaurant on the 18th floor offers a panoramic view of the city. First opened in 1934 and completely renovated in 1985, this 505-room hotel has a huge lobby featuring white brick, natural woods, brass, and contemporary glass chandeliers. All rooms are nicely appointed and come with TV with CNN broadcasts (bilingual TVs are available upon request) and refrigerator. Singles here range from ¥10,500 ($84) to ¥14,300 ($114), twins run ¥20,000 ($160) to ¥28,000 ($224), and doubles cost ¥21,000 ($168) to ¥28,000 ($224).

Just west of Nagoya Castle is the **Hotel Nagoya Castle,** 3-19 Hinokuchi-cho, Nishi-ku (tel. 052/521-2121). This 253-room hotel boasts an indoor swimming pool (fee charged), shops, restaurants serving Western, Japanese, and Chinese food, and bars. Guest rooms come equipped with the usual TV with CNN broadcasts (bilingual TVs available) and refrigerator, and those facing east have a wonderful view of Nagoya Castle. Singles, none of which face the castle, start at ¥10,500 ($84). Twins and doubles, most of which have castle views, range from ¥19,800 ($158) to ¥32,000 ($256) and ¥19,800 ($158) to ¥27,000 ($216), respectively.

The Medium-Priced Range

About a five-minute walk from Nagoya Station, the **Nagoya Miyako Hotel,** 4-9-10 Meieki, Nakamura-ku (tel. 052/571-3211), is one of the best hotels in this price category. As in all Miyako hotels, service is excellent, and all guest rooms have recently been refurbished. Built more than two decades ago, the hotel has an attractive white marble lobby, a rooftop beer garden open in summer, Chinese, Japanese, and Western restaurants, and an underground shopping arcade with passageways to

Meitetsu Bus Station, Kintetsu Station, and Nagoya Station. Rooms are comfortable, with wooden furniture, fridge, hot-water thermos, TV with video and CNN, clock, and radio. Rates are based on room size: ¥8,500 ($68) to ¥11,000 ($88) for singles, ¥15,500 ($124) to ¥20,000 ($160) for twins, and ¥17,500 ($140) to ¥20,000 ($160) for doubles. Most of the singles face an inner courtyard—no view, but the rooms are quiet. Japanese-style rooms, some of which have bathtubs made of cypress, range from ¥20,000 ($160) to ¥27,000 ($216).

The **Meitetsu Grand Hotel,** 1-2-4 Meieki, Nakamura-ku (tel. 052/582-2211), is conveniently located right above Meitetsu Station. The check-in desk is on the 11th floor. Built in 1967, this 242-room hotel offers easy access to shops on the third and fourth floors, three restaurants, one lounge, and a beer garden open in the summer. Singles here are ¥9,300 ($74), comfortably decorated with semidouble bed, desk, chair, and table. All rooms have TV and refrigerator. Twins range from ¥11,000 ($88) to ¥22,000 ($176); the most expensive is a large room featuring an entry foyer, separate vanity area, semidouble beds, and a sitting area with couch, chairs, and table separated from the sleeping area by a glass partition. Doubles here start at ¥13,000 ($104) and Japanese-style rooms are ¥22,000 ($176).

Hotel Castle Plaza, 4-3-25 Meieki, Nakamura-ku (tel. 052/582-2121), a six-minute walk from Nagoya Station, is a sister hotel to the first-class Hotel Nagoya Castle. About seven years old, this 262-room hostelry has twelve restaurants, a shopping plaza, gym, heated swimming pool, sauna, and jogging track. The pool, sauna, gym, and jogging facility can be used for ¥2,700 ($21.60). The hotel is decorated in classy contemporary designs of glass and mauve coloring, and the rooms are bright and cheerful. Singles range from ¥7,500 ($60) to ¥10,000 ($80), and twins are ¥11,500 ($92) to ¥20,000 ($160). The most expensive twins have good views of the city plus a separate entrance foyer and semidouble beds. Doubles start at ¥13,200 ($106).

Mont Blanc Hotel, 3-14-1 Meieki, Nakamura-ku (tel. 052/541-1121), is less than two minutes away from Nagoya Station on foot. It's a business hotel, so most of its 281 rooms are singles, but it does have 47 twins and 12 doubles. Built in 1980 and renovated in 1985, it's clean and bright and has both Western and Japanese restaurants. Rooms—which start at ¥6,500 ($52) for a single, ¥11,000 ($88) for a twin, and ¥11,800 ($94) for a double—come with radio, clock, TV with pay video, and fridge. Bathtubs in the cheapest singles are extremely narrow; if you're a big Westerner you may have trouble taking a bath in one of these.

Opened in 1985, **Hotel Sunroute Nagoya,** 2-35-24 Meieki, Nakamura-ku (tel. 052/571-2221), is one of Nagoya's newest business hotels. A handsome brick building located about a three-minute walk from Nagoya Station, it features a spacious lobby with an atrium and marbled pool and restaurants serving Japanese and Western food. More than 200 of its 276 rooms are singles, ranging in price from ¥6,800 ($54) to ¥8,800 ($70). Twins start at ¥11,500 ($92), while doubles start at ¥14,300 ($114). White walls make the rooms bright and pleasant, while TV with pay video, refrigerator, radio, alarm, and hot water with tea add to the comfort.

The Budget Category

Western Style: The **Nagoya Daini Washington Hotel,** 3-22-12 Nishiki, Naka-ku (tel. 052/962-7111), is located close to Sakae and its restaurants and bars. Unlike most business hotels, which have few facilities, this hotel features four restaurants serving Japanese, Chinese, and Western food; there is also a sauna. Singles range from ¥4,800 ($38) to ¥6,600 ($53); the cheapest rooms manage to maintain an atmosphere of cheerfulness even though they're small and without windows. Twins and doubles range from ¥11,000 ($88) to ¥13,200 ($106), and are small but functional, coming with single and narrow beds, a small writing area, and two chairs. Machines selling soda and beer are located on the fifth and eighth floors.

Also located in Sakae, about a three-minute walk from the Sakae subway station, is the **Nagoya Plaza Hotel,** 3-8-21 Nishiki, Naka-ku (tel. 052/951-6311), a business hotel with just the basics but relatively cheap prices. More than 15 years old, the decor could use some updating but the staff is friendly and the location convenient. Rooms come with coin-operated TV, refrigerator, and desk. Singles start at ¥5,200 ($42) and run to ¥6,000 ($48); the cheapest is rather bare, with just a bed and wall hooks for clothes. Twins are ¥9,500 ($76); doubles range from ¥8,800 ($70) to ¥10,000 ($80). The hotel's one restaurant serves only breakfast, with prices running ¥750 ($6). Room rates here include tax and service charges.

Japanese Style: Oyone Ryokan, 2-2-112 Aoi, Higashi-ku (tel. 052/936-8788), is a member of the Japanese Inn Group and offers inexpensive tatami rooms ranging from ¥3,800 ($30) to ¥4,400 ($35) for one person, ¥7,000 ($56) to ¥8,000 ($64) for two persons, and ¥10,000 ($80) to ¥11,000 ($88) for three. The building itself is rather characterless, but rooms are clean and come with air conditioner, heater, and coin-operated TV. Breakfasts are available starting at ¥500 ($4), while Japanese dinners start at ¥1,500 ($12). To reach Oyone, take the Higashiyama subway line from Nagoya Station to Chikusa Station (about a seven-minute ride), from which it's a five-minute walk. You can also reach Oyone by taking the JR Chuo Line (bound for Kozoji) to Chikusa Station.

Ryokan Meiryu, 2-4-21 Kamimaezu, Naka-ku (tel. 052/331-8686), is another Japanese Inn Group member, this one located near Kamimaezu subway station. It's been a family-owned operation for more than 40 years, but the present building is cement—a no-nonsense, business-type accommodation. In fact, most of its customers are Japanese businessmen, some of whom have lived here for years during the week, commuting home to their families on weekends. None of the 23 rooms here have private bathrooms, but they do come with the basics: telephone, TV, safe for valuables, cotton kimono, and combination air conditioner/heater. The men's public bath also has a sauna (they don't have many female guests at this ryokan, but there is a separate public bath in case the lone female makes an appearance). Singles are ¥4,400 ($35), twins are ¥8,200 ($66), and triples are ¥11,500 ($92). Japanese breakfasts are ¥500 ($4) and dinners start at ¥1,500 ($12).

Youth Hostels: The **Nagoya Youth Hostel**, 1-50 Kameiri, Tashiro-cho, Chikusa-ku (tel. 052/781-9845), is 16 minutes from Nagoya Station by subway (subway stop: Higashiyama Koen), followed by ten minutes on foot. The charge for both members and nonmembers is ¥1,600 ($12.80) per night. Breakfast is an additional ¥400 ($3.20) and dinner runs ¥600 ($4.80). As in most youth hostels, life is fairly regimented: the front doors close at 9 p.m., lights out at 10 p.m., and rising time is 6:30 a.m.

It's also worth a try calling to see whether there's room at the **Youth Hostel Aichi-ken Seinen-Kaikan**, 1-18-8 Sakae (tel. 052/221-6001), but it's so centrally located that it's usually full. Reached in ten minutes by bus from Nagoya Station and three minutes on foot, it charges ¥2,300 ($18.40) for members and ¥3,900 ($31) for nonmembers. A dinner menu has choices ranging from ¥700 ($5.60) to ¥2,000 ($16). Breakfast is ¥500 ($4).

WHERE TO DINE

One of Nagoya's specialties is *kishimen* noodles (white noodles). It's also famous for its *miso nikomi udon,* which are udon noodles served in a bean-paste soup and flavored with such ingredients as chicken and green onions. There are also fine restaurants serving kaiseki, tempura, and other Japanese cuisine.

Around Nagoya Station

Shoufukuro ⑬⑨, 2-14-19 Meieki Minami (tel. 586-0005), is a kaiseki restaurant with a sweeping view of the city. Located on the 26th floor of the Sumitomo Building, about a ten-minute walk south of Nagoya Station, this tiny restaurant consists of only eight tables and very simple furnishings, using the dramatic backdrop of e city and its own food arrangements as the focal points for decoration. Service is tentive and gracious from kimono-clad waitresses. The menu changes monthly according to what's in season, and it's best to make a reservation, especially if you want to come for dinner. Kaiseki meals cost ¥11,000 ($88), ¥14,300 ($114), ¥16,500 ($132), and ¥22,000 ($176); the differences in price reflect the number of dishes and the type of food served. There's also a ¥5,500 ($44) mini-kaiseki available for lunch. Hours are 11:30 a.m. to 3 p.m. and 5 to 9 p.m.; closed Sunday and national holidays.

For outdoor dining, there's the Miyako Hotel where the beer garden is open during the summer months from 5 to 9 p.m. Pop music plays from a loudspeaker, and there's a plastic-food display case to help in making your selection of everything from frankfurters to sushi. Teppanyaki (strips of beef that you grill at your table) is available for ¥3,500 ($28) per person and includes all the beer or juice you can consume. If you go the à la carte route, beer starts at ¥600 ($4.80).

Yamamoto-ya Honten ⑭ is a chain noodle shop specializing in miso nikomi udon. Its noodles, all handmade, are thick, hard, and chewy and are served in a type of bean paste special to Nagoya. If you like your noodles spicy, you can add a mixture of spices to your food from the large bamboo container on your table. A bowl of udon in soup costs ¥600 ($4.80). With chicken (called *Kashiwa iri nikomi udon*) it costs ¥880 ($7.04). A Yamamoto-ya Honten shop is located just a three-minute walk from Nagoya JR Station near Hotel Castle Plaza (see above for location) on Sakura Dori Street in the basement of the Horiuchi Building (tel. 565-0278). If you want to try these noodles in Sakae, there's another shop just a couple minutes from the Sakae subway station in the basement of the Chu-Nichi Building (tel. 263-7519). Both shops open at 11 a.m.; the noodle shop on Sakura Dori takes its last order at 7:40 p.m., while the Sakae shop remains open until 8:30 p.m.

For a wide choice of inexpensive dining, a good bet is the ninth floor of the **Meitetsu** department store, which is that shiny, white building right next to Nagoya Station. Approximately ten small restaurants are scattered along the ninth floor, offering everything from noodles and sushi to Chinese cuisine, tempura, eel, and spaghetti. You can dine here every day except Thursday from 10:30 a.m. to 7 p.m. for ¥600 ($4.80) to ¥1,500 ($12).

In Sakae

A good choice in Sakae's nightlife and restaurant district is **Yaegaki Tempura House** ⑭, 3-17-28 Nishiki, Naka-ku (tel. 951-3250). This well-established tempura restaurant has been serving fresh seafood and vegetables for more than half a century and features open kitchens so guests can watch the action. The staff here is very friendly and there's an English menu for the offerings in season, which may include shrimp, oyster, smelt, Japanese trout, gingko nuts, or lotus root. It's easiest to order the set dinner, which consists of hors d'oeuvres, four shrimp, six pieces of varied seasonal fish, vegetables, rice, soup, pickled vegetables, and fruit for ¥7,000 ($56). Set lunches start at ¥4,400 ($35.20). This tempura restaurant is open from 11:30 a.m. to 2 p.m. and 5 to 9 p.m.; closed Sunday and national holidays. Reservations are recommended if you want to eat dinner here.

Kisoji ⑭, 3-20-15 Nishiki, Naka-ku (tel. 951-3755), is a restaurant in Sakae specializing in shabu-shabu. In business for more than 20 years, it evokes a countryside atmosphere with traditional, comfortable decor. You can dine either at tables or on tatami. There's an English menu, but the kimono-clad waitresses are unable to elaborate on what the various courses entail, so choose according to your budget. Set lunches start at ¥1,400 ($11.20). Most dinners range from ¥5,200 ($41.60) to ¥9,000 ($72). The Shabu-Shabu Special includes hors d'oeuvres, shabu-shabu, rice, pickles, and ice cream, while the Shabu-Shabu Keyaki features hors d'oeuvres, shabu-shabu, sashimi, tempura vegetables, rice, pickles, and dessert. It's open from 11:30 a.m. to 3 p.m. and 5 to 10 p.m. (noon to 9:30 p.m. on Sunday).

Kishimentei ⑭, 3-20-4 Nishiki, Naka-ku (tel. 951-3481), is a small hole-in-the-wall that has been offering Nagoya's specialty for more than 70 years—kishimen noodles. It even sells packages of noodles in case you want to take some home with you. There's no English menu, but plastic food is displayed in the window. Meals range from ¥600 ($4.80) to about ¥1,700 ($13.60) and include kishimen noodles with pork, tempura shrimp, or vegetables. It's open Monday through Saturday from 11 a.m. to 8 p.m.

2. Ise-Shima National Park

Blessed with subtropical vegetation, many small islands dotting its shoreline, and the most revered Shinto shrine in all of Japan, Ise-Shima National Park merits a one- or two-night stopover if you're anywhere near the vicinity of Nagoya. Located on Shima Peninsula and covering 200 square miles, this national park is also the home of the Mikimoto pearl, Japan's famous women divers, and thousands of oyster rafts in its many bays and inlets. Although you could conceivably cover the major attractions on a day's outing from Nagoya, I've included some recommended accommodations in case you'd like to take in the sights at a more leisurely pace.

ORIENTATION

Ise-Shima's major attractions are concentrated in the small towns of Ise, Toba, and Kashikojima, all in Mie Prefecture. Ise, for example, is where you'll find the Ise Jingu Shrines; Toba contains the Mikimoto Pearl Island, with a pearl museum and demonstrations by women divers; and in Kashikojima you can visit the Shima Marineland or take boat trips around Ago Bay, considered to be the most scenic spot in the national park.

The easiest way to get to Ise-Shima is from Nagoya on the private Kintetsu Ise-Shima Line (Kinki Nippon Railway), which departs about every 30 minutes or so from the Kintetsu Station right next to the Japan Railways' Nagoya Station. It takes about an hour and 20 minutes to reach Ise (Ujiyamada Station), about one hour and 30 minutes to reach Toba, and two hours to reach Kashikojima. A ticket from Nagoya to the end of the line in Kashikojima costs ¥3,000 ($24) one way. There are also Kintetsu lines to Shima Peninsula from both Kyoto (two hours and 15 minutes to Toba) and from Osaka's Kintetsu Station in Namba (two hours to Toba).

If you're on a JR rail pass, you might be interested to know that you can also reach Ise-Shima by JR, though the trains are not as frequent or convenient. There is only one train from Kyoto, and if you're coming from Nagoya you'll have to change trains in Taki. Note that JR trains pass through Ise (Iseshi Station) and terminate in Toba. If you want to go onward to Kashikojima, therefore, you'll have to switch in Toba to the Kintetsu private line.

Transportation inside Ise-Shima National Park is either by local train or by bus. You might also consider joining a sightseeing tour. Although they're conducted in Japanese only, tours provide a convenient way of seeing the park's far-flung attractions.

Be sure to drop by the Tourist Information Center in Tokyo or Kyoto to pick up the free leaflet *Ise-Shima*. It lists train schedules from Osaka, Kyoto, and Nagoya, and gives information on the national park's main attractions.

THE SIGHTS

The easiest way to see the sights of Ise-Shima National Park is to start in Ise and work your way down the peninsula to Kashikojima.

Ise Jingu Shrines

Ise, the northern gateway to Ise-Shima National Park, is famous for the Ise u Shrines, also called the Grand Shrines of Ise. The shrine grounds consist of the er Shrine, the Inner Shrine, and more than 100 minor shrines.

The **Outer Shrine** (*Geku*) is just a ten-minute walk from either Ujiyamada or Iseshi Station. Founded in 478, it's dedicated to the Shinto goddess of harvest and agriculture. The **Inner Shrine** (*Naiku*) was founded a few centuries earlier and is dedicated to Amaterasu, the sun goddess. Since the shrines lie about four miles apart, you should walk first to the Outer Shrine and then take a bus to the Inner Shrine. Buses make runs between the two shrines about every 15 minutes and the fare is ¥340 ($2.72).

The Ise Jingu Shrines are one of the few Shinto shrines in Japan that do not show any Chinese Buddhist influences. Constructed of plain cypress wood with thick thatched roofs, the shrines are starkly simple and do not have any ornamentation save some gold and copper on the facing of their beams and doors. In fact, if you've come all the way to Shima Peninsula just to see the shrines you may be disappointed—there is nothing much to see. The shrines are considered so sacred that no one is allowed close to them—that is, no one except members of the imperial family and high Shinto priests. Both shrines are surrounded by four wooden fences and we lesser mortals are allowed only as far as the third gate. Because of the fences you can't see much of the shrines, but that doesn't stop the estimated six million Japanese who come here annually. They come because of what the shrines represent, which is an embodiment of the Japanese Shinto religion itself. The Inner Shrine is by far the more important of the two shrines because it's dedicated to the sun goddess, who is considered the legendary ancestress of the imperial family. It contains the Sacred Mirror (*Yata-no-Kagami*), one of the Three Sacred Treasures of the emperor.

According to legend, the sun goddess sent her grandson to Japan so that he and his descendants could rule over the country. Before he left she gave him three insignia—a mirror, a sword, and a set of jewels. As she handed him the mirror, she is said to have remarked, "When you look upon this mirror, let it be as if you look upon me." The mirror, therefore, is considered to embody the sun goddess herself and is regarded as the most sacred object in the Shinto religion. The mirror is kept in the deep recesses of the Inner Shrine in a special casket and is never shown to the public. As for the other two treasures, they are also kept locked away. The sword is in the Atsuta Shrine in Nagoya and the jewels are in the Imperial Palace in Tokyo.

Even though you can't see much of the shrines themselves, they're still the most important things you should see in Ise-Shima. The Inner Shrine is surrounded by old cypress trees. Watch how the Japanese stop after crossing the second small bridge on the approach to the shrine to wash and purify their hands and mouth with water from the Isuzu River. Its source lies on the Inner Shrine grounds itself and it's considered to be a sacred stream. You'll also see a couple of white royal horses, kept near the shrine for the use of the sun goddess. Perhaps the most amazing thing about the Outer and Inner Shrines is that even though they were founded centuries upon centuries ago, the buildings themselves are not more than 20 years old. Every twenty years they are completely torn down and rebuilt exactly as they were on neighboring sites. With workers employing the old methods of dowels and interlocking joints, no nails are used. The present buildings were built in 1973 for the 60th time. Keep in mind that no photographs of the shrines themselves are allowed.

Ise-Shima Skyline Highway

Not far from the front entrance of the Inner Shrine are the buses that depart for Toba traveling on the Ise-Shima Skyline highway. About ten miles long, it rises up over Mount Asama, on top of which is **Kongoshoji Temple**. If you want you can get off the bus here, visit the temple, and then catch the next bus on to Toba. Kongoshoji Temple is renowned for the vermillion-painted Moon Bridge, which forms a circle as it reflects in a pond, and for a huge footprint said to be Buddha's. Behind the temple is a pathway lined with poles erected in memory of departed loved ones. The entire ride from the Inner Shrine to Toba takes about 45 minutes and costs ¥1,000 ($8).

Toba

Toba's best-known attraction is the **Mikimoto Pearl Island,** just a few minutes' walk from Toba Station and connected to the mainland via a short bridge. Open daily from 8:30 a.m. to 5 p.m. (from 9 a.m. to 4:30 p.m. November 20 to February 28) and charging ¥850 ($6.80), it's geared entirely toward tourists but is still quite enjoyable—especially if you have a weakness for pearls or are interested in how they're cultivated. In addition to a pearl museum and a shop, there's a demonstration hall where the process of culturing pearls and the steps involved in sorting and stringing them are explained in live demonstrations. You'll learn more about pearls than you ever thought possible—and possibly more than you ever wanted to know. Most fascinating in my opinion is the **Mikimoto Memorial Hall,** chronicling in flawless English the attempts, failures, and final success of Kokichi Mikimoto to cultivate pearls. The son of a noodle-shop owner, Mikimoto went to Yokohama as a young man and was surprised to see stalls selling pearls with great success. Pearls were produced naturally by oysters around his hometown of Toba. Mikimoto reasoned that if oysters produced pearls as the result of an irritant inside the shell, why couldn't man introduce the irritant himself and thereby induce oysters to make pearls?

It turned out to be harder than it sounded. Oysters used in Mikimoto's experiments kept rejecting the foreign material and dying. It wasn't until 1893, five years after he started his research, that Mikimoto finally succeeded in cultivating his first pearl. In 1905 Mikimoto was able to cultivate his first perfectly round pearl, after which he built what is probably the most successful pearl empire in the world. Mikimoto, who died at the age of 93, was a remarkable man and a real character. His favorite expressions included "Have you anything worth talking about?" and "Make the most of it." Nothing disgusted him more than wastefulness. I'm particularly fond of this quote: "Wisdom is indispensable to success. As is good fortune. But life is the most necessary ingredient of all." I certainly can't argue with that. Mikimoto's most famous line, however, was probably what he said to Emperor Meiji in 1905: "I want to adorn the neck of every woman in the world with a pearl necklace."

As for the **Pearl Museum,** it examines the relationship between mankind and pearls since ancient times. On the second floor you'll find various models made with pearls. The Pearl Pagoda, for example, has 12,760 Mikimoto pearls and took 750 craftsmen six months to complete, after which it was exhibited at the Philadelphia World Exhibition in 1926. The Liberty Bell, one-third the size of the original, has 12,250 pearls and was displayed at the New York World's Fair in 1939.

Also at Mikimoto Pearl Island are frequent demonstrations given by women divers. Wearing traditional white diving outfits, these divers demonstrate how women of Shima Peninsula have dived through the ages in search of abalone, seaweed, and other edibles. At one time there used to be thousands of women divers and they were known for their skill in diving to great depths for extended periods of time. Today's tourist brochures say that there are still 2,500 of these women divers left—but the only places I've ever seen divers at work were at demonstrations given for tourists. If you happen to see women divers working in earnest, consider yourself lucky.

If you have more time in Toba, other things to do here include visiting **Toba Aquarium** with its otters, seals, and sea cows, and **Brazil Maru,** a moored ship that took Japanese immigrants to Brazil from 1954 to 1974.

ımigaura

If you're at all sentimental, you might want to make a trip to Futamigaura, h you can reach by either bus or train from Ise or Toba. There you'll find a pair of large rocks that jut out of the sea not far from shore. Known as the **Wedded Rocks,** they are considered to represent man and wife and are joined by a thick braided rope, the same kind you see extended from torii gates at Shinto shrines. If you're an early riser, the best time to visit the rocks is at dawn. In this Land of the Rising Sun, the spectacle of the sun rising between these two rocks is a favorite among Japanese.

Kashikojima

At the southern end of Shima Peninsula and the last stop on the Kintetsu Line is Kashikojima. Here you can visit **Shima Marineland,** open from 8:30 a.m. to 6 p.m. in summer and 9 a.m. to 5 p.m. the rest of the year. It describes the fish and plant life of the region and beyond and also has demonstrations given by women divers. Although explanations are in Japanese only, it's a fun place for children to visit. Entrance is ¥850 ($6.80) for adults, ¥400 ($3.20) for children. The main attraction of Kashikojima, however, is its **boat cruises of Ago Bay.** Vessels leave from the boat dock about a two-minute walk from the train station. The cost of the cruise is ¥1,500 ($12), and you'll pass oyster rafts, fishing boats, and many small islands along the way. The trip lasts approximately one hour, with boats departing every hour or so between 9 a.m. and 3:30 p.m. in the summer. For more information or inquiries about the winter schedule, call the Kintetsu Shima Kanko Kisen Co. at 05994/3-1023.

If you're desperate for a dip in salt water, the most popular beach in the area is **Goza.** The boat from Kashikojima to Goza takes about 25 minutes and costs ¥550 ($4.40) one way, passing oyster rafts, their cultivators, and the sweeping mountainous terrain of the region. The boat ride is very enjoyable but the beach itself is, well, a bit disappointing after coming all that distance. There are certainly prettier beaches in the world, but this one is okay for a quick fix.

FOOD AND ACCOMMODATIONS

There are resort and hotel establishments throughout Shima Peninsula, which offer the best in seafood dining as well.

In Kashikojima

Sitting atop a hill above Ago Bay with its many oyster rafts, the **Shima Kanko Hotel** in Kashikojima (tel. 05994/3-1211) is a resort hotel with a large outdoor swimming pool and fine Western and Japanese restaurants. A hotel in the old tradition, it boasts impeccable service. Although it's just a few minutes' walk from the train station, hotel buses meet each incoming Kintetsu train. Rooms are spacious, and though they have recently been remodeled, they retain a healthy old-fashioned atmosphere with shoji screens and wooden furniture. Some of the twins here have balconies, and rooms that face the bay have splendid views of oyster rafts, watercraft, and islands. There are no single rooms. Standard twins range from ¥20,000 ($160) to ¥27,000 ($216), semi-doubles are ¥14,300 ($114), and doubles are ¥20,000 ($160). Japanese-style rooms accommodating up to four persons are available for ¥20,000 ($160) to ¥25,000 ($200). If you come during the peak tourist seasons of July and August or New Year's, expect to pay about ¥3,000 ($24) more than the prices quoted above.

Since Kashikojima is surrounded by water, you can safely assume that the seafood here is fresh and excellent. The Shima Kanko Hotel's **La Mer** French restaurant has a well-deserved reputation for serving its own delightful recipes created by its well-known chef. Its specialty is lobster, served in a Western dining hall with chandeliers, wooden floor, white tablecloths, and tables overlooking the bay and oyster rafts. A lobster menu for ¥22,000 ($176) includes abalone, while meals for ¥25,000 ($200) and ¥29,000 ($232) include steak as well. The small à la carte menu offers entrées of lobster, shrimp, or beef, most in the ¥5,500 ($44) to ¥8,000 ($64) range. Lunch set courses range from ¥6,500 ($52) to ¥13,000 ($104), with either beef or seafood as the main dish. In any case, if you want one of the set dinner courses, you should make a reservation beforehand. Incidentally, if you've never had abalone, this is a great, albeit expensive, place to try it. Hours here are 11:30 a.m. to 2 p.m. and 5 to 9 p.m.

The Shima Kanko Hotel has a couple of Japanese restaurants as well, open only in the evenings. **Hamayu** is designed like a country lodge with a high slanted roof of thick beams supported by large pillars and a wooden floor. Open from 6 to 8:30 p.m., it serves a kaiseki dinner from ¥8,800 ($70.40). Other seafood dishes, such as abalone, lobster, shrimp, sashimi, and fried fish, average about ¥2,500 ($20) to ¥7,000 ($56).

The hotel also has a sushi bar called **Tsubaki,** open from 6:30 to 10 p.m. The best deal here is the ¥5,500 ($44) set meal, which offers a variety of seafood in season.

If you're looking for an inexpensive place to stay, a good choice is **Ishiyama-So** ⑭, Yokoyama-jima, Kashikojima (tel. 05995/2-1527). It's located on a small island just a stone's throw from the Kashikojima pier, and the only way to get there is in Ishiyama-So's own private boat. If you call ahead they'll even come fetch you at the train station and lead you to their boat. In any case, the trip over the water takes only two minutes, and you pull up right at the ryokan's front door. Although the building itself is concrete, the rooms in this family-run establishment are tatami and feature an air conditioner, heater, TV, and a safe for valuables. Three of the 12 rooms have their own private bathroom and go for ¥5,500 ($44) per person; other rooms, 3 of which have their own toilet, are ¥4,400 ($35.20) per person. Prices include breakfast. Japanese dinners start at ¥1,500 ($12). If you want you can swim right off the dock here, and footpaths cross the small island. One of the family members here speaks good English.

In Toba

A good choice in Toba is the **Toba Hotel International,** 1-23-1 Toba (tel. 0599/25-3121). Perched atop a hill about a 20-minute walk or 5-minute taxi ride from Toba Station, it has twin and Japanese-style rooms that go for ¥18,500 ($148) off-season, rising to ¥24,000 ($192) in July and August. Combination rooms with both Western-style beds and a separate tatami area go for ¥50,000 ($400). Some rooms have balconies with great views of the water, oyster rafts, fishing boats, and islands.

Facilities here include an outdoor swimming pool and French and Japanese restaurants. Most unique, perhaps, is its floating seafood restaurant, **Shioji,** which features a large fish tank in the middle of its dining room. Your fish couldn't be fresher. The dinner menu, served from 5:30 to 8 p.m., has courses that start at ¥8,800 ($70.40). The Shioji dinner, for example, includes an appetizer, sashimi, tempura, both broiled and boiled shellfish, soup, and fruit. If you're on a budget, consider coming for lunch, served from noon to 2 p.m. from ¥2,700 ($21.60) for a set menu.

A conveniently located ryokan in Toba is **Kimpokan** ⑭, 1-10-38 Toba (tel. 0599/25-2001), just a couple of minutes' walk from Toba Station. With 100 years of history under its belt, it's the oldest ryokan in Toba. The present white concrete building, however, is much more recent, now catering largely to Japanese groups. All 45 rooms face the water, but because it's located on a little inland the views aren't ⁓⁓⁓ grand. Rooms come with private bath and Western-style toilet, refrigerator, a ⁓⁓ or valuables, TV with pay video, and shoji screens. Western breakfasts are ⁓ d on request. Rates here range from ¥11,000 ($88) to ¥22,000 ($176) per ⁓ n, including two meals, and service.

In Futamigaura

Futamikan, 569-1 Ko, Futami-cho (tel. 05964/3-2003), is a grand, traditional Japanese-style inn which has even played host to the imperial family. The oldest part of the ryokan is more than 100 years old and features beautifully carved transoms and sitting alcoves overlooking the garden. Since they didn't make private bathrooms back then, you might prefer one of the rooms in the newer annex, which also have the additional advantage of a small balcony—ask for a room on the fifth floor, where you have a sweeping view of the sea. But no matter where you stay, be sure to explore. On the second floor of the old building is one of the most beautiful banquet rooms I have ever seen—it has wooden railings outside its sliding glass windows, chandeliers, and 120 tatami mats. As for the town itself, it's small and peaceful. The famous Wedded Rocks are only a five-minute walk away. Rates here range from ¥14,000 ($112) to ¥33,000 ($264) per person.

In Ise

Not considered as much a resort area as Toba and Kashikojima, Ise has more reasonably priced accommodations. One of the most interesting architecturally is **Yamadakan** ⑭, 13-1 Honmachi (tel. 0596/28-2532). Built more than 60 years ago, it features old wooden corridors that circle an inner courtyard. There are 28 rooms in all, 6 of which are in a newer annex and have their own bathrooms. Always the romantic, I prefer the older rooms without bathrooms. Rates here range from ¥7,500 ($60) to ¥16,500 ($132) and include two meals. Yamadakan is conveniently located about a three-minute walk from Iseshi Station on the road leading to the Outer Shrine.

Catering to a young traveling crowd, **Hoshidekan** ⑭, 2-15-2 Kawasaki (tel. 0596/28-2377), is less than a ten-minute walk from either Ujiyamada or Iseshi Station. This 70-year-old ryokan has only 13 rooms, all without toilet and bath. Some of the rooms have windows framed with gnarled roots and bamboo (they simply don't make windows like that anymore). Room rates do not include meals: ¥3,300 ($26.40) for one person and ¥6,000 ($48) for two. This inexpensive ryokan is run by a group of women who are strong advocates of **macrobiotic vegetarian cooking,** which they serve in a simple tatami room connected to the ryokan. Open from 11 a.m. to 2 p.m. and 5 to 8 p.m. every day except Sunday, it offers a vegetarian course (*Genmae teishoku*) for ¥750 ($6), vegetarian pilaf for ¥550 ($4.40), and such other choices as noodles, tempura, tofu dishes, raw wheat beer, and natural raw sake.

Of the business hotels in the area, your best bet is **Ise City Hotel** ⑭, 1-11-31 Fukiage (tel. 0596/28-2111). Located between Ujiyamada and Iseshi stations (it's about a three-minute walk from each) and situated right beside the railroad tracks, it opened in 1985. The adequately sized rooms are clean and cheerful, with flowered wallpaper and tiled bathrooms. Amenities include a radio, TV with pay video, clock, push-button phone, and hot water with tea. Single rooms, all of which feature a semidouble bed, go for ¥6,400 ($51) for one and ¥9,900 ($79) if you can squeeze in two. Twins are ¥12,300 ($98). Prices include tax and service.

Youth Hostels

Youth Hostel Taikoji ⑭, 1659, Ei, Futami-cho (tel. 05964/3-2283), is in a temple four minutes by bus from Futamigaura Station and then five minutes on foot. Tatami mats here accommodate up to 28 persons. The price for card-carrying members is ¥1,800 ($14.40), ¥2,400 ($19.20) for nonmembers. Breakfast and dinner are available for an additional ¥1,000 ($8).

Ise-Shima Youth Hostel ⑮, at 1219-80 Anagawa, Isobe-cho (tel. 05995/5-0226), is seven minutes on foot from Anagawa Station and charges ¥2,300

($18.40) for an overnight stay. The rules say you have to have a membership card. Breakfast costs ¥450 ($3.60), while dinner is ¥700 ($5.60).

---

3. Kanazawa

Located on the northwest coast of Honshu on the Sea of Japan, Kanazawa serves as a gateway to the rugged and sea-swept Noto Peninsula. The second-largest city after Kyoto to escape bombing during World War II, some of the old city has been left intact, including a few samurai houses, old geisha quarters, and tiny narrow streets that run crooked without rhyme or reason, apparently to confuse any enemies foolish enough to attack. Kanazawa is most famous for its Kenrokuen Garden, one of the most celebrated gardens in all of Japan. Considering all its assets, therefore, it's little wonder that Kanazawa has become one of the most popular new destinations for foreigners in Japan. If your time in Japan is limited, however, and you're mainly interested in traditional Japanese buildings and neighborhoods, my own opinion is that Kyoto or Takayama in the Japan Alps has more to offer. On the other hand, if you are a big fan of Japanese gardens, Kenrokuen is one of the best. It's the main reason people come here.

Kanazawa first gained notoriety about 500 years ago when a militant Buddhist sect joined with peasant fanatics to overthrow the feudal lord and establish its own autonomous government, an event unprecedented in Japanese history. The independent republic survived almost 100 years before it was attacked by an army of Nobunaga Oda, who was trying to unite Japan at a time when civil wars wracked the nation. Kanazawa was subsequently granted to one of Nobunaga's retainers, Toshiie Maeda. The Maeda clan continued to rule over Kanazawa for the next 300 years, amassing wealth in the form of rice paddies and encouraging development of the arts. All through the Tokugawa shogunate era the Maedas remained the second most powerful family in Japan after the Tokugawas themselves and controlled the largest domain in the country. About a million *koku* of rice (equaling five million bushels of rice) was produced here annually. The arts of Kutani ware, Yuzen silk dyeing, and Noh theater flourished and enjoy success and popularity even today.

ORIENTATION

The **tourist information window** is located just outside Kanazawa Station as you exit from the east side (tel. 0762/31-6311). Open from 8 a.m. to 8 p.m. (8:30 a.m. to 7:30 p.m. in winter), it distributes a map in English and will also book hotel rooms for you. Before leaving Tokyo, be sure to pick up the flyer *Kanazawa and Noto Peninsula* at the Tourist Information Center.

Kanazawa's attractions spread south and southeast from the station (take the station's east exit). Kenrokuen Garden, for example, is 1½ miles southeast of Kanazawa Station, easily reached by bus 10, 11, or 12 from the station. You can also take a bus from the station to the Kosen Pottery Kiln. Other attractions can be covered on foot in one day.

The **telephone area code** for Kanazawa is 0762. Kanazawa serves as the capital of Ishikawa Prefecture.

THE SIGHTS

Much of Kanazawa's charm lies in the atmosphere of its old neighborhoods. Be sure to wear your good walking shoes, since the best way to explore the city is via your own two feet.

rokuen Garden and Vicinity

At one time Kanazawa possessed an impressive castle belonging to the powerful a clan. Unfortunately, the castle was destroyed by fire in 1881. One of the few structures left standing is the **Ishikawamon Gate,** which used to be the south entrance to the castle. Looking at how big and grand the gate is, you can gain at least a little appreciation of how mighty the Maeda castle once was.

Just south of Ishikawamon Gate is **Kenrokuen Garden,** Kanazawa's main attraction. Along with Kairakuen Garden in Mito and Korakuen Garden in Okayama, Kenrokuen is considered to be one of the best three landscape gardens in Japan. As the largest of the three, it's also considered by many to be the best. Its name can be translated as "a refined garden incorporating six attributes," which are: spaciousness, careful arrangement, seclusion, antiquity, elaborate use of water, and scenic charm. What this all means is that ponds, trees, streams, rocks, mounds, and footpaths have all been combined so aesthetically that the effect is quite spellbinding. No matter the season, you're bound to be captivated by its beauty. Altogether it took about 150 years to complete the garden. The fifth Maeda lord started construction in the 1670s, and through the years each successive lord added to the garden according to his own individual tastes. The garden as we now see it was finished by the 12th Maeda lord in 1822. As the private garden of the Maeda clan, it wasn't until after the Meiji Restoration that the garden was opened to the public in 1875. Admission to the garden is ¥300 ($2.40) and hours are 6:30 a.m. to 6 p.m. daily (8 a.m. to 4:30 p.m. in winter).

As a side note, it may be worth it to arrive either at dawn or near the end of the day, since the garden is a favorite destination of Japanese tour groups, led by guides who explain everything in detail—through loudspeakers. I don't know how they affect you, but loudspeakers drive me to absolute distraction.

In the southeast corner of Kenrokuen Park, and charging a separate admission of ¥500 ($4), is **Seisonkaku Villa,** built in 1863 by the 13th Maeda lord as a retirement home for his widowed mother. Of elegant and graceful workmanship, this villa is decidedly feminine in nature with its carved-wood transoms and shoji screens painted with various designs. The villa's bedroom is decorated with tortoises painted on the shoji wainscoting (tortoises were associated with long life, and it must have worked, since the mother lived to be 84). Closed on Wednesday, it's open the rest of the week from 8:30 a.m. to 4:30 p.m.

Next to Seisonkaku Villa is the **Ishikawa Prefectural Museum for Traditional Products and Crafts,** open daily from 9 a.m. to 4:30 p.m.; closed every third Thursday from April through November and every Thursday from December through March. Admission is ¥200 ($1.60). Opened in 1984, it houses a good collection of various locally produced lacquerware, woodcarvings, folk toys, pottery, silk, washi (Japanese paper), and hats and baskets made from cypress. You can see the famous Kutani pottery here as well, first produced under the patronage of the Maeda clan in the 1600s. There are also displays of Yuzen dyeing, with its bold and clear picturesque designs. A pamphlet and explanations of the various displays in English make a visit here worthwhile.

South of Kenrokuen Park and not far from Seisonkaku Villa are a scattering of more museums to visit if you like museums and you're interested in learning more about Kanazawa's past. The **Ishikawa Prefectural Art Museum (Ishikawa-ken Bijutsukan),** open daily from 9:30 a.m. to 4:30 p.m. and charging a ¥300 ($2.40) admission, houses a small collection of antique Kutani pottery, samurai costumes, and decorative art, most dating from the Edo Period. Several rooms are also devoted to modern and contemporary paintings, sculptures, and other artwork by local artists, with exhibitions changed monthly. Close by is the **Honda Museum,** which displays samurai outfits, weapons, artwork, and the personal effects of the Honda clan, one of Lord Maeda's chief retainers. Open daily from 9 a.m. to 5 p.m. (closed on Thursday from November through February), it charges ¥500 ($4). A third museum, the **Ishikawa Prefecture History Museum (Reikishi Hakubutsukan),** exhibits artifacts dealing with the history of the prefecture from prehistoric to modern times. Housed in a handsome red-brick building that was built to stock guns and gunpowder before the turn of the century, it contains archeological finds from the region items from the Edo Period, and folkloric objects. There are even samurai outfits you can try on for size—they weigh up to 44 pounds. Open every day from 9 a.m. to 5 p.m., it charges ¥250 ($2).

Since it would be tiring (and expensive) to visit all the museums described above, you might want to limit your selection to one or two. My own personal favorite is the Prefectural Museum for Traditional Products and Crafts.

Nagamachi Samurai District

About a 20-minute walk west of Kenrokuen Garden is an area known as the Nagamachi Samurai District. This place should be visited more for absorption of atmosphere than anything else, since most of the homes are still privately owned and are not open to the public. Furthermore, despite the name, many of these homes were built during the Meiji era and never belonged to samurai at all.

The Nagamachi Samurai District is basically just one street, lined with beautiful wooden homes hidden behind gold-colored mud walls. An unhurried stroll in the neighborhood is the main source of entertainment here—perhaps not so different from many neighborhoods in Japan, but certainly different from neighborhoods back home. One home that is open to the public is the **Nomura Samurai House,** open daily from 8:30 a.m. to 5 p.m. (4:30 in winter) and charging ¥400 ($3.20) admission. Its drawing room is of Japanese cypress with elaborate designs in rosewood, and its shoji screens are painted with landscapes. There's also a small, charming garden with a miniature waterfall, a winding stream, and stone lanterns.

Another old home in the Nagamachi Samurai District open to the public has been converted into a Yuzen silk center, where you can watch artists at work painting intricate designs on silk. Closed on Thursday and open the rest of the week from 9 a.m. to noon and 1 to 4:30 p.m., the **Yuzen Silk Center (Saihitsu-an)** charges ¥500 ($4) admission, which includes a welcoming tea and a sweet. A video shows the process of Yuzen dyeing, and an English pamphlet describes the steps in detail. It can take up to six months to make one kimono of Yuzen hand-painted silk.

From the Nagamachi District it's just a few minutes' walk to **Oyama Jinja Shrine,** built in 1599 in dedication to the first Maeda lord, Toshiie Maeda. It possesses a three-story gate designed by a Dutchman in 1875, with stained-glass windows on the third floor.

Other Sights

If your interest lies in pottery, it's worth a visit to the **Kosen Pottery Kiln (Kutani Kosengama),** 20 minutes by bus from Kanazawa Station to the Nomachi bus stop (tel. 41-0902). It's the only kiln within Kanazawa and shows the entire process of producing Kutani ware. Admission is free, and it's open daily from 9 a.m. to 5 p.m.

Myoryuji Temple, 15 minutes by bus from Kanazawa Station to the Nomachi-Hirokoji bus stop and then a five-minute walk, is popularly known as the Ninja-dera (or Temple of the Secret Agents) because of its secret chambers, hidden stairways, tunnels, and trick doors. Although it's very interesting, you must make a reservation to see it (tel. 41-2877) and admission is ¥500 ($4). To make sure you don't get lost (which would be quite easy because of all the trick doors), you will be grouped with other visitors and led by a guide who unfortunately describes everything only in Japanese. The tour lasts about 30 minutes and you'll probably be able to make a reservation on the same day of your call. The temple was constructed to serve as an escape route for the Maeda lord in case the castle was attacked. A well at the temple was supposedly connected to the castle via a secret tunnel.

If you're in Kanazawa for more than one day, you should consider taking an ⸍g to Yuwaka Spa, where you'll find the **Edo-Mura Village.** About a 40-minute ⸍le from Kanazawa Station, this is an open-air architectural museum with a col⸍ of some 20 buildings from the Edo Period, including a samurai mansion, ⸍ouses, and shops. This museum provides unique insight into how the various social classes lived back in the feudal days. Open daily from 8 a.m. to 6 p.m. (to 5 p.m. in winter), it charges ¥1,100 ($8.80).

If you're interested in seeing the **Noto Peninsula,** there are many JR trains and buses that provide transportation throughout the area. The main attraction is the landscape, and various fares and timetables are provided in T.I.C.'s *Kanazawa and Noto Peninsula.*

SHOPPING

The most famous products of Kanazawa are its Kutani pottery, known for its bright five-color overglaze patterns, and its hand-painted Yuzen silk. Kanazawa also produces toys, lacquerware, and wooden products. For one-stop shopping, visit the **Ishikawa Prefectural Kanko Bussankan** (tel. 22-7788), located close to Kenrokuen Garden (if you're arriving at Kenrokuen Garden via bus 10, 11, or 12 from Kanazawa Station, you'll get off the bus just a few steps away from the Bussankan). The ground and basement floors sell local products, the second floor is a restaurant, and the third floor houses the Ishikawa Prefectural Museum of Handicrafts, which charges a ¥200 ($1.60) admission to see artisans produce crafts of the area, including Kutani pottery, Japanese cakes, and lacquerware. Hours are from 9 a.m. to 6 p.m.; closed Thursday during the winter.

WHERE TO STAY

Most of Kanazawa's hotels are clustered conveniently around Kanazawa Station. There are also a few ryokan in the city, located in the older sections of town.

The Upper Bracket

Western Style: Conveniently located right in front of Kanazawa Station's east exit is the **Kanazawa Miyako Hotel,** 6-10 Konohanacho (tel. 0762/31-2202). First established in the 1960s and remodeled in 1984, it's part of the famous Miyako hotel chain and features 200 comfortable rooms, all well designed with attractive wood furniture and large windows. Each room comes with hot-water pot, alarm clock, double glass windows to shut out offending traffic noise, bilingual TV, and fridge. Singles start at ¥8,500 ($68); doubles at ¥14,000 ($112); and twins at ¥16,000 ($128). A shopping arcade is connected to the hotel, there are both Western and Japanese restaurants, and there's a beer garden on the roof in the summer.

Right next door, **Holiday Inn Kanazawa,** 1-10 Horikawa-cho (tel. 0762/23-1111), is similar to most Holiday Inns in Asia and foreigners should feel readily at home. Single rooms with double-size bed begin at ¥8,200 ($66); if you want a single room with a queen-size bed, the cost is ¥11,000 ($88). Twins and doubles range from ¥14,300 ($114) to ¥16,500 ($132), and Japanese-style rooms for one to five persons are available for ¥26,000 ($208). All rooms have TV, refrigerator, a good-size bathroom, and a water heater and tea bags. Built in the late 1970s, this 174 room hotel has four restaurants, including a Western-style restaurant and bar on the 14th floor with good views of the city, where piano music serenades every evening except Monday.

Opened in 1985, the **Kanazawa Tokyu Hotel** is one of the newest places to stay in town. A 16-story brick building rising from the heart of the city at 2-1-1 Kohrinbo (tel. 0762/31-2411), it's located close to Kanazawa's nightlife and department stores and is within walking distance of both the Nagamachi Samurai District and Kenrokuen Garden. The lobby and front desk are up on the second floor. Rooms are small and simple but pleasant, with V-shaped windows providing good views of the city. Rates are based on room size as well as height and range from ¥9,300 ($74) to ¥12,000 ($96) for a single, ¥19,000 ($152) for a double, and ¥20,000 ($160) for a twin. Regardless of which price category you select, ask for the highest floor available where the views are much better.

The absolute newest place in town, however, is the **ANA Hotel Kanazawa,** 16-3 Showa-machi (tel. 0762/24-6111), scheduled to open in June 1990. Located right next to Kanazawa Station, it features 255 rooms, a huge atrium lobby, and Western, Chinese, and Japanese restaurants. Room rates weren't available at press time, but I expect them to be comparable or a bit higher than those cited for the above hotels.

Japanese Style: South of Kanazawa Station in the heart of the city, **Miyabo** ⑮, Shimo Kakinokibatake 3 (tel. 0762/31-428), is close to Katamachi Shopping Street and within walking distance of Kenrokuen Garden. It boasts one of the oldest private gardens in Kanazawa, and part of the ryokan used to be the private tea house of Kanazawa's first mayor after the feudal age came to an end. Most of the ryokan's building dates from before World War II, although there is also a newer section. Per-person rates including two meals (but excluding tax) range from ¥13,000 ($104) to ¥30,000 ($240); the lowest price is for a room in the newer section, while the top price is for rooms with private views of the garden and more elaborately prepared meals. My favorite room is the one that used to be the mayor's tea ceremony room. Named "Bunte," with maroon walls, it's off by itself, secluded from the rest of the ryokan right in the middle of the garden. This room usually runs about ¥27,000 ($216) per person with two meals.

The Medium-Priced Range

Located across from the train station next to the Miyako Hotel, the **Garden Hotel,** 2-16-16 Honcho (tel. 0762/63-3333), caters primarily to Japanese business-men. This 147-room hotel opened in the mid-1980s and has a small contemporary lobby with a restaurant that serves breakfast, lunch, and dinner. It offers tiny but nicely decorated singles with semidouble beds for ¥5,700 ($46) to ¥6,500 ($52), doubles for ¥8,500 ($68) to ¥10,000 ($80), and twins for ¥11,000 ($88) to ¥12,000 ($96). Rooms are equipped with refrigerator, hot-water pot and tea, TV with adult video, music, alarm clock, windows that can be opened, and panels that can be closed for complete darkness.

Just 1½ blocks south of the Garden Hotel with rooms that are similarly equipped is the **Hotel New Kanazawa,** 2-4-10 Honmachi (tel. 0762/23-2255). Another business hotel, this decade-old establishment has a small but homey lobby, a restaurant serving both Japanese and Western food, and a cozy lounge area on the second floor. Vending machines are located on the fifth and eighth floor. Rooms are rather plain but comfortable, and start at ¥6,000 ($48) for singles, ¥10,000 ($80) for doubles, ¥12,000 ($96) for twins, and ¥13,200 ($106) for triples.

The Budget Category

Western Style: A practical and attractive business hotel about a three-minute walk from Kanazawa Station, **Kanazawa Castle Inn** ⑮, 10-17 Konohanamachi (tel. 0762/23-6300), offers 96 simple but cheerful rooms. The bathtubs are minia-ture, but otherwise you'll find comfort in the refrigerator, hot-water pot and tea, and TV with adult video. The cheapest singles, which offer a semidouble bed, begin at ¥5,400 ($43), while twins and doubles begin at ¥11,000 ($88). Prices include tax and service.

Less than a block away from Castle Inn and offering the same basic amenities is the **Oka Hotel,** 5-2 Horikawa (tel. 0762/63-5351). Although the front-desk staff doesn't speak much English, they are accommodating and friendly. This simply dec-orated business hotel, which opened in the early 1980s, offers singles without bath-room for ¥4,000 ($32) and singles with a private bathroom for ¥5,300 ($42) and ¥5,900 ($47). Doubles, all with bathroom and semidouble bed, are ¥9,600 ($77), while twins range from ¥8,300 ($66) for those without bathroom to ¥11,800 ($94) for those with. Triples, in case you're interested, start at ¥15,800 ($126). The hotel's one restaurant serves both Japanese and Western selections, and there's a public bath. All rates include service, but tax is extra.

Japanese Style: A 12-minute bus ride from Kanazawa Station and then a three-minute walk, **Ryokan Murataya,** 1-5-2 Katamachi (tel. 0762/63-0455), is in the heart of Kanazawa not far from Katamachi Shopping Street and within walking distance of Kenrokuen Garden. A member of the Japanese Inn Group, it's modern-looking and rather uninteresting from the outside, but comfortable and pleasant on the inside. All 12 rooms are without bath or toilet and cost ¥4,000 ($32) for a single, ¥7,700 ($62) for a twin, and ¥9,900 ($79) for a triple. All rooms come with TV, air conditioning, and heating. Japanese breakfasts only are served, and cost ¥800 ($6.40). As the owner pointed out, there are plenty of coffeeshops nearby if you need your morning coffee to perform.

Yogetsu ⑮, 1-13-22 Higashiyama (tel. 0762/52-0497), is a delightful little minshuku in the middle of the old Higashiyama geisha district. This district of plain wooden buildings was set aside in the 1820s by the local government as a place where geishas could entertain. Yogetsu is a 100-year-old house that used to belong to a geisha and has only five guest rooms. Run by a jovial woman, it charges ¥6,000 ($48) per person for an overnight stay with two meals and ¥4,900 ($39) without meals. The rooms are rather plain, but the quiet and quaint atmosphere of the surrounding district more than make up for the lack of decor. It's located either a 20-minute walk or a 10-minute bus ride from Kanazawa Station.

Youth Hostels: The **Kanazawa Youth Hostel** ⑭, 37 Suehiro-cho (tel. 0762/52-3414), is a 25-minute bus ride away from Kanazawa Station and a bit far from all the attractions, but it has a nice location. Rooms here are both tatami and Western, and cost ¥3,500 ($28) for members and ¥4,000 ($32) for nonmembers. Note that nonmembers are not accepted during the busy summer season. Prices include breakfast and dinner.

About 20 minutes from Kanazawa Station is the **Matsui Youth Hostel** ⑮, 1-9-3 Kata-machi (tel. 0762/21-0275). Take bus 20 to the Katamachi bus stop. It sleeps 30 persons in tatami rooms (about six people to a room) for ¥2,300 ($18) per person. Nonmembers pay ¥700 ($5.60) more. Breakfast costs ¥450 ($3.60).

WHERE TO DINE

Kanazawa's local specialties are known collectively as *Kaga no aji* and consist of seafood (such as tiny shrimp and winter crabs) as well as freshwater fish and mountain vegetables.

Around Kenrokuen Garden

A great place to try the local Kaga cuisine is right in Kenrokuen Garden itself at the **Miyoshian** ⑯ (tel. 21-0127). This restaurant was built about 100 years ago and consists of three separate wooden buildings, the best of which was built extending over a pond. This is where you'll probably dine, seated on tatami with a view of an ancient pond and giant carp swimming in the murky waters below. Kaga cuisine here ranges from ¥5,500 ($44) to ¥11,000 ($88). You can also order à la carte for such dishes as *jibuni* stew (a chicken and vegetable stew eaten primarily in winter) for ¥770 ($6.16) and shrimp sashimi for ¥550 ($4.40). Set obento lunches range from ¥1,600 ($12.80) to ¥3,300 ($26.40). A jibuni teishoku, which includes chicken stew, sashimi, pickled vegetables, rice, and soup, is available for ¥1,600 ($12.80). Miyoshian is open from 10 a.m. to 3 p.m.

Another restaurant serving Kaga specialties is **Tozan** ⑰ (tel. 63-8666), located just outside the north entrance of Kenrokuen Garden. Open from 11 a.m. to 3 p.m. and catering largely to Japanese groups, it has a dining hall on the second floor and features tatami mats, shoji screens, and a wooden ceiling. Outside the front door you'll see the dishes named in English, so ordering is easy here. Meals range from ¥2,200 ($17.60) to ¥5,500 ($44). A jibuni stew course is served for ¥2,000 ($16).

Also located close to the north entrance of Kenrokuen Garden is an inexpensive udon noodle shop called **Takeda** ⑮ (tel. 21-3662). A simple restaurant with a few tables and tatami seating, it's located between Kenrokuen Garden's north entrance and the Ishikawa Prefectural Kanko Bussankan. Look for the black curtains hanging at its front door and a plastic-food display case of noodles. Noodles here start at ¥600 ($4.80). Hours are 10:30 a.m. to 5 p.m.; closed Friday.

The second floor of the **Kanko Bussankan** also features a traditionally decorated restaurant with reasonably priced Japanese food, starting at ¥1,300 ($10.40) for such set courses as sashimi, tempura, noodles, and other common Japanese dishes, including Kaga cuisine. Its most popular set lunch is the Kaga Sanmi with local cuisine priced at ¥2,000 ($16). Although the menu is only in Japanese, there are pictures of set meals and a plastic display case. It's open from 10 a.m. to 6 p.m.; closed Thursday from November to March.

Katamachi Area

Just east of the Saigawa Ohashi Bridge is an area of restaurants and drinking establishments radiating out from the Katamachi Shopping and Chuo Dori streets. One of Kanazawa's best-known and most exclusive restaurants is **Zeniya** ⑲, 2-29-7 Katamachi (tel. 33-3331). It serves seasonal kaiseki meals of local specialties in cool, elegant surroundings for ¥11,000 ($88) to ¥16,500 ($132). Lunch is less expensive, with obento meals starting at ¥5,500 ($44) and mini-kaiseki offerings for ¥8,800 ($70.40). The presentation of each dish, naturally, is spectacular, and meals are by reservation only. Lunch is served from 11 a.m. to 2 p.m. and dinner from 5 p.m.; closed last Sunday of the month.

Located right down the street from Zeniya on the opposite side of the street is **Hamacho** ⑯, 2-31-32 Katamachi (tel. 33-3390). Open only in the evenings from 5 to 11 p.m. every day except Sunday and holidays, it offers seafood and vegetables in season. The menu, written on a blackboard but unfortunately only in Japanese, changes according to what's fresh and available and may include *imo* (Japanese potatoes), freshly picked mushrooms, vegetables, various seafood selections, and sashimi. Courses are available beginning at ¥4,000 ($32), with most averaging ¥6,000 ($48). Just tell Mr. Ishigami, the owner and chief chef, how much you want to spend and he'll do the rest. If there's anything you don't like, be sure to tell him. Sit at the counter where you can watch your set course being prepared, which may include grilled fish or shrimp, noodles, tofu, sashimi, soup, and vegetables.

A bit kinder to the traveler's purse is the moderately priced **Kitama** ⑯, 2-3-3 Katamachi (tel. 61-7176). Sitting on tatami mats, you have a pleasant view of a small, moss-covered 100-year-old garden of tiny pines, stone lanterns, and rocks. I ordered the jibuni teishoku, which came with chicken stew, clear soup, pickled vegetables, rice, and hors d'oeuvres for ¥1,300 ($10.40). My friend opted for the Kojitsu Obento, served in an upright lunchbox; it featured such delicacies as sashimi, small pieces of pork and fish, fried shrimp, soybean patty, and various seasonal vegetables. Most meals here cost less than ¥3,000 ($24). The restaurant is closed Wednesday, but open the rest of the week from 11:30 a.m. to 9:30 p.m.

Even cheaper is **Kaga Tobi** ⑯, located in the Kohrinbo 109 department store beside the Tokyu Hotel (tel. 62-0535). To reach the restaurant, don't enter the department store but, rather, walk around the building to the tiny back street flanking a narrow canal. Open every day except Wednesday from 11 a.m. to 2 p.m. and 5 to 10 p.m., it serves very reasonable set lunches. For ¥850 ($6.80) you can choose a main course of sashimi, tempura, or eel, which will come with side dishes. If you'd like to try Kaga cuisine, order the Shokado Teishoku for ¥2,200 ($17.60). Mini-kaiseki is only ¥2,700 ($21.60).

Part of a nationwide chain of inexpensive drinking establishments, **Irohanihoheto** ⑯, 2-23-7 Katamachi (tel. 21-1683), is located on the ground floor of the Prince Hotel. Decorated with crafts and heavy ceiling beams that are the trademarks of this chain, it's open daily from 5:30 p.m. to a respectable 4 a.m. Most items on the menu are less than ¥400 ($3.20) and include yakitori, grilled tofu, nikujaga (beef-and-potato stew), grilled fish, pizza, and salads. Beer starts at ¥380 ($3.04).

In case you feel like going out after dinner, next door to the Prince Hotel is **Ivory Coast** (tel. 22-1212), located in the basement of the Sunrose Katamachi Building. Cashing in on the latest craze for '50s and '60s American music, it features Japanese groups that imitate the real thing, with music ranging from Paul Anka, Neil Sedaka, and the Eagles to the Beatles. The place is open nightly from 7 p.m., and showtime begins at 8 p.m. The admission fee varies but averages ¥2,200 ($17.60) for males and ¥1,500 ($12) for females. Beer costs ¥500 ($4), and cocktails start at ¥650 ($5.20).

Around Kanazawa Station

The Kanazawa Miyako Hotel, 6-10 Konohanacho (tel. 31-2202), has both Japanese and Western restaurants on its seventh floor, each with large windows overlooking the city. **Kakitsubata** serves Japanese kaiseki meals for ¥6,600 ($52.80) and ¥11,000 ($88) and sashimi or tempura set courses starting at ¥3,300 ($26.40). You can also come here for lunch, when eel, sashimi or tempura, and obento box lunches are served for ¥1,600 ($12.80) to ¥3,300 ($26.40). Ordering is easy because the menu is in English.

Miyako's Western restaurant, the **Belle Vue**, is decorated in soft plum colors, with comfortable cushioned chairs and chandeliers providing a romantic setting. Piano music serenades on Saturday and Sunday nights. Dinners here are reasonable, starting at ¥4,400 ($35.20) and going up to ¥8,800 ($70.40). If you want to select your own combination of dishes, most entrées cost from ¥2,500 ($20) to ¥3,500 ($28) and include sole, steak, veal, lamb chops, and other seasonal choices. Set lunches range from ¥1,500 ($12) to ¥4,500 ($36). Hours for both Miyako restaurants are 11:30 a.m. to 2 p.m. and 5 to 10 p.m.

Incidentally, if you're more interested in downing a few pints rather than food, there's a beer garden atop the Miyako Hotel open from mid-May to the end of August every day except rainy ones from 5 to 9 p.m. Beer starts at ¥800 ($6.40) and the view is great.

If you're traveling on a budget, the **Shoan**, on the first floor of the Hotel New Kanazawa, 2-4-10 Honmachi (tel. 23-2255), serves both Western and Japanese dishes from 7:15 a.m. to 9:30 p.m. daily. Comfortably small with brilliant red walls, it offers everything from kaiseki, sashimi, and sukiyaki to pork cutlet, lamb, spaghetti, and fish. Most dishes run from ¥800 ($6.40) to ¥2,000 ($16). It also serves Kaga cuisine for ¥3,800 ($30.40) and up.

You can save even more money by going underground. There's an underground passageway leading from the train station to the nearby bus depot and to the Miyako Hotel, but the entrance is a bit difficult to find in the station itself, so look for the stairway outside the station or in front of the Miyako Hotel. You'll also find a slew of tiny holes-in-the-wall and diners here serving tempura, noodles, sushi, spaghetti, and the usual train-station fare designed to meet the needs of hurried commuters. You can easily dine for less than ¥1,000 ($8), but don't expect much in the way of atmosphere except that provided by the locals.

---

4. Osaka

Although it's history stretches back about 1,500 years, Osaka first gained prominence when Hideyoshi Toyotomi built Japan's most magnificent castle here in the

16th century. To develop resources for his castle town, he persuaded merchants from other parts of the nation to resettle in Osaka. During the Edo Period the city became an important distribution center as feudal lords from the surrounding region sent their rice to merchants in Osaka. The merchants in turn sent the rice to Edo (present-day Tokyo) and other parts of the nation. As the merchants prospered, the town grew and such arts as Kabuki and Bunraku flourished. With money and leisure to spare, the merchants also developed a refined taste for food.

Nowadays Osaka is an industrial city with a population of almost 2.8 million, making it the third-largest city in Japan (after Tokyo and Yokohama). With inklings of its merchant beginnings still present, Osakans are usually characterized as being rather money-minded, and often greet one another with a saying that translates as "Are you making any money?" Today Osaka has a reputation throughout Japan for its food, its castle, and Bunraku puppet theater.

ORIENTATION

Osaka lies on the southern coast of western Honshu about three hours from Tokyo by Shinkansen bullet train. If you arrive in Osaka by Shinkansen, you'll find yourself at Shin-Osaka Station, at the city's northern edge. To get from Shin-Osaka Station to Osaka Station and other points south, the most convenient mode of public transportation is the Midosuji subway line. The name of the subway stop at Osaka Station is called Umeda Station. JR trains also make runs between Shin-Osaka and Osaka stations. Note that if you need to turn in your voucher for your Japan Rail Pass, you can do so only at Osaka Station, at the JR Travel Service Center, from 10 a.m. to 6 p.m.

If you arrive by plane at **Osaka International Airport,** you can take one of the airport limousine buses that make frequent runs to Shin-Osaka, Osaka, and Namba stations. The trip to Osaka (Umeda) Station takes about a half hour and costs ¥380 ($3.04).

For getting around Osaka, there's a convenient **subway** network that's easy to use because all lines are color-coded and the station names are in English. The Midosuji Line is the most important one for visitors. It passes through Shin-Osaka Station and then goes to Umeda (close to Osaka Station), Shinsaibashi, Namba, and Tennoji. There's also a JR train called the Osaka Kanjo Line, which passes through Osaka Station and makes a loop around the city; take it to visit Osaka Castle.

With regard to hotels, shopping, restaurants, and nightlife, Osaka can be divided into two distinct parts: **Kita,** the North ward, which embraces the area around Osaka and Umeda stations; and **Chuo-ku,** the Middle ward, which is in the center of the JR loop train line and includes the Shinsaibashi shopping district and a lively eating and entertainment district clustered around a narrow street called Dotonbori. Connecting the two areas is a wide boulevard lined with gingko trees called Midosuji Dori Avenue. It runs from Osaka Station south all the way to Namba Station.

The **Osaka Tourist Information Office** (tel. 06/345-2189) is located at the east exit of Osaka Station and is open from 8 a.m. to 7 p.m. Its staff speaks English, gives out good maps of the city, and will also help in securing hotel rooms. Another tourist office is located near the central exits of Shin-Osaka Station, on the third floor (tel. 06/305-3311). Note that if you're arriving by Shinkansen, you'll be up on the fourth floor, so simply go down one flight to the tourist office. It's open daily from 8 a.m. to 8 p.m.

For information on what's going on in Osaka, pick up a copy of *Kansai Time Out,* a monthly magazine with information on sightseeing, festivals, restaurants, and other items of interest pertaining to Osaka, Kobe, and Kyoto. Costing ¥300 ($2.40), it's available at bookstores, restaurants, and places frequented by English-speaking tourists. Another good source of information is *Discover Kinki!,* available for free at the tourist offices and at many hotels.

The **telephone area code** for Osaka is 06. Osaka is in Osaka Prefecture.

WHAT TO SEE AND DO

Osaka does not have many tourist sights, which means that you can cover the basics of the city in a one- or two-night stay. Top priority on your list here should be Osaka Castle, Bunraku, and dining.

Osaka Castle

Osaka Castle was built in the 1580s upon the order of Hideyoshi Toyotomi. In constructing the castle he requisitioned materials from his feudal generals, the most conspicuous of which were huge stones. The largest stone measures 19 feet high and 48 feet long, and is known as the "Higo-ishi." Upon its completion Osaka Castle was the largest castle in all of Japan, a magnificent structure used by Hideyoshi as a military stronghold as he waged war against rebellious feudal lords. By the time he died in 1598, Hideyoshi had succeeded in crushing his enemies and unifying Japan under his command.

After Hideyoshi's death, Ieyasu Tokugawa seized power and established his shogunate government in Edo. Toyotomi's heirs, however, still had ideas of their own and, considering Osaka Castle impregnable, they plotted to overthrow the Tokugawa government. In 1615 Ieyasu sent troops to Osaka, where they not only defeated the Toyotomi insurrectionists but destroyed Osaka Castle. Although the Tokugawas rebuilt the castle, they burned it down again in 1868 during the Meiji Restoration as they made their last retreat.

The present Osaka Castle dates from 1931. Built of ferroconcrete, it's not as massive as the original but is still quite large and impressive. Its eight-story donjon, or keep, rises to a height of 130 feet and houses a museum with displays relating to the Toyotomis and old Osaka, including armor, fans, and personal belongings. Hours are 9 a.m. to 4:30 p.m. and admission is ¥400 ($3.20). To reach Osaka Castle, take either the Kanjo loop line to Morinomiya or Osakajokoen Station or the subway to Temmabashi, Tanimachi 4-chrome, or Morinomiya Station.

Since you're in the area, you might consider doing a few things in the vicinity of Osaka Castle. Just a few minutes' walk from the castle is the **O-Kawa River,** one of the many waterways that once served as an important avenue for transportation back in Osaka's merchant days. Although O-Kawa doesn't look anything like it used to, glass-enclosed boats (air-conditioned in summer) ply the river throughout the year, departing from a dock close to the castle. Rides last one hour and cost ¥1,500 ($12). Boats depart once an hour (at last check on the hour, but it would be wise to double-check) from 10 a.m. to 4 p.m. (longer hours in summer). The trip is beautiful (and therefore crowded) during the cherry-blossom season. For more information or to make reservations, call the Osaka Aqua Liner at 444-5000.

Also just a few minutes' walk from Osaka Castle are the Twin 21 buildings, easy to spot because they are two identical-looking buildings that tower over everything. On the second floor of one of them, called National Tower Building, is **Panasonic Square,** a hall filled with electronics of various fields, including electronic communications (such as the TV telephone) and electronic games. Although it's designed for the Japanese (with most things explained in Japanese), there's enough to interest everyone, especially children. A robot, for example, can draw your portrait, while a periscope mounted on the building's roof lets you scan Osaka's panorama. Panasonic Square is open every day except Wednesday from 10 a.m. to 6 p.m., and admission is ¥200 ($1.60). For more information call 949-2122.

Bunraku

The **National Bunraku Theater,** 1-12-10 Nipponbashi, Chuo-ku (tel. 212-2531), was completed in 1984 and presents traditional puppet theater six times a year, with most productions running a three-week stretch. Tickets usually range from ¥3,000 ($24) to ¥4,000 ($32). To find out whether a performance is being held, contact the Osaka Tourist Office. The National Bunraku Theater is located

about a ten-minute walk from Namba Station on the Midosuji subway line or a few minutes from Nipponbashi Station.

Shitennoji Temple

First built in 593 at the order of Prince Shotoku, Shitennoji Temple is considered one of the oldest Buddhist temples in Japan (it was founded more than a decade before Horyuji Temple, outside Nara, was constructed). Popularly known as Tennoji Temple, it has been destroyed by fire many times through the centuries so that none of the original structures remain. Southwest of the temple is **Tennoji Park,** where you can visit a zoo, botanical gardens, and the Municipal Art Museum with both ancient and modern Oriental art.

Takarazuka

Takarazuka is the name of a town northwest of Osaka, but its name is synonomous with the all-female **Takarazuka Troupe.** Founded back in 1914 to attract vacationers to Takarazuka, the troupe proved instantly popular with the general public, which had slowly been turning away from more traditional forms of Japanese drama in favor of lively Western musicals and entertainment. Combining both Japanese and Western elements in its performances, the Takarazuka Troupe today consists of about 400 women divided into four different groups that perform musicals, classical Japanese drama, folk dances, and modern revues in Takarazuka and Tokyo and on tours around the world.

Performances are held at the Takarazuka Revue hall most days throughout the year, with tickets ranging from about ¥750 ($6) to ¥3,900 ($31.20). Note, however, that the Revue hall is located on the grounds of an amusement park called Takarazuka Family Land, admission to which is an additional ¥1,000 ($8) and includes access to a zoo and botanical garden. It takes approximately 45 minutes to reach Takarazuka Station from Umeda Station via the private Hankyu Line. For more information, call 0797/84-0321.

Shopping

Osaka must rank as one of the world's leading cities in underground shopping arcades. The **Umeda Chika Center** is a huge underground shopping mall that connects Osaka and Umeda stations to a number of buildings, including the Hanshin and Hankyu department stores, Hankyu Sanbangai, and the Hankyu Grand Building. It caters primarily to the people working in the area and is so massive and complicated that you'll probably get lost in the maze. Other shopping areas include the underground mall at **Namba** and an aboveground covered shopping street near Shinsaibashi subway station. Paralleling Midosuji Dori Avenue to the east, it runs south all the way past Dotonbori and on to Namba.

Den Den Town is Osaka's electronics shopping region, similar to Tokyo's Akihabara (*Den* is short for "electric"). The nearest subway station is either Nipponbashi or Ebisucho.

Nightlife

Osaka's liveliest—and most economical—nightlife district radiates from a narrow pedestrian lane called **Dotonbori,** which flanks the south bank of the Dotonbori River. About a five-minute walk from Namba Station or less than a ten-minute walk from Shinsaibashi Station, it's lined with restaurants and drinking establishments.

The best place to begin an evening of carousing, however, is not in Dotonbori itself but in the nearby Nikko Hotel, 1-3-3 Nishishinsaibashi (tel. 244-1111), which is located on Midosuji Dori Avenue right above Shinsaibashi Station. Head for the 32nd floor to the **Jet Stream**, where you have a dynamite view of the city, perfect for watching the sun go down and the lights of the city come on. More than 360 feet high, the Nikko Hotel is the tallest building in the area. Romantic with soft candlelight, it offers what it calls its Twilight Dinner every day from 5 to 7 p.m. A bargain at just ¥2,200 ($17.60), it offers a choice of entrée, salad, bread, and coffee.

From 7:30 to 11 p.m., Jet Stream features live jazz and popular music, for which it levies a ¥1,000 ($8) cover charge on most weekdays. On weekends the cover charge climbs to ¥2,000 ($16) to ¥4,500 ($36) depending on the visiting band and event. Beer starts at ¥700 ($5.60) and most cocktails average ¥1,100 ($8.80). Food is also available, with most entrées averaging between ¥2,000 ($16) and ¥5,500 ($44) for such items as fried chicken, steak teriyaki, fish and scallops au gratin with mushroom sauce. There are also set dinners for ¥5,500 ($44), ¥8,800 ($70.40), and ¥11,000 ($88).

At the more frenzied end of the scale is **Maharaja,** located on the fifth floor of the Diamond Building, 1-5-12 Shinsaibashisuji, (tel. 213-7090). Serving the needs of disco maniacs, it's open daily from 5:30 p.m. to midnight, charging ¥5,000 ($40) for males and ¥4,500 ($36) for females; on Saturday night and the eve before a holiday, rates go up ¥500 ($4) for males only. The entrance fee buys you ten tickets, which you then trade in for drinks; the drinks average about two tickets each. The music is loud, and there are lots of mirrors so you can watch yourself dance. Maharaja is located on the first street paralleling Dotonbori River to the north, identified by a big sign that says "Soemon-Cho."

If all you want to do is drink, the **Pig and Whistle,** on the second floor of the Is Building at 2-1-32 Shinsaibashisuji (tel. 213-6911), is probably the best-known expatriate bar in Osaka. However, because there aren't that many foreigners living in the city, the majority of customers here are Japanese. It's open from 4 p.m. to midnight (to 1 a.m. on weekends). A large beer here costs ¥650 ($5.20), and whisky and water is ¥500 ($4). Munchies include pizza and fish and chips.

That futuristic black, chrome, and glass building rising up from the banks of the Dotonbori River is Kirin Plaza Osaka, 2-46-1 Shinsaibashisuji. Owned by the Kirin beer company, it features **Kirin City** (tel. 212-6572) on the second floor, one of a chain of modern beer halls seemingly found in every hamlet of the country. This one is open daily from 11 a.m. to 11 p.m., and its beer—Kirin naturally—starts at ¥450 ($3.60).

A casual, trendy bar is **Newz Bar,** 2-6 Shinsaibashisuji (tel. 212-6063). It's located right on Midosuji Dori Avenue, just north of the Holiday Inn on the same side of the street, in a building called intriguingly enough Gourmet Tower Across—but across from what remains a mystery. Fashionable, with bare white walls, a marbled floor from Italy, and outdoor sidewalk tables, it's a good place from which to observe the world go stumbling by. Open from 11 a.m. to a formidable 6 a.m., it offers beer starting at ¥650 ($5.20), cocktails at ¥750 ($6), and wine from ¥650 ($5.20) a glass. Its food, mostly in the ¥900 ($7.20) to ¥1,500 ($12) price range, includes spaghetti, steaks, salmon steak, and snacks.

For more outdoor drinking in the summertime, walk down the street from Newz Bar to the **Holiday Inn,** where you'll find a beer garden on a third-floor patio. It's open from 5 to 9 p.m. from the end of May to the end of August.

Part of a chain that has 14 locations in Japan, the **Wine Bar,** on the third floor of the Awajiya Building, 2-4-5 Shinsaibashisuji (tel. 211-7736), serves wine by the glass beginning at ¥500 ($4) and is popular with young Japanese. It's located on the first street paralleling the Dotonbori River to the north (on the same street as Maharaja described above) and is open daily from 5 p.m. to 1 a.m. Along with wines from France, Germany, and California, it also offers such dishes as grilled spareribs, salads, pizza, and snacks.

Meanwhile, down in the basement of the same building is **Irohanihoheto,** an inexpensive yakitori-ya where beer and snacks are dispensed, with most prices under ¥600 ($4.80). Opening at 5:30 p.m., it closes at 3:30 a.m. on weekdays and 5 a.m. weekends. It bills itself as an "Antique Pub" and is decorated with traditional memorabilia. Part of a chain of drinking establishments, it's popular with younger Japanese.

If you happen to be much farther north, in the vicinity of Osaka Station, try **Studebaker's,** 2-4-12 Nakazakinishi (tel. 372-1950), located next to Umeda Center. Open daily from 11:30 a.m. to 5 p.m. and again from 5:30, p.m. to midnight, it's an enthusiastic re-creation of an American 1950s diner, complete with lots of chrome, red, white, and blue, as well as booths and counters. A sister shop to similar diners in Houston and Dallas, it offers a buffet lunch for ¥850 ($6.80) until 2 p.m. After 5:30 p.m. there's a ¥1,000 ($8) admission charge (¥1,500 on weekends), which until 7:30 p.m. includes an all-you-can-eat buffet. A disc jockey plays golden oldies, and in an attempt to make this diner upscale, only persons older than 23 are admitted and jeans, sweat shirts, and tennis shoes are not allowed.

WHERE TO STAY

Like Tokyo, Osaka has a wide range of hotels, from first-class accommodations to business hotels. The majority are concentrated around Osaka Station, while the rest stretch to the south and around Shin-Osaka Station.

The Upper Bracket

Opened in 1984, the **ANA-Sheraton Hotel,** 1-3-1 Dojimahama, Kita-ku (tel. 06/347-1112), is a sleek white first-class hotel about a 15-minute walk south of Osaka Station. Its architectural philosophy is based on the concepts of running water, greenery, and ample sunlight, evident as soon as you enter the impressive lobby. An inner courtyard stretches up to a skylight on the sixth floor, from which water trickles along extended chains to a pond below. Facilities include a number of fine restaurants, a swimming pool and sauna (which cost ¥3,000, or $24, to use), and an excellent guest relations desk where the staff will help in everything from directions to recommending nightspots in the vicinity. During July and August you can down beer on the hotel's outdoor patio. Its guest rooms are large and comfortably designed, and feature bilingual TV with an English channel of sightseeing information and news, plug-in hot-water thermos, English-language newspapers delivered both morning and afternoon, and excellent room service. Single rooms range from ¥14,000 ($112) to ¥17,600 ($141), twins run ¥24,000 ($192) to ¥30,000 ($240), and doubles cost ¥24,000 ($192) to ¥28,000 ($224).

The **Miyako Hotel Osaka,** 6-1-55 Uehommachi, Tennoji-ku (tel. 06/773-1111), opened in autumn 1985. Located close to Uehommachi Station of the Kintetsu Line, it was designed by the well-known Japanese architect Togo Murano, renowned for his ability to combine Japanese simplicity and tradition with modern efficiency. He recently died at the age of 91, so this Miyako Hotel was his last complete architectural achievement. It's a sister hotel to the famous Miyako Hotel in Kyoto, and the service is excellent. Facilities include a health club (charge begins at ¥4,000, or $32) with swimming pool, racquetball courts, sauna, and 13 restaurants serving everything from Japanese to Chinese to French cuisine. La Mer is an exclusive and expensive seafood restaurant specializing in seafood, while the Ciel Bleu up on the 21st floor offers French dishes and a view. In the basement are inexpensive restaurants, including those specializing in buckwheat noodles, tofu, and okonomiyaki, a local dish described later in the dining section. Guest rooms come with all the comforts you'd expect from a first-class hotel, including bilingual TV with CNN cable broadcasts from the United States, packets of soup and coffee along with tea, a stocked refrigerator, delivery of English-language newspapers twice a day, and semidouble beds in most rooms. Beds are decked with quilts instead of the usual heavy blankets. Rates start at ¥13,000 ($104) for a single, ¥22,000 ($176) for a double, and ¥23,000 ($184) for a twin.

Another new hotel—and Osaka seems to have a lot of them—is the **Hotel New Otani Osaka,** 1-4 Shiromi, Chuo-ku (tel. 06/941-1111), located close to Osaka Castle. Everything about this hotel is visually pleasing, right down to the elevators. The marbled lobby boasts a four-story atrium with a clever use of mirrors and skylights to give it an added airiness. Its fitness club facilities include indoor and outdoor swimming pools and four tennis courts, and although as with most hotel sports clubs a fee is charged (a base rate of ¥3,500, or $28), hotel guests can use the outdoor pool free during weekdays in the summer. Rooms are pleasant and comfortable and are equipped with semidouble beds, bilingual TV with CNN newscasts from the United States, radio, minibar, hairdryer, and windows that open. Rates are based on room size and whether you get a view of the castle. Singles range from ¥15,500 ($124) to ¥18,500 ($148), twins from ¥26,000 ($208) to ¥40,000 ($320), and doubles from ¥24,000 ($192) to ¥32,000 ($256). Among its many restaurants is the ever popular Trader Vic's.

Not to be outdone is the **Osaka Hilton International,** 1-8-8 Umeda, Kita-ku (tel. 06/347-7111), which opened in 1986. Conveniently located just a five-minute walk from the Central Exit of Osaka Station in the heart of the city, it has 553 double, twin, and suite rooms, with rates based on height and therefore view. Single occupancy ranges from ¥20,000 ($160) to ¥28,000 ($224), while double occupancy ranges from ¥25,000 ($200) to ¥34,000 ($272). Decorated in subtle blends of Japanese and Western styles, rooms feature soothing color combinations of pale peach and celadon green, shoji screens, bilingual TV with CNN newscasts and remote control, radio, minibar, and large full-length mirrors. Facilities include a fitness center (charge: ¥3,000) with pool, tennis court, sauna, and gym; a multitude of restaurants; and an adjoining shopping arcade.

Just a few years older than the newer hotels, the elegant **Hotel Nikko Osaka,** 1-3-3 Nishi-Shinsaibashi, Chuo-ku (tel. 06/244-1111), is owned by Japan Airlines. Located on fashionable Midosuji Boulevard above Shinsaibashi subway station, it has a striking architectural design with slanted walls. It's only a seven-minute walk from the hotel to Dotonbori Street, the heart of Osaka's nightlife district with its many restaurants. The hotel's service is excellent and there's a guest relations desk to answer any questions you may have regarding Osaka or the hotel. About 30% to 40% of hotel guests are foreigners, mainly Americans. Rooms are equipped with bilingual TV featuring CNN, with movies shown on weekends. On the 27th floor are rooms designed by Hanae Mori, one of Japan's best-known fashion designers. Rates range from ¥14,000 ($112) to ¥20,000 ($160) for a single, ¥24,500 ($196) to ¥30,000 ($240) for a twin, and ¥24,000 ($192) to ¥29,000 ($232) for a double.

One of Osaka's most established hostelries is the **Royal Hotel,** 5-3-68 Nakanoshima, Kita-ku (tel. 448-1121). First opened more than 40 years ago but now completely remodeled, it's located on an island called Nakanoshima in the middle of a river in the heart of Osaka. One of the largest hotels in Osaka, it boasts 1,200 guest rooms, almost two dozen restaurants, a beautifully designed swimming pool (charge: ¥2,000, or $18), and a shopping arcade with more than 40 boutiques. The lobby has views of a waterfall surrounded by trees. Its rooms sport large windows, bilingual TV with CNN, and English-language newspapers delivered twice daily. Singles start at ¥11,000 ($88), twins from ¥23,000 ($184) and doubles from ¥22,000 ($176). The nearest subway stop is Yodoyabashi Station on the Midosuji Line; free shuttle buses make runs between this station and the hotel every 15 minutes.

The **Plaza,** 2-2-49 Oyodo-Minami, Kita-ku (tel. 06/453-1111), was one of Osaka's first deluxe hotels (it opened in 1970). It's about a seven-minute taxi ride west of Osaka Station. Facilities here include an outdoor swimming pool (free of charge), six restaurants, one lounge, and two bars. Its Rendezvous French restaurant on the 23rd floor is one of Osaka's best. Foreigners constitute about 30% of the hotel's guests. Rooms are large and come with the usual amenities of hot-water pot, bilingual TV with CNN, minibar, and radio. Rates begin at ¥12,000 ($96) for a single, ¥23,000 ($184) for a twin, and ¥25,000 ($200) for a double.

The Medium-Priced Range

Since it's right beside Osaka Station, the **Osaka Terminal Hotel,** 3-1-1 Umeda, Kita-ku (tel. 06/344-1234), is very convenient for a one-night stay in the city. But because its lobby is on the ground floor with doors that open right into the train station, it's also very hectic and busy. Thankfully, its 665 guest rooms are located above all this confusion up on the 21st to 26th floors. Opened in 1983, this tourist hotel caters to a 10% foreign clientele and has nine restaurants and bars, many of them located on the 19th floor with grand views of the city. Rooms are cheerful and have double-pane windows, a pot for heating water, radio, alarm clock, refrigerator, and TV with CNN and pay video. The cheapest singles and twins face an inner courtyard—they're quieter, but you're missing a great view of the city. Rates range from ¥10,000 ($80) to ¥13,000 ($104) for a single, ¥17,500 ($140) to ¥26,000 ($208) for a double, and ¥20,000 ($160) to ¥28,000 ($224) for a twin.

Hotel New Hankyu, 1-1-35 Shibata, Kita-ku (tel. 06/372-5101), opened in 1964 but is so well maintained it doesn't seem nearly that old. As part of the conglomerate that owns Hankyu Railways, Hankyu department stores, restaurants, and even Takarazuka Family Land, this hotel is located just north of Hankyu Station next to Osaka Station. There are almost 1,000 rooms here, all with TV with CNN and pay video, clock, music, and double-pane windows. Vending machines dispense soda and beer. The decor is simple and resembles that found in business hotels. Altogether there are 23 bars and restaurants in the hotel and in the neighboring Hankyu complex. You'll pay ¥9,300 ($74) to ¥16,500 ($132) for a single, ¥16,000 ($128) to ¥38,000 ($304) for a twin, and ¥17,500 ($140) to ¥25,000 ($200) for a double. Triples are available for ¥25,000 ($200) and Japanese-style tatami rooms start at ¥22,000 ($176) for double occupancy.

Part of a nationwide hotel chain, the **Osaka Tokyu Inn,** 2 Doyama-cho, Kita-ku (tel. 06/315-0109), is your typical standard business hotel. Its one restaurant serves Western food, and its 402 rooms are quiet and clean, featuring clock, desk, TV with pay video, fridge, and small bathroom. Vending machines are on the seventh floor. Singles start at ¥8,500 ($68), and twins and doubles at ¥14,800 ($118), tax and service included. The Tokyu is about a ten-minute walk east of Osaka Station, but it's a bit confusing to find because the most direct way to get there is via an underground passageway lined with shops. Follow the signs that say "Ogimachi" until they bring you above ground at the W31 exit—you should be able to spot the Tokyu from there.

Also about a ten-minute walk east of Osaka Station is the much older and cheaper **Hotel Kitahachi,** 7-16 Doyama-cho, Kita-ku (tel. 06/361-2078). Opening as a ryokan back in 1946 and then converting to a Western-style hotel in the early 1980s, this small, personable hotel has only 38 rooms, 19 of them singles with semidouble-size beds. Its singles are often fully occupied, but twins are usually available. Rooms are larger than those of most business hotels and are more tastefully furnished as well. A plus is that all rooms have double doors to block out corridor noise and are equipped with coin-operated TV, radio, clock, phone, fridge, and hot-water pot. The only disadvantage is that at last check, no one here spoke any English—try to have a Japanese make your reservation. Rates start at ¥6,000 ($48) for a single, ¥11,000 ($88) for a double, and ¥12,000 ($96) for a twin.

The **Holiday Inn Nankai,** 2-5-15 Shinsaibashisuji Chuo-ku (tel. 06/213-8281), has a very convenient location close to Dotonbori and Osaka's nightlife district right on Midosuji Dori Avenue. The lobby is on the fifth floor, and the rooftop pool, open free to hotel guests during the summer months, is a plus. There's also an outdoor beer garden on the third floor, open daily from 5 to 9 p.m. from the end of May to the end of August. Four restaurants serve French, Chinese, American, and Japanese cuisine. As with all Holiday Inns, all beds are doubles, even those in single rooms, and the rooms are large. Rates for one person start at ¥12,500 ($100), for two persons, at ¥16,000 ($128).

Hotel Osaka Grand, 2-3-18 Nakanoshima, Kita-ku (tel. 06/202-1212), is a fine medium-priced hotel located on the island of Nakanoshima in a river in the heart of Osaka. Dating from 1960, it's also one of Osaka's older hotels and has aged gracefully. The lobby is small and cozy and evokes an atmosphere of decades past with its high ceiling and old decor. Its 348 rooms start at ¥10,200 ($82) for a single, ¥17,600 ($141) for a twin, and ¥18,000 ($144) for a double. As proof of its age, the bathrooms are covered with tile instead of the usual plastic, and all rooms come with radio, clock, TV with CNN and with bedside control buttons, and a pot for hot water. I prefer the rooms that face the river—although there's little traffic on the river and there's nothing to see, it at least affords a bit of spaciousness.

The **Tennoji Miyako Hotel,** 10-48 Hidein-cho, Tennoji-ku (tel. 06/779-1501), is a medium-priced tourist hotel belonging to the Miyako hotel chain. It's right over the train tracks of Tennoji Station, which you can reach via the Midosuji subway line from either Shin-Osaka or Osaka Station. The front desk is on the fifth floor. A small hotel with only 150 rooms, it first opened in 1960 but has been renovated frequently. Even the single rooms here are spacious. Bathrooms are tiled and large, and wide windows let in a lot of sunshine. Decor is simple but tasteful, and rooms are equipped with a pot for hot water, TV, clock, and double-pane windows. The hotel's two restaurants serve Western food. Rooms without private bathroom are ¥6,000 ($48) for a single and ¥12,000 ($96) for a twin. Rooms with private bathroom start at ¥9,300 ($74) for a single; ¥16,500 ($132) for a twin, double, or Japanese-style room.

Hotel California, 1-9-30 Nishishinsaibashi, Chuo-ku (tel. 06/243-0333), tries to evoke images of sunny California through its use of whites and greens, plants, and brass railings. Rooms are cheerfully decorated in soft pastels with rattan furniture and come with TV with pay video, radio, clock, hot-water pot, and refrigerator. Rates start at ¥6,600 ($53) for a single, ¥10,000 ($80) for a double, and ¥12,000 ($96) for a twin. The California is conveniently located in Chuo-ku, not far from the Nikko Hotel and Shinsaibashi subway station.

There are a few hotels located close to Shin-Osaka Station, but because the area is unexciting and industrial I suggest staying at one of the hotels listed above. If you find it more convenient to stay close to the Shinkansen station, however, try the **New Osaka Hotel,** 5-14-10 Nishi-Nakajima, Yodogawa-ku (tel. 06/305-2345). It's about a two-minute walk from the central exit of the station and caters almost exclusively to Japanese businessmen (most of its 304 rooms are singles). Rooms are simply decorated and come with refrigerator and TV with pay video. Because the building is sandwiched in between two other buildings, all but 76 of the rooms face a wall. If you want to have more of a view, be sure to ask. Singles range from ¥6,000 ($48) to ¥7,500 ($60), twins are ¥12,000 ($96), doubles are ¥11,500 ($92), and Japanese-style rooms are ¥13,000 ($104). A restaurant on the 13th floor serves Chinese and Western food.

One of the newest business hotels to open near Shin-Osaka Station is the **Shin-Osaka Station Hotel,** 1-16-6 Higashi-Nakajima, Higashiyodogawa-ku (tel. 06/325-0011). To reach it, take the central exit from the station and continue over the pedestrian bridge that crosses the railroad tracks. Don't confuse this hotel with the much older, smaller one just in front of it with the exact same name (the older hotel is identified only in Japanese, while the newer one has an English sign). Rooms are small but adequate, coming with TV with pay video, fridge, clock, and hot-water pot. Rates start at ¥5,000 ($40) for a single, ¥10,000 ($80) for a double, and ¥11,000 ($88) for a twin. Note, however, that no credit cards are accepted here.

If you find yourself with a stopover at Osaka International Airport, try the **Osaka Airport Hotel,** located right in the airport terminal building (tel. 06/855-4621). There are 105 rooms here, and they come with TV, fridge, and a pot for hot water. Singles start at ¥10,000 ($80), twins at ¥16,500 ($132), and doubles at ¥19,000 ($152).

The Budget Category

Hotel Hokke Club ⑯, 12-19 Togano-cho, Kita-ku (tel. 06/313-3171), first opened about 37 years ago and is one of Osaka's oldest business hotels. Located about a ten-minute walk east of Osaka Station, it only has rooms without private bathrooms, but there are large, separate public baths for men and women. Rooms are small but clean and adequate. If you're taking a single, request a corner room, since the other singles face an inner courtyard and are dark. Rooms are available in either Western or Japanese style, and go for ¥6,500 ($52) for a single and ¥10,500 ($84) for a twin. Prices include tax, service, and buffet-style breakfast. If you elect to take your breakfast elsewhere, rates are ¥1,000 ($8) cheaper.

Ebisu-so, 1-7-33 Nipponbashi-Nishi, Naniwa-ku (tel. 06/643-4861), is a Japanese-style inn located a 10-minute walk from the Kintetsu Nipponbashi Station, a 15-minute walk from Namba Station, or a 5-minute walk from the Ebisu-cho subway station. A member of the Japanese Inn Group, it's more cluttered and run-down than most (it's been an inn for 35 years and no one speaks English). There are 13 tatami rooms, all without private bathroom, but of course there's a public bath. This inn reminds me of a small apartment house where young single Japanese often live—a narrow corridor flanked on both sides with 4½- and 6-tatami rooms. I have friends who say they like living in a 4½-tatami room because they can reach everything without having to move. At any rate, rates here are certainly cheap: singles go for ¥3,300 ($26); twins, for ¥6,600 ($53); and triples, for ¥9,900 ($79). Rooms come with coin-operated TV, fan, and heater.

Two subway stops north of Shin-Osaka Station on the Midosuji Line is Esaka Station, where you'll find two business hotels under the same ownership. The oldest of these is **1 Sunny Stone Hotel,** 10-3 Hiroshiba-cho, Suita City (tel. 06/385-1281), just a couple of minutes' walk from the station. About 20 years old, it shows its age and offers very simple rooms. The cheapest rooms are those with toilet but no bath, going for ¥3,500 ($28) for a single and ¥6,500 ($52) for a twin. Note, however, that all of these face another building, so that if you're claustrophobic, you may want to spring for one of the Western- or Japanese-style rooms with bath and toilet. These cost ¥4,500 ($36) for one person, ¥7,900 ($63) for two, and ¥11,200 ($90) for three.

Catercorner from hotel 1 is **2 Sunny Stone Hotel,** 1-22-4 Esaka-cho, Suita City (tel. 06/386-3200), which opened in the mid-1980s. Rooms here are slightly larger and all have private bathrooms; they cost ¥5,500 ($44) for a single and ¥8,800 ($70) for a twin. Six of the twins feature bunk beds that have curtains for more privacy, reminding me of train sleeping compartments. At any rate, be warned that neighboring buildings have been built only a few feet from the hotel itself, obstructing any and all views.

If you want to stay near Shin-Osaka Station, **Shin-Osaka Sen-i City** ⑯, 2-2-17 Nishi-Miyahara, Yodogawa-ku (tel. 06/394-3331), is a very simple business hotel with 70 rooms. It's about an eight-minute walk north of the station, and is easy to spot with its green-and-blue sign and clock on the top of the building. The lobby is on the sixth floor and guest rooms are on the sixth and seventh floors. The rooms are a few decades away from being modern, but they're clean, good for the price, and fairly large as far as business hotels go. They come with refrigerator and coin-operated TV with pay video. All the singles and most twins are bathless, and go for ¥4,500 ($36) and ¥7,700 ($62), respectively, but there are public baths. Eight twins with Western-style toilet and Japanese-style bathtub are ¥8,300 ($66).

A business hotel about a five-minute walk from Osaka International Airport is **Kurebe,** 1-9-6 Kuko, Ikeda-shi (tel. 06/843-7201). A lot of business people stay here if they have an early-morning flight. Simple, with just the basics of a bed, bathroom, and TV, singles here range from ¥6,000 ($48) to ¥7,700 ($62). Twins run ¥11,000 ($88) to ¥14,300 ($114), and doubles are ¥14,300 ($114).

Youth Hostels: The **Osaka-Shiritsu Nagai Youth Hostel** ⑯, 450 Higashinagai-cho, Higashi-sumiyoshi (tel. 06/699-5632), is located on municipal sports grounds. You don't have to have a membership card to stay here, and the overnight price of ¥1,900 ($15.20) is the same for both members and nonmembers. Sheets rent for ¥200 ($1.60), while air conditioning costs are an additional ¥250 ($2). Breakfast costs ¥350 ($2.80) and dinner is ¥600 ($4.80). To reach the youth hostel, take the Midosuji subway line to Nagai Station (about a 20-minute ride from Umeda Station, 30 minutes from Shin-Osaka); from there it's a 15-minute walk.

Hattori Ryokuchi Youth Hostel ⑯, 1-3 Hattori-ryokuchi, Toyonaka-shi (tel. 06/862-0600), is a 45-minute subway ride on the Midosuji Line from Umeda Station. Get off at Ryokuchi-koen Station and from there it's a ten-minute walk. Both members and nonmembers are charged ¥1,500 ($12) for an overnight stay. Breakfast costs ¥300 ($3.20) and dinner is ¥700 ($5.60). Sheets are an extra ¥200 ($1.60). This youth hostel is located in the Hattori-Ryokuchi Park, which has a swimming pool and an open-air museum of old Japanese farmhouses.

WHERE TO DINE

There's a saying among Japanese that whereas a Kyotoite will spend his last yen on a fine kimono, an Osakan will spend it on food. You don't have to spend a lot of money to enjoy good food in Osaka, however. Most of Osaka's restaurants are found either in Kita-ku near Osaka Station or in Minami-ku or near Dotonbori Street. The best Western-style restaurants are in Osaka's first-class hotels. Be sure to check the many restaurant/bars described in the nightlife section above.

In Kita-ku

Japanese Style: Part of the Suehiro chain of steak restaurants in Japan, **Suehiro Asahi** ⑯, 1-5-2 Sonezaki-shinchi (tel. 341-1610), is conveniently located about a seven-minute walk south of Osaka Station. Serving Matsuzaka beef as well as beef imported from the United States, it offers shabu-shabu and sukiyaki specials ranging from ¥6,500 ($52) to ¥11,000 ($88). Prices for steak range widely depending on the weight and cut. Sirloin from the U.S. starts at ¥2,700 ($22), while tenderloin steak starts at ¥4,000 ($32). If you come for lunch you can also order such dishes as fried shrimp, beef stew, beef or pork cutlet, a hamburger, or fried fish, priced from ¥600 ($4.80) to ¥1,800 ($14). Hours here are 11 a.m. to 10 p.m. except on Saturday, when it closes at 9 p.m., and on Sunday when it doesn't open until noon.

Serving everything from sushi to tempura to shabu-shabu, **Unkai,** on the sixth floor of the ANA-Sheraton Hotel, 1-3-1 Dojimahama (tel. 347-1112), is a good place to go if you can't decide on just one type of cuisine. Open daily from 11:30 a.m. to 2:30 p.m. and 5:30 to 10 p.m., this simple and pleasant restaurant has both a sushi and a tempura counter where the food is prepared in front of the guests, as well as individual tables and chairs. Tempura set meals range from ¥8,000 ($64) to ¥9,900 ($79), while the sushi runs from ¥800 ($6.40) to ¥2,000 ($16) for two pieces. A sushi teishoku set meal is served at lunch only for ¥3,700 ($29.60); obento lunch boxes are ¥2,200 ($17.60). Shabu-shabu is available for ¥7,700 ($61.60), and kaiseki dinners range from ¥8,800 ($70.40) to ¥16,500 ($132).

A specialty of Osaka is *okonomiyaki*, which literally means "as you like it." Its origins date from about 1700, when a type of thin flour cake cooked on a hot plate was served during Buddhist ceremonies. The cake was filled with a bean paste called *miso*. It wasn't until this century that it became popular among the masses, primarily during food shortages. At first it was a simple dish consisting only of flour, water, and a sauce, but gradually other ingredients such as pork, egg, and vegetables were added.

Osaka is literally riddled with okonomiyaki restaurants offering very inexpensive dining. One of the best-known establishments in **Botejyu,** a chain store with one shop located in the second basement of the Hankyu Sanbangai Building, next to Osaka Station (tel. 374-2254), open from 10 a.m. to 10 p.m. (except the third Wednesday of the month). Most of its dishes range from ¥650 ($5.20) to ¥1,200 ($9.60). Its window display shows okonomiyaki filled with pork and egg, squid, shrimp, noodles, and pork, and many other ingredients in various combinations. I tried the *omu soba*, a type of omelet filled with cabbage, wheat noodles, and pork and smothered in ketchup and mayonnaise. Cooking is done on a hot griddle right in front of you, and dishes are served on sheets of aluminum foil.

Probably a bit easier to find is **Okonomiyaki Madonna,** located in the second basement of the Hilton Plaza next to the Hilton Hotel, 1-8-8 Umeda (tel. 347-7371). Following the recent trend of modern and with-it okonomiyaki restaurants, Madonna is open daily from 11 a.m. to 11 p.m. Ingredients for its okonomiyaki change with the seasons but may include pork, beef, squid, octopus, shrimp, potato, mushroom, or oyster. Okonomiyaki with one ingredient is ¥1,000 ($8), with two it's ¥1,250 ($10), and with three it's ¥1,500 ($12). Fried noodles are also available. Madonna is located across from Victoria Station, described later in this chapter.

If you want inexpensive dining with a view, there are many restaurants on the top four floors of the **Hankyu Grand Building** (also called 32 Bangai) near Osaka Station. On the 28th floor, for example, there are Japanese restaurants serving everything from shabu-shabu to tonkatsu (pork cutlet) to noodles to tempura and sashimi. Prices are generally low, with most meals costing about ¥1,000 ($8) to ¥2,000 ($16). All the restaurants have plastic-food displays, so ordering is no problem. Hours for most of the restaurants on the 28th floor are 11 a.m. to 8:45 p.m., but some restaurants on other floors remain open until 11 p.m. On the 29th and 31st floors you'll find mainly Western-food restaurants.

Western Style: The ANA-Sheraton Hotel's **Rose Room,** 1-3-1 Dojimahama (tel. 347-1112), is an elegant French restaurant serving nouvelle cuisine and is popular with local Osakans. Its chef, Tomoyoshi Yokota, studied French cooking in France for six years and worked as a chef at the well-known Le Rendezvous in the Osaka Plaza Hotel before joining the Sheraton as grand chef in 1984. Small, with seating for only 59 diners, the restaurant features a huge bouquet of roses as its focal point and makes dining intimate with low lighting and candles. You might want to start your meal with one of the hotel's specially made cocktails. Rose d'Or uses a mixture of three different kinds of wines, while Symphonie en Rose is made from Campari and white wine.

For dinner you might want to start out with Norwegian smoked salmon with capers, followed by chilled lobster soup with sour cream. The seafood selection includes turbot with sea urchin, fresh seasonal fish, and lobster au gratin with spinach. Entrées include hashed duck and sweetbread with mashed potatoes, roasted rack of lamb, pigeon, and steak. Expect to spend about ¥15,000 ($120) and up per person for dinner. There are also set dinners ranging from ¥10,000 ($80) to ¥17,600 ($140.80). Set lunches start at ¥5,500 ($44). The Rose Room is open daily from 11:30 a.m. to 2:30 p.m. and 5:30 to 10 p.m.

Another popular and well-known French restaurant in Osaka is **Le Rendezvous,** on the 23rd floor of the Plaza Hotel, 2-2-49 Oyodo-Minami, Kita-ku (tel. 453-1111). Advising on its creations are internationally known chefs Paul Bocuse and Louis Outhier. Outhier is the owner and chef of L'Oasis on the Côte d'Azur, which has a three-star rating from Michelin. Le Rendezvous is the only Asian member of Traditions et Qualité, a prestigious gastronomical association of French restaurants. With windows overlooking Osaka, this restaurant serves such à la carte selections as Kobe sirloin and tenderloin steaks, duck, sole stuffed with artichoke and basil, and young rabbit leg, with meals running as much as ¥20,000 ($160) per person and more. Le Rendezvous is open daily only for dinner from 5:30 to 10:30 p.m.

One of the most popular new forms of cuisine to hit the Japanese culinary scene in recent years is French food presented in the Japanese kaiseki manner. That is, the food is French, but each course is served separately using Japanese plates and dishes, and guests use chopsticks instead of forks. Each plate is chosen to enhance the food that's on it, according to color, texture, and the seasons. One of these restaurants serving French kaiseki cuisine is **Kaen** ⑯, on the third floor of the Steak Ron Building, 1-10-2 Sonnezaki-shinchi (tel. 344-2929). Located about a ten-minute walk south of Osaka Station not far from the Hilton, this refined, modern restaurant combines elegance with tradition, and since only full courses are offered, ordering is easy. The menu is changed twice a month, with lunch courses ranging from ¥2,700 ($21.60) to ¥5,500 ($44) and dinner courses ranging from ¥10,000 ($80) to ¥16,500 ($132). It's essential to make reservations in advance. Closed on Sunday, it's open the rest of the week from 11:30 a.m. to 2 p.m. and 5 to 9 p.m.

If you're looking for more casual and cheaper dining, **Victoria Station**, in the second basement of the Hilton Plaza next to the Hilton Hotel (tel. 347-7470), serves a mean hamburger with a trip to the salad bar for ¥1,000 ($8) daily until 5 p.m. Other lunch selections include teriyaki beef steak beginning at ¥880 ($7.04), sirloin steak beginning at ¥1,700 ($13.60), and seafood quiche, beef, and chicken, all for ¥1,200 ($9.60) with salad bar. The dinner menu also includes steaks, roast prime rib, and chicken, most under ¥2,200 ($17.60). Set dinner courses, which include a trip to the salad bar, soup, and more, start at ¥3,500 ($28). Victoria Station is open daily from 11 a.m. to 11 p.m.

There are a couple of medium-priced hotels that have inexpensive lunch buffets at very good prices. Up on the 19th floor of the Osaka Terminal Hotel, 3-1-1 Umeda, above Osaka Station (tel. 344-1234), is a daily smörgåsbord at the **Pub Restaurant Ab**, from 11 a.m. to 2 p.m. with a wide selection of dishes. Very popular with Osaka's residents, it costs only ¥1,000 ($8). You can dine here with a great view of the city, but get here by 11:30 a.m. if you don't want to wait for a table.

The Osaka Grand Hotel, 2-3-18 Nakanoshima (tel. 202-1212), offers both lunch and dinner buffets in its **Grand Sky** restaurant on the 14th floor. The lunch smörgåsbord, served from 11:30 a.m. to 2 p.m. every day except Sunday and national holidays, costs ¥2,200 ($17.60). A dinner buffet is served daily from 5 to 9:30 p.m., costing ¥5,400 ($40).

Chuo-ku

Dotonbori Street, a narrow pedestrian lane flanking the south bank of the Dotonbori River, is lined with restaurants and drinking establishments. One of the best-known restaurants on Dotonbori is **Kuidaore** ⑰, 1-8-25 Dotonbori (tel. 211-5300). It's famous for its clown model outside the front door, which has been beating a drum and wiggling its eyebrows ever since the place first opened in 1949. There's an extensive plastic-food display case by the front door, which is one good indication of the wide variety of food this restaurant serves, including tempura, sashimi, charcoal-broiled beef, shabu-shabu, udon, eel, sukiyaki, yakitori, noodles, and even Western food. Altogether there are eight floors of dining, with prices increasing the higher up you go. On the ground floor is a family-style, modern dining area, where you can order such things as spaghetti, sushi, tempura, and noodles, with most prices around ¥1,000 ($8). On the second floor is a *nomiya*, or pub, where you can order a beer, yakitori, and snacks. The third floor is for nabe (one-pot stews), while the fourth floor is where you'll go for a sukiyaki experience. Prices for sukiyaki start at ¥3,800 ($30.40). Hours are from 10:30 a.m. to 10:30 p.m. daily, except for the second-floor pub, which is open from 4 p.m. to midnight.

Also on Dotonbori is another well-known restaurant, **Kani Doraku** ⑰, 1-6-18 Dotonbori (tel. 211-8975). Open from 11 a.m. to 11 p.m. daily, its specialty is *kani* (crab). You can't miss this place, because it has a huge model crab on its façade which moves its legs and claws. The restaurant is part of a chain originating in Osaka a couple of decades ago, with more than 55 stores now spread throughout Japan. Its dishes range from crab-suki and crab-chiri (a kind of crab sukiyaki) for ¥4,400

($35.20) to fried crab dishes starting at ¥2,700 ($21.60). Other offerings include set meals of boiled hairy crab with vinegar starting at ¥4,000 ($32), crab tempura starting at ¥1,300 ($10.40) and various combinations of crab sushi.

Under the same ownership as Kani Doraku, but specializing in shrimp, **Ebi Doraku** (172) is also on Dotonbori Street at 1-6-2 Dotonbori (tel. 211-1633). *Ebi* is the Japanese word for shrimp. Opened about 20 years ago, this restaurant has a big wriggling shrimp on its façade and a dining room overlooking the canal and its fountains. There's no English menu here, so make your selections from the plastic-food display case. It's open daily from 11 a.m. to 11 p.m. Most dishes range from ¥1,500 ($12) to ¥4,500 ($36) and include *ebi-shi* (a shrimp sukiyaki), ebi tempura, fried shrimp, and shrimp sushi. If you feel like overdosing on shrimp, the kaiseki ebi teishoku for ¥3,800 ($30.40) features nine different kinds of shrimp dishes.

Located on Dotonbori Street almost directly in front of Kuidaore and beside Kani Doraku, the Dohton Biru Building, 1-6-15 Dotonbori, has several different kinds of restaurants. On the second floor is another **Botejyu** (tel. 211-3641), selling okonomiyaki from 12 a.m. to 10:30 p.m. daily. Also on the second floor is a **Shakey's** (tel. 213-7624) pizza parlor with its all-you-can-eat lunch special from 11 a.m. to 3 p.m. Monday through Saturday for ¥600 ($4.80). On the third floor is **Moti** (tel. 211-6878), an Indian restaurant open daily from 11:30 a.m. to 10 p.m., with various meat and vegetable curries from ¥1,100 ($8.80) and tandoori from ¥1,400 ($11.20).

Near the Castle

If you find yourself in the vicinity of the castle come lunchtime, a good choice is **Trader Vic's,** open daily from noon to midnight in the New Otani Hotel, 1-4 Shiromi (tel. 941-1111). It serves a daily luncheon special until 3 p.m. for ¥2,000 ($16), as well as a champagne brunch on Sunday for ¥4,400 ($35.20). Dinners offer a wider selection, including salads, a good selection of vegetable side dishes, curries, steaks, seafood, and Chinese dishes.

5. Kobe

Blessed with the calm waters of the Seto Inland Sea, Kobe has served Japan as an important port town for centuries. Even today its port is the heart of the city, its raison d'être, and the people of Kobe seem to be proud and content with their city, satisfied with where they are. As one of the first ports to begin accepting foreign traders in 1868 following Japan's 200-some years of isolation, Kobe is quite cosmopolitan, with 45,000 foreigners living in this vibrant city of 1.5 million inhabitants. There are a number of fine restaurants serving Western, Japanese, Chinese, Korean, and Indian food, not to mention the many steakhouses offering the famous Kobe beef. Equally famous is Kobe's wonderful nightlife, crammed into a small, navigable, and rather intimate quarter of neon lights, cozy bars, brawling pubs, and sophisticated nightclubs. As one resident of Kobe told me, "We don't have a lot of tourist sights in Kobe, so we make up for it in nightlife."

ORIENTATION

Squeezed in between hills rising in the north and the shores of the sea in the south, Kobe stretches long and thin along the coastline. The city is about 18 miles from east to west—but in many places less than two miles wide—and is made up of many wards (*ku*), such as Nada-ku, Chuo-ku, and Hyogo-ku. The heart of the city lies around the Sannomiya and Motomachi stations in the Chuo-ku ward. It's here that you'll find the city's nightlife, its port, its restaurants and shopping district, and most of its hotels. Many of the major streets here have names with signs posted in English. Because the city is not very wide, you can walk to most points north and south of Sannomiya Station. South of Sannomiya Station are the Sannomiya Center Gai covered-arcade shopping street and a flower-lined road leading straight south, towards the port—called appropriately enough Flower Road. North of Sannomiya Station are bars and restaurants clustered around narrow streets like Higashimon Street and Kitano-Zaka. About a ten-minute walk west of Sannomiya Station is Motomachi Station, south of which lies Chinatown.

Only 3½ hours from Tokyo, 34 minutes from Kyoto, and 15 minutes from Osaka by Shinkansen bullet train, Kobe's Shinkansen station is called Shin-Kobe, which lies about a mile northwest of Sannomiya Station. Shin-Kobe is easily linked to Sannomiya Station via a three-minute subway ride (or a 20-minute walk). If you're arriving in Kobe from nearby Osaka, Himeji, or Okayama, however, it's easiest to take a local commuter train that stops directly at Sannomiya Station. Incidentally, there are several terminals in Sannomiya, including stations for JR, Hankyu, and Hanshin. There are also buses from Sannomiya bound for Osaka International Airport, leaving approximately every 20 minutes. The trip takes 40 minutes and costs ¥680 ($5.44).

There are **tourist information offices** in both Shin-Kobe (open from 10 a.m. to 6 p.m.) and Sannomiya stations (open from 9 a.m. to 6 p.m.), where you can pick up a map and ask for directions to your hotel. (The tourist office at Sannomiya Station is on the second floor of the Kobe Kotsu Center and is rather difficult to find; if you get lost, the telephone number is 392-0020.) Current information on Kobe's sights, festivals, and attractions appears in a monthly magazine called *Kansai Time Out*, which you can pick up at bookstores, restaurants, and tourist-oriented locations for ¥300 ($2.40).

If you're calling from outside Kobe, the **telephone area code** is 078. Kobe lies in Hyogo Prefecture.

THE SIGHTS

I find Kobe's port fascinating. Unlike many harbor cities where the port is located far away from the center of town, Kobe's port is right there, demanding attention and getting it. For a bird's-eye view of the whole operation, go to Naka Tottei Pier where you'll find **Port Tower**. Opened in 1963, it's designed to resemble a Japanese drum, a cylindrical shape with the middle squeezed together. Almost 600 feet tall, its glass-enclosed, five-story observatory can be reached by two elevators. It's open from 10 a.m. to 9 p.m. Right beside the Port Tower is the newly developed **Meriken Park,** along with the **Kobe Maritime Museum,** which has a roof shaped like a ship. Open every day except Monday from 10 a.m. to 5 p.m., the museum's exhibits show the history of Kobe's port, as well as ports and harbors around the world. Models of port activities spring to life with a push of a button, along with a spoken commentary in English. A combination ticket for both the Port Tower and the Maritime Museum is ¥700 ($5.60). If you buy the tickets separately, they're ¥500 ($4) each. The closest station is Motomachi Station.

Next to Port Tower are boats offering **cruises of the harbor.** Costing ¥1,000 ($8), the trip lasts 50 minutes and takes you to Kawasaki and Mitsubishi shipyards, the container yard, Port Terminal, and Port Island. Although the commentary is only in Japanese, it's well worth it. Departures are every hour on the hour from 10 a.m. to 4 p.m. on weekdays, and every 30 minutes on Sunday and holidays. For more information, call 391-8633.

Another interesting way to see the harbor is by taking the unmanned, computer-controlled **Portliner monorail** from Sannomiya Station out to **Port Island.** Port Island is an artificial island complete with amusement park, luxury hotel, high-rise condominiums, exhibition grounds, and convention halls. This is a great ride even if you don't get off the monorail. It takes about a half hour to make the whole loop around the island, passing bridges, ships, tankers, tugboats, barges, and stacked containers along the way. If you're up to an outing, I suggest you get off at Shimin Hiroba Station and go to the Portopia Hotel for a meal or cup of coffee. It's

quite an interesting hotel with a dramatic lobby. From there you can walk to the amusement park. The monorail costs ¥210 ($1.68) no matter how far you go, and announcements are in English.

If you want to learn more about the history of Kobe, visit the **Kobe City Museum,** located next to the Oriental Hotel about a 10-minute walk south of Sannomiya Station. Open from 10 a.m. to 5 p.m. every day except Monday, it displays the history and folklore of Kobe, including Japanese paintings and art objects of the 16th and 17th centuries showing decidedly European influences. Admission here is ¥200 ($1.60). Chinese bronzes, ceramics, and lacquerware are displayed at the **Hakutsuru Art Museum,** a 15-minute walk from Mikage Station on the Hankyu Line, while the **Hyogo Prefecture Ceramic Museum,** with a collection of Japanese ceramics, is just a 3-minute walk from Motomachi Station.

Another point of interest are some **wooden houses in Kitano-cho,** north of Sannomiya Station, where foreigners used to live after Kobe became an international port. Although it may not hold much interest for foreigners who have come to see Japan, Kitano-cho is very popular with the Japanese, particularly young girls, who flock here in droves. There are a number of houses (most unauthentic) that have opened in the past couple of years and are based on a particular national theme—there are, for example, the Holland House, the Persian House, the American House, and the Meiji-kan (German), where costumes are rented out for picture-taking sessions. Seeing a young Japanese girl decked out in a turn-of-the-century long dress, apron, and blonde wig may be reason enough for making the trip here. Entrance fees, however, are quite high, so it's best just to walk around the steep and narrow roads and take a quick spin through the Kazamidori-no-ie (Weathervane House), built in 1909 by a German trader and open to the public for free.

You might also want to travel to **Sakagura,** where you can visit the Sawanotsuru Collection Hall, once a sake cellar and now a museum displaying tools used in sake brewing during the Edo Period. This hall, open free to the public, is close to Oishi Station on the Hanshin Line. It's closed on Wednesday and open the rest of the week from 10 a.m. to 4 p.m.

Farther away, **Mount Rokkosan** is a resort high among the peaks, with hiking, golfing, eating, and relaxation the main forms of entertainment. Serving mainly as an escape for residents of Osaka and Kobe, it has little of interest to the short-term visitor but is worth a day's outing if you're here for an extended length of time. More convenient for a quick getaway are the hills directly behind Shin-Kobe Station. Hiking trails lace through an area of woods and streams. You can reach Nunobiki Falls (called *Nunobiki-no-taki* in Japanese) in less than an hour.

NIGHTLIFE

Kobe has a wide selection of English-style pubs, bars, expatriate hangouts, and nightclubs. All the establishments below are easily accessible to foreigners and are within walking distance of Sannomiya Station. Have fun!

Live Music

The **Casablanca Club,** 3-1-6 Kitano-cho on Yamamoto Dori Avenue (also called Ijinki Dori Avenue) (tel. 241-0200), is actually a membership club with a great dinner special available also to nonmembers for slightly more. As a nonmember you pay a ¥1,000 ($8) cover charge, but the dinner is only ¥2,200 ($17.60) and includes your choice of chicken, fish, veal, or beef, plus soup, salad, rice or pita bread, dessert, and coffee. The interior is an elegant cool white with a grand piano, palm trees, and pictures of Bogart and Bacall. There's nightly entertainment and dancing. Hours are 5 p.m. to midnight on weekdays, until 1 a.m. on weekends.

Much older and more established is **Sone,** 1-24-10 Nakayamate Dori on Kitano-zaka Street (tel. 221-2055), which has been a jazz hangout for more than 20 years. It has its own in-house jazz band, which plays mainly classics and well-known tunes to an appreciative Japanese audience. Open daily from 5:30 p.m. to 2 a.m.

(until midnight on Sundays), it offers beer for ¥750 ($6) and cocktails starting at ¥900 ($7.20), as well as snacks and sandwiches. Music charge is ¥200 ($1.60).

With more than 20 locations in Japan, **Kento's,** 3-10-18 Shimoyamate Dori (tel. 392-2181), has been a great hit among the Japanese, with live bands playing oldies but goodies from the 1950s and '60s. Located on Tor Road just north of where it intersects with Ikuta Shinmichi Street (near the Washington Hotel), it's open daily from 5 p.m. to 4 a.m. and charges a ¥1,300 ($10.40) music and table fee. Guests must buy at least one drink and one food item; beer starts at ¥650 ($5.20) and dishes of spaghetti, salads, seafood, desserts, and snacks average ¥900 ($7.20).

Pubs and Bars

King's Arms, 4-2-15 Isobedori (tel. 221-3774), is an English-style pub popular with Kobe's foreigners. Located south of Sannomiya Station on Flower Road not far from New Port Hotel, it started out in 1950 as an exclusive club for American and British military personnel. After it went public it became a favorite hangout for sailors and travelers passing through town, and has since mellowed into a cozy and well-established eating and drinking spot catering to all kinds of people, including the businessmen who stop here after work for a drink and a study of the daily newspaper. Its walls are decorated with beer coasters, bills of various currencies from around the world (including a U.S. $2 bill), and business cards of former patrons. Churchill's portrait gazes sternly down upon the bar, where beer starting at ¥450 ($3.60) and cocktails at ¥800 ($6.40) are dispensed to customers. While the first floor is for serious drinking, the second floor is for dining—on steaks, stewed beef, grilled chicken, roast beef sandwiches, and such. À la carte entrées are in the ¥1,650 ($13.20) to ¥2,500 ($20) range. Lunch specials begin at ¥1,000 ($8). Hours here are 11:30 a.m. to 11 p.m. (till 10 p.m. on Sunday and holidays), with the last order for food taken at 9 p.m.

An English-style pub popular with the Japanese, **Danny Boy,** located north of Sannomiya Station at the corner of Hunter-Zaka and Yamate Kansen roads at 2-10-1 Nakayamate Dori (tel. 231-6566), is a quiet place to escape the noisy crowds of Kobe's nightlife. There's an English menu here with such choices as pizza, teriyaki steak, and beef Stroganoff starting at ¥1,000 ($8). Beer starts at ¥600 ($4.80) and cocktails at ¥770 ($6.16). A respectable and somewhat plush establishment, it's open daily from 11:30 a.m. until 1 a.m.

Another pleasant retreat in Kobe's nightlife district is **The Studio,** on the sixth floor of the Palais de Kitanozaka, 4-7-11 Kano-cho (tel. 392-3908), on Kitano-zaka Street. The owners here are a Canadian-Japanese couple and a mother-in-law, and with its comfortable and cozy atmosphere and mellow music, this is a good place to relax and reminisce. The owners consider their bar an "extension of their homes." Highly recommended, the Studio is open daily from about 7 or 8 p.m. to whenever, which is sometimes as late as 1 a.m. Table charge is ¥550 ($4.40), beer starts at ¥650 ($5.20) and cocktails are ¥880 ($7.04) and up.

The Attic, 4-1-12 Kitano-cho (tel. 222-1586), is located in the Ijinkan Club Building on the—where else—top floor. It's crammed with all kinds of things often relegated to the attic and then promptly forgotten—tennis shoes, racquets, football helmets, license plates, an American flag, a cello, guitars, and assorted junk. It's owned by local celebrity Marty Kuehnert, a broadcaster of English-language sport shows. This is also a membership club, so as a nonmember a 20% service charge will be added to your bill, and on weekends there's an additional ¥500 ($4) cover charge. Munchies include hamburgers, barbecued chicken, and steak sandwiches, with most entrées about ¥1,000 ($8). Hours here are from 6 p.m. to 2 a.m. daily.

If you're a sports fanatic and you'd kill to see your favorite U.S. basketball, baseball, or football team in action, your best bet is to wander across the street (Ijinkan Dori) from The Attic, where catercorner you'll find **Attic Junior.** The latest games and play-offs are zoomed in by satellite, and the whole place is plastered with old

Sports Illustrated covers and Americana sports memorabilia. Hours are the same as at The Attic, but nonmembers pay only 10% more.

If your ambition is to stay up until dawn, head toward **Second Chance,** second floor of the Takashima Building at 2-1-12 Nakayamate Dori (tel. 391-3544), on Yamate Kansen Road. Open from 6 p.m. to 5 a.m., this all-nighter is a small, one-room bar favored by young night owls who don't mind the rather sparse furnishings. I must admit my own recollections of this place are a bit fuzzy, but I do remember music ranging from the Doors to the Talking Heads. This is where people congregate when the other bars have had the good sense to close down for the night. Cocktails start at ¥750 ($6).

Nightlife Miscellany

One of Kobe's most famous entertainment hot spots is **Copacabana,** 2-1-13 Nakayamate Dori (tel. 332-6694), in the basement of the Akai Fusha-no-Aru Building on Yamate Kansen Road north of Sannomiya Station (next to Second Chance). It features Brazilian and other Latin American music, but the real draw is probably the almost-nude female dancer who entertains the large number of sailors who come here. The place is small with a brightly colored interior. Open from 6 p.m. to 3 a.m. except for a day of rest on Sunday, it charges a ¥770 ($6.16) entrance fee and a ¥330 ($2.64) obligatory table snack. Beer starts at ¥770 ($6.16) and cocktails are ¥1,100 ($8.80).

A Japanese interpretation of a German beer hall can be found at the **Asahi Bierhaus,** located north of the Hankyu Sannomiya Station in the basement of the Eki Mae Building (tel. 332-0593). It's a good place for a hearty beer or two, with prices starting at ¥400 ($3.20) for a small mug. The hall is designed to resemble a German establishment with all kinds of corny statements in German—one translation reads "In heaven there's no beer, that's why I drink it here." German beer-garden music serenades in the background and the waitresses here even wear dirndls. If you're hungry, the menu includes roulade, sausage and sauerkraut, German fried potatoes, and pizza, with most items under ¥1,300 ($1.04). It's open daily from noon to 10 p.m., except from November through April, when it closes the third Monday of every month.

Located just north of Hankyu Sannomiya Station on a small side street is an inexpensive yakitori-ya called **Irohanihoheto,** 1-9-17 Kitanagasa Dori (tel. 321-1688). One of a chain of drinking establishments that cater primarily to young Japanese, it's identified outside its door with a sign that says "Antique Pub Restaurant," but there's nothing antique about it. Its prices are cheap, with most dishes of fish, sashimi, soup, yakitori, and much, much more available for less than ¥400 ($3.20). Beer starts at ¥400 ($3.20). Hours here are from 5:30 p.m. to 3:30 a.m. for those who like to party late.

If you've had your fill of alcohol, **Nishimura,** 1-26-3 Nakayamate Dori (tel. 221-1872), is a good place to go for a cup of coffee. Located on the corner of Hunter-Zaka and Yamate Kansen roads, it's open from 8:30 a.m. to 11 p.m., with coffee starting at ¥380 ($3.04) for such blends as Colombian, mocha, and Jamaican. In addition to this branch there are six other Nishimura coffeehouses in Kobe.

WHERE TO STAY

Most of Kobe's tourist and business hotels radiate north and south of Sannomiya Station within easy reach of Kobe's many restaurants and bars.

The Upper Bracket

Kobe's most famous and ritziest hotel is the **Kobe Portopia Hotel,** 6-10-2 Minatojima, Nakamachi, Chuo-ku (tel. 078/302-1111). Opened in 1981, this first-class hotel on Port Island is sleek, tall, and white, looking like some futuristic ship slicing through the landscape. With waterfalls, fountains, lots of brass, marble, plants, and 27 name-brand shops like Nina Ricci and Givenchy, this impressive hotel flaunts space and brightness. It offers visitors 15 restaurants, lounges, and coffeeshops, plus indoor and outdoor swimming pools, a gym, and tennis courts. The most dramatic way to arrive at the hotel is via monorail. Otherwise, it's about a 15-minute taxi ride from Shin-Kobe Station or a 10-minute ride from Sannomiya Station.

Its 778 rooms, whose large windows face either the sea or Kobe city (some even have balconies), are elegantly designed with all the amenities and plushness you'd expect from a first-rate hotel, including bilingual TVs with CNN satellite newscasts from the United States. Singles range from ¥9,300 ($74) to ¥13,000 ($104), twins run ¥19,800 ($158) to ¥26,500 ($212), and doubles cost ¥22,000 ($176) to ¥26,000 ($208). There are also Japanese-style rooms available for ¥35,000 ($280) for two persons.

"Grand," "stunning," and "numbing" are words that come to mind in trying to describe the **Shinkobe Oriental Hotel,** 1-chome Kitano-cho, Chuo-ku (tel. 078/291-1121), one of Kobe's newest deluxe hotels. Soaring like a steeple on a hill above the city right next to Shin-Kobe Station, this hotel is huge, with 600 well-appointed rooms, 10 restaurants and bars—and a whole "city" underneath with almost 200 additional shops and restaurants. Indeed, the scope of its facilities is staggering, with so much to do that it would be easy never to leave the hotel. You can swim in the indoor pool, sweat it out in the gym or sauna (which costs, however, a pretty stiff ¥5,000, or $40), shop until 10 p.m., and then drink until 4 a.m. This hotel is so popular that it has been almost solidly booked every Saturday night since it opened in 1988. And since it's located right next to the Shinkansen station, you can be in Osaka in 15 minutes or Kyoto in 34.

As for the hotel itself, it is decorated with finesse in art deco style, with what must have cost a fortune in furnishings and lighting. Each of the hotel's own restaurants, for example, is decorated to complement the food served, whether French, Chinese, or Japanese. The hotel proper starts on the fourth floor, with rooms offering great views of the city. Equipped with bilingual TV complete with CNN newscasts and remote control, radio, fridge, hot-water pot, and newspapers delivered daily, rooms run ¥10,000 ($80) to ¥18,500 ($148) for a single, ¥22,500 ($180) to ¥38,000 ($304) for a twin, and ¥22,500 ($180) to ¥32,500 ($260) for a double. Incidentally, the hotel complex is linked to Shin-Kobe Station via a covered walkway; Kobe's one subway line has a station right in the basement.

The **Oriental Hotel,** at 25 Kyomachi Street, Chuo-ku (tel. 078/331-8111), is about a 5-minute taxi ride or 15-minute walk south of Sannomiya Station. A handsome brick building, it's one of Kobe's older hotels and has aged well. It has 190 rooms and seven restaurants, serving everything from Italian to Chinese to French to kaiseki cuisine. Its guest rooms are small but comfortable and pleasant, and come with TV, fridge, clock, and radio. Room rates begin at ¥8,800 ($70) for a single and ¥16,500 ($132) for a twin or double.

The Medium-Priced Range

You can't get any closer to Sannomiya Station than the **Sannomiya Terminal Hotel,** Kumoi-Dori 8-chome, Chuo-ku (tel. 078/291-0001). Located practically on top of the JR Sannomiya Station, it's a very convenient and upper-scale business hotel with check-in at 1 p.m. instead of 3 p.m. as with most business hotels. Singles start at ¥7,900 ($63), doubles at ¥14,300 ($114), and twins at ¥15,400 ($123). Rooms are fairly large and spotlessly clean, and feature TV with CNN cable and pay video, radio, a pot for heating water, and double-pane windows to shut out noise from train traffic. Long-staying guests in deluxe twins and doubles are provided with scales—perhaps so they can monitor their weight gain as they gorge themselves on Kobe's scrumptious food in the Japanese and French restaurants. Only the twins, doubles, and deluxe singles have refrigerators, but there are vending machines in case you're searching for liquid other than water.

As part of a nationwide business hotel chain, the **Kobe Washington Hotel,** 2-

11-5 Shimoyamatedori, Chuo-ku (tel. 078/331-6111), is a reliable and high-quality business hotel about a seven-minute walk northwest of Sannomiya Station on Ikuta Shinmichi Street. The rooms are tiny but nicely decorated with modern furniture and come with refrigerator, TV with pay video (bilingual in twins and doubles), clock, and piped-in music. Panels on the windows slide shut for complete darkness. Three restaurants serve Japanese and Western food. Rates for single rooms start at ¥6,000 ($48); twins start at ¥11,000 ($88) and doubles at ¥12,000 ($96).

Opened in 1986, **Hana Hotel,** 4-2-7 Nunobiki-cho, Chuo-ku (tel. 078/221-1087), is a cheerful, airy business hotel located just a two-minute walk north of JR Sannomiya Station. *Hana* means flower in Japanese, and that's the motif here. A small, personable business hotel with only 6 rooms on each floor, its 42 rooms are nicely furnished with refrigerator, radio, TV with pay video, alarm clock, hairdryer, and windows that open. The front desk is on the second floor, and the staff is accommodating and courteous. Singles are ¥7,700 ($62), doubles are ¥12,000 ($96), and twins are ¥13,900 ($111). Note that prices include tax and service.

Remodeled in 1985, the **Kitagami Hotel** ⑰, 3-2-3 Kano-cho, Chuo-ku (tel. 078/391-8781), started out primarily as a business hotel but is trying to change its image to attract tourists—most of the 42 rooms are twins that go for ¥11,500 ($92) to ¥16,500 ($132). Triple rooms start at ¥15,500 ($124). Prices include tax and service. Western-style breakfasts are available for ¥800 ($6.40). Rooms are simple but bright, with large windows. The Kitagami is less than a five-minute walk north of Sannomiya Station.

Kobe Union Hotel, 2-1-9 Nunobiki-cho, Chuo-ku (tel. 078/222-6500), is located between Sannomiya and Shin-Kobe stations, about a ten-minute walk to each. It's next to Lawson Food Store, a 24-hour convenience store. They're used to foreigners here and have one Western restaurant. Rooms are small and simple but pleasant with large double-pane windows that open, TV with video, hairdryer, fridge, and hot-water pot. Check-in is at 2 p.m. Rates are ¥6,000 ($48) for a single and ¥10,500 ($84) for a twin, excluding tax and service.

There's not a lot you can say about the Green Hill Hotels 1 and 2 except that they're both located between Sannomiya and Shin-Kobe stations and are your typical clean and sparsely furnished business hotels. **Green Hill Hotel 1,** 2-5-16 Kano-cho, Chuo-ku (tel. 078/222-1221), is slightly older and cheaper, with singles beginning at ¥6,600 ($53) and twins and doubles at ¥12,000 ($96). **Green Hill Hotel 2,** 2-8-3 Kano-cho (tel. 078/222-0909), sports more modern rooms, which feature shoji screens, refrigerator, and TV with pay video. Singles here are ¥7,600 ($61), while twins begin at ¥13,900 ($111). All rates include tax and service. Green Hill Hotel 2 even has a chapel and Japanese wedding room in case you want to tie the knot while staying there (weddings constitute a big part of the business in Japanese hotels, sometimes as much as 25% of the hotel's profit).

The Budget Category

A good choice in this category, **Tor Ryokan,** 3-12-11 Kitanagasa Dori, Chuo-ku (tel. 078/331-3590), is a member of the Japanese Inn Group. It has a great location, just a three-minute walk from Motomachi Station or a seven-minute walk from Sannomiya Station, just off Tor Road. Owned by an older couple, this small establishment has 12 rooms. Half have their own private bathroom and two of them come with beds instead of futons. If you can do without a private bathroom, room rates are ¥4,700 ($38) for one person and ¥9,400 ($75) for two. Rooms with a bathroom go for ¥5,500 ($44) for one person and ¥11,000 ($88) for two. Rates include tax and service charge. Rooms are simple with a tatami, futons, a low table, a coin-operated TV, and a clothes rack and mirror. There's a public bath and coin-operated washer and dryer in the hotel. A bell at the front door signals your coming and going, at which point one of your hosts appears to either take your shoes or give them back. Some may not like the attention; others welcome the homey atmosphere.

The **Kobe YMCA Hotel,** 2-7-15 Kano-cho, Chuo-ku (tel. 078/241-7205), between Sannomiya and Shin-Kobe stations, is sandwiched in between the two Green Hill Hotels. Used primarily for banquets, weddings (yes, you can get married here at the YMCA), and for teaching classes, it has only four single rooms beginning at ¥5,500 ($44) and nine twins starting at ¥10,500 ($84), including breakfast, tax, and service charge. Rooms have a bare, dormitory look to them, but all have a minuscule bathroom, a coin-operated TV, and a pot for heating water. Men, women, and families are welcome, and if you're a YMCA member you get a ¥300 ($2.40) discount.

Youth Hostels: There are no conveniently located youth hostels in Kobe. **Youth Hostel Kobe Mudoji** ⑰, 100 Shinchi, Fukuchi, Yamada-cho, Kita-ku (tel. 078/581-0250), is reached via bus from Minotani Station followed by ten minutes on foot. The cost is ¥2,800 ($22) for members and ¥3,300 ($26) for nonmembers, including two meals.

WHERE TO DINE

In addition to the many Japanese and Western restaurants listed below, be sure to read the nightlife section. Many bars serve meals and snacks that are sometimes cheaper than those served at restaurants.

Japanese Food

Kobe is famous for its beef, and one of Kobe's most famous steakhouses is **Misono**, 1-7-6 Kitanagasa Dori (tel. 331-2890). It claims to have originated teppanyaki steak back in 1945, a style of cooking that uses flat hot plates. Today teppanyaki steak is a favorite not only in Japan but in other countries as well. Misono uses Kobe beef from cattle raised in mountain villages about 40 miles north of the city.

Unlike Western countries where cattle graze in open fields, in these mountain villages the cattle are hand-fed barley, corn, rice, bran, molasses, rapeseed oil, and soybean meal. The rumor that cattle are fed beer is untrue—they may, however, get one bottle each as a farewell present just before being sent off to the slaughterhouse. There are only a few head of cattle per household, so each gets a lot of individual attention. For exercise the cattle are used for labor, and after the workout are washed and massaged with water and straw brushes.

Misono serves its teppanyaki steaks from 11:30 a.m. to 2 p.m. and again from 5 to 10 p.m. (open throughout the day on Sunday). As you sit around a small table, your chef will prepare your steak right before your eyes. Set dinners cost ¥11,000 ($88) to ¥18,000 ($144), while special lunch menus are available for ¥2,200 ($17.60). Misono is located a couple minutes northwest of Sannomiya Station on Ikuta Shinmichi Street, across from Higashimon Street.

Iroriya, 3-chome Kitano-cho (tel. 231-6777), a rather formal establishment, is another well-known restaurant serving Kobe beef but specializing in shabu-shabu and sukiyaki. Here you take off your shoes at the front entryway, where a man will quickly whisk them out of sight. Then a kimono-clad woman will lead you through this rather large restaurant to your dining table with your own private hearth. All interior artwork is done by the owner of the restaurant. Meals begin at ¥4,500 ($36) for sukiyaki or shabu-shabu and ¥2,800 ($22.40) for *udon suki* (noodles, seafood, and vegetables cooked together and eaten straight out of the pot). Iroriya is about a 10- to 15-minute walk north of Sannomiya Station on Kitano-zaka Road, and is open daily from noon to 10 p.m. (last order at 9:30 p.m.).

Okagawa, 1-115-2 Kitano-cho (tel. 222-3511), occupies a rather new and dignified building up on the bluffs of Kitano not far from Shin-Kobe Station and about a five-minute taxi ride from Sannomiya Station. It specializes in tempura, offered for ¥4,400 ($35.20) at lunch and ¥8,800 ($70.40) at dinner. You can also order shabu-shabu or sukiyaki for ¥7,700 ($61.60) and a kaiseki menu for ¥11,000 ($88). Okagawa is in a modern building that follows the traditional Japanese design of simplicity with latticed wood, shoji screens, and flower arrangements—coolly elegant. In addition to various tatami rooms, its two tempura counters command good views of the city. Hours here are 11 a.m. to 9 p.m. daily.

Budget Selections: If you want to eat teppanyaki steak but can't afford the high prices of Kobe beef, one of the cheapest places you can go is **Steakland Kobe** ⑰, 1-8-2 Kitanagasa Dori (tel. 332-1787), on the street facing the north side of Hankyu Sannomiya Station. Lunch specials, served from 11 a.m. to 3 p.m., begin at only ¥1,300 ($10.40) for steak cooked on the hot plate in front of you, miso soup, rice, Japanese pickles, and a vegetable. At dinner, served until 10 p.m., you can have steaks beginning at ¥1,800 ($14.40). If you opt for Kobe beef, these steak set dinners begin at ¥4,400 ($35.20).

Yamada no Kakasi, 3-9-6 Sannomiya-cho (tel. 391-0363), is a cozy kushikatsu restaurant on the western edge of the Sannomiya Center Gai covered shopping arcade. A very narrow and small establishment, it consists of a long counter and some tables in the back. All the wood gleams with a shine, and added touches of pottery make you feel you're in the country instead of in the middle of Kobe. The man who has been operating this eatery for the past quarter of a century makes 25 different kinds of kushikatsu, the kinds dependent on the season. Skewers here average ¥150 ($1.20) to ¥270 ($2.16), but the easiest thing to do is simply to order the "Kakasi Course" set menu for ¥1,500 ($12), which consists of ten sticks. Your man behind the counter will select the ingredients himself, and since the food is supposed to be eaten hot, he'll serve one stick at a time. If you're still hungry at the end of the meal, you can always order a few skewers more. The specialty here is the delicately breaded shrimp and garlic skewer. Other morsels include asparagus wrapped in bacon, mushrooms, potatoes with cheese, chicken wrapped in mint leaf, and lotus root. Closed on Tuesday, it's open from 11 a.m. to 3 p.m. and 5 to 9 p.m. every day except Sunday and holidays, when it stays open throughout the day.

Popular with Kobe's younger generation is the cozy and intimate **Three Little Pigs,** 4-7-14 Kano-cho (tel. 321-5858), located just southeast of the Yamate Kansen and Kitano-zaka intersection. Cavern-like, with three tiny floors of dining, it offers an eclectic selection of cuisine, from salads and rice onigiri rolls to omelets and various seafood dishes. At any rate, both Japanese and Western food is available, but since the menu is only in Japanese, it's best to look around at what others are eating. Most items are under ¥1,000 ($8), with set meals starting at ¥3,000 ($24). Hours are 5 to 10:30 p.m.; closed every third Tuesday of the month.

A well-known noodle restaurant in Kobe, **Masaya Honten,** 1-8-21 Nakayamate Dori (tel. 331-4178), is a few minutes' walk north of Sannomiya Station on Kitano-zaka. It has been dishing out noodles for more than 30 years and is easy to spot by the waterwheel outside its front door and its plastic-food display case of noodles (there's another display case inside). Since the menu is in Japanese only, make your choice from one of these cases before sitting down. Dishes available include tempura with noodles (*tempura soba*), pork cutlet with noodles (*tonkatsu soba*), and curry noodles, each less than ¥1,000 ($8). Sukiyaki served with noodles is available for ¥3,800 ($30.40). A good place for night owls, it's open daily from 11 a.m. to 1 a.m.

International Restaurants

French and Continental Cuisine: For elegant French dining, **Alain Chapel,** on the 31st floor of the Portopia Hotel, 6-10-2 Minatojima, on Port Island (tel. 302-1111), is an excellent choice. In a stately drawing-room setting of square pillars, chandeliers, flowers, and white tapered candles on each table, this restaurant serves the creations of French chef Alain Chapel. Set lunches, served from 11:30 a.m. to 2 p.m., are priced at ¥6,600 ($52.80), while set dinners, offered from 5 to 9:30 p.m., range from ¥11,000 ($88) to ¥17,600 ($141). If you decide to dine à la carte, you might start with lobster salad and then try either Kobe beef or duck in foie gras. Average dinner checks including wine, tax, and service are generally around ¥17,000 ($136) per person. Top off your meal with a drink or coffee at **Plein**

d'Etoiles, which is a floor below Alain Chapel. This lounge features piano music and a band every night, for which it charges a ¥650 ($5.20) cover charge. Cocktails, served until 11:50 p.m., start at ¥800 ($6.40).

Another fine Western restaurant is the **Sky Restaurant,** on the 11th floor of the Oriental Hotel, on Kyomachi Street (tel. 331-8111). Open from noon to 2 p.m. and 5 to 10 p.m., the restaurant has three walls of glass, letting the port and city serve as the decorative background. Piano music nightly adds to the mood. Set dinner menus start at ¥5,500 ($44), but for steaks with truffle sauce and lobster, expect to spend ¥13,200 ($106). If you're ordering à la carte, I recommend the roast rib of Kobe beef. Other dishes include seafood, chicken, veal, and lamb. If you order from the menu, expect to spend about ¥11,000 ($88). Set lunch specials start at ¥2,200 ($17.60).

One more place with a view is **Kitano,** 1-5-7 Kitano-cho (tel. 222-5123), located on a hill overlooking the city about a ten-minute walk from Shin-Kobe Station. Lunches, served daily from 11 a.m. to 2:30 p.m., include set steak meals for ¥5,500 ($44) and the daily lunch special, known as the Queen's Lunch, for ¥3,300 ($26.40). It's especially popular with middle-aged Japanese women, but, yes, you guys can order it too. Open for dinner from 5 to 10:30 p.m., Kitano serves sole, turbot, lobster, chicken, filet mignon, scallops, and steaks, with set courses starting at ¥7,000 ($56).

Underneath the Shinkobe Oriental Hotel next to Shin-Kobe Station is a huge shopping complex with more than 30 food and beverage outlets. Called **OPA** (short for Oriental Park Avenue), this modern-day maze offers everything from Tex-Mex, sushi, and Japanese nouvelle cuisine to Italian, Chinese, and seafood cuisine. I can't claim to have tried them all (I never would have made it to the rest of this book), but I can vouch for the salad bar at **Central Station,** second floor (tel. 262-2731), decorated in a train motif. A trip through the salad bar (one of the best I've seen in Japan) costs ¥740 ($5.92), though it drops to only ¥400 ($3.20) if you buy an entrée as well. The specialty here is steak, with a steak cooked with either ginger or garlic sauce priced at ¥640 ($5.12). These are prices for lunch, which you can order until 4 p.m. Dinner prices are slightly higher. Other items on the menu include turkey, chicken, prawns, fish, and lobster. Hours are 11 a.m. to 2 a.m. daily (last order at 11:30 p.m.).

Indian Restaurants: With a sizable Indian population, Kobe has a number of excellent Indian restaurants. One of the best known is **Gaylord,** in the basement of the Meiji Seimi Building at 8-3-7 Isogami Dori (tel. 251-4359), on Flower Road between the Sanwa and Kyowa banks and across from the Flower Clock. With its low lighting, candles, wood-paneled ceiling, Indian artwork, and piped-in sitar music, this place is classier than your usual Indian restaurant. Other franchise Gaylord restaurants are in Bombay, New Delhi, Hong Kong, London, San Francisco, and Los Angeles. It has an extensive menu, with such delights as shrimp cooked in mild gravy with coconut, marinated lamb pieces cooked in cream and spices, and tandoori fish, chicken, or mutton. Vegetarian selections include saffron-flavored rice with nuts and fruit, Bengal beans cooked in sharp spices, spiced lentils cooked with cream, and spinach and cheese cooked in spices. Most dishes range from ¥1,400 ($11.20) to ¥2,000 ($16), and it's customary to order one dish per person and then share. If you're by yourself, a good way to sample various dishes is to order one of the set menus starting at ¥3,300 ($26.40). Since that was my case, I ordered the mini-tandoori set course, which came with fish and chicken tandoori, shish kebab, Indian bread, salad, chicken curry, a dry vegetable dish (in this case potato and cabbage), rice, and tea or coffee. Lunch specials are served every day except Sunday and holidays starting at ¥1,300 ($10.40). The restaurant is open daily from 11:30 a.m. to 2:30 p.m. and 5 to 9:30 p.m., except on Saturday, Sunday, and holidays, when it remains open throughout the day.

Raja, 2-7-4 Sakaemachi Dori (tel. 332-5253), is located south of Motomachi Station and just west of Chinatown. Open every day except Wednesday from 11:30 a.m. to 2:30 p.m. and from 5 to 9 p.m., this small establishment is rather trendy in its simplicity; my only complaint is that the tables are squeezed too closely together. Perhaps it's just a reflection of the demand. At any rate, the menu offers the usual tandoori chicken, seafood, mutton, and vegetable curries, with most priced around ¥1,200 ($9.60). Set lunch courses start at ¥1,000 ($8), while set dinner courses begin at ¥2,700 ($21.60).

Gandhara, on the fourth floor of the Nikaku Building, 1-2-3 Kitanagsa Dori (tel. 391-4975), is an Indian restaurant conveniently located just north of Sannomiya Station next to Shakey's. Its portions are not as generous as those described above, but it is easy to find and the curries are slightly cheaper, with most averaging around ¥1,000 ($8). Set dinners range from ¥2,700 ($21.60) to ¥5,500 ($44), but the best deal is the lunch special for ¥1,650 ($13.20), which comes with chicken curry, vegetable curry, rice, Indian bread, shish kebab, salad, and dessert. Decorated with Indian knickknacks you never see in restaurants in India, this place is open daily from 11 a.m. to 10 p.m. Another Gandhara restaurant in Kobe is located in Kitano.

Thai Food: Claiming to be the first Thai restaurant in the Kansai area (which encompasses Kobe, Osaka, and Kyoto), **Wang Thai,** on the second floor of the President Arcade at 2-14-22 Yamamoto Dori Avenue (tel. 222-2507), offers an extensive menu in English with almost 100 items. With most dishes priced between ¥1,000 ($8) and ¥1,900 ($15.20), it serves pork, beef, seafood, rice, noodle, and vegetarian selections. Most popular is the chicken wrapped in bamboo leaf, but I found the chicken curry with peanuts, potatoes, and herbs equally delicious. Closed Wednesday except on national holidays, it's open the rest of the week from 11 a.m. to 2:30 p.m. and from 5:30 to 9:30 p.m. It's located across the street from the Casablanca Club.

Chinese Food: Chinatown, called Nankinmachi by the locals, is located south of Motomachi Station. Occupying the former hot spot of sailor bars and pubs, this pedestrian-laned area boasts about 30 restaurants, most with plastic-food displays outside their doors. Simply walk around and pick one.

For dining in Sannomiya, **Kinrykaku** (tel. 221-1616) is located on the seventh floor of the Kobe Shinbun Kaikan Building just southwest of Sannomiya Station. The English translation of its name is "Golden Dragon," and it's more luxurious than the usual Chinese restaurant. It serves Cantonese food from 11:30 a.m. to 8:30 p.m. daily. The chef is Chinese and the dishes include many different varieties of pork, chicken, seafood, vegetables, and noodles. Set dinner courses for two persons start at ¥8,800 ($70.40). Much cheaper is the set lunch menu available every day except Sunday and holidays for ¥1,000 ($8), which allows you to select two main dishes from a list of ten, plus pickles, soup, and rice. Since most à la carte dishes are meant for two to three persons, ask for the Japanese menu if you're dining alone—it offers smaller portions with dishes averaging ¥700 ($5.60).

Budget Selections: Kobe also has its share of inexpensive fast-food joints. **Shakey's,** which serves an all-you-can-eat lunch from 11 a.m. to 3 p.m. every day except Sunday and holidays for only ¥600 ($4.80), is located just north of Sannomiya Station. In the same vicinity is a **McDonald's.**

---

6. Mount Koya

The sacred mountain of Mount Koya is the place to go if you've harbored visions of wooden temples nestled in among the trees whenever you've thought of Japan. It's all there—head-shaven monks, religious chantings at the crack of dawn, the wafting of incense, temples, towering cypress trees, tombs, and early-morning mist rising above the treetops. Mount Koya, called Koyasan by the Japanese, is one of Japan's most sacred places and is the mecca of the Shingon Esoteric sect of Buddhism. Standing 3,000 feet above the world, the top of Mount Koya is home to about 120 Shingon Buddhist Temples scattered through the mountain forests. Some 50 of these temples offer accommodations to visitors, making it one of the best places in Japan to observe temple life firsthand.

Koyasan became a place of meditation and religious learning more than 1,170 years ago when Kukai, known posthumously as Kobo Daishi, was granted the mountaintop by the imperial court in 816 as a place to establish his Shingon sect of Buddhism. Kobo Daishi was a charismatic priest who spent two years in China studying Esoteric Buddhism and introduced the Shingon sect in Japan upon his return. Revered for his excellent calligraphy, his humanitarianism, and his teachings, Kobo Daishi remains today one of the most beloved figures in Japanese Buddhist history. When he died in the ninth century, he was laid to rest in a mausoleum on Mount Koya. His followers believe that Kobo Daishi is not dead but is simply in a deep state of meditation, awaiting the arrival of the last Bodhisatva (Buddha messiahs). According to popular belief, priests opening his mausoleum decades after his death found his body still warm. Through the centuries many of Kobo Daishi's followers, wishing to be close at hand when the great priest awakens, have had huge tombs or tablets constructed close to Kobo Daishi's mausoleum, and many have had their ashes interred here. Pilgrims over the last thousand years have included emperors, nobles, and common people, all climbing to the top of the mountain to pay their respects. Women, however, were barred from entering the sacred grounds of Koyasan until 1872.

ORIENTATION

The easiest way to get to Koyasan is from Osaka. Ordinary express (*kyuko*) trains of the Nankai Line depart from Osaka's Namba Station every half hour and cost ¥1,060 ($8.48) one way. The trip south takes about one hour and 40 minutes. If you want to ride in luxury you can also take one of the limited express cars with reserved seats. These cost an extra ¥700 ($5.60) and take about one hour and 20 minutes. After the train ride (the last stop is called Gokurakubashi) you continue your trip to the top of Mount Koya by cable car. The price of the cable car is included in your train ticket.

At the top of Koyasan is Koyasan Eki Station, where you'll find a booth of the **local tourist office.** Stop by for a map of Koyasan, and here you can also book a room in a temple. Outside the station you can board a bus that goes through the main street of Koyasan all the way to the Okunoin-mae or Ichinohashi bus stop. It passes almost all the sites along the way as well as most temples accommodating visitors. It also passes the **Koyasan Tourist Association**'s main office (tel. 0736/56-2616), located approximately in the center of Koyasan. Here you can also pick up an English brochure with a map and arrange for accommodation in a temple if you have not already done so. Both tourist offices are open daily from 8:30 a.m. to 5 p.m., with slightly shorter hours in winter.

The **telephone area code** for Mount Koya is 0736. Mount Koya is located in Wakayama Prefecture, the complete address for which is 600 Koya-san, Koya-cho, Ito-gun, Wakayama Prefecture.

THE SIGHTS

The most awe-inspiring and magnificent of Koyasan's many structures and temples, **Okunoin** contains the mausoleum of Kobo Daishi. The most dramatic way to approach Okunoin is from the Ichinohashi bus stop, where a pathway leads one mile to the mausoleum. Swathed in a respectful darkness of huge cypress trees that form a canopy overhead are monument after monument, tomb after tomb, all belonging to faithful followers from past centuries. I don't know whether being here will affect you the same way, but I was awestruck by the hundreds of tombs, the iridescent green moss, the shafts of light streaking through the treetops, the stone lanterns, and the gnarled bark of the old cypress trees. Together they present a dramatic picture representing a thousand years of Japanese Buddhist history—a picture that has engraved itself upon my mind forever. If you're lucky you won't meet many people along this pathway. (Tour buses fortunately park at a newer entrance to the mausoleum at the bus stop called Okunoin-mae. I absolutely forbid you to take this newer and shorter route, since its crowds lessen the impact of this place considerably. Rather, make sure you take the path to the farthest left, which begins near Ichinohashi bus stop. Much less traveled, it's also much more impressive). At any rate, be sure to return to the mausoleum at night—the stone lanterns are lit (now electrically), creating an effect both mysterious and powerful.

At the end of the pathway is the **Lantern Hall,** which houses about 11,000 lanterns. Two sacred fires which have been burning reportedly since the 11th century are kept safely inside. The mausoleum itself is *behind* the Lantern Hall. Buy a white candle, light it, and wish for anything you want. Then sit back and watch respectfully as Buddhists come to chant and pay respects to one of Japan's greatest Buddhist leaders.

As for other things to see, **Kongobuji Temple** ⑯ is close to the tourist office and is the headquarters of the Shingon sect in Japan. The entrance fee of ¥350 ($2.80) allows you to wander around the old wooden structure. On the temple grounds is a large and magnificent rock garden. Imagine the effort spent in getting those huge boulders to their present site. If it's raining, consider yourself lucky—the wetness adds a sheen and color to the rocks.

Another important site is the **Danjogaran Complex,** an impressive sight with a huge main hall (*kondo*); a large vermillion-colored pagoda (*daito*) which many consider to be Koyasan's most magnificent structure; and the oldest building on Mount Koya, the Fudodo, built in 1198. Next to the complex is the **Reihokan Museum** ⑰, with such treasures of Koyasan on display as wooden Buddha sculptures, scrolls, art, and implements. It's open from 9 a.m. to 4 p.m. (until 5 p.m. in summer), and admission is ¥500 ($4).

A little out of the way from the other sites are the **Tokugawa Mausolea,** where two Tokugawa shoguns were laid to rest. There's nothing spectacular about them.

FOOD AND LODGING

Because about 7,000 people live on Mount Koya, the community has the usual stores, schools, and offices of any small town. However, what is unusual is the fact that there are no hotels here—the only place you can stay at is a temple, and I strongly suggest you do so. Japanese who come here have almost always made reservations beforehand, so you should do the same. You can make a reservation by calling the temple directly or through travel agencies such as JTB. You can also make reservations upon arrival in Koyasan at the tourist association offices described above, but that may be a bit risky during peak travel seasons. At last check, the Koyasan Tourist Association indicated it would make reservations only for those who come in personally to its office.

Prices for an overnight stay, including two vegetarian meals, are the same for all temples on Koyasan and range from ¥7,500 ($60) to ¥11,000 ($88) per person.

Your room will be tatami and may include a nice view of a garden. Living at the temple are high school students and college students attending Koyasan's Buddhist university, who will bring your meals to your room, make up your futon, and clean your room. The morning service is at 6 a.m. (You don't have to attend but I recommend that you do.) Both baths and toilets are communal, and meals are at set times. Because the students must leave for school, breakfast is usually served by 7:30 a.m. Incidentally, Buddhist monks are vegetarians, not teetotalers, and because beer and sake are made of rice and grain, they're readily available at the temples for an extra charge. Below are just a few of the dozens of temples open for overnight guests.

Shojoshinin ⑱ (tel. 0736/56-2006) has a good location right at the beginning of the tomb-lined pathway to Okunoin, making it convenient for your late-night stroll to the mausoleum. The present temple buildings date from about 150 years ago, but the temple was first founded about 1,000 years ago. A large wooden structure with rooms overlooking a small garden and pond, it's usually full in August and peak seasons, so make reservations early.

Also located near Shojoshinin near the Ichinohashi bus stop is **Ekoin** ⑰ (tel. 0736/56-2514). This 100-year-old temple has beautiful grounds and is nestled in a wooded slope.

Fumonin Temple ⑱ (tel. 0736/56-2224) is centrally located close to the tourist association and has a small but beautiful garden created by the same person who designed the garden at Nijo Castle in Kyoto. (Other temples with famous gardens include Hosenin and Tentokuin.)

Rengejoin Temple ⑱ (tel. 0736/56-2233) is owned by a priest whose wife and son speak English, so a lot of foreigners are directed here and it's a good place to meet people. There's also a nice garden here, and this is one of the few temples that will probably take you in if you show up without a reservation.

Even the **Henjoson-in Youth Hostel** ⑱ (tel. 0736/56-2434) is located in a temple, about 50 years old. An overnight stay here for members is ¥3,500 ($28); nonmembers pay ¥500 ($4) more. Breakfast and dinner are included. Reservations can be made by postcard only. The address is 303, Koyasan, Koya-cho, Ito-gun, Wakayama-ken 648-02.

---

7. Himeji

The main reason tourists come to Himeji is to see its beautiful castle, which embodies better than any other the best in Japan's military architecture.

ORIENTATION

Himeji is located about four hours from Tokyo, one hour from Kyoto, and a half hour from Okayama by the Shinkansen bullet train. The **Himeji City Tourist Information Center** (tel. 0792/85-3792) is at a central exit of the station's north side to the left after you exit from the ticket gate. It's open daily from 9 a.m. to 5 p.m. and offers maps in English. If you're stopping in Himeji only for a few hours to see the castle, deposit your luggage in the coin lockers just beside the tourist office or underneath the Shinkansen tracks. Himeji Castle is about a ten-minute walk straight north of the station. You can see it immediately upon leaving the station.

The **telephone area code** for Himeji is 0792. Himeji is in Hyogo Prefecture.

THE SIGHTS

Perhaps the most beautiful castle in all of Japan, Himeji Castle is nicknamed White Heron Castle in reference to the fact that its white walls stretching out on either side of the main donjon resemble a white heron poised in flight over the plain. Whether it looks to you like a heron or just a castle, the view of the white five-story donjon under a blue sky is striking. It is also one of the few castles in Japan that has remained virtually undamaged since its completion centuries ago, surviving even the World War II bombings that laid Himeji city in ruins.

Originating as a fort in the 14th century, Himeji Castle took a more majestic form in 1581, when a three-story donjon was built by Hideyoshi Toyotomi during one of his military campaigns in the district. In the early 1600s the castle became the residence of Terumasa Ikeda, one of Hideyoshi's generals and a son-in-law of Ieyasu Tokugawa. He remodeled the castle into its present five-story structure. With its extensive gates, three moats, and turrets, it had one of the most sophisticated defense systems in Japan. The maze of passageways leading to the donjon was so complicated that intruders would find themselves trapped in dead ends. The castle walls were constructed with square or circular holes to allow muzzles of guns to poke •through; the rectangular holes were for archers. There were also drop chutes where stones or boiling water could be dumped on enemies trying to scale the walls.

Open daily from 9 a.m. to 4 p.m. (5 p.m. in summer), the castle charges a ¥500 ($4) admission fee. On weekends there are sometimes volunteer guides hanging around the ticket office who are willing to give you a guided tour of the castle for free. It gives them an opportunity to practice their English. Often college students, they can tell you the history of the castle and relate old castle gossip. But even if you go on your own, you won't have any problems learning about the history of the castle, since the city of Himeji has done a fine job in placing English explanations throughout the castle grounds. Allow about 1½ hours to see the castle.

Just behind Himeji Castle to the northeast is the **Hyogo Prefectural Museum of History.** If you're coming here from the castle, take the Karamete Exit from the castle, follow the circular drive to the right, and then turn left in front of the red-brick building (the city art museum). The history museum is straight ahead. Open every day except Monday from 10 a.m. to 5 p.m. and charging a ¥200 ($1.60) admission, it exhibits materials from prehistorical times to the present day, with many explanations in English. Some of the displays allow hands-on experience, such as traditional Japanese toys and Bunraku puppets with strings you can pull to move eyebrows and other facial features. If you're here on Sunday or a national holiday, you can even try on a samurai period costume (samurai outfits were amazingly heavy). Displays include those devoted to castles in Japan and around the world, with videos in English describing the structure and layout of Himeji Castle; children's games of yesteryear; and Shoshazan Enkyoji, a famous temple complex on nearby Enkyo Mountain.

If you're at all interested in Japanese flower arrangement, tea ceremony, or the proper way to wear a kimono, you'll want to take advantage of the free cultural classes held Monday through Friday from 1:30 to 3:30 p.m. at the **Himeji Shimin Kaikan,** 112 Sosha Honmachi (tel. 84-2800). It's located east of the main road leading from the train station to Himeji Castle. Classes are offered on an alternating basis, so the best thing to do is drop by the tourist office in the train station for an English leaflet complete with a schedule and a map of how to get there.

If you have time for an excursion, board bus 6 or 8 from in front of Himeji Station (to the right after exiting from the station's central exit) and ride it for 25 minutes to **Shoshazan Enkyoji.** Founded in the Heian Period (12th century), this large complex of temples contains a thousand years of Buddhist history in its precincts, including the Kongo Satta Buddha sculpted in 1395 and the Yakushido, the oldest surviving structure dating from the Kamakura Period (early 14th century). The easiest way to reach the temple complex from the bus stop (called Shosha) is by ropeway, which costs ¥300 ($2.40) one way. There are also horse-drawn carriages available for the same price.

WHERE TO STAY

Himeji lacks an adequate supply of good accommodations. In fact, some of the worst hotels I've seen in Japan are in Himeji. Your safest bet is to stick to the recommendations listed below.

Banryu ⑱, 135 Shimodera-machi (tel. 0792/85-2112), is a traditional ryokan about a 10-minute taxi ride from Himeji Station and about a 15-minute walk to Himeji Castle. Surrounded by a wood-and-stone wall and possessing a modest but peaceful garden, this Japanese-style inn has 20 rooms and is used to catering to foreigners. A pleasant place with large rooms and some antiques, it's about 30 years old. Rates per person, including two meals, start at ¥13,000 ($104) for rooms without a bathroom and ¥16,500 ($132) for rooms with a bathroom and views of the garden. Western breakfasts are served upon request.

Himeji Castle Hotel, 210 Hojyo (tel. 0792/84-3311), opened in 1975, is considered to be one of Himeji's best tourist hotels. A ten-minute walk from the south exit of the station (which is also the Shinkansen exit), it charges ¥6,600 ($53) to ¥10,000 ($80) for a single, ¥16,500 ($132) for a double, and ¥13,200 ($106) to

¥21,000 ($168) for a twin. I especially like the cheapest twins—they were made by joining two single rooms together, with the result that beds are in one room, a couch in the other, and there are two bathrooms and two television sets. Who knows, this could be a lifesaver for couples or friends who have been traveling together a bit too long. Facilities include an outdoor swimming pool, which unfortunately charges ¥1,500 ($12) for a dip, and a Western restaurant called Chateau, which serves lunches starting at ¥1,500 ($12) and dinners at ¥2,200 ($17.60).

If swimming is part of your daily routine (or you wish it were), walk down the street from the Castle Hotel to **Hotel Okuuchi,** 3-56 Higashi Nobusue (tel. 0792/ 22-8000). It has an indoor swimming pool guests can use for free all year. A little more than half of this business-type hotel's 318 rooms are singles, which start at ¥5,500 ($44). Most of the rest are twins, which start at ¥10,000 ($80). Tax and service are extra. Rooms are small but are equipped with push-button phone, alarm clock, radio, fridge, hot-water pot, and TV with pay video. Because of the construction of the building, most rooms have absolutely no view—if that's important to you, be sure to specify your wishes. The hotel's two restaurants serve Japanese and Chinese cuisine.

A business hotel, **Hotel Himeji Plaza,** 158 Toyozawa-cho (tel. 0792/81-9000), is your best bet for a good hotel close to the station. Located about a minute away from the south exit of the station, it's a white building with a clock on top of the front façade. Its 230 rooms are bright and cheerful and come with minibar, hot-water pot for tea, TV with pay video, clock, and semidouble beds. The windows are glazed but can be opened. Singles start at ¥6,400 ($51) and twins and doubles begin at ¥10,500 ($84), all with a private bathroom. There are also cheaper singles for ¥6,000 ($48) with a toilet but no bathtub. Prices include tax and service. There's a coin-operated laundry in the hotel, a public bath and sauna (for men only), soda and beer machines, and one Western-style restaurant. The staff is friendly and courteous.

Hotel Sunroute Himeji ⑱, 195-9 Ekimae-cho (tel. 0792/85-0811), is a white building located within a minute's walk to the right after exiting from Himeji Station's central exit on the north side. The front desk and lobby are up on the fourth floor. Opened in the mid-1970s, it features rooms with heavy curtains that can be drawn to shut out any light, a hot-water pot for tea, refrigerator, and TV with pay video. Rooms facing the railroad tracks are fitted with double-pane windows to screen out train noises. During summer months there's a rooftop beer garden here open daily from 5 to 9 p.m., with mugs of beer starting at ¥500 ($4). The hotel's one restaurant serves Japanese food, plus a Western-style buffet breakfast for ¥1,000 ($8). Room rates begin at ¥7,200 ($58) for a single, ¥12,000 ($96) for a twin, ¥14,300 ($114) for a double, and ¥16,000 ($128) for a triple. Prices include service but not tax.

Hotel Sunroute New Himeji ⑱, 241 Ekimae-cho (tel. 0792/23-1111), opened in 1983, when it took over an existing hotel. Facilities have recently been renovated, including a Chinese restaurant and cheerful coffeeshop. Windows are large, with sliding panels for complete darkness, and rooms are equipped with the usual alarm clock, refrigerator, hot-water pot and tea, and TV with pay video. The cheapest singles have tiny glazed windows that can't open, so if sunshine is important to you, pay the higher price. Rates are ¥5,500 ($44) to ¥6,600 ($53) for a single, ¥13,000 ($104) to ¥14,300 ($114) for a twin, and ¥13,200 ($106) for a double. Japanese-style rooms start at ¥14,300 ($114) for two. Tax and service extra. This hotel is located right across the street from Himeji Station's central exit. During summer months there's a rooftop beer garden here open daily from 5 to 9 p.m.

Youth Hostel Tegarayama Seinen-no-le, 58 Nishi-nobuse (tel. 0792/93-2716), is very inexpensive at only ¥1,200 ($9.60) a night. However, no meals are served, no one here speaks English, and the woman I talked to was not very receptive. If you're still undaunted (or broke), you can reach this youth hostel by taking a bus from Himeji Station for ten minutes and then walking for another ten minutes.

Youth hostel cards aren't required. Note that this youth hostel is closed every second and fourth Monday.

WHERE TO EAT

Paralleling and to the right of the main drag from Himeji Station to the castle is a covered shopping arcade called **Miyukidori,** with lots of restaurants and coffeeshops. There's even a McDonald's if you're interested.

I suggest, however, that you try **Fukutei** ⑱, 75 Kameimachi (tel. 23-0981). If you're walking from the station, it's about halfway down the arcade on a side street. If you have the English map from the tourist office, it's indicated by number 77 and is wrongly spelled "Hukutei" (unless they've corrected the map by the time you get there). This restaurant offers a wide assortment of Japanese food, including sashimi, tempura, noodles, eel, and sushi. A meal here will probably cost you between ¥1,000 ($8) and ¥2,000 ($16). A great deal is the hearty teishoku obento lunch for around ¥900 ($7.20), served until 2 p.m. It usually includes sashimi, tempura, soup, rice, and pickled vegetables. A refuge for shoppers, Fukutei has soothing Japanese instrumental music playing in the background. It's closed on Thursday and is open the rest of the week from 11 a.m. to 10 p.m.

About a five-minute walk from Himeji Station is a small neighborhood noodle shop called **Minato-an** ⑱, Tatemachi (tel. 22-1171), identified by number 69 on the tourist office map. It's on a back street to the west of the main street leading from the station to the castle. Across from a tiny neighborhood shrine and located on a corner, the restaurant has pictures of a black-and-red bucket, as well as a plastic-food display case, outside. The specialty here is udon noodles served in a wooden bucket. Other noodle dishes include somen, ramen, tempura udon, and curry udon, with most in the ¥500 ($4) to ¥650 ($5.20) price range. The menu is only in Japanese, so make your choice from the plastic goodies on display. Hours here are from 11 a.m. to 9 p.m.; closed Wednesday.

Mampuku ⑱, Hakurocho (tel. 22-3901), is a small and plain-looking restaurant located on the left-hand side of the street leading from the station to the castle. It's just before the last stoplight leading to the castle grounds. It has blue curtains in front of its door and a plastic-food display case. It's an eel shop, but also has noodles, sushi, tempura, and other Japanese food, with most dishes priced below ¥1,500 ($12). This place is open from 10 a.m. to 5 p.m.; closed Thursday.

Beside Mampuku is an obento counter selling box lunches of eel, curry rice, hamburgers, and more for about ¥450 ($3.60) per lunch. You might want to buy your lunch here for a picnic on the castle's park grounds.

Not far from the Miyukidori shopping arcade and across from Taiyo Kobe Bank is **C.P. News,** Gofukumachi 16 (tel. 82-7510 and 84-1774), one of the trendiest restaurant/bars in town. It looks like it was imported from Tokyo, with its sparse, art deco style, triangular tables, young staff, and young clientele. Open from 11:30 a.m. to midnight, it offers sandwiches, spaghetti, pizza, salads, curry rice, and more, all for around ¥600 ($4.80) to ¥800 ($6.40). It also serves coffee, tea, beer, and alcoholic concoctions.

And finally, if you're here during the summer months, there are **beer gardens** located on the roofs of Hotel Sunroute Himeji, Hotel Sunroute New Himeji, and Festa department store, which is right above Himeji Station itself. Hours for all are 5 to 9 p.m., and snacks are available in addition to beer.

---

8. Okayama

With the opening of the Seto Ohashi Bridge in the spring of 1988, Okayama Prefecture has leaped into the tourism spotlight. Japanese from all over the country have come to marvel over this bridge measuring almost six miles in length and connecting Okayama Prefecture on Honshu island with Sakaide on Shikoku island. Whereas it used to take one hour by ferry to reach Shikoku, the double-decker bridge for trains and cars cuts travel time down to just 15 minutes. For the Japanese, the Seto Ohashi Bridge is one of the most important attractions of Okayama Prefecture and the Seto Inland Sea.

For those of you less interested in bridges, Okayama is important for other reasons as well. In Okayama city, there's a garden considered to be one of the most beautiful in Japan. In nearby Kurashiki, covered later in this chapter, there's an old section of the town that's one of the most picturesque places in the country. And scattered through Okayama Prefecture are so-called International Villas, built by the prefecture especially for foreigners and located primarily in rural areas, with rates that are amazingly low.

ORIENTATION

Okayama lies on the Shinkansen line about four hours from Tokyo and 1½ hours west of Kyoto. The **Okayama Tourist Office** (tel. 0862/22-2912) is inside the Okayama Station building, located near the central exit of the east side (look for the signs). The tourist office window is well marked in English and is open daily from 8:30 a.m. to 8 p.m. They're well prepared for foreign visitors with brochures and a map in English.

Okayama's sights are all clustered within walking distance of each other and are located to the east of Okayama Station. The easiest way to sightsee is to take a streetcar from Okayama Station bound for Higashiyama, and to disembark after about eight minutes at the Shirojita tram stop. From there you can walk to the Orient Museum and then Korakuen Park, Okayama Castle, the Yumeji Art Museum, and the Hayashibara Art Museum. It should take about four or five hours to tour all of these sights. Before leaving Tokyo, stop by the T.I.C. and pick up a leaflet called *Okayama and Kurashiki*.

If you're calling from outside of Okayama, the **telephone area code** for the city is 0862. Okayama city is located in Okayama Prefecture.

THE SIGHTS

Okayama's claim to fame is its **Korakuen Park**, considered to be one of Japan's three most beautiful landscape gardens (the other two are in Kanazawa and Mito). Completed in 1700 after 14 years of work, its 28 acres are graced with a pond, running streams, pine trees, plum and cherry trees, bamboo groves, and tea plantations. The surrounding hills, as well as Okayama's famous black castle, are incorporated into the design of the garden. The garden's name, Korakuen, means "the garden for taking pleasure later," which has its origins in an old saying: "Bear sorrow before the people; take pleasure after them." This garden is different from most gardens in that it has large expanses of grassy open areas, a rarity in crowded Japan. Entrance to Korakuen is ¥250 ($2) and it's open from 7:30 a.m. to 6 p.m. April through September, from 8 a.m. to 5 p.m. October through March.

Across the river from Korakuen Park and over a footbridge, **Okayama Castle,** open from 9 a.m. to 5 p.m. daily, was originally built in the 16th century. Destroyed in World War II and rebuilt in 1966, this unique castle has earned the nickname of Crow Castle because of its black color. It seems that the lord of this castle had some sense of humor, since he deliberately painted his castle black to contrast with neighboring Himeji's famous White Heron castle. At any rate, like most castles this one houses swords, samurai gear, and palanquins. Unlike castles of yore, however, this one comes with an elevator that whisks you up to the top floor of the donjon, from which you have a view of the park and the city beyond. If you feel like indulging in whimsical fantasies deserving of children's fairy tales, you can rent paddleboats in the shape of swans or tea cups in the river below the castle. Admission is ¥200 ($1.60).

The **Orient Museum,** open every day except Monday from 9 a.m. to 4:30 p.m., exhibits about 2,000 items of artwork from the ancient Orient, including pottery, glassware, and metalwork from Asia, Iran, Syria, and ancient Mesopotamia. Admission is ¥200 ($1.60). Another museum worth visiting is the **Hayashibara Art Museum,** about a five-minute walk from Okayama Castle. Open daily from 9 a.m. to 5 p.m. and charging an entrance fee of ¥300 ($2.40), it contains relics belonging to the former feudal owners of the castle, the Ikeda clan, including furniture, swords, pottery, lacquerware, and armor. And finally, north of Korakuen Park and across the river is the **Yumeji Art Museum,** dedicated to the works of Takehisa Yumeji. Born in Okayama Prefecture in 1884, Yumeji is sometimes referred to as Japan's Toulouse-Lautrec and is credited with developing the fin de siècle art nouveau movement in Japan. This museum is open every day from 9 a.m. to 6 p.m., except from November through March, when it closes an hour earlier and is closed all day on Monday. Admission is ¥500 ($4).

SHOPPING

A sampling of products and crafts made in Okayama Prefecture can be seen at the **Okayama Prefectural Product Center (Okayama-ken Bussan Tenjijo)** ⑱⑨, 1-3-1 Tamachi (tel. 25-4765), about a ten-minute walk from Okayama Station. It features Bizen pottery, rush-grass mats (*igusa*), woodcarvings, colorful wooden masks, spirits and papier-mâché toys, and more. Closed Sunday and holidays, it's open the rest of the week from 9 a.m. to 5 p.m.

For general shopping, at Okayama Station there's a large underground shopping arcade called **Ichibangai** with boutiques selling clothing, shoes, and accessories, and across from the station is the Takashimaya department store. In addition, in the heart of the city is also the **Omotecho** covered shopping arcade, where you'll find Tenmaya, Okayama's largest department store.

WHERE TO STAY

A Western-style hotel with a resort-like holiday atmosphere, the **Okayama Kokusai Hotel,** 4-1-16 Kadota Honmachi (tel. 0862/73-7311), is located above the city on a wooded hill about a 15-minute taxi ride from the station. It features a rooftop beer garden with romantic views of the city lights, open from the end of June through August; and an outdoor swimming pool, open from mid-July to the end of August. Built in 1973, this hotel also has the most psychedelic elevators I've ever seen—their walls are lined with fabric of colorful silk threads in wavy patterns. Rooms face either the city or the woods—with the view of the city being the most dramatic. The cheapest single and double rooms face the woods, but all twins and higher-priced doubles have views of the city. Rates range from ¥8,800 ($70) to ¥12,000 ($96) for a single, ¥17,600 ($141) to ¥18,500 ($148) for a double, and start at ¥16,500 ($132) for a twin. Rooms are comfortable and feature a radio, free English newspapers, an alarm clock, and a refrigerator stocked with everything from beer to "titbits"—which turn out to be nuts. The television has a video channel you can view for an extra charge, including movies in English, sports, and adult movies that the management assures "can be put off at your inconvenience." Ah, the joys of Japanese English. The staff here is friendly and courteous, and restaurants serve Japanese, French, and Chinese cuisine.

Hotel New Okayama, 1-1-25 Ekimae-cho (tel. 0862/23-8211), is a spacious hotel located right across from Okayama Station's east exit. The large lobby is on the sixth floor. Rooms are luxuriously appointed, with large windows covered with shoji-like screens, semidouble beds, minibar, radio, refrigerator, and alarm clock. Rates here range from ¥11,000 ($88) to ¥14,300 ($114) for a single, ¥17,600 ($141) to ¥26,000 ($208) for a twin, and are ¥17,600 ($141) for a double. The cheapest singles face an inner courtyard and have absolutely no view, so it may be worth it to spring for the higher-priced rooms. The hotel has both Japanese and Western restaurants, and from May to mid-August there's a beer garden on the hotel's roof from 5 to 9 p.m.

Located right beside Okayama Station to the right as you exit from the east side is the **Okayama Terminal Hotel,** 1-5 Ekimoto-cho (tel. 0862/33-3131). Your average business hotel, this white building houses rooms with TV, hot water for tea, radio, and clock, which begin at ¥6,200 ($50) for a single, ¥11,000 ($88) for a twin, and ¥11,600 ($93) for a double. The front desk is on the third floor, and rooms feature double-pane windows to shut out traffic noise.

Opened in 1988, **Washington Hotel,** 3-6 Honmachi (tel. 0862/31-9111), is about a five-minute walk from the station on Momotaro Odori. Its lobby is up on the second floor, and 167 of its 210 rooms are singles that range in price from ¥6,000 ($48) to ¥6,800 ($54), all of which feature semidouble beds. Twins and doubles start at ¥11,500 ($92). Rooms are pleasant, with windows that open, bilingual TV (operated by a bedside control panel), radio, push-button phone, and refrigerator. Toilets are even equipped with bidet-like jets of water, the latest in Japanese technology. Facilities here include a Chinese restaurant and a live-music house in the basement called Kento's, which features "oldies but goodies," tunes from the '50s and '60s.

Hotel Sunroute ⑲, 1-3-12 Shimoishi (tel. 0862/32-2345), is a chain business hotel about a ten-minute walk from the station. Look for a red-brick building. Rooms are basic, coming with TV with pay video, clock, hot-water pot, and tea bags. Singles start at ¥5,700 ($46), doubles and twins run ¥9,900 ($79), and triples cost ¥15,500 ($124).

About a five-minute taxi ride from the station, **Culture Hotel,** 1-3-2 Gankunan-cho (tel. 0862/55-1122), is an excellent choice for a modestly priced hotel. It is a rather striking white building, which opened in 1983, and its lobby uses white bricks in a number of imaginative ways—chipped to form patterns, buckled, or pulled out from the wall in relief. Water from an inside fountain empties into a stream that runs through the lobby lounge to an outside waterfall and small garden. I wish other hotels in this price category would take their cue from this establishment and put as much excitement into their designs as this one does.

Rooms here are pleasantly decorated with cheerful flowered wallpaper and have a clock, radio, and hot-water pot. They cost ¥6,500 ($52) for a single, ¥12,000 ($96) for a twin or double. There are also eight Japanese-style rooms that range from ¥13,000 ($104) to ¥16,500 ($132). Used primarily by wedding parties in preparation for elaborate receptions held at the hotel, some of them look onto a small private garden. The hotel's one restaurant serves Western food.

Okayama Plaza Hotel, 2-3-12 Hama (tel. 0862/72-1201), is right next to Korakuen Park, about a ten-minute taxi ride from the station. The lobby features a gigantic wind chime—glass chandeliers in front of the main door which sway in the breeze and make a music of their own. Rooms are large with semidouble beds, but the bathrooms are fairly small. You'll pay ¥6,500 ($52) and up for a single, ¥12,000 ($96) for a twin, and ¥13,200 ($106) for a double.

The Budget Category

Matsunoki ⑲, 19-1 Ekimotocho (tel. 0862/53-4111), is located just a two-minute walk from the west side of Okayama Station. A gleaming white building that was built in 1987, it's situated behind the New Station Hotel. Owned and managed by a friendly family, it has 15 Japanese-style tatami rooms and 5 Western-style singles and twins. All rooms are equipped with deep Japanese tub, Western toilet, hairdryer, TV, and air conditioning, and those that face east toward the station even have their own little balcony. Rates are on a per-person basis and are ¥6,900 ($55) with two meals and ¥4,900 ($39) without meals. If there are two or more of you sharing a room, the rate without meals drops to ¥4,000 ($32) per person. Meals are served in a cheerful, communal dining hall. Incidentally, there are 10 more Japanese-style rooms in an older annex next door. All without private bathroom, these nevertheless go for about the same price.

The **Youth Hostel Okayama-ken Seinen Kaikan** ⑫, 1-7-6 Tsukura-cho (tel.

0862/52-0651), is about a 20-minute walk from Okayama Station. Its 13 Japanese-style rooms sleep three to ten persons per room, for a total capacity of 65 persons. Members are charged ¥2,000 ($16) and nonmembers pay ¥2,750 ($22). Breakfasts cost ¥400 ($3.20) and dinners, ¥650 ($5.20).

International Villas

Although they're not located within the city limits of Okayama, you might consider treating yourself to a few days in the country by staying at an International Villa. Financed and maintained by the Okayama prefectural government, these small country inns are the brainstorm of Okayama's governor, who wished to repay the kindness he had received from foreigners during his trips abroad as a youth. Thus, these villas are open only to foreigners, though accompanying Japanese guests are welcome. The cost of staying at one of the villas is only ¥3,000 ($24) per person for nonmembers and ¥2,000 ($20) for members, but it's worth becoming a member because all you have to do is pay an initial ¥500 ($4) application fee—for which you receive a telephone card worth ¥500 in phone calls that you can use anywhere! Each villa is small, with only a half dozen or so guest rooms, and is outfitted with the latest in bathroom and kitchen facilities. You can cook your own food or visit one of the local restaurants.

So far, three villas have been opened, with two more slated for completion by the time you read this. One of the completed villas, modeled after a traditional soy-sauce warehouse, is located in a mountain village named **Fukiya,** an old copper-mining town that has changed little since the mid-19th century. In **Koshihata,** accommodations are in an old but renovated thatched farmhouse, and in **Ushimado** guests stay in a modern, open-beamed villa with sweeping views of the Seto Inland Sea. In short, these villas are remarkable—and maybe other prefectures will take their cue from Okayama and start building inexpensive lodging. For more information on the International Villas, call the Okayama Prefectural Government's **International Exchange Section** at (0862)24-2111, ext. 2805.

WHERE TO DINE

As with all cities in Japan, you won't have any problems finding restaurants in Okayama. Many Japanese restaurants are clustered around Okayama Station, while the best Western restaurants are located in the hotels.

Japanese Food

If you're hungry for sushi, you can't go wrong with **Gonta-Zushi** ⑲, 1-2-1 Nodaya-cho (tel. 23-6442). The prices are reasonable, the food is excellent, and the atmosphere is typical sushi bar with a long counter and sushi experts dressed in traditional garb with twisted headbands. Sushi set meals range from ¥880 ($7.04) to ¥2,700 ($21.60). I had the Nigiri Matsu for ¥1,850 ($14.80), which came with nigiri-zushi of conger eel, shrimp, squid, sea bream, tuna, and fish from the Seto Inland Sea, and three *norimaki* (edible seaweed rolled around rice and pickled vegetables). If you order sushi à la carte, it will be served to you on large shiny leaves. Other choices include seafood kaiseki starting at ¥5,000 ($40) and the Okayama Barazushi set for ¥1,400 ($11.20). Traditionally served during festive occasions, this Okayama specialty consists of a rice casserole laced with shredded ginger and cooked egg yolk and topped with a variety of goodies, including conger eel, shrimp, fish, lotus root, and bamboo. They also sell sushi to go here starting at ¥500 ($4). Hours are 10:30 a.m. to 11 p.m.; closed the second and fourth Mondays of the month. This sushi bar is about a five-minute walk from Okayama Station. To reach it, take the Ekimae Shotengai covered shopping arcade from the station, walk all the way through, and after emerging from the arcade you'll come to a busy street. Gonta-Zushi is across this street on the left corner, recognizable by its white lanterns hanging in front of the door and green sign.

There are lots of inexpensive restaurants in the basement of the Dai-ichi Central

Building across from Okayama Station's east exit. Among the restaurants selling pizza, plus Chinese and Japanese cuisine, is **Suishin** ⑲ (tel. 32-5101), which specializes in kamameshi (rice casserole dishes), with prices starting at ¥660 ($5.28). This is a chain restaurant with headquarters in Hiroshima. Being a great fan of eel dishes, I chose the eel kamameshi, which came laced with bits of conger eel, ginger, and boiled egg yolk with Japanese pickles on the side. The Japanese menu shows pictures of other dishes served, including cold shabu-shabu, tempura, and sushi. Most dishes cost under ¥2,000 ($16). A simply furnished and popular place, it gets quite busy at lunchtime. It's open from 11 a.m. to 9 p.m.; closed Wednesday.

Although it sounds as if it should be French, **C'est La Vie** ⑲, located in the basement of the Honmachi Building, Honmachi (tel. 31-6155), is a Japanese restaurant specializing in kaiseki meals beginning at ¥10,000 ($80) and vegetarian offerings beginning at ¥5,500 ($44). You can also order elaborate obento meals, which come in large round lacquered boxes for ¥2,700 ($21.60) and up. Closed Wednesday, it's open for dinner from 5 to 9 p.m. During lunch hours, from 11 a.m. to 2:30 p.m., it serves teishoku specials ranging from ¥1,650 ($13.20) to ¥4,400 ($35) for tempura, tofu, sashimi, or eel. This restaurant is located about a three-minute walk from Okayama Station.

In the heart of town just off the Omotecho covered shopping arcade is **Okabe** ⑲, 1-10-1 Omotecho (tel. 22-1404), a very popular and informal eatery specializing in tofu it makes itself. Open every day except Sunday and national holidays from 11 a.m. to 3 p.m. and 5 to 9 p.m., it offers a great lunchtime Okabe Teishoku for ¥650 ($5.20), which consists mainly of tofu dishes along with rice and pickled vegetables. Seating is along one long counter, behind which an army of women scurry to get out orders. This is one of Okayama's best-known restaurants.

Western Food

For relaxed and intimate dining, head for the Okayama Kokusai Hotel, 4-1-16 Kadota Honmachi, to eat at its French restaurant on the 13th floor. Called **L'Arc en Ciel** (tel. 73-7311), it has sweeping views of the city (beautiful at sunset) and is open daily from 11:30 a.m. to 2 p.m. and 5 to 10 p.m. If you order à la carte for such dishes as filet of steak or lobster, you can expect to spend about ¥7,000 ($56) per person for a full-course meal. Dishes here are imaginative and fun. I once had filet of sole in white cream sauce and was surprised to see it arrive with small squid, a shrimp, and shredded crab and carrots on top. There are also set meals ranging from ¥5,500 ($44) to ¥11,000 ($88) and lunch specials from ¥2,200 ($17.60).

Akatogarashi ⑲, 6-27 Togiya-cho (tel. 25-7966), means "hot pepper" in Japanese and is the name of an inexpensive Italian restaurant about a ten-minute walk from Okayama Station. To reach it, walk east from the station on Momotaro Dori Street (the street on which the streetcar runs). Akatogarashi is on a side street—the third right after crossing over the canal (there's a stoplight on the corner). A one-room place with white stucco walls, heavy ceiling beams, and Italian wine bottles as decoration, it's small and personable, and for some reason attracts mainly young Japanese females, who the manager here figures make up about 80% of its clientele. Open every day except every third Sunday and every Monday from 11 a.m. to 3 p.m. and 5 to 10 p.m., it serves different kinds of spaghetti starting at ¥800 ($6.40), pizzas from ¥850 ($6.80), and entrées of chicken, beef, lamb, and fish that average ¥1,400 ($11.20) to ¥2,000 ($16). There are also set dinners ranging from ¥2,700 ($21.60) to ¥5,500 ($44) and a lunch teishoku for ¥800 ($6.40).

For inexpensive French dining, try **Petit ("Puchi") Marie** ⑲, 6-7 Nishikimachi (tel. 22-9066), located about a five-minute walk east of Okayama Station. In this tiny one-room establishment that's so popular customers line up outside, the interior is kind of corny but the food is fun, with most of the dishes costing less than ¥2,500 ($20). A beef stew cooked in red wine is popular, as is the set lunch, which costs ¥700 ($5.60). Hours here are from 11:15 a.m. to 2:45 p.m. (last order) and from 5 to 9 p.m. (last order). It's closed on Wednesday.

If you're in the vicinity of Korakuen Park, you might want to try the ninth-floor restaurant of the **Okayama Plaza Hotel** (tel. 72-1201), open daily from 7 a.m. to 9 p.m. Its huge windows give this Western restaurant a bright and spacious look. The à la carte menu includes steaks, sole, and scallops, as well as spaghetti, pilaf, and curry rice. Best bet is the Chef's Suggestion, a changing full-course meal that usually costs about ¥5,500 ($44). There are also special Western and Japanese set lunches for ¥1,650 ($13.20) and up.

9. Kurashiki

If I were forced to select what I consider to be the most picturesque town in Japan, Kurashiki would certainly be a top contender. In the heart of the city clustered around a willow-fringed canal is a delightful area of old buildings and ryokan perfect for camera buffs. As an administrative center of the shogunate in the 17th century, Kurashiki blossomed into a prosperous marketing town where rice, sake, and cotton were collected from the surrounding region and shipped off to Osaka and beyond. Back in those days wealth was measured in rice, and large granaries were built in which to store the mountains of granules passing through the town. Canals were dug so that barges laden with grain could work their way to ships anchored in the Seto Inland Sea. "Kurashiki," in fact, means Warehouse Village. It's these warehouses still standing that give Kurashiki its distinctive charm. In addition, Kurashiki is known throughout Japan for its many art museums.

ORIENTATION

Before leaving Tokyo, pick up the leaflet *Okayama and Kurashiki* at the Tourist Information Center. In Kurashiki, the **tourist information office** (tel. 26-8681) at Kurashiki Station passes out maps in English and will point you in the right direction to your hotel. It's located on the second floor of the station near the ticket wicket and is open daily from 9 a.m. to 5:30 p.m.

The willow-lined canal with all the museums is only a ten-minute walk south of Kurashiki Station. There's another tourist information office, called the **Kurashiki-Kan** (tel. 22-0542), located right on the canal, which also has maps and brochures. It's open from 9 a.m. to 5:30 p.m. (to 5 p.m. in winter) and is the only Western-looking wooden building in the area.

Note that if you're arriving in Kurashiki by Shinkansen (which takes about 4½ hours from Tokyo and almost 2 hours from Kyoto), you'll arrive at Shin-Kurashiki Station, which is about six miles west of Kurashiki Station and the heart of the city. The local train between the stations runs about every 20 minutes. If you're coming to Kurashiki from the east, it's easier to disembark from the Shinkansen in Okayama and transfer to a local train for the 17-minute ride directly to Kurashiki Station.

The **telephone area code** for Kurashiki is 0864, and the town is located in Okayama Prefecture.

THE SIGHTS

Called the Bikan Area, Kurashiki's old town is small, consisting of a canal lined with graceful willows and 200-year-old granaries. The granaries are made of black-tile walls topped with white mortar, and many of them have been turned into museums, ryokan, restaurants, and boutiques selling hand-blown glass, papier-mâché toys, and mats and handbags made of igusa (rush grass). Street vendors sell jewelry, their wares laid out beside the canal, and healthy young boys stand ready to give visitors rides in rickshaws. "I hear they're imported from Hong Kong," explains a resident who feels impelled to stop and point out Kurashiki's museums spread out along the canal. He's anxious that I don't miss a thing. Another Kurashiki resident advises me that because of the crowds that descend upon Kurashiki during the day (about four million tourists come here a year), I should get up early in the morning before the shops and museums open and explore this tiny area while it's still under the magic of the early-morning glow. "Real lovers of Kurashiki come on Monday," he adds, "because that's when most everything is closed and there are less people." But no matter when you come you're likely to fall under the city's spell. Even rain only enhances the contrasting black and white of the buildings. In other words, one of the most rewarding things to do in Kurashiki is simply to explore.

The Museums

A highlight of Kurashiki's old town is its many fine museums. Foremost in this cultural oasis is the **Ohara Art Museum,** which first opened in 1930 and is located right on the canal. The main building, a two-story stone structure that looks like a transplanted Greek temple, is small but manages to contain the works of such European greats as Picasso, Matisse, Vlaminck, Chagall, Manet, Monet, Degas, Pissarro, Sisley, Toulouse-Lautrec, Gauguin, Cézanne, El Greco, Renoir, Corot, and Rodin. The founder of the museum, Magosaburo Ohara, believed that people even in remote Kurashiki should have the opportunity to view great works of art. Other galleries on the museum grounds hold modern Japanese paintings, contemporary Japanese and Western art, ceramics, and woodblock prints, including prints by the famous Japanese artist Shiko Munakata, paintings by Ryusei Kishida, and ceramics by Shoji Hamada. The entrance fee of ¥600 ($4.80) allows entry to all galleries, and hours are 9 a.m. to 5 p.m. Note that along with most museums in Kurashiki, this one is closed on Monday.

Incidentally, after visiting the Ohara Art Museum you might wish to stop in at **El Greco coffeehouse** (tel. 22-0297) next door. An ivy-colored stone building, it's Kurashiki's most famous coffeeshop and is simply decorated with a wooden floor, wooden tables and benches, and vases of fresh flowers. It serves coffee, green tea, milkshakes, ice cream, and cake from 10 a.m. to 5 p.m. Like the museums, it's closed Monday.

Continuing along the same side of the canal as the Ohara Art Museum and rounding the curve to the right, you'll come to the **Kurashiki Museum of Folkcraft,** easily identified by its sign in English. With the slogan "Usability Equals Beauty," the museum contains folkcrafts not only from Japan but from various countries around the world, giving a unique glimpse at the similarities and differences in cultures as reflected in the items they make and use in daily life. There are baskets, for example, made of straw, bamboo, willow, and other materials from such diverse cultures as Taiwan, Hawaii, Mexico, Sweden, Indonesia, England, Portugal, Germany, and Japan. There are also ceramics, glass, textiles, and woodwork. The displays are housed in three old rice granaries, virtual museum pieces in themselves. Admission is ¥400 ($3.20), and hours are 9 a.m. to 5 p.m. (to 3 p.m. December through February); closed Monday.

Almost next to the Folkcraft Museum is the **Japanese Rural Toy Museum,** a delightful and colorful display of traditional and antique toys from all over Japan, as well as dolls from various countries (the United States is represented by the cornhusk doll). Included in the museum are miniature floats, spinning tops, masks, and kites—2,000 items in all. It's open every day from 8 a.m. to 5 p.m., which means you can drop by even on a Monday, and admission is ¥300 ($2.40). A store at the entrance sells toys in case your appetite has been whetted by all those wonderful creations.

Other museums worth exploring include the **Archeological Museum,** with objects unearthed in the surrounding region as well as relics of the Incas and Chinese, and the **Ohashi House,** built in 1796 by a wealthy merchant family that made its fortune in rice and salt. The **Kurashiki City Art Museum (Shiritsu Bijutsukan)** is on the second floor of what used to be city hall and houses works of art by Yoson

Ikeda and other Kurashiki artists. Many visitors stop by just to see the building itself, designed by famous architect Kenzo Tange in 1960 and one of the first buildings to use bare concrete as decoration.

Ivy Square

A few minutes' walk from the canal and museums is a complex called Ivy Square. Built as a cotton mill by a local spinning company in 1888, this handsome red-brick complex shrouded in ivy has been renovated into a hotel, restaurants, museums, and a few boutiques and galleries selling crafts. It's especially romantic in the evening, when from the end of June to the end of August there's a beer garden in the inner courtyard open daily from 5:30 to 9:30 p.m. Classical music wafts from loudspeakers built into the brick floors of the courtyard.

As for museums at Ivy Square, the **Kurabo Memorial Hall** shows the history of the old spinning company, a company that was Kurashiki's biggest employer for decades, providing jobs for many young women in the area. Perhaps the most interesting thing to see in this museum is a tape made more than 70 years ago showing life at the factory, including the women's dormitory where many of the single women lived. The tape is located toward the end of the museum and is activated with the push of a button.

Nearby is **Ivy Gakkan,** a museum with a curious mixture of reproductions of the world's famous paintings (perhaps for art students who can't afford trips to see the real thing) and a section devoted to the history of Kurashiki. Interesting here are photographs of the city taken in the early 1900s.

Finally, the **Kojima Memorial Hall** contains more Western art of the Ohara collection, as well as paintings by Torajiro Kojima, who was responsible for going to Europe and purchasing most of the pieces in the Ohara museums. The Oriental Room of the Memorial Hall (it has its own separate entrance) contains vases, pottery, glass, and some sculpture from ancient Egypt, Iran, Turkey, and other early cultures.

Entrance to Kurabo Memorial Hall, Ivy Gakkan, and Kojima Memorial Hall costs ¥400 ($3.20) for a combined ticket. Hours for all are 9 a.m. to 5 p.m., but note that the Kojima Memorial Hall is closed on Monday.

Kurabo Orchid Center

Near Ivy Square is the Kurabo Orchid Center, which displays 200 different varieties of orchids in every conceivable shape, color, and size. Hours here are 9 a.m. to 6 p.m. daily and admission is ¥300 ($2.40).

WHERE TO STAY

One of the great things about staying in Kurashiki is that it offers some really interesting places to stay with a wide selection of choices in all price ranges. The hard part is in selecting just one of them to stay in.

Ryokan

The best place to stay to get a feeling of old Kurashiki is right in the heart of it in one of the old warehouses. **Ryokan Kurashiki** ⑲, 4-1 Honmachi (tel. 0864/22-0730), is made up of an old mansion and three converted rice-and-sugar warehouses more than 250 years old. Located right on Kurashiki's picturesque willow-lined canal and filled with antiques, this ryokan has long, narrow corridors, nooks and crannies, and the peaceful sanctuary of an inner garden. There's no other ryokan in Japan quite like this one—it's fun simply walking through the corridors and looking at all the antiques. No two rooms are alike, and at the Terrace de Ryokan Kurashiki you can sip ceremonial green tea while looking out over a small garden. Even if you don't stay at this ryokan, you may wish to come treat yourself to green tea, which costs ¥500 ($4). Those of the ryokan's 20 rooms without their own private bath and toilet start at ¥16,500 ($132) per person, including two meals, while rooms with their own bathroom start at ¥30,000 ($240). It goes without saying that there are public communal baths. Western-style breakfasts are available.

A Note on Japanese Symbols

Many hotels, restaurants, and other establishments in Japan do not have signs showing their names in English letters. Appendix II lists the Japanese symbols for all such places appearing in this guide. Each establishment name in Japanese symbols is numbered, and the same number appears in an oval in the text following the boldfaced establishment name. For example, in the text Osaka's **Hotel Hokke Club** ⑯₄ is number 164 in the Japanese symbol list in Appendix II.

Another old building located right on the canal that has been converted into a ryokan is **Tsurugata** ⑳₀, 1-3-15 Chuo (tel. 0864/24-1635). About 240 years old, it was once a merchant's house and shop selling rice, cotton, and cooking oil. All 13 rooms here have their own toilet but only three come with bath as well. There are public baths, however, with instructions in English on how to use them, indicating that they're accustomed to foreign guests here. Rustic furniture, gleaming wood, and high ceilings are trademarks of this ryokan. Rates per person range from ¥17,500 ($140) to ¥36,000 ($288), including Japanese breakfast and dinner. The kaiseki dinners here are lovely, beautifully arranged on various dishes and as delicious as they look. Tsurugata also maintains its own small restaurant, serving kaiseki, tempura, and sashimi. Open from 11 a.m. to 2 p.m. and 5 to 7 p.m., it's a good place to stop off for lunch. Mini-kaiseki starts at ¥3,300 ($26.40), while sashimi teishoku is ¥1,600 ($12.80).

Minshuku

Kamoi ㉑₁, 1-24 Honmachi (tel. 0864/22-4898), is a minshuku located on a slope leading toward Tsurugatayama Park and Achi Shrine. About a 15-minute walk from Kurashiki Station, this pleasant establishment can be found right beside the stone torii gate leading to Achi Shrine. Charging only ¥5,500 ($44) per person, including two meals (Western breakfast served upon request), this one is popular among young people and its fourth-floor rooms have good views of the city. Since the owner of this minshuku is also owner and chef of a restaurant (described later), you can be assured that the food served here is especially good. Although the building was built about a decade ago, it follows an architectural style befitting old Kurashiki. Rooms are simple, with coin-operated TV, and are without private bathroom. If you take your meals elsewhere, the charge for a room only starts at ¥3,500 ($28).

Located on a tiny side street just off the Kurashiki canal and not far from the Rural Toy Museum, the **Minshuku Kawakami** ㉒₂, 1-10-13 Chuo (tel. 0864/24-1221), has eight Japanese-style rooms. Rooms are simple and without private bathroom, but they have coin-operated TVs and are air-conditioned. Rates per person here are ¥5,500 ($44) with two meals (Western-style breakfasts available) and ¥3,800 ($30) without.

Another minshuku which caters mainly to young Japanese is **Tokusan Kan** ㉓₃, 6-21 Honmachi (tel. 0864/25-3056), located near the canal and Ivy Square.

Rooms are divided into two separate buildings, one 90 years old and the other 200 years old, but both interiors have been totally renovated and are modern. Both buildings serves lunches to tour groups of Japanese, which can be quite noisy, assuming you want to hang around in your room. There are a total of 19 Japanese-style rooms, all but one without private bathroom. The per person charges here are ¥5,500 ($44) with two meals and ¥4,500 ($36) without.

If you prefer to stay closer to the station, **Kokumin Ryokan Ohguma,** 3-1-2 Achi (tel 0864/22-0250), is located just across from Kurashiki Station. The entry to this small establishment with 13 Japanese-style rooms is through a narrow, pedestrian-covered shopping arcade (located to the right of the main road leading from the station, not the more obvious, large arcade located to the left). The ryokan first opened more than 60 years ago, but most of the building dates from about 15 years ago. Rooms with two meals start at ¥7,000 ($56) per person, while room-only rates start at ¥4,400 ($35) per person. One of the rooms has its own private bathroom, which without meals goes for ¥5,200 ($42) per person.

Hotels

The Top Choice: If you prefer to sleep in a bed rather than on a futon, the **Kurashiki Kokusai Hotel,** 1-1-44 Chuo (tel. 0864/22-5141), is Kurashiki's most popular Western-style hotel—and it's easy to see why. This delightful 106-room hotel built in 1963 blends into its surroundings, with walls of black tiles set in white mortar. Inside the hotel's lobby are two huge woodblock prints by Japanese artist Shiko Munakata. Commissioned by the hotel, the work is titled *Great Barriers of the Universe* and constitutes his largest piece. The atmosphere of the hotel is decidedly a little old-fashioned, which only adds to the charm. If you prefer more modern surroundings, however, ask for a room in the much newer annex, which features mainly twins with slightly upgraded facilities. The hotel is located behind the Ohara Art Museum about a ten-minute walk from Kurashiki Station, and its back rooms have a pleasant view of the museum, greenery, and the black-tile roofs of the old granaries. It's a convenient location for exploring the old town, and facilities include a pleasant Western-style restaurant, a Japanese-style restaurant with a tempura corner, a bar, and a beer garden in the backyard from mid-July to the end of August. All rooms come with radio, TV, refrigerator, hot-water pot, and tea bags. Rates range from ¥8,000 ($64) to ¥9,500 ($76) for a single, ¥13,000 ($104) to ¥14,000 ($112) for a double, and ¥13,500 ($108) to ¥18,700 ($150) for a twin. The more expensive rooms are those that face the back of the hotel, which have the most pleasant views.

The Medium-Priced Range: Another interesting place to stay, and a good choice in this price category, the **Ivy Hotel,** 7-2 Honmachi (tel. 0864/22-0011), is located in the converted cotton mill on Ivy Square. The hotel opened in 1974 with 180 rooms that have a somewhat stark but country feel to them. Much of the architectural style of the old mill has been left intact. Rooms come with the usual TV, fridge, clock, and hot water for tea, and all rooms have a toilet. Singles without a bathtub start at ¥6,500 ($52), while those with bath are ¥8,800 ($70). Twins without bath start at ¥10,500 ($84), and those with bath begin at ¥13,700 ($110). All doubles have baths and are ¥16,500 ($132), while triples are without bath and start at ¥12,500 ($100). The best rooms are those that face a tiny expanse of green grass and an ivy-covered wall.

Not far from the Ohara Museum and the Bikan area is **El Paso Inn,** 1-9-4 Chuo (tel. 0864/21-8282). I'm not sure why it has the name it does, but at any rate it opened in 1987 and appeals mainly to the younger generation. Having only 31 rooms, it features a pleasant and contemporary restaurant with seating under a glass-domed inner courtyard. Rooms are simple, with fridge, phone, TV, and tiny unit bathroom. Those on the third floor facing north have the best view. Rates, which include service but not tax, are ¥6,000 ($48) for a single, ¥10,900 ($87) for two in a semidouble bed, ¥12,000 ($96) for a twin, ¥17,500 ($140) for a triple, and

¥24,000 ($192) for a quadruple. You can rent bicycles here for ¥250 ($2) for the whole day.

If you prefer to stay in a place close to Kurashiki Station, you can't get any closer than the **Hotel Kurashiki,** 1-1-1 Achi, a business hotel located right above the train station (tel. 0864/26-6111) and part of the Japan Railways group. To find it, take the south exit from the station, go outside, and turn right. The entrance to the hotel is on the ground level, and check-in time is 2 p.m. The rooms in this modern, spotless, and attractive hotel are pleasantly decorated with flowered bedspreads and cheerful pastels of green or pink and have nicely tiled bathrooms instead of the usual one-unit cubbyholes of most business hotels. Windows are of double-pane glass to shut out noise, and there are both Japanese and Western restaurants. Singles here are ¥7,200 ($58), twins begin at ¥12,000 ($96), and triples are ¥16,500 ($132).

Another business hotel close to the station is the **Kurashiki Terminal Hotel** ㉔, 1-7-2 Achi (tel. 0864/26-1111). After emerging from the south exit of Kurashiki Station, look for the red-brick building immediately to the right with the name of the hotel written at the top of the building. The lobby is on the ninth floor, and its 212 rooms are spread between the 10th and 12th floors. The rooms come with TV with pay video, minibar, alarm clock, and double-pane windows. On the ninth floor is a restaurant serving both Japanese and Western food, as well as a buffet-style breakfast costing ¥1,000 ($8). Vending machines dispense beer and soda, and hot water for tea is free. Room rates start at ¥6,000 ($48) for one person, ¥12,000 ($96) for two, and ¥17,000 ($136) for three.

The Budget Category: If all the hostelries suggested above are full, you might try a rather different kind of place called **Young Inn Kurashiki,** 1-14-8 Achi (tel. 0864/25-3411). A red-brick building about a one-minute walk from the south exit of Kurashiki Station behind the Terminal Hotel, it has a youth-hostel feel to it and reminds me more of places in Europe than in Japan. Painted in bright primary colors, it looks as though it might have been rather chic at one time but has faded somewhat with neglect. Informal, it caters mainly to young people, with two to three beds per room; the beds are arranged on different levels in bunk-bed style. In fact, the three-bed rooms on the fifth floor have to be seen to be believed—the third bed is about ten feet off the floor and you have to climb a ladder to reach it. Definitely for the nimble unafraid of heights. There are no single rooms here, but single occupancy rates are ¥3,600 ($29) for a twin without a bathroom and ¥5,200 ($42) for one with a bathroom. Double occupancy rates per person are ¥3,100 ($25) and ¥4,600 ($37), respectively.

The **Kurashiki Youth Hostel,** Mukoyama (tel. 0864/22-7355), has a policy of accepting card-carrying members only, but has been known to let in unknowing foreign nonmembers who show up forlornly on their doorstep. What you do with that bit of information is up to you. It's located 30 minutes from the station—on foot, there are no buses that go there. There are eight persons to a room with 80 beds total. The price is ¥2,300 ($18.40) per night, ¥700 ($5.60) for dinner, and ¥450 ($3.60) for breakfast. If you don't have a membership card and they accept you, expect to spend about ¥500 ($4) more for your overnight stay.

WHERE TO DINE

Kamoi ㉕, 1-3-17 Chuo (tel. 22-0606), is a sushi restaurant run by the man who has a minshuku of the same name. It's located in a 200-year-old rice granary along Kurashiki's willow-fringed canal across from the Ohara Art Museum. Inside, the stark-white walls and dark wooden beams are decorated with such antiques as cast-iron teapots, old rifles, gourds, and samurai hats. Since the menu is in Japanese, you can select from the plastic display outside the front door. Set meals range from ¥1,000 ($8) to ¥2,000 ($16), and in addition to sushi there's also tempura, eel, and *daikonzushi,* a local rice dish covered with vegetables and seafood commonly served during festivals. During winter the same dish is served warm and is called *nukuzushi.* The cost of both rice casseroles is ¥750 ($6). Closed, along with the museums, on Monday, it's open the rest of the week from 9 a.m. to 7:30 p.m. (last order is 6 p.m.).

Kiyutei, 1-2-20 Chuo (tel. 22-5141), is also located across from the main entrance of the Ohara Art Museum at the head of the canal. Enter through the front gate, pass through the small courtyard, and enter a small room dominated by a counter with cooks grilling steaks, the specialty of the house. Steak dinners, which come with soup, salad, and rice or roll, range from ¥2,200 ($17.60) to ¥5,500 ($44). The English à la carte menu lists such dishes as grilled lobster or salmon, stewed beef with soup, hamburger steak, spaghetti, fried shrimp, and grilled chicken, with most dishes around ¥1,000 ($8) to ¥2,000 ($16). Closed on Monday, it's open other days from 11 a.m. to 9 p.m. (last order is 8 p.m.).

For more Western dining close to the canal, **Wisteria** (tel. 22-5141), in the Kurashiki Kokusai Hotel, offers a pleasant setting with large windows. Lunch, served daily from 11 a.m. to 2 p.m., includes such selections as seafood, salads, spaghetti, sandwiches, and beef or shrimp curry, with most dishes between ¥1,000 ($8) and ¥1,800 ($14.40). Lunch set meals begin at ¥1,400 ($11.20). Dinner, served from 6 to 9:30 p.m., includes seafood, roasted duck with peach, stewed beef, grilled salmon, lobster, and steaks. If available, try the *sawara* in champagne, a locally caught fish. Set dinner courses begin at ¥4,500 ($36).

In Ivy Square you might try **Tsuta** (tel. 22-0011), which means "ivy" in Japanese. It serves local Kurashiki specialties, including special rice dishes, fish, obento, sukiyaki, shabu-shabu, and farm products. Set in the converted spinning factory, it has high ceilings and is airy and bright. Most set meals here range from ¥1,500 ($12) to ¥5,000 ($40). The most popular dish consists of rice with red beans, sashimi, fried tofu, and vegetables and is called *obento rikyu*. It's open daily from 11:30 a.m. to 2 p.m. and 5 to 9 p.m.

Next to Tsuta in Ivy Square is **Restaurant Ivy** (tel. 22-0011), which serves Western fare. It's open every day from 11:30 a.m. to 9 p.m. Decorated on an ivy theme, even the tablecloths and napkins are green with designs of vines. It also has the high ceiling of the original factory. Set menus start at ¥2,000 ($16) for a hamburger course, going up to ¥4,500 ($36) for sirloin or tenderloin steak dinners. À la carte entrées average ¥2,000 ($16) and include salmon or shrimp, scallops, chicken, pork ginger, beef teriyaki, or beef Stroganoff. Less expensive dishes include beef or shrimp curry, mixed pilaf, spaghetti, and sandwiches for ¥1,000 ($8) to ¥1,500 ($12).

---

10. Matsue

With a population of about 140,000, Matsue lies near the northern coast of western Honshu. It's off the beaten track of most foreign tourists, who keep to a southerly route in their travels toward Kyushu. The Japanese, however, are quite fond of Matsue, and a fair number of them choose to spend their summer vacation at this pleasant small town. I'll always remember Matsue as the place where the local schoolchildren greet foreigners with *"konnichiwa"* (good afternoon) instead of the usual *"haro"* (hello), testimony to the fact that foreigners are still few and far between. At last check with the Japan National Tourist Organization, only one of the more than 130 group tours organized by foreign tour operators included Matsue in its itinerary of Japan. And yet Matsue, hugging the shores of Lake Shinji, has a number of cultural assets that make a trip here worthwhile.

ORIENTATION

The easiest way to reach Matsue is from Okayama via a three-hour train ride. There's also one daily express to Matsue directly from Hiroshima (a beautiful ride, by the way). Upon arrival at Matsue Station, stop off at one of the **tourist informa-**

tion offices. One is located inside the station itself and is open daily from 8:30 a.m. to 7 p.m. An additional information office is located to the left after you leave the station by the north exit, and it's open daily from 9:30 a.m. to 5:30 p.m. Both locations have an English brochure with a good map of the city. If you have any questions, call the tourist office (tel. 27-2598).

Matsue's attractions lie to the north of the station, and although buses run virtually everywhere, you can easily cover the distances on foot. At the Tokyo or Kyoto T.I.C. be sure to pick up the leaflet *Matsue and Izumo-Taisha Shrine.*

The **telephone area code** for Matsue is 0852. Matsue is located in Shimane Prefecture.

THE SIGHTS

Although Matsue's sights are concentrated in one area of town and are easy to find on your own, you may wish to apply for a "goodwill guide" to show you around, especially if you're going to Izumo-Taisha Shrine. Established by the Japan National Tourist Organization, the goodwill guide network is composed of volunteers with foreign-language abilities who act as guides in their city. All you have to do is pay their entrance fees into museums, etc., and it's nice if you buy them lunch too. If you wish to have guides (they're always assigned in pairs), apply the day before at one of the tourist information offices listed above before 4 p.m.

First built in 1611 and partly reconstructed in 1642, **Matsue Castle** was the only castle along this northern stretch of coast built for warfare rather than merely as a residence. It's also one of Japan's few original castles—that is, it's not a reconstruction as many castles are. Rising up from a hill with a good view of the city about one mile northwest of Matsue Station, the five-story donjon (which actually conceals six floors to give its warriors a fighting advantage) houses the usual daimyo and samurai gear, including armor, swords, and helmets. Lafcadio Hearn, a European who lived in Matsue in the 1890s, adopted Japanese citizenship, and wrote extensively about Japan and the Japanese, wrote this about Matsue Castle: "Crested at its summit, like a feudal helmet, with two colossal fishes of bronze lifting their curved bodies skyward from either angle of the roof and bristling with horned gables and gargoyled eaves and tilted puzzles of tiles roofing at every storey, the creation is a veritable architectural dragon, made up of magnificent monstrosities." As you walk through the castle up to the top floor, notice the staircase. Although it looks sturdy, it's light enough that it could be pulled up to halt enemy intrusions back in the feudal days. And to think that the castle almost met its demise during the Meiji Restoration, when the ministry of armed forces auctioned it off. Luckily, former vassals of the clan pooled their resources and bought the castle keep. In 1927 the castle grounds were donated to the city. It is open daily from 8:30 a.m. to 5 p.m.; admission is ¥300 ($2.40).

Just south of Matsue Castle is the **Matsue Cultural Museum (Matsue Kyodokan)** ⑳⑥, a white Western-style building erected in honor of Emperor Meiji in 1903. Open daily from 8:30 a.m. to 5 p.m. and charging ¥150 ($1.20) admission, it displays crafts, utensils, and implements of everyday life from the Meiji era beginning in 1868 through the early part of this century. There are old photographs, manuscripts, old obento lunch boxes, combs and hairpins, and tea ceremony objects.

If you walk from Matsue Castle north along its moat, in about five minutes you'll come to a number of attractions. Stop off at **Teahouse Meimei-an** ⑳⑦, one of Japan's most renowned and well-preserved thatch-roofed tea houses, which was built in 1779. It's located at the top of a flight of stairs from which you have a good view of Matsue Castle. For the entrance fee of ¥150 ($1.20) and an additional ¥300 ($2.40), you can have the bitter Japanese green tea and sweets served to you before moving off to your next destination. It's open daily from 9 a.m. to 5 p.m.

Buke Yashiki ⑳⑧, a few minutes' walk from the tea house, is an ancient samurai house open daily to the public from 8:30 a.m. to 5 p.m. Facing the castle moat, it was built in 1730 and belonged to the Shiomi family, one of the chief retainers of the feudal lord residing in the castle. High-ranking samurai, the Shiomi family lived pretty much like kings themselves, with a separate servants' quarters and even a shed for their palanquin. As you walk around this house, peering into rooms with their wooden walls slid open to the outside breeze, you'll see furniture and objects used in daily life by samurai during the Edo Period. Admission is ¥200 ($1.60).

On the same street as this samurai house are two more attractions. The **Tanabe Art Museum** ⑳, is a modern building housing changing exhibits of ceramics and artwork, open every day from 9 a.m. to 5 p.m. except Monday and days of exhibit changes. Its admission ranges from ¥500 ($4) to ¥750 ($6), depending on the exhibit. The **Hearn Memorial Hall (Hearn Kinenkan)** contains memorabilia of writer Lafcadio Hearn (1850–1904), including his desk, manuscripts, and smoking pipes. The Japanese are fascinated with this man who married a Japanese, took out Japanese citizenship, and adopted the name Koizumi Yakumo. Writing a number of books about Japan, he was one of the first writers to give the Japanese the chance to see themselves through the eyes of a foreigner. His books still provide insight into Japanese life at the turn of the century and are available at all bookstores in Japan with an English section. Since most Japanese will assume it's out of respect for Hearn that you've come to Matsue, you may want to read one of his books before coming here. His volume *Glimpses of Unfamiliar Japan* contains an essay called "In a Japanese Garden," in which he gives his impressions of Matsue, where he lived for 15 months before moving to Kumamoto to teach English. This memorial is open daily from 8:30 a.m. to 5 p.m. and admission is ¥200 ($1.60). Near the memorial is a Japanese-style house where Hearn lived. Charging ¥100 (80¢), it's open from 9 a.m. to 4:30 p.m. (until 5 p.m. in summer); closed Wednesday.

About a 15-minute walk west of Matsue Castle is **Gesshoji Temple** ⑩, the family temple of the Matsudaira clan. It was established back in 1664 by Naomasa Matsudaira, whose grandfather was the powerful Ieyasu Tokugawa. Generations of the Matsudaira clan are buried here. It's open daily from 8 a.m. to 6 p.m. (5 p.m. in winter), and admission is ¥300 ($2.40).

The most important religious structure in the vicinity of Matsue, however, is **Izumo-Taisha Shrine.** It takes 55 minutes from Matsue-onsen Station to Izumo-Taisha-mae Station, with a change of trains required at Kawato Station. The shrine is important, however, because its site is the oldest in Japan and is probably the most popular attraction in the area. But as with most things in Japan, the present shrine buildings date only from 1744 and 1874. Dedicated to the Shinto deity responsible for medicine and farming, the shrine is constructed in an ancient style, simple and dignified.

SHOPPING

For one-stop shopping for locally crafted goods, visit the **Shimane Souvenir and Handcraft Center (Shimane-ken Bussankanko-kan)** ㉑, Tonomachi (tel. 22-5758), located just southeast of Matsue Castle close to the Ichibata department store in the Kenmin Kaikan Building. It sells everything from ceramics to furniture to toys and foodstuffs, all products of Shimane Prefecture. It's open daily from 9:30 a.m. to 6 p.m.

More products of Shimane Prefecture are for sale at the **Matsue Folk Art Center (Matsue Meisan Center)** ㉒, Chidori-cho (tel. 21-5252), located next to Ichibata Hotel in an area of town called Matsue Onsen. Open daily from 9 a.m. to 9 p.m., it also features a stage on the third floor where shows of music, dance, and other traditional performing arts are given four times every day except December. The cost is ¥400 ($3.20). Inquire at the tourist office for current showtimes.

FOOD AND LODGING

Accommodations in Matsue include ryokan, tourist hotels, and business hotels, most of them within walking distance of Matsue Station.

Ryokan

Minami-kan ㉑㉓, located off the Kyomise covered shopping arcade at 14 Suetsugu Honmachi (tel. 0852/21-5131), has 12 Japanese-style rooms facing Lake Shinji, 9 of which come with a private bathroom. Completely remodeled in 1985, its modern rooms come with TV and fridge, and cost ¥16,500 ($132) to ¥27,000 ($216) per person. As with most ryokan, prices include two meals, tax, and service charge. Western breakfasts are available. If you want to feel special, there are two rooms in a separate little house right beside the lake that cost up to ¥22,000 ($176) per person.

Minami-kan is also renowned for its restaurant, which overlooks a gravel garden and the water of the lake beyond. Open daily from 11:30 a.m. to 2:30 p.m. and 5 to 9 p.m., it serves lunch menus beginning at ¥1,600 ($12.80). I particularly recommend the mini-kaiseki Hanagoromo set lunch for ¥2,500 ($20) with its various dishes of bite-size morsels. For dinner there are set meals of various local specialties ranging from ¥3,300 ($26.40) to ¥8,800 ($70.40).

An older ryokan tucked away on a side street not far from Matsue Castle, the 50-year-old **Horaiso** ㉑㉔, Tonomachi (tel. 0852/21-4337), is guarded by a wall, an imposing wooden gateway, and a pine tree. It has ten rooms, each one different and facing an inner courtyard garden. Rates here, per person, including two meals, range from ¥11,000 ($88) to ¥22,000 ($176). This is one of the few ryokan that doesn't mind if you want to take your meals elsewhere, in which case it's ¥8,000 ($64) to ¥10,000 ($80) per person, depending on the room. The higher-priced rooms are those with a private bathroom.

Much cheaper than the above two is **Kiraku Ryokan,** Isemiya Machi (tel. 0852/21-5549). Located about a seven-minute walk from Matsue Station (the tourist office has a map with directions), it's in the midst of Matsue's nightlife district. There are eight traditional Japanese rooms here, all without private bathroom. This family-run establishment has been around more than 30 years and it's spotless. Highly recommended. Rates per person here are ¥3,500 ($28) without meals and ¥5,500 ($44) for two meals served in a communal dining room.

Hotels

Tokyu Inn, 590 Asahimachi (tel. 0852/27-0109), one of Matsue's newer business hotels and part of a national chain, is located across the street from Matsue Station's north exit. Its 181 rooms are of adequate size and come with TV and clock. Vending machines dispense beer, cold coffee, soda, and whisky. The front desk is courteous and facilities include the Shangri-La restaurant, which serves both Western and Japanese dishes. It's open from 11 a.m. to 2 p.m. and 5 to 9 p.m. and offers seafood, steaks, spaghetti, tempura, and sandwiches. Japanese-style obento lunch boxes cost ¥850 ($6.80). If you're on a budget or like sitting outside, Tokyu Inn also has a rooftop beer garden open in summer from 5:30 to 9 p.m. Beer starts at ¥550 ($4.40), and the food menu includes yakitori, fried noodles, and chicken steak. Singles at this hotel begin at ¥7,000 ($56), and twins and doubles at ¥13,000 ($104), service included.

Matsue Urban Hotel ㉑㉕, 590-3 Asahimachi (tel. 0852/22-0002), is a red building located to the right of the Tokyu Inn. Its 60 single rooms go for ¥4,800 ($38) and its 10 twins for ¥8,800 ($70). Although the single rooms are rather small, with tiny windows, all beds are semidouble in size, and the twin rooms are all corner rooms with large windows. Rooms are pleasant, with a fridge, clock, and TV with pay video, but large people may have trouble fitting into the tiny tubs. There's a Japanese restaurant as well as a Western restaurant that serves spaghetti and pilaf. The front desk is located up on the second floor.

If there are two of you and you want to sleep in the same bed, you're welcome to one of the semidouble singles mentioned above if you can fit into them, for which the price is ¥7,000 ($56). You're probably better off, however, moving to the

Urban's new annex building next door, which offers 211 single and double rooms. Single rates here are the same as in the older building; doubles are ¥7,700 ($62). The phone number is the same as the one for the main hotel.

Matsue's best-known tourist hotel is the **Hotel Ichibata,** 30 Chidori-cho (tel. 0852/22-0188), located in a part of town called Matsue Onsen, a hot-spring spa. It's not very conveniently located, since it's about a 30-minute hike or 15-minute bus ride from the station and a 20-minute walk to Matsue Castle. In addition, it's seen better days (it was built in 1968). Still, it does have hot-spring public baths on the seventh floor with views over the lake. Right next to Lake Shinji, it also has a summertime beer garden on its front lawn and one restaurant serving both Japanese and Western fare. Rooms, equipped with TV, clock, refrigerator, radio, and hot-water pot for tea, begin at ¥6,500 ($52) for a single and ¥12,000 ($96) for a double—but none of these face the lake. Twins facing the lake begin at ¥17,500 ($140), while those that face inland start at ¥12,000 ($96). All the Japanese-style rooms, which begin at ¥17,500 ($140) for two, have views of the lake, as do the combination-style rooms for ¥18,700 ($150) for two.

There are a couple of business hotels located at the south exit of Matsue Station. The **Matsue Plaza Hotel** ⑯, 469-1 Asahimachi (tel. 0852/26-6650), is a red-brick and brown building across the street from the station. The front desk is located on the second floor. The carpets here are a little worn and the rooms are small, but they're cheap—beginning at ¥4,000 ($32) for a single and ¥7,700 ($62) for a double or twin. On weekends, when business traffic is at its slowest, the price for single rooms drops a couple of hundred yen. No rooms have a great view, but those on the top floor are best. All rooms have a private bathroom, windows that open, coin-operated TV with pay video, clock, and hot-water pot. Both Japanese and Western restaurants are located in the hotel building.

To the right of Plaza Hotel is a white building on a corner that contains the **Matsue Minami Guchi Hotel** ⑰, 470-1 Asahimachi (tel. 0852/27-2000). Its name means "South Exit Hotel." The people working the front desk (on the second floor) are accommodating, and the guest rooms are typical business hotel rooms with TV, bathroom, fridge, and clock, beginning at ¥4,400 ($35) for one person and ¥8,200 ($66) for two.

Youth Hostel

The **Matsue Youth Hostel** ⑱, 1546 Kososhicho (tel. 0852/36-8620), is located about a ten-minute walk from Furue Station, with instructions in English on how to get there available at the Matsue tourist offices at the train station. Rates are ¥3,500 ($28) with two meals, ¥2,500 ($20) if you take your meals elsewhere. Nonmembers pay ¥450 ($3.60) more.

More Dining

For dining outside hotel or ryokan facilities, try **Kaneyasu** ⑲, Otesemba-cho (tel. 21-0550). Located about two minutes directly north of Matsue Station, this is an unpretentious and modest one-counter place with good food run by motherly women bustling behind the counter and back in the kitchen. It's been around for more than 20 years, and about 80% of its customers are local working people. It has a great lunch teishoku for ¥550 ($4.40) that includes a piece of yakizakana (grilled fish), vegetable, soup, tofu, rice, and tea. It's served from 10:30 a.m. to "whenever"; I came at 3 p.m. and still got the lunch special. Since it's popular with local regulars, avoid the noontime rush. If you come for dinner and indulge in sake, sashimi, and grilled fish, expect to spend about ¥3,000 ($24). Hours here are 10 a.m. to 9 p.m.; closed Sunday and holidays.

Also just a few minutes' walk from Matsue Station is **Ginsen** ⑳, Asahimachi (tel. 21-2381), located on the street that runs right in front of the station's north side. One of Matsue's best-known and popular restaurants, it's open every day except Sunday from 11 a.m. to 10 p.m. Its specialty is kamameshi (rice casseroles), which change with the season and may include such toppings as red snapper, oysters, eel, and other delicacies. The Hakozen teishoku, which includes kamameshi, sashimi, soup, rice, and numerous side dishes, begins at ¥2,700 ($21.60), but kamameshi alone costs less than ¥1,000 ($8).

A wonderful place to stop off for lunch if you're sightseeing north of Matsue Castle, **Yagumoan** ㉑ (tel. 22-2400) is located between the Buke Yashiki samurai house and the Tanabe Art Museum on the road bordering the castle moat. Open daily from 9 a.m. to 6 p.m. this lovely soba shop with a tea house–like atmosphere is surrounded by bamboo, bonsai trees, a Japanese garden, and a pond. The noodles here are all handmade and start at ¥500 ($4). Surrounded by a stone wall with a large wooden entryway, part of this restaurant is 200 years old and is a former samurai residence. A plastic-food display case is located to the left as you step through the entryway.

A good choice of an inexpensive evening eatery is **Orochidaiko** ㉒, located right in the Kyomise shopping arcade (tel. 27-4440). It's easy to spot, with its red-paper lantern hanging outside the front door and a mock thatched roof. Open every day except Sunday from 5 to 11 p.m., it offers lots of dishes for less than ¥400 ($3.20), including yakitori, sashimi, tempura, and salads.

11. Hiroshima

With a population of approximately one million, Hiroshima looks just like any other up-and-coming city in Japan. Modern buildings, industry, the manufacture of cars and ships—the city is full of vitality and purpose, with a steady flow of both Japanese and foreign businessmen in and out of the city.

But unlike other cities, Hiroshima's past is clouded: it has the unfortunate distinction of being the first city ever destroyed by an atomic bomb (the second city, and hopefully the last, was Nagasaki). It happened one clear summer morning, August 6, 1945, at 8:15, when three B-29s approached Hiroshima from the northeast. One of them passed over the central part of the city, dropped the bomb, and then sped off at full speed. The bomb exploded 43 seconds later at an altitude of 1,900 feet in a huge fireball, followed by a mushroom cloud of smoke that rose 29,700 feet in the air.

There were approximately 400,000 people living in Hiroshima at the time of the bombing and about half of them lost their lives. The heat from the blast was so intense that it seared people's skin, while the pressure caused by the explosion tore clothes off bodies and caused the rupture and explosion of intestines and other internal organs. Flying glass tore through flesh like bullets, and fires broke out over the city. But that wasn't the end of it. Victims who survived the blast were subsequently exposed to huge doses of radioactivity. Their hair fell out, their gums bled, their white blood cells decreased, and many died of leukemia or other forms of cancer. Even people who showed no outward signs of sickness suddenly died, creating a feeling of panic and helplessness in the survivors. And today people still continue to suffer from the effects of the bomb, including a high incidence of cancer, disfigurement, scars, and keloid skin tissue. Hiroshima's most important event is the peace demonstration held here every year on August 6.

ORIENTATION

Before leaving Tokyo, pick up a copy of the leaflet *Hiroshima and Miyajima* at the T.I.C. The Hiroshima city tourist offices are located both at Hiroshima Station (open daily from 9 a.m. to 5:30 p.m.) and in the Rest House at the north end of Peace Memorial Park (open daily from 9:30 a.m. to 6 p.m. April through September and from 8:30 a.m. to 5 p.m. October through March). Both locations have a brochure and map in English. If you have any questions, call the tourist office at 082/ 249-9329.

There are tram and bus lines running through the city, but you can make the circuit between Shukkei-en Garden, Hiroshima Castle, and Peace Memorial Park on foot. Shukkei-en Garden is 15 minutes from Hiroshima Station; Hiroshima Castle is five minutes from the garden; and from the castle to the park it's another 15-minute walk, passing the A-Bomb Dome on the way. The Hondori covered shopping arcade and its neighboring streets are considered the heart of the city and are located to the east of Peace Park. Close by is Nagarikawa, Hiroshima's nightlife district.

The **telephone area code** for Hiroshima is 082, and Hiroshima is located in the prefecture of the same name.

THE SIGHTS

As you walk around Hiroshima today, it's hard to imagine that it was the scene of such widespread horror and destruction 45 years ago. On the other hand, Hiroshima does not have the old buildings, temples, and historical structures other cities have. But even though there are not many tourist sights in Hiroshima, it draws a steady flow of travelers who come to see Peace Memorial Park, the city's best-known landmark. Hiroshima is also the most popular gateway for cruises of the Seto Inland Sea and for trips to Miyajima, a jewel of an island covered later in this chapter.

Peace Memorial Park

The main focus of Peace Memorial Park, located in the center of the city, is **Peace Memorial Museum.** The exhibit begins by describing the atomic bomb used to destroy the city, the route of the American B-29s, and the intensity of the blast's epicenter. It then goes on to show in graphic detail the effects of the blast on bodies, buildings, and materials. Most of the photographs in the exhibit are of burned and seared skin, charred remains of bodies, and people with open wounds. There's a bronze Buddha that was half melted in the blast and melted glass and ceramics. There are also some granite steps that show a dark shadow where someone had been sitting at the time of the explosion—the shadow is all that remains of that person's life.

Opening at 9 a.m., the museum closes at 6 p.m. May through November and at 5 p.m. December through April. Note that the ticket window closes a half hour before closing time. Admission fee is ¥50 (40¢). The exhibits all have excellent explanations in English.

Next to the museum is the **Peace Memorial Hall,** where two documentaries in English are shown throughout the day on the second floor. One focuses on Hiroshima and the results of the bombing, while the second film takes a more scientific look at the atomic bombs in both Hiroshima and Nagasaki.

To the north of the museum is the **Memorial Cenotaph,** designed by Japan's famous architect Kenzo Tange (who also designed Tokyo's Akasaka Prince Hotel). Shaped like a figurine clay saddle found in ancient tombs, it shelters a stone chest, which in turn holds the names of those killed by the bomb. An epitaph, written in Japanese, carries the hopeful phrase, "Repose ye in Peace, for the error shall not be repeated." If you stand in front of the cenotaph, you have a view through the hollow arch of the Peace Flame and the Atomic-Bomb Dome. The **Peace Flame** will continue to burn until all atomic weapons vanish from the face of the earth and nuclear war is no longer a threat to mankind. The **A-Bomb Dome** is the skeletal ruins of the former Industrial Promotion Hall—it was left as a visual reminder of the death and destruction caused by the single bomb.

Also in the park is the **Statue of the A-Bomb Children,** dedicated to the war's most innocent victims, who died instantly in the blast or afterward from the effects of radiation. The statue is of a girl with outstretched arms, and rising above her is a crane, symbol of happiness and longevity in Japan. The statue is based on the true story of a young girl who suffered from the effects of radiation after the bombing in

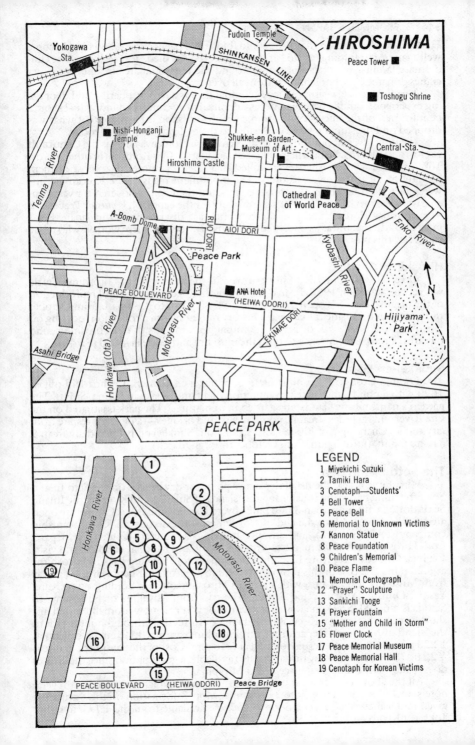

HIROSHIMA

Peace Tower ■

Toshogu Shrine ■

Fudoin Temple

SHINKANSEN LINE

Yokogawa Sta.

Tenma River

Nishi-Honganji Temple

Hiroshima Castle

Shukkei-en Garden · Museum of Art

Central Sta.

Cathedral of World Peace

A-Bomb Dome

RIJO DORI

AIOI DORI

Peace Park

Enko River

Kyobashi River

ANA Hotel (HEIWA ODORI)

PEACE BOULEVARD

Motoyasu River

EKIMAE DORI

N

Hijiyama Park

Asahi Bridge

Honkawa (Ota) River

PEACE PARK

Honkawa River

Motoyasu River

PEACE BOULEVARD (HEIWA ODORI)

Peace Bridge

LEGEND

1 Miyekichi Suzuki
2 Tamiki Hara
3 Cenotaph—Students'
4 Bell Tower
5 Peace Bell
6 Memorial to Unknown Victims
7 Kannon Statue
8 Peace Foundation
9 Children's Memorial
10 Peace Flame
11 Memorial Centograph
12 "Prayer" Sculpture
13 Sankichi Tooge
14 Prayer Fountain
15 "Mother and Child in Storm"
16 Flower Clock
17 Peace Memorial Museum
18 Peace Memorial Hall
19 Cenotaph for Korean Victims

Hiroshima. She believed that if she could fold 1,000 paper cranes she would become well again. After folding her 964th crane, however, she died. Today all Japanese children are familiar with her story, and around the memorial are streamers of paper cranes donated by schoolchildren from all over Japan.

Needless to say, visiting Peace Memorial Park is a rather sobering and depressing experience, but it's perhaps a necessary one. Every concerned individual should be informed of the effects of an atomic bomb and should be aware that what was dropped on Hiroshima is small compared to the hydrogen bombs of today.

Incidentally, just outside Peace Park across the Honkawa River is the **Cenotaph for Korean Victims.** It's a little-publicized fact that 20,000 Koreans (in other words, 10% of those who perished) were killed that fateful summer day, most of them brought to Japan as forced laborers. The monument reads, "The Korean victims were given no funerals or memorial services and their spirits hovered for years unable to pass on to heaven . . ." It's significant that the cenotaph is *outside* Peace Park —even today Koreans and their descendants face discrimination in Japan. But I must also add that it was a concerned and conscientious Japanese woman who made sure I saw this monument.

Hiroshima Castle

Originally built in 1593 but destroyed in the atomic blast, Hiroshima Castle was reconstructed in 1958. Its five-story donjon, or keep, is a faithful reproduction of the original one. It's open from 9 a.m. to 5:30 p.m. (to 4:30 p.m. from October through March). Inside the castle is a history museum with a collection focusing on Japan's feudal days, with displays of samurai gear, models of old Hiroshima, and pictures of the past. Entrance to both the museum and castle is ¥300 ($2.40).

Shukkei-en Garden

Located close to Hiroshima Station, Shukkei-en Garden was first laid out in 1620 with a pond constructed in imitation of a famous lake in China, Si Hu. The garden's name means "landscape garden in miniature." The park is situated on the Ota River and includes streams, ponds, islets, and bridges—a pleasant respite from city traffic. Charging a ¥200 ($1.60) admission, Shukkei-en is open daily from 9 a.m. to 6 p.m. (until 5 p.m. from October through March).

The Seto Inland Sea

Hiroshima is also the usual departure point for day cruises on the Seto Inland Sea. Stretching between Honshu and the islands of Shikoku and Kyushu, the Inland Sea is dotted with more than 3,000 pine-covered islands and islets. Cruises are operated daily from March to the end of November by the Setonaikai Kisen steamship company (tel. 253-1212), and advance booking is required. One cruise departs from Hiroshima at 9:30 a.m. on Saturday, Sunday, and national holidays, and visits Etajima, Ondonoseto, Kure Bay, and Enoshima before arriving back in Hiroshima at 3:20 p.m. The cost of this tour is ¥11,500 ($92). Another boat leaves every day from Miyajima at 8:30 a.m. with a stop in Hiroshima before heading on to Kure, Yasura, Omishima Island, and Setoda. The trip from Miyajima or Hiroshima to Setoda is ¥6,500 ($52) one way. If it's winter or you're simply more interested in a shorter cruise, Setonaikai Kisen also offers three cruises daily throughout the year to the island of Miyajima. Departures from Hiroshima are at 10:10 a.m. and again at 12:20 p.m., with a sunset cruise offered at 6:45 p.m. Cost of the round-trip cruise is ¥2,100 ($16.80). One-way tickets are also available, a good option since the cruises do not allow any time for sightseeing on Miyajima.

All the above cruises must be booked in advance, which you can do at several hotels, including the ANA Hotel Hiroshima. More information on these cruises is given in a leaflet called *Inland Sea and Shikoku,* available from the T.I.C. in either Tokyo or Kyoto.

WHERE TO STAY

The most common accommodations in Hiroshima are Western-style hotels. There are also a few Japanese-style inns.

The Upper Bracket

Western Style: Opened in 1983, the **ANA Hotel Hiroshima,** 7-20 Nakamachi (tel. 082/241-1111), is on wide Peace Boulevard (*Heiwa Odori*) just a few minutes' walk from Peace Memorial Park. The lobby, overlooking a tiny garden with waterfalls, is carpeted and subdued, with a menagerie of glass birds hanging from the ceiling. Some 20% of the hotel's guests are foreigners, the majority of them Americans. Therefore, rooms have facilities Westerners will appreciate, such as bilingual TV with pay video and with one channel devoted to Kyodo news service in English, FEN English radio station, and free delivery of the *Japan Times*. Rooms are large and comfortable, with all the amenities you'd expect from a first-class hotel. Singles here range from ¥9,500 ($76) to ¥11,000 ($88); doubles, from ¥15,200 ($122) to ¥17,800 ($142); and twins, from ¥16,800 ($134) to ¥19,500 ($156). There are also four Japanese suites for ¥34,000 ($272), which sleep up to four persons. Facilities at the hotel include Japanese, Chinese, teppanyaki steak, and Western restaurants and a rooftop beer garden (open in summer months from 5:30 to 9 p.m.). There are two bars on the 22nd floor, one of which features live piano music nightly. The hotel's health club charges ¥5,500 ($44) for use of its swimming pool, exercise equipment, and sauna. Use of the pool alone is ¥2,200 ($17.60).

One of Hiroshima's newest hotels is the **Hiroshima Terminal Hotel,** 1-5 Matsubara-cho, Minami-ku (tel. 082/262-1111), located right beside the Shinkansen exit of Hiroshima Train Station. Despite its rather ordinary name, it's a first-class hotel, with a spacious marbled lobby and each of the 440 rooms offering a push-button phone, alarm clock, TV with pay video, radio with FEN, hot-water pot, and hairdryer. Facilities include 12 restaurants and bars, including a high-class okonomiyaki eatery, a good sushi bar, and a popular disco in the basement called Maharaja. The teppanyaki steak house on the 14th floor offers dining with a view. Rates here range from ¥8,800 ($70) to ¥12,000 ($96) for a single, ¥14,000 ($112) to ¥16,500 ($132) for a double, and ¥16,500 ($132) to ¥19,500 ($156) for a twin.

Japanese Style: The nine-room **Mitakiso** ㉓, 1-7 Mitaki-cho, Nishi-ku (tel. 082/237-1402), offers visitors the memorable experience of staying in a traditional Japanese inn. The oldest part of the ryokan is more than 70 years old, and its rooms are spread along an exquisite landscape garden with stunted pines, ponds, tiny maple trees, stone lanterns, and meandering streams. Well known for its excellent cuisine, it charges ¥18,000 ($144) to ¥38,000 ($304) per person, including two meals, tax, and service charge. The best rooms are elegant and private, with sliding doors that open onto the garden. The least expensive rooms face away from the garden toward the street, but if you're traveling off-season you may be upgraded to a room with a garden view. Rooms come with toilet only, but there are public baths. The ryokan is about a 15-minute taxi ride from Hiroshima Station, and entrance is past a high stone wall and a massive stone lantern.

The Medium Range

Western Style: Part of a nationwide chain of business hotels, the **Tokyu Inn,** 3-17 Komachi (tel. 082/244-0109), is a good and reliable medium-priced hotel. About 80% of its clientele are Japanese businessmen. Located close to Peace Memorial Park not far from the ANA Hotel, it has 284 rooms, which start at ¥6,700 ($54) for a single and ¥11,000 ($88) for a twin, service charge included. The hotel's restaurant serves a buffet-style Japanese and Western breakfast for ¥1,000 ($8), lunches for ¥550 ($4.40) to ¥2,800 ($22.40), and dinners from about ¥1,500

($12). Because *Tokyu* means "109," there are special lunches served on the 19th of each month, consisting of sirloin steak, rice or bread, salad, and coffee for just ¥1,090 ($8.72). Served from 11 a.m. to 2 p.m., they're real bargains. To reach Tokyu Inn from Hiroshima Station, take streetcar no. 1 and disembark at the stop called Jugoku-denryoku-mae, a trip that takes about 15 minutes. The hotel is located close to the Rijo Dori and Peace Boulevard interjunction.

Hotel Silk Plaza, 14-1 Hatchobori (tel. 082/227-8111), is located on Hakushima Dori Avenue close to three department stores. You can reach it in about ten minutes from Hiroshima Station by taking streetcar no. 1, 2, or 6 and getting off at the Hatchobori stop. A locally owned hotel rather than part of a chain, it started out in 1974 as a business hotel, but after five years began catering to wedding receptions and now attracts foreign tourists as well. Singles, all with semidouble-size bed, range from ¥5,800 ($46) to ¥6,000 ($48); doubles and twins are ¥11,000 ($88). The cheaper singles are not recommended, since they open toward another wall with windows of other guest rooms just two feet away. They also tend to be dark. The rooms facing the outside are much better. All rooms are very simple—TV with pay video, clock, refrigerator, and phone. There are both Western and Japanese restaurants, and a buffet-style breakfast is served for ¥1,000 ($8).

Built in 1966, the **Hiroshima Kokusai Hotel,** 3-13 Tatemachi (tel. 082/248-2323), is a well-known and established hotel in the center of Hiroshima. Rooms are rather crowded in appearance, but they're comfortable and come with refrigerator, TV with pay video, clock, and radio. Room charges begin at ¥6,300 ($50) for a single ¥11,000 ($88) for a twin, and ¥12,000 ($96) for a double. If two of you can fit onto a semidouble-size bed, you can have it for ¥9,600 ($77). Japanese rooms are available beginning at ¥7,100 ($57) for one person and ¥9,600 ($77) for two. There are both Japanese and Western restaurants, and smörgåsbord breakfasts are served for ¥1,000 ($8).

If you prefer to stick close to Hiroshima Train Station, a good bet is **Hiroshima City Hotel,** 1-4 Kyobashi-cho, Minami-ku (tel. 082/263-5111), just a three-minute walk from the station. Take the Minami Guchi exit, walk straight through the underpass and then over the bridge. The hotel is on your right, across from the Century City Hotel (you can see the Century City Hotel's sign from the train station if you look hard enough). At any rate, even though this business hotel opened in the 1970s, it has been renovated and looks so new it stopped me in my tracks (people think I'm weird, crying out at the sight of a new business hotel). Half of the rooms are singles, which range in price from ¥6,000 ($48) to ¥7,700 ($62). The cheapest singles are the smallest I've seen (which, in Japan, says quite a lot), but all rooms come with bathroom, TV with the adult-oriented pay video, radio, and alarm clock. Doubles are ¥11,000 ($88), and twins begin at ¥11,500 ($92). If you want a view, ask for a room above the ninth floor. Vending machines are on the fifth floor; you'll also find both a Western and a Japanese restaurant on the top floors.

Japanese Style: A modern ryokan, **Sera Bekkan** ㉒㉔, 4-20 Mikawa-cho (tel. 082/248-2251), is located in the center of the city just off Namiki Dori Avenue. All 35 rooms are Japanese style with the usual shoji screens, TV, and safe for valuables. Although there are large public baths, all rooms have a private bathroom. Dinner and breakfast are served in your room and Western-style breakfasts are available. Charges per person range from ¥13,000 ($104) to ¥27,000 ($216), depending on the meal you order for dinner and the number of people staying in the rooms.

The Budget Category

An excellent place to stay at if there's room is **Rijyo Kaikan** ㉒㉕, 1-5-3 Otemachi (tel. 082/245-2322). Located close to the Hondori covered shopping arcade and Peace Memorial Park, it's intended primarily as lodging for government office employees, but anyone can stay here. Opened in 1985, it's a modern structure of glass and brown tiles in an unusual shape—because of a sloping side wall it looks like a triangle when viewed from the front. Check-in isn't until 4 p.m. here, and the front counter is located to the left as you enter the building. Per-person rates range from ¥4,400 ($35) to ¥5,500 ($44) for a single, and ¥4,000 ($32) to ¥6,600 ($53) for a twin. An extra bed is ¥2,000 ($8). The rooms here are great for the price—bright, white, and cheerful with hot-water pot, phone, radio, TV, clock, toilet, and deep tub. There are both Japanese and Western restaurants and a self-service cafeteria named Maple, where you can get a cup of coffee for only ¥200 ($1.60). Breakfast, consisting of ham and eggs, bread, soup, salad, and coffee, is served for ¥700 ($5.60). If you want to stay here, it's safest to make a reservation two months in advance. The weekends are usually fully booked, but weekdays are generally not so full.

Mikawa Ryokan, 9-6 Kyobashi-cho, Minami-ku (tel. 082/261-2719), is about a seven-minute walk from Hiroshima Station. A member of the Japanese Inn Group, this 13-room establishment prefers advance reservations. Rooms are simple tatami and come with coin-operated TV, telephone, heater, and air conditioning. Singles are ¥3,300 ($26), doubles are ¥6,000 ($48), and triples run ¥9,000 ($72). Check-in is at 5 p.m. and the front doors close at 11 p.m. A Japanese breakfast is available for ¥500 ($4).

Youth Hostel: Just 15 minutes from Hiroshima Station by bus, the **Hiroshima Youth Hostel** ㉖, 1-13-6 Ushitashi-machi (tel. 082/221-5343), is very easy to find. The bus even announces the youth-hostel stop in English, from which there are signs directing you to the hostel. Located partway up a hill with good views, it accepts nonmembers. An overnight stay is ¥2,000 ($16) in spring. The price includes sheets. Breakfast is ¥400 ($3.20) and dinner is ¥600 ($4.80). The staff all speak English, and they're enthusiastic about accepting foreigners (reservations in summer a must). Doors close at 9:30 p.m., but it's worth it to get back by 9 p.m., when a movie in English is shown every night.

WHERE TO EAT

In addition to the Japanese and Western restaurants listed below, the hotel section above also gives some information about buffets and meals.

Japanese Food

Amagi ㉗, 10-10 Kaminobori-cho (tel. 221-2375), is a well-known modern restaurant specializing in kaiseki meals. It offers informal dining up on the second floor in a setting of cool and simple elegance. The lunch menu, available from 11 a.m. to 2 p.m., includes obento lunch boxes from ¥3,300 ($26), with full kaiseki courses starting at ¥6,600 ($52.80). Dinner, served from 5 to 9 p.m. (last order at 8 p.m.), offers kaiseki courses beginning at ¥11,000 ($88). If you feel like splurging, you can reserve your own private tatami room in the back of the restaurant in what used to be a ryokan years ago. You should make reservations for kaiseki meals here, which start at ¥11,000 ($88) for lunch and ¥16,500 ($132) for dinner, at least three days in advance; charges for your own private room are ¥1,000 ($8) per person. Amagi is closed the last Sunday of every month and every Monday.

Unkai, on the fifth floor of the ANA Hotel, 7-20 Nakamachi (tel. 241-1111), is a Japanese restaurant overlooking a garden of stunted pine trees, azalea bushes, neatly arranged stones, and a pond full of golden carp. The arrangement of this garden is said to resemble that of Shukkei-en Garden. There's an English menu here, with such à la carte choices as tempura shrimp, abalone in butter served in its own shell, sashimi, rice porridge, and even the head of red snapper boiled in soy sauce, costing between ¥1,500 ($12) and ¥3,000 ($24). There are also set meals ranging from ¥4,400 ($35) to ¥15,000 ($120) for such fare as shabu-shabu, tempura, kaiseki, and red snapper sashimi, delivered still jumping and twitching to your table. I had the Miyajima Course, which came with sashimi, sardines, clear soup, eggs of red snapper, a locally caught fish from the Seto Inland Sea, tempura, vegetables, bean-paste soup, Japanese pickles, rice, and fruit. A lunch teishoku, served until 2 p.m. for

¥3,000 ($24), offers soup, sashimi, tempura, pickles, rice, and dessert. There are also other set lunches ranging from ¥1,800 ($14.40) to ¥3,800 ($30.40) for such dishes as noodles, Japanese steak, and obento lunch boxes. The restaurant is open daily from 11:30 a.m. to 10 p.m.

Right next to the ANA Hotel (in the direction of Peace Park) is a teppanyaki steak restaurant called **Atago,** 7-20 Nakamachi (tel. 241-1111). It is strikingly modern with its marble tables and geometric lines, but kimono-clad waitresses bring drinks while chefs prepare steak and seafood before your eyes. Best are the lunch time set courses for ¥2,200 ($17.60), which offer sirloin steak, vegetables, miso soup, rice, Japanese pickles, and sherbet. Hours are 11:30 a.m. to 2 p.m. and 5 to 10 p.m. daily.

There are 10,000 rafts cultivating oysters in Hiroshima Bay with a yearly output of 30,000 tons of shelled oysters. Needless to say, oysters are a Hiroshima specialty, and one of the best places to enjoy them is at **Kanawa** ㉒ (tel. 241-7416), a houseboat moored on the Motoyasu River just off Peace (Heiwa) Boulevard not far from Peace Memorial Park. Although winter is the best time to enjoy fresh oysters, the owner of this restaurant has his own oyster rafts and freezes his best stock in January so that he's able to serve excellent oysters even in summer. This floating restaurant has been here more than 25 years, and dining is in tatami rooms with views of the river. The English menu lists oysters cooked about any way you like or can imagine. À la carte dishes range from ¥900 ($7.20) to ¥2,200 ($17.60) for the popular baked oyster in its shell with lemon, tempura oyster, or oyster soup. Set menus range from ¥5,500 ($44) to ¥11,000 ($88); one course features just oysters cooked in various ways, including in the shell, fried, in soup, and steamed. Open from 11 a.m. to 3 p.m. and 5 to 9 p.m., this restaurant is closed every first and third Sunday except in December (peak oyster season).

Suishin ㉒ 6-7 Tatemachi (tel. 247-4411), is the main shop of a locally owned restaurant chain specializing in kamameshi (rice casseroles). First opened in 1950, this chain now has five locations in Hiroshima alone. The main shop, in the middle of town, has five floors of dining, and though the decor is rather simple, this place is very popular for its rice casseroles topped with such Hiroshima delicacies as oysters, mushrooms, sea bream, sea eels, shrimp, and chestnuts. It sells about 800 kamameshi per day, a number that swells to as many as 2,000 on Sunday. To deal with the demand, the restaurant owner invented his own conveyor-belt oven, which can cook 180 kamameshi in one hour. Kamameshi starts at ¥650 ($5.20). Other dishes include oysters, eel, globe fish, flatfish, and sardines. Most choices range from ¥1,000 ($8) to ¥2,500 ($20). Lunch specials change daily and are available for ¥600 ($4.80) from 11:20 a.m. to 1:30 p.m. There are also take-out boxes of seafood and vegetables for ¥1,000 ($8) to ¥3,800 ($30.40), making this a good place to buy your picnic lunch. Closed on Wednesday, the restaurant is open the rest of the week from 11:20 a.m. to 10 p.m. (last order is 9 p.m.).

Masui, located close to Chugoku Bank, which is close to the Silk Plaza Hotel in the middle of town (tel. 227-2983), is a very inexpensive and popular restaurant serving beef dishes. Individual small servings of shabu-shabu, for example, start at only ¥750 ($6) for pork and ¥1,300 ($10.40) for beef, while sukiyaki goes for ¥880 ($7.04) and ¥1,400 ($11.20). Steaks start at ¥2,000 ($16). This two-story restaurant is especially crowded during lunchtime, when it churns out plate after plate of teishoku specials. The ¥700 ($5.60) teishoku gets you a hamburger patty, ham, omelet, pork cutlet, and rice, but if that's too expensive you can forgo the hamburger and get the other items for ¥600 ($4.80). Open from 11 a.m. to 9 p.m., it's closed every Wednesday and the second Tuesday of the month.

Although the people of Osaka claim to have made *okonomiyaki* popular among the masses, the people of Hiroshima claim to have made it an art. In any case, okonomiyaki is a kind of Japanese pancake, filled with cabbage, meat, and other fillings. Whereas in Osaka the ingredients are all mixed together, in Hiroshima each layer is prepared separately, which means the chefs have to be quite skilled at keeping the whole thing together. At any rate, the best place in town to witness these short-order cooks at their trade is at **Okonomi-Mura** ㉚, 5-21 Shin-tenchi (tel. 241-8758). Its name means "okonomiyaki village" and that's what it is—a ramshackle building with two floors of about 14 individual stalls each dishing out okonomiyaki (the food still remains a dish for the masses). All stalls offer basically the same menu —just sit down at one of the counters and watch how the chef first spreads pancake mix on a hot griddle, then follows it with a layer of cabbage and bean sprouts, bacon, and then an egg on top. If you want, you can have yours with udon (thick white noodles) or soba (thin yellow noodles). All are less than ¥700 ($5.60) and helpings are enormous. Okonomi-Mura is open daily from 11 a.m. to 9 p.m.—but some stalls stay open past midnight. You'll find the place just off the Hondori shopping arcade near Shakey's. Highly recommended, it's one of Hiroshima's most beloved establishments.

Western Food

Castle View, on the 22nd floor of the ANA Hotel, 7-20 Nakamachi (tel. 241-1111), is named for the view you have here of the castle, but you have to look pretty hard to find it. Still, this is the second-tallest building in Hiroshima and you *do* have a fine view of the city. A small and elegant restaurant decorated in gold and light pink, with comfortable chairs and a single rose on each table, this establishment has set steak and seafood dinners for ¥6,000 ($48) and ¥13,200 ($105.60) and a lunch for ¥2,750 ($22). Expect to spend about ¥5,000 ($40) to ¥10,000 ($80) and up per person if you order from the à la carte menu. Hours here are 11:30 a.m. to 2:30 p.m. and 5:30 to 10 p.m.

Le Train Blue, on the 14th floor of the Kokusai Hotel, 3-13 Tatemachi (tel. 248-2323), is Hiroshima's only revolving restaurant, making a full turn every hour. It is fashioned after the dining car of a train (supposedly the Oriental Express), and each table is placed beside the window, making for privacy with a view. Reasonably priced, Le Train Blue's à la carte menu lists steak, seafood, lamb, veal, and duck; but the best bargain is the weekly set lunch course for ¥1,500 ($12), offered daily from 11:30 a.m. to 2 p.m. Set dinner courses start at ¥4,400 ($35.20). You can also come here for just a drink; cocktails are ¥750 ($6) and beer starts at ¥550 ($4.40). Hours here are 11:30 a.m. to 2 a.m. (until midnight on Sunday and national holidays).

For other hotel dining, the Hotel Silk Plaza's **Caspi** restaurant, 14-1 Hatchobori (tel. 227-8111), serves a good lunch bargain daily from 11 a.m. to 2 p.m. for ¥850 ($6.80). Its menu changes daily, but when I was there the special consisted of soup, salad, pork cutlet with vegetables, and coffee, with unlimited portions of salad.

Rijyo, in the Rijyo Kaikan, 1-5-3 Otemachi (tel. 245-2322), described under budget accommodations, is a bright and modern restaurant made cheerful by colorful wall hangings. It serves a variety of inexpensive dishes, including salmon steak, hamburger steak, roast beef, sirloin and tenderloin steaks, beef curry, pizza toast, sandwiches, and spaghetti. Lunches start at ¥660 ($5.28) and dinners at ¥1,650 ($13.20). It's open daily from 9 a.m. to 9 p.m.

Anderson Kitchen, 7-1 Hondori (tel. 247-2403), is located on a corner of the Hondori covered shopping arcade not far from Peace Park. It's a popular cafeteria on the second floor above its own bakery with the same name. There are several counters serving different types of food. One counter, for example, sells drinks, while other counters specialize in salads and sandwiches, fried dishes such as grilled chicken, or desserts. Just pick up a tray and select the items you want. You pay at the end of each counter. Most items are between ¥500 ($4) and ¥1,000 ($8). Closed the third Tuesday of every month, it's open otherwise from 11 a.m. to 7:30 p.m. A small corner of the restaurant with waitress service stays open until 10 p.m., serving French and Chinese food.

Incidentally, at the Hondori shopping arcade you'll also find a number of inexpensive and fast-food places, including McDonald's, Shakey's, and Mister Donut.

12. Miyajima

Easily reached in about 45 minutes from Hiroshima, Miyajima is a treasure of an island only 1.2 miles off the mainland in the Seto Island Sea. No doubt you've seen pictures of its most famous landmark—a huge red torii, or shrine gate, rising up out of the water. Erected in 1875 and made of camphor wood, it's the largest torii in Japan, measuring more than 53 feet tall, and guards Miyajima's main attraction, Itsukushima Shrine.

Miyajima is considered one of the most scenic spots in Japan. It is an exceptionally beautiful island that has been held sacred since ancient times. In the olden days no one was allowed to do anything so human as to give birth or die on the island, with the result that both the pregnant and the ill were quickly ferried across to the mainland. Even today there's no cemetery on Miyajima. Covered with cherry trees that illuminate the island with their snowy petals in spring and maple trees that emblazon it in reds in autumn, Miyajima is home to tame deer that roam freely through the village and to monkeys that swing through the woods. It's a delightful island on which to stroll around—but avoid coming on a weekend.

ORIENTATION

Before leaving Tokyo or Kyoto, drop by the T.I.C. for a copy of *Hiroshima and Miyajima*. You can reach Miyajima directly by ferry from Hiroshima Ujina Port. The **Setonaikai Kisen steamship company** (tel. 253-1212), for example, offers several cruises daily throughout the year aboard its Galaxy luxury boat complete with French and seafood restaurants. Cost of the round-trip cruise is ¥2,100 ($16.80). Unfortunately, none of the cruises allows much of a stopover, but one-way tickets are also available. You may wish to take the early cruise to Miyajima and return with the afternoon boat or else return to Hiroshima by a different route.

You can, for example, also travel from Hiroshima by train, streetcar, or bus, all of which deposit you at Miyajimaguchi, from which it's just a ten-minute ferry ride to the island of Miyajima. If you have a JR rail pass, you can ride free on the JR ferry, which leaves from the pier right in front of the train station.

In Miyajima stop off at the **Tourist Information Office** (tel. 44-0008), located in the JR ferry terminal. Open every day from 8:30 a.m. to 5 p.m., it has a brochure in English with a map.

The **telephone area code** for Miyajima is 0829, and Miyajima is located in Hiroshima Prefecture.

THE SIGHTS

Itsukushima Shrine is less than a ten-minute walk from the ferry pier along a narrow street lined with souvenir shops and restaurants. Founded back in 592 to honor three female deities, the shrine is built out over the water so that when the tide is in it appears as though the shrine is floating. A brilliant vermillion, it contrasts starkly with the wooded hills in the background and the blue of the sky above, casting its reflection in the waters below. The majority of the buildings are thought to date from the 16th century, preserving the original style of 12th-century architecture. Since the shrine is made of wood, it's been repaired repeatedly through the centuries. Most of the buildings of the shrine are closed, but from 6:30 a.m. to 6 p.m. daily (5 p.m. in winter) and for ¥200 ($1.60), you can walk along the 770-foot covered dock that threads its way past the outer part of the main shrine and the oldest Noh stage in Japan. From the shrine you have a good view of the red torii standing in the water. If you're lucky you might get to see *bugako* put on for one of the many tour groups which pass through. An ancient musical court dance, bugako was introduced to Japan centuries ago from India through China and Korea. The costume of the dancer is orange, matching the shrine around him.

Incidentally, I should also add that . . .
Shrine when the tide is in and it's seemingl . . .
yourself very lucky indeed. Most of the tim . . .
ing more glamorous than mud. That's whe . . .

As you exit from the shrine, you'll fi . . .
Treasures, which contains replicas of nat . . .
locked away), old books, armor, and househ . . .
Miyajima Municipal History and Folklore . . .
shrine. This one has explanations in Englisl . . .
house, which once belonged to a wealthy m . . .
p.m., it features farm equipment, water jar . . .
furniture, and items used in daily life. Admi . . .

Other attractions on Miyajima include . . .
Misen, the largest peak on the island a . . .
Momijidani Park; and beaches for swimmin; . . .

30 rooms of this people's lodg . . .
futon yourself. Sheets, cotto . . .
ply decorated rooms wit . . .
bathrooms are ¥6,90 . . .
charge are extra.

Fujitaya ㉟ . . .
the road leadi . . .
Shrine. It's . . .
though t . . .
tainin; . . .
cou . . .

FOOD AND LODGING

Although you can visit Miyajima in a day from Hiroshima, it's a pleasant experience to stay overnight in a ryokan (there are no Western-style hotels).

The most famous ryokan on the island is **Iwaso Ryokan** ㉛, (tel. 0829/44-2233), which has a history spanning more than 130 years since it became the first ryokan to open on the island. Most of its rooms range in price from ¥16,500 ($132) to ¥30,000 ($240) per person, including two meals, tax, and service charge, with the price determined by the room, its view, and the meals you select. There are four price levels of dinners, and Western breakfasts are served on request. The newest part of the ryokan was built in 1981, and though some of its rooms have very peaceful and relaxing views of a stream and woods, I prefer the rooms dating from about 50 years ago (they have more individuality than the newer rooms). But if you really want to splurge and live in style, there are also a couple of separate cottages more than 70 years old that are exquisitely decorated and come with old wooden tubs. You can open your shoji screens here to see maples, a gurgling brook, and woods, all in utter privacy. You'll be treated like royalty here, but of course you have to pay for it—these cottages cost up to ¥40,000 ($320) per person.

Even if you don't stay at Iwaso, you can stop off for lunch at its restaurant, **Momiji** ㉜, open from 11 a.m. to 2 p.m. This is a very pleasant modern restaurant with clusters of paper-covered lanterns hanging from the ceiling and windows opening onto woods and a stream below. The specialty here is mini-kaiseki lunches for ¥2,000 ($16) and ¥3,300 ($26.40). Momiji also serves an *anagomeshi* (barbecued conger eel on rice) teishoku for ¥1,000 ($8).

The **Miyajima Grand Hotel** (tel. 0829/44-2411) was completely renovated and reopened in 1985 with 67 rooms, 10 of which are combination rooms with both twin beds and separate tatami areas. This ryokan doesn't differ from other modern ryokan, except that in its lobby there's a rather unusual mix of green, light purple, and pink in the decor. Rates here average about ¥18,000 ($144) per person (cheaper weekdays and in winter), and Western breakfasts are served on request.

If you're looking for a ryokan that's a bit more moderately priced, a good choice is **Jyukeiso** ㉝ (tel. 0829/44-0300). Although it's about a 20-minute hike from the ferry pier (located in the same vicinity as Miyajima Lodge listed below), it has the advantage of sitting atop a small hill, with some pleasant views of Miyajima. In addition, the owner here speaks English. The ryokan was started some 50 years ago by his grandmother, though the present building is much more modern. All but one of the rooms are Japanese tatami rooms, and two have their own private bathroom. Rates here, which include two meals (Western breakfast on request), tax, and service, range from ¥10,000 ($80) to ¥13,000 ($104) per person.

For lower-priced accommodations, try **Miyajima Lodge** ㉞ (tel. 0829/44-0430). Located about a 25-minute walk from Miyajima Pier beside Omoto Park, the

are the do-it-yourself kind in which you lay out your
kimono, and TV are provided in each room. The sim-
out private bathroom are ¥5,500 ($44), and those with
($55) per person, including two meals. Tax and service

(tel. 44-0151) is a pleasant restaurant located on the right side of
toward Mount Misen and Daishoin as you exit from Itsukushima
open daily from 11 a.m. to 5 p.m. It has a history of 80 years, but al-
building itself is recent, the management has done a good job of main-
a traditional atmosphere with a wooden ceiling, shoji lamps, and a back
tyard with a maple tree, moss-covered rocks, and water running from a bamboo
pe into a pool carved into a flat rock. I had the house special here, anagomeshi
(barbecued conger eel on rice). Costing ¥1,400 ($11.20), it comes with pickled
vegetables, soup, and tea. There's also a sashimi lunch for ¥2,200 ($17.60) and
noodles or rice with chicken for around ¥650 ($5.20).

SHIKOKU

1. TAKAMATSU
2. MATSUYAMA

The smallest of Japan's four main islands, Shikoku is also one of the least visited by foreigners making a trek through Japan. That's surprising considering the natural beauty of its rugged mountains, its mild climate, and its most famous monuments —88 sacred Buddhist temples. It's the wish of many Japanese to make a pilgrimage to all 88 temples at least once in their lifetime as a tribute to the great Buddhist priest Kobo Daishi, who was born in Shikoku in 774 and who founded the Shingon sect of Buddhism. Such a pilgrimage has been popular since the Edo Period in the belief that a successful completion of the tour releases Buddhist followers from having to go through rebirth. It used to take several months to visit all 88 temples on foot, and even today you can see the pilgrims making their rounds dressed in white—only now they go by bus, which cuts traveling time down to two weeks. Many Japanese make the trip upon retirement.

I suggest you visit Shikoku on your travels through southern Japan. You could, for example, travel through Honshu to Kyushu and from Kyushu start back north via Shikoku, or vice versa. Ferries connect Shikoku to Beppu on Kyushu island, as well as to Tokyo, Osaka, Kobe, and Hiroshima on Honshu island. In fact, for centuries the only way of reaching Shikoku was by boat, but the completion of one of the longest bridges in the world changed all that. Opened in 1988, the Seto Ohashi Bridge measures 5.83 miles from shore to shore and connects Kojima on Honshu with Sakaide on Shikoku. Those of you aboard the Shinkansen, therefore, need only change trains in Okayama for trains bound for either Takamatsu or Matsuyama on Shikoku. Whereas the journey from Tokyo Station to Shikoku used to take six to seven hours, you can now cover the same distance in about 4½ hours. Incidentally, the Seto Ohashi Bridge took ten years to construct and actually consists of six separate bridges that connect various islands of the Seto Inland Sea. The people of Shikoku are very proud of this bridge connecting their once-isolated island with Honshu and consider it one of their major tourist attractions. Since the bridge is double-decker and can also accommodate cars, buses, and trucks, in addition to trains, this easier access to Shikoku will undoubtedly change the nature of the island and open it up to further development.

1. Takamatsu

Shikoku's second-largest town, Takamatsu is on the northeastern coast of the island overlooking the Seto Inland Sea. Takamatsu means "high pine," and the city served as the feudal capital of the powerful Matsudaira clan from 1642 until the

Meiji Restoration in 1868. Takamatsu's most famous site is Ritsurin Park, one of the most outstanding gardens in Japan.

ORIENTATION

The Takamatsu train station is located on the coast of the Seto Inland Sea, only a few minutes' walk from the pier where ferries depart for Honshu and Shodo islands. The **Takamatsu City Information Office** (tel. 0878/51-2009) is located directly in the train station and is open every day except New Year's from 9 a.m. to 5 p.m. Stop here for an English map of the city and directions to your hotel. If you want more detailed information on Shikoku, be sure to drop by the Tourist Information Center in Tokyo or Kyoto for a leaflet called *Inland Sea and Shikoku*.

All of the hotels and restaurants listed below, as well as Ritsurin Park, are located south and southeast of the train station. Chuo-dori Street is the town's main avenue and runs south from the train station past Ritsurin Park, passing Takamatsu Grand Hotel, Tokyu Inn, and Hotel Rich on the way. Buses and trams depart from in front of the station. The tram station, called Kotoden Chikko Station, is located across the street from the train station right beside the Takamatsu Grand Hotel. If you're taking the tram to Ritsurin Park, get off at the stop called Ritsurin-koen.

The **telephone area code** for Takamatsu is 0878. If you're writing to one of the hotels in Takamatsu, add Kagawa Prefecture 760 to the addresses given below.

THE SIGHTS

The main attractions of Takamatsu are spread out in the city but are easily reached by bus, tram, or train from the train station.

Ritsurin Park

Ritsurin Park was once the summer retreat of the Matsudaira family. Work on the park began in the 1600s, and it took about 100 years to complete. Using the backdrop of adjacent Mount Shiun in a principle known as "borrowed landscaping," the park incorporates the mountain into its overall design. Basically the garden can be divided into two parts: a traditional, classical southern garden and a modern northern garden with wide grassy lawns.

The southern garden holds the most interest to visitors. Arranged around the prescribed six ponds and 13 scenic mounds, it represents what is called a strolling garden in which each bend of the footpath—indeed, every new step—brings another perspective into view, another combination of rock, tree, and mountain. The garden is absolutely exquisite, and when I was there a mist was rolling off Mount Shiun, lending a mysteriousness to the landscape. After all, what better fits the image of traditional Japan than mist and pine trees? Altogether there are 1,500 pine trees and 500 cherry trees in Ritsurin Park, which you should tour in a counterclockwise fashion to appreciate fully the changing views.

Also in the park are a museum of local folk art and handcrafts, a zoo, and a shop where local products of Kagawa Prefecture are sold, including kites, masks, woodcarvings, umbrellas, fans, and bamboo vases. Be sure also to stop off at the park's tea house for a cup of frothy green tea. Called Kikugetsu-tei, the tea house dates from feudal days. There's a separate entrance charge of ¥300 ($2.40); a cup of ceremonial tea costs another ¥300.

Ritsurin Park is open every day of the year from sunrise to sunset, which is approximately from 7 a.m. to 5 p.m. in winter and 5:30 a.m. to 7 p.m. June through August. The admission fee to the park is ¥300 ($2.40), and the park is located about ten minutes from Takamatsu train station by bus or tram. If you have a Japan Rail Pass, you might even consider going by JR train traveling in the direction of Tokushima; get off at Ritsurin-koen Kita Guchi, which is near the north entrance to the park.

Shikoku Mura Village

Shikoku Mura Village is an open-air museum of 21 houses dating from the Edo Period and brought to Takamatsu from all parts of Shikoku. The houses, which are picturesquely situated on the slope of Yashima Hill, include thatch-roofed homes of farmers and fishermen, a 150-year-old rural Kabuki stage, a tea ceremony house, and sheds for pressing sugar and for producing paper out of mulberry bark. There's also a suspended bridge made of vines, a familiar sight in Shikoku as a means for crossing the island's many gorges and ravines—if you look closely, however, you'll see that this one is reinforced by cables.

It takes at least an hour to stroll through the village, which is open daily from 8:30 a.m. to 4:30 p.m. (until 5 p.m. in summer). The admission fee is ¥500 ($4). I heartily recommend this village if you have not had the opportunity to see similar villages in Takayama or Kawasaki, since they convey better than anything else what it must have been like to live in rural Japan in centuries past. Shikoku Mura Village is about a 20-minute tram ride from the Kotoden Chikko tram station, which is across the square from Takamatsu Station. You can also get there by JR train traveling in the direction of Tokushima. In any case, the station for both is called Yashima.

Other Sights

From Yashima Station close to Shikoku Mura Village you can take a cable car to the top of Yashima Plateau, where you'll find **Yashimaji Temple,** 84th of Shikoku's 88 sacred temples. Yashima is also famous as the site of a 12th-century battle between the rival clans of Taira and Minamoto as they fought for control over Japan. The Minamoto clan eventually won and established its shogunate court in Kamakura.

If you have some extra time and want to rest a few minutes, visit **Tamamo Park,** which is located behind the Takamatsu Grand Hotel close to the Takamatsu train station. The moats, gardens, and several three-story turrets are all that remain of what used to be an imposing castle belonging to the local warlords. There isn't a lot to see, but it's a pleasant place for a stroll or a picnic lunch if you're waiting for the next train.

One of Takamatsu's newest attractions is the **Takamatsu City Museum of Art,** which opened in 1988 in a light and airy modern building located at Konyamachi 10-4 (tel. 23-1711). It's about a ten-minute walk south of Takamatsu Station: simply walk along Chuo-dori Street past the Hyogomachi covered shopping arcade, turning left a couple of blocks later onto Bijutsukan Dori. The museum features a permanent exhibition of postwar Japanese art, as well as changing exhibitions of both Japanese and Western artists. Cost of the permanent exhibit is ¥200 ($1.60) and the museum's hours are 9 a.m. to 5 p.m. every day except Monday.

If you're spending several days in Takamatsu, there are several attractions in the surrounding countryside worthy of your attention. **Shodo Island** (called *Shodoshima* in Japanese) is the second-largest island in the Seto Inland Sea and is easily reached from the ferry pier close to the Takamatsu train station in about an hour. Most visitors come to Shodo Island to see its natural wonders, including Kankakei Gorge, which measures 3.7 miles long, a monkey park with more than 700 wild monkeys, and Shihozashi Lookout with its panoramic views of the Inland Sea. An extensive network of public buses crisscrosses the island, but if you're on a tight schedule, you may wish to join one of the full or half-day sightseeing tours available. More information on Shodo Island can be obtained by calling the Shodoshima Tourist Office at 0879/62-1111.

If your interests run more along the lines of history, one of the best side trips you can take is to **Kotohira,** home of Kotohiragu Shrine as well as the oldest Kabuki theater in Japan. It takes about an hour to reach Kotohira by train from Takamatsu Station, but that isn't the end of it—the shrine itself is at the top of 785 granite steps. If that's too much for you, you can hire porters who will take you only to the main gate (called *Omon* in Japanese), which is reached after climbing 365 steps. The cost of riding in one of these palanquins is ¥4,500 ($36) if you ride it one way and ¥5,500 ($44) if you're carried back down.

At any rate, the long trek up to Kotohiragu Shrine begins by exiting from the Kotohira train station's only exit, taking a left after passing under the first torii gate, and then right on a narrow, shop-lined street. Presently you'll reach the first flight of stairs. If you're making a detour to the Kabuki theater described below, turn left after the twenty-second step, from which the theater is only a 3-minute walk away; otherwise, continue climbing upwards—you should reach the main shrine after a 30-minute workout. You'll be rewarded with a sweeping view of the surrounding countryside, as well as the shrine itself. Popularly known as Kompira-San, Kotohiragu Shrine was originally founded in the 11th century but has been rebuilt many times, with the main shrine buildings re-erected about 100 years ago. Considered one of the biggest and oldest Shinto shrines in the country, it's a popular shrine for fishermen, who come here to pray for safe journeys at sea. Part of the shrine complex is filled with boat models and photographs of ships that have been placed under the deity's care. Notice also the paper cranes, symbolizing good luck, as well as the small slats of wood hanging from the beams. If you wish, you can buy one of these slats and write a wish upon it. On my last visit, I saw a plea for a better profit in a family's business, as well as a wish to become smarter.

Since you're in the vicinity, I highly recommend a visit to **Kompira Grand Playhouse,** known as **Kompira O-Shibai** ⑳ in Japanese. Open every day except Tuesday from 9 a.m. to 5 p.m. and charging an admission fee of ¥300 ($2.40), it is stunning in its simplicity and delightful in its construction. Since there was no electricity back in 1835, when it was built, the sides of the hall are rows of shoji screens and wooden coverings, which could be opened and closed to control the amount of light reaching the stage. Notice the tatami seating, the paper lanterns, and the revolving stage, which was turned by eight men sweating it out in the basement. You can also tour the various makeup and dressing rooms behind the stage. Most curious is the fact that although all actors in Kabuki are men, there's a separate dressing room for the actor who impersonated and played the part of a woman. Actual Kabuki plays are staged once a year in April, but as you may well imagine, tickets are hard to come by. I'm sure it's a beautiful and moving sight.

WHERE TO STAY

Because Takamatsu is not a big tourist destination, it doesn't have a wide selection of accommodations. Prices for rooms, however, are much lower here than in most cities in Japan.

Hotels

In terms of location, price, and view, one of the best deals in town is the **Takamatsu Grand Hotel,** 1-5-10 Kotobuki-cho (tel. 0878/51-5757). A striped building on Chuo-dori Street, it's conveniently located about a minute's walk from Takamatsu Station, the main artery for trains to the rest of Shikoku and for ferries from Honshu and Kyushu. Built in 1971 and having 136 rooms, the hotel sits on the edge of Tamamo Park, formerly the site of Takamatsu Castle and now an oasis of pine trees, three-story turrets, moats, and a classical garden. Both the lobby on the third floor and the Yashima Sky Restaurant on the seventh floor command sweeping views of the park, a welcome respite after a day of sightseeing. Rooms were recently renovated and come equipped with a minibar, clock, and TV. Singles range from ¥6,900 ($55.20) to ¥17,000 ($56), twins run ¥12,000 ($96) to ¥22,000 ($176), while doubles are ¥12,500 ($100). The higher-priced rooms face the park and have the nicest views. There are nine restaurants as well as a shopping arcade located in the hotel complex.

The **Takamatsu Tokyu Inn,** 9-9 Hyogo-machi (tel. 0878/21-0106), was built in 1982 and still remains one of the newest hotels in town. A brown building, it's about a seven-minute walk from Takamatsu train station on Chuo-dori Street, beside the Hyogomachi covered shopping arcade. The lobby is on the second floor, and its one restaurant serves Western fare. Its 181 rooms begin at ¥7,000 ($56) for a single, ¥14,200 ($114) for a twin, and ¥14,000 ($112) for a double. Rooms are clean, simple, and small but have all the usual business-hotel amenities, including clock, TV, and cotton kimono. Rooms facing Chuo-dori Street are fitted with double-pane glass to shut out traffic noise. None of the views are spectacular, but given a choice I'd choose a room on a top floor facing the west and the distant sea.

Located almost directly across the street from Tokyu Inn on Chuo-dori Street is **Hotel Rich,** 9-1 Furujinmachi (tel. 0878/22-3555). A beige-brick building, it features three restaurants serving Japanese, Chinese, and French cuisine, as well as a bar. Rooms are similar to those in Tokyu Inn and range from ¥6,000 ($48) to ¥7,900 ($63) for a single and ¥12,000 ($96) to ¥17,600 ($141) for a double or twin.

If the above hotels are full, **Takamatsu Plaza Hotel** ㉘, 7-Banchi, Tamamocho (tel. 0878/51-3655) is an inexpensive, ten-story business hotel just a five-minute walk from Takamatsu train station near the ferry docks. Rooms are of adequate size, with the difference in price based on room size—so I recommend you ask for a room on a higher floor with a view of either the sea or Tamamo Park. Singles here are ¥5,200 ($42), doubles and twins are ¥8,800 ($70). The twin rooms don't have closets; instead there are hooks on the wall for hanging clothes, just like in olden days in Japan.

A Note on Japanese Symbols
Many hotels, restaurants, and other establishments in Japan do not have signs showing their names in English letters. Appendix II lists the Japanese symbols for all such places appearing in this guide. Each establishment name in Japanese symbols is numbered, and the same number appears in an oval in the text following the boldfaced establishment name. For example, in the text Osaka's **Hotel Hokke Club** ⑯ is number 164 in the Japanese list in Appendix II.

Ryokan
Hotel Kawaroku, Kyakken-cho (tel. 0878/21-5666), first opened as a ryokan 110 years ago, was destroyed during an air raid in World War II, and is now a modern structure with 49 Japanese-style rooms and 21 Western-style rooms. A ten-minute walk from Takamatsu Station, it's located close to the Mitsukoshi department store and several shopping arcades right in the heart of the city. All rooms come with private bathroom, safe, minibar, and TV. The Western-style rooms are white, bright, and clean, while the Japanese-style rooms are simply furnished and have that wonderful earthy smell of tatami. The hotel's one restaurant serves French cuisine (described in detail below); if you want Japanese food, it will be served in your room. The rate per person, including Japanese dinner and breakfast, is ¥14,300 ($14). If you decide to take your meals elsewhere, the room charge for Western-style rooms begin at ¥6,600 ($53) for a single and ¥11,000 ($88) for a twin, while Japanese-style rooms begin at ¥6,500 ($52) for one person and ¥10,000 ($80) for two.

A traditional Japanese ryokan, **Tokiwa Honkan** ㉙, 1-8-1 Tokiwa-cho (tel. 0878/61-5577), has a delightful inner courtyard reminiscent of those found around tea houses, with a pond, dwarf pine trees, golden carp, stone lanterns, wooden passageways, and vermillion railings. The ryokan is topped with a donjon, making it look like a shogun's castle. Built in 1954, the ryokan at first catered almost exclusively to foreigners, but as Western-style hotels began making their appearance, it lost many of its foreign customers. Now the ryokan receives only about 20 foreign guests a year. Rooms were completely renovated in 1987, with the result that all now have a private toilet. Only half the rooms are equipped with a private bathtub, but public baths are located on each floor. There are also large communal baths separated for men and women. Prices here range from ¥13,200 ($106) to ¥22,000 ($176) per person, including two meals.

Youth Hostel

The **Takamatsu Yuai-Sanso Youth Hostel** ㉓㊉ is just a ten-minute walk from Takamatsu Station at 2-4-14 Nishiki-cho (tel. 0878/22-3656). It's small—only six rooms accommodating 32 persons. Rates are ¥1,900 ($15), with an additional ¥200 ($1.60) charged in summer and winter for heating or air conditioning expenses. Breakfasts are available for ¥450 ($3.60) and dinners for ¥750 ($6). If you're not a card-carrying youth hostel member, you can still stay here, though you'll be charged an extra ¥500 ($4) per night.

WHERE TO DINE

Takamatsu is known throughout Japan for its *sanuki udon,* which are thick white noodles made from wheat flour. With Takamatsu as the center of the industry, there are as many as 400 sanuki manufacturers and more than 2,000 noodle shops in Kagawa Prefecture. It's been estimated that about 10% of the population eats sanuki noodles every day, a percentage that's about five times higher than in any other area of Japan. Takamatsu also has a fresh supply of fish from the Seto Inland Sea.

Japanese Food

If you want to watch sanuki udon being made, the best place to observe it is at **Kanaizumi** ㉔⓪, Daikumachi (tel. 21-6688), located about a 15-minute walk from Takamatsu Station. It's a bit classier than your usual noodle shop, and is easily recognizable from the outside by a huge paper lantern hanging in front of the restaurant and a front window where sanuki noodles are being made by hand. Although the menu is in Japanese, pictures accompany each set meal, making it easy to order. These come with noodles and a combination of various vegetables and meats, and range from ¥550 ($4.40) to ¥3,000 ($24). If you want just a bowl of noodles without side dishes, it will cost about ¥380 ($3.04). I had a set meal called Niku-nabe Udon, which cost ¥1,000 ($8) and consisted of a bowl of noodles, leeks, thin slices of beef, and rice cake in hot broth. Before eating each morsel I dipped it first into a mixture of raw egg, just as one does with sukiyaki. It was good, but rice cakes take forever to chew. Be prepared also for slippery noodles and all that good-natured slurping that accompanies a meal in a noodle shop. Hours here are 10 a.m. to 1 a.m.; closed the second and third Mondays of the month.

Another noodle restaurant you might want to try—especially if you're going to Shikoku Mura Village—is **Zaigoudon-waraya** (tel. 43-3115). It's located next to and just below the village in a 100-year-old thatched house (look for the water wheel and tables for outdoor seating) and is open daily from 10 a.m. to 7 p.m. Its handmade udon ranges in price from ¥450 ($3.60) to ¥2,500 ($20). The combination udon and tempura dish is especially popular.

A well-known tempura and sushi restaurant in town is **Tenkatsu** ㉔①, Hyogomachi (tel. 21-5380). To reach it from Takamatsu Station, walk south on Chuo-dori Street until it intersects with a large covered pedestrian shopping arcade called Hyogomachi. Turn right, walk all the way through the arcade, and upon emerging you'll find the restaurant immediately on your left. It's a modern-looking building with a plastic-food display case and a window where a chef prepares sushi. Inside the restaurant are tatami mats and tables, but I suggest sitting at the counter, which encircles a large pool filled with fish, mainly flatfish. As customers order their meals, fish are swooped out of the tanks with nets—they certainly couldn't be fresher. In fact, I saw some customers served a fish that was still quivering even though it had been sliced for sashimi. Although the menu here is in Japanese only, there are pictures accompanying some of the tempura and sushi courses. Most dishes range from ¥1,000 ($8) to ¥2,000 ($16). If you feel like splurging, there's a meal for ¥3,500 ($28) that features Japanese food in season, changing every month. Another specialty of the house is wine, served every month with something different in it, usually flower petals. In March, for example, it's peach blossoms and in April cherry blossoms. Hours are 11 a.m. to 10 p.m. daily.

Hansuke ② is located just around the corner from Tokyu Inn in the Hyogomachi shopping arcade (tel. 51-5653). Unlike many of the other shops in the covered arcade, this yakitori-ya has been in operation in this same spot for more than 30 years, making it one of the oldest—if not the oldest—yakitori shops in town. Simple and cheap, it's a greasy spoon in the true sense of the word; the grill looks like it's been here from the beginning. The yakitori, however, is excellent and costs ¥350 ($2.80) for four skewers of chicken wedged between slices of onion. The establishment also serves eel, with kabayaki, a filet of eel, costing ¥1,300 ($10.40). The real specialty of Hansuke, however, is its namesake, *hansuke,* which according to the shop owner means "heads of eel stuck on a skewer." Both I and the Japanese I was with thought it was one of the most unappetizing sights we had ever seen, but in a spontaneous burst of adventure we decided to try it. I don't want to spoil your own experiences by telling you what it was like, but be prepared for lots of bones. A skewer of hansuke is a bargain at only ¥80 (64¢) a stick. This locale is open every day except Sunday and national holidays from 11:30 a.m. to 1 p.m. and again from 4 to 10 p.m.

Although technically a drinking establishment because of the fact that it's open only in the evenings from 5 to 11 p.m. (closed Sunday), **Maruichi** ㉓, 1-4-13 Tokiwa-cho (tel. 61-7623), is also a great place for an inexpensive meal. Located about a 15-minute walk from Takamatsu Station or only a minute from the Kotoden Kawaramachi tram station, it's a cozy, friendly place decorated with colorful kites, heavy wooden beams, and a stone floor. A Westerner living in Takamatsu introduced the place to me and said it's a good place to meet the natives. In any case, an English menu lists such delectables as octopus sashimi (if you've never tried it, this is a good place to do so), kimchi (Korean spiced cabbage) with pork, mushrooms with melted cheese, salads, and, of course, yakitori. An evening of eating, drinking, and merriment here should cost about ¥2,000 ($8) per person. Maruichi is easy to spot from the outside by its huge red lantern and blue curtains hanging in front of the door inscribed with "Yakitori Izaka."

Western Food

If you want Western food in Takamatsu, your best bet is to dine at a hotel. **Le Bon 6** is a French restaurant located on the ground floor of the Hotel Kawaroku, Hyakken-cho (tel. 21-5666). The Japanese chef here studied and worked for many years in both France and Belgium and, representing Japan, won a gold medal in 1982 at a world food contest held in Luxembourg. The emphasis at this restaurant is on food rather than on decor, and the menu includes seafood, beef, and lamb dishes. Entrées range from about ¥2,300 ($18.40) to ¥6,000 ($48) for most dishes. The chef takes special pride in his creations for the set meals, which change monthly and cost ¥6,500 ($52) and ¥8,800 ($70.40). These dishes are so beautifully arranged you almost hate to eat them. If you're on a budget, consider coming for one of the set lunches priced from ¥1,000 ($8) to ¥3,000 ($24). Hours here are 11 a.m. to 2 p.m. and 5 to 8:30 p.m. daily.

On the seventh floor of the Takamatsu Grand Hotel, 1-5-10 Kotobuki-cho, is the **Yashima Sky Restaurant** (tel. 51-5757). Enclosed on three sides by glass, it affords panoramic views of Tamamo Park and the harbor full of boats and ferries coming and going. Lunch, served from 11:30 a.m. to 2 p.m., has set meals available for ¥900 ($7.20), ¥2,200 ($17.60), and ¥2,750 ($22). Dinners, served from 5 to

8:30 p.m. range from ¥2,750 ($22) to ¥6,000 ($48). The à la carte menu is varied with such items as fondue, steak tartare, lobster thermidor, tenderloin and sirloin steaks, filet mignon, wienerschnitzel, shrimp pilaf, and sandwiches. Most dishes are in the ¥1,500 ($12) to ¥3,000 ($24) price range.

The **Takamatsu Plaza Hotel,** 7-Banchi, Tamamo-cho (tel. 51-3655), also has a restaurant, this one on the tenth floor with views of the harbor. It's open from 11 a.m. to 2 p.m. and 5 to 9 p.m. Dishes are slightly cheaper and include spaghetti, pork, beef, and chicken entrées averaging ¥1,000 ($8).

2. Matsuyama

Although Matsuyama is Shikoku's largest town, with a population of more than 420,000, it has the relaxed atmosphere of a small town. Located on the island's northwest coast, about a three-hour train ride from Takamatsu, Matsuyama features one of Japan's best-preserved feudal castles and what I consider to be the most delightful public bathhouse in the country.

ORIENTATION

Since the completion of the Seto Ohashi Bridge in the spring of 1988, the easiest way to reach Matsuyama is by train from Okayama on Honshu island. Matsuyama is also linked to various ports, including Beppu on Kyushu and Hiroshima on Honshu.

The **Matsuyama City Tourist Information Office** (tel. 0899/31-3914) is located inside the Matsuyama JR Train Station and can be spotted easily with its sign in English. Open daily from 8:30 a.m. to 7:30 p.m., it has an excellent pamphlet and map in English. The train station itself is situated on the west end of town, with most points of interest spreading to the east. Streetcars depart from the front of the station to such places as Dogo Spa and the Okaido Shopping Arcade, a covered pedestrian passageway lined with restaurants and shops, considered to be the heart of the city. Matsuyama Castle lies just northwest of Okaido. Many buses and commuter trains bound for the suburbs depart from Matsuyama City Station, called *Shi-eki* in Japanese, which is linked to Matsuyama JR Train Station via streetcar. More information on how to reach Matsuyama and places of interest can be obtained in a leaflet called *Inland Sea and Shikoku,* available at the T.I.C. in either Tokyo or Kyoto.

The **telephone area code** for Matsuyama is 0899. Matsuyama lies in Ehime Prefecture, and its postal code is 790.

THE SIGHTS

Matsuyama Castle crowns the top of Katsuyama Hill right in the heart of the city. It was built by feudal lord Kato Yoshiakira about 385 years ago, later falling into the hands of the powerful Matsudaira family. Like most structures in Japan, Matsuyama Castle has suffered fire and destruction through the ages, but unlike many other castles (such as those in Osaka and Nagoya) this one is the real thing rather than a replica made of ferroconcrete. There's only one entrance to the castle, a pathway leading through a series of gates that could be swung shut to trap attacking enemies. The three-story donjon houses a museum where you can see armor and swords that used to belong to the Matsudaira family. Surrounding the castle is a park, and if you're feeling energetic you can walk to the castle in about 15 minutes. Otherwise, there's a chair lift and a cable car on the east side of Katsuyama Hill. A ticket for ¥550 ($4.40) includes the round-trip ride to the top of the hill and entrance to the castle; otherwise admission is ¥250 ($2). The castle is open daily from 9 a.m. to 4:30 p.m.

Dogo Spa, with a history of 3,000 years, claims to be the oldest hot-spring spa in Japan, certainly an impressive record. Located in the northeast part of the city about a 20-minute tram ride from Matsuyama Station (take streetcar 5), Dogo Spa can accommodate about 9,000 people in 62 hotels and ryokan, which means that the narrow streets resound at night with the clatter of geta (wooden shoes) as vacationers go to the various bathhouses.

Most of the hotels and ryokan in Dogo have their own *onsen* (hot-spring bath), but I suggest that no matter where you stay you make at least one trip to **Dogo Onsen Honkan** (tel. 21-5141), a wonderful three-story public bathhouse built in 1894. A wooden structure with shoji screens, tatami rooms, creaking wooden stairways, and a white heron topping the crest of the roof, Shinrokaku is as much a social institution as it is a place to soak and scrub. On busy days as many as 4,000 people will pass through its front doors. The water here is transparent, colorless, tasteless, and alkaline. The hottest spring water coming into the spa is 120°F and coolest is 70°F—but don't worry, the waters are mixed to achieve a comfortable 108°F.

Bathing, however, is just a small part of the experience here. Most people come to relax, socialize, and while away an hour or more, and I suggest that you do the same. Although you can bathe for as little as ¥250 ($2), it's worth it to pay extra for the privilege of relaxing on tatami mats in a communal room on the second floor, dressed in a rented yukata (kimono), drinking tea from a lacquered tea set, and eating Japanese sweets. If the weather is fine, all the shoji screens are pushed open to let in a breeze, and as you sprawl out on the tatami, drinking your tea and listening to the clang of the streetcar and the clatter of wooden shoes, you can almost imagine you've somehow landed in ancient Japan. To my mind the whole scene resembles an old woodblock print that has suddenly sprung to life. Cost of the bath, yukata, sweets, and tea is ¥660 ($5.28). Use of a smaller and therefore more private bath and lounging area where tea and sweets are also served costs ¥1,000 ($8). And if you really want to splurge, you can rent your own private tatami room on the third floor, which also comes with tea, sweets, and yukata, for ¥1,300 ($10.40).

Connected to the spa is another building built in 1899 for the imperial family, and you can take a tour of these rooms for a couple hundred yen. The spa is open from 6:30 a.m. (which is the arrival time of the first streetcar) until 11 p.m., but you must enter by 10 p.m. The ticket window for sweets, yukata, and tea closes at 9 p.m.

After your bath, you may want to visit **Ishiteji Temple,** about half a mile east of Dogo. Built in 1318, it's the 51st of Shikoku's 88 sacred temples and is a good example of architecture of the Kamakura Period with its blend of Chinese and Japanese styles. Notice the many straw sandals hanging on the temple gate. They are placed there by older Japanese in hopes of regaining new strength in their legs. There are, incidentally, seven other temples in Matsuyama that belong to the sacred 88, but Ishiteji is the most important and popular.

Crafts and Culture

Matsuyama is famous for several crafts, one of which is *Iyo Kasuri,* a cotton cloth dyed with Japanese indigo and worn traditionally as working clothes by farm housewives. The history of the cloth stretches back to the early 1800s, when it was originated by a woman named Kana Kagiya. If you're interested in seeing firsthand how this cloth is produced, then and now, you can visit **Mingei Iyo Kasuri Kaikan** ㉔, Kumanodai 1165 (tel. 22-0405), a small factory you can reach by bus from the JR Train Station. Open daily from 8 a.m. to 5 p.m., it charges a small admission fee of ¥50 (40¢) and displays the process of dyeing, machine weaving, and hand-weaving the blue cloth. You can even dye your own handkerchief for an extra ¥800 ($6.40). A shop sells various products made from Kasuri cloth, including pillowcases, purses, clothing, hats, and bolts of cloth.

Another product of Ehime Prefecture is Tobe pottery, called *Tobe-yaki* in Japanese. Noted for its thick white porcelain painted with cobalt-blue designs, Tobe pottery is produced in the town of Tobe, which you can reach by bus in about 40 minutes from Matsuyama Shi-eki. There are several kilns open to the public, the most well known of which is **Umeno-Seito-jo** ㉕, tel. 62-2311. It's open every day except Monday from 9 a.m. to 5 p.m. Founded back in 1882 and now in its fourth generation of the Umeno family, it employs more than 100 people, whom you can observe busy at their crafts. That is, you can watch all of the artisans except those who do the actual painting of the designs—the technique is a closely guarded secret. In any case, inside the shop be sure to check out the bargain corner, where pieces with slight imperfections go for about half price. Another place you can shop for Tobe-yaki is at **Tobe-yaki Kanko Center** ⑳, tel. 62-2070, with the same open hours, but open Monday too. At both places you can try your hand in a workshop.

If you'd like to see Kasuri cloth or Tobe-yaki but don't have the time to visit the places where they are made, you can see both at the **Ehime Prefectural Products Hall (Ehime no Bussan)** ⑳, located at Ichibancho 4-chrome not far from the ANA Zenniku Hotel at Kencho-mae tram stop (tel. 41-7584). Open every day from 8:30 a.m. to 5 p.m. except Saturday afternoon, Sunday, and national holidays, it sells the products of Ehime Prefecture, including such foodstuffs as sweets and honey, as well as Tobe-yaki, Kasuri cloth, masks, bamboo vases, lacquerware, cultivated pearls, and dolls. Notice how the dolls are shaped in an oval. Known as the princess doll, they are made in the image of Empress Jingu, who came to Dogo Spa way back in the second century when she was pregnant.

Incidentally, for less esoteric shopping, take a spin through the covered shopping arcade. I don't think there's a Japanese city left without one, but this arcade is especially long. It starts with the Okaido arcade next to Mitsukoshi department store, which eventually runs into the Gintengai covered arcade, which in turn dips underground into the Matsuchika Town underground shopping center near Shieki. You'll find a bewildering number of shops, boutiques, and inexpensive restaurants selling everything from hamburgers to tempura and sushi.

If you're interested in the performing arts, you should check whether there's anything going on in the newly opened **Ehime Prefectural Convention and Cultural Hall.** Designed by Kenzo Tange, this bright, modern hall has frequent concerts, dramas, and other performances. Check with your hotel or the tourist office for information on current productions.

And finally, if you're a devoted fan of Japanese swords and samurai armor, head straight for the hydrofoil that will whisk you to **Omishima** in about an hour. Here, on this unpretentious and rather neglected island, is Japan's most important sword and armor collection. As much as 80% of Japan's national treasure of swords and armor is kept at the shrine here, just as it has been for centuries. Many of the pieces were donated by the owners themselves, including armor once worn by Yoritomo Minamoto 800 years ago. You can also see the armor worn by female warrior Tsuruhime, a kind of Japanese Joan of Arc.

Uchiko

If you have time for a side trip around Ehime Prefecture, I strongly recommend an excursion to the village of Uchiko. With a population of less than 13,000, it has some fine old homes and buildings dating back to the Edo Period and the turn of the century. Whereas about 70% of Matsuyama was destroyed during World War II, Uchiko was left intact and a tiny part of the old city is a living memorial to the days of yore. Even the train ride from Matsuyama JR Station is enjoyable as you weave through valleys of wooded hills. The train trip takes about 50 minutes. Be sure to pick up a map of the village at the Uchiko train station, even though it's in Japanese. A walk through the old part of town, known as *Yokaichi,* should take about an hour or two, depending on how often you stop along the way. Most of the older homes are clustered along one narrow street—there isn't a whole lot to see, but the walk is pleasant and some of the scenes make good photo essays. Note that most museums and buildings in Uchiko are closed on Wednesday.

The first important building on a walking tour of the city is **Uchikoza** ⑳, which is a Kabuki theater built back in 1916. It was recently restored, and though it's not as grand as the one near Takamatsu described earlier in this chapter, it's a good example of how townspeople used to enjoy themselves years ago. It features a revolving stage and many windows that can be opened and closed to control the amount of light reaching the stage.

Other places of interest in Yokaichi include **Machi-ya Shiryokan** and **Kamihaga House,** old homes that have been restored and are open to the public. Built in 1894, Kamihaga House is especially grand, having once belonged to a merchant who made his fortune by exporting wax. During the Edo Period, Uchiko gained fame as a center of candlemaking and wax production, used both for lighting and for the styling of elaborate hairdos. Later the wax was applied to thread used in weaving and as an ingredient in vanishing cream, pomade, and shoe polish. At the world fairs of 1894 in Chicago and 1900 in Paris, Uchiko wax won first prize for quality.

Today only one man carries on this wax making tradition, a man named Omori Yataro, who represents the fifth generation of candlemakers. Following the same techniques as those developed by his ancestors 200 years ago, he even collects his own *haze* berries (a kind of sumac) and makes his candles by hand. His workshop is open to the public, and in the mornings you can observe him at work.

FOOD AND LODGING

There are plenty of choices of both hotels and ryokans in Matsuyama and in Dogo Spa.

The Top Choice

Matsuyama's premier hotel is the **ANA Zenniku Hotel,** 3-2-1 Ichiban-cho (tel. 0899/33-5511). About a ten-minute taxi ride from the train station, it is in a good location for visiting both Matsuyama and Dogo Spa. It's only a five-minute walk to the cable car going up to the castle, and streetcars heading for Dogo pass right in front of the hotel. Built in 1979, the hotel is spacious, cheerfully decorated, and offers 55 boutiques on four floors for shopping (including one selling Tobe-yaki). Its 334 rooms, which start at ¥7,000 ($56) for singles and ¥15,500 ($124) for twins and doubles, are large and well appointed with TV, minibar, radio, clock, and desk.

The hotel also offers a good selection in dining. The **Unkai** is a Japanese restaurant offering a variety of food, including sukiyaki, shabu-shabu, tempura, and sashimi. Although the menu is in Japanese only, there are pictures accompanying most of the set meals, which average about ¥7,500 ($60). À la carte dinners usually run about ¥5,000 ($40) per person; lunches start at ¥1,500 ($12). The restaurant overlooks a small garden with a stream that is lit up at night.

If you'd rather have Western food, the **Castle Grill,** on the 14th floor, serves seafood and steaks, with the cost of an average dinner coming to about ¥6,000 ($48) to ¥8,000 ($64). There are also dinner specials for ¥5,500 ($44) to ¥11,000 ($88). Dinner is romantic, with candles and flowers on each table and a view in the valley below of a European-style castle built by a former lord. Lunch courses start at ¥1,500 ($12).

ANA Zenniku's Chinese restaurant, **Tohen,** is decorated in soothing peach tones and warm woods. The most popular time to come is at lunch, when quick service will bring you set meals starting at ¥1,000 ($8). The dinner menu lists set courses for two people beginning at ¥7,000 ($56). The à la carte menu offers shrimp, pork, beef, liver, kidney, duck, and chicken dishes that come in two sizes. If there are two of you, the practice is to order three small dishes and share.

Tohen, Unkai, and Castle Grill are open daily from 11:45 a.m. to 2:30 p.m. and 5 to 9:30 p.m. Located next to Castle Grill is a bar where you can retire for drinks after dinner.

If you're on a budget or simply want to sit out under the sun or stars, try the ANA Zenniku's **rooftop beer garden.** Open May to September from 5 to 9:30 p.m., this place serves snacks and dishes at about ¥550 ($4.40) to ¥800 ($6.40) a plate. Choices include chicken, pizza, and Japanese dishes. Mugs of beer go for

¥500 ($4) and ¥850 ($6.80), and cocktails are ¥600 ($4.80). Buy your food and drink tickets at the front counter. After you seat yourself, the waiter will collect your ticket and deliver your order.

A Medium-Priced Hotel

A small and pleasant medium-priced hotel not far from the ANA Zenniku Hotel at the Okaido tram stop, the **Kokusai International Hotel,** 1-13 Ichiban-cho (tel. 0899/32-5111), has 80 rooms with radio, clock, TV, minibar, and large windows that let in lots of light. Rooms start at ¥6,000 ($48) for one person and ¥7,300 ($58.40) for two. Even single rooms here have double beds, and some rooms have views of Matsuyama Castle. **Yoshicho,** the hotel's Japanese restaurant, serves such specialties as kushikatsu, sashimi, sukiyaki, and tempura, with the average meal costing ¥3,000 ($24) to ¥5,000 ($40). Restaurant hours are 11:30 a.m. to 9:30 p.m. daily. The hotel's Western restaurant, open from 7 a.m. to 10 p.m., offers sandwiches, fish, beef curry, spaghetti, and set meals, as well as teppanyaki steaks. Expect to spend about ¥3,000 ($24) for a meal.

Ryokan

If you want to stay in a ryokan, head for Dogo. A good choice here is **Funaya** ㉔, Dogo Yunamachi (tel. 0899/47-0278). Although it doesn't look like much from the outside, the inside is comfortable and pleasant. The present building dates from 1963 but the ryokan itself has a history extending almost 140 years. This is where the imperial family stays on visits to Dogo. The lobby and many of its rooms look out onto a garden. Of the ryokan's 43 rooms, 38 are tatami, two are furnished with twin beds, and three are combinations with both beds and tatami areas, which is ideal if you want the feel of a ryokan but don't relish sleeping on the floor. Rates here are ¥24,000 ($192) per person, which includes breakfast, dinner, tax, and service charge.

Another ryokan in Dogo is **Kasugaen** ㉕, 3-1 Saigidani-cho (tel. 0899/41-9156). It has both Japanese-style rooms as well as rooms fitted with both twin beds and tatami. Amenities include minibar, TV, and safe. The price of a room, which includes two meals, tax, and service charge, is ¥20,000 ($160) per person.

The Budget Category

A red-brick building about a five-minute walk from the Matsuyama JR Train Station, **Hotel Sunroute,** Miyatacho (tel. 0899/33-2811), opened in 1986 with a total of 110 rooms. Its rooms are reasonably priced and feature TV with coin-operated videos, radio, clock, hot-water pot for tea, and double-pane windows to shut out noises from the train station. The best views are from those rooms on the top floors facing east, which have a glimpse of the distant castle. Singles are ¥6,500 ($52), while doubles and twins begin at ¥10,500 ($84). On the hotel's roof is a covered beer garden, open rain or shine from 5 to 9 p.m. March through September. After paying an initial charge of 2,700 ($21.60), you can eat and drink as much as you like.

Taihei Business Hotel ㉖, 3-1-15 Heiwa Dori (tel. 0899/43-3560), is a rather interesting establishment located at the northern base of Katsuyama Hill about a 15-minute taxi ride from Matsuyama Station. Unlike the plastic impersonal atmosphere of most business hotels, this one is rather eccentric—most rooms are decorated with old-fashioned wallpaper, worn flowered bedspreads, curtains, and shaggy rugs. The effect is cozy and pleasant, and rooms are great for the price. Singles are ¥4,300 ($34.40) to ¥5,500 ($44), twins are ¥7,700 ($61.60) to ¥10,000 ($80), doubles run ¥8,800 ($70.40), and triples go for ¥13,000 ($104) and up. There are also Japanese-style rooms available for ¥4,000 ($32) per person. All rooms have bathrooms. Buffet breakfasts for ¥500 ($4) and dinners for ¥1,000 ($8) are served in a cheerful dining area. There's a public bath and sauna, but it's only for men. If women happen to be in the majority, it becomes a women's-only facility, but I have the feeling that happens only rarely.

The **Matsuyama Shinsen-en Youth Hostel** ②⑤②, 22-3 Dogohimezaka Otsu (tel. 0899/33-6366), is an eight-minute walk from Dogo Spa Station. A one-night's stay here costs ¥2,200 ($17.60), breakfast is ¥440 ($3.52), and dinner runs ¥650 ($5.20). If you're not a youth hostel member, you can still stay here but you'll be charged an extra ¥500 ($4) per night.

More Dining

Hyakumi ②⑤③, 2 Sanbancho (tel. 45-1893), is just off Okaido pedestrian shopping lane close to the ANA Zenniku Hotel. Although it doesn't have an English menu, it has a plastic-food display case outside showing tempura, shabu-shabu, somen, kamameshi, and other dishes. Most items are ¥800 ($6.40) to ¥2,700 ($21.60). I've had the Bochan Teishoku, a rice casserole dish served with fish, soup, egg custard, and tea, for ¥1,850 ($14.80). The topping for your rice casserole is your choice—how about crab, shrimp, or fish? I've also tried the Higawari Teishoku, which means daily special and which changes every day. It's available until 2 p.m. every day except Sunday and national holidays and costs ¥900 ($7.20). It usually consists of a variety of small dishes, and included soup, sashimi, tempura, pickled vegetables, beef, egg custard, and rice during my last visit. The ground floor provides counter seating, but I find the little cubicles with either tatami or table seating on the first floor much more festive. The hours here are from 11:30 a.m. to 9:30 p.m.; closed on Tuesday. If Tuesday is a national holiday, the restaurant stays open but closes the following Wednesday.

Shinhamasaku ②⑤④, Sanbancho 4-chome (tel. 33-3030), is a modern restaurant serving fresh seafood from the Seto Inland Sea and other local specialties, as well as shabu-shabu, kamameshi, and crab and eel dishes. The menu is in Japanese only but has pictures of the various set courses, most of which range from ¥1,000 ($8) to ¥3,000 ($24). Popular is the *Seiro bento* with tempura for ¥2,700 ($21.60), which includes about 20 different bite-size morsels, all served in a wooden box. It's open daily from 11 a.m. to 3 p.m. and from 4:30 to 8:30 p.m. and is located in the heart of town near the Matsuyama Central Post Office.

KYUSHU

1. FUKUOKA
2. BEPPU
3. MOUNT ASO
4. KUMAMOTO
5. NAGASAKI
6. UNZEN
7. KAGOSHIMA
8. IBUSUKI
9. MIYAZAKI

As the southernmost of Japan's four main islands, Kyushu offers a mild climate, hot-spring spas such as Beppu and Ibusuki, beautiful countryside, national parks, and warm, friendly people. Historians believe that Japan's earliest inhabitants lived in Kyushu before gradually pushing northward, and according to Japanese legend it was from Kyushu that the first emperor, Jimmu, began his campaign to unify Japan. Kyushu is therefore considered to be the cradle of Japanese civilization. And because Kyushu is the island closest to Korea and China, it has served through the centuries as a point of influx for both people and ideas from abroad, including those from the West. Christian missionaries such as St. Francis Xavier succeeded in converting many Kyushu Japanese to Christianity. And in Nagasaki, small communities of Dutch and Chinese merchants were allowed to remain throughout Japan's 200-some years of isolation from the West. In short, Kyushu should be high on the list of any visitor to Japan. From its hot sand baths to its volcanic peaks to its beaches and cosmopolitan cities, Kyushu offers some of the best attractions in Japan.

1. Fukuoka

With a population of more than one million, Fukuoka is Kyushu's largest city and serves as a major gateway to the island, both internationally and domestically. With international direct flights from Pusan, Seoul, Taipei, Manila, Hong Kong, and Honolulu, Fukuoka is also the last stop on the Shinkansen bullet train from Tokyo, about seven hours away; Hiroshima is just 1½ hours away.

During Japan's feudal days, Fukuoka was actually divided into two distinct towns separated by the Nakagawa River. Fukuoka was where the samurai lived, since it was the castle town of the local feudal lord. Across the river in Hakata was where the merchants lived, making it the commercial center of the area. Both cities were joined into one town in 1889 under the common name of Fukuoka. Fukuoka's main train station, however, is in Hakata and is therefore called Hakata Station.

In Japanese history books, Fukuoka's main claim to fame lies in the 13th century, when it was selected by Mongol forces under Kublai Khan as the most convenient place to invade Japan. The first invasion occurred in 1274, but the Japanese were able to repel the enemy. The second attempt came in 1281, but the Japanese had not been idle and were well prepared for the attack. They had built a stone wall along the coast almost ten feet high. Not only did the Mongols find the wall impossible to scale, but a typhoon blew in and destroyed the entire Mongol fleet. The Japanese called this gift from heaven "divine wind," or kamikaze, a word that took on quite a different meaning when young Japanese pilots crashed their planes into American ships during World War II in an attempt to turn the tide of war in Japan's favor.

As an industrial and business center of Kyushu, Fukuoka is not considered much of a destination on the tourist circuit. However, you may find yourself making a one-night stopover here after an international flight or a day's train ride from Tokyo.

ORIENTATION

Before leaving Tokyo or Kyoto, drop by the Tourist Information Center to pick up a leaflet called *Fukuoka*. It lists the major sights of the city.

The **Fukuoka Tourist Information Office** (tel. 431-3003) is in Hakata Station. Open from 9 a.m. to 7 p.m., it has maps in English. If you're going to spend any amount of time in Fukuoka Prefecture, pick up a copy of *Fantastic Fukuoka*, available for ¥300 ($2.40) at the Fukuoka Kotsu Center on the fourth floor next to Hakata Station. By the way, an **international post office** is also located next to Hakata Station.

Although Hakata Station is the terminus for the Shinkansen bullet train and has most of Fukuoka's hotels clustered in its vicinity, the heart of Fukuoka is actually in an area of town called **Tenjin**. Serving as the business center for the city, it's also home to several department stores, a large underground shopping arcade, coffeeshops, and restaurants. Less than a ten-minute walk from Tenjin is **Nakasu,** Fukuoka's largest nightlife district with lots of bars, restaurants, and small clubs.

As for getting around Fukuoka, the easiest method of transportation is by subway. One convenient subway line, for example, runs from Hakata Station to Tenjin (the third stop), passing Nakasukawabata on the way, which is the stop for the Nakasu nightlife district. If you stay on this same line, it will also take you to Ohori-Koen Park. Fukuoka also has bus lines; the city's two bus terminals are located in Tenjin and at Hakata Station. And whereas Hakata Station serves as the terminus for the Shinkansen and JR trains departing for the rest of Kyushu, Tenjin has its own station, called the Nishitetsu Fukuoka Station. This is where you board the train if you're going to Dazaifu.

The **telephone area code** for Fukuoka is 092, and Fukuoka is located in the prefecture of the same name.

THE SIGHTS

Shofukuji Temple is just a ten-minute walk northwest of Hakata Station. Thought to be the oldest Zen Buddhist temple in Japan, it was founded in 1195 by a priest named Eisai, who was the first to introduce Zen and tea seeds into Japan after studying four years in China.

Located about 15 minutes by foot from Hakata Station is **Sumiyoshi-jinja Shrine.** With buildings dating from about 400 years ago, it's one of Kyushu's oldest

Shinto shrines and is dedicated to the guardians of seafarers. As it's favored by the Japanese as a good place for wedding ceremonies, you may be lucky and witness a traditional wedding in progress.

If you feel like being completely and wickedly lazy, take the subway line from Hakata Station to the Ohori-Koen subway stop, just ten minutes away. There you'll find **Ohori-Koen Park,** built on part of the outer defenses of the former Fukuoka Castle. Laid around a lake with small islands connected with bridges, it's a perfect place to relax with a picnic lunch. On the south side of the park is a traditional Japanese garden—constructed not centuries ago but in 1984.

If you start feeling guilty for being so lazy, visit the nearby **Fukuoka City Art Museum (Fukuoka Shiritsu Bijutsukan),** in the southeastern part of the park facing the lake. It contains modern and Buddhist art as well as tea ceremony utensils, ancient weapons, and armor. Closed on Monday, it's open the rest of the week from 9:30 a.m. to 5:30 p.m. Admission is ¥150 ($1.20).

If you have time, the most popular thing to do in Fukuoka is to take a side trip to **Dazaifu Temmangu Shrine,** which you can reach in 35 minutes by taking the Nishi Nippon Tetsudo Line (called Nishitetsu for short) from Nishitetsu Fukuoka Station in Tenjin. Trains depart every 30 minutes and the station stop is called Dazaifu Station. Dazaifu Temmangu Shrine was established in 905, although the present main hall dates from 1590. It's dedicated to the god of scholarship, which is one reason why the shrine is so popular—high school students flock here to pray that they pass the tough entrance exams into universities. Planted with lots of plum trees, camphor trees, and irises, the extensive grounds surrounding the shrine can be explored on a rented bicycle.

SHOPPING

You don't have to venture far from Hakata Station to go shopping. In fact, the Izutsuya department store is located right above the station itself. Incidentally, on top of the department store is a rooftop beer garden open mid-April through August from 5 to 10 p.m. Radiating out from the station are underground shopping arcades. Deitos is located under the Shinkansen tracks and is comprised of various souvenir shops selling cakes, woven handbags, and Hakata's famous clay *ningyo* dolls.

Another large shopping area is in Tenjin, third stop on the subway line from Hakata Station. There's a huge underground shopping mall here, called Tenjin Chikagai, which stretches some 1,300 feet north to south. There are also many boutiques, department stores, specialty shops, coffeeshops, and restaurants in the area.

FOOD AND LODGING

Because most people make a stopover in Fukuoka for only one night, I've listed accommodations conveniently located within walking distance of Hakata Station.

The Upper Bracket

One of the finest places to stay in town is the **ANA Zenniku Hotel Hakata,** 3-3-3 Hakata-ekimae (tel. 092/471-7111). It's about a five-minute walk from what is called the Hakata Guchi Exit of the station. A modern and sparkling-clean first-class hotel, it has everything you'd expect from a hotel of this stature. Its lobby is large and spacious and its 363 rooms are bright and comfortable, with the usual pay video channels on TV, minibar, radio, and large bathroom. Singles range from ¥9,900 ($79) to ¥14,300 ($114), doubles run ¥14,800 ($118) to ¥22,000 ($176), and twins cost ¥18,500 ($148) to ¥28,000 ($224). Japanese-style suites with all the modern conveniences cost ¥25,000 ($200) and sleep two to three persons.

The ANA Zenniku Hotel also offers fine dining. Most hotels feature Western restaurants on their top floors, but this hotel has given its Japanese restaurant, **Tsukushino,** the premier spot on the 15th floor. A beautifully sculpted bonsai pine graces the entrance to the restaurant, constructed in such a fashion that it looks like the lane of a village. Overhanging eaves topped with traditional tiled roofs extend down from the ceiling above the walls, and in the center of the restaurant is a glass-enclosed courtyard with raked gravel and bushes. As soon as you can tear your eyes away from your immediate surroundings, you'll notice the city spread beyond the windowpanes. The English menu describes each dish. Mizutaki, for example, is a Fukuoka specialty described as chicken boiled in light broth with various Japanese vegetables and tofu. Kaiseki offerings, which change every two months, are ¥6,600 ($52.80) to ¥16,500 ($132). There are also shabu-shabu, sashimi dishes, and a separate tempura counter. Most set meals cost ¥6,000 ($48) and up, but you can do it much cheaper if you come here for lunch, served until 2 p.m. Teishoku specials begin at ¥1,000 ($8). The most popular is the Tsukushino obento box lunch for ¥2,700 ($21.60), which includes sashimi, boiled vegetables, and lots more. The restaurant is open daily from 11:30 a.m. to 10 p.m.

Other facilities at the hotel include an outside sidewalk café open from 5 to 9:30 p.m. during summer months; a health club with pool, sauna, and exercise equipment which you can use for ¥4,500 ($36); cocktail lounges; and Chinese and Western restaurants.

The **Hakata Miyako Hotel,** 2-1 Hakata-eki Higashi (tel. 092/441-3111), is just in front of the Shinkansen bullet train exit of Hakata Station, on the south side. With the good name and legendary service of the Miyako hotel chain behind it, this hostelry has well-appointed rooms (some with bilingual TV) beginning at ¥8,400 ($67) for a single, ¥14,500 ($116) for a twin, and ¥14,800 ($118) for a double. The hotel's six Japanese-style rooms, used most often as waiting rooms before wedding ceremonies and receptions held at the hotel, have cypress bathtubs and cost ¥17,500 ($140).

Western dining at the Miyako Hotel is done in style at the 12th-floor **Starlight,** open only for dinner from 5 to 10:30 p.m. There's music nightly from the large white piano and at one end of the restaurant is a cocktail bar, where you can retire for drinks after dinner. Set courses range from ¥5,500 ($44) to ¥11,000 ($88). If you order seafood or steak entrées from the large leather-bound menu, expect to spend about ¥10,000 ($80) per person.

With the Miyako chain's most famous hotel located in Kyoto, it's not surprising that this hotel's Japanese restaurant, **Shikitei,** specializes in Kyoto-style dishes. Set meals start at ¥3,300 ($26.40) for sashimi, tempura, and mizutaki and rise to ¥6,500 ($52) for shabu-shabu and ¥5,500 ($44) for sukiyaki. Kyoto kaiseki selections start at ¥6,600 ($52.80). During lunch there are also obento lunchbox specials for ¥1,400 ($11.20) and ¥2,200 ($17.60). Shikitei is open from 11:30 a.m. to 2 p.m. and 5 to 9:30 p.m.

The Medium-Priced Range

One of Fukuoka's newest hotels is **Clio Court,** 5-3 Hakataeki-Chuogai (tel. 092/472-1111), which is located beside the Shinkansen exit of Hakata Station. In this sleek modern hotel with lots of chrome, mirrors, and white marble, the lobby is up on the third floor and the 203 guest rooms are doubles and twins decorated in art deco styles. Few of the rooms—the creation of well-known female architect Rei Kurokawa—have the same interior design. Rooms are large; even the bathrooms are roomy. Single occupancy rates range from ¥7,700 ($62) to ¥12,000 ($96) for double rooms and ¥8,800 ($70) to ¥16,500 ($132) for twins. Double occupancy rates range from ¥8,800 ($70) to ¥14,300 ($114) for double rooms and ¥10,000 ($80) to ¥19,800 ($158) for twins. The cheapest rooms, however, don't have any windows.

Restaurants in the hotel serve French, Chinese, or Japanese cuisine. In the basement is an interesting setup called **Clio Seven,** which is essentially one large room cleverly divided into seven different bars and restaurants, including a sushi bar, a yakitori-ya, and an English-style pub. Clio Seven is open daily from 5 p.m. to 1 a.m.

Another new hotel in Fukuoka is **Hotel Centraza Hakata,** 4-23 Hakataeki-Chuogai (tel. 092/461-0111), located just across the square from Clio Court. Its spacious and marbled lobby is up on the second floor, and all its rooms are equipped with semidouble- or double-size beds, a TV control panel beside the bed, radio, clock, refrigerator, and hot-water pot. There's a small outdoor swimming pool. Singles here begin at ¥7,700 ($62), doubles at ¥11,000 ($88), and twins at ¥14,300 ($114).

In the basement of Hotel Centraza is **Gourmet City,** with approximately a dozen establishments offering everything from sushi, Chinese food, and steaks to ice cream and beer. All of the restaurants, open daily from 11 a.m. to 11 p.m., have plastic-food displays, with lunch specials offered for less than ¥1,500 ($12). Restaurants are chic and well-designed, a welcome addition to the dining scene around Hakata Station.

On the other side of Hakata Station are several more business hotels, among them the **Chisan Hotel Hakata** ⑤, 2-8-11 Hakata-ekimae (tel. 092/411-3211). To reach it, take the Hakata Guchi exit, keep walking straight ahead for about seven minutes, and look for a light-tiled triangular building to your right. It's an efficient and dependable hotel with good service and a friendly staff, and the rooms come with TV with pay video, radio, clock, minibar, and hot-water pot for tea. The hotel's one restaurant serves a buffet breakfast of Japanese and Western food for ¥900 ($7.20). With tax and service charge included, rates here are ¥6,500 ($52) for a single, ¥9,600 ($76.80) for a double, and ¥11,000 ($88) to ¥13,000 ($104) for a twin. The best rooms are the higher-priced twins. Located in the curve of the hotel's front façade, they offer large rounded windows and lots of space.

Next to Chisan Hotel is another business hotel, the **Mitsui Urban Hotel** ⑤, 2-8-15 Hakata-ekimae (tel. 092/451-5111). Part of a nationwide hotel chain, this one was built more than a decade ago but still looks relatively new. The rooms are small but the windows are large. Singles start at ¥6,500 ($52) and doubles and twins are ¥11,500 ($92), tax and service charge extra.

Toyo Hotel, 1-9-36 Hakata-eki Higashi (tel. 092/474-1121), is a comfortable business hotel a few minutes' walk from the Shinkansen exit of the station. All beds in the hotel are semidoubles, and prices include tax and service charge. Singles are ¥5,700 ($45.60), doubles are ¥7,700 ($62), and twins run ¥9,500 ($76). The sofa in the twin rooms can be made into an extra bed for a third person, in which case the room goes for ¥12,000 ($96). Some of the twin rooms on lower floors face another building, making them rather dark. Ask for a room higher up; those facing north have the best view. Since this is a Japanese businessman's hotel, don't be too surprised to find vending machines selling magazines of questionable taste.

Not far from the Toyo Hotel are the **Hakata Green Hotels 1 and 2,** 4-4 Hakataeki-Chuogai (tel. 092/451-4111), a minute's walk from the station. Green Hotel 1 is slightly older and has mainly singles starting at ¥4,900 ($39). In my opinion it's worth it to spend the extra couple of bucks to stay in the newer Green Hotel 2. It also has mainly singles, but some twins and doubles are available. Prices here are ¥5,500 ($44) for a single, ¥7,900 ($63) for a twin, and ¥7,200 ($58) for a double, including tax and service. Rooms, tiny and without closets, are white, bright, and clean, and come with coin-operated TV, clock, a plug-in pressing board to keep businessmen's pants nicely pressed (you can also use it on skirts), and large windows that open. There's a tiny drying rack in the bathrooms to hang up wet clothes. Machines in the hallway dispense free hot tea.

On the ground floor is a Japanese restaurant called **Ginroku.** Decorated with Japanese kites and traditional decor, it has music that's most likely to be modern pop. Open daily from 11 a.m. to 2 p.m. and 5 to 11 p.m., it offers such dishes as yakitori, sashimi, baked potatoes, flatfish, and corn on the cob. You can eat here for less than ¥1,000 ($8).

The Budget Category

As for youth hostels in the area, there isn't one in Fukuoka itself. The **Dazaifu Youth Hostel** ⑤, 1553-3 Oaza-Dazaifu, Dazaifu-machi (tel. 092/922-8740), is about a 12-minute walk from Dazaifu Station. An overnight stay costs ¥2,300 ($18.40), breakfast is ¥450 ($3.60), and dinner runs ¥750 ($6). If you're a non-member, you can stay here but you'll be charged extra for a one-night guest card, which is ¥600 ($4.80). There's another youth hostel about a 50-minute bus ride from Nishitetsu-Fukuoka Bus Center in Tenjin called the **Yakiyama Youth Hostel,** Yakiyama, Izuka City (tel. 09482/2-6385).

More Dining

A Japanese restaurant specializing in Japanese seafood, **Gyosai** ⑳, 3-chome Hakata-ekimae (tel. 441-9780), is located across the street from the Chisan Hotel about a seven-minute walk from Hakata Station (its sign says "Oki Doki"). Actually it's one of four Gyosai restaurants in Fukuoka—two are in the Tenjin shopping area and another one is located not far from Hakata Station. There's even a Gyosai in New York City. You can get a plate of assorted sashimi here for ¥1,550 ($12.40); most other dishes of fried fish and more sashimi cost between ¥900 ($7.20) and ¥2,200 ($17.60). The menu is in Japanese only, so the easiest thing to do is order a set meal. There's a brochure with pictures of dishes ranging from ¥4,000 ($32) to ¥7,000 ($56). The lunch teishoku, served from 11:30 a.m. to 1:30 p.m., is very reasonable at ¥600 ($4.80) and consists of fried and raw fish, vegetables, pickles, soup, and rice. Hours are 11:30 a.m. to 1:30 p.m. and 5 to 11 p.m.; closed Sunday.

---

2. Beppu

Twelve million people come to Beppu every year to relax and rejuvenate themselves, and they do so in a number of unique ways. They sit in mud baths up to their necks. They bury themselves in hot black sand. They soak in hot springs, and on New Year's they bathe in water filled with floating orange peels. With more than 3,000 hot springs spewing forth 140,000 tons of water daily, and a total of 168 public bathhouses, Beppu is one of Japan's best-known spa resorts. Whether it's in mud, sand, or water, bathing reigns supreme here—and I suggest you join in the fun. After all, visiting Beppu without enjoying the baths would be like going to a famous restaurant with your own TV dinner.

Beppu itself, not a very large town, is situated on Kyushu's east coast in a curve of Beppu Bay. Its 150,000 inhabitants are bounded on one side by the sea and on the other by steep hills and mountains. Steam rises everywhere throughout the city, escaping from springs and pipes and giving the town an otherworldly appearance. Indeed, eight of the hot springs look so much like hell that that's what they're called—Jigoku, the Hells. But rather than a place most people try to avoid, the Hells are a major tourist attraction. In fact, everything in Beppu is geared toward tourism, and if you're interested in rubbing elbows with Japanese on vacation, this is one of the best places to do so.

ORIENTATION

The Tourist Information Centers in Tokyo and Kyoto have a free leaflet called *Beppu and Vicinity* with information on this area of Kyushu as well as on transportation in the area. The trip from Tokyo takes about seven to eight hours, with the usual route involving a change of trains in Kokura from the Shinkansen to a limited express bound for Beppu. The nearest airport is Oita, an hour's bus ride away; ANA flights can reach it from Tokyo's Haneda airport in about 1½ hours. There are also ferries making regular runs to Beppu from Osaka, Hiroshima, Kobe, and Matsuyama.

Once in Beppu be sure to stop by the **Beppu Tourist Information Office** (tel.

0977/24-2838), which is located at Beppu Station and is open daily from 9 a.m. to 6 p.m. You can pick up an excellent brochure called *The Smile of Japan—Beppu,* with such useful information as what to see in the area, which local buses to take, the opening and closing hours for the major sights, and a map of the city. Another information office, called the **Foreign Tourist Information Service,** is located about a two-minute walk from Beppu Station on the second floor of the Frosen Building (tel. 23-1999). It's operated by English-speaking volunteers and offers tourist information and advice.

The easiest ways to get around Beppu are bus and taxi. If you plan on doing a lot of sightseeing by bus, there's a one-day bus pass with the strange name of "My Beppu Free," which nonetheless costs ¥700 ($5.60) and allows unlimited travel on Kamenoi Company buses within the city. If you're short of time you may want to join one of the many organized tours.

The **telephone area code** for Beppu is 0977. Beppu is located in Oita Prefecture and the postal code is 874.

WHAT TO DO

There are many kinds of springs and baths with various mineral contents that help in ailments from rheumatism to skin disease. If all you want is a quick dip in a hot-spring bath in between train rides, you have no farther to go than **Eki-mae Onsen,** which is just a minute's walk from Beppu Station's main exit and which also features a Jacuzzi. If you have a specific ailment, call the hot-springs section of the tourist office (tel. 21-1111) to ask which baths would help you most. The pamphlet *The Smile of Japan,* described above, also has information on the various baths and their specific benefits. Otherwise, if you're simply here for the experience of the baths, there are two I particularly recommend.

Suginoi Palace

Most of the Japanese inns, hotels, and even private homes are tapped into Beppu's hot springs, but no matter where you stay you should visit Suginoi Palace, which adjoins the Suginoi Hotel. This is one of the most fantastic and fantasy-provoking baths in all of Japan, and also one of the largest. Housed in gigantic affairs that look like airplane hangars are two separate bathing areas, one for men and one for women. Filled with lush tropical plants and pools of various sizes and temperatures, one of the baths features a benevolent-looking Buddha sitting atop a giant fish bowl full of carp, while the other bath boasts a large red torii gate similar to ones you see at Shinto shrines. If you come two days in a row you can see both baths as men and women alternate facilities daily. Other features of the baths here include a steam room, a sauna, an outdoor pool, a Korean-style heated floor upon which you can lie down and relax, a pit with hot sand in which to bury yourself, and even a so-called "coffee bath" with real coffee in it, thought to aid the complexion.

The baths are open daily to the public from 9 a.m. to 9 p.m. The cost is ¥1,750 ($14) Monday through Saturday and ¥2,000 ($16) on Sunday. If you're staying at the Suginoi Hotel, you can use the baths daily for free from 7 a.m. to 10:30 p.m.

In addition to its huge bathhouses, Suginoi Palace offers quite a few other diversions as well, including an outdoor waterfall and pond filled with greedy carp (buy some fish food and you'll see what I mean—they almost jump out of the water in their feeding frenzy). There's also a small landscaped garden, a beautiful display of bonsai plants, a play area with amusement-park rides for children, a miniature golf course, and bowling lanes. There's even a variety show with two performances daily. (*Note:* The variety show is included in the admission price to the baths, but occasionally big-name entertainers appear and admission prices go up regardless of whether or not you attend the show. To avoid having to pay extra, it might be prudent to check the price). Especially good is the **Suginoi Museum,** which charges a separate admission fee of ¥500 ($4). Its collection is worth more than ¥10 billion and includes a varied selection of samurai armor, Japanese antique weapons, toilet sets, ceramics, lacquerware, religious artifacts, clocks, and other items dating from the Edo Period. The museum is small but gives a good overview of objects used in Japan in centuries past.

A Hot-Sand Bath

One of the unique things you can do in Beppu is take a bath in hot sand, and one of the best places to do it is at **Takegawara Bathhouse**. Built in 1879, it's one of the oldest public baths in the city. The inside of the building resembles an ancient gymnasium. Bathing areas are separate for men and women, and are dominated by a pit filled with black sand. The attendants are used to foreigners here and will instruct you to strip, wash yourself down, and then lie down in a hollow they've dug in the sand. You should bring your own towel, which you should use to cover your vital parts. An attendant will then shovel sand on top of you and pack you in until only your head and feet are sticking out. I personally didn't find the sand all that hot, but it is relaxing as the heat soaks into your body. You stay buried for ten minutes, contemplating the wooden ceiling high above and hoping you don't get an itch somewhere. When the time is up, the attendant will tell you to stand up, shake off the sand, and then jump into a bath of hot water. The cost of this bathing experience is ¥600 ($4.80), and hours are 6:30 a.m. to 9 p.m. daily.

Open-air sand baths are also offered at **Beppu Beach**, known as *Shoningahama* in Japanese and reportedly good for muscle pain, rheumatism, and neuralgia. You keep on your yukata for the burial here, and the experience also costs ¥600 ($4.80). Hours are 8:30 a.m. to 6 p.m., with slightly shorter hours in winter. You can reach Beppu Beach via bus 24 or 26, departing from the main exit on the east side of Beppu Station; you can also reach it on a local commuter train to Daigoku Station.

The Hells

As for sightseeing, you might as well join everyone else and go to the Hells. These Hells are actually boiling ponds created by volcanic activity. Six of them are clustered close together in the Kannawa area within walking distance of each other and can be toured in about an hour or so. One ¥1,200 ($9.60) ticket allows entrance to all eight Hells. Otherwise, the separate entrance fee to each one is ¥250 ($2). You can also join a two-hour tour of the Hells for ¥2,900 ($23.20), but it's conducted in Japanese only. Each Hell has its own attraction. Umi Jigoku, or Sea Hell, has the color of sea water. Chinoike Jigoku, the Blood-Pond Hell, is blood-red in color because of the red clay dissolved in the hot water. Yama Jigoku features animals living in its hot spring and Oniyama Jigoku is where crocodiles are bred. Tatsumaki Jigoku, Waterspout Hell, has one of the largest geysers in Japan, and with a temperature of 221°F it's hotter than any other hot spring in Beppu.

Takasakiyama Mountain

On Beppu's southern border, about a 15-minute bus ride from Beppu Station, rises Takasakiyama Mountain. Its peak is home to more than 1,800 monkeys, which come down every day to feed, returning to their home by late afternoon. They wander freely among the visitors, and humans are advised not to challenge them by looking directly into their eyes. Admission to this attraction is ¥300 ($2.40), and hours are 8:30 a.m. to 5 p.m. in winter, 8 a.m. to 5:30 p.m. in summer.

African Safari

If you have children traveling with you or simply are fond of zoos, you may be interested in visiting African Safari, a drive-through nature park with a road that winds through bare grassland. Bears, baboons, elephants, rhinos, zebras, camels, bison, giraffes, lions, tigers, and other exotic animals are allowed to roam in their own restricted areas, separated by fences so that they don't eat each other. Humans are confined to their cars or special buses.

Entrance to the park is ¥2,000 ($16), while bus rides through the park cost

¥400 ($3.20). Best, however, is to pay extra for the ¥1,000 ($8) caged bus that features slots of food for the various animals so that you can watch them eat at close range. The prices for children are ¥1,000 ($8) for admission and ¥750 ($6) for the caged bus. The zoo, which features 1,300 animals belonging to 69 different species, is open every day from 9 a.m. to 5 p.m. (9:30 a.m. to 4 p.m. from November 16 to March 15).

To reach African Safari, take bus no. 41 or 43 from Beppu Station. The trip takes about 50 minutes. Incidentally, the bus passes through an interesting part of Beppu called Myoban, where you'll notice a number of straw huts along the side of the road. These huts are built above hot springs and protect the formation of white powder-like sulphur deposits called *yunohana* in Japanese. You can buy the powder and add it to your bath at home for an instant hot-spring experience.

WHERE TO STAY

Since Beppu is a resort town, there are many accommodations in all price ranges, including hotels, ryokan, and minshuku.

The Top Choices

Probably the best-known hotel in Beppu is the **Suginoi Hotel**, Kankaiji (tel. 0977/24-1141), famous for its gigantic baths. A huge complex situated on a wooded hill with a sweeping view of the city and sea below, it's one of the most popular places to stay for both Japanese and foreign visitors. Popular also with group tours, it's a lively and noisy hotel filled with good-natured vacationers. In other words, if you like being in the middle of the action, this is the place for you. Although this place calls itself a hotel, only 88 of its 590 rooms are Western style. The rest are all Japanese tatami rooms. The drawback to Western-style rooms is that they face inland, though some combination-style rooms that feature both beds and a separate tatami area are also available that have fantastic views of the sea.

Room rates without meals are ¥11,000 ($88) for one person and ¥13,200 ($106) for two in Western-style rooms, while in the Japanese-style rooms they begin at ¥15,400 ($123) and ¥17,500 ($140), respectively. If you want rates that include breakfast and dinner served buffet style in both Japanese and Western restaurants, Western rooms go for ¥13,200 ($106) per person if there are two of you and ¥17,500 ($140) if you're alone. Japanese-style rooms with meals start at ¥24,000 ($192) for one person and ¥16,500 ($132) per person for two. All rooms are modestly furnished and come with private bathroom, TV, and a safe for valuables. Note that rates with meals include tax and service charge, as do those in a ryokan, while room-only rates do not.

If it's peace and quiet you're searching for, **Kannawaen** ㉕⑨, Kannawa (tel. 0977/66-2111), is a wonderful ryokan hidden away on a lushly landscaped hill not far from the Hells. It actually consists of six separate houses spread around its grounds, and its tatami rooms with shoji screens look out onto carefully tended gardens, hot springs, bamboo, streams, bonsai, stone lanterns, and flowers. This is the perfect place to escape the crowds and to relax in an open-air bath set among rocks and trees. Rates range from ¥18,000 ($144) to ¥30,000 ($240) per person, depending on the room, and include breakfast, dinner, tax, and service charge. Rooms do not have private bathrooms, but the beauty of the surrounding countryside more than makes up for it. I highly recommend this place. Incidentally, if the ryokan itself is too expensive for you, you can come here just to use its open-air bath, open to the public from noon to 4 p.m. for ¥500 ($8). Since it's close to the Hells, you might want to come here after battling the crowds.

A much more reasonably priced ryokan is **Tenjuso** ㉖⓪, Minami-soencho 6 Kumi (tel. 0977/23-0131). Located about a five-minute taxi ride from the station, this traditional inn is more than 50 years old and is hidden from the rest of the world by an old stone wall. Each of the 20 tatami-style rooms here are different and 8 have private bathrooms, but in any case you'll want to try the hot-spring public bath.

Rates per person including two meals are ¥5,500 ($44) to ¥15,000 ($120), with the more expensive rooms offering bathrooms and views of the sea.

Minshuku

If you're on a budget, one of the best places to stay is near the Hells at **Sakaeya** ㉑, Ida, Kannawa (tel. 0977/66-6234), a minshuku with an 82-year history and the oldest minshuku in the city. The oldest rooms date from the Meiji Period (1868–1912) and are furnished with old radiators heated naturally from hot springs. Another relic is the stone oven in the open courtyard which utilizes steam from hot springs for cooking (many older homes in Beppu still use such ovens). Use of the oven is free in case you want to cook your own meals; there's also a modern kitchen you can use. There are 30 rooms here, all with TV, air conditioner, and kimono; most have sinks as well and five have bathrooms. Room rates here are ¥3,000 ($24) to ¥5,500 ($44) per person. Meals, cooked with natural steam, are especially good, with set Japanese courses available for ¥2,500 ($20) to ¥5,500 ($44). Western or Japanese breakfasts cost ¥1,000 ($8). Sakaeya is about a ten-minute taxi ride from Beppu Station, but as you might imagine, this establishment is popular with Japanese, especially during Golden Week at the beginning of May and during New Year's. If the minshuku is full, the owner here says he'll be happy to relocate you in another minshuku close by.

About a two-minute walk from Beppu Station is **Kokage,** 8-9 Ekimaecho (tel. 0977/23-1753). In operation for 20 years, it is run by a friendly older gentleman who speaks a few words of English and welcomes foreign guests. There are 11 Japanese-style rooms, 1 combination room with bed and tatami area, 3 twin rooms, and 1 double room. Rooms are old and a bit worn but are furnished with kimono, towels, hot water for tea, coin-operated heaters and air conditioners, telephones and televisions, and 10 rooms have private bathrooms. In any case there's a public hot-spring bath and prices are unbeatable. Rates for rooms only are ¥3,300 ($26), while rates with two meals are ¥6,000 ($48) per person. Meals are served in a homey dining room with a cluttered but interesting collection of hanging lamps and clocks.

READER'S SUGGESTION: "I stayed at the **Minshuku Kokage,** and for those on a budget I would highly recommend it just because of the large hot-spring bath. Just around the corner from Kokage is a small restaurant with a red-and-white dragon over the door that had a delicious and most filling set dish (displayed in the front window) consisting of a large piece of shrimp tempura, two pieces of vegetable tempura, a bowl of soba, and a bowl of rice for ¥500 ($4)" (Gene Smith, Tigard, Oreg.).

Budget Hotels

About a ten-minute walk from Beppu Station, **Nippaku Hotel,** 26-12-3 Kitahama (tel. 0977/23-2291), is a reasonably priced tourist hotel. Welcoming more than 1,000 foreign guests a year, they're used to foreigners here and the front-desk staff speak English. Rooms are nicely but modestly furnished, and facilities include a restaurant and hot-spring public baths. Both Japanese- and Western-style rooms are available. Those without private bathroom are ¥6,200 ($50) for one person and ¥10,600 ($85) for two. Rooms with private bathroom are ¥7,800 ($62) for one person and ¥11,800 ($94) for two. Prices include tax and service.

Green Business Hotel ㉒, 1-3-11 Kitahama (tel. 0977/25-2444), is a relatively new business hotel located just a couple of minutes' walk from Beppu Station, with rooms much larger than those of the average business hotel. All 56 rooms come with coin-operated TV, radio, and private bathroom and cost ¥4,400 ($35) for a single, ¥6,000 ($48) for a double, and ¥7,500 ($60) for a twin. Rooms facing the front of the hotel have tiny balconies.

And now for the super-budget choice and what is probably the best deal in all of Beppu—the **Kagetsu,** Tanoyucho 7-22 (tel. 0977/24-2355). A room here costs only ¥2,500 ($20) per person, which is about the lowest I've come across in my travels through Japan. Even more astonishing: each of the ten rooms, both Western and Japanese style, comes with its own private bathroom, television, and central heating and air conditioning. And as if that's not enough, Mrs. Takayama gives out free tickets to the local public bath, even though her own water is supplied from the natural hot springs. Finally, it's conveniently located just a minute's walk from the train station: take the west exit and turn left. No meals are served, but there are plenty of restaurants in the area. I wish every city had a Kagetsu.

Youth Hostel

The **Beppu Youth Hostel** is close to the Suginoi Hotel at Kankaiji 2 (tel. 0977/ 23-4116), about a 20-minute bus ride from Beppu Station. Accommodations cost only ¥2,200 ($17.60) if you have a youth hostel card and ¥2,900 ($23) if you don't. Breakfasts are ¥400 ($3.20) and dinners are ¥700 ($5.60). Obviously, since you have to fork out money for the bus ride, you're much better off staying at the Kagetsu, described above. In any case, there's room here for 138 people, both in tatami rooms and those with bunk beds. Facilities include hot-spring baths and a coin laundry.

WHERE TO DINE

An economically priced restaurant, **Chikuden** ㉖, 1-6-1 Kitahama (tel. 25-2277), is about a ten-minute walk from Beppu Station's main exit. It serves a variety of sashimi, including fugu, sea bream, and abalone, and is a good place to go if you want to sample a variety of raw seafood without spending a small fortune. The menu is in Japanese only, but if you want a plate with a variety of sashimi, ask for the *Mori-a-wa-se*, which costs ¥2,700 ($21.60) per person. A plate of fugu costs ¥2,700 ($21.60). Sukiyaki is also served. The ground floor has tatami and counter seating, while the second floor has four private tatami rooms for groups. The restaurant is open every day of the week from 5 p.m. to 1 a.m.

In addition to fugu, another specialty of Beppu is flat noodles. A popular noodle restaurant, **Amamijaya** ㉔, 1-4 Jissoji (tel. 67-6024), means "Sugar Tea House." Filled with local crafts and toys hanging on its walls, this inexpensive shop is about a 15-minute walk from the cluster of six Hells. Most items on the Japanese menu are ¥350 ($2.80) to ¥500 ($4), and all the noodles are made by hand by the owner. Dishes include *dangojiro* (flat noodles and vegetable soup), *yaseiuma* (a sweet dish of flat noodles covered with powdered soy beans and sugar), *mochi* (Japanese rice cake), and *zosui* (rice porridge with plums). Closed on Wednesday, it's open the rest of the week from 10 a.m. to 10 p.m.

If you're simply looking for a quick, inexpensive meal near the train station, you'll find plenty of them in and around the main exit. One of these is **Jin** ㉕, 1-15-7 Kitahama (tel. 21-1768), about a five-minute walk from the main exit. Simply walk straight down the shop-lined street under the awnings all the way to the end. Jin is across the street from the modern Tokiwa department store and has a row of red lanterns hanging from its eaves. It offers several lunch teishoku, all for ¥600 ($4.80). I had tonkatsu with rice, vegetables, soup, and custard during my visit, but other choices included grilled fish or fresh oysters. Jin is open daily from 11:30 a.m. to midnight, but note that the teishoku is available only until 2 p.m. An English menu lists fish and various meat and vegetable skewered delicacies.

---

3. Mount Aso

In the center of Kyushu between Beppu and Kumamoto is the **Mount Aso National Park.** The park encompasses two groups of mountains, volcanic Mount Aso and Mount Kuju, as well as grasslands, forests, and hot springs. Although Mount Kuju is the largest mountain on the island, the chief attraction of the park is Mount

Aso—it has the honor of possessing the largest crater basin in the world. Measuring 11 miles from east to west, almost 15 miles from north to south, and 74½ miles in circumference, Mount Aso must have been one mighty mountain before blowing its stack, larger even than Mount Fuji. Today five volcanic cones sit in the Mount Aso crater basin. One of them, Nakadake, is still active, constantly spewing forth high-temperature gas and sulfurous fumes. Every once in a while it even explodes (the latest eruption occurring in 1979). At the base of Nakadake at Aso West Station is the **Mount Aso Volcanic Museum.** The entrance fee is ¥800 ($6.40), and the highlights are two cameras that have been placed on the walls of the active volcanic cone so that you can see the latest activity. There's also a 15-minute show depicting Mount Aso National Park during the various seasons.

ORIENTATION
There are several resort towns at Mount Aso circling Nakadake, including Aso, Takamori, and Aso-Shimoda. If you're interested in going to the top of Nakadake, the approach is from Aso Station in Aso. Aso Station is an hour from Kumamoto and 2½ hours from Beppu. From Aso Station you can board a bus for the 40-minute ride to Aso West Station (Asosan Nishi), from which you can take a ropeway to the top of the crater. There are nine buses daily running both ways between Aso Station and Aso West Station. The last bus departs Aso West Station at 5 p.m., but you'd be wise to check on this.

Trans-Kyushu Highway
Although you can reach Aso by rail, the most popular and pleasant route is by bus along the 186-mile-long Trans-Kyushu Highway, which links Beppu with Mount Aso, Kumamoto, and Nagasaki. Sightseeing buses departing several times daily from both Kumamoto and Beppu are operated by the Kyushu Kokusai Kanko Bus Company. A timetable for buses departing from both Beppu and Kumamoto is provided in the leaflet *Kumamoto and Mt. Aso,* available at the Tourist Information Centers in Kyoto and Tokyo.

The buses pass through rice paddies, tobacco and wheat fields, and bamboo groves, and skirt around waterfalls, streams, and hot springs. They all stop at Aso Station and allow a half hour for sightseeing at Mount Aso's West Station. Since this is hardly enough time to visit both the museum there and take the cable car to the summit, if you're a volcano buff you may want to purchase a one-way ticket to Mount Aso, spend an hour or two at the top, and then take one of the local buses back down to Aso Station.

FOOD AND LODGING
Because of its high altitude Mount Aso National Park is an ideal summer retreat, with a number of hot-spring resorts spread throughout the Aso crater basin.

In Aso and Vicinity
About a ten-minute ride from Aso Station, **Ryokan Mimura** ㉖, Uchinomaki, Aso-machi (tel. 0967/32-0835), is a new and elegant ryokan that spreads along the ridge of a hill. This peaceful 17-room establishment is the epitome of simplified beauty—flower arrangements in each room, wooden beams. Four rooms have twin beds with separate tatami areas for those who prefer to sleep in beds. Some of the rooms also have Japanese-style deep wooden tubs, which smell wonderful when filled with piping hot water. There are also separate hot-spring baths for men and women, with large windows overlooking the countryside below.

Rooms here cost ¥16,500 ($132) to ¥45,000 ($360) per person, depending on the meals you order for breakfast and dinner. But no matter the price range, the food served is as elegant as the ryokan itself and is the highlight of a stay here. The meals are beautifully displayed using items from nature—a sprig from an azalea bush may serve as a chopstick holder, while cedar leaves or a delicate maple leaf may be used to enhance individual dishes. My sashimi came in a small ice igloo complete with pebbles in the bottom. My meal also included *basashi* (raw horse meat), considered a great delicacy in Kyushu. Diced crab was served in its shell, which acted as its bowl, and fish was fried on a hot flat stone. Each plate that arrived was another culinary and visual surprise.

If the above ryokan is too expensive, too full, or for some reason you want to stay closer to Aso Station, you might want to try **Aso no Tsukasa Villa Park Hotel,** Kurokawa, Aso-machi (tel. 0967/34-0811). Located about three minutes by taxi or ten minutes on foot from Aso Station, this modern brick hotel first opened more than 20 years ago but was completely rebuilt and renovated in 1984. It charges ¥11,000 ($88) to ¥36,000 ($288) per person including two meals and service, with the difference in price reflected in room size, furnishings, and meals. The cheapest rooms have no private bathroom, while the most expensive ones feature a wooden tub. Most of the 128 rooms are Japanese style, but there are also combination rooms with a bedroom, living room, and separate tatami area, large enough for the whole family.

Facilities at the hotel include hot-spring baths, tennis courts, an outdoor pool, and horses for rent. There's also a restaurant where you might want to go for lunch called **Steak House Ban,** which features local beef from the Aso area, known as "Higo beef." This restaurant buys whole cows so that it can slice the beef itself. The texture of the meat is unique, and is much different from the beef back home. The menu is in Japanese only, with steak courses starting at ¥3,000 ($24), which includes soup, rice, and salad. If you want to go à la carte and add your own soup and salad, tenderloin starts at ¥3,600 ($28.80) for 150 grams, while sirloin starts at ¥3,800 ($30.40) for 200 grams. Also available is raw Higo beef and smoked salmon. This restaurant is open daily from 11 a.m. to 9 p.m.

Not far from Aso near a small town called Uchinomaki are a dozen or so Western-style pensions. They differ from minshuku in that their rooms contain beds instead of futons, but they are also small, family-run affairs with only a handful of rooms. The owner of **Pension Aso no Tokei-dai,** Uchinomaki, Aso-machi (tel. 0967/32-2236), speaks some English and will refer you to one of the other nearby pensions if his place is full. Rooms in all the pensions average about ¥7,000 ($56) per person, including two meals, tax, and service. This "Pension Mura," as the locals call it (it means Pension Village), is located about five minutes by taxi from Uchinomaki Station, but if you call from the station, someone from the pension will come pick you up.

Also in Aso is the **Aso Youth Hostel** ㉖⑦, 9222-2 Bochu, Aso-machi (tel. 0967/34-0804), about a five-minute walk or five-minute bus ride from Aso Station. Accommodating 64 people, it charges ¥2,000 ($16) per night without meals and ¥3,000 ($24) if you want breakfast and dinner for both members and nonmembers.

In Takamori

On the other side of Mount Aso is another resort town called Takamori. Since there's no bus service from here to the summit, this place is better for those who appreciate the beauty of massive volcanoes from afar.

In Takamori is a National Vacation Village called **Minami Aso Kokumin Kyuka Mura** ㉖⑧ (tel. 0967/62-2111). Popular with school groups and families because of the great view it commands of Mount Aso, it features tennis courts, bikes for rent, public baths, and a botanical garden. The rooms are typical of national vacation villages—simple tatami rooms with TV, futon and sheets, yukata cotton kimono, and private bathroom. The cost of a room per person starts at ¥2,700 ($21.60) for rooms without a bathroom and run to ¥4,400 ($35.20) for those with. Add another ¥3,000 ($24) if you opt for meals. The 81 rooms are usually packed during July and August, but otherwise you should be able to get a room. It's wise to make reservations in advance.

A wonderful restaurant in Takamori is **Dengaku no Sato** ㉖⑨ (tel. 62-1899), about a five-minute taxi ride from Takamori Station. Housed in a 120-year-old thatched farmhouse, this rustic restaurant has tatami seating around individual hibachis built into the wooden floor. Its specialty is *dengaku* (food skewered on sticks). You cook your dengaku yourself by sticking the skewers into the ashes surrounding the blaze in your hibachi. Order the dengaku teishoku for ¥1,500 ($12), and you'll have a variety of skewered items, including fish, taro, tofu, and mountain crabs that you pop whole into your mouth—delicious and crunchy. You can also order *kappozake* (sake heated in a hollow bamboo) beside your fire. Hours are 10 a.m. to 8 p.m.

In Aso-Shimoda

Near Aso-Shimoda you'll find a People's Lodge, the **Minami Aso Kokumin Shukusha** ㉗⓪ (tel. 0967/67-0078). Its rates are cheaper than the National Vacation Village described above: an overnight's stay per person, including two meals, comes to ¥5,400 ($43.20). If you don't want meals it's only ¥2,800 ($22.40). There are only three buses daily from Aso-Shimoda Station, so it might be best to take a 15-minute taxi ride. All the rooms have balconies, some with splendid views, and come with coin-operated TV, yukata cotton kimono, sheets, and futon. Not far from the lodge is a picturesque open-air bath beside a pounding waterfall. Men and women bathe together here.

---

4. Kumamoto

Located roughly in the middle of Kyushu about 1½ hours south of Fukuoka, Kumamoto boasts a fine castle and a landscape garden, both with origins stretching back to the first half of the 17th century. Once one of Japan's most important castle towns, Kumamoto today is a progressive city with a population of more than half a million. In an effort to attract both domestic and foreign enterprises, the city is planning a technopolis—a technological research city—to be built close to its airport by 1995. With other technopolises being planned for such cities in Kyushu as Kagoshima, Oita, and Miyazaki, the island has given itself a nickname: Silicon Island.

ORIENTATION

Upon arrival at Kumamoto Station, stop by the **tourist information center** in front of the station (tel. 096/352-3743) to pick up a good English map and brochure of the city. It's open daily from 9 a.m. to 5:30 p.m.

The leaflet *Kumamoto and Mt. Aso* distributed by the Tourist Information Centers in Kyoto and Tokyo contains information on how to get to Kumamoto and places of interest in the city.

Kumamoto Station is not in the city's downtown section but it's easy to get there by streetcar 2, which departs from in front of the station. Downtown is considered to be the area south and southeast of Kumamoto Castle, centered around several covered shopping streets called Shimotori and Sunroad Shinshigai. There are many shops, bars, and restaurants in the area. Nearby is Kotsu Center, from which all buses in the city depart, and the location of several business hotels listed below. Streetcar 2, which runs from Kumamoto Station and passes Kotsu Center, will also take you to both the castle (stop: Kumamoto-jo-mae) and the Suizenji Garden (stop: Suizenji-Koen-mae).

The **telephone area code** for Kumamoto is 096, and the city is located in Kumamoto Prefecture.

THE SIGHTS

Completed in 1607, **Kumamoto Castle** is massive—it took seven years to build. It was constructed under the direction of Kiyomasa Kato, a great warrior who fought alongside Ieyasu Tokugawa in a battle in 1600 and who was rewarded for his loyalty with land in what is today Kumamoto. To make the castle walls impossible for enemies to scale, they were built with curves and topped with an overhang. Furthermore, the castle was built atop a hill and had three main buildings, 49 towers, 29 gates, and 18 two-story gatehouses. Passing into the possession of the Hosokawa family in 1632, the castle remained an important stronghold for the Tokugawa shogunate throughout its 250 years of rule, particularly in campaigns against powerful and independent-minded lords in southern Kyushu.

Unfortunately, much of the castle was destroyed in 1877 during the Seinan Rebellion led by Takamori Saigo. A samurai disgruntled with the new policies of the Meiji government in which ancient samurai rights were rescinded, Saigo led a troop of samurai in an attack on the castle and its imperial troops. The battle raged for 50 days before government reinforcements finally arrived and quelled the rebellion. When the smoke cleared, most of the castle lay in smoldering ruins, ravaged by fire.

The castle was reconstructed in 1960 of ferroconcrete and although it's not nearly as massive as before, it's still quite impressive. The interior houses a museum with elaborately decorated palanquins, armor of feudal lords, swords, former possessions of both Kiyomasa Kato and the Hosokawa family, and artifacts from the Seinan Rebellion. There are also displays of such locally made products as pottery and toys. Open from 8:30 a.m. to 5:30 p.m. (until 4:30 p.m. in winter), it charges an admission of ¥200 ($1.60) for the castle grounds. If you want to go inside the castle, it costs ¥300 ($2.40) more.

Not far from the castle are two museums worth seeing. The **Kumamoto Prefectural Art Museum (Kumamoto Kenritsu Bijutsukan),** open every day except Monday from 9:30 a.m. to 4:30 p.m., displays fine art, as well as replicas of burial tombs that have been excavated in the prefecture. Nearby is the **Kumamoto Municipal Museum (Kumamoto Shiritsu Hakubutsukan),** open every day except Monday from 9 a.m. to 4:30 p.m. It houses collections devoted to the humanities and the natural and physical sciences, and also contains a planetarium.

Suizenji Garden, laid out in 1632 by the Hosokawa family, wraps itself around a cold spring-fed lake. Incorporated into the design of the garden are famous scenes in miniature from the 53 stages of the ancient Tokaido Highway, which connected Kyoto and Tokyo and which were immortalized in Hiroshige's famous woodblock prints. Most recognizable is cone-shaped Mount Fuji. Considering the fact that the real Mount Fuji is often cloaked in clouds, this reproduction may be the closest you'll get to seeing the famous peak. The park is small—almost disappointingly so. One wishes it stretched on and on. To assuage disappointment, stop off at the 400-year-old thatch-roofed tea house beside the pond, transported from the imperial grounds in Kyoto. Inside, ceremonial green tea is served while you sit and contemplate the view. If you want to sit on tatami inside the tea house, it costs ¥500 ($4). If you're content sitting outside at a table under the shelter of trees, it costs ¥400 ($3.20). Entrance to the park is ¥100 (80¢) between 7:30 a.m. and 6 p.m. (from 8:30 a.m. and 5 p.m. in winter); after that it's free, but only the main gate remains open. If you want to do some moon gazing, this is the place.

Although it's located on the outskirts of Kumamoto, about 30 minutes by bus from Kotsu Center, if you're at all interested in handcrafted items used in everyday life from various countries around the world, you'll enjoy the **Kumamoto International Folk Art Museum,** Tatsuda machi-Kamitatsuda (tel. 096/338-7504). Located in a 140-year-old sake warehouse that once stood in Okayama, this museum displays furniture, pottery, weavings, toys, and other handcrafted items from such diverse countries as India, Peru, Greece, Korea, Mexico, Egypt, and Japan. As items used in everyday life both now and in former times, many of them are rustic but beautifully made. The museum is open every day except Monday from 9 a.m. to 4 p.m. and charges an admission of ¥300 ($2.40). If you're going by bus, get off at Sannomiya bus stop.

SHOPPING

One of Kumamoto's most famous products is its damascene, in which gold and silver are inlaid on an iron plate to form patterns of flowers, bamboo, and other designs. Originally used to adorn armor, damascene today is used in such accessories as jewelry and tie clasps. Another Kumamoto product is the Yamaga lantern, made of gold paper and used during the Yamaga Lighted Lantern Festival held in August. Other products include Amakusa pearls, pottery, toys, and bamboo items.

A wonderful place to see Kumamoto Prefecture's products and learn about their production is the **Kumamoto Traditional Crafts Center** ㉛, located at 3-35 Chiba-jo (tel. 324-4930), next to Kumamoto Castle, not far from Kumamoto Castle Hotel. Confusingly enough, it's identified on the English map given out by the tourist office as the Industrial Art Museum—hopefully someone will get around to correcting this someday. A spacious and attractive brick building constructed in 1982, the center has a second floor devoted to handmade craftwork from all over the prefecture, along with displays on how the items are made. The displays are so well laid-out and the room is so bright and cheerful that it doesn't matter that the explanations are only in Japanese. By looking at the display on the bow and arrow, for example, you can see for yourself the intricate steps involved in its production. Wander around and look at pottery, bamboo products, fans (haven't you ever wondered how they're made?), bows and arrows, toys, furniture, wooden rice barrels, damascene, and kitchen knives sharp enough to chop through bone. The products are so well designed that you can't help but gain a wider appreciation of the beauty and simplicity of Japanese design. Most items aren't hidden away behind glass but are out in the open. Entrance here is ¥150 ($1.20) and worth every yen.

The first floor of the Traditional Crafts Center is free and serves as a gallery at which locally made products are sold, including those wonderful kitchen knives, furniture, ceramics, toys, paper lanterns, and damascene. Unfortunately, the center can ship only purchases that have a total value less than ¥60,000 ($480) and even then only to about eight large cities in the United States. The center is open from 9 a.m. to 5 p.m.; closed Monday.

Another place selling local products is the **Display Hall of Kumamoto Products (Kumamoto-ken Bussankan)** ㉜, on the third floor of the Sangyo Bunka Kaikan Building downtown next to the Kotsu Center. This store, open from 10 a.m. to 6:30 p.m. (except on the second and fourth Mondays of the month), sells pottery, toys, knives, paper lanterns, damascene, Amakusa pearls, spirits, and confectioneries.

For more shopping, in the heart of downtown there are covered shopping arcades, called **Shimotori** and **Sunroad Shinshigai,** where you'll find the usual clothing boutiques, gift shops, shoe stores, restaurants, and coffeeshops.

WHERE TO STAY

Accommodations in Kumamoto are hotels rather than ryokan. Many of the hotels, however, have Japanese-style rooms in case you'd rather sleep on futon and tatami. There are also some inexpensive minshuku.

The Upper Bracket

A 25-story high-rise about a ten-minute walk from Kumamoto Station, **New Sky Hotel,** 2 Higashiamidaji-cho (tel. 096/354-2111), is one of Kumamoto's best hotels. Its 358 rooms are divided between an older west wing and a more modern east wing. Its guest rooms are stocked with a lot of thoughtful amenities: a laundry rope in the bathroom (a welcome sight if you've been on the road a while), a hot-water pot for tea, bilingual TV (in the new wing only), minibar, alarm clock, radio, bedside control panels, an extra phone in the bathroom, and the *Japan Times* delivered to your room in the morning (it's always a day late in Kyushu). Facilities of the hotel itself include Japanese, Chinese, and Western restaurants, a beauty salon and a barbershop, and a health club with workout equipment and indoor swimming pool. The health club is rather expensive at an extra ¥3,000 ($24), but if it's only the 25-meter pool you want to use, it costs ¥700 ($5.60). The hotel also has a sauna and public bath you can use for free. Single rooms, which are located only in the older west wing, begin at ¥7,400 ($59), while twins begin at ¥16,500 ($132). Doubles are ¥14,300 ($114). There are also 40 Japanese-style rooms available for ¥12,000 ($96) for two people.

The **Kumamoto Castle Hotel,** 4-2 Joto-cho (tel. 096/326-3311), is a tall brick building next to the Kumamoto Castle grounds, which means that some of its rooms have good views of the city's most famous landmark. A more subdued, quiet, and conservative hotel than the New Sky, it offers rooms with the usual TV (Japanese only), fridge, and hot-water pot; they start at ¥8,200 ($66) for a single, ¥11,800 ($94) for a double, and ¥14,800 ($118) for a twin. Japanese-style rooms are ¥27,000 ($216). Restaurants in the hotel serve Western, French, and Chinese cuisine.

Business Hotels

There are several medium- and budget-priced business hotels located in the downtown section close to Kotsu Center bus depot. Newest of these and first on my list is **Chisan Hotel Kumamoto,** 4-39 Karashimacho (tel. 096/322-3911), which opened in 1984 as part of the Chisan hotel chain. Its lobby is pleasantly decorated with marble, brass railings, and stained glass, and the rooms are simply but tastefully decorated and come with stocked fridge, TV, and hot-water pot for tea. The electricity in the room works only when you insert your key into a pocket beside the door (this not only saves energy but saves time searching for misplaced keys). The hotel's one restaurant, decorated with masks from Africa, serves Western food. It offers a buffet lunch on Tuesday and Thursday from 11:30 a.m. to 2 p.m. at a price of ¥1,000 ($8) per person. Room rates begin at ¥6,500 ($52) for a single, ¥9,500 ($76) for a double, and ¥12,000 ($96) for a twin.

Tokyu Inn, 7-25 Shinshigai (tel. 096/322-0109), is a business hotel located across the street from the Kotsu Center right next to the Sunroad Shinshigai covered shopping arcade. Its rooms are small but contain everything you need, including TV, refrigerator, and cotton kimono. Single rooms are ¥6,500 ($52), doubles are ¥7,900 ($63), and twins are ¥9,500 ($76). There's a Western as well as a Japanese/Korean restaurant.

Located right in the Kotsu Center itself is the **Kotsu Center Hotel,** 3-10 Sakuramachi (tel. 096/354-1111). Its lobby is on the third floor above the bus center and is usually buzzing with activity from Japanese group tours. There's a French and a Chinese Szechuan restaurant, and from April to September there's a rooftop beer garden open daily from 5 to 9:30 p.m. Rooms are basic but comfortable, and have recently been renovated with new wallpaper and upgraded in quality with the addition of refrigerators, televisions with pay videos, hairdryers, and hot-water pots for tea. Singles range from ¥5,000 ($40) to ¥7,700 ($62), but the lowest-priced rooms don't have windows and aren't recommended. Doubles are ¥10,000 ($80), twins begin at ¥11,000 ($88), and triples run ¥14,200 ($114). There are eight Japanese-style rooms that go for ¥7,400 ($59) for one person, ¥11,500 ($92) for two, and ¥14,200 ($114) for three.

For a business hotel close to Kumamoto Station, the **Kumamoto Station Hotel** ㉗, 1-3-6 Nihongi (tel. 096/325-2001), is a three-minute walk from the station. A typical business hotel, its 50 single rooms go for ¥5,000 ($40), its 21 twins and doubles run ¥9,000 ($72), and its three Japanese-style rooms cost ¥11,000

($88) for two people and ¥14,300 ($114) for three. Breakfast is available for ¥550 ($4.40). To reach this business hotel, walk straight out from Kumamoto Station, pass over the bridge you see in front of you, and then turn immediately right. Kumamoto Station Hotel is the first building to your right and is located right beside the small river.

Inexpensive Japanese Style

A member of the Japanese Inn Group, **Maruko Hotel**, 11-10 Kamitori-cho (tel. 096/353-1241), is larger than most members of this group, with a total of 45 rooms. Completely renovated in 1985, this brick building is located in the heart of the city just off the Kamitori covered shopping arcade. To reach it, take streetcar 2 from Kumamoto Station, disembarking at Torichosuji stop, from which it's an eight-minute walk through Kamitori. Owned and managed by a petite, gracious woman who is happy to receive foreign guests, it charges ¥6,300 ($50) for single occupancy, ¥11,500 ($92) for a double, and ¥13,600 ($109) for a triple. Forty-one of its rooms are Japanese tatami rooms, with a pleasant sitting alcove next to large windows. There are also a couple of Western-style rooms and a couple of combination rooms with both beds and tatami. All rooms come with private bathroom, TV with video, hot water for tea, a safe for valuables, refrigerator, kimono, and air conditioning. Both breakfast and dinner are available.

Just a minute's walk to the left after exiting from Kumamoto Station, **Tsukasa Besso** ㉔, 1-12-20 Kasuga (tel. 096/354-3700), is a family-run minshuku with a total of 12 rooms, most of them Japanese style. The family members here are very friendly, and the daughter speaks English. Although the building itself is a bit old, the atmosphere makes up for it, as does the price at ¥6,000 ($48) per person, which includes two meals, tax, and service charge. About half of the rooms have their own private toilet, and some of them have a private tub as well. In any case, there are two public baths. Meals are served in a communal dining hall.

Youth Hostels

Suizenji Youth Hostel ㉕, 1-2-10 Hakusan (tel. 096/371-9193), can be reached by taking tram 2 from the station to tram stop Misotenjin, about a 25-minute ride. From there it's a 2-minute walk. It has six Japanese-style rooms with a total capacity of 22 people. A one-night stay is ¥2,100 ($16.80) if you're a card-carrying member and ¥2,800 ($22.40) if you're not. Breakfast is ¥400 ($3.20).

Located in a residential area, **Kumamoto Shiritsu Youth Hostel** ㉖, 5-15-55 Shimazaki-machi (tel. 096/352-2441), can be reached by taking a bus leaving from platform 36 of the Kotsu Center bus terminal. Get off at the Kuriyama Youth Hostel Mae bus stop, 50 minutes later. The price here is the same whether you're a youth hostel member or not: room charges are ¥1,600 ($12.80), breakfasts are ¥400 ($3.20), and dinners are ¥600 ($4.80). In summer and winter you'll be charged an extra ¥200 ($1.60) for air conditioning or heating. This hostel has 32 beds for women and 32 beds for men. Incidentally, on the map issued by the tourist office, this establishment is identified as the Municipal Youth Hostel, and the man in charge here speaks English.

WHERE TO DINE

Kumamoto's special dishes include *dengaku* (delicacies such as fish, taro, and tofu coated with bean paste and grilled at a fire), *karashi renkon* (lotus root that has been boiled, filled with a mixture of bean paste and mustard, and then deep-fried), and *basashi* (raw horse meat that is sliced thin and then dipped in soy sauce flavored with ginger or garlic).

Japanese Food

You can try Kumamoto's local dishes at **Senri** ㉗ (tel. 384-1824), located right in Suizenji Garden. A good place to stop off for lunch or dinner while visiting the famous garden, it's open every day from 11 a.m. to 9 p.m. Although the menu is in Japanese only, there's a pamphlet available with pictures. Teishoku set lunches cost ¥2,000 ($16) each and choices include eel, river fish, tempura, or basashi. Along with your choice of main dish are side dishes of a vegetable, soup, rice, and tea. Dinners cost ¥3,500 ($28) and up and include the same items as in the lunch teishoku, plus extra dishes. Dining is in small tatami rooms, located to the right after you enter the front door. The choice rooms face the garden. It's best to make a reservation to dine here. Incidentally, connected to this restaurant is its cheaper dining room (to the left if you face the building, with a plastic-food display case outside in front), which offers the same eel, river fish, tempura, and basashi lunch teishoku for about ¥500 ($4) less than in the private tatami rooms described above.

Just a few steps away from Senri and also located in Suizenji Garden is **Kimura-so** ⑳ (tel. 384-1864). Open daily from 11 a.m. to 9 p.m., it features inexpensive dining outside in a pavilion built over a pond, with a partial view of the garden. Carp is its specialty, which you can have raw or fried for ¥500 ($4). Also on the menu are grilled shrimp, eel, tonkatsu, and basashi.

Everyone in Kumamoto knows **Aoyagi** ⑳, 1-2-10 Shimotori (tel. 353-0311), just off the Shimotori shopping arcade in downtown Kumamoto. It has a plastic-food display case outside its front door with dishes of sushi, tempura, basashi, and kamameshi (rice casseroles). Set meals range from ¥1,300 ($10.40) to ¥2,500 ($20). You can also take out box lunches of sushi for ¥1,200 ($9.60) and up. Hours are 11:30 a.m. to 11 p.m. daily, and there are three floors of dining.

Located in the same vicinity is **Goemon** ⑳, 1-7-3 Shimotori (tel. 354-2266). Since it's open only in the evening from 5 p.m. to 2 a.m., this is technically a drinking establishment, but it serves a variety of inexpensive dishes and is popular with a lively young crowd, especially on weekends. À la carte dishes of dengaku, flatfish, sashimi, green-tea noodles, and much more range from a mere ¥100 (80¢) for rice balls to ¥500 ($4) for raw tuna. Most items cost ¥200 ($1.60) to ¥400 ($3.20). There are also set meals for ¥1,300 ($10.40) to ¥2,750 ($22). The menu is only in Japanese but it has some pictures; the best thing to do is simply to look around at what others are eating. This establishment has a rustic feel to it, and although it's tatami seating, some of the tables have leg wells underneath for your feet. Take off your shoes at the front door and deposit them in a locker, just as you would at a bathhouse.

The New Sky Hotel, 2 Higashiamidaji-cho, has an excellent Japanese restaurant called **Kohrin** (tel. 354-2111), open from 11:30 a.m. to 2 p.m. and 5 to 10 p.m. The menu is in Japanese only, but set meals range from ¥3,300 ($26.40) to ¥11,000 ($88) and include sushi, tempura, and seasonal kaiseki dishes. I highly recommend the course of *seishoho-yaki*— Japanese steak wrapped in bamboo and served with side dishes of basashi, mustard lotus, sashimi, red snapper, pickled vegetables from the region of Mount Aso, and rice. For an after-dinner drink, top off your meal with shochu, for which Kumamoto is famous. If you come here for lunch, you can have noodles—try the tempura soba for ¥1,000 ($8). Another good lunchtime choice is the Kohrin teishoku, for ¥2,000 ($16), which includes sashimi, tempura, sushi, soba noodles, and side dishes.

Another hotel restaurant serving Japanese food, **Ginnan** (tel. 326-3311) is located in Kumamoto Castle Hotel, 4-2 Joto-cho. A fish tank at the restaurant's entrance displays shrimp, flatfish, and eels happily swimming around, unaware of their impending fate. The Japanese menu has pictures of its offerings, most of which range from ¥3,000 ($24) to ¥6,000 ($48). The tempura dinner is most popular. Set teishoku lunches run ¥1,000 ($8) to ¥3,800 ($30.40).

If the weather's warm and you're more interested in drinking beer while sitting outside, head for the roof of the **Kotsu Center Hotel** (tel. 354-1111), conveniently located at the Kotsu Center bus depot. Open from April to mid-September from 5 to 9:30 p.m., this beer garden has its share of fake palm trees and Astro-turf, but it also offers panoramic views of the city. Beer starts at ¥450 ($3.60) and snacks include grilled chicken, sausage, french fries, *edamame* (soybeans), and other fare, most of it under ¥500 ($4).

Western Food

For elegant dining, go to **Leodor,** the New Sky Hotel's tower restaurant on the 25th floor at 2 Higashiamidaji-cho (tel. 354-2111). A white piano (with nightly entertainment from 7 to 8:30 p.m.) dominates the powder-blue room. Elaborate tableware and flowers on every table enhance meals of steak, fish, or lamb, with most entrées ranging from ¥2,750 ($22) to ¥7,000 ($56). Expect to spend about ¥10,000 ($80) per person for dinner, including wine. There are also set dinners for ¥6,600 ($52.80) and ¥7,700 ($61.60), and a set lunch menu for ¥3,800 ($30.40). Hours are 11:30 a.m. to 2 p.m. and 5 to 10 p.m.

Another place to go for Western food is the **Loire,** on the 11th floor of the Kumamoto Castle Hotel, 4-2 Joto-cho (tel. 326-3311). While dining here you can look out over Kumamoto Castle. The menu is short, offering primarily set meals ranging from ¥4,200 ($33.60) to ¥11,000 ($88). The offerings are changed every four months to match the changing seasons, but usually include seafood and beef dishes. Dinner is served from 5 to 10 p.m. From 11:30 a.m. to 2 p.m. set lunches are served, ranging in price from ¥1,000 ($8) to ¥5,500 ($44).

5. Nagasaki

Unlike Kumamoto, Kagoshima, or many other well-known cities in Japan, Nagasaki does not have a castle or famous landscape garden. Rather, Nagasaki's charm is much more subtle, lying in the city itself. Many people in Japan—including foreign residents—consider Nagasaki one of the country's most beautiful cities. It's a town of hills rising from the harbor, of houses perched on terraced slopes, of small streets, distinctive neighborhoods, and a people extremely proud of their city. Without a doubt it's one of Japan's most liveable cities.

Perhaps to the untrained foreign eye Nagasaki may look like any other modern Japanese town. In truth, however, there's no other city in Japan quite like Nagasaki. In a nation as homogeneous as Japan, Nagasaki from a historical perspective is its most cosmopolitan city, with a unique blend of outside cultures interwoven into its architecture, food, and festivals. Centuries ago, Nagasaki's bay, sheltered by islands, made it a natural as a safe place to anchor ships. It opened its harbor to European vessels in 1571 and became a port of call for Portuguese and Dutch ships. Chinese merchants moved here and set up their own community. Along with traders came Christian missionaries, primarily from Portugal and Spain, who found many converts among the Japanese in Nagasaki. And during Japan's more than 200 years of isolation, only Nagasaki was allowed to conduct trade with the outside world and thus served as the nation's window on the rest of the world. Even today Japanese come to Nagasaki for a dose of the city's intermingled cultures.

If you're looking for a typical Japanese city, Nagasaki isn't the place. If you're searching for something more than just typical—something special—then Nagasaki won't disappoint you.

ORIENTATION

Nagasaki lies on the northwest coast of Kyushu about 2½ hours from Fukuoka and 9½ hours from Tokyo by train. At Nagasaki Station the **Nagasaki City Office of Tourist Information** (tel. 0958/22-1954 or 23-3631) maintains an information window, located just ahead after you exit from the ticket gate, which distributes maps in English. It's open daily from 9 a.m. to 5 p.m. An even better map, however, is available just across the street from the train station in the **Nagasaki Prefecture Tourist Federation** office (tel. 0958/26-9407), on the second floor of the Kotsu Sangyo Building. This office can provide information on all of Nagasaki Prefecture, including Unzen. More information on Nagasaki and its attractions is given in *Nagasaki and Unzen,* available at the Tourist Information Centers in Tokyo and Kyoto.

Nagasaki Station is not considered the downtown part of the city. Rather, the majority of nightspots, shops, and restaurants are located southeast of the station, clustered around an area that contains Shianbashi, Kanko Dori Street, and the Hamanomachi shopping arcade. Peace Park and its museum on the atomic bomb are located north of Nagasaki Station.

The easiest way to get around the city is by streetcar. Four lines run through the heart of the city and most stops are written in English. The streetcars are ancient, one-wagon affairs, retired to Nagasaki from other cities that considered them too slow and old-fashioned a mode of transportation. And yet in Nagasaki streetcars have their own lanes of traffic, so that during rush hour they're usually the fastest things on the road. It costs a mere ¥100 (80¢) to ride one; pay at the front when you get off. You can also buy a ¥500 ($4) ticket at major hotels that allows unlimited rides for one day on the city's streetcars. If you're buying individual tickets, you're allowed to transfer to another line only at Tsukimachi Station. Otherwise, you must buy a separate ticket each time you board a tram.

You can also get around Nagasaki easily by foot, certainly the most intimate way to experience the city and its atmosphere. You can walk from the Hamanomachi shopping district to Glover Garden, for example, in 15 to 20 minutes, passing Chinatown, Dejima, and the Dutch Slope on the way. Shianbashi Dori, located just off the streetcar stop of the same name, is just a few minutes' walk from Hamanomachi shopping arcade.

In any case, along with Kobe and Sapporo, Nagasaki is one of Japan's most navigable cities, and there are lots of signs in English that point the way to attractions. Nagasaki also has buses, but destinations are only in Japanese and who knows where the heck they're going. Stick to the streetcars.

The **telephone area code** for Nagasaki is 0958, and the prefecture is Nagasaki Prefecture.

THE SIGHTS

All of Nagasaki's major attractions are connected with the city's diversified and sometimes tragic past. The city is perhaps best known as the second city—and, we hope, the last city—to be destroyed by an atomic bomb.

Nishizaka Hill

After Nagasaki opened its port to European vessels, Christian missionaries began coming to the city to convert the Japanese to Christianity. Gradually, however, the Japanese rulers began to fear that these Christian missionaries would try to exert influence in Japan through their converts. After all, Christian churches in Europe held vast political and financial power in Europe, and who wasn't to say that conversion to Christianity was just the first step toward colonialization? So in 1587 the shogun Hideyoshi Toyotomi officially banned Christianity. In 1597, 26 Christians (20 Japanese and 6 foreigners) were arrested in Kyoto and Osaka, marched through the snow to Nagasaki, and crucified on Nishizaka Hill as examples of what would happen to offenders. Through the ensuing years there were more than 600 documented cases of Christians being put to death in the Nishizaka area. In 1862 the 26 martyrs were named saints by the pope. Today on Nishizaka Hill, about a three-minute walk from Nagasaki Station, there's a monument dedicated to the saints with statues of the 26 martyrs carved in stone relief. There's also a small museum housing artifacts relating to the history of Christianity in Japan and ashes of three of the saints. Perhaps most amazing about the history of Christianity in Japan is that the religion was practiced secretly by the faithful throughout Japan's isolation

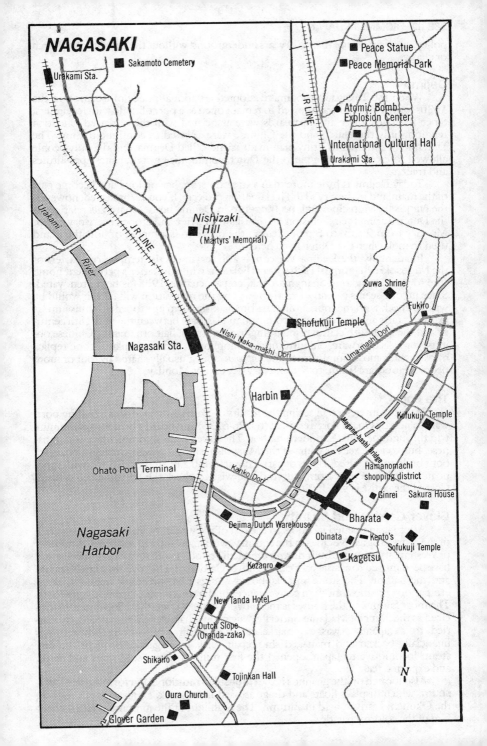

policy, surviving more than 200 years underground without the benefits of a church or clergy.

Dejima

When the Tokugawa shogunate adopted a national policy of isolation in the 1630s, only Nagasaki was allowed to remain open as a port of trade with foreigners. Since the Portuguese and Spaniards were associated with the outlawed Christian religion, only the Dutch and the Chinese were allowed to continue trading. The Dutch were confined to a tiny man-made island called Dejima, and the only people allowed to cross the bridge into the Dutch community were Japanese prostitutes and traders.

Today Dejima is little more than a streetcar stop, having long ago become part of the mainland in the city's land reclamation projects. If you're interested, however, the **Nagasaki Municipal Dejima Museum** in Dejima houses materials relating to the Dutch during their seclusion on the island. It's free and is open every day except Monday from 9 a.m. to 5 p.m. Behind the museum is a model of how the island used to look when the Dutch lived here.

Incidentally, the Dejima Museum is also serving as the temporary quarters of the **Nagasaki Museum of History and Folklore** while the latter's permanent home (the former Hongkong Shanghai Bank, constructed in 1908) is being renovated. Since no one seems to know exactly how long the renovation will take, it would be wise to check with the tourist office before making a trip just to see this museum. It exhibits crafts and daily utensils common in Nagasaki between the mid-18th century and the mid-20th century, including hand mirrors, hair ornaments, Chinese objects, some lacquerware, old furniture, gramophones, and even a plastic-food replica of Nagasaki's most famous meal, the *shippoku*, a feast usually shared by four or more people. Hours are 9 a.m. to 5 p.m. every day except Monday.

The Port

If you're interested in seeing the results of Nagasaki's history as a trading port, walk to nearby Ohato Port Terminal (tel. 26-6236) and board a boat for a 50-minute trip through the town's modern harbor. The never-ending commentary is in Japanese, but you can see for yourself the Mitsubishi shipyards where massive boats are both built and repaired. Boats depart daily at 11:40 a.m. and 3:15 p.m., with more boats added in peak season, but you'd be wise to check the schedule beforehand. Cost of the cruise is ¥750 ($6).

Glover Garden and Vicinity

After Japan opened its doors to the rest of the world, Nagasaki emerged as one of the more progressive cities in the country, with many foreign residents. A number of Western-style houses built during the Meiji Period (1868–1912) still survive and have been moved to a large park called Glover Garden on a hill overlooking Nagasaki and the harbor. The stone and clapboard houses have sweeping verandas, Western parlors, the most modern conveniences of the time—and Japanese-style roofs. The most famous of the houses is the **Glover Mansion,** built in 1863 and romanticized as the home of Madame Butterfly (a fictitious character). Thomas Glover, married to a Japanese, was a remarkable Englishman who among other things financially backed and managed ship-repair yards in Nagasaki, brought the first steam locomotive to Japan, opened the first mint in Japan, sold guns and ships, and exported tea.

Also located on the grounds is the **Nagasaki Traditional Performing Arts Museum,** which displays floats and dragons used in Nagasaki's most famous festival, the Okunchi Festival, held in autumn. The highlight of the museum is an excellent film of the colorful parade.

Entrance to Glover Garden and the museum is ¥600 ($4.80), and hours are 8 a.m. to 6 p.m. (8:30 a.m. to 5 p.m. December through February). After entering the grounds you might be a little shocked to see moving escalators carved into the hillside. While an outdoor escalator in a garden might seem a little bizarre, the Japanese point out that it's there for the benefit of senior citizens who might find the climb up the hill too strenuous. At any rate, the views from here are among the best in the city, offering a good look at both the town, its harbor, and the shipyards.

Next to Glover Garden is the **16th Mansion (Jurokuban-kan Mansion),** built in 1860 by the American government as the first mansion in Japan for its consular staff. It houses many relics of Nagasaki's early years, including glassware, chinaware, and religious objects. Some of the pieces of Imari chinaware on display have pictures of Europeans on them. Destined for Western markets, they prove that the Japanese were willing and able to adapt their products for an outside market even then. The entrance fee is ¥400 ($3.20), and hours are 8:30 a.m. to 5 p.m. daily.

Within a few minutes' walk from Glover Garden are the **Oura Catholic Church,** Japan's oldest Gothic wooden church, built in 1865 to commemorate the 26 Christian martyrs, and **Dutch Slope (Oranda-zaka),** a cobbled road lined with wooden houses built by former Dutch residents.

Temples, Shrines, and Bridges

The legacy left by Nagasaki's many Chinese residents is best enjoyed at the city's many Chinese restaurants (refer to the dining section) and best seen at its Chinese-style temples. Not far from the Oura Church mentioned above are the colorful **Confucius Shrine** and the **Historical Museum of China,** which charges an admission of ¥500 ($4) to see its artifacts, on loan from the Chinese National Museum of History in Beijing. Nagasaki's most famous temple, however, is **Sofukuji Temple,** which dates back to 1629 and is known for its Ming Dynasty architecture. It's located about a seven-minute walk from the Hamanomachi downtown shopping district. From Sofukuji Temple I recommend a pleasant 20-minute walk north along narrow streets to **Kofukuji Temple,** the first Obaku-Zen Buddhist temple in Japan, founded by a Chinese priest in 1629.

Although the Okunchi Festival has Chinese roots, it's celebrated at **Suwa Shrine,** a Shinto shrine that was built to promote Shintoism when the feudal government was trying to stamp out Christianity. Today the shrine symbolizes better than anything else the spiritual heart of the Japanese community. When Japanese women turn 33 and men turn 40, they come here to pray for good health and a long life. The shrine sells fortunes in English. If you're satisfied with your fortune, keep it. If you're not, tie it to the branch of a tree and the fortune is conveniently negated.

In addition to the temples described above, the Chinese also left their mark on Nagasaki with the construction of several bridges. Most famous of these is the so-called **Megane-bashi,** or **Spectacles Bridge,** named after the reflection the two-arched bridge casts in the water. I wouldn't know, however, because I've never seen the Nakashima River larger than a trickle. It does occasionally flood, as in 1982, when it wiped out several old bridges. These have now been reconstructed, along with a promenade complete with benches and children's playgrounds. Since it's only a five-minute walk from the Hamanomachi shopping arcade, you might wish to come here with some take-out sushi and enjoy a picnic. The Megane-bashi, by the way, was built in 1634 by a Chinese Zen priest named Mozi of Kofukuji Temple. It's the oldest stone-arched bridge in Japan and is one of Nagasaki's most photographed objects.

Peace Park

On August 9, 1945, at 11:02 a.m., American forces dropped an atomic bomb over Nagasaki, three days after they had dropped a bomb over Hiroshima. Exploding 1,600 feet above ground, it destroyed about one-third of the city, killed an estimated 75,000 people, and injured 75,000 more. Today Nagasaki's citizens are among the most vigorous peace activists in the world, and Peace Park, located north of Nagasaki Station, serves as a reminder of that fateful day and as a warning to the destructiveness of the atomic bomb. Every year on the anniversary of the bombing a peace demonstration is held in Peace Park. As the director of the Peace Park's museum told me, "When the atomic bomb was produced, human beings entered an era when they should stop killing each other. If a nuclear war breaks out, humans will be annihilated. The problems of starvation, religion, and education are all connected to peace."

At one end of Peace Park a black stone pillar marks the exact epicenter of the atomic blast. Ironically enough, the bomb exploded almost directly over a Catholic church. At the other end of the park is the Peace Statue, a 30-foot-high statue of a male deity. Although the exact meaning of the statue is left to individual interpretation, one hand points to the sky from whence the bomb came (meant as a warning?) and the other hand points to the horizon (representing the future?).

Next to Peace Park is a museum, the **Nagasaki International Cultural Hall** (popularly called the **Atomic Bomb Museum**). It contains objects, photos, and artifacts showing the devastation caused by the atomic bomb. It's by no means pleasant, but something every concerned individual should see. An estimated one million people visit the museum every year, including about 50,000 foreigners. The International Cultural Hall is open from 9 a.m. to 6 p.m. April through October, closing one hour earlier November through March. Entrance fee is ¥50 (40¢). Located in the basement of the same building but containing an entirely different kind of collection is the **Nagasaki Municipal Museum,** which charges a ¥100 (80¢) admission. It features artifacts relating to Nagasaki's history and the saga of Japanese Christianity, especially the Edo Period and Japanese Christianity. Peace Park can be reached by streetcar 1 or 3; disembark at Matsuyama tram stop.

Nagasaki Holland Village

If you're in Nagasaki for more than one day and you want to take a side trip, you might want to visit one of Nagasaki's newest attractions—Nagasaki Holland Village, a living proof of how adept the Japanese are at imitation. They have reconstructed a replica of a Dutch village, with each building a faithful copy of an original back in the Netherlands. Although I was a bit skeptical about visiting an imitation Dutch village in Japan, I must admit that the grounds and craftsmanship are beautifully done. Even Holland itself doesn't always look this pristine. Contained in the village are a porcelain museum, with an exact replica of a room in West Berlin's Charlottenburg Palace that has an elaborate display of china made in both China and Arita, Japan; a museum dedicated to the Dutch in Nagasaki's history; churches; and an abundance of shops. There are china shops, craft shops, souvenir boutiques, and more. There's even a cheese shop selling Dutch imports—it once managed to sell three tons of cheese in one day. That could well be a world record.

At any rate, Nagasaki Holland Village is one hour away by bus from Nagasaki Station. Admission is a bit steep at ¥2,500 ($20), and bus fare is ¥600 ($4.80). At Nagasaki Station there's a special information office for the Holland Village where you can buy your ticket, called a "passport." The best time to visit is of course in the spring, when—what else?—it's tulip season.

SHOPPING

Locally made Nagasaki products include cultured pearls, coral objects, and tortoiseshell jewelry. Keep in mind, however, that U.S. Customs forbids tortoiseshell imports. At any rate, a convenient place to shop for Nagasaki products is the **Local Products Hall (Nagasaki-ken Bussankan),** across the street from Nagasaki Station on the second floor of the Kotsu Sangyo Building. Look for the sign outside that says "Nagasaki Prefecture Tourist Federation."

Another good place for shopping is the **Hamanomachi shopping arcade,** close to the Nishi-Hamanomachi and Kanko Dori streetcar stops. Located centrally downtown, this covered arcade has clothing boutiques, restaurants, accessory stores, and shops specializing in tortoiseshell products and other local handcrafts.

Another famous product of Nagasaki is its castella (*kasutera*), a spongecake with Portuguese origins. Japanese visitors to Nagasaki can't leave Nagasaki without buying castella for co-workers and friends back home. There are cake shops throughout the city. The most famous one is **Fukusaya,** 3-1 Funadaiku-machi (tel. 21-2938), not far from the Hamanomachi shopping arcade. Fukusaya is located in a 200-year-old building and has a history that stretches back even further. It's open from 8:30 a.m. to 8 p.m.; closed the second Thursday of each month.

WHERE TO STAY

Nagasaki has very reasonably priced hotels. The busiest time of the year is in May, when Nagasaki is brimming with busloads of schoolchildren who come here on class excursions from other cities.

The Upper and Medium-Priced Range

Nagasaki's newest and most deluxe hotel is **Hotel New Nagasaki,** 14-5 Daikoku-machi (tel. 0958/26-8000), which opened in 1988 and is conveniently situated right next to the Nagasaki train station. Its marble lobby is light and airy, and rooms are outfitted with TV, hot-water pot, hairdryer, and cable radio with more than 400 stations. Many rooms also have connections for facsimile machines. All seven restaurants, which range from Western to Chinese and Japanese, including a Kobe steakhouse, are hotel-managed. Prices for the 149 rooms here begin at ¥11,000 ($88) for singles, ¥18,700 ($150) for twins, and ¥20,900 ($167) for doubles.

Nagasaki Grand Hotel, 5-3 Manzai-machi (tel. 0958/23-1234), is a fine older hotel conveniently located not far from the Hamanomachi shopping district. Its 126 rooms are soothingly decorated in soft pastels of mauve or pea green and come with what you'd expect from a hotel of this category—TV, hot-water pot, alarm clock, and minibar. The single rooms, with unusual layouts utilizing space to its utmost, are especially pleasant. In addition to three restaurants, there's also a great beer garden right outside the lobby that is surrounded by palm trees and azaleas. It's open mid-April to the end of August from 5 to 10 p.m. Rooms in this hotel start at ¥7,300 ($58) for singles and ¥14,300 ($114) for doubles and twins. There are also three Japanese-style rooms, starting at ¥24,000 ($192) for one person and ¥25,000 ($200) for two.

Hotel New Tanda, 2-24 Tokiwa-machi (tel. 0958/27-6121), is a brick hotel located at the bottom of Dutch Slope about a seven-minute walk to either Glover Garden or the Hamanomachi shopping district. Popular with foreign visitors, it has one Western-style restaurant as well as a beer garden on its roof (open in summer), where you can look out over the harbor. Room rates, which are based on location, view, and furnishings, range from ¥7,300 ($58) to ¥8,800 ($70) for a single, ¥12,000 ($96) to ¥16,500 ($132) for a double, and ¥14,300 ($114) to ¥17,000 ($136) for a twin. Triples are ¥18,200 ($146).

Also located close to Glover Garden is the **Nagasaki Tokyu Hotel,** 1-18 Minamiyamate-machi (tel. 0958/25-1501). Although the lobby is sparsely furnished (with its bare white walls and stained-glass windows, it reminds me of the inside of a church—which fits in with Nagasaki's history), the rooms are comfortable and come with tiny balconies and bilingual TVs. Since rates are based on room size rather than view, ask for a room facing Glover Garden. Singles start at ¥10,000 ($80), and twins and doubles start at ¥18,500 ($148). Restaurants in the hotel serve Western, Japanese, and Chinese cuisine.

Opened in 1984, the **Holiday Inn,** 6-24 Doza-machi (tel. 0958/28-1234), is conveniently located just off Kanko Dori Street close to the Hamanomachi shopping arcade. You can walk from the hotel to most sites, including Glover Mansion and Sofukuji and Kofukuji temples. All 84 rooms have double-, queen-, or king-size beds, and start at ¥7,500 ($60) for one and ¥9,900 ($79) for two. Rooms are large and bright, and come with the usual TV, fridge, and alarm clock. The hotel restaurant serves Japanese and Western food.

Park Side Hotel, 14-1 Heiwa-machi (tel. 0958/45-3191), is a pleasant and small hotel located next to Peace Park. Long-term guests like the place because it's quiet and because they can jog early in the morning in the park. The Western-style restaurant has big windows overlooking the greenery of the park, which is ablaze with cherry blossoms in spring. Since this hotel is the tallest building in the area, its rooftop beer garden (open May to the end of August from 5 to 9 p.m.) gives a good view of the vicinity and of the surrounding hills radiating into the distance. The 56 rooms have semidouble beds and double-pane windows. Single rooms are ¥6,200 ($50), twins are ¥12,000 ($96), and doubles run ¥11,000 ($88).

Hotel Station Ajisai ㉛, 7-3 Daikoku-machi (tel. 0958/22-2222), a modern brick building across the street from Nagasaki Station, is a cross between a business and a tourist hotel. It is locally owned by a Japanese who has eight hotel properties in Nagasaki, and its 82 rooms come with just the basics, including double-pane windows to shut out train traffic. Singles here are ¥6,500 ($52), doubles cost ¥9,900 ($79), and twins start at ¥12,000 ($96). The most expensive twins are large corner rooms with big windows that open onto a balcony and offer sweeping views. The best deal, however, is a Japanese-style room. It's large, has two beds plus a separate tatami area, and is good for a family, large group, or the entertaining of friends. Rates for this room are ¥15,400 ($123) for two people and ¥24,000 ($192) for four persons. The hotel has one coffeeshop and one Japanese-style restaurant.

Nagasaki Washington Hotel, 9-1 Shinchi-machi (tel. 0958/28-1211), is a chain hotel located on the edge of the city's tiny Chinatown, about two minutes' walk from the Hamanomachi shopping district. The rooms in this ten-story brick building are slightly more expensive than those in the average business hotel, but the rooms are large and come equipped with TV, alarm clock, fridge, radio, and Japanese-style deep tub. Panels in the windows can be closed for complete darkness. To save energy, electricity is generated only when the key card is inserted into the bedside panel. Singles here start at ¥6,000 ($48), doubles begin at ¥13,000 ($104), and twins go up from ¥14,300 ($114).

If you want to stay in a ryokan, **Sakamoto-ya** ㉜, Kanaya-machi (tel. 0958/26-8211), is a beautiful 90-year-old ryokan located right in the heart of the city, about five minutes from the station—a wonderful place to stay. In this, Nagasaki's oldest ryokan, most of the 19 rooms have Japanese-style bathtubs made of wood, as well as artwork on the walls. The best room is the Pine Room (Matsu No Ma), which even has its own private little garden. Rates here vary according to the room and the meals served, and range from ¥13,200 ($106) to ¥27,000 ($216) per person, including tax and service charge. If you want you can order shippoku, a Nagasaki specialty consisting of a variety of dishes showing European and Chinese influences, for ¥5,000 ($40) more. Western breakfasts are also served.

The Budget Category

Hotel Ibis, 8-19 Kabasima-machi (tel. 0958/24-2171), is a reasonably priced business hotel about a ten-minute walk from Nagasaki Station. Rooms are simple, and rates start at ¥4,700 ($38) for a single, ¥8,300 ($66) for a double, ¥9,200 ($74) for a twin, and ¥14,500 ($116) for a triple. Western breakfasts are served for ¥750 ($6).

Another business hotel you might try is the **Nishikyushu Daiichi Hotel** ㉓, 2-1 Daikoku-machi (tel. 0958/21-1711), located across the street from Nagasaki Station. Rooms are comfortable, with the usual TV with pay video for adult entertainment and alarm clock, but the bathrooms are minuscule. Singles start at ¥4,800 ($38), but because the windows are shaded by an adjoining building, you're better off paying ¥5,700 ($46) for singles with more light. These higher-priced singles come with either a sofa or a semidouble bed. I suggest taking the larger bed, since the sofas are uselessly tucked away in a corner and simply make the rooms more crowded. Twins and doubles here start at ¥9,000 ($72), and triples are ¥12,500 ($100). The hotel's restaurant serves a Western breakfast for ¥800 ($6.40).

Incidentally, if you're male and are content with just the basics, behind the Daiichi Hotel is **Capsule Inn Nagasaki** ㉔, 2-11 Daikoku-machi (tel. 0958/21-1099). This is one of those functional capsule hotels, with each unit no larger than a coffin but outfitted with a TV nevertheless. As you might guess, noisy neighbors are the main setback, though at only ¥2,700 ($21.60) you might not care.

An inexpensive ryokan about a five-minute walk from Nagasaki Station, **Terada** ㉕, 1-7 Goto-machi (tel. 0958/22-6178), is more than 20 years old and has a rather unusual feature—a dusty shell museum on the ground floor. The owner here speaks English and is glad to initiate foreigners into the intricacies of staying in a Japanese-style inn. All 18 rooms are tatami, and 2 are equipped with Japanese-style toilets; 8 have bathtubs as well. Rates per person are ¥3,800 ($30) on weekdays and ¥4,900 ($39) on weekends, but in the off-season they're willing to bargain here. Rates do not include meals, but the ryokan has a small and informal Japanese seafood restaurant that serves set meals from ¥2,200 ($17.60).

Another inexpensive Japanese-style accommodation just a few minutes' walk from Nagasaki Station is **Sansui-so** ㉖, 2-25 Ebisu-machi (tel. 0958/24-0070). All of its 29 rooms have private bathrooms, and the charge here on weekdays is ¥4,900 ($39) per person without meals and ¥8,800 ($70) with breakfast and dinner. On weekends and on holidays, the rates go up to ¥6,000 ($48) and ¥11,000 ($88), respectively. Six of the rooms are Western style, and all rooms are outfitted with coin-operated TV, heater, and air conditioner. Facilities include a public bath and a laundry machine.

If you're on a tight budget or prefer the intimacy of a minshuku, one of the best places to stay is **Minshuku Siebold** (sometimes pronounced "Shibolt" by the Japanese), 1-2-11 Sakurababa (tel. 0958/22-5623). There are only five Japanese-style rooms here, all without private bathrooms, and rates are low at only ¥3,300 ($26) per person for rooms without meals, ¥3,800 ($30) including breakfast, and ¥5,000 ($40) with two meals. The woman who runs the place doesn't speak much English, but her husband, who works at a travel agency, does and is happy to recommend inexpensive yakitori-ya in the neighborhood. To reach Siebold, take streetcar 3 from the station and disembark at Shindaiku Machi, which is the fourth stop. Siebold is just a minute's walk from the tram stop on a back street.

Youth Hostels

There are four youth hostels in Nagasaki. The most conveniently located is the **Nagasaki Kenritsu Youth Hostel** ㉗, 2 Tateyama-cho (tel. 0952/23-5032), about a 12-minute walk from Nagasaki Station. There are 90 beds, and you don't have to be a youth hostel member to stay here. A one-night stay costs ¥2,000 ($16) for both members and nonmembers, breakfast is ¥400 ($3.20), and dinner runs ¥600 ($4.80). Sheets can be rented for ¥200 ($1.60).

Nagasaki Oranda-Zaka Youth Hostel, ㉘, 6-14 Higashiyamate-cho (tel. 0952/22-2730), can accommodate 50 persons and is located about a three-minute walk from the Ishibashi streetcar stop. Members are charged ¥3,400 ($27) per night, which includes breakfast and dinner, while nonmembers are charged ¥3,900 ($31).

Other youth hostels in Nagasaki are **Uragami-ga-oka Youth Hostel,** 6-14 Miyoshi-machi (tel. 0952/47-8473), and **Nagasaki Nanpoen Youth Hostel,** 320 Hamahira-cho (tel. 0952/23-5526), both about 20 minutes from Nagasaki Station by bus.

WHERE TO EAT

Nagasaki's most famous food is actually a whole meal of various dishes with Chinese, European, and Japanese influences. Called shippoku, it's a feast generally shared by a group of four or more persons and includes such dishes as fish soup, sashimi, and fried, boiled, and vinegared seasonal delicacies from land and sea. Another Nagasaki specialty is *champon,* a thick Chinese noodle usually served in soup.

Japanese and Chinese Food

A wonderful but very expensive place to try shippoku, **Kagetsu** ㉙, Maruyama-cho (tel. 22-0191), was first established in 1618 and is one of Japan's longest-running restaurants. The oldest part of the present building is about 300 years old. A wooden structure set back from the road, which is the center of Nagasaki's night scene of sailors' bars and strip cabarets, Kagetsu is an oasis of dignified old Japan, with kimono-clad waitresses shuffling down wooden corridors and serving guests in tatami rooms. Formerly a geisha house, it even has a stone-floored room designed for a table and chairs where foreign patrons could be entertained. In the back of the restaurant is a 300-year-old garden. I'll never forget my evening stroll here as a half moon rose above gnarled stunted pines. The back of the restaurant, consisting mainly of glass, was all lit up so I could see into a multitude of private tatami rooms all on different levels. Guests were seated on the floor on cushions, and women in kimonos were playing the gracious hostess, pouring drinks and laughing behind their hands, and from the eaves outside the wooden restaurant hung lighted lanterns. If it weren't for the fact that the men were in business suits, I would have sworn it looked exactly like a woodblock print of old Japan.

Needless to say, this restaurant is very popular and reservations should be made at least a week in advance, though sometimes it is booked up to a full month in advance. There must be at least two of you if you want to eat shippoku. Lunch or dinner of either shippoku or kaiseki cuisine usually costs about ¥20,000 ($160) per person, including tax and service charge. It's open from noon to 8 p.m. and is usually closed the second and fourth Sundays of the month.

Another elegant old wooden restaurant, **Fukiro** ㉚, 146 Kami Nishiyama-machi (tel. 22-0253), sits perched on a small cliff not far from Suwa Shrine. In a building 180 years old, it specializes in shippoku served in private, tatami rooms. It's open only for lunch (from 11 a.m. to 3 p.m.), which costs ¥5,000 ($36). The restaurant is open daily and reservations are a must.

If sitting on the floor puts your legs to sleep, you can enjoy a shippoku meal in Western surroundings at the **Dejima Restaurant,** on the seventh floor of the Grand Hotel, 5-3 Manzai-machi (tel. 23-1234). Open from 11 a.m. to 9 p.m., it has set meals of steak, daily specials, and shippoku, all starting at ¥6,000 ($48). If you order the shippoku here, you'll get swordfish in diced soybean sauce, various seasonal hors d'oeuvres, minced veal soup, fresh seafood, brisket of pork, seafood and vegetable fritter, chicken hollandaise, cold beef, Chinese pilaf, dessert, and coffee.

Another hotel restaurant serving shippoku is the **Ohura** restaurant in the Tokyu Hotel, 1-18 Minamiyamate-machi (tel. 25-1501). It also serves Japanese and Chinese selections, including tempura, fried sweet-and-sour pork, shredded pork with green pepper, and assorted fried noodles Nagasaki style. Shippoku courses start at ¥3,100 ($24.80) for a small selection of dishes and go to ¥9,900 ($79.20) for an all-out feast. Colorful pictures depict each course. Ohura is open daily from 11:30 a.m. to 2:30 p.m. and 5 to 9:30 p.m. Located just a few minutes' walk from Glover Garden, it's a convenient and quiet place to stop for a meal if you're in the area.

Another inexpensive place to try shippoku is at a modern restaurant called **Hamakatsu** ㉛, 6-50 Kajiya-machi (tel. 26-8321), located just a minute's walk from the Hamanomachi covered shopping arcade. There must be at least two of you to order shippoku meals, which start at ¥4,100 ($32.80) per person. If you're by yourself you can order a smaller set menu for ¥2,750 ($22) that will give you a variety of local specialties including tempura with green tea noodles, fried and boiled dishes, sashimi, and more. Set meals are served on the second floor; the first floor is devoted to inexpensive à la carte dishes of both Japanese and Chinese origin, with most items under ¥700 ($5.60). Although the menu is in Japanese and changes seasonally, each dish is accompanied by a photo and may include such items as steamed dumplings, tofu dishes, cold chicken, raw beef, or chili shrimp. Opening daily at 11:30 a.m., this restaurant's second floor takes last orders at 8:30 p.m., but the inexpensive first floor serves food until 8:50 p.m.

If you're interested in eating champon Chinese noodles, **Shikairo,** 4-5 Matsugae-cho (tel. 22-1296), is the Chinese restaurant that created these Nagasaki noodles. First opened back in 1899, it moved into its present building in 1973. Located close to the Tokyu Hotel and Glover Garden, it's a large white building topped with a rounded dome and offering four floors of dining. It can accommodate as many as 1,500 people, and caters to large groups and receptions. Knowing where to go for a meal would be confusing if it weren't for the welcoming committee on the ground floor, who are eager to point the way. Come to think of it, however, you might still be confused because the numbers for floors in the elevator are written in kanji only. Assuming that you do eventually end up in the right dining hall, you'll find yourself in a large and noisy room surrounded by lots of other hungry souls.

Champon starts at ¥700 ($5.60) and dinner courses start at about ¥2,700 ($21.60). There are more than 30 items on the English menu, including barbecued pork, braised shark fin with shredded meat, chicken with bamboo shoots and onion, fried noodles, and, of course, champon. Hours here are 11:30 a.m. to 9:30 p.m. daily, with the last orders taken at 8 p.m.

Another popular Chinese restaurant is **Kouzanrou** ㉜, 12-1 Shinchi-machi (tel. 21-3735), located in the heart of Nagasaki's small Chinatown. Most of its foreign clientele is Chinese (which speaks highly of the restaurant), and its most popular dish is champon, ranging in price from ¥600 ($4.80) to ¥800 ($6.40). If you order such à la carte dishes as spring rolls, champon, or sweet-and-sour pork, most of which are under ¥1,200 ($9.60), you'll dine in the restaurant's simply furnished ground-floor dining area of tables and chairs. You may wish to order a set meal of various dishes, which range in price from ¥2,200 ($17.60) to ¥8,800 ($70.40), in which case you have the option of being escorted upstairs to your private tatami room. Kouzanrou is open daily from 11 a.m. to 9 p.m., with last orders taken at 8:30 p.m.

Kouzanrou is so successful that it's opened a smaller shop right next to the Nagasaki train station (to the right after exiting from the station). Very modern and sleek in design, it also offers champon and is open daily from 10:30 a.m. to 9 p.m.

If you're hungering for raw fish, it doesn't come any fresher than at **Tokiwa,** a Japanese restaurant within the Nagasaki View Hotel, 2-33 Oura-machi (tel. 24-2211), conveniently located between Hamanomachi and Glover Garden. Tokiwa features a wooden counter surrounding a pool filled with live fish. When it's number is up, a fish is scooped out of the water and then prepared right before your very eyes. Sometimes the fish is gutted and fileted, with only the head, heart, and skeleton left intact, so that the sashimi can be arranged around the alive and still-quivering animal and delivered to the customer's table. Barring that, you might opt for one of the lunch teishoku available from 11 a.m. to 2 p.m.; they begin at ¥1,000 ($8) and include sashimi and other delicious bite-size morsels. Tokiwa is also open daily for dinner, from 5 to 9 p.m.

Much less dramatic is **Yagura-Sushi** ㉝, located in the Hamanomachi covered shopping arcade on the stretch closest to Megane-bashi (tel. 22-1813). Look for its traditional-looking store front, with a window showing the sushi experts at work and a sign in English saying "Try our delicious sushi for one." The sushi teishoku here is only ¥650 ($5.20). There's a small dining area; most people you'll see standing in line, however, are waiting for take-out orders, with lunch boxes starting at ¥500 ($4). This is a good place to buy a picnic lunch, and you can eat it near Megane-bashi bridge. Closed on Thursday, the restaurant is open the rest of the week from 9 a.m. to 9 p.m.

Nagasaki's nightlife district centers on a small street near Hamanomachi known as Shianbashi Dori, which begins just off the streetcar stop of the same name and is easily recognizable by its neon arch of a bridge and palm trees. Lined with pink plastic flowers, this street shimmers with the lights of various drinking establishments and yakitori-ya, which are often the cheapest places to go for a light dinner. **Yagura-chaya** ⑳, 6-38 Motoshikkui-machi (tel. 22-0984), is one such place and is located right next to a live-music house called Kento's. Open daily from 5 p.m. to midnight (to 2 a.m. on Saturday), Yagura-chaya sports dark-stained heavy wooden beams that give it a respectable farmhouse feeling, an atmosphere amplified by the dolls, straw sandals, kites, paper lanterns, umbrellas, and other things suspended from the walls and ceiling. The menu is extensive but unfortunately written only in Japanese, and includes baked fish, skewers of yakitori, chicken nuggets, sashimi, baked corn, pizza, sashimi, salads, tofu, and much more. Most dishes are priced under ¥600 ($4.80); beer starts at ¥400 ($3.20) and shochu at ¥300 ($2.40).

Incidentally, **Kento's** (tel. 21-3453) next door features "oldies but goodies," primarily American hits from the 1950s and '60s, sung by Japanese bands. Admission fee is ¥1,200 ($9.60), after which each customer is required to buy at least one food dish and one drink. Dishes range from ice cream to spaghetti and salads, all under ¥1,000 ($8). This place is open daily from 6 p.m. to 2 a.m., and the music is loud.

Foreign Restaurants

Established in 1959, **Harbin**, 2-27 Kozen-machi (tel. 22-7443), is a family-run restaurant serving a unique blend of French and Russian cuisine. The owner, Mitsuru Kubota, was born in Manchuria and named his restaurant after a town close to his birthplace that was once an international city of Russian, Chinese, and Japanese residents. The restaurant itself looks as if it belongs to another era. It has the atmosphere of an old house, mellowed and comfortable with age, with dark-wood paneling and antiques. You might start your dinner here with borscht, followed by skewered lamb, beef Stroganoff, scallops and shrimp in curry sauce, filet of duck in orange sauce, or lamb chops in cumin sauce. À la carte dinners generally run about ¥8,000 ($64) per person. Set dinners range from ¥4,900 ($39.20) to ¥8,500 ($68). The inexpensive set lunches, at ¥1,000 ($8) to ¥2,700 ($21.60), are a good bargain. The restaurant is open from 11:30 a.m. to 2:30 p.m. and from 5:30 to 9 p.m. (last order). It's closed every Sunday, except during March and December, when it remains open every day of the week. Incidentally, Harbin has a small branch on the sixth floor of Daimaru department store in Hamanomachi, serving sandwiches, soups, and light meals.

Another Western-style restaurant with a solid reputation and a faithful clientele, **Ginrei**, 2-11 Kajiya-cho (tel. 21-2073), is close to the Hamanomachi shopping district on Kajiya-machi Street. Open daily from 10 a.m. to 9 p.m., it resembles an English country cottage, packed full of antique glass and pottery the owner spent half a century collecting. The building itself is 100 years old and from the outside looks like a miniature castle covered in ivy. Although the menu is in Japanese only, there's a lighted display board at the restaurant's entrance with pictures of various dishes. Steaks are the specialty here, with tenderloin and sirloin dishes running about ¥5,000 ($40) to ¥6,000 ($48). Steak courses start at ¥3,500 ($28).

One of my favorite restaurants, **Obinata**, 3-19 Funadaiku-machi (tel. 26-1437), has a warm, earthy feel to it, due perhaps to its heavy wooden beams, large bouquets of flowers, candelabra, and classical music playing softly in the background—an oasis of old Europe in the heart of Kyushu. The atmosphere is cozy and the service is a delight. The menu lists such entrées as steaks, Southern fried chicken with bacon, filet of beef goulash, Japanese steak, spaghetti, lasagne, and pizza. Dishes are creative and fun, the restaurant's own interpretations. Expect to pay about ¥6,000 ($48) if you go all out and order appetizers, entrées, and wine (there's a wide selection of Bordeaux, Moselle, and Rhine wines), but you can eat more cheaply if you stick to pastas, which range from ¥900 ($7.20) to ¥1,300 ($10.04). It's open daily from 5 p.m. to 1 a.m. and is located behind the Fukusaya castella shop, just off the nightlife street called Shianbashi Dori.

Although it's one of Nagasaki's newer and trendy restaurants, **Sakura House,** 6-15 Kajiya-machi (tel. 26-0229), resembles a much older establishment from the 1930s or '40s. Decorated with half-paneled walls, wooden floors, and a wooden bar counter, it's located close to Hamanomachi not far from Ginrei and Hamakatsu, described above. Its menu lists soups, salads, seafood, chicken, duck, beef, pork, and lamb selections, most under ¥2,000 ($16), with set dinner courses starting at ¥2,700 ($21.60). Lunches start at ¥1,000 ($8). Since it calls itself a restaurant/bar, you can also come here for just a drink and listen to background music of jazz or swing. It's open daily from 11:30 a.m. to 1 a.m., but the last order is taken at midnight.

A craving for hot and spicy food can be satisfied at **Bharata,** 2-10 Yasaka St., Aburaya-machi (tel. 24-9194), located close to the Hamanomachi shopping arcade just off Kajiya-machi Street on the second floor of a brick building. An inexpensive establishment with modest decor, it serves Indian food; curry dishes of beef, chicken, kofta (meatballs), shrimp, or fish run about ¥1,000 ($8), including Indian bread or pilaf, chutney, and salad. There's a set vegetarian meal with various small dishes for ¥1,300 ($10.40) and a nonvegetarian set meal for ¥2,500 ($20).

On weekdays this restaurant is open from 11:30 a.m. to 3 p.m. and 5 to 10 p.m., while on weekends it's open the whole day from 11 a.m. to 10 p.m. It's closed the first and third Thursdays of the month.

And finally, if you're having a Big Mac attack, you'll find **McDonald's** on Kanko Dori Avenue next to the Holiday Inn in the Hamanomachi shopping district.

6. Unzen

Unzen Spa is a small resort town 2,385 feet above sea level in the pine-covered hills of the Shimabara Peninsula. Because of its high altitude and cool mountain air, its great scenery and hot sulfur springs, Unzen became popular as a summer resort for foreigners back in the 1880s. American and European missionaries, businessmen, and government officials and their families came from as far away as Shanghai, Hong Kong, and Singapore to escape the oppressive humid summer heat. They arrived in Unzen by bamboo palanquin from Obama, seven miles away. The fact that there were foreigners here explains why Unzen has one of Japan's oldest golf courses, dating from 1913.

ORIENTATION

Before leaving Tokyo or Kyoto, be sure to pick up the free leaflet *Nagasaki and Unzen,* which describes places of interest in Unzen and the Shimabara Peninsula. The easiest way to get to Unzen is by Kenci Bus from Nagasaki. Buses leave about every hour or so from the bus terminal across the street from Nagasaki Station. The ride takes about two hours and costs ¥1,700 ($13.60) one way. The **Unzen tourist office** (tel. 0957/73-3434) is located in the heart of Unzen Spa not far from the

Hells. Open daily from 9 a.m. to 5 p.m., it has a rudimentary but adequate map in English of Unzen and the surrounding area. Not far away is the **Unzen Visitor's Center** with natural history displays of the national park.

The **telephone area code** for Unzen is 0957, and Unzen is located in Nagasaki Prefecture.

THE SIGHTS

In 1934 the area around Unzen became **Unzen National Park,** named after an extinct volcano, Mount Unzen. Unzen Spa itself, however, still bubbles with activity as sulfurous hot springs erupt into surface cauldrons of scalding water in an area known as the Hells (Jigoku). Indeed, in the 1600s these cauldrons were used for hellish punishment as Christians were boiled alive here after Christianity was outlawed in Japan. Today Unzen Spa has more than 30 solfataras and fumaroles. The Hells are a favorite hangout of huge black ravens, and the barren land has been baked a chalky white through the centuries. There are pathways leading through the hot springs where sulfur vapors rise thick to veil pine trees on surrounding hills. Old women in bonnets sell eggs that have been boiled in the hot springs for ¥50 (40¢) apiece. They also sell corn on the cob for ¥350 ($2.80) an ear.

I like Unzen Spa because it's small and navigable. It consists basically of just a few streets with hotels and ryokan spread along them, a welcome relief if you've been spending a few hectic weeks rushing through big cities and catching buses and trains. Only 1,700 people live here, and from the town a number of hiking paths wind into the tree-covered hills. If you feel like taking an excursion, buses leave about every hour for **Nitta Pass,** about a 20-minute ride away. The fare is ¥330 ($2.64) one way. From Nitta Pass you can take a ropeway up higher to **Mount Myoken** for a better view, but the best thing to do in my opinion is to take the footpath that runs from Nitta Pass and skirts the mountain along a tree-shaded path. The first 15 or 20 minutes of the path is fairly easy, and that's all you may care to exert yourself. If you're ready for some real climbing, however, continue along the path for another half hour or so where it leads starkly uphill to the summit of **Mount Fugen,** Unzen's highest peak at 4,462 feet above sea level. There on a clear day you'll be rewarded with splendid views of other volcanic peaks as far away as Mount Aso in the middle of Kyushu. Also on Mount Fugen is Fugen Shrine, which is about a 20-minute hike from the peak. Allow at least two hours for the hike from Nitta Pass to Mount Fugen and back.

For sports, you can play golf at Unzen's famous and Japan's oldest public golf course (tel. 73-3368), open from 8 a.m. to 5 p.m. Total charge for the nine-hole course, including greens fees, tax, and caddy, is ¥7,300 ($58.40) on weekdays and ¥9,500 ($76) on weekends and holidays. There's also a shorter nine-hole course (good for beginners) charging ¥2,900 ($23.20). Unzen Spa also has public tennis courts that are free—your only obligation is to rake the dirt court when you finish playing.

Keep in mind that, as with many resort areas in Japan, Unzen tends to be crowded during Golden Week in early May, during New Year's, and in July and August. The best times of year are late April to June, when the azalea bushes are in glorious bloom, and in late October and early November, when the maple leaves turn brilliant reds.

FOOD AND LODGING

If you're the least bit of a romantic, you won't be able to resist staying at the **Unzen Kanko Hotel** (0957/73-3263). Built in 1935, a year after the establishment of Unzen National Park, it's an old-fashioned mountain lodge of stone and wood covered in ivy. The rooms are rustic and old-fashioned too, with heavy ceiling-to-floor curtains tied back to reveal a balcony, brass doorsills, high ceilings, and wooden beams. There are 50 Western-style rooms here starting at ¥8,800 ($70.40) for a single and ¥13,000 ($104) for a double or twin. There are also eight newer

Japanese-style tatami rooms starting at ¥22,000 ($176), and two combination rooms that come with both bed and tatami area for ¥22,000 ($176). Facilities at the hotel include hot-spring sulfur baths, billiard tables, table tennis, and electronic games. The hotel also has a couple of racquets you can use in case you want to swing at balls down at the public tennis courts.

Even if you don't stay at the hotel, you may want to come here for a meal. The dining hall is large, with wooden paneling and wooden floors, white tablecloths, and flowers on each table. Open for lunch from noon to 1:30 p.m. and for dinner starting at 6 p.m., with last orders taken at 8 p.m., it serves set menus of both Japanese and Western selections starting at ¥4,400 ($35.20). The Western set meal for ¥6,500 ($52), for example, will bring you hors d'oeuvres, soup, lobster, the main entrée and vegetables, a salad, ice cream, a roll or rice, and coffee or tea. There's also a small à la carte menu that includes such dishes as filet mignon, chicken, pork cutlets, lobster, sole, fried shrimp, and spaghetti. Spaghetti costs ¥850 ($6.80).

Also on the hotel grounds is a tempura restaurant called **Gyo En**, located just to the right as you enter the hotel's cedar-lined driveway. A small house with one room for dining, it's open daily from 5 to 8:30 p.m., with set meals ranging from ¥4,400 ($35.20) to ¥6,500 ($52).

Miyazaki Ryokan ㉙ (tel. 0957/73-3331) is one of the largest Japanese inns in Unzen, a modern structure with a lobby overlooking a manicured traditional garden and hills and sulfur vapors rising in the background. All 107 rooms come with TV with pay video, a safe for valuables, alarm clock, fridge, and private bathroom. Japanese-style rooms start at ¥16,500 ($132) per person. There are also combination rooms with twin or double bed and a separate tatami area for ¥25,000 ($200) per person. Rates include two excellent meals, tax, and service charge. Breakfasts (Western style, if desired) are served in a communal dining area, but dinners are served in the individual guest rooms in true ryokan fashion. Room prices are the same regardless of which direction the rooms face, so I'd advise one facing the hot springs and wooded hills rather than the village. The views from these rooms are among the best in Unzen. As expected, this ryokan has large hot-spring public bath facilities.

First opened during the Meiji Period about 100 years ago by the present owner's grandfather, **Yumei Hotel** (tel. 0957/73-3206) is a moderately priced ryokan in Unzen. With the present building constructed in 1973 and renovated in 1987, rates begin at ¥13,000 ($104) per person on weekdays and at ¥16,500 ($132) on weekends and during peak season. All rooms come with private bathroom, a safe for valuables, refrigerator, and TV with adult video. Rooms on the fifth floor have the extra advantage of a large balcony. Although most of the 72 rooms are Japanese style, 20 of the rooms are combination style, with both beds and a separate tatami area, going for ¥16,500 ($132) to ¥20,000 ($160) per person. Dinners are served in each guest's room, while breakfasts are served in a communal dining room. Facilities include hot-spring baths open 24 hours a day, a pool open from July through August, a bowling alley, and public tennis courts next door.

A more economically priced ryokan, **Kaseya Ryokan** ㉖ (tel. 0957/73-3321) charges ¥6,600 ($53) to ¥11,000 ($88) per person, including two meals (Western-style breakfasts available), tax, and service charge. The ryokan, which dates back to 1909, has been totally remodeled so that it appears new and modern. All 13 rooms are Japanese style and are simply decorated, with high ceilings and flower arrangements in each room. There are three communal public sulfur baths, one each for men and for women, and a smaller bath for families.

Formerly a youth hostel, **Seiunso Kokumin Shukusha** ㉗ (tel. 0957/73-3273) still offers the least expensive accommodations in Unzen Spa. Because it is about a 30-minute walk from the spa, the staff will pick guests up if they telephone from the bus stop in Unzen. It has 52 tatami-style rooms, which range in price from ¥5,500 ($44) to ¥6,500 ($52) per person, including two meals, tax, and service charge. The higher-priced rooms have their own private bathroom and balcony, but the view from the cheaper rooms is no less grand. There's a hot-spring public bath (there's also a public outdoor bath not far from Seiunso). The most crowded times of the year here are during New Year's and in August, during which times you should try to make reservations three months in advance.

7. Kagoshima

With a population of more than half a million, Kagoshima in southern Kyushu is a city of palm trees, flowering trees and bushes, wide avenues, and people that are like the weather—warm, mild-tempered, relaxed, and easygoing. In addition, because of its relative isolation at the southern tip of Japan far away from the capitals of Kyoto and Tokyo, Kagoshima through the centuries has developed a mind of its own, an independent spirit that fostered a number of great men and accomplishments. Foremost in Kagoshima's history is the Shimazu clan, a remarkable family that for 29 generations (695 years) ruled over Kagoshima and its vicinity before the Meiji Restoration in 1868. Much of Japan's early contact with the outside world was via Kagoshima, first with China and then with the Western world. Japan's first contact with Christianity, for example, occurred in Kagoshima when St. Francis Xavier landed here in 1549. Although he stayed only ten months, he converted more than 600 Japanese to Christianity.

By the mid-19th century, as the Tokugawa shogunate began losing strength and the confidence of the people, the Shimazu family was already looking toward the future and the modernization of Japan. In the mid-1850s the Shimazus built the first Western-style factory in the country, employing 200 men to make cannons, glass, ceramics, landmines, ships, and farming tools. In 1865, while Japan's doors were still officially closed to the outside world and all contact with foreigners was forbidden, the Shimazus smuggled 17 young men to Britain so that they could learn foreign languages and technology—certainly an act of defiance in the first degree. After these men returned to Japan, they became a driving force in the Meiji Restoration and the modernization of Japan.

Another historical figure who played a major role during the Meiji Restoration was Takamori Saigo, who was born in Kagoshima Prefecture. A philosopher, scholar, educator, and poet, he helped restore Emperor Meiji to power, but because he was also a samurai he subsequently became disillusioned when the ancient rights of the samurai class were rescinded and the wearing of swords was forbidden. He led a force of samurai against the government in what is called the Seinan Rebellion, but suffered defeat. He then withdrew to Shiroyama in Kagoshima, where he committed suicide in 1877. Today Saigo has many fans among the Japanese, and on Shiroyama hill you can visit the cave where he committed suicide.

ORIENTATION
Information on Kagoshima is given in *Southern Kyushu*, a leaflet distributed by the Tourist Information Centers in Tokyo and Kyoto. In Kagoshima there are **tourist information centers** at both Nishi Kagoshima Station (tel. 0992/53-2500) and Kagoshima Station (tel. 0992/22-2500), as well as at the airport. The staffs speak English and have good English maps of the city. Tourist information centers are open every day from 8:30 a.m. to 5 p.m.

Kagoshima's international airport connects Kyushu with Hong Kong, Singapore, and Guam, while domestic flights give easy access to such cities as Tokyo, Nagoya, Osaka, and Hiroshima. Travel by train takes about 12 hours from Tokyo, 8 hours from Osaka, and about 5 hours from Fukuoka. All trains passing through Kagoshima make two stops, at both Kagoshima Station and Nishi Kagoshima Station. Kagoshima Station is the closest station to Iso Garden, the Sakurajima Ferry Terminal, Shigetomiso, Hirayama Ryokan, and Shiroyama Kanko Hotel, listed below. If you're heading for any of the other hotels described below, you should get off the train at Nishi Kagoshima Station, where you'll also find an international post office.

The downtown section of Kagoshima is the area between Nishi Kagoshima and Kagoshima stations, with Tenmonkan Dori Street (a covered shopping arcade) serving as the heart of the city. You can walk from one station to the other in less than 30 minutes, but there is also a streetcar connecting the two. If you think you'll be doing a lot of traveling by streetcar, you might want to invest in a one-day pass for ¥500 ($4), valid for travel on trams and some city buses and which gives a 20% discount in the admission fee at Iso Garden.

The **telephone area code** for Kagoshima is 0992, and Kagoshima is located in Kagoshima Prefecture.

THE SIGHTS

With ties to Naples, Italy, as its sister city, Kagoshima bills itself as the "Naples of the Orient." That's perhaps stretching things a bit too far, but Kagoshima is balmy most of the year and it even has its own Mount Vesuvius—**Mount Sakurajima,** an active volcano across Kinko Bay, continuously puffs steam into the sky and occasionally covers the city with fine soot and ash. In 1914 Sakurajima had a whopper of an eruption in which it belched up three billion tons of lava. When the eruption was over, the townspeople were surprised to discover that the flow of lava had been so great that it blocked the 1,666-foot-wide channel separating the volcano from a neighboring peninsula. Sakurajima, which had once been an island, was now part of the mainland.

Magnificent from far away and impressive if you're near the top, Sakurajima can be visited by a ferry that leaves every 15 minutes from a pier close to Kagoshima Station. It takes 15 minutes to reach Sakurajima. Oddities of Sakurajima include the fact that its rich soil produces both the world's largest radishes and the world's smallest oranges. Although Sakurajima radishes average about 37 pounds, occasionally they weigh more than 80 pounds. The oranges, on the other hand, are only 1.2 inches in diameter.

There are walking paths through lava fields close to Sakurajima's ferry pier, but because Sakurajima is sparsely populated, with only limited public transportation, you might want to join a tour operated by Japan Railways that visits lava fields and lookouts around the volcano in one hour and 45 minutes. JR buses depart three times daily at 9:45 a.m., 10:45 a.m., and 2:30 p.m. from the ferry dock on Sakurajima. It would be prudent to check the departure times to make sure they haven't changed. Price of the tour is ¥1,360 ($10.88), but if you have a Japan Rail Pass, you can go for free.

Whereas Sakurajima, rising dramatically across the bay, is Kagoshima's best-known landmark, **Iso Garden** (tel. 47-1791) is its most widely visited attraction. These gardens of the Shimazu clan were laid out more than 300 years ago with Sakurajima and Kinko Bay incorporated into the design scheme. Open daily from 8:30 a.m. to 5:30 p.m. (until 5 p.m. in winter) with an admission fee of ¥500 ($4), the garden features a particularly idyllic spot where the 21st lord of the Shimazu family held famous poem-composing garden parties. Guests seated themselves on stones beside a gently meandering rivulet and were requested to have completed a poem by the time a cup filled with sake came drifting by on the tiny brook. Ah, those were the days!

Next to Iso Garden, and included in its entrance fee, is the **Shokoshuseikan Museum,** built in the mid-1850s as Japan's first modern factory. It houses about 300 items relating to the almost 700-year history of the Shimazu clan, including palanquins used to carry lords to far-away Edo (present Tokyo). There are also everyday items the family used and photographs. I find the photographs showing the Shimazu family dressed in Western-style fashions particularly interesting. Iso Garden is located about 10 minutes by bus from Kagoshima Station and 30 minutes by bus from Nishi Kagoshima Station.

Another museum worth visiting is the **City Art Museum (Kagoshima Shiritsu Bijutsukan)** (tel. 24-3400), which has a collection of contemporary paintings by artists born in Kagoshima Prefecture, including Seiki Kuroda, Takeji Fujishima, and Wada Eisaku. A small selection of paintings by Western artists is also displayed, as well as pottery, glass, bronzes, and other works of art. The permanent exhibition is small, but special exhibitions are also held here. Hours here are 9 a.m. to 5 p.m.; closed Monday. Admission is ¥200 ($1.60).

Only a few minutes' walk away is the **Kagoshima Prefectural Museum of Culture (Reimeikan)** (tel. 22-5100), also open from 9 a.m. to 5 p.m. every day except Monday. It's one of the finest prefectural museums in the country and was built on the former site of Tsurumaru Castle, of which only the moat remains. The museum traces the history of the people of Kagoshima over the last 40,000 years, with exhibits devoted to topography and natural history, archeological finds, and the society and culture of old Satsuma. Admission here is also ¥200.

Chiran

If you have an extra morning or afternoon, I suggest taking an excursion to Chiran, a small village 19 miles south of Kagoshima. Surrounded by wooded hills and rows of neatly cultivated tea plantations, it's one of the 102 castle towns that once bordered the Shimazu kingdom during the Edo Period. Although the castle is no longer standing, six old gardens and samurai houses have been carefully preserved by descendants.

Apparently, the village headman of Chiran had the opportunity to travel with his lord Shimazu to Kyoto and Edo in the mid-1700s, taking along with him some of his local samurai as retainers. The headman and his retainers were so impressed with the sophisticated culture of Kyoto and Edo that they invited gardeners to Chiran to construct a series of gardens on the samurai estates surrounding the castle.

Some of these gardens remain intact, and are located on a delightful road called Samurai Lane, which is lined with moss-covered stone walls and hedges. Since descendants of the samurai are still living in the houses, only the gardens are open to the public. There are three types of gardens here: the miniature artificial hill style, in which a central pond symbolizes the sea and rocks the mountains; the "dry" garden, in which the sea is symbolized not by water but by white sand that is raked to give it rippling movements of water; and the "borrowed scenery" garden, in which surrounding mountains and scenery are incorporated into the general garden design. Although the gardens are small, they are exquisite and charming. Notice, for example, how the tops of hedges are cut to resemble rolling hills, blending with the shapes of mountains in the background.

The six gardens open to the public are indicated by a white marker in front of each entry gate. All six can be visited for ¥300 ($2.40), and it should take about an hour to see them all. Pay the entry fee for all six at the first garden you visit; you'll be given a pamphlet containing a map and a description of the gardens in English.

Chiran can be reached in about 75 minutes from Yamagataya Bus Station next to the Yamagataya department store in downtown Kagoshima. Although Chiran is located midway between Ibusuki and Kagoshima, there are unfortunately no buses going onward to Ibusuki. If you want to visit Chiran and continue on to Ibusuki, it's best to join one of the organized tours that depart from Kagoshima, stop briefly in Chiran, and end in Ibusuki. The cost of such a tour, conducted in Japanese only, is ¥3,800 ($30.40). Tour buses depart from Nishi Kagoshima Station at 10:10 a.m. and include stops at Lake Ikeda and Mount Kaimon, at a thought-provoking museum dedicated to the kamikaze pilots of World War II, and at the Ibusuki Jungle Bath (part of the Ibusuki Kanko Hotel), in addition to the short walk through Chiran. The bus reaches the Ibusuki Jungle Bath at around 5 p.m., where you can soak at leisure—your tour ticket includes local bus transportation to Ibusuki Station, which you can use when you want.

SHOPPING

If you're interested in shopping in Kagoshima, local products include *oshima pongee*, Japanese silk made into such items as clothing, handbags, and wallets; shochu, an alcoholic drink made from such ingredients as sweet potatoes and drunk either cold on the rocks or mixed with boiling water; furniture, statues, and chests made from *yaku* cedar; and Satsuma pottery. Satsuma pottery is probably Kagoshima's most famous product. It's been produced in the Kagoshima area for more than 380 years, first by Korean potters brought here to practice their trade. Satsuma pottery comes in two styles—black and white. White Satsuma pottery is more elegant and was used by former lords; the black pottery, on the other hand, was used by the townspeople in everyday life.

In Kagoshima's downtown area are several department stores—Yamagataya, Mitsukoshi, and Takashimaya—where you can shop for local products. There are also souvenir shops in the downtown area, including a covered shopping arcade called Tenmonkan-Dori.

Another good place to shop for local items is the **Display Hall of Kagoshima Products** in the Sangyo Kaikan Building, 9-1 Meizancho, (tel. 25-6120). Open Monday to Friday from 8:30 a.m. to 5 p.m. and on Saturday until 12:30 p.m., this one-room shop is located in Kagoshima's downtown and sells such goods as tinware, handmade knives, Satsuma pottery, glassware, oshima pongee, yaku cedar, shochu, and other items from Kagoshima Prefecture. Incidentally, the **Kagoshima Prefectural Tourist Office** is located in the same building up on the fourth floor (tel. 23-5771); here you can obtain information on the city as well as the prefecture, including Ibusuki and Chiran.

If you're interested in pottery, there are many Satsuma pottery factories in the Kagoshima area. Most easily accessible is **Kinko Togei** ㉘, 2-2-3 Taniyamako (tel. 61-0037). Open daily from 8:30 a.m. to 5:15 p.m., it can be reached by train or tram from Nishi Kagoshima Station. If you're going by train, get off at Sakanoue Station; from there it's either a 20-minute walk or a 5-minute taxi ride. If you want to go by streetcar, get off at Taniyama Station; from there it's a 10-minute taxi ride. You can observe production of Satsuma pottery here and make purchases from its showroom. The factory will ship or airmail your purchases home.

FOOD AND LODGING

In addition to accommodations, hotels in Kagoshima offer a good selection of dining for both Japanese and Western cuisine. In case you wish to eat a few meals outside a hotel, more restaurants are listed at the end of this section, along with recommendations of local food specialties you should try.

The Upper Bracket

Japanese Style: One of Kagoshima's most beautiful ryokan is **Shigetomiso** ㉙, 31-7 Shimazu-machi (tel. 0992/47-3155), once a villa for the ruling Shimazu clan. Spreading along a gentle slope of a hill in a profusion of flowering plants, with a garden and a waterfall, this enchanting ryokan overlooks the bay in a storybook setting. Its oldest rooms date from the 1820s, and through the decades a number of stories, myths, and legends have arisen to add to its mystique. One room, for example, is said to have belonged to the lord's mistress; here you can see a wooden pillar marred by tiny holes—apparently made by the mistress as she stabbed it with her hairpin out of frustration caused by the lord's too infrequent visits. Another room is colored a unique reddish tinge, derived from the blood of pigs brought from Okinawa. There's a closet where the clan could hide during attack, and the ceiling of one hallway was constructed deliberately low to thwart downward blows of enemy swords. In more recent history, the James Bond movie *You Only Live Twice* has a sequence filmed in one of the ryokan's rooms. In short, the whole ryokan is a museum in itself and contains antiques that once belonged to the Shimazu family. All rooms come with private bathroom, peace, and tranquillity for ¥20,000 ($160) to ¥38,000 ($304) per person, including two meals, tax, and service charge. Highly recommended if you can afford it.

Western Style: Kagoshima's foremost hotel is the **Shiroyama Kanko Hotel,** 41-1 Shinshoin-cho (tel. 0992/24-2211), which sits 353 feet high on wood-covered Shiroyama hill and commands a fine view of the city below and Sakurajima across the bay. Rooms start at ¥7,700 ($62) for a single, ¥12,000 ($96) for a double, and ¥14,800 ($118) for a twin, with the best rooms facing the volcano. Rooms are pleasant and comfortable, although the singles are slightly small. Facilities at the hotel include a pool and sauna (free for guests); souvenir shops selling such locally made products as silk pongee, Satsuma pottery, yaku cedar, and confectioneries; an art gallery; a pleasant outdoor beer garden open during the summer months; and Japanese, Western, and Chinese restaurants.

The **Sky Lounge,** on the seventh floor of the Shiroyama Kanko Hotel, is open from 11 a.m. to 11:30 p.m. Its à la carte selections include fried or grilled shrimp, sole filet, lobster thermidor, green pepper steak, veal cutlet, spaghetti, and sandwiches. Most entrées run between ¥1,300 ($10.40) and ¥3,000 ($24). There are also set dinner menus from ¥5,500 ($44). Complete lunch courses begin at ¥1,300 ($10.40). The restaurant affords a good view of the city and volcano, especially at dusk as the lights come on below and Sakurajima slowly fades into darkness.

Taki-no-Chaya is Shiroyama Kanko Hotel's Japanese restaurant, serving sashimi, tempura, shabu-shabu, sukiyaki, kaiseki, and Japanese barbecued dishes from 11 a.m. to 10 p.m., with a beautiful view of a garden. Most dishes cost ¥2,000 ($16) to ¥5,000 ($40). If you feel like splurging, one section of the restaurant, called Kappo Lakusui, serves local selections of seafood and vegetables. The setting here is impressive, with an indoor pond and individual tatami rooms constructed as though they were tiny huts in a village. Dinners here run anywhere from ¥6,500 ($52) and up, and you should make a reservation if you want to dine in this section. Lunch courses start at ¥3,300 ($26.40).

The Medium-Priced Range

Kagoshima Tokyu Hotel, 22-1 Shinmachi, Kamoike (tel. 0992/57-2411), is a first-rate medium-priced hotel located in a new section of town that sports immaculate, modern buildings and wide avenues. Its only drawback is that it's a bit far from the center, but city buses departing from Nishi Kagoshima Station reach the hotel in 15 minutes. Built right on the waterfront with a good view of the volcano, its 206 rooms range from ¥7,500 ($60) to ¥9,600 ($77) for a single, ¥13,700 ($110) to ¥16,000 ($128) for a twin, and ¥17,000 ($136) for a double. The twins and doubles face the water and have verandas, great for sitting out in the morning and watching the sun rise over Sakurajima. Singles all face inland and do not have balconies. There's an outdoor swimming pool open during the warmer months (usually from about May to September) and an outdoor Jacuzzi, both fed by natural hot springs and open year-round.

The hotel's Japanese restaurant, **Yamabuki,** serves tempura, sashimi, and local dishes; its Western restaurant, **Hibiscus,** serves steak, lobster, sandwiches, curries, and pilaf. If you're in the mood for teppanyaki steak, try the hotel's **Steak House Fresia,** where the chef prepares your food before your very eyes. Steaks here cost between ¥4,000 ($32) and ¥8,000 ($64), but steak set lunches are only ¥1,000 ($8).

Kagoshima Sun Royal Hotel, 1-8-10 Yojiro (tel. 0992/53-2020), is also located in the new section of Kagoshima, not far from the Tokyu Hotel. Its rooms come with TV with pay video, clock, music, and refrigerator, and all the double, twin, and Japanese-style rooms face the sea and have balconies. Singles, which face only inland and do not have balconies, start at a low ¥3,800 ($30) for those without bathtub or shower but with toilet and sink; those with bathroom start at ¥6,300

($50). Twins are ¥7,300 ($58) without bathroom and ¥13,200 ($106) with bathroom. The doubles all have bathrooms and cost ¥16,500 ($132). I personally prefer the Japanese-style rooms with their tatami sitting alcoves beside the balcony. They go for ¥14,300 ($114) and up. There's a great *onsen* (hot-spring bath) on the 13th floor, separated for men and women. You can look out over Mount Sakurajima as you bathe.

For meals with a view, try the **Phoenix Sky Lounge** on the 13th floor, open from 11:30 a.m. to 2 p.m. and from 5:30 p.m. to 11:30 p.m. It's very pleasant, with a drawing-room ambience in colors of pale pink and green. Set lunches start at ¥1,500 ($12), while dinner set menus begin at ¥2,700 ($21.60). It's famous for its beef curry, and other entrées include grilled chicken, steak, beef Stroganoff, fish, grilled lobster, pilaf, and spaghetti.

The hotel also has a Japanese restaurant, where kaiseki and local dishes are served for about ¥2,500 ($20) to ¥6,000 ($48).

Located right in the heart of downtown near the Tenmonkan-Dori arcade, the **Kagoshima Hayashida Hotel**, 12-11 Higashisengoku-cho (tel. 0992/24-4111), is about a ten-minute walk from either Nishi Kagoshima or Kagoshima Station. Following what appears to be a Space Age theme, it's built around an inner garden atrium called Space Garden, and the inside guest rooms possess views of the atrium through one-way mirrors. Although these rooms facing the inside tend to be dark, they're much quieter than those facing the outside streets. Rooms are of modern design, though small, and are equipped with TV, clock, and radio. All have a private bathroom. Single rooms start at ¥6,900 ($55), doubles begin at ¥9,350 ($75), and twins run ¥11,550 ($92) and up.

Inside the Space Garden, with its sunroof, plants, and trees, are four restaurants serving Japanese, Cantonese, French, and Western cuisine. Meals average about ¥3,000 ($24) and up, and hours are 11 a.m. to 2:30 p.m. to 5 to 10 p.m. daily. A Filipino band performs in the center of the atrium in the summer.

The Budget Category

The past few years have witnessed the opening of a number of business hotels in Kagoshima, most of them located close to Nishi Kagoshima Station. **Park Hotel** ⑨⑩⑩, 15-24 Chuo-cho (tel. 0992/51-1100), is one of these and can be reached in two minutes on foot from the station. All of its 70 rooms are Western style and come with semidouble-size beds, TV with adult videos, windows that can be opened, hot water for tea, and bathrooms that are larger than in most business hotels. All but 12 of its rooms are single, which are ¥6,000 ($48). There are six doubles, which go for ¥9,700 ($78), and six twins, which cost ¥11,000 ($88). Tax and service are included. Its one restaurant serves both Western and Japanese food, with selections including shabu-shabu, obento lunch boxes, spaghetti, sirloin steak, and hamburger steak.

Also about a two-minute walk from Nishi Kagoshima Station but older is **Station Hotel New Kagoshima**, 6-5 Chuo-cho (tel. 0992/53-5353). Its 210 rooms are basic but adequate, and all come with a private bathroom. Single rooms start at ¥5,200 ($42), doubles begin at ¥8,200 ($66), and twins go for ¥8,800 ($70) and up, tax and service charge included. Eight Japanese-style rooms are also available beginning at ¥8,800 ($70) for two. A restaurant on the eighth floor called Star Dust serves both Japanese and Western food; there's also a Chinese restaurant. The ninth floor boasts a beer garden (open in summer).

About a three-minute walk from Nishi Kagoshima Station is **Business Hotel Gasthof**, 7-3 Chuo-cho (tel. 0992/52-1401). Although it looks rather uninteresting from the outside, the lobby is quite another story. It reminds me of some forgotten pawnshop, with glass cases packed with antiques (some several centuries old), old knives, ceramics and pottery, and fish tanks. More likely than not three small dogs will greet you from atop the check-in counter. None of the stuff is for sale—it's all there simply for your viewing pleasure. The rooms are very basic and a bit worn,

but are adequate enough and come with a bathroom. For one person the charge is
¥3,700 ($30). Doubles are ¥4,400 ($35), twins are ¥6,400 ($51), and triples are
¥9,600 ($77). Charges include tax and service, and breakfasts are available for
¥400 ($3.20).

Close to the city's other train station, Kagoshima Station, is **Hirayama** ③, 6-7
Meizancho (tel. 0992/22-4489), about five minutes away. All 18 rooms here are
Japanese style without private bathroom. The building is old and the hallways could
use a good vacuuming, but the tatami rooms are fine and come with coin-operated
TV and air conditioning. Rates are on a per-person basis and are ¥3,300 ($26) for a
room without meals, ¥3,800 ($30) for a room with breakfast, and ¥5,500 ($44)
including two meals. Meals are Japanese and are served in a dining hall.

If you're a youth hosteler, try **Kagoshima Fujin Kaikan Youth Hostel** ③,
Shimoarata 2-27-12 (tel. 0992/51-1087). To reach it, take bus 13 from Nishi Kagoshima Station and get off at bus stop Shimoatara Fujin Kaikan Mae. There are eight
Japanese-style rooms here, in a beautiful, traditional-style house more than 55 years
old. The price including two meals is ¥2,900 ($23). Nonmembers can stay for
¥3,400 ($27).

Another youth hostel is the **Sakurajima Youth Hostel** ③, Hakama-goshi (tel.
0992/93-2150). It's on the slope of the Sakurajima volcano, about a five-minute
walk from the ferry terminal. The charge of ¥3,000 ($24) brings you bed, breakfast,
and dinner and is the same for both members and nonmembers.

More Dining

While in Kagoshima, be sure to try its local dishes, known as *Satsuma* cooking
(Satsuma was the original name of the Kagoshima area). This style of cooking supposedly has its origins in food cooked on battlefields centuries ago, but if that's the
case I'm sure it's improved greatly since then.

A good place to try local Satsuma dishes is **Kumasotei** ④, 6-10
Higashisengoku-cho (tel. 22-6356), located in the center of town between Nishi Kagoshima and Kagoshima stations. Hours here are 11 a.m. to 10 p.m. daily. This restaurant is well known in Kagoshima and reminds me more of a private home or
ryokan, since dining is in individual tatami rooms. As soon as you enter you are
ushered into its recesses, and if there isn't a crowd you'll probably have your own
private room; otherwise, you'll share. The main menu is in Japanese, but there's a
smaller menu in English listing courses for ¥3,000 ($24) that feature Satsuma
cooking. There are also kaiseki courses starting from ¥2,000 ($16) for lunch and
Satsuma specialties including *Satsuma-age* (ground fish that has been deep-fried),
torisashi (raw chicken, and not as bad as it sounds), *tonkotsu* (pork that has been
boiled for several hours in shochu and brown sugar—absolutely delicious),
zakezushi (rice that has been soaked in sake all day and is then mixed with such
things as vegetables and shrimp), bonito baked with salt, *awameshi* (rice mixed with
wheat and undoubtedly very healthy), and *Satsume-jiru* (miso soup with chicken
and locally grown vegetables). *Kibinago* is a small fish belonging to the herring family caught in the waters around Kagoshima. A silver color with brown stripes, it is
often eaten raw arranged on a dish so that it looks like a chrysanthemum.

A more modestly priced restaurant serving Satsuma food, **Satsuma** ⑤, 10-4
Chuo-chu (tel. 52-2661), is right across the street from Nishi Kagoshima Station.
Look for a tiny restaurant with a large red lantern and white curtains outside its
door. Open from 10 a.m. to 3 p.m. and from 5:30 to 10 p.m. every day except Monday, this cozy and wonderfully cluttered establishment has room for about only ten
people on its ground floor and another ten people on the second floor. Such items as
torisashi, kibinago, Satsuma-jiru soup, Satsuma-age, and tonkotsu cost between
¥500 ($4) and ¥1,000 ($8), and there are also set meals ranging from ¥550
($4.40) to ¥2,750 ($22).

Another popular and inexpensive dining place is **Noboruya** ⑥, 2-15 Horie-
cho (tel. 26-6690). This is Kagoshima's best-known ramen, or noodle, shop, and

since there's only one dish there's no problem ordering. Costing ¥800 ($6.40), a big bowl of ramen comes with noodles (made fresh every day) and slices of pork and is seasoned with garlic. You also get pickled radish (supposedly good for the stomach) and tea. Open from 11 a.m. to 7 p.m. every day except Sunday, it's in the center of town about a 15-minute hike from Kagoshima Station. As you eat your ramen at the counter, you can watch women peeling garlic and cooking huge pots of noodles over gas flames.

---

8. Ibusuki

Located about an hour from Kagoshima by train at the southern tip of the Satsuma Peninsula, Ibusuki (pronounced "ee-*boo*-ski"), with a population of 33,000, is southern Kyushu's most famous hot-spring resort. With a pleasant average temperature of 64.5°F, it's a region of lush vegetation, flowers, and palm trees—and of course, hot springs.

ORIENTATION

Be sure to get the leaflet *Southern Kyushu* from the T.I.C. in Tokyo or Kyoto. Upon arrival in Ibusuki, stop by the **tourist information counter** (tel. 0993/22-4114) at Ibusuki Station to pick up a map in Japanese with some English on it. There's also an English brochure available with a brief rundown of sightseeing attractions in the area around Ibusuki. The information counter is open daily from 9 a.m. to 7:30 p.m.

The town of Ibusuki is spread along the coast, and there are public buses that run through the main streets. In any case, the town isn't large, and taxis are readily available.

The **telephone area code** for Ibusuki is 0993. Ibusuki is located in Kagoshima Prefecture.

WHAT TO DO

The most popular thing to do is to have yourself buried up to your neck in hot black sand, and the best place to do this is at **Surigahama Public Beach,** located about five minutes from Ibusuki Station by bus. After paying ¥500 ($4) you'll be supplied with a yukata cotton kimono and towel. Change into the yukata in the changing room and then walk down to the beach. One of the women there will dig you a shallow grave. Lie down, arrange your yukata so that no vulnerable areas are left exposed, and then lie still while she piles sand on top of you. It's quite a funny sight, actually, to see nothing but heads sticking out of the ground. Bodies are heated by hot springs that surface close to the ground before running into the sea. It's best to go when the tide is low so you can get closer to the sea. The water is alkali saline, a hot 185° Fahrenheit, and helps in gastroenteric troubles, neuralgia, and female disorders. Many of the older people you see here are not tourists but are living in Ibusuki and come here every day for treatment. After your sand bath, go indoors for a hot-spring bath. The Surigahama sand baths are open every day from 8:30 a.m. to 9 p.m. (until 8 p.m. in the winter).

Other hot-spring and sand baths are found in the spa hotels spread along Ibusuki's six-mile-long beach. The biggest indoor baths are the **Ibusuki Kanko Hotel's Jungle Bath,** a huge affair with pools of various shapes and sizes surrounded by tropical plants. If you've been to Beppu's Suginoi Palace baths, however, this one may be somewhat of a letdown. The women's baths are much smaller than the men's, although no one objects if women want to use the men's baths instead. Use of the Jungle Bath is free to hotel guests; all others must pay a ¥600 ($4.80) entrance fee. There are also indoor hot-sand baths here, for which everyone (including hotel guests) must pay an extra ¥1,000 ($8).

To visit the area surrounding Ibusuki, it's best to either join a tour group (conducted in Japanese only) or rent a car. Public bus lines are neither extensive nor frequent. Popular destinations include **Nagasakibana Point,** Kyushu's southernmost point and the location of a bird and animal park with variety shows; and **Lake Ikeda,** Kyushu's largest lake. It has a depth of 265 meters (820 feet), not to mention gigantic eels. Some of these eels weigh 33 pounds and measure about six feet in length. If you're interested in seeing these creatures, souvenir shops and stops along the lake have some on display in big tanks.

Another destination is **Kaimon Natural Park,** located at the foot of Mount Kaimon. There's a rest house here serving snacks and inexpensive food, and an 18-hole golf course. Greens fees are ¥8,300 ($66.40) on weekdays, ¥12,400 ($99.20) on Saturday, and ¥15,200 ($121.60) on Sunday and holidays. For more information on golfing, call the golf course at 32-3141.

FOOD AND LODGING

Most of Ibusuki's hotels are located along its six-mile beach. Because this is a resort area, accommodations are more expensive than in the cities.

Ibusuki's best-known spa hotel is the **Ibusuki Kanko Hotel,** 3755 Juni-cho (tel. 0993/22-2131). It's a self-contained resort with everything from outdoor swimming pools to tennis courts, a bowling arcade, a shopping arcade, its own private beach, and the huge hot-spring baths described above. It even has a delightful small art museum called the Iwasaki Museum of Art, and the collection contains French and Japanese paintings by such artists as Henri Matisse, Seiki Kuroda, and Takeji Fujishima. Next to the art museum and connected to it by an underground passageway is a newly opened museum featuring art and antiques from Japan and China, including cloisonné, ivory, and ceramics. The architecture of the two buildings is innovative and impressive, with an imaginativeness and creativity rarely expressed in bare concrete. The museums are open daily from 8 a.m. to 6 p.m.

As for the hotel itself, it's situated on 125 acres of lush tropical grounds with pleasant walking trails throughout. The hotel is very popular with Japanese tour groups and is a good place to rub elbows with Japanese on vacation. It tries to look as much as possible as though it's in Hawaii—the staff even wears Hawaiian shirts to help create the mood. The hotel has 460 Western-style twin rooms (there are no singles) and 167 Japanese tatami rooms. Twins range from ¥10,000 ($80) to ¥18,000 ($144) for single occupancy and ¥12,000 ($96) to ¥20,000 ($160) for a double. All the rooms have either a full or partial view of the sea and come with balconies—the best rooms in my opinion are the ones that face the acres of garden. The Japanese-style rooms, which are located in an older building with a less magnificent view, are ¥10,000 ($80) for those without bathrooms and ¥14,500 ($116) for those with bathrooms, with rates based on double occupancy.

Nights at the Kanko Hotel are nice, with the sound of the waves and the frogs croaking in the lotus pond.

Altogether the hotel has nine food-and-beverage outlets. For Western dining, try the **Sky Lounge** on the tenth floor, with a sweeping panoramic view of the water. Open from 7 a.m. to 11:20 p.m., it serves a variety of dishes including salmon, lobster, sole, and sirloin steak. The average dinner costs about ¥5,000 ($40). The Japanese restaurant, **Okonomi,** serves tempura, sushi, and local dishes. A particularly entertaining place to dine is the **Jungle Park Restaurant Theater.** It features live variety shows usually from—you guessed it—Hawaii. Although a new theater may be built in the near future, the present one is massive, holding up to 1,500 people in an airplane-hangar-size building filled with tropical plants. The Japanese guests show up in an outfit provided in the hotel rooms—blue-flowered pajama-like shirts and shorts for the men and pink-flowered shifts for the women. If you really want to join in the fun, wear the same. Most of the Japanese here are with tour groups. The food is Japanese barbecue style, and you cook your thin slices of beef and vegetables at your table on a hot griddle over a gas flame. Dinner begins at ¥4,000 ($32) and showtime is 6:30 to 8 p.m. Another dinnertime show, the Mexican Acapulco Diving Show, features platform divers from Mexico who plunge more than 100 feet through the air into the sea. Diners watch the spectacle from a glass-enclosed restaurant-theater right on the beach, and the price here is also ¥4,000 ($32) for the show and dinner.

If you want to stay in a ryokan, **Shusuien** ⑳, 5-27-27 Yunohama (tel. 0993/ 23-4141), is renowned both for its excellent service and its cuisine. In 1987 and 1988 competitions held by Japanese travel agencies in which 100 top accommodations were rated, Shusuien won first prize for its cooking, third for its service, and third overall. Although it has only 41 rooms, Shusuien employs a staff of 120.

This is a good place to stay if you want to be pampered and don't want to spend your holidays with group tours of jovial vacationers. Rates per person range from ¥17,800 ($142) to ¥63,000 ($504), including two meals and service charge. The most expensive rooms face the sea, have balconies, and are higher up. The less expensive rooms face inland and have no balconies. Needless to say, this ryokan is elegant yet refined in its setting. Used to foreign businessmen, it serves Western-style breakfasts on request.

Hotel Hakusuikan ⑳, Tarahama-kaigon (tel. 0993/22-3131), has a driveway lined with pine trees, which immediately sets the mood for this modern and elegant Japanese-style inn on the beach. On the hotel grounds are two swimming pools, an indoor hot-sand bath, a beer garden (open in summer), a practice golf course, and a beautifully constructed outdoor hot spring, with separate areas for men and women. Of the 210 rooms, 40 are Western-style twin rooms and 71 are combination rooms with both beds and separate tatami areas. The rest are Japanese-style tatami rooms. Rates range from ¥8,800 ($70) to ¥38,000 ($304) per person, two meals included. Breakfasts are Western-style buffets. This is a very pleasant place to stay.

An inexpensive place to stay is **Hotel Kairakuen,** 5-26-4 Yunohama (tel. 0993/ 22-3121). About a 20-minute walk from Ibusuki Station or a five-minute taxi ride, it's located right next to the Surigahama sand baths on the beach. Of its 61 rooms, two are Western style and four are combination rooms with both beds and tatami areas. Although the hotel's building is old and a bit run-down, the price is right at ¥8,000 ($64) per person, including two meals, tax, and service. Since rates are the same for all rooms, be sure to request a room facing the sea. The best room of all is room 408, which is located on a corner of the building with lots of windows and features both beds and a tatami area, making it perfect for families. All rooms have private baths that feature water directly from the hot springs, and rooms facing the sea have windows above the tubs so you can look out on the water as you bathe. Dinner is served in your room, while Japanese breakfasts are served in a communal dining area.

Even less expensive is **Marutomi** ⑳, 5-24-15 Yunohama (tel. 0993/22-5579). It's also located close to the Surigahama sand baths, on a tiny road that leads inland just across the street from the baths. This establishment is a family-run minshuku, and since the owner here is a fisherman, you can count on fresh seafood. Rates here are ¥5,000 ($40) per person including two meals. There are only seven Japanese-style rooms, all without private bathroom but featuring coin-operated TV, coin-operated air conditioners, and chips of camphor wood to give the rooms a pleasant, outdoor smell. There's a coin-operated laundry machine and a small tiled bathtub with water from a hot spring.

Another place to try if you're on a budget is **Ibusuki Kokumin Kyuka-son** ⑳, Higashikata, Shiomi-cho (tel. 0993/22-3211), a National People's Village. It's located right at the water's edge and is very reasonable, charging ¥6,500 ($52) per person, including meals, for rooms with toilets only and ¥8,000 ($64) for those with baths. You can do it even cheaper if you don't take meals here and your room is without a bathroom—that costs only ¥3,500 ($28) per person. With tennis courts, rental bikes, and hot-spring baths, this place is very popular and is full during the summer vacation months of July and August, on New Year's, in March during spring vacation, and in May during school trips. Otherwise, you can probably get a room here. Rooms are basic, with TV, and some that face the sea even have balconies. Eight of the 65 rooms are Western style. You can reach the village by the village's own bus, recognizable by three circles of green, red, and blue, which is the symbol of National People's Villages. Buses depart from in front of Ibusuki Station following every train arrival. Otherwise, it's about a ten-minute taxi ride.

A ten-minute walk from the station, the **Ibusuki Youth Hostel,** 12-Cho 836 (tel. 0993/22-2758), recently moved into these new quarters, with a total of five rooms that each have air conditioning, heater, and TV. Prices, which include two meals, are ¥3,500 ($28) for members and ¥4,400 ($35) for nonmembers.

If you're looking for a place to eat lunch, the best place in town is probably **Shimazu-han,** located in Shusuien ryokan, described above (tel. 23-4141). In fact, Shimazu-han is so well known among the Japanese that visitors staying in other ryokan in Ibusuki will request room-only rates so that they can enjoy dinner here at Shimazu-han. Shusuien has won awards for its cuisine, and though the food served in its restaurant is not as extensive or expensive as that served to its ryokan guests, meals here are a pleasure, served in private tatami rooms on plates that have been chosen with care to match both the seasons and the food displayed. Dishes are served in courses rather than all at once and start at ¥1,500 ($12) for lunch and ¥2,500 ($20) for dinner. Since there are only eight small rooms, you should make a reservation. Although the menu is in Japanese only, there are photos for each course. The most popular set meal is the Shimazu Gozen for ¥3,300 ($26.40), which includes sashimi, tempura, fish, soup, egg custard, vegetables, rice, and other dishes. Be sure to order a cup of plum shochu (*ume shu*)—it's the best shochu I've ever had. Shimazu-han is open from noon to 2 p.m. and from 6 to 11 p.m.

If you're adventurous, there's a very fun restaurant in the countryside called **Chozyuan** ⑪, Kaimon-cho, Tosenkyo (tel. 22-3155). Eight buses depart daily from Ibusuki Station and the ride lasts about 30 minutes. This restaurant is also a lunch stop for some of the organized tours of the area (including the Kagoshima-to-Ibusuki bus tour described in the previous section). This restaurant is a unique *somen,* or cold noodle place. Seating is under a pavilion beside a man-made waterfall, so you eat to the accompaniment of running water and Japanese traditional music playing in the background. In the middle of your table is a large round container with water swirling around in a circle. When you get your basket of noodles (only ¥450, or $4), dump them into the cold water; then fish them out with your chopsticks, dip them in soy sauce, and enjoy. There are also four set menus starting at ¥1,000 ($8), which come with such things as grilled trout, vegetables, and soup. You can also try carp sashimi. Be sure to keep the wrapper your chopsticks came in— it can be used as a bookmark. Hours are 9 a.m. to 9 p.m. July and August, 9 a.m. to 7 p.m. May and June, and 9 a.m. to 5:30 p.m. September through April.

For an inexpensive meal closer to Ibusuki Station, **Aoba** ⑫, 1-2-11 Minato (tel. 22-3356), is less than a minute's walk away. Take a left out of the train station and look for a small shop on the main street with white curtains over its door and a display of plastic food. Open daily from 11 a.m. to 9:30 p.m., this pleasant and informal eatery offers tempura, eel, local specialties, noodles, and more, with most items priced under ¥1,000 ($8). There's a lunch teishoku offered until 2 p.m. for ¥1,000 ($8).

9. Miyazaki

With a population of 280,000, Miyazaki is one of the largest and most important cities in southern Kyushu and serves as the government seat of Miyazaki Prefecture. Yet Miyazaki feels isolated and somewhat neglected by the rest of Japan. Tokyo seems far away, and most foreigners who happen to land at Kagoshima's international airport tend to head north for Kumamoto, missing Miyazaki altogether. Japanese honeymooners, who used to favor Miyazaki over most other destinations a decade ago, are now flocking to the shores of Hawaii and Australia.

And yet Miyazaki is a perfect place to relax, swim in the Pacific Ocean, get in some rounds of golf, and savor some of the local delicacies. Temperatures here are the second-warmest in Japan, after Okinawa, and flowers bloom throughout the year. You won't see many foreigners here, and the natives will treat you warmly and kindly. If you want to unwind and pamper yourself for a few days, Miyazaki is a good place to do it. And if you have the energy for sightseeing, Miyazaki Prefecture has some historical and natural attractions to occupy your time.

ORIENTATION

It takes more than 12 hours to reach Miyazaki from Tokyo by train. The trip by plane takes only 1½ hours, after which it's about a 15-minute ride to the center of town.

For a map of the city in English, stop off at the **tourist information centers** at either the airport or JR Miyazaki Station, open from 9 a.m. to 6 p.m. Monday through Friday and from 9 a.m. to 5 p.m. on Saturday.

The main street in town is Tachibana-dori Street, lined with shops, department stores, and restaurants. Many buses serving other parts of town as well as Miyazaki Prefecture make stops along this main thoroughfare. There's also a large bus terminal south of the Oyodo River close to Minami Miyazaki Station.

For detailed information on Miyazaki Prefecture, drop by the **prefectural tourist office** (called *kankyo kyokai* in Japanese), located just off Tachibana-dori Street at 1-6 Miyata-cho (tel. 0985/25-4676). Open from 8:30 a.m. to 5 p.m. Monday through Friday and from 8:30 a.m. to 12:30 on Saturday, it has information on Aya, Aoshima, Udo Shrine, and other attractions. This is also a good place to shop for locally made products in its adjoining shop. You can purchase wooden trays, bowls, ceramics, masks, haniwa clay reproductions, swords, lacquerware, and other crafts made in Miyazaki Prefecture.

Before leaving Tokyo or Kyoto, be sure to pick up the leaflet *Miyazaki and Vicinity*, which has information on Miyazaki. The **telephone area code** for Miyazaki is 0985.

THE SIGHTS

Although all of the sights listed below are accessible by public transportation, they are quite spread out. You may, therefore, want to join an organized tour even though it will be conducted only in Japanese. At least it gets you to each destination and you won't have to worry about time schedules and bus stops. A tour operated by Miyazaki Kotsu Bus Company that departs at 8:50 a.m. daily from the bus terminal near Minami Miyazaki Station visits Miyazaki Shrine, Haniwa Garden, Aoshima island, Horikiri Pass, Cactus Park, and Udo Shrine. The tour lasts seven hours and costs ¥4,650 ($37.20).

The most important shrine in town is **Miyazaki Shrine,** dedicated to the first emperor of Japan, Emperor Jimmu, who was the first leader of the Yamoto courts. Peacefully surrounded by woods and cedar trees and about a 15-minute bus ride from Tachibana-dori Street, the shrine is austerely plain and is built from cedar. Be sure to visit the nearby **Miyazaki Prefectural Museum (Miyazaki-ken Sogo Hakubutsukan),** open every day except Monday from 8:30 a.m. to 5 p.m. Its collections of ancient clay images, stone implements, ancient pottery, folklore, and other items depict the natural history, ancient history, and arts of Miyazaki Prefecture.

Archeological digs in Miyazaki Prefecture have unearthed a multitude of ancient burial mounds and clay figures known as *haniwa*. Replicas of both these ancient mounds and haniwa clay figures can be seen in **Haniwa Garden,** most easily reached by taxi in about 15 minutes from Miyazaki Station. Approximately 400 of these clay figures have been placed between trees on mounds covered with moss. Even though they are replicas, the impact of seeing so many images together is quite effective. I especially like the haniwa with the simple face and body and the O-shaped mouth; it's said to represent a dancing woman. A one-room exhibition house displays some items found in ancient burial mounds, and if you want you can buy a small clay replica to take home with you.

Heiwadai Garden is located in a large park called Heiwadai Park, in which you'll also find the **Tower of Peace.** Having a pedestal built with stones donated from countries around the world, it was constructed with the help of volunteers and was finished—ironically enough—in 1940.

If you want to see real burial mounds, head for Saitobaru, where there are more than 300 ancient tombs constructed mostly in the 5th and 6th centuries. Most of the mounds are now covered with grass and trees, so there isn't a lot to see. There is, however, the **Saitobaru Museum,** with a display of excavated artifacts taken from the tombs, including swords, mirrors, bead jewelry, clay pots, stone coffins, tools, and haniwa. The haniwa were buried along with deceased lords to symbolize court retainers who would serve him after death. There are also scale models of several of the burial mounds, including models of the two largest mounds, where the emperor's ancestors were buried. Saitobaru can be reached in about an hour by bus from the bus terminal near Minami Miyazaki Station or from downtown.

Also an hour's bus ride from Miyazaki is **Aya,** a village of 7,300 people. Known for its production of traditional handicrafts, Aya boasts about 13 kilns, more than 10 woodcarving shops, 2 bamboo-craft makers, and 3 weaving shops. All these products are now gathered under one roof in a recently constructed crafts center, which, with its native wooden beams and clay walls, is just as interesting as the products for sale. Next to the crafts center is a workshop where you can make your own pottery piece for ¥1,000 ($8), which includes the price of shipment of your masterpiece to the United States. There's also a weaving workshop, where you can fashion your own coaster for about ¥300 ($2.40).

Next to the crafts center is **Aya Castle,** a reproduction of the original Aya castle built 650 years ago. Made of fir trees, the castle is tiny compared to most in Japan and contains just a few artifacts, such as samurai uniforms and swords. Because both the castle and the crafts center are small and are located an hour away from Miyazaki, I suggest you visit Aya only if you have a special interest in crafts or have no other chance to see a Japanese castle. Both the center and castle are located about a ten-minute walk from the center of Aya town on top of a peaceful wooded hill. Hours are 9 a.m. to 5 p.m. and the entrance fee is ¥200 ($1.60).

One of the most famous sights associated with Miyazaki is **Aoshima,** a tiny island less than a mile in circumference and connected to the mainland via a walkway. Although Aoshima is located about 25 minutes south by train from Miyazaki Station, it's considered part of Miyazaki city. There's a small shrine on the island, and the beaches nearby are the most popular among the people of Miyazaki for swimming. It seems everything in Japan has its own special season, and the season for swimming here is July and August.

If you follow the coast from Aoshima farther south, you'll come to **Nichinan Coast,** famous for its eroded, rippling waves of rock, which resemble a washboard. There's a local bus from Miyazaki that travels along this beautiful coastline (and passes through Aoshima), going all the way to Udo in about 1½ hours (the name of the bus stop is "Udo"). Here you'll find **Udo Shrine,** located about a 15-minute walk from the bus stop. Dedicated to the father of Emperor Jimmu, this vermillion-colored shrine is actually located in a cave beside the ocean, and the view, in my opinion, is exhilarating. Udo Shrine is famous among young couples who come here to pray for success and harmony in marriage. Up until 60 years ago, the trek to the shrine was not so easy, requiring climbs over mountain passes and along beaches. At any rate, behind the shrine are cave formations thought to resemble breasts, and milk candy is a specialty of the shops near the shrine.

FOOD AND LODGING

The most relaxing and luxurious places to stay in Miyazaki are Sun Hotel Phoenix and Seaside Hotel Phoenix, located side by side about a 15-minute taxi ride from Miyazaki Station at 3083 Hamayama Shioji. Under the same ownership, both of the hotels are isolated, surrounded by many acres of land and by the sea. Facilities include tennis courts, bowling lanes, a zoo, a children's playground, an outdoor swimming pool (open in summer only), a golf course, and a public bath. The 27-hole golf course is famous in Japan and is much cheaper than courses near Tokyo. Greens fees including tax and caddy are ¥20,000 ($160) on weekdays, ¥24,000 ($192) on Saturday, and ¥26,000 ($208) on Sunday. Club rentals are about ¥2,000 ($16). The hotel has a much cheaper course in the mountains, where weekday fees including caddies are ¥9,600 ($76.80). Next to the hotel complex is a wonderful area of woods and ponds, and bicycles are available for rent.

Built about 15 years ago, the **Sun Hotel Phoenix** (tel. 0985/39-3131) is the more expensive of the two hotels, with rates per person beginning at ¥17,500 ($140) per person including buffet-style breakfast and dinner, tax, and service. Room-only rates are also available, beginning at ¥17,500 ($140) for two persons in the Western-style rooms and ¥21,000 ($168) for two in the Japanese-style rooms. Higher prices are charged for rooms facing the sea. Western-style rooms are roomy, with bedside reading lamps, a hairdryer, stocked fridge, clock, radio, and kimono.

The Sun Hotel Phoenix's **Restaurant Ski Blue,** up on the ninth floor, has unobstructed views of the Pacific, pine woods, and the golf course below. Open from 11 a.m. to 3 p.m. and 5 to 10 p.m., it offers lunch courses starting at ¥2,000 ($16) and dinner courses from ¥3,300 ($26.40) for steaks or seafood. The à la carte menu includes gratin, sandwiches, seafood, stewed beef, pilaf, curry, and spaghetti. The hotel's Japanese restaurant on the second floor features seafood and sashimi, with teishoku beginning at ¥3,300 ($26.40).

Two years older is **Seaside Hotel Phoenix** (tel. 0985/39-1111), with both Western and Japanese rooms. Rates including two meals, tax, and service begin at ¥16,500 ($132). Rooms without meals start at ¥8,800 ($70.40) for a single and ¥11,000 ($88) for a double, while Japanese rooms start at ¥14,300 ($114).

Also under the same ownership, but in town, is the **Hotel Phoenix,** 2-1-1 Matsuyama (tel. 0985/23-6111), located right beside the Oyodo River about a seven-minute taxi ride from Miyazaki Station. Its Western-style rooms begin at ¥7,700 ($62) for a single and ¥11,500 ($92) for a double, while Japanese-style rooms start at ¥13,200 ($106) for two. Rooms that face the river cost slightly more. There's a small outdoor pool open in July and August, which is unfortunately located right outside the lobby's window, so there's no hiding those extra pounds. A beer garden on the roof, open from June to September 15 from 5:30 to 9 p.m., has a great view of the river, city, and the hills beyond. Beer starts at ¥600 ($4.80).

If you're looking for a business hotel, the **Miyazaki Oriental Hotel,** 2-10-22 Hiroshima (tel. 0985/27-3111), is just a two-minute walk from Miyazaki Station. Built in 1975, its rooms are a bit old but are reasonable at ¥5,000 ($40) for a single, ¥8,000 ($64) and ¥9,000 ($72) for a twin. Ninety of its 104 rooms are single, and rates with meals are also available. There's someone at the front desk who speaks English, and the hotel's one restaurant serves Chinese food. Single rooms come with stocked fridge, hairdryer, a pants-presser, and clock, while some of the twins have a separate toilet and shower area.

If you're a sun worshipper, you may want to stay at the **Aoshima Kokumin Shukusha** ⑬, located at 2-12-36 Aoshima (tel. 0985/65-1533) right next to the tiny island. All of its rooms face the ocean, and the beach for swimming is only a five-minute walk away. All of its 45 Japanese-style rooms (5 of which have private bathrooms) have balconies, but its 8 Western-style rooms do not. Popular with Japanese families, this kokumin shukusha is heavily booked during New Year's, Golden Week in May, and July and August, so book ahead if you plan to travel during these times. Rates per person begin at ¥3,500 ($28) for Japanese rooms without bathroom and ¥5,000 ($40) for Japanese rooms with bath and for Western rooms. Breakfasts are ¥750 ($6), while suppers begin at ¥1,600 ($12.80). Aoshima can be reached in about 25 minutes by train from Miyazaki Station, after which it's about a three-minute walk.

More Dining

Miyazaki's subtropical climate is conducive to the growth of a number of vegetables and fruits, including sweet pumpkins, oranges, cucumbers, green peppers, shiitake mushrooms, and chestnuts. Especially popular is shochu, made from sweet potatoes, buckwheat, or corn. Both of the restaurants listed below specialize in dishes made with locally grown vegetables, fruit, and other produce, used imaginatively in unique creations by their own chefs. They are located close together just off Tachibana-dori Street near the prefecture tourist office, about a 15-minute walk from JR Miyazaki Station.

Although the stairwell doesn't look like much as you walk down into the basement of the Shokokaikan Building, **Gyosantei** ㉞, Higashi 1-chome (tel. 24-7070), is an attractive restaurant with wooden floors, tatami mats, leg wells under the tables, and waitresses dressed in kimonos. Notice the two little mounds of salt on either side of the restaurant's door—they symbolize purification. Just as in the olden days, there's a split length of bamboo inside the leg well on which to rest your stockinged feet, and the menu is written on a scroll. I suggest you order one of the courses featuring local food, which range from ¥3,800 ($30.40) to ¥7,500 ($60). The *Himukazen* course, for example, which means "facing the sun," changes according to what's in season and what the cook decides to create, but it always includes as its main course a pumpkin filled with chicken and radish and topped with hard-boiled egg yolk, with a raw yolk plopped on top (which nevertheless slowly cooks from the heat)—meant to resemble the sun. Side dishes might include salmon rolled inside Japanese radish, raw flying fish served with freshly grated wasabi (horseradish), fried prawn with dried mushrooms used as a coating instead of flour, or Miyazaki melon. It's truly a restaurant of culinary surprises, making dining here a pleasure and an experience. It's open from 11:30 a.m. to 2 p.m. and from 5 to 10 p.m.; closed Sunday.

Not far away is **Sugi no Ko** ㉟, Tachibana-dori 2-1-4 (tel. 22-5798), located up on the third floor. The owner of this restaurant creates all his own dishes and has even produced a book with his recipes. The dining area displays haniwa dolls and other crafts of Miyazaki Prefecture, and there are also private tatami rooms. The menu is written in Japanese only, and lists lunch teishoku for ¥1,000 ($8) to ¥2,200 ($17.60) and dinner courses from ¥3,800 ($30.40) to ¥10,000 ($80). The lunch Miyazaki Gyuu Teishoku, for example, comes with Miyazaki beef seasoned with soy sauce and served with four different sauces, vegetables, soup, rice, and fruit. One of the side dishes featured during my visit was delicate tofu filled with pungent mustard. Sugi no Ko is open from 11:30 a.m. to 2 p.m. and 4 to 11 p.m.; closed every Sunday.

NORTHERN JAPAN

Because so many of Japan's historical events took place in Kyoto, Tokyo, and other cities in southern Honshu, most tourists to Japan never venture farther north than Tokyo. True, northern Japan does not have the temples, shrines, gardens, and castles of southern Japan. It does have spectacular scenery, however. Matsushima, about three hours north of Tokyo, is considered one of Japan's most scenic spots, with pine-covered islets dotting its bay. Farther north is Hokkaido, the northernmost of Japan's four main islands.

HOKKAIDO

Hokkaido's landscape is strikingly different from any other place in Japan. With more than 30,000 square miles, Hokkaido makes up about 21% of Japan's total land mass and yet it has only 5% of Japan's population. In other words, Hokkaido has what the rest of Japan doesn't, and that's space. Considered Japan's last frontier, Hokkaido didn't begin opening up to development until after the Meiji Restoration in 1868, when the government began encouraging Japanese to migrate to the island. Even today Hokkaido has a frontier feel to it, attracting lots of young Japanese who come here to backpack, ski, camp, and tour across the countryside on motorcycles or bicycles. There are dairy farms and silos and broad fields of flat land clothed in wheat, corn, potatoes, and rice. Then the land puckers up to craggy and bare volcanoes, gorges, and hills densely covered with trees. There are clear spring lakes, mountain ranges, rugged wilderness, wild animals, and rare plants. About 7% of Hokkaido is preserved as national and prefectural parks. An English photographer I know who has lived in Japan for six years and traveled the length and breadth of the country says that Hokkaido is her favorite place in all of Japan.

With winters that are long, cold, and severe, Hokkaido has its main tourist season in August, when days are cool and pleasant with an average temperature of 70°F. And while the rest of the nation is under the deluge of the rainy season, Hokkaido's summers are usually bright and clear. However, even winter is not an idle time in Hokkaido. Ski enthusiasts flock to slopes near Sapporo and to resorts such as Daisetzusan National Park. And February marks the annual Sapporo Snow Festival, with its huge ice and snow sculptures.

As for the people of Hokkaido, they are considered to be as open and hearty as the wide expanse of land around them. Hokkaido is also home of the Ainu, the native inhabitants of the island. Not much is known about their origins, but the Ainu arrived in Hokkaido approximately 800 years ago. It's not even clear whether they're Asian or Caucasian, but at any rate they're of different racial stock than the Japanese. They are round-eyed and light-skinned, and Ainu males can grow thick beards and mustaches. Traditionally the Ainu lived as hunters and fishermen, but after Hokkaido opened up to development they were gradually assimilated into Japanese society, taking Japanese names and adopting the Japanese language and clothing. Like American Indians, they were often discriminated against and their culture was largely destroyed. Today there are an estimated 15,000 Ainu still living in Hokkaido. Some of them earn their living from tourism, selling Ainu woodcarvings and other crafts, and performing traditional dances and songs.

TRAVELING AROUND HOKKAIDO

Getting around Hokkaido is by train and bus. In addition to regular bus lines, there are also sightseeing buses linking national parks and major attractions. Although they are more expensive than trains and regular buses, they offer unparalleled views of the countryside. Keep in mind that bus schedules fluctuate with the seasons, as some lines cease operations altogether during the snowy winter months.

If you plan to do a lot of traveling in Hokkaido and you are not traveling by Japan Railpass, you can purchase a special pass issued by Japan Railways that allows unlimited travel on its trains and buses in Hokkaido. The pass can be purchased in Japan, and there are several options available. A 20-day Hokkaido JR Pass, for example, costs ¥43,000 ($344) and includes a round-trip ticket from the place of departure (say, Tokyo) to Hokkaido. A 5-day pass costs ¥14,500 ($116) and a 10-day pass costs ¥23,000 ($184). These allow 20% discounts on round-trip tickets from the place of departure to Hokkaido.

Because distances are long and traffic is rather light, Hokkaido is one of the few places in Japan where driving your own car is actually recommended. Because it's expensive, however, it's economical only if there are several of you. The rate for three days of car rental generally starts at about ¥18,000 ($144) for the first 260 miles. After that it's about ¥20 (16¢) per kilometer. Car-rental agencies are found throughout Hokkaido as well as at Chitose Airport outside Sapporo.

Incidentally, travel to Hokkaido by land is generally via Shinkansen bullet train from Tokyo to Morioka, followed by limited express from Morioka to Aomori on the northern tip of Honshu island. For centuries the only way to continue from Aomori to Hokkaido was by boat, but the opening of the Seikan Tunnel (April 1988) now allows the entire trip to be made by train. Whereas the ferry ride to Hakodate, on Hokkaido, used to take four hours, the train ride by tunnel takes less than three —45 minutes of which is in the tunnel. At any rate, the entire trip from Tokyo to Hakodate via train should take about eight hours. The fastest way to reach Hokkaido, of course, is to fly.

1. Matsushima

Because the trip to Hokkaido is such a long one, the most pleasant way to travel is to break up the journey with an overnight stay in Matsushima in northern Honshu. Matsushima means "Pine-clad Islands," and that's exactly what this region is. More than 200 pine-covered islets and islands dot Matsushima Bay, giving it the appearance of a giant pond in a Japanese landscape garden. Twisted and gnarled pines sweep upward from volcanic tuff and white sandstone, creating a wonderland of bizarre and beautiful shapes. Matsushima is so dear to Japanese hearts that it is considered one of the three most scenic spots in Japan (the other two are Miyajima in Hiroshima Bay and Amanohashidate on the north coast of Honshu). Basho (1644–1694), the famous Japanese haiku poet, was so struck by Matsushima's beauty that it's almost as though he were at a loss for words when he wrote: "Matsushima, Ah! Matsushima! Matsushima!"

I have no doubt that Matsushima was indeed awesomely and strikingly beautiful during Basho's time, as well as during the time it was selected as one of Japan's three most scenic spots about 270 years ago in a book written by a Confucian philosopher of the Edo government. But motorboats have been invented since then, and although they offer the closest view of the islands, all those boats plying the water somehow detract from the mood that evoked such ecstasy in Basho long ago. Still, Matsushima itself is a pleasant small town on the waters of Matsushima Bay and makes a worthwhile stop if you're on your way north to Hokkaido.

ORIENTATION

Before leaving Tokyo, be sure to pick up from the T.I.C. a sheet called *Sendai, Matsushima, and Hiraizumi*. It has a map of Matsushima Bay and tells of attractions in and around Matsushima. From Tokyo you can take the Tohoku Shinkansen from Ueno Station to Sendai, which will take from 2 to 2½ hours, depending on the number of stops your train makes. In Sendai, change to the JR Senseki Line—it's well marked in English, so you shouldn't have any difficulty changing trains in Sendai. It takes about 25 minutes by express train to reach Matsushima Kaigan Station, which is where you disembark. You can also arrive in Matsushima by boat (described in the sightseeing section below).

Once in Matsushima, stop off at one of the **Matsushima Tourist Association Offices,** located at both Matsushima Kaigan train station and at Matsushima Kaigan Pier (tel. 022/354-2618). You can pick up a brochure with a map in English and get directions to your hotel. Hours for both are 8:30 a.m. to 5 p.m. daily. The train station and pier are about a ten-minute walk apart. As for Matsushima itself, all its major attractions are within walking distance of both the train station and the pier. You can cover the whole area on foot in half a day of leisurely sightseeing.

The **telephone area code** for both Matsushima and Sendai is 022, and both are located in Miyagi Prefecture.

WHAT TO SEE

Your sightseeing trip around Matsushima can begin even before you reach your destination. A popular way to get to Matsushima is to take the Senseki Line from Sendai only as far as Hon-Shiogama (about 18 minutes by express). From there you can catch a **sightseeing boat** to Matsushima Kaigan Pier. Passing pine-covered islands and oyster rafts along the way, it's a good introduction to the bay and costs ¥1,500 ($12) for the one-hour trip. Unfortunately, the commentary is in Japanese only (a good time to break out the Walkman unless you've become oblivious to noise by now). And believe it or not, a couple of the boats have been disguised as either a peacock or a dragon. Boats leave from both Hon-Shiogama and Matsushima Kaigan piers about every half hour between 8 a.m. and 4 p.m. in summer, but only once an hour in winter. If you're going in the off-season, be sure to check the schedule (tel. 022/362-2431).

Even if you don't arrive by boat, you might still want to take a boat trip in the bay (if you can't beat 'em, join 'em, right?). Regular sightseeing boats make 40-minute trips around the bay and back and charge ¥1,500 ($12) per person. You can also charter smaller motorboats—which, judging by the number of them leaving the pier every few minutes, seems to be the most popular way to see Matsushima. Charter motorboats cost ¥4,500 ($36) for a tour lasting 20 minutes, ¥11,000 ($88) for 60 minutes, and ¥16,500 ($132) for two hours. You can see more of the islands on these smaller craft than you can on the regular sightseeing boats.

In addition to the boat trips, there are four spots spread around Matsushima Bay historically considered the best for viewing Matsushima's islands. These spots are called Otakamori, Tomiyama, Tamonzan, and Ogidani. The closest is **Ogidani,** a ten-minute taxi ride away from the pier. However, I personally don't think it's worth the time or effort to make it to each of these four lookouts. You can get as much a feel for Matsushima's beauty simply by visiting the more easily accessible attractions listed below. If you feel like hiking to a lookout, **Sokanzan Lookout** is about a 30-minute walk from Matsushima Kaigan Pier and offers a panoramic view of the region.

Matsushima's best-known structure is **Zuiganji Temple** ⑯, the most famous Zen temple in the northern part of Japan. Located right in front of Matsushima Kaigan Pier just a few minutes' walk away, its entrance is shaded by tall cedar trees. On the right side of the pathway leading to the temple are caves and grottoes dug out by priests long ago. Adorned with Buddhist statues and memorial tablets, they were used for practicing zazen (sitting meditation). Zuiganji Temple was founded in 1606 by the order of Masamune Date, the most powerful and important lord of northern Honshu. Unifying the region known as Tohoku, Date built his castle in nearby Sendai and today almost all sites in and around Sendai and Matsushima are tied to the Date family. At any rate, it took hundreds of workers six years to build the temple, which was constructed in the *shoin-zukuri* style typical of the Momoyama Period. The temple served as the family temple of the Date clan.

An adjoining treasure hall, the **Seiryuden,** displays items belonging to the temple and the Date family, while the main hall contains elaborately carved wooden doors, transoms, and painted sliding doors—and this is one of the few temples that still allows flash photography (in its outer corridor). Admission is ¥500 ($4) and hours vary according to the season. The longest hours are from April to mid-September, when it's open from 7:30 a.m. to 5 p.m. In winter, hours are reduced to 8 a.m. to 3:30 or 4 p.m.

Next to Zuiganji Temple (to the left if you're facing Zuiganji) is **Entsuin** ⑰, a lesser-known temple also built more than 300 years ago by the Date clan. Open from 8 a.m. to 5 p.m. throughout the year and charging a ¥300 ($2.40) admission, it features a small rock garden, a beautiful rose garden, and a small temple housing an elaborate statue of Lord Mitsumune Date, grandson of Lord Masamune Date who founded the Sendai fief. Depicted here on horseback, Mitsumune was reportedly poisoned and died at the tender age of 19. The statues surrounding him represent retainers who committed ritual suicide to follow their master into death. At any rate, the statues and small temple are located at the back of the temple grounds, past the rose garden. Tour groups seem to bypass this temple, making it a peaceful retreat away from the crowds that sometimes descend on Matsushima.

Under the supervision of Zuiganji Temple is **Godaido,** a small wooden worship hall on a tiny island not far from the pier. Connected to the mainland by a short bridge, it's open night and day and is free, but there's not much to see. The interior is closed to the public, open only every 33 years. (It won't be open again until August 20, 2006.) Godaido is often featured in brochures of Matsushima, making this delicate wooden temple one of the town's best-known landmarks.

Kanrantei, the "Water-Viewing Pavilion," is just a short walk from the pier. A simple wooden tea house, it was used by generations of the Date family for such aesthetic pursuits as viewing the moon and watching the ripples on the tide. Originally it belonged to warlord Hideyoshi Toyotomi as part of his estate at Fushimi Castle near Kyoto, but he presented it to the Date family at the end of the 16th century. Kanrantei is open from 8 a.m. to 5 p.m. The entrance fee is ¥200 ($1.60). For an additional ¥300 ($2.40) you can drink ceremonial green tea while seated upon the tatami of the tea house and contemplating the bay, its islands, and the boats carving ribbons through the water. After drinking your tea, wander through the small museum, which contains artifacts belonging to the Date family. I found particularly interesting a screen painted long ago showing Matsushima—even then there were boats winding between the islands. Realizing how quaint those wooden boats powered by men in straw hats look to us now, it occurred to me that the Matsushima of today with its motorboats may one day look quaint and old-fashioned to generations hence.

Just a couple of minutes beyond Kanrantei on the southern edge of Matsushima is **Oshima,** a small island once used as a retreat by priests. At one time there used to be many caves with carvings of scriptures, Buddhist images, and sutras, but today the island and its remaining stone images and structures are rather neglected and forgotten. There's no fee, no gate, and the island never closes. It's a nice quiet spot to sit and view the harbor. While you're sitting here, think about the fact that because it was a Buddhist retreat, women were forbidden to enter Oshima until after the Meiji Restoration in 1868. Think also about the fact that if a place like this were left unguarded in America, it would have long ago been vandalized.

Next to Oshima is an aquarium called **Marine Pier** ㉘, open from 9 a.m. to 5 p.m. and charging ¥1,100 ($8.80) for adults and ¥550 ($4.40) for children (tel. 354-2020). Although rather small, it has a variety of freshwater and saltwater fish and animals, including penguins, turtles, crocodiles, octopi, sea otters, moray eels, and ocean sunfish. This place appeals mainly to kids, and with them in mind there are also such attractions as a miniature train, carousel, and monorail.

At the other end of Matsushima is **Fukuurajima,** another island connected to the mainland, this time by a long red concrete bridge with orange-colored railings. It's a botanical garden of sorts, with several hundred labeled plants and trees, but mostly it's unkempt and overgrown—which comes as a surprise in cultivated Japan. It takes less than an hour to walk completely around the island. Between the hours of 8 a.m. and 6 p.m. (4 p.m. in winter) you must pay ¥100 (80¢) admittance; after hours you can enter for free.

As for destinations outside Matsushima, if you have time you may want to visit **Kinkazan Island,** accessible in about two hours by ferry from Ishinomaki. Kinkazan is small with a pyramid-shaped mountain on it and has woods inhabited by deer and monkeys. A shrine called Koganeyama is located halfway up the mountain.

FOOD AND LODGING

Because this is a tourist town, accommodations in Matsushima are not cheap, especially during the peak months of May through November. During the Tanabata Festival, held August 6 to 8 in Sendai, and the Toronagashi Festival, held August 15 and 16 in Matsushima, rooms are usually fully booked a half year in advance. Rates are generally cheaper during the off-season months (from December through April). Almost all accommodations here are in ryokan, which means you're generally expected to take your dinner and breakfast at the ryokan. Unless otherwise stated, all prices quoted below include two meals. Because Matsushima tends to be expensive, I've included some budget accommodations in nearby Sendai at the end of this section.

In Matsushima

Accommodating 1,500 people, **Taikanso** ㉙, 10-76 Aza Inuta (tel. 022/354-2161), sprawls atop a plateau surrounded by pine-covered hills and offers the best view in town. Even its public baths overlook the island-studded bay, so you can wash contemplating the beauty of Matsushima. The hotel, located 5 minutes by taxi or 15 minutes on foot from Matsushima Kaigan Station, has a nightclub with floor shows nightly and an outdoor swimming pool. Both Western- and Japanese-style rooms are available, most with private bathroom. Pleasantly bright, they come with fridge, TV with pay video, and a safe for valuables. Rates vary according to the season and whether your room faces the sea or the wooded mountains (which are also quite nice), has tatami or beds. Rates during the tourist season (May through November) start at ¥20,000 ($160) for Japanese-style rooms (all of which face the sea); Western-style twins start at ¥16,500 ($132) for those facing the mountains and ¥18,500 ($148) for those with views of the sea. Combination-style rooms with both beds and tatami areas start at ¥16,500 ($132). On Saturday night and evenings just before public holidays during peak season, you should expect to spend about ¥3,000 ($24) more than the rates quoted above. During off-season months, however, prices are ¥3,000 ($24) less than the quoted rates. Prices are per person and include two meals.

Restaurants in Taikanso include a noodle shop with noodle dishes starting at ¥700 ($5.60), a Japanese seafood restaurant serving sashimi and tempura ranging in price from about ¥1,000 ($8) to ¥2,200 ($17.60), and a Western restaurant, called **Shiosai,** on the seventh floor with fine views of both Matsushima Bay and the surrounding pine-covered hills. In fact, the view from here is probably the best in town and is worth the 30-minute walk from Matsushima's pier. The food itself is nothing to write home about but is reasonably priced, with entrées of curry, pilaf, spaghetti, and seafood and Japanese dishes priced at less than ¥2,000 ($16). Steak and lobster dinners start at ¥6,500 ($52), while a daily lunch special is available for ¥1,600 ($12.80). Hours are 11 a.m. to 9 p.m.

Matsushima Century Hotel, 9 Aza Senzui (tel. 022/354-4111), is a glittering white hotel that opened on the shore of Matsushima in 1984. A cool oasis in the middle of town with a convenient location between the pier and Fukuurajima Island, it's a sleek hotel appealing especially to the young. Its **karaoke bar** (where people sing to the taped instrumental music to a variety of songs) charges a ¥2,700 ($21.60) cover, which includes one free drink. Another plus of this hotel is its outdoor swimming pool, and its modern and beautiful public baths and sauna, all of which overlook the bay.

A Note on Japanese Symbols

Many hotels, restaurants, and other establishments in Japan do not have signs showing their names in English letters. Appendix II lists the Japanese symbols for all such places appearing in this guide. Each establishment name in Japanese symbols is numbered, and the same number appears in an oval in the text following the boldfaced establishment name. For example, in the text Osaka's **Hotel Hokke Club** ⑯⑭, is number 164 in the Japanese symbol list in Appendix II.

The rooms here are sunny and cheerful and decorated in pastels and white. The Japanese-style rooms, all of which face the bay and have balconies, cost ¥22,000 ($176) per person with two meals during tourist season and ¥16,500 ($132) during the winter months. Western-style rooms, which face only inland and have no balconies, are very reasonable. Prices for these rooms do not include meals and run ¥6,000 ($48) for a single and ¥11,000 ($88) to ¥14,000 ($112) for a twin all year round.

The Century Hotel is also a good place to come for lunch or dinner at **La Saison.** Open from 11 a.m. to 1:30 p.m. and from 5 to 8:30 p.m., this Western seafood restaurant is decorated with white latticed wood and ferns. You can order such dishes as sole, fried shrimp, scallops, steak, and beef Stroganoff à la carte, but especially good are the set lunch courses starting at ¥1,300 ($10.40).

Hotel Sohkan, Isozaki, Aza Hama 1-1 (tel. 022/354-2181), is a modern and comfortable ryokan located on the edge of Matsushima about a five-minute taxi ride from the pier. Catering mainly to Japanese groups, it offers a koto concert in the early evening in its lobby, played by a woman in a traditional kimono. Facilities include public baths, a couple of golf holes for practice or beginners, and a 210-foot-high tower from which for ¥350 ($2.80) you can have a view over all of Matsushima. Its bar is a fun place to watch the Japanese enjoying themselves—there's even karaoke here, in which people from the audience stand up and sing while accompanied by taped instrumental music to a variety of songs. There are a total of 76 rooms, all with private bathroom. Two of the rooms are Western style, can sleep four people, and even have bilingual TV. Rates per person at this ryokan range from ¥14,000 ($112) to ¥22,000 ($176) during peak season and ¥11,000 ($88) to ¥16,500 ($132) during the off-season. You have your choice of Japanese or Western breakfast and dinner.

If you want to stay in an old-fashioned ryokan, the best choice in town is the **Matsushima Kanko Hotel** ⑳, near Matsushima Kaigan Pier (tel. 022/354-2121), popularly called Matsushima-jo, which means Matsushima Castle. Indeed, as Matsushima's oldest ryokan (built about 100 years ago), it does rather resemble a castle with its sloping tiled roof, white walls, and red railings. Inside it's airy and delightful, with old wooden banisters polished from decades of human hands. Its walls are decorated with woodblock prints by the famous artist Hiroshige, as well as photographs of stern-faced Japanese who have stayed here in the past. Because the building was built before the advent of modern plumbing, only eight of the 28 rooms have bathrooms, and the communal toilets are Japanese style. Keep in mind also that rooms come only with fans, not air conditioning, and tend to be drafty in winter. However, rooms do have a sink, coin-operated TV, and fridge, and those on the third floor are high enough to see over the rooftops to the water beyond. It has a convenient location directly behind Godaido worship hall just a minute from Matsushima Kaigan Pier. Rates throughout the year range from ¥8,800 ($70.40) to ¥27,000 ($216) per person with two meals. Off-season you can also stay here without taking meals, in which case rates begin at only ¥6,500 ($52) per person. The public bath is unique: it mixes underground salt water with tap water. Western breakfasts are served on request.

Konnoya ㉑, 38-1 Fugendo (tel. 022/354-3006), is a moderately priced, clean, modern ryokan about a 5-minute walk inland from the pier and a 15-minute walk from Matsushima Kaigan train station. All 26 rooms are Japanese style and come with a safe for valuables, telephone, coin-operated TV, and refrigerator. Per-person rates with two meals are ¥14,000 ($112) for rooms with private bathroom and ¥13,000 ($104) for those without. During winter, rates are ¥2,000 ($16) less.

Ryokan Kozakura ㉒, near Matsushima Kaigan Pier on the town's main street (tel. 022/354-2518), is a simple concrete Japanese-style inn with inexpensive rooms. About a ten-minute walk from the train station, it has a total of 12 tatami rooms, some with their own private bathroom that go for ¥11,000 ($88) per person including two meals; rooms without their own bathroom are ¥6,500 ($52). If you want to take your meals elsewhere, you can stay here for as little as ¥3,800 ($30.40) per person. In summer months and on Saturday night, rates increase by ¥2,000 ($16). Rooms are simple but come with TV, air conditioner, heater and refrigerator, and meals are served in your own room.

The **Matsushima Youth Hostel** ㉓ is located not in Matsushima itself but on Miyato Island, Narusei-cho (tel. 0225/88-2220). From Matsushima Kaigan Station take the Senseki Line 15 minutes to Nobiru Station. From there it's about a 15-minute walk. The hostel sleeps on the average eight persons per room in bunk beds. Members pay ¥2,000 ($16), while nonmembers pay ¥700 ($5.60) more. Breakfast costs ¥450 ($3.60) and dinner is ¥700 ($5.60).

Since all ryokan serve breakfast and dinner, the only meal you probably have to think about is lunch. There are several restaurants in Matsushima and you shouldn't have any trouble locating one. If you want a specific recommendation, however, **Okunohosomichi** ㉔, Zuiganji Tenrin-in (tel. 354-5806), is a small and attractive restaurant located on a street running behind Kanrantei not far from Tenrin-in Temple. The menu is in Japanese only, but includes sashimi, sushi, fried shrimp, fried oysters (winter only), obento, various fish, and eel. Most teishoku range from about ¥1,650 ($13.20) to ¥3,000 ($24). Hours are 11 a.m. to 9 p.m.; closed the first and third Wednesdays of the month except during summer, when it remains open throughout the week. A convenient place for a light, inexpensive lunch is **Donjiki Chaya** ㉕, located right across the street from Entsuin Temple (tel. 354-5855). Easy to spot because of its thatched roof, it was built about 300 years ago and offers tatami seating and sliding doors pushed wide open in the summertime. It serves noodles beginning at ¥300 ($2.40) as well as its specialty of *odango,* which are pounded rice balls covered with sesame, red-bean, or soy sauce. Open daily in the summer from 9:30 a.m. to 5 p.m., in the winter it's open only on weekends and holidays.

In Sendai

Although Matsushima is where most of the attractions are, because it's a resort area it may be too expensive for your budget. In that case the most convenient alternative would be to spend the night in Sendai and make a day trip to Matsushima, only 25 minutes away. There are two inexpensive ryokan close to Sendai Station, which offer basically the same facilities of tatami rooms at moderate prices, coin-operated TV, and public baths. Members of the Japanese Inn Group, both are happy to receive foreigners. Rates are for room charge only and do *not* include meals.

A five-minute walk from the station is **Isuzu Ryokan,** 1-148 Kakyoin (tel. 022/222-6430), which has nine Japanese-style rooms. Rates here start at ¥3,300 ($26.40) for a single, ¥6,000 ($48) for a twin, and ¥8,000 ($64) for a triple. The ryokan will also serve a tempura or sukiyaki dinner for ¥1,650 ($13.20). **Japanese Inn Aisaki,** 5-6 Kitame-machi (tel. 022/264-0700), is a ten-minute walk from the station behind the Sendai Central Post Office. It has both Japanese- and Western-style rooms, starting at ¥3,800 ($30.40) for a single and ¥7,000 ($56) for a twin.

There are also four youth hostels in Sendai: **Sendai Chitose Youth Hostel,** 6-3-8 Odawawra (tel. 022/222-6329), 10 minutes by bus from Sendai Station and then 3 minutes on foot; **Youth Hostel Sendai Akamon,** 61 Kawauchi-Kawamae-cho (tel. 022/264-1405), 15 minutes by bus from Sendai Station and then a 5-minute walk; **Sendai Onai Youth Hostel,** 1-9-35 Kashiwagi (tel. 022/234-3922), 15 minutes by bus and 2 minutes on foot; and **Sendai-Dochuan Youth Hostel,** 31 Kitayashiki, Onoda (tel. 022/247-0511), 12 minutes by subway from the station and 8 minutes on foot. Count on spending about ¥3,300 ($26.40) per person per night, including two meals. Nonmembers pay ¥700 ($5.60) more.

HOKKAIDO

The southern gateway to Hokkaido, Hakodate is about as far as you can get in one day if you're arriving in Hokkaido from Tokyo by train. Not a destination in and of itself, Hakodate makes a good one-night stopover because it has one nighttime attraction and one early-morning attraction, which means that you can easily see a little of the city before setting out to your next destination.

2. Hakodate

ORIENTATION

Connected by rail to northern Honshu with the completion of the Seikan Tunnel in the spring of 1988, Hakodate can be reached in less than nine hours by train from Tokyo and about four hours by train from Sapporo, Hokkaido's largest town. The **Hakodate tourist office** (tel. 0138/23-5440) is just to the right after you exit from the Hakodate train station. Open from 9 a.m. to 7 p.m. (to 5 p.m. in winter), the tourist office has information and an excellent map of Hakodate written in English. Before leaving Tokyo or Kyoto, be sure to pick up a flyer called *Southern Hokkaido.* Its strolling tours include Hakodate's old Western-looking buildings constructed back in the days when the town first opened as an international port.

The **telephone area code** for Hakodate is 0138.

THE SIGHTS

Hakodate is probably most famous for its night view from atop **Mount Hakodate,** which rises 1,100 feet just 1¾ miles southwest of Hakodate Station. Few vacationing Japanese spend the night in Hakodate without taking the cable car to the top of this lava cone, which was formed by the eruption of an undersea volcano. From the peak, the lights of Hakodate shimmer and glitter like jewels spilled on black velvet. You can reach the foot of Mount Hakodate via streetcar from Hakodate Station. The name of the stop is Jyujigai, and it's a five-minute trip from the station. From there you can take the cable car to the top for ¥1,200 ($9.60) round trip. From mid-April to mid-October it runs every 10 minutes from 9 a.m. to 10 p.m., with shorter hours during the cold winter season. On the peak is an informal restaurant where you can indulge in a drink or snack while admiring the spectacular view, as well as the usual souvenir shops.

The next morning you can get up and visit the **morning market** before taking the train out of town. The market spreads out just south of the train station every morning except Sunday from about 5 a.m. to noon. Walk around and look at the variety of food for sale, especially the hairy crabs for which Hokkaido is famous.

If you have more time on your hands and are interested in renovated buildings dating from before the turn of the century, continue walking from the morning market in the direction of Mount Hakodate until you come to a group of brick warehouses that have been converted into shops and restaurants (refer to the food and lodging section for more information on dining). In succession you'll find Union Square, Bay Hakodate, and History Plaza, all well done with exposed beams and original walls. I'm ecstatic to see this revitalization of Hakodate's waterfront, since all too often old buildings in Japan are simply torn down.

And finally, if you have some extra time, you might consider a one-hour boat trip around the harbor. Hakodate, along with Nagasaki, Kobe, and Yokohama, was one of the first ports open to foreigners in 1859. Boats leave three times a day from the end of April to the end of October and cost ¥1,340 ($10.72). At last check, boats left at 11 a.m., 1 p.m., and 3 p.m., but contact the tourist office to confirm this.

FOOD AND LODGING

Because it's not a major tourist destination, Hakodate does not have a lot in the way of accommodations. Most of its hotels are near the train station.

The Top Choices

Although located in a part of town full of junkyards and roads with potholes, the **Hakodate Kokusai Hotel,** 5-10 Otemachi (tel. 0138/23-8751), is the city's most expensive hotel. About a five-minute walk from the station close to the water's edge, it has both Japanese- and Western-style rooms that are a good value for the money. Singles range from ¥8,200 ($66) to ¥12,000 ($96), twins run ¥15,500 ($124) to ¥22,000 ($176), and doubles cost ¥17,600 ($141) to ¥22,000 ($176). Tatami rooms range from ¥13,200 ($106) to ¥18,700 ($150). All rooms come with their own bathroom, TV, clock, radio, and refrigerator. This is also one of the few hotels to have air conditioning (most hotels in Hokkaido forgo air conditioners because it's hot only one month of the year). The most expensive twins and doubles are deluxe rooms facing the busy harbor, are larger in size than standard rooms, and offer semidouble-size beds in the twin rooms.

On the eighth floor of the Kokusai Hotel are both a Japanese and a Western restaurant, both with good views of the harbor. **Matsumae,** open from 11:30 a.m. to 9:30 p.m. (last order), is a Japanese seafood restaurant offering a variety of dishes from sashimi to tempura to broiled flatfish and squid, with à la carte prices starting at about ¥900 ($7.20). There are also lots of Hokkaido specialties, such as spring salmon, crab, and shrimp. In any case, there's an English menu, so you shouldn't have any difficulty ordering. Special lunch teishoku, served until 2 p.m., range from about ¥750 ($6) to ¥1,600 ($12.80) and may include tempura or sashimi in addition to side dishes. Set dinners start at ¥1,600 ($12.80).

If you feel like eating Western food, try the hotel's **Vue Mer,** which also has a great view and an extensive wine and cocktail menu. In fact, it's the perfect place to come for a late dinner because it's open from 5 p.m. to 12:30 a.m. (last order). You might want to come here after an evening stroll atop Mount Hakodate. Its à la carte menu lists seafood, steaks, and pastas ranging from ¥1,000 ($8) to ¥3,300 ($26.40). Set dinner courses start at ¥3,300 ($26.40).

One of Hakodate's newest hotels, **Harborview Hotel,** 14-10 Wakamatsu-cho (tel. 0138/22-0111), is the tall brick building located just to the right as you exit from Hakodate Station. Despite its name, none of its 190 rooms squarely face the harbor, though those closest to the waterfront do afford views of the water. Rooms are small but pleasant, complete with refrigerator, TV, thermos water and tea, and tiled bathroom. Rates, based on room size, are ¥8,800 ($70) to ¥9,000 ($72) for a single, ¥12,000 ($96) to ¥13,000 ($104) for a double, and ¥15,500 ($124) to ¥22,000 ($176) for a twin. Ask for a room on one of the top floors, where you have a view of the whole city. On the thirteenth floor are both a bar (open from 6 p.m. to 2 p.m.) and a Western restaurant. Other outlets include Japanese and Chinese restaurants.

A Medium-Range Hotel

Just a three-minute walk from Hakodate Station is a very reasonably priced place to stay called the **Hotel Kikuya,** 8-23 Wakamatsu-cho (tel. 0138/26-1144). The front desk is on the second floor and various kinds of rooms are available. Singles in peak season (April through October) are ¥5,700 ($46); in winter, ¥4,900 ($39). Twins are ¥9,900 ($79); in winter they're ¥8,800 ($70). Japanese-style rooms start at ¥11,000 ($88). Rooms are small but adequate, and come with private bathroom, coin-operated TV, and clock. The hotel's small restaurant serves both Japanese and Western food.

The Budget Category

A conveniently located minshuku is **Minshuku Fukuiso** ㉖, 30-16 Wakamatsu-cho (tel. 0138/26-8239). It's about a five-minute walk from Hakodate Station. To reach it, turn left on the road in front of the station (the one with the tram rails). Fukuiso is a couple of blocks down on the left side, past the crossroad with the planted median strip. There are 12 rooms here, all Japanese style without private bathroom; they are simply decorated and with the basics of air conditioning, heater, coin-operated TV, and cotton kimono. Fukuiso charges ¥3,800 ($30) per person for a room only. If you want to dine here, the rate starts at ¥5,500 ($44) per person with breakfast and dinner. Although the proprietor here doesn't speak much English, things are pretty self-explanatory. The minshuku has its own public baths.

For even cheaper accommodations, a great place to stay is **Akai Boshi,** 3-22 Asahi-cho (tel. 0138/26-4035). The charge here is only ¥2,500 ($20) per person, and the owner, Miyako Yamada, speaks good English. There are only three rooms, two of which are Japanese style for one or two persons, while a third has beds to accommodate up to four persons. Spotlessly clean and cheerful, it has both a shower and a bathtub and coin-operated washing machine. No meals are served, but friendly Yamada-san is happy to recommend restaurants in the vicinity; you're also allowed to eat store-bought food in your room. The only disadvantage is that it's a 13-minute walk from the station or a ¥400 ($3.20) taxi ride, there being no public transportation, but it's worth the extra effort.

More Dining

As mentioned earlier, there are several restaurants in the renovated brick warehouses along the waterfront, about a ten-minute walk from the train station. In the History Plaza, for example, there's the **Hakodate Beer Hall** (tel. 27-1010), which serves both dark and regular Sapporo beer along with seafood, sausages, fried noodles, and a range of other dishes displayed in its plastic-food case. It's open daily from 11:30 a.m. to 10:30 p.m.

My favorite is **Bay Restaurant and Market** (tel. 22-1300), an airy locale with exposed ceiling beams, brick walls, and simple but hip furniture. Serving mainly seafood (the chef worked in the States for 17 years), it offers set lunches for ¥850 ($6.80) to ¥2,700 ($21.60) from 11:30 a.m. to 2 p.m., as well as a large selection of à la carte dishes from a menu unfortunately only in Japanese. Try the teriyaki chicken or seafood grill set meals. Better yet, how about the all-you-can eat salad bar for only ¥550 ($4.40)? From the dinner menu, served from 5:30 to 10 p.m., you might want to try fried shrimp with chili sauce, spicy tofu salad Chinese style, or tuna salad with coconut milk. There's also a raw seafood bar where you can choose from the fresh seafood on display and then specify how you want it cooked (for example, grilled, fried, or even simply raw as is). An average dinner here costs ¥3,000 ($24). There are even tables outside by a canal for dining in fine weather.

3. Sapporo

Sapporo is one of Japan's newest cities. Unlike other Japanese towns such as the centuries-old Kyoto, Osaka, and Nagasaki, Sapporo was, just a little more than a century ago, nothing more than a scattering of huts belonging to a handful of Ainu and Japanese families. All of Hokkaido, in fact, was a vast wilderness, untamed, largely unsettled, rich in timber and land. With the dawning of the Meiji Era, however, the government decided to colonize the island and established the Colonization Commission in 1869. The area of Sapporo, which comes from the Ainu word meaning "big, dry river," was chosen as the site for the new capital from which to administer the land. In 1871 construction of the city began.

During the Meiji Era Japan looked eagerly toward the West for instruction in technology, for ideas and education, and Hokkaido was no exception. Foreign technicians and experts who had had experience in colonization were brought to this Japanese wilderness to aid in the island's development. Between 1871 and 1884, 76 foreigners were brought to Hokkaido to share their expertise, including 46 Americans. Sapporo was laid out in a grid pattern of uniform blocks similar to that of American cities. In 1875 the Sapporo Agricultural College was founded to train youths in skills useful to Hokkaido's colonization and development. Among the Americans invited to Hokkaido was Dr. William S. Clark, who taught one year at the agricultural college. He is most remembered for what he said upon leaving: "Boys, be ambitious."

Ambitious they were. The Sapporo of today has grown to 1.5 million residents, making it the largest city north of Tokyo. In 1972 Sapporo was introduced to the world when the Winter Olympics were held here. Its many fine ski slopes continue to attract winter vacationers, and its annual Snow Festival, with its mammoth snow and ice sculptures, has attracted visitors from around the world. In August, when the rest of Japan is sweltering under uncomfortably humid temperatures, Sapporo stays pleasantly cool. With its nearby Chitose Airport, Sapporo serves as a springboard to Hokkaido's national parks and lakes. And yet despite all Sapporo has to offer and despite its size and importance, I've seen few foreigners in Sapporo even in August. For most visitors to Japan, Sapporo and the rest of Hokkaido remain virtually undiscovered.

ORIENTATION

After the jumble of most Japanese cities with their incomprehensible address systems, Sapporo will come as a welcome surprise. Because its streets are laid out in a grid pattern, Sapporo ranks as one of the easiest Japanese cities in which to find your

way around. Addresses in Sapporo refer to blocks that follow one another in logical, numerical order. The center of Sapporo is considered to be Odori (Main Street), a tree-lined avenue that bisects the city into north and south sections. North 1st, therefore, refers to the street one block north of Odori as well as the entire block to the north of that street. Addresses in Sapporo are generally given by block. N1 W4, for example, is the address for the Sapporo Grand Hotel and means that it's located a block north of Odori and four blocks west of West 1st Street. (West 1st Street runs along the west bank of the Soseigawa River while East 1st Street runs along the east bank.) If you want to be more technical about it, the entire, formal address of the hotel would read N1-jo W1-chome. "Jo" runs from north to south, while "chome" goes from east to west. Street signs are in English.

Most of Sapporo's attractions and hotels lie south of Sapporo Station. Transportation in Sapporo is via bus, a few subway lines, and one streetcar line. Sapporo is also easy to cover on foot. You can, for example, walk south from Sapporo Station to Odori Park in less than ten minutes and on to Susukino, Sapporo's nightlife district, in another seven or eight minutes.

If you're arriving at Sapporo's Chitose Airport, you can reach downtown Sapporo by either the airport limousine bus or by train from JR's Chitose Airport Station.

For information on Sapporo, be sure to pick up a flyer called *Sapporo and Vicinity* from the T.I.C. in either Tokyo or Kyoto. There is a Sapporo **tourist office** at Sapporo Station, located in the underground passageway of the south exit, near the subway station. Hours are from 9 a.m. to 5 p.m. daily, and there's an excellent brochure in English titled *Welcome to Sapporo,* with a very good map, information on sightseeing, and other helpful advice. If you have any questions during your stay, call the **Sapporo Tourism Department** at 211-2376.

Also of service to foreigners is the **Sapporo International Communication Plaza,** located on the third floor of the MN Building across from the Clock Tower (tel. 211-2105). In addition to providing information on Sapporo, it also maintains a staff of volunteer interpreters from 9 a.m. to 5 p.m. every day except Sunday. The Plaza also stocks a number of foreign publications, including *The New York Times, Time,* and *Newsweek.* For information on subways and buses in Sapporo, drop by the **Sapporo Transportation Information Office** located underground at the Odori Station concourse. Open daily from 8 a.m. to 7 p.m., it also has maps of the city and can answer sightseeing inquiries.

The **telephone area code** for Sapporo is 011.

WHAT TO SEE AND DO

One of the first things you should do in Sapporo is simply walk around. Starting from Sapporo Station, take the street leading directly south called **Eki-mae Dori Street** (which is also West 4). This is one of Sapporo's main thoroughfares, and takes you through the heart of the city. Four blocks south of the station, turn left on N1 and after a block you'll find Sapporo's most famous landmark, **Clock Tower.** This Western-style wooden building was built back in 1878 as a drill hall for the Sapporo Agricultural College (present Hokkaido University). The large clock at the top of the tower was made in Boston and was installed in 1881. Chiming away ever since, during the summer months it attracts tourists even at night; they hang around the outside gates just to listen to it strike the hour. Inside the tower is a local history museum with some old photographs of Sapporo and displays outlining the city's development. Although the explanations are only in Japanese, the museum is free—so you might as well go in and pay your respects. It's open from 9 a.m. to 4 p.m. every day except Monday and national holidays.

If you continue walking one block south of the Clock Tower, you'll reach **Odori,** a wide boulevard stretching almost a mile from east to west. In the middle of the boulevard is a wide median strip that has been turned into a park with trees, flower beds, and fountains. This is where much of the Sapporo Snow Festival is held in early February, when snow is packed together and then carved to form statues, palaces, and fantasies. One snow structure may require as much as 300 six-ton truckloads of snow, brought in from the surrounding mountains. The Snow Festival also displays intricate ice carvings, done with such a flourishing degree of detail that it's almost a crime the carvings must melt. First begun in 1950 to add a bit of spice and life to the cold winter days, the Snow Festival now features about 150 large and small snow statues and draws about 1.9 million visitors a year. The festival is always held from the first Wednesday to the following Sunday in February.

Odori Park is also the scene of the Summer Festival, celebrated with beer gardens set up the length of the park from mid-July to mid-August every evening beginning at 5 p.m. Various Japanese beer companies set up their own booths and tables under the trees, while vendors set up stalls selling fried noodles, corn on the cob, and other goodies. Stages with live bands serenade the beer drinkers under the stars. It all resembles the cheerful confusion of a German beer garden, which isn't surprising considering the fact that Munich is one of Sapporo's sister cities (Portland, Oregon, is another one).

From Odori Park you can continue your walk either above or below ground. Appreciated especially during inclement weather and during Hokkaido's long cold winters are two underground shopping arcades. Underneath Odori Park from Odori Subway Station all the way to the TV tower in the east is **Aurora Town,** with its boutiques and restaurants. Even longer is **Pole Town,** 1,300 feet of shop after shop, almost 100 in all. Pole Town extends from Odori Subway Station south all the way to Susukino, Sapporo's nightlife amusement center, where you can find many restaurants and pubs (refer to the dining section). Before reaching Susukino, however, you may want to emerge at **Sanchome** (you'll see escalators going up), where you'll find more shopping at the Tanuki-koji covered shopping arcade.

Backtracking now toward the station, your last stop should be the **Botanical Garden (Shokubutsu-en),** the entrance to which is at N3 W8. Open every day except Monday from 9 a.m. to 4 p.m. from April 29 to September 30 and until 3:30 p.m. from October 1 to November 3, it has 5,000 varieties of plants arranged in marshland, herb, and alpine gardens, a greenhouse, and other sections. With lots of trees and grassy lawns, it's a good place for a summer afternoon picnic. Admission is ¥360 ($2.88). In winter, only the greenhouse is open.

On the Botanical Garden grounds is the **University Museum,** a natural history museum with collections of stuffed animals, plants, and minerals of Hokkaido.

Other Things to See

Although it's not within easy walking distance of Sapporo Station, you should make the **Sapporo Beer Factory** part of your sightseeing itinerary. You can reach the beer factory which is directly east from Sapporo Station in about ten minutes by bus. Sapporo Beer is famous throughout Japan, and the brew has been produced here in Sapporo ever since the first factory opened in 1876. Tours are held daily throughout the year, with the first tour starting at 8:40 a.m. and the last at 4:45 p.m. during peak summer months. It's best to make reservations beforehand to avoid having to wait (tel. 731-4368). Although tours are conducted only in Japanese, a few of the guides speak English, so ask whether it's possible to have an English interpreter at the time you make your reservation. Free of charge, tours last approximately one hour.

More than 200,000 people tour the brewery each year, and during peak time in August as many as 3,000 people may come in one day. The tour begins with a walk through the brewery, where you'll be struck by how empty the whole factory is of human help. The process is fully automated in assembly lines—the main human function is merely to watch to make sure nothing goes haywire. Following the brewery tour is a short stop in the **Sapporo Museum,** where you'll see old beer posters, photographs, and other memorabilia. Then comes the fun part—you get to sample the brew. If after the tour you want to stick around and drink more of it (it often seems to work that way), you'll find the Sapporo Beer Hall on the grounds, and in summer months there's even an outdoor beer garden. Refer to the dining section for more mouthwatering details.

If you have time you should also consider visiting **Nopporo Forest Park (Nopporo Shinrin Koen)**, where you'll find a 330-foot tower (built in 1970 to commemorate Hokkaido's centennial) and two other attractions. The **Historical Museum of Hokkaido (Kaitaku Kinenkan)** houses collections detailing Hokkaido's development from prehistoric to modern times (including Ainu artifacts). The admission charge is ¥250 ($2) and hours are 9 a.m. to 4:30 p.m.; closed Monday and national holidays. The **Historical Village of Hokkaido (Kaitaku-no-Mura)** is an open-air museum of various houses from the pages of Hokkaido's history, including homes, farmhouses, a school, hostel, and shrine. With the same hours as the Historical Museum, it charges ¥510 ($4.08) admission (¥410 [$3.28] in winter). You can reach Nopporo Park via the JR bus from Sapporo Station in 50 minutes.

Skiing

The slopes around Sapporo offer skiing from early December to late April. Since you can fly directly to Sapporo from many cities in Japan, it's a popular winter destination. The **Teine Olympia Ski Grounds** are located about an hour from Sapporo by bus. This was the site of the alpine, bobsled, and toboggan events in the Sapporo Winter Olympic Games of 1972. Other skiing areas within 30 minutes of Sapporo are **Mount Moiwa, Mount Arai,** and **Maruyama.** Most sites provide ski-rental equipment for approximately ¥3,500 ($28) per day, but keep in mind that sizes are generally smaller than in the West.

ACCOMMODATIONS

Because of the 1972 Olympics held in Sapporo, the city has a large selection of fine hotels in various price categories. Sapporo's heaviest tourist season is during the summer months and during the annual Snow Festival held in early February. If you plan to attend the Snow Festival, book your hotel room at least six months in advance. At other times during the year you should have no problem finding a room, but if you're coming in August you'd be wise to make a reservation. During winter (excluding the time of the Snow Festival) some upper- and medium-priced hotels lower their room rates, sometimes as much as 40%. That should come as welcome news to you ski enthusiasts. Be sure to ask for a discount. Unless otherwise stated, rooms come with private bathroom.

The Upper Bracket

Sapporo Grand Hotel, N1 W4 (tel. 011/261-3311), is usually where VIPs stay when they come to Sapporo. About a six-minute walk south of Sapporo Station, this dignified hotel with more than 50 years of excellent service behind it has an exceptional French restaurant, a beer hall, several bars, Japanese restaurants, and a shopping arcade. Rooms in the newer annex (which opened in 1984) are very chic, with contemporary furniture, a minibar built into a wood cabinet, bilingual TV with pay video, large desks with lots of working space, semidouble beds, and tiled bathrooms with marble-topped counters. These rooms go for ¥14,000 ($112) for a single and ¥23,000 ($184) for a twin. Rooms in the older part of the hotel are also very nice and are less expensive, going for ¥12,000 ($96) for a single, ¥19,000 ($152) for a double, and ¥20,000 ($160) for a twin. Eight Japanese-style rooms are available for ¥23,000 ($184).

Opened in 1988, **Sapporo Korakuen Hotel,** Odori W8 (tel. 011/261-0111), is located right on Odori, the heart of the city. In fact, this would be the place to be during the Snow Festival (no single rooms, however, face the park). Its lobby flaunts space with an inner atrium that stretches 14 stories high (I can just imagine what the heating bills must be; this is, after all, the cold north). Facilities include a sports club with workout equipment and sauna available to hotel guests for a fee of ¥3,000

($24), and there are Japanese, Chinese, and Western restaurants. Rooms are rather feminine, with a decor of soft pastels, and include all the amenities you'd expect such as TV with remote control. Singles start at ¥13,000 ($104); doubles and twins at ¥20,000 ($160).

Less than a five-minute walk from Sapporo Station, the **ANA Hotel Sapporo** (in Japanese, the **Zenniku Hotel**) ㉗, N1 W3 (tel. 011/221-4411), is a gleaming white building rising high in the skyline of Sapporo. It has the kind of rooms travelers can appreciate: five lamps in its larger rooms so you don't have to read in the dark, bilingual TVs that swivel and have pay video, an extra phone in the bathroom, two layers of curtains for complete darkness, and such amenities as a minibar, hot-water pot for tea, radio, and alarm clock. Rates here range from ¥11,500 ($92) to ¥16,000 ($128) for a single, ¥18,500 ($148) to ¥25,000 ($200) for a twin, and ¥20,000 ($160) for a double. Facilities include Japanese and French restaurants on the 25th and 26th floors with views of the city. Also on the 26th floor is the sky lounge Sapporo View, where there's piano music every night except Sunday starting at 7:30 p.m.; cocktails here start at ¥850 ($6.80).

Next to the ANA Hotel is the **New Otani**, N2 W1 (tel. 011/222-1111). Also a five-minute walk from the train station, it has a wide range of facilities, including a medical center, the Asahi Culture Center (with traditional art exhibitions), and two restaurants. One restaurant, The Four Seasons, offers French, Chinese, and Japanese cuisine, while the other one, Rendezvous, is a convenient lobby coffeeshop open from 7 a.m. to 10:30 p.m. (the hot tuna sandwich, by the way, is delicious). Also available at the New Otani are rental bicycles, golf clubs, and skis. Rooms, decorated in soothing pastels, have bilingual TV with pay video, radio, alarm clock, fridge, and double-pane windows that open; their bathrooms have larger-than-average tubs. Singles start at ¥13,000 ($104), while twins and doubles start at ¥23,000 ($184).

Just a few minutes west of Sapporo Station, the **Keio Plaza Hotel**, N5 W7 (tel. 011/271-0111), is a graceful hostelry that made its debut in 1982. Its white and light-green lobby gives way to bold colors in the bedrooms, which are accented with striped bedspreads in primary colors. It features 11 bars and restaurants, and a sauna and indoor pool hotel guests can use for ¥2,900 ($23.20). Rooms are what you'd expect in an upper-class hotel, including double-pane windows to block out noise, TV with pay video, minibar, hot-water pot, clock, and radio. The sink area has lots of room to spread out. It's an attractive hotel all around. Singles start at ¥11,000 ($88), twins at ¥20,000 ($160), and doubles at ¥23,000 ($184). Winter rates are as much as 40% lower than in summer.

The Medium-Priced Range

The **Century Royal Hotel**, N5 W5 (tel. 011/221-2121), has an excellent location, right next to the train station—which is the main selling point of the hotel. Another selling point is its revolving restaurant on the 23rd floor. Otherwise, rooms are fairly basic, with fridge, TV, music, and alarm clock, and windows have double panes to shut out noise. Rates throughout the year start at ¥10,500 ($84) for a single, ¥18,500 ($148) for a twin, and ¥20,000 ($160) for a double.

Part of a reliable national hotel chain, the Washington Hotel has two locations in Sapporo, both close to the train station. **Washington Hotel 2**, N5 W6 (tel. 011/222-3311), is the newer of the two and therefore a bit nicer and more pleasant in its facilities. The hotel is a three-minute walk southwest of the station, and its guest rooms have rattan furniture, TV with video, fridge, hot-water pot, music, and alarm clock. Unlike most business hotels with check-in at 3 or 4 p.m., the Washington's check-in is 2 p.m. Singles start at ¥9,000 ($72), and twins and doubles begin at ¥17,000 ($136), including tax and service. Winter rates are about ¥1,000 ($8) less.

Washington Hotel 1, N4 W4 (tel. 011/251-3211), is right across the street from the station. Its lobby is on the second floor up the escalator. Although the cheapest singles go for a low ¥6,000 ($48), I don't advise them unless you hate sunshine (they have no windows and are extremely dark). Singles for ¥8,200 ($66) face a rather drab inside courtyard, but at least you have a window. Why not splurge and go for the best singles in the house for ¥9,000 ($72), which are larger and face toward the outside? Twins start at ¥16,500 ($132); doubles, at ¥17,500 ($140). All rates include tax and service charge. Rooms have TV with pay video, hot-water pot and tea, and a tiny bathroom; those that face the station have double-pane windows to shut out noise. Vending machines in the hallways dispense beer, snacks, and soft drinks.

Opened in 1986, the **Hotel Sunroute New Sapporo,** S2 W6 (tel. 011/251-2511), is a pleasant modern business hotel located on the Tanuki-koji covered shopping street. Sporting a souvenir shop and Japanese and Western restaurants, it offers typical business-type rooms with TV and adult video, music, fridge, alarm clock, and hot-water pot. Its 334 rooms are priced starting at ¥7,500 ($60) for a single, ¥14,800 ($118) for a double, and ¥16,000 ($128) for a twin. Tax and service charges are extra.

Chisan Hotel Sapporoshinkan, N2 W2 (tel. 011/222-6611), opened in 1984 as an annex to an older Chisan hotel. It is a pleasant business hotel about a five-minute walk from Sapporo Station; its rooms, all with bathroom, come with the usual dark furniture and purple- and pink-striped bedcover that is the trademark of Chisan chain hotels. Panels close over the windows for darkness, and other facilities include TV with pay video, fridge, and semidouble beds. Prices here are ¥8,200 ($66) for a single and ¥16,000 ($128) for a twin, going down to ¥6,200 ($50) and ¥12,000 ($96) respectively, in winter. Tax is extra. The hotel contains one Japanese restaurant.

Don't confuse this hotel with the older **Chisan,** where prices are ¥6,200 ($50) for a single and ¥12,000 ($96) for a twin. Winter rates here are ¥1,000 ($8) less per person. Located just 30 seconds from the newer branch, it has rooms that are more dated and less cheerful. If you can afford it, therefore, you're better off staying in the newer Chisan.

If you want to be close to the nightlife action in Susukino, the **Sapporo Tokyu Inn,** at S4 W5 (tel. 011/531-0109), is your best choice in the area. A member of the Tokyu hotel chain, this red-brick business hotel is only a one-minute walk from the Susukino subway station. Altogether there are 18 restaurants in the hotel and the adjoining basement shopping arcade. The guest rooms are spotlessly clean and tastefully decorated in muted browns, and come with TV and clock. Vending machines with beer and soda are located in the hallways. Prices remain the same year round: ¥7,700 ($62) to ¥8,300 ($66) for a single; ¥14,800 ($118) to ¥16,500 ($132) for a double, and ¥15,000 ($120) to ¥17,000 ($136) for a twin. Rates include only service charge. Notice the tiny dots beside each door, which are the room number in Braille. They're for the hotel's masseurs, who are often blind in Japan.

If you want to stay in a ryokan, **Nakamuraya Ryokan** ㉘, N3 W7 (tel. 011/241-2111), is a comfortable and modern Japanese inn located about a seven-minute walk southwest of Sapporo Station next to the entrance of the Botanical Garden. It has 32 rooms, mostly Japanese style, all of which come with bathroom, fridge, TV, and clock. I prefer the Japanese rooms to the Western ones—their simplicity is in sharp contrast to the old carpeting and odd color combination in the Western rooms. Rates for Western or Japanese rooms are ¥18,500 ($148) for one person and ¥26,000 ($208) for two, including two meals. Those are the rates, anyway, that Japanese pay. This ryokan is a member of the Japanese Inn Group, so if you make a booking in advance and mention Japanese Inn Group, you'll receive a much lower rate as a foreigner. In this case rooms start at ¥6,000 ($48) for one person and ¥11,000 ($88) for two. Prices do not include meals, but there's a cafeteria in the ryokan and Japanese dinners are served starting at ¥3,000 ($24). Although rooms have their own tubs, you might want to take advantage of the public baths here.

Located in the heart of the Susukino nightlife district, **Hotel Sunflower Sapporo,** S5 W3 (tel. 011/512-5533), is a good place to stay if you like carousing through the bars at night—it's not far to crawl back to your hotel. Based on its facilities and atmosphere, I would classify this establishment as strictly a business hotel, but because of its location it caters to both businessmen and tourists. The rooms are tiny and unexciting, coming with TV with pay video and a minuscule bathroom. The single rooms have glazed windows, so you can't see out; but even if you open the windows there isn't much to see, so I guess it doesn't matter. The hotel serves a popular and good buffet dinner, which offers a variety of Western, Japanese, Chinese, and local Hokkaido specialties for only ¥2,400 ($19.20) from 5 to 9 p.m. Rates here are ¥7,000 ($56) for a single, ¥9,000 ($72) for a double, and ¥13,000 ($104) for a twin. Prices include tax and service and are about 10% lower in winter.

The Budget Category

Hotel New Frontier ㉙, N1 W9 (tel. 011/231-7533), is about a 15-minute hike or 5-minute taxi ride from Sapporo Station, but it has a central location between the Botanical Garden and Odori. Though clean and simple, this business hotel is unimaginative, resembling a college dormitory. The only rooms with private bathrooms are the three doubles; the majority of rooms are bathless singles and Japanese-style tatami rooms. Western-style rooms do have sinks, and all rooms come with heater, phone, coin-operated TV, tea service, and yukata. The public bath is open 24 hours (the men even get a sauna), and the one restaurant serves Japanese and Western fare. Rates are ¥4,700 ($38) for a single, ¥8,800 ($70) for a twin, ¥9,400 ($75) for a double, and ¥8,800 ($70) for two in a tatami room. Tax is extra. Rates are the same year-round, but in winter they also include breakfast. The closest youth hostel to Sapporo Station is **Sapporo House Youth Hostel**, N6 W6 (tel. 011/726-4235), about a seven-minute walk from the station. The sign outside this white concrete building is in Japanese only, but look for the sign with "YH" on it. More than 200 people can be accommodated here in both tatami and Western-style rooms, and even in August they often have space. Prices are ¥2,300 ($18.40) for members and nonmembers. Breakfast is ¥460 ($3.68) and dinner runs ¥610 ($4.88).

If the above youth hostel is full, there are a couple alternatives in the vicinity of Sapporo. **Sapporo Miyagaoka Youth Hostel**, N1 14-chome Miyanomori (tel. 011/611-9016), can be reached by subway and bus from Sapporo Station in about 30 minutes. Closed from October through June, it charges both members and nonmembers ¥3,300 ($26.40) for an overnight stay including two meals. If you eat elsewhere, the rate is only ¥2,200 ($17.60). **Sapporo Shiritsu Lions Youth Hostel**, N1 18-chome Miyanomori (tel. 011/611-4709), is about 40 minutes away from Sapporo Station by bus and subway. Open throughout the year, it charges ¥2,200 ($17.60) for members and ¥2,900 ($23.20) for nonmembers. Breakfast is ¥450 ($3.60) and dinner is ¥700 ($5.60).

WHERE TO DINE

Hokkaido's specialties include crab, corn on the cob, potatoes, Genghis Khan (also spelled "Jingisukan"), Chinese noodles, salmon, and *Ishikari Nabe*. Genghis Khan is a dish of mutton and vegetables that you grill yourself, while Ishikari Nabe is a stew of salmon and other Hokkaido vegetables, also cooked at your table. As for Western food, your best bet is to dine in one of the many fine restaurants in Sapporo's top hotels.

Japanese Food

I can't imagine going to Sapporo without dropping by the **Sapporo Bier Garten**, N6 E9 (tel. 742-1531). Open from June through August every day from 5 to 9 p.m., the beer garden is spread out under broad-leafed acacia trees. If it's winter or early in the day, you can dine in the Sapporo Beer Hall, an old ivy-covered brick building built in 1889 as the Sapporo brewery. The interior is also brick with a wood floor and wood beams, making for a very congenial atmosphere. I personally prefer the second floor of this establishment, where you dine underneath a huge old mash tub once used in brewing beer. Since the eatery is on the grounds of Sapporo brewery itself, you can raise your mugs unabashedly here. By the way, though I haven't seen it myself, the management tells me that from January 20 to mid-February there's a snow igloo built outside in which you can sit and drink beer too—that is, if it's cold enough so the snow doesn't melt. Anyway, if it gets too cold for you there's sure to be a roaring fire inside the hall itself, which is open daily from 11:30 a.m. to 9 p.m.

The specialty of the house is Genghis Khan, which you cook yourself on a hot skillet at your table. Look at the skillet closely. Recognize the shape? It's a map of Hokkaido. The best deal in the house is the King Viking, which for ¥2,900 ($23.20) gives you as much Genghis Khan and as much draft beer as you can consume in a two-hour period. If you don't feel like gorging yourself for two hours, a regular serving of Genghis Khan is ¥1,000 ($8). Other dishes include such Hokkaido favorites as buttered corn on the cob, potatoes, and crab. Draft beer starts at ¥450 ($3.60) for a small mug.

Not to be outdone is **Suntory,** which opened its own Suntory Beer Benizakura Garden at Sumikawa 389-769, Minami-ku (tel. 582-4411), in 1985. It's located on the south edge of town just a five-minute taxi ride from the Makomanai Subway Station on the Nanboku Line. Buses run between the subway station and the beer garden every 30 minutes. Open daily from 11:30 a.m. to 9 p.m., this establishment also offers Genghis Khan for ¥1,000 ($8), and Suntory beer starts at ¥450 ($3.60). For ¥2,900 ($23.20) you can eat all the Genghis Khan and drink as much beer as you want over a two-hour time period. Sauces for dipping morsels of mutton and vegetables are available either mild or spicy. Although the building itself is bright and airy, dining outside by the lotus pond is great in fine weather. Be sure to wander through the gardens, which extend back behind the restaurant. Created about 30 years ago, they consist of ponds and a waterfall, a pleasant respite from the city.

Another well-known restaurant in Sapporo is **Hyosetsu-no-Mon** ㉚, S5 W2 (tel. 521-3046), which specializes in giant king crab caught in the Japan Sea north of Hokkaido. Actually there are three restaurants here side by side in Sapporo's Susukino nightlife district. The main shop is the one farthest west (the first one you'll reach if you're walking from the Susukino subway station). The menu is easy enough—it's almost entirely of king crab, which comes in a variety of styles with prices to match. Set courses start at ¥4,400 ($35.20) which includes a cooked crab, sashimi, crab soup, crab tempura, and vegetables. Other meals range all the way up to ¥13,200 ($105.60), increasing the portion of crab and number of side dishes. You can also order à la carte for fried king crab claws, deep-fried king crab, tempura king crab, grilled king crab, and crabmeat chowder, with average meals ranging from ¥3,000 ($24) to ¥6,000 ($48). Other à la carte selections include various sashimi, raw sea urchin, salmon eggs, and raw crab organs. This main shop is open daily from 11 a.m. to 11 p.m.

Next to the main restaurant is its Western restaurant, which serves king crab à la carte dishes ranging from ¥1,000 ($8) to ¥3,300 ($26.40), including crab fondue and crab gratin. Other dishes include spaghetti, steak, sausage, pork, and potatoes, with prices mostly under ¥1,500 ($12).

A small band provides entertainment nightly. The interior of this place is imitation European, although exactly which country it's imitating is hard to say. Hanging on its walls are menus collected from various countries by the manager, who has a passion for easy-to-read menus. His menus here all come with photographs so that foreigners have no problems ordering. Open 5 p.m. to midnight.

The third Hyosetsu-no-Mon restaurant serves the same food as in the main shop, but this one has a floor show as well. There are two shows nightly, and it's best to make a reservation. One show starts at 6 p.m. and the second show is at 8. The show costs only ¥900 ($7.20), so it's worth coming here for dinner. This establishment is filled with Japanese tourists on holiday in Hokkaido and is great fun. You sit on the floor here to eat your meal in a dining hall reminiscent of old Kabuki theaters. The show starts off with a classical dance followed by contemporary and folk dances.

Another good nightspot in the Susukino area is **Irohanihoheto** ㉛, S5 W4 (tel. 521-1682). Open from 5 p.m. to 12:30 a.m. daily (until 3 a.m. on Saturday), this eating and drinking establishment is part of a chain that originated in Sapporo and has since spread all over Japan. It's popular everywhere with young Japanese because of its low and affordable prices. As in most Irohanihoheto shops, this one is decorated in a rustic country style with heavy wooden beams and folkcraft hanging from the rafters. The menu is in Japanese only, but there are some pictures; an alternative is to look at what others are eating around you. There are nearly 100 items on the menu, most within the ¥200 ($1.60) to ¥500 ($4) price range, so you don't have to worry that what you order will bankrupt you. Beer starts at ¥380 ($3.04). Items include yakitori, tofu dishes, oden, sashimi, vegetables, sausage, nikujaga (potato and beef stew), salads, buttered corn, fried fish, and more. Other Irohanihoheto branches in Sapporo can be found at S4 W2 and at S6 W3, both in the Susukino area, and at N3 W3 just a few minutes' walk south of Sapporo Station.

Sapporo is famous for its ramen (Chinese noodles), and the most popular place to eat them is on a tiny, narrow street in Susukino popularly known as **Ramen Yokocho.** Located just one block east of Susukino subway station before you get to the Hotel Sunflower, it's an alleyway of noodle shop after noodle shop—16 in all. It doesn't matter which one you choose—just look to see where there's an empty seat. The shops are all very small affairs consisting of a counter and some chairs. Most are open from 11 a.m. to 4 a.m. and their closed days are staggered, so you're sure to find some open. Noodles generally begin at ¥600 ($4.80) for a steaming bowlful.

Closer to Sapporo Station, in the basement of the ANA Hotel (the Zenniku), N1 W3 (tel. 221-4411), is a restaurant called **Satohoro** ㉜ serving Hokkaido specialties at reasonable prices. Simply decorated with wood and bamboo, it serves such items as frozen salmon *(benishake ruibe),* potatoes in butter *(imo batta),* crab salad, local fish, and other dishes, starting at ¥800 ($6.40). There are also set meals starting at ¥5,000 ($40). Hours are 11:30 a.m. to 10 p.m.

If you want to dine in more elegant surroundings with a view of the city, the Zenniku's 25th floor has both a Japanese and a Chinese restaurant. **Kurumaya,** the Japanese restaurant, has an English menu and includes such things as a shabu-shabu dinner course for ¥5,300 ($42.40), a sukiyaki meal for ¥5,800 ($46.40), or broiled Matsuzaka beef with Japanese peppers for ¥3,800 ($30.40). Other items include tempura, sashimi, salmon, noodles, rice porridge, and kaiseki. You can pay as little as ¥800 ($6.40) or as much as ¥12,000 ($96), according to what your pocketbook dictates. Hours here are 11:30 a.m. to 10 p.m.

Non-Japanese Food

On the 26th floor of the ANA Hotel (the Zenniku) is a French restaurant called **Top of Sapporo,** open only for dinner from 5 to 11 p.m. This small, intimate, and tastefully decorated restaurant has meals beginning at ¥7,400 ($59.20), which change every two months and which include Hokkaido delicacies cooked in a French style. À la carte dishes, for which you'll probably spend ¥8,000 ($64) for a complete meal, include broiled lobster, cream style king crab with sea urchin, roast lamb, and steaks.

Another excellent French restaurant in town is the **Grand Chef,** located in the Grand Hotel, N1 W4 (tel. 261-3311). Elegantly and cheerfully decorated in pink, white, and gray, this superb restaurant specializes in Hokkaido food cooked Western style. Lunch is served from 11:30 a.m. to 2 p.m. with various courses available for ¥3,300 ($26.40) and up. Dinner, served from 5 to 10 p.m., has an à la carte menu that changes annually but always includes selections of seafood such as scallops, sole, or salmon; steaks; and lamb; chicken; and duck. The average dinner will cost around

¥6,500 ($52) to ¥11,000 ($88). There are also special dinner courses for ¥8,800 ($70.40) to ¥16,500 ($132).

If you're fond of revolving restaurants, there's one atop the Century Royal Hotel next to Sapporo Station, N5 W5 (tel. 221-2121), on the 23rd floor. Called **Rondo,** it's open from 11:30 a.m. to 11 p.m. and has an English menu complete with photos. It revolves a complete turn in one hour, and tables are all located at windows so that everyone gets the best view in the house. Even if you don't eat here, it's a good place to come on a fine clear day for a cup of coffee or an evening cocktail. The varied menu includes spaghetti, sandwiches, curry rice, grilled half chicken, pork chops, steak, crab gratin, and lobster gratin. Set lunches start at ¥2,200 ($17.60). Cocktails are ¥880 ($7.04).

Serving North Indian food, **Taj Mahal** has two convenient locations. Its main shop is at S1 W2 (tel. 231-1168) near Odori and Mitsukoshi department store, while a branch is located at N2 W3 about a five-minute walk from Sapporo Station near the Grand Hotel. Hours for both are from 11 a.m. to 10 p.m. (last order). In addition to its tandoori and kabobs are chicken, lamb, and vegetable curries (no beef or pork is served). Set lunches start at ¥750 ($6); curries are mostly in the ¥900 ($7.20) to ¥1,300 ($10.40) range.

---

4. The National Parks of Hokkaido

Much of Hokkaido's wilderness has been set aside in national parks. Of these, Shikotsu-Toya, Daisetsuzan, and Akan national parks are the best known, offering a wide range of activities from hiking to skiing to bathing at hot-spring resorts.

SHIKOTSU-TOYA NATIONAL PARK

If you have only a couple of days to spare to visit a national park in Hokkaido, Shikotsu-Toya National Park is the closest to Sapporo and therefore the easiest for the short-term visitor. It's also the first national park you'll reach if you've entered Hokkaido via train to Hakodate. With 381 square miles, this national park encompasses lakes, volcanoes, and the famous hot-spring resorts of Toyako Spa and Noboribetsu Spa. In the village of Shiraoi a museum and village have been erected commemorating the native Ainu and their culture.

Be sure to pick up a copy of *Southern Hokkaido,* put out by the Tourist Information Center in either Tokyo or Kyoto. It lists places of interest throughout the national park. As for traveling to and within the park, there's a bus from Sapporo that goes directly to Toyako Spa on Lake Toya. From Toyako Spa you can then proceed by bus to Noboribetsu and then back to Sapporo; from Noboribetsu you can also take a train to Shiraoi and back to Sapporo. There are also JR trains that run directly from Hakodate to Toya Station (from Toya Station it's a 15-minute bus ride to Lake Toya), and on to Noboribetsu, Shiraoi, and Sapporo.

Toyako Spa

Hugging the shores of Lake Toya, Toyako Spa (also called Toyako Onsen; *onsen* means spa in Japanese) is a small resort town with a sprinkling of ryokan, souvenir shops, and not much more. However, you don't come here for Toyako Spa itself. Rather, you come here for what it gives access to, which is **Lake Toya,** the shining blue jewel of Shikotsu-Toya National Park. Surrounded on all sides by hills, Lake Toya is almost perfectly round. It is a typical caldera lake—that is, a lake that has formed within the collapsed crater of an extinct volcano. Approximately 590 feet deep, Lake Toya is invitingly clear and cool and never freezes over even in the dead of winter. In the middle of the lake are four thickly wooded islets, casting mirror images of themselves in the water below.

Orientation: If you're arriving by train from Sapporo (about two hours) or from Hakodate (a little over two hours), you'll arrive at Toya Station. Toyako Onsen on Lake Toya is located about 4½ miles northwest of Toya Station, easily reached by bus in about 15 minutes. If you decide to splurge and take a taxi, the fare from Toya Station to Toyako Onsen is about ¥2,000 ($16). You can also reach Toyako Onsen directly by either Donan or Jotetsu Bus Company from Sapporo. The trip takes two hours and 40 minutes and costs ¥2,800 ($22.40).

Since there is no train station in Toyako Onsen itself, you'll arrive by bus at Toyako Onsen bus terminal. The **tourist association** (tel. 01427/5-2446) is down the hill toward the lake about a minute's walk away from the bus terminal. It's open from 9 a.m. to 5 p.m. and can help with room reservations. Unfortunately, there's no map in English, but the spa is so small you shouldn't have any difficulty finding your way around. Your own two feet are your best mode of transportation. The town stretches along one main road, which follows the curve of the lake. Buses for Showa-Shinzan and Takinoue Camp depart from the bus terminal, so inquire there about the schedule. Buses aren't very frequent, so if you find yourself stuck somewhere, stick out your thumb. Hitching in Hokkaido is safe and easy, especially since people realize that public transportation is sometimes a bit inconvenient out here in the "wilderness."

Most people stay in Toyako Onsen only one night. It's enough time to relax and do the few things the place has to offer. If you happen to stay two nights, you'll find your ryokan deserted after check-out time until the next crowd arrives at check-in time.

The **telephone area code** is 01427.

The Sights: With the water such a strong lure, it's probably no surprise that the most popular thing to do is take a **boat ride** across the clear lake to a couple of the islands in the middle. Charging ¥1,000 ($8), the boat pulls into two small docks, the first at an island where there are some deer and winding footpaths, the second at another island where there's a natural history museum (which, unfortunately, has explanations only in Japanese and is therefore of little interest to foreign visitors). If you decide to disembark at either of these islands, you can catch the next boat in about a half hour. Otherwise, if you don't disembark but simply stay on the boat for the entire trip, it takes about an hour. Along the shore of Toyako Spa are also several docks where you can rent rowboats and paddleboats.

If it's August and hot, the temptation to simply jump into the lake and cool off will be almost too hard to resist. To your astonishment, however, you won't find any swimming facilities in Toyako Spa itself. In fact, hardly any lakes in Hokkaido allow swimming, the reason being that they are considered too cold and dangerous for humans. Desperate for a swim and unwilling to leave the lake until its coolness swallowed me up, I took a bus ride 20 minutes around the lake to **Takinoue Camp** (tel. 01426/6-2121), one of the few places where swimming is allowed. There's a small sandy beach here and a few parents playing with their children, making it a good place to jump in and play too. Incidentally, you can also camp here for ¥300 ($2.40) per person. There are even tents for rent at ¥850 ($6.80), but you must have your own sleeping bag and camping supplies.

A bit closer to home are the huge **public baths** of the Sun Palace Hotel, located on the edge of Toyako Spa and described in the hotel section. Open to the general public every day from 10 a.m. to 4 p.m. (and only to hotel guests after 4 p.m.), they feature a huge indoor pool filled with hot-spring water and complete with artificial waves and even water slides. You wear your swimming suit here, but there are also hot-spring bathing facilities (separated for men and women) that include saunas. Incidentally, the swimming pool also has an outdoor area where you can sun yourself. In any case, if you've never been to one of Japan's huge public baths, it's worth the ¥2,000 ($16) entry fee, which becomes ¥2,500 ($20) on Sunday and public holidays. Hotel guests get to use the facilities for free.

There are two very active volcanoes on the shores of Lake Toya not far from Toyako Spa. **Mount Usu,** which towers up above the tiny spa, erupted in August

1977, blanketing 80% of Hokkaido in volcanic ash and dumping enough ash on Toyako Onsen itself that the people literally had to dig their way out of it. Chronicling Mount Usu's eruption is the **Abuta Volcano Science Museum (Abuta Kazan Kagaku-kan)** (tel. 01427/5-4400), conveniently located right above the Toyako Onsen bus terminal. Open from 8:30 a.m. to 5 p.m. and charging ¥400 ($3.20) admission, it depicts the 1977 eruption with photographs and lava rocks displays, and even exhibits the mayor's car covered in rubble. Although explanations are in Japanese, a pamphlet is available in English explaining important facts. The most interesting aspect of the museum is the "experience room," which seats 350 persons around a large panoramic model of Lake Toya and Mount Usu. At the beginning of the "experience" the lights are turned out and a rumbling begins directly below you, followed by vibrations so that your whole seat shakes and shimmies. Then the model begins erupting, the vibrations continue, and the rumbling gets louder, giving at least a little insight into what it must feel like to see a volcano blow its top. Following is a film (again, only in Japanese) showing the Usu eruption, the evacuation of Toyako Onsen, and the ashes covering the town. The whole experience brings home the fact that all of Japan is basically volcanic in origin and that its people have lived in the shadows of volcanoes and earthquakes from the beginning of time.

The other famous volcano in the vicinity is **Showa-Shinzan,** somewhat of an upstart, which made its debut only in 1945. Before then it was nothing more than a flat farm field. Over a period of two years, however, the ground began to rise, volcanic eruptions shook the area, and lava rose, resulting in the fledgling volcano. Showa-Shinzan still spouts billowing clouds of smoke. If you're interested in getting a closeup view, you can reach Showa-Shinzan by buses that depart from the Toyako Onsen bus terminal. A small museum at the foot of the volcano documents its birth. You can also catch a glimpse of the volcano from afar if you take the boat ride out onto Lake Toya.

One other thing worth mentioning are the nightly **fireworks** displays put on by the town of Toyako Onsen from June through August—that is, if they're still going on. Although the town has managed to put on fantastic shows the past few years, such displays are extremely costly and as of now it's not certain whether they'll be carried on during the summers of 1990 and 1991. If so, however, they're worth seeing. The show begins at about 8:40 p.m. and fireworks are set off from boats in the lake.

Where to Stay: Because the town of Toyako Spa itself is not very interesting, the best rooms are those that face the lake (with its picturesque islands in the middle). Of course, these rooms are also the most expensive. This being a resort town for the Japanese, accommodations are largely Japanese-style inns in which you're expected to take your dinner and breakfast at the ryokan. So all prices given below include two meals, unless otherwise stated. The busiest tourist season is from May to October; rates are generally higher during these months.

The **Sun Palace Hotel** (tel. 01427/5-4126) is the most elaborate and conspicuous hotel in Toyako Onsen. Isolated on the edge of the small town on the shores of the lake, it's about a 30-minute walk from the bus terminal. Since buses are infrequent, the easiest way to reach it if you have baggage is by taxi. Its lobby features a spectacular light fixture made of gold-colored twisted metal sheets that rise out of a pond and spread up and out into the ceiling. This resort hotel also has the largest public bath in town, described in the sightseeing section. Its hot baths meander both indoors and out, and have waterslides and other play objects for kids. There's also a large indoor pool. The children I saw here were racing excitedly about, obviously enthralled with the whole setup. For older kids there's an electronic game room with sophisticated machinery, while for adults there's a disco. This is a good family hotel that appeals widely to both adults and kids. Its 459 rooms are in both Japanese and Western style, and you don't have to worry about a lake view here—all rooms face the lake. Rooms come with TV, a safe for valuables, and a fridge. The cheapest rooms are quite simple, while the more expensive ones are larger and more nicely furnished. The main thing you're paying for at this hotel is its public facilities. Rates per person range from ¥17,000 ($136) to ¥26,000 ($208). In the off-season, rooms go down to as little as ¥13,000 ($104) per person.

Another first-class hotel in town, **Manseikaku** ③③③ (tel. 01427/5-2171) is a large, handsome brown-brick building at the water's edge. Rooms are modern and comfortable, and some even have balconies. Most of the rooms are Japanese-style tatami. There are also Western-style rooms with beds; most of these rooms face inland. The hotel has its own tennis court, an indoor pool, and large indoor and outdoor public baths. In fact, there's a woman's bath on the eighth floor that even features a small outdoor hot-spring bath (called *rotenburo* in Japanese), which, if you ask me, would be a perfect spot from which to watch the fireworks. Other facilities include a small disco and a karaoke bar where guests sing along to their favorite tunes. Breakfast is served buffet style, and for dinner you have a choice of a Japanese meal served in your room or a Western-style buffet in the hotel's European restaurant.

Right beside the hotel is a boat dock where you can rent paddleboats and take charter motorboats around the lake. High-season rates range from ¥16,500 ($132) to ¥40,000 ($320) per person, decreasing to ¥11,000 ($88) to ¥36,000 ($288) October through April.

Less than a five-minute walk from the bus terminal, the waterside **Park Hotel** (tel. 01427/5-2445) boasts tennis courts, a pleasant public bath filled with tropical plants, a game room, bowling lanes, and a bar with laser shows. Half the rooms facing the water have verandas of sorts—but you have to crawl over the windowsill to get outside. The other rooms have only windows. Since the hotel's Western-style rooms—all twins—face only inland, the Japanese rooms here are better by far, especially since they're the same price. You're much better off going native. All with private bathroom, they're ¥11,000 ($88) on weekdays, rising to ¥16,500 ($132) per person on weekends. There are also bathroom-less Japanese rooms facing inland for as little as ¥8,800 ($70). During the off-season, rooms are available for about ¥2,000 ($16) to ¥4,000 ($32) less.

A somewhat older medium-range ryokan is the **Toyako Onsen Hotel** (tel. 01427/5-2222). The only facilities for guests are rather nice public baths, and rooms were recently renovated with new wallpaper and tatami mats. The big plus here is that all rooms facing the lake have balconies, perfect for watching the summertime fireworks. All rooms have toilets, and a few rooms have tubs as well. Although 15 Western-style rooms are available, none of them face the lake; a few combination rooms with both beds and tatami area, however, do have lake views. Prices here are ¥14,000 ($112) to ¥16,500 ($132) in summer season, ¥8,800 ($70) to ¥11,000 ($88) in the off-season.

If you want to stay in Toyako Onsen but can't afford a hotel on the lake's edge, you might try **Takatsu Ryokan** ③③④ (tel. 01427/5-3088), which is located a block inland just a two-minute walk from the bus terminal. No English is spoken, but the proprietress says she gets by with hands and feet. There are ten rooms altogether, all Japanese style except for one twin, and two of the rooms have private bathroom facilities. All rooms come with TV and fridge. Per-person rates here with two meals are ¥6,500 ($52) to ¥10,000 ($80).

Another inexpensive accommodation is the **Hotel New Toyako** ③③⑤, (tel. 01427/5-2818), located a block downhill from the bus depot. A combination business hotel/minshuku, its 15 rooms are very clean and basic and consist of a dozen Japanese-style rooms, two twins, and one double. Only the twin rooms have a private bath and toilet. Rates are the same for all rooms the whole year round: ¥5,500 ($44) to ¥8,800 ($70) per person, including two meals.

The closest youth hostel is the **Showa-Shinzan Youth Hostel** ③③⑥, 103 Sobetsu-onsen, Sobetsu-cho (tel. 01427/5-2283). Sleeping some 60 people on tatami, it's about a seven-minute bus ride from Toyako Onsen bus terminal. Get off at the Showa-Shinzan Toza-an Guchi bus stop. Members pay ¥3,200 ($25.60), which entitles them to two meals, while nonmembers pay ¥700 ($5.60) more. Included in the price is free use of the hostel's hot-spring bath. In winter, a ¥200 ($1.60) heating fee is levied.

Where to Dine: Since you'll be taking dinner and breakfast at your hotel, you have only lunch to worry about. **Oshima** ③③⑦ (tel. 5-4111) is on the second floor of the Wakasaimo Honten Building on the water's edge just west of the main boat dock. In this pleasant and attractive modern restaurant you sit on tatami beside huge windows overlooking the lake. The menu is in Japanese only, but you can make your selection from the plastic-food display case. This is primarily a tempura and soba restaurant, with a variety of other selections as well. Set meals average about ¥1,100 ($8.80) to ¥1,600 ($12.80), with such main dishes as shrimp tempura, salmon teishoku, obento box lunch, and tempura soba. Hours here are 11 a.m. to 8 p.m. (11 a.m. to 6 p.m. in winter) daily.

Another good choice is **Nagisa,** a floating houseboat moored outside the Sun Palace Hotel (tel. 5-4126). Open from 11 a.m. to 2 p.m. and 6 to 10 p.m., it's a light, airy, bright place for a meal. The specialties here are Genghis Khan (strips of mutton and vegetables) for ¥1,600 ($12.80) and barbecued meat dishes starting at ¥2,700 ($21.60), all of which you cook at your own tabletop grill. The barbecued meat dishes include mountains of fresh vegetables and seafood, enough to feed a small army.

Not far from the tourist office, **Boyotei** (tel. 5-2311) is a rather interesting-looking café set back from the town's main road behind an overgrown garden. A wooden sign hanging outside over the sidewalk says "Kafe Restaurant." Opened more than 40 years ago before the large hotels across the street were built to block the view, it now seems rather hidden and forgotten. The interior looks as if it hasn't changed much over the decades, and is filled with knickknacks. A good, cozy place for a morning coffee, lunch, or an evening drink, it's open daily from 10 a.m. to 10 p.m. (until 7 p.m. in winter) and even has some tables and chairs outside. The menu includes pork chops, hamburger steak, fried salmon, macaroni chicken gratin, macaroni crabmeat gratin, beef curry, spaghetti, and sandwiches, with prices ranging from ¥700 ($5.60) to ¥1,750 ($14). There are also set lunches and dinners for ¥1,400 ($11.20) to ¥5,500 ($44). Various kinds of coffees start at ¥380 ($3.04), and beer starts at ¥550 ($4.40). They even have Guinness.

One more inexpensive place for lunch is **Restaurant Park** on the second floor of the Park Hotel (tel. 5-2445). Open only from 10 a.m. to 3 p.m., this informal and simply decorated place serves hamburger steak, curry dishes, noodles, sandwiches, and other choices for ¥700 ($5.60) to ¥1,650 ($13.20).

Noboribetsu

Famous for the variety of its hot-water springs, Noboribetsu Spa (called *Noboribetsu Onsen* in Japanese) is one of Japan's best-known spa resorts. It boasts 11 different types of hot water and gushes 10,000 tons a day. With temperatures ranging between 113° and 197° Fahrenheit, the waters contain all kinds of minerals, including sulfur, salt, iron, and gypsum, and are thought to help relieve such disorders as high blood pressure, rheumatism, arthritis, eczema, and even constipation. Noboribetsu gets its name from the Ainu word meaning simply "white muddy river."

Orientation: Noboribetsu Onsen is about a 15-minute bus ride from the town of Noboribetsu and its Noboribetsu Station, which is where you'll arrive if you come by train. There are also direct buses from Sapporo and Toyako Onsen to Noboribetsu Onsen.

The **tourist office** (tel. 0143/84-3311) is on Noboribetsu Onsen's main street just a minute north of the bus depot. It's open daily from 9 a.m. to 6 p.m. There's a pamphlet and map in English, but you may not encounter anyone here who speaks English. Luckily, the town is so small that you shouldn't have any problem getting around. The busiest tourist season is May to October and during New Year's, which is when hotel rates are at their highest.

The **telephone area code** for Noboribetsu Onsen is 0143.

What to Do: Although all the spa hotels and ryokan have their own taps into the spring water, the most famous hotel bath in town is at the **Daiichi Takimotokan,** a monstrous bathing hall with more than a dozen pools containing different mineral contents at various temperatures. Recently remodeled, it's an elaborate affair with hot-spring baths both indoors and out, a Jacuzzi, saunas, steam rooms, and waterfall massage (the waterfall massage is one of my favorites—you simply sit under the shooting water and let it pummel your neck and shoulders). The baths are separated for men and women, but there's an indoor pool with mixed bathing, so be sure to bring your swimsuit. My only complaint is that the workers cleaning the walls and floors of the bathhouses are men, a couple of whom were none too discreet in their stares. The Japanese women paid them no attention, so I guess we're supposed to do the same. At any rate, visiting the baths here is the best favor you can do yourself while in Noboribetsu. If you're staying at the Daiichi Takimotokan hotel, you can use the baths free of charge at any time. Otherwise, the baths are open to the public only from 9 a.m. to 3 p.m. (that is, you must enter by 3 p.m.). The charge is ¥2,000 ($16).

To get an idea of what all this hot water looks like, visit **Hell Valley (Jigokudani),** at the north edge of town past the Daiichi Takimotokan hotel. A volcanic crater 1,485 feet in diameter, the huge depression is full of bubbling and boiling hot water and rock formations of orange and brown. If you walk along the concrete path that winds along the left side of the crater (called Hell Valley Promenade) and follow it as it swings farther to the left, you'll soon see a picnic area with a narrow footpath that leads off to the right through lush woods. If you follow it for about ten minutes, you'll come to a lookout point overlooking a large pond of hot bubbling water called Ohyunuma (the lookout is across the highway). If you want to take a different route back, follow the path that leads to the right just as you recross the highway. This pathway, called Funamiya Promenade, traces the backbone of several ridges all the way back into town, passing a number of small stone deities on the way.

Another attraction is **Lake Kuttara.** It's an unspoiled caldera lake a few miles from Noboribetsu Onsen and is ranked the second clearest in Japan (the clearest is considered to be Masshu in Akan National Park). Because the water is very cold, swimming is forbidden, but you can rent rowboats. The water is beautiful and wooded hills rise on all sides. There's also a small restaurant where you can eat ramen, tempura, soba, and trout. Unfortunately, there are only three buses a day that come here from Noboribetsu Onsen, leaving the onsen at 9:30 a.m., 11 a.m., and 3:20 p.m. Each bus makes a 25-minute stop at the lake before returning to Noboribetsu Onsen. If this isn't enough time for you, you might want to take the early bus to the lake and return on a later one. Be sure to check on the latest schedule. Buses run from June 1 to October 22 only.

Incidentally, you'll also see advertisements for a bear park and Ainu village attraction. The best thing about this place is the trip via ropeway—the bear park occupies one of the tallest hills around. The hundred or so bears, however, are crowded together in a cement pen, and the Ainu "village" is mainly for souvenirs. I personally think you're better off spending your money elsewhere.

If you find yourself at Noboribetsu Station with some time on your hands, you might want to check out the Hokkaido Marine Park, about ten minutes from the station on foot. Scheduled for opening sometime in the summer of 1990, it is one of the largest aquariums in eastern Japan.

Food and Lodging: Because of its large bathing hall with the various pools, the **Daiichi Takimotokan** (tel. 0143/84-2111) is Noboribetsu Onsen's best-known ryokan and first opened 130 years ago. Guests are entitled to use the pools free anytime night or day. The ryokan's present modern structure houses 336 rooms: 8 rooms have beds, and the rest are all Japanese-style tatami. As with most first-class ryokan in Hokkaido's resort areas, rooms come with fan, TV with pay video, fridge, and a safe for valuables. Rates here during peak season average ¥20,000 ($160) per person in both twin and tatami rooms, including two meals. Off-season, Japanese rooms with toilets only cost ¥16,000 ($128), while twin rooms are ¥18,000 ($144) per person.

Across the street from Daiichi Takimotokan is its Western-style counterpart, **Takimoto Inn** (tel. 0143/84-2205). A small, comfortable, and moderately priced hotel, it has only 47 rooms, all twins. Rooms are colorfully decorated—some with larger-than-life-size flowers splashed onto the wallpaper—but otherwise are fairly basic, with a small bathroom and TV with pay video. The main advantage to staying here is that you can use Daiichi Takimotokan's famous baths for free. From late spring through early autumn, all weekends, and during New Year's, rooms cost ¥12,000 ($96) per person including two meals, decreasing to ¥10,000 ($80) other times of the year. If you'd rather not take your meals here, rooms are available for about 30% less.

Rivaling Daiichi Takimotokan in terms of size, facilities, and comfort is the **Grand Hotel** (tel. 0143/84-2101). Spreading along the slope of a hill just above the bus terminal, it has 259 rooms, 92 of which are twins. Per-person rates for these Western-style rooms are ¥13,000 ($104) including two meals, or ¥16,500 ($132) for two persons without meals. Japanese rooms are ¥15,000 ($120) per person for rooms with a private bathroom and two meals. Rates are the same throughout the year, although they increase by about ¥1,000 ($8) per person on Saturday night. This hotel sports a nice public bath. Though not as large as Takimotokan's, it is more elegant. The men's section has baths both indoors and outdoors, complete with waterfall and Roman goddess statues. As for the women's section, sorry—no outdoor pool, waterfall, or goddesses. However, it's large and bright, and there are saunas for both sexes.

A small, reasonably priced, and very friendly ryokan is **Kiyomizu** (tel. 0143/84-2145). Located on Noboribetsu Onsen's main street just a couple of minutes' walk from the bus terminal, its 20 Japanese-style rooms are modestly furnished and are all without bathroom. Singles range from ¥4,400 ($35.20) to ¥6,500 ($52), twins run ¥8,000 ($64) to ¥10,000 ($88), and triples cost ¥11,500 ($92) to ¥15,000 ($120). Prices are room rates only, without meals. If you opt for food, Japanese or Western breakfasts cost an additional ¥800 ($6.40), while dinner ranges from ¥1,600 ($12.80) to ¥2,200 ($17.60). Meals are served in your room. The owner, Mr. Iwai, speaks very good English and can answer your questions regarding Noboribetsu and the surrounding area. There are small hot-spring baths in the ryokan and the public toilets are Japanese style. Incidentally, Mr. Iwai plans to add another 40 rooms in a nearby annex. Slated for completion by the summer of 1990, it will feature both a hot-spring bath on the seventh floor with views of the surrounding countryside and an open-air bath. Rates here for tatami rooms will start at around ¥10,000 ($80).

Although they're a bit far from Noboribetsu Onsen, if you're on a budget you might consider staying at either Kikusui or Noboribetsu-so. Both are minshuku run by families who also manage adjoining temples. **Kikusui** ⓷⓸⓼ (tel. 0143/84-2437) is run by a woman whose husband is a Buddhist monk. There are a total of nine tatami rooms here, all without bath. Close by is **Noboribetsu-so** ⓷⓸⓽ (tel. 0143/84-3352), smaller, with only five tatami rooms, all without bath. Both minshuku charge ¥6,000 ($48) per person, including two meals. Note that these two minshuku are located on the route of the bus that travels between Noboribetsu Station and Noboribetsu Onsen, so if you're coming from the train station, there's no need to go all the way to the spa—get off at "Chugaku-mae." Buses are rather infrequent, so check the schedule. Since these minshuku do not have hot-spring baths, you'll have to hike into town (about 30 minutes) to Takimotokan if you want the real thing. Personally, I rather like the isolation of these minshuku.

There are three youth hostels in Noboribetsu Onsen, the first two with hot-spring baths. **Kannonji** ③④⓪ (tel. 0143/84-2359) is run by a very friendly group of people who delight in receiving foreign guests. Accommodating 25 persons in tatami rooms, it has its own hot-spring bath, and coffee is available free in the small dining room. Members are charged ¥2,100 ($16.80) and nonmembers pay ¥2,800 ($22.20). Japanese breakfasts cost ¥400 ($3.20), while dinners are ¥700 ($5.60). The dinners are especially good—notably a one-pot stew with chicken, egg, and vegetables called nabe. Kannonji is located about a seven-minute walk from the bus terminal.

Another good choice in youth hostels is **Akashiya Youth Hostel** ③④① (tel. 0143/84-2616). Just a couple of minutes' walk from the bus terminal, it sleeps 55 persons in both beds and tatami. The charge of ¥3,200 ($25.60) for members and ¥3,900 ($31) for nonmembers includes two meals.

If these two places are full, there's another youth hostel located a few minutes farther out of town called **Youth Hostel Ryokan Kanefuku** ③④② (tel. 0143/84-2565), with prices similar to those given above. Unfortunately, there is no hot-spring bath here—only baths with water of the regular kind.

If you find yourself looking for a place to stop for lunch, or a draft beer, or coffee, the Takimoto Inn's **Poplar Restaurant** serves inexpensive Western dishes from 11 a.m. to 2 p.m. The Japanese menu with pictures lists such choices as beefsteak, pork chops, hamburger steak, fried shrimp, fried scallops, sandwiches, curry rice, shrimp gratin, and spaghetti. All are in the ¥650 ($5.20) to ¥1,600 ($12.80) range.

Shiraoi

On your way between Sapporo and Noboribetsu you might wish to visit Shiraoi, where a mock Ainu village has been set up. The village consists of thatched houses in which demonstrations and dances are performed by Ainu. Particularly interesting is the museum, which contains crafts, utensils, and clothing of the Ainu. Explanations are in English and the displays realistically depict what life was like for the Ainu before the Japanese assimilated them into their society. If you want to know more about the Ainu, pick up a booklet called *The Ainu Museum* (¥400 [$3.20]), which describes their lifestyle, religious beliefs, and customs. Entrance fee to the Ainu village is ¥515 ($4.12), and hours are 8 a.m. to 5:30 p.m. daily (8:30 a.m. to 4:30 p.m. November through March).

DAISETSUZAN NATIONAL PARK

Although I find it difficult to rank nature in terms of beauty, there are some who maintain that Daisetsuzan National Park is the most spectacular of Hokkaido's parks. With its tall mountains covered with fir and birch trees and sprinkled with wildflowers, its river gorge laced with waterfalls and hiking trails throughout, Daisetsuzan National Park is the perfect place to come if you've been itching to get some exercise in a relatively unspoiled countryside. Lying in the center of Hokkaido, this national park, Japan's largest, contains three volcanic mountain groups, including the highest mountain in Hokkaido, Mount Asahi, at 7,513 feet. Hiking in summer and skiing in winter are the primary pursuits of the region.

The perfect base for exploring the national park is Sounkyo Onsen, nestled at the very edge of Sounkyo Gorge, Daisetsuzan's most famous natural attraction. A tiny village of ryokan and minshuku, it's a good starting point for seeing both the gorge and for ascending the mountains. Although the town itself is rather unattractive, with its cluster of souvenir shops and unimaginative buildings, its soothing hot springs and magnificent scenic backdrop make coming here worthwhile. Not only that, Sounkyo Onsen serves as the starting point for bicycle trips along Sounkyo

Gorge and for the cable car trip to the top of a neighboring peak. Sounkyo is one of my favorite places in all of Hokkaido.

Orientation

The only way to reach Sounkyo Onsen by public transportation is by bus. If you're coming from Sapporo, take the train as far as Kamikawa (2½ hours) and from there transfer to a bus for a 30-minute ride that will take you directly to Sounkyo. There are also buses connecting Sounkyo Onsen with Asahigawa and Rubeshibe, both about a 2-hour ride away. The **tourist information office** is located in a modern-looking wooden building downhill from the bus station. You can see it from the bus depot, and it's called the PR Center (tel. 01658/5-3350). No one speaks English here and maps of the village are in Japanese only, but the staff can point you in the direction of your ryokan or even make ryokan reservations for you. They also have a brochure in English describing the national park and its attractions. The office is open daily from 9 a.m. to 5 p.m. (from 10 a.m. to 4 p.m. November through April). In any case, the village is so tiny you won't have any difficulty getting around.

The **telephone area code** for Sounkyo Onsen is 01658.

What to Do

Sounkyo Gorge is a river valley hemmed in on both sides by rock walls rising almost 500 feet high. Almost perpendicular in places, the gorge extends for about 12 miles, offering spectacular views with each bending curve. The best way to see the gorge is on a bicycle, which you can rent from stalls beside the bus terminal and a number of other places for ¥1,200 ($9.60) a day. There's a designated route you're supposed to follow, and altogether the trip to the end of the route and back should take no longer than 2½ hours. The first part of the trip by bicycle is unfortunately on a sidewalk next to a highway strung with cars. (Since you probably already think I'm degenerate, I might as well tell you that I wore my Walkman while riding on the sidewalk here to block out traffic noise. What the heck, I was by myself anyway and had no one else to talk to.) The highway winds along a rushing river past a couple of waterfalls until finally the highway disappears into a dark tunnel—which is where I'm convinced it belongs anyway. At this point the gorge belongs to cyclists and hikers, and becomes quite narrow. You then pass through a tunnel yourself and emerge at the turning point of your trip where you'll find—what else?—souvenir shops, soda machines, and vendors selling corn on the cob. This is where tour buses pull in for a quick look.

If you're interested in hiking, or even if you're not, take the cable car from Sounkyo Onsen to the lofty peak of **Kuro-dake Mountain.** The trip takes seven minutes and costs ¥750 ($6) one way. From the cable-car station, walk a few minutes farther up the mountain where you'll come to a chair lift. This costs ¥220 ($1.76) one way and takes 15 minutes, swinging you past lush forests of fir and birch. At the end of the lift where the hiking paths begin, there's a hut where you sign your name and give your route so that tabs can be kept on people who are on the mountain. If you're not feeling overly ambitious, you can hike an hour and reach the peak of Kuro-dake, 6,500 feet high, where if the weather is clear you'll be rewarded with views of the surrounding mountain ranges.

If you feel like taking a day's hike, there's a circular path along the top of mountain ridges that you can hike in about seven hours. And if you're really into hiking and wish to carry your backpack with you, a popular route is to walk from the Sounkyo chair lift over Mount Asahi, Hokkaido's tallest mountain, and on to another chair lift that will take you down to Asahidake Onsen, a spa where you can spend the night. This trip takes eight to ten hours, so set out early. Be sure to pick up a map showing the hiking trails. It's in Japanese only, but since the trails are also marked in Japanese only, having an English map wouldn't do you much good. The hiking path isn't considered that strenuous, but you do need sturdy walking shoes.

If you're going for just a short hike, tennis shoes are fine. The tops of the mountains are really beautiful here, covered with wildflowers and alpine plant life. It would be a shame to come to Sounkyo and not spend at least a few hours amid its lofty peaks.

During the winter season the mountains become a skier's haven from November to May. Although you can rent skis up on the mountain at the cable-car station, keep in mind that your feet may be too big. Skis and boots rent for ¥3,300 ($26.40) and up. A day's cable-car and chair-lift ticket costs ¥2,800 ($22.40). The lift operations vary according to the month, but are open from about 8 or 9 a.m. to 4 or 4:30 p.m. in winter and from 6 a.m. to 7 p.m. in summer months. Please note that the lifts shut down entirely for two weeks beginning in mid-February for maintenance work.

If you have time to kill, you might also consider dropping in on the **Sounkyo Museum Daisetsuzan National Park.** Its explanations are in Japanese only, and you'll see some aerial reliefs of the area, stuffed animals, butterflies, insects, and birds. Admission is ¥200 ($1.60).

Food and Lodging

As in all resort areas in Japan, Sounkyo Onsen's hotels, ryokan, and minshuku all include breakfast and dinner in their rates. Unless otherwise stated, therefore, all prices quoted below are on a per-person basis and include two meals. If you want to stay here in August, make reservations in advance. Incidentally, most families who live here run several operations that might include a ryokan, an adjoining restaurant, and a souvenir shop. As for the army of young Japanese college-age guys you see waiting tables, hustling customers at the bicycle stalls, and working in ryokan kitchens and souvenir shops in the summertime, they're not locals. Rather, they come from other parts of Japan and are working in Sounkyo for a summer job. They may not know a lot about the area, but most of them speak some English.

If you can get a room on a top floor facing the gorge, one of the best places to stay in town is the **Taisetsu Hotel** (tel. 01658/5-3211). A large white hotel atop a hill above the town, this 250-room property is about a seven-minute walk from the bus terminal. Depending on the size of your room and its view, rates here range from ¥9,000 ($72) to ¥16,500 ($132) per person; rates are about 20% cheaper in the wintertime. The most expensive rooms face the gorge, while the cheapest rooms have toilets but no baths. Western breakfasts are available on request. Most rooms are tatami, but four Western-style rooms are also available. The hot-spring public baths here are large and consist of several different pools. As is often the case, however, the men's bath commands a better view than the women's.

Just across the street from the Taisetsu is the **Sounkyo Prince Hotel Choyotei** (tel. 01658/5-3241), which made its debut in 1987. Boasting a good view of the gorge from its location atop a ridge, it offers 271 rooms, all with private bathroom. With both Japanese-style and combination rooms available, its rooms are pleasant and elegantly simple and come with refrigerator, a safe for valuables, and TV with adult video. Rates average ¥16,500 ($132) to ¥22,000 ($176) per person with two meals, with the higher rates charged for rooms with views of the gorge. Rates are about 20% cheaper in winter. Facilities include a modern, comfortable lobby with views of a rock garden, an electronic-game room, a souvenir shop, noodle and sushi counters, and public baths on the top floor overlooking the gorge.

Situated beside the highway that runs through Sounkyo Gorge, the **Grand Hotel** ③ (tel. 01658/5-3111) is an older hotel that recently received a much-needed face-lift. The lobby, with its marbled pillars and white walls, is cheerful though a bit overdone; the public spa baths are quite nice, with large windows, white tile, and stone. There are also outdoor baths, separated for men and women. All of its 191 rooms come with private bathroom and start at ¥11,000 ($88), with ¥20,000 ($160) the average price paid for a room on a top floor with a view of the surrounding mountain ranges. During winter the rates are about 10% lower.

Pension Yukara ③ (tel. 01658/5-3216) opened in 1985, its spotlessly clean, white, bright, and cute style meant to appeal to young Japanese girls. Its seven rooms, all without bathroom, include both twins and tatami rooms and are decorated with pastel-colored wallpaper, feminine furniture, and lots of pink. There's a coin laundry here, but the drawback to this place is that it doesn't have a hot-spring bath—just regular bath water. Breakfast and dinner are Western style. Rates are ¥7,500 ($60) throughout the year except in August, when they're ¥10,000 ($80).

Tsuchiya �345 (tel. 01658/5-3517) prides itself on being the largest minshuku in Hokkaido, for whatever that's worth. It has 50 rooms in a main building and an annex, all without bathroom. It charges ¥6,000 ($48) throughout the year. Facilities include hot-spring baths, coin laundry, and very clean rooms. Western breakfasts are available.

A simple minshuku with only eight Japanese-style rooms, a few minutes' walk from the bus terminal, **Onozuka** �346 (tel. 01658/5-3308) does have its own hot-spring baths, as well as a coffeeshop on the ground floor. None of the rooms come with private bathroom, and the year-round rate here is ¥5,500 ($44) to ¥6,000 ($48) per person. Western-style breakfasts are available if ordered the night before.

Kitagawa �347 (tel. 01658/5-3515 and 5-3231) is another minshuku that attracts mainly young Japanese. Located above a souvenir shop and restaurant of the same name, it has 12 Japanese-style rooms without bathroom facilities. It has both a coin laundry and hot-spring baths. Clean and pleasant, it charges ¥5,800 ($46.40) per person.

There are two youth hostels in Sounkyo Onsen. **Sounkyo Youth Hostel** �348 (tel. 01658/5-3418) is located on top of a hill past the Taisetsu Hotel, about a ten-minute walk from the station, a pleasant location. It has both beds and futons and charges ¥3,500 ($28) including two meals, for both members and nonmembers. Unfortunately, it doesn't have hot springs. The other youth hostel, **Ginsenkaku Youth Hostel** �349 (tel. 01658/5-3003), is located in town just a few minutes' walk from the bus terminal. It charges ¥3,500 ($28) for hostel members, while nonmembers pay ¥700 ($5.60) more. Prices include two meals. This youth hostel also has its own hot-spring bath, for which it charges an extra ¥150 ($1.20).

AKAN NATIONAL PARK

Spreading through the eastern end of Hokkaido, Akan National Park features volcanic mountains, dense forests of subarctic primeval trees, and three caldera lakes, including Lake Akan. The best place to stay in the park is at Akanko Onsen, a small hot-spring resort on the edge of Lake Akan. It makes a good base from which to explore both the Akan National Park and the Red-Crested Crane National Park nearby.

Orientation

Because Akan National Park lies at the eastern extremity of Hokkaido, you may wish to fly back to Tokyo. **Kushiro Airport** is one hour and 20 minutes away by bus from Akanko Onsen. The plane trip from Kushiro to Tokyo takes about 1½ hours.

Since there's no train station at Akanko, transportation to the resort town is by bus from Kushiro or Bihoro. Sightseeing buses are the best way to see the park, described in more detail below. If you have any questions concerning Akan National Park, drop by the **Visitor's Center,** with displays (unfortunately only in Japanese) of natural wonders pertaining to the park. You can also stop at the **tourist association** (tel. 0154/67-2254), located just a minute's walk from the bus terminal in the direction of the lake. You can pick up an English pamphlet about Akan National Park here and make reservations for hotels, ryokan, and minshuku. It's open daily from 9 a.m. to 7 p.m. There's also a small tourist window next to the boat pier where you buy tickets for boat rides on Lake Akan.

As for Akanko Onsen itself, it's small and walking is the best way to get around. It consists primarily of one main street that snakes along the lake, with ryokan and souvenir shops on both sides.

The **telephone area code** for Akanko Onsen is 0154.

What to Do

Your sightseeing in Akan National Park should begin before reaching Akanko Onsen, which lies in the southern part of the park. The best way to see the park, if you're not renting a car, is to board an **Akan sightseeing bus** in Bihoro, which is north of the park. That way you'll travel all the way through the park and see the most important natural wonders. The bus trip takes five hours, making stops at several scenic spots along the way, including Kussharo and Mashu lakes. Kussharo is one of Japan's largest mountain lakes, while Mashu is considered to be one of the most beautiful. A deep crater lake with the clearest water in Japan, Mashu was called "lake of the devil" by the Ainu because of the mysterious fact that no water flows either into it or out of it. Surely Mashu is one of Japan's least-spoiled lakes—because of the steep, 660-foot-high rock walls ringing the lake, it has remained inaccessible to mankind (the bus stops at two observation platforms high above the lake). The bus trip costs ¥5,360 ($42.88) and is called the Panorama Course. At last check buses departed from Bihoro three times daily, at 8:40 a.m., 11 a.m., and 12:40 p.m. from the end of April to the end of October. During the winter months, only one bus departs daily. In any case, be sure to check departures ahead of time, since bus schedules change. In addition to sightseeing buses, there are also regular, direct buses that travel between Bihoro and Akan in about 70 minutes. For more information, call 0152/3-4182.

As for things to do in Akanko, the most popular activity is to take a **boat cruise** around **Lake Akan.** Lake Akan is famous for its very rare spherical green weed, called marimo. It's a sponge-like ball of duckweed that grows two to five inches in diameter. Found in only a few places in the world, marimo is formed when many separate and stringy pieces of weed at the bottom of the lake roll around and eventually come together to form a ball. The ball grows larger and larger until sooner or later it breaks apart, whereby the whole process starts over again. On your boat cruise you'll make a stop at a small island on the lake where a marimo museum has been set up, consisting of duckweed in a few tanks, together with explanations of how they're formed. Supposedly, when the sun shines the marimo rises to the surface of the water, giving Lake Akan a wonderful green shimmer. However, the only marimo I ever saw was in the museum's tanks and in tanks of souvenir shops around town—even though the sun was shining. Perhaps you'll have better luck. The boat trip takes 1½ hours and costs ¥1,020 ($8.16).

While you're out on your boat trip, you'll notice two cone-shaped **volcanoes,** O-Akandake to the east and Me-Akandake to the south. Both are popular destinations for hikers. O-Akandake is dormant and it's about a 4½ hour hike to the summit from Akanko Onsen. Me-Akandake, the highest mountain in the Akan area, is active and is covered with primeval forests of spruce and fir. There's a trail leading to Me-Akandake from the west end of the town, and it takes about four hours to reach the top, from which you have panoramic views of the surrounding area.

A shorter hike follows a trail to Mount Hakutozan, from which you also have a good view of the town and lake. It takes about two hours to reach Akan's skiing area and another 30 minutes to reach Mount Hakutozan, a grassy and moss-covered knobby hill that remains warm throughout the year because of thermal activity just below the surface. The woods of birch and pine here are beautiful, and what's more, you'll probably find yourself all alone.

Incidentally, behind the Visitor's Center described under the orientation section is a catwalk leading through marshy woods and connecting with a trail that terminates on the lake's shore. Here you'll find some bubbly hot-mud ponds, a grassy area good for picnics, and a rock-enclosed hot-spring that empties right into the lake.

If you're in Akan in the winter, you may want to take advantage of its artificial snow atop the town's one skiing hill. The season runs from about the end of November until May and the two runs are good for beginners.

If you haven't seen any Ainu dances yet, you might want to pay a visit to **Ainu Kotan Village** (tel. 67-2727). Actually, this isn't a village at all. It's a souvenir-shop-lined street leading to a thatch-roofed lodge where you can see Ainu performing traditional dances. Costing ¥600 ($4.80), shows are performed about six times a day from May to the end of October and last half an hour.

By the way, since Akanko Onsen is a hot-spring spa, it would be a shame to come all this way and not partake of its waters. If you're staying somewhere that doesn't have hot springs, you can visit the public hot springs, called **Marimo Onsen,** located across the street from the main boat dock. Open from 9 a.m. to 10 p.m. (until 9 p.m. in winter), Marimo Onsen charges a ¥260 ($2.08) admission.

Red-crested cranes are the prefectural birds of Hokkaido, and south of Akan is a breeding ground for these graceful and beautiful animals. **Tancho-zuru Shizen Koen (Red-crested Crane Natural Park)** (tel. 0154/56-2219) is a marshy area set aside for breeding and raising the crane. Open throughout the year from 9 a.m. to 5 p.m. (to 4 p.m. in winter), it charges ¥300 ($2.40) for visitors to observe the birds behind high mesh fences. You'll be surprised at how large these birds actually are. The crane park is one hour and 15 minutes by bus from the Akanko Onsen bus terminal; get off at the Tsuru-koen bus stop. By the way, this is the same bus that goes from Akanko to Kushiro Airport. The bus makes a 15-minute stop at this park, which is enough time to jump out and take a quick look at the birds before continuing on to the airport.

If you happen to be in Akan in the winter, you'll have the extra delight of visiting **Tancho-no-Sato,** private grounds where red-crested cranes court, mate, and live in the winter months from November to March. This is the best place to photograph the birds in action. It's a 42-minute bus ride from Akanko Onsen bus terminal.

Food and Lodging

Unless otherwise stated, all prices include two meals and are per person.

Ryokan and Hotels: Situated on a shady spot beside Lake Akan, the **New Akan Hotel** (tel. 0154/67-2121) is a 296-room property winding along the curve of the lake in a series of wings built at various stages in the past 20 years. The newest addition is the Annex Crystal, with very pleasant rooms featuring bay windows looking out on shade trees and the lake beyond. Rooms cost about ¥27,000 ($216) per person in summer and ¥20,000 ($160) in winter. These rooms have nicely finished tile bathrooms, plus hairdryers and the usual fridge, radio, clock, hot-water pot, TV with coin video, and even a pants presser for pants and skirts. Both Japanese-style and Western-style rooms are available. Rooms in the older wings are more modestly priced, beginning at ¥17,500 ($140) per person for rooms facing the lake and ¥13,000 ($104) for those facing inland.

Facilities at the hotel include souvenir shops, large public hot-spring baths, a bar, and a few restaurants. **Crystal Restaurant** in the Annex Crystal is a good place to come for lunch. Its English menu offers sandwiches, spaghetti, beef curry, shrimp or crab pilaf, noodles, and more, at ¥700 ($5.60) to ¥1,500 ($12) for most items, as well as daily specials for ¥2,200 ($17.60). The restaurant has a very nice view of shade trees and lake and is open from 11 a.m. to 9 p.m.

Located right next to the boat dock on the water's edge, **Hotel Akankoso** (tel. 0154/67-2231) has a variety of Japanese-style rooms, as well as combination rooms, with and without bathroom, all with a variety of prices to match. The best rooms face the lake and come with a private bathroom, at ¥17,500 ($140) while the least expensive are Western-style twins or Japanese-style rooms without a bathroom that face inland and cost ¥15,400 ($123). During winter, rates drop down to ¥9,000 ($72) and ¥6,500 ($52), respectively. The hotel's large communal hot-spring baths on the fifth floor are nicely laid out in brick and have views of the lake.

Opened in 1984, the **Akan View Hotel** (tel. 0154/67-3131) is the spa's newest place to stay and, despite its name, one of the few hotels without a view of the lake. It's back from the waterfront, more inland than the other hotels, and 200 rooms are Western-style twins with private bathrooms. There are also 28 Japanese-style rooms. Rates here range from ¥11,000 ($88) to ¥16,500 ($132) per person during peak season, dropping down to ¥6,600 ($53) in winter. One of the best things about this hotel is that it has large indoor pools, one for swimming laps and one for children, as well as the usual hot-spring baths, open from 7 a.m. to 9 p.m. Even if you're not staying at the hotel, you can use the facilities for ¥750 ($6) on weekdays and ¥1,100 ($8.80) on weekends and holidays. Other facilities include tennis courts and bicycles for rent. Although none of the rooms has a view of the water, the best rooms, in my opinion, are those that face east, where there are some woods and a creek.

A much older hotel, the **Hotel Ichikawa** ③⑤⓪ (tel. 0154/67-2011) is an 89-room ryokan that opened back in 1961. Located right on the water's edge, it's a very reasonably priced place to stay and the front-desk personnel are nice and friendly. One advantage to staying here is Shigeru Dameon Takada, a young Japanese man who studied in Canada and speaks very good English. Since this ryokan is a family-run affair, he told me, he would be staying here the rest of his life. He also said he'd be very happy to help foreigners with any questions they might have regarding Akan —which could be quite useful, since hardly anyone in Akan speaks English. All rooms are Japanese style except two twins, and rates are ¥8,000 ($64) per person for rooms facing inland and ¥13,000 ($104) for those with a view of the lake. During winter the rates go down to ¥7,000 ($56) and ¥11,000 ($88), respectively. Rooms on the top (sixth) floor command the best views. The hot-spring public baths on the first floor are very modern and face the lake. If you're here in summer, be sure to go out on the hotel's tatami-floored boat, gaily decorated with lanterns. It goes out for about 40 minutes at night serenaded by Japanese music. The trip costs ¥1,500 ($12) per person and includes one drink with a snack.

The hotel also maintains a pontoon boat for two-hour sunset cruises on the lake, complete with barbecue dinner and a glass of wine for ¥3,300 ($26.40) per person. The hotel can make arrangements for fishing, waterskiing, or snow skiing and will even tailor day trips to other lakes and hiking destinations to your own desires.

Right next to Ichikawa is the **Akan Grand Hotel** ③⑤① (tel. 0154/67-2531), also right on the water's edge. This white hotel has Japanese-style tatami and combination rooms, all with bathroom. Rooms with a lake view cost ¥13,000 ($104) to ¥22,000 ($176), while those facing inland are ¥11,000 ($88) to ¥20,000 ($160). Winter rates are ¥2,000 ($16) to ¥4,000 ($32) lower. Rooms are modern and clean, and come with the usual TV with pay video, fridge, and clock. The public baths here are fairly unique and have a large fish tank built into the wall.

Minshuku: In addition to the large hotels and ryokan there are a number of inexpensive minshuku in Akanko Onsen. Rooms are simple and are without private bathroom but offer good value for the money. The charge for all the minshuku listed below is ¥5,500 ($44) per person, with two meals.

Minshuku Yamaguchi ③⑤② (tel. 0154/67-2555) is located on the west edge of town. As with most minshuku, this family-run lodge is small, with just ten Japanese-style rooms. The advantage to staying here is that it has a hot-spring communal bath. Rooms come with coin-operated TV and are simple but cozy. From the dining room you have a peaceful view of some woods and, in winter when the leaves are gone, a view of the lake.

Across the street from Yamaguchi is **Minshuku Ginrei** ③⑤③ (tel. 0154/67-2597). There are nine rooms here, again simple, with coin-operated TV. There's no view and no hot-spring bath, but the man who runs this place is used to foreigners and welcomes them.

One more minshuku is **Minshuku Kiri** (tel. 0154/67-2755), located across the street from the Hotel Ichikawa. Look for the wooden sign hanging above the door with the English written very small. The nine Japanese-style rooms are simple, with coin-operated TV. The bathtubs here are wooden and the water is from hot springs.

Youth Hostels: The **Akankohan Youth Hostel** (tel. 0154/67-2241) is right next to the boat sightseeing dock. Old and a bit run-down and open only July and

August, it charges ¥3,500 ($28) for hostel members, including two meals, while nonmembers pay ¥700 ($5.60) more. Its sign is in English, and it's conveniently located about a four-minute walk from the bus terminal. More than 25 years old, it has a rather uncertain future, so it would be wise to call beforehand to make sure it's still in operation.

The **Angel Youth Hostel** ⑤④ (tel. 0154/67-2309) is farther out of town, about a 15- to 20-minute walk from the bus terminal, but the building is newer and in better shape. If you call from the bus terminal, someone will come pick you up. There are also bicycles for rent here, making it easy to get back and forth to town. Rates here with two meals are ¥3,500 ($28) for members and ¥4,200 ($33.60) for nonmembers. The place has its own hot-spring bath.

PART TWO

HONG KONG

ENJOYING HONG KONG

Every time I go to Hong Kong I feel as though I've wandered onto a movie set. Perhaps I'm an incurable romantic, but whenever I stand at the railing of the famous Star Ferry as it glides across the harbor, crouch upon the wooden bench of a rickety old tram as it winds its way across Hong Kong Island, or clutch the side of the funicular as it groans its way up to Victoria Peak, I can't help but think I must have somehow landed in the middle of an epic drama where the past has melted into the present. So many images float by—wooden boats bobbing up and down in the harbor beside huge ocean liners; narrow streets and old crumbling buildings standing next to modern high-rises; abacuses being sold alongside pocket calculators. There are neon lights, markets, crowds of people, and noise. Certainly it's one of the most vibrant cities in the world. But that doesn't say it all.

A British colony, Hong Kong was founded as a place to conduct business and to trade, and that has been its raison d'être ever since. The world's third-largest financial center after New York and London, Hong Kong is the Wall Street of Asia, with banking, international insurance, advertising, and publishing among its biggest concerns. Hong Kong is also the world's leading exporter of toys and garments and is one of the largest manufacturers of watches and electronics.

A duty-free port, Hong Kong attracts more than five million tourists a year, making tourism its third-largest industry. Shopping is one of the main reasons people come here, and at first glance Hong Kong does seem rather like one huge department store. But there's much more to Hong Kong than shopping. Whether it's dining, wining, sightseeing, or relaxing that you're looking for, one thing is certain—the more you search, the more you'll find. And before long you too will be swept up in the drama.

1. Introducing Hong Kong

GEOGRAPHY

Located at the southeastern tip of the People's Republic of China, Hong Kong is just south of the Tropic of Cancer, at the same latitude as Mexico City, the Bahamas, and Hawaii. Covering 404 square miles, Hong Kong can be divided into four distinct parts: Hong Kong Island, Kowloon Peninsula, the New Territories, and 235 outlying islands.

Hong Kong Island is where the colony's financial and business district is located, in a modern area known as the Central District. East of the Central District are Wanchai, formerly the reputed haunt of the fictitious Suzie Wong and women of the night, and Causeway Bay, an area of restaurants and shops. Victoria Peak crowns the center of the island, and on the southern coast can be found Aberdeen with its boat population, Repulse Bay with its long stretch of beach, and Stanley with its famous market.

North across the harbor from Hong Kong Island is Kowloon Peninsula, the tip of which is called Tsimshatsui (also written Tsim Sha Tsui). This is where most of Hong Kong's tourist hotels, shops, and restaurants are located. The New Territories stretch north of Kowloon to the border of China. Once a vast area of peaceful little villages, fields, and duck farms, in the past decade the New Territories have witnessed a remarkable mushrooming of satellite towns with huge public-housing estates.

HISTORY

Records show that Hong Kong Island has been inhabited since ancient times, evidenced by the recovery of stone, bronze, and iron artifacts, and more than 100 Neolithic and Bronze Age sites have been identified on Hong Kong and its 235 islands.

Hong Kong's modern history, however, begins in 1841, when Hong Kong Island was ceded to the British as a spoil of the first Opium War. The Opium War was fought basically because the British were determined to sell bars of opium to the Chinese, while the Chinese emperor was determined to keep the British from doing so. Opium, after all, was damaging Chinese society and was draining the country of silver traded to support the drug habit. China lost the struggle, however, and in a treaty it never recognized, was forced to cede in perpetuity Hong Kong Island to the British.

Kowloon Peninsula and Stonecutters Island were added to the colony in 1860 as a result of the second Opium War, and in 1898 the New Territories, including the 235 outlying islands, were leased to Britain for 99 years.

When the British moved in to occupy Hong Kong Island in 1841, it was so empty that the British Lord Palmerston described it as "a barren island with hardly a house upon it." It didn't stay that way for long. The British were interested in Hong Kong Island as a trade and warehousing center as well as a stronghold in Asia, and by 1846 the population was an astonishing 24,000. By the turn of the century the number had swelled to 300,000.

Hong Kong's growth this century has been no less astonishing, in terms of both its trade and its population. In 1911 the overthrow of the Manchu Empire in China sent a flood of refugees into Hong Kong, followed in 1938 with an additional 500,000 Chinese refugees. Another mass influx of Chinese refugees took place after the fall of Shanghai to the Communists in 1950. From this wave of immigrants emerged the beginnings of Hong Kong's now-famous textile industry.

In 1978 Vietnamese refugees started pouring into Hong Kong at the rate of 600 a day, and a year later more than 550,000 Vietnamese were living in camps around the colony. Finding itself no longer able to support additional refugees, Hong Kong now has a policy whereby illegal immigrants from China are immediately sent back and Vietnamese are sent elsewhere as soon as possible.

THE PEOPLE

With a population of 5½ million, Hong Kong is one of the most densely populated areas in the world. The vast majority—98%—are Chinese, more than half of whom were born in Hong Kong. The other 2%, known in Cantonese as *gwailo*—which literally means "foreign devils"—are primarily British, followed by Americans, Australians, Canadians, Indians, and other Asians.

The Chinese are by nature a very hard-working, pragmatic people. There are many stories of refugees who arrived with nothing in their pockets, set up a small sidewalk business, worked diligently until they had their own store, and then expanded it into a modest chain. In such a business-oriented society, success is everything and failure accounts for nothing.

People often ask me whether there is much difference between the Japanese and the Chinese. There probably couldn't be two more dissimilar peoples. While the Japanese tend to be quiet, reserved, restrained, and restricted, the Chinese are noisy, less inhibited, less orderly, and probably more gregarious. Many Japanese have told me that Hong Kong is too much for them—accustomed to orderliness, they find Hong Kong too chaotic, too confusing, and too unpredictable. And it is for exactly these reasons that I like it.

RELIGION

The practical nature of the Chinese is also evident in the role religion plays in their lives. Most Hong Kong Chinese are both Taoist and Buddhist, something they do not find incongruous. There are about 360 Chinese temples scattered throughout Hong Kong.

Whereas Buddhism is concerned with the afterlife, Taoism is a folk faith that believes in luck and in currying its favor. In Taoism gods must be worshipped and spirits appeased, and the most popular of these is Tin Hau, goddess of the sea and protectress of fishermen. There are at least 24 temples erected in her honor in Hong Kong.

Another Taoist belief is that before a house can be built, a tree chopped down, or a boulder moved, a specialist must be called in to make certain that the spirits inhabiting the place are not disturbed. In New Year's celebrations, door gods are placed on the front door for good luck and all lights are switched on to ward off monster spirits. On New Year's Day, the house is not swept for fear of whisking away good luck.

THE FUTURE

As a Crown Colony governed by the British, Hong Kong has always lived very much in the present. However, with the expiration of the 99-year lease on the New Territories in 1997, the future of Hong Kong is on everyone's mind.

On July 1, 1997, Britain will transfer all of capitalist Hong Kong to Chinese Communist rule. According to the pact drawn up for the transfer, China guarantees that it will preserve Hong Kong's capitalist lifestyle and social system for at least 50 years after 1997. But whether Hong Kong nonetheless will undergo a great change once China takes over is a subject of hot debate in the Crown Colony, especially in

HONG KONG AND ENVIRONS

Shataukok

Mirs Bay

Fanling

Tai Po

CANTON RR

Tolo Harbor

.University Station

Shatin

Sai Kung

g Dynasty
age

Kowloon Peak

Port Shelter

Kai Tak Airport

wloon City

Kowloon
Bay

hatsui

North Point

arbour Tunnel

Leiyuemon

Central

WANCHAI

CAUSEWAY BAY

Hong Kong

Clear Water Bay

erdeen

chau

Ta: Tam
Bay

Repulse Bay

Stanley
Bay

nd I.

Chunghumkok

N

Potoi Island

Canton

PEOPLE'S REPUBLIC
OF CHINA

Kwantung   Province

Pearl River

Hong Kong

Macau
(Port.)

SOUTH CHINA SEA

| 0 | Miles | 20 |
| 0 | Kilometers | 30 |

light of the brutal manner in which the Communist authorities quashed the student rebellion in 1989. Thus, as Britain pulls out, many of Hong Kong's foreign community will go with her. Many Chinese who can afford to emigrate have already searched for viable new homes, with Singapore and North America high on the list. As one Hong Kong Chinese told me, his family fled China to escape Communist rule—why remain after 1997?

The vast majority of Chinese, however, will stay. They point out that Hong Kong has had a strong relationship with China for a long time and is dependent on the mainland for much of its food and even its water. China, they hope, has much to gain by keeping Hong Kong as it is, especially since China is opening up more and more to foreigners and seems eager to compete in the world market.

---

2. Getting There and Getting Around

GETTING THERE

Most likely you'll arrive in Hong Kong by plane, unless you've joined a luxury liner or are trekking across China. As described in Chapter I in the section on getting to Japan, the best thing to do if you plan to visit both Japan and Hong Kong is to purchase a ticket to Hong Kong that allows stopovers in Japan. The airlines that will allow you to do this from the U. S. are *Japan Airlines* (tel. 800/525-3663), *Northwest Airlines* (tel. 800/225-2525), *Singapore Airlines* (tel. 800/742-3333), and *United Airlines* (tel. 800/241-6522). *Cathay Pacific Airways* (tel. 800/233-2742), however, flies directly from the West Coast to Hong Kong. The fares listed below are for **Japan Airlines,** and all flights originating in North America stop in Japan before continuing on to Hong Kong. The fares quoted are as of fall of 1989 and are subject to change. Be sure to contact a travel agent or the airlines once you've decided on your itinerary for up-to-date information.

Plane Fares

If you want to travel in luxury, JAL's first-class round-trip ticket to Hong Kong is $4,580 from New York, $4,578 from Chicago, and $3,880 from Seattle, San Francisco, or Los Angeles. The business class, all-year round-trip fare is $2,720 from New York, $2,718 from Chicago, and $2,138 from airports on the West Coast. The all-year economy round-trip fare with no restrictions is $2,350, $2,348, and $1,768, respectively.

If you're traveling on a budget, you can save money by purchasing a Super Saver ticket. Reservations, ticketing, and payment must be completed prior to departure. There is no minimum period of stay and the trip must be completed within one year. Two stopovers are permitted along the way for regular Super Saver fares, but no stopover is permitted (except at the point of turnaround) for midweek Super Saver fares. There is a 25% cancellation penalty. You should check with your travel agent for any other restrictions or changes. Rates vary according to whether it's peak season (June through August and again from the middle to the end of December), low season (January through March), or in between (April and May and again from September to the middle of December). Each season also has different rates for both weekday and weekend flights. These fares can run as high as $1,459 for flying on a weekend in high season from New York to as low as $935 during the week in low season from the West Coast.

See Chapter 1 for information about discount travel.

Kai Tak Airport

Hong Kong's Kai Tak Airport (tel. 7697531) is located in densely populated Kowloon Peninsula and has one of the most spectacular runways in the world—

built right out into the middle of the bay. From the airport it's about a 20- to 30-minute ride to Tsimshatsui and a 40-minute ride to the Central District; though during rush hours (8 to 9:30 a.m. and again from 4 to 6:30 p.m.) it can take as long as an hour.

The cheapest and one of the easiest ways to travel between the airport and Hong Kong's major hotels is by **Airbus**. There are three different routes, with buses traveling every 15 minutes between 7 a.m. and 11 p.m. Airbus A1 goes to East Tsimshatsui and Tsimshatsui and costs HK$6 (78¢), delivering passengers to such hotels as the Ambassador, Empress, Grand, Holiday Inn Golden Mile, Holiday Inn Harbour View, Hyatt Regency, Imperial, International, Kowloon, Miramar, New World, Park, Peninsula, Ramada Inn Kowloon, Regent, Shangri-La, Sheraton, and YMCA (Salisbury Road).

Airbus A2, which costs HK$8 ($1.04), travels through Wanchai and Central before terminating at the old Macau Ferry Pier, making stops at or near the Furama, Harbour, Harbour View International House, Hilton, Mandarin, New Harbour, Ramada Inn Hong Kong, and Victoria along the way. Airbus A3 also charges HK$8 for the trip to Causeway Bay and makes stops at the Caravelle, Excelsior, Lee Gardens, and Park Lane. Note that the Airbus requires exact fare, so be sure to ask for coins when exchanging money at the airport.

There are also **hotel shuttle buses** that pick up arriving passengers at Kai Tak and deliver them to major hotels. Fares differ depending on how far you're going, but it cost me HK$30 ($3.90) to get to Tsimshatsui.

Since these shuttle buses do not make regular and continuous rounds to hotels, you should use the Airbus or a taxi to get back to the airport. A taxi to the airport costs about HK$30 ($3.90) from Tsimshatsui and HK$60 ($7.79) from the Central District. Departure tax at the airport is HK$100 ($12.99) for adults and HK$50 ($6.49) for children aged 2 to 11.

GETTING AROUND

If you've been traveling in Japan, getting around in Hong Kong will seem like a breeze. For one thing, the streets here have names, they're written in English, and fares for public transport are generally quite low. In addition, public transportation is extensive and varied, and even the novice traveler should have no problem getting around. One thing you should keep in mind, however, is that buses and trams require the exact fare. It's therefore imperative to have a lot of loose change with you whenever you go out. Even though the ferries and subways will give change, you'll find it more convenient if you have the exact change, especially during rush hours. If you plan to do a lot of traveling by public transport, pick up a brochure called *Places of Interest by Public Transport,* available free at Hong Kong Tourist Association offices.

By Ferry

Without a doubt the ferries of the **Star Ferry Company** are among the most famous and celebrated boats in the world. And well they should be. Carrying passengers back and forth between Hong Kong Island and Kowloon ever since 1898, these boats have come to symbolize Hong Kong itself, and are almost always featured in travel articles on Hong Kong.

The familiar white-and-green ferries ply the waters daily from 6:30 a.m. to 11:30 p.m. between Hong Kong Island's Central District and the tip of Kowloon's Tsimshatsui, offering a seven-minute ride that is one of the best in the world, and certainly one of the cheapest. It costs only HK$.60 (8¢) for ordinary (second) class; if you really want to splurge, first class is HK$.80 (10¢). First class is on the upper deck and is a good idea if it's raining because it has glass windows surrounding it. Otherwise I find ordinary class much more colorful and entertaining because it's the one the locals use. Signs admonish passengers to watch out for pickpockets, to refrain from spitting on the deck, and to remain seated until the ferry docks.

To ride the ferry, simply drop your money into the ancient-looking turnstile, follow the crowd in front of you down the ramp, walk over the gangway, and find a seat on one of the polished wooden benches. A whistle will blow, a man will haul up the gangway, and you're off, dodging fishing boats, tugboats, and barges as you make your way across the harbor. Except for early in the morning or late at night, ferries depart every few minutes.

In addition to the Star Ferry, there are also many ferries to other parts of the colony. Ferries from the Central District, for example, also go to Kowloon's Hung Hom, where the railway station is located, and to the Yaumatei Ferry Pier, close to Jordan Road. If you want to go to one of Hong Kong's outlying islands, most ferries to the islands depart from the Outlying Islands Ferry Pier located west of Central's Star Ferry Terminal. Operated by the Hong Kong Ferry Company Ltd. (HKF), these boats vary in fares and departure times. The latest schedules and fares are available in a list compiled by the Hong Kong Tourist Association (HKTA) or by calling HKF at 5423081. One thing to keep in mind is that on weekends the ferries are unbelievably crowded and fares often go up. It's best, therefore, to travel on a weekday.

By Tram

Another colorful way to get around is by tram, and these are found only on Hong Kong Island. Set up in 1904, these are old, narrow, double-decker affairs that clank their way slowly along the northern part of the island from Kennedy Town in the West to Shau Kei Wan in the east, with one branch making a detour to Happy Valley. Passing through the Central District, Wanchai, and Causeway Bay on Des Voeux, Queensway, and Hennessy roads, they can't be beat for atmosphere and are easy to ride, since most of them go on only one line (those branching off to Happy Valley are clearly marked).

Enter trams from the back and go immediately up the winding stairs to the top deck. Try to get a seat at the very front of the tram and from there you'll have an unparalleled view of Hong Kong: laundry hanging from second-story windows, markets down side streets, crowded sidewalks, and people darting in front of the tram who you'll swear couldn't have made it. When you've had enough, go downstairs to the front of the tram and pay the exact fare of HK$.60 (8¢) into a little tin box next to the driver as you exit. Trams run from 5:40 a.m. to 1 a.m.

By Subway

Hong Kong's **Mass Transit Railway (MTR)** is modern, efficient, clean, and easy to use. The only hard thing about it is trying to remain seated on its slick stainless-steel seats (you may laugh now, but wait till you've tried it). Built primarily to transport commuters to and from work, it runs under the harbor to link Hong Kong Island with Kowloon and has replaced ferries, trams, and buses as the fastest way to travel. Lines begin on Kowloon at Tsuen Wan and Kwun Tong, run down the length of Nathan Road through Tsimshatsui, go underneath the harbor, and emerge on Hong Kong Island at Admiralty. From there they either go one stop west to the Central District and then to Sheung Wan or go east through Wanchai and Causeway Bay to Chai Wan.

Buy your plastic credit-card-size ticket at a vending machine at the station, where signs in English will tell you how much to pay. The fare begins at HK$2.50 (32¢), and no change is given. If you don't have the right amount, there are change machines close by for coins and information desks for bills. As you enter the turnstile, insert your ticket into a slot and pick it up after it shoots out the other end of the turnstile. Be sure to save your ticket for the end of your journey, when you will again insert your ticket, but this time you won't get it back.

If you think you're going to be doing a lot of traveling on the MTR, then buy the **MTR Tourist Ticket,** available upon presentation of your passport at HKTA offices or at the minibanks located in many of the subway stations. It costs HK$20

($2.60) and gives you HK$20 worth of transportation on the subway. Used just like a regular ticket, it's valid for a year, and the computerized gate will show how much you have left on your ticket as you exit the station. Remember to collect your ticket as you leave.

The subway is in operation from 6 a.m. to 1 a.m. Also, take note that there are no public toilets at any of the stations or on the trains, and that smoking, drinking, and eating are prohibited.

By Bus

Buses are good for traveling to places where other forms of public transport don't go, such as to the southern part of Hong Kong Island or up into parts of Kowloon and the New Territories. Depending on the route, buses run from about 6 a.m. until midnight, and fares range from HK$1.20 (16¢) to HK$9 ($1.17). You must have the exact fare, which you pay as you get on. Drivers often do not speak English, so you may want to have someone at your hotel write down your destination in Chinese. You can pick up leaflets indicating bus routes to some of the major tourist spots at HKTA offices.

By Minibus

These are a bit confusing for the tourist. Although the destination is written in both Chinese and English, you almost need a magnifying glass to identify the English, and by then the minibus has probably already whizzed past. There are two types of minibuses, distinguishable by color, and they both hold up to 14 persons. The green-and-yellow ones follow fixed routes, range in price from HK$1 (13¢) to HK$4 (52¢), depending on the route, and are paid for as you enter.

The red-and-yellow minibuses follow no fixed route and can be hailed from almost anywhere except in some restricted areas in the Central District. Fares usually range from HK$2 (26¢) to HK$6 (78¢) and you pay as you exit. Just yell when you want to get off.

By Taxi

As a rule taxi drivers in Hong Kong are strictly controlled and are fairly honest. If they're free to pick up passengers, a red "For Hire" flag will be raised in the windshield or at night their "Taxi" sign will be lighted on the roof. You can hail them from the street, but since most drivers do not speak English, it's a good idea to have your destination written in Chinese. Taxis are generally abundant anytime except rainy days, during shift change (which is usually at 4 p.m.), and on horse-racing days.

Taxis on **Hong Kong Island and Kowloon** are red and start at a low HK$6.50 (84¢), plus HK$.80 (10¢) for each 275 yards. Waiting time is HK$.80 (10¢) for every 60 seconds, and if you go through the harbor tunnel, you'll be charged an extra HK$20 ($2.60). The luggage charge is HK$2 (26¢) per piece.

Taxis in the **New Territories** are green and white, and rates begin at HK$5.5 (72¢) at flag fall.

If you have a complaint about a taxi driver, call the police at 5277177, but make sure you have the taxi's license number.

By Rental Car

Rental cars are not advisable in Hong Kong. For one thing, nothing is so far away that you can't get there easily and quickly by taxi or public transport. In addition, there will probably be no place to park once you get there. If you want a chauffeur-driven car, many of the major hotels have their own private fleet you can hire. But if you are still determined to rent, the familiar self-drive firms have branches here—**Avis, Budget,** and **Hertz**—along with a couple of dozen local firms. A valid driver's license is required.

By Train

There's only one train line in Hong Kong and it goes from Hung Hom in East Tsimshatsui in Kowloon up to Sheung Shui in the New Territories. That is, Sheung Shui is where you have to get off if you don't have a visa to go any farther into China; if you do have a visa, you can continue to the border, change trains, and travel into the mainland. Known as the Kowloon–Canton Railway, it passes through Mongkok, Kowloon Tong, Tai Wai, Shatin, Fo Tan, University, Tai Po Market, and Fanling before reaching Sheung Shui. The whole journey takes about a half hour on Hong Kong's new electric trains and costs HK$5.40 (70¢) one way for ordinary (second) class and HK$11 ($1.43) for first class.

By Rickshaw

Once the most common form of transport in the colony, rickshaws are almost a thing of the past—no new licenses are being issued. A few ancient-looking men hang around the Star Ferry Terminal in the Central District, but usually they're either snoozing or reading the paper. I've never once seen them hauling a customer. They'll charge you about HK$50 ($6.49) to HK$100 ($12.99) to take you around the block, clearly the most expensive form of transportation in Hong Kong, and by the look of them that's about as far as they can go. Probably the most humane thing you can do is take their picture—they'll charge you about HK$20 ($2.60) to HK$50 ($6.49) just for that. If you still want to take a ride, be sure to settle the price before climbing in.

---

3. The ABCs of Hong Kong

Arriving in a new city is never very easy, especially if it's at the other end of the earth where the language, culture, and people are different from your own. This section is designed to answer some questions you might have before departing on your trip, to make your immersion into Hong Kong life easier, and to help you with unforeseen questions or emergencies that might arise during your stay.

Remember that the concierge of your hotel is usually a valuable source of information for everything from where the nearest bank is to how to get to a certain destination. The Hong Kong Tourist Association (HKTA) is also very proficient in answering visitors' questions.

AMERICAN EXPRESS: The most convenient office in the Central District is opposite Jardine House at 8 Connaught Rd. in the Swire House (tel. 5243151). On the Kowloon side it's 119 Nathan Rd. (tel. 7391542). Hours for both are 9:30 a.m. to 4 p.m. Monday through Friday and 9:30 a.m. to noon on Saturday.

BABYSITTERS: Most of the upper-class hotels have babysitting services. For a full list of hotels providing this service, contact the Hong Kong Tourist Association.

BANKING HOURS: The average banking hours are 9:30 or 10 a.m. to 3 p.m. Monday through Friday and 9:30 a.m. to noon on Saturday. However, some branches stay open longer. Hongkong Bank and Standard Chartered Bank, Hong Kong's two major banks, stay open from 9 a.m. to 4:30 p.m. weekdays and from 9 a.m. to 12:30 p.m. on Saturday.

BUS TERMINALS: The two major bus terminals are at both ends of the Star Ferry, in the Central District on Hong Kong Island and in Tsimshatsui in Kowloon. HKTA has a free leaflet helpful for getting around on buses: *Places of Interest by Public Transport,* which tells how to get to such major destinations as Stanley or Aberdeen.

CLIMATE: Because of its subtropical location, Hong Kong's weather is generally mild in winter and hot and humid in summer. Peak tourist seasons are spring and autumn, a time when many hotels raise their rates and when accommodations become tight. Late September to early December is considered the most pleasant time of year, with clear skies and temperatures ranging in the 70s. January and February are the coldest months, when temperatures in the 50s mean you should bring along a jacket or sweater. In spring the humidity rises, the temperature goes up to about 70, and it's often cloudy and misty. By summer temperatures are in the 90s, humidity is 90%, and there's little or no relief even at night. Summer is also typhoon season, but Hong Kong has a very good warning system so there's no need to worry. Most of Hong Kong's rain falls in summer, but it's a good idea to bring along an umbrella any time of year.

CONSULATES: The **American Consulate** is at 26 Garden Rd., Central District (tel. 5239011). Hours are 8:30 a.m. to 12:30 p.m. and 1:30 to 5:30 p.m. weekdays. If you need to go to the passport section, it's open weekdays only from 8:30 a.m. to noon and again from 1:30 to 5 p.m. The **Canadian Consulate,** Tower One, Exchange Square, Connaught Road, Central District (tel. 8104321), is open Monday through Friday from 8 a.m. to 4:30 p.m. The **Australian Consulate** is on the 23rd and 24th floors of Harbour Centre, 25 Harbour Rd., Wanchai, on Hong Kong Island (tel. 5731881), and is open weekdays from 9 to 11:30 a.m. and 1 to 4 p.m. Matters pertaining to **Britain** are c/o Overseas Visa Section, Hong Kong Immigration Dept., Upper Basement, Mirror Tower, 61 Mody Rd., East Tsimshatsui (tel. 7333111). Hours here are 8:45 a.m. to 4:30 p.m. Monday to Friday and 9 to 11:30 a.m. on Saturday.

CREDIT CARDS: Most shops accept international credit cards, although some of the smaller ones may not. Look to see whether there are credit-card signs in the shop. Credit cards readily accepted include American Express, VISA, and MasterCard. American Express cardholders also have access to Jetco automated-teller machines and can withdraw local currency and traveler's checks at Express Cash automated tellers. Holders of VISA cards can obtain local currency from the Hongkong Bank automated-teller machines at the airport and approximately ten other convenient locations.

CRIME: Hong Kong is relatively safe for the tourist, especially if you use common sense and stick to such tourist areas as Tsimshatsui or Causeway Bay at night. However, you do have to guard against pickpockets. Although on the decline, they often work in groups to pick men's pockets or slit open a woman's purse, quickly taking the valuables and then relaying them on to accomplices who disappear in the crowd. Japanese tourists, used to the safety in their own country, are easy targets since they usually carry large amounts of cash with them, and favored places are Tsimshatsui, Causeway Bay, and Wanchai. To be on the safe side, keep your valuables in your hotel's safety deposit box.

CURRENCY: The basic unit of currency in the colony is the **Hong Kong dollar.** Notes are issued by two local banks for HK$10, HK$20, HK$50, HK$100, HK$500, and HK$1,000. In 1985 new notes began circulation and are smaller than the older notes, which are still being used. Coins are minted in England in bronze for 5-, 10-, 20-, and 50-cent pieces and in silver for HK$1, HK$2, and HK$5.

Throughout Hong Kong the dollar sign ("$") refers to Hong Kong dollars, but the same symbol is most familiar to readers of these guides as indicating U.S. dollars. In order to prevent confusion, *in this guide Hong Kong dollars are always identified by the symbol "HK$."*

Although rates fluctuate, all conversions in this book are based on HK$7.7 to $1 U.S. If the exchange rate has changed drastically, plan your budget accordingly.

The best deal for money exchange is at banks, since they don't charge a commission, except on traveler's checks. Hotels give a slightly less favorable exchange rate but are convenient. Money changers are found in the tourist areas, especially in Tsimshatsui. Avoid them if you can. They often charge a commission or a "changing fee." If you exchange money at Kai Tak Airport, you'll be charged a 5% service fee. If you want to exchange cash or cash American Express traveler's checks at the American Express office, therefore, change at the airport only what you need to get into town—$10 (U.S.) should be enough.

CUSTOMS: You're allowed to bring into Hong Kong duty-free a one-liter (34-ounce) bottle of alcohol, 200 cigarettes or 50 cigars, and a reasonable quantity of cosmetics and perfumes in opened bottles for personal use.

DRUGSTORES: There are no 24-hour drugstores in Hong Kong, so if you need something urgently in the middle of the night you should contact one of the hospitals listed below.

One of the best-known pharmacies in Hong Kong is **Watson's,** which first opened in the 1880s. Today there are more than 30 Watson's drugstores in Hong Kong, most of them open from 10 a.m. to 7:30 or even 9 p.m. Locations for some of them are Star House next to the Star Ferry on the Kowloon side (tel. 7301832); Haiphong Road in Tsimshatsui (tel. 3686381); Paterson Plaza on Paterson Street, Causeway Bay (tel. 8954008); the Hilton Hotel and the Pedder Building on Pedder Street (tel. 5215531), both in the Central District.

ELECTRICITY: The electricity used in Hong Kong is 200 volts, alternating current (AC), 50 cycles. Most hotels have adapters to fit shavers of different plugs and voltages, but for other gadgets you'll need transformers and plug adapters. Better yet, buy travel hairdryers or irons that can be used both in the United States and abroad.

EMERGENCIES: All emergency calls are free—just **dial 999** for police, fire, or ambulance.

FIRST FLOOR: The floors of Hong Kong buildings are under the British system. That is, what we would call the first floor in the United States is called the ground floor in Hong Kong. Our second floor, therefore, is called the first floor in Hong Kong.

HOLIDAYS: The Chinese New Year, which falls according to the Chinese lunar calendar in either late January or in February, is the only time of year when most shops close in Hong Kong. They stay closed for two to four days, but some restaurants and shops do stay open to cater to tourists.

HOSPITALS: The following hospitals can help you around the clock: **Queen Mary Hospital**, Pokfulam Road, Hong Kong Island (tel. 8192111); **Hong Kong Adventist Hospital**, 40 Stubbs Rd., Hong Kong Island (tel. 5746211); **Queen Elizabeth Hospital**, Wylie Road, Kowloon (tel. 7102111).

LANGUAGES: Both Chinese and English are spoken in Hong Kong, with Cantonese the most common Chinese dialect. Although English is understood in the hotels and tourist shops, few Chinese understand it outside these areas, including taxi drivers, bus drivers, and waiters in many Chinese restaurants. To avoid confusion, have someone in your hotel write out your destination in Chinese so that you can show it to the taxi or bus driver.

LAUNDRY: Most hotels provide same-day laundry service.

LITERATURE: If you want to know something about Hong Kong before setting out on your trip, I recommend reading *A History of Hong Kong* by G. B. Endacott, which gives a thorough account of the history of the colony. A more intimate view of Hong Kong is given in *Borrowed Place, Borrowed Time* by Richard Hughes, a *Sunday Times* correspondent who has lived in Hong Kong for several decades. Fictional accounts that depict the flavor of Hong Kong are Richard Mason's *The World of Suzie Wong* and James Clavell's *Taipan*. Finally, few writers can capture the essence of a place as accurately and poetically as Jan Morris, whose *Hong Kong* is one of the best books to come out on the British colony in recent years. Tracing the evolution of Hong Kong from its birth during the Opium Wars up to the present, she provides a unique insight into the workings of the colony and gives a wealth of information. Good and fascinating armchair reading.

MAIL DELIVERY: If you don't know where you're going to be staying in Hong Kong, you can still receive mail. Have it sent to you c/o *Post Restante* at the **General Post Office**, 2 Connaught Pl., Central District, Hong Kong Island, which is located just to the right as you exit from the Star Ferry. They'll hold your mail for you here for two months, and the counter is on the ground floor.

NEWSPAPERS: Five English-language newspapers are printed in Hong Kong: *South China Morning Post, Hong Kong Standard, Asian Wall Street Journal,* and *International Herald Tribune.*

PASSPORTS AND VISAS: Visas are not necessary for most tourists entering Hong Kong, only a valid passport. Americans can stay up to one month without a visa. Australians, Canadians, and other British Commonwealth citizens can stay for three months, while those from the United Kingdom can stay for six months without a visa. If you have any questions regarding visas once you're in Hong Kong, contact the **Hong Kong Immigration Dept.**, 61 Mody Rd., East Tsimshatsui (tel. 7333111).

POST OFFICES: Post offices are open from 8 a.m. to 6 p.m. Monday through Saturday; closed on Sunday and holidays. On Hong Kong Island the **main post office**

is at 2 Connaught Pl.—next to the Star Ferry concourse—where stamps are sold on the first floor (what we would call the second floor in the United States). On the Kowloon side, post offices are located at 405 Nathan Rd. between the Jordan and Yaumatei subway stations, and at 10 Middle Rd., which is one block north of Salisbury Road.

SHOP HOURS: Most shops are open seven days a week, although some department stores are closed on Sunday. Shops in the Central District are generally open from 10 a.m. to 6 p.m.; in Causeway Bay and Wanchai from 10 a.m. to about 9:30 p.m.; in Tsimshatsui from 10 a.m. to 9 or 10 p.m., some even later than that; and in East Tsimshatsui from 10 a.m. to 7:30 p.m.

STUDENT INFORMATION: If you're a student, the **Hong Kong Student Travel Bureau** can help you with sightseeing tours of the city, visas and trips to China, cheap flights to other destinations, and even rail passes for both Europe and Japan. Even if you're not a student you can take advantage of some of their services. They have two conveniently located offices: on the tenth floor of Star House in Tsimshatsui next to the Star Ferry (tel. 7303269), open from 9 a.m. to 7 p.m. Monday through Saturday, and on the 13th floor of the Entertainment Building, 30 Queen's Rd., Central District (tel. 8107272), open the same hours.

TAXES AND SERVICE CHARGES: Hotels will add to your bill a 10% service charge and a 5% government tax. Restaurants and bars will automatically add a 10% service charge. There's an airport departure tax of HK$100 ($12.99) for adults and HK$50 ($6.49) for children aged 2 to 11. If you're taking the boat to Macau, you have to pay a Hong Kong departure tax of HK$17 ($2.21).

TELEPHONES AND TELEGRAMS: Telephones are free for local calls made from homes, offices, shops, restaurants, and most hotel lobbies, so don't feel shy about asking to use the phone. From some hotel lobbies, hotel rooms, and in public phone booths a local call costs HK$1 (13¢).

Hong Kong used to have **telephone prefix numbers,** similar to our area codes. However, these have recently been discontinued. All telephone numbers now have seven digits. But if you still see a number with a 3-, 5-, or 0- as a prefix, count the digits in the telephone number itself; disregard the prefix if the number has seven digits, but incorporate the prefix if it has six digits (for example, 3-1234567 becomes simply 1234567, while 5-123456 becomes 5123456).

Most hotels in Hong Kong will handle overseas calls and offer direct dialing. Otherwise **long-distance calls and telegrams** can be made from Cables and Wireless offices. Open 24 hours a day including public holidays, the Cables and Wireless office is at Room 102A, Exchange Square Tower I, Connaught Place, Central District. On the Kowloon side there's an office in the Hermes House, Middle Road, Tsimshatsui. There are also international direct-dialing public phones that accept coins or telephone cards. They are located on both sides of the harbor near the Star Ferry and at the airport.

If you want to make a **collect call,** you can make one from any public or private phone by dialing 011. For **international customer service,** call 013. For **directory assistance,** dial 108.

TIPPING: Even though restaurants and bars will automatically add a 10% service charge to your bill, you're still expected to leave your small change for the waiter. A general rule of thumb is to leave 5%, but in most Chinese restaurants, where the prices of meals are usually low, it's acceptable to leave change up to HK$2 (25¢).

You're also expected to tip taxi drivers, bellboys, barbers, and beauticians. For taxi drivers, simply round up to the nearest HK$1 or add a HK$1 (13¢) tip. Tip people who cut your hair 5% or 10%, and give bellboys HK$10 ($1.30) to HK$20 ($2.60), depending on the number of bags.

TOURIST INFORMATION: The **Hong Kong Tourist Association** is a well-organized and efficient outfit designed to make your trip to Hong Kong pleasant and enjoyable. If you'd like information and literature before leaving on your trip, contact one of the HKTA offices in the United States: 590 Fifth Ave., New York, NY 10036-4706 (tel. 212/869-5008); Suite 2400, 333 N. Michigan Ave., Chicago, IL 60601 (tel. 312/782-3872); Suite 404, 360 Post St., San Francisco, CA 94108 (tel. 415/781-4582); Suite 1220, 10940 Wilshire Blvd., Los Angeles, CA 90024 (tel. 213/208-4582).

Once you arrive in Hong Kong you will find four HKTA offices ready to serve you. In Hong Kong's **International Airport at Kai Tak** in the arrival hall, the HKTA is open from 8 a.m. to 10:30 p.m. daily. The **Kowloon Information Centre** is in the Star Ferry Terminal and hours here are 8 a.m. to 6 p.m. daily. In East Tsimshatsui there's a new office in the Royal Garden Hotel, 69 Mody Rd., open daily from 9 a.m. to 6 p.m. (to 1 p.m. on Saturday and Sunday).

The **main HKTA office** is on Hong Kong Island in the basement of Jardine House, Shop 8, in the Central District to the right as you exit the Star Ferry (tel. 5244191). It's closed on Sunday and public holidays, but is open Monday through Friday from 8 a.m. to 6 p.m. and on Saturday until 1 p.m.

The HKTA also operates a **hotline** to answer any questions you might have. Call 7225555 from 8 a.m. to 6 p.m. daily. If you call after office hours, an answering machine should ask for your telephone number and the staff will return your call the next day.

There's quite a bit of **free literature** available on Hong Kong you can pick up at HKTA offices, which should help you during your stay. I recommend *The Quick Guide to Hong Kong, Places of Interest by Public Transport, Museums & Arts & Crafts, Outlying Islands* and *The Official Guide to Shopping, Eating Out and Services in Hong Kong.*

You can also ask HKTA for a **free map** of Tsimshatsui and northern Hong Kong Island. *The Official Hong Kong Guide,* published monthly, is available free in most upper- and medium-range hotels, and has a lot of practical information and sightseeing advice on the colony. It's also available at HKTA offices for HK$10 ($1.30).

Two tourist tabloids distributed free in hotel lobbies and tourist places are *Hong Kong* and *Orient.* Although they're filled mostly with advertisements, they're published weekly and have some information on what's going on in Hong Kong. *Hong Kong Visitor,* published by the *South China Morning Post,* is also valuable for information on what's happening in the colony.

TRIPS TO CHINA: Hong Kong is a major gateway for travelers going to the People's Republic of China. Most visitors join organized tours to the mainland that last anywhere from one day to a week or more. **China Travel Service** is probably the biggest and best-known company organizing tours to China. On Hong Kong Island its office is at 77 Queen's Rd., Central District (tel. 5252284). On the Kowloon side its office is at 27-33 Nathan Rd. (tel. 7211331). Office hours are from 9 a.m. to 5:30 p.m. Monday through Friday, from 9 a.m. to 5:30 p.m. on Saturday. The Kowloon office is also open from 9 a.m. to 1 p.m. and again from 2 to 5 p.m. on Sunday and holidays. CTS can arrange for your visa, but be sure to make your visa application at least two working days prior to departure.

4. Accommodations

For many years hotel managers in Hong Kong were in the enviable position of having too many guests and not enough rooms to accommodate them. Because of this high demand and low supply, prices for hotel rooms skyrocketed a few years back, with many hotels raising their room rates as much as 20% each year. A surplus in visitors to Hong Kong also led to a flurry of new hotel projects. In December 1985, the Hong Kong Tourist Association reported a total of 18,180 hotel rooms in the colony. By the end of 1991, when the last of the new hotels has been completed, this figure is expected to rise to an astounding 38,121.

Luckily for tourists, this mushrooming of new hotels has caused fierce competition among the existing hotels. Room rates have stabilized, first-class hotels are offering all kinds of incentives, and medium-priced hotels are all remodeling and upgrading their facilities. Admittedly, the price of hotel rooms in Hong Kong is not inexpensive and can be compared to hotel prices of major cities around the world. On the brighter side, however, dining and shopping in Hong Kong remain very much a bargain.

Although the biggest hotel crunches occur twice a year, from March to early June and again from October to early December, you'd be wise to reserve your room at least two months in advance no matter when you come. If you're traveling off-season, it doesn't hurt to bargain for a cheaper rate, or at the very least to ask whether you can be upgraded to a better room.

Generally speaking, the price of a room in Hong Kong is governed by the view and location. Not surprisingly, rooms with a view of the famous Victoria Harbour are the most expensive, as well as those on higher floors. In contrast to Japan, room size often has little to do with price, and rooms here are much larger than they are in Japan. You should also note that prices listed in this section are for *room rates only*—with the exception of some of the budget hotels, a 10% service charge and 5% government tax will be added to your hotel bill.

Most of the hotels I am including in this section are members of the **Hong Kong Hotel Association (HKHA).** All of Hong Kong's deluxe and upper-range hotels are members of this organization, as well as the best of the medium range. The benefit of staying in one of these hotels is that if you have a complaint, you can lodge it directly with the Hong Kong Tourist Association. In addition, the HKHA maintains a counter at Kai Tak Airport where you can reserve a room in one of its member hotels at no extra charge.

Realizing that HKHA hotels are among the first to fill up during peak season, I am also including what I consider to be a few good alternatives in the budget range, as well as some rock-bottom recommendations. Unless otherwise specified, all rooms in the deluxe through budget categories are air-conditioned and come with private bath.

Incidentally, new hotels opening in the latter half of 1989 and 1990 include the New World Harbour View and the Grand Hyatt in Wanchai on the grounds of the new Hong Kong Convention and Exhibition Centre, and the Conrad Hotel on Queensway. Since room rates were unavailable at the time this book went to press, consult a travel agency or contact the Hong Kong Tourist Association if you're interested in staying in one of these new hotels.

KOWLOON

Kowloon Peninsula, including its tip, known as Tsimshatsui, has the greatest concentration of hotels in Hong Kong. Many travelers prefer to stay in this area because it abounds in shops of all kinds, restaurants, and nightlife. In any case, Hong Kong Island is just across the harbor, a short subway or ferry ride away. Unless a subway station or bus route is given, you can assume that the hotels listed below are within walking distance of the Star Ferry and Tsimshatsui MTR station.

The Deluxe Hotels

The Peninsula, Salisbury Road (tel. 3666251), is to Hong Kong what Raffles is to Singapore. An imposing and grand edifice facing Victoria Harbour, the Peninsula has remained Hong Kong's most famous and most elegant hotel ever since it was built back in 1928, and it exudes more of a colonial atmosphere than any other hotel in Hong Kong. This is where you should stay if you are an incurable romantic, have a penchant for the historical, and have enough money to afford its high prices. The hotel prides itself on service, and room attendants will even draw your bath if you ask them. All rooms were recently renovated, with additional wings opening in 1992.

Rooms for both single and double occupancy range from HK$2,400 ($312) to HK$3,300 ($429), with the higher rate charged for rooms with a harbor view. Sadly enough, however, that view has all but disappeared with the construction of the Space Museum on reclaimed land across the street. That's progress Hong Kong style, but the Peninsula is worth a visit even if you don't stay here. Lobby-sitting at the Peninsula has always been high on the list of things to do in Hong Kong, so put on your finest and go for a cup of coffee in a lobby reminiscent of a Parisian palace with high gilded ceilings, pillars, and ferns. The Peninsula is also famous for its restaurant, Gaddi's, described in the dining section.

The Regent, Salisbury Road (tel. 7211211), has replaced the Peninsula as the deluxe hotel with the best view of the water. In fact, you can't get much closer to the water than at the Regent—the hotel is located on a projection of reclaimed land and sits on more than 120 pylons sunk into the harbor. Seventy percent of the hotel's 548 rooms command sweeping views of the harbor, and all come with sunken bathtubs, separate rooms for both shower and toilet, three phones, and a butler for every six rooms.

Special features of the hotel, built in 1981, include a magnificent free-standing staircase of white Carrara marble, a large outdoor heated swimming pool, and lobby and restaurants with great views of the harbor. Although the Regent is a relative newcomer, many of the people staying here are repeat guests, which speaks highly of the hotel's service and facilities. Rates here, the same for single or double occupancy, begin at HK$1,680 ($218). Rooms with a view of the harbor begin at HK$2,250 ($292).

Shangri-La, 64 Mody Rd., East Tsimshatsui (tel. 7212111), is a deluxe hotel designed for business travelers, who make up a large percentage of the hotel's guests. A Westin hotel, it is situated on the waterfront of East Tsimshatsui and features large and luxuriously appointed rooms with ceiling-to-floor bay windows overlooking the harbor, a health club with free use of the swimming pool and whirlpool, an executive business center with secretarial services, and five superb restaurants. The hotel also has a nonsmoking floor, where even the room attendants are nonsmokers. Service throughout the hotel is discreet and excellent. Rooms here begin at HK$1,800 ($234) for a single and HK$1,950 ($253) for a double, increasing to HK$2,700 ($351) and HK$2,850 ($370), respectively, for rooms with harbor views.

The Upper Bracket

Falling somewhere between the deluxe and upper-bracket groups of hotels, the **Ramada Renaissance Hotel,** 8 Peking Rd. (tel. 3113311), may be rightly called a deluxe upper-class accommodation with well-decorated rooms. One of Kowloon's newest hotels, it is also one of the colony's most technically advanced. A sophisticated bedside control panel allows guests to operate lights and curtains, adjust air-conditioning levels, select a TV or radio program, call up messages or the hotel bill on the television screen, and switch on a "Do Not Disturb" light (which also disconnects the door chime). As an extra safety precaution, each guest receives an electronic key with a new combination, and staff keys are programmed for specific times only, thereby barring them from entering rooms after their shifts. A printer records all hotel employee use, indicating when each key was used, where, and by whom. Other room features include electronic safes and two hands-free phones, while hotel facilities include a rooftop swimming pool and a health club, a business center, and restaurants that include an excellent Italian outlet and the Bostonian Seafood Restaurant. What's more, the hotel is just a few minutes' walk from the Star Ferry. Rates here start at HK$1,500 ($195), rising to HK$2,000 ($260) for a deluxe with a harbor view. The 11th and 12th floors feature the Renaissance Club with its own private lounge, complimentary breakfast and afternoon cocktails, and other advantages to the business traveler. Rooms here start at HK$2,280 ($296). All rates are the same for single and double occupancy.

Located on Nathan Road only a five-minute walk from the Star Ferry and a one-minute walk from the Tsimshatsui subway station, the **Hyatt Regency Hong Kong,** 67 Nathan Rd. (tel. 3662321), was established in 1969 as Hyatt's first property in Asia. All 723 of its rooms were recently renovated and feature colors of apricot and celadon along with natural teakwood furniture. Hints of local culture are represented with a lacquered Chinese chest housing a television, and there are Chinese brush paintings on the walls. Special features of the new rooms include double-glazed windows and insulated walls to reduce outside noise, minibars, and telephones in the bathroom and at the bedside, with an extra plug-in socket at the desk; in all rooms there are safe-deposit boxes large enough for a briefcase. Bathrooms, designed with Italian marble, all come equipped with hairdryers. The hotel boasts five food-and-beverage outlets, including the original Hugo's, and a fortune-teller in the lobby who will read your palm between noon and 6 p.m. every day except Sunday—if you've always wanted to have your palm read, this is the place to do it. A room here starts at HK$1,100 ($143).

The **Royal Garden,** 69 Mody Rd., East Tsimshatsui (tel. 7215215), is a small hotel with a lot of architectural surprises. The middle of the lobby looks down on an open area of fountains and water, while from the 3rd to the 15th floors an open atrium reaches up to the ceiling. Plants hang down from balconies ringing the atrium, glass-enclosed elevators glide up the wall, a piano sits on an island in the middle of a pool, and the sound of rushing water adds a freshness and coolness.

With only 433 rooms, the Royal Garden is one of the best choices in this category, but is also one of the most expensive. Its rooms, which begin at HK$1,260 ($164) for a standard single or a double and rise to HK$1,980 ($257) for a room with a partial harbor view, are decorated in an Oriental theme with Chinese furniture and dark russet colors. (In case you're wondering, "a partial harbor view" means either that other buildings are obstructing part of your view or that your windows do not squarely face the water.) Facilities at the hotel include both Chinese and Western restaurants and a disco that charges HK$100 ($12.99) on weekdays and HK$130 ($16.88) on weekends.

One of East Tsimshatsui's newest hotels is the **Hotel Nikko,** 72 Mody Rd. (tel. 7391111), which opened at the end of 1986. Affiliated with Japan Airlines, it features 461 rooms and suites decorated with furniture carved from American maple and with either Japanese works of art or Dutch maps of the Far East. An electronic bedside panel enables guests to set the alarm clock, control the television, and open or shut the curtains. Bathrooms, finished in black-veined white Italian Carrara marble, come equipped with separate bathtubs and showers, hairdryers, and bathrobes and cotton kimonos.

Rates for single occupancy start at HK$1,320 ($171), with HK$2,220 ($288) charged for rooms with a view of the harbor. Double occupancy is an extra HK$100 ($13) added to the rates above. Restaurants serve Chinese, Japanese, and French cuisine, while the Sky Lounge on the fifteenth floor offers drinks, dancing, and a view of Hong Kong's lights.

The **Sheraton Hong Kong Hotel,** 20 Nathan Rd. (tel. 3691111), is an attractive hotel situated on the waterfront at the corner of Nathan and Salisbury roads—certainly one of the choicest spots on Kowloon Peninsula. Its rooms are tastefully decorated in bright earth tones and come with the usual radio, fridge, and color TV. Although single rooms are available, they are small and face an inner courtyard. A rooftop swimming pool, heated in winter, is free to hotel guests. There's also a health club. Rooms here start at HK$1,020 ($132) for a single and HK$1,140 ($148) for a double, with HK$1,600 ($208) and HK$1,800 ($234) charged respectively for rooms with a harbor view. If you feel like splurging, rooms on the 16th and 17th floors are known as the Sheraton Towers and include such extras as complimentary continental breakfast, evening cocktails, personalized stationery, and their own check-in lounge. Rates for these rooms begin at HK$1,200 ($156) for a single and HK$1,800 ($234) for a double, with harbor views costing HK$2,000 ($260) and HK$2,100 ($273), respectively.

Holiday Inn Harbour View, 70 Mody Rd., East Tsimshatsui (tel. 7215161), is one of the farthest of a string of hotels that stretches from the Star Ferry through East Tsimshatsui. Because it's close to Hong Kong's coliseum, a number of stars have stayed here, including David Bowie, Elton John, and John McEnroe. Its rooms are comfortable and cheerful, although the least expensive ones, which begin at HK$1,250 ($162) for one person and HK$1,350 ($175) for two, have windows that open rather unceremoniously onto a facing windowless wall. Those with a harbor view start at HK$1,800 ($234) for a single and HK$1,900 ($247) for a double. Some of the rooms come equipped with sofa beds in consideration of female executives who might feel uncomfortable about hosting a business meeting in a hotel room. A plus in this hotel is its rooftop swimming pool.

Another member of this chain in Hong Kong is the **Holiday Inn Golden Mile,** 50 Nathan Rd. (tel. 3693111), named after the so-called Golden Mile of shopping on Nathan Road. Very clean and decorated with modern furnishings, the rooms start at HK$960 ($125) for single or double occupancy. Within the hotel complex are three floors of shopping arcades, a rooftop swimming pool, restaurants, bars, and a delicatessen. The hotel lobby is used as a departure point for a number of tours throughout the colony, which means that it's convenient if you want to join tours during your stay but rather noisy and bothersome if you don't.

The **Hotel Regal Meridien,** 71 Mody Rd., East Tsimshatsui (tel. 7221818), is a French-owned hotel that does a good job of blending the East and the West. In the lobby and elsewhere in the hotel, reproduction 18th-century French antiques and Louis XV–style furniture stand alongside Chinese works of art. Its 589 rooms, all soundproof and containing two phones, a minibar, color TV, clock, and radio, are decorated in variations of soft pastels of peach and celadon green. A French restaurant and a brasserie are among the eating establishments in the hotel. Room rates start at HK$1,100 ($143) for a single or a double, but these rooms have no view at all, since they face another building. Deluxe rooms, some of which have a partial harbor view, go for HK$1,800 ($234) for a single or a double.

The **Omni Hongkong Hotel,** 3 Canton Rd. (tel. 7360088), is the closest hotel to the Star Ferry. It's connected to three shopping centers by air-conditioned walkways and sports an outdoor pool, 11 restaurants and bars, and 750 guest rooms. Its marbled lobby is spacious and comfortable and its rooms combine both Western and Eastern decor in muted colors. Rooms without a harbor view start at HK$1,300 ($169) for single or double occupancy. The deluxe room, which offers a partial view of the harbor that is better if you get a room on a higher floor, is HK$1,750 ($227). A full harbor view here will cost HK$2,100 ($273) and offers a great look at harbor activity, including the ocean liners that sometimes dock right next door.

The **Omni Marco Polo,** Harbour City, Canton Road (tel. 7360088), offers no views from its windows, but it's a comfortable hotel located in the middle of the Harbour City shopping complex, a shopping mall of 600 shops and boutiques not far from the Star Ferry. It caters mainly to business travelers, so the rooms feature desks with a large work space, stocked refrigerators, and large bathrooms. With a friendly and efficient staff, this hotel prices its rooms according to height—but note that those that face Canton Road tend to be somewhat noisier. Rates start at HK$1,300 ($169) for singles and doubles for rooms on the lower floors and go to HK$1,500 ($195) for deluxe rooms at the top. There is no swimming pool in the hotel itself, but since it's part of the Omni group of hotels, guests are free to use the pool at the nearby Hongkong Hotel.

Another Omni hotel, the **Prince Hotel,** Harbour City, Canton Road (tel. 7361888), is also located in the huge Harbour City shopping complex. It's a small hotel with a gleaming white marble lobby, and its 400 rooms all feature queen-size beds, even in the twin rooms. The economy rooms, which cost HK$1,300 ($169) for single or double occupancy, are on the lower floors. Deluxe rooms are higher up and therefore quieter, and go for HK$1,500 ($195); a few of these rooms even give minute glimpses of the harbor at no extra cost, so ask for the highest room with a view. As with the Marco Polo, guests wishing to swim will have to go to the sister Hongkong Hotel.

One of Tsimshatsui's newest hotels, the **Royal Pacific Hotel and Towers,** 33 Canton Rd. (tel. 7361188), encompasses two properties, each with its own lobby, concept, and room rates. The Royal Pacific Hotel is geared to tour groups from Japan, Korea, and Taiwan, while the Towers caters to individual travelers and businesspeople and offers more personalized services at higher rates. Both properties sit practically on top of the new China Ferry Terminal, making it a convenient place to stay if you're traveling to China or Macau via ferry. Otherwise, it's a bit far from the Star Ferry, about a 15-minute walk. Rates in the lower-priced hotel complex start at HK$920 ($119) for a single and HK$980 ($127) for a double, which are rooms on the lower floors, and rise to HK$1,100 ($143) and HK$1,170 ($152), respectively, for the highest rooms with views of Kowloon Park. If you want the luxury of staying in the more spacious Tower rooms, expect to pay HK$1,300 ($169) to HK$2,220 ($288) for a single or a double.

Farther up Nathan Road across from Kowloon Park is the **Hotel Miramar,** 130 Nathan Rd. (tel. 3681111). It's strategically located in the midst of a shopping area, including the relatively new Park Lane shopping arcades. An older hotel once known for its showy exterior and flashy gold-colored decor, it has joined the recent trend in renovating and updating its facilities and guest rooms, a process that will take several years. Catering primarily to group tourists from Japan, it charges HK$1,020 ($132) to HK$1,380 ($179) for singles and HK$1,150 ($149) to HK$1,500 ($195) for twins.

If you have only one or two nights to spend in Hong Kong and you'd rather stay close to the airport, the **Regal Meridien Airport Hotel,** San Po Road, Kowloon (tel. 7180333), is as close as you can get. Linked directly to the airport by an air-conditioned conveyor-belt walkway, this hotel features rooms with soundproof windows and TV screens with flight information. A free shuttle-bus service transports guests to the Star Ferry about every half hour. Rates for single occupancy range from HK$780 ($101) to HK$1,550 ($201); doubles are HK$780 ($101) to HK$1,680 ($218).

The Medium Bracket

Opened in 1986 and under the same management as the Peninsula Hotel, **Kowloon Hotel,** 19-21 Nathan Rd. (tel. 3698698), is a modern, glass-walled structure situated right behind the older edifice of the Peninsula. Although its 742 rooms are fairly small, they're built at such an angle that their V-shaped bay windows allow unobstructed views up and down the street. Conceived with the business executive in mind, the hotel features what it calls a "Telecenter" in each room, which is a combination television and computer. Equipped with a simplified keyboard, it allows access to pages of computerized information files, including airline telephone numbers, the weather report, and tourist sightseeing information. At the touch of a button, guests can also call up any messages they may have received as well as their hotel bills. Single occupancy begins at HK$880 ($114), doubles are HK$920 ($119). Rooms on the top floors are high enough to offer views of the harbor and cost HK$980 ($127) for a single and HK$1,040 ($135) for a double.

The **Ramada Inn Kowloon,** 73-75 Chatham Rd. (tel. 3111100), is a 206-room middle-range hotel that opened in 1988. Popular with the individual business traveler, it offers a convenient location, a business center, one restaurant and one bar/lounge, and rooms that feature TV with remote control, minibar, fridge, and hairdryer. The electricity is activated in your room when you insert your key into a special slot by the door. Rates are the same for single and double occupancy, and begin at HK$910 ($118).

Also opened in 1988 is the **Windsor Hotel,** 39-43A Kimberley Rd. (tel. 7395665), which is a bit less convenient because of the 15-minute walk to the Star Ferry. However, it's a pleasant hotel, with a spotless white interior, marbled lobby, and pastel-colored rooms that offer the usual TV, radio, telephone with a bathroom extension, a minibar, and laundry rope in the bathroom. Restaurants serve Western and Chinese cuisine. Single and double occupancy ranges from HK$900 ($117) to HK$1,100 ($143).

Another relatively new hotel is the **Guangdong Hotel,** 18 Prat Ave. (tel. 7393311), located about a ten-minute walk from the Star Ferry. Its rooms are pleasant and clean, with rates based on size. If you want to be away from the din of traffic, ask for a room on a higher floor. Its marbled lobby is spacious and bare, reflecting the latest look in Hong Kong's hotels. Singles and doubles here are HK$840 ($109), while twins range from HK$960 ($125) to HK$1,080 ($140). Restaurants serve Japanese and Chinese food.

The **New World Hotel,** 22 Salisbury Rd. (tel. 3694111), is a 720-room hotel that is part of the New World complex, which includes more than 400 shops and boutiques. But even though it's situated in a prime location right on the waterfront, not one of its rooms faces the harbor. Resembling a Japanese business hotel with economy rooms not much larger than its beds, the New World is modern, clean, and functional, and is conveniently located. Facilities include an outdoor swimming pool, restaurants and cocktail lounges, and Faces, a popular disco in Tsimshatsui. The smallest economy rooms cost HK$790 ($103) for a single and HK$860 ($112) for a double. The hotel's largest deluxe rooms go for HK$1,500 ($195) for a single and HK$1,620 ($210) for a double.

The **Ambassador,** 4 Middle Rd. (tel. 3666321), has a great location between the Sheraton and Holiday Inn hotels on Nathan Road and is a good choice in this category. Its rooms are bright, cheerful, and roomy, and come with the usual color TV, fridge, phone, radio, and desk. The staff is young and friendly, and dim sum are served daily in one of its restaurants. Its cheaper rooms, which are HK$1,170 ($152) for single occupancy and HK$1,300 ($169) for double, all face the back of the hotel and are the same no matter which floor you're on. Rooms that face toward the front of the hotel are larger and have views of Nathan Road, starting at HK$7,530 ($199) for single occupancy and HK$1,650 ($214) for double.

Almost right next door to the Ambassador is the **Imperial Hotel,** 30-34 Nathan Rd. (tel. 3662201). Conveniently located, its rooms are simple but come with radio, fridge, phone, color TV, desk, and large bathroom. Its standard rooms, which cost HK$700 ($91) for a single and HK$740 ($96) for a twin or double, face the back side of Chungking Mansion, notorious for its cheap and often uninviting rooms. Although the view is not what you'd call stunning, it is enlightening, with laundry strung everywhere and garbage piled up below, apparently tossed unconcernedly from the windows up above. If that doesn't appeal to your sense of adventure, some of the moderate rooms face Nathan Road and begin at HK$780 ($101) for a single and HK$830 ($108) for a double or twin. Some standard rooms also face Chungking Mansion, so if the view is important to you, be sure to ask for one of them. Be aware, however, that rooms that face the road get the brunt of the traffic noise below. Rooms high enough to offer a glimpse of the harbor are HK$900 ($117) for a single and HK$950 ($123) for a double or twin.

Although located a good 20-minute hike from the Star Ferry, the **Ritz Hotel,** 122 Austin Rd. (tel. 3692282), is one of the best choices among hotels of comparable price. In 1984 it became one of the first medium-range hotels to renovate its rooms with modern facilities in both rooms and bathrooms, setting an example for other hotels that have since followed suit in the face of stiff competition. With only 60 rooms, the Ritz is small and personable and is a favorite with visiting businessmen from Japan and Southeast Asia. In fact, it's such a popular choice with a high number of repeat guests that it's almost mandatory to reserve a room here at least two months in advance during peak season. Rates start at HK$720 ($94) for a single and HK$820 ($106) for a double. The closest MTR subway station is Jordan Station, about two minutes away.

Built in the early 1960s, the **Park Hotel,** 61-65 Chatham Rd. South (tel. 3661371), is one of the best-known medium-priced hotels on Kowloon. Especially popular with Australians, it has what are probably the largest rooms in this category, certainly a plus if you're tired of cramped quarters. What's more, all guest rooms received a much-needed face-lift in 1987, so that now it doesn't even look like the same hotel. You can't go wrong staying in this comfortable and clean hotel. Singles range from HK$840 ($109) to HK$1,200 ($156), and twins run HK$960 ($125) to HK$1,300 ($169).

The **Grand Hotel,** 14 Carnarvon Rd. (tel. 3669331), is another older hotel built in the early '60s, with rooms refurbished in 1985. Guest rooms come with a minibar, digital clock, radio, and color TV and are bright and cheerful. Located in the heart of Tsimshatsui off Nathan Road, this hotel serves a popular lunch buffet for HK$70 ($9.09) from noon to 3 p.m. and a dinner buffet for HK$130 ($16.88) from 6 to 10:30 p.m. Depending on the size and location of the room, a person traveling alone will pay from HK$790 ($103) to HK$1,130 ($147) for accommodation, while two people can expect to spend HK$860 ($112) to HK$1,200 ($156). Triples are available for HK$1,800 ($234).

Located at the corner of Chatham and Mody roads about a ten-minute walk from the Star Ferry, the **Empress Hotel,** 17-19 Chatham Rd. (tel. 3660211), is a 189-room property that is slowly being renovated. An older hotel, it boasts a good location and a personable staff. Its deluxe rooms are a good bargain at HK$1,080 ($140) for single occupancy and HK$1,140 ($148) for double; they feature a large balcony with glass sliding doors and a view of the harbor. Otherwise, rooms begin at HK$720 ($94) for a single and HK$780 ($101) for a twin. Incidentally, if you want to sit outside on the deluxe room balcony, you can request outdoor chairs from housekeeping.

Farther up Nathan Road a few blocks past the Jordan subway station is the **Hotel Fortuna,** 355 Nathan Rd. (tel. 3851011), where 22 single rooms are available for HK$600 ($78). Although they're nicely furnished, some people may find them too claustrophobic because they don't have windows. Much larger rooms with windows are available beginning at HK$780 ($101) for single occupancy and HK$840 ($109) for double. This hotel is more than a quarter-century old, but it's been so artfully renovated that you can't tell. The clean, bright lobby is of marble with art deco lighting, and the hotel's one restaurant serves dim sum and Taiwanese food. Since the hotel is owned by the Wing On corporation, hotel guests are entitled to a discount at the Wing On department store next door.

Located across the street from Hotel Fortuna north of the Jordan subway station, **Nathan Hotel,** 378 Nathan Rd. (tel. 3885141), is another older hotel that has been completely renovated. Its 186 rooms are fairly large and come with color TV, alarm clock, fridge, push-button phone (plus a phone in the bathroom). Singles range from HK$600 ($78) to HK$720 ($93), twins from HK$780 ($101) to HK$960 ($125), and triples from HK$960 ($125) to HK$1,020 ($132).

Located close to the Jordan subway station, the **Shamrock Hotel,** 223 Nathan Rd. (tel. 3-662271), is an older hotel built in the early 1950s that caters mainly to visitors from Asia. It's a pioneer member of the HKHA. The most remarkable thing about this hotel is its lobby—although small, the ceiling is covered with about two dozen chandeliers and lights of all different designs. You don't have to worry about darkness here. Guest rooms are rather small, but high ceilings give them a bit more feeling of spaciousness. Singles begin at HK$450 ($58), doubles at HK$660 ($86), and twins at HK$540 ($70).

Off Nathan Road on a quiet side street not far from the Shamrock, the 70-room **Bangkok Royal Hotel,** 2-12 Pilkem St. (tel. 3679181 and 7359181), not surprisingly considering its name, has a popular Thai restaurant. The only drawback to this hotel is that its bathrooms are quite small and its sinks minute. In an attempt to upgrade itself, however, the hotel is slowly renovating the rooms. During peak season, singles range from HK$420 ($55) to HK$600 ($78) and twins from HK$550 ($71) to HK$740 ($96), with the higher rates charged for renovated rooms. Off-season rates are slightly cheaper.

The **International Hotel,** 33 Cameron Rd. (tel. 3663381), is more than 35 years old and looks it. However, the hotel is well located—only 15 minutes or so away from the Star Ferry—and the size of its rooms is adequate. Only international guests (that is, no Hong Kong residents) are accepted at the International, and all rooms come with the usual color TV, radio, phone, and desk, and some have a fridge. Some of the double rooms even have balconies, although the view is nothing to write home about. Rooms that face towards the back of the hotel have glazed windows. Depending on the season and the size of the room, single rates range from HK$450 ($58) to HK$810 ($105) and double rates run HK$600 ($78) to HK$1,050 ($136).

The Budget Category

The overwhelmingly number one choice in this category is the **YMCA** on Salisbury Road (tel. 3692211), which has the good fortune of being right next door to the Peninsula on the waterfront. Note, however, that the YMCA is in a state of flux until the middle half of 1991, when a new facility with an additional 263 rooms will make its debut. Until then the YMCA is operating with only 135 twin rooms, all of which have the comforts of a private bathroom, TV, room safe, and refrigerator and go for HK$470 ($61). You can expect that rooms in the new addition will be more expensive, but there will be dormitory rooms for about HK$100 ($12.99). The YMCA welcomes families, men, and women, and has an inexpensive, popular restaurant.

Caritas Bianchi Lodge, 4 Cliff Rd., Yaumatei (tel. 3881111), is another good choice in this price range. Although it's a bit far from the Star Ferry, it's close to the Yaumatei subway station and is located next to the Salvation Army. Its 90 rooms come with minibar, color TV, phone, and a private bath, and most rooms face a cliff with a small park and a few trees, certainly a more pleasant view than most hotels can boast. Try to get a room on a higher floor. Rates here including continental breakfast are HK$330 ($43) for a single, HK$450 ($58) for a double or twin, and HK$540 ($70) for a triple.

Right down the street from Caritas Bianchi Lodge is the Salvation Army, where you'll find the **Booth Lodge** up on the seventh floor, 11 Sing Sing Lane, Yaumatei (tel. 7719266). Its 33 rooms are all doubles and twins and come with private bathroom, color TV, small fridge, and telephone. It's close to the Yaumatei subway station, and an easy walk to the Jade Market and the Temple Street night market. Standard rooms are HK$380 ($49) for single or double occupancy, while more deluxe rooms start at HK$430 ($56).

Fuji Hotel, 140-142 Austin Rd. (tel. 3678111), has 60 rooms with bath, color TV, and phone, and is not a member of HKHA. A bit run-down, it caters mainly to a younger Asian crowd, including many Japanese, and has a young staff as well. Only those rooms facing the front street have a window, and although they are certainly brighter, they are also much noisier. Single rooms here cost HK$410 ($53), while doubles are HK$440 ($57). Twin rooms are slightly larger and go for HK$470 ($61). Continental breakfast is free. This hotel has a variety of different rooms, so if you don't like the one you're shown, ask to see another one. All have a private bathroom. The nearest subway station is Jordan Station.

Located near the Yaumatei subway station, **King's Hotel,** 473 Nathan Rd. (tel. 7801281), is just a basic hotel with no frills, its rooms supplied with color TV, stocked fridge, phone, and bath. It caters primarily to Asians, including mainland Chinese, and has a good Thai restaurant. Singles begin at HK$400 ($52) and twins at HK$480 ($62).

Although not a member of HKHA, **Jade Hotel,** 23 Cameron Rd. (tel. 3697491), is conveniently located in the middle of Tsimshatsui and is worth a try if other hotels are full. The wallpaper, shag carpeting, and rattan furniture are a bit old, but the prices are reasonable: HK$360 ($47) to HK$480 ($62) for a single, HK$480 ($62) to HK$600 ($78) for a twin or double. Prices are slightly lower off-season.

The **YMCA International House,** 23 Waterloo Rd. (tel. 7719111), is near the Yaumatei subway station and accepts both males and females. It seems to appeal more to Asians (most Westerners seem to opt for the YMCA on Salisbury Road.) All rooms come with air conditioning and private bathroom, costing HK$370 ($48) for a single and HK$400 ($52) for a double.

Inconveniently located but with reasonable prices, the **YWCA Guest House,** 5 Man Fuk Rd., Waterloo Hill (tel. 7139211), can be reached by bus 8 from the Star Ferry. Both men and women are welcome, and all rooms are air-conditioned. Singles without private bathroom are HK$230 ($30), while those with are HK$430 ($56). Double rooms, all with bathroom, also are HK$430 ($56).

Rock-Bottom Choices

Getting down to the rock-bottom choices, most notorious is **Chungking Mansion,** which occupies a prime spot at 40 Nathan Rd. between the Holiday Inn and the Imperial Hotel. Actually a huge and meandering concrete high-rise rather than one single hotel, Chungking Mansion consists of an extensive and cheap shopping arcade on the ground floor and a variety of eating and sleeping establishments on the many floors above, many of which seem to be owned by Indians living in Hong Kong. Some of the so-called hotels are passable; many are not.

I stayed in Chungking Mansion on my first trip to Hong Kong a few years back, living in a neon-colored cell that contained only two sagging beds, a night table, and a closet. In the shared bathroom down the hall lived the biggest spider I have ever seen, a hairy thing that nevertheless behaved itself quite well whenever I was there— it never moved an inch the whole time I took a shower, but when I returned the next night it was always motionless in another part of the room. I figured it survived only by being unobtrusive and I wouldn't be surprised if it's still there. I shared my room with another women and we paid about $5 (U.S.) each.

These are the kinds of places that have made Chungking notorious, but luckily not all are quite as colorful as where I stayed (too bad I didn't have this book). Whereas ten years ago there weren't many guest houses from which to choose, the past couple of years have witnessed a virtual mushrooming of sleeping establishments throughout the rabbit-warren maze of Chungking Mansion. A security guard I talked to estimated that there were 200 guest houses in all, most of them small affairs with a handful of rooms, but I myself counted about 70. At any rate, there are a lot, and if you simply show up and start searching, you're bound to find something. For the less daring, A Block is probably the easiest to manage, since its elevator is the one nearest the front entrance—after the shops of the arcade close, it can be a bit disconcerting to walk down the deserted corridors to reach the elevators of the blocks farther to the back. What follows are a few of the better guest houses. If these are full or you want to save money, check the guest houses toward the back of the building.

Best known in the building is **Chungking House** (tel. 3665362), on the fourth and fifth floors of A Block (Chungking Mansion is divided into sections A through E, each with its own elevator). It's the only one in the building that's a member of HKHA, and all rooms here have private bath, air conditioning, phone, and TV. It's a bit dreary, but prices are reasonable. Often fully booked, rooms here start at HK$180 ($23) a single and HK$220 ($29) for a double.

My own personal favorite is the **Peking Guest House,** located on the 12th floor of A Block (tel. 7238320). Since it has been open only since 1988, it is newer, brighter, and more cheerful than most of the older establishments. There are nine rooms altogether, six of them with private bathroom. All rooms have TV, air conditioning, and windows, and four rooms face Nathan Road (which is infinitely more uplifting than a view of the back side of Chungking). A person alone pays HK$100 ($12.99) for a room without bath and HK$120 ($15.59) for a room with; two people pay HK$165 ($21.42) and HK$175 ($22.73) to HK$260 ($33.77), respectively.

Another good choice is the **Welcome Guest House,** on the seventh floor of A Block (tel. 7217793), which is managed by a friendly young couple. Altogether they manage 35 rooms scattered throughout the A Block, more than half of which face Nathan Road. They provide laundry service and can help arrange a visa for China. Rooms without private bathroom go for HK$77 ($10) for those with bunk beds and HK$90 ($11.69) for those with a double-size bed, regardless of whether there are one or two of you. A single with bathroom starts at HK$120 ($15.59), while a double with bathroom is HK$155 ($20.13). A family room big enough for four or five persons starts at HK$200 ($25.97).

On the 13th floor of B Block is the **New Washington Guest House** (tel. 3665798), which has ten rooms and has been in operation for more than 20 years. Rooms are simple and clean, but don't have private bathrooms. The cheapest rooms go for HK$100 ($12.99) and come with TV and fan, while air-conditioned rooms are priced at HK$130 ($16.88). This establishment is one of the best in its price category.

New Asia Guest House (tel. 7240426) is located on the eighth floor of A Block and offers a variety of rooms ranging from HK$130 ($16.88) to HK$220 ($28.57), most with private bathroom and air conditioning. Rooms are clean and the owners are friendly.

Popular with the backpacking crowd, the **Traveller's Hostel** is on the 16th floor of A Block (tel. 3682505) at Chungking Mansion. A dormitory bunk bed costs HK$33 ($4.28), singles go for HK$75 ($9.74), and doubles run HK$90 ($12.86). Toilets and showers are shared. Traveller's Hostel is basic, but the fact that it's so high up and has so many windows means that it's bright and sunny. Perhaps the main drawback is that it's a bit messy, with everyone's belongings strewn everywhere. On the other hand, it's a good place to stay if you want to meet other travelers, and there's even a travel service here that specializes in arranging trips to China.

If staying in Chungking Mansion doesn't appeal to you, another option is **Great Wall Hotel,** located on the corner of Nathan and Jordan roads near the Jordan subway station at 300 Nathan Rd. (tel. 3887675). Located up on the 14th floor, its rooms are old but they're clean and have private bathroom, air conditioning, and TV. The premises are orderly, not cluttered like many guest houses tend to be. The woman running the place doesn't understand English, but she does understand "single," which costs HK$250 ($32.47), and "double," which runs HK$280 ($36.36).

One other rock-bottom place worth mentioning is the **International Youth Accommodation Centre,** on the sixth floor at 21A Lock Rd. (tel. 3663419), behind the Hyatt Regency. Not for the squeamish, it's a chaotic but mellow place with backpacks, belongings, and unidentifiable objects strewn all over the place. It certainly could be cleaner, but people who have stayed here swear that it has the best atmosphere in town. Of course, it should be mentioned that these are long-term travelers, mostly Europeans, who have been roughing it for who knows how many years. There are 26 bunk beds here that rent for HK$33 ($4.28) a night.

READER'S ROCK-BOTTOM SUGGESTION: "May I suggest a clean, inexpensive $20 (U.S.) hostel in Hong Kong called **Promise Land Hostel**, 38 Bute St., Mongkok (tel. 7891080). It is run by two Chinese who really make an effort to help" (Mike Clark, Chicago, Ill.).

WANCHAI/CAUSEWAY BAY

If the thought of jostling elbows with other tourists in Kowloon in an area that is obviously tourist-oriented does not appeal to you, then consider staying in a hotel across the harbor in Wanchai or Causeway Bay on Hong Kong Island. This is where the locals themselves come to shop and to eat. Prices are lower, and the area has much more of a Chinese feel to it. Although redevelopment is slowly gobbling up old neighborhoods here too, there are still old buildings, side streets with markets, street vendors, and narrow, winding roads.

The Upper Bracket

The **Excelsior,** Causeway Bay (tel. 5767365), is the most exclusive hotel in the area. A Mandarin Oriental Associate hotel, it sits on the waterfront with a view of the Hong Kong Yacht Club and Kowloon across the harbor. Although it doesn't have a swimming pool, it has rooftop tennis courts and seven restaurants and bars, including the comfortable Dickens Bar and the Talk of the Town disco. All rooms are the same size with the same decor, but those with a harbor view are more expensive.

Comfortably decorated with small sofas in front of the windows, a large desk area, and a black-and-white tiled bathroom, each room costs the same regardless of single or double occupancy, starting at HK$1,080 ($140). Superior rooms, which have partial harbor views, cost HK$1,300 ($169). The best of these face the Central District and Victoria Peak. If you want a full harbor view, expect to pay HK$1,600 ($208).

Park Lane Radisson Hotel (formerly called the Park Lane Hotel), 310 Gloucester Rd., Causeway Bay (tel. 8903355), is popular with visiting groups from Japan. All rooms have recently been renovated and feature marble tabletops and marble bathrooms. Room rates, which vary according to location (the lower floors are cheapest), begin at HK$1,250 ($162) for both single and double occupancy. If you feel like splurging, the hotel's deluxe rooms, which go for HK$1,800 ($234), are located on the top floors and have views of either the harbor or Victoria Park.

Another hotel that caters mostly to Japanese and Taiwanese groups is **Lee Gardens,** Hysan Avenue, Causeway Bay (tel. 8953311), located a bit inland. The prices of its rooms are based on size, decor, and floor number rather than view. Decorated on a South Pacific theme with bamboo furniture and soothing colors of beige and bisque, the rooms are pleasant and bright, and run HK$960 ($125) to HK$1,400 ($182) for single or double occupancy. Restaurants in the hotel serve Chinese, Korean, Japanese, and Western food, and a shuttle bus transports guests to the Central District.

The Medium-Priced Bracket

One of three Ramada properties to open in Hong Kong in the latter half of the 1980s, the **Ramada Inn Hong Kong,** 61-73 Lockhart Rd. (tel. 8611000) in Wanchai, is a business hotel with 340 rooms, rooftop swimming pool, sauna, restaurant, and bar. Rooms are small but adequate and come complete with radio, TV with free in-house movies, alarm clock, fridge, and telephone. There are only 16 rooms that go for HK$900 ($117); the others are deluxe rooms for HK$980 ($127). Prices are the same for single and double occupancy.

Totally renovated and reopened in 1986 under a new name, **Hotel New Harbour,** 41-49 Hennessy Rd. (tel. 8611166), is a pleasant hotel catering largely to tour groups from China. Although the hotel is located on a busy street in the heart of Wanchai, rooms are quiet and come with stocked refrigerator, TV, and direct-dial telephone service. Rates are based on both room size and height, with the cheapest singles going for HK$630 ($82) and doubles for HK$690 ($90). Deluxe rooms are on the 18th floor, and some of these offer glimpses of the harbor at a price of HK$930 ($121) for single occupancy and HK$1,020 ($132) for double.

The **New Hong Kong Cathay Hotel,** 17 Tung Lo Wan Rd., Causeway Bay (tel. 5778211), is a 229-room hotel built in 1967 and renovated in 1989. Rooms are large, bright, and modestly furnished with the basics of color TV, stocked refrigerator, and large desk. Rates begin at HK$620 ($81) for single occupancy and HK$700 ($91) for double. By far the best rooms here are the deluxe twins on the tenth floor—they come with large balconies that are great for looking out on the city below and cost HK$840 ($109).

Harbour Hotel, 116-122 Gloucester Rd. (tel. 5748211), sits slightly back from the waterfront and offers some harbor-view rooms at a reasonable price. A place popular with groups of visiting businessmen from mainland China, its cheapest economy rooms rent for HK$510 ($66) single or double, and come with color TV, phone, radio, desk, and private bath, but they're small and windowless and a bit claustrophobic. Next up the scale are singles for HK$670 ($87) and doubles or twins for HK$810 ($105) that feature windows opening onto a quiet back street. The largest rooms are deluxe twins with a partial harbor view, which rent for HK$1,020 ($132) and come with a small fridge. There are 16 of these rooms and since they're all the same price, ask for one on a higher floor where the view is better.

If you've come to Hong Kong primarily for the horse races, the **Caravelle Hotel,** 84 Morrison Hill Rd., Happy Valley (tel. 5754455), is where you may want to stay. It's located just across the street from Happy Valley racetrack and its front rooms even have views of the racecourse. It's a small hotel with only ten rooms on each floor and the corridors are dimly lit, but there's an attendant on every floor. The rooms are bright enough and come with the usual color TV, radio, empty fridge, desk, and phone, though furnishings are old. Most guests here are Japanese and British. Singles begin at HK$540 ($70) and twins or doubles at HK$600 ($78). Rates are the same for those facing the track, so if you're interested in the races, be sure to ask.

The Budget Category

Opened in 1986, the **Harbour View International House,** 4 Harbour Rd., Wanchai (tel. 5201111), is owned and operated by YMCA and occupies a prime spot right by the harbor. Located next to the Hong Kong Arts Centre, it's a 20-story building with 320 rooms, each simply decorated but very functional with TV, carpeting, international direct-dial telephone, refrigerator, radio and in-house music, and a tiny but private bathroom. Facilities include a coffeeshop, one restaurant with a view of the harbor, room service, laundry service, and telex. But the best thing about the hotel is that more than half of its rooms face the harbor and go for HK$600 ($78) for a twin and HK$660 ($86) for a double (there are no single rooms). Twin rooms facing inland are HK$520 ($67).

CENTRAL DISTRICT

The business area of Hong Kong, the Central District has only a few hotels and tends to empty out and shut down after dark, but it serves as a good base for exploring the rest of Hong Kong. Trams, most Hong Kong Island buses, Victoria Peak tram, the Star Ferry, the subway, and ferries to the outlying islands pass through or begin in the Central District.

Deluxe Choices

Famed for its service and consistently rated as one of the top hotels in the world, the **Mandarin Oriental,** 5 Connaught Rd. (tel. 5220111), maintains a staff of 1,000 for its 545 rooms. Located in front of the Star Ferry, it caters to a primarily business clientele and its rooms are the most expensive on Hong Kong Island. Spacious and decorated on an Oriental theme, all rooms have balconies and range from HK$1,800 ($234) for those facing inland and HK$2,200 ($286) to HK$2,800 ($364) for those with a view of the harbor. Rooms have an understated elegance and include all amenities you could possibly want—but if you are still in need of something, the staff will make every effort to fulfill your wishes. The lobby is decorated with a stunning glass light fixture and woodcarvings from China. Several of its restaurants have well-deserved reputations for serving excellent cuisine, including the Mandarin Grill for seafood, Man Wah for Cantonese food, and the Pierrot for specialties from France.

The Upper Bracket

Hong Kong Hilton, 2 Queen's Rd. (tel. 5233111), is at the junction of Queen's and Garden roads not far from the Victoria Peak tram. One of the few hotels on Hong Kong Island with an outdoor heated swimming pool, the Hilton has 751 rooms plus eight restaurants and bars. All rooms, decorated in mauve or smoky green, have large windows extending the full width of the exterior wall, three phones, a marble bathroom, a well-stocked minibar, and a sitting area with settee and desk. Singles range from HK$1,740 ($226) for a standard to HK$2,100 ($273) for a deluxe room on a top floor with a harbor view, while twins or doubles begin at HK$1,840 ($239) and go up to HK$2,290 ($297) for a deluxe overlooking the water. Special features of the Hilton include six floors of "Executive Rooms" (priced the same as deluxe rooms) with their own reception desk, and free breakfast and cocktails; a business center; packing and mailing service; a health club you can use at an extra charge; and an 110-foot brigantine, a faithful reproduction of British piratechasers of the 1840s. Service at the hotel is excellent.

Joining Hong Kong's hotel boom is the **Hong Kong Marriott,** 88 Queensway (tel. 8108366), which made its debut in 1989. Its lobby is rather grandiose, with a three-story atrium, a staircase waterfall, large windows looking out on Hong Kong, and a jungle of fake plants. Rooms are designed with right-angled "saw-tooth" windows for a maximum view, and when you wake up in the morning, all you have to do is push a button by the bed to open curtains to the morning light. Rooms are elegantly appointed and facilities include an outdoor swimming pool, a fitness center, and a business center. The hotel is connected to a shopping arcade. Rates for single or double occupancy start at HK$1,650 ($214), with harbor-view rooms going for HK$2,200 ($286).

The lobby of the **Hotel Furama,** 1 Connaught Rd. (tel. 5255111), is on the second floor and faces beautiful Chater Garden. Famous for its revolving restaurant, La Ronda, on the 30th floor, this hotel equips all its guest rooms with a safe, bathrobe, hairdryer, and minibar. Rooms begin at HK$1,350 ($175) for single or double occupancy, while rooms with a harbor view are HK$1,900 ($247).

Opened in 1986, **Hotel Victoria,** Shun Tak Centre, Connaught Road (tel. 5407228), is located in the same complex that also houses the Macau Ferry Terminal and the entrance to the Sheung Wan MTR subway station. You can walk all the way from Hotel Victoria to the Star Ferry Terminal in the heart of Central via an elevated walkway in about 15 to 20 minutes. Occupying the top 15 floors of a 40-story building, Hotel Victoria offers 540 rooms with spacious sitting areas close to the large windows, large writing tables (reflective of the hotel's high percentage of business clientele), and marbled bathrooms with lots of room to spread out. Rates range from HK$1,550 ($201) for rooms facing inland to HK$1,900 ($247) for deluxe rooms with great views of the harbor. Facilities include an outdoor swimming pool, two floodlit tennis courts, a business center, and restaurants serving Cantonese and Western cuisine.

YOUTH HOSTELS AND CAMPSITES

Hong Kong and its territories have a number of youth hostels and camping sites available, offering the cheapest rates around. The most conveniently located youth hostel is **Ma Wui Hall,** located on the top of Mount Davis on Hong Kong Island (tel. 8175715). As with all the other youth hostels in Hong Kong, it charges HK$18 ($2.38) a night, with nonmembers paying HK$15 ($1.95) more. Seven other youth hostels are spread on some of the outlying islands and in the New Territories. For more information on Hong Kong's youth hostels, contact the **Hong Kong Youth Hostels Association,** 1408A Watson's Estate, Causeway Bay (tel. 5700985 or 5706222). You may also purchase a youth hostel card here for HK$90 ($11.69).

There are **camping** facilities on some of the outlying islands, ranging in price from free to about HK$33 ($4.28). You must bring your own tent, but some of the camps provide sheets and blankets. The more primitive campsites lack water or latrine facilities—but they're free. For more information on campsites, contact the HKTA.

---

5. Where to Dine

With an estimated 19,000 restaurants, Hong Kong has what is probably the greatest concentration of Chinese restaurants in the world. In fact, the food is so good and the prices are so reasonable that dining out ranks high as one of *the* things to do while in Hong Kong.

Traditionally speaking, Chinese restaurants tend to be noisy and crowded affairs, the patrons much more interested in food than decor. Recent years, however, have witnessed an explosion in chic, trendy, and fashionable Chinese restaurants, outfitted in styles reminiscent of art deco. In any case, dining is usually in large groups; the basic rule is to order one dish for each person and then to share each dish as it comes. If you want to be correct about it, a Chinese meal usually begins with a cold dish, followed by dishes of beef, pork, vegetables, seafood, soup, and noodles or rice. Many of the dishes are accompanied by sauces, the most common being soy sauce, chili sauce, and hot mustard. Tea is often provided whether you ask for it or not (if you want more tea, simply take the lid off the teapot—someone will come around to refill it), and the beginning and end of your meal is heralded with a round of hot towels, a wonderful custom that you'll soon grow addicted to and wish would be imported to restaurants in the United States.

The most common styles of Chinese cooking in Hong Kong are Cantonese, Peking, Szechuan (also called Sichuan), Shanghai, and Chiu Chow, though Cantonese is by far the most popular: most Hong Kong Chinese are originally from the area of Canton in China. It's also the most common style of Chinese cooking around the world and is probably the one with which you're most familiar. **Cantonese food** is either steamed or fried and prepared without spices in the belief that the natural flavor of the various ingredients should be prevalent and enjoyed. Popular dishes include roast duck or pigeon, pan-fried lemon chicken, shark's-fin soup, slices of garoupa (a local fish) with ham and bamboo shoots, and sweet-and-sour pork.

Another popular Cantonese dish is *dim sum,* which means "light snack" and is eaten for breakfast and lunch and with afternoon tea. Dim sum consists primarily of finely chopped meat, seafood, and vegetables wrapped in thin dough and then either steamed, fried, boiled, or braised.

Many Cantonese restaurants offer dim sum from about 7:30 a.m. until 4 p.m., served from trolleys wheeled between the tables. Just point at what you want. Some of my favorite dishes are *shiu mai* (steamed minced pork and shrimp dumpling), *har gau* (steamed shrimp dumpling), *au yuk* (steamed minced beef balls), *fun gwor* (steamed rice-flour dumpling filled with pork, shrimp, and bamboo shoots), and *tsun guen* (deep-fried spring roll filled with shredded pork, chicken, mushrooms, bamboo shoots, and bean sprouts). A serving of dim sum usually comes three to four on a plate and averages about HK$5 (65¢) to HK$10 ($1.30). Your bill is figured at the end of your meal by the number of plates on your table or by a card that was stamped each time you ordered a dish.

Peking food, much of which originated in the imperial courts of emperors and empresses, uses a liberal amount of peppers, garlic, ginger, leek, and coriander. Noodles and dumplings are more common than rice, the food is richer than Cantonese cuisine, and roasting is the preferred method of cooking. Most famous among Peking-style dishes is Peking or (or Beijing) duck, which is air-dried and then coated with a mixture of syrup and soy sauce before roasting. It's best to have at least four people to order this dish, and it's served by wrapping thin slivers of duck in a thin pancake together with spring onion, radish, and sweet plum sauce.

Other popular cuisine includes "drunken chicken," a cold dish of chicken in wine sauce; "beggar's chicken," a whole chicken stuffed with mushrooms, pickled Chinese cabbage, herbs, and onions, sealed in clay and baked all day; sautéed beef with spring onions served on a sizzling platter; and Mongolian hotpots, with dumplings, meat, noodles, and vegetables.

Szechuan food is my favorite Chinese cuisine, as it's the spiciest, hottest, and most fiery style of cooking. Seasoning is done with chili-bean paste and peppercorns, and Szechuan specialties include pan-fried shrimp in spicy sauce, sour-and-peppery soup, smoked duck with camphor and tea flavoring, and sautéed diced chicken in chili-bean paste.

Shanghai food is heavier, richer, sweeter, and oilier than either Cantonese or Peking food (technically speaking, Shanghai does not have a cuisine of its own; rather, the food is a composite of various cooking styles). Some dishes are rather heavy on the garlic, and portions tend to be enormous. The most popular Shanghai dish in Hong Kong is freshwater hairy crab, flown in from Shanghai in autumn. Other foods you might consider trying include eel, sautéed shrimp in spicy tomato sauce over crispy rice, and sautéed shredded beef and green pepper.

One other type of Chinese food worth mentioning, which is not very well known, is **Chiu Chow.** The name refers to the people, dialect, and food of the area of Swatow in southeast Canton. The food is rich in protein, light and tasty, and sauces are liberally applied. Dishes include steamed lobster, deep-fried shrimp balls, sautéed slices of whelk, fried goose blood, and bird's nest in coconut milk. Chiu Chow tea, popularly called Iron Buddha, is probably the world's strongest and bitterest tea. Drink some of this stuff and you'll be humming for hours.

Of course, there are many other dishes you can eat in addition to the ones I've mentioned above. It's said that the Chinese will eat anything that swims, flies, or crawls, and though that may not be entirely true, if you're adventurous enough you may want to try such delicacies as snake soup, pig's brain, bird's nest soup (derived from the saliva of swallows), or eel heads simmered with Chinese herbs.

If you want to know more about the great variety of Chinese food available, there's an excellent booklet called *Visitor's Guide to Chinese Food in Hong Kong* available at HKTA offices. You're safe eating almost anywhere in Hong Kong, but residents warn foreigners never to eat local oysters—there have been too many instances of oyster poisoning. Eat oysters only if they're imported, say, from Australia. The good restaurants will clearly stipulate in the menu that their oysters are imported.

Another thing you should watch in eating Chinese food is your reaction to monosodium glutamate (MSG), used to enhance flavor in Chinese cooking. Some people react strongly to this spice, reporting bouts of nausea and headaches and a feeling of being bloated. Although you can try requesting dishes without MSG, much of the food has been prepared beforehand and may already include liberal doses. Fortunately, however, in the past couple of years there has been an increased awareness in Hong Kong about the detrimental side effects of MSG, with the result that most of the top and medium-range Chinese restaurants (especially those in hotels) have either cut down in its usage or stopped using it altogether.

In addition to Chinese restaurants, I've also included a good selection of Western restaurants that could easily stand on their own anywhere in the world. Keep in mind, however, that Western restaurants tend to be more expensive than Chinese ones, and that wine is especially expensive. To keep costs down, stick with beer: the two most popular brands are San Miguel or Tsingtao.

In addition to the restaurants listed below, there are also bars and pubs in the "Hong Kong After Dark" section that serve food. In any case, keep in mind that, in addition to the prices I've given below, a 10% service charge will be added to your bill. You're also expected to leave your small change or 5% of the bill for your waiter.

THE UPPER BRACKET

By far Hong Kong's best and most exclusive restaurants, both Chinese and Western, are in the hotels. That's not surprising when you realize that first-class hotels are used to catering to well-traveled visitors who demand high quality in service, cuisine, and decor.

Chinese Food

The **Man Wah,** on the 25th floor of the Mandarin Oriental Hotel, 5 Connaught Rd., Central District (tel. 5220111), is the place to go if you're tired of the usual noisy Chinese restaurant and feel like splurging on elegant dining with a good view of the harbor. A 600-year-old screen from the Ming Dynasty, woodcarvings, pink tablecloths, exquisite chinaware, fresh flowers and candles on every table, and Chinese instrumental music playing softly in the background set the mood for a romantic dinner of Cantonese cuisine.

Although the menu changes often, dishes might include such specialties as braised pigeon with bamboo shoots and mushrooms in oyster sauce, deep-fried scallops with minced shrimp, sautéed diced chicken with chili, roast duck Peking style (order it in advance), sweet-and-sour pork, shark's-fin soup with crab roe, or spicy pork spareribs. For soup I can personally recommend the spicy-and-sour soup, piquant and full of noodles, tofu, and mushrooms. Dinner here averages about HK$380 ($49.35) à la carte. Lunch is served from noon to 2:30 p.m. and dinner from 6:30 to 10:30 p.m. Seating is for 55 people only, and if you want to be assured of having a window seat, be sure to say so when you call for reservations.

Perched on the top floor of the Hilton hotel at 2 Queen's Rd. (tel. 5233111) is the **Eagle's Nest,** from which you have a bird's-eye view of the Central District around you and Kowloon across the harbor. Decorated with art deco lamps and accented with fresh flowers and candles on every table, it looks like a European restaurant—only the chopsticks betray the fact that the Eagle's Nest dishes out superb Cantonese cuisine. Open daily from 7 p.m. to 1 a.m. (last order is at 10:30 p.m.) to the accompaniment of a small dance band, it serves a wide selection of abalone, chicken, pigeon, duck, beef, pork, seafood, and vegetarian dishes. Specialties of the restaurant include Vagabond (beggar's) chicken, fresh lobster salad, roast duck with plum sauce, double-boiled shark's fin with shredded chicken, baked stuffed sea whelk in the shell with curry sauce, steamed garoupa, and roasted Peking duck. An especially good deal is the special menu for HK$270 ($35.06) per person, which allows you to select as many dishes as you want from a list of about 70 items. A vegetarian dim sum platter is available for lunch for HK$60 ($7.79), served from noon to 2 p.m.

One more Cantonese restaurant worth mentioning on the Hong Kong side is **The Bloom,** located in the basement of an elegant colonial-style building in the heart of the Central District at 12 Pedder St. (tel. 5218421). Smartly decorated in an art deco style with warm woods and flowers on the tables, it's a chic place that attracts everyone from businesspeople to artists and writers. Although the food is Cantonese with an emphasis on fresh seafood, the presentation and preparation of some of the dishes border on nouvelle Chinese cuisine. Specialties are shark's fin soup, crispy roast Lung Kong chicken, abalone with bamboo piths, flambéed drunken prawns, and braised noodles with shredded abalone. On Sunday, dim sum is served until 3 p.m. Otherwise, you can expect to spend HK$200 ($25.97) to HK$300 ($38.96) for dinner, excluding drinks. The Bloom is open daily from 11 a.m. to midnight (to 10 p.m. on Sunday).

One of the most elaborately decorated Chinese restaurants in Hong Kong is the **Shang Palace** in the Shangri-La Hotel, 64 Mody Rd., East Tsimshatsui (tel. 7212111). The entrance to the restaurant is past rows of red columns, which are cleverly multiplied with the use of mirrors to give the illusion of a long corridor. The walls are of red lacquerware carved in designs, and Chinese lanterns hang from the ceiling.

The menu is quite extensive, with a large variety of seafood, chicken, duck, pigeon, beef, and pork cooked Cantonese style. Most dishes are for two to four persons, and average HK$50 ($6.49) to HK$100 ($12.98). If you really want to splurge, you can order bamboo fungus with crabmeat or bird's nest, which are priced at HK$200 ($25.97) or more. Other specialties include shark's-fin soup, barbecued pork, Peking duck, and pan-fried minced pigeon with lettuce. Expect to spend about HK$270 ($35.06) per person for dinner, served daily from 6:30 to 11 p.m.

Shang Palace also serves lunch from noon to 3 p.m. (from 11 a.m. on Sunday and holidays), and although the menu changes every two weeks, it always includes more than a dozen varieties of dim sum for about HK$13 ($1.69) per plate. Because the menu is in English, this is a great place to try dim sum for the first time, not to mention the fact that it's also some of the best dim sum in town. There's also a set lunch for two for HK$129 ($16.75), a particularly good deal.

Lai Ching Heen, in the Regent, on Salisbury Road, Kowloon (tel. 7211211), is a deluxe Cantonese restaurant that emphasizes the beauty of stark simplicity. Bonsai trees and a color scheme of rose and pale gray offset beautiful jade table settings and ivory and silver chopsticks. Dishes are traditional Cantonese as well as creations of the executive chef that border on Chinese nouvelle cuisine. Lunch is served from noon to 3 p.m. and dinner from 6 to 11:30 p.m. Dinner will probably be about HK$400 ($51.95) and lunch about HK$300 ($38.96). The menu changes with each lunar month.

Opened in 1986 on the sixth floor of the Hongkong Hotel at 3 Canton Rd. (tel. 7226565) in Kowloon, the **Golden Unicorn Restaurant** is one of the forerunners of the recent trend to uplift Chinese food into a modern and more formal setting. Serving Cantonese cuisine with a Western flair, this restaurant uses Wedgwood china and Christofle silverware in its presentation of such specialties as drunken shrimp, deep-fried chicken, duck, pork, and seafood selections. Ordering à la carte will probably amount to a bill of HK$550 ($71.43), but if you're by yourself you'll probably want to order the set menu (which changes monthly) for HK$218 ($28.31). Hours here are from noon to midnight daily.

Western Food

Gaddi's, in the Peninsula Hotel, on Salisbury Road in Kowloon (tel. 3666251), has long had a reputation for being the best European restaurant in town. Although that is now being challenged by some pretty stiff competition from other hotels, the service is still excellent, the waiters are all professionals, and the food is always beyond reproof. The atmosphere is that of an elegant dining room, with two crystal-and-silver chandeliers, a pure wool Tai Ping carpet in royal blue, and plenty of space between the tables. There's live music and dancing at night, and although the menu changes every six months, it always includes steak and seafood. A full-course dinner here, excluding wine, will set you back about HK$650 ($84.41) per person, but it's definitely worth it if you can afford it, since Gaddi's is as much a part of Hong Kong as the Peninsula Hotel. If you don't want to splurge for dinner, come for the Squire set lunch menu at HK$160 ($20.78). Hours are noon to 3 p.m. and 7 to 11 p.m. daily. Jacket and tie required for dinner.

I personally prefer the **Verandah Grill,** also located in the Peninsula Hotel. It's less pretentious than Gaddi's and is the restaurant you see under the light-blue-and-green canopy on the second floor if you walk past the front of the hotel. Its big windows wrap themselves around the U-shaped front façade of the hotel, offering a view of the harbor that is unfortunately blocked to some extent by the Space Museum. An airy, bright, and cheerful place that does give an illusion of being a veranda, this place offers seafood, grilled steaks, and veal dishes beginning at HK$150 ($19.48). If you want to splurge, you can order fresh beluga caviar or lobster soup, but the best deal is undoubtedly the light luncheon set menu for HK$130 ($16.88), which includes a salad or soup, entrée, dessert, and coffee or tea. Otherwise, meals here average about HK$270 ($35.06) per person. The Verandah is open for business from 7 to 11 a.m., noon to 3 p.m., and 6:30 to 11 p.m. Dress is casual during the day, but jacket and tie are recommended for dinner.

The Hyatt Regency's **Hugo's,** 67 Nathan Rd., Tsimshatsui (tel. 3662321), was the first Hugo's to open in Asia. A good example of a great restaurant in a hotel, this place is noted for its superb continental cuisine and excellent service. The decor is very masculine, with swords on the walls, huge leather-bound menus, and big green water glasses. Needless to say, men need a coat and tie here. Filipino musicians serenade in the evenings, and the specialty of the house is U.S. prime rib of beef, with the rest of the menu changing every six months. If lobster bisque is on the menu, you can't go wrong ordering it, and the desserts are always spectacular. Depending on the wine you choose, dinner will range from about HK$500 ($64.93) to HK$650 ($84.41) and is served from 7 to 11 p.m. You can do it cheaper if you go for lunch between noon and 2:30 p.m. and order the set meal for HK$145 ($18.83).

Serving continental food with an emphasis on French nouvelle cuisine, **Margaux,** in the Shangri-La Hotel, 64 Mody Rd., East Tsimshatsui (tel. 7212111), is decorated with Viennese chandeliers and teakwood and has an inspiring view of the harbor. Margaux offers the usual beef, veal, and seafood dishes, with an innovative menu that changes often. Dinner, by candlelight and requiring both coat and tie, will cost about HK$450 ($58.44) if you don't order wine. The wine list is fairly extensive; Château Margaux is widely featured, so it may be hard to resist. There's a three-course dinner priced at HK$380 ($49.35) and a lunch special for a reasonable HK$108 ($14.03). Lunch is considerably more casual, but jeans are frowned upon. Lunch is served from noon to 3 p.m. every day except Sunday, and dinner is from 7 to 11:30 p.m. daily.

Some people consider the **Plume,** in the Regent Hotel, on Salisbury Road in Kowloon (tel. 7211211), to be the best European restaurant in Hong Kong. Certainly it feels like a great restaurant, sitting right over the water with a grand view of Hong Kong Island and serving nouvelle cuisine.

It's open only for dinner from 7 to 11 p.m. The evening here begins with a complimentary glass of champagne Mir (champagne with a hint of blackberry liqueur), Indian bread, and goose-liver pâté. The menu, which contains only original creations, is printed anew every day but always includes the house specialty: a delicate cream of artichoke with beluga. Most entrées run around HK$180 ($23.38), but a full dinner with appetizer, soup, and dessert may cost up to HK$500 ($64.93), excluding wine. As expected, coat and tie are required.

The Mandarin Oriental's **Pierrot** on the 25th floor, 5 Connaught Rd., Central (tel. 5220111), was the first hotel restaurant to introduce Hong Kong gourmets to a year-round menu of nouvelle cuisine and has remained one of the city's favorites.

With its name and decor inspired by Picasso's painting of his son in a Pierrot costume, this restaurant offers a great view of the harbor and a menu that changes twice a year. Selections may include such dishes as marinated Scotch salmon and beluga caviar served with potato galette; pan-fried goose liver; garoupa; poached chicken accompanied by a truffle sauce; and white chocolate mousse. Dinners here average about HK$500 ($64.93). Hours here are from noon to 3 p.m. every day except weekends and holidays and from 7 p.m. to midnight daily. After dinner you may wish to retire to the Harlequin Bar for a cocktail; the bar is open from 11 a.m. to midnight.

For exclusive Italian dining, head for the **Capriccio** in the Ramada Renaissance, 8 Peking Rd., Kowloon (tel. 3113311). This is the hotel's premier restaurant (unusual because most top restaurants in hotels are French) and is quite elegant with its beautiful flower arrangements, wonderful lighting, and a color scheme of gray and yellow. All the pasta is homemade, and the menu itself is enough to make my mouth water. The dishes change often, but if it's available you might want to try the lobster served with eggplant, tomato, and Genovese pesto. Dinners average HK$500 ($64.93), but business lunches are available. Hours are noon to 2:30 p.m. and 7 to 11 p.m. Coat and tie are required.

If you absolutely refuse to dine in a hotel, then **Au Trou Normand**, 6 Carnarvon Rd., Tsimshatsui (tel. 3668754), may be for you. With prices slightly lower than the hotel restaurants listed above, dinner here will run about HK$270 ($35.06), including wine. There's a lunch special for HK$88 ($11.43), which includes a buffet appetizer table, choice of entrée, dessert, and a glass of wine. The French owner and chef, Bernard Vigneau, is always there and makes frequent appearances, a plus for any restaurant. It's decorated in the style of a farmhouse in Normandy, and the menu includes such things as pork and duck liver, grilled steaks, sautéed frogs' legs, an excellent cheese board, and sublimely superb chocolate mousse. A mainstay in Hong Kong since it opened back in 1964, this restaurant serves food from noon to 3 p.m. and 7 to 11 p.m.

On the other side of the harbor is **Café de Paris,** 30-32 D'Aguilar St., Central District (tel. 5247521). Decorated like a Parisian café with white tablecloths, candles, and fresh flowers, it's a traditional French restaurant. The owner, Maurice W. Gardett, is also the chef, and he says he doesn't compromise. Outgoing and gregarious, he claims to have the only real French restaurant in town and says, "People who ask for ketchup are thrown out." The menu changes every four months but always includes a pepper steak, pâté, and chateaubriand. Dinners average about HK$270 ($35.06) and lunches about HK$200 ($25.97). There are also fixed lunches starting at HK$95 ($12.34). Since there are only 24 tables, reservations are a must. It's open every day except Sunday from noon to 3 p.m. and from 7 p.m. to midnight.

With a cheeky reference to Hong Kong's future, **Ninety-Seven,** 9 Lan Kwai Fong, Central District (tel. 5260303), is a high-tech café/restaurant/bar that offers a pleasant place to while away the evening. Located up on the first floor, it sports a ceiling covered with draped cloth, which gives the place a cozy, tent-like atmosphere, while artwork of local and overseas artists is exhibited on the walls. Open daily from noon to 2 p.m. and from 7 to 11 p.m., this place offers a fun and innovative menu, with delights that may include sole stuffed with crabmeat, grilled pigeon with ginger curry sauce, and vegetarian couscous. There are separate lunch and dinner menus, with lunches averaging about HK$90 ($11.69) and dinners about HK$320 ($41.56).

If you can't decide whether you want Western or Chinese food, then head for **La Ronda** (tel. 5255111) for its buffet lunch or dinner. Located on the 30th floor of the Furama Hotel at 1 Connaught Rd., Central District, this is a revolving restaurant with stunning views of Hong Kong Island, the harbor, and Kowloon. Taking about 70 minutes to make a complete turn, La Ronda features Chinese, Indian, Japanese, and Western dishes, and charges HK$150 ($19.49) for lunch served from noon to 3 p.m. and HK$215 ($27.92) for dinner from 7 to 11 p.m. There's a live band and dancing in the evenings, and if you want a window table, be sure to call ahead for reservations.

As part of London's famous chain of seafood restaurants, **Bentley's** opened in 1987 in the basement of the Prince's Building, Statue Square, in the Central District (tel. 8680881). It specializes in oysters (from Scotland and Australia), including oysters on the half shell or served with sauces like curry and tomato or tomato, chili, and bacon. Also on the menu are selections of soups, lobster bisque, Dover sole, scallops, and baked crab. Expect to spend at least HK$300 ($38.96) per person. It's open every day except Sunday and holidays from noon to 3 p.m. and from 6 to 10:30 p.m. (last order).

THE MEDIUM-PRICED RANGE

Most of Hong Kong's better restaurants outside hotels fall into this category, which means that you don't have to spend a lot of money to have a good meal. Although the decor in many of the Chinese restaurants may not be very exciting, good food in generous portions more than makes up for it. The Western restaurants, on the other hand, go much more for atmosphere and are pretty much the same as what you'd find back home. In addition to the restaurants listed below, there are some in the upper bracket above that offer very reasonable lunches, including Shang Palace, Gaddi's, Hugo's, Verandah Grill, Margaux, Au Trou Normand, and La Ronda. If you feel like splurging, lunch in an expensive restaurant may be the way you want to go.

Chinese Food

One Chinese restaurant that rates high on both food and decor is **Luk Yu Tea House,** 24-26 Stanley St., Central District (tel. 5235464). With ceiling fans, individual wooden booths for couples, marble tabletops, wood paneling, and stained-glass windows, Luk Yu is the most famous tea house remaining in Hong Kong (it originally opened in 1925 and moved to its present site a few years back). It's one of the best places to try a few Chinese teas. *Bo lai* (a black tea) is the favorite drink with dim sum. Other teas here include jasmine, *lung ching* (a green tea), and *sui sin* (narcissus or daffodil).

A Cantonese restaurant, Luk Yu is well known for its dim sum, which is served from 7 a.m. to 5 p.m. Although dishes are very reasonable at HK$9 ($1.17) to HK$20 ($2.60) a plate, the problem here is that the place is always packed during the day with regular customers who all have their own special places to sit. And if you come after 11 a.m., dim sum is no longer served by trolley but from a menu, which is written only in Chinese. If you want to come during the day (certainly when it's at its most colorful), try to get a Chinese to go with you.

Otherwise, consider going for dinner, which is served from 5 to 10 p.m. There are more than 200 items on the English menu, which includes all the Cantonese favorites. Dishes start at HK$40 ($5.19) and you can probably have dinner here for less than HK$140 ($18.18).

No doubt you've heard about Hong Kong's floating restaurants in Aberdeen. Although they are often included in Hong Kong's nighttime organized tours, they are no longer touted by the tourist office as one of the places every tourist has to see—there are simply too many other restaurants that are less touristy, more authentic, better priced, with better food. However, if it's been your lifetime fantasy to eat in a floating restaurant in Aberdeen, try **Tai Pak Seafood Restaurant** (tel. 5525953). The atmosphere here is of a huge, high-ceilinged dining room with traditional Chinese decor. The Cantonese menu is diverse with lots of choices, and portions are hearty. Specialties include shark's-fin soup, baked lobster with onion sauce, braised garoupa (a local fish), sautéed scallops, crabmeat omelet, sliced beef in oyster sauce, and steamed chicken with vegetables. Dinner here will cost at least HK$150 ($19.48) per person. Hours here are from 11 a.m. to 11 p.m. daily.

Decorated in stark black and white with a blend of art deco and modern Chinese decor, **The Chinese,** in the Hyatt Regency, 67 Nathan Rd. in Kowloon (tel. 3662321), features walls lined with wooden booths, reminiscent of Chinese tea houses of the 1920s. Serving dim sum and Cantonese favorites, it's open from noon to 3 p.m. and from 6:30 to 11 p.m. Recommended is the dim sum lunch special, which gives you four different varieties for HK$60 ($7.79). A seasonal menu lists selections of beef, pork, pigeon, chicken, duck, shellfish, fish, abalone, and vegetables, with most dinners averaging about HK$160 ($20.78). If available, deep-fried crispy chicken skin, minced pigeon with butter lettuce, and fried lobster balls are all equally delicious.

A popular restaurant for decades, **Yung Kee Restaurant,** 32-40 Wellington St., Central District (tel. 5221624), started out as a small shop selling roasted goose. Its goose became so much in demand that it was transformed into a Cantonese restaurant specializing in roasted goose with plum sauce. Other specialties include bean curd combined with shrimp, shredded chicken, or other delicacies; filet of garoupa sauté; and hundred-year-old eggs (which come automatically with each meal). Meals here average about HK$70 ($9.09) and are served up on the first floor. If all you want is a bowl of congee or other rice dishes, join the office workers who pour in for a quick meal on the ground floor. Hours here are from 11 a.m. to 11:30 p.m. daily, with dim sum served only in the afternoon from 2 to 5:30 p.m.

Fook Lam Moon Restaurant in Tsimshatsui has an address of 31-35A Mody Rd. (tel. 3660286), but its entrance is around the corner on Hart Avenue. With an old-fashioned, 1940ish appearance and atmosphere, it dishes out traditional Cantonese food served by waiters who are at best indifferent—which is also characteristic of the old Hong Kong (Hong Kong's Chinese waiters used to be notorious for their indifference). Open daily from 11:30 a.m. to 11:30 p.m., it offers the usual bird's-nest, abalone, seafood, chicken, frog, pork, chicken, pigeon, and beef selections. Shark's fin, however, is the obvious specialty, with 19 different renditions listed on the menu. If you feel like splurging, prices for a half bowl of shark's fin begin at HK$125 ($16.23). There's another Fook Lam Moon Restaurant on the Hong Kong side, at 35-45 Johnston Rd., Wanchai (tel. 8660663).

With its pink tablecloths and modern decor, **Full Moon,** 102 Barnton Court in Harbour City, just off Canton Road in Tsimshatsui across from Silvercord (tel. 7309131), is another one of Hong Kong's newer and trendier Chinese restaurants. Opened in 1985, it offers more than 100 items on its Cantonese menu. Its specialty is drunken prawns, which are supposedly drowned in Chinese yellow wine and then cooked in a soup at HK$110 ($14.29) for two persons; but it's not on the menu, so you'll have to ask for it. Barbecued Beijing duck is HK$130 ($16.89). Dim sum, served only during lunch, costs HK$13 ($1.69) a plate. Hours are 11:30 a.m. to 3 p.m. and 5:30 p.m. to midnight every day except Sunday and holidays, when it opens at 10 a.m. Full Moon has a second location in East Tsimshatsui in the lower ground floor of the Empire Centre, 68 Mody Rd. (tel. 7392868).

United Restaurant, conveniently located on the sixth floor of United Centre above the Admiralty MTR subway station on Queensway in the Central District (tel. 5295010), is a gigantic Cantonese restaurant with seating for 2,400 persons. Popular for large banquets and private parties, it has many private rooms for the Chinese game of mah-jongg. The decor is simple but the food is good, and dinners average about HK$100 ($12.99). Open daily from 7 a.m. to midnight, the place has specialties that include barbecued whole suckling pig, baked lobster in supreme soup, and deep-fried shrimp balls.

Popular with local Chinese on a night out on the town, **Food Street** in Causeway Bay is a pedestrian lane bordered on both sides by restaurant after restaurant serving all kinds of different food, from Chinese to Japanese to Western to fast foods. Altogether there are about 28 food outlets, so there's lots to choose from. A good Cantonese restaurant here is **Riverside Restaurant** (tel. 5779733), located at the end of Food Street at 13-15 Cleveland. Open from 11 a.m. to 3 p.m. and 5:30

p.m. to midnight Monday through Friday and from 11 a.m. straight through to midnight on weekends and holidays, this restaurant has a trendy Chinese feel to it, with black chairs and screens. I recommend the roasted chicken, steamed shrimp with garlic sauce, deep-fried stuffed crab claws, boneless duck with mashed lotus taro, or garoupa balls sauté. Dim sum is available for lunch. Otherwise lunches average about HK$50 ($6.49), while dinners are usually around HK$130 ($16.88).

Another restaurant in the area that enjoys popularity with the locals is the **Cleveland Szechuan Restaurant,** 6 Cleveland St. (tel. 5763876). A favorite of families with children, this spicy Szechuan restaurant has rather plain decor but very good prices, with meals here running from about HK$70 ($9.09) to HK$100 ($12.99). The main specialty of the house is its smoked duck with camphor tea. Other dishes highly recommended are fried king shrimp on a sizzling plate, fried diced chicken with black beans and pepper, deep-fried fish with sweet-and-sour sauce, and beef filet with hot garlic sauce served on a hot plate. Most dishes come in two sizes, small and medium: the small one is good for 2 people, the medium for 4. Hours are from 11 a.m. to 2:30 p.m. and again from 5:30 p.m. to midnight Monday through Friday; open throughout the day on weekends.

One of my favorite Szechuan restaurants in Hong Kong is the **Red Pepper,** 7 Lan Fong Rd. in Causeway Bay (tel. 5768046), which has a large following among the colony's expatriates. It's a very relaxing, smaller restaurant, though its decor is fairly elegant: Chinese lanterns, Chinese straight-backed chairs, and a red ceiling with gold dragon motifs. Since it's so popular with Western residents living in Hong Kong, I strongly recommend that you make reservations for this place if you want to come for dinner. Open since 1970, Red Pepper specializes in fried shrimp with chili sauce on a sizzling platter, sour-pepper soup, smoked duck, and dry fried string beans. Hours are noon to midnight daily, and you can expect to spend HK$130 ($16.88) to HK$160 ($20.78) for a meal.

Sze Chuen Lau Restaurant is located at 466 Lockhart Rd. in Wanchai (tel. 8919027) and is open daily from 11:30 a.m. to midnight. If you order à la carte to sample such Szechuan specialties as chili shrimp on a sizzling plate, smoked duck, smoked pigeon, braised eel, or cold chicken with chili-sesame sauce, your meal will come to about HK$100 ($12.99) per person.

Reportedly one of the most expensive Szechuan restaurants in Hong Kong, **Sichuan Garden** (tel. 5214433) is located on the third floor of the chic Landmark Building in the Central District, which probably explains why the restaurant is so expensive (somebody has to pay the rent). In its defense, though, it should also be said that the food here is excellent, the service attentive, and the atmosphere bright and elegantly simple. Open every day from 11:30 a.m. to 3 p.m. and again from 6 p.m. to midnight, it's a very popular restaurant and almost always crowded. The hot-and-spicy dishes are indicated on the 150-item menu to help the uninitiated, with small plates beginning at HK$45 ($5.84) and medium at HK$70 ($9.09). You might try the hot-and-sour soup, fried shrimp with chili sauce, shredded pork in hot garlic sauce, or the pigeon smoked in camphor wood and tea leaves. I had the last and found it quite good, but I was unprepared for the decapitated pigeon head that came on the platter as decoration (at least I assumed it wasn't for consumption). Dinner here can cost HK$180 ($23.38) per person, though you can do it for about half that if you select your dishes with care and don't drink alcohol.

A relatively new Szechuan restaurant with a modern decor is **Lotus Pond,** 15 Harbour City, Canton Road in Tsimshatsui (tel. 7308688). Open daily from 11 a.m. to 3 p.m. and from 5:30 to 11:30 p.m., it lists more than 100 dishes on its menu, including such specialties as fried shrimp in chili sauce, fried chicken Szechuan style, smoked duck, and shark's-fin soup. Average checks here range from about HK$100 ($12.99) to HK$200 ($25.97), though you can eat for less if your wallet dictates. Small dishes are available for less than HK$50 ($6.49). Dim sum starts at HK$6 (78¢).

Spring Deer Restaurant, 42 Mody Rd. in Kowloon (tel. 3664012), offers excellent Peking food at reasonable prices and is an old standby favorite in Hong Kong. Nothing fancy, the restaurant is likely to give you a table with a cloth that is clean but has some holes in it, but that doesn't deter the fans who come here obviously to enjoy themselves. Spring Deer is cheerful and very easy and accessible to foreigners, and is one of the best places to come if you want to try its specialty—Peking duck. Since you'll probably have to wait 40 minutes for the duck if you order it during peak time (between 7:30 and 9:30 p.m.), it's best to arrive either before or after the rush (the restaurant is open daily from noon to 3 p.m. and from 6 to 11 p.m.). Chicken dishes are also well liked, including the deep-fried chicken in soy sauce, and the handmade noodles are excellent. Most dishes come in small, medium, and large sizes, and meals range from HK$120 ($15.58) to HK$150 ($19.48) per person.

Despite its name, the **American Restaurant,** 20 Lockhart Rd., Wanchai (tel. 5271000), is another restaurant serving Peking food. Easily spotted from the outside by its bright green-and-red façade, this restaurant is popular with both Chinese and Western residents as well as with visitors, and is an updated version of one of the few original Peking restaurants (it opened in the 1940s after World War II). The waiters don't speak English and tend to be gruff, but the menu, with almost 200 dishes, is in English and includes barbecued Peking duck, beggar's chicken, and various beef, chicken, pork, and seafood dishes. Open every day from 11:30 a.m. to 11:30 p.m., the restaurant serves its selections in three sizes: most small dishes good for one person range from HK$24 ($3.12) to HK$40 ($5.19); medium, from HK$35 ($4.54) to HK$60 ($7.79); and large, from HK$40 ($5.19) to HK$80 ($10.39). Peking duck comes in one size only—at HK$140 ($18.18)—and can be shared between two or more persons.

Established in 1958, the **Great Shanghai** at 26-36 Prat Ave. (tel. 3662693) is a well-known restaurant in Tsimshatsui serving Shanghai food. A big dining hall with bright lights, white tablecloths, and plenty of waiters in white shirts and black bow ties, this restaurant has more than 300 items on its menu, including chop suey with fried noodles, shrimp in chili sauce, diced chicken with cashew nuts, cold chicken in wine sauce, hot-and-sour soup, Peking duck, and beggar's chicken. Although the restaurant is open daily from 11 a.m. to 11 p.m., beggar's chicken is available only at night and it's necessary to call in your order by midafternoon. Being by myself, I could manage only one dish, braised eel, which was cooked in an oily garlic sauce that I found excellent. Average cost of a meal here will be HK$90 ($11.69) to HK$140 ($18.18).

Another popular restaurant serving Shanghai cuisine is **Wu Kong,** the address for which is 27 Nathan Rd. but whose entrance is around the corner on Peking Road (tel. 3667244). Usually packed during mealtimes, it's open daily from 11:30 a.m. to midnight and with its soothing green-and-white color scheme is more upscale than most Shanghai restaurants. Its menu includes a variety of shark's-fin dishes, as well as the usual pigeon in wine sauce, sautéed fresh shrimp, braised shredded eels, and other dishes common to Shanghai cuisine. Dinner here will average about HK$100 ($12.99) to HK$150 ($19.48).

On the other side of the harbor is **Shanghai Garden,** located in the Hutchison House next to the Furama Hotel in the Central District (tel. 5238322). Although it's primarily a restaurant specializing in Shanghai food, it also serves dishes from Peking, Nanking, Sichuan, and Hangchow. The menu is extensive, including such soups as hot-and-sour shredded meat and fish soup, such cold dishes as spiced duck or sautéed shredded eels in garlic sauce, and such entrées as sautéed shrimps with tea leaves, quick-fried shredded eels with ginger, stewed shrimps with tomato sauce and crispy rice, and fried noodles Shanghai style. The average check here is HK$150 ($19.48), and hours are 11 a.m. to 3 p.m. and 6 to 11 p.m. (last order) daily.

If you want to try the little-known Chiu Chow cuisine, **City Chiuchow Restaurant,** in the East Ocean Centre at 98 Granville Rd., East Tsimshatsui (tel. 7236226), is a spacious dining room overlooking the gardens that lead down to a major promenade. With seating for 500, it's decorated in gold and red and features a big tank with fresh fish to choose from.

Famous dishes here include Chiu Chow shark's-fin soup, much thicker and stronger tasting than the Cantonese style; double-boiled shark's-fin-and-chicken soup, not as strong but equally popular; sliced soy goose, fried chicken with a black spicy sauce; and seafood dishes, including lobster. I particularly recommend the cold sliced lobster in a special honey sauce—it's not on the menu but it's available year-round. This restaurant also serves Chiu Chow and Cantonese dim sum until 3 p.m. Monday through Saturday and 5 p.m. on Sunday at HK$10 ($1.29) for a plate of six pieces. Hours for the restaurant are 11 a.m. to midnight, but during weekdays it closes for afternoon siesta from 3 to 5 p.m. Expect to spend about HK$200 ($25.97) if you have drinks, HK$100 ($12.99) if you don't.

If you're a vegetarian or simply have a craving for vegetarian fare, head for **Vegi Food Kitchen** on Cleveland Street in Causeway Bay, commonly known as Food Street (tel. 8906603 or 8906660). Its famous for its Buddhist Carnival of assorted vegetables, as well as its vegetable shark's-fin soup made with vermicelli and shredded mushrooms. For another soup you might try white fungus with sweet corn or asparagus, and other dishes include mushrooms, fungus, nuts, bean curd, and seasonal vegetables as their staples. The place is open daily from 11 a.m. to midnight, and a meal here ranges from HK$50 ($6.49) to HK$100 ($12.99).

Western and Non-Chinese Food

Well known for its lunch buffet, the **Jade Lotus** in the Hilton Hotel, 2 Queen's Rd., Central District (tel. 5233111), serves a variety of Western, Chinese, Indian and vegetarian foods. This is a real bargain at HK$140 ($18.18)—but don't forget the automatic 10% service charge—and is served from noon to 2:30 p.m.

The Hilton Hotel also has another lunch buffet at the **Dragon Boat** from noon to 2:30 p.m. Monday through Friday, including such choices as roast beef, Peking duck, and salad bar, as well as desserts. The price is HK$108 ($14.03).

Another popular buffet lunch is served in **Nathans** at the Hyatt Regency, 67 Nathan Rd. in Kowloon (tel. 3662321), from noon to 2:30 p.m. daily. The specialty here is Indian tandoori and international dishes, and it's all reasonably priced at HK$88 ($11.43).

Another great buffet available for both lunch and dinner is **The Spice Market,** located on the third floor of Harbour City in Tsimshatsui near the Hongkong Hotel (tel. 7306238). Pleasantly decorated with rattan furniture and large Chinese umbrellas hanging upside down from the ceiling, it offers a great view of the harbor, including the coming and going of the Star Ferry. Passenger ships dock right next door. Its buffet is a culinary voyage through Asian lands, with food from Malaysia, Singapore, Thailand, Indonesia, the Philippines, India, and China. You can fill your plate with everything from Indian bread and tandoori to Singaporean fried noodles or vegetable curry in coconut milk. The lunch buffet, served from noon to 2:30 p.m., costs HK$75 ($9.74) on weekdays and HK$90 ($11.69) on Saturday, Sunday, and holidays. The dinner buffet, available from 6:30 to 9:30 p.m., costs HK$90 ($11.69) on weekdays and HK$100 ($12.99) on Saturday, Sunday, and holidays.

For Italian food, **Rigoletto,** 14-16 Fenwick St. in Wanchai (tel. 5277144), is one of the old standbys frequently recommended by Hong Kong residents. The presence of Italian owner and musician Ugo Conta gives the restaurant its special Italian flair, and even though the decor is a bit overdone with Italian pendants and souvenirs hanging around and rather loud orange and green tablecloths, the lighting is pleasantly dark and wide windows offer an interesting perspective on the action of Wanchai on Fenwick and Lockhart roads.

Dinner here might open with one of the spaghettis which begin at HK$45 ($5.84), lasagne at HK$50 ($6.49), risottos at HK$60 ($7.79), or pizza at HK$45 ($5.84). Entrées consist mainly of northern Italian dishes and include calves' liver, veal, steaks, and seafood. A full-course dinner here will run about HK$180

($23.38). Rigoletto is open for lunch every day except Sunday from noon to 3 p.m. and for dinner daily from 6 p.m. to midnight.

First opened more than two decades ago, **La Taverna,** 24-30 Ice House St., Central District (tel. 5238624), is Italian-owned and employs an Italian chef to cook up its daily specials, as well as such favorites as homemade pasta, thinly sliced beef tenderloin in olive oil and rosemary dressing, veal, chicken, seafood, and pizza. A guitar player serenades in the evenings, while candles on all the tables bathe the restaurant in a warm, soft glow. Set lunches are available starting at HK$70 ($9.09) for soup and pasta or pizza and are served daily from 11:30 a.m. to 3 p.m. Dinner, served from 6:30 to 11 p.m., averages about HK$200 ($25.97). If you're on the Kowloon side, another La Taverna is located at 24-30 Ashley Rd., Tsimshatsui (tel. 3691945), with the same opening hours.

Serving nouvelle Italian cuisine, **Seasons,** 17 On Lan St., Central District (tel. 5268429) is a trendy restaurant decorated with artwork, marble-top tables, and high-tech lighting. The innovative menu changes frequently but pasta is its specialty. A business lunch is available for HK$80 ($10.39), while dinners average HK$200 ($25.97). From 5 to 8 p.m. there's a happy hour when you can buy two drinks for the price of one. Food is served every day except Sunday from 11 a.m. to 3 p.m. and from 6 to 11 p.m.

First opened in 1928, **Jimmy's Kitchen** had several homes before moving to its present site—1-3 Wyndham St. in the Central District (tel. 5265293)—in the 1960s. The atmosphere here reminds me of an American steakhouse, with white tablecloths, dark-wood paneling, and grocery-store music, but it's a favorite with foreigners living in Hong Kong and serves dependably good European food.

Open from noon to 11 p.m. every day, it features daily specials written on a blackboard and a large à la carte menu offering seafood, steak, salads and soups, chicken, spaghetti, and curries. You can have oysters imported from the U.S., New Zealand, and Australia, and there's a large selection of seafood, including sole, scallops, and the local garoupa. A glass of house wine or beer begins at HK$20 ($2.59). If you have the works, dinner here will range from HK$170 ($22.08) to HK$250 ($32.47). A second Jimmy's Kitchen is located across the harbor at 29 Ashley Rd., Tsimshatsui (tel. 3684027), with the same menu. Hours for both are noon to 11 p.m. seven days a week.

Landau's, owned by the same company as Jimmy's Kitchen, first opened in 1976 and is located at 30 Harbour Rd. in Wanchai (tel. 8912901). Blackboards throughout the place announce daily specials, but a general meal may begin with a soup such as chilled cream of avocado, lobster bisque, cream of tomato, or baked onion, ranging from HK$25 ($3.25) to HK$30 ($3.90). Entrées, which generally cost HK$80 ($10.39) to HK$100 ($12.99), include such specialties as black pepper steak, port wine duck, New Zealand lamb chops, wienerschnitzel, beef Stroganoff, Australian rock oysters, paprika veal goulash, and corned beef and cabbage. House wine begins at HK$20 ($2.60) a glass. The management estimates that the cost of an average meal here, including wine, runs about HK$250 ($32.47). Landau's is open for business from noon to 3 p.m. and from 7 p.m. to midnight.

One of the joys of traveling to the village of Stanley on Hong Kong Island (apart from the obvious pleasure of shopping) is a meal at **Stanley's Restaurant,** 86-88 Stanley Main St. (tel. 8138873). Located on the edge of the famous market, it's a charming and refined French restaurant housed in what used to be a residential home. Dining is in small and cozy rooms, some of which have views of the water. Its specialties include smoked salmon pâté or Caesar salad for starters, zucchini-and-dill soup, and such entrées as sautéed Tasmanian scallops and calamaries in lemon garlic butter, blackened filet of pomfret, roast whole spring chicken, rack of lamb, and blackened prime rib eye of beef with Cajun hollandaise. Don't neglect the daily specials. Expect to spend at least HK$100 ($12.99), but it will be closer to HK$200 ($25.97) if you partake of an appetizer, soup, entrée, and wine. Reservations are a must. It opens every day at 10 a.m. for breakfast, followed by lunch from noon to 3 p.m., afternoon tea from 3 to 5 p.m., and dinner from 7 to 10:30 p.m. Absolutely charming. And very romantic.

Although located in the elegant Regent hotel, on Salisbury Road, **Harbour Side** (tel. 7211211) is an informal dining hall with a view of the harbor and is open daily from 6 a.m. to midnight. Rather plain and bare with a brick floor and wooden chairs, it serves hamburgers, seafood, chicken and shrimp curry, and other dishes listed on a menu printed daily. Most entrées are between HK$50 ($6.49) and HK$100 ($12.99), a cup of coffee is HK$20 ($2.60), and cocktails average HK$38 ($4.93).

Thai food is very popular in Hong Kong these days, and one of the better-known Thai restaurants is the **Golden Elephant Thai Restaurant,** located in Harbour City toward the back of Barnton Court near the cinemas (tel. 7350733). A member of HKTA and affiliated with Thai Airways, this restaurant serves both spicy and mild foods in meals that will probably cost less than HK$150 ($19.48) per person. A lunch buffet is a good bargain at HK$75 ($9.74), but if you opt for an à la carte meal, perhaps you want to start out with such appetizers as Thai crispy rice served with minced pork and shrimp sauce or Thai shrimp crackers. Main courses include such delectables as boiled beef with satay sauce, fried diced chicken with red chili and hot basil leaf, Thai fish cake, steamed fish with plum sauce and ginger, and fried beef with chili sauce. Hours here are noon to 3 p.m. and 6 to 11 p.m. daily.

THE BUDGET CATEGORY

Hong Kong has an almost endless number of inexpensive restaurants, food stalls, and tiny holes-in-the-wall where you can eat quite well and quite a lot at very reasonable prices. Keep in mind that in addition to the restaurants listed below, there are a number of Cantonese restaurants that serve dim sum through much of the day, a real bargain for those on a budget. Restaurants listed in the medium-range section above serving dim sum are The Chinese, Full Moon, United Restaurant, City Chiuchow Restaurant, and Luk Yu Tea House.

Chinese Food

Dim Sum Kitchen (tel. 5777286) is one of the many restaurants located on Food Street in Causeway Bay, described earlier in the medium-priced restaurant section. Simple and cheap, this cafeteria serves dim sum beginning at HK$6 (78¢), as well as such other dishes as barbecued pork with rice or soy-sauce chicken, both of which costs HK$20 ($2.60). Simply pay for what you want beforehand at the ticket window and then present your food ticket to someone at the counter. Hours here are from 7:30 a.m. to midnight.

Offering what is probably the cheapest dim sum in Tsimshatsui is the **Capital Restaurant,** located in Chungking Mansion at 40-44 Nathan Rd. (tel. 3681844). Serving dim sum from 7 a.m. to 5 p.m., it charges HK$6 (78¢) to HK$14 ($1.81) a plate. Dim sum is served up on the second floor (which would be the third floor in the United States). The dining room is large and noisy, just like a dim sum place should be. There used to be a lot of Cantonese restaurants like this one, but in the fervor of modernization most of them have closed down. This is one of the few oldtimers left in Tsimshatsui.

If you want your dim sum in a more refined and civilized setting, down the street is the Ambassador Hotel on Nathan Road (located between the Sheraton and the Holiday Inn), where up on the 16th floor is the **East Ocean** (tel. 3671133). Cheerful and modern with a view of Hong Kong, it serves dim sum from 11 a.m. to 2:30 p.m. Servers wheel trolleys between the tables, calling out the dim sum names. Simply choose the bamboo container that looks the most appetizing. Dim sum ranges mostly from about HK$10 ($1.30) to HK$15 ($1.95). If you're starving, you can also order from the English menu.

A rather bare-looking but popular and usually crowded Szechuan restaurant, **Fung Lum Restaurant, 23** Granville Rd. in Tsimshatsui (tel. 3678919), is a small place seating only about 80 persons. It's been here more than a quarter of a century, so far surviving the onslaught of clothing stores that now occupy sites of former restaurants that used to line the street. It's open daily from noon to 11 p.m., with specialties that include Szechuan chicken, shrimp with chili and garlic sauce, sliced pork in garlic and chili sauce, beef filet with pepper and hot garlic sauce, scallops in garlic and onion sauce, and frogs' legs with chili. Small dishes average about HK$35 ($4.54) to HK$60 ($7.79), and larger ones run up to HK$80 ($10.39).

One of Hong Kong's oldtimers, **Wishful Cottage Vegetarian Restaurant,** 336-340 Lockhart Rd., Wanchai (tel. 5735645), opened in 1967. Under the watchful gaze of a Buddhist statue, it serves seasonal vegetables, noodles, and bean-curd dishes. The most expensive thing on the menu is bamboo fungus for HK$270 ($35.06), but otherwise you should be able to eat here for about HK$50 ($6.49) per person. It's open daily from 10 a.m. to 10 p.m.

If you don't know very much about Chinese food, feel that you should try it, but still aren't very keen on the idea, head for one of the **Jade Garden Chinese** restaurants. There are seven of these Cantonese restaurants altogether, the most convenient being: Swire House, Central District (tel. 5239966); Star House, fourth floor, Kowloon (tel. 7226888); and 25-31 Carnarvon Rd., Kowloon (tel. 3698311). Geared toward the Chinese-food novice, these places have the traditional decor of reds and blacks that one would expect of a Chinese restaurant and offer fine food at reasonable prices.

Generally open daily from 11:30 a.m. to midnight, each restaurant serves the typical dim sum lunch, with women offering steaming bamboo bowlfuls of rice, shrimp in wonton, and many other dishes, as well as sautéed-to-order pork cakes, shrimp tofu, tripe stew, and other items. Most dim sum here average between HK$8 ($1.04) and HK$12 ($1.59). Lunch at these places can be rather a free-for-all: you watch for the carts, look, and then order fast. An alternative is to order dishes from the menu, but you have to find the waiter. Specialties include braised shark's fin, sautéed chicken with oyster sauce, barbecued Peking duck, braised abalone in oyster sauce, roasted pigeon, beggar's chicken, and sweet-and-sour pork.

Popular with the locals and tourists is the **Can Do Restaurant,** located near the Park Hotel at 37 Cameron Rd. in Tsimshatsui (tel. 7218183). It advertises "bloody good cheap Chinese and Western food at fair dinkum prices" and is open daily, breakfast through dinner, from 7 a.m. to 1 a.m. It's simple and informal and resembles an American diner, except that it's much more packed. Most likely you'll be seated at a table with someone else—people come here to chow down, not socialize. Its English menu lists Cantonese dishes that include sweet-and-sour pork, chicken with cashews, beef in oyster sauce, seafood, mixed vegetables in curry sauce, and fried noodles. There's also Western fare like fish-and-chips, sandwiches, and spaghetti. You can dine here for less than HK$50 ($6.49), but most popular is the daily special for HK$20 ($2.60). An American breakfast costs HK$25 ($3.25).

Western and Non-Chinese Food

If you're looking for spaghetti or pizza cooked American style, the **Spaghetti House** is your best bet. There are nine locations in Hong Kong, including 5 Sharp St. East, Causeway Bay (tel. 7952245); Hennessy and Luard roads, Wanchai (tel. 5290901); Malahon Centre, 10 Stanley St., Central District (tel. 5231372); 3B Cameron Rd., Tsimshatsui (tel. 3688635); and Barnton Court, ground floor, Harbour City, Tsimshatsui (tel. 3735060). Similar to American pizza parlors in atmosphere and decor, these restaurants have 14 different kinds of spaghetti beginning at HK$21 ($2.69), pizza beginning at HK$25 ($3.25), chili con carne, sandwiches, fried chicken, and lasagne. Hours are 11 a.m. to 11 p.m. daily.

Although it calls itself **Beverly Hills Deli,** its menu says it's "Hong Kong's only New York style deli." In any case, this informal diner serves a wide selection of sandwiches, including overstuffed sandwiches, triple-deckers, and open-faced hot sandwiches, plus traditional deli fare. You can also get a decent burger, Texas chili, Middle East specialties (how did they slip in here?), pizza, spaghetti, fettuccine, and vegetarian selections. Most sandwiches, meals in themselves, cost HK$50 ($6.49) to HK$60 ($7.79). Beverly Hills Deli has two locations, and if it proves popular you can expect more to open. On Hong Kong Island it's at 2 Lan Kwai Fong, Central District, in the heart of the nightlife area (tel. 5265800), and hours here are 11 a.m. to midnight every day except Sunday and holidays, when it closes an hour earlier. On the Kowloon side, you'll find the deli on the second level of the New World Centre on Salisbury Road (tel. 3698695), where it's open every day from 11 a.m. to 10 p.m.

One of the cheapest places for a filling meal in Tsimshatsui is at the **Salisbury** restaurant in the YMCA on Salisbury Road (tel. 3692211). It offers a buffet breakfast from 7 to 10:30 a.m. for HK$42 ($5.45). A lunch buffet is spread out every day from noon to 2:30 p.m. and costs HK$38 ($4.93) on weekdays and HK$55 ($7.14) on Saturday and Sunday. And dinner, served from 6 to 9 p.m., offers a set meal for HK$42 ($5.45). There's also an à la carte menu for soups, salads, steak, chicken, pork chops, and seafood, as well as for Asian dishes like satay, fried noodles, and Szechuan-style shrimp.

If you're in Causeway Bay, there's inexpensive dining in the second basement of the **Sogo Department Store,** located right beside the Causeway Bay subway station. Open daily from 10 a.m. to 10 p.m., it offers counter after counter of inexpensive, simple dishes. Simply walk around and choose what looks best. Once you've decided, go to the cashier and then return to the counter with your ticket to pick up your selection. Selections may include beef curry with rice, chicken leg with rice, salads, Chinese noodles, satay, spaghetti, *congee* (a rice pudding), and Japanese foods (Sogo, after all, is a Japanese department store). Top off your meal with Häagen-Dazs ice cream. It should all cost less than HK$25 ($3.25).

As its name implies, the **SMI Curry Restaurant,** 81-85 Lockhart Rd. (tel. 5273107 or 5299111), specializes in various international curries of Asia. The SMI of its name stands for Singapore, Malaysia, and India, but its selection ranges much more widely than that. Consider chicken, which comes in such styles as dry tandoori, dry masala, East Indies chicken curry, Southeast Asian hot chicken curry, Tamil chicken curry, Pakistan chicken curry, chicken korma, and Ceylon white chicken curry. And then there are also selections of beef, mutton, prawns, and vegetables—if you're a curry freak, you'll go crazy trying to make a decision. This place is popular, crowded, very informal, and fun, and you should be able to eat for around HK$50 ($6.49).

Considering the fact that many of the shops and hostels in Chungking Mansion are run by Indians, you'd expect that the complex would contain at least a few cheap Indian restaurants. **Sheri Punjab Club Mess,** Block B, on the third floor of Chungking Mansion at 36-44 Nathan Rd. (tel. 3680859), is one of the most popular among travelers on a tight budget. It consists of a bare, clean, and simple room, with some tables and chairs as the only decorations. The menu consists of things like chicken curry, mutton masala, mutton vindaloo, mixed vegetable, tandoori, and muglai chicken, with prices ranging from HK$15 ($1.95) to HK$35 ($4.54) a plate. You'll need to order at least two plates per person, and the plates here are plastic. Hours are 11 a.m. to 3:30 p.m. and 6 to 11:30 p.m.

The local fast-food chain in Hong Kong is **Maxim's,** branches of which can be found all over Hong Kong. You can eat in or take out, and the hours are generally 7:30 a.m. to 9 p.m. The menu offers such items as chicken legs, hamburgers, and sandwiches, with prices averaging HK$8 ($1.04) and less. A lunch box for HK$10 ($1.30) changes every day.

In case you're interested, there are also plenty of **McDonald's** available. A hamburger costs HK$3.50 (45¢) and a Big Mac is HK$8 ($1.03).

---

6. What to See and Do

THE FOUR MUSTS

There are four things every visitor to Hong Kong should do, and they all involve the colony's public transportation system. They are: ride the Star Ferry across the harbor; take a rickety old tram on Hong Kong Island; go up to Victoria Peak in the Peak tram; and ride one of the ferries to the outlying islands. Nothing can beat the thrill of these four experiences, nor give better insight into the essence of Hong Kong and its people; these rides on the ferries and trams are trips in themselves and all are inexpensive.

For tips on using the Star Ferry and Hong Kong's tram system, refer to the "Getting Around" section of this chapter. The Peak tram will be described later in this section, while ferries to outlying islands are outlined in "Exploring the Territories and Environs." You might also want to pick up two free brochures at Hong Kong Tourist Association (HKTA) offices called *Places of Interest by Public Transport* and *Outlying Islands*.

JUST WALKING AROUND

Surprisingly compact, Hong Kong is an easy city to explore by foot. Walking affords a more intimate relationship with your surroundings, allows chance encounters with the unexpected, and lets you discover that vegetable market, temple, or shop you otherwise never would have seen. If, for example, you're in the Central District and want to eat dinner on Food Street in Causeway Bay, you can walk there in less than an hour, passing through colorful Wanchai on the way. Causeway Bay is good for unstructured exploring, since it's full of little sidewalk markets, street vendors, restaurants, and shops patronized by the locals. A walk up Nathan Road from the harbor to the Yaumatei subway station takes less than 30 minutes, although it would be hard to resist all the shops and department stores you pass on the way. If you don't mind dishing out HK$15 ($1.92), you can purchase a nifty booklet put out by the Hong Kong Tourist Association called *Central and Western District Walking Tour*. Complete with detailed maps, it describes a three-hour walk through Hong Kong Island's Central and Western districts, including Cloth Alley, with its stalls selling fabrics; Egg Street, with its variety of eggs bound for Hong Kong's restaurants; Bonham Strand, with Chinese medicinal shops; and Cat Street, with its junk and antiques. The booklet explains things you'll see on the way and is highly recommended.

CHINESE CULTURAL SHOWS

The HKTA provides **free cultural entertainment** for visitors throughout the month. The program and location of the shows vary. Programs may be demonstrations of Chinese magic and acrobatics, folk songs and dances, Fukienese glove and rod puppetry, Chinese martial arts, Chinese instrumental music, or shadow puppetry. The shows, which last an hour, take place at two locations: Taikoo Shing's Cityplaza on Hong Kong Island and New World Centre on Kowloon. For information on what's being shown, times, and locations, contact the HKTA.

Chinese opera, with its elaborate costumes and stage settings, has a worldwide

reputation. Unfortunately, this ancient form of entertainment is so popular in Hong Kong that it is almost impossible for visiting tourists to get tickets. The best performers are from mainland China, and tickets sell out well in advance.

If you're still determined to see a performance, contact the HKTA to see whether anything is going on or check with the weekly *Hong Kong,* a tourist publication available free in hotels and at HKTA offices.

Other cultural activities in which you may be interested include performances by the **Hong Kong Philharmonic Orchestra** or entertainment at the **Arts Center and Academy for Performing Arts** at Wanchai, which offers everything from live theater and pop concerts to avant-garde films. Another venue for entertainment and the performing arts is the new **Hong Kong Cultural Center** on the waterfront of Tsimshatsui near the Star Ferry. It boasts a concert hall, theaters, exhibition areas, restaurants, and bars. Hong Kong also has two arts festivals, one in February and one in October.

For information on what's going on, check Hong Kong's two **newspapers,** the *South China Morning Post* and the *Hong Kong Standard;* the two tourist newspapers, *Orient* and *Hong Kong;* and the *Official Hong Kong Guide.*

HONG KONG ISLAND

With about 30 square miles, Hong Kong Island holds the most attractions for the visitor. This is where the colony's history began, and there's everything here from the high-rises of the Central District to the beaches on the southern coast.

Victoria Peak

At 1,308 feet, Victoria Peak is the island's tallest hill and offers the best and most spectacular views of Hong Kong. It's always been one of the colony's most exclusive places to live, since in the days before air conditioning the peak was usually a few degrees cooler than the sweltering city below. A hundred years ago the rich reached the peak after a three-hour trip in sedan chairs (which were carried to the top by coolies). Then, in 1888, the **peak tram** opened, cutting the journey from three hours to eight minutes.

The easiest way to reach the peak tram, located on Garden Road just behind the Hilton Hotel, is to take one of the free shuttle buses that operate between the tram terminal and the Star Ferry. Shuttle buses run between 9 a.m. and 7 p.m. daily at 20-minute intervals.

As for the peak tram, it costs HK$6 (78¢) one way, HK$10 ($1.30) round trip. The new tram cars (imported from Switzerland) depart every ten minutes and are in operation daily from 7 a.m. to midnight. The tram climbs almost vertically to the top of the peak and—don't worry—there's never been an accident. At the top there's the **Peak Tower,** where you will find a restaurant, observation deck, and the Peak Tower Village, with more than 30 booths selling Chinese arts and crafts from 9:30 a.m. to 7 p.m. daily.

If you want to do some walking, there are a couple of possibilities. A footpath beside the Peak Tower snakes along the side of the cliff, offering great views of the Central District down below, the harbor, and Kowloon. If you want a look in the opposite direction, you can circle the top of the peak in about an hour on Lugard and Harlech roads. Although in my opinion the views are not as spectacular as those on the Central District side, on really clear days you can see past Aberdeen and the islands of Cheung Chau, Lantau, and Lamma all the way to Macau. If you're feeling really energetic, you might want to hike up Mount Austin Road to where the governor's summer lodge used to stand. Only the formal gardens remain, but it's a pleasant respite from the crowdedness of Hong Kong down below.

Central and Western Districts

The Central District used to be called Victoria and had elegant colonial-style buildings with sweeping verandas and narrow streets filled with pigtailed men pulling rickshaws. That's hard to imagine if you look at it now. Today it's Hong Kong's financial and business center, with high-rise office buildings of glass and concrete. There's almost nothing to remind one of the olden days, but it's still interesting walking around here a bit.

If it's summer, begin your trip in the Central District by stopping off for a relaxing drink or snack on the upper deck of the public **Blake Pier,** located just west of the Star Ferry Terminal. This is one of the cheapest places to enjoy a great view of the harbor and of the Star Ferry as it comes and goes. Popular at lunchtime with office personnel, the snackbar here sells sandwiches, spaghetti, and salads as well as ice cream, beer, coffee, and soft drinks. As you sit there soaking up some of the waterfront ambience, consider the fact that the waterfront used to be much farther back, at Queen's Road. In the 1800s land reclamation added first Des Voeux Road and then Connaught Road. Land reclamation has also been carried on extensively across the harbor on Kowloon—all of East Tsimshatsui is reclaimed land. One Hong Kong local I met joked that so much land was being reclaimed it wouldn't be long before you could walk across the harbor.

Next on your tour of the Central District could be the **Hong Kong Museum of Art,** on the 10th and 11th floors of City Hall (tel. 5224127), just east of Star Ferry Terminal. Open every day except Thursday from 10 a.m. to 6 p.m. (from 1 p.m. on Sunday and holidays), the museum features changing exhibitions that may include ceramics, Chinese art and antiquities, including jade, cloisonné, lacquerware, or paintings. Included in the museum are works by contemporary Hong Kong artists. Admission is free.

Another museum worth your time is the **Flagstaff House Museum of Teaware,** located off Cotton Tree Drive up the hill from Chater Garden (tel. 5869690). Flagstaff House is the oldest colonial building in Hong Kong—it was built in 1844 as the home of the commander of the British forces. Open daily except Wednesday from 10 a.m. to 5 p.m., the museum is free and displays 500 pieces of Chinese tea ware of various dynasties from the 7th century on.

From Flagstaff House, retrace your steps to Queensway Road, where you'll find the tram tracks. Take a left and follow the tracks onto **Des Voeux Road Central.** As you walk along Des Voeux, you'll pass smart-looking fashion boutiques, banks, and office buildings as well as the Landmark with its designer shops and restaurants. Presently you'll reach **Li Yuen Street East** and **Li Yuen Street West,** which rise up steeply to your left and are packed with street vendors selling clothing and accessories. After you've explored these two streets, continue walking down Des Voeux until you reach **Central Market,** a four-story Victorian-looking square building where fresh produce—everything from vegetables and eels to live chickens—is sold. It's open from 6 a.m. to 2 p.m. and again from 4:30 to 8 p.m.

The next interesting place to look for is **Wing On Street,** locally known as Cloth Alley because of the long string of stalls selling fabrics from around the world. Next comes **Wing Sing Street,** also called Egg Street, which is the first left off Wing Lok Street. All different kinds of eggs are sold here in the morning, from century-old eggs to salted eggs. Century-old eggs are actually only a few weeks old, having first been treated with tea leaves, salt, and chemicals before being covered with mud and rice husks.

At the end of Wing Sing Street, take a right onto Queen's Road Central, and keep going straight onto Bonham Strand. From here take an immediate left onto Jervois Street. On **Jervois Street** and **Hillier Street** you'll find snake shops. Eaten in autumn as protection against the winter cold, snakes are favored also for their gall bladders, which are mixed with Chinese wine as cures for rheumatism. The mixture is also believed to be an aphrodisiac.

Back on Bonham Strand, you'll pass several rattan shops, followed by Chinese herb and medicinal shops on Bonham Strand West, where you'll see everything from ginseng to deer antlers for sale. From Bonham Strand cut back inland (south) until you reach **Hollywood Road.** Hollywood Road is a strange mixture of shops selling coffins and other things for funerals and those selling furniture, curios, and antiques (real antiques as well as excellent imitations). Next to Ladder Street, an extremely steep flight of stairs, is **Man Mo Temple,** Hong Kong Island's oldest and most famous temple. It was around this area that the movie *The World of Suzie Wong* was shot. The temple, which dates back to 1847 and is open daily from 7 a.m. to 5 p.m., is dedicated to two deities, a 3rd-century statesman representing the god of literature and a 2nd-century soldier, the god of war. Two ornately carved sedan chairs kept in the temple are used to carry the two gods around during festivals. Incidentally, the deity representing the soldier is said to find patronage among members of the underworld—as well as the police force.

If you follow the steps leading downhill on Ladder Street, you'll see **Upper Lascar Row** leading off to the left, better known as Cat Street. Pleasant with potted palms, this pedestrian lane offers a fantastic study in junk, with most dealers laying their wares out on the street. Browse here for old bits of china, snuff bottles, watches, pictures, and other odds and ends.

Zoological and Botanical Gardens

Established in 1864, these gardens are located on the side of Victoria Peak past the Hilton on Garden Road. They are free to the public, and exploring them is a pleasant way to spend an hour or so if you're tired of the Central District and its traffic. Flowers are almost always in bloom, from azaleas in spring to wisteria and bauhinea in summer and fall. In addition to jaguars, orangutans, and monkeys, there's an aviary with about 800 birds representing 300 species. Included are Palawan peacocks, birds of paradise from Papua New Guinea, cranes, and Mandarin ducks.

Aw Boon Haw Gardens (Tiger Balm Gardens)

These are probably the most bizarre gardens you'll ever see. Built in 1935 by Chinese millionaire Aw Boon Haw, who made his fortune with a cure-all called Tiger Balm, the 7½ acres of these gardens feature colorfully painted statues from Chinese mythology. Some of the figures are rather grotesque, especially those depicting unfortunate souls being tortured in hell. However, the place is free and is open daily from 10 a.m. to 4 p.m. Because the gardens are so colorful you can get some great photographs here to show the folks back home. Aw Boon Haw Gardens is located off Tai Hang Road in Causeway Bay, which you can reach by bus 11 from the Central Bus Terminal.

Noon Day Gun

It's not worth going out of your way for, but if you're in the neighborhood of the Excelsior Hotel in Causeway Bay, look for a small garden opposite the hotel with a gun planted in it. Fired every day at noon, this gun was immortalized in Noël Coward's "Mad Dogs and Englishmen": "In Hong Kong they strike a gong and fire off the noon day gun." The tradition started in the last century when the Jardines trading company fired off a double-gun salute to returning bosses. This so perturbed a British senior naval officer that, as punishment, he ordered Jardines to fire the gun every day at noon.

Aberdeen

A naturally protected harbor on the south side of Hong Kong Island, Aberdeen used to be a charming fishing village famous for its several thousand junks and boat people. Many of the boat people, however, have been moved to massive housing projects, and the waterfront surrounding Aberdeen is crowded with high-rises. Still, Aberdeen continues to be popular with the tourist crowd because of its remaining boat population and floating restaurants. Women operating sampans will vie for your dollars to tour you around the harbor, which is definitely worth the cost, since it's about the only thing to do here and is the best way to see the junks. A 30-minute tour will cost HK$80 ($10.39) per person and is offered daily between 8 a.m. and 6 p.m. You'll pass huge boats housing extended families and you'll see men repairing fishing nets, women hanging out their laundry, dogs barking and children playing, families eating, and people fishing in the murky waters. There was a time when a boat person could be born, live, marry, and die on board without ever setting foot on shore. Nowadays, however, young people are moving to shore to take advantage of job opportunities.

Ocean Park

If you're a kid or a kid at heart, you'll love Ocean Park and its attractions, open every day from 10 a.m. to 6 p.m. except on Sunday and holidays, when it opens earlier at 9 a.m. Situated along a rocky and dramatic coastline on the island's southern shore, the park is divided into "lowland" and "highland" areas, which are linked together by a spectacular ten-minute ride by cable car. The lowland boasts a botanical garden, a butterfly house, and the Golden Pagoda, with more varieties of goldfish than you ever imagined possible, most of them from China. For children there's a children's **Adventure World** with its animals and things to climb on.

The highland area has an artificial wave cove that is home to seals, walruses, sea lions, and penguins, as well as various thrill rides that include a roller coaster that turns upside down. Ocean Theatre features shows by talented dolphins, sea lions, and a killer whale. But most impressive of all, in my opinion, is the Atoll Reef, the world's largest aquarium. The observation passageway circles three stories around the outside of the aquarium, giving you views from different angles of everything from giant turtles to schools of tropical fish. Ocean Park's most recent additions are its impressive aviary, with approximately 150 species of birds and a shark aquarium.

Even newer is the fantastical **Middle Kingdom,** a small, re-created village of China's past with full-size temples, shrines, pavilions, pagodas, street scenes, and public squares. Its streets lead visitors past 13 dynasties of Chinese history, with craftsmen re-creating the beauty of the various periods. Visitors can watch papermaking, iron-casting, silk-weaving, pottery-making, and glass-manufacturing demonstrations; shops sell a variety of Chinese products, from writing instruments to tea, engravings, and incense. A bit Disneyesque, but a welcome addition to Ocean Park.

Entrance fee to Ocean Park is HK$100 ($12.99) for adults, half price for children. The separate admission fee for the Middle Kingdom is HK$140 ($18.20) for adults, half price for children. For more information, call 5520291.

Water World

This attraction is located next to Ocean Park and is a good place to cool off on a hot summer's day. Open daily from 10 a.m. to 10 p.m. (until 5 p.m. in spring and autumn), Water World is a conglomeration of several pools with various slides and diving platforms, and it even has a pool with a sandy beach and real waves. Open from April to the end of October only, it costs HK$45 ($5.84). Be sure to bring your bathing suit.

KOWLOON

Kowloon gets its name from *Gau Lung,* which means "nine dragons." Legend has it that about 800 years ago a boy emperor counted eight hills on Kowloon and remarked that there must be eight dragons living here, since dragons were known to inhabit hills. His prime minister answered that in actuality there must be nine dragons, since an emperor is also considered to be a dragon.

You'd have a lot of trouble trying to find eight hills in Kowloon today. Most of the peninsula has been taken over by housing and industrial estates, and doesn't offer much to the tourist other than shopping. However, there are a few attractions you may wish to visit, especially if it's a humid or rainy day and you're looking for some respite.

Space Museum

Located on Salisbury Road in front of the Peninsula Hotel on the Tsimshatsui waterfront, this museum is easy to spot, with its white-domed planetarium. The museum is divided into three parts—the Space Theatre's planetarium, where the film is projected onto the 75-foot domed roof; the Hall of Solar Sciences on solar phenomena; and an exhibition hall that explores man's progress in astronomy and space. Shows at Space Theatre are held throughout the afternoon and early evening and cost HK$15 ($1.95) per person. English headsets with simultaneous translations are provided free of charge for the hour-long show. Space Museum is open every day except Tuesday until 9:30 p.m., opening at 2 p.m. on weekdays, at 1 p.m. on Saturday, and 10:30 a.m. on Sunday. Call 3721361 for more information on show times.

Museum of History

In Kowloon Park, the Museum of History (tel. 3671124) outlines the history of the colony through displays of archeological finds, ethnographic collections, and historical photographs. The museum is free of charge and open every day except Friday from 10 a.m. to 6 p.m. (on Sunday and holidays from 1 to 6 p.m.).

Jade Market and Yaumatei

Every morning at 10 a.m. and continuing until 3:30 p.m., buyers, traders, and sellers of jade converge on Kansu Street in Kowloon's Yaumatei District. Laying out their wares on everything from cloth spread out on the sidewalk to satin-lined display cases, vendors sell jade to Chinese who know the market. In other words, unless you know what you're looking for and can tell good jade from worthless, you're better off coming here just for a look. It's possible to infuse jade with color so that inferior stones acquire the brightness and translucence associated with more expensive jade. If you want a souvenir, pick up a pendant or bangle but don't spend more than a few dollars for it. Pearls are also sold.

Jade has long been important to the Chinese, who consider it a symbol of youth and regeneration. Jade comes in a variety of colors, including, red, white, and black. Green, however, is the color you usually see. Watch how the Chinese bargain at the market—they do it secretly so that no one standing around and watching will know the final price. More information is available in a free pamphlet put out by HKTA called *Yau Ma Tei & Jade Market*.

If you want to explore the area around the Jade Market more fully, you'll want to purchase the *Yau Ma Tei Walking Tour* booklet for HK$15 ($1.95), available at HKTA offices. This one-hour do-it-yourself tour leads visitors through a nearby produce and fruit market and past a variety of traditional shops selling everything from incense and snakes to chinaware, embroidery, and herbal teas. In the evenings, nearby Temple Street transforms itself into an interesting night market.

Sung Dynasty Village

This is a re-creation of how a village might have looked in China 1,000 years ago during the Sung Dynasty. Built at a cost of two million U.S. dollars, it took five years to construct the village with close attention given to architectural detail. The village consists of various open-fronted wooden shops, stalls, and buildings grouped around a willow-lined stream. Staffed by villagers dressed in Sung Dynasty cos-

tumes, each shop is based on a different theme and each offers a different product, from almond cookies and Chinese tea to hand-painted fans and incense. Demonstrations are given to show how the items are made. There are a rice-wine shop, a herbal medicine shop, a Chinese restaurant, and a replica of a rich man's house. There's also entertainment, from a monkey show to Chinese acrobatics and opera.

Included in the village is Hong Kong's largest wax museum, with famous personalities from Chinese history. Be sure to read the explanations that accompany each figure—they're quite entertaining. We learn, for example, that Pao Szu, the favorite concubine of Emperor Chou Yu, was a great beauty but that it was very difficult to make her laugh. Kou Chien, who lived around 421 B.C., suffered defeat by his enemies and as self-punishment "he slept on faggots and constantly tasted gall." It must have worked because we're told that after 20 years he finally succeeded in defeating his enemy.

If you're interested in visiting Sung Dynasty Village, it's best to join an organized tour, the information for which is given below. Otherwise, if you want to go on your own, you can do so only on Saturday or Sunday from 12:30 to 5 p.m. Admission is HK$50 ($6.49) for adults and HK$30 ($3.90) for children, and to get there take either bus 6A from the Star Ferry or the Mass Transit Railway (MTR) to Mei Fou Station.

ORGANIZED TOURS

Hong Kong is well developed in the organized-tour department, and if you're pressed for time this is the best way to go. The **Hong Kong Island Tour,** for example, is a three- to four-hour trip offered both morning and afternoon to such places as Victoria Peak, Tiger Balm Gardens, Repulse Bay, and Aberdeen. **Watertours** is the largest tour organizer of boat and junk cruises around the harbor and to outlying islands, offering about 20 various trips from which to choose. There's even a one-hour harbor cruise aboard a Star Ferry that includes complimentary drinks. There are also tours of factories making everything from clothing to brassware, porcelain, and silk. For information on night tours, refer to Section 8, "Hong Kong After Dark." You can contact Watertours directly through your hotel or call 5254808 or 5263538.

Another tour operator, **The Gray Line,** offers a variety of tours to Hong Kong Island, Kowloon and the New Territories, Macau, and China, with tour outlets at most first- and medium-class hotels. The Hilton even offers its own cruise aboard its 110-foot brigantine named the *Wan Fu,* built in Taiwan in 1959. Breakfast, luncheon, dinner, and sunset cruises are offered. For more information, call the Hilton at 5233111.

If you're interested in Chinese junks, you might want to board the *Duk Ling* (tel. 3311611) for a 1½-hour cruise of Victoria Harbour. Built 35 years ago in Hong Kong, the *Duk Ling* is typical of traditional junks that used to sail the seas 150 years ago. There are four cruises leaving from Queen's Pier in the Central District every day except Sunday and the cost is HK$150 ($19.48), which includes unlimited drinks on board.

Since the Sung Dynasty Village is open to individual visitors only on weekends, you might consider joining an organized tour of this replica of a thousand-year-old Chinese village, especially if you're in Hong Kong only on a weekday. Tours to the village that include lunch or dinner are HK$190 ($24.67) for adults and HK$128 ($16.62) for children. Afternoon tours, including a snack only, are HK$145 ($18.83) and HK$105 ($13.64), respectively. An interesting HKTA tour is **"The Land Between" Tour,** which takes guests via air-conditioned motorcoach on a trip through the New Territories. This seven-hour trip includes lunch in a Cantonese restaurant and visits to a Buddhist temple and a produce market at HK$220 ($28.57) for adults and HK$170 ($22.08) for children under 12.

You can also join an HKTA tour for a visit to the racetrack on Wednesday, Saturday, and an occasional Sunday from September through May. This is an exciting trip if you get in on the betting, and you don't have to bet much—HK$10 ($1.30) per race is enough. This tour costs HK$250 ($32.47), includes lunch or dinner, and is limited to tourists over 18 who have been in Hong Kong fewer than 21 days.

Sports enthusiasts may want to take advantage of the **Sports and Recreation Tour,** which involves a day spent at the Clearwater Bay Golf and Country Club. The tour price of HK$240 ($31.17) for adults and children includes transportation to and from the club, lunch, and the admission fee to the club. Facilities at the club include golf courses, tennis courts, swimming pool, saunas, and a Jacuzzi. There's a greens fee of HK$320 ($41.56) charged for golf, tennis courts rent from HK$33 ($4.29) per hour, and both clubs and racquets are available for hire. Use of the pool, saunas, and Jacuzzi is free.

All tours can be booked through your hotel, a travel agent, or HKTA.

SPORTS

Despite the fact that Hong Kong is rather small with a sizable population, there's enough open space to pursue everything from golf to hiking to windsurfing. For the hard-working Chinese and expatriates, recreation and leisure are important for winding down after a tiring week. With that in mind, try to schedule your golfing, swimming, or hiking trips on weekdays unless you enjoy jostling elbows with the crowds.

Horse Races

If you'd rather watch sports than play, and if you're in Hong Kong anytime from September through May, join the rest of Hong Kong at the horse races. Horse racing got its start in the colony in Happy Valley more than 100 years ago, making the **Happy Valley Racetrack** the oldest racecourse in Asia outside China. Without a doubt, horse racing is by far the most popular sporting event in Hong Kong. The Chinese love to gamble and there are even off-course betting offices around the city for those unable to make it to the races. There are two tracks in Hong Kong, the older one in Happy Valley and a new, modern one in Shatin in the New Territories, with races held at one or the other on Wednesday nights and on Saturday and Sunday afternoons.

The cheapest admission fee is HK$10 ($1.30), which is for the general public and is standing room only. If you want to watch from the Hong Kong Royal Jockey Club members' stand, are over 18 years old, and have been in Hong Kong fewer than 21 days, you can purchase a member's badge for HK$50 ($6.49). It's available upon display of your passport at either the Badge Enquiry Office at both tracks' main entrance to the members' private enclosure or at the off-course betting center near the Star Ferry concourse in the Central District. Tickets are sold on a first-come, first-served basis. If you don't want to go to the races but would still like to bet on the outcomes, you can place bets at one of the many off-course betting centers. Two convenient off-course centers are near the Star Ferry concourse in the Central District and 2-4 Prat Ave. in Tsimshatsui. On the other hand, the most effortless way to see the races is to join an HKTA tour to the horse races, described in the tour section above.

Golf

The **Royal Hong Kong Golf Club** welcomes visitors during weekdays at courses in both Fanling and Deep Water Bay. There are three 18-hole courses at Fanling, with greens fees at HK$800 ($103.90). Deep Water Bay charges HK$200 ($25.97) for its nine holes (weekdays only), with clubs renting for HK$100 ($12.99). For more information, call the Royal Hong Kong Golf Club at 0901211.

The **Discovery Bay Golf Club** (tel. 9877271) on Lantau Island has a beautiful 18-hole course developed by Robert Trent Jones, Jr., with great views of the water. Visitors are allowed to play here from Monday to Friday with the exception of public holidays, and greens fees are HK$350 ($45.45).

Another scenic course is operated near Sai Kung by the **Clearwater Bay Golf and Country Club** (tel. 7192454). Visitors' greens fees are HK$400 ($51.95). On weekends, guests must be signed in by a member, but greens fees remain the same. If you're interested in playing golf here but want to let someone else worry about arranging transportation, contact HKTA for its Sports and Recreation Tour, described in the organized tour section above.

Beaches

There are about 40 beaches in Hong Kong open for public use, most of which have lifeguards on duty in the summer, changing rooms, and snack stands or restaurants. Even on Hong Kong Island itself you can find a number of beaches, including Big Wave Bay and Shek O on the east coast, and Stanley, Deep Water Bay, and Repulse Bay on the south coast. Repulse Bay is by far the most popular beach in Hong Kong and gets unbelievably crowded on a summer weekend. Prettier beaches are found on the outlying islands, including Hung Shing Ye on Lamma, Tung Wan on Cheung Chau, and Cheung Sha on Lantau. However, it's advisable to check the condition of the water before going for a swim.

Windsurfing boards can be rented at many of the beaches, including Stanley and Tung Wan. Although prices may vary slightly, cost of a board for one hour is HK$45 ($5.85) to HK$60 ($7.79) at Stanley.

Hiking

There are many trails of varying levels of difficulty throughout Hong Kong. Serious hikers, for example, may want to consider the MacLehose Trail in Sai Kung in the New Territories, which stretches about 60 miles through eight country parks, or Lantau Trail, a 43-mile circular trail on Lantau Island. The Lantau Trail begins and ends at Mui Wo (also called Silvermine Bay), passing several popular scenic spots along the way. Both the MacLehose and Lantau trails are divided into smaller sections of varying difficulty, which means you can tailor your hike to suit your own abilities. For more information about hiking in Hong Kong, contact HKTA.

FESTIVALS

Hong Kong has 17 public holidays a year. Although some of them are British holidays, the majority are Chinese and follow the Chinese lunar calendar, which means that they do not fall on the same date each year. Most shops and restaurants stay open during holidays, with the exception of Chinese New Year. Below are a few of the most popular festivals.

Chinese New Year

The most important Chinese holiday, this is a family festival with visits paid to friends and relatives. Falling in either late January or February, it's a time for settling debts, visiting fortune tellers, and worshipping ancestors. Shops close down for two to three days, streets are decorated, and a fireworks display is held over the harbor. Since this festival is a family affair, it holds little interest to the tourist. In fact, you should remember that if you're planning a side trip into China, this is the worst time to go, since all routes to the mainland are clogged with Chinese going back to their homeland to visit relatives. Dates for the Chinese New Year are January 27 in 1990 and February 15 in 1991.

Tin Hau Festival

This is one of Hong Kong's most colorful festivals. Tin Hau, Hong Kong's most popular deity among fishing folk, is goddess of the sea. Legend has it that she was a fisherman's daughter who guided a fishing fleet to shore in the midst of a terrible storm. To pay tribute to Tin Hau, fishing boats are decorated with colorful flags, and family shrines are carried to shore to be blessed by Taoist priests. This festival falls on April 18 in 1990 and on May 7 in 1991.

Cheung Chau Bun Festival

Held in May on the island of Cheung Chau, this three-day affair is to appease restless ghosts and spirits. Activities include street parades and prayers in the temples, and in front of Pak Tai Temple three scaffolds holding buns are erected. These buns supposedly bring good luck to those who receive them. The 1990 and 1991 dates for this festival have not been set as we go to press. Check with HKTA for dates.

Dragon Boat Races

Races of long and narrow boats gaily painted and powered by oarsmen are held every year around June. It's an exciting event, and tour operators run cruises so that visitors can watch the events from a junk, ferry, or cruiser. Upcoming dates are May 28, 1990, and June 16, 1991.

Mid-Autumn Festival

Held in early autumn, this festival celebrates the harvest and the brightest moon of the year. In honor of the event, locals light lanterns and eat mooncakes. The Urban Council organizes lantern carnivals in parks on both Hong Kong Island and Kowloon, where you can join the Chinese for strolls under hundreds of lanterns. This festival falls on September 3, 1990, and September 22, 1991.

---

7. Where to Shop

One of the main reasons people come to Hong Kong is to shop. In fact, Hong Kong is such a popular shopping destination that many luxury cruise liners dock longer in Hong Kong than they do anywhere else on their tour. According to the Hong Kong Tourist Association (HKTA), visitors to the colony spend approximately 50% of their money on shopping. As a duty-free port, all imported goods are free of duty in Hong Kong with the exception of tobacco, alcohol, perfume, cosmetics, cars, and some petroleum products. This means that you can get many items cheaper in Hong Kong than you can in the country where they were made. There is also no sales tax.

However, Hong Kong is a buyer-beware market. Name brands are sometimes fakes and equipment may not work. To make things worse, goods usually are not returnable and deposits are not refundable. To be on the safe side, try to make your major purchases at HKTA member stores, which display the HKTA logo (a round circle with a red junk in the middle). They are required to give accurate representation of the products they sell and prompt rectification of justified complaints. Altogether there are more than 750 member shops, listed in a directory provided free by HKTA offices called *The Official Guide to Shopping, Eating Out and Services in Hong Kong*. This booklet gives the names, addresses, and phone numbers of shops for everything from audio-video equipment to musical instruments and hairpieces. If you have any complaints against a member store, contact the Membership Department of HKTA, 35th floor, Jardine House, Central District (tel. 5244191, ext. 278).

In any case, if you're buying an imported good such as a camera or electronic item, be sure to ask for a guarantee, which should include a description of the model and serial number, date of purchase, name and address of the shop where you bought it, and the shop's official stamp. You should also ask for a receipt detailing a description of your purchase.

And before you buy anything, be sure to shop around. Unless you're in a department store or an expensive boutique you'll probably be able to bargain—and prices for items can vary drastically.

WHAT TO BUY

If you've looked at the labels of clothes sold in your own hometown stores and shopping malls, you've probably noticed that "Made in Hong Kong" is a common label. It shouldn't come as a surprise, therefore, to learn that Hong Kong is one of the best places in the world to buy clothes. Both custom-made and designer clothes are a real bargain in Hong Kong, including three-piece business suits, leather outfits, furs, and jeans. Other good buys include shoes, jewelry, watches, clocks, stereo equipment, leather goods, luggage, handbags, briefcases, shoes, Chinese herbs, and eyeglasses. And, of course, if you're interested in fake name-brand watches, handbags, or clothing to impress the folks back home, you've come to the right place. Although illegal, fake name-brand items were still being sold at Hong Kong's night markets during my last visit. The vendors are simply a little more cautious, ready to flee at the first sight of officials.

Sometimes products from the People's Republic of China, including porcelain, jade, cloisonné, silk clothing, jewelry, and artwork, are cheaper in Hong Kong. Hong Kong is also the center for arts and crafts from other parts of Asia, including Indonesia, the Philippines, India, and Thailand.

SHOPPING DISTRICTS

Tsimshatsui has the greatest concentration of shops in Hong Kong. **Nathan Road,** which extends up the backbone of Kowloon for 2½ miles from the harbor to the border of the New Territories, is lined with stores selling clothes, jewelry, cameras and electronic goods, crafts from China, shoes, handbags, luggage, watches, and more. There are tailors, tattoo artists, and even shops that will carve your name into a wooden chop, a stamp used in place of a signature on official documents. (I saw a sign that was probably more truthful than most when it advertised "chop craving.") There are also department stores and shopping arcades. Be sure to explore the side streets radiating off Nathan Road, as well as the three huge shopping malls spread along the waterfront of Tsimshatsui, which are described under their own section below.

Another shopping district is **Causeway Bay** on Hong Kong Island. In contrast to Tsimshatsui, it caters more to a local market rather than to tourists, and prices are generally quite low. In addition to small shops selling everything from shoes to clothing to Chinese herbs, there are Japanese department stores, a Lane Crawford department store, and the China Products store with imports from mainland China. On the other side of Hong Kong Island is Stanley Market, a fun, interesting, and inexpensive shopping destination described in more detail later in this chapter.

TAILORS

The 24-hour suit is a thing of the past, but you can still have clothes made to fit in a few days. Tailors in Hong Kong will make anything you want, from business suits to evening gowns and wedding dresses. Some stores will let you bring in your own fabric, while others require that you buy theirs. Take a picture or drawing along with you to show what you want. As for price, it will cost about the same as and sometimes less than what you'd pay for it ready-made back home, but the difference, of course, is that this one should fit you perfectly. If it doesn't, the tailor should make alterations—but make sure beforehand that they're included in the original price. If you still don't like the finished product, you don't have to accept it. However, you'll forfeit the deposit that you were required to pay before the tailor began working, usually about 50% of the total cost.

With more than 2,500 tailoring establishments in Hong Kong, it shouldn't be any problem finding one. If your hotel has a shopping arcade, you may even be able to find one there. Otherwise, check the list in the *Official Guide to Shopping, Eating Out and Services in Hong Kong.*

EXPENSIVE DESIGNER BOUTIQUES

If you're looking for international name brands and don't care about price, check out the boutiques in the Peninsula Hotel in Tsimshatsui and the **Landmark, Swire House,** and **Prince's Building** in the Central District. The Landmark, for example, has shops for Gucci, Hermès, Louis Vuitton, Givenchy, Lanvin, Christian Dior, Wedgwood, and Bally. The Swire House has Japanese fashions from such designers as Matsuda, Kenzo, Issey Miyake, and Yohji Yamamoto. The Prince's Building, located across from the Mandarin Oriental Hotel, showcases boutiques by Aquascutum, Dunhill, Cartier, Cerruti, Chanel, Christian Dior, Daks Simpson, and Diane Freis, while the Peninsula Hotel across the water boasts a shopping arcade with designer boutiques by Charles Jourdan, Louis Vuitton, Loewe, Bally, Chanel, and Dunhill, to name only a few. Expect to pay a lot of money.

FACTORY OUTLETS

Shoppers in the know head for Hong Kong's factory outlets to buy their clothes. Most outlets are either in the Central District on Hong Kong Island or in Hung Hom and Tsimshatsui in Kowloon. Clothes sold here are excess stock, overruns, and quality control rejects that sell at unbelievably low prices. Because they are made for the export market, sizes are Western. HKTA puts out a pamphlet listing some of the factory outlets. Most shops are open from about 9 a.m. to 5:30 or 6 p.m. Monday through Friday, and some shops are also open on Saturday and Sunday. Bargains include clothes made of silk, cashmere, leather, cotton, and wool, and some outlets have men's clothing as well. These are great places to buy well-tailored and expensive-looking business outfits.

DEPARTMENT STORES

Department stores in Hong Kong sometimes have great sales. Wing On and Lane Crawford are two up-market chain department stores with a good selection of clothing, accessories, local and imported designer fashions, gift items, and cosmetics. Japanese department stores have also made great headway in Hong Kong and are very popular with the locals. In Causeway Bay, for example, there are Daimaru, Matsuzakaya, Sogo, and Mitsukoshi stores, while Kowloon has Isetan and Tokyu department stores.

For addresses of department stores, consult the *Official Guide to Shopping, Eating Out and Services in Hong Kong.*

SHOPPING MALLS

Kowloon has the largest shopping mall in Asia. Called **Harbour City,** it's only a minute's walk away from the Star Ferry on Canton Road and encompasses **Ocean Terminal, Ocean Galleries,** and **Ocean City.** All interconnected by air-conditioned walkways, the entire complex has shops selling clothing, accessories, jewelry, cosmetics, antiques, electronic goods, furniture, housewares, Asian arts and crafts, etc. Altogether there are 600 outlets in the whole complex, enough to keep you occupied on a rainy or humid day when you'd rather be inside than out. Most shops are open from about 10 a.m. to 7 or 8 p.m. Another shopping mall is located in the **New World Centre** in East Tsimshatsui. And finally, there's another huge shopping mall called **Taikoo Shing Cityplaza,** which boasts 260 shops and restaurants, as well as an ice-skating rink, roller-skating rink, bowling center, and a playground for children. It's on Hong Kong Island, near the Taikoo subway station.

CHINESE PRODUCTS

Three names to watch out for if you're looking for imports from China are Chinese Products Co., Chinese Arts & Crafts Ltd., and Yue Hwa Chinese Products Emporium Ltd. As I said before, you can buy some products from China more cheaply in Hong Kong than in China itself.

Chinese Arts & Crafts Ltd. is the top upper-end shop for Chinese arts and crafts. This is probably the best and safest place to buy jade, and you can also buy silk dresses and blouses, antiques, carpets, cloisonné, furs, Chinese medicine, rosewood furniture, and embroidered linen tablecloths or pillowcases. There are several stores in Hong Kong, including those located in the New World Centre and the Star House next to the Star Ferry in Tsimshatsui and at Queen's Road and Wyndham Street in the Central District. This chain's largest store is in the Silvercord Building, located across from the Harbour City complex in Tsimshatsui on Canton Road. This three-story shop claims to be the largest emporium of China-made goods in Hong Kong. In addition to traditional jade and rosewood carvings, antique Chinese jewelry, paintings, and silk fashions, there are also garments by Pierre Cardin manufactured in a factory in China. The Silvercord shop is open from 10 a.m. to 6:30 p.m. every day except Sunday, when it's open from noon to 6 p.m.

China Products Co. sells more ordinary everyday household items, including household goods and appliances, kimonos, porcelain, clothes, shoes, and furniture. **Yue Hwa** is more of the same. It was here that I bought some friends a gag wedding gift—Chinese whisky with preserved lizards in it, all for only HK$25 ($3.25). Definitely a bargain.

Check *The Official Guide to Shopping, Eating Out and Services in Hong Kong* for the many addresses of these stores.

MARKETS

These are where you can get some of the best deals in Hong Kong, though a lot depends on how well you can bargain. If you're good at it, you might be able to get items for 25% off the originally quoted price.

Li Yuen Street East and West

These two streets are pedestrian lanes in the Central District. They're packed full with stalls selling handbags, clothes, scarves, sweaters, toys, bolts of cloth, knickknacks, and even brassieres. They're popular with locals, and sometimes human traffic is quite slow. Don't neglect the open-fronted shops behind the stalls. Some of these are boutiques selling fashionable but cheap clothing as well as shoes, purses, and accessories.

Stanley Market

Stanley Market is probably the most popular market in Hong Kong and it's a trendy place for foreign residents to live. Located on the southern coast of Hong

Kong Island on a small peninsula, it's a great place to pick up jeans and clothing for a song. Some of the shops are remodeling and becoming more chic, but you can still find good bargains in silk clothing as well as arts and crafts. It seems as though no one who comes here can leave without bundles and bags of purchases. Most shopkeepers seem reluctant to bargain but it's still worth a try, especially if you're purchasing more than one item. To reach Stanley, take bus 6 or 260 from the Central Bus Terminal by the Star Ferry. The bus ride to Stanley takes approximately 30 minutes.

Night Markets
Both **Temple Street** in Kowloon and **Poor Man's Nightclub** on Hong Kong Island are night markets that open up when the sun goes down. They sell the usual stuff street vendors sell, including T-shirts, jeans, watches, lighters, socks, jewelry and jewelry boxes, cassette tapes, sweaters, and imitation Lacoste shirts. Be sure to bargain fiercely, and check products to make sure they're not faulty or poorly made. Temple Street is the bigger of the two.

ANTIQUES
In addition to the Chinese products department stores, you can also find antiques in the Hollywood Road area above the Central District. There are shops selling porcelain, silver, rosewood and blackwood furniture, as well as fakes and curios. **Cat Street Galleries** on neighboring Lok Kwu Road has arts and crafts and expensive antiques.

For serious Oriental antiques lovers and buyers with deep pockets, don't miss **Charlotte Hortsmann and Gerald Godfrey,** a large, high-quality shop at Ocean Terminal. Even if you haven't a pence to your name, it's worth a visit. If you find yourself enthralled, ask to see their basement warehouse.

---

8. Hong Kong After Dark

Hong Kong's nightlife, although not as varied and extensive as Tokyo's, does offer the visitor a steady stream of British pubs, topless bars, discos, and cocktail lounges from which to choose. Keep in mind that one of the finest traditions in Hong Kong is its "happy hour," when some bars offer drinks at half price, two for the price of one, or simply at lower prices. Happy hour generally is from 5 to 7 p.m., sometimes longer. Remember also that a 10% service charge will be added to your bill.

COCKTAIL LOUNGES
The Sheraton Hotel's **Sky Lounge,** 20 Nathan Rd. in Kowloon (tel. 3691111), has what I consider to be the best and most romantic view of Hong Kong Island glittering across the harbor. Take the glass-enclosed capsule elevator up to the 18th floor just as dusk approaches, grab a window seat, and watch the colors of the day fade as lights turn on one by one in the Central District and Wanchai. Open from 11 a.m. to 1 a.m. daily (to 2 a.m. on Friday and Saturday), the Sky Lounge charges HK$25 ($3.25) for most of its beers and HK$33 ($4.29) for most of its cocktails. Unfortunately, there's no happy hour here, and from 8 p.m. onward there's a minimum drink charge of HK$77 ($10) per person if you're not a hotel guest. Soft, live music begins at 5:30 p.m. and serenades until midnight, 1 a.m. on weekends.

Another cocktail lounge on the Kowloon side is the **Tiara,** on the 21st floor of the Shangri-La, 64 Mody Rd., East Tsimshatsui (tel. 7212111). Tiara is open daily from 5 p.m. to 2 a.m., and it's best to get here right when it opens if you want to be assured of a window seat overlooking the harbor. Piano music sets the mood for this intimate and cozy lounge where beer and cocktails average HK$35 ($4.54). There's a minimum drink charge here of HK$95 ($12.34) per person after 8 p.m.

On the Hong Kong side, a lounge offering spectacular closeup views of the Central District and of the harbor and Kowloon beyond is **La Ronda Bar,** on the 30th floor of the Furama Hotel, 1 Connaught Rd. (tel. 5255111). Although it's located next to a revolving restaurant, the bar itself is stationary. With cocktails averaging HK$40 ($5.19), it's open from 5:30 p.m. to 11 p.m. every day.

PUBS AND BARS

One of the most interesting developments in Hong Kong's night scene in recent years is the modest mushrooming of some bars and pubs in the area of Lan Kwai Fong and D'Aguilar streets in Hong Kong Island's Central District. Catering more to Hong Kong's foreign and Chinese young residents than to tourists, who tend to stick to Tsimshatsui, it's a welcome relief in the Central District, which has always tended to shut down as soon as the offices close up. One of the most chic bars here is **California,** Lan Kwai Fong (tel. 5211345), whose owner is, nonetheless, Canadian. This is the place to see and be seen, the place of the young nouveaux riches in search of a definition. The atmosphere is modern and sophisticated, with silent TV screens showing movies almost everywhere you look. It's open from noon to 1 a.m. every night except Wednesday, Friday, and Saturday, when California turns into a disco from 11:30 p.m. until 4 a.m. Cover charge for the disco is HK$108 ($14.02), which includes two drinks, but on Wednesday women can get in for free. Otherwise, drinks here begin at HK$33 ($4.29) for beer and HK$49 ($6.36) for cocktails, except during happy hour, from 5 to 7 p.m., when you can get two drinks for the price of one. If you're interested in lunch or dinner, the menu lists everything from hamburgers (the house specialty) to pastas, seafood, and chicken.

Close to Lan Kwai Fong is **MadDogs,** 33 Wyndham St. (tel. 5252383), one of Hong Kong's most pleasant English pubs, which caters to a mellow and professional working crowd. A favorite with local expatriates who drop by on their way home from work, MadDogs is located in an old building and consists of a ground floor, basement, and small patio courtyard out back. With traditional decor that includes a stern picture of Queen Victoria, cane chairs, and ceiling fans, the pub is open for business from 11:30 a.m. to 1 a.m. (2 a.m. on Friday and Saturday), and offers a small glass of beer for less than HK$10 ($1.29) and snacks of sandwiches, meat pies, and salads. If you want to get away from Queen Victoria's gaze, the downstairs area is a little less staid, the music tends to be louder, and the atmosphere a bit livelier. Incidentally, the easiest way to get to MadDogs is via the side-door entry just off D'Aguilar and Lan Kwai Fong streets, especially if you're walking from the nightlife area around Lan Kwai Fong.

Serving German draft beers, sauerkraut, sausages, and other German fare, **Schnurrbart** is a serious drinking establishment located at 29 D'Aguilar St. (tel. 5234700). Popular with German expatriates, it's open from noon to 2 a.m. every day except Sunday. German beer starts at HK$20 ($2.60), and the food menu changes weekly. By the way, a second Schnurrbart (which means "moustache" in German) is located across the harbor at 6-6A Hart, Tsimshatsui (tel. 3723982).

The **Bull and Bear,** on the ground floor of Hutchinson House at 10 Harcourt Rd., Central District (tel. 5257436), was one of the first English pubs to open in Hong Kong back in 1974, and it has been notorious from the beginning. A huge, sprawling place with dart boards and waitresses in long skirts and frilly white blouses, this pub gets pretty rowdy on weekend nights, and draws everyone from businessmen in suits to servicemen on leave. Having had to fight off the attentions of a rather inebriated sailor with tattoos up and down his arms, I can state that it's not a particularly comfortable place for a woman alone; however, for those who are interested, there are definitely more men here than women. (You may also be interested in knowing that a British woman living in Hong Kong described this place as a meat market.) If that's what you're looking for, HK$11 ($1.43) will buy you a small beer, and in case you're so uncultured as to ask for a cocktail in an English pub, they average HK$27 ($3.51). Hours are 7:30 a.m. to midnight every day except Sunday and bank holidays, when it remains closed. The menu includes items like chili con carne, steak-and-kidney pie, salads, sandwiches, and daily specials—as well as an English breakfast, available until 10:30 a.m. for HK$38 ($4.93).

Another long-time favorite in the Central District is the **Godown,** which had a home in the Sutherland House for 20 years before moving to the Admiralty Tower 2 Building in 1988, next to the Admiralty subway station (tel. 8661166). Decorated like an old godown (warehouse) with exposed beams and wooden barrels, this popular expatriate bar is open daily from 9 a.m. to 2 a.m. Its lunch menu lists steak-and-kidney pie, Irish stew, lasagne, liver, seafood, fish-and-chips, steak, and salads. Set lunches, which include a trip through the salad bar, are HK$80 ($10.39). During happy hour, from 5 to 7 p.m., you get two drinks for the price of one. Each Wednesday night there's live jazz from 9:30 p.m. to 12:30 a.m.; on other nights you can dance to disco tunes.

A much quieter and more refined English pub, **The Jockey,** on the first floor of the Swire House, Central District (tel. 5261478), is popular with bankers, lawyers, and office people. Its theme is obviously racing and jockeys, with a very masculine decor. Open every day except Sunday from 11 a.m. to 11 p.m., the Jockey prices its beer from HK$15 ($1.95) to HK$28 ($3.64), and cocktails run HK$30 ($3.90).

Rivaling the Jockey for elegance is **Dickens Bar,** located in the basement of the Excelsior Hotel, Causeway Bay (tel. 5767365). A classy place with dark-wood paneling, softly lit lamps, and live music from 9 p.m. to 1 a.m., this English pub serves snacks of soups and sandwiches as well as a curry buffet lunch from noon to 2 p.m. every day except Saturday and public holidays for HK$65 ($8.44). Draft beer begins at HK$13 ($1.69) for a half pint and cocktails start at HK$29 ($3.77). Particularly recommended is a jazz band that plays every Sunday afternoon from 3 to 6 p.m.

The **Captain's Bar,** on the ground floor of the Mandarin Oriental Hotel, 5 Connaught Rd. in the Central District (tel. 5220111), is popular with Hong Kong's professional working crowd. Seating is at the bar or on couches, and live music begins nightly at 9. It's open from 11 a.m. to 2 a.m. every day. Cocktails are HK$40 ($5.19) and beer starts at HK$22 ($2.86).

Old China Hand, 104 Lockhart Rd. in Wanchai (tel. 5279174), is an informal English pub with dart boards, a picture of Queen Elizabeth, and a lot of kitsch on the walls. A sign warns customers: "Sorry, we don't serve women—you have to bring your own." A small draft here starts at HK$10.50 ($1.36) and spirits at HK$17 ($2.21). In the tradition of the pub lunch, meals are also served, including steak-and-kidney pie, fish-and-chips, sandwiches, salads, chili con carne, and moussaka, with most items costing less than HK$35 ($4.54). It's open daily from 11 a.m. to 2 a.m.

Not far away in Wanchai is one of the most popular *gwaile* (foreigner) hangouts, **Joe Bananas,** 23 Luard Rd. (tel. 5291811). Commonly called JB's by the locals, it's managed by the same people who brought you MadDogs. A bar/restaurant that transforms itself into a disco every night, it's open from noon to 2 a.m. Monday through Thursday and to 5 a.m. on Friday and Saturday; on Sunday it's open from 6 p.m. to 2 a.m. Decorated like an American diner with a jukebox, posters, and memorabilia of movie stars and rock 'n' roll greats, it serves burgers, hot dogs, salads, and sandwiches, as well as a weekdays-only set lunch for HK$60 ($7.79). Happy hour is every day from 3 to 8 p.m., when you get two for the price of one; cocktails range from HK$28 ($3.64) to HK$48 ($6.23). On Monday and Wednesday, you can get two cocktails for the price of one from 3 p.m. until closing time. On Friday and Saturday nights after 9 p.m., there's a cover charge of HK$65 ($8.44), which includes two drinks. Joe Bananas is just a two-minute walk from the Wanchai subway station.

White Stag, 72 Canton Rd., Tsimshatsui (tel. 3661951), is an English-style pub that caters to a large Chinese clientele. A nice, quiet place where you can actually hear yourself talk, this place sports wooden tables and a few deer heads and antlers, with beer beginning at HK$12 ($1.59) for a half pint. A blackboard tells of entrées for the day, which might include such things as corned beef hash and eggs, spring rolls, Shanghai fried noodles, or tuna-fish salad, and it's open for business from 10 a.m. to 2 a.m. daily.

Just down the road at 70 Canton Rd. is **Beefy's Cabin** (tel. 7214689), open 24 hours. With no money wasted on decor, it looks like any bar anywhere. Happy hour is from 5 to 9 p.m., when you can get two drinks for the price of one. A pint of San Miguel is HK$24 ($3.12). If you're hungry, there's beef stew, bacon and eggs, burritos, beef satay, chili, Mexican pizza, spaghetti, spring rolls, and other snacks on the menu. A live Filipino band plays from 5 p.m. to 5 a.m.—and there's no cover or music charge. As you might guess, the action here starts late.

Ned Kelly's Last Stand, 11A Ashley Rd. in Tsimshatsui (tel. 3660562), is an Australian pub with live Dixieland jazz or swing nightly from 9 p.m. to 2 a.m. Resembling a saloon, it opens its doors at 11:30 a.m. and serves beer beginning at HK$11 ($1.43) until 7 p.m., after which it costs HK$16 ($2.08). The food here ranges from HK$25 ($3.25) to HK$60 ($7.79) and includes juicy pork sausages from Australia served with mashed potatoes and onion gravy; stew; hamburgers; liver, bacon, and fried onions; chicken; Australian sirloin steak; and meat pie with mashed potatoes and onion gravy.

One of Tsimshatsui's most popular watering holes is **Someplace Else,** located in the basement of the Sheraton Hotel, 20 Nathan Rd. (tel. 3691111). It's standing room only from 4 to 7 p.m., when you can buy two drinks for the price of one. Most drinks are priced at HK$33 ($4.29), while draft beer starts at HK$17 ($2.21). Open from 11 a.m. to 1 a.m. daily (until 2 a.m. on weekends), this establishment is divided into two levels and decorated with stained-glass lampshades and ceiling fans. If you're hungry, there's a great menu with everything from satay, samosas, and tacos to fish-and-chips, spareribs, and hamburgers. From 11 a.m. to 3 p.m. there's a salad bar available for HK$33 ($4.29).

One of my favorites is **Rick's Café,** 4 Hart Ave., Tsimshatsui (tel. 3672939). Taking its name from the movie *Casablanca,* it sports potted palm trees, ceiling fans, and posters of Humphrey Bogart and Ingrid Bergman. Although it's more of a bar than a restaurant, it also serves great tacos, enchiladas, chili con carne, sandwiches, Moroccan kebab, African ribs, and other exotic fare for HK$30 ($3.90) to HK$45 ($5.84) per plate. Drinks are a little steep, with cocktails starting at HK$39 ($5.06) and a half pint of beer at HK$16 ($2.08), but until 9 p.m. there's a happy hour when you can get two for the price of one. Rick's has a small dance floor, and after 9 p.m. there's a disk jockey. The hours of this place are 3 p.m. to 3 a.m. every day except Sunday, when it's open from 6 p.m. to 2 a.m.

THE TOPLESS BARS AND HOSTESS CLUBS

Wanchai was the world of Suzie Wong, a world of bars and two-bit hotels, narrow streets, and dark alleyways, where men came to drink and to brawl and spend money for women. Sailors came here when they landed in port, followed by American soldiers on leave from Vietnam, and it was a place of neon lights and buzzing activity, excitement, the unspoken and the whispered.

Much of the nightlife district has given way to new buildings and high-rises. However, it's still interesting to walk around Wanchai along Lockhart Road, where you'll find food stalls, tattoo parlors, neon lights galore, and plenty of nighttime activity.

Much of Hong Kong's nightlife, however, has moved to Tsimshatsui, where topless bars, so-called nightclubs, and hostess establishments try to part customers from their dollars. Japanese men are big customers here, perhaps because they're used to hostess bars in their own country. At any rate, you've been warned.

The best place to go if you want to go to a topless joint is **Bottoms Up,** 14 Hankow Rd., Tsimshatsui (tel. 3675696). Despite the lewd pictures in the entranceway, this place is actually rather innocuous and welcomes tourists, couples, men, and women. Used as a location shot in the James Bond movie *Man with the Golden Gun,* it features four round counters with a topless waitress in the middle of each, with soft, red lighting. I don't know what was in the men's bathroom, but the women's room had some posters of Burt Reynolds in sexy poses. Open from 4 p.m. to 3 a.m. daily (5 p.m. to 3 a.m. Sunday), it has one of the longest happy hours in Hong Kong—from 4 to 9 p.m., when beer is HK$18 ($2.34) and other drinks average about HK$24 ($3.12). After 9 p.m. prices double.

The largest hostess club in the colony—and maybe the world—is **Club Volvo,** located in the Mandarin Plaza in Tsimshatsui East (tel. 3692883). Open daily from 2 p.m. to 4 a.m., it features nightly stage shows, with a stage that rotates so that all guests get a chance to ogle the performers. There's also a large dance floor. This place is so big that an electric Rolls-Royce delivers drinks and guests to their tables. There's a minimum charge of HK$110 ($14.29) during the day and HK$165 ($21.43) at night, which includes two drinks. Furthermore, every six minutes you sit at a table during the day costs HK$14 ($1.82), and a hostess joining you for small talk and dancing costs HK$380 ($49.35) for three hours. At night, these charges go up to HK$180 ($23.38) per hour at a table, while time spent with a hostess is HK$45 ($5.84) for every 15 minutes.

DISCOS

Disco fever hit Hong Kong in the late 1970s and the first to cash in on the craze was **Disco Disco,** 38 D'Aguilar St., Central District (tel. 5248809). Now under new management, it may change its name and its image to keep up with the stiff competition, but at last check the establishment drew a wide mixture of clientele, including gays, straights, expatriates, and Chinese. From Sunday through Thursday it's open from 10 p.m. to 3 a.m. and charges a HK$70 ($9.09) cover; women can get in for free on Wednesday and Friday; men get in free on Tuesday and Thursday. On Friday and Saturday nights, the cover charge increases to HK$95 ($12.34). Included in the cover charge are two standard drinks. After that, beer and cocktails are HK$35 ($4.54). There are separate rooms for dancing and drinking, and the dance floor is surrounded with mirrors so you can watch yourself if so inclined.

Not far away is **Club 97,** located on the ground floor under the restaurant Ninety-Seven at 9 Lan Kwai Fong (tel. 5810933). This small, rather eclectically decorated disco opens its doors at 10 p.m., closing at 4 a.m. Sunday through Thursday and 6 a.m. on weekends. There's an entrance fee of HK$55 ($7.14) Thursday through Saturday. Cocktails are around HK$45 ($5.84).

Also on Hong Kong Island but over in Causeway Bay is **Talk of the Town,** on the 30th floor of the Excelsior Hotel (tel. 5767365). This disco, decorated in art deco style, has a fantastic view of the harbor and Kowloon and features a Filipino band. If you're a hotel guest there's no cover charge; otherwise it costs HK$99 ($12.86) on weekdays and HK$110 ($14.29) on weekends, which includes two free drinks. Talk of the Town is also open for happy hour from 5 to 8:30 p.m., when beers go for HK$22 ($2.86) and cocktails run HK$29 ($3.77).

On the other side of the harbor is another popular hotel disco that caters to a young and trendy crowd. Called **Hollywood East,** it's located in the basement of the Regal Meridien at 71 Mody Rd. in Tsimshatsui (tel. 8936460). Decorated on a Hollywood theme with backlighting fixtures, posters of movie stars, and 12 screens that depict the history of Hollywood, this disco charges HK$95 ($12.34) at the door but it includes two drinks. Hours are 9:30 p.m. to 2 a.m. (to 3 a.m. on the weekends).

One of Hong Kong's hottest and most innovative discos is **Canton,** located next to the Prince Hotel on Canton Road in Harbour City, Tsimshatsui (tel. 7350209). It changes its look often so that the locals keep coming back—and judging by the crowds, it's highly successful. Complete with a dance cage where you can watch a professional performer go at it, TV video screens with Canton's own in-house videos, and Chinese poster advertisements from the 1920s, it boasts a dance floor with lots of technical gadgets and lights. Open from 9 p.m. until 3 a.m. on weekdays and 4 a.m. on Friday and Saturday, it charges a cover of HK$95 ($12.34) on weekdays and HK$108 ($14.03) on weekends, which includes two drinks. After that, concoctions cost HK$48 ($6.23).

Down the road is **Hot Gossip,** also located in Harbour City on Canton Road (tel. 7306884). The ground floor is a high-tech restaurant and bar, while the disco is located in the basement. The disco is huge, with laser shows nightly, and the entrance charge of HK$96 ($12.47) on weekdays and HK$108 ($14.03) on weekends includes two drinks. On Sunday and Monday women are admitted free. The disco is open from 9 p.m. to 2:30 a.m. (until 3:30 a.m. weekends), but the restaurant, which serves soups, salads, sandwiches, burgers, spaghetti, and more, opens at noon (5 p.m. on Sunday).

Boobs, 35-39 Hankow Rd., Tsimshatsui (tel. 3683829), is the place a lot of people gravitate to after the other establishments close. Open from 10 p.m. until 5 a.m., it's at its peak after midnight, after which things can become quite wild and hectic. Admittance for males is HK$88 ($11.43), while females are charged HK$45 ($5.84), which includes one drink. This place is popular with people in their 20s, including Chinese, Filipinos, Westerners, and other expatriates.

The **Music Room,** in the Shangri-La Hotel, 64 Mody Rd., East Tsimshatsui (tel. 7212111), is the place to go if you think you're too old for the discos described above but aren't quite ready for the rest home. Aiming for an older, sophisticated crowd, it's designed more for socializing and conversation than for wild partying. It's a relaxing place that looks like a living room, with plush carpets and sofas, and the music is concentrated on the dance floor. Open daily from 5 p.m. to 2 a.m., it charges an entrance fee of HK$107 ($13.90) on Friday and on Saturday after 9 p.m. Cocktails cost HK$30 ($3.90) to HK$40 ($5.19).

NIGHT MARKETS

Shopping is one of the things you can do in Hong Kong in the evenings, since many shops stay open until 10 p.m. But if you're looking for some atmosphere, head for one of the night markets. **Temple Street market** on the Kowloon side extends for several blocks and has stalls selling clothing, accessories, toys, cassettes, household items, and much more. Bargain fiercely here, and be sure to check the merchandise to make sure it isn't going to fall apart in two weeks. Be sure also to follow Temple Street to its northern end and beyond, where you'll find palm readers, musicians, and street singers. Cantonese pop songs and operas are among the favorites in their repertoire.

Another market is the **Poor Man's Nightclub** on Hong Kong Island, which was unfortunately drastically reduced in size with the completion of the Macau Ferry Terminal next to it. Still, you can pick up some good buys here, with stalls selling everything from imitation Lacoste shirts to belts, jeans, wallets, jewelry boxes, and noodle soup. The night markets are open from approximately 6 to 11 p.m.

NIGHT STROLLS

One of the most beautiful night views in the world is that afforded of Hong Kong from Victoria Peak. For an inexpensive evening out, take the peak tram to the top and make a right out of the Peak Tower Building, where you'll find a footpath that skirts the side of the steep hill. If you want, you can stroll in a circular route on Lugard and Harlech roads in about an hour or so.

On the Tsimshatsui side, there's a promenade along the waterfront popular with young Chinese couples. Another interesting stroll is through the Temple Street night market, as outlined above.

NIGHT TOURS

If you have only one or two nights in Hong Kong, I suggest taking an organized night tour. **Watertours** offers eight different tours of Hong Kong by night, combining harbor cruises with various land activities. The tram and dinner cruise, for example, starts out with a tram ride from Causeway Bay through Wanchai to the Central District, followed by a stroll through Poor Man's Nightclub and then either a Chinese dinner and cruise through the harbor or a Western buffet meal in La Ronda revolving restaurant. The price for this tour is HK$345 ($44.80). Other tours might include a trip up Victoria Peak, dinner in an Aberdeen floating restaurant, a cruise in a traditional Chinese junk, or a ride in an open-top bus. You can make reservations for tours through your hotel or by calling Watertours directly at 5254808.

If you like having some guidance in making your plans but prefer to carry them out on your own, you might want to take advantage of a do-it-yourself night tour organized by the HKTA that lets you select from a number of discos, pubs, bars, and establishments that are members of HKTA. You decide which ones to visit, when, and for how long, though there are some restrictions. Two options are available. With the Grand Tour, you receive two coupons for your choice of two pubs, bars, or nightclubs, where you can have one or two standard drinks free as well as one disco coupon good for one standard drink. Cost of the Grand Tour is HK$165 ($21.43). If you opt for the De Luxe Tour package for HK$290 ($37.66), you receive one coupon good for one or two standard drinks at a pub, bar, or nightclub as well as one hostess club coupon good for two standard drinks, a fruit plate, and one hour with a hostess. For more information, contact HKTA.

9. Exploring the Territories and Environs

Mention Hong Kong and most people think of Hong Kong Island and Kowloon, of shops, nightclubs, and neon signs. What they don't realize is that Hong Kong Island and Kowloon are rather minute in the scheme of things—the New Territories and outlying islands make up a whopping 90% of the colony.

If you have a day or two to spare, or even just an afternoon, I suggest spending it on a trip outside the city in one of Hong Kong's rural areas. After all, it's in the small villages and in the countryside that you have the chance to glimpse an older and a slower way of life, where traditions still reign supreme and where lifestyles have a rhythm of their own.

THE NEW TERRITORIES
Before the 1980s the New Territories were a peaceful countryside, with duck farms, fields, and old villages. No longer. A vast area that stretches 281 square miles between Kowloon and the border of China, the New Territories is Hong Kong's answer to its population and refugee crunch. Huge government housing projects have mushroomed throughout the Territories, turning once-sleepy villages into satellite concrete jungles.

However, the Territories is so big that not all of it has been turned into housing, and it still makes an interesting day trip for first-timers to the colony. For information on transportation in the New Territories, drop by a HKTA office to pick up *Round New Territories by Bus,* which tells which bus to take and where to get off for some of the major destinations.

"The Land Between" Tour
The easiest and best way to get a roundup view of the New Territories is to join a tour organized by the Hong Kong Tourist Association called "The Land Between." A seven-hour trip via air-conditioned coach, the tour takes you past satellite towns into a countryside dotted with ponds, duck farms, and small vegetable gardens planted with Chinese kale, chives, onions, and tomatoes. Every inch of land in the

valley is used; only the barren hills are empty. Stops on the tour include Cheuk Lam Sim Yuen, a Buddhist monastery housing three of the largest "precious Buddha" statues in Hong Kong, and the indoor market of Luen Wo in Fanling.

Lunch is at Yucca de Lac Restaurant, a pleasant establishment built on a hill overlooking Tolo Harbour. The food is Cantonese, with lots of dishes that might include fried chicken with lemon sauce, diced pork with cashew nuts, or fried filet of garoupa with green pepper. Cost of the tour, which is operated on weekdays only, is HK$220 ($28.57) for adults and HK$170 ($22.08) for children.

Kowloon–Canton Railway

For years the thing every visitor did in the New Territories was to take the train to the border for a look into forbidden and mysterious China. Now, of course, it's easy to get permission to enter China, so the border lookout has lost its appeal and the view was never very exciting anyway. Still, you might want to take the train up into the New Territories just for the experience. Starting from the Kowloon railway station, the Kowloon–Canton Railway will take you along 20 miles of track, passing through towns like Shatin, University Station, Tai Po Kau, and Fanling before reaching Sheung Shui about a half hour later. Sheung Shui is your last stop unless you have a visa to go farther into China. Altogether the train makes eight stops along the way, making it possible to get out and do some exploring on your own.

Shatin: Shatin is Hong Kong's prime example of a budding satellite town. It's also home to Hong Kong's new and modern racetrack. The most interesting thing for the tourist here, though, is the **Temple of 10,000 Buddhas,** located on a hill west of the Shatin railway station. It will take you about a half hour to walk there, and be prepared for the more than 300 stairs you have to climb to get to the top. The temple was founded by a monk named Yuet Kai, who is still there. Well, he's kind of still there—he's been embalmed in gold leaf and sits behind a glass case for all to see. The other attraction of the temple is the Buddha statues. Actually there are more than 10,000 of them. There are 12,800 Buddha statues lining the walls, and no two are exactly alike. Included on the grounds is a nine-story pink pagoda. The temple affords a good view of the surrounding countryside.

University Station: This stop serves students going to Chinese University. It's also where you get off if you want to go to the Art Gallery. From the train station, catch a bus going to Chinese University and get off at the second stop, called Science Centre. There you will find the **Art Gallery** (tel. 6952218), a museum that contains more than 1,000 paintings and examples of calligraphy from the Ming Period to the present. Also in the collection are bronze seals, jade flower carvings, and Chinese ceramics. The museum is open daily from 10 a.m. to 4:30 p.m. (from 12:30 to 4:30 p.m. on Sunday), and admission is free.

University Station is also where you get off if you want to take a **ferry around Tolo Harbour.** From the station it's a five-minute walk to Ma Liu Shui, where you board the ferry for a leisurely trip to six villages around the harbor. The ferry leaves only two times a day, at 7:25 a.m. and at 3:15 p.m. Since the first ferry may be a little too early for you and doesn't allow you to disembark for sightseeing, I suggest taking the afternoon cruise. The ferry makes a stop at Tap Mun at 4:50 p.m., goes on to some other villages, and then returns to Tap Mun about 45 minutes later. This gives you time to do some sightseeing, but make sure you make it back to the ferry by 5:45 p.m. because there are no hotels here. The ferry gets back into Ma Liu Shui at 7:10 p.m.

Tai Po Market: The **Tai Ping Carpet Factory** allows visitors to come watch the intricate process of producing its beautiful carpets. Visiting hours are 2 to 4 p.m. only, Monday through Thursday. You have to make an appointment here, which you can do by calling 6565161, extension 211. The factory is located on Lot No. 1687, Tai Ping Industrial Park, Ting Kok Road, Tai Po Market.

Fanling: The **Luen Wo Market** in the middle of Fanling (included in "The Land Between" Tour) is interesting if you've never seen a Chinese country market.

Covering one square block, this indoor market is a maze of tiny passageways and various stalls selling everything from live chickens to deer heads (honest).

Sheung Shui: Sheung Shui Heung is an ancient village located about 300 yards north of the main town. Although much of its charm has been lost with the construction of modern buildings all around it, it's still more peaceful than other old villages that are more on the beaten path. A home belonging to a prominent family, the Liu family, has recently been renovated and is open to the public.

Kam Tin Walled Village

During the Ming Dynasty (1368–1644), some of the clans in the area of the New Territories built walls around their homes to protect themselves against roving bandits and invaders. Six of these walled villages still exist today. The most famous of these is **Kut Hing Wei,** popularly known as **Kam Tin.** About 400 descendants of the Tang clan who built the village back in the 1600s still live here. Although it's the best preserved of the walled villages, it's crowded with souvenir stands and the locals don't like it if you wander off the main passageway. Kam Tin is located near the town of Yuen Long. To reach it, take the MTR subway to Tsuen Wan and then board bus 51, getting off at the last stop.

Incidentally, before boarding bus 51 in Tsuen Wan you should first visit the **Sam Tung Uk Museum,** located just a few minutes' walk from the Tsuen Wan MTR subway station (there's a map in the station that can point you in the right direction). The museum is actually a restored Hakka walled village. Built in the 18th century by members of the Hakka Chan clan, it's a tiny oasis of tiled-roof houses in the midst of modern high-rises. On display are farm implements and traditional Chinese furniture. Visiting the museum before a trip to one of the walled villages where the Hakka still live will make the experience more enriching. The museum, open from 9 a.m. to 4 p.m. every day except Tuesday, is free.

Other villages in the area are Shui Tau, Kam Hing Wai, Kam Tsin Wai, and Shek Tsin Wai. They are inhabited by Hakka people, and Hakka women are easily recognizable by their straw hats with hanging black fringe. They hate to have their photographs taken because they think it steals something from their spirit, so it might be a good idea to show respect for their beliefs by putting away your camera when visiting these villages. On the other hand, some Hakka have realized that there's money to be made by posing for the tourists' cameras. Be sure to settle on a price before you start clicking away.

Where to Eat

I suggest that you eat at the same restaurant HKTA selected for its "The Land Between" Tour, **Yucca de Lac Restaurant,** in Ma Liu Shui (tel. 6921835). The easiest way to get here is by taxi from Shatin Station. You can sit outside on a terrace overlooking the harbor, which gives it a slightly European atmosphere. The Cantonese menu has more than 200 items, including duck, pigeon, pork, beef, chicken, seafood, and tofu dishes. Selections average HK$38 ($4.93) to HK$90 ($11.69) and the restaurant is open daily from 11 a.m. to 11 p.m.

OUTLYING ISLANDS

In addition to Hong Kong Island there are 235 outlying islands, most of them barren and uninhabited. Because construction in the New Territories is booming, the islands of Hong Kong now offer the best opportunity for observing rural Chinese life. Three of the most accessible islands are Lantau, Cheung Chau, and Lamma. Ferries are cheap (less than HK$12, or $1.56) and depart about every hour from the Outlying Districts Services Pier for Lantau and Cheung Chau and from the Central Harbour Services Pier for Lamma. Both piers are located about a five-minute walk from the Star Ferry concourse in Hong Kong Island's Central District. Ferries to Lantau and Cheung Chau have an open area in the back of the first-class deck, which is a great place to sit when the weather is fine, enjoy a beer or coffee, and watch

Hong Kong and the harbor float past. Remember to avoid going to the islands on a Sunday, when ferries are packed with city folks on family outings.

Be sure to pick up the *Outlying Islands* leaflet provided free by HKTA. HKTA also has information on the latest ferry schedules. If you plan on doing some extensive hiking on the islands, inexpensive maps are available at the Government Publications Centre, located just west of the Central District Star Ferry Terminal.

Lantau

Twice the size of Hong Kong Island, Lantau is the colony's largest island. But whereas Hong Kong Island has a population of more than a million, Lantau has about 16,000 residents.

Taking a ferry from Hong Kong Island, you'll arrive in **Silvermine Bay,** known as Mui Wo in Chinese. There's not much of interest here, but in front of the ferry pier is where you can catch buses around the island.

If you've arrived in time for lunch, first stop on your itinerary should be **Po Lin Monastery** (tel. 9855113), largest and most famous of the 135 Buddhist monasteries located on Lantau. Situated on the plateau of Ngong Ping at an elevation of 2,460 feet, this place has what many consider to be the best vegetarian meals in Hong Kong. The big dining hall serves steaming dishes of vegetables and rice daily from noon to 6 p.m. for HK$33 ($4.29).

If you don't mind rather austere surroundings, you can also spend the night here. For HK$145 ($18.83) you can sleep on a hard mat and eat three vegetarian meals. No matter that lunch and dinner look pretty much the same, that lights are out at 6:30 p.m. (at least the night I was there), and that breakfast is served at 7:30 a.m. The landscape around the monastery is empty and peaceful, good for long solitary walks, and if you want you can climb to Lantau Peak (3,064 feet above sea level) to watch the sunrise. Close to the monastery is a tea plantation you might want to visit, and that monstrosity they're building on the side of the hill is Southeast Asia's tallest Buddha, more than 100 feet tall and costing HK$60 million ($7.8 million). They've been working on it for several years, so maybe it will be finished by the time you see it.

From Po Lin Monastery you can catch a bus, or, as I suggest, walk the two hours to the village of **Tai O,** Lantau's most interesting village. Tai O wraps itself around the muddy waters of a bay on the west coast of the island. There are no cars on the narrow, twisting streets, no neon signs, no high-rises of concrete and steel. Instead there are one-story wooden houses resting on stilts above the mud of the bay. Life is unhurried and relaxed. You can hear the click-clicking of adults playing mah-jongg all day long.

There are several temples in Tai O, the best known of which is Kwan Ti, on Market Street. There are also some fish-processing shops and open-fronted stores selling Chinese herbs and hardware. The village is divided in two by a creek, and the only way to get across is by a flat-bottomed boat that is pulled along a rope strung across the water.

From Tai O the bus back to Silvermine Bay takes about 45 minutes. You might want to cool off here with a swim at **Cheung Sha beach,** a two-mile-long white sandy beach with changing rooms, showers, and toilets. Cheung Sha is about ten minutes away from Silvermine Bay by bus.

Where to Eat: In addition to the vegetarian meals served at the Po Lin Monastery described above, there are a couple of other places you might want to try. In Silvermine Bay, Cantonese dishes are served at the **Silvermine Beach Hotel** (tel. 9848295) from 7:30 a.m. to 10 p.m. daily. There's an English menu with various shark's-fin, bird's-nest, abalone, pigeon, seafood, chicken, duck, pork, beef, and vegetable dishes, most within the HK$40 ($5.19) to HK$60 ($7.79) range.

If you like to dine outdoors in a festive setting, a great place is **Sang Lee,** Chung Hau Road (tel. 9848478) in Silvermine Bay. To reach it, take a right out of the ferry dock and follow the sidewalk next to the water. Sang Lee will be on your left, easily recognizable by its string of white lights. Open all year from 11 a.m. to midnight daily, it specializes in fresh seafood, including barbecued fish, squid fried with spiced salt, fried rice Singapore style, steamed fish, and crab and clams. Prices for most dishes are between HK$15 ($1.95) and HK$30 ($3.90).

At the other end of the island in Tai O, there's the **Tai O Seafood Restaurant,** 15 Wing On St. (tel. 9857094), open from 5 a.m. for all those early-rising fisherfolk until midnight. Serving Cantonese food as well as seafood, it specializes in clam dishes, and there's an English menu to choose from. There are tables outside for dining where you have a view of some fish ponds. A meal here will range from HK$60 ($7.79) to HK$130 ($16.88).

Cheung Chau

If you have only a few hours to spare and don't want to worry about catching buses and finding your way around, Cheung Chau is your best bet. It's a tiny island only a square mile in area, but 50,000 people live here in a thriving fishing village. There are no cars on the island, making it a delightful place for walking around and exploring.

The waterfront where the ferry lands, known as the **Praya,** buzzes with activity as vendors sell fish, lobsters, and vegetables. About 10% of Cheung Chau's people live on junks in the harbor, and one of the things to do here is to take a *kai do,* or water taxi, past the junks to **Sai Wan.** I like this harbor more than Aberdeen, and I find it amazing how many families keep dogs on board their boats. At Sai Wan there's a temple dedicated to Tin Hau, goddess of the sea, from which it's about a 30-minute walk back to the Praya.

As for the village itself, it's threaded through with tiny alleys and with shops offering noodles and rice, teakwood coffins, and haircuts. Through open doors you can see tailoring, basket weaving, soy sauce manufacturing, and jade carving. Junks are built on Cheung Chau after a design hardly changed in centuries, entirely from memory and without the aid of blueprints. If you walk down narrow Tung Wan Road, you'll pass lots of open-fronted shops, finally reaching **Tung Wan Beach,** the most popular beach on the island.

Food and Lodging: If you want to spend a few nights away from the hustle and bustle of Hong Kong to unwind and relax, the **Warwick Hotel** (tel. 9810081) is the best place to do it. It's located on the south end of Tung Wan Beach. Although its 70 rooms are slightly small, they are tastefully decorated in a tropical theme and come with color TV, clock, radio, phone, air conditioning, marble-top counter, and balcony. Although rooms facing the beach are slightly more expensive at HK$520 ($67.53), they're worth it. Those that don't have water views go for HK$460 ($59.77). Prices are 10% to 15% higher on weekends. Facilities at the hotel include a bar/disco, windsurfing boards and paddleboats that rent for HK$25 ($3.25) an hour, and a swimming pool with sunken stools and a bar in the water.

The Warwick is also a good place to come for a meal. Its two restaurants serve Western and Chinese food, and you can sit outside on a veranda with a good view of the beach for either a meal or cocktails. The Western restaurant, open from 7 a.m. to 10:30 p.m., serves spaghetti, curries, chicken, and sandwiches for lunch and such dishes as coconut shrimp, sole, garoupa, and steak for dinner. The Chinese restaurant, open from noon to 3 p.m. and 6 to 10:30 p.m., offers sautéed chicken with soybeans and chili, roasted crisp chicken, sautéed sliced beef in oyster sauce, sautéed shrimp with garlic, and more. Cost of a meal at the Warwick averages about HK$85 ($11.04) at both restaurants.

The **Sea Pearl** (tel. 9818153) is a gaily painted floating restaurant anchored in Cheung Chau's harbor. It specializes in fresh Cantonese seafood, but also serves such dishes as roasted chicken or pigeon, sweet-and-sour pork, or sliced beef with noodles. You can spend as little as HK$30 ($3.90) or as much as HK$110 ($14.29). Very popular with vacationing Chinese, it's open daily from noon to 9 p.m. To reach the restaurant, take the free shuttle service from the public pier (located to the right as you disembark from the ferry from Hong Kong Island). The shuttle boat won't have any English sign on it, but look for the yellow flag with red Chinese characters written on it that it flies on its roof.

Easy to find right on Cheung Chau's waterfront (and located just to the right as you disembark from the Hong Kong Island ferry), **Amego Café**, at 31 Praya St. (tel. 9810710), is open daily from 11:30 a.m. to 11 p.m. It serves easy-to-prepare snacks and Western dishes, including sandwiches, spaghetti, omelets, milk shakes, and daily specials, most priced under HK$16 ($2.08).

Not far away is **King's Café** (tel. 9810878), 25 Praya St., to the left as you disembark from the Hong Kong Island ferry. Like the Amego Café described above, it serves Western-style food and snacks such as spaghetti, curry rice, soups, omelets, salads, ice cream, shakes, and beer. Although the food isn't great, prices are cheap: most dishes average HK$11 ($1.43) to HK$35 ($4.54), and there are some tables and chairs outside where you have a wonderful view of the action on the Praya and on the junks anchored close by. Closed on Wednesday, it's open the rest of the week from noon to midnight.

The local foreigner hangout is **The Garden Café/Pub,** located on the main pedestrian thoroughfare that links the Praya with the beach at 84 Tung Wan Rd. (tel. 9814610). It's a simple café, but the best things about it are its tables outside and the small beer garden across the street. Open from 10 a.m. to midnight, it serves European grub like steak-and-mushroom pie, pork pie, sandwiches, and fish-and-chips. An American breakfast is HK$33 ($4.29).

On the same road at 16 Tung Wan Rd. is the **Bor Kee Restaurant** (tel. 9812328). With its open façade and cafeteria-like appearance, it doesn't look like much, but what it lacks in character is more than made up for by its Cantonese-style seafood. It has a long menu in English, but most prices aren't given; it's best just to ask what's fresh and available. Expect to pay about HK$50 ($6.50) for a meal. It's open every day from 10 a.m. to 10 p.m.

Although it's actually located on nearby Lantau Island, the **Frog and Toad,** Tai Long Village (tel. 9892300), is a restaurant/bar most easily reached via a 20-minute sampan ride from Cheung Chau. Simply tell the sampan driver "Tai Long Wan," which means Big Wave Bay. Cost of the trip will be about HK$50 ($6.49), but be sure to bargain and settle the fee beforehand. You'll find yourself deposited at a pier on a seemingly deserted beach, but if you follow a trail leading inland from the middle of the beach (where you'll also see a sign), you'll soon come to a tiny settlement and the Frog and Toad. Owned by several expatriates, this mellow establishment serves as a day-trip getaway for people in the know, many of whom come here to relax in the rural setting. Open from 11 a.m. until the last customer leaves, it serves a barbecue for HK$60 ($7.79), including ribs, chicken wings, sausage, and salad. If you want fresh seafood, you can order it by calling beforehand—it will then be bought in Cheung Chau. In fact, it might be a good idea to call beforehand anyway, simply to make sure they're open. This place is so far out of the way you might well be the only customer. There's a veranda where you can sit outside on fine days, and when you're ready to leave, simply tell the man behind the bar. He'll call Cheung Chau and have a sampan sent on its way.

Lamma

If you want to do some pleasant hiking, Lamma is the island to visit. The closest of the outlying islands, Lamma is Hong Kong's third-largest island and has a population of only 3,000, with much of its area still undeveloped. There are no cars on the island and a two-hour hiking trail connects Lamma's two main villages, Sok Kwu Wan and Yung Shue Wan.

From Sok Kwu Wan the hiking trail winds around the harbor through lush and verdant valleys and over barren and windswept hills. Large "armchair" graves dot the hillsides, and as you get closer to Yung Shue Wan, the grasses give way to vegetable patches and green quilts of neatly cultivated fields. Watch for the villagers who water their fields by swinging back and forth two watering cans balanced on a pole slung across their shoulders.

There are a number of good beaches on Lamma. **Hung Shing Ye Beach** is the island's most popular, and is located about 20 minutes outside Yung Shue Wan on the hiking path described above. It has changing facilities, showers, and toilets, and lifeguards are on duty during the summer.

You might also want to try out **Mo Tat Wan Beach,** about a 20-minute walk east of Sok Kwu Wan, but there are no lifeguards on duty here. While you're in the area, check out the village of **Mo Tat,** about 400 years old and the oldest settlement on the island. It consists of a handful of crumbling old houses inhabited mainly by old people and sits picturesquely amid banana trees and lush countryside.

Where to Eat: Try to schedule your outing on Lamma so that you can eat in Sok Kwu Wan. A fishing village, Sok Kwu Wan is well known for its seafood restaurants, many of which sit over the water on stilts with views of the harbor. I suggest you just walk along the waterfront and choose one that strikes your fancy, but if you want a specific recommendation, try **Shum Kee Restaurant,** 26 1st St. (tel. 9828241). Facing the sea and partly built on stilts, it offers outside dining in a covered area with a view of the harbor. It's open from 10 a.m. until late in the evening (usually about 11 p.m.) and serves Cantonese-style seafood. An English menu is available and specialties include spicy shrimp and chili crab dishes. The average cost of a meal is about HK$85 ($11.04).

Another waterfront restaurant you might try is **Peach Garden Sea Food Restaurant,** 11 Sok Kwu Wan (tel. 9828581). Open from 10 a.m. to 10 p.m., it also has outside dining with a view of the water and serves seafood Cantonese style. Try its baked, buttered lobster or spicy squid. A meal here costs about HK$80 ($10.39).

If you end up in Yung Shue Wan and decide to eat there instead, a restaurant with a variety of seafood and Cantonese dishes is **Man Fung Restaurant,** 5 Yung Shue Wan St. (tel. 9820719). This restaurant also has outdoor seating where you have a view of the sea, and there's an English menu available with such specialties as pigeon, locally caught seafood, and dim sum. It's open from 6 a.m. for dim sum to 10 p.m. Meals run about HK$60 ($7.79).

---

10. Macau

Presently under Portuguese rule but reverting to Chinese authority in 1999, Macau is located on the southeastern coast of China and has a total land area of only six square miles. Although Portuguese is the official language, 98% of its 400,000 residents are Cantonese, which means that you hardly ever hear the official language.

Portugal first landed its ships in Macau in 1513, acquiring it from the Chinese in 1557. It became Portugal's most important trading center in Asia and was once the Orient's greatest port. As Hong Kong came onto the scene, however, Macau lost its importance and slowly sank into obscurity. Today its main attractions are its casinos, and Hong Kong residents and foreigners alike flock here to try their luck at the gambling tables.

With its mixture of Portuguese and Chinese influences, Macau has a charm all its own and boasts a number of churches, temples, and government buildings that reflect Portugal's 400 years of rule. The most famous structure is the ruin of St. Paul's, which was designed by an Italian Jesuit and built with the help of Japanese Christians who had fled persecution in Nagasaki in the 1600s. In 1835 during a typhoon the church caught fire and burned to the ground, leaving its now-famous façade.

Before leaving for Macau, visit the **Macau Tourist Information Bureau** at the Macau Terminal, 305 Shun Tak Centre Shopping Mall, 200 Connaught Rd., Central District (tel. 5408180). Open from 9 a.m. to 1 p.m. and from 2 to 5 p.m. Monday through Friday and from 9 a.m. to 1 p.m. on Saturday, the bureau can supply you with a map and brochures outlining Macau's historical and architectural attractions.

Located only 40 miles from Hong Kong, Macau is easily accessible by jetfoil, jetcat, hydrofoil, or ferry, all of which leave from the Macau Ferry Terminal on Hong Kong Island. On the Kowloon side there's the new China Hong Kong Terminal, where boats depart for Macau as well as China. It's located on Canton Road, next to the Royal Pacific Hotel.

No visas are required for Americans, Canadians, Australians, or the British, but you will have to pay a HK$17 ($2.21) departure tax upon leaving Hong Kong. Although the pataca is Macau's official currency, you can use your Hong Kong dollars everywhere in Macau, even in buses and for taxis. Hotels will add a 10% service charge and 5% government tax to room prices, while restaurants will add a 10% service charge to your bill.

WHERE TO STAY

The **Macau Oriental,** Avenida da Amizade (tel. 567888), is a Mandarin International Hotel and one of Macau's most expensive hotels, but it's still much cheaper here than in Hong Kong. Rooms begin at HK$670 ($87), and those facing the sea go for HK$910 ($118). Opened in 1984, the Oriental is elegantly decorated throughout with imports from Portugal, including blue and white tiles, chandeliers, tapestries, and artwork. Recreation facilities include an outdoor swimming pool, two tennis courts, two air-conditioned squash courts, and a health center with sauna and massage. There's also a small casino in the hotel.

Opened in 1983, the **Hyatt Regency Macau** on Taipa Island (tel. 27000) has 356 rooms that were shipped in units from the United States and assembled in Macau like a jigsaw puzzle. Rooms are bright with all the usual amenities, and begin at HK$750 ($97), HK$860 ($112) for rooms with ocean views. The Hyatt has the island's most popular disco, the Green Parrot, and a fantastic sports and recreational center that includes an outdoor swimming pool (heated in winter), jogging track, tennis and squash courts, gym, spa with Jacuzzi and sauna, and a small lake.

The **Pousada de São Tiago,** Avenida da República (tel. 78111), is a delightful small hotel built around the ruins of the Portuguese Fortress da Barra, which dates from 1629. The entrance to the hotel is quite dramatic—a flight of stairs leads through a cave-like tunnel with a small stream running alongside. There are only 23 guest rooms in the hotel, and all bedroom furniture is imported from Portugal, including the carved-wood beds. Rooms begin at HK$970 ($126); those with balconies cost HK$1,100 ($143). With a staff of more than 100, service here is excellent. There's an outdoor pool.

One of Macau's new medium-range hotels is the **Hotel Guia,** Estrada do Engenheiro (tel. 513888), which opened in 1989. It's located on a hill near the Guia Lighthouse. Although it's a bit far from the action, there's a free shuttle bus that makes runs about every half hour to and from the boat pier and the Lisboa Hotel. In any case, it's a quiet and peaceful part of town; and the hotel, with only 89 rooms, is small and personable. Its one restaurant serves Cantonese food, including dim sum and fresh seafood. Rooms are small but adequate, and the higher-priced ones have views of the water. Rates are the same for single or double occupancy and start at HK$380 ($49) for a standard, rising to HK$550 ($71) for those with a small balcony and a view of the sea.

If you're coming to Macau to gamble, you can't get much closer to the action than at the **Hotel Lisboa,** Avenida da Amizade (tel. 77666). Its large casino, the most popular in town, is open 24 hours a day. Built in 1969, the hotel is a bit on the garish side and seems old-fashioned by today's standards. Rooms are large but the furniture is a bit old, and bathrooms are overdone in pink. Still, this is the place to be if you want to be in the thick of it. Singles begin at HK$230 ($30) and twins start at HK$370 ($48).

A hostelry of a bygone era, the **Bela Vista,** 8 Rua do Comendador Kou Ho Neng (tel. 573821), built in 1892, is an old, rambling eccentric-looking hotel standing on a hill overlooking the water. Although its carpets are worn, its walls are cracking, and its paint is blistering, the Bela Vista is rather like a museum piece and is the place to stay if you're at all nostalgic. There are only 23 rooms in this two-story hotel: singles are priced at HK$250 ($32) and doubles or twins start at HK$310 ($40). The best room in the hotel, and the one I'd recommend, is Room 39, a corner room with a dramatically high ceiling and its own private veranda overlooking the water. It costs HK$410 ($53).

WHERE TO EAT

Macau's best dining is in the hotels, and its cuisine shows Portuguese, African, and Indian influences. Specialties include caldeirada (seafood stew), spicy giant shrimp, grilled Macau sole, and feijoada (pork with red beans). Portuguese wine is inexpensive and a great bargain here.

Afonso's, in the Hyatt Regency, specializes in Portuguese food, with an emphasis on fresh seafood. In addition to the daily specials and dessert buffet, Afonso's also serves such authentic dishes as plain grilled fresh tuna steak with seasonal vegetables and marinated pork with clams, coriander, and paprika. Lunch is served from noon to 3 p.m. and dinner from 7 to 11 p.m., and there is live music every evening to set the mood. A meal here will average about HK$80 ($10.39) to HK$200 ($25.97) depending on what you order and what you drink.

Decorated in hot pink is **Flamingo,** located also in the Hyatt Regency Macau on Taipa Island. It has a great Mediterranean-like ambience, with ceiling fans, a terrace overlooking a pond, and swaying palms. It specializes in Macanese cuisine, along with Portuguese favorites. For an appetizer you might try the Portuguese sausage flambé, followed by spicy king shrimp with chili sauce or the crab curry. And of course there's the ever-popular African chicken. Flamingo is open from noon to 3 p.m. and from 7 to 11 p.m., with live entertainment accompanying diners in the evening.

The **Grill Fortaleza,** in the Pousada de São Tiago, is a pleasant place to come for lunch or dinner because it's small and intimate, with seating for only 40 persons. A half-oval room with heavy red curtains drawn back to reveal a full view of the ocean, the Grill Fortaleza serves both Portuguese and continental cuisine, with most dishes ranging from HK$55 ($7.15) to HK$100 ($13). The menu includes shredded cod, spicy king shrimp, duck terrine with cherry sauce, spicy African chicken, Macau sole, and grilled U.S. sirloin. Hours here are noon to 3 p.m. and 7 to 11 p.m. daily.

A good place to dine in the Macau Oriental is in **The Grill,** decorated in old-world colonial elegance and affording a view of the water. A small restaurant with only 60 seats and very attentive waiters, it serves French and international cuisine. Steak and seafood are the prime dishes served. You might want to start your meal with sliced beef carpaccio with tomatoes, mozzarella cheese, and olive oil dressing, or how about homemade noodles with fresh goose liver, wild mushrooms, and parmesan cheese? The mousseline of lobster with sweetbread croutons is particularly delightful, and you'd be foolish to pass up the hot soufflé (your choice of ginger, passion fruit, or almond). You could easily spend HK$350 ($45.45) here excluding wine, but you can eat more cheaply if you order the Executive Luncheon, which changes monthly and starts at HK$108 ($14.02) for two courses. Closed on Monday, it's open the rest of the week from 12:30 to 3 p.m. and from 6:30 to 11 p.m.

A good place for lunch when the weather is balmy is the **Bela Vista,** which offers outside dining on its veranda and terrace with sweeping views of the ocean, tugboats, and barges. A great place to while away the afternoon, it offers chicken, seafood, and curry dishes. Most dishes range from about HK$55 ($7.14) to HK$80 ($10.39). It's open daily from noon to 3 p.m. and from 6 to 10:30 p.m.

If you don't feel like dining out in a hotel, try **Henri's Galley Maxim's,** 4 Avenida da República (tel. 76207). Open daily from 11 a.m. to 11 p.m., it's owned by Henri Wong, who used to be a chief steward on a galley at sea. A jovial and friendly man who speaks English well, he has decorated his café-like restaurant with things reminiscent of a galley. The staff is attentive and there are a few seats outside under umbrellas. Specialties of the house include fried Macau sole, African chicken, Portuguese baked chicken, fresh crab curry, and stuffed crabmeat in its shell. The average meal will cost about HK$100 ($12.99) per person.

JAPANESE VOCABULARY

Needless to say, it takes years to become fluent in Japanese, particularly in written Japanese with its thousands of *kanji*, or Chinese characters, and many *hiragana* and *katakana* characters. Knowing just a few words of Japanese, however, is not only useful but will also delight the Japanese you meet during your trip.

In pronouncing the following vocabulary, keep in mind that there's very little stress on individual syllables (pronunciation of Japanese is often compared to Italian). Here is an approximation of some of the sounds of Japanese:

a,	as in f*a*ther
e	as in p*e*n
i	as in s*ee*
o	as in *o*h
oo	long o as in *ooo*h
u	as in b*oo*k
g	as in *g*ift at the beginning of words; like *ng* in si*ng* in the middle or at the end of words

Vowel sounds are always short unless they are pronounced double, in which case you hold the vowel a bit longer. Similarly, double consonants are given more emphasis than only one consonant by itself. *Okashi,* for example, means "a sweet," whereas *okashii* means "strange." As you can see, even slight mispronunciation of a word can result in confusion or hilarity. Incidentally, jokes in Japanese are nearly always plays on words.

GENERAL WORDS AND PHRASES

Good morning	**Ohayo gozaimasu**
Good afternoon	**Kon-nichi-wa**
Good evening	**Kon-ban-wa**
Good night	**Oyasumi-nasai**
Hello	**Haro (or Kon-nichi-wa)**
Good-bye	**Sayonara (or bye-bye!)**
Excuse me, I'm sorry	**Sumimasen**
Thank you	**Domo arigatoo**
You're welcome	**Doo-itashi-mashite**
Please (go ahead)	**Doozo**
Yes	**Hai**
No	**I-ie**
Foreigner	**Gaijin**
Japanese person	**Nihonjin**
Japanese language	**Nihongo**
American person	**Amerikajin**

English language	**Eigo**
Do you understand?	**Wakarimasu ka?**
I understand	**Wakarimasu**
I don't understand	**Wakarimasen**
Just a minute, please	**Chotto matte kudasai**
How much?	**Ikura desu ka?**
Where?	**Doko desu ka?**
When?	**Itsu desu ka?**
Expensive	**Takai**
Cheap	**Yasui**
I like it	**Suki desu (pronounced "ski")**

TRAVELING

Train station	**Eki**
Airport	**Kuukoo**
Subway	**Chika-tetsu**
Bus	**Bus-u**
Taxi	**Takushi**
Airplane	**Hikooki**
Ferry	**Ferri**
Train	**Densha**
Bullet train	**Shinkansen**
Limited express train	**Tokkyu**
Ordinary express train	**Kyuko**
Local train	**Futsu**
Ticket	**Kippu**
Exit	**Deguchi**
Entrance	**Iriguchi**
North	**Kita**
South	**Minami**
East	**Higashi**
West	**Nishi**
Left	**Hidari**
Right	**Migi**
Straight ahead	**Massugu (or zutto)**
Far	**Toi**
Near	**Chikai**
Can I walk there?	**Aruite ikemasu ka?**
Street	**Dori (or michi)**
Tourist information office	**Kanko annaijo**
Map	**Chizu**
Police box	**Koban**
Post office	**Yubin-kyoku**
Stamp	**Kitte**
Bank	**Ginko**
Hospital	**Byooin**
Toilet	**Toire**
	Ben joh
	Goh fu joh
	O teh ahmai
Spa	**Onsen**
Bath	**Ofuro**
Public bath	**Sento**

FOOD AND LODGING

Restaurant	**Resutoran**
I'd like to make a reservation	**Yoyaku onegai shimasu**
For one person	**Hitori**
For two people	**Futari**
Menu	**Menyu**
Tea	**Ocha**
Coffee	**Koohi**
Water	**Mizu**
Lunch or daily special	**Teishoku**
Delicious	**Oishii**
Thank you for the meal	**Gochisoo-sama deshita**
Hotel	**Hoteru**
Japanese-style inn	**Ryokan**
Youth hostel	**Yusu hosuteru**
Cotton kimono	**Yukata**
Room	**Heya**
Does that include meals?	**Shokuji wa tsuite imasu ka?**
Key	**Kagi**
Balcony	**Baranda**

TIME

Now	**Ima**
Later	**Ato de**
Today	**Kyoo**
Tomorrow	**Ashita**
Day after tomorrow	**Asatte**
Yesterday	**Kinoo**
Which day?	**Nan-nichi desu ka?**
Daytime	**Hiruma**
Morning	**Asa**
Night	**Yoru**
Afternoon	**Gogo**
Sunday	**Nichiyoobi**
Monday	**Getsuyoobi**
Tuesday	**Kayoobi**
Wednesday	**Suiyoobi**
Thursday	**Mokuyoobi**
Friday	**Kinyoobi**
Saturday	**Doyoobi**
January	**Ichi-gatsu**
February	**Ni-gatsu**
March	**San-gatsu**
April	**Shi-gatsu**
May	**Go-gatsu**
June	**Roku-gatsu**
July	**Shichi-gatsu**
August	**Hachi-gatsu**
September	**Kyuu-gatsu**
October	**Juu-gatsu**
November	**Juuichi-gatsu**
December	**Juuni-gatsu**

NUMBERS

1	Ichi
2	Ni
3	San
4	Shi
5	Go
6	Roku
7	Shichi (or nana)
8	Hachi
9	Kyuu
10	Juu
11	Juuichi
12	Juuni
20	Nijuu
30	Sanjuu
40	Shijuu (or yonjuu)
50	Gojuu
60	Rokujuu
70	Nanajuu
80	Hachijuu
90	Kyuuju
100	Hyaku
1,000	Sen

JAPANESE SYMBOL LISTINGS

In Japan, many hotels, restaurants, and other establishments do not have signs showing their names in English letters. This appendix lists the Japanese symbols for all such places appearing in this guide.

Each establishment name in Japanese symbols is numbered, and the same number appears in an oval in the text following the boldfaced establishment name. For example, in the text Osaka's **Hotel Hokke Club** ⑯₄ is number 164 in this list.

TOKYO

1. Seifuso
   聖富荘

2. Shimizu Bekkan
   しみず別館

3. National YWCA of Japan
   日本 YWCA

4. Tokyo YWCA Sadowara
   Hostel
   東京 YWCA 砂土原ホステル

5. Keiunso Ryokan
   景雲荘

6. Takamura
   篁

7. Kakiden
   柿伝

8. Tamura
   田村

9. Kinsen
   金扇

10. Hayashi
    はやし

11. Shirakawago
    白川郷

12. Inakaya
    田舎家

13. Fukuzushi
    福鮨

14. Sushiko
    寿司幸

15. Zakuro
    ざくろ

16. Sushi Sei
    寿司清

17. Edogin
    江戸銀

18. Tentake
    天竹

19. Hassan
    八山

20. Shabu Zen
    しゃぶ禅

21. Chinya
    ちんや

22. Komagata Dojo
    駒形どじょう

23. Mugitoro Shiori
    むぎとろ栞り

24.	Gonin Byakusho 五人百姓		43.	Keyaki 欅
25.	Hayashi はやし		44.	Donto どんと
26.	Ohmatsuya 大松屋		45.	Yabu-Soba やぶそば
27.	Tsunahachi つな八		46.	Tanuki Soba 狸穴そば
28.	Suehiro スエヒロ		47.	Namiki 並木薮
29.	Kushi Colza 串コルザ		48.	Ichioku 一億
30.	Ganchan がんちゃん		49.	Tenmi 天味
31.	Seiyo Hiroba せいよう広場		50.	Negishi ねぎし
32.	Tatsumiya 東南屋		51.	Kuremutsu 暮六つ
33.	Irohanihoheto いろはにほへと		52.	Ichimon 一文
34.	Uogashi 魚がし		53.	Club Maiko クラブ舞妓
35.	Sushi Dai 寿司大		54.	Lupin ルパン
36.	Genrokusushi 元禄寿司		55.	Yagura Chaya 櫓茶屋
37.	Torigin 鳥ぎん		56.	Volga ボルガ
38.	Atariya 当りや			
39.	Torijoh 鳥上		**KAMAKURA**	
40.	Kushinobo 串の坊		57.	Raitei 檑亭
41.	Tonki とんき		58.	Monzen 門前
42.	Izu'ei 伊豆栄		59.	Miyokawa 御代川
			60.	Kayagi-ya 茅木屋

61. Nakamura-an
なかむら庵
62. Kamakura Hotel
鎌倉ホテル

YOKOHAMA

63. Kaseiro
華正楼
64. Janomeya
じゃのめや

HAKONE

65. Kappa Tengoku
かっぱ天国
66. Ichinoyu
一の湯
67. Hakone Prince Hotel
箱根プリンスホテル
68. Ryuguden
龍宮殿
69. Sugiyoshi Ryokan
杉よし旅館

ATAMI

70. Kiunkaku
起雲閣
71. Hotel New Akao
ホテルニューアカオ

SHIMODA

72. Haji
はじ

DOGASHIMA

73. Ginsuiso
銀水荘
74. Kaikomaru
海晃丸

KYOTO

75. Kinmata
近又
76. Ryokan Rikiya
力弥
77. Takigawa
たき川
78. Yuhara
ゆはら
79. Rokuharaya Inn
六波羅屋
80. Myorenji Temple
妙蓮寺
81. Minoko
美濃幸
82. Nakamuraro
中村楼
83. Awata Sanso
粟田山荘
84. Hyotei
瓢亭
85. Okutan
奥丹
86. Koan
高庵
87. Goemonjaya
五衛ェ門茶屋
88. Mikaku
みかく
89. Beniya
紅屋
90. Isobe
いそべ
91. Chorakukan
長楽館
92. Izumoya
いづもや

93. Tagoto
田ごと

94. Ganko Sushi
がんこ寿司

95. Kuru Kuru Zushi
くるくるずし

96. Gontaro
権太呂

97. Misogi-gawa
禊川

98. Sancho
サンチョ

99. Izusen
泉仙

100. Kodaiji Rakusho Tea Room
洛匠

101. Tanakaya
田中弥

102. Miyawaki Baisen-an
宮脇売扇庵

103. Suishin Honten
酔心本店

104. Zu Zu
厨厨

105. Taku Taku
磔磔

106. Irohanihoheto
いろはにほへと

107. Kikusui
菊水

NARA

108. Kikusuiro
菊水楼

109. Furuichi
古市

110. Harishin
はり新

TAKAYAMA

111. Ryokan Hishuya
飛州屋

112. Hida Gasshoen
飛驒合掌苑

113. Kinkikan
金亀館

114. Seiryu
清龍

115. Asunaro
あすなろ

116. Hachibei
八兵衛

117. Kakusho
角正

118. Suzuya
寿々屋

119. Bandai Kado Mise
萬代角店

120. Kofune
小舟

121. Jizake-ya
地酒屋

SHIRAKAWA-GO

122. Seikatsu Shiryokan
生活資料館

123. Myozenji
明善寺

124. Doburoku Matsuri no Yakata
どぶろく祭りの館

125. Magoemon
孫右ェ門

126. Kandaya
かんだ屋

127. Yosobe
よそべえ

128. Otaya
大田屋

129. Juemon
十右ェ門

130. Irori
いろり

131. Kitanosho
基太の庄

MATSUMOTO

132. Matsumoto Folkcraft
Museum (Mingei-kan)
松本民芸館

133. Hotel Ikyu
一休

134. Nishiya Ryokan
西屋旅館

135. Kajika
かじか

136. Shikimi
しき美

MAGOME AND TSUMAGO

137. Tsumago
妻籠

138. Magome
馬籠

NAGOYA

139. Shoufukuro
招福楼

140. Yamamoto-ya Honten
山本屋本店

141. Yaegaki Tempura House
八重垣

142. Kisoji
木曽路

143. Kishimentei
きしめん亭

ISE-SHIMA NATIONAL PARK

144. Ishiyama-So
石山荘

145. Kimpokan
錦浦館

146. Yamadakan
山田館

147. Hoshidekan
星出館

148. Ise City Hotel
伊勢シティホテル

149. Youth Hostel Taikoji
ユースホステル 太江寺

150. Ise-Shima Youth Hostel
伊勢志摩ユースホステル

KANAZAWA

151. Miyabo
みやぼ

152. Kanazawa Castle Inn
キャッスルイン金沢

153. Yogetsu
陽月

154. Kanazawa Youth Hostel
金沢ユースホステル

155. Matsui Youth Hostel
松井ユースホステル

156. Miyoshian
三芳庵

157. Tozan
東山

158. Takeda
竹田

159. Zeniya
銭屋

160. Hamacho
浜長

226. Hiroshima Youth Hostel
広島ユースホステル

227. Amagi
あまぎ

228. Kanawa
かなわ

229. Suishin
酔心

230. Okonomi-Mura
お好み村

MIYAJIMA

231. Iwaso Ryokan
岩惣旅館

232. Momiji
もみじ

233. Jyukeiso
聚景荘

234. Miyajima Lodge
宮島ロッジ

235. Fujitaya
ふじたや

TAKAMATSU

236. Kompira O-Shibai
金毘羅大芝居

237. Takamatsu Plaza Hotel
高松プラザホテル

238. Tokiwa Honkan
常磐本館

239. Takamatsu Yuai-Sanso
Youth Hostel
高松友愛荘ホステル

240. Kanaizumi
かな泉

241. Tenkatsu
天勝

242. Hansuke
半助

243. Maruichi
まるいち

MATSUYAMA

244. Mingei Iyo Kasuri
Kaikan
民芸伊予かすり会館

245. Umeno Seito-jo
梅野精陶所

246. Tobe-yaki Kanko Center
砥部焼観光センター

247. Ehime no Bussan
愛媛の物産

248. Uchikoza
内子座

249. Funaya
ふなや

250. Kasugaen
春日園

251. Taihei Business Hotel
ビジネスホテル泰平

252. Matsuyama Shinsen-en
Youth Hostel
松山神泉園ユースホステル

253. Hyakumi
佰味

254. Shinhamasaku
新浜作

FUKUOKA

255. Chisan Hotel Hakata
チサンホテル博多

256. Mitsui Urban Hotel
三井アーバンホテル

257. Dazaifu Youth Hostel
太宰府ユースホステル

258. Gyosai
魚菜

BEPPU

259. Kannawaen
神和苑

260. Tenjuso
天寿荘

261. Sakaeya
サカエ屋

262. Green Business Hotel
グリーン ビジネス ホテル

263. Chikuden
ちくでん

264. Amamijaya
甘味茶屋

265. Jin
仁

MOUNT ASO

266. Ryokan Mimura
旅館みむら

267. Aso Youth Hostel
阿蘇ユースホステル

268. Minami Aso Kokumin
Kyuka Mura
南阿蘇国民休暇村

269. Dengaku no Sato
田楽の里

270. Minami Aso Kokumin
Shukusha
南阿蘇国民宿舎

KUMAMOTO

271. Kumamoto Traditional
Crafts Center
熊本県伝統工芸館

272. Kumamoto-ken
Bussankan
熊本県物産館

273. Kumamoto Station Hotel
熊本ステーションホテル

274. Tsukasa Besso
司別荘

275. Suizenji Youth Hostel
水前寺ユースホステル

276. Kumamoto Shiritsu
Youth Hostel
熊本市立ユースホステル

277. Senri
泉里

278. Kimura-so
きむら荘

279. Aoyagi
青柳

280. Goemon
五右衛門

NAGASAKI

281. Hotel Station Ajisai
ホテル ステーション あじさい

282. Sakamoto-ya
坂本屋

283. Nishikyushu Daiichi
Hotel
西九州第一ホテル

284. Capsule Inn Nagasaki
カプセル イン 長崎

285. Terada
てらだ

286. Sansui-so
山水荘

287. Nagasaki Kenritsu Youth
Hostel
長崎県立ユースホステル

288. Nagasaki Oranda-Zaka
Youth Hostel
長崎オランダ坂ユースホステル

289. Kagetsu
花月

323. Matsushima Youth
Hostel
松島ユースホステル

324. Okunohosomichi
奥の細道

325. Donjiki
どんじき茶屋

HAKODATE

326. Minshuku Fukuiso
民宿ふく井荘

SAPPORO

327. Zenniku Hotel
全日空ホテル

328. Nakamuraya Ryokan
中村屋旅館

329. Hotel New Frontier
ホテル ニューフロンティア

330. Hyosetsu-no-Mon
氷雪の門

331. Irohanihoheto
いろはにほへと

332. Satohoro
さとほろ

**SHIKOTSU-TOYA
NATIONAL PARK**

333. Manseikaku
万世閣

334. Takatsu Ryokan
多佳津旅館

335. Hotel New Toyako
ホテルニュー洞爺湖

336. Showa-Shinzan Youth
Hostel
昭和新山ユースホステル

337. Oshima
大島

338. Kikusui
菊水

339. Noboribetsu-so
のぼりべつ荘

340. Kannonji
観音寺

341. Akashiya Youth Hostel
あかしやユースホステル

342. Youth Hostel Ryokan
Kanefuku
ユースホステル旅館金福

**DAISETSUZAN NATIONAL
PARK**

343. Grand Hotel
グランドホテル

344. Pension Yukara
ペンション ユーカラ

345. Tsuchiya
つちや

346. Onozuka
おのづか

347. Kitagawa
北川

348. Sounkyo Youth Hostel
層雲峡ユースホステル

349. Ginsenkaku Youth Hostel
銀泉閣ユースホステル

AKAN NATIONAL PARK

350. Hotel Ichikawa
ホテル市川

351. Akan Grand Hotel
阿寒グランドホテル

352. Minshuku Yamaguchi
民宿山口

353. Minshuku Ginrei
民宿ぎんれい

354. Angel Youth Hostel
エンジェル ユースホステル

INDEX

JAPAN

HONG KONG

N O W !
ARTHUR FROMMER LAUNCHES HIS SECOND TRAVEL REVOLUTION
with

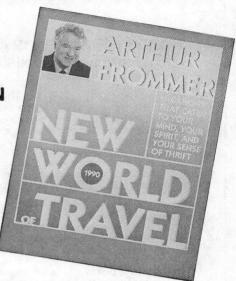

The New World of Travel

The hottest news and latest trends in travel today—heretofore the closely guarded secrets of the travel trade—are revealed in this new sourcebook by the dean of American travel. Here, collected in one book that is updated every year, are the most exciting, challenging, and money-saving ideas in travel today.

You'll find out about hundreds of alternative new modes of travel—and the many organizations that sponsor them—that will lead you to vacations that cater to your mind, your spirit, and your sense of thrift.

Learn how to fly for free as an air courier; travel for free as a tour escort; live for free on a hospitality exchange; add earnings as a part-time travel agent; pay less for air tickets, cruises, and hotels; enhance your life through cooperative camping, political tours, and adventure trips; change your life at utopian communities, low-cost spas, and yoga retreats; pursue low-cost studies and language training; travel comfortably while single or over 60; sail on passenger freighters; and vacation in the cheapest places on earth.

And in every yearly edition, Arthur Frommer spotlights the 10 GREATEST TRAVEL VALUES for the coming year. 448 pages, large-format with many, many illustrations. All for $16.95!

ORDER NOW
TURN TO THE LAST PAGE OF THIS BOOK FOR ORDER FORM.

NOW, SAVE MONEY ON ALL YOUR TRAVELS!
Join Frommer's™ Dollarwise® Travel Club

Saving money while traveling is never a simple matter, which is why the **Dollarwise Travel Club** was formed 31 years ago. Developed in response to requests from Frommer Travel Guide readers, the Club provides cost-cutting travel strategies, up-to-date travel information, and a sense of community for value-conscious travelers from all over the world.

In keeping with the money-saving concept, the annual membership fee is low —$18 (U.S. residents) or $20 (residents of Canada, Mexico, and other countries)— and is immediately exceeded by the value of your benefits, which include:

1. Any TWO books listed on the following pages.
2. Plus any ONE Frommer City Guide.
3. A subscription to our quarterly newspaper, *The Dollarwise Traveler*.
4. A membership card that entitles you to purchase through the Club all Frommer publications for 33% to 50% off their retail price.

The eight-page *Dollarwise Traveler* tells you about the latest developments in good-value travel worldwide and includes the following columns: **Hospitality Exchange** (for those offering and seeking hospitality in cities all over the world); **Share-a-Trip** (for those looking for travel companions to share costs); and **Readers Ask . . . Readers Reply** (for those with travel questions that other members can answer).

Aside from the Frommer Guides, the Serious Shopper Guides, and the Gault Millau Guides, you can also choose from our Special Editions. These include such titles as **California with Kids** (a compendium of the best of California's accommodations, restaurants, and sightseeing attractions appropriate for those traveling with toddlers through teens); **Candy Apple: New York with Kids** (a spirited guide to the Big Apple by a savvy New York grandmother that's perfect for both visitors and residents); **Caribbean Hideaways** (the 100 most romantic places to stay in the Islands, all rated on ambience, food, sport opportunities, and price); **Honeymoon Destinations** (a guide to planning and choosing just the right destination from hundreds of possibilities in the U.S., Mexico, and the Caribbean); **Marilyn Wood's Wonderful Weekends** (a selection of the best mini-vacations within a 200-mile radius of New York City, including descriptions of country inns and other accommodations, restaurants, picnic spots, sights, and activities); and **Paris Rendez-Vous** (a delightful guide to the best places to meet in Paris whether for power breakfasts or dancing till dawn).

To join this Club, simply send the appropriate membership fee with your name and address to: Frommer's Dollarwise Travel Club, 15 Columbus Circle, New York, NY 10023. Remember to specify which single city guide and which two other guides you wish to receive in your initial package of member's benefits. Or tear out the next page, check off your choices, and send the page to us with your membership fee.

FROMMER BOOKS
PRENTICE HALL TRAVEL
15 COLUMBUS CIRCLE
NEW YORK, NY 10023
212-373-8125

Date_____

Friends:
Please send me the books checked below:

FROMMER™ GUIDES

(Guides to sightseeing and tourist accommodations and facilities from budget to deluxe, with emphasis on the medium-priced.)

☐ Alaska	$14.95	☐ Germany	$14.95
☐ Australia	$14.95	☐ Italy	$14.95
☐ Austria & Hungary	$14.95	☐ Japan & Hong Kong	$14.95
☐ Belgium, Holland & Luxembourg	$14.95	☐ Mid-Atlantic States	$14.95
☐ Bermuda & The Bahamas	$14.95	☐ New England	$14.95
☐ Brazil	$14.95	☐ New York State	$14.95
☐ Canada	$14.95	☐ Northwest	$14.95
☐ Caribbean	$14.95	☐ Portugal, Madeira & the Azores	$14.95
☐ Cruises (incl. Alaska, Carib, Mex, Hawaii, Panama, Canada & US)	$14.95	☐ Skiing Europe	$14.95
☐ California & Las Vegas	$14.95	☐ South Pacific	$14.95
☐ Egypt	$14.95	☐ Southeast Asia	$14.95
☐ England & Scotland	$14.95	☐ Southern Atlantic States	$14.95
☐ Florida	$14.95	☐ Southwest	$14.95
☐ France	$14.95	☐ Switzerland & Liechtenstein	$14.95
		☐ USA	$15.95

FROMMER $-A-DAY® GUIDES

(In-depth guides to sightseeing and low-cost tourist accommodations and facilities.)

☐ Europe on $40 a Day	$15.95	☐ New York on $60 a Day	$13.95
☐ Australia on $30 a Day	$12.95	☐ New Zealand on $45 a Day	$13.95
☐ Eastern Europe on $25 a Day	$13.95	☐ Scandinavia on $60 a Day	$13.95
☐ England on $50 a Day	$13.95	☐ Scotland & Wales on $40 a Day	$13.95
☐ Greece on $35 a Day	$13.95	☐ South America on $35 a Day	$13.95
☐ Hawaii on $60 a Day	$13.95	☐ Spain & Morocco on $40 a Day	$13.95
☐ India on $25 a Day	$12.95	☐ Turkey on $30 a Day	$13.95
☐ Ireland on $35 a Day	$13.95	☐ Washington, D.C. & Historic Va. on $40 a Day	$13.95
☐ Israel on $40 a Day	$13.95		
☐ Mexico on $35 a Day	$13.95		

FROMMER TOURING GUIDES

(Color illustrated guides that include walking tours, cultural and historic sites, and other vital travel information.)

☐ Australia	$9.95	☐ Paris	$8.95
☐ Egypt	$8.95	☐ Scotland	$9.95
☐ Florence	$8.95	☐ Thailand	$9.95
☐ London	$8.95	☐ Venice	$8.95

TURN PAGE FOR ADDITONAL BOOKS AND ORDER FORM.

FROMMER CITY GUIDES

(Pocket-size guides to sightseeing and tourist accommodations and facilities in all price ranges.)

☐ Amsterdam/Holland	$7.95	☐ Minneapolis/St. Paul	$7.95
☐ Athens	$7.95	☐ Montréal/Québec City	$7.95
☐ Atlantic City/Cape May	$7.95	☐ New Orleans	$7.95
☐ Barcelona*	$7.95	☐ New York	$7.95
☐ Belgium	$7.95	☐ Orlando/Disney World/EPCOT	$7.95
☐ Boston	$7.95	☐ Paris	$7.95
☐ Cancún/Cozumel/Yucatán	$7.95	☐ Philadelphia	$7.95
☐ Chicago	$7.95	☐ Rio	$7.95
☐ Denver/Boulder*	$7.95	☐ Rome	$7.95
☐ Dublin/Ireland	$7.95	☐ San Francisco	$7.95
☐ Hawaii	$7.95	☐ Santa Fe/Taos/Albuquerque	$7.95
☐ Hong Kong*	$7.95	☐ Seattle/Portland*	$7.95
☐ Las Vegas	$7.95	☐ Sydney	$7.95
☐ Lisbon/Madrid/Costa del Sol	$7.95	☐ Tokyo*	$7.95
☐ London	$7.95	☐ Vancouver/Victoria*	$7.95
☐ Los Angeles	$7.95	☐ Washington, D.C.	$7.95
☐ Mexico City/Acapulco	$7.95	*Available June, 1990	

SPECIAL EDITIONS

☐ A Shopper's Guide to the Caribbean	$12.95	☐ Manhattan's Outdoor Sculpture	$15.95
☐ Beat the High Cost of Travel	$6.95	☐ Motorist's Phrase Book (Fr/Ger/Sp)	$4.95
☐ Bed & Breakfast—N. America	$11.95	☐ Paris Rendez-Vous	$10.95
☐ California with Kids	$14.95	☐ Swap and Go (Home Exchanging)	$10.95
☐ Caribbean Hideaways	$14.95	☐ The Candy Apple (NY with Kids)	$12.95
☐ Honeymoon Destinations (US, Mex & Carib)	$12.95	☐ Travel Diary and Record Book	$5.95

☐ Where to Stay USA (Lodging from $3 to $30 a night) $10.95
☐ Marilyn Wood's Wonderful Weekends (Conn, Del, Mass, NH, NJ, NY, Pa, RI, VT) $11.95
☐ The New World of Travel (Annual sourcebook by Arthur Frommer for savvy travelers) $16.95

SERIOUS SHOPPER'S GUIDES

(Illustrated guides listing hundreds of stores, conveniently organized alphabetically by category.)

☐ Italy	$15.95	☐ Los Angeles	$14.95
☐ London	$15.95	☐ Paris	$15.95

GAULT MILLAU

(The only guides that distinguish the truly superlative from the merely overrated.)

☐ The Best of Chicago	$15.95	☐ The Best of Los Angeles	$14.95
☐ The Best of France	$16.95	☐ The Best of New England	$15.95
☐ The Best of Hong Kong	$16.95	☐ The Best of New York	$14.95
☐ The Best of Italy	$16.95	☐ The Best of Paris	$16.95
☐ The Best of London	$16.95	☐ The Best of San Francisco	$14.95

☐ The Best of Washington, D.C. $14.95

ORDER NOW!

In U.S. include $2 shipping UPS for 1st book; $1 ea. add'l book. Outside U.S. $3 and $1, respectively.
Allow four to six weeks for delivery in U.S., longer outside U.S.
Enclosed is my check or money order for $_____

NAME _____

ADDRESS _____

CITY _____ STATE _____ ZIP _____